HISTORY
YEAR BY YEAR

هشتم
هفتم
ششم
پنجم

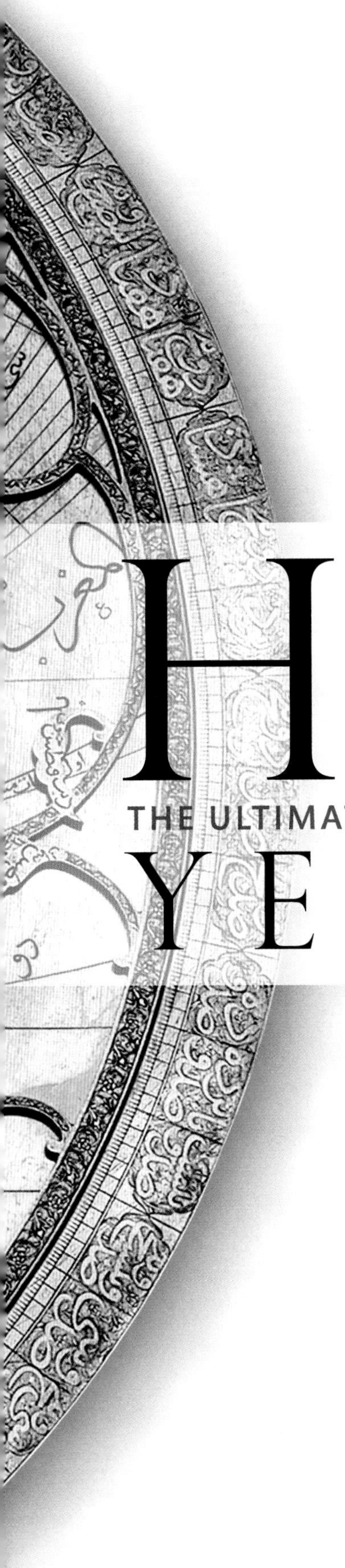

HISTORY

THE ULTIMATE VISUAL GUIDE TO THE EVENTS THAT SHAPED THE WORLD

YEAR BY YEAR

LONDON, NEW YORK, MELBOURNE,
MUNICH, AND DELHI

DORLING KINDERSLEY

Senior Art Editor
Ina Stradins

Project Art Editors
Paul Drislane, Alison Gardner,
Anna Hall, Francis Wong

Designers
Riccie Janus, Fiona Macdonald,
Duncan Turner

Production Editor
Ben Marcus

Senior Production Controller
Mandy Inness

Creative Technical Support
Adam Brackenbury

Jacket Designers
Mark Cavanagh

Cartographer
Encompass Graphics Limited

Managing Art Editor
Michelle Baxter

Art Director
Phil Ormerod

Senior Editors
Angeles Gavira Guerrero,
Peter Frances, Janet Mohun

Project Editors
Lara Maiklem, Ruth O'Rourke-Jones,
Peter Preston, David Summers

Editors
Corinne Masciocchi, Lizzie Munsey,
Martyn Page, Laura Palosuo,
Gill Pitts, Steve Setford,
Nikki Simms, Alison Sturgeon,
Miezan van Zyl, Laura Wheadon,
Victoria Wiggins

Editorial Assistant
Sam Priddy

Indexer
Hilary Bird

Picture Researchers
Ria Jones, Liz Moore

Managing Editor
Sarah Larter

Publisher
Jonathan Metcalf

DK INDIA

Design Manager
Arunesh Talapatra

Senior Designers
Sudakshina Basu, Balwant Singh

Designers
Anjana Nair, Mini Dhawan,
Pallavi Narain

Assistant Designers
Showmik Chakraborty,
Arushi Nayar,
Neha Sharma

Production Manager
Pankaj Sharma

Senior DTP Designers
Dheeraj Arora, Jagtar Singh

Managing Editor
Rohan Sinha

Senior Editor
Soma B. Chowdhury

Editor
Rahul Ganguly

Assistant Editors
Sudeshna Dasgupta,
Himanshi Sharma

DTP Manager
Balwant Singh

DTP Designers
Arjinder Singh, Rajesh Singh
Adhikari, Tanveer Abbas Zaidi,
Shankar Prasad

SMITHSONIAN INSTITUTION

Project Co-ordinator
Ellen Nanney

First published in Great Britain in 2011
by Dorling Kindersley Limited
80 Strand, London WC2R 0RL
Penguin Group (UK)

2 4 6 8 10 9 7 5 3
007 - 178147 - Oct/2011

A CIP catalogue record for this book is available from
the British Library.

ISBN: 978 1 4053 6712 7

Colour reproduction by Alta Images, London

Printed and bound in China by Hung Hing

Discover more at
www.dk.com

CONTRIBUTORS

HUMAN ORIGINS
Dr Fiona Coward
Research Fellow at Royal Holloway University of London; contributed to DK's *Prehistoric*.
Additional text by Dr Jane McIntosh

EARLY CIVILIZATIONS
Dr Jen Green
Author of over 250 books on a range of subjects, from history and geography to nature and the environment.
Additional text by Dr Jane McIntosh

THE CLASSICAL AGE
Philip Parker
Historian and writer; books include *The Empire Stops Here* and *DK Eyewitness Companion to World History.*

TRADE AND INVENTION
Joel Levy
Writer specializing in history and scientific history; books include *Lost Cities* and *Lost Histories*.

REFORMATION AND EXPLORATION
Thomas Cussans
Author and contributor to *The Times* newspaper; previous titles for DK include *Timelines of World History* and *History*.
Additional text by Frank Ritter

THE AGE OF REVOLUTION
Dr Carrie Gibson
Writer who has contributed to *The Guardian* and *Observer* newspapers; gained a doctorate in 18th- and 19th-century history from the University of Cambridge, UK.

TECHNOLOGY AND SUPERPOWERS
R.G. Grant
History writer who has published more than 20 books, including *Battle*, *Soldier*, *Flight*, and *History* for DK.

Sally Regan
Contributor to several books for DK including *History*, *World War II*, and *Science*; award-winning documentary maker whose films include *Shell Shock* and *Bomber Command* for Channel 4.

GLOSSARY
Richard Beatty

CONSULTANTS

Dr Jane McIntosh
8MYA–700BCE
Senior Research Associate, Faculty of Asian and Middle Eastern Studies, University of Cambridge, UK

Professor Neville Morley
700BCE–599CE
Professor of Ancient History, School of Humanities, University of Bristol, UK

Dr Roger Collins
600–1449
Honorary Fellow, School of History, Classics, and Archaeology, University of Edinburgh, UK

Dr David Parrott
1450–1749
Fellow in History and University Lecturer, New College, University of Oxford, UK

Dr Michael Broers
1750–1913
Fellow and Tutor, Lady Margaret Hall, University of Oxford, UK

Professor Richard Overy
1914–present
Professor of History, University of Exeter, UK

SMITHSONIAN INSTITUTION

Smithsonian contributors include historians and museum specialists from:

National Air and Space Museum
The Smithsonian's National Air and Space Museum is one of the world's most popular museums. Its mission is to educate and inspire visitors by preserving and displaying aeronautical and space flight artifacts.

National Museum of American History
The Smithsonian's National Museum of American History dedicates its collections and scholarship to inspiring a broader understanding of the American nation and its many peoples.

National Museum of Natural History
The Smithsonian's National Museum of Natural History is the most visited natural history museum in the world and the most visited museum in the Smithsonian complex.

CONTENTS

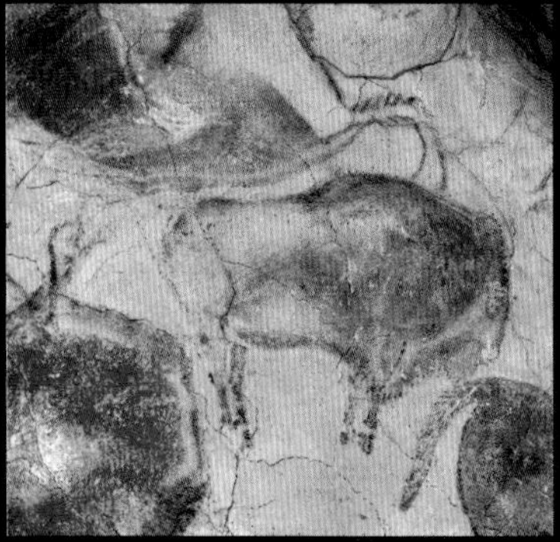

Foreword

Like many people, my early enthusiasm for history focused on particular dates and events: 1588 and the defeat of the Spanish Armada; the battle of Waterloo in 1815; the fall of Constantinople in 1453. Some had personal connections: 1st July 1916, when my grandfather, serving as an artilleryman, had lost several of his closest friends on the first day of the Somme offensive.

From the earliest times history had been cast as a grand chronicle of events and actions, the work of often larger-than-life protagonists, and was intended to enthral and capture the imagination in the same way as a great novel. But during the 20th century academic historians grew sceptical about the "history of the event". Most often the events were battles, treaties, and political struggles, a narrative which excluded the lives of the great majority of men, women, and children. In reaction to this, historians focused on cultural, social, and economic continuities, looked for their evidence in everyday objects, trading records, accounts of childhood and old age. The result was certainly a richer and more diverse account of human experience, but one that often left little sense of change over time.

As the present book shows, history constructed on a timeline does not have to be a narrow account of war and conquest, treaties and treason. All of these feature here, but so do the dates of intellectual and technological innovations, the creation of key works of art, crucial shifts in patterns of agriculture, exploration and commerce. This is an exhilarating and comprehensive account of human creativity as much as its destructiveness, of discovery and understanding as well as natural disasters and human folly. Spectacularly illustrated and succinctly explained, key events in history from the first beginnings of agriculture to the most recent astrophysical discoveries are laid out along what is probably the most comprehensive timeline ever assembled.

No less exciting for me in helping to compose this book and to choose from all facets of human history to build up the timeline, is the contribution that *History Year by Year* makes to an understanding of global history. Throughout the book events, discoveries, and achievements occurring in Europe and North America are set against the equally momentous and significant events in the Middle and Far East, India, Africa, or South America and the Pacific Rim. This is a history which stimulates awareness of a wider world by placing events from across that world side by side and reminding us that progress and discovery, feats of social organization, and challenges to a political status quo are no monopoly of the Western world, but as likely to originate in India or Egypt as in France and Spain.

The design of this book offers a unique opportunity to appreciate a global history of mankind in all its facets. I hope that you enjoy reading *History Year by Year* and using it as a source of reference as much as we enjoyed planning and writing it.

DAVID PARROTT
University of Oxford

Lost city of the Incas
Perched 2,430m (7,970ft) above sea level, in the Peruvian Andes, the Inca citadel of Machu Picchu was probably constructed in the 15th century, and abandoned in the 16th.

1

HUMAN ORIGINS

8 MYA–3000 BCE

Our earliest ancestors lived in Africa almost eight million years ago. Over seven million years later, we appeared and developed the skills – including sophisticated tool-making and agriculture – that allowed us to colonize the world.

Olduvai Gorge in Tanzania is a site of great archaeological significance and it is sometimes referred to as the "Cradle of Mankind". At least two species of early hominin are associated with this area.

THE DIFFERENCES BETWEEN HUMAN AND OTHER APES DNA and blood proteins suggest that our lineage separated from that of the chimpanzees between 8 and 6 million years ago (MYA). Only a few fossil specimens date to this time: ***Sahelanthropus tchadensis*** (7–6 MYA), ***Orrorin tugenensis*** (6.1–5 MYA), and two species of ***Ardipithecus***, *kadabba* (5.8–5.2 MYA) and *ramidus* (4.4 MYA). While all of these species seem to have **walked on two legs** like us, it is not certain whether any were actual ancestors of humans. Because species are **constantly evolving**, and individuals of those species can vary, it is difficult to tell from isolated and often poorly preserved fossils which species they should be assigned to, or how these are related to one another. However, these fossils do tell us a great deal about what the **last common ancestor** we shared with chimpanzees was like.

7 MYA THE TIME WHEN **THE FIRST** HUMAN **ANCESTOR** APPEARS

SEVERAL DIFFERENT AUSTRALOPITHECINE species lived in Africa between 4.2 and 2 MYA. Although they walked on two legs most of the time, they were rather **small and ape-like** and still lived partially in trees. Their brains were about the size of those of modern chimpanzees, but some australopithecines seem to have **used tools**. The earliest stone tools come from Ethiopia and date to **2.6 MYA**, but bones with cut marks made by stone tools have been found associated with ***Australopithecus afarensis*** nearby, and date to 3.4 MYA. The australopithecines' descendants followed two distinct modes of life: members of the genus ***Paranthropus*** had huge jaws and big teeth for eating tough vegetable foods; meanwhile, ***Homo rudolfensis*** and ***H. habilis*** seem to have eaten **more protein**, using tools to get at the protein-rich marrow inside long-bones by scavenging from carnivore kills.

Lucy
This unusually complete skeleton of Australopithecus afarensis*, discovered in Kenya in 1974, was named after the Beatles' song "Lucy in the sky with diamonds".*

ULTIMATELY, THE PARANTHROPINES' WAY OF LIFE was unsuccessful and they became **extinct** after about **1.2 MYA**, while their cousins *Homo habilis* and *H. rudolfensis* survived. These early *Homo* species were not very different from australopithecines.

It was with ***Homo ergaster*** (1.8 MYA) that our ancestors started to **look much more familiar**. *H. ergaster* was tall and slender, and may have been the first hominin (a term used to describe humans and their ancestors) without much body hair. Their **brains were larger** than those of their ancestors, and they lost the last of their adaptations to tree-climbing to become fully adapted to walking and running.

TOOLS

Many animal species use natural objects as tools, but the manufacture of stone tools is unique to hominins. The earliest are simply sharp flakes broken off stone cobbles by striking them with a "hammerstone". These are known as "Oldowan" tools, after Olduvai Gorge where they were first found. Later tools, such as Acheulean handaxes, required more skill. Our manufacture of tools might be one explanation for the evolution of the human brain.

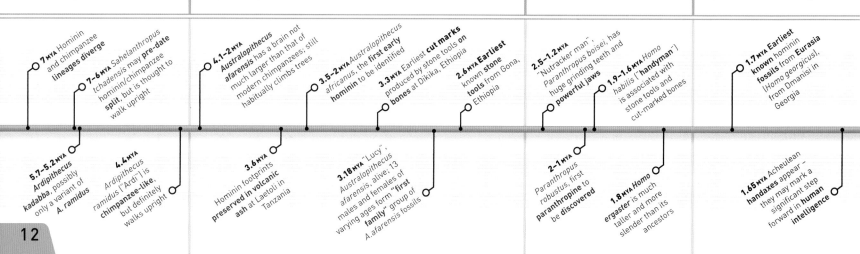

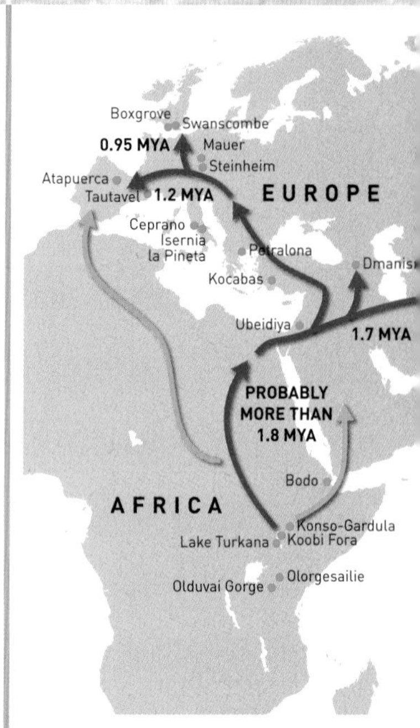

NOT LONG AFTER THE APPEARANCE of *Homo ergaster*, hominins expanded their range **beyond Africa** for the first time. A species called ***H. georgicus*** appeared in Dmanisi in Georgia by **1.7 MYA**. Another close relative of *Homo ergaster*, ***Homo erectus***, lived in China and Indonesia perhaps not long afterward. Some archaeologists believe that earlier groups of hominins may also have left Africa, as some of the skulls from Dmanisi and from the much later site of Liang Bua in Flores in Indonesia (currently known as ***Homo floresiensis***) resemble those of *Homo habilis* and *Homo rudolfensis*.

Living further north would have required a **different way of life**

7 MYA Hominin and chimpanzee **lineages diverge**

7–6 MYA *Sahelanthropus tchadensis* may **pre-date** hominin/chimpanzee **split**, but is thought to walk upright

5.7–5.2 MYA ***Ardipithecus kadabba***, possibly only a variant of ***A. ramidus***

4.4 MYA *Ardipithecus ramidus* ("Ardi") is **chimpanzee-like**, but definitely walks upright

4.1–2 MYA ***Australopithecus afarensis*** has a brain not much larger than that of modern chimpanzees; still habitually climbs trees

3.6 MYA Hominin footprints **preserved in volcanic ash** at Laetoli in Tanzania

3.5–2 MYA *Australopithecus africanus*, the **first early hominin** to be identified

3.3 MYA Earliest **cut marks** produced by stone tools **on bones** at Dikika, Ethiopia

3.18 MYA "Lucy", *Australopithecus afarensis*, alive; 13 males and females of varying ages form **"first family"** group of *A.afarensis* fossils

2.6 MYA Earliest known **stone tools** from Gona, Ethiopia

2.5–1.2 MYA "Nutracker man", *Paranthropus boisei*, has huge grinding teeth and **powerful jaws**

2–1 MYA *Paranthropus robustus*, first **paranthropine** to be **discovered**

1.9–1.6 MYA *Homo habilis* (**"handyman"**) is associated with stone tools and cut-marked bones

1.8 MYA *Homo ergaster* is much taller and more slender than its ancestors

1.7 MYA Earliest known hominin **fossils** from **Eurasia** (*Homo georgicus*), from Dmanisi in Georgia

1.65 MYA Acheulean **handaxes** appear – they may mark a significant step forward in **human intelligence**

> **"** ALL LIVING HUMANS **DESCENDED FROM COMMON ANCESTORS** WHO LIVED IN AFRICA LESS THAN 200,000 YEARS AGO. **"**
>
> **Stephen Jay Gould, American palaeontologist**, from *I have Landed: the end of a beginning in natural history*, 2002

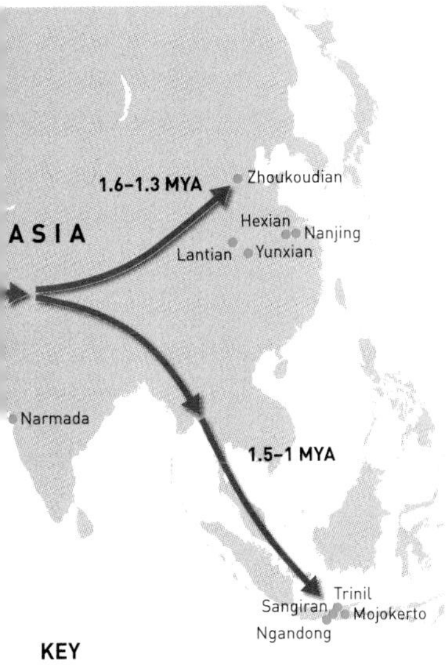

KEY
- Site of fossil finds
- More likely route
- Less likely route

Hominins beyond Africa
Our earliest ancestors evolved in Africa. Possible dispersal routes from Africa are shown on this map, with dates referring to the earliest fossils known from each region.

to life in the African savanna. The climate was cooler and environments were more seasonal, with significant variation in food resources over the course of a year. Fewer edible plants meant that hominins would have had to rely more on harder-to-find and fiercely competed-for **animal protein** for food. They needed to move over greater distances and **work together** to share resources and information to **survive** in these regions.

ACHEULEAN HANDAXES made by *Homo ergaster* and *H. erectus* were produced across most of Africa and Eurasia, and demonstrate the ability to learn **complex skills** from one another and pass them down over generations. To make these tools, knappers had to think several steps ahead in order to select a suitable stone and to prepare and place each strike. Handaxes were used for a wide range of activities, including butchery, but they might also have been important for **personal or group identity**, demonstrating their makers' strength and skill.

While Homo Erectus continued to thrive in Asia, ***Homo antecessor*** had appeared as far west as northern Spain and Italy by 1.2 MYA. Marks on their bones at the site of **Atapuerca** in Spain suggest they practised **cannibalism**. However, these early colonists may not have thrived in these unfamiliar landscapes, as very few sites are known. By 600,000 years ago, a new hominin species, ***Homo heidelbergensis***, had spread much more widely across Europe. *H. heidelbergensis* seem to have been good hunters, or at least proficient scavengers.

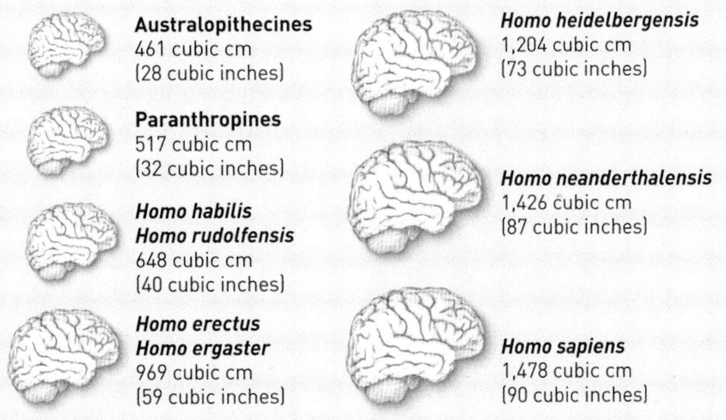

HOMININ BRAIN SIZES

Humans have a disproportionately large brain for a primate of their size, but archaeologists disagree about how and why this expansion happened. Switching to fatty and calorific foods such as bone marrow and meat may have "powered" brain growth, and also demanded more complex tools and effective hunting and foraging skills. Social skills were also a part of this process, as increasing group co-operation and pair-bonding were necessary to sustain the longer periods of childhood that infants needed for their larger brains to develop.

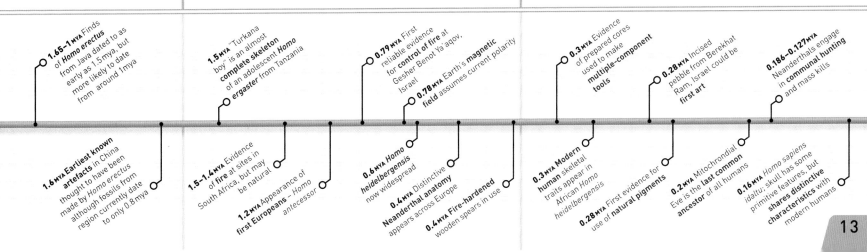

Burying the dead
Neanderthals often disposed of their dead with care. Some were buried in graves, as here at Kebara Cave in Israel, which dates to 60,000 BCE.

BY AROUND 350,000 YEARS AGO, while *Homo erectus* continued to hold sway over eastern Asia, *Homo heidelbergensis* in Europe and Western Asia had evolved into ***Homo neanderthalensis***.

Neanderthals were **stockier and stronger** than modern humans, and their brains were as large or even larger, although shaped slightly differently. Neanderthals were almost certainly very accomplished hunters. They were also **highly skilled** at making stone tools and heavy thrusting spears with which they tackled even large and dangerous animal prey, such as horses and bison.

However, despite burying their dead – which may have indicated ceremonial practices or belief in an afterlife – Neanderthals do not seem to have created more than the most **limited art** or used any symbols, as all modern humans do. Whether or not they spoke in a similar way to modern humans is also difficult to establish. Although their throat and voice box anatomy suggests that a **Neanderthal language** may have been limited compared to that of humans, they must have communicated in some fashion, perhaps by combining a **less complex** form of vocalization with expressive miming.

200,000
THE NUMBER OF YEARS THE **NEANDERTHAL DOMINATED** EUROPE AND WESTERN ASIA

1.65–1 MYA Finds of ***Homo erectus*** from Java dated to as early as 1.5 mya, but more likely to date from around 1 mya

1.6 MYA Earliest known artefacts in China thought to have been made by *Homo erectus* although fossils from region currently date to only 0.8 mya

1.5 MYA "Turkana boy" is an almost **complete skeleton** of an adolescent ***Homo ergaster*** from Tanzania

1.5–1.4 MYA Evidence of **fire** at sites in South Africa, but may be natural

1.2 MYA Appearance of **first Europeans** – *Homo antecessor*

0.79 MYA First reliable evidence for **control of fire** at Gesher Benot Ya'aqov, Israel

0.78 MYA Earth's **magnetic field** assumes current polarity

0.6 MYA *Homo heidelbergensis* now widespread

0.4 MYA Distinctive **Neanderthal anatomy** appears across Europe

0.4 MYA Fire-hardened wooden spears in use

0.3 MYA Evidence of prepared cores used to make **multiple-component tools**

0.3 MYA Modern human skeletal traits appear in African *Homo heidelbergensis*

0.28 MYA Incised pebble from Berekhat Ram, Israel could be **first art**

0.28 MYA First evidence for use of **natural pigments**

0.2 MYA Mitochrondial Eve is the **last common ancestor** of all humans

0.186–0.127 MYA Neanderthals engage in **communal hunting** and mass kills

0.16 MYA *Homo sapiens idaltu*; skull has some primitive features, but **shares distinctive characteristics** with modern humans

COLONIZING THE PLANET

THE SPREAD OF MODERN HUMANS ACROSS THE WORLD

Skeletal and DNA evidence suggests that our species, *Homo sapiens*, evolved in Africa and then spread across the globe. The first traces of modern humans beyond Africa come from fossils in Israel and possibly from stone tools found in Arabia. They date to before 100,000 years ago.

Homo sapiens' colonization of the globe involved many stops, starts, and sometimes retreats, as well as waves of different groups of people in some areas. *Homo sapiens* may have moved into Eurasia via the Mediterranean coast of western Asia, spreading into Western Europe by 35,000 years ago (YA). Archaeological evidence suggests that people may also have taken a "southern route" across Arabia into southern Asia. There may also have been movement eastward, perhaps much earlier, as stone tools have been found in India from 77,000 YA and Malaysia from 70,000 YA. Some possible *Homo sapiens* finds from southern China are dated to 68,000 YA (Liujiang), and even 100,000 YA (Zhirendong). However, these finds remain controversial, and most scholars favour later dates here. In Australia, widespread colonization probably did not occur until 45,000 YA, though some sites have been dated to as early as 60,000 YA.

Further north, *Homo sapiens* first spread across northern Eurasia around 35,000 YA. However, they may have retreated during the last Ice Age, and not re-colonized the region until after 14,000–13,000 YA. Genetically, the North American colonists are likely to have originated in East Asia. They probably travelled across the plain of "Beringia" – now beneath the Bering Straits between Siberia and Alaska, but exposed by low sea levels at the height of the last Ice Age. Distinctive "Clovis" spear points (flaked on both sides) are found across North America around 12,000 YA, so modern humans were widespread at that point, but earlier sites are also known, including South American sites such as Monte Verde (15,500–15,000 YA).

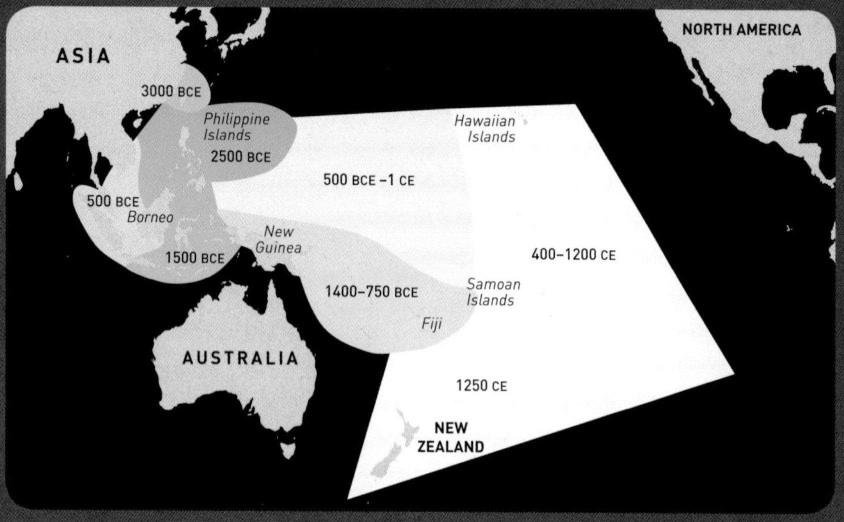

LATE ARRIVALS

The islands of Oceania were some of the last parts of the globe to be colonized, via the Philippines, by Austronesian-speaking early farmers from Taiwan. The more remote northern and eastern islands of Micronesia and Polynesia remained uninhabited until after 700 CE, and New Zealand was populated as late as 1250 CE.

Tracking language
The spread of languages can often be tracked to reflect the movement of people. This map shows the spread of Austronesian speakers across Oceania. Earlier settlers were already present in some western areas.

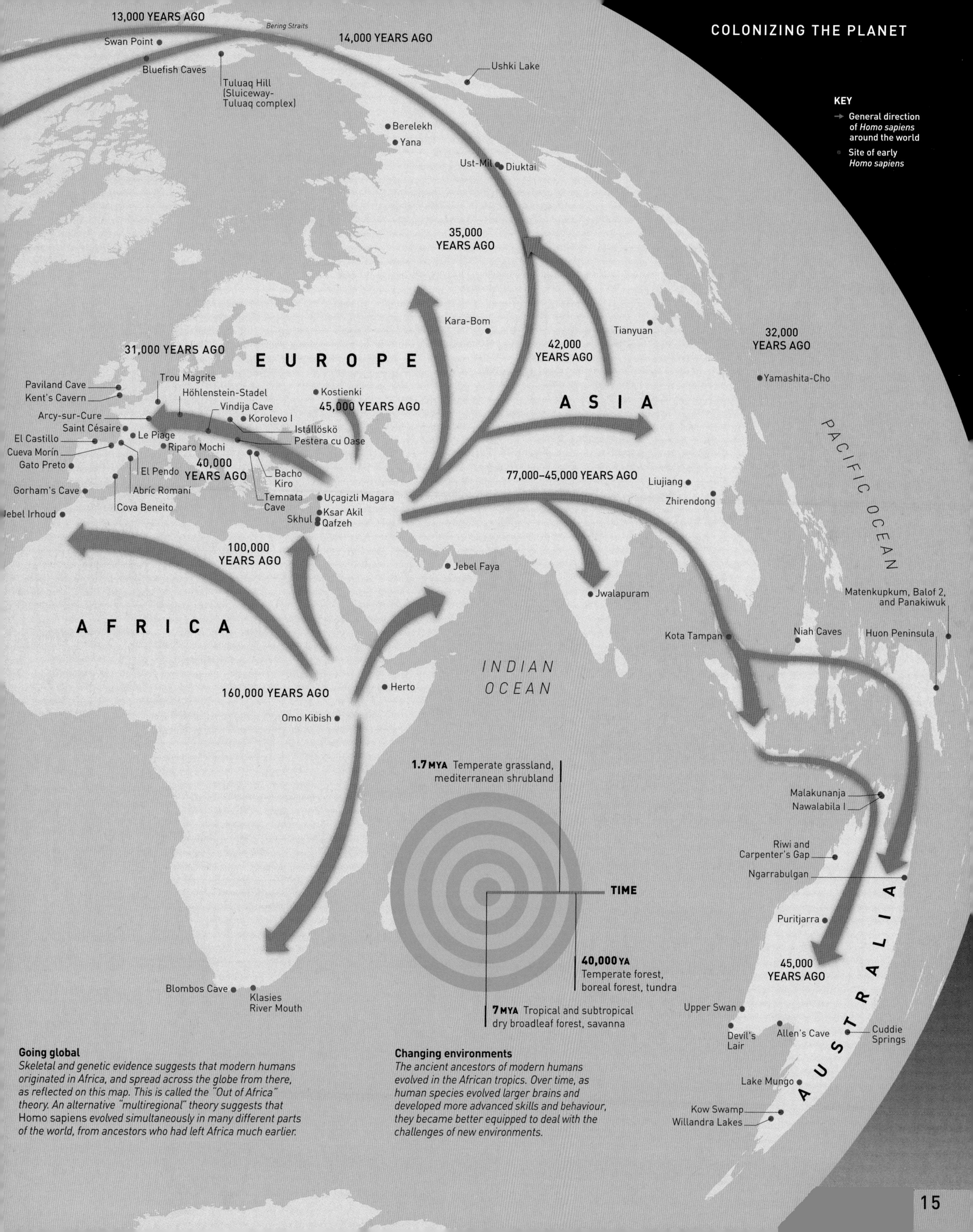

Going global
Skeletal and genetic evidence suggests that modern humans originated in Africa, and spread across the globe from there, as reflected on this map. This is called the "Out of Africa" theory. An alternative "multiregional" theory suggests that Homo sapiens evolved simultaneously in many different parts of the world, from ancestors who had left Africa much earlier.

Changing environments
The ancient ancestors of modern humans evolved in the African tropics. Over time, as human species evolved larger brains and developed more advanced skills and behaviour, they became better equipped to deal with the challenges of new environments.

160,000–45,000 YA

45,000–35,000 YA

35,000–28,000 YA

These cave paintings from Lascaux in France date to around 17,000 years ago. Most cave paintings are from a similar period, though some were created by the earliest *Homo sapiens* to arrive in western Europe, around 32,000 years ago.

IN AFRICA, HOMININ FOSSILS gradually began to reveal the characteristic skeletal traits of *Homo sapiens* from around 400,000 YA: smaller brow ridges, higher and rounder skulls, and chins. DNA analysis of living humans suggests that the **common ancestors of all living humans** (known as Mitochondrial Eve) lived in Africa around 200,000 YA. An Ethiopian fossil

250,000 YEARS AGO WHEN **HOMO SAPIENS** FIRST APPEARED

skull from 160,000 YA is almost modern in shape; this has been identified as a subspecies of modern humans, *Homo sapiens idaltu*. Humans moved north into Western Asia some time before 100,000 YA, but they do not seem to have stayed there for long.

It is debated whether uniquely human behaviours such as **language and the ability to use symbols** evolved before or after modern human anatomy. One theory is that such behaviours became vital only after 74,000 YA, when the massive eruption of **Mount Toba** in Indonesia triggered a global **"volcanic winter"**. DNA analysis suggests that many human groups died out at this

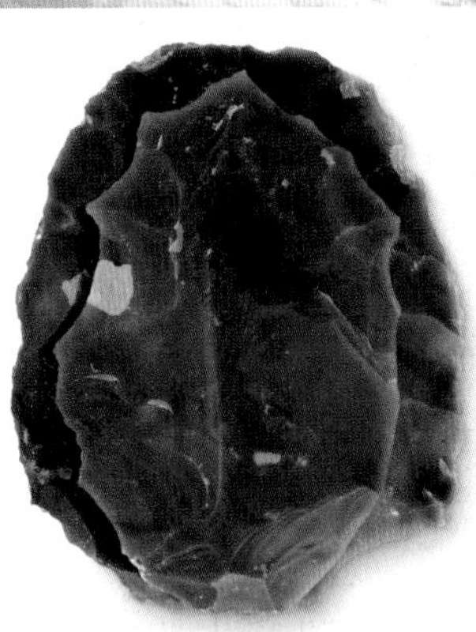

Prepared core and flake
Neanderthals and other hominins prepared a stone core before striking off a sharp flake to use. In Europe this technology is known as the "Mousterian".

time and, in such harsh conditions, complex modern language and symbolism would have allowed groups to **exchange resources and information** with one another, which could have made the difference between survival and extinction. However, others argue that the impact of the eruption of Mount Toba has been exaggerated, and that achaeology in Africa suggests complex hunting practices and the development of symbolism even before this.

It is not clear when **modern humans first spread into Eurasia**. Some researchers argue they left Arabia before 74,000 YA. Others say the major migration occurred later, 50,000 YA, and via western Asia, after developing a new form of stone-tool technology that involved producing long, thin flint "blades", which probably formed part of composite tools.

HUMANS SPREAD RAPIDLY across Europe and Asia. In **Europe**, modern humans appeared in Turkey from 40,000 YA, and in western Europe shortly afterwards. In Asia, fossils of *Homo sapiens* in **Indonesia** and **China** date to at least 42,000 YA, and the sea crossing to **Australia** occurred before 45,000 YA. These dates suggest that the earliest modern humans in Asia may have encountered groups of *Homo erectus*, who survived in China until at least 40,000 years ago. In Indonesia the picture was even more complicated. Fossils found on the **island of Flores** date to less than 38,000 years ago, and seem to represent specialized, extremely small forms of *Homo erectus*, or perhaps even the descendants of earlier hominins. More evidence comes from **Denisova Cave** in Russia – DNA analysis of bones found here reveals **genetic material** distinct from that of both modern humans and Neanderthals, dated to around 40,000 YA. It seems increasingly likely that several groups descended from hominins who left Africa before *Homo sapiens* may have **coexisted in Eurasia** at this time.

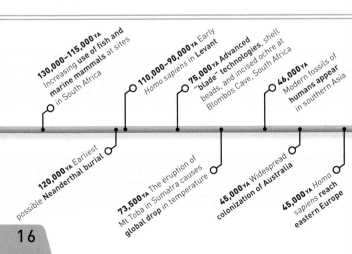

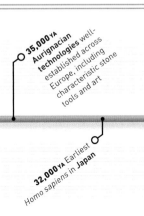

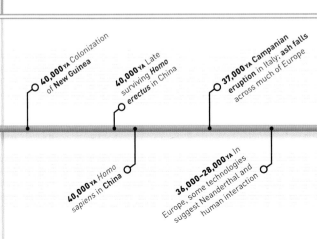

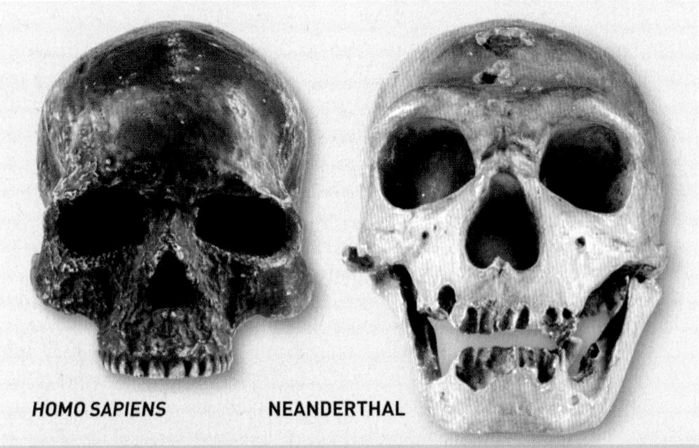

MODERN HUMANS AND NEANDERTHALS

Neanderthal skulls (right) were about the same size as anatomically modern human skulls (left), but they had lower, more sloping foreheads and a double arch of bone over their eyes that created heavy brow ridges. Their lower faces jutted out and they did not have chins. Overall, Neanderthal skeletons reveal that they were much more muscular than modern humans, as well as being extremely physically active and well-adapted to cold climates.

> “THE NEANDERTHALS **WERE NOT APE-MEN**… THEY WERE **AS HUMAN AS US**, BUT THEY REPRESENTED A **DIFFERENT BRAND OF HUMANITY.**”
>
> **Chris Stringer and Clive Gamble**, from *In Search of the Neanderthals*, 1993

IN EUROPE, MODERN HUMANS overlapped with Neanderthals, who survived until at least 30,000 years ago. How and why **Neanderthals died out** is one of the most intensely debated topics in archaeology. There is little evidence of violent interactions between the species, and comparison of DNA increasingly suggests that there may have been some exchange of **mating partners** between the groups.

Early humans may have **outcompeted** their relatives for **food and raw materials** in the rapidly changing environmental conditions. Environments at the time were highly unstable, so even a slight increase in competition could have been significant. However, populations were small and spread out, and co-existed for up to 10,000 years in Europe, and more than 30,000

130,000–115,000 YA Increasing **use of fish and marine mammals** at sites in South Africa

120,000 YA Earliest possible **Neanderthal burial**

110,000–90,000 YA Early *Homo sapiens* in **Levant**

75,000 YA Advanced "blade" technologies, shell beads, and incised ochre at Blombos Cave, South Africa

73,500 YA The eruption of Mt Toba in Sumatra causes **global drop** in temperature

46,000 YA Modern fossils of **humans appear** in southern Asia

45,000 YA Widespread **colonization of Australia**

45,000 YA *Homo sapiens* **reach eastern Europe**

40,000 YA Colonization of **New Guinea**

40,000 YA Late surviving ***Homo erectus*** in China

40,000 YA *Homo sapiens* in **China**

37,000 YA Campanian eruption in Italy; **ash falls** across much of Europe

36,000–28,000 YA In Europe, some technologies suggest Neanderthal and human interaction

35,000 YA Aurignacian technologies well-established across Europe, including characteristic stone tools and art

32,000 YA Earliest *Homo sapiens* in **Japan**

28,000–21,000 YA | 21,000–18,000 YA | 18,000–12,000 YA

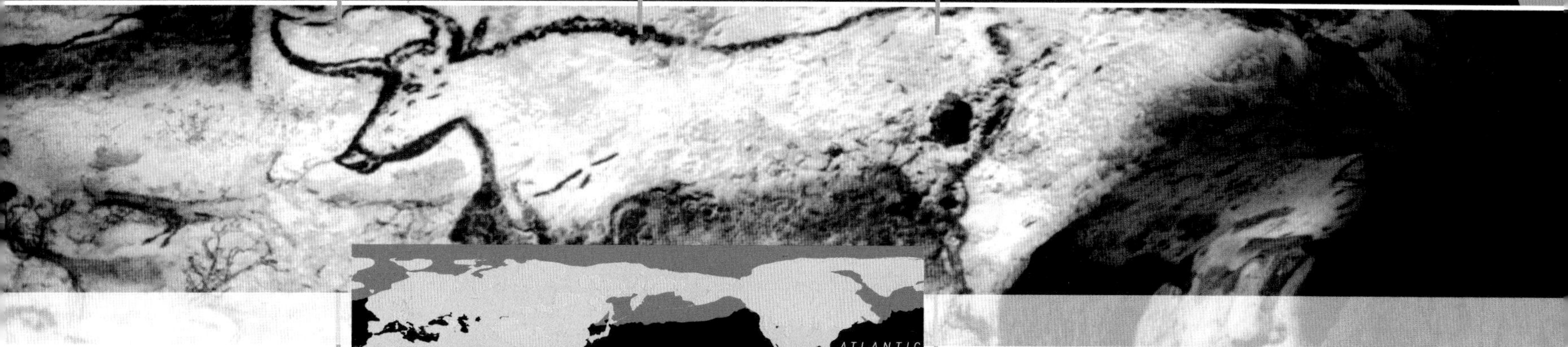

in Indonesia. Alternatively, the **exchange of resources and information** allowed by modern humans' language and symbol use, and their planned and flexible technologies made *Homo sapiens* better able to withstand climatic downturns than Neanderthals.

Others believe that these behaviours were not unique to modern humans. Hominins would have needed to **use rafts or boats** to reach the island of Flores in Indonesia by 800,000 YA. Some late Neanderthal sites also contain elements of technologies normally associated with *Homo sapiens*, although it is possible that Neanderthals may have copied, traded with, or even stolen from modern humans.

A combination of environmental unrest and increased competition is currently considered to be the most likely explanation for **Neanderthal extinction**.

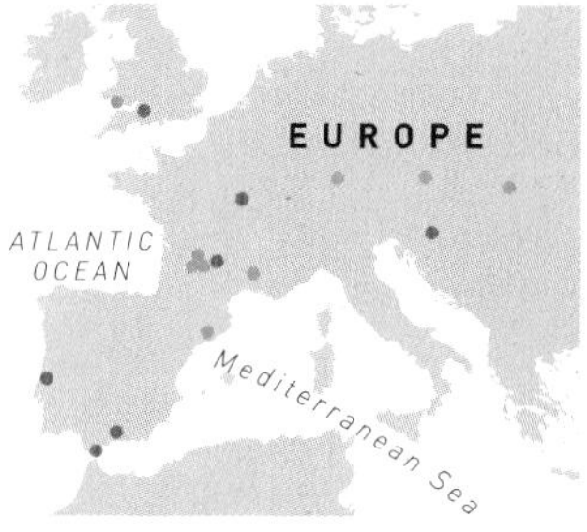

Neanderthal and human ranges
Modern humans and Neanderthals co-existed for several thousand years. Sites appear to show evidence for interaction between the groups.

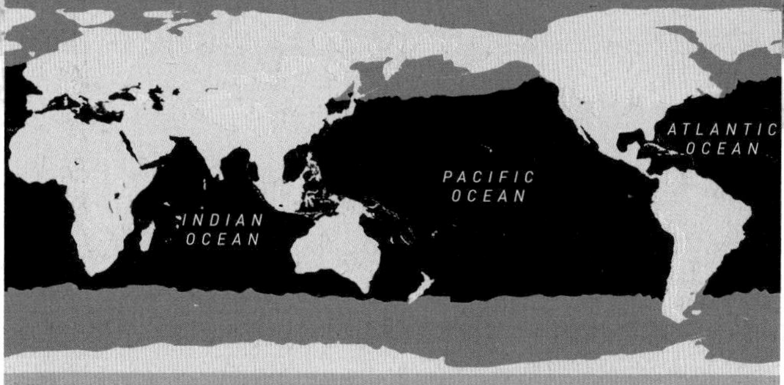

THE MAXIMUM EXTENT OF THE LAST ICE AGE

European climates after 23,000 BCE grew steadily cooler, and during the "Last Glacial Maximum" (21,000–18,000 YA) ice-caps covered most of northern Europe. Further south huge areas of grassland with few trees offered good hunting for groups of humans able to survive the cold.

THE "GRAVETTIAN" CULTURE OF Europe and Russia (28,000–21,000 YA) is known for its elaborate sites, which often have complex structures and burials, as well as large amounts of shell jewellery, and sculpted bone and antler. Also found at Gravettian sites are some of the earliest known clay objects, including some of the famous **"Venus" figurines**. These may have been fertility or religious charms, or part of a system of exchange between social networks across the region as the **Ice Age intensified**.

"Venus" statuette
This figurine from Willendorf in Austria depicts a stylized pregnant or obese female figure.

AT THE HEIGHT OF THE GLACIAL Maximum, when the ice caps were at their maximum extent, people living in more northerly and mountainous areas retreated to **"refuge" areas** such as – in Europe – northern Spain and southwest France, where this period is known as the "Solutrean". Globally, **many groups probably died out**, but some held on in more sheltered regions. To survive the harsh conditions, much time and effort was invested in hunting. Weapons include beautifully worked points known as "leaf-points". Although little evidence survives beyond finely worked bone needles, people probably developed **sophisticated clothing** to keep them warm. Perhaps more importantly, hunters would have worked hard to predict and intercept the movements of herds of large animals, ensuring the **hunting success** that was the difference between life and death.

IN EUROPE, SOPHISTICATED BONE and antler points, needles, and harpoons characterize the **"Magdalenian"** technologies that were used to hunt a wide range of species, especially reindeer.

The Magdalenian (18,000–12,000 YA) is famous for its beautiful art objects, engravings, and cave paintings. There are many theories about what these mean and why they were produced. As most depict animals that were hunted, the paintings may represent a magical means of ensuring hunting success, or show information about the best ways to hunt different species. Paintings of imaginary half-human, half-animal creatures and the inaccessibility of some cave art suggests that painting may have been a magical or ritual activity, perhaps practised by shamans or during initiation or religious ceremonies. Alternatively paintings and art objects may have helped establish group identities and territories, as the number of archaeological sites in this period suggests that populations were growing, and competition for rich and localized resources may have been intensifying.

A rise in temperature led to the **retreat of the ice sheets** that had covered northern Europe, and these areas were rapidly recolonized, with **groups expanding** as far north as Siberia by around 14,000–13,000 YA. Some groups later moved on into Alaska and the Americas. Further east in China and in the Jomon culture of Japan, some of the first pots manufactured from clay appeared between 18,000 and 15,000 YA.

Altamira cave paintings
This Paleolithic cave painting of bison was discovered at the Altamira cave site in Spain.

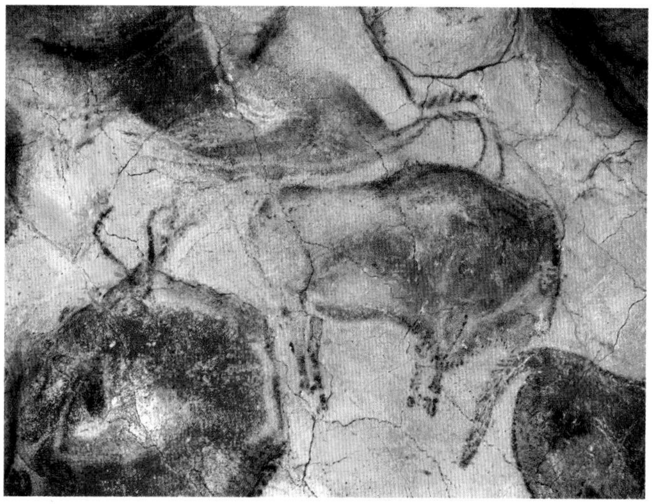

32,000 YA Chauvet cave paintings, France

28,000 YA Youngest known **Neanderthal sites**

28–21,000 YA Gravettian culture

27,000 YA Complex hunter-gatherer sites on the **Russian plains**

21,000 YA Solutrean technologies appear

21–18,000 YA Last glacial maximum

18,000 YA Magdalenian technologies appear

18,000 YA Date of the controversial *Homo floresiensis* specimen, **"the hobbit"**

17,000 YA Earliest known atlatl, or spear-thrower, from **Combe Sauniere**, France

16–15,000 YA Beginning of recolonization of areas of northern **Europe abandoned** during worst climatic conditions

17,000 YA Lascaux cave paintings, France

15,000 YA **Monte Verde**, Chile, a South American site with controversially early dates

14,000 YA Earliest **domesticated dog**

Megalithic (large stone) architecture was used for monumental tombs in Neolithic Europe. Developments around 3300 BCE included the construction of stone circles, such as this example at Castlerigg in northern England.

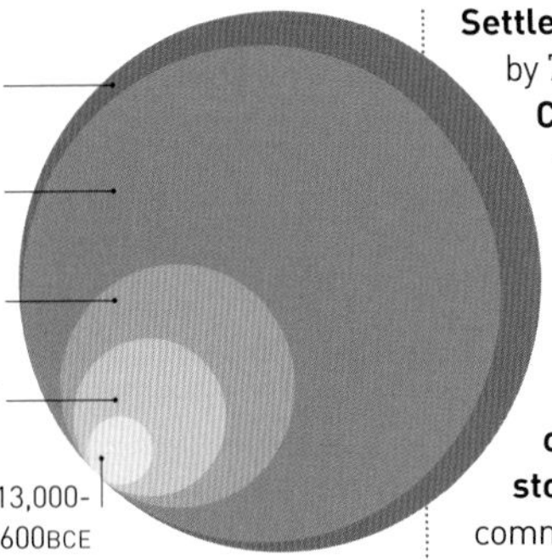

Population density
The population in western Asia grew rapidly from 13,000 to 6400 BCE.

AS STEEPLY RISING TEMPERATURES between 12,700 and 10,800 BCE **melted the northern ice sheets,** global sea-levels rose, lakes formed, and rainfall increased, promoting the **spread of forests and grasslands** and providing new opportunities for hunter-gatherer communities. Coastal areas drowned by rising sea levels were **rich sources of aquatic foods**, as were lakes and rivers. Grasslands sustained large herds of animals, while forest margins provided abundant plant foods and game. **Most hunter-gatherers moved seasonally** to exploit the resources of different areas, but particularly favoured places such as river estuaries could support people year round. One such region was coastal Peru and Chile, where the cold Humboldt current provides especially rich fisheries.

Settled communities lived here by 7000 BCE, including the **Chinchorro** who created the world's first mummies (see panel, opposite).

Another area with favourable conditions was West Asia. Here, vegetation included **wild cereals that could be stored**, sustaining communities throughout the year when supplemented by other wild foods such as gazelle. A period of cold, arid conditions from 10,800 to 9600 BCE led to a steep decline in the availability of wild cereals. This prompted some West Asian villagers to turn to cultivation, planting cereals.

Agriculture began in many parts of the world at different times, using local resources. Domesticated plants and animals spread by trade between neighbouring groups and when farming communities colonized new areas. Agriculture was not a discovery: hunter-gatherers had a deep knowledge of the plants and animals on which they depended, and often took actions to **increase productivity**. Farming was therefore a choice that people made, increasing local productivity, often at the cost of increasing work and risk. Their reasons for farming may have included extending their period of residence in a settled village, providing extra food for feasting or to support a growing population, and boosting the supply of preferred or declining foodstuffs.

Cereals were common staples of early agriculture. Wheat and barley were domesticated in West Asia, spreading into North Africa, Europe, and Central and South Asia. Broomcorn and foxtail millet were domesticated in the Yellow River valley and rice in the Yangzi valley in China, from where they spread through East and Southeast Asia. In Africa, other millets and African rice were domesticated after 3000 BCE. In the Americas, maize was the principal cereal. However, although it was cultivated by 6000 BCE, it was not until 2000 BCE that maize was sufficiently productive to support permanently settled villages.

Pulses and vegetables were grown alongside cereals in many parts of the world.

Tubers, such as manioc and yams, and **treecrops** were cultivated in moist tropical regions, beginning at an early date in the New Guinea highlands and the rainforests of Central America and northern South America.

Domestic sheep, goats, pigs, and cattle were raised across Eurasia and Africa, initially just for meat. However, in the Americas only the Andes had animals suitable for domestication: guineapigs, llamas, and alpacas. **Birds**, particularly chickens,

Lepinski Vir "fish god"
Abundant fish supported a settled hunter-gatherer village on the Danube in Serbia. Its inhabitants carved fish-human sculptures, probably representing gods.

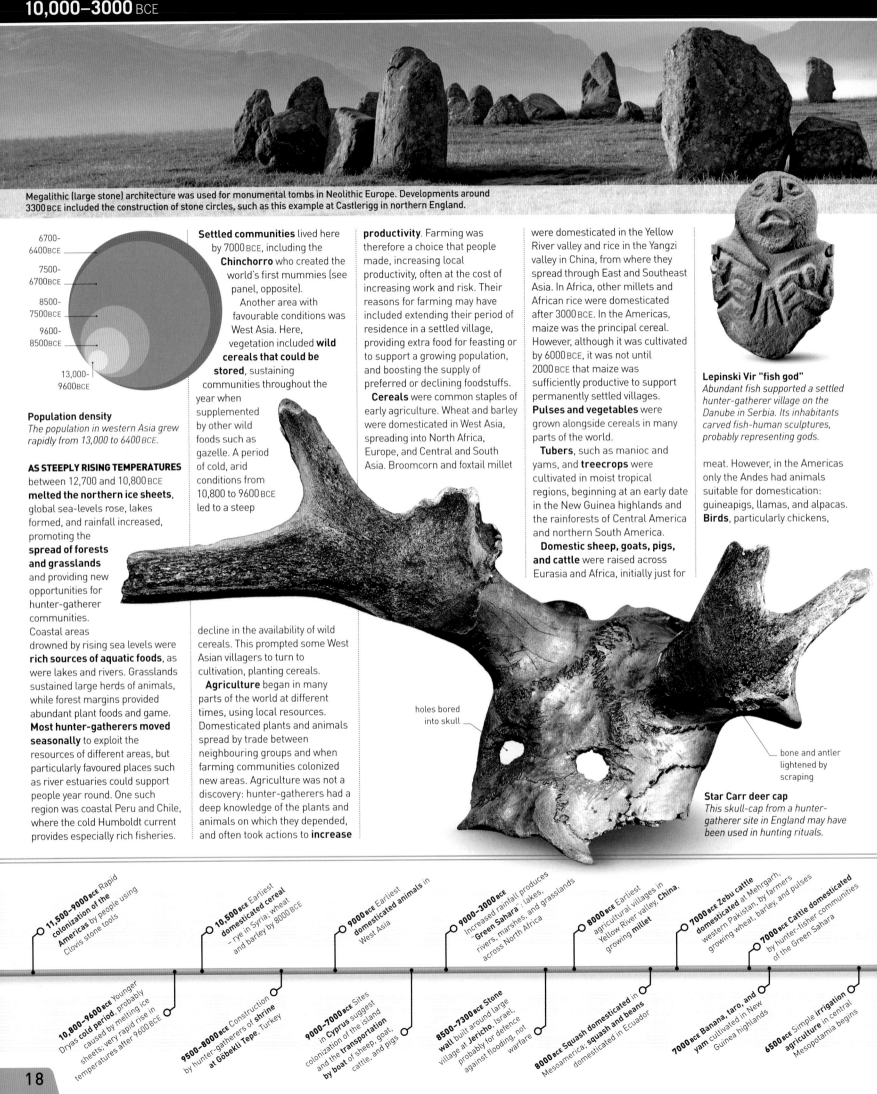

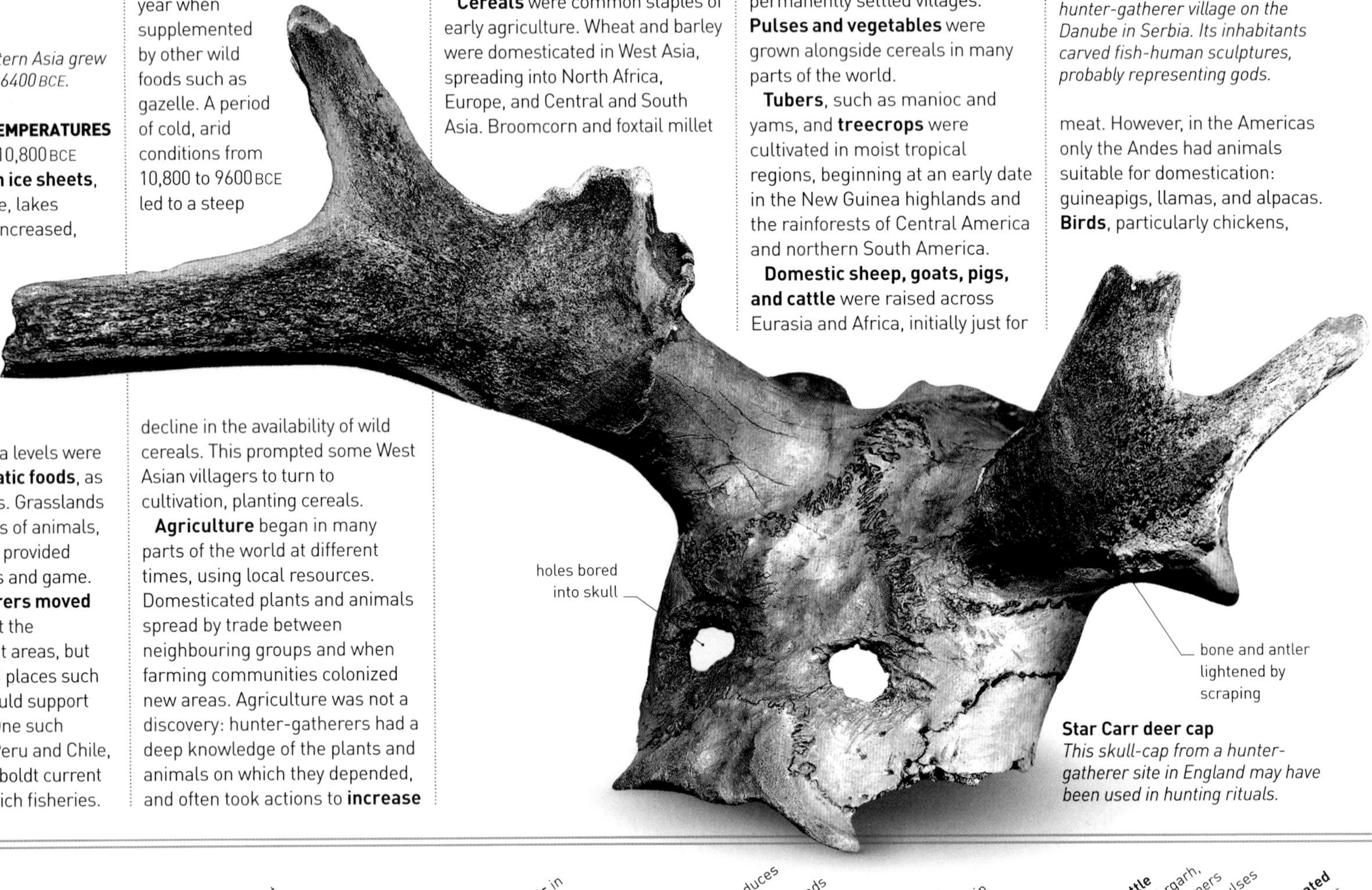

Star Carr deer cap
This skull-cap from a hunter-gatherer site in England may have been used in hunting rituals.

11,500–9000 BCE Rapid **colonization of the Americas** by people using Clovis stone tools

10,800–9600 BCE Younger Dryas **cold period**, probably caused by melting ice sheets; very rapid rise in temperatures after 9600 BCE

10,500 BCE Earliest **domesticated cereal** – rye in Syria; wheat and barley by 8000 BCE

9500–8000 BCE Construction by hunter-gatherers of **shrine at Göbekli Tepe**, Turkey

9000 BCE Earliest **domesticated animals** in West Asia

9000–7000 BCE Sites in **Cyprus** suggest colonization of the island and the **transportation by boat** of sheep, goat, cattle, and pigs

9000–3000 BCE Increased rainfall produces **"Green Sahara"**: lakes, rivers, marshes, and grasslands across North Africa

8500–7300 BCE Stone wall built around large village at **Jericho**, Israel, probably for defence against flooding, not warfare

8000 BCE Earliest agricultural villages in Yellow River valley, **China**, growing **millet**

8000 BCE Squash domesticated in Mesoamerica; **squash and beans** domesticated in Ecuador

7000 BCE Zebu cattle domesticated at Mehrgarh, western Pakistan, by farmers growing wheat, barley, and pulses

7000 BCE Banana, taro, and yam cultivated in New Guinea highlands

7000 BCE Cattle domesticated by hunter-fisher communities of the Green Sahara

6500 BCE Simple **irrigation agriculture** in central Mesopotamia begins

ducks, and turkeys, were also kept by Old and New World farmers. By 5000 BCE cattle, sheep, and goats were **raised for milk** as well as meat, while cattle were used to pull **ploughs**, enabling people to cultivate much larger areas. **Wool-bearing sheep** were bred in West Asia in the 4th millennium BCE, and rapidly spread into Europe and Central Asia. The use of **pack animals** such as llamas and donkeys allowed long-distance transport.

Agriculture was more productive than foraging and could support **larger communities**. Settled life also encouraged **population growth**. Many early farming villages in West Asia grew to a considerable size. Most remarkable was **Çatalhöyük** in Turkey, occupied around 7400–6200 BCE, which housed as many as 8,000 people. Its tightly packed houses were entered from the roof by ladders, and were decorated with paintings and modelled animal heads.

After 7000 BCE **farmers spread** from Turkey into southeast and central Europe, while Mediterranean hunter-gatherers gradually turned to agriculture, using imported West Asian crops and animals. By 3500 BCE most of Europe had adopted farming.

Megaliths – stone chambered tombs of which a wide variety were built, often with earthen mounds – were constructed in western and northern Europe from the early 5th millennium BCE. Most housed the bones of a number of individuals.

Native (naturally occurring pure) **copper and gold** were being shaped into small objects by cold hammering before 8000 BCE in West Asia. Around 7000 BCE, **ores were smelted** here to extract metal and by 6000 BCE copper and lead were also cast. Metals were initially made into small personal objects that could enhance prestige and status. Later, however, copper began to be used for **tools**, and by 4200 BCE copper ores containing arsenic were deliberately selected to produce a harder metal. The addition of tin created a stronger alloy, **bronze**, which was in use in West Asia by 3200 BCE.

The development of **water-control techniques** enabled West Asian farmers to colonize the southern **Mesopotamian plains**, where agriculture depended entirely on irrigation but was highly productive. By the mid 4th millennium BCE, this region was densely populated, and villages were developing into **towns**, with craft specialists. There was a growing demand for raw materials, including metal ores, which often came from distant sources. A **trading network** developed that stretched from Egypt through West Asia to the mountainous borderlands of South Asia, with towns controlling sources of materials and strategic points along the routes. **Sumer** (southern Mesopotamia) was at the forefront of this development, but social, religious, economic, and political complexity was also emerging in **Elam** (southwest Iran) and **Egypt**. All three regions developed **writing systems** before 3000 BCE, which they used to record and manage economic transactions and the ownership of property. The earliest known pictographic writing, around 3300 BCE, comes from **Uruk** in Sumer, a huge and complex settlement that is deservedly known as the **world's first city**.

> “ THE **NEOLITHIC** WAS… A POINT IN A CONTINUOUS STORY OF **GREATER ECONOMIC CONTROL** OVER RESOURCES… FROM **SCAVENGING** TO… **FARMING.** ”
>
> **Clive Gamble,** from *Origins and revolutions: human identity in earliest prehistory,* 2007

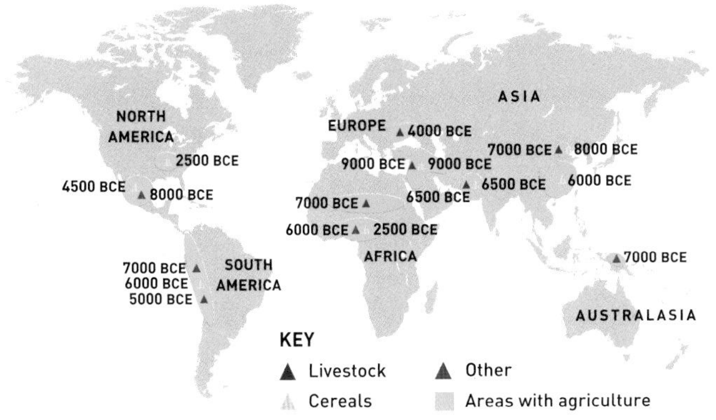

The spread of agriculture
Humans began to cultivate plants and manage animals independently, in different areas at different times, across the world.

CHINCHORRO MUMMIES

The earliest mummies come not from Egypt, but from coastal northern Chile, an arid region where natural mummies occur from 7000 BCE. After 5000 BCE the Chinchorro began artificial mummification. They removed the flesh, reassembled and reinforced the skeleton, stuffed the skin with plant material, coated it in clay, and painted it with black manganese or red ochre. Only some individuals, particularly children, were mummified.

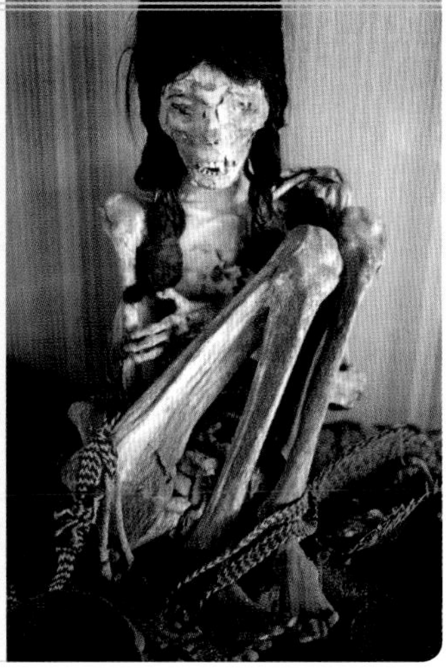

Copper axe heads
Gold and copper were the first metals to be worked. They became widespread in Europe around 2500 BCE.

6200 BCE First **farming communities** established in Euphrates valley of southern Mesopotamia

6000 BCE Villages in Yangzi valley (China) **fish**, grow **rice**, and raise **pigs** and **chickens**

6000 BCE Domestic **maize** develops from wild teosinte in Mexico

5500 BCE Independent development of **copper** metallurgy in the Balkans

5100 BCE Copper mining at Aibunar, Bulgaria

5000–1000 BCE **Old Copper Culture**, a major industry and trade network based on locally mined, cold-hammered native copper, flourishes in Great Lakes region of North America

5000 BCE Domestic animals kept for **milk and pulling ploughs**, as well as for meat, in West Asia, North Africa, and Europe

5000 BCE Domesticated **llama, alpaca, and probably guineapig** in the Andes; range of crops grown in Andes, Andean coast, and tropical lowlands of northeast South America

4000 BCE Domestication of **vine and olive** in eastern Mediterranean

4000 BCE Wet-rice cultivation in ploughed, flooded paddy fields in China begins

3500 BCE Wheeled transport emerges, spreads rapidly through Eurasia – used for local transport and military purposes

3500 BCE Stamp seals begin to be used in West Asia for administrative and economic purposes

3300 BCE Writing invented in southern Mesopotamia

3200 BCE Uruk emerges as first city

3200 BCE Beginning of Egyptian **writing**

3200 BCE First **bronze** manufactured in West Asia

3100–2900 BCE Proto-Elamite script (early Bronze Age **writing system**) across the Iranian plateau

3000 BCE Metallurgy reaches western China

Pottery shard
4000 BCE • ROMANIA
Different cultures can be identified by their unique ways of decorating objects – this shard is typical of the Cucuteni-Tripolye culture.

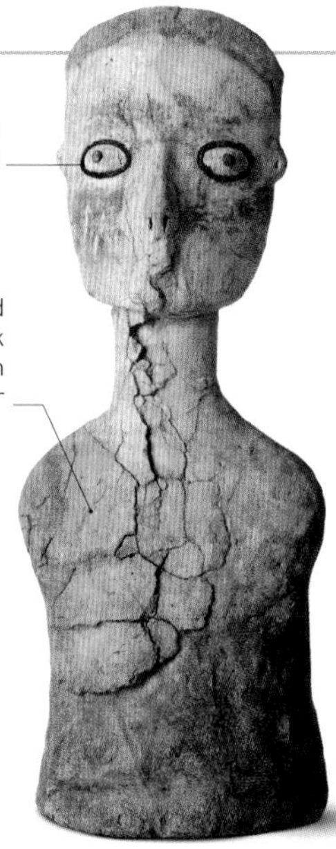

Human figurine
6750–6500 BCE • JORDAN
This large statue from Ain Ghazal is one of several from sites in the Near East that may have represented ancestors or gods.

Schist plaque
4000 BCE • PORTUGAL
It is unclear what Neolithic engraved plaques, like this one from Alentejo, symbolized, but they seem to have been made for burial with the dead.

Engraved bone
13,000–8000 BCE • FRANCE
Paleolithic artists often carved as well as painted their depictions of animals, as with this scene of a bison being chased, from Laugerie-Basse.

PREHISTORIC PEOPLES

EARLY HUMANS ARE DEFINED BY THE RAW MATERIALS THEY USED TO FASHION TOOLS, WEAPONS, AND ORNAMENTS

Prehistory is traditionally divided into the Stone, Bronze, and Iron ages, but many other kinds of raw materials such as wood, hide, and plant fibres were also used in early technologies. Little evidence of these survives.

As well as being functional aids to survival and subsistence, the objects made by prehistoric peoples would also have been important in their social lives. Different groups develop their own ways of manufacturing and decorating objects, and distinctive designs may become badges of identity or status symbols. The trade and exchange of objects is another vital way in which individuals and groups establish social relationships and hierarchies.

Oldowan tool
2.6–1.7 MYA • AFRICA
The earliest stone tools were simple, sharp-edged flakes of stone, made by striking a stone cobble with a hard "hammerstone".

Blades and core
100,000 BCE ONWARDS • WIDESPREAD
Early modern humans produced uniform, narrow blades that would have been fitted to wooden and antler handles or held in the hand, as tools for many different purposes.

Flint hand-axe
200,000 BCE • UK
Hand-axes, such as this one from Swanscombe, were skilfully made and used for a wide range of activities, including woodworking and butchery.

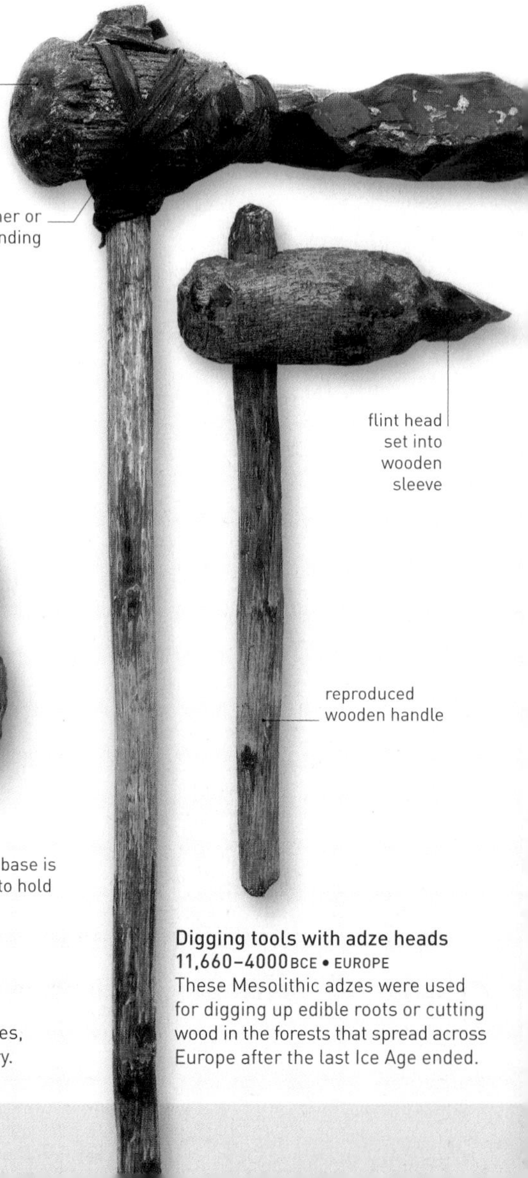

Digging tools with adze heads
11,660–4000 BCE • EUROPE
These Mesolithic adzes were used for digging up edible roots or cutting wood in the forests that spread across Europe after the last Ice Age ended.

Antler harpoon
8000 BCE • UK
This harpoon head is attached to a long handle for spearing fish – a key source of food when sea levels rose as the last Ice Age ended.

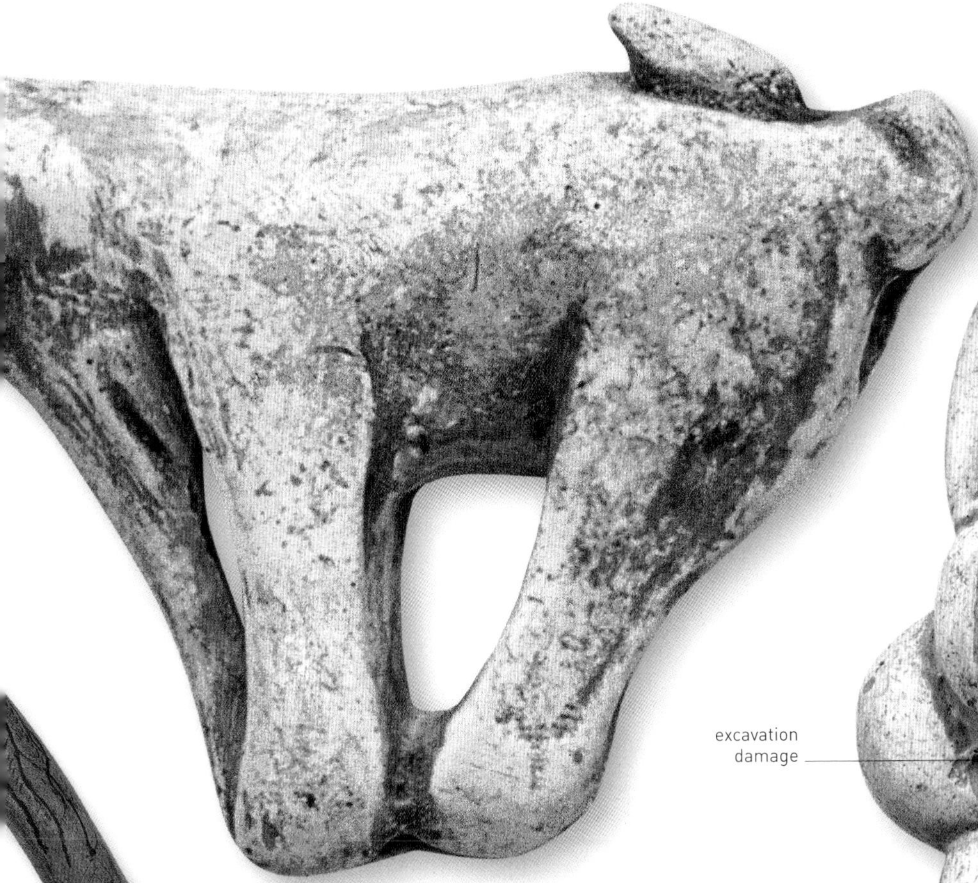

Carved spear-thrower
10,500 BCE • FRANCE
Spear-throwers, such as this one from Montastruc, were often carved into animal shapes – here, a woolly mammoth made from antler. They enabled hunters to throw spears further and with greater force.

Lespugue Venus
24,000–22,000 BCE • FRANCE
This ivory figurine from Lespugue in the Pyrenees is one of many "Venus" figurines – depicting women who are pregnant or obese, or whose female features are greatly exaggerated.

Clay burial chest
4000 BCE • NEAR EAST
One Chalcolithic ("copper age") burial practice involved leaving the dead out to decay, then collecting the bones and placing them in clay chests like this one.

Mummified head
7000–3000 BCE • PERU
In very dry climates, bodies can become mummified. Some of the earliest mummies have been found in Peruvian deserts.

Agricultural tools
9500 BCE–1834 CE • WIDESPREAD
First wild and later domesticated cereals were harvested using sickles like these, until they were superseded in most places by the invention of the combine harvester.

Gold jewellery
4700–4200 BCE • BULGARIA
At the cemetery of Varna in Bulgaria, more than 3,000 pieces of some of the earliest gold jewellery have been found, mainly buried with elite males.

Neolithic seal
7500–5700 BCE • ANATOLIA
Seals such as this one from the settlement of Çatal Höyük were used during the Neolithic to stamp decorative designs on to skin or cloth.

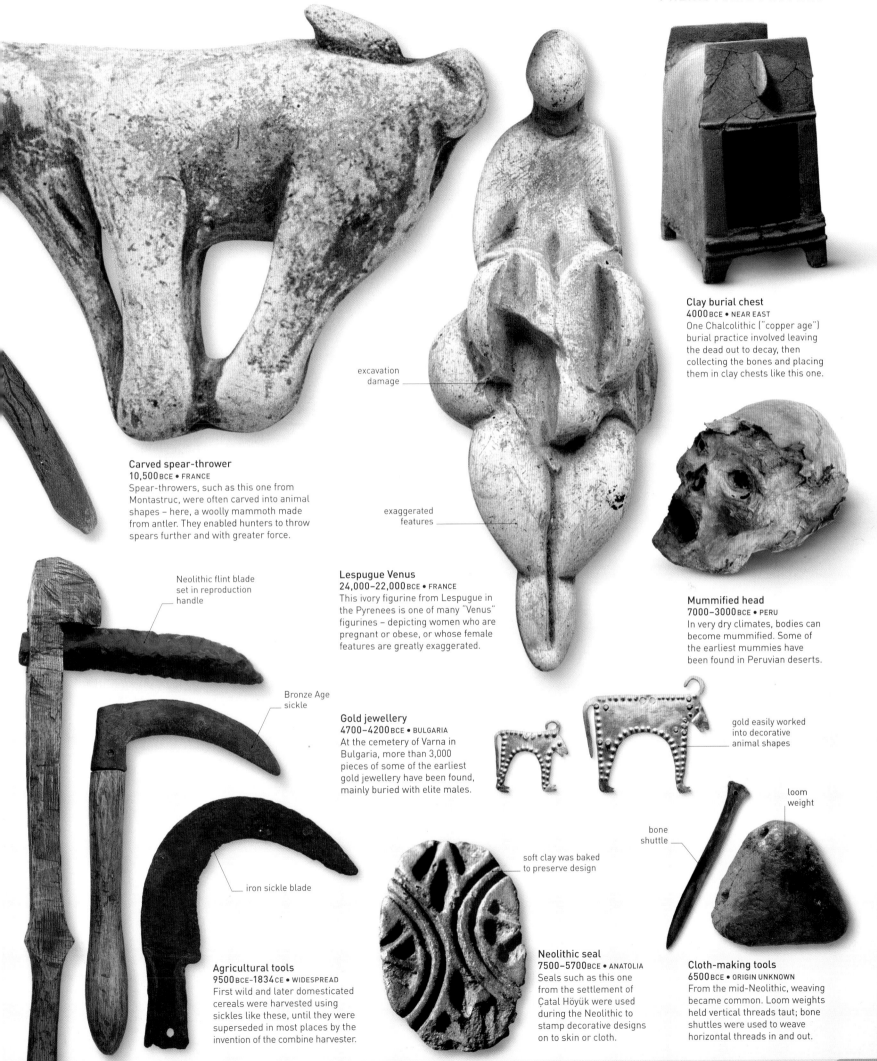

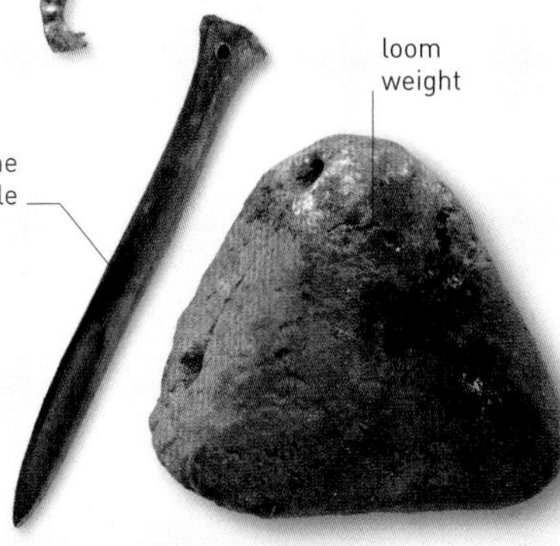

Cloth-making tools
6500 BCE • ORIGIN UNKNOWN
From the mid-Neolithic, weaving became common. Loom weights held vertical threads taut; bone shuttles were used to weave horizontal threads in and out.

2

EARLY CIVILIZATIONS 3000–700 BCE

This period saw the emergence of complex civilizations. Communities flourished and trade developed in the fertile valleys of Egypt, India, western Asia, and China. Europe, and Central and South America also flourished during this time.

Stonehenge in western Britain was a ceremonial site from around 3100 BCE. An early earth enclosure and a circle of wooden posts was later replaced by the outer circle of stones seen here.

DURING THE LAST HALF OF THE FOURTH MILLENNIUM BCE, the world's first civilizations arose, first in Western Asia, then North Africa and South Asia. Civilization also appeared in China in the early second millennium BCE. By 3000 BCE, **the world's first urban culture** had begun to develop in southern **Mesopotamia**, in what is now Iraq. The lower Euphrates River plains had been farmed from *c.*6200 BCE, after the development of irrigation systems – the Greek word "mesopotamia" means "land between the rivers". By 3500 BCE, farming communities were growing into towns and then cities such as Ur, Uruk, and Eridu. Over the next 300 years, each city came to dominate its surrounding area, forming a group of city-states in the land called Sumer in southeast Mesopotamia.

Metalworking had begun in Mesopotamia around 6000 BCE. Around 3200 BCE, Sumerian smiths began **manufacturing bronze**. The plough had been in use since about 5000 BCE, wheeled carts from around 3500 BCE, and such advances made farming more productive. The resulting food surplus freed some people from the farming life, allowing **specialization into professions** such as priesthood, crafts, trade, and administration. The **world's first tiered society** developed, headed by kings sometimes known as lugals.

50 THOUSAND THE POPULATION OF THE CITY OF URUK *c.*2800 BCE

In **Egypt**, one of the world's **most complex ancient civilizations** was forming along the banks of the River Nile by 3100 BCE. The Nile formed a narrow strip of cultivatable land, floodplain, as the river's annual flood (known as the inundation) spread black silt along its banks. The Egyptian farming year began in autumn when the inundation subsided, and farmers cultivated wheat, barley, beans, and lentils in the fertile soil.

By the end of the 4th millennium BCE, farming communities had evolved into two kingdoms: **Upper Egypt** in the south and **Lower Egypt** in the north. **King Narmer** united the two kingdoms *c.*3100 BCE. After Narmer came **Menes**, although historians are unsure whether Menes was Narmer's successor or a different name for Narmer himself. Menes is credited with founding the Egyptian capital at Memphis and Egypt's first dynasty.

As in Mesopotamia, efficient agriculture produced prosperity and specialism, allowing **arts, crafts, engineering, and early medicine** to develop.

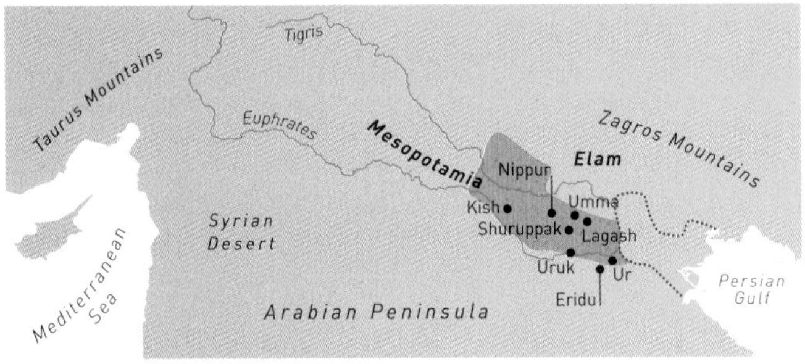

Ancient cities of Mesopotamia
Sumer in southern Mesopotamia was the location of the world's first urban civilization from c.2900 BCE as agricultural success led to a complex society.

KEY
Extent of Early Dynastic city-states
Ancient coastline

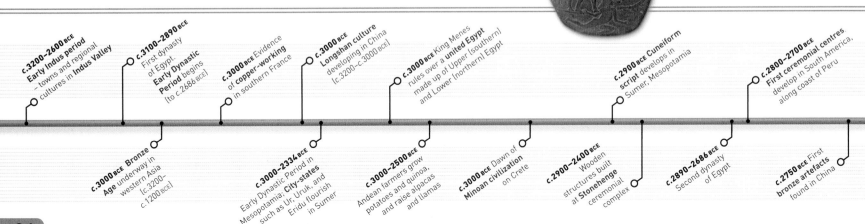

Narmer Palette
This carved piece of green siltstone records the triumph of the legendary King Narmer of Upper Egypt over his enemies.

The Early Dynastic Period (*c.*3100–2686 BCE) was already characterized by many of the celebrated aspects of Egyptian culture: **hieroglyphic** writing, a sophisticated **religion** (including belief in an afterlife), and preserving the dead using **mummification**. A complex hierarchical society developed, with the king at the apex accorded semi-divine status. Egyptian kings – later known as **pharaohs** – ruled with the help of a chief minister, or vizier, regional governors (nomarchs), and a huge staff of lesser officials including priests, tax collectors, and scribes.

In China, civilization originated in the valleys of eastern rivers such as the Huang He (Yellow River), where the rich loess soil made the land fertile. As early as 8000 BCE, millet had been cultivated in the area around Yangshao in Henan Province. Around *c.*2400 BCE, the neighbouring Dawenkou culture developed into the **Longshan culture** of Shangdong Province. Longshan farmers grew rice after developing irrigation systems. As in other early civilizations, agricultural success allowed the development of an elaborate society. Chinese craftsmen were making **bronze tools** *c.*3000 BCE, **jade vessels** *c.*2700 BCE, and **silk weaving** had begun by 3500 BCE.

The **Bronze Age** was underway in western Asia by 3000 BCE, and possibly considerably earlier. The Bronze Age in Europe seems to have developed separately from around 2500 BCE, using ore sources from the Carpathian Mountains in Central Europe. This era also saw the beginnings of the **Minoan civilization** on the Greek island of Crete around 2000 BCE, with trading links to the nearby Cyclades Islands and the wider Mediterranean. In Western Europe, the earlier tradition of megalithic tomb building and a growing interest in astronomical observation gave rise to a new **megalithic tradition** of erecting stone circles, stone rows, standing stones, and tombs including astronomical features. **These include** Newgrange in Ireland, Stonehenge in England, and Carnac in France.

- ***c.*3200–2600 BCE** **Early Indus period** – towns and regional cultures in **Indus Valley**
- ***c.*3000 BCE** **Bronze Age** underway in western Asia (*c.*3200–*c.*1200 BCE)
- ***c.*3100–2890 BCE** First dynasty of Egypt. **Early Dynastic Period** begins (to *c.*2686 BCE)
- ***c.*3000 BCE** Evidence of **copper-working** in southern France
- ***c.*3000–2334 BCE** Early Dynastic Period in Mesopotamia; **City-states** such as Ur, Uruk, and Eridu flourish in Sumer
- ***c.*3000 BCE** **Longshan culture** developing in China (*c.*3200–*c.*3000 BCE)
- ***c.*3000 BCE** King Menes rules over a **united Egypt** made up of Upper (southern) and Lower (northern) Egypt
- ***c.*3000–2500 BCE** Andean farmers grow potatoes and quinoa, and raise alpacas and llamas
- ***c.*3000 BCE** Dawn of **Minoan civilization** on Crete
- ***c.*2900–2400 BCE** Wooden structures built at **Stonehenge** ceremonial complex
- ***c.*2900 BCE** **Cuneiform script** develops in Sumer, Mesopotamia
- ***c.*2890–2686 BCE** Second dynasty of Egypt
- ***c.*2800–2700 BCE** **First ceremonial centres** develop in South America, along coast of Peru
- ***c.*2750 BCE** First **bronze artefacts** found in China

2.3 MILLION THE NUMBER OF **BLOCKS** USED TO BUILD THE GREAT **PYRAMID** OF GIZA

The three pyramids at Giza were built for the pharaohs Khufu, Khafra, and Menkaura between 2575 and 2465 BCE. They are guarded by the statue of the Sphinx, which may bear the features of King Khafra.

Standard of Ur
This box-like object has two side panels – one depicting war, the other (shown here) times of peace.

SOUTHERN MESOPOTAMIA was a patchwork of over 40 city-states, among which Ur, Uruk, Nippur, and Kish were the most important. **Trade flourished** using a network of rivers and canals, and trade links extended to Anatolia (modern-day Turkey), Iran, and Afghanistan, with grain, minerals, timber, tools, and vessels traded. The **Sumerian** population was unique in being **predominantly urban**. In Ur, Uruk, and other centres, people lived in clustered mud-brick houses. At the heart of the city, the **ziggurat** – a terraced temple mound – provided the focus for religious ceremonies, and grain was stored in storerooms within the temple precincts. From around 2500 BCE, some citizens of Ur were buried in **tombs** along with treasures such as the **Standard of Ur**. The purpose of its intricate side panels is still a mystery; they may have formed the soundbox of a lyre.

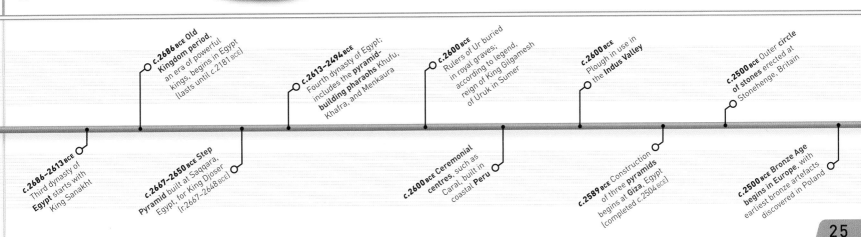

Cuneiform tablet
Over time, the inventory of signs regularly used in cuneiform script was greatly reduced.

Arising from the need to keep economic and administrative records, the **first pictographic writing** developed in **Sumer** (*c.*3300 BCE). Pictographs (pictorial writing representing a word or phrase) evolved into a script called **cuneiform** *c.*2900 BCE, in which scribes pressed sharpened reeds into soft clay to leave wedge-shaped impressions.

Southern Mesopotamia became densely populated, putting pressure on natural resources. This led to **conflicts** over land and water, and alliances between cities were forged and broken.

The first signs of **civilization in the Americas** appeared along the coast of Peru and in the Andes *c.*2800 BCE. **Andean farmers** grew potatoes and the cereal quinoa, and raised alpacas and llamas. There were fishing communities on the coast, while inland towns became ceremonial centres, built around mud-brick temple platforms. An exceptional example is **Caral**, about 200km (125 miles) from Lima and dating from *c.*2600 BCE. Another, **Aspero**, had six platform mounds topped by temples. Cotton was grown in the region, and maize was cultivated from around 2700 BCE.

The **Indus Valley civilization** began to emerge in South Asia in the fourth millenium BCE, as **flood control technology** developed. By 2600 BCE, the Indus Plain contained dozens of towns and cities. Of these, **Mohenjo-daro** on the River Indus, and **Harappa**, to the northeast, were pre-eminent, with populations of around 100,000 and 60,000 respectively.

In **Egypt**, King Sanakht acceded to the throne in the year 2686 BCE, marking the beginning of the Third dynasty and the **Old Kingdom** era – a time of strong, centralized rule and **pyramid-building**. These magnificent monuments were built as **royal tombs**. In Early Dynastic times, kings had been buried beneath rectangular mud-brick platforms called mastabas. Around 2650 BCE, the first pyramid, the **Step Pyramid of Saqqara**, was completed for King Djoser. Designed by the architect Imhotep, it resembled six stone mastabas on top of one another.

Straight-sided pyramids appeared soon after, the greatest of which were the **three pyramids at Giza**. These incredible feats of engineering were constructed not by slaves as was once thought, but by a staff of full-time craftsmen and masons supplemented by farmers performing a type of national service during the Nile floods. Enormous blocks of stone (lower stones of 6–10 tonnes; higher ones of 1–2 tonnes) were cut from local quarries, hauled on site using sleds, and then heaved up ramps, which grew ever-higher as construction progressed.

- ***c.*2686–2613 BCE** Third dynasty of **Egypt** starts with King Sanakht
- ***c.*2686 BCE Old Kingdom period**, an era of powerful kings, begins in Egypt (lasts until *c.*2181 BCE)
- ***c.*2667–2650 BCE Step Pyramid** built at Saqqara, Egypt, for King Djoser (r.2667–2648 BCE)
- ***c.*2613–2494 BCE** Fourth dynasty of Egypt; includes the **pyramid-building pharaohs** Khufu, Khafra, and Menkaura
- ***c.*2600 BCE** Rulers of Ur buried in royal graves; according to legend, reign of King Gilgamesh of Uruk in Sumer
- ***c.*2600 BCE Ceremonial centres**, such as Caral, built in coastal **Peru**
- ***c.*2600 BCE** Plough in use in the **Indus Valley**
- ***c.*2589 BCE** Construction of three **pyramids** begins at **Giza**, Egypt (completed *c.*2504 BCE)
- ***c.*2500 BCE** Outer **circle of stones** erected at Stonehenge, Britain
- ***c.*2500 BCE Bronze Age begins in Europe**, with earliest bronze artefacts discovered in Poland

2500–2350 BCE

The ruined citadel of Mohenjo-daro was made up of various buildings. It was built on a platform to guard against flooding of the River Indus.

IN THE SECOND HALF OF THE 3RD MILLENNIUM BCE, civilizations continued to develop in western Asia, Egypt, and and southern Asia, and complex societies were emerging in China, Europe, and South America.

In southern Asia, the **Indus civilization** (see 2700–2500BCE) emerged in its mature form around 2500BCE, stretching 1,700km (1,060 miles) from east to west and 1,300km (800 miles) from north to south. The region's prosperity was based on farming, mining, crafts, and trade. More than 100 sites have been excavated, including the cities of Mohenjo-daro, Harappa, and Dholovira.

Mohenjo-daro and **Harappa** were **well-planned** cities laid out on a grid system. Each city was protected by brick walls and dominated by a **citadel** overlooking a "lower town" of public buildings and residential **town houses** of one or two storeys. The residential areas were seemingly divided by industry, such as pottery, bead-making, and metalworking.

Indus cities and towns had the most **advanced plumbing** system in the ancient world, with enclosed wells and covered drains. Latrines emptied waste into drains, which ran below the streets.

These urban centres were also connected by extensive **trade links**. Merchants supplied craft products from the valleys to the surrounding regions in return for metal ores, precious stones, and timber. Long-distance trade routes reached as far as Mesopotamia and Afghanistan.

By around 2500 BCE, an **Indus script** of hundreds of signs appeared on seals and pottery. Attempts to decipher the script have failed; hence, many aspects of this culture remain a mystery.

In western Asia, **Mesopotamia** (see 2700–2500BCE) remained a patchwork of small but **powerful city-states**, each controlling the surrounding farmlands where barley, pulses, and date palms were grown. To the west, city-states were developing in Syria and the Levant. A **trade network** linking Mesopotamian towns suggests co-operation between states, but there was **frequent warfare** as well.

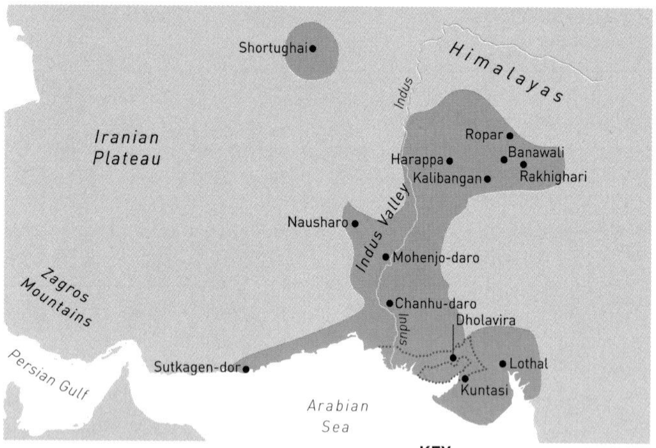

Indus civilization
Excavations suggest that the Indus civilization covered an area far larger than Mesopotamia and Egypt combined.

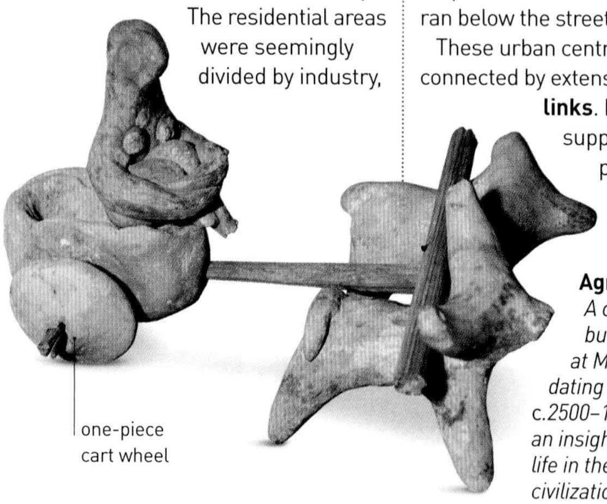

Agrarian lives
A clay model of a bullock cart found at Mohenjo-daro, dating back to c.2500–1900BCE, gives an insight into farming life in the Indus civilization.

2350–2200 BCE

Silbury Hill in Wiltshire, England, is one of the tallest man-made chalk mounds in Europe. These mounds probably had a social or cultural function.

A NEW POWER AROSE IN MESOPOTAMIA c.2334BCE, **King Sargon** (c.2334–2215BCE) from the northern region of **Akkad** defeated Lugalzagesi of Umma to become the ruler of Sumer. Through subsequent campaigns to the Levant, Syria, and Anatolia, Sargon carved out the **world's first empire** – the Akkadian Empire – stretching from the eastern Mediterranean to the Gulf.

Sargon's exploits were recorded in several documents, such as the *Sumerian King List*. His name means "**legitimate king**", which led some scholars to believe that he took power through force. Sargon spoke Akkadian, a Semitic language that replaced Sumerian as the official language of the empire.

> “UNDER HIM **ALL COUNTRIES** LAY [CONTENTED] IN THEIR MEADOWS, AND THE **LAND REJOICED.**”
>
> **Lugalzagesi, king of Sumer,** defeated by Sargon c.2316BCE

Akkadian rule was enforced through regional governors who collected tributes and taxes. The **empire's weakness** lay in its lack of defensible **borders**, and it came under regular **attacks** from neighbouring **hill tribes**. Sargon's grandson, Naram-Sin, extended the empire, but it lasted for only four generations before falling to attacks. Sargon's rule established a practice of statewide bureaucratic controls and standardization in many aspects of economic life.

In **Egypt**, this period saw a **weakening** of the power of the **Old Kingdom** rulers (see 2700–2500BCE), in favour of regional governors called **nomarchs**, who administered different parts of the Nile valley and delta. To the south of the first cataract on the Nile, the kingdom of Nubia also grew **more powerful**. Nubia was centred around the city of Kerma at the third cataract. By the end of the **Sixth dynasty** (c.2184BCE), the

BRONZE AGE EUROPE

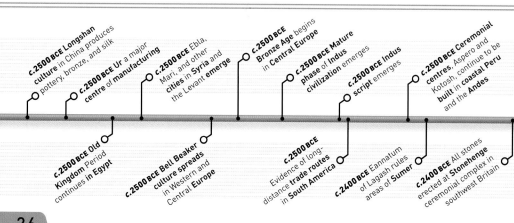

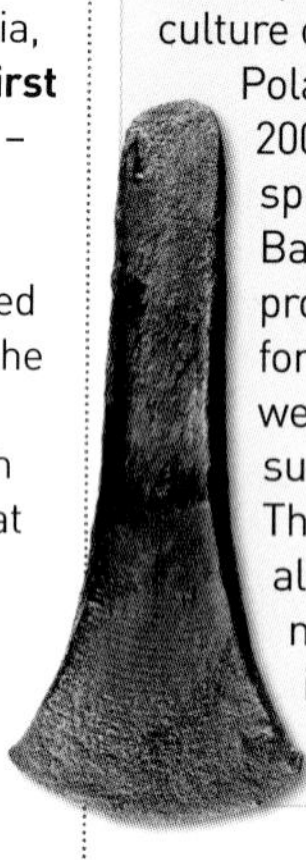

Bronze-working had begun in West Asia c.3200BCE (see 10,000–3000BCE). It was developed by the Únětice culture of Bohemia and Poland c.2500BCE, and 200 years later had spread to Italy and the Balkans. Bronze provided a hard metal for forging armour, weapons, and tools such as this hand axe. The bronze industry also increased trade, making Europe more interconnected than ever before.

- **c.2500 BCE Longshan culture** in China produces pottery, bronze, and silk
- **c.2500 BCE** Old Kingdom Period continues **in Egypt**
- **c.2500 BCE Ur** a major **centre of manufacturing**
- **c.2500 BCE** Ebla, Mari, and other **cities in Syria** and the Levant **emerge**
- **c.2500 BCE Bell Beaker culture spreads** in Western and Central **Europe**
- **c.2500 BCE Bronze Age** begins in **Central Europe**
- **c.2500 BCE Mature phase of Indus civilization** emerges
- **c.2500 BCE** Evidence of long-distance **trade routes** in **South America**
- **c.2500 BCE Indus script** emerges
- **c.2400 BCE** Eannatum of Lagash rules areas of **Sumer**
- **c.2500 BCE Ceremonial centres**, Aspero and Kotosh, continue to be **built** in **coastal Peru** and the **Andes**
- **c.2400 BCE** All stones erected at **Stonehenge** ceremonial complex in southwest Britain
- **c.2350 BCE Lugalzagesi** of Umma **unites all Sumer**
- **c.2345–2181 BCE Sixth dynasty** of Egypt **founded**
- **c.2334–2316 BCE Sargon of Akkad** conquers Sumer to create **world's first empire**

Relief sculptures in Egyptian tombs represented everyday life and religious rituals. This carving from the Sixth dynasty shows boys with sticks, on the left, and youths wrestling, on the right.

authority of the Egyptian rulers had steadily eroded.

In **Western Europe**, the **Bell Beaker culture** flourished. Named after the distinctive shape of **pottery vessels** found in graves, this culture emerged by *c.*2600 BCE in France, Spain, and the Netherlands. Over the next three centuries, it spread to Germany and Britain. Around 2300 BCE, **bronze technology** from Mediterranean regions and from Central Europe started to **spread** northwards **along** the **Rhine** and **Danube**. The increasingly militaristic societies used bronze to create weapons, triggering the appearance of **small chiefdoms** across Europe.

As populations grew, **competition** over **land** and **resources** intensified. Fields were enclosed, farming expanded, and boundary walls built. Imposing structures such as **chalk mounds** were constructed in many areas.

In **South America**, societies continued to develop in two distinct regions: the upland **valleys** and **high plains** of the **Andes**, and along the **Pacific coast** and inland valleys. Andean cultures were based on **farming** and **herding**. **Coastal settlements** such as Aspero (Peru) were unique in their dependence on **fishing** rather than on agriculture. The coastal people grew cotton for textiles, and gourds, which were used as fishing floats.

Akkadian warrior king
This bronze cast of an Akkadian ruler may depict Sargon I or his grandson, Naram-Sin, who extended Sargon's empire.

THE MOUNTAIN PEOPLE OF GUTIUM ATTACKED the Akkadian Empire *c.*2150 BCE. **Sumerian states** such as Kish, Ur, and Lagash took the opportunity to **reassert** their **independence**. For the next 80 years, the city-states vied for control in Mesopotamia. In 2112 BCE, **Ur** under Ur-Nammu (r.2112–2095 BCE) gained ascendancy. The armies of Ur overran eastern Mesopotamia and Elam, and regained much of Sargon's empire.

Ur-Nammu founded the **Third dynasty of Ur**, which witnessed a **revival of Sumerian power**, as well as an artistic and cultural **renaissance**. Sumerian scholars devised a method of counting, based on units of 60. This system is reflected in our modern division of hours into 60 minutes, minutes into 60 seconds, and a circle into 360 degrees.

Ur-Nammu also commissioned the **first ziggurat** in Ur – an imposing stepped platform topped with a temple. The ziggurats later became a characteristic of ancient western Asian architecture.

In *c.*2181 BCE, Egypt's **Old Kingdom collapsed** following a series of natural disasters, including famine. This undermined the authority of the king, who was believed to secure the annual floods that brought fertility to the Nile valley. The rule of Memphis, the capital city of the Old Kingdom, was overthrown as nomarchs and nobles seized control of the provinces. This ushered in a time of **unrest** called the **First Intermediate Period**, the first of the three eras of uncertainty in Egyptian history. For 140 years, kingdoms such as Herakleopolis in central Egypt vied for control with Thebes in the south. In *c.*2040 BCE, the Theban ruler Nebhepetre **Mentuhotep** defeated his rivals and **united Egypt** once more, beginning the start of what came to be known as the **Middle Kingdom**.

In China, the Neolithic **Longshan culture** (see 3200 BCE) continued to develop along the Yellow River in Shandong province. According to Chinese historical tradition, the **first dynasty**, **Xia** (Hsia), was **founded** by Yu the Great. However, **no archaeological evidence** has been found to confirm the existence of **a centralized state** in China at this time.

100 THOUSAND
THE LIKELY **POPULATION** OF **UR** *c.*2100

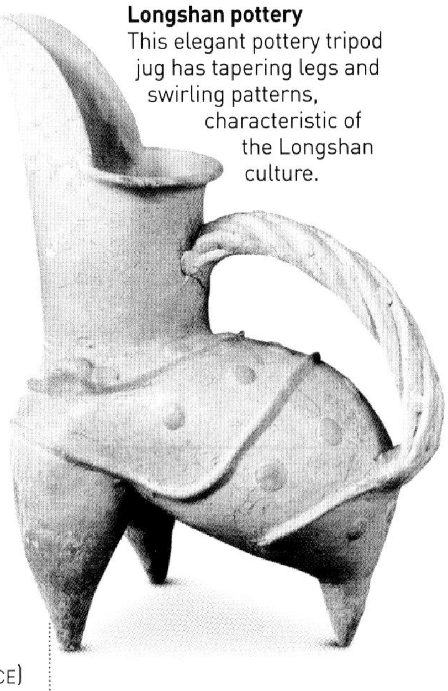

Longshan pottery
This elegant pottery tripod jug has tapering legs and swirling patterns, characteristic of the Longshan culture.

By the end of the 3rd millennium, **Europe's first civilization** was emerging on the Mediterranean island of **Crete**, which lay at the heart of Mediterranean trade routes. Known as the **Minoan civilization**, it grew prosperous through **trade** and **farming**. Cretan farmlands produced wheat, olives, wine, and wool, which could be easily transported by sea. The Minoans also made bronzework, pottery, and dyes for export. By 2000 BCE, Crete was home to several small kingdoms.

c.2300 BCE Bronze Age begins in southern Europe, in Italy and the Balkans

2278–2184 BCE Reign of **Pepy II** of the Sixth dynasty in **Egypt**

c.2205 BCE Xia dynasty founded in eastern **China** by Yu the Great, according to Chinese tradition; said to have ruled until 1766

c.2181 BCE Sixth dynasty and Old Kingdom period **ends** in **Egypt** after natural disasters weaken authority of ruler

c.2181 BCE First Intermediate Period begins in Egypt (to 2040 BCE)

c.2150 BCE Gutians defeat Akkadians; **city-states** of **Mesopotamia**, such as Lagash, **reassert independence**

c.2150 BCE Nubian kingdom emerges south of Egypt, based at Kerma on Third Cataract of Nile

c.2112–2095 BCE Reign of **Ur-Nammu** of Ur reunites much of Mesopotamia; rebuilds Ur's temple as a ziggurat

2112 BCE Third Dynasty of Ur, founded by Ur-Nammu (to 2004 BCE)

c.2050 BCE Emergence of the **Minoan palace civilization**, Crete

c.2040 BCE Nebhepetre **Mentuhotep** of Thebes defeats rivals to **unite Egypt**

c.2040 BCE Mentuhotep founds a new **capital** at Itj-Towy near Memphis; **Middle Kingdom begins**

2004 BCE City of **Ur falls** to Elamites, ending **dynasty of Ur**

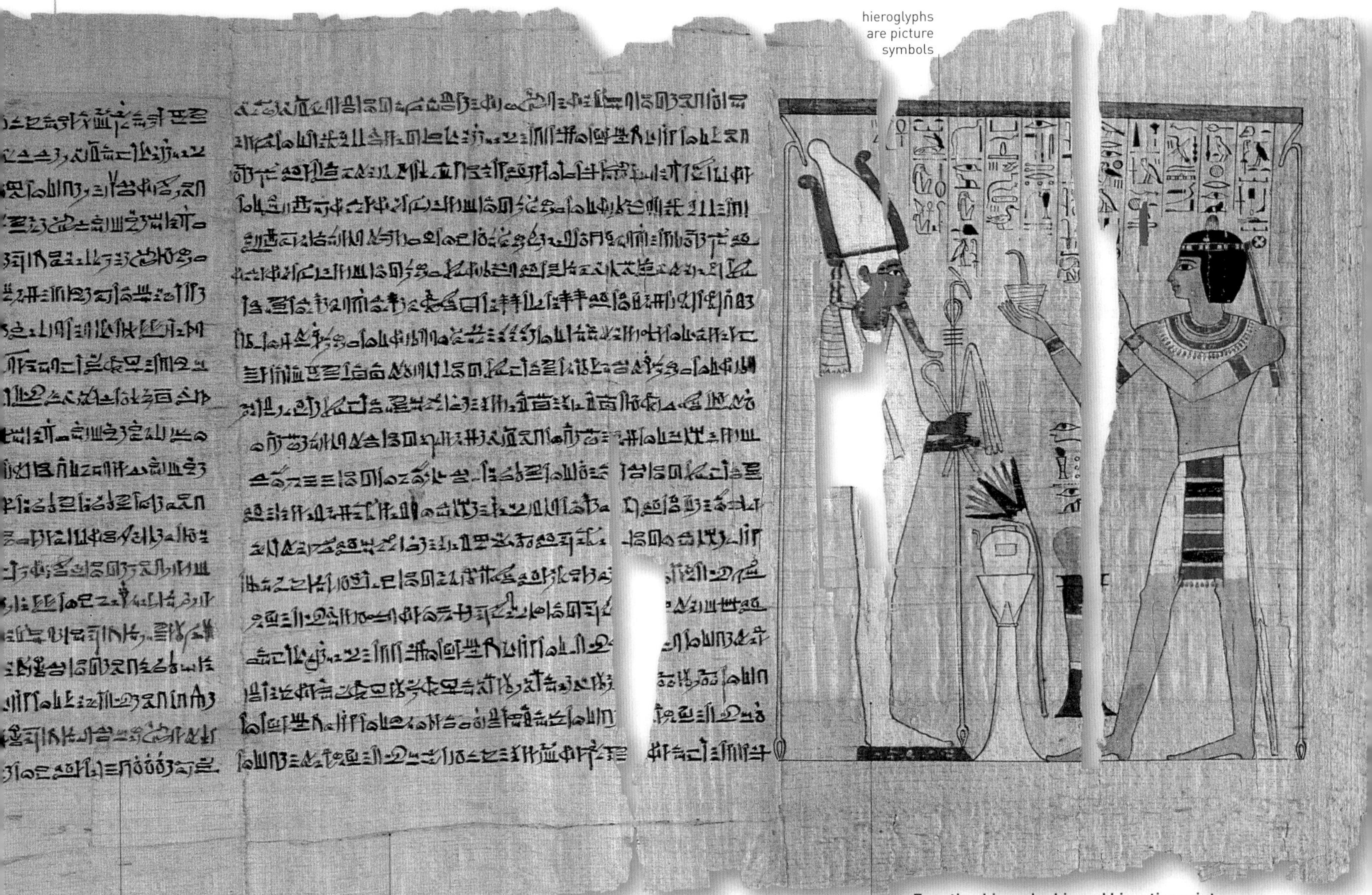

Egyptian hieroglyphic and hieratic script
This ancient Egyptian papyrus manuscript shows two forms of Egyptian writing: hieratic script (left) and hieroglyphic script (right) above the two figures. Hieroglyphic is an elaborate script in which signs take a highly pictorial form, while hieratic is a simplified version of hieroglyphic for ease of speed and writing.

Prehistory
Pictograms
Pictures painted on walls of caves up to 25,000 years ago are considered a precursor to writing, recording information that could then be understood by others.

Cave images by Anasazi Indians

3300 BCE
Cuneiform
The first proper written script is developed by the Sumerians of Mesopotamia. Writing with a reed stylus creates a wedge-shaped impression on tablets of wet clay, which then dry hard.

Mesopotamian tablet

***c.*3200 BCE**
Egyptian hieroglyphs
Egyptian writing develops 100 years after cuneiform. This script begins as a form of picture writing, and includes signs for words and also sounds. It remains in use until the 4th century CE.

***c.*1900 BCE**
Chinese writing
The first surviving Chinese writing appears on oracle bones, used in divination. This ancient script is still in use today. Chinese script involves 50,000 characters that stand for words.

Chinese paper scroll

8th century BCE
The Greek alphabet
The first alphabets, using only consonants, develop in the Levant by *c.*1150 BCE. They include the Phoenician alphabet, which spreads to the Greeks through trade, who add vowels.

Greek wax tablet

***c.*6th century BCE**
Parchment
Made from dried and processed animal skins, parchment becomes a popular medium for writing around the 6th century BCE, taking over from papyrus, a paper made from reeds.

Chinese parchment scroll

100
The Roman alphabet
The Romans adapt the Greek script to write Latin. Through the Roman Empire, this alphabet spreads across Europe and is used for personal as well as official correspondence.

THE STORY OF WRITING

FROM CAVE PAINTINGS TO THE DIGITAL AGE, WRITING IN ITS VARIOUS FORMS HAS ALWAYS BEEN AN IMPORTANT PART OF OUR CIVILIZATION

The development of writing was an amazing breakthrough as it allowed people to communicate over distance and record information for posterity. Writing evolved separately in different cultures: in Mesopotamia, Egypt, and the Indus Valley before 2500 BCE and later in Crete, China, and Mesoamerica.

Some scholars consider that prehistoric cave paintings featuring images and symbols constitute a form of writing. The first proper script was developed by the Sumerians of Mesopotamia (now Iraq) around 3300 BCE. Soon, a number of different ancient cultures had developed writing, usually to keep economic records or track of time. As writing developed, it was commonly used to reinforce the authority of rulers. Many early texts, including monumental ones in stone, glorify the deeds of kings and attribute their success to divine approval.

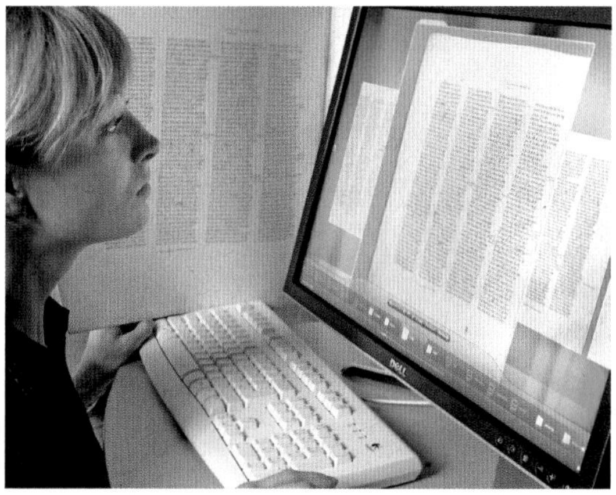

Writing systems can be divided into three types, according to the function of the signs used: logographic, syllabic, and alphabetic. However, some scripts make use of two types of signs. In logographic scripts, each sign stands for a whole word; Chinese writing is an example, although it also uses syllabic signs. The drawback is that a very large number of symbols are needed (Chinese has 50,000 characters). In syllabic scripts, signs stand for syllables. A smaller but still large number of signs are needed – 700 in Babylonian cuneiform. In alphabetic scripts, each sign stands for a sound. Far fewer symbols are needed – usually around 26. The first alphabets developed in the Levant between 1450 and 1150 BCE. For years, the spread of writing was limited by the labour involved in hand-copying texts, but this changed with the invention of printing. In the late 20th century, writing became electronic with the invention of word processors. In the 1990s, the spread of information was again revolutionized by the arrival of the Internet.

Ancient texts in the digital world
Nowadays, ancient texts can be viewed digitally. Here, a student examines a digitized page of the Codex Sinaiticus, *handwritten in Greek over 1,600 years ago.*

Roman mosaic

Modern sign

PICTOGRAPHIC SYMBOLS

Pictograms, or picture signs, are an ancient form of communication. Some scholars do not consider pictograms to be "true" writing, since the symbols do not convey the sounds of words in any language. For example, the pictures above – from a house in Roman Pompeii dating to 79 CE, and a modern sign – convey the same warning. The symbol can be read in any language, for example as *canis*, *chien*, *Hund*, or dog. Those words convey the same idea but reproduce the sounds of different languages – Latin, French, German, and English. Pictograms have limited use but remain widespread, appearing for example on street signs, maps, and clothes labels.

4th century
The codex
The codex, or manuscript in book form, gradually supersedes the roll of parchment. Originally developed by the Romans, the use of codices spreads with the Christian religion.

7th century
Arabic script
The Arabic alphabet is used to write down the Qur'an, the holy book of Islam. Its use spreads with the Islamic faith to become one of the world's most widely used scripts.

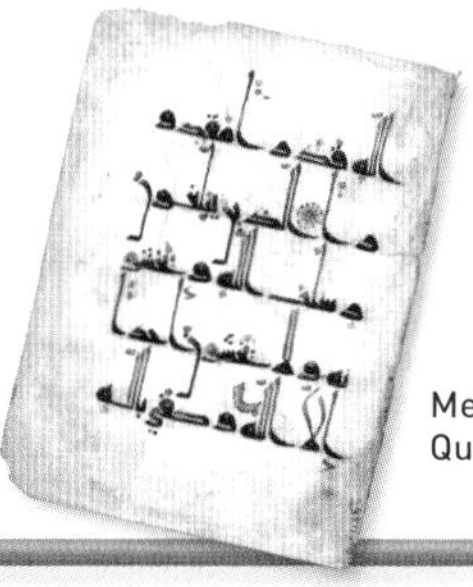

Medieval Qur'an

7th–9th centuries
Illuminated manuscripts
In early medieval times, the use of writing spreads through the copying of Christian texts. Illuminated manuscripts are highly decorative, with ornate capital letters and marginal illustrations.

Book of Durrow

c.1450
Invention of printing
In medieval times, the laboriousness of copying by hand limits the spread of writing. The invention of printing using moveable type makes writing far more accessible. In 1500, an estimated 35,000 texts are in print.

1867–1868
The typewriter
American inventor Christopher Latham Sholes helps to build the first practical typewriter. The patent is sold to Remington, who puts the first typewriters on sale in 1874.

The Remington Model I

1884
The fountain pen
The first practical fountain pen is produced by American inventor L.E. Waterman, and quickly replaces the quill pen. Biros, invented by László Bíró, are in use by the 1940s.

Waterman fountain pen

1971
Writing enters the digital age
In 1971, Ray Tomlinson sends the first electronic message (email) from one computer to another. Emails become popular with the spread of personal computers in the 1980s.

1990–present
Text messaging
In the 1990s, the first text messages are sent via mobile phones. Texting becomes very popular in the 2000s. In 2009, more than 1.5 trillion text messages are sent.

Smartphone

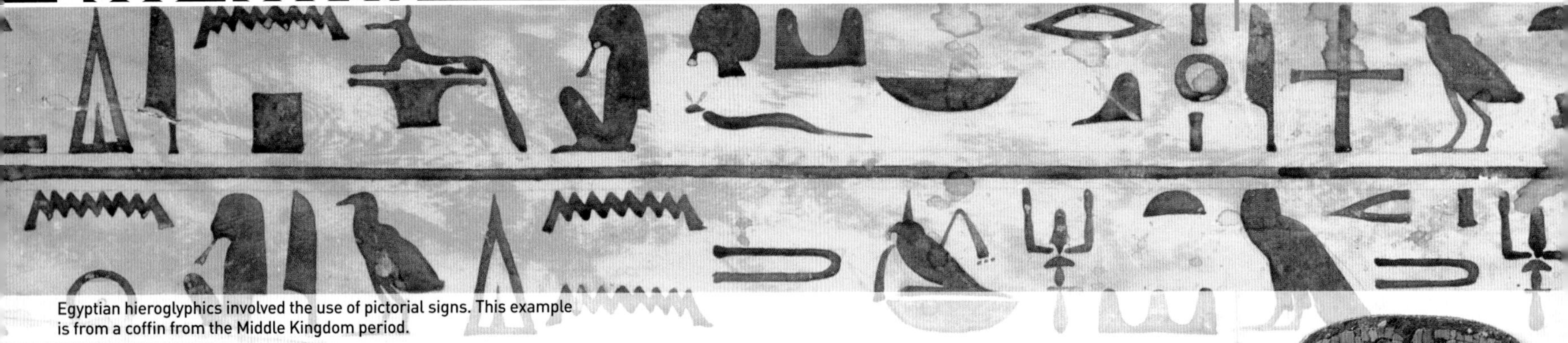

Egyptian hieroglyphics involved the use of pictorial signs. This example is from a coffin from the Middle Kingdom period.

THE MINOAN CIVILIZATION, named after the legendary King Minos, **flourished** on the **Aegean island** of **Crete** in the early 2nd millennium, reaching its peak between 2000 and 1600 BCE. It is thought that Crete's **prosperity** was based on the **export** of **pottery**, **gold**, and **bronze**, as well as possibly grain, wine, and oil, to Egypt, Cyprus, and Palestine. The Minoans established colonies in many parts of the Aegean, including the islands of Kythera, Thera, Melos, and Rhodes, and at Miletos on the Turkish mainland.

The farmlands of Crete were ruled from cities with **central palaces** that housed workshops, the administration, religious facilities, and state storerooms. Those at Knossos, Phaestos, Mallia, and Zakros were particularly impressive, judging by their remains. Around 1700 BCE, these palaces were burnt down, and only **Knossos** was **rebuilt**, on a more magnificent scale than before, suggesting its dominance over the entire island. The palace was five storeys high, with rooms opening onto inner courtyards. This maze-like complex is thought to have given rise to the labyrinth in the **legend** of the **Minotaur**, a bull-headed monster.

Bulls certainly featured in Minoan ceremonies. The **deities** worshipped in Minoan shrines seem to have been **female**, with a **goddess of nature** being the most popular. However, details of Minoan culture remain obscure since the Minoan scripts, known as Cretan hiroglyphic and Linear A, have yet to be undeciphered.

In Egypt, King Mentuhotep had reunited the country at the end of the 3rd millennium (see 2350–2000 BCE). Yet, the second of Egypt's eras of strong, centralized rule only **began with** the reign of **Amenemhet I**, from about 1985 BCE, during the Middle Kingdom. In 1965 BCE, his successor **Senwosret I** conquered the land of **Nubia** to the south, extending Egypt's borders as far as the second cataract of the Nile. Nubia yielded gold, copper, and slaves to swell the ranks of Egypt's army. Around a century later, **Senwosret III** also made **Levant** a vassal state of Egypt.

Middle-Kingdom Egypt was **more democratic** than it was during the Old Kingdom period. Rulers presented themselves as shepherds of the state rather than absolute monarchs. The process of **mummification**, once confined to kings, was now **permitted for ordinary citizens**. In order to preserve it as a permanent home for the spirit, the body was dried in natron salt, its vital organs were removed, and it was stuffed with linen and wrapped in bandages.

40

THE NUMBER OF **DAYS** IT TOOK **TO MUMMIFY** A **BODY**

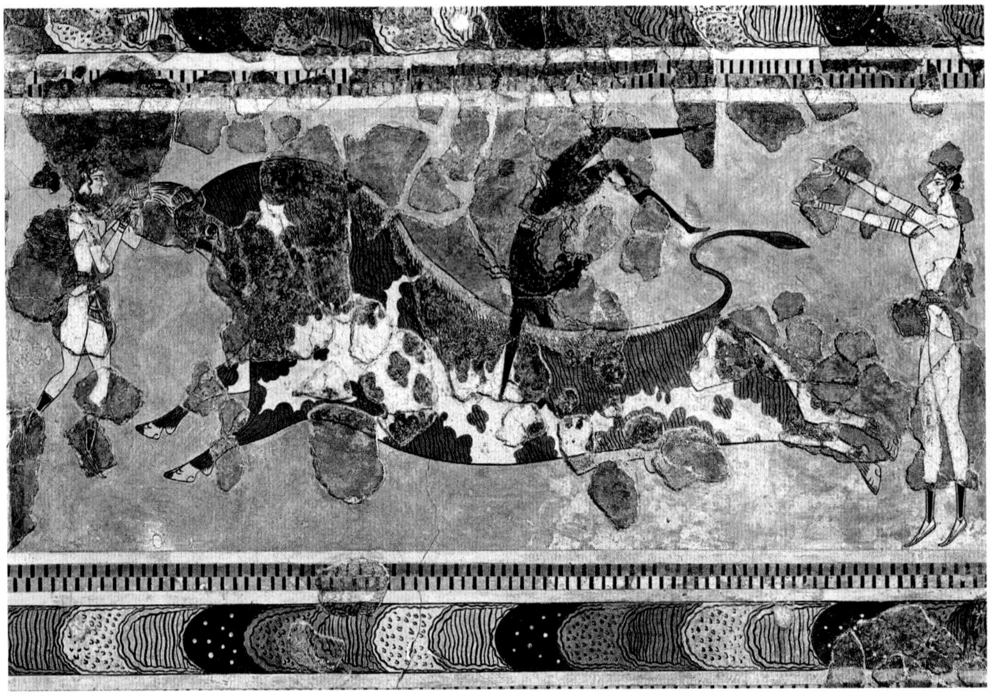

Charging bull

Minoan rituals included a bull-leaping ceremony, in which athletes grasped the bull's horns and vaulted over its back. This Knossos fresco dates back to c.1500 BCE.

Shang bronze

This bronze plate was found at Erlitou, and is of the Xia period. It is inlaid with turquoise mosaic, believed to represent a dragon's scales.

IN CHINA, THE SHANG CIVILIZATION developed along the **Yellow River** by 1850 BCE. According to legend, China's first dynasty was the Xia, but current archaeological evidence points to **Shang** as the **first dynasty**. At Erlitou in Henan province, archaeologists have uncovered a **palace complex** built on a

20,000

THE NUMBER OF **CLAY TABLETS** SO FAR FOUND AT **MARI**

c.2000 BCE City of **Ashur** becomes dominant in northern **Mesopotamia**

c.2000 BCE Maize, beans, and squashes cultivated in southwestern North America; long-distance trade routes in place

c.2000–1750 BCE **Arctic Small Tools population**, ancestors of the Inuit, spread from Alaska across Canada to settle Greenland

c.2000–1600 BCE **Minoan** civilization of Crete reaches height

c.1985–1955 BCE King Amenemhet I brings stability to Egypt during **Middle Kingdom** period

c.1984 BCE Founding of first dynasty of **Babylon**

c.1965–1920 BCE Reign of **Senwosret I** of Egypt

1960 BCE **Senwosret I** of Egypt defeats Nubia and extends his kingdom as far as second cataract on Nile

c.1900 BCE Towns and small kingdoms developing in **Anatolia**

c.1900 BCE City of **Erlitou** constructed around Yellow River, China

c.1900–1700 BCE **Indus civilization declines**; its cities gradually abandoned

1813–1781 BCE Reign of Shamshi-Adad; conquers northern Mesopotamia to establish **Kingdom of Upper Mesopotamia**, with its capital at Shubat-Enlil

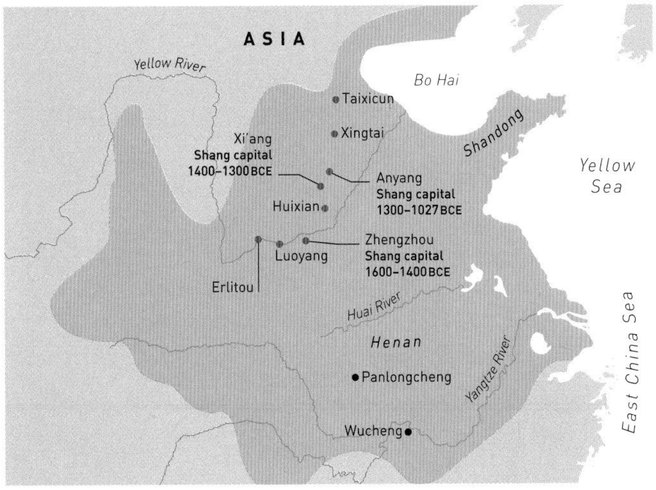

Shang China
The middle course of the Yellow River was the heartland of the Shang civilization from c.1800–1100 BCE. From here, Shang influence, such as bronze-working, spread elsewhere.

platform of compressed earth. They have also unearthed bronze vessels. Evidence suggests that many features that were to characterize Chinese society later, such as a strong **bureaucracy** and the **worship of ancestors**, date back to this time.

In southern Asia, the **Indus civilization**, which had thrived during the 3rd millennium (see 2500–2350 BCE), went into a **decline** by around 1800 BCE. Scholars believe that this was partly caused by the changes in the regimes of the rivers that provided water for irrigation. Cities seem to have been **ravaged by diseases** such as cholera and malaria. Trade with Mesopotamia also declined. Meanwhile, new crops such as millet and rice were introduced. All these factors seem to have led to a **decline in urban culture**, characterized by writing and a centralized bureaucracy, in favour of a **rural-based culture**.

In South America, large-scale cultivation was taking place along the Pacific coast by about 1800 BCE. Substantial settlements such as **El Paraiso** and **Sechin Alto** in Peru were dominated by **massive temple complexes**. Long-distance trade routes linked coastal towns with communities in Andean valleys to the east and beyond. This allowed for the **spread of pottery** from Colombia to Peru by 1800 BCE. Meanwhile, in North America, crops such as sunflowers and gourds began to be cultivated in the east.

In Western Asia, the fall of the Ur III Empire led to the **rise of** two states – **Assyria** in the north and **Babylon** in the southeast – which were to dominate Mesopotamia for the next 1,500 years. The first dynasty of Babylon was established in c.1894 BCE. In the north, the city of **Ashur** became an important trading centre in the 20th century BCE. In 1813 BCE, it was taken over by the Amorite king **Shamshi-Adad**, who **carved out a kingdom** in northern Mesopotamia. This kingdom was a forerunner of the **Greater Assyrian Empire** of the 9th century BCE (see 900–800 BCE).

Clay tablets recovered from Mari in central Mesopotamia hold records of trade and tributes levied by Assyria from vassal-states. Writing from this period included copies of the earliest surviving work of literature, *The Epic of Gilgamesh.*

Sumerian hero
Tablets and stone carvings from the Old Babylonian period provide a record of the Epic of Gilgamesh, *previously passed down in the oral tradition.*

> **“ IF A MAN PUTS OUT THE EYE OF AN EQUAL, HIS EYE SHALL BE PUT OUT. ”**
>
> Law Code of Hammurabi, king of Babylon

WHEN THE ASSYRIAN KING SHAMSHI-ADAD died in 1781 BCE, he was succeeded by his son Ishme-Dagan. During his reign, **Assyria declined**, allowing the state of Babylon to come to the fore. During the reign of Shamshi-Adad, Babylon was probably a vassal state of Assyria, but as Assyria declined, **King Hammurabi** of Babylon saw his chance to seize a wider kingdom. From 1760 BCE, Hammurabi embarked on a series of conquests, which made **Babylon** the **region's foremost state**. Between 1763–1762 BCE, he defeated Elam to the east and Larsa, which controlled Sumer, to the south. Between 1757–1755 BCE, King Hammurabi conquered much of northern Mesopotamia and took the city of Eshnunna after diverting its water supply.

Hammurabi introduced the Babylonian law code in the region under his control. Its 282 laws covered property, family, trade, and business practices. The **Law Code of Hammurabi** is famous for punitive laws which meted out punishments in the same measure as the crime committed – "an eye for an eye". However, it is thought that the law code was more of a moral statement of principle than an enforced judicial system. As such, the code bound the powerful and wealthy as well as ordinary people; the strong were exhorted to refrain from oppressing the weak.

Set in stone
Hammurabi's code was inscribed on stone pillars called stele. This stele shows the god of justice Shamash (right) dictating laws to the king.

c.1800 BCE Shang civilization begins in China

c.1800 BCE Ceremonial centre of **La Florida** built in **Peru**

1792–1750 BCE Reign of **Hammurabi** of Babylon; establishes **Babylonian Empire** in Mesopotamia and promulgates a lawcode for use throughout his empire

1766 BCE Traditional date for founding of **Shang dynasty** by King Tang, according to Chinese history

c.1750 BCE Large ceremonial complex of **Sechin Alto** constructed in **Peru**

c.1750 BCE Linear A script comes into use in Crete

c.1725 BCE Middle Kingdom in Egypt torn by unrest; start of **Second Intermediate Period** (to c.1540)

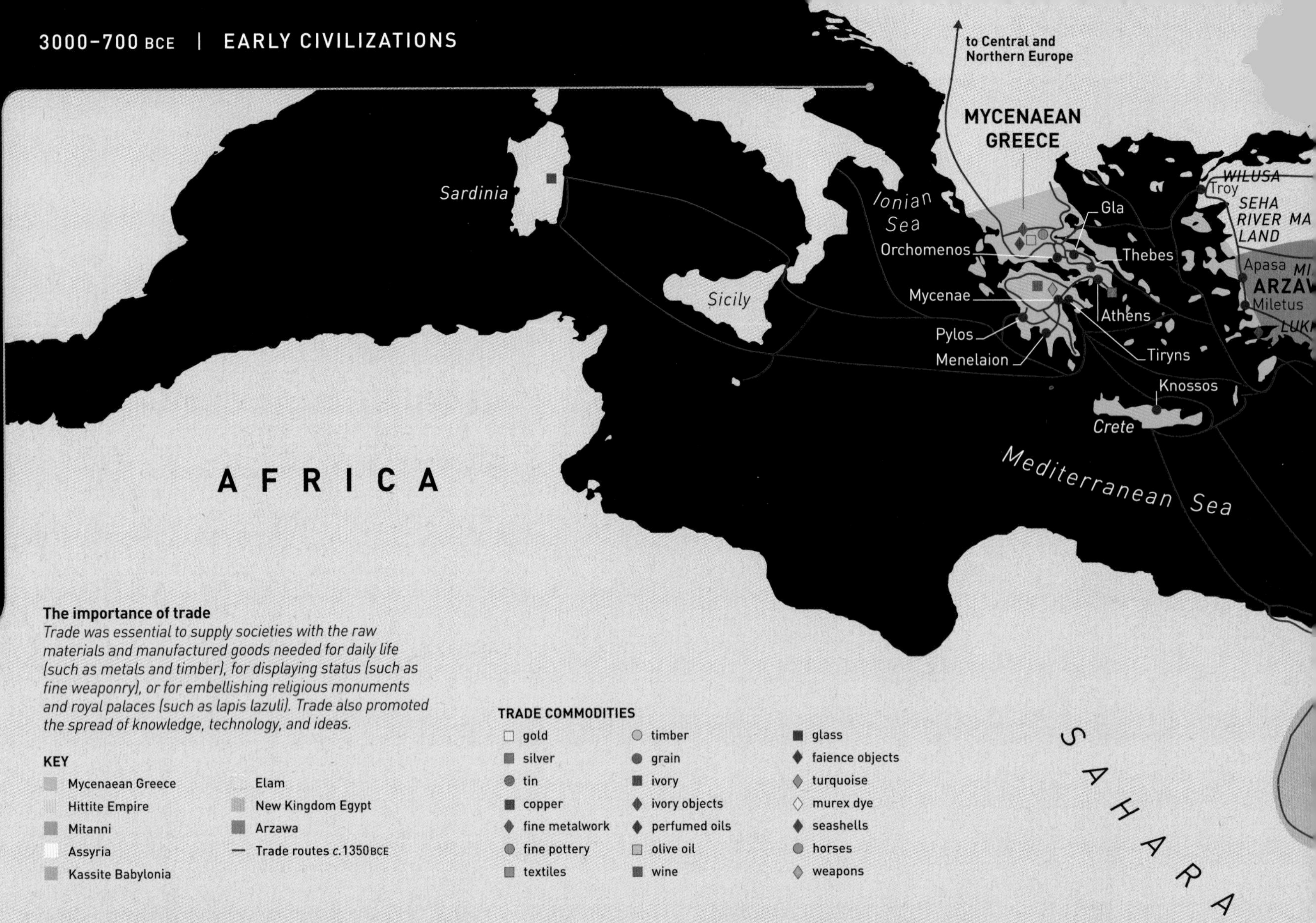

The importance of trade
Trade was essential to supply societies with the raw materials and manufactured goods needed for daily life (such as metals and timber), for displaying status (such as fine weaponry), or for embellishing religious monuments and royal palaces (such as lapis lazuli). Trade also promoted the spread of knowledge, technology, and ideas.

ANCIENT EMPIRES

THE BIRTH OF ADVANCED SOCIETIES

In the 3rd millennium BCE, states emerged in Egypt, Mesopotamia, and the Indus. Urban society was consolidated in Western Asia in the 2nd millennium, and powerful states vied for control of lands; in contrast, in South Asia, towns disappeared. Complex societies emerged in China and the Americas.

The exceptional agricultural productivity of the Nile, Euphrates, Indus (see p.26), and Yellow River (see p.31) valleys undoubtedly played a part in the precocious emergence of civilizations in these regions. So did international trade, which was also important in the development of the first New World civilizations. Trade also enabled many neighbouring societies to achieve prosperity: through time they developed complex cultures increasingly focused on urban centres, and came into competition for resources and markets. High-level diplomacy was essential to the smooth operation of international trading networks and to success in inter-state power struggles. Royal letters found in the Egyptian capital, Akhetaten (Amarna), provide a fascinating picture of relations between the 14th-century BCE rulers of the rival great states of the eastern Mediterranean.

“ FOR A **LONG TIME** WE HAVE HAD GOOD RELATIONS BETWEEN US **KINGS...** ”

Babylonian king Burnaburiash II to Egyptian pharaoh Akhenaten, from the Amarna letters, 14th century BCE

THE WORLD PICTURE

Urbanism and complex societies became more widespread during the 2nd millennium BCE. While they shared many features such as trade, high agricultural productivity, dense populations, and their managerial needs, urban societies took many different forms. In the Americas, large ceremonial complexes with residential suburbs provided the focus for the communities of the wider region, strongly connected by shared religion and trade.

Advanced centres
This map shows established and emerging civilizations in the later 2nd millennium BCE. Societies of farmers and hunter-gatherers occupied other regions.

KEY
- Chavín
- Olmec
- Shang
- Mycenaeans
- Egypt
- Babylonia
- Assyria
- Hittites
- Mitanni
- Elam

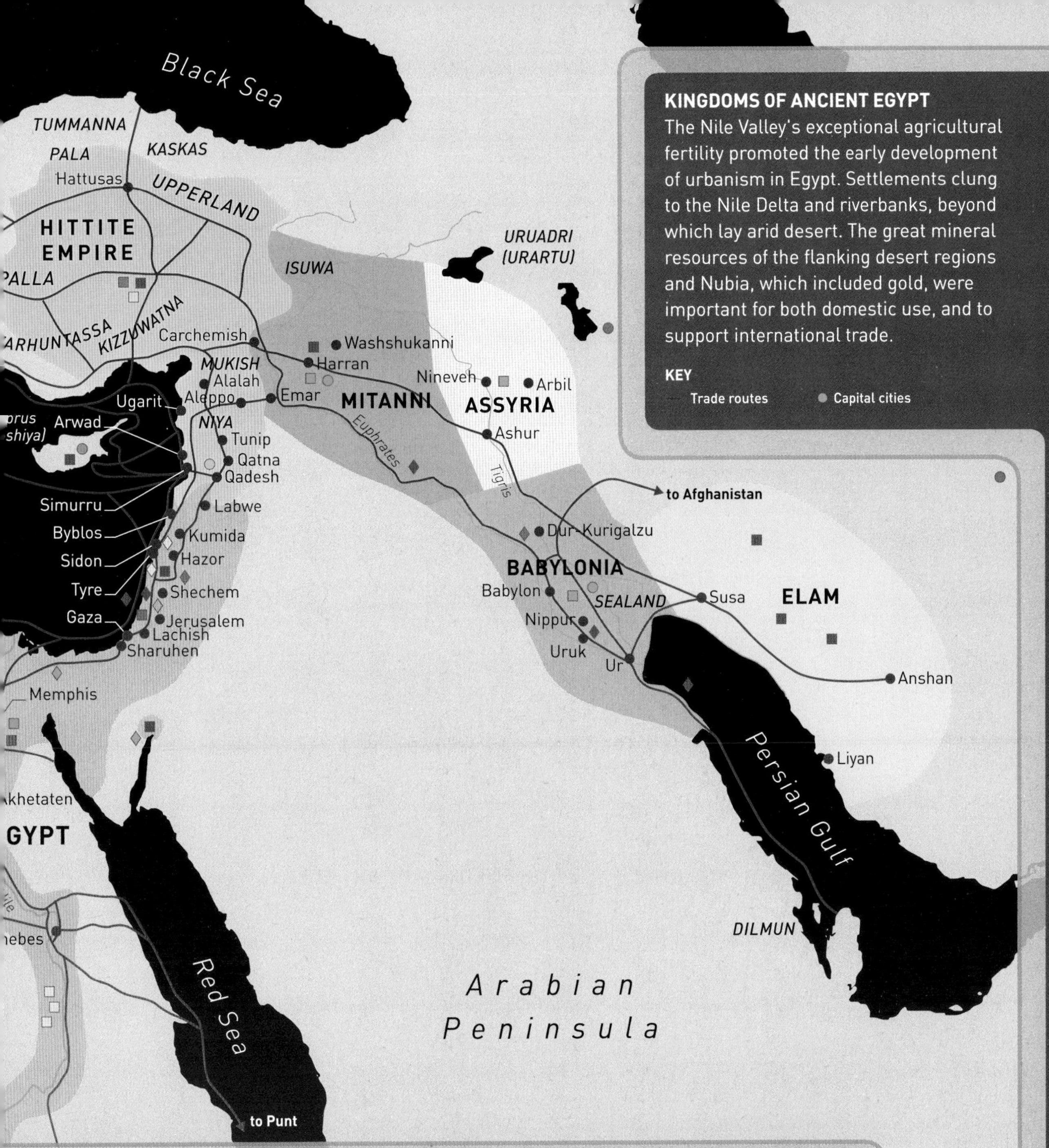

KINGDOMS OF ANCIENT EGYPT

The Nile Valley's exceptional agricultural fertility promoted the early development of urbanism in Egypt. Settlements clung to the Nile Delta and riverbanks, beyond which lay arid desert. The great mineral resources of the flanking desert regions and Nubia, which included gold, were important for both domestic use, and to support international trade.

KEY

Trade routes

Capital cities

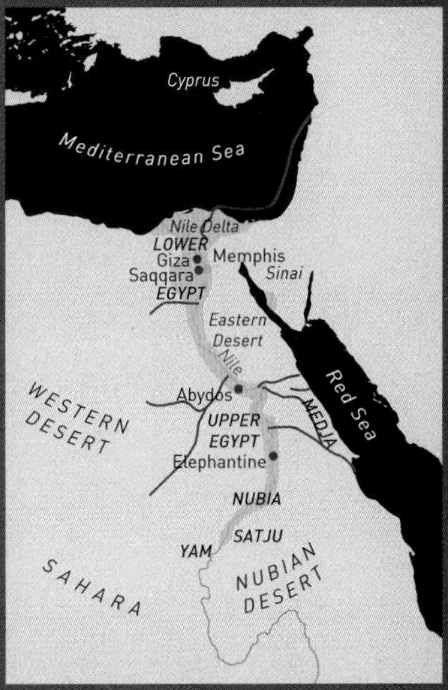

Old Kingdom ***c.*****2686–2181 BCE**
Rulers exercised centralized control and commanded impressive resources, as shown by the pyramids at Giza.

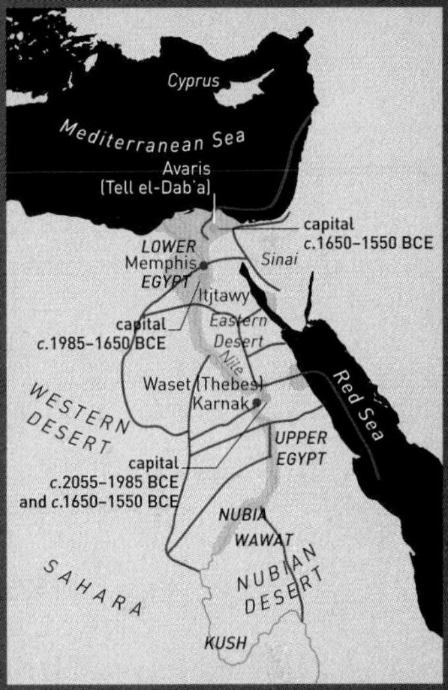

Middle Kingdom ***c.*****2040–1640 BCE**
Decorated tombs record prosperous life under the stable 12th dynasty, but the state disintegrated under later rulers.

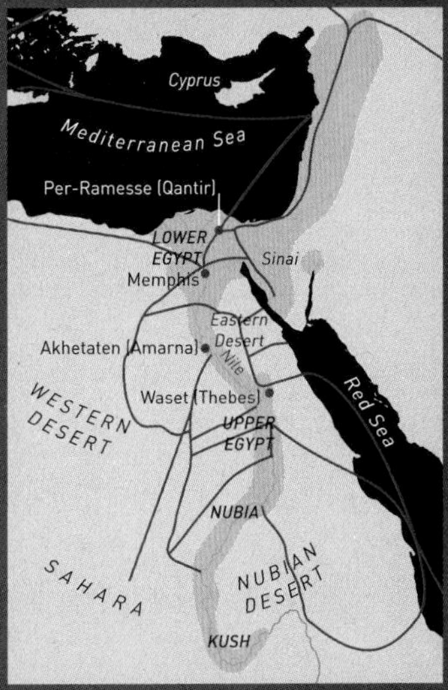

New Kingdom ***c.*****1550–1069 BCE**
Egypt reached its greatest power and prosperity, conquering Nubia and the Levant, and building several temples.

1650–1550 BCE

Hattusas, the Hittite capital, was founded by Hattusalis I in 1650 BCE and destroyed in 1180 BCE.

AFTER HAMMURABI'S DEATH in 1750 BCE, the Babylonian Empire (see 1850–1790 BCE) declined. At the same time, other powers were on the rise, such as the **Hurrians** of Mitanni in Syria, and the **Hittites** of Anatolia in Turkey. By 1650 BCE, the Hittites had built an extensive kingdom in central Anatolia, with its capital at Hattusas. The Hittites had developed advanced bronze- and **iron-working** skills and they were also known to be **fierce fighters**. In 1595 BCE, the Hittite king **Mursilis** (r.1620–1590 BCE) **raided Babylon** and expanded his empire. However, he was killed soon after, and the empire shrank back for about a century.

In Egypt, the **Middle Kingdom** (see 2000–1850 BCE) was **waning** by 1670 BCE, partly due to erratic floods in the Nile. As regional governors became more powerful, **civil war** broke out.

Outsiders soon took advantage of the unrest. The **Nubians** won back lands that the Egyptians had taken earlier (see 2000–1850 BCE). In 1650 BCE, the **Hyksos** from the Levant seized Lower Egypt, but Upper Egypt remained under the control of Egyptian kings.

IRON-WORKING

The Hittites developed iron smelting by *c.*1500 BCE. At first iron was used only in luxury objects, such as in the decoration of this box from Acemhoyek. Later, as technology developed, iron was used to create superior weapons. Though the Hittites traded iron goods, they kept this technology secret for about 300 years. Around 1200 BCE, iron-working spread to Greece, and then to Central Europe by *c.*750 BCE – the dawn of the Iron Age.

Man and beast
The Hittite Empire was known for its bronze craftsmanship. Bronze weapons and artefacts fetched a high price. This statuette of a man and a horse was probably a commission.

1550–1400 BCE

Built over 300 years, the temple complex at Karnak, Egypt, includes the world's largest temple, dedicated to Amun-Re, the patron deity of the pharaohs.

IN *c.*1550 BCE, THE THEBAN KING Ahmose I (r.1550–1525 BCE) **drove** the **Hyksos** from Lower Egypt, ushering in the third period of settled rule in Egypt, known as the **New Kingdom** (*c.*1550–1070 BCE). During this time, **Egyptian rulers** assumed the **title "pharaoh"**, meaning "great house". A succession of warrior kings campaigned to expand Egypt's boundaries once more. **Tuthmosis I** (r.1504–1492 BCE) **drove** the **Nubians** back in the south and recaptured Sinai and parts of Syria and Palestine. Under **Tuthmosis III** (r.1479–1425 BCE), Egypt controlled a strip along the Mediterranean coast and north of the Euphrates (see p.33).

The conquered states paid huge annual tributes to Egypt, a part of which was spent building one of the world's largest **religious sites at Karnak** and the impressive mortuary temple **of Queen Hatshepsut** (r.1473–1458 BCE).

2000
THE NUMBER OF **NAMES** FOR **GODS** AND **GODDESSES** IN **ANCIENT EGYPT**

Egyptian religion was very complex. Every village, town, and district had its own patron deity. In paintings and sculptures, many deities were shown with animal heads, representing their most important attributes. For example, the falcon god Horus protected the king, while the ibis-headed Thoth was the patron god of scribes.

By 1600 BCE, a new civilization emerged on the Greek mainland. Its people are now known as the **Mycenaeans**, after the fortress-palace of Mycenae, believed to be the home of the mythical king Agamemnon from Homer's *Iliad*. However, the Mycenaeans

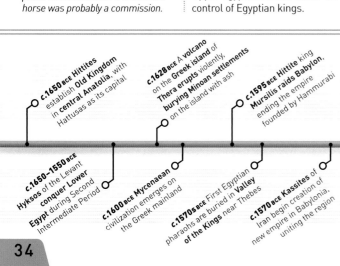

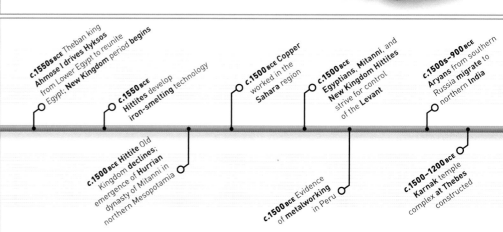

Mask of gold
German archaeologist Heinrich Schliemann found this funerary mask at a grave in Mycenae, and claimed it belonged to King Agamemnon.

- ***c.*1650 BCE Hittites** establish **Old Kingdom** in **central Anatolia**, with Hattusas as its capital
- ***c.*1650–1550 BCE Hyksos** of the Levant **conquer Lower Egypt** during Second Intermediate Period
- ***c.*1628 BCE** A **volcano** on the **Greek island** of **Thera erupts** violently, **burying Minoan settlements** on the island with ash
- ***c.*1600 BCE Mycenaean** civilization emerges on the Greek mainland
- ***c.*1595 BCE Hittite** king **Mursilis raids Babylon**, ending the empire founded by Hammurabi
- ***c.*1570s BCE** First Egyptian pharaohs are buried in **Valley of the Kings** near Thebes
- ***c.*1570 BCE Kassites** of Iran begin creation of new empire in Babylonia, uniting the region
- ***c.*1550s BCE** Theban king **Ahmose I drives Hyksos** from Lower Egypt to reunite Egypt; **New Kingdom** period **begins**
- ***c.*1550 BCE Hittites** develop **iron-smelting** technology
- ***c.*1500 BCE Hittite** Old Kingdom **declines**; emergence of **Hurrian** dynasty of Mitanni in northern Mesopotamia
- ***c.*1500 BCE Copper** worked in the **Sahara** region
- ***c.*1500 BCE** Evidence of **metalworking** in Peru
- ***c.*1500 BCE Egyptians**, **Mitanni**, and **New Kingdom Hittites** strive for control of the **Levant**
- ***c.*1500s–900 BCE Aryans** from southern Russia **migrate** to northern **India**
- ***c.*1500–1200 BCE Karnak** temple complex **at Thebes** constructed

Tutankhamun was buried with fabulous treasure. This detail from the pharaoh's throne shows him being anointed by his wife Ankhesenamun.

probably called themselves Ahhiyawa. They had **migrated from** the **Balkans** or Anatolia about 500 years earlier. Their **lands** were a **patchwork of small kingdoms**, each later dominated by a palace-citadel such as the ones at Mycenae, Tiryns, and Pylos. They spread their influence through trade. After the collapse of the Minoan Empire in *c.*1450 BCE, the Mycenaeans took over several sites formerly occupied by the Minoans, including Knossos. After *c.*1400 BCE, they also took over Minoan trade networks and **established settlements** on Rhodes, Kos, and the Anatolian mainland.

The Mycenaeans inherited Minoan arts and crafts, adapting the **Linear A script** to write an early form of Greek known as the **Linear B script**. They were **great traders**, and ventured out to Sicily and Italy. A ship believed to be of Canaanite origin, wrecked off Uluburun on the coast of Turkey, was found to contain tin from Iran or Afghanistan, copper and pottery from Cyprus, ivory and jewellery from Egypt, and Mycenaean swords.

The **late Bronze Age** was a time of **unrest** in **Western Asia**. From 1550–1400 BCE, there was a **struggle between various powers** in the region, including the Hurrians, Hittites, Elamites, Egyptians, and the Kassites. In the 1570s BCE, the Kassites had gained control of Babylon. However, by **1450 BCE**, the **Hittite New Kingdom** was **growing** in **influence**, partly due to an alliance with Egypt. Around this time, the Mitanni dominated Syria, but by the 1400s, the Hittites were fighting for control of the region.

In China, the **Shang civilization** (see 1850–1790 BCE) **flourished** around 1500 BCE, with its rulers dominating a large area of central China. However, the Shang had to regularly fend off threats to their kingdom from nomadic tribes to the north. **Shang capitals** were surrounded by **defensive walls**. Kings and nobles were buried in tombs, which held fabulous grave goods. The Shang capital moved several times during this period. Shang society was believed to be well organized and extremely hierarchical. Writing began around 1900 BCE. Most examples of **early writing** took the form of **oracle bones**, attesting to the Shang rulers' practice of consulting their ancestors on important decisions. Questions concerning the future were inscribed on the bone of an ox or on a turtle shell, which was then struck with a hot metal tool. The way the bone cracked was believed to provide the answer.

Aegean civilizations
Around 1450 BCE Mycenaean influence spread throughout the Aegean, including to several sites that had been part of the Minoan Empire.

IN *c.*1352 BCE, AMENHOTEP IV, a religious reformer, became **Egypt's pharaoh**. He broke with the traditional religion, with its pantheon of gods, and **initiated** the **worship of a single god, Aten**, or sun-disk. He changed his name to Akhenaten, meaning "living spirit of Aten", and founded a **new capital** between Thebes and Memphis. He named it Akhetaten, meaning "horizon of Aten".

Akhenaten's religious reforms were believed to have been unpopular, especially with the influential priestly elite. After his death in *c.*1336 BCE, his son **Tutankhamun** ascended the throne at the age of nine. He restored the old gods and abandoned the new capital. Tutankhamun is believed to have died under mysterious circumstances at 18, and was hastily buried in a minor tomb. It was thought for years that Tutankhamun died of a blow to the head, but the latest evidence suggests he died of blood poisoning after breaking his leg in a chariot crash while out hunting in the desert.

Since the 1570s BCE, Egypt's pharaohs had been buried in rock-cut tombs in the **Valley of the Kings**, on the west bank of the Nile. Rulers hoped their tombs would be safe from robbers, but almost all the **tombs** were **robbed** of their rich goods. However, in 1922, British archaeologist Howard Carter discovered **Tutankhamun's tomb** virtually **intact**. The shrine room had four gilded shrines, holding the king's **coffin and mummy** with a solid gold mask. The other rooms contained jewellery, furniture, golden statues, and musical instruments.

Sun worship
Akhenaten instituted the worship of the sun disk Aten. In this relief carving found at Akhetaten (modern el-Amarna), he is seen worshipping the sun with his wife Nefertiti.

- **c.1400s BCE Bronze working spreads** to Vietnam and Thailand
- **mid-1400s BCE Lapita** people migrate eastward from Melanesia to **colonize Pacific** islands
- **c.1450 BCE Mycenaean trading** network stretches from Sicily to the Levant
- **c.1450 BCE** Minoan palaces on **Crete** destroyed; **Mycenaeans** take **control** of the island
- **c.1400 BCE Shang** capital moves from **Zhengzhou to Xi'ang** in China
- **c.1300s BCE** Hittite king **Suppiluliumas I** (r.1380–1334 BCE) briefly **conquers Syria**, rivalling Egypt in size
- **c.1352–1336 BCE** Reign of **Amenhotep IV**, breaks with Egypt's old religion to worship the sun-disk Aten and takes the name Akhenaten
- **mid-1300s BCE** City of Ashur breaks free from Mitannian rule; **rise of Assyrian** power
- **c.1336–1327 BCE** Brief **reign** of the boy-king **Tutankhamun**; old Egyptian religion restored and Akhetaten abandoned

1300–1200 BCE

The facade of the temple of Ramesses II at Abu Simbel features four colossal seated statues of the pharaoh, but the statue second from left has perished.

TOWARDS THE END OF THE 2ND MILLENNIUM BCE, the eastern Mediterranean and Western Asia were a **mosaic of empires**, which comprised Egypt, Babylonia, Elam, Assyria, and the Hittites in Anatolia. Borders fluctuated as each kingdom strove to gain ascendancy over its neighbours through conquest or diplomacy. In war and peace, **vital trade routes**, through which tin and copper for **bronze** reached the region, remained intact.

A frequent flashpoint for conflict was the **Levant** (modern Syria and Lebanon), which Egypt had lost to the Hittites following the reign of Akhenaten (see 1350 BCE). In the 13th century BCE, Pharaoh Seti I and his son **Ramesses II** campaigned to win it back. Ramesses' 67-year reign (r.1279–1213 BCE) was a time of **stability and prosperity** for Egypt. Through a combination of war, diplomacy, and strategic marriage, Ramesses sought to extend Egyptian influence to Western Asia. In the 1270s BCE, he fought a series of wars with the Hittite king, Muwattalis II, of which the most famous was the **Battle of Qadesh** (c.1274 BCE). Although Ramesses claimed victory at Qadesh, the battle is believed to have been inconclusive, and the Hittites held on to the region.

> “ YOU ARE A **GREAT WARRIOR** WITHOUT EQUAL, **VICTORIOUS** IN SIGHT OF THE WHOLE WORLD. ”
>
> Inscription commemorating the victory of Ramesses II at Qadesh

Ancient propaganda
A detail from the temple of Ramesses II at Abu Simbel shows the king firing an arrow, taking on the Hittite army single-handed at the Battle of Qadesh.

In 1259 BCE, after further campaigns in Syria, Ramesses tried a different tactic, and negotiated a **pioneering peace treaty** with the new Hittite king, **Hattusilis III**. Ramesses also took two Hittite princesses in marriage (he had about seven wives in total). Following the treaty, Ramesses kept up a friendly correspondence with the Hittite ruler, which was recorded on clay tablets in Akkadian cuneiform script.

Ramesses also embarked on an extensive programme of **monument-building**. On Egypt's southern border with Nubia he constructed the magnificent temple of **Abu Simbel**. He founded a new capital at **Per-Ramesses** in Lower Egypt, although Thebes in Upper Egypt remained an important centre. West of Thebes he built a vast mortuary temple, which doubled as a palace, court, and centre of learning.

The late 2nd millennium BCE saw the resurgence of Ashur, in what is now called the **Middle Assyrian Empire** (1350–1000 BCE). Following the death of Shamshi-Adad in 1781 BCE (see 1850 BCE), Ashur had become a vassal, first of Babylon, then of Mitanni. A revival of Ashur's fortunes began under **Ashur-uballit I** (r.1363–1328 BCE), who broke free of Mitannian rule and carved out a kingdom in northern Iraq. His later successors, Shalmaneser I and Tukulti-Ninurta I, continued to gain territory, expanding the kingdom's borders west to conquer eastern Mitanni and briefly, from 1225–1216 BCE, southeast to Babylonia.

In the Aegean, the **Mycenaean** palace-kingdoms of the Greek mainland **continued to thrive.**

1200–1100 BCE

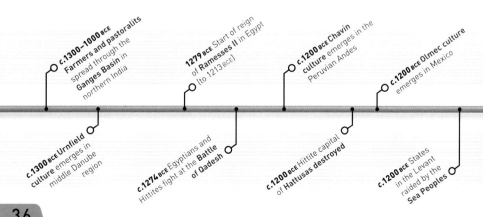

The boulders used to make these walls, now in ruins, at Mycenae on the Greek mainland were so huge, later civilizations believed they were built by giants.

BETWEEN 1250 AND ABOUT 1050 BCE, many of the **powers** that had dominated Western Asia for centuries **went into decline**, and some disappeared altogether. The eastern Mediterranean entered a **time of turmoil**, and many coastal cities were laid waste by unknown invaders – written records of the period give few clues as to their identity. First to succumb were the Hittites, whose capital **Hattusas** was **sacked** and abandoned c.1200 BCE. By c.1180 BCE, Hittite possessions in the Levant were lost and the **empire fragmented**.

These conflicts were most likely instigated by the waves of migrants known collectively as the **Sea Peoples**. These warlike peoples came from many different areas, including Sicily, Sardinia, Greece, Libya, and Anatolia. Whatever their origins, their movements through the eastern Mediterranean in c.1200–1100 BCE led to attacks on Cyprus, Egypt, Anatolia, and Canaan and Syria in the Levant. In 1178 BCE, the Egyptian pharaoh **Ramesses III** drove the Sea Peoples from Lower Egypt, but could not prevent them from colonizing the Levant.

Around 1200 BCE, the **Mycenaean kingdoms** entered a time of upheaval, a result of both internal disintegration and external threats. The defences of many Mycenean palaces were strengthened. Records at Pylos show the inhabitants feared attack from the sea. By 1100 BCE, most of the Mycenaean palaces had been sacked and abandoned. This triggered the so-called **Dark Age of Greece**, when writing fell out of use, not to be reintroduced until the Homeric age (see 800 BCE).

In the late Bronze Age, parts of Europe came to be dominated by the **Urnfield Culture** – named after the practice of cremating the dead and burying the remains in funerary urns, sometimes accompanied by rich grave goods. This culture originated in the **Danube region** in 1300 BCE, and spread to Italy and central and eastern Europe in the following centuries.

Between 1200 and 700 BCE **iron technology** spread northwards from Greece to Central Europe.

> “ THEY CAME **BOLDLY SAILING** IN THEIR WARSHIPS FROM THE **MIDST OF THE SEA,** NONE BEING ABLE TO WITHSTAND THEM… ”
>
> An inscription by **Ramesses II** (r.1279–1213), referring to the Sea Peoples

- **c.1300–1000 BCE** Farmers and pastoralits spread through the **Ganges Basin** in northern India
- **c.1300 BCE Urnfield culture** emerges in middle Danube region
- **1279 BCE** Start of reign of **Ramesses II** in Egypt (to 1213 BCE)
- **c.1274 BCE** Egyptians and Hittites fight at the **Battle of Qadesh**
- **c.1200 BCE Chavín culture** emerges in the Peruvian Andes
- **c.1200 BCE** Hittite capital of **Hattusas destroyed**
- **c.1200 BCE Olmec culture** emerges in Mexico
- **c.1200 BCE** States in the Levant raided by the **Sea Peoples**
- **c.1184 BCE** Reign of **Ramesses III**, Egypt's last great pharaoh, starts (to 1153 BCE)
- **c.1180 BCE Hittite Empire** collapses
- **c.1150 BCE** Mycenaean defences strengthened, indicating **fear of attack**

1100–1000 BCE

“WHEN ALL LONGINGS THAT ARE IN THE HEART VANISH, THEN A MORTAL BECOMES IMMORTAL...”

Krishna Yajur Veda

Iron rapidly replaced bronze in tools and weapons, signalling the end of the **Bronze Age**.

In Mesoamerica, the region's first great civilization, the **Olmec**, was emerging in the lowlands of Mexico's southern Gulf coast. The Olmecs built ceremonial centres, including San Lorenzo, constructed temples and houses on earthen mounds, and carved huge stone heads clad in helmets. They also established long-distance trade routes. Meanwhile, **other cultures** were **emerging**, such as at Cerro Sechin, in what is now Peru.

Stone warrior
Monumental carvings from temples at Cerro Sechin on the Peruvian coast show warriors, torture victims, and human sacrifices.

THE CLOSE OF THE 2ND MILLENIUM SAW MAJOR CHANGES in the power politics of West Asia In 1070 BCE, the Egyptian New Kingdom ended and Egypt entered a time of unrest called the **Third Intermediate Period**, which lasted until 747 BCE (see 800–700 BCE). Historians believe that the power of the pharaohs had been eroded by a priestly elite who had gained control of many areas. By 1000 BCE, all the territories won by New Kingdom pharaohs had been lost.

In **Mesopotamia**, there were **frequent wars** between the Babylonians, Assyrians, and Elamites; the region was also subjected to devastating raids by Aramaean nomads from the west.

Meanwhile, other powers were rising in the region. A Semitic-speaking people, who called themselves **Canaanites**, had inhabited the Levant for centuries, living in city-states that controlled the surrounding territory. They were skilled seafarers and played a major role in international trade. By 1100 BCE, Canaanite port cities such as Arwad, Byblos, Tyre, and Sidon were expanding their operations, establishing trading posts and colonies throughout the eastern Mediterranean. They traded cedarwood from Lebanon, glass- and ivory-ware, metal ores, and most important, an expensive purple dye made from murex shellfish. It was this luxury commodity that caused them to be known by their more familiar Greek name, the **Phoenicians**, after *phoinix*, the Greek for purple.

In China, a new dynasty replaced the Shang in 1027 BCE, when King Wu of the Zhou defeated the last Shang ruler, Di-Xin. The **Zhou dynasty** was to **rule China for 700 years**. This long era is usually divided into two periods: the Western and Eastern Zhou. During the first era the Zhou capital was Zongzhou. This was a **time of prosperity** and strong central control. Zhou territory was divided into fiefs held by trusted noblemen, in return for military allegiance. But many aspects of Chinese tradition already present in the Shang period continued in the Zhou, including ancestor worship and the use of oracle bones for divination.

Meanwhile in Japan, the **Jomon culture**, named after the cord patterns (*jomon*) that decorate its pottery, continued. The Jomon people were still hunter-gatherers, albeit prosperous and sedentary.

In northern India, small groups of nomadic pastoralists had been migrating into the **Ganges basin** from Central Asia since the 1500s BCE. By the 1100s BCE, most had begun to **settle and cultivate crops**. They spoke **Sanskrit**, which became the language of early Indian sacred writings. Sanskrit, an Indo-European language related to Iranian and almost all European languages, is also the ancestor of modern languages such as Hindi and Urdu.

Sacred writings called **the Vedas** were transmitted orally in Sanskrit for many centuries. Although the Vedas are largely religious writings and hymns, the geographical information that they contain not only describes the gradual spread of farmers and pastoralists from the Punjab to the Ganges basin, but also gives some information about conflicts with other groups, and local life at the time. For example, the **division of society** into **varnas** or **castes** is described in the Vedas, first appearing in Book X of *Rigveda*, although there is nothing in the text to suggest that the system was hereditary at the time.

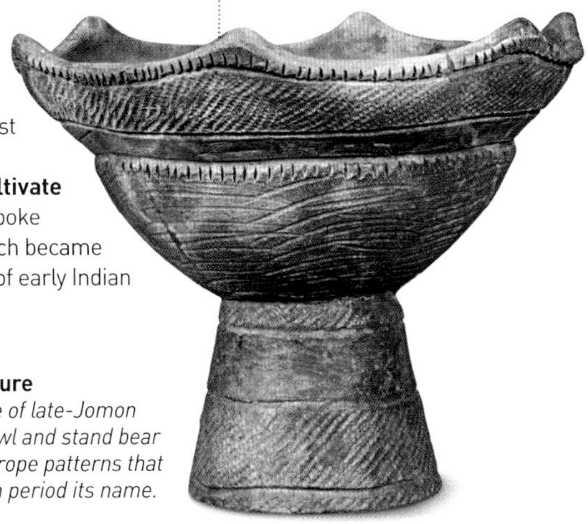

Mark of a culture
In this example of late-Jomon pottery, the bowl and stand bear the distinctive rope patterns that give the Jomon period its name.

c.1100 BCE Mycenaean period ends and **Dark Age of Greece** begins

1069 BCE Start of **Third Intermediate Period** in Egypt

1027 BCE King Wu claims Shang king has forfeited **Mandate of Heaven** to rule

1006 BCE David succeeds Saul as **king of the Hebrews** (Israelites)

c.1000 BCE Phoenicians establish colonies and ports around the Mediterranean

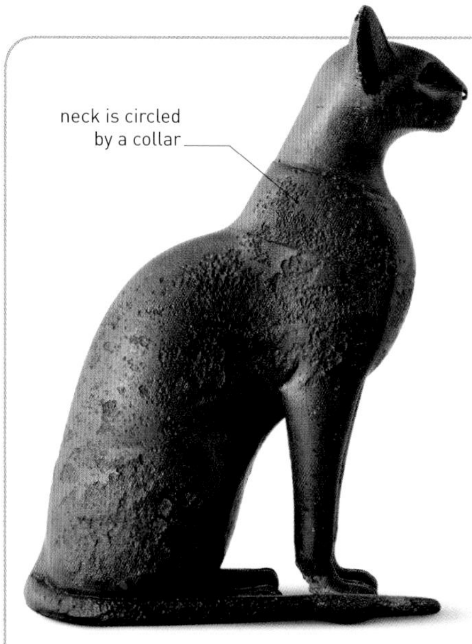

Cat figurine
*c.*600 BCE
This copper alloy figurine sits on a wooden base. Cats were linked with the goddess Bastet, who protected the pharaoh. A hole through the nose originally held a ring.

Statue with stele
*c.*1360 BCE
A carved figure representing a high-priest of Amun holds a stele, or carved slab. These slabs were used as grave or commemorative markers. The inscription is a hymn to the Sun god and lists local dignitaries.

Decorated box of Perpauty
*c.*1370 BCE
This sycamore box belonging to a man called Perpauty may have held linen. All four sides are painted with scenes. This side shows Perpauty and his wife being offered gifts by their son and three daughters.

Duck-shaped flask
*c.*1700 BCE
This jar is carved in the shape of a duck, which appears to be trussed and plucked. It probably held cosmetic paste, such as eye-paint, which was likely removed and applied using a stopper-cum-applicator, now lost.

ANCIENT EGYPT

A REMARKABLE CIVILIZATION REVEALED THROUGH EVERYDAY ITEMS AND TREASURES

Artefacts manufactured over some 2,000 years bear witness to the skills of Egyptian craft workers. They also reflect Egypt's wealth and its trade network, through which ebony, lapis lazuli, and turquoise were imported.

Many of the objects shown here were used in daily life by well-to-do Egyptians. They reflect belief in the afterlife and the practice of burying possessions that it was believed would be used by the dead person's spirit in the afterlife. The ruling classes were buried with great wealth, but almost all of their tombs were stripped of their riches either in antiquity or more recently.

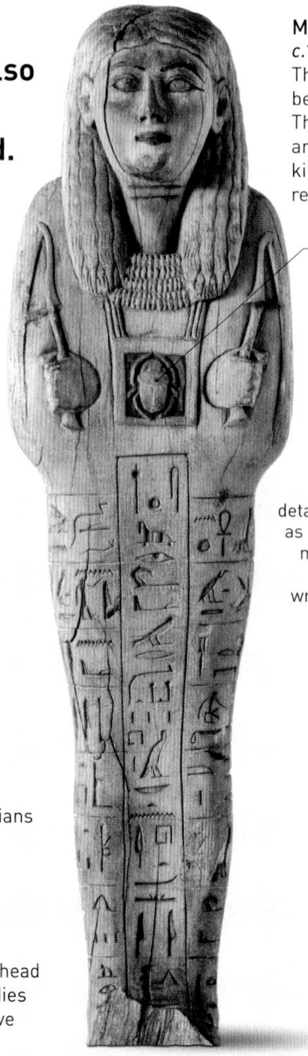

Mummiform shabti
*c.*1300 BCE
This large shabti figure has been carved from wood. The tools the figure carries are traditional symbols of kingship, while the scarab represents the god Khepri.

Shabtis
1292–1190 BCE
Statuettes of servant-figures called shabtis were commonly placed in tombs. The Egyptians believed they would come alive to serve the dead person's spirit in the life to come.

Funerary mask
*c.*1500 BCE
This mask would have been placed over the head of a mummy. The Egyptians mummified bodies because the deceased spirit could not survive unless there was a body for it to return to.

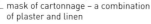

Mummified jackal or dog
*c.*600 BCE
Jackals and, from the 8th century BCE onwards, also dogs were mummified in honour of the jackal-headed god Anubis, who presided over funerals and embalmings.

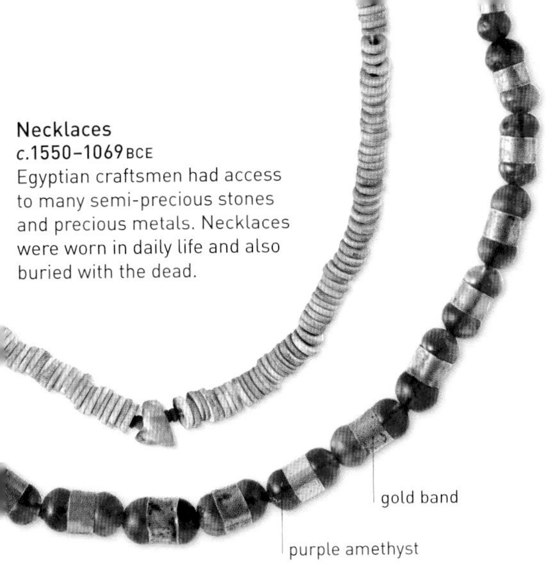

Necklaces
*c.*1550–1069 BCE
Egyptian craftsmen had access to many semi-precious stones and precious metals. Necklaces were worn in daily life and also buried with the dead.

Ear studs and earring
*c.*1550–1069 BCE
Once the basic shapes for these studs and earring were made, strands of glass in a contrasting colour were wound around them. The studs required large perforations in the wearer's lobes.

Wooden comb
*c.*300 BCE
This double-sided comb has a row of longer and shorter teeth. Many Egyptians had short hair and wore wigs. Combs were used to keep both natural hair and wigs tidy.

Cosmetic spoon
*c.*1360 BCE
This spoon for cosmetic paste has been carved from schist in the shape of an ibex, with its head bent over its back, so that its straight horns touch the bowl.

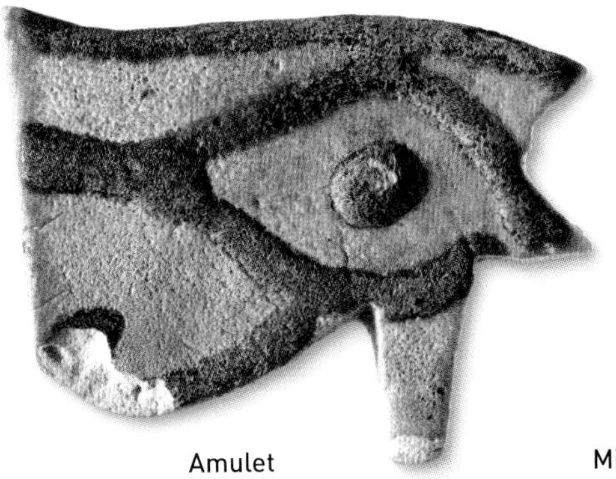

Amulet
912–343 BCE
The wedjat eye symbolizes the eye of the god Horus. This charm was placed on mummies to protect the dead person's spirit in the afterlife. It also symbolized regeneration.

Mirror handle
*c.*1360 BCE
This hardwood mirror setting originally held a polished bronze mirror disc. The handle is carved in the shape of a papyrus column topped with the god Bes – a popular deity.

Scarab pectoral
*c.*1361–52 BCE
This magnificent chest ornament represents the scarab god Khepri rolling the red sun-disk. It was found in the tomb of King Tutankhamun.

Male figure amulet
*c.*2200 BCE
This golden charm shows a kneeling male god clasping two palm ribs. He is probably the god Heh, who symbolized eternity. The palm ribs are notched, representing years.

Frog amulets
*c.*1360 BCE
Frogs were a symbol of life and fertility. Women wore frog amulets for luck. These charms are made of blue faience (pottery) with details picked out in gold.

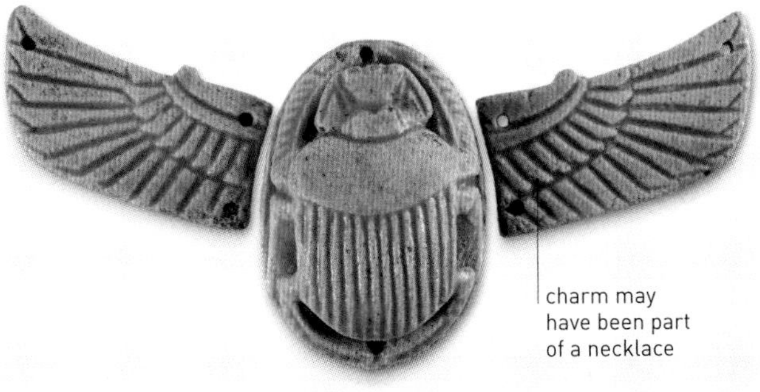

Winged scarab
644–322 BCE
Scarabs were common lucky charms. The scarab beetle was a symbol for rebirth and was worn as jewellery in ancient Egypt.

1000–900 BCE

In the mid-10th century BCE, during the reign of King Solomon, Megiddo (in modern Israel) was an important Israelite fortress and administrative centre.

IN THE 10TH CENTURY BCE, THE PERIOD OF DECLINE in the major powers of Western Asia continued. Egypt, Babylon, and Assyria had weakened, enabling the rise of the short-lived but historically significant **Kingdom of Israel**. The Israelites were Semitic-speaking pastoralists who, according to the Bible, migrated into the land of Canaan in the 1200s BCE. There, they came into conflict with the local Philistines and Canaanites. Around 1000 BCE **King David** (r.1006–965 BCE) **united the Israelite tribes**, and established his capital at **Jerusalem**. David's son **Solomon** (r.*c.*965–928 BCE) increased Israelite territory and built a magnificent palace and temple in the capital, but on his death the kingdom split in two. Eventually Israel and, later, Judah became part of the Assyrian Empire.

Meanwhile, **Assyria** began to re-emerge as a **major power in Mesopotamia**. King Ashur-dan II (r.934–912 BCE) boosted agriculture, bringing prosperity. His successor Adad-nirari II increased Assyria's territory, regaining lands that had been held by the Middle Assyrian Empire in the 13th century BCE.

SHALMANESER III (858–824 BCE)

In the 9th century BCE, King Shalmaneser III of Assyria greatly expanded his empire, with campaigns against Mesopotamian tribes, Israel and Judah, Syria, Urartu, and Anatolia. This black limestone obelisk commemorates his deeds and those of his commander-in-chief, Dayyan-Assur. It details, in cuneiform, the enforced tributes paid by the people he conquered.

Etched in gold
This golden plaque showing the protective wedjat *eye symbol dates from the reign of Psusennes I of the 21st dynasty, when Egypt was divided.*

900–800 BCE

The jaguar featured in many Mesoamerican and South American religions. Here it is depicted in a stone carving from Chavín de Huántar.

THE OLMEC CULTURE CONTINUED TO DEVELOP IN MESOAMERICA in the 9th century BCE. After San Lorenzo was destroyed in *c.*900 BCE, **La Venta** to the northeast became the **main Olmec centre**. This larger settlement was dominated by a 34m (111ft) high pyramid, the forerunner of Mayan temples. The Olmecs also devised a script of **glyphs** – the first in the region. Their influence spread across Mesoamerica, impacting on other cultures that were starting to emerge at this time – the **Zapotecs** and the **Maya**.

In eastern North America, the **Adena culture** was developing in the Ohio Valley. It was characterized by ritual earthworks and burial mounds containing objects of fine craftsmanship.

Far to the south, the **Chavín culture** had appeared in the Peruvian Andes by *c.*1200 BCE and spread to the coast. The Chavín were **skilled engineers** and **architects** who built canals and levelled slopes for farming and construction. The main settlement, **Chavín de Huántar**, was high in the Andes, and seems to have been a pilgrimage centre for a cult of supernatural beings that were part-human, part-animal. The main god, the "Staff God", is usually depicted with fangs.

In **Europe**, **iron** was gradually **replacing bronze** as the metal of choice for tools and weapons. The area around **Hallstatt** in Austria became a centre for an early Iron Age culture which developed from the Urnfield culture (see 1200 BCE). Hallstatt chieftains dominated local salt-mining and iron working. They lived in hilltop forts and were buried with rich grave goods.

During the 9th century BCE, the **Phoenicians** were becoming a major power in the Mediterranean. Their trading ships, previously confined to the eastern sea, now plied the western Mediterranean. Colonies were set up in Cadiz, in Spain, on the Balearic Islands, and, most notably, on the North African coast at Carthage (in modern Tunisia). Through this trading network, the Phoenician **alphabet** became known throughout the Mediterranean.

In Western Asia, the **Neo-Assyrian Empire** began to expand, and, one by one, Israel, Judah, and the small states of nearby Syria and Phoenicia were brought under Assyrian control.

Grave goods
This Iron Age brooch was discovered in a grave at Hallstatt in Austria. The type of jewellery found suggests that a woman was buried there.

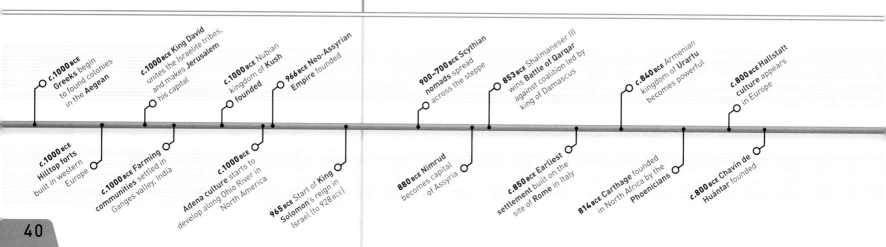

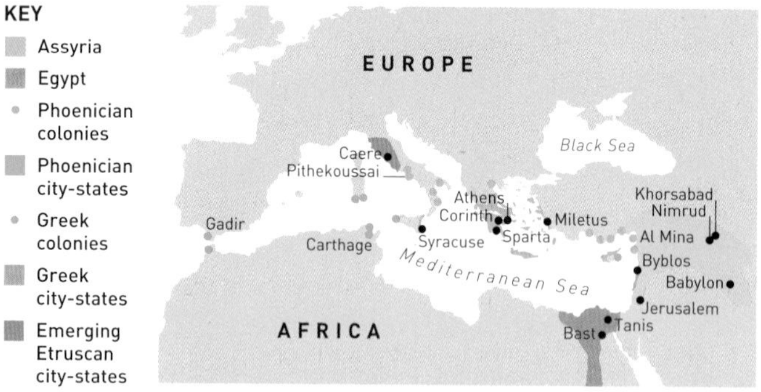

Mediterranean region
This map of the Mediterranean region in the 8th century BCE shows the colonies established by the dominant civilizations of the period, including the Phoenicians and Greeks.

c.1000 BCE Greeks begin to found colonies in the **Aegean**

c.1000 BCE Hilltop forts built in western Europe

c.1000 BCE King David unites the Israelite tribes, and makes **Jerusalem** his capital

c.1000 BCE Farming communities settled in Ganges valley, India

c.1000 BCE Nubian kingdom of **Kush founded**

c.1000 BCE Adena culture starts to develop along Ohio River in North America

966 BCE Neo-Assyrian Empire founded

965 BCE Start of **King Solomon**'s reign in Israel (to 928 BCE)

900–700 BCE Scythian nomads spread across the steppe

880 BCE Nimrud becomes capital of Assyria

853 BCE Shalmaneser III wins **Battle of Qarqar** against coalition led by king of Damascus

c.850 BCE Earliest settlement built on the site of **Rome** in Italy

c.840 BCE Armenian kingdom of **Urartu** becomes powerful

814 BCE Carthage founded in North Africa by the **Phoenicians**

c.800 BCE Hallstatt culture appears in Europe

c.800 BCE Chavín de Huántar founded

In 705 BCE, the Assyrian capital moved to Nineveh. This stone relief shows the Assyrian king and his queen feasting in the gardens of the royal palace there.

ASSYRIA CONTINUED ITS POLICY OF AGGRESSION through the 8th century BCE, conquering rival states in Western Asia and reducing them to provinces. Assyrian success was based on a **disciplined**, technically advanced **army** and an **efficient bureaucracy**. Conquered peoples had to pay costly tributes, and revolts were ruthlessly crushed. Particularly troublesome nations suffered forced deportations – large numbers of people were resettled in Assyria.

Following a period of weak rule in the first half of the 8th century BCE, Tiglath-Pileser III (r.744–727 BCE) recouped Assyria's losses. His successor **Sargon II** (r.722–704 BCE) campaigned in Iran and Anatolia, conquering Babylon and, in 714 BCE, defeating the Armenian state of Urartu. He also defeated the Israelites and transported the "ten lost tribes" of Israel to northern Mesopotamia.

Ritual container
Zhou smiths were highly skilled metal-workers. This bronze bowl dates from the 8th century BCE, the time of the Eastern Zhou dynasty.

In **China**, the Zhou capital moved east to Luoyang in 770 BCE, marking the start of the earlier part of the **Eastern Zhou era**, which lasted until about 480 BCE (see 500 BCE). Royal control had weakened, as the lords who held large fiefdoms had grown more powerful. Now central control disintegrated, and **rival warlords** fought one another. Despite the chaos, this era was a time of technical and cultural advancement. Iron tools increased efficiency in agriculture and food production. Populations and cities grew, and **philosophy, the arts**, and **literature** began to **develop**.

In Egypt, the unrest of the Third Intermediate Period continued. Since 850 BCE, the country had been embroiled in a destructive civil war, and was now divided into small states. In the 8th century BCE, the Kushite ruler of Nubia to the south, **Piye** (r.747–716 BCE), **conquered** both Upper and Lower **Egypt**, and united them under **Kushite rule**.

In the Mediterranean, Phoenician influence continued to spread, as the city of **Carthage** in North Africa **grew powerful**. Greece, meanwhile, was starting to emerge from the Dark Age that had followed the Mycenaeans' downfall. City-states or ***poleis*** were forming on the Greek mainland, centred on hilltop citadels. To increase their territory, the *poleis* founded colonies around the shores of the Aegean. Although rivalry between cities was often intense, a **distinct Greek identity and culture** was emerging. All Greeks were identified as "Hellenes". In 776 BCE the first pan-Hellenic games were held in honour of Zeus at **Olympia**. By the mid-700s BCE the Greeks had adapted the Phoenician alphabet for their own language, and not long after, Homer's epic poems the *Iliad* and the *Odyssey* – hitherto transmitted orally – were probably written down.

In the 8th century BCE, **central Italy** was a mosaic of small states ruled by the dominant **Etruscans** – Italy's first indigenous civilization – and Italic tribes such as the Latins, Umbrians, and Sabines. **Rome** is thought to have been founded by the Latin chief **Romulus** in 753 BCE. In its early days, the city, built on seven hills, was ruled by various peoples, including the Etruscans, Latins, and Sabines.

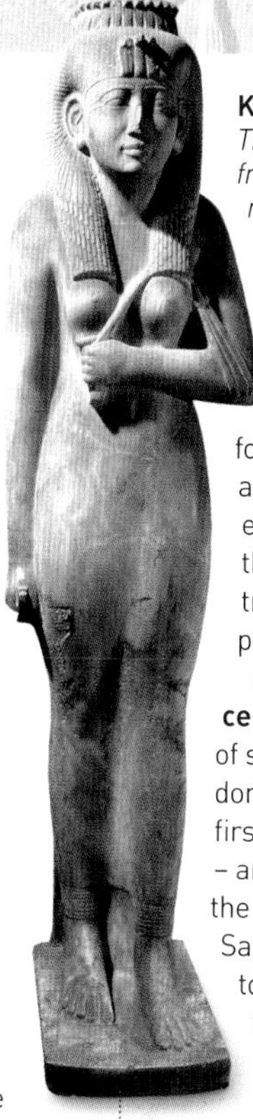

Kushite statue
This alabaster statue dates from the period of Kushite rule in Egypt. Amenirdis I, sister of Shabaka (r.c.716–702 BCE), is shown holding a flail – a traditional symbol of Egyptian rule.

Twin discovery
This painting by Charles de La Fosse depicts the legend of Romulus and Remus, who were abandoned as babies and suckled by a she-wolf, before being rescued by shepherds.

> "SUCH A **GREAT TASK** IT WAS **TO FOUND** THE **ROMAN RACE.**"
>
> **Virgil**, from *Aeneid* 1:33

776 BCE First pan-Hellenic **games** held at **Olympia** in Greece, and every four years thereafter

c.775 BCE Start of **Greek colonization** of **Mediterranean**

771 BCE Zhou capital moves east to **Luoyang**, marking beginning of **Eastern Zhou** period

753 BCE Traditional date for **founding of Rome** by **Romulus**

c.750 BCE Kushite rulers of Nubia send armies into **Egypt, conquering** it by 747 BCE

c.750 BCE Homer's *Iliad* and *Odyssey* written down

c.744 BCE Tiglath-Pileser III of Assyria's reign begins (to 727 BCE)

c.722 BCE Sargon II takes Assyrian throne (to 705 BCE)

714 BCE Sargon II defeats **Urartu** and sacks its major sacred site of Musasir

705 BCE Assyrian capital moves to **Nineveh**

701 BCE Assyrians invade **Judaea**

3

THE CLASSICAL AGE

700 BCE–599 CE

Culturally dynamic civilizations emerged in Greece, Rome, Persia, India, and China, marking the beginning of the Classical Age. The impact of Classical developments in science, art, and politics is still felt to this day.

HE EVERYWHERE SOUGHT EXCUSES FOR STIRRING UP WAR.

Livy, from *Histories* book I, xxi, on Tullus Hostilius, third King of Rome

IN CHINA, THE CITY OF LUOYANG HAD FALLEN TO THE SHEN in 771 BCE, and the Western Zhou capital was transferred east to Chengzhou. From there, the Eastern Zhou dynasty presided over the **fragmentation of China** into as many as 148 states. From around 700 BCE the Zhou were ruled by puppet-emperors, while real power lay with the **ba** ("senior one") among nearby states. Under **Qi Huan Gong** (r.685–643 BCE) the state of Qi had supremacy. After Huan Gong's death the **competition for power** between his five sons weakened Qi, and **Jin Wen Gong** (r.685–643 BCE), the ruler of Jin, rose to become ba. By the end of the century, power in China alternated between the **states of Qi, Jin, Qin, and Chu**.

Nubian Pharoah
Taharqa ruled Egypt for 19 years before an Assyrian invasion forced him to return to Nubia in 671 BCE.

7 THE NUMBER OF KINGS OF ROME

In Italy, the **city-state of Rome** was beginning to acquire an urban heart, and the **first forum** was constructed. The second king of Rome, **Numa Pompilius** (r.716–674 BCE) is believed to have established the main Roman priesthoods and a calendar.

In the Near East, the **Assyrians continued their expansion**, confronting Egypt, whose intermittent support for rebels against Assyrian rule in Syria had long been a source of tension. In 671 BCE, the Assyrian ruler Esarhaddon invaded, **capturing the Egyptian royal capital** of Memphis. However, Assyrian control over Egypt was weak, and the Nubian pharaoh **Taharqa** drove the invaders out.

The **Etruscans** expanded southwards from modern Tuscany and Umbria around 700 BCE. Their language remains undeciphered, but lavish tombs indicate a **rich material culture**. During their expansion, the Etruscans founded cities such as Capua, but came into **conflict** with Greek colonies and with Rome. Although more powerful at first, the Etruscans were **politically disunited**, and a **long series of wars** with the Romans turned against them.

Pyramids from the cemetery at Nuri, Sudan, which was the burial site of the Napatan and Meroitic kings from around 650 BCE.

IT TOOK A CONCERTED CAMPAIGN BY ASHURBANIPAL (r.668–627 BCE) in 664–663 BCE to defeat the Egyptians who had rebelled against Assyrian rule, and to push Assyrian control as far south as Thebes (modern Luxor). This was not the last rebellion against the Assyrians – only ten years later, the vassal king of Saïs, **Psammetichus I** (r.664–610 BCE), revolted against his Assyrian masters, driving them out and founding the 26th Dynasty, under which **Egypt's independence was restored**. After the final collapse of Assyrian power, in 609 BCE, Egypt was able to establish a foothold in Palestine under **Pharaoh Necho II** (610–595 BCE).

In Greece, the **rise** to pre-eminence of a number of **city states** began, notably **Athens**, **Sparta**, and **Corinth**. In Corinth, a new type of ruler, the "tyrant", emerged with the overthrow of the Bacchiadae kings in 658 BCE.

TAHARQA THE GODLESS CAME OUT TO TAKE EGYPT.

Ashurbanipal's account of the conquest of Egypt, 664 BCE

The new ruler, **Cypselus** (reign *c.*657–627 BCE) relied on force of personality rather than divine sanction, and established a dynasty under whom Corinth enjoyed a **seven-decade period of dominance**, creating colonies throughout the western Mediterranean.

On the fringes of the Greek world, in western Asia Minor, the **kingdom of Lydia** was increasing in power under **Gyges** (685–647 BCE), its first great king. He allied with Ashurbanipal of Assyria to see off a joint threat to their two lands by Cimmerian raiders in 668–665 BCE, but then assisted Psammetichus I of Egypt in his revolt against the Assyrians. He also adopted an aggressive stance towards his neighbours, the Ionian Greeks of Miletus and Smyrna.

According to Japanese tradition, the first emperor, **Jimmu Tenno**, a descendant of the sun goddess **Amaterasu**, ascended to the throne in 660 BCE. The stories of his migration from southern Honshu eastwards to establish his kingdom near Nara are legendary, but may echo real events of the Japanese **Yayoi** period after 100 BCE, when tribal chieftains began to **consolidate their territories**.

The third king of Rome, **Tullus Hostilius** (r.673–642 BCE) was more martially inclined than his precedessor Numa Pompilius, and

ASHURBANIPAL (r.668–627 BCE)

Ashurbanipal initially shared rule over Assyria with his brother, Shamash-shuma-ukin. After defeating his brother's revolt in 648 BCE he greatly expanded the Assyrian domains. As well as annexing Egypt, he attacked Elam, sacking its capital, Susa, in 647 BCE. His latter years saw none of the military successes of his early reign. At his death a dispute between his two sons further weakened the Assyrian Empire.

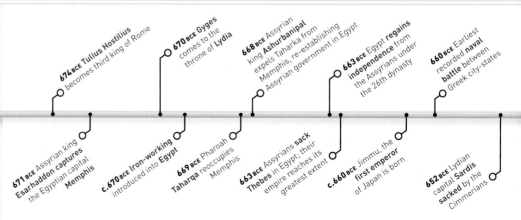

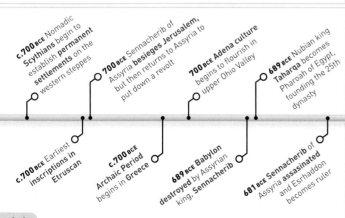

30,000 THE NUMBER OF CLAY TABLETS UNCOVERED IN ASHURBANIPAL'S LIBRARY

c.700 BCE Nomadic Scythians begin to establish **permanent settlements** on the western steppes

c.700 BCE Earliest **inscriptions in Etruscan**

700 BCE Sennacherib of Assyria **besieges Jerusalem**, but then returns to Assyria to put down a revolt

c.700 BCE Archaic Period begins in **Greece**

700 BCE Adena culture begins to flourish in upper Ohio Valley

689 BCE Babylon destroyed by Assyrian king, **Sennacherib**

689 BCE Nubian king **Taharqa** becomes Pharoah of Egypt, founding the 25th dynasty

681 BCE Sennacherib of Assyria **assasinated** and Esrhaddon becomes ruler

674 BCE Tullus Hostilius becomes third king of Rome

671 BCE Assyrian king **Esarhaddon captures** the Egyptian capital **Memphis**

670 BCE Gyges comes to the throne of **Lydia**

c.670 BCE Iron-working introduced into **Egypt**

669 BCE Pharoah **Taharqa** reoccupies Memphis

668 BCE Assyrian king **Ashurbanipal** expels Taharka from Memphis, re-establishing Assyrian government in Egypt

663 BCE Egypt **regains independence** from the Assyrians under the 26th dynasty

663 BCE Assyrians **sack Thebes** in Egypt; their empire reaches its greatest extent

c.660 BCE Jimmu, the **first emperor** of Japan is born

660 BCE Earliest recorded **naval battle** between Greek city-states

652 BCE Lydian capital **Sardis sacked** by the Cimmerians

650–601 BCE

A lion frieze from the Processional Way in Babylon, which was built around 600 BCE and ran through the heart of the city to the Ishtar Gate.

The Assyrian Empire
From its core around Assur and Nineveh, the Assyrian empire grew to encompass Babylonia, Media, Elam, Urartu, Syria, and Egypt.

led the war against neighbouring Alba Longa, which ultimately led to that city's destruction and the deportation of its population to Rome, in the **first major Roman expansion**. The fourth king, **Ancus Marcius** (641–617 BCE), expanded Roman territory towards the coast, and founded Rome's great port of Ostia at the mouth of the Tiber. His successor, **Tarquinius Priscus** (616–578 BCE) was the fifth king of Rome and one of the city's greatest kings. He came from an Etruscan background, a sign of the high level of Etruscan influence over the early city of Rome. Tarquinius Priscus won a series of victories over the Sabines, the Latins, and the Etruscans, who all competed with Rome for dominance over central Italy. He is also said to have established the public games in Rome.

THE ASSYRIANS HAD FINALLY CONQUERED BABYLON in 691 BCE, partially destroying the city. Reconstruction work began under Esarhaddon (680–669 BCE), and by 652 BCE Babylon had recovered its importance and became the centre for a **major revolt** led by Shamash-shuma-ukin against his younger brother Ashurbanipal. It took **four years of war** to suppress the Babylonians and their Elamite allies, and the fighting drained Assyria's ability to hold on to its empire. By 630 BCE, Assyria had lost Egypt and Palestine, and in 626 BCE the **Babylonians regained their independence**. By 616 BCE Babylon was strong enough to invade Assyria, aided by the Medes (whose base was in northwestern Iran). In 612 BCE the Babylonians, Medes, and Scythians sacked the Assyrian capital of Nineveh. The **Assyrian empire crumbled**. A remnant of the Assyrian army regrouped and established a small kingdom around Harran, but by 609 BCE this, too, had fallen.

The **Scythians** formed part of a culture of **nomadic horsemen** which held a large territory on the steppes north of the Caucasus from around 800 BCE. In 652 BCE they forced the Medes to submit to them and the Scythian King Bartatua was even sufficiently influential to be given an Assyrian princess as his wife. The **alliance with Assyria** survived into the reign of his son Madyes, but around 615 BCE the Scythians switched sides and played a **key role in Assyria's destruction**. Their Median subjects soon turned on them and around 590 BCE the Scythians retreated north.

In the Greek world, there was a growing movement to **establish colonies** in the Mediterranean. Among the earliest were in Italy, including **Syracuse**, founded around 733 BCE. In North Africa, Greek settlers founded **Cyrene** (in Libya) in about 630 BCE, and **Massilia** (Marseilles) around 600 BCE. New cities were established as far west as Spain, and around the Black Sea coast.

In Greece itself, the **city-state of Sparta** was establishing its dominance in the Peloponnese. A defeat by the city-state of Argos, in 669 BCE, was followed by military reforms and victory against the Messenians (660–650 BCE). By 600 BCE, **Sparta had conquered** almost all the southern Peloponnese and established a stratified social system.

Sparta's future rival, **Athens**, gradually united the area surrounding Attica under its rule in the 8th century BCE. The hereditary monarchy was replaced by nine "archons", chosen annually. Shortly after a damaging popular uprising by Cylon in 632 BCE, Athens received its first law code, drafted by Draco in 621 BCE. The **Draconian law** was later known for the severity of the punishments it prescribed.

To the south of Egypt the **state of Napata** became a power of the first order, conquering Egypt under Piankhy (751–716 BCE) and controlling it under after the death of Taharqa (690–664 BCE).

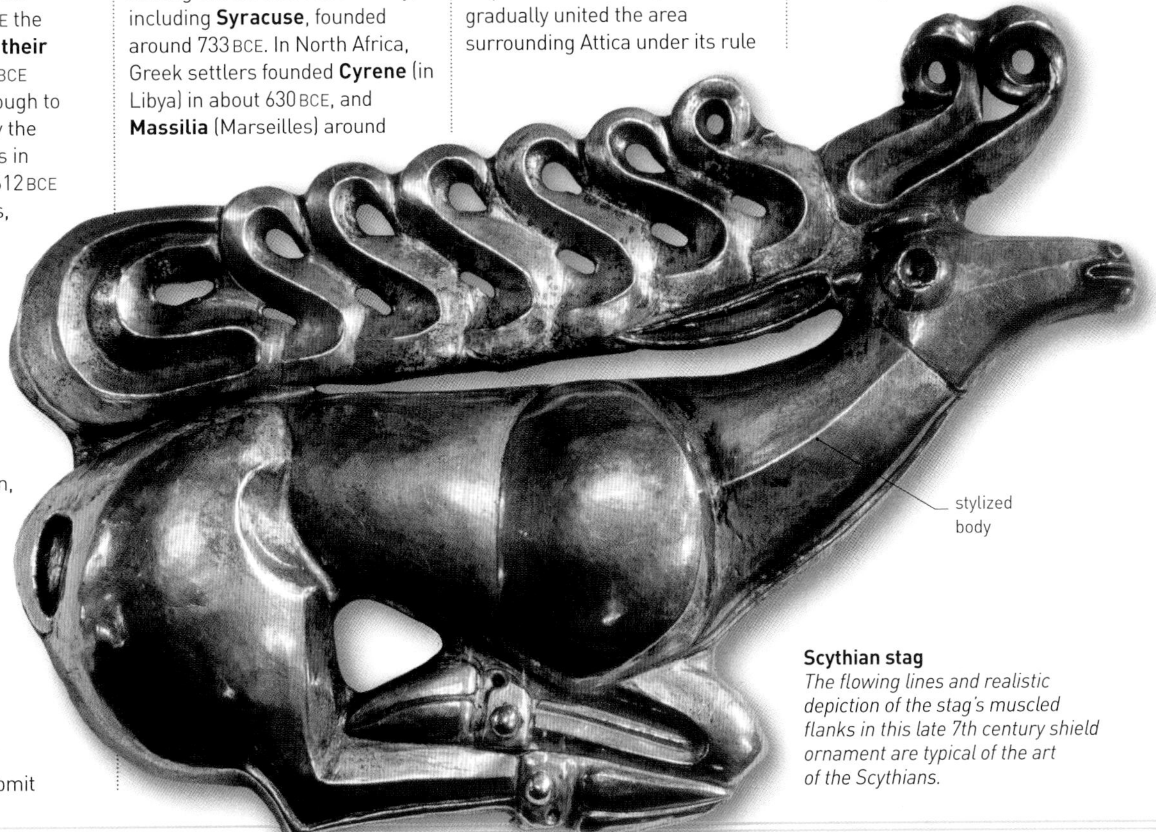

Scythian stag
The flowing lines and realistic depiction of the stag's muscled flanks in this late 7th century shield ornament are typical of the art of the Scythians.

652 BCE Babylonian rebellion threatens Assyrian rule, but is put down (ends 649 BCE)

c.650 BCE Age of **"tyrants"** begins in many Greek states

c.650 BCE Iron technology reaches **Zhou China**

650 BCE First coins minted in **Lydia**

650 BCE Meroe founded (in modern Sudan)

648 BCE Babylon surrenders to Ashurbanipal

647 BCE Ashurbanipal **sacks Susa**

631 BCE Ashurbanipal dies

630 BCE Sparta wages **war** against the **Messenians**

630 BCE Greek colony of **Cyrene founded** (in modern Libya)

626 BCE Nabopolassar becomes ruler of Babylon, founding Neo-Babylonian dynasty

625 BCE Periander takes power as Tyrant in Corinth

621 BCE First Athenian law code, **Code of Draco**

620 BCE Foundation of Greek colony of **Tartessus** in Spain

616 BCE Tarquin, an Etruscan, becomes **king of Rome**

615 BCE The **Medes**, an emerging power, **defeat** the **Scythians**

612 BCE Assyrian empire collapses in face of attacks from Medes and Babylonians

609 BCE Residual Assyrian state, **Harran**, captured by Babylonians and Medes; Assyrian state disappears forever

608 BCE Necho II of Egypt **invades Judah**

605 BCE Nebuchadnezzar II succeeds to the throne of Babylon

604 BCE Traditional date for the birth of **Lao Tzu**, the founder of **Taoism**

600–551 BCE

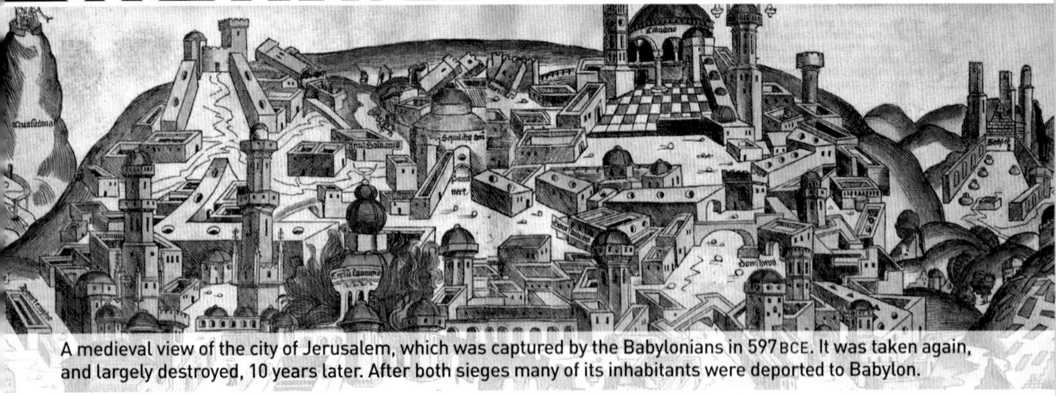

A medieval view of the city of Jerusalem, which was captured by the Babylonians in 597 BCE. It was taken again, and largely destroyed, 10 years later. After both sieges many of its inhabitants were deported to Babylon.

HAVING HELPED DESTROY THE ASSYRIAN EMPIRE, Nabopolassar (r.626–605 BCE), first king of the **neo-Babylonian dynasty**, embellished the city of Babylon. His son Nebuchadnezzar (r.605–562 BCE) defeated the Egyptians in 605 BCE, repaired Babylon's main ziggurat, and ordered the building of the famous "Hanging Gardens". The last neo-Babylonian king, **Nabonidus** (r.556–539 BCE), moved his royal court to the Arabian oasis of Tema, but **discontent rose** among the Babylonians during his reign.

The Medes of northwest Persia (Iran), consolidated their kingdom under **Cyaxares** (r.624–585 BCE) and took part in the destruction of the Assyrian Empire in 612 BCE. Under the last Median king, Astyages (r.584–549 BCE), Median armies campaigned in Azerbaijan and controlled land as far west as Lydia (Turkey). But by the 550s BCE, Media was under pressure from the Babylonians to the south and the new power of Persia.

The kingdom of Judah had long acted as a block to Assyrian and Babylonian expansion to the west. In **597 BCE**, Nebuchadnezzar **took Jerusalem** and deposed King Jehoiakim. The king they installed in his place, Zedekiah, turned against the Babylonians, and in **587 BCE** there was **another siege**. Much of the city was burnt, the Jewish Temple destroyed, and many of its inhabitants deported to a **life of exile** in Babylon.

The powerful city-state of **Athens** experienced reforms under **Solon** about 600 BCE, notably a **law code** that protected the property rights of the poor, forbade debt-slavery, and moderated the more extreme parts of the **Draconian laws** (see 650-601). Around 560 BCE, Pisistratus seized power and began to rule as a **tyrant** (dictator). Driven out once, he returned in 547 BCE and established a stable regime.

The **Greek city** of Miletus saw the beginnings of **philosophical thought** from about 600 BCE. Thales (born *c.*624 BCE) tried to understand the basic nature of the universe and thought its fundamental element was water.

Lawgiver and reformer
This image shows the Greek statesmen and lawgiver Solon teaching. His reforms began to undermine the power of the aristocracy in Athens.

- **600 BCE Iron-working** in Nok region, **West Africa**
- **600 BCE** First **Greek coins issued** in Ionia
- **600 BCE Olmec culture** of **Mexico** still flourishing
- **600 BCE Aryan** kingdoms dominate **northern India**
- **597 BCE** Nebuchadnezzar of Babylon **captures Jerusalem**
- **594 BCE Solon** becomes archon (ruler) of Athens
- **590 BCE** First **drainage system** is built in Rome
- **589 BCE** Apries becomes Egyptian **pharaoh**
- **585 BCE** Thales of Miletus predicts a **solar eclipse**
- **578 BCE** Servius Tullius becomes **king of Rome**; builds Rome's first wall
- **563 BCE** Possible birth date of Siddhartha Gautama, the **Buddha**
- **562 BCE Nebuchadnezzar II dies**, and is succeeded by Amelmarduk
- **560 BCE Pisistratus** becomes **Tyrant of Athens**
- **560 BCE Croesus** succeeds to **throne of Lydia** and begins its expansion
- **559 BCE Cyrus** the Great becomes **ruler** of **Anshan**

550–501 BCE

Central Asia became a stronghold of Buddhist beliefs. These cave paintings at Dunhuang in China illustrate a variety of Buddhist parables.

CYRUS, RULER OF THE SMALL KINGDOM OF PERSIS (also called Pars) in the west of Persia (Iran), **revolted** against his Median overlords in **559 BCE**. By 550 BCE he had conquered the Median capital of Ecbatana and overthrown their ruler, King Astyages. Afraid of the **increasing power of Persia**, the Lydians under **King Croesus** opposed Cyrus, but he struck west and in 547 BCE, on the River Halys, defeated the Lydian army and annexed western Asia Minor.

In 539 BCE **Cyrus captured Babylon**, acquiring most of Mesopotamia and making the **Persian Empire** the greatest in the Middle East. **Cyrus died in** 530 BCE while fighting in what is today Turkmenistan, and was succeeded by his son **Cambyses**.

In 526 BCE Cambyses sent his **armies south into Egypt**. The Pharaoh Amasis had just died and his successor Psammetichus III was not well established. Cambyses defeated the Egyptian army at Pelusium in 525 BCE and then **captured the royal capital at Memphis**. He installed himself as the pharaoh and then subdued south Egypt. Persian rule in Egypt lasted until 402 BCE.

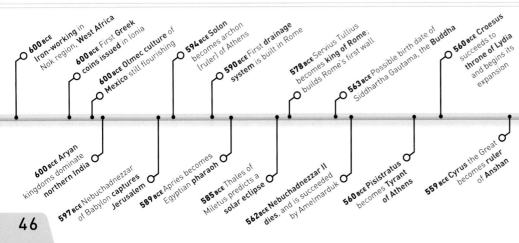

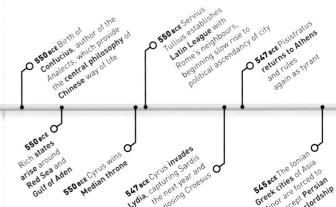

Darius the Great
King Darius is shown enthroned and bearing symbols of power in this frieze. His son Xerxes succeeded him.

Cambyses died in 522 BCE and after the brief rebellion of Bardiya, who was either the younger brother of Cambyses or someone impersonating him, **Darius**, a Persian noble, took over as king. Widespread revolts broke out, including in Media, but Darius put them all down. He then **expanded the Persian Empire** by annexing lands in central Asia and on the borders of India from 519 to 515 BCE. In **India**, the political power had coalesced around the **Mahajapanadas**, a group of around 16 powerful

> “I HAVE **FOUGHT 19 BATTLES IN ONE YEAR**… I HAVE **WON** THEM.”
>
> The Behistun inscription of **Darius**

- **550 BCE** Birth of **Confucius**, author of the *Analects*, which provide the **central philosophy** of **Chinese** way of life
- **550 BCE** Rich **states arise** around **Red Sea** and **Gulf of Aden**
- **550 BCE** Cyrus wins **Median throne**
- **550 BCE** Servius Tullius establishes **Latin League** with Rome's neighbours, beginning slow rise to political ascendancy of city
- **547 BCE** Cyrus **invades Lydia**, capturing Sardis the next year and deposing Croesus
- **547 BCE** Pisistratus **returns to Athens** and rules again as tyrant
- **545 BCE** The Ionian **Greek cities** of Asia Minor are forced to accept **Persian overlordship**

> **"EVEN DEATH IS NOT TO BE FEARED BY ONE WHO HAS LIVED WISELY"**
>
> **Gautama Siddharta (Buddha)**, 563–483 BCE

482

THE NUMBER OF **YEARS** OF THE **ROMAN REPUBLIC**

kingdoms. Of these, Magadha was the most important state. Afterwards, Darius subdued most of the Greek city-states of Ionia, before he **crossed into Europe** in 513 BCE to conquer Thrace.

In Italy, Servius Tullius (r.578–534), the **sixth king of Rome** and said to be a former slave, had succeeded Tarquinius Priscus in 578 BCE. During his reign he implemented **important reforms**, fixing the formal boundaries of the city by dividing the Romans into four "tribes", a system that would be extended as Roman territory grew, and also into classes that were **graded by wealth**. The population was divided by what equipment they could afford and what role they played in the Roman army. The wealthiest class fought as cavalry, the higher classes as heavy infantry, and the poor as light auxiliary troops.The votes of the richer classes carried much greater weight in the popular assembly. **The last king of Rome**, Tarquinius Superbus (r.534–509 BCE) was an Etruscan. Concerned at the **growing tyranny** of his rule, a group of Roman aristocrats led by Lucius Junius Brutus and Lucius Tarquinius Collatinus (the king's cousin) won over the army and barred the gates of the city to the king, who was deposed. The coup leaders then **established a republic** in which supreme authority was held by two magistrates called **consuls**. The power of the consuls was limited by the fact that **new consuls were elected** by the popular assembly each year.

Some time around 530 BCE, **Gautama Siddharta**, a Hindu prince of Kapilvastu (now in Nepal), had a religious revelation and rejected his noble upbringing to embark on a quest for "enlightenment". Six years later he received it and began to preach a way of moderate asceticism to gain release from the suffering of material life. He is known as the Buddha (which means the "awakened one" in Sanskrit) and his followers, who became known as **Buddhists**, spread his ideas throughout South Asia and, in the late 3rd century CE into China and thence to Korea, Japan, and Southeast Asia.

Confucius (or Kong Fuzi) was born around 551 BCE, in a period of political instability during China's **Spring and Autumn period**. From the age of 15 he devoted himself to scholarship, and the **political philosophy** he developed reflects the turbulent times. He taught that the righteous man (or junzi) must have regard to others and **inflict no unnecessary harm**. His philosophy, as developed by his disciples, taught respect for elders and became a cornerstone of the later imperial system.

CYRUS THE GREAT
(r.559–539 BCE)

Little is known about the early life of Cyrus. He was the ruler of the kingdom of Pars when he led a revolt against his Median overlord Astyages. By defeating Astyages, Cyrus became king of the Medes. He then continued to expand Persian influence with the conquest of Lydia. Cyrus adapted local ideas about kingship to cast himself as an ideal ruler in the cities he conquered. Cyrus died in 539 BCE.

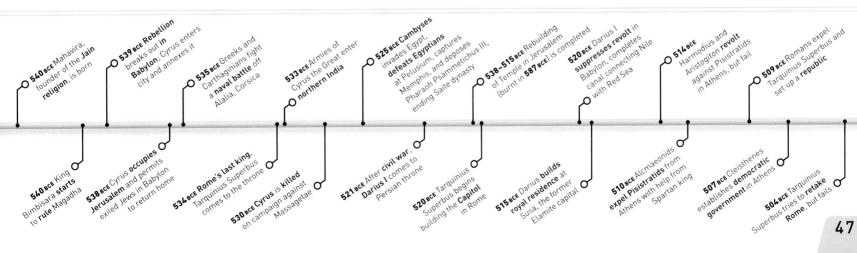

Persian elite
These archers from the palace of Darius at Susa were the elite of the Persian army, which included representatives from provinces as far off as Ethiopia and Afghanistan.

- **540 BCE** Mahavira, founder of the **Jain religion**, is born
- **540 BCE** King Bimbisara **starts** to **rule** Magadha
- **539 BCE Rebellion** breaks out **in Babylon**; Cyrus enters city and annexes it
- **538 BCE** Cyrus **occupies Jerusalem** and permits exiled Jews in Babylon to return home
- **535 BCE** Greeks and Carthaginians fight a **naval battle** off Alalia, Corsica
- **534 BCE Rome's last king**, Tarquinius Superbus comes to the throne
- **533 BCE** Armies of Cyrus the Great enter **northern India**
- **530 BCE Cyrus** is **killed** on campaign against Massagetae
- **525 BCE Cambyses** invades Egypt, **defeats Egyptians** at Pelusium, captures Memphis, and deposes Pharaoh Psammetichus III, ending Saite dynasty
- **521 BCE** After **civil war**, **Darius I** comes to Persian throne
- **538–515 BCE** Rebuilding of Temple in Jerusalem (burnt in **587 BCE**) is completed
- **520 BCE** Tarquinius Superbus begins building the **Capitol** in Rome
- **520 BCE** Darius I **suppresses revolt** in Babylon, completes canal connecting Nile with Red Sea
- **515 BCE** Darius **builds royal residence** at Susa, the former Elamite capital
- **514 BCE** Harmodius and Aristogiton **revolt** against Pisistratids in Athens, but fail
- **510 BCE** Alcmaeonids **expel Pisistratids** from Athens with help from Spartan king
- **509 BCE** Romans expel Tarquinius Superbus and set up a **republic**
- **507 BCE** Cleisthenes establishes **democratic government** in Athens
- **504 BCE** Tarquinius Superbus tries to **retake Rome**, but fails

Medusa antefix
DATE UNKNOWN
This terracotta antefix – an ornament placed at the cornice of buildings or at roof eaves – is in the form of Medusa, the mythical creature whose gaze turned people to stone.

Corinthian helmet
600–500 BCE
The Corinthian helmet, made from a single bronze sheet, was the most common type in Greece, from around 750–300 BCE.

Spearhead
600–400 BCE
Greek hoplites (armed infantry soldiers) carried a large thrusting spear, of which this is the tip.

ANCIENT GREECE

FROM THE FUNCTIONAL TO THE DECORATIVE, THE GREEKS PRODUCED ART OF GREAT BEAUTY

While the Greeks created magnificent monumental art, smaller items such as jewellery, musical instruments, weaponry, and vases show the Greek love of intricate forms and decorative adornment throughout all periods of their history.

Greek art underwent a series of phases that were reflected in all aspects of artistic production, but particularly on vases. In the Geometric phase (*c.*850–700 BCE), decoration was mainly composed of geometric forms, replaced in the Orientalizing phase (*c.*700–600 BCE) with floral and animal themes, followed by the more naturalistic representations of the Classical phase (from 600 BCE).

Bronze mirror
490–460 BCE
This mirror is richly adorned with an image of Aphrodite flanked by cupids.

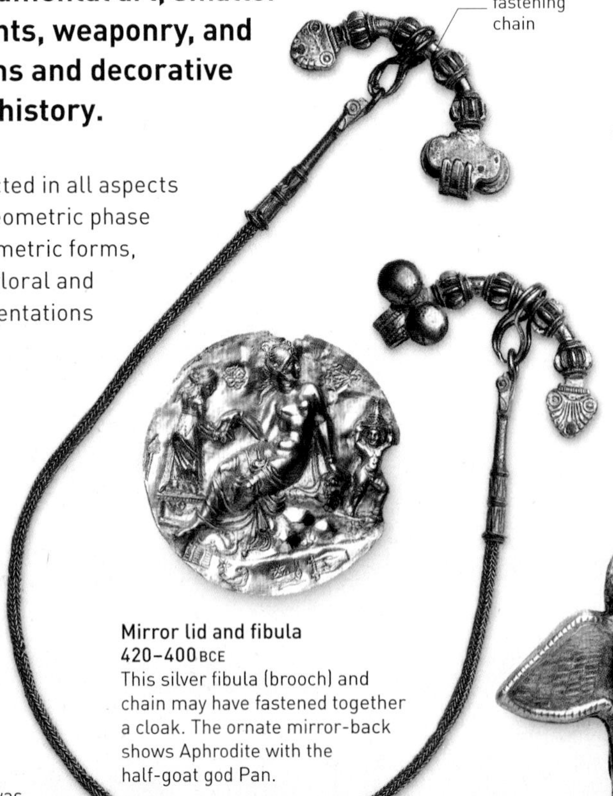

Gold earrings
420–400 BCE
These delicate gold filigree earrings depict boats containing sirens, mythical creatures whose beautiful voices lured unwary seafarers to their doom.

Bronze cymbals
500–400 BCE
Greek cymbals are bell- or cup-shaped, and are often depicted on vases being held by fauns or satyrs, or by women in Bacchanalian revels.

Mirror lid and fibula
420–400 BCE
This silver fibula (brooch) and chain may have fastened together a cloak. The ornate mirror-back shows Aphrodite with the half-goat god Pan.

Gold brooch
650–600 BCE
This hawk-shaped brooch dates from a period in which Oriental (and particularly Egyptian) influences were strong in Greece.

Aulos
400 BCE
This wind instrument was originally a double one (one wooden pipe has been lost), played through a reed.

Boeotian horse and rider figurine
550 BCE
The depiction of this horse and rider has an archaic feel about it, in contrast to the production of Boeotian terracotta workshops over 200 years later (see right).

Boeotian figurine
400–200 BCE
This terracotta figurine of a woman holding a jar comes from Boeotia, where a tradition of such sculptures began as early as the 8th century BCE.

Ostrakon
*c.*475–470 BCE
In Athens, influential politicians could be ostracized (exiled) by public vote. The name of the politician each voter wished to be banished was inscribed on a piece of pottery.

Discus
600–500 BCE
This fine bronze discus belonged to an athlete called Exoidas. After he won a victory in a sporting contest using it, he dedicated the discus to the gods Castor and Pollux.

Attic askos
425–400 BCE
The askos was a type of vessel for pouring liquids such as oil, shaped in the form of a traditional wine sack. The design is in the red-figure style that became popular around 530 BCE.

Athenian amphora
540–530 BCE
An amphora was a type of vessel used for storing wine. This one is decorated using the black-figure technique, which pre-dates the red-figure method.

Attic skyphos
525–500 BCE
This drinking vessel shows a couple at their wedding standing in a chariot. The vase is painted in the black-figure style.

Apulian pyxis
500–400 BCE
A pyxis was often used for storing small items of jewellery and cosmetics. This south-Italian example is decorated with geometrical shapes.

Attic lekythos
480–470 BCE
Greek vases were often painted with mythological scenes. This black-figure vase shows the goddess Athena beating a giant to his knees.

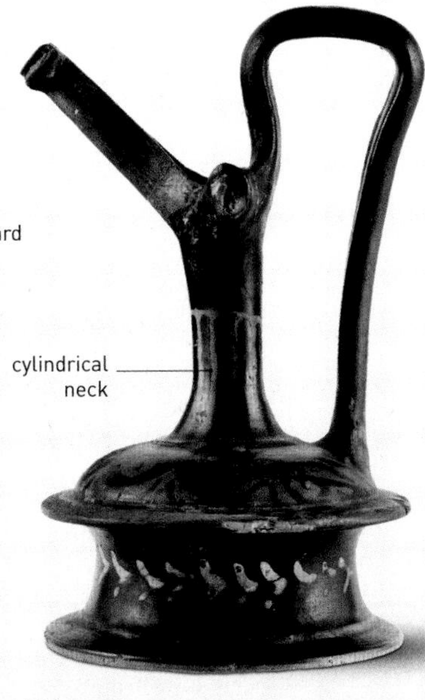

Epichysis
375–340 BCE
The long-spouted epichysis was a vessel used for pouring wine. This south-Italian vase has its base decorated with a pattern of white chevrons.

“ THIS IS **GOOD NEWS** … IF THE PERSIANS **HIDE THE SUN,** WE SHALL DO BATTLE **IN THE SHADE.** ”

Herodotus, ancient Greek historian, quoting words attributed to Dieneces, a Spartan, on being told that the Persian archers shot so many arrows they would conceal the Sun; from *Histories*

This 19th-century painting shows the Spartan king Leonidas I (centre, facing) and his men at the Battle of Thermopylae in 480 BCE. Thermopylae became a byword for heroic defiance against overwhelming odds.

Plebeians withdraw from Rome
The departure of the plebeians (on the left in this engraving) threatened to split Rome irreparably, so the patricians (right) ceded some political power.

THE GREEK CITY-STATES OF IONIA in western Anatolia had been subjects of the Persian Empire since Cyrus conquered Lydia, their previous overlord, in 547 BCE (see 550–501 BCE). In 499 BCE, **Aristagoras**, the ruler of Miletus, set out to mainland Greece to recruit allies for a **planned uprising** against the Persians. Sparta rejected his pleas, but only Athens and Eretria sent forces. A failed attack on Sardis led the Athenian forces to return home. The Ionians gradually lost ground to a **Persian land offensive** from 497 BCE. The fall of Miletus to the Persians that year and the death of Aristagoras undermined Ionian unity and, after a great naval defeat at the **Battle of Lade** in 494 BCE, the revolt fell apart.

In Italy, the **young Roman Republic** was rocked by **social dissent** in 494 BCE when the plebeians (the lower social groups) withdrew from Rome en masse in protest at their treatment by the patricians (the higher social groups); they threatened to set up an alternative state. They were persuaded back only by official recognition of their own representatives (tribunes).

The Battle of Lade
The Ionian Greek navy fought hard at Lade, but the pre-arranged defection of the Samians to the Persians led to its utter defeat.

THE KINGDOM OF MAGADHA emerged as an important state in northern India under the rule of **Bimbisara** (r.543–491 BCE), friend and protector of Gautama **Buddha** (c.563–c.486 BCE), who founded Buddhism (see 550–501 BCE). Bimbisara's son Ajatashastru (r.491–461 BCE) strengthened the royal capital at Rajagirha and **built a centre at Pataligrama** on the Ganges, which later became **Pataliputra, the Mauryan royal capital** By conquering Kosala and Kashi, and annexing the Vrijji confederacy, Ajatashastru turned Magadha into the **dominant power** on the Ganges Plain.

In China, the political system of the Spring and Autumn period evolved into the **Warring States period** (481–221 BCE), in which seven main states engaged in a constant round of diplomatic manoeuvres to weaken each other, periodically interrupted by outbreaks of war.

In 490 BCE, **Darius I** (548–486 BCE) of Persia decided to take revenge on the mainland Greeks for their support of the Ionian revolt. Darius despatched a **huge naval expedition** under Artaphernes and Datis, which sailed from Cilicia, landing first at Naxos before seizing Eretria, which had aided the Ionians in 499 BCE. Although the **Athenians** appealed to Sparta for aid, the only help they received came from Plataea, which sent 1,000 reinforcements. The Athenians opted to march out to meet the **Persians** rather than wait for a siege, on the advice of their general, Miltiades (550–489 BCE). In 490 BCE at

7

THE **NUMBER** OF **WARRING STATES**

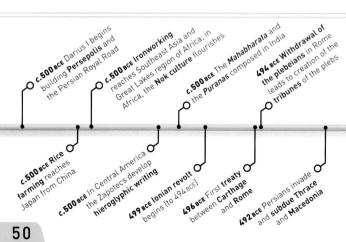

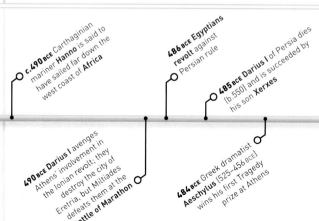

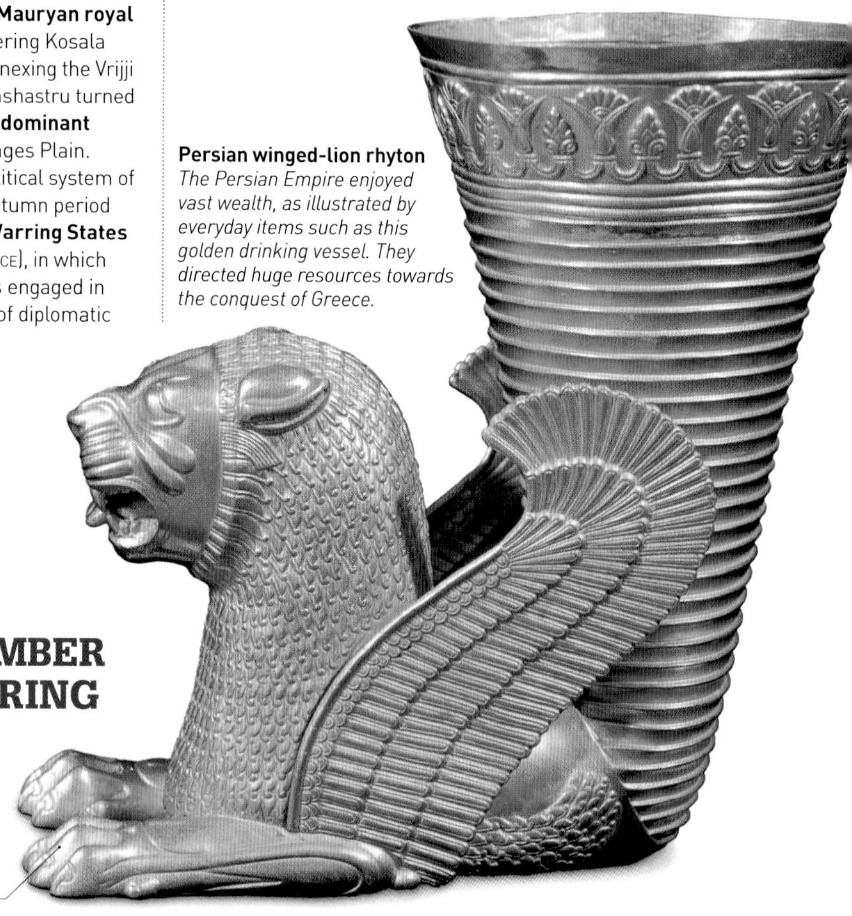
animals were often the inspiration for a rhyton's shape

Persian winged-lion rhyton
The Persian Empire enjoyed vast wealth, as illustrated by everyday items such as this golden drinking vessel. They directed huge resources towards the conquest of Greece.

- **c.500 BCE** Darius I begins building **Persepolis** and the Persian Royal Road
- **c.500 BCE Rice farming** reaches Japan from China
- **c.500 BCE Ironworking** reaches Southeast Asia and Great Lakes region of Africa; in Africa, the **Nok culture** flourishes
- **c.500 BCE** In Central America the Zapotecs develop **hieroglyphic writing**
- **c.500 BCE** The ***Mahabharata*** and the ***Puranas*** composed in India
- **499 BCE Ionian revolt** begins (to 494 BCE)
- **496 BCE** First **treaty** between **Carthage** and **Rome**
- **494 BCE Withdrawal of the plebeians** in Rome leads to creation of the **tribunes** of the plebs
- **492 BCE** Persians invade and **subdue Thrace** and **Macedonia**
- **c.490 BCE** Carthaginian mariner **Hanno** is said to have sailed far down the west coast of **Africa**
- **490 BCE Darius I** avenges Athens' involvement in the Ionian revolt; they destroy the city of Eretria, but Miltiades defeats them at the **Battle of Marathon**
- **486 BCE Egyptians revolt** against Persian rule
- **485 BCE Darius I** of Persia dies (b.550) and is succeeded by his son **Xerxes**
- **484 BCE** Greek dramatist **Aeschylus** (525–456 BCE) wins his first Tragedy prize at Athens
- **483 BCE Athenians** begin to **build a fleet** on the proceeds of the new silver mines at Mount Laurium
- **483 BCE Buddha** dies (b.c.563 BCE)

Marathon, the Greek hoplite (heavy infantry) formation advanced head-on against a far more numerous Persian force to win **an unlikely victory**.

Chastened, the Persian expeditionary force withdrew from Greece after Marathon, but in 481 BCE **Xerxes I** (519–465 BCE) despatched another huge Persian army, which crossed over the Hellespont (near modern-day Istanbul) and proceeded south towards Athens. Many northern Greek states chose to submit, but Athens and Sparta patched together a league of southern states. In 480 BCE, a **heroic defence** of the pass at **Thermopylae** by the Spartan king Leonidas I, in which he and all his 10,000 soldiers died, bought time for the Athenians to evacuate. The Persians burnt the city, but soon after, under the command of **Themistocles** (see panel below), the Athenian fleet inflicted a serious defeat on Xerxes's naval force at **Salamis**. Further Greek victories followed in June 479 BCE, on land at Plataea in Boeotia and at sea at Mycale off the Ionian coast. The Greeks then took the offensive, and during 478–477 BCE won a string of victories in Ionia and Cyprus, which **reversed most of the Persians' gains**.

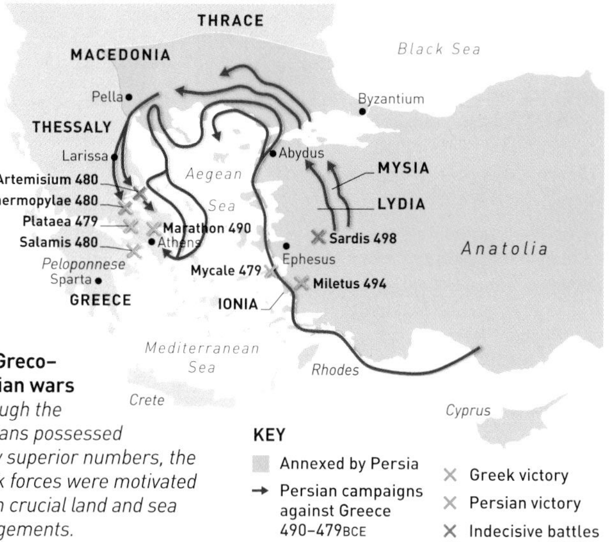

The Greco–Persian wars
Although the Persians possessed vastly superior numbers, the Greek forces were motivated to win crucial land and sea engagements.

After the initial defeats of the Persians in 480–479 BCE, Athens sought to formalize the **league of anti-Persian allies**. A treasury was set up on the island of Delos in around 477 BCE. The league's funds were to be deposited here and regular meetings were to take place. But this **Delian League** soon became little more than an Athenian empire, and Sparta and its allies refused to take part.

THEMISTOCLES (c.524–460 BCE)

A clever politician and strategist, Themistocles persuaded the Athenians to use the wealth of a silver mine discovered at Laurium in 483/2 BCE to double their fleet. However, after the naval victory at Salamis, he became the object of increasing jealousy from political rivals. In about 470 BCE Themistocles was ostracized from Athens (exiled by public vote).

> **“ THE GREAT STRUGGLE HAS COME. ”**
>
> **Herodotus, ancient Greek historian**, quoting Pausanias, the Spartan commander, before the Battle of Plataea in 479 BCE; from *Histories*

THE ATHENIANS ENJOYED EARLY SUCCESS under the direction of Cimon (510–450 BCE), wresting Eion on the Strymon river (in Anatolia) from the Persians in 476 BCE and then attacking Carystos on Euboea (which had submitted to the Persians) in 470 BCE. An attempt by the island of Naxos to leave the Delian League around the same time led to an Athenian expeditionary force that powerfully suppressed the breakaway movement. In 469 BCE, Athenian forces won a great **victory over the Persians** at the River Eurymedon on the south coast of Anatolia, establishing Athenian supremacy in the Aegean.

Pericles (c.495–429 BCE), the Athenian statesman largely responsible for making Athens the political and cultural focus of Greece, tried but failed to prosecute Cimon in 463 BCE, on a charge of having neglected a chance to conquer Macedonia. From this manoeuvre, **Pericles' vision** and ideas of expansion for Athens were already evident. When the leading figure among the democrats, Ephialtes, was assassinated in 461 BCE, Pericles, his protégé, swiftly took his place.

Periodically, the Persians had tried to bribe the Spartans into diversionary attacks on Athens but initially to little effect. In 464 BCE, a **revolt of the Messenian Helots** (unfree men) in the western Peloponnese further distracted the Spartans from any attempt to stem the rising power of the Delian League. The Messenians received little outside assistance, and by 462 BCE their last stronghold at Ithome had been reduced. Soon after, open conflict broke out between Sparta and Athens and their respective allies. The **First Peloponnesian War** was inconclusive. It ended in 451 BCE with a five-year truce, extended in 446 BCE to a **Thirty Years Peace** between the two sides.

Meanwhile, the western part of the Greek world was becoming increasingly important, marked by the **rise of** the Sicilian city-state of **Syracuse**. Under a series of able rulers (tyrants) that began with **Gelon** (r.485–478 BCE) and his brother **Hieron** (r.478–467 BCE), Syracusan forces subdued the neighbouring city of Acragas and expanded territory around Catana. Although Hieron's younger brother **Thrasybulus** was driven out in 466 BCE, the Syracusans retained their dominant position in Sicily beyond the 450s BCE.

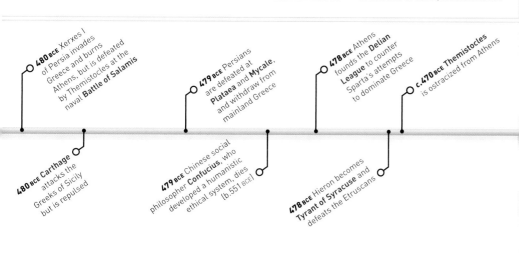

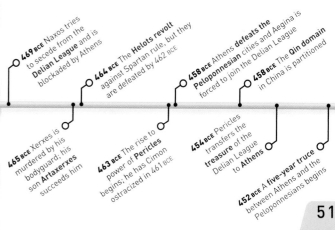

Athenian treasury at Delos
All members of the Delian League had to deposit funds at treasuries on Delos, but the contribution of Athens was the most important.

- **480 BCE** Xerxes I of Persia invades Greece and burns Athens, but is defeated by Themistocles at the naval **Battle of Salamis**
- **480 BCE Carthage** attacks the Greeks of Sicily but is repulsed
- **479 BCE** Persians are defeated at **Plataea** and **Mycale**, and withdraw from mainland Greece
- **479 BCE** Chinese social philosopher **Confucius**, who developed a humanistic ethical system, dies (b.551 BCE)
- **478 BCE** Athens founds the **Delian League** to counter Sparta's attempts to dominate Greece
- **478 BCE** Hieron becomes **Tyrant of Syracuse** and defeats the Etruscans
- **c.470 BCE Themistocles** is ostracized from Athens
- **469 BCE** Naxos tries to secede from the **Delian League** and is blockaded by Athens
- **465 BCE** Xerxes is murdered by his bodyguard; his son **Artaxerxes** succeeds him
- **464 BCE** The **Helots revolt** against Spartan rule, but they are defeated by 462 BCE
- **463 BCE** The rise to power of **Pericles** begins; he has Cimon ostracized in 461 BCE
- **458 BCE** Athens **defeats the Peloponnesian** cities and Aegina is forced to join the Delian League
- **458 BCE** The **Qin domain** in China is partitioned
- **454 BCE** Pericles transfers the **treasure** of the Delian League to **Athens**
- **452 BCE** A **five-year truce** between Athens and the Peloponnesians begins

450–431 BCE

430–404 BCE

In the late 5th century, the Mexican city of Monte Albán began to build its public buildings – the ancestors of its later magnificent pyramids, shown here.

IN THE ROMAN REPUBLIC, the two social classes – the patricians and the plebeians (see 500–491 BCE) – were still divided. The two sides came to an agreement in 451 BCE, appointing a group of ten men (**the decemviri**) to govern Rome outside the normal constitution. In 449 BCE, the decemviri produced the **Laws of the Twelve Tables**, which formed the basis of all Roman law codes.

Around 450 BCE in Central Europe, a **new Celtic culture emerged** called **La Tène**, which supplanted the earlier dominant Halstatt culture. Ruled over by a warrior aristocracy that buried its dead with swords, spears, and funerary chariots, La Tène had important centres in Bohemia (in what is now the Czech Republic) and around the Marne and Moselle rivers (in modern France).

In Oaxaca on Mexico's Pacific Coast, a new centre arose shortly before 450 BCE at **Monte Albán**. This proto-city, on a hill top above the Oaxaca Valley, drew people from the surrounding agricultural villages. Monte Albán's centre housed **large-scale public buildings** – including truncated pyramids, great plazas, and ballgame courts – as well as elaborate burial tombs. Within 150 years, the population of Monte Albán would swell to around 17,000, making it the **largest city in Mesoamerica**.

12

THE NUMBER OF **TABLES** OF **ROMAN** LAW

Zapotec figure from Monte Albán
This elaborate ceramic deity is typical of the production of Monte Albán, which became Mexico's premier site in the 5th century BCE.

ATHENS AND SPARTA HAD FOUGHT EACH OTHER BEFORE (see 451 BCE). The Athenian Empire had the **naval advantage** as it included most of the island and coastal states around the northern and eastern shores of the Aegean Sea. Meanwhile, the city-state of Sparta led an alliance of independent states from the Peloponnese and central Greece, as well as Corinth, and had the **strongest army**. Despite the Thirty Years Peace of 446 BCE, tensions remained high between Athens and Sparta. The events that led to **renewed hostilities** in 430 BCE began three years earlier, when Athens had intervened on behalf of Corcyra in a dispute with Corinth; the Spartans took it as a sign that Athens had breached the peace. An attack by Thebes, a Spartan ally, on Plataea, which supported Athens, was similarly taken by the Athenians to indicate Sparta was fixed on war. Athens, led by Pericles, achieved early success in the **Peloponnesian War** (431–404 BCE). In 426 BCE, **the Athenians invaded the Peloponnese**, and the following year landed a large force at Pylos southwest of Sparta. Yet neither side could land a fatal blow and in 421 BCE they agreed the **Peace of Nicias**, which was supposed to last for 50 years.

The truce soon began to unravel. Corinth refused to recognize its authority, a pro-war leadership emerged in Sparta, and a complex set of political manoeuvres by **Alcibiades** (450–404 BCE), the newly dominant politician in Athens, led to the **renewal of the war** in 419 BCE. The following year, Sparta's allies won a **key victory at Mantinea**. Athens struck back

> “ THE **EMPIRE** YOU POSSESS IS BY NOW **LIKE A TYRANNY** – PERHAPS WRONG TO ACQUIRE IT, BUT CERTAINLY **DANGEROUS** TO LET IT GO. ”

Thucydides, ancient Greek historian, relating a speech by Pericles to the Athenians; from *History of the Peloponnesian War*, II.63

SOCRATES (469–399 BCE)

One of the greatest Greek philosophers, Socrates served on the Athenian Council in 406 BCE, but his challenges to conventional morality at a time of political uncertainty gained him powerful enemies. He refused to mount a conventional defence against charges of corrupting the Athenian youth and was sentenced to die by drinking the poison hemlock.

c.450 BCE La Tène culture emerges in Central Europe

c.450 BCE Steppe nomad **burials** at Pazyryk and Noin-Ula in Siberia

c.450 BCE Construction begins of Zapotec city of **Monte Albán** in Mexico

449 BCE Peace of Callias struck between Greeks and Persians

449 BCE The **Twelve Tables of the Law** officially adopted in Rome

449 BCE Pericles begins **building the Long Wall** between Athens and its port, Piraeus

448 BCE Construction of a **new Parthenon** begins (finished 432 BCE)

433 BCE Athens intervenes for **Corcyra** in its quarrel with **Corinth**, inviting Spartan retaliation

431 BCE Quarrel between Plataea and Thebes leads to another **Peloponnesian War** between Athens and Sparta

430 BCE Sparta invades Attica; Athens stricken with **plague**, killing many thousands

c.428 BCE Birth of Greek philosopher **Plato** (d.c.347 BCE)

427 BCE City of Plataea, an Athenian ally, surrenders to Sparta

423 BCE Darius II becomes Persian king after assassination of Artaxerxes I

423 BCE One-year truce in the war between Athens and Sparta (extended in 422 BCE)

421 BCE Peace of Nicias between Athens and Sparta puts temporary halt to Peloponnesian War

The Great Peloponnesian War
The period of 431 to 404 BCE saw the destruction of the Athenian Empire at the hands of a coalition of Sparta and its allies.

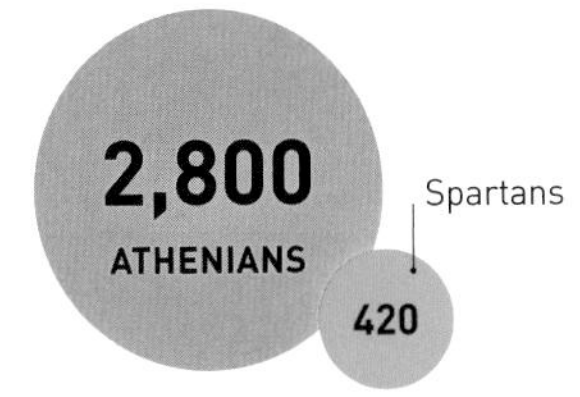

BATTLE OF SPHACTERIA 425 BCE

BATTLE OF DELIUM 424 BCE

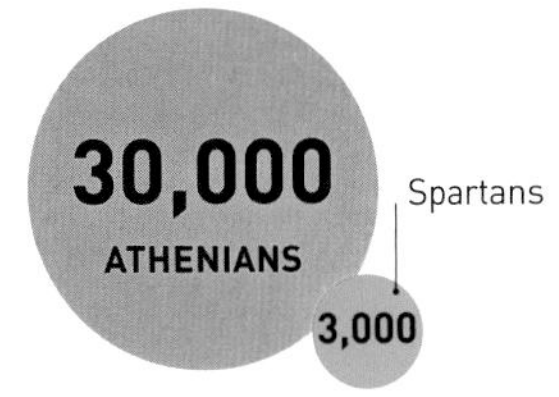

SIEGE OF SYRACUSE 415–413 BCE

in 416 BCE by capturing Melos – the only main Aegean island not in its possession – but fatally over-reached itself in 415 BCE with an expedition to Sicily, ending in the **total destruction** of the Athenian force by **the Syracusans** in 413 BCE. The Spartans, meanwhile, established a fort at Decelea in Attica, which denied the Athenians access to the rich silver mines. An alliance with Persia further strengthened Sparta's position in 412 BCE, and a year later the democratic regime in Athens was briefly overthrown. Democracy was restored the following year, and, though the Athenians won victories at Cyzicus in 410 BCE and Arginusae in 406 BCE, the **total destruction of their fleet at Aegospotami** off Ionia in 405 BCE left Athens defenceless. The Spartans blockaded the city, and, despite a determined resistance, the **Athenians were forced to surrender**. Athens was deprived of its fleet and in 404 BCE a pro-Spartan Council of Thirty was installed to govern it.

In Magadha in **India** the Haryanka dynasty founded by Bimbisara was replaced *c.*413 BCE after the death of Ajatashatru (*c.*459 BCE) and a series of ineffectual rulers. **Shishunaga founded a new dynasty**, which was responsible for overseeing the final transfer of the Magadha royal capital to **Pataliputra**. The Shishunaga dynasty lasted only 500 years.

AFTER ITS VICTORY IN THE PELOPONNESIAN WAR, Sparta found itself embroiled in a quarrel with Persia over whether the Ionian Greek cities should regain their autonomy. Through the 390s BCE, sporadic fighting and abortive peace talks diverted Sparta from a weakening position in mainland Greece. The "**King's Peace**", a definitive treaty with Persia in 386 BCE, deprived the Ionians of autonomy but allowed the Spartans to quash any threats to its supremacy. In 385 BCE, they attacked Mantinea in the central Peloponnese and in 382 BCE occupied Thebes. Spartan power seemed unassailable.

In Persia, the **death of Darius II** (r.423–404 BCE) was followed by a **brief civil war**, when Cyrus the Younger tried to overthrow his older brother **Artaxerxes II** (r.404–358 BCE). Cyrus was defeated and killed at the **Battle of Cunaxa** in 401 BCE, but in its aftermath some 10,000 Greek mercenaries were left trapped in northern Mesopotamia. Under **Xenophon**, the Greeks marched to the Black Sea coast and safety near Trapezus (Trabzon in modern-day Turkey), a feat their commander immortalized in his book *Anabasis*.

In Italy, the **Romans widened their territory** and annexed the city of Veii in 396 BCE, whose submission represented the **end of any Etruscan threat**. However, *c.*390 BCE, an army of Celts, who had been attacking the Etruscan city of Clusium, turned south, defeated a Roman army at the Battle of the Allia, and then **took Rome** itself. This disaster haunted the Romans for centuries.

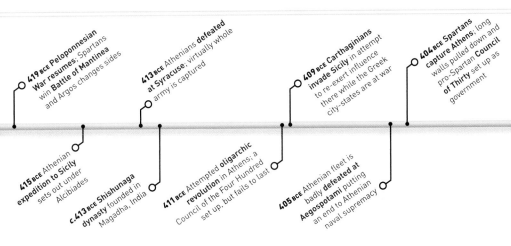

Etruscan tomb painting
The Etruscan language has never been deciphered, so it is through the frescoes in their tombs that much has been learnt of their culture.

- **419 BCE Peloponnesian War resumes**; Spartans win **Battle of Mantinea** and Argos changes sides
- **415 BCE** Athenian **expedition to Sicily** sets out under Alcibiades
- **413 BCE** Athenians **defeated at Syracuse**; virtually whole army is captured
- ***c.*413 BCE Shishunaga dynasty** founded in Magadha, India
- **411 BCE** Attempted **oligarchic revolution** in Athens; a Council of the Four Hundred set up, but fails to last
- **409 BCE Carthaginians invade Sicily** in attempt to re-exert influence there while the Greek city-states are at war
- **405 BCE** Athenian fleet is badly **defeated at Aegospotami** putting an end to Athenian naval supremacy
- **404 BCE Spartans capture Athens**; long walls pulled down and pro-Spartan **Council of Thirty** set up as government
- **403 BCE** Council of Thirty in Athens dissolved; **democracy restored**
- ***c.*400 BCE Moche culture** emerges in Peru
- **401 BCE Xenophon** leads 10,000 Greek mercenaries supporting a Persian rebellion from Babylon to the Black Sea
- **399 BCE** Greek philosopher **Socrates executed**
- **399 BCE Egypt breaks away** from Persia and begins its 29th dynasty
- **398–397 BCE Dionysius of Syracuse** wins war against Carthaginians
- **396 BCE** Romans capture Etruscan **city of Veii**
- **386 BCE** Sparta and Persia sign the **"King's Peace"**
- **384 BCE Plato** completes his ***Symposium*** and founds his Academy
- **383 BCE** War restarts between **Carthage** and Dionysius of **Syracuse**

Sutton Hoo buckle

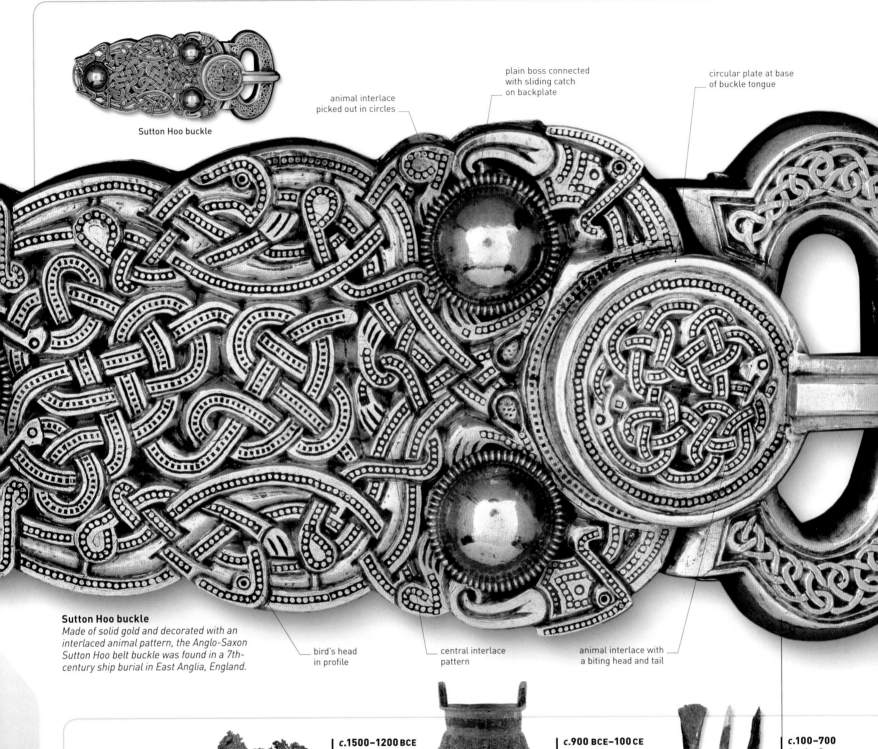

Sutton Hoo buckle
Made of solid gold and decorated with an interlaced animal pattern, the Anglo-Saxon Sutton Hoo belt buckle was found in a 7th-century ship burial in East Anglia, England.

Prehistory
Use of copper ore
In western Iran and Anatolia, copper ore is ground or beaten into shape to make small objects such as beads.

Copper ore

2600–2400 BCE
Use of beaten copper plate
Early copper smelting methods are refined, allowing the beating of copper while still hot into more complex shapes.

Sumerian copper bull

c.1500–1200 BCE
Refinement of bronze casting
New techniques are developed for casting and adorning bronze vessels, such as decorating them by beating on the inside.

Shang cauldron

c.1500–30 BCE
Purifying gold
The ancient Egyptians learn how to separate pure gold from silver in around 1500 BCE and begin to use it more extensively for decorative purposes.

Funeral mask of Tutankhamun

c.900 BCE–100 CE
Using iron
Ironworking spreads from western Anatolia, reaching Greece around 900 BCE and West Africa about 400 BCE, enabling stronger tools and weapons to be made.

Weapon heads

c.640–500 BCE
Metal as money
Metal coins (made of an alloy of gold and silver) are first used in Lydia (in present-day Turkey) around 640 BCE. The ancient Greeks adopt the idea and spread it around the Mediterranean.

c.100–700
Anglo-Saxon metalworking
The Anglo-Saxons bring a new level of sophistication to metalworking, often using animal forms as decoration.

Greek coin

THE STORY OF METALWORKING

FROM EVERYDAY OBJECTS TO COMPLEX MACHINES, METALS ARE VITAL FOR OUR CIVILIZATION

Since their earliest known use in the 8th millennium BCE, metals have played a crucial role in the production of a vast range of objects, and even today, with the availability of sophisticated polymers and composites, they still permeate every aspect of modern civilization.

Around 7000 BCE, naturally occurring metals, notably copper, began to be used for small items such as pins in western Iran and eastern Anatolia. These were made by simply grinding or beating the metal into shape. Heating copper to make it more malleable was probably discovered by accidentally dropping the metal in fire, but it was the introduction of smelting in a crucible around 3800 BCE that led to the large-scale use of metals.

THE DEVELOPMENT OF ALLOYS

About 3000 BCE, the first alloy – bronze – was produced. Made by smelting tin and copper together in a crucible, bronze is stronger and more easily worked than either of its individual constituents, and it remained the principal metal for tools and weapons until the invention of ironworking around 1250 BCE. The technology to melt pure iron was not invented until the 19th century, so early iron objects were made by first smelting iron ore to an impure iron "bloom", then separating out the iron pieces and welding them together in a furnace. This method of production continued until the introduction of blast furnaces in Europe in the 15th century. The Industrial Revolution in the 18th century brought new techniques and the use of coking coal in blast furnaces, but it was English inventor Henry Bessemer's invention of the Bessemer converter in 1856 that permitted the large-scale production of steel, a strong, high-quality, iron–carbon alloy. Later in the Industrial Revolution, further advances made it possible to produce other metals, such as aluminium, magnesium, and titanium, whose light weight and strength played a vital role in the development of the aviation and space industries.

1,083°C

THE **MELTING POINT** OF **COPPER.** WHEN COPPER IS **ALLOYED** WITH **TIN**, THIS **DROPS** TO **950°C**

HOW ALLOYS ARE MADE

An alloy is a mixture of metals or of a metal with a non-metal (such as iron with carbon in steel). Many metals occur naturally in alloyed form, but synthetic alloys were not produced until around 3000 BCE, when copper was melted with tin to produce bronze. The technique spread, reaching Mesopotamia soon after 3000 BCE and Egypt by 2000 BCE or possibly earlier.

700–800
Sword-making
In Europe, sword-makers develop stronger swords by welding together successive layers of iron with carbon added, or by beating out thin iron strips then welding them together.

Viking sword

800–1300/1450
Christian objects in precious metals
Medieval Christians make sacred objects, such as crucifixes and reliquaries, from gold and other precious metals, sometimes encrusted with gemstones.

The Verdun Altar

***c.*15th century**
Weapons from cast metal
Cast iron is developed. Because it is strong and can be used to make shapes such as tubes, it finds an immediate use in making artillery.

Medieval cannon

1810
Tin can
English inventor Peter Durand patents the tin can for preserving food. His patent was for a can made of iron and coated with tin to inhibit rusting of the iron.

1856
Bessemer converter
Englishman Henry Bessemer invents a converter that enables large-scale production of high-quality steel.

Bessemer converter

Lockheed Blackbird

1910
Aluminium foil
The first aluminium foil is produced. It was made possible by the invention in 1886 of a method of mass-producing the metal by passing an electric current through molten ore.

1950s
Titanium aircraft
Because of its high strength-to-weight ratio, titanium starts to be extensively used in military aircraft. It is now also widely used in commercial aircraft.

380–371 BCE

A carving showing the pharaoh Nectanebo I, founder of the 30th Dynasty, making offerings to gods, including the crocodile-headed Sobek.

EGYPT HAD BROKEN AWAY FROM Persian control after the revolt of Amyrtaeus, who founded the 28th Dynasty in 404 BCE. However, the **Persians** had not given up on Egypt. **Nectanebo I** established the 30th Egyptian Dynasty in 380 BCE. He was able to repel a force sent by the Persians and their Greek allies in 373 BCE. Persia was diverted from further attempts to bring Egypt to heel by the **Great Rebellion of the Satraps** in the 360s BCE. This rebellion was partially aggravated by the campaigns of Tachos, son of Nectanebo I, in Persian-ruled Palestine from 361–360 BCE. **Nectanebo II** (r.360–343 BCE) succeeded Nectanebo I, and continued to meddle in the Persian civil wars. In an ill-judged intervention in 346 BCE, he sent troops to aid an uprising in Sidon (Lebanon). In response, **Artaxerxes III of Persia** marched into the Nile Delta region in 343 BCE, and Egypt was defeated within two years. Now under Persian rule, Egypt was never again ruled by a native dynasty.

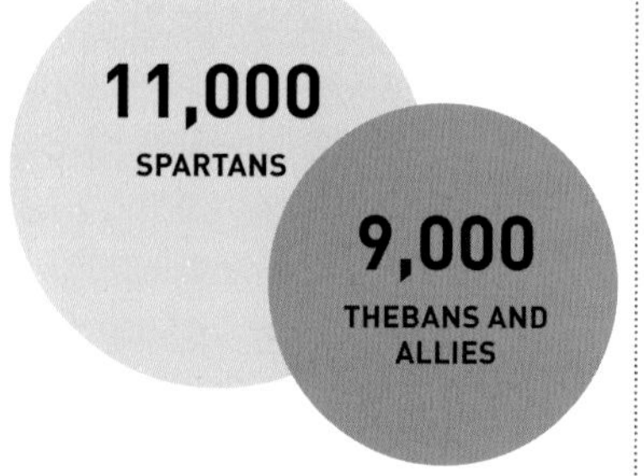

Battle of Leuctra
At Leuctra in central Greece, the Thebans exploited the tendency of the Spartans to shift right by concentrating their attack on the left, enabling them to defeat an enemy with larger numbers than theirs.

150 COUPLES FORMED THE ELITE MILITARY UNIT THE **SACRED BAND OF THEBES**

In Greece, the **Spartan occupation of Thebes,** which had begun in 382 BCE, was short-lived. In 379 BCE, the Spartan **polemarch** (governor) of Thebes was assassinated, and the Thebans drove out the Spartan garrison with the aid of two Athenian generals who arrived on their own initiative to help. In retaliation, the **Spartans mounted an expedition** under King Cleombrotus (r.380–371 BCE). This expedition failed to retake Thebes, but it so alarmed the Athenians that they executed one general and exiled the other, and temporarily abandoned the alliance with Thebes. The **Spartans invaded the region of Boeotia** in 378–377 BCE but made little headway, although the Athenians were alarmed enough to revive the Theban alliance and try to establish a **Second Athenian Confederacy** in opposition to Sparta. In 375 BCE the Thebans, Athenians, and Spartans signed a "Common Peace", but it broke down almost immediately. The Thebans then took the offensive, aided by a new elite force of citizen soldiers, the **Sacred Band**, which consisted of 150 male couples. The Sacred Band supplemented the mercenaries who largely fought Greek city-states' wars by this period. Theban attempts to conquer the region of Phocis and retain dominance in Boeotia rankled with Sparta, and scuppered Athenian attempts to broker a peace in 372 BCE. At **Leuctra** in 371 BCE, the Theban army under the general **Epaminondas** fought a tactically brilliant battle to smash the Spartan phalanx. At Sparta's mercy just eight years before, **Thebes** was now the **dominant power in Greece**.

In Sicily, **Syracuse** continued to flourish under the strong rule of **Dionysius I** (402–367 BCE), who fought the third in a series of wars against the Carthaginians from 383 to 375 BCE. At first, the war went badly for Dionysius, whose fleet was wrecked in a storm. Carthaginian efforts to mount an expedition to Sicily were hampered by plague in 379 BCE and a revolt by subject cities in Libya, so that it was only in 377 BCE that an army was landed. Dionysius, who had been campaigning against Carthage's allies in southern Italy, returned to Sicily and **crushed Mago's force** – 10,000 are said to have died. Dionysius allowed the remnants to slip away, and they regrouped and returned the following year under Mago's son Himilco to deliver a stinging defeat to the Syracusans. Both sides were war-weary and in 375 BCE **made peace**, leaving Dionysius in possession of most of eastern Sicily and parts of southern Italy.

Temple of Thoth
Situated at Hermopolis in Upper Egypt, the temple of Thoth dates from the New Kingdom but was renovated in the 4th century BCE.

370–356 BCE

The ruins of Thebes, Greece's dominant city-state in the 360s BCE.

ALTHOUGH THE ATHENIANS brokered a **general peace** in Greece in 371 BCE, the Thebans did not participate. Thebes built up a coalition of allies and **invaded Sparta** in 370–369 BCE. As a result, Messenia was finally detached from Spartan control, but further Theban success was hampered by the temporary deposition of **Epaminondas**, who was tried for allegedly sparing the city of Sparta in exchange for a bribe. Once Epaminondas was back in control, the Thebans won Persian backing for their anti-Spartan alliance in 367 BCE, and a further **invasion of the Peloponnese** in 366 BCE gained recruits for the Theban coalition. However, Theban successes relied too narrowly on the personality of one man, and when Epaminondas

Ancient theatre
The Odeon was a temple built in the town of Messene, which was founded by Epaminondas of Thebes in 367 BCE.

c.380 BCE Farming and **iron metallurgy** is spread by Bantu-speaking people in the **Western Zambezi** region of Africa

380 BCE The **Servian Wall** is built around Rome

380 BCE Nectanebo becomes the first pharaoh of Egypt's 30th Dynasty

378 BCE Exiled Theban democrats under **Epaminondas** lead an **uprising** against the pro-Spartan ruling party. The Spartan garrison abandons the city of Thebes

373 BCE Artaxerxes II is defeated after invading Egypt in attempt to bring it back under Persian control

371 BCE Athens and Sparta make **peace**, ending an eight-year conflict

371 BCE Theban general Epaminondas wins the **Battle of Leuctra** against Sparta, and the Arcadians revolt against Spartan rule

370 BCE Foundation of the **Nanda dynasty** in India

369 BCE Epaminondas invades **Messenia**

360 BCE Revolt of the satraps (governors) begins in the Persian empire

362 BCE Battle of Mantinea marks final eclipse of Spartan power

> **“** AN ARMY OF DEER **LED BY A LION** IS MORE TO BE FEARED THAN AN ARMY OF LIONS **LED BY A DEER. ”**

Attributed to **Philip II, king of Macedonia,** 4th century BCE

was killed in battle in 362 BCE, Theban power was rapidly eclipsed.

In India, the **Nanda dynasty** began its **expansion** in the 370s BCE, and continued to expand until it was able to take power from the Shishunaga in 345 BCE. The dynasty's founder **Mahapadma Nanda** conquered much of north India, building up a huge army. He operated an efficient administrative system with centrally appointed tax collectors and undertook irrigation works. However, the deposition of Dhana Nanda in 321 BCE was followed by the **absorption of the Nanda empire into the Mauryan empire**.

The **state of Chu** was the most southerly of China's **Warring States**, centred on the Middle Yangzi river. Throughout the 5th century BCE it annexed a number of states, becoming the dominant power by 380 BCE. In 366 BCE a resounding victory by the state of **Qin** against the armies of **Hann** and **Wei,** followed by another defeat of Wei at the **battle of Shimen** in 364 BCE led to Chu's decline and the shift eastwards of Wei's royal centre to Daliang. A rejuvenated Wei was strong enough to force the rulers of four other Warring States to attend its court in 356 BCE. Wei's supremacy was short-lived, and defeats inflicted on it by Qi armies at Guiling in 353 BCE and Maling in 341 BCE reduced it to a Qi vassal.

88

THE AGE OF **MAGAPADMA NANDA** AT HIS DEATH

IN 359 BCE PERDICCAS III OF Macedonia died and his successor, **Philip II** (r.359–336 BCE) began to transform the position of what had been regarded by other Greeks as a very minor kingdom. In 357 BCE, he made his first major conquest, Amphipolis in Thrace. He became involved in the **Third Sacred War** (356–346 BCE), which was fought over perceived violations by Sparta and Phocis of the sacred oracle at Delphi, using this to cement his position as an important player in the power politics of central Greece and the Peloponnese. In the 340s, Philip strengthened his position in Thessaly and became involved in petty disputes between the city-states, as rival factions turned either to him or to Athens for support. In 340 BCE **open war** broke out between Philip and the Athenian-Theban alliance. Just two years later, at Chaeronea in Boeotia, **Philip defeated the Athenians** and annihilated the Theban Sacred Band (see 380–371 BCE). Macedonian power in Greece was now unchallenged.

Rome's steady expansion in central Italy had caused alarm among her neighbours. This led to a bitter six-year struggle with the town of Tibur from 360 BCE, among other conflicts. In 340 BCE, a general **war broke out between Rome and the Latins,** who inhabited the modern region of Lazio around Rome. The Romans had just emerged from a war with the Samnites, a people who inhabited the central Apennines, and the Latins took advantage of Rome's exhausted state to launch an attack. During the first year of the war, at a battle near Vesuvius, the consul Publius Decius Mus is said to have dedicated his body to the gods of the underworld and then undertaken a suicidal charge against the Latin ranks which turned the tide of battle in the Roman's favour. By 338 BCE, the **Romans had defeated the Latin League.** The peace terms were favourable, with many Latins being granted Roman citizenship. The League was then dissolved, and many of the former Latin cities were absorbed into the Roman state, moving Rome further towards complete dominance of central Italy.

In Peru, the **Nazca culture** began around 350 BCE. These people created mysterious geoglyphs, huge lines in the desert creating animal and abstract shapes, which cannot be made out from the ground.

PHILIP OF MACEDONIA (382–336 BCE)

Philip II reformed the Macedonian army and forced the Greek states to join a League of Corinth under Macedonian control. After his return to Macedonia, he took a new wife, Cleopatra, but was stabbed to death at his wedding feast, possibly on the orders of his son, Alexander the Great, who stood to lose his position if Cleopatra bore another heir.

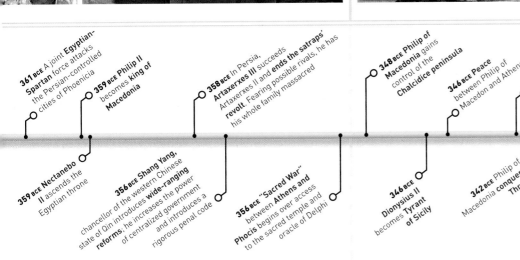

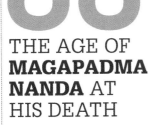

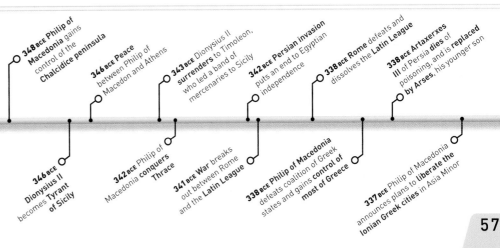

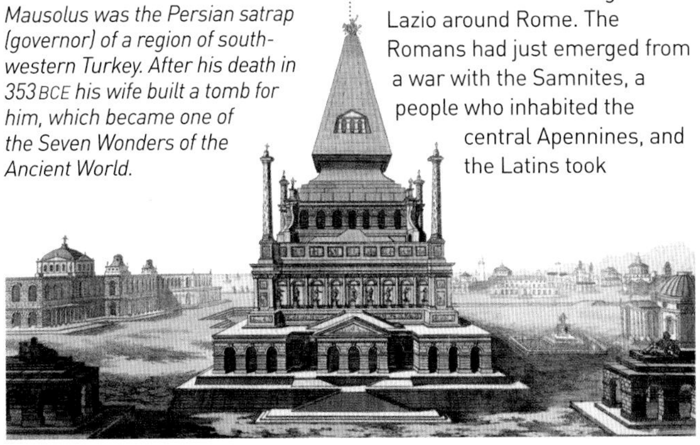

Mausoleum of Halicarnassus
Mausolus was the Persian satrap (governor) of a region of south-western Turkey. After his death in 353 BCE his wife built a tomb for him, which became one of the Seven Wonders of the Ancient World.

361 BCE A joint **Egyptian-Spartan** force attacks the Persian-controlled cities of Phoenicia

359 BCE Nectanebo II ascends the Egyptian throne

359 BCE Philip II becomes **king of Macedonia**

358 BCE In Persia, **Artaxerxes III** succeeds Artaxerxes II and **ends the satraps' revolt.** Fearing possible rivals, he has his whole family massacred

356 BCE Shang Yang, chancellor of the western Chinese state of Qin introduces **wide-ranging reforms**; he increases the power of centralized government and introduces a rigorous penal code

356 BCE "Sacred War" between Athens and Phocis begins over access to the sacred temple and oracle of Delphi

348 BCE Philip of Macedonia gains control of the **Chalcidice peninsula**

346 BCE Dionysius II becomes **Tyrant of Sicily**

346 BCE Peace between Philip of Macedon and Athens

343 BCE Dionysius II **surrenders** to Timoleon, who led a band of mercenaries to Sicily

342 BCE Philip of Macedonia **conquers Thrace**

342 BCE Persian invasion puts an end to Egyptian independence

341 BCE War breaks out between Rome and the **Latin League**

338 BCE Philip of Macedonia defeats coalition of Greek states and gains **control of most of Greece**

338 BCE Rome defeats and dissolves the **Latin League**

338 BCE Artaxerxes III of Persia **dies** of poisoning, and is **replaced by Arses,** his younger son

337 BCE Philip of Macedonia announces plans to **liberate the Ionian Greek cities** in Asia Minor

Despite being heavily outnumbered at Issus, Alexander the Great, depicted here on his horse Bucephalus, made brilliant use of his cavalry to win a stunning victory over King Darius III.

Ruins of Persepolis
The Persian ceremonial capital of Persepolis was burnt to the ground by Alexander's troops in 330 BCE.

AFTER THE ASSASSINATION OF PHILIP OF MACEDONIA in 336 BCE (see 355–337 BCE), his 20-year-old son Alexander (often referred to as Alexander the Great) became commander of the major Greek city states. The next year Alexander invaded Thrace, but a rumour that he had been killed caused a major revolt centred on the Greek city of Thebes, supported by **Darius III of Persia** (r.336–330 BCE). Alexander reacted swiftly; the Thebans were defeated and their city razed to the ground. The other states soon submitted. In 334 BCE, Alexander hurried to Anatolia, where a Macedonian army was already established, totalling perhaps 43,000 infantry and 6,000 cavalry. Although this figure was dwarfed by the forces of the local Persian satraps (governors), Alexander's cavalry smashed the lines of the **satrap Arsites** at the River Granicus in northwest Turkey. He pushed on towards the heart of the Persian Empire. In 333 BCE, at Issus, northern Syria, he routed an army led by Darius III himself. In 331 BCE, the Macedonians defeated Darius III again at **Gaugamela** (in modern Iraq). The next year Darius was stabbed to death by **Bessus**, one of his generals. Alexander now seemed to have acquired the whole of the vast Persian Empire.

Aristotle
The philosopher Aristotle was employed by Philip of Macedonia as Alexander the Great's tutor.

AFTER HIS MURDER OF DARIUS, Bessus declared himself the new king of Persia (as **Artaxerxes V**), but some of the Persian satraps submitted to Alexander instead of Bessus. During 330–329 BCE, Alexander pursued Bessus into the easternmost regions of the Persian Empire, beyond the Hindu Kush and into Bactria. Finally, in Sogdiana, north of the River Oxus, the local nobles, led by the Sogdian warlord **Spitamenes**, betrayed Bessus and handed him over to Alexander. Once Alexander had continued his march north, however, Spitamenes revolted. It took Alexander a year of bitter campaigning to relieve the **siege of Macaranda** (Samarkand) and pacify Sogdiana, although the fortress of the "Sogdian Rock" managed to hold out against the Macedonian forces until 327 BCE. Alexander then crossed into the Kabul Valley and the following year, at the river Hydaspes, he overcame the local ruler **Porus**. His plans to push further into India were stymied by his soldiers who, demoralized and disease-ridden, mutinied and demanded to go home. Part of the army returned home by sea under Nearchus, but a detachment under Alexander marched through the harsh Gedrosian desert, suffering heavy losses. His army reached central Persia early in 324 BCE, but Alexander, still planning new expeditions into Arabia, died of a fever at Babylon in May 323 BCE, aged 33.

In central Italy, the Samnites of the central-southern Apennines, who had lost a war against the Romans in 342–340 BCE, fought them once more in the **Second Samnite War** (326–304 BCE). The advance of the Romans into Campania after their abolition of the **Latin League** in 338 BCE alarmed the Samnites, and the Roman placing of a colony in their land in 328 BCE and tensions over the control of Neapolis (Naples) led to the **outbreak of war** in 326 BCE. In 321 BCE, the Samnites defeated a Roman army at the Caudine Forks. The **Romans were humiliated** by being forced to bow down and "pass under the yoke" (an arch made from their captured spears). Four years of peace followed before the Romans renewed the war and, despite dogged resistance by the Samnites, finally emerged victorious in 304 BCE.

Alexander the Great's conquests
Alexander penetrated the farthest corners of the Persian empire. To cement his rule he founded a series of new cities, almost all named after himself, notably Alexandria in Egypt.

CONQUEST OF ALEXANDER
Macedonian Empire 336-323 BCE
→ Route taken by Alexander's forces

30
THE AGE OF ALEXANDER'S **FAVOURITE HORSE, BUCEPHALUS,** WHEN IT DIED

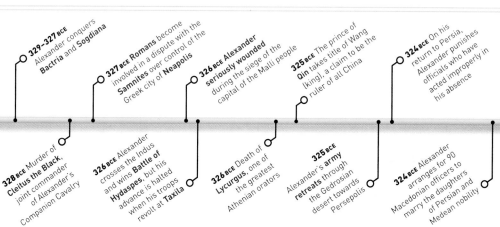

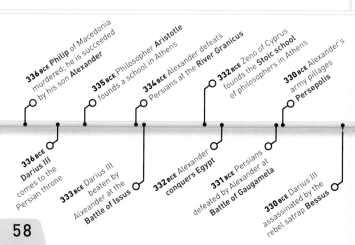

336 BCE Philip of Macedonia murdered; he is succeeded by his son **Alexander**

336 BCE Darius III comes to the Persian throne

335 BCE Philosopher **Aristotle** founds a school in Athens

334 BCE Alexander defeats Persians at the **River Granicus**

333 BCE Darius III beaten by Alxeander at the **Battle of Issus**

332 BCE Zeno of Cyprus founds the **Stoic school** of philosophers in Athens

332 BCE Alexander **conquers Egypt**

331 BCE Persians defeated by Alexander at **Battle of Gaugamela**

330 BCE Alexander's army pillages **Persepolis**

330 BCE Darius III assassinated by the rebel satrap **Bessus**

329–327 BCE Alexander conquers **Bactria** and **Sogdiana**

328 BCE Murder of **Cleitus the Black**, joint commander of Alexander's Companion Cavalry

327 BCE Romans become involved in a dispute with the **Samnites** over control of the Greek city of **Neapolis**

326 BCE Alexander seriously wounded during the siege of the capital of the Malli people

326 BCE Alexander crosses the Indus and wins **Battle of Hydaspes**, but his advance is halted when his troops revolt at **Taxila**

326 BCE Death of **Lycurgus**, one of the greatest Athenian orators

325 BCE The prince of **Qin** takes title of Wang (king), a claim to be the ruler of all China

325 BCE Alexander's **army retreats** through the Gedrosian desert towards Persepolis

324 BCE On his return to Persia, Alexander punishes officials who have acted improperly in his absence

324 BCE Alexander arranges for 90 Macedonian officers to marry the daughters of Persian and Medean nobility

“ TO THE STRONGEST! ”

Alexander the Great, on his deathbed in reply to a question about who would succeed him

Samnite-style helmet
The Romans admired the Samnites as fighters. This gladiator helmet is based on the Samnite style of armour.

ALEXANDER THE GREAT had not provided for an orderly succession after his death in 323 BCE, and his most experienced generals were also dead – except for Antipater who had been left as regent in Macedonia. Alexander's wife Roxane was pregnant, and he had a half-brother Arrhidaeus, who was, unfortunately, mentally unstable. **A clique of generals** who were present at Alexander's deathbed – **Ptolemy**, **Cassander**, **Seleucus**, and **Lysimachus** – engineered a solution by which Roxane's newborn son Alexander IV (323–310 BCE) notionally shared power with Arrhidaeus, who became **Philip III**. In reality, this military clique carved up the empire between themselves and four other generals. **Perdiccas** emerged as the main power in the centre; **Antipater** and **Craterus** took Europe; **Antigonos Monopthalmos** ("the one-eyed") was given Phrygia; **Ptolemy** got Egypt; and **Seleucus** and **Cassander** were promoted to senior military commands.

These generals, who became known as the **Diadochoi** ("successors"), then fought a long series of wars for dominance in Alexander's former empire, at first pitting the others against Perdiccas, who was assassinated in 320 BCE. Antipater rose to power next, but he died of natural causes in 318 BCE, leaving Antigonos to make a bid for power

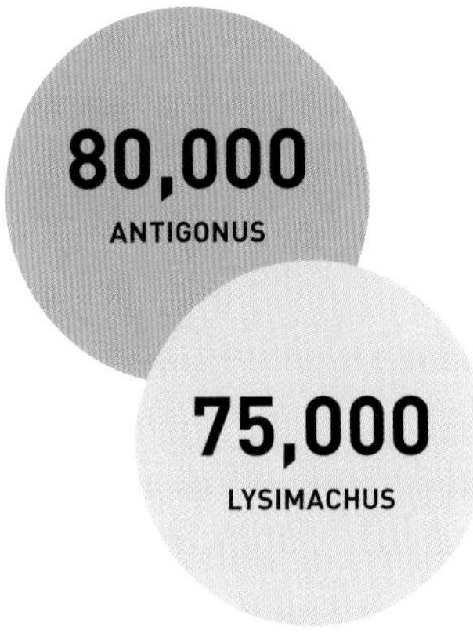

Battle of Ipsus
Although slightly outnumbered, Lysimachus deployed his archers against his enemy's flank, causing Antigonus's infantry to flee in panic.

against the four remaining principal players: Cassander in Macedonia, Ptolemy in Egypt, Lysimachus in Thrace, and Seleucus in Babylon. War between the parties raged inconclusively until 311 BCE. But when it was renewed again in 308 BCE, it looked as if Antigonus might overcome all the others. Then, in 301 BCE, **Lysimachus crushed the Antigonid army** at Ipsus, and annexed most of Antigonus's former territories, so cementing a **tripartite division** of Alexander's empire between himself, Ptolemy, and Seleucus.

In India, in around 320 BCE, **Chandragupta Maurya** (r.c.320–297 BCE) overthrew the last of the Nandas (see 370–356 BCE) to become ruler of Magadha and the Ganges plain. An energetic ruler, he then gradually absorbed the outlying regions of the Nanda Empire, pushing his control as far as Gujarat and the Punjab. In 305 BCE, he began a campaign against one of Alexander's successors, **Seleucus**, which ended in a treaty in 303 BCE, by which the Greeks ceded control of eastern Afghanistan and Baluchistan to Chandragupta. Having established the **Mauryan Empire** in 307 BCE, Chandragupta decided to abdicate in favour of his son **Bindusara** (r.297–272 BCE). He then retired to become a Jain monk, ultimately starving himself to death.

In China, **Meng Zi** (or Mencius) (*c*.372–289 BCE) arrived at the Wei court around 320 BCE and rapidly earned himself a reputation as the "second sage" of the **Confucian tradition**. His surviving work, the ***Shi Ji***, is written in the form of dialogues with several contemporary kings. Meng Zi stresses the value of *de* (virtue) for a king and, more practically, recommends lower taxes, less harsh punishments, and ensuring the people have enough to eat. He believed that if a king acted benevolently, everyone would want to be ruled by him, and he would have no need of conquest. Meng Zi's benevolent view of human nature had a widespread appeal, and politically his views were most influential in the time of the **Song dynasty** (960–1279 CE).

ALEXANDER THE GREAT (356–323 BCE)

Aged 20, Alexander inherited much of Greece from his father; by his death just 13 years later, he had extended this to cover a vast area from the Indus River in the east to Illyria in the west. He was a brilliant general but prone to acts of impetuous violence. His adoption of Persian court ritual alienated many native Macedonians, and his not naming an heir proved catastrophic.

323 BCE Alexander dies in Babylon; his empire begins to disintegrate among warring factions

323 BCE Outbreak of the **Lamian (or Hellenic) War** between Athens and her allies and the Macedonians in Thessaly

321 BCE Roman army defeated by Samnites at the **Caudine Forks**

321 BCE Athens defeated by **Antipater**; peace terms entail the end of **Athenian democracy**

320 BCE Ptolemy annexes Judaea and Syria

315 BCE Olympias, the mother of Alexander, murdered

312 BCE Rome's first aqueduct built by **Appius Claudius**

311 BCE Alexander's successors agree on **division of the empire**

310 BCE Alexander IV, son of Alexander the Great, dies

308 BCE Last royal burial of a **Kushite king**, Natasen, takes place at Napata

307 BCE Athens falls under **Macedonian** control

306 BCE Ptolemy I of Egypt **defeated** off Salamis (Cyprus) by Greeks under Demetrius

305 BCE Seleucus establishes himself in Persia and Anatolia, founding the **Seleucid Dynasty**

304 BCE Second Samnite War ends; Rome wins but gains no territory

302 BCE Chandragupta Maurya signs a **peace treaty** with Seleucus

301 BCE At the **Battle of Ipsus**, Lysimachus and Seleucus **defeat Antigonus**, who is killed

300–281 BCE

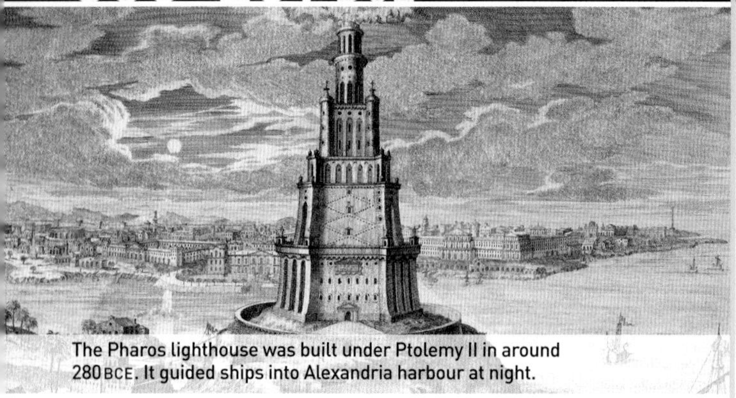

The Pharos lighthouse was built under Ptolemy II in around 280 BCE. It guided ships into Alexandria harbour at night.

IN ITALY, A THIRD WAR broke out between the **Romans and Samnites** in 298 BCE, apparently provoked by Samnite harassment of their neighbours, the Lucanians. Despite two Roman victories in 297 BCE, the Samnites, this time allied with the Gauls, could still field a huge army against the Romans at **Sentinum** in 295 BCE.

275

THE NUMBER OF YEARS THE **PTOLEMAIC DYNASTY** RULED EGYPT

The equally vast Roman army – at 45,000, the largest they had ever fielded – was threatened with defeat until the Roman consul **Publius Decius Mus** (d.295 BCE) dedicated himself and the enemy army as sacrificial victims to the gods of the underworld and led a **suicidal charge** that shattered the Samnite line. A string of **Roman successes** followed in 293 and 292 BCE, and two years later the Samnites finally surrendered and their lands were annexed. Roman territory now stretched across the Italian peninsula to the Adriatic Sea.

Demetrius Poliorcetes (c.337–283 BCE), the son of Antigonus (see 322–301 BCE), was now rebuilding his strength from bases in the Aegean islands and in Cyprus. He was able to exploit the need of **Seleucus**, in Babylon, for allies against the now over-mighty **Lysimachus**. In 294 BCE, Demetrius **invaded Macedon**, whose ruler Cassander had died three years before, leaving his two young sons to engage in a **bitter civil war**. Demetrius then attacked Lysimachus's Asian territories, but in 292 BCE he was brought back to Greece by a revolt in Aetolia. By 289 BCE, Demetrius had suppressed the revolt, but he had lost most of his island bases to Ptolemy's Egyptian fleet. He retreated to Asia, and died in 283 BCE, a captive of Seleucus.

Of Alexander's successors, Ptolemy inherited the weakest position. A naval defeat in 306 BCE by Demetrius Poliorcetes confined his ambitions temporarily to Egypt. Yet here he shrewdly chose to exploit the existing mechanisms of power, establishing himself as a pharaoh in the old style and setting up an administration that melded the best of Greek and Egyptian traditions. By 295 BCE, Ptolemy's naval forces had recovered and conquered much of the Aegean. In Egypt, Ptolemy's position was sufficiently secure that, at his death in 283 BCE, aged 84, he passed the kingdom on to his son Ptolemy II Philadelphos (r.283–245 BCE), the second king of a Ptolemaic dynasty that would rule Egypt until 30 BCE.

280–266 BCE

“ ANOTHER SUCH VICTORY AND **WE ARE UNDONE.** ”

Pyrrhus, king of the Greek state of Epirus, 279 BCE

IN 281 BCE, THE APPEAL by envoys from the southern Italian city of Tarentum for protection against the Romans provided **Pyrrhus**, the king of the Greek state of Epirus, with a perfect excuse for fulfilling his ambitions and intervening there. He arrived with an army more than 25,000 strong, including war elephants. He beat the Romans at the **River Siris** in 280 BCE, but the Roman senate refused to make peace. Pyrrhus vanquished another Roman army at **Asculum** the next year, but his losses were so severe that it seemed more like a defeat. After invading Sicily, Pyrrhus retreated back to **Epirus** in 275 BCE, nursing huge losses in troops and having made no territorial gains.

The defeat and **death of Lysimachus** in 281 BCE in battle

Pyrrhus of Epirus
Despite his many campaigns, when Pyrrhus died he ruled little more than the kingdom he had inherited.

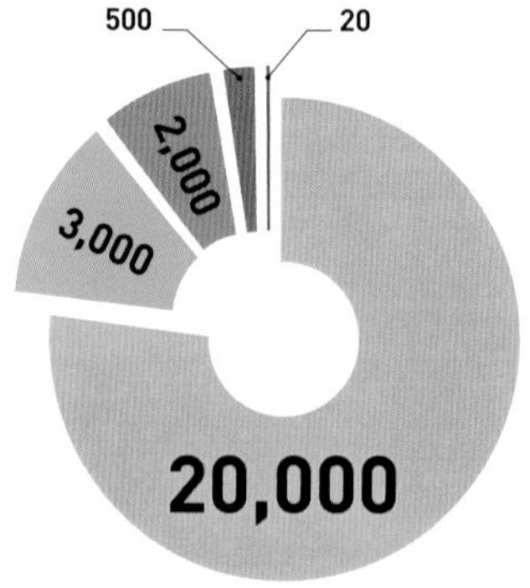

Pyrrhus's army
The army that Pyrrhus took over to Italy included a small number of war elephants whose presence caused the Roman cavalry to panic and flee.

against Seleucus, and the latter's assassination, soon led to instability on the frontier between the **Seleucid Empire** (now ruled by his son Antiochus I) and the Egyptian ruler **Ptolemy II Philadelphos**. Finally, in 274 BCE the **First Syrian War** broke out between them. The Egyptians emerged victorious, annexing parts of the Syrian coast and southern Anatolia. This position was in part reversed by Egyptian losses in the **Second Syrian War** (260–253 BCE) and then renewed in the **Third Syrian War** (246–241 BCE), which was fought between the Seleucid **Antiochus II** and **Ptolemy III**. These three debilitating wars left the Seleucids particularly vulnerable to the now growing power of **Parthia**.

265–241 BCE

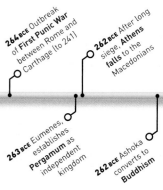

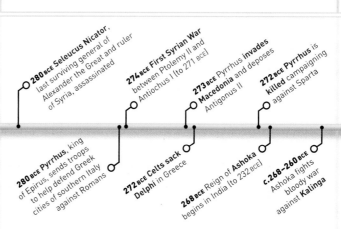

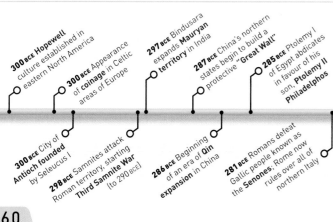

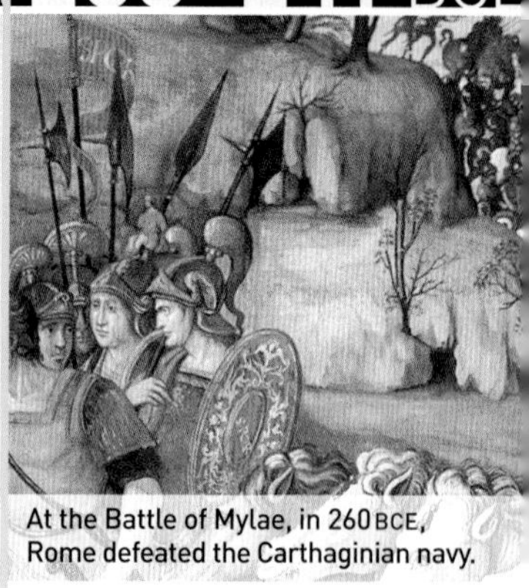

At the Battle of Mylae, in 260 BCE, Rome defeated the Carthaginian navy.

IN INDIA, the accession of **Ashoka** (c.294–232 BCE) to the throne in 268 BCE had marked a watershed for the **Mauryan Empire**. On his father Bindusara's death (see 322–301 BCE), Ashoka had to fight a four-year **civil war** with his brothers before he was enthroned. Around eight years later, he launched a campaign against **Kalinga** (modern Orissa), which was so bloody that around 100,000 people are said to have died. So struck with remorse was Ashoka at this slaughter, that he ever after rejected war and promoted the Buddhist concept of **dharma**, meaning mercy or piety. He set up a series of edicts carved in rock throughout the empire – many of them on pillars topped with a lion – promoting his adherence to dharma. Under his patronage the **Third Buddhist Council** met at Pataliputra around 250 BCE, and Ashoka sought to export his ideas abroad, exchanging diplomatic missions with foreign rulers, such as **Antiochus II of Syria** and **Ptolemy II of Egypt**. At his death in 232 BCE, the Mauryan empire had reached its greatest extent and seemed securely established.

In China, **Zhao Zheng** succeeded his father to the throne of Qin in 246 BCE. From 228 BCE, ably advised by **chancellor Li Si**, Zhao Zheng unleashed a final war of conquest against the remaining **Warring States** (see 370–356 BCE). Zhao and Yan soon fell to his forces, the Qin armies captured Wei and, in 223 BCE, overcame Chu. Only Qi still held out but, in 221 BCE, Zhao Zheng finally annexed it, leaving

300 BCE Hopewell culture established in eastern North America

300 BCE City of **Antioch founded** by Seleucus I

300 BCE Appearance of **coinage** in Celtic areas of Europe

298 BCE Samnites attack Roman territory, starting **Third Samnite War** (to 290 BCE)

297 BCE Bindusara expands **Mauryan territory** in India

287 BCE China's northern states begin to build a protective **"Great Wall"**

286 BCE Beginning of an era of **Qin expansion** in China

285 BCE Ptolemy I of Egypt abdicates in favour of his son, **Ptolemy II Philadelphos**

281 BCE Romans defeat Gallic people known as the **Senones**; Rome now rules over all of northern Italy

280 BCE Seleucus Nicator, last surviving general of Alexander the Great and ruler of Syria, assassinated

280 BCE Pyrrhus, king of Epirus, sends troops to help defend Greek cities of southern Italy against Romans

274 BCE First Syrian War between Ptolemy II and Antiochus I (to 271 BCE)

272 BCE Celts sack Delphi in Greece

273 BCE Pyrrhus **invades Macedonia** and deposes Antigonus II

268 BCE Reign of **Ashoka** begins in India (to 232 BCE)

272 BCE Pyrrhus is **killed** campaigning against Sparta

c.268–260 BCE Ashoka fights bloody war against **Kalinga**

264 BCE Outbreak of **First Punic War** between Rome and Carthage (to 241)

263 BCE Eumenes, establishes **Pergamum** as independent kingdom

262 BCE After long siege, **Athens falls** to the Macedonians

262 BCE Ashoka converts to **Buddhism**

23 YEARS THE LENGTH OF THE **FIRST PUNIC WAR**

ROMAN RELIGION

Early Roman religion combined the worship of the great gods, such as Neptune (shown here), with that of more local deities. There were several different types of priest: *haruspices* made predictions from the entrails of sacrificed animals; *augures* determined the divine will from signs, such as the flight of birds; and *pontifices* controlled the complex calendar of religious festivals. In their homes, Romans had shrines to household gods and the spirits of their ancestors.

him the master of all China. The same year he proclaimed himself the "First Emperor" as Qin Shi Huangdi, and the first ruler of the new **Qin dynasty**.

In Persia, the Greek Seleucid dynasty, which had inherited the region after Alexander the Great's death in 323 BCE, faced a series of nomad incursions after 280 BCE. **Antiochus I** (reign c.292–261 BCE) expelled the nomads, but wars with Egypt (280–272 BCE and 260–253 BCE) overstretched the kingdom's resources. On the death of **Antiochus II** (r.261–246 BCE), civil war broke out between the king's widow Berenice and his former wife Laodice. This led to the **breakaway of Bactria under Diodotus and Parthia under Andragoras**. Taking advantage of this instability, the nomadic Parni, led by **Arsaces**, entered Parthia in the mid-240s BCE.

Rivalry over Sicily, where the Carthaginians had possessed colonies since the 8th century BCE, was at the root of the **First Punic War** (264–241 BCE), a conflict between Rome and the North African power of Carthage. In 264 BCE, the Romans sent an army to help the **Mamertines** – a group of south-Italian mercenaries occupying the Sicilian city of Messana – in their conflict with the city of Syracuse, which was in turn aided by Carthage. The Carthaginian's resistance was so stubborn that the Romans made little headway. However, after they had built their first ever fleet, the Romans' fortunes changed. In 260 BCE, they won an important victory over the Carthaginians at **Mylae**. A Roman invasion of North Africa in 256 BCE failed to capture Carthage only through the ineptitude of the consul, Regulus. On land, the Romans took the Carthaginian strongholds in Sicily one by one until, by 249 BCE, only **Drepana**, in western Sicily, held out against them. A massive **Carthaginian naval victory** there set back the Roman cause, but in 241 BCE, a new Roman fleet appeared off Drepana, took it, and the next year smashed a Carthaginian fleet at the **Aegades Islands**. This defeat caused **Hamilcar Barca**, the Carthaginian general, to sue for peace. The peace terms involved the Carthaginians leaving Sicily. The two sides' spheres of influence remained uncomfortably overlapping, creating the seeds of two future conflicts.

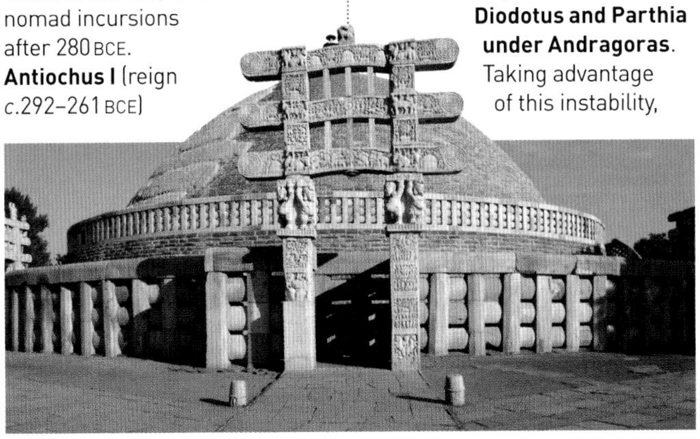

Great Stupa at Sanchi
This Buddhist stupa in central India was begun by the Mauryan ruler Ashoka in the 3rd century BCE.

> “ IF THEY **WILL NOT EAT**, LET THEM **DRINK!** ”
>
> **Publius Claudius Pulcher, Roman consul and general**, ordering the drowning of the sacred chickens when they refused to eat grain before the Battle of Drepana, 249 BCE

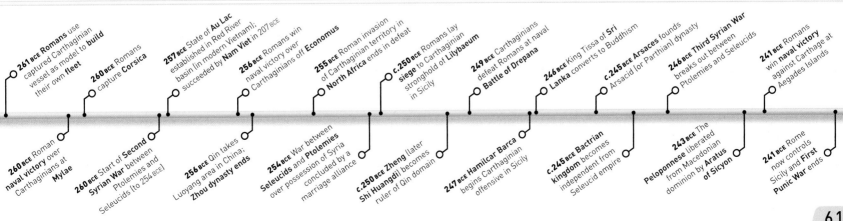

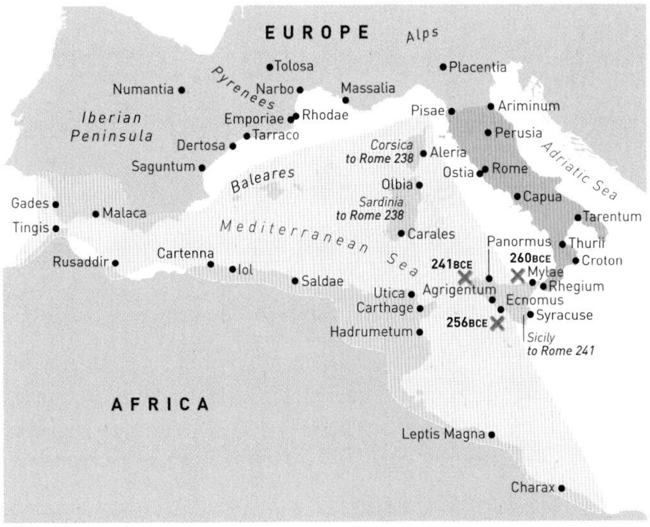

KEY
Carthaginian Empire in 264 BCE
Roman gains by 264 BCE
Roman gains by 238 BCE
× Roman victory

The First Punic War
The two decades of fighting was concentrated around Sicily, but also saw Roman invasions of North Africa and Sardinia.

261 BCE Romans use captured Carthaginian vessel as model to **build** their own **fleet**

260 BCE Roman **naval victory** over Carthaginians at **Mylae**

260 BCE Romans capture **Corsica**

260 BCE Start of **Second Syrian War** between Ptolemies and Seleucids (to 254 BCE)

257 BCE State of **Au Lac** established in Red River basin (in modern Vietnam); succeeded by **Nam Viet** in 207 BCE

256 BCE Romans win naval victory over Carthaginians off **Economus**

256 BCE Qin takes Luoyang area in China; **Zhou dynasty ends**

255 BCE Roman invasion of Carthaginian territory in **North Africa** ends in defeat

254 BCE War between **Seleucids** and **Ptolemies** over possession of Syria concluded by a marriage alliance

c.250 BCE Romans lay **siege** to Carthaginian stronghold of **Lilybaeum** in Sicily

c.250 BCE Zheng (later **Shi Huangdi**) becomes ruler of Qin domain

249 BCE Carthaginians defeat Romans at naval **Battle of Drepana**

247 BCE Hamilcar Barca begins Carthaginian offensive in Sicily

246 BCE King Tissa of **Sri Lanka** converts to Buddhism

c.245 BCE Arsaces founds Arsacid (or Parthian) dynasty

c.245 BCE Bactrian kingdom becomes independent from Seleucid empire

246 BCE Third Syrian War breaks out between Ptolemies and Seleucids

243 BCE The **Peloponnese** liberated from Macedonian dominion by **Aratus of Sicyon**

241 BCE Romans win **naval victory** against Carthage at Aegades Islands

241 BCE Rome now controls **Sicily** and **First Punic War** ends

36 THE NUMBER OF COMMANDERIES (REGIONS) SET UP BY EMPEROR QIN SHI HUANGDI

IN 221 BCE, QIN SHI HUANGDI, the first emperor of China, divided his empire into 36 commanderies on the advice of his minister **Li Ssu**. The dispossessed aristocrats and nobles of Qin's former enemies were moved to the capital Xianyang to keep them under close control. To further encourage a sense of unity, Li Ssu commissioned a single script and a standardized system of weights and measures for China. Further conquests were made to the north and south in 219 and 214 BCE, and thousands of colonists were sent to the new territories. Shi Huangdi dealt firmly with opposition. In 213 BCE, he ordered the "**burning of the books**", by which the writings of philosophers opposed to the Qin state were burnt, and in 212 BCE he had many intellectuals who opposed him brutally killed.

Suppressing opposition
This watercolour-on-silk painting shows Shi Huangdi, China's first emperor, overseeing the burning of books and the execution of scholars.

In the aftermath of the **First Punic War** (see 264–241 BCE), with Sicily and Sardinia lost, Carthage turned its attention to **Spain**. In 238 BCE, **Hamilcar** was sent there, and he soon conquered almost the whole of southern Spain. He died in battle against the **Oretani**, a Celtic tribe, in 229 BCE, but by then he had won both a **new empire** for Carthage and a strong power base for his family, the **Barcids**.

Despite their victory in the First Punic War, the Romans' position in northern Italy was still weak. In 225 BCE, the Celtic **Insubres and Boii tribes** tried to drive them out. At the **Battle of Telamon**, the Celts were trapped between two Roman armies and routed. Although the Boii accepted defeat in 224 BCE and the Insubres sued for peace two years later, the Romans rebuffed them and pushed on for total victory. The king of the Boii was killed in single combat against a Roman consul, and their capital **Mediolanum** (Milan) captured. The Romans established colonies in the Celtic territories in 218 BCE, including at Piacenza.

A revolt led by **Arsaces** (see 265–241 BCE) in Parthava – a former satrapy in the northeast of the Seleucid Empire – could not be quelled by Seleucus II (r.246–225 BCE), and a separate **Parthian kingdom emerged** in the region of modern Iran. The Parthians gradually annexed more territory to the west, especially under **Mithridates I** (r.171–138 BCE). By the early 1st century BCE, only a small area of Syria was under Seleucid control.

This rendition of Hannibal's crossing of the Alps is attributed to Italian artist Jacopo Ripanda. Amazingly, all 37 elephants survived the mountain passage.

Second Punic War
There were three principal theatres of conflict: Spain, Italy, and North Africa. By 203 BCE, the Carthaginians were confined to Africa.

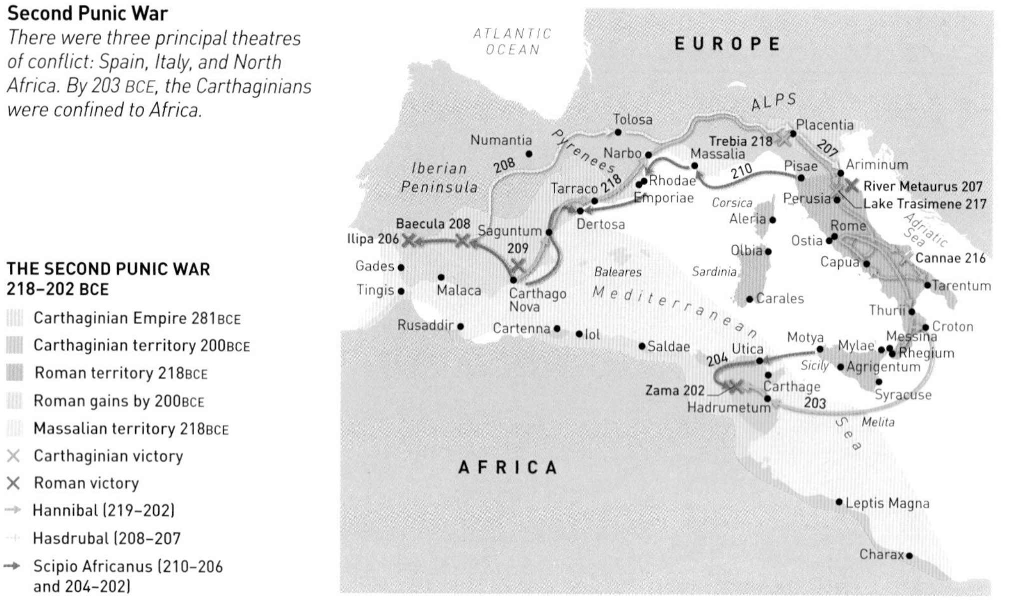

ALARMED AT CARTHAGINIAN EXPANSION IN SPAIN, in 226 BCE the Romans sent an embassy to **Hasdrubal** – son of Hamilcar and the new Barcid commander there – and secured an agreement that the Carthaginians would not move north of the Ebro River. In return, the Romans pledged not to move south – although they did forge alliances with cities in the south, such as Saguntum. In 221 BCE, Hasdrubal was assassinated; two years later, **Hannibal**, his brother and successor, attacked Saguntum, rapidly leading to the **Second Punic War** (219–201 BCE).

With the prospect of the Romans sending one army to Spain and another via Sicily to invade North Africa, Hannibal decided to strike first. He marched with 50,000 infantry, 9,000 cavalry, and 37 elephants into northern Spain, across the Pyrenees, through southern Gaul and – to the Romans' astonishment – **crossed the Alps**. Although he now had only around half the force he had started with, his presence encouraged the north Italian Celts to revolt and, at **Trebia** in late 218 BCE, he routed a Roman army. The following year he smashed another large Roman force at **Lake Trasimene**, killing 15,000 Romans – including one of the consuls. Faced with many **defections** among the allied cities, the Romans turned to delaying tactics to hold Hannibal at bay. But this was a temporary measure, and the Romans suffered one of their worst ever defeats at **Cannae** in 216 BCE, when Hannibal's army massacred up to

Battle of Canae
Some 35,000 Romans survived the battle of Cannae, but half of those were captured by the Carthaginians, and many were sold into slavery.

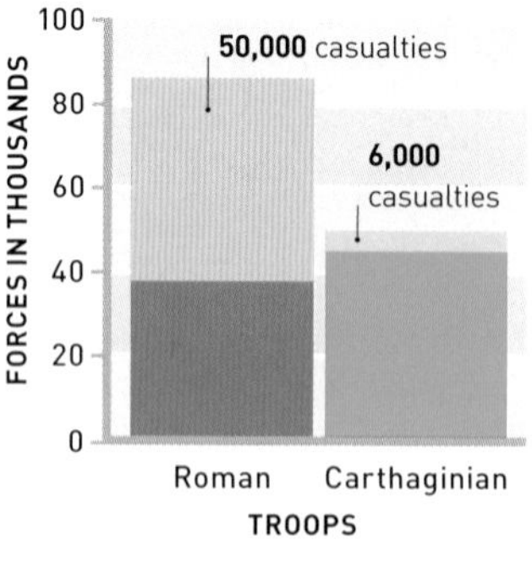

238 BCE Hamilcar Barca **re-establishes Carthaginian rule** in Spain

232 BCE Mauryan Empire starts to break up after Ashoka's death

231 BCE Seleucus II defeated by Tiridates of Parthia

225 BCE Gallic tribes defeated by Romans at **Telamon**

222 BCE Gallic stronghold of **Mediolanum** (Milan) taken by the Romans

223 BCE Antiochus III ascends to Seleucid throne

221 BCE The first emperor (Shi Huangdi) unites China under the **Qin Dynasty**

221 BCE Hannibal becomes **Carthaginian commander** in Spain

220 BCE Philip V becomes **king of Macedonia**

219 BCE Fourth Syrian War breaks out between Ptolemies and Seleucids over possession of Phoenecia

219 BCE Hannibal besieges Saguntum in Spain, beginning the **Second Punic War**

218 BCE Hannibal **crosses the Alps** to invade Italy

217 BCE Hannibal triumphs over the Romans at **Lake Trasimene**

217 BCE Egyptians, led by Ptolemy IV Philopator, **crush the Seleucid army** under Antiochus III at Raphia, Palestine

216 BCE Hannibal defeats the Romans at **Cannae**

215 BCE Romans counterattack against the Carthaginians in Spain

215 BCE Philip V of Macedonia invades Illyria, starting the **First Macedonian War** (to 205 BCE)

212 BCE Antiochus III campaigns in the east in an unsuccessful attempt to conquer **Bactria** and **Parthia**

212 BCE In China, the **Qin ban non-scientific books**; standardization and simplification of **Chinese script**

After his death, the First Qin Emperor was buried in a vast mausoleum, in which an army of 8,000 terracotta warriors, each around 2 m (6 ft 6 in) tall, was placed.

HANNIBAL (247–182 BCE)

A brilliant tactician, Hannibal's string of victories against the Romans from 218 BCE was not matched by the strategic judgement to convert them into final victory. Following the surrender of Carthage in 201 BCE, Hannibal served as the city's suffete (chief magistrate) until the Romans had him exiled in 195 BCE. He then offered his service to a succession of Rome's enemies before poisoning himself in Bithynia.

50,000 of them. But Hannibal did not march immediately on Rome, and his campaign lost momentum. Although Hannibal captured much of southern Italy, including the key city of Capua in 211 BCE, by 212 BCE the Romans had raised 25 fresh legions and stood ready to carry the war back to the Carthaginians.

WHEN THE FIRST QIN EMPEROR DIED IN 210 BCE, resentment against his autocratic rule erupted in a series of peasant revolts. A number of new kingdoms broke away from the centre, while the anti-Qin forces found a talented military leader in **Xiang Yu**. In 208 BCE, Li Ssu was executed and a new army, led by **Liu Bang**, a man of peasant origins, emerged to challenge the Qin. By 206 BCE, the **Qin Empire** was fragmented and Xiang Yu and Liu Bang were at war with one another. In 202 BCE, Xiang Yu committed suicide after being defeated at **Gaixia**. With no one left to oppose him, Liu Bang had himself declared emperor as **Gaozu**, the first ruler of the **Han dynasty** (see 200–171 BCE).

With Hannibal making little headway in **southern Italy**, the Romans embarked on a policy of picking off the allies of Carthage. Their first target was **Philip V of Macedonia**, whose attacks on Illyria in 215 BCE had provoked the **First Macedonian War** (215–205 BCE) with Rome. In 211 BCE, the Romans allied with the Aetolians, who fought the Macedonians on land while the Romans launched naval attacks. Philip's invasion of **Aetolia** in 207 BCE forced the Aetolians to sue for peace the next year, and though the Romans sent fresh forces in 205 BCE, the war ended with a recognition of the **status quo** between the two sides.

In Spain, the Romans had retaken **Saguntum** in 212 BCE, but a disastrous defeat the following year in which both consuls died looked set to destroy the Roman position there. The Roman senate sent the young general **Publius Cornelius Scipio** (*c.*236–183 BCE) to Spain, where he captured the Carthaginian capital of **Carthage Nova**. In 206 BCE, he crushed a large Carthaginian force at **Illipa**.

In 207 BCE, Hannibal's brother **Hasdrubal** was defeated and **killed** at the **River Metaurus** in northern Italy, denying Hannibal crucial reinforcements. By 204 BCE, many of Hannibal's south-Italian allies had deserted him, and when Scipio landed with a Roman army at **Utica** in North Africa, the Carthaginians recalled Hannibal to head off a threat to **Carthage** itself. The Romans offered relatively lenient peace terms, but the Carthaginians rejected them, and Scipio captured their towns one by one. Aided by the Numidian prince, Massinissa, **Scipio defeated Hannibal's last army** at Zama in 202 BCE. The peace terms the Carthaginians now had to accept were much harsher. All of their territory was forfeit save a band around Carthage itself; their fleet was reduced to a mere 10 ships; they were not allowed to make war outside Africa at all, and inside it they needed Roman permission to do so. An annual tribute of 10,000 talents payable to the Romans completed the humiliation of what had once been Rome's greatest enemy.

The Continence of Scipio
Scipio was noted for his mercy. In this 19th-century painting, he is seen handing back a captured Carthaginian woman to her fiancé.

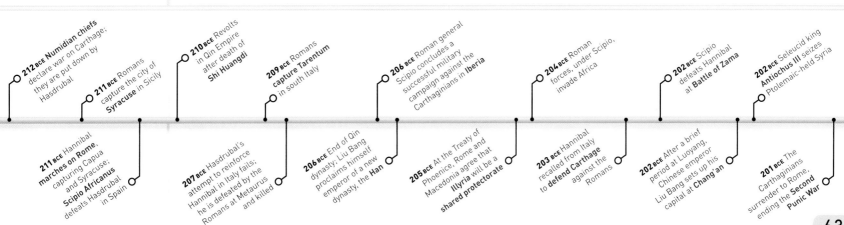

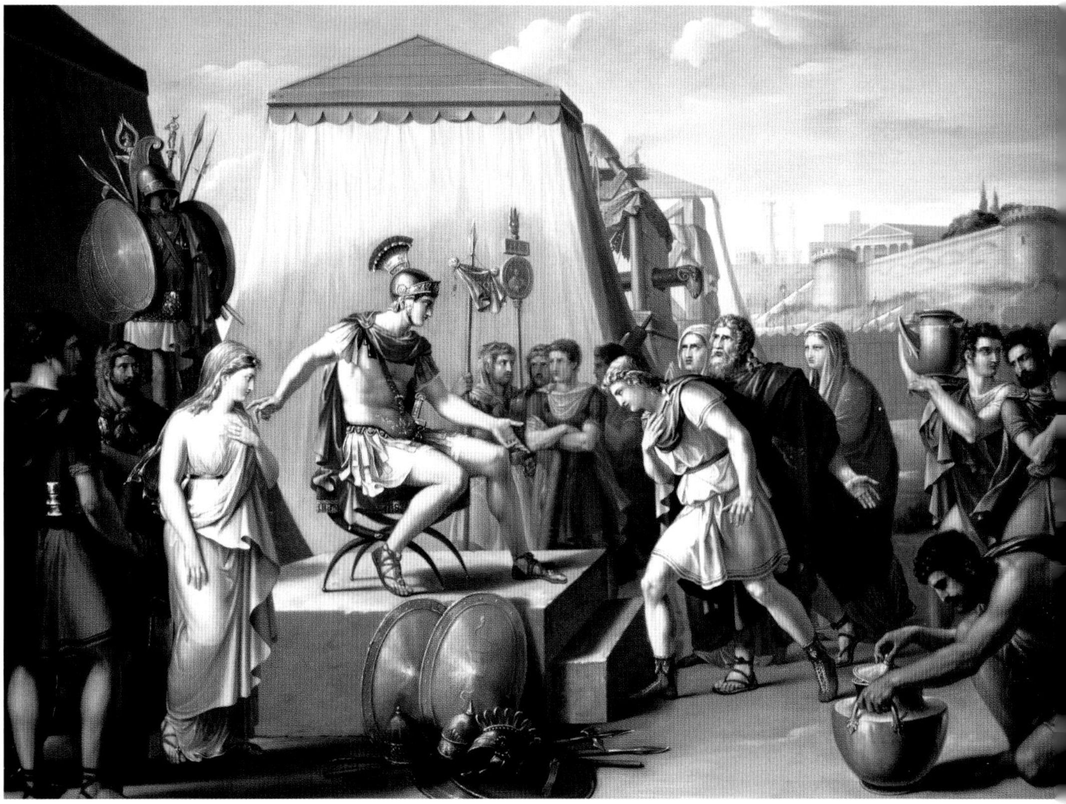

- **212 BCE Numidian chiefs** declare war on Carthage; they are put down by Hasdrubal
- **211 BCE** Hannibal **marches on Rome**, capturing Capua and Syracuse; **Scipio Africanus** defeats Hasdrubal in Spain
- **211 BCE** Romans capture the city of **Syracuse** in Sicily
- **210 BCE** Revolts in Qin Empire after death of **Shi Huangdi**
- **207 BCE** Hasdrubal's attempt to reinforce Hannibal in Italy fails; he is defeated by the Romans at Metaurus and killed
- **209 BCE** Romans **capture Tarentum** in south Italy
- **206 BCE** End of Qin dynasty; Liu Bang proclaims himself emperor of a new dynasty, the **Han**
- **206 BCE** Roman general Scipio concludes a successful military campaign against the Carthaginians in **Iberia**
- **205 BCE** At the Treaty of Phoenice, Rome and Macedonia agree that **Illyria** will be a **shared protectorate**
- **204 BCE** Roman forces, under Scipio, invade Africa
- **203 BCE** Hannibal recalled from Italy to **defend Carthage** against the Romans
- **202 BCE** Scipio defeats Hannibal at **Battle of Zama**
- **202 BCE** After a brief period at Luoyang, Chinese emperor Liu Bang sets up his capital at **Chang'an**
- **202 BCE** Seleucid king **Antiochus III** seizes Ptolemaic-held Syria
- **201 BCE** The Carthaginians surrender to Rome, ending the **Second Punic War**

Athenian coin
The Athenian silver tetradrachm has an image of an owl on one side and a helmeted head on the other. It was also stamped with the Greek letters for "ATHE" to identify the city of its origin.

Prehistory
Cattle as capital
Prehistoric people use cattle as money, with animals such as sheep or chickens sometimes acting as small change.

Cattle

1200 BCE
Shells as money
Beginning from the Maldives, the use of cowrie shells as money spreads throughout the Pacific, and, by the 19th century, into Africa.

Cowrie shells

1000–500 BCE
Tool money
In China, common tools are cast in metal, punched with holes (for stringing several together), and used as money.

Knife money

c.640–630 BCE
First true coins
The state of Lydia produces the first true coins, made of electrum (an alloy of gold and silver) and stamped with an image of a lion or stag.

Lydian coins

465–454 BCE
Greek coins
Almost every Greek city-state issues its own coinage, often with the name of the state inscribed on it. Silver replaces electrum as the main metal used.

27 BCE–14 CE
Augustan aureus
Emperor Augustus reforms the Roman coinage system and issues a new version of the standard gold coin, the aureus, worth 25 silver denarii.

Gold aureus

THE STORY OF MONEY

THE ADOPTION OF MONEY ENABLED EARLY SOCIETIES TO FLOURISH AND GROW INTO COMPLEX CIVILIZATIONS

As societies became more complex, a need arose for a uniform medium of exchange to acquire goods. Money was created to fulfil this role, and it evolved from cattle to precious metals, and finally, to coins and notes. Today, money is exchanged more abstractly, through credit cards or electronic transfers.

The earliest forms of money – used in ritual exchanges (for example, as a dowry) and in paying fines – included physical items such as cattle. In the 4th millennium BCE, the growth of trade in Egypt and Mesopotamia led to more compact and portable forms of money. For thousands of years, precious metals were used, often in the forms of bars and ingots. Babylonian king Hammurabi's law code mentions loans paid in silver. In 640 BCE, in the kingdom of Lydia in Asia Minor, the development of money went a stage further with the invention of coinage, which later spread to the Greek world. By the Roman era, a tri-metallic system had been adopted, with coins of gold, silver, and bronze (of least value) circulating across the empire. All had the head of the ruler stamped on them, for propaganda as well as fiscal use.

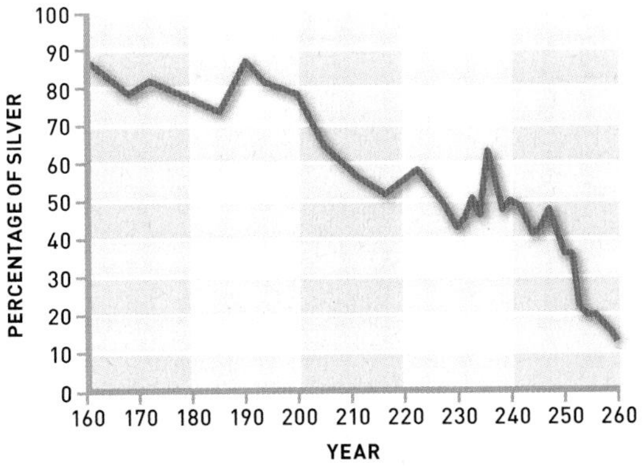

The debasement of Roman coins
Due to inflation, excessive expenditure, and weak control of minting, the purity of the Roman denarius fell from around 90 per cent silver under Marcus Aurelius (r.161–180) to 4 per cent during Gallienus's rule (r.260–268).

EXCHANGE NOTES

In 1189, paper money came into use in China during Jin rule. Notes could express larger denominations and, therefore, were more convenient than coins. Gradually, government-backed banks began to issue notes, which were, in theory, exchangeable for an equivalent amount in bullion (a system known as the Gold Standard). However, the economic crisis following World War I forced countries to abandon the Gold Standard. Subsequently, the "real" value of notes and coins became nominal, relying instead on a sense of trust that they could be exchanged for goods. The growth of credit cards from 1950 took this a stage further, as the purchaser passed on nothing save the promise of payment at a later date.

TRADE AND PAPER MONEY

The growth in paper money in Europe after the Middle Ages was fuelled by the needs of merchants. Traders would deposit funds in a bank in one city and receive a promissory note, which allowed them to withdraw the amount in any other city where the bank had a branch. Great Italian banking houses, such as the Medici, were rich enough to fund the military campaigns of European kings through their loans.

806–821
Paper money
In China, Emperor Xianzong issues the earliest bank notes during a period of copper shortage. The Jin dynasty issues the first true bank notes around 1189.

Song dynasty note

1158
Making change
Henry II of England creates high-quality coinage, based on a silver penny, with a cross design that will last over the next 100 years.

Henricus penny

1519
Thalers
Coin minted from silver found in the Joachimsthal mine, Bohemia, becomes standard in the Spanish and Austrian Habsburg empires.

Joachimsthal thaler

17th century
Modern cheque
By the 17th century, the use of cheques, often backed by goldsmiths, becomes widespread in Europe.

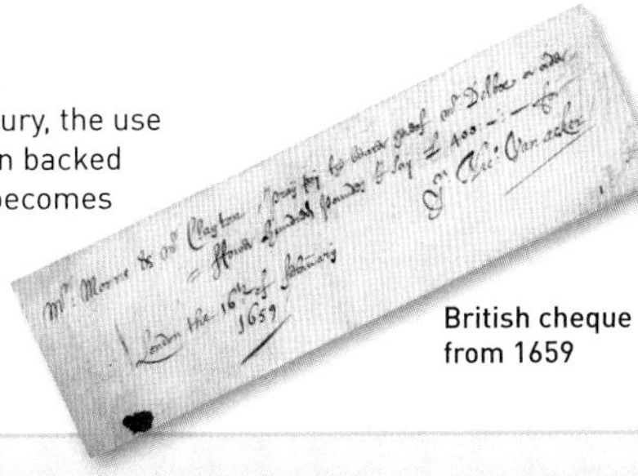

British cheque from 1659

1694
First bank note
The Bank of England is founded to fund England's growing national debt. It issues its first bank notes, backed by the bank's own gold reserves.

1862
First dollar bill
The US Treasury issues the first dollar bills for national circulation. These are known as "greenbacks" for their vivid green colour.

First one dollar bill

1949
Credit and debit cards
The first credit cards appear in the US in 1949. By the 1980s, debit cards, which operate as electronic cash (without deferred payment) appear.

Credit cards

The royal entourage of Gaozu, the first emperor of the Han, depicted in the mountains of China. Gaozu was one of the few Chinese rulers to come from a peasant background.

THE FIRST HAN EMPEROR OF CHINA, GAOZU, died in 195 BCE, when his successor, Hui Ti, was just 15. Hui Ti fell under the sway of his mother, the empress Lu, who took power for herself on his premature death in 188 BCE. Under her rule **China was invaded** by the Hsiung-nu from the north and the kingdom of Nan-yueh to the south, and it was only under Gaozu's grandson Wen Ti (r.180–157 BCE) that **stability was restored**. By 143 BCE, the number of commanderies (regions) under central Han control had risen from 13 to a total of 40.

In Japan, the **Middle Yayoi** period (*c.*200–100 BCE) saw an increase in population – possibly to as high as 600,000 people – and the beginnings of **political consolidation in central Japan**, especially around the lower Nara basin (near Osaka).

In **India,** the **Sunga dynasty** took power in Magadha in 185 BCE, when its founder Pusyamitra Sunga (r.185–151 BCE), a former Mauryan general, assassinated the last Mauryan ruler (see 265 BCE). He is said to have persecuted Buddhists, marking the beginning of the religion's decline in its Indian homeland. He also fought a **long series of wars** with Magadha's neighbours, including the **Satavahanas,** the **Kalingas,** and the **Indo-Greek** kingdoms of Bactria.

Bactria (in modern Afghanistan) had broken away from Seleucid control around 275 BCE, but a series of Greek kings continued to rule there, starting with Diodotus around 250 BCE. Another **Indo-Greek dynasty** emerged in India, and became powerful under **Menander I** (*c.*165–130 BCE), an important patron of Buddhism. Under the Indo-Greek kings, a new **school of art** emerged around Gandhara, which fused Buddhist iconography and Greek naturalism. Gradually, these easternmost Greeks came under pressure from Scythian and Yuezhi nomads and in 125 BCE Bactria collapsed. The last Indo-Greek kingdom of the Punjab survived until 10 CE.

The Roman victory against Philip V of Macedon (see 210 BCE) in the **Second Macedonian War** (200–197 BCE) did not lead to permanent acquisitions in Greece, and the Romans withdrew their army in 194 BCE. After the death of Philip V in 179 BCE, his son Perseus presided over worsening relations with Rome, and in 171 BCE a **Third Macedonian War** broke out. Initial Roman campaigning achieved little except the alienation of their Greek allies, but a more disciplined approach under the consul **Aemilius Paullus** (see 170 BCE) yielded better results.

13
THE NUMBER OF **REGIONS** THAT MADE UP **HAN CHINA**

Yayoi vase
The Yayoi period in Japanese history (c.300 BCE to 250 CE) is named for the site near Tokyo where its pottery was first found.

This wall painting shows Judah Maccabee's revolt in Jerusalem.

THE THIRD MACEDONIAN WAR ended In 168 BCE, when Paullus defeated Perseus at the **Battle of Pydna.** A purge of anti-Roman elements swept through the Greek cities, and Macedonia was broken up into four republics to prevent it recovering its strength.

In 150 BCE, Spartan attempts to get the Romans to intervene in a quarrel with the **Achaean League** (a group of Greek city-states) coincided with an **anti-Roman revolt** in Macedonia. By 148 BCE, the Macedonians had been defeated and the Romans turned their attention to the Achaeans. The Roman consul L. Mummius quickly routed the Archaeans and took Corinth, which he razed to the ground. The various leagues of Greek cities were dissolved and **Greece lost its independence**, becoming the Roman province of **Achaea**.

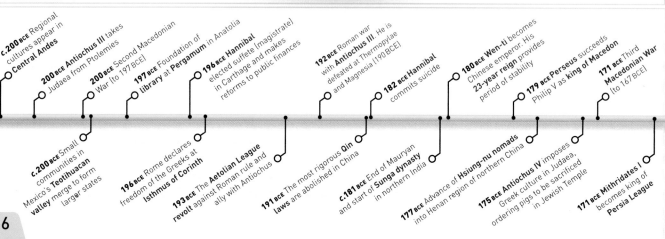

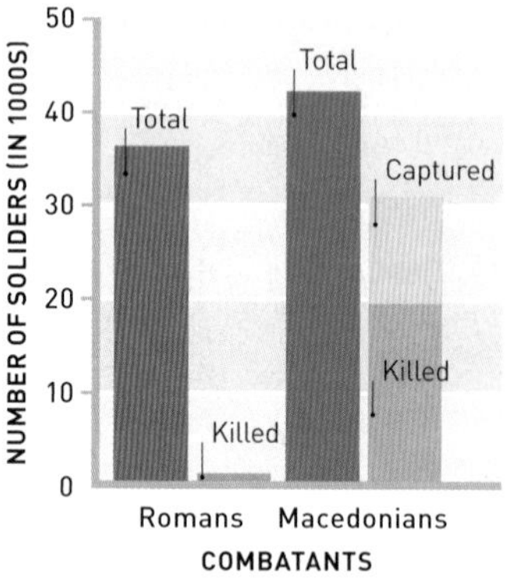

Battle of Pydna
The Macedonian army led by Perseus was destroyed at the Battle of Pydna. The Romans killed 20,000 Macedonians and captured 11,000.

c.200 BCE Regional cultures appear in **Central Andes**

c.200 BCE Small communities in Mexico's **Teotihuacan valley** merge to form larger states

200 BCE Antiochus III takes Judaea from Ptolemies

200 BCE Second Macedonian War (to 197 BCE)

197 BCE Foundation of **library** at **Pergamum** in Anatolia

196 BCE Rome declares freedom of the Greeks at **Isthmus of Corinth**

196 BCE Hannibal elected suffete (magistrate) in Carthage and makes reforms to public finances

193 BCE The **Aetolian League revolt** against Roman rule and ally with Antiochus

192 BCE Roman war with **Antiochus III.** He is defeated at Thermopylae and Magnesia (190 BCE)

191 BCE The most rigorous **Qin laws** are abolished in China

182 BCE Hannibal commits suicide

c.181 BCE End of Mauryan and start of **Sunga dynasty** in northern India

180 BCE Wen-ti becomes Chinese emperor. His **23-year reign** provides period of stability

177 BCE Advance of **Hsiung-nu nomads** into Henan region of northern China

179 BCE Perseus succeeds Philip V as **King of Macedon**

175 BCE Antiochus IV imposes Greek culture in Judaea, ordering pigs to be sacrificed in Jewish Temple

171 BCE Third **Macedonian War** (to 167 BCE)

171 BCE Mithridates I becomes king of **Persia League**

c.165 BCE First official examination for the selection of Chinese **civil servants**

164 BCE Judah Maccabee enters Jerusalem

161 BCE Judah Maccabee is **killed in battle**

160 BCE The city of **Pergamum,** ruled by King Eumenes II, becomes a renowned cultural centre

The ruins of Carthage, which was burnt and ritually cursed after its capture in 146 BCE. A new Roman town was founded near the city around 48 BCE.

After the end of the Second Punic War, in 202 BCE, the Romans had allowed their ally King Massinissa of Numidia to encroach on Carthaginian territory. The peace conditions that ended the war forbade the Carthaginians to wage war without Roman approval. Unable to act, the Carthaginians were reduced to sending **embassies to Rome** to protest at Massinissa's behaviour. However, Rome sided with its ally, and one Carthaginian embassy in 162 BCE even resulted in Carthage being made to pay an annual fine of 500 talents. In 151 BCE, the Carthaginian government sent a military force to relieve a town that had been besieged by Massinissa, and the Romans reacted by **declaring war**. This was the **Third Punic War** (149–146 BCE). Rome's war was encouraged by the anti-Carthaginian senator **Cato the Elder**, who made a series of speeches to the Senate calling for the destruction of Carthage.

> “**CARTHAGE** MUST BE **DESTROYED.**”
>
> **Cato the Elder, Roman statesman**

Carthaginean tophet
A memorial stone from the tophet (cemetery) at Carthage, showing Tanit, the goddess of the heavens.

The first two years of the Third Punic war saw ineffective Roman attacks on towns around Carthage. In 147 BCE, a new commander was appointed, **Scipio Aemilianus**, who transformed Rome's fortunes in the war within a year.

In 167 BCE, the Seleucid ruler **Antiochus IV** outlawed Jewish religious practices in Judaea, leading to the **revolt of Judah Maccabee** and his brothers in 164 BCE. Judah Maccabee entered Jerusalem, reconsecrated the temple, and re-established Judaism. The **Seleucid kingdom** then continued to decline (see also 280 BCE), with the overthrow of its ruler Demetrius I in 150 BCE by Alexander Balas rapidly leading to the **loss of the key satrapies** (provinces) of Media and Susiana.

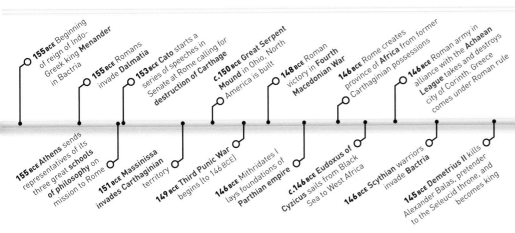

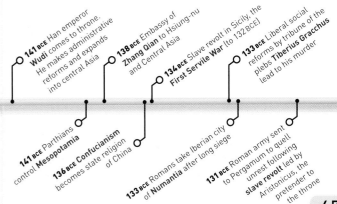

THE ROMAN REPUBLIC

After the overthrow of the last king in 507 BCE, Rome became a republic, ruled by two annually elected consuls. Over time the consuls came to be supported by other magistrates (praetors and quaestors), and tribunes of the plebs who had a special role in protecting the rights of the lower orders. Later elections for the consulate became bitterly contested as the office provided great potential for enrichment and personal and family glory. After Augustus became emperor in 27 BCE the office of consul lost any real power, being increasingly awarded to imperial favourites.

> “I SHUDDER TO THINK THAT **ONE DAY** SOMEONE MAY GIVE THE SAME ORDER **FOR ROME.**”
>
> **Scipio Aemilianus, Roman general and consul,** on giving the order to burn Carthage, from Plutarch's *Apophthegmata*

IN CHINA, RAIDS BY NOMADIC HSIUNG-NU TRIBES from 177 BCE gravely threatened the Han dynasty's northern borders. In 139 BCE the imperial envoy, Zhang Qian, set out to Central Asia to seek out **possible allies** against the Hsiung-nu. His epic journey helped scout the way for Chinese expansion as far as Dunhuang, and the foundation of a number of **new Central Asian commanderies** by 104 BCE. Zhang Qian was held captive by the Hsiung-nu for some years during his journey before he was able to make an escape. Under emperor Wu (141–87 BCE) the Chinese launched **several offensives** against the **Hsiung-nu**, particularly in 121 BCE and 119 BCE, after which the frontier was quiet for almost 20 years.

In the Near East, the shrunken and near-helpless **Seleucid realm** (see 170 BCE) was riven by civil wars and prey to interference from the Parthians, the Hasmonaeans, and, increasingly, the Romans. In 142 BCE, the Maccabees succeeded in wresting Jerusalem from Seleucid control and established a **Hasmonaean kingdom**, with Jerusalem as its capital, under which a Jewish dynasty ruled until Jerusalem was captured by the Romans in 63 BCE.

In the **Iberian Peninsula**, the Romans had conquered most of southern Spain and parts of Portugal (where the Lusitanians vigorously resisted them) by 174 BCE. A revolt by the Lusitanian leader Viriathus from 147 BCE was joined by several Celtiberian tribes in 144 BCE. This rebellion petered out after Viriathus was murdered in 140 BCE. In 133 BCE, Numantia, the main centre of the revolt, finally fell to the Romans after a bitter siege. Its population was sold into slavery and Rome was left in control of all of Iberia, except the far north of Spain.

The **Third Punic War** came to an end when Scipio Aemilianus blocked Carthage's harbour then launched a **successful attack** on the city itself in spring 146 BCE. The last Carthaginian defenders died in an inferno in the city's main temple. The defeat of Carthage brought its 118-year struggle against Rome to an end. The Romans burnt the whole city and deported its population to prevent any Carthaginian revival.

- **155 BCE** Beginning of reign of Indo-Greek king **Menander** in Bactria
- **155 BCE Athens** sends representatives of its three great **schools of philosophy** on mission to Rome
- **155 BCE** Romans invade **Dalmatia**
- **151 BCE Massinissa invades Carthaginian** territory
- **153 BCE Cato** starts a series of speeches in Senate at Rome calling for **destruction of Carthage**
- **149 BCE Third Punic War** begins (to 146 BCE)
- **c.150 BCE Great Serpent Mound** in Ohio, North America is built
- **146 BCE** Mithridates I lays foundations of **Parthian empire**
- **148 BCE** Roman victory in **Fourth Macedonian War**
- **146 BCE** Rome creates province of **Africa** from former Carthaginian possessions
- **c.146 BCE Eudoxus of Cyzicus** sails from Black Sea to West Africa
- **146 BCE** Roman army in alliance with the **Achaean League** takes and destroys city of Corinth. Greece comes under Roman rule
- **146 BCE Scythian** warriors invade **Bactria**
- **145 BCE Demetrius II** kills Alexander Balas, pretender to the Seleucid throne, and becomes king
- **141 BCE** Han emperor **Wudi** comes to throne. He makes administrative reforms and expands into central Asia
- **141 BCE** Parthians control **Mesopotamia**
- **138 BCE** Embassy of **Zhang Qian** to Hsiung-nu and Central Asia
- **136 BCE Confucianism** becomes state religion of China
- **134 BCE** Slave revolt in Sicily, the **First Servile War** (to 132 BCE)
- **133 BCE** Liberal social reforms by tribune of the plebs **Tiberius Gracchus** lead to his murder
- **133 BCE** Romans take Iberian city of **Numantia** after long siege
- **131 BCE** Roman army sent to Pergamum to quell unrest following **slave revolt** led by Aristonicus, the pretender to the throne

> **"** HOWEVER MUCH YOU MAY **TRY TO DELAY,** YOU ARE **FATED TO MEET** THE **SAME DEATH** AS I DID. **"**

Tiberius Gracchus, Roman official, speaking in a dream to his brother Gaius; from an account by Cicero

This 17th-century silk painting from a history of Chinese emperors shows the Emperor Wudi greeting a scholar.

SAKA (SCYTHIAN) TRIBESMEN invaded Punjab, northern India, in **about 125 BCE**. They gradually **occupied more territory**, ending a brief period of Indo-Greek unity (see 200–171 BCE) under the reign of Antialcidas around 110 BCE. Led by **King Maues**, the Sakas took the kingdom of Gandhara and its capital Taxila in about 80 BCE. After Maues died (*c.*60 BCE), the Saka kingdom collapsed, but it was revived under his son **Azes I** (r.58–*c.*30 BCE), who conquered much of northwest India. The Sakas held this region until the rise of the Kushan Empire during the 1st century CE.

Amravati relief carving
This carving depicts the life of the Buddha. It comes from Amravati in Andra Pradesh, southeast India, one of the capitals of the Satavahanas.

In southern and central India, the **Satavahanas** began their rise to power after the breakup of the **Mauryan Empire** in the 2nd century BCE (see 200–171 BCE). From his capital in the Deccan, the third Satavahana king, **Satakarni**, extended his sway considerably around 50 BCE, although he and later Satavahana rulers struggled to contain the Saka and Kushan threats from the northwest.

In **Rome**, social turmoil had erupted over the distribution of public land held by the Senate. **Tiberius Gracchus**, who was tribune of the plebs in 133 BCE, sought to ensure that plots of this land would be handed over to poorer families. When the Senate obstructed his plans, he tried to extend his tribunate so that he could pursue his aim. A **mob organized by senators** opposed to the plans beat him to death in the Forum. Tiberius's brother **Gaius became tribune in 123 BCE** and tried to carry on his brother's work. He also reduced the Senate's role in dispensing justice, and pushed through a law to allow the sale of subsidized grain to the poor. In 122 BCE, the Senate declared **Gaius an enemy of the state**, due to his plans to extend Roman citizenship more widely in Italy. He killed himself, and thousands of his political supporters were executed.

IN PALESTINE, THE HASMONEAN KINGDOM (see 146–131 BCE) had continued its expansion until the **fall of Jerusalem** to the Seleucid Antiochus VII in 131 BCE. However, during the reign of John Hyrcanus (r.134–104 BCE) it recovered much of the ground that had been lost. **Alexander Jannaeus** (r.103–76 BCE) enlarged the kingdom until it occupied most of modern Israel and the West Bank. After defeats by the Nabataean king Aretas III in 84 BCE and internal strife following Alexander's death, the Hasmoneans were increasingly vulnerable to Roman interference.

In **North Africa**, the Romans faced a serious challenge when Micipsa, the son of their former ally Massinissa of Numidia (see 170–147 BCE), died in 118 BCE. The Romans ordered the kingdom be divided between Micipsa's nephew **Jugurtha** and his sons. Jugurtha rejected this, killing one cousin and attacking the other, Adherbal, who fled to Rome. After a brief division of Numidia between Jugurtha and Adherbal, Jugurtha renewed his attack on his cousin and the Romans became involved.

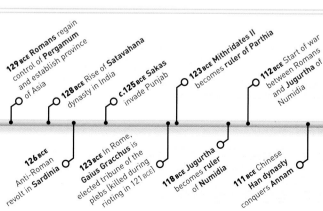

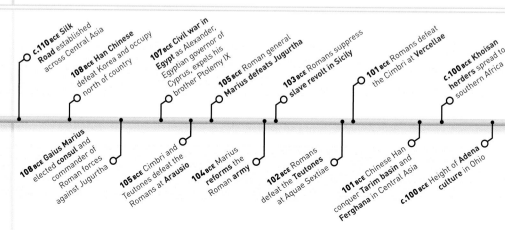

ROMAN MILITARY REFORMS

By the late 2nd century BCE, the Roman army was experiencing difficulty recruiting from the traditional propertied classes. Gaius Marius changed this by opening the army to those who fell below the normal property qualification. The eagle became the universal legionary standard for the first time, and the legions themselves were reformed as a heavy infantry force. From this point onward Roman light infantry and cavalry were organized into "auxiliary" units, which were recruited from non-citizens.

> **"** YOU DO WELL TO **CONSIDER THE OFFICE YOUR OWN,** FOR **YOU BOUGHT IT. "**

Julius Caesar's father chastising the future dictator Sulla for having corruptly bought office in 94 BCE; from *Lives* by **Plutarch**

Following several disastrous years of campaigning from 111 BCE, the Romans sent **Quintus Caecilius Metellus**, who captured Jugurtha's strongholds one by one. In **108 BCE**, **Gaius Marius** replaced Metellus. Finally, trapped in the far west of his territory, Jugurtha was handed to the Romans by his father-in-law **Bocchus of Mauretania**.

In Gaul, two Germanic tribes, the **Cimbri** and **Teutones**, had been defeating the Romans since 107 BCE, notably at Arausio in 105 BCE, where **Roman losses** reached 80,000. Marius took command of the defence against the Germans on his return from North Africa, and in 102 BCE vanquished the Teutones at Aquae Sextiae in Gaul. He next crushed the Cimbri at the **Battle of Vercellae** in 101 BCE. He was rewarded with an unprecedented sixth consulship in 100 BCE.

In China, **Emperor Wudi** (r.141–87 BCE) strengthened the **Han Empire's** administrative

- **129 BCE Romans** regain control of **Pergamum** and establish province of Asia
- **128 BCE** Rise of **Satavahana** dynasty in India
- **126 BCE** Anti-Roman revolt in **Sardinia**
- **c.125 BCE Sakas** invade Punjab
- **123 BCE** In Rome, **Gaius Gracchus** is elected tribune of the plebs (killed during rioting in 121 BCE)
- **123 BCE Mithridates II** becomes **ruler of Parthia**
- **118 BCE Jugurtha** becomes **ruler of Numidia**
- **112 BCE** Start of war between Romans and **Jugurtha** of Numidia
- **111 BCE** Chinese **Han dynasty** conquers **Annam**
- **c.110 BCE Silk Road** established across Central Asia
- **108 BCE Gaius Marius** elected **consul** and commander of Roman forces against Jugurtha
- **108 BCE Han Chinese** defeat Korea and occupy north of country
- **107 BCE Civil war in Egypt** as Alexander, Egyptian governor of Cyprus, expels his brother Ptolemy IX
- **105 BCE** Cimbri and Teutones defeat the Romans at **Arausio**
- **105 BCE** Roman general **Marius defeats Jugurtha**
- **104 BCE Marius reforms** the Roman **army**
- **103 BCE** Romans suppress **slave revolt in Sicily**
- **102 BCE** Romans **defeat the Teutones** at Aquae Sextiae
- **101 BCE** Romans defeat the Cimbri at **Vercellae**
- **101 BCE** Chinese Han conquer **Tarim basin** and **Ferghana** in Central Asia
- **c.100 BCE Khoisan herders** spread to southern Africa
- **c.100 BCE** Height of **Adena culture** in Ohio

Maiden Castle hill-fort in Britain underwent several phases of rebuilding after it was begun around 600 BCE, reaching its final form about 500 years later.

Captured in stone
The Danzante carvings at Monte Alban, Mexico, were once thought to be of dancers, but they are now believed to represent the mutilated bodies of enemies captured in war.

system by beginning **civil service examinations**. Official positions for academics had been established in 136 BCE, consolidating the ruling house's stranglehold on the intellectual life of China. In 106 BCE, **Wudi appointed 13 regional inspectors** to monitor the behaviour of government officials, raised taxes, and forbade private coin-minting. His armies pushed deep into Central Asia. By 108 BCE, the Han Empire had reached its **largest extent**.

In **Mexico**, the population of **Monte Albán** had reached about 17,000 by around 100 BCE. Monte Albán's control began to reach beyond the immediate vicinity of the **Valley of Oaxaca**, and many large stone platforms and public monuments were built in the city.

AFTER HIS VICTORY AT VERCELLAE, (see 110–91 BCE) Marius became Rome's dominant politician, but the brutal behaviour of his ally Saturninus, tribune of the plebs, provoked the Senate. **Political violence** flared, and in 100 BCE Marius had to march an army into Rome. Saturninus was killed in the ensuing riot. As Marius's power waned, discontent rose among Italians without Roman citizenship. In 91 BCE, this erupted into the **Social War**. A protégé of Marius, **Lucius Sulla** (c.138–78 BCE), took a key role in suppressing the revolt, which was **largely over by 88 BCE**, albeit with some concessions offered by Rome to the rebels.

Sulla was elected consul in 88 BCE. That same year, while waiting to sail with his army to Greece to counter the threat posed by the king of Pontus, **Mithridates VI** (134–63 BCE), Sulla heard that the Senate had voted to put Marius in charge of the campaign. Enraged, Sulla entered Rome with his troops and siezed power. He moved against Mithridates in 89 BCE, and had driven him out of Greece by 84 BCE. Sulla returned to Rome, defeated his remaining opponents (including the aged Marius), and was **appointed dictator** in 82 BCE.

Sulla took savage revenge on the Marians, packed the Senate with his supporters, and curtailed the powers of the tribunes. Anti-Sullan forces regrouped around **Quintus Sertorius**, who had fled to Spain. After Sulla died in 78 BCE, the Senate sent **Pompey** to deal with Sertorius. His military efforts were ineffective; only the assassination of Sertorius allowed Pompey to return victorious to Italy in 71 BCE.

In 73 BCE, a **slave revolt** led by the gladiator **Spartacus**, broke out near Naples and grew into the most serious revolt Rome had ever faced. Eventually, the rebel slaves were trapped in southern Italy and defeated by the Roman General **Marcus Licinius Crassus** in 71 BCE.

By the 1st century BCE, the Celtic peoples of southern Britain had started to expand their existing **hill-forts** into *oppida* ("towns") that were defended by extensive fortifications. The greatest *oppida* were formidable obstacles to attackers and some were royal capitals, complete with palaces.

The rebellion by Spartacus
Crassus crucified slaves along the Appian Way, which led to Rome, as a warning to any others who might plan a similar insurrection.

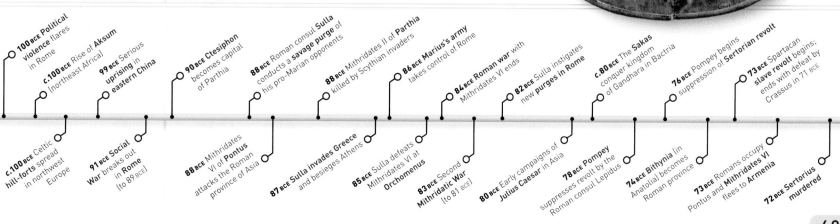

Sacred offering
This 1st-century BCE British Celtic shield was discovered in the River Thames, where it had probably been thrown as an offering to a river god.

- **100 BCE Political violence** flares in Rome
- **c.100 BCE** Rise of **Aksum** (northeast Africa)
- **c.100 BCE** Celtic **hill-forts** spread in northwest Europe
- **99 BCE** Serious **uprising** in **eastern China**
- **91 BCE Social War** breaks out in **Rome** (to 89 BCE)
- **90 BCE Ctesiphon** becomes capital of Parthia
- **88 BCE** Roman consul **Sulla** conducts a **savage purge** of his pro-Marian opponents
- **88 BCE** Mithridates VI of **Pontus** attacks the Roman province of Asia
- **88 BCE** Mithridates II of **Parthia** killed by Scythian invaders
- **87 BCE Sulla invades Greece** and besieges Athens
- **86 BCE Marius's army** takes control of Rome
- **85 BCE** Sulla defeats Mithridates VI at **Orchomenus**
- **84 BCE Roman war** with Mithridates VI ends
- **83 BCE** Second **Mithridatic War** (to 81 BCE)
- **82 BCE** Sulla instigates new **purges in Rome**
- **80 BCE** Early campaigns of **Julius Caesar** in Asia
- **c.80 BCE** The **Sakas** conquer kingdom of Gandhara in Bactria
- **78 BCE Pompey** suppresses revolt by the Roman consul Lepidus
- **76 BCE** Pompey begins suppression of **Sertorian revolt**
- **74 BCE Bithynia** (in Anatolia) becomes Roman province
- **73 BCE** Spartacan **slave revolt** begins; ends with defeat by Crassus in 71 BCE
- **73 BCE** Romans occupy Pontus and **Mithridates VI** flees to **Armenia**
- **72 BCE Sertorius murdered**

Mound City, Ohio, USA, contains a cluster of more than 20 Hopewell earthwork burial mounds.

A reconstruction of the Roman ramparts at Alesia, where Caesar forced Vercingetorix to surrender.

AFTER POMPEY'S RETURN TO ITALY (see 90–71 BCE), he was elected **consul** for the year, despite still being below the legal minimum age. When war broke out with **Mithridates of Pontus** again, the Romans, under general **Lucullus**, forced Mithridates to retreat to Armenia, which was ruled by his son-in-law Tigranes. However, Lucullus's **troops mutinied in 68 BCE**, and **Pompey** was sent to replace him. Tigranes surrendered and Mithridates retired north of the Black Sea. Having achieved his aim, Pompey entered Syria, where he deposed the last Seleucid king, and then **captured Jerusalem**.

In China, the **Han Dynasty** retreated from modernizing policies under **Zhaodi** (r.87–74 BCE) and **Xuandi** (r.74–49 BCE). The **Huo family**, which had dominated the government for decades was removed from power, and its leading members executed. Government expenditure was cut, and aggressive expeditions in Central Asia were replaced by the establishment of **small, permanent colonies.**

In **Mexico**, the city of **Cuiculco** in the south of the Valley of Mexico was destroyed by a **volcano** some time in the 1st century BCE. Its disappearance opened the way for **Teotihuacán**, to assert its control over the whole valley and become Mexico's dominant power for more than 500 years.

By the end of the 1st century BCE, the **Adena peoples** of Ohio, in eastern North America, were beginning to develop into the **Hopewell culture**. These people lived by hunting and gathering, but they also built large, elaborate burial mounds for their chieftains.

3

THE NUMBER OF **MILITARY TRIUMPHS** AWARDED TO **POMPEY**

Hopewell bird
Clay pipes, often in the shape of birds, are one of the most characteristic products of the Hopewell culture.

GAIUS JULIUS CAESAR BECAME CONSUL OF ROME for the first time in 59 BCE. Having served a term as governor of Spain, he was popular among the equestrians (wealthy non-senators), but resistance to him from the Senate (and the obstructiveness of his co-consul Bibulus) led him to join with **Pompey** and **Crassus**, and the three dominated Rome until 53 BCE as the **"First Triumvirate"**.

In 58 BCE, Caesar was appointed governor of Narbonensis, the Roman-occupied area of southern Gaul. He took advantage of the migration of the Germanic **Helvetii** across Gaul towards Italy to cross over the Alps and defeat **Ariovistus**, the Helvetian king. Caesar returned to Rome, but his deputy, Labienus, stayed in Gaul and the following year he pressed on to conquer the **Belgae** of northwestern Gaul. By 55 BCE, Caesar had subdued most of Gaul and had acquired a vast new province for Rome, without ever receiving any approval from the Senate.

In 56 BCE, an **anti-Roman revolt** broke out among the **Veneti** of northern Gaul, apparently supported by the Celtic tribes of Britain. Caesar responded by crossing over to Britain in 55 BCE with two legions. A storm

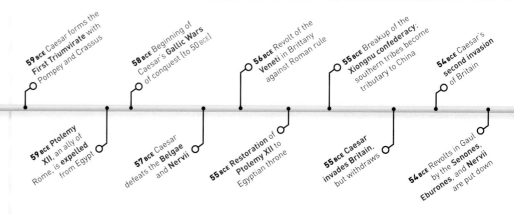

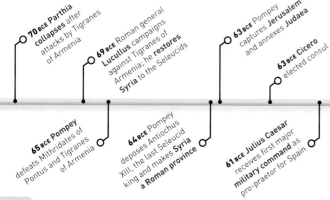

Caesar at the Louvre
Wearing the laurel wreath of a victorious general, this statue is part of Caesar's cult of personality.

70 BCE Parthia collapses after attacks by Tigranes of Armenia

69 BCE Roman general **Lucullus** campaigns against Tigranes of Armenia; he **restores Syria** to the Seleucids

65 BCE Pompey defeats Mithridates of Pontus and Tigranes of Armenia

64 BCE Pompey deposes Antiochus XIII, the last Seleucid king and makes **Syria a Roman province**

63 BCE Pompey captures **Jerusalem** and annexes **Judaea**

63 BCE Cicero elected consul

61 BCE Julius Caesar receives first major **military command** as pro-praetor for Spain

59 BCE Caesar forms the **First Triumvirate** with Pompey and Crassus

59 BCE Ptolemy XII, an ally of Rome, is **expelled** from Egypt

58 BCE Beginning of Caesar's **Gallic Wars** of conquest (to 50 BCE)

57 BCE Caesar defeats the **Belgae** and **Nervii**

56 BCE Revolt of the **Veneti** in Brittany against Roman rule

55 BCE Restoration of **Ptolemy XII** to Egyptian throne

55 BCE Breakup of the **Xiongnu confederacy**; southern tribes become tributary to China

55 BCE Caesar invades Britain, but withdraws

54 BCE Caesar's **second invasion** of Britain

54 BCE Revolts in Gaul by the **Senones**, **Eburones**, and **Nervii** are put down

> **“…[CAESAR] DREAMT** THAT HE WAS **FLYING ABOVE THE CLOUDS,** AND NOW THAT HE WAS **CLASPING THE HAND OF JUPITER.”**

Suetonius, recounting Julius Caesar’s dream the night before his murder in the Senate House in 44 BCE; from *Lives of the Caesars*

prevented the arrival of reinforcements, causing him to retreat, but he returned the next year with five legions (around 30,000 men). The Britons did not resist at first, but later, led by **Cassivelaunus**, chief of the Catuvellauni, they vigorously opposed the Romans all the way to the River Thames. When Cassivelaunus’s stronghold at Wheathampstead fell, he sued for peace, and Caesar returned to Rome with hostages and the promise of tribute.

At the end of 54 BCE, shortly after Caesar’s second expedition to Britain, another **revolt** in Gaul, this time led by the **Senones**, wiped out much of the Roman force there. After putting down the revolt, Caesar’s attentions were diverted to Rome, where **political violence** had resulted in the murder of his former ally Clodius, and where Pompey had been elected sole consul in 52 BCE, rupturing the Triumvirate. Emboldened by the turmoil in Rome, the **Carnutes** revolted in Gaul. They were joined by the Averni, led by **Vercingetorix**, who won several skirmishes against Labienus. Vercingetorix also defeated Caesar himself at Gergovia, but was then trapped at **Alesia** in September 52 BCE. The Romans constructed an encircling rampart around the Gauls’ position and managed to beat off a Gaulish relief force. With no hope left, **Vercingetorix surrendered** and was taken back to Rome, where he was strangled in 46 BCE after appearing in Caesar’s triumphal parade.

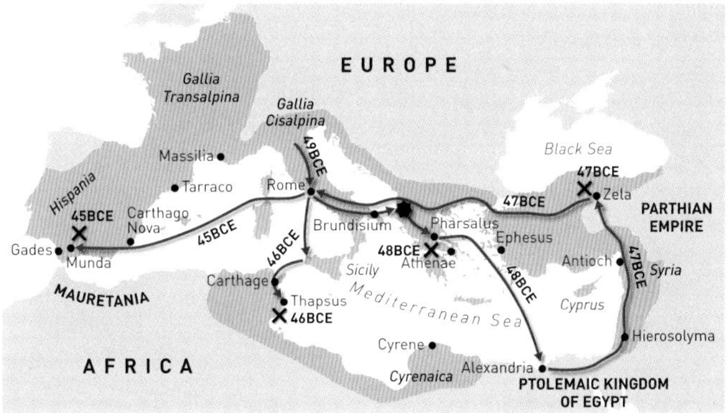

Roman Civil Wars
Caesar won Italy easily, but he had to fight hard to overcome Pompey in his Greek stronghold, and then Pompey’s sons and remaining supporters in Africa and Spain.

CAESAR ENDED THE GALLIC REVOLT by the end of 51 BCE, but by this point the **Triumvirate** had ended: Pompey’s supporters had turned against Caesar, and Crassus had been killed in battle in 53 BCE. The Senate ordered Caesar to disband his army or be declared an enemy of the state. Instead, he **crossed the Rubicon River** into Italy with his troops in 49 BCE. This was illegal, constituting a **declaration of war** against the Senate.

As **Caesar marched towards Rome**, town after town submitted to him. Fearing Caesar, **Pompey** left Rome and **fled to Greece**. Caesar turned first to Spain, where seven legions had declared for Pompey. In August

> **“THE DIE IS CAST.”**

Julius Caesar to his troops on crossing the Rubicon in 49 BCE; from Plutarch’s *Parallel Lives*

49 BCE, he forced the Pompeians there to surrender. In December, Caesar set off for Greece in pursuit of Pompey. A military engagement at **Dyrrachium** in July went against Caesar, but he fought back before Pompey’s support could grow, and won a resounding victory at **Pharsalus**. Pompey took refuge in Egypt, where he was murdered on the orders of **Ptolemy XIII**, who hoped (in vain) to ingratiate himself with Caesar.

After a short time in Egypt, **Caesar returned to Rome**, where he raised money by confiscating property from the supporters of Pompey. In late 47 BCE, Caesar set sail for Africa, where he defeated a new Pompeian army at **Thapsus** (in modern Tunisia). Pompey’s sons Gnaeus and Sextus escaped to Spain to continue the resistance from there, and Caesar annexed the kingdom of King Juba of Mauretania, who had supported them. Caesar then proceeded to Spain, where in March 45 BCE he defeated Gnaeus Pompey at **Munda**, effectively ending the civil war.

Caesar was now all-powerful. He was made **dictator in 48 BCE**, and in 44 BCE he was given the office for life. Concerns over Caesar’s power – in particular, fears that he planned to make himself king – led a group of about 60 conspirators to form around senators **Cassius** and **Marcus Brutus**. They **murdered Caesar** on the **Ides of March** (14 March) just before a session of the Senate. If they had hoped to seize power, the conspirators were disappointed: **Mark Antony**, one of Caesar’s leading supporters, came to the fore in Rome, while Caesar’s great-nephew and adoptive son **Octavian** received widespread support in a bid to take up the mantle of his father.

In India, **Kalinga** (modern Orissa), which had been a client kingdom of the Mauryas (see 200–171 BCE), rose to prominence under **Kharavela** in the mid-1st century BCE. Kharavela expanded Kalinga far to the north and east, conquering the Sunga capital of Pataliputra in Magadha. A strong patron of the Indian religion of Jainism, Kharavela established **trading contacts** as far afield as southeast Asia.

Murder of Caesar
Conspirators struck Caesar down with daggers. As he fell, Caesar saw Marcus Brutus, a former protégé, and cried out “you too, child?”.

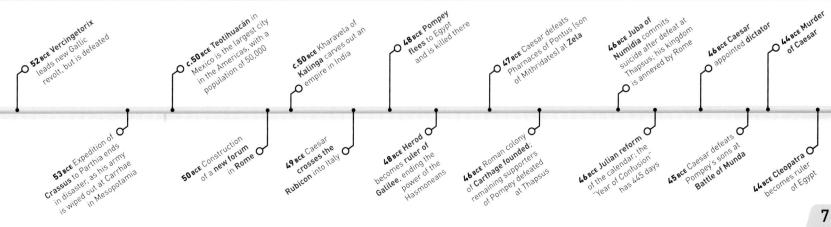

52 BCE Vercingetorix leads new Gallic revolt, but is defeated

53 BCE Expedition of **Crassus** to Parthia ends in disaster, as his army is wiped out at Carrhae in Mesopotamia

c.50 BCE Teotihuacán in Mexico is the largest city in the Americas, with a population of 50,000

50 BCE Construction of a **new forum** in **Rome**

c.50 BCE Kharavela of **Kalinga** carves out an empire in India

49 BCE Caesar **crosses the Rubicon** into Italy

48 BCE Pompey flees to Egypt and is killed there

48 BCE Herod becomes **ruler of Galilee**, ending the power of the Hasmoneans

47 BCE Caesar defeats Pharnaces of Pontus (son of Mithridates) at **Zela**

46 BCE Roman colony of **Carthage founded**; remaining supporters of Pompey defeated at Thapsus

46 BCE Juba of Numidia commits suicide after defeat at Thapsus; his kingdom is annexed by Rome

46 BCE Julian reform of the calendar; the “Year of Confusion” has 445 days

46 BCE Caesar appointed **dictator**

45 BCE Caesar defeats Pompey’s sons at **Battle of Munda**

44 BCE Murder of Caesar

44 BCE Cleopatra becomes ruler of Egypt

43–28 BCE

This 18th-century painting shows Mark Antony fleeing from the battle scene at Actium in 31 BCE. Many of his supporters defected to Octavian's side as a result.

IN ROME, THE PERIOD AFTER THE ASSASSINATION of **Julius Caesar** saw rising tensions between **Mark Antony** and **Octavian**, whom many viewed as Caesar's rightful heir. The two almost came to blows early in 43 BCE, when Octavian marched to raise the **siege of Mutina** (Modena, Italy), where Mark Antony was besieging Decimus Brutus, one of Caesar's assassins. Mark Antony was forced to retreat to Gaul. When the Senate voted to transfer Octavian's legions to Decimus Brutus, Octavian realized he was being sidelined and formed a three-way alliance with Mark Antony and **Marcus Lepidus**, the governor of Transalpine Gaul. This became the **Second Triumvirate**.

The Triumvirate conducted a war against **Cassius and Marcus Brutus**, two more of Caesar's assassins, who had seized much of the territory in the east. In 42 BCE, Mark Antony and Octavian defeated them at **Philippi**, in northern Greece, after which Cassius committed suicide. Three weeks later, they destroyed the remnants of Marcus Brutus's army. Mark Antony stayed in the east until 40 BCE, when he returned to Italy to try to undermine the **growing power of Octavian**. Their two armies refused to fight, and a de facto **division of the Roman world** was agreed, with Mark Antony ruling the east and Octavian governing the west; Lepidus had to make do with Africa. The **Triumvirate was renewed** in 38 BCE for a further five years, but it was clear that conflict between Octavian and Mark Antony could not long be postponed.

10
THE NUMBER OF YEARS THE SECOND TRIUMVIRATE RULED ROME

However, Mark Antony was occupied with a **war against the Parthians**, who allied with remnants of Cassius's army and **attacked Syria** in 39 BCE. In 36 BCE, Mark Antony **invaded Parthia** itself – ostensibly to recover the legionary eagles captured by the Parthians at the **Battle of Carrhae** (see 53 BCE) – and advanced to the capital Phraata, but he did not have sufficient resources to besiege it.

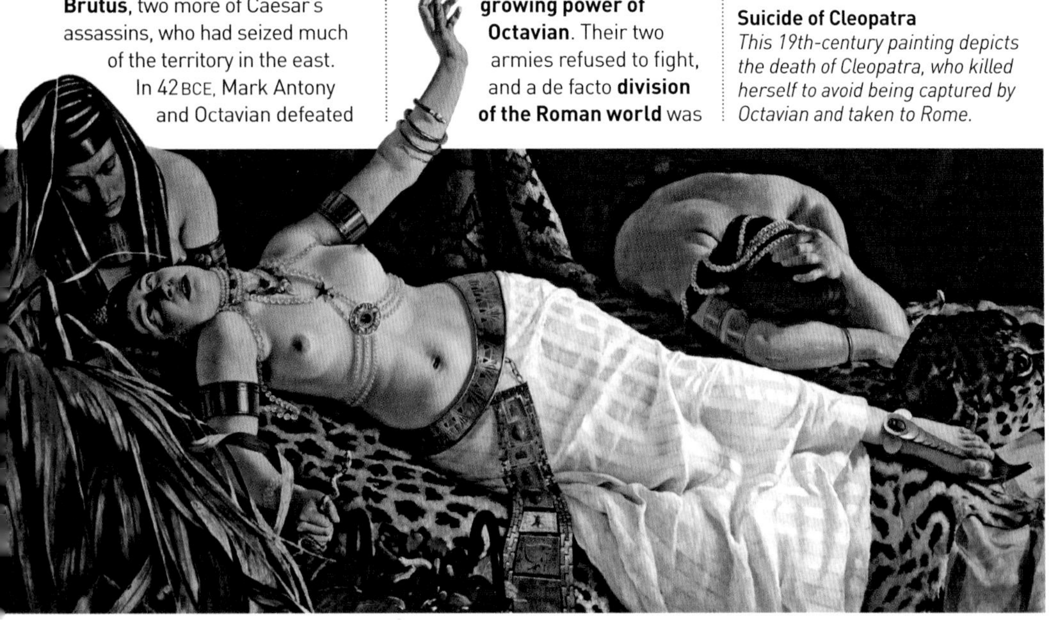

Suicide of Cleopatra
This 19th-century painting depicts the death of Cleopatra, who killed herself to avoid being captured by Octavian and taken to Rome.

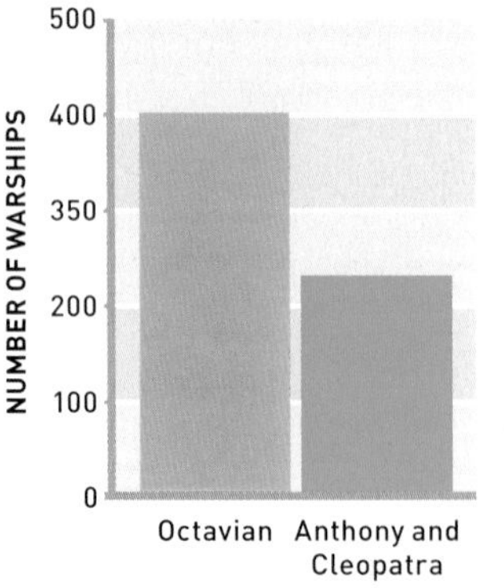

Battle of Actium
Octavian's fleet outnumbered that of Mark Antony and Cleopatra, with smaller more manoeuvrable ships, and fresher, better trained crews.

In 33 BCE, the **Triumvirate expired** and Octavian had the Senate declare Mark Antony a **public enemy**. The latter had lost popularity through his relationship with **Cleopatra**, the Egyptian queen, and Octavian quickly rallied public opinion to himself. A fleet was rapidly assembled, and this destroyed Mark Antony's naval force at **Actium**, off western Greece, in September 31 BCE. Mark Antony's land army then **defected** to Octavian, and Antony and Cleopatra **fled to Greece**, where Octavian caught up with them in the summer of 30 BCE. The Roman warlord and the Egyptian queen both **committed suicide**, and Egypt was annexed to the Roman empire. **Octavian** was now the **unchallenged master** of the whole Roman world.

27–20 BCE

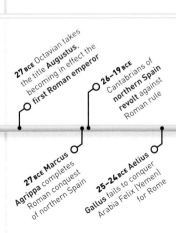

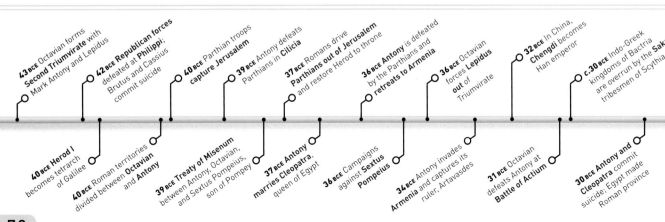

Augustus built a new Forum at Rome, with an imposing new temple to Mars.

HAVING DEFEATED HIS ENEMIES, Octavian did not take on the title of dictator, as Julius Caesar had. He instead ruled informally as the *princeps* – the **first man of the state**. Having acquired control of Antony's legions, he now had an army of about 500,000 men. He disbanded more than half of these, retaining 28 legions (about 150,000 soldiers), settling the remainder in colonies in Italy and abroad. In 27 BCE, Octavian gave up all his powers, ostensibly **restoring the Republic**. The Senate responded by granting him personal control of Egypt, Gaul, Germany, Spain, and Syria. He was also given the title "**Augustus**" and, cementing his position further, he was consul each year from 27 to 23 BCE. Over time, the Senate voted Augustus **further powers**, including that of *imperium maius* in 23 BCE, which gave him supreme authority in the provinces he had not previously governed, and the permanent powers of a **tribune of the plebs** in 23 BCE. Although the Senate was, in theory, the supreme authority in Rome, in practice no-one could match Augustus's power, and he is seen as the **first Roman emperor**.

North Africa had been a centre of strong resistance to both Julius Caesar and Augustus, who settled many army veterans there. In 25 BCE, Augustus gave Mauretania (western North Africa) to **Juba II of Numidia**. Juba, whose wife was the daughter of Mark Antony and Cleopatra, proved a reliable **Roman ally**. Augustus still sent a legion to garrison North Africa, where it stayed for over 300 years.

- **43 BCE** Octavian forms **Second Triumvirate** with Mark Antony and Lepidus
- **42 BCE Republican forces** defeated at **Philippi**; Brutus and Cassius commit suicide
- **40 BCE Herod I** becomes tetrarch of Galilee
- **40 BCE** Roman territories divided between **Octavian** and **Antony**
- **40 BCE** Parthian troops **capture Jerusalem**
- **39 BCE** Antony defeats Parthians in **Cilicia**
- **39 BCE Treaty of Misenum** between Antony, Octavian, and Sextus Pompeius, son of Pompey
- **37 BCE** Romans drive **Parthians out of Jerusalem** and restore Herod to throne
- **37 BCE Antony marries Cleopatra**, queen of Egypt
- **36 BCE Antony** is defeated by the Parthians and **retreats to Armenia**
- **36 BCE** Campaigns against **Sextus Pompeius**
- **36 BCE** Octavian forces **Lepidus out** of Triumvirate
- **34 BCE** Antony invades **Armenia** and captures its ruler, Artavasdes
- **32 BCE** In China, **Chengdi** becomes Han emperor
- **31 BCE** Octavian defeats Antony at **Battle of Actium**
- **c.30 BCE** Indo-Greek kingdoms of Bactria are overrun by the **Saka** tribesmen of Scythia
- **30 BCE Antony and Cleopatra** commit suicide; Egypt made Roman province
- **27 BCE** Octavian takes the title **Augustus**, becoming in effect the **first Roman emperor**
- **27 BCE Marcus Agrippa** completes Roman conquest of northern Spain
- **26–19 BCE** Cantabrians of **northern Spain revolt** against Roman rule
- **25–24 BCE Aelius Gallus** fails to conquer Arabia Felix (Yemen) for Rome

In western Asia, the ruler of Galilee, **Herod I**, was allowed to retain his position by **Octavian**, even though he had supported Mark Antony. He was even **given extra territories**, including parts of Syria and Gaza. Herod had been appointed by Mark Antony in 42 BCE, and by 37 BCE he had conquered the remains of the **Hasmonean kingdom** (see 146–131 BCE). Herod remained a reliable **ally of Rome** until his death in 4 BCE.

Emperor Augustus
Augustus, seen here dressed as a priest, acquired the title of pontifex maximus *(chief priest) on the death of Lepidus in 12 BCE.*

20–10 BCE

La Maison Carré, in Nîmes, southern France, is one of the finest surviving Roman temples. It was built around 16 BCE by Marcus Vipsanius Agrippa.

> “ HE COULD **JUSTLY BOAST** THAT HE HAD FOUND IT **BUILT OF BRICK** AND LEFT IT **IN MARBLE.** ”

Suetonius, on Augustus's embellishment of the city of Rome; from *Lives of the Caesars*

AUGUSTUS'S MILITARY AND POLITICAL SUCCESSES had relied largely on the abilities of **Marcus Vipsanius Agrippa**, who rose from a minor family to become consul in 37, 28, and 27 BCE. After Agrippa had married Augustus's daughter Julia, he received numerous promotions, including tribune of the plebs in 18 BCE. Augustus's own appointed heir had died in 25 BCE, so he **adopted Agrippa's children**, renaming them **Gaius** and **Lucius Caesar**. Agrippa seemed likely to succeed Augustus, but in 12 BCE he died unexpectedly, throwing open the **question of succession**.

By threatening to **invade Parthia** in 20 BCE, Augustus had engineered the return of legionary standards captured by the Parthians at **Carrhae** (see 53 BCE). In 16 BCE, the Roman governor of Macedonia began pushing towards the River Danube, and from 12 BCE **Tiberius**, Augustus's stepson, the son of his second wife Livia, moved north from Illyria to create the Roman province of **Pannonia** (modern Austria and Hungary). Tiberius's brother **Drusus** pushed Roman control across the Rhine towards the Elbe between 12 and 9 BCE, when he died. Around this time, the Romans annexed the provinces of **Raetia** (in modern Switzerland) and **Noricum** (between the Alps and the Danube), **moving the empire's frontiers** almost to a line along the Rhine and the Danube.

Supporters of Tiberius, now the most **high-profile general**, tried to have him displace Lucius and Gaius Caesar as Augustus's heir. Augustus himself did little to resolve the question of succession.

ROMAN LITERATURE AT THE TIME OF AUGUSTUS

The end of the Republic and the reign of Augustus saw a golden age in Latin literature. The orator Cicero and the historian Sallust marked the height of late Republican literature. After Augustus's rise to power, the poets Virgil (right; 70–19 BCE), author of the *Eclogues* and the epic poem *The Aeneid*, and Horace (65–8 BCE), author of the *Odes* and *Carmen Saeculare*, both flourished under the patronage of Maecenas, a close confidant of Augustus.

9–1 BCE

> “ THOSE **WHO SLEW MY FATHER I DROVE INTO EXILE...** AND... **DEFEATED THEM** IN BATTLE. ”

Augustus, from the *Res Gestae Divi Augusti*, the testament of Augustus, in Ankara, Turkey

BY 9 BCE, DRUSUS HAD DEFEATED THE MAIN GERMAN TRIBES and had reached the River Elbe. After his death, Augustus appointed **Tiberius** to replace him. Tiberius won a series of victories in 8 BCE, but then mysteriously **resigned his offices** and went into exile in Rhodes. This left Gaius and Lucius Caesar (both underage) as **heirs apparent** to the Roman Empire.

In China, the **reign of Yuandi** (49–33 BCE) saw the economic retrenchment begun under **Xuandi** (see 70–61 BCE) continue. Some semi-independent kingdoms that the early Han had suppressed began to reappear. Yuandi and his successors **Chengdi** (r.33–7 BCE) and **Aidi** (r.7–1 BCE) also created numerous **marquisates**, many of which were granted to the sons of the new kings, weakening the state's central control. Chengdi lacked a **male heir**, resulting in the succession of his half-nephew Aidi in 7 BCE. This caused **dissent** among nobles whose candidates for the throne had been overlooked.

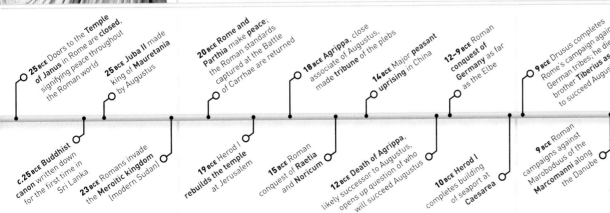

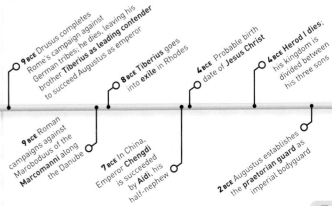

Khazneh at Petra
The Khazneh is one of Petra's finest monuments. Carved out of a sheer cliff-face, it was probably a royal tomb – perhaps of Aretas IV (c.9 BCE–40 CE).

The **Nabataean kingdom** of northern Arabia grew rich on its control of the spice trade from southern Arabia, reaching its height in the mid-1st century BCE under **Malichos I** (*c.*59–*c.*30 BCE). It then faced a growing threat on its northern borders from **Herod I**. A disputed succession in 9/8 BCE between **Aretas IV** and his chief minister **Syllaeus** led the Romans to take an interest in the area. An expedition led by Gaius, grandson of Augustus, may even have briefly annexed Nabataea in 3–1 BCE, but the Romans pulled back, allowing Nabataea another century of independence.

- **25 BCE** Doors to the **Temple of Janus** in Rome are **closed**, signifying peace throughout the Roman world
- **c.25 BCE Buddhist canon** written down for the first time in Sri Lanka
- **25 BCE Juba II** made king of **Mauretania** by Augustus
- **23 BCE** Romans invade the **Meroitic kingdom** (modern Sudan)
- **20 BCE Rome and Parthia** make **peace**; the Roman standards captured at the Battle of Carrhae are returned
- **19 BCE** Herod I **rebuilds the temple** at Jerusalem
- **18 BCE Agrippa**, close associate of Augustus, made **tribune** of the plebs
- **15 BCE** Roman conquest of **Raetia** and **Noricum**
- **14 BCE** Major **peasant uprising** in China
- **12 BCE Death of Agrippa**, likely successor to Augustus, opens up question of who will succeed Augustus
- **12–9 BCE** Roman **conquest of Germany** as far as the Elbe
- **10 BCE Herod I** completes building of seaport at **Caesarea**
- **9 BCE** Drusus completes Rome's campaign against German tribes; he dies, leaving his brother **Tiberius as leading contender** to succeed Augustus as emperor
- **9 BCE** Roman campaigns against Maroboduus of the **Marcomanni** along the Danube
- **8 BCE Tiberius** goes into **exile** in Rhodes
- **7 BCE** In China, Emperor **Chengdi** is succeeded by **Aidi**, his half-nephew
- **4 BCE** Probable birth date of **Jesus Christ**
- **4 BCE Herod I dies**; his kingdom is divided between his three sons
- **2 BCE** Augustus establishes the **praetorian guard** as imperial bodyguard

THE RISE OF THE ROMAN EMPIRE

FROM CITY, TO REPUBLIC, TO DOMINANT EUROPEAN EMPIRE

Soon after its foundation in 753 BCE, the city of Rome began fighting its neighbours to gain new territory. Gradually the Romans became entangled in campaigns in the Italian Peninsula and beyond. By the 1st century CE, the Roman Empire had become the largest Europe had ever seen.

The early growth of Roman territories was slow, with wars against neighbours often threatening the survival of Rome itself. By 290 BCE the Romans dominated central Italy, and began expanding into the Italian Peninsula. Rivalry with Carthage led to the three Punic Wars between 264 and 146 BCE, but victories brought the acquisition of territory in Sicily, Sardinia, Spain, and then North Africa itself.

In the early 2nd century BCE the Romans fought campaigns in the Balkans, leading to the annexation of most of Greece in 146 BCE. The pace of acquisition quickened in the later years of the Republic, as generals competed for political power and used their military successes to bolster their position in Rome. It was in this period that Pompey annexed Syria and Julius Caesar conquered much of Gaul, between 58 and 51 BCE.

The collapse of the Roman Republic and the accession of the first emperor, Augustus, in 27 BCE did not end the empire's expansion. The quest for security along the existing frontiers resulted in the frontiers being pushed even further forward. Rome's final large-scale acquisitions were made in the reigns of Claudius, who oversaw the invasion of Britain in 43 CE, and Trajan, who conquered new provinces in Dacia (modern Romania) and Mesopotamia between 106 and 117 CE.

> “TO THE **ROMANS** I SET **NO BOUNDARIES** IN TIME OR SPACE.”

Virgil, Roman poet (70–19 BCE), the god Jupiter, prophesying the future greatness of Rome, from the *Aeneid*

7:1 **Roman population**
Around 1 CE, the Roman Empire contained just under one seventh of the world's population – 45 million out of 300 million people.

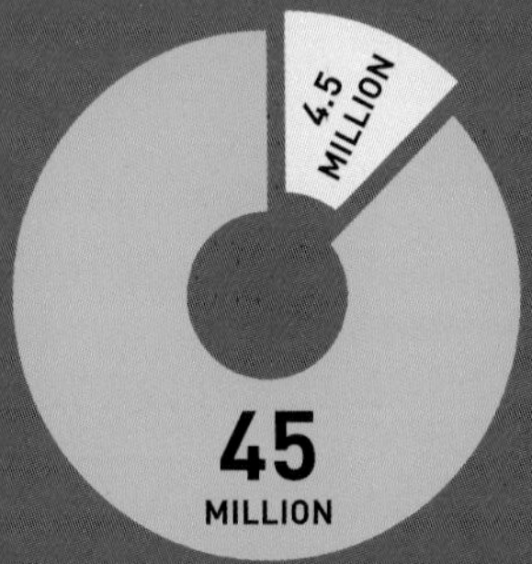

An empire of non-citizens
In 1 CE, only a tenth of the Roman population were full citizens. The rest were slaves or had limited civic rights.

Expanding empire
Between the accession of Augustus and the death of Trajan, the Roman Empire almost doubled in size, acquiring vast new territories in northwestern Europe and western Asia.

KEY
Roman territory

100 CE
By around 100 CE, the Mediterranean had become a Roman "lake", and the acquisition of territories in northwest and Central Europe had brought the northern Roman frontier as far as the Rhine and the Danube.

A GROWING EMPIRE

It took the Romans nearly 500 years to complete the conquest of Italy, but only half that time to enlarge their territories to include Spain, Gaul, parts of Germany, most of the Balkans, much of North Africa, and large parts of western Asia. Over the following 100 years they acquired Morocco, Britain, and Dacia, and made small advances into western Asia, but the empire began to contract after 250 CE.

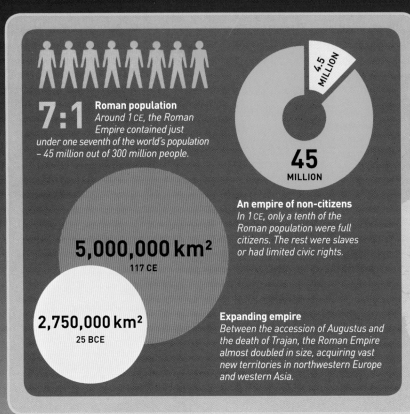

240 BCE The Romans dominated most of the Italian Peninsula. Victory in the First Punic War (264–241 BCE) brought new territory in Sicily, but the Romans still faced resistance to their rule in northern Italy.

10,000 KILOMETRES

THE APPROXIMATE LENGTH OF THE **ROMAN FRONTIERS** AT THEIR **MAXIMUM EXTENT**

200 BCE The Roman defeat of Carthage in the Second Punic War brought new possessions in Spain and Sardinia. By 200 BCE, a toehold had also been gained in northwestern Greece.

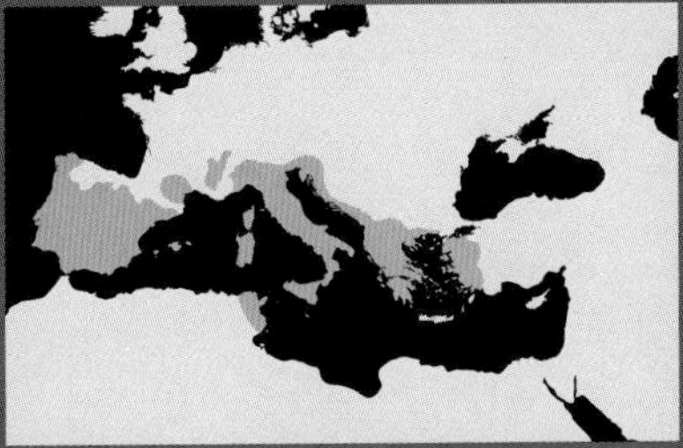

120 BCE Most of Spain had fallen into Roman possession, as well as Carthaginian territory in North Africa. Greece and parts of western Anatolia were also acquired.

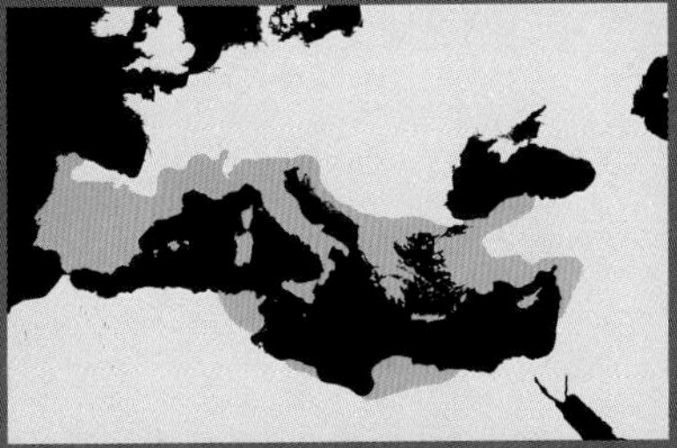

60 BCE New North African territories were gained in 96 BCE, and in 63 BCE Syria and parts of Palestine were annexed. The frontiers in Anatolia were also pushed forward.

14 CE The Roman borders had expanded to include Gaul beyond the Alps, as well as new provinces in Raetia and Noricum (Switzerland, south Germany, and Austria), and Pannonia (Hungary).

“ QUINCTILIUS VARUS, GIVE ME BACK MY LEGIONS. ”

Emperor Augustus, on hearing of the Roman defeat in the Teutoberg Forest, 9 CE

Consolidating ruler
Rather than extending Roman territory through foreign conquests, Tiberius concentrated on strengthening the existing empire.

WANG MANG WAS IN CHARGE OF BOTH THE CHINESE ARMY and the government under **Emperor Ping Di** (r.1 BCE–6 CE). He strengthened his influence by marrying his daughter to the young emperor. On Ping Di's death, many of the nobility rejected Wang Mang's choice of successor and rose up in **revolt**. Wang Mang easily put them down, and in 9 he took the title of **first Xin emperor**. He reissued the currency, forbade the selling of private slaves, reorganized the commanderies (China's administrative regions), and reimposed several state monopolies. Serious floods on the Yellow River in 4–11 led to **famine and revolts** in rural areas. In 23, the peasant rebels called the "**Red Eyebrows**" joined forces with Han loyalists and overwhelmed Wang Mang's armies. When the capital Chang'an fell, **Gengshi** became the first emperor of the **restored Han dynasty**. One of his first acts was to make Luoyang his capital.

28
THE NUMBER OF DIFFERENT **TYPES** OF **COIN** ISSUED BY **WANG MANG**

In Europe, **Tiberius** (see 20–2 BCE) returned to Germany in 4 to subdue the tribes there. The **Marcomanni resisted**, but a planned attack on them in 6 was postponed because of a revolt in Pannonia, which took three years to quell. A new Roman commander, **Quinctilius Varus**, was sent to Germany, but his **corrupt rule** angered the German tribes. In 9, Varus was ambushed in the **Teutoberg Forest**, and his three legions were annihilated. Augustus then ordered a **withdrawal to the Rhine**, where the Roman frontier remained for the next 400 years.

When Emperor Augustus (see 20–2 BCE) died in 14, **Tiberius** was his obvious heir (Lucius and Gaius Caesar having died). Tiberius already possessed most of Augustus's powers and had the **loyalty of the Praetorian Guard** – the elite army unit based in Rome, which Augustus had established. Although there were moves in the senate to **restore the Republic**, Tiberius rapidly squashed them. His reign (to 37) was quiet at home. **Germanicus**, Tiberius's nephew, campaigned extensively in Germany up to 16, but his efforts led to no permanent reacquisition of territory beyond the Rhine and he died of poisoning in 19. After Drusus, Tiberius's son, died in 23, the **emperor tired of public life** and retired to the island of Capri, off Naples. **Sejanus**, head of the Praetorian Guard, took day-to-day power, but his rule was tyrannical and in 31 Tiberius suddenly reasserted himself and had Sejanus executed.

Ponte di Tiberio, Rimini, Italy
Completed in the reign of Tiberius, this bridge carried the Via Aemilia (which ran from Riminia to Piacenza) across the River Marecchia.

GENGSHI'S REIGN AS CHINESE EMPEROR WAS SHORT. He alienated the Red Eyebrows and angered many of China's nobility and bureaucrats by moving the capital from Luoyang back to **Chang'an**. Much of China had already slipped from Gengshi's grasp by 25, when Chang'an was sacked by the Red Eyebrows. The emperor was deposed and replaced by **Guang Wudi** (25–57), who is regarded as the first **Eastern Han** emperor. The new ruler had first to face a **civil war**; by 27, he had defeated the Red Eyebrows, but it took him until 36 to overcome the last of the **warlords** who opposed him. In 37, he abolished all except three of the kingdoms that had sprung up

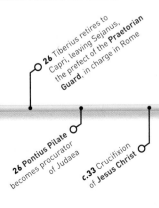

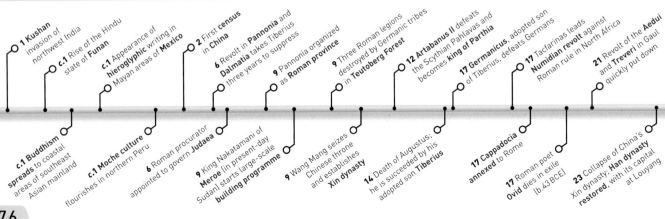

Chinese Han Empire
When Guang Wudi began the Eastern Han Dynasty in 25, Chinese control extended deep into Central Asia. Much of this territory had been won under the Western Han Dynasty.

- **1 Kushan** invasion of northwest India
- **c.1** Rise of the Hindu state of **Funan**
- **c.1 Buddhism spreads** to coastal areas of southeast Asian mainland
- **c.1** Appearance of **hieroglyphic** writing in Mayan areas of **Mexico**
- **c.1 Moche culture** flourishes in northern Peru
- **2** First **census** in **China**
- **6** Revolt in **Pannonia** and **Dalmatia** takes Tiberius three years to suppress
- **6** Roman procurator appointed to govern **Judaea**
- **9** Pannonia organized as **Roman province**
- **9** King Nakatamani of **Meroe** (in present-day Sudan) starts large-scale **building programme**
- **9** Three Roman legions destroyed by Germanic tribes in **Teutoberg Forest**
- **9** Wang Mang seizes Chinese throne and establishes **Xin dynasty**
- **12 Artabanus II** defeats the Scythian Pahlavas and becomes **king of Parthia**
- **14** Death of Augustus; he is succeeded by his adopted son **Tiberius**
- **17 Germanicus**, adopted son of Tiberius, defeats Germans
- **17** Tacfarinas leads **Numidian revolt** against Roman rule in North Africa
- **17 Cappadocia annexed** to Rome
- **17** Roman poet **Ovid** dies in exile (b.43 BCE)
- **21** Revolt of the **Aedui** and **Treveri** in Gaul quickly put down
- **23** Collapse of China's Xin dynasty; **Han dynasty restored**, with its capital at Louyang
- **26** Tiberius retires to Capri, leaving Sejanus, the prefect of the **Praetorian Guard**, in charge in Rome
- **26 Pontius Pilate** becomes procurator of Judaea
- **c.33** Crucifixion of **Jesus Christ**

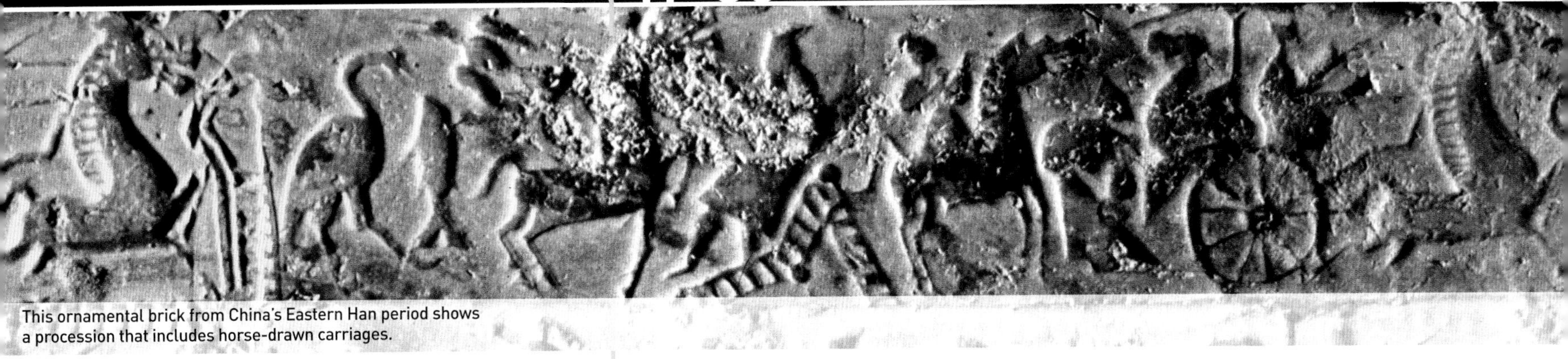

This ornamental brick from China's Eastern Han period shows a procession that includes horse-drawn carriages.

JESUS CHRIST (*c.*4 BCE–33 CE)

Jesus, a carpenter from Nazareth, began his ministry in his early 30s. He taught in the Jewish tradition, calling for the reform of the Temple and for the love of one's neighbour to take precedence over the strict observance of religious law. Jesus gathered a group of twelve disciples around him, but was targeted by Jewish conservatives afraid of his growing influence. In 33, the Roman authorities in Judaea executed Jesus by crucifixion, but the disciples, convinced that Jesus had risen from the dead, continued his teaching.

under his predecessors, and reinstated Luoyang as the capital. He faced renewed tension with the **Hsiung-nu** on China's northern frontier, but failed to take advantage of their split into two **rival chiefdoms** in 49.

The **Roman Empire** once again faced an **unclear succession** at the death of Tiberius in 37. He had named two heirs, but Gemellus was soon pushed aside because Gaius, nicknamed **Caligula** ("little boots"), was popular with the senate and the army. Caligula's behaviour as emperor became increasingly erratic – he had Gemellus executed, and had many of Tiberius's supporters killed. He also had his sister's husband – his heir apparent – condemned to death. After visiting the Rhineland legions in 39, Caligula marched them to the coast opposite Britain to launch an invasion; when they got there, he merely had them collect seashells along the beach.

Independent **Jewish kingdoms** in Palestine **collapsed** as Roman power grew, creating a powerful ferment of religious change. **John the Baptist** preached in the 20s, followed in around 30 by a new preacher, **Jesus**. After Jesus's death in 33, his disciples began to spread his message more widely. By around 50, communities of Christians, as Jesus's followers were known, would be established throughout Western Asia, with particularly large groups in Antioch and the first appearance of **Christians in Rome**.

IN INDIA, GROUPS OF YUEZHI NOMADS occupying land in Bactria united under Kujula Kadphises (30–80), who founded the **Kushan Empire** and conquered parts of Gandhara. Although few details of Kujula's reign are known, he **minted coins** in imitation of both Greek and Roman models, demonstrating that Bactria and northwestern India remained very much a **cultural crossroads**.

In northwestern Europe, a group of disgruntled officers of Rome's Praetorian Guard **assassinated Caligula** in January 41, tired of his cruel and irrational behaviour (see 24–40). In 43, the new emperor, **Claudius** (r.41–54), sent an invasion force of four legions led by **Aulus Plautius**, governor of Pannonia, to **conquer Britain**. The Romans landed unopposed at Richborough, pushed on to London, and then captured Colchester, the capital of the principal British resistance leader, **Caractacus**. Claudius himself made a brief appearance at the fall of Colchester, before returning to Rome to bask in the glory of having **acquired a new province**. In 47, the Romans paused briefly in their conquest of Britain, having reached a line roughly between the River Humber in the east and the River Severn in the west. They began **establishing legionary fortresses** in their new province, including at Exeter and Lincoln. Aulus Plautius's replacement, **Ostorius Scapula** invaded Wales, where Caractacus was continuing the resistance. In 50, he defeated an army of Silurian and Ordovician tribesmen, and Caractacus fled to the imagined safety of the Brigantes tribe in northern England. However, the Brigantian queen, **Cartimandua**, handed Caractacus over to the Romans, and Roman Britain remained relatively trouble free during the following decade.

Christian catacomb, Rome
At first, Roman Christians did not have their own cemeteries. Later, they buried their dead in underground complexes called catacombs.

The 40s saw a struggle in the early **Christian community** between those who wanted to remain within the Jewish tradition and those, led by **Paul**, who favoured the inclusion of gentiles (non-Jews) in the Christian church. Paul began a series of **missionary journeys** in 46 which led him through Anatolia and Greece to Rome, where he was **martyred** around 62. A charismatic preacher, Paul also wrote a powerful series of **epistles** (letters) to various fledgling Christian groups. In appealing to a wider group than the Jews within the Roman empire, Paul ensured that **Christianity spread** sufficiently to help it weather the storms of **persecution** that began under the Emperor Nero in 64. By the late 4th century, Christianity would be the **majority religion** within the Roman Empire.

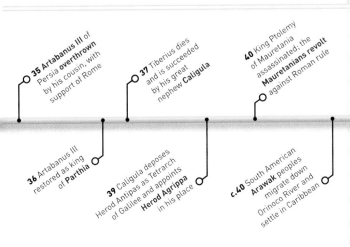

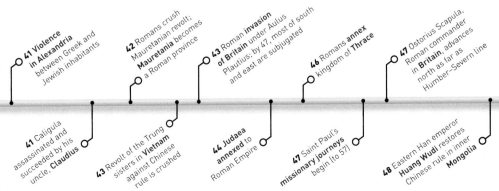

EMPEROR CLAUDIUS
(10 BCE–54 CE)

Caligula's uncle, Claudius, was an unlikely candidate for Roman emperor. However, he turned out to be intelligent and forceful, putting down two revolts in 42, after which he executed more than 300 senators. He was unfortunate in his choice of wives: he had his wife Messalina executed after she had an affair, and her successor Agrippina (Caligula's sister) is reputed to have poisoned him.

35 Artabanus III of Persia **overthrown** by his cousin, with support of Rome

36 Artabanus III restored as king of **Parthia**

37 Tiberius dies and is succeeded by his great nephew **Caligula**

39 Caligula deposes Herod Antipas as Tetrarch of Galilee and appoints **Herod Agrippa** in his place

40 King Ptolemy of Mauretania assassinated; the **Mauretanians revolt** against Roman rule

c.40 South American **Arawak** peoples migrate down Orinoco River and settle in Caribbean

41 Violence in Alexandria between Greek and Jewish inhabitants

41 Caligula assassinated and succeeded by his uncle, **Claudius**

42 Romans crush Mauretanian revolt; **Mauretania** becomes a Roman province

43 Roman **invasion of Britain** under Aulus Plautius; by 47, most of south and east are subjugated

43 Revolt of the Trung sisters in **Vietnam** against Chinese rule is crushed

44 Judaea annexed to Roman Empire

46 Romans **annex** kingdom of **Thrace**

47 Saint Paul's **missionary journeys** begin (to 57)

47 Ostorius Scapula, Roman commander in **Britain**, advances north as far as Humber-Severn line

48 Eastern Han emperor **Huang Wudi** restores Chinese rule in inner **Mongolia**

70 THOUSAND THE NUMBER OF PEOPLE **KILLED** BY **BOUDICCA'S ARMY** DURING THE **ICENI REVOLT**

WHEN CLAUDIUS DIED IN 54, the Roman imperial throne fell to **Nero** (37–68), his adopted son and son-in-law. The young emperor's reign began well when he promised the senate he would avoid making any arbitrary measures. However, the first sign of Nero's tyranny surfaced in 59, when he had his mother **Agrippina** (15–59) murdered. In 62, a new praetorian prefect (commander of the imperial bodyguard), **Tigellinus** (*c.*10–69), took office. Tigellinus pandered to the less desirable side of Nero's personality, whose rule became increasingly despotic. Following a **fire** that destroyed much of Rome in 64, Nero is said to have taken terrible retribution on Rome's small Christian population, who proved convenient scapegoats. Later, during the reconstruction of Rome, Nero alienated senators by seizing their land to build himself a new palace. He also ordered additional taxes in Palestine, which sparked a **Jewish revolt** in 66.

In **Britain**, the Romans faced a serious **Iceni** revolt in 60. When the king of the Iceni died, he left his lands to his queen, **Boudicca**. The revolt was triggered when the Roman procurator (chief financial official) ruled that Boudicca could not inherit her lands, and that they would be annexed by Rome. Boudicca raised an army and marched on Camulodunum (Colchester). **Suetonius Paullinus**, the governor of Britain, was away on campaign in Wales, and by the time he returned, Camulodunum had been sacked by the Iceni. The rebels then burnt Londinium (London) and Verulamium (St Albans) before they were finally trapped and defeated by Paullinus. It is said the Iceni lost 80,000 warriors and Boudicca herself was captured, though she died, possibly poisoned, soon after.

Boudicca
This statue of Boudicca stands outside the Houses of Parliament in London, a city that the Iceni queen razed to the ground.

The ruins at Masada, the last outpost of the Jewish revolt against the Romans, which began in 66.

IN THE EAST, Rome faced further troubles with **Parthia** over the border region of **Armenia**, where the Parthian king had installed his own candidate, **Tiridates**, as king in 53. A Roman force invaded Armenia in 59, took its capital cities of Artaxata and Tigranocerta and put in place a pro-Roman king, **Tigranes VI.** His ill-advised invasion of a Parthian ally in 61 led to his removal, and Tiridates was restored. A new Roman army was then roundly beaten by the Parthians in 62, and only a Roman push into Armenia the following year ended the war.

Tiridates was allowed to keep the throne, as long as he travelled to Rome to seek Nero's approval, which he eventually did in 66.

Nero's position as emperor became increasingly precarious when **Calpurnius Piso** led a conspiracy in 64, which prompted Nero to order further executions, including those of many senators. In early 68, a revolt broke out, led by **Gaius Julius Vindex**, governor of Gallia Lugdunensis. Shortly after the revolt of Vindex, the legion based in Spain proclaimed the governor, **Sulpicius Galba**, as emperor. Vindex's revolt was put down by **Verginius Rufus**, the governor of Germany, but **Nero** panicked and **committed suicide**, believing Rufus would be the next to try to claim his throne.

After Nero's suicide, four men became emperor in rapid succession, making 69 the **"Year of the Four Emperors"**. First, the praetorian guard recognized **Galba** (3 BCE–69 CE) as emperor, but he made himself unpopular by refusing to give the praetorians the donative, a customary bonus payable on the accession of a new emperor. In January 69, the governor of Upper Germany, **Aulus Vitellius**, revolted, and one of Galba's former supporters, **Salvius Otho** (32–69), angered when Galba recognized another senator as his heir, had the emperor murdered and took the throne. In April 69, the armies of Otho and Vitellius clashed at Bedriacum near Cremona in northern Italy, and the Vitellian army won. Otho committed suicide, but Vitellius soon faced a further conspiracy when T. Flavius Vespasianus

Roman invasion
When the Romans finally breached the walls of Masada, all except seven defenders committed suicide rather than fall into Roman hands.

51 Romans capture **Caractacus**, leader of the British resistance

52 Saint Paul begins spreading Christianity in Greece

53 Vologases of Parthia puts his brother **Tiridates** on the throne of Armenia, fuelling tensions with Rome

54 Roman emperor **Claudius** is murdered and succeeded by his stepson **Nero**

57 An ambassador from Japan arrives at the **Han capital** of Luoyang

58 Armenia becomes a Roman protectorate

59 Suetonius Paulinus becomes governor of Britain

c.60 Mark begins writing the first of the **gospels** recounting the life of Jesus Christ

c.60 Kushans under Kujula Kadphises advance into northern India, starting the **Kushan Empire**

60 Nero sends an expedition to explore **Meroe** on the east bank of the Nile

60 The **Iceni revolt against the Romans** in Britain

63 Peace of Rhandeia between Rome and Parthia; **Tiridates** is returned to the Armenian throne

64 Great **Fire of Rome**; Nero blames the Christians and many are martyred

c.65 Buddhism reaches China

66–70 Jewish revolt against Roman rule

A fresco from Pompei – many of Pompei's elaborate frescoes survived for nearly 2,000 years buried under the ash.

Jewish revolts between 66 and 74
Although the Jewish rebels of 66 initially managed to gain control of a large part of Palestine, by 69 they had lost control of all but the area around Jerusalem.

(Vespasian) (9–79) – the general in charge of suppressing the Jewish revolt – set himself up as yet another rival emperor. The whole of the East and the Balkans defected immediately to Vespasian. At a second **battle near Cremona** in October, Vitellius's forces were crushed. By December Vespasian's army had taken Rome and Vitellius was executed shortly afterwards. Rome had an **unchallenged ruler** once again.

Vespasian moved quickly to re-establish the loyalty of the army, dismissing Vitellius's praetorian guard and recruiting another. He also had to face a serious revolt along the Rhine, where **Julius Civilis**, a noble of the Batavian people, joined forces with dissident legionaries and almost established an independent **Gallic empire**.

Judaea had been under direct Roman rule since the death of King Agrippa I in 44. Foreign rule and Roman insensitivity towards Jewish laws caused great discontent. In 60, the rebuilding of the Temple that Herod had ordered built decades before was finished, and 20,000 unemployed workmen added to the rising tension. The Roman procurator of Judaea aggravated these feelings with his **heavy-handed rule**, and in 66 an uprising broke out. Although the commanders of the uprising were competent, it lacked political leadership and the Jewish strongholds were gradually reduced, first by Vespasian and then by his son Titus (39–81). In 70, **Jerusalem** came under siege, and in late August the city fell and the Temple was destroyed. Perhaps as many as 200,000 people died, many sacred Jewish treasures were taken to Rome, and thousands of Jews were enslaved. Resistance continued at **Masada** until 74, when it fell after a two-year siege.

BY THE MID-70S, CIVILIS'S REVOLT had fizzled out and the rest of Vespasian's reign was largely peaceful. With a reputation for frugality, he restored the empire's finances, imposing levies on a number of provinces, including Egypt. By the time he died in 79, **stability had been restored** to such an extent that the succession of his eldest son, **Titus** (r.79–81), was unopposed.

Two months after the accession of Titus as Roman emperor, on 25 August 79 the city of **Pompeii**, near modern Naples, was destroyed by a volcanic eruption. Showers of ash came raining down from **Vesuvius**, and those who did not escape in time were overwhelmed by the pyroclastic flow (a fast-moving mass of hot gases, ash, and debris) from the volcano. Perhaps a tenth of the population of 20,000 died, including the naturalist Pliny the Elder, who was commanding a naval unit nearby and perished in a failed rescue attempt.

Figure from Pompeii
The bodies of those who died in the Pompeii eruption were coated in volcanic ash, which then solidified, leaving their outlines behind.

In **Britain**, the Roman-controlled area continued to expand, with governor Petillius Cerialis (71–74) occupying the northern English kingdom of **Brigantia**. Julius Frontinus (74–77) completed the subjugation of Wales, defeating the Silures, but it was left to Julius Agricola (77–83/4) to send Roman armies far into Scotland, until a final defeat of the Caledonii at **Mons Graupius** (possibly near Aberdeen) made it likely the whole of Scotland would be annexed. But emperor **Domitian** (81–96) was facing trouble on the Danube and a legion was withdrawn from Britain around 86, leaving an insufficient force to garrison northern Scotland, which was evacuated.

Domitian had managed to fend off the threat from the **Sarmatians, Marcomanni, and Quadi** along the **Danube** by 84, but war then erupted with the **Dacians** (of modern Romania) who crossed the Danube and killed the governor of Roman Moesia. By 86, Domitian had defeated the Dacians, under their new king, **Decebalus**. Dacia was not occupied by Rome, leaving Decebalus in place to cause the Romans further trouble.

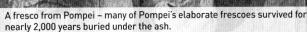

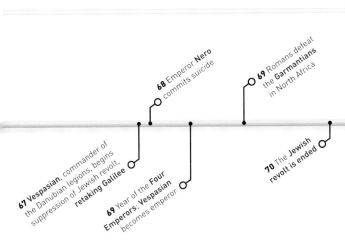

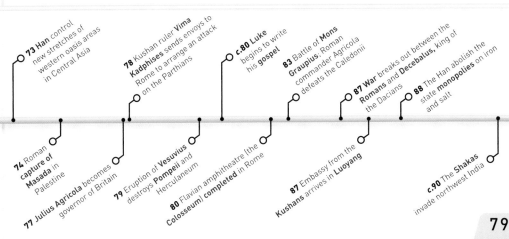

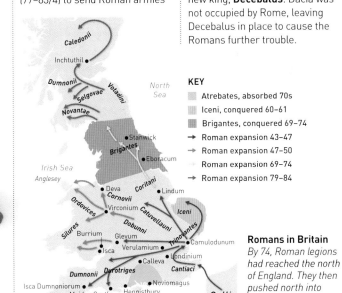

Romans in Britain
By 74, Roman legions had reached the north of England. They then pushed north into Scotland until 83.

67 Vespasian, commander of the Danubian legions, begins suppression of Jewish revolt, **retaking Galilee**

68 Emperor **Nero** commits suicide

69 Year of the **Four Emperors**; **Vespasian** becomes emperor

69 Romans defeat the **Garmantians** in North Africa

70 The **Jewish revolt is ended**

73 Han control new stretches of western oasis areas in Central Asia

74 Roman **capture of Masada** in Palestine

77 Julius Agricola becomes governor of Britain

78 Kushan ruler **Vima Kadphises** sends envoys to Rome to arrange an attack on the Parthians

79 Eruption of **Vesuvius** destroys **Pompeii** and Herculaneum

c.80 Luke begins to write his **gospel**

80 Flavian amphitheatre (the **Colosseum**) **completed** in Rome

83 Battle of **Mons Graupius**; Roman commander Agricola defeats the Caledonii

87 Embassy from the **Kushans** arrives in **Luoyang**

87 War breaks out between the **Romans** and **Decebalus**, king of the Dacians

88 The Han abolish the state **monopolies** on iron and salt

c.90 The **Shakas** invade northwest India

“[AN EMPEROR] UNDER WHOM **EVERYBODY** WAS **PERMITTED** TO DO **EVERYTHING.**”

Fronto, Roman orator, on Emperor Nerva, from Cassius Dio's *History of Rome*

Emperor Domitian
Domitian's reign began well, but his descent into tyranny proved too much for his opponents, who had him assassinated.

DOMITIAN (51–96) BECAME ROMAN EMPEROR after the unexpected death of his brother, Titus (39–81). Domitian had never commanded armies and was unprepared for the exercise of supreme power. He had some success in his early campaigns, but he over-extended himself against the Dacians, and in putting down a legionary revolt led by **Saturninus**, the governor of Germania Superior. This distraction allowed **Decebalus, King of the Dacians** (r.87–106), to renew his war against Rome, and Domitian was forced to pay off the Dacians with an annual subsidy.

The conspiracy of Saturninus led Domitian to become paranoid and he had many senators executed for treason. In September 96, he was murdered in a palace conspiracy and the Senate chose the aged **M. Cocceius Nerva** (30–98) to replace him. The Senate then voted to destroy all statues of Domitian and to recall those he had exiled. However, in 97 Nerva faced a mutiny of the praetorian guard, who demanded the punishment of Domitian's murderers. Nerva was forced to give in, weakening his authority. His position was further diminished by his lack of an heir. To rectify this he adopted M. Ulpius Traianus **(Trajan)**, the governor of Upper Germany, a man with a strong military backing. Nerva died soon afterwards and Trajan became emperor.

In Central Asia, the northern Hsiung-nu confederation (see 146–131 BCE) collapsed in 89, allowing the Han to make large gains in the region, led by **general Ban Chao** (32–102). Ban Chao became protector-general of the Western Regions in 92, and re-established control over the key oases along the **Silk Route.** By the time he retired in 102 the Han controlled most of the Tarim Basin. **Chinese state organization** became very complicated under the Han. Three supreme officials supervised large, complex departments. Each of these was subdivided into nine ministries. Governors oversaw each region, with regions divided into over 1,000 counties, each supervised by a magistrate. Eunuchs became increasingly influential at the Han court.

Trajan's Column, in Rome, gives a visual account of Trajan's campaigns against Decebalus in the Dacian Wars.

EMPEROR TRAJAN (98–117) WAS FROM A ROMAN FAMILY who had settled in Spain – he was the first emperor to come from a Roman province rather than Italy. Having returned to Rome from Germany in 100 to claim his throne, he started a new **Dacian War** against Decebalus in 101. From a base at Viminacium (in modern Serbia), he pushed into central Dacia, and fought a major engagement at Tapae, in which both sides suffered serious losses. When Trajan's legions neared the Dacian royal capital at **Sarmizegetusa Regia**, Decebalus sued for peace, agreeing to give up his army's weapons and siege equipment, and to demolish his remaining forts. The Roman army did not withdraw totally, establishing a legionary base near the mountains and building a bridge across the Danube at Drobeta to allow easier access across the river. Three years later, in 105, the Senate declared that Decebalus had violated the treaty, and Trajan embarked on his **Second Dacian War**. This time the legions reached, and took, Sarmizegetusa in 106. Decebalus fled and then committed suicide to avoid capture. The Romans acquired an enormous amount of treasure in Dacia, which allowed Trajan to embark on a building spree, including the construction of a **new Forum** in Rome. Dacia was annexed as Rome's first province across the Danube. It remained in imperial hands for over 160 years.

Some time around 106 the Roman governor of Syria annexed the **Nabataean kingdom**, which became the Roman province of Arabia. It was not Trajan's last acquisition in the east – in 113 he set off on a campaign against **Parthia**. He began by attacking Armenia in 113–114, but it was his campaign against Parthia itself that gave him greater success in the east than any previous Roman emperor. By late 114 the Armenians had submitted to him, and he pushed into Mesopotamia, capturing the Parthian capital of **Ctesiphon**. By the end of 115, Trajan had reached the Persian

Sacred city
This ruined temple is in the Dacian capital, Sarmizegetusa Regia (in modern-day Romania). It contained the kingdom's most sacred shrines.

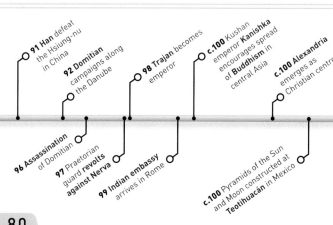

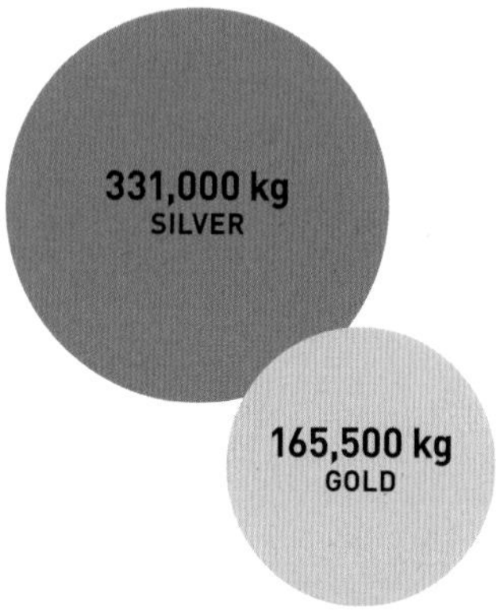

The Dacian Fortune
The large amount of treasure Trajan acquired in Dacia allowed him to build impressive monuments to commemorate his Dacian victory.

91 Han defeat the Hsiung-nu in China

92 Domitian campaigns along the Danube

96 Assassination of Domitian

97 Praetorian guard **revolts against Nerva**

98 Trajan becomes emperor

99 Indian embassy arrives in Rome

c.100 Kushan emperor **Kanishka** encourages spread of **Buddhism** in central Asia

c.100 Alexandria emerges as Christian centre

c.100 Pyramids of the Sun and Moon constructed at **Teotihuacán** in Mexico

101 Trajan invades **Dacia** (to 102)

105 Trajan's **Second Dacian War**

c.105 Paper invented in China

106 Following defeat of Decebalus, his kingdom is annexed as the Roman province of **Dacia**

106 The Nabataean kingdom is annexed by Rome and becomes **province of Arabia**

109 Pliny the Younger appointed governor of Bithynia

c.110 Buddhist council in northern India leads to division into two branches, **Mahayana** and **Hinayana**

113 Trajan completes building of a **new Forum** at Rome

114 Trajan annexes **Armenia** and invades **Parthia**

The remains of Hadrian's Wall in northern England. The central portion of the wall occupies a high position that vastly enhances its defensive value.

Gulf near modern Basra, Iraq, where he is said to have remarked that, had he been younger, he might have pressed on to India. The newly conquered territories were organized as the provinces of **Mesopotamia** and **Assyria**, but they were already in revolt when Trajan returned home in 117. The Parthians rejected Trajan's **puppet king Parthamaspates**, and by the time Trajan died in August 117 almost all of his gains in the east had been lost. On his death-bed Trajan adopted Publius Aelius Hadrianus (**Hadrian**), the governor of Syria, effectively appointing Hadrian as his successor.

In 109, Trajan appointed the historian **Pliny the Younger** (61–*c.*112) as his personal representative to govern **Bithynia-Pontus** on the Black Sea coast of Anatolia. This was a controversial move, as Bithynia-Pontus was theoretically a senatorial province. The provinces of the empire had been divided between the emperor and the senate at the accession of Augustus in 27 BCE, with the emperor receiving only the provinces that held legionary garrisons. This division of the provinces persisted into the time of Trajan. Pliny stayed in Bithynia-Pontus for at least two years, trying to sort out the finances of the main cities, which had fallen into confusion. His letters to Trajan are an invaluable insight into the imperial government of the time.

TRAJAN'S SUCCESSOR HADRIAN (r.117–135) rejected his predecessor's policy of expansion and concentrated on better defence of the **imperial frontiers**. In 122, Hadrian visited Britain, where there had been frontier troubles. He ordered the building of a huge barrier from the Solway Firth in the west to the River Tyne in the east. It took governor **Aulus Platorius Nepos** two years to complete **Hadrian's Wall** (part in stone, and part in turf), which ran 76 Roman miles (113 kilometres), and was equipped with a series of forts and milecastles for its garrison. Hadrian's Wall acted as the northern frontier line of Roman Britain for the next 40 years.

The **Parthian kingdom** was left in some confusion by the campaigns of Trajan. His puppet king, Parthamaspates, was expelled in 117, but the Parthian kingdom then seems to have been divided between **Vologeses III** (r.105–147) who ruled the eastern portion, and **Osroes** (r.117–129) then **Mithridates IV** (r.129–140) in the west. There was no further conflict between Parthia and Rome for the time being.

985

THE NUMBER OF **VILLAGES RAZED** DURING THE **BAR-KOCHBA REVOLT**

In India, the **Kushan empire** expanded enormously under **Kanishka** (127–140), who conquered Magadha and campaigned against the Chinese in Central Asia; his inscriptions are found from the Oxus river in Afghanistan to as far south as Varanasi and Sanchi. He was a strong patron of Buddhism and presided over the **fourth Buddhist Council**, as well as building a great stupa at his capital Purushapura (Peshawar).

Hadrian's ban on circumcision, his plan to turn Jerusalem into the Roman town of Aelia Capitolina, and his intent to ban Jewish religious practices in Jerusalem caused a furious **revolt in Jerusalem** in 132, as religious Jews rose up against religious reforms. Led by **Shimon Bar Kochba**, the rebels had early successes against Rome. They set up the beginnings of an independent government and minted their own coins. In response, Hadrian summoned **Julius Severus**, the governor of Britain, to conduct a war against the rebels. Severus commanded an army formed of detachments from 12 legions. The rebels had no large towns under their control, and so adopted **guerrilla warfare** while still attempting to defend the smaller forts they held. In 135, the rebel's last main stronghold at **Bethar was captured** amid great slaughter, after which the revolt petered out. Hadrian proceeded with his plan to **outlaw Judaism** in Palestine, and many of the Jews who had survived the rebellion fled abroad.

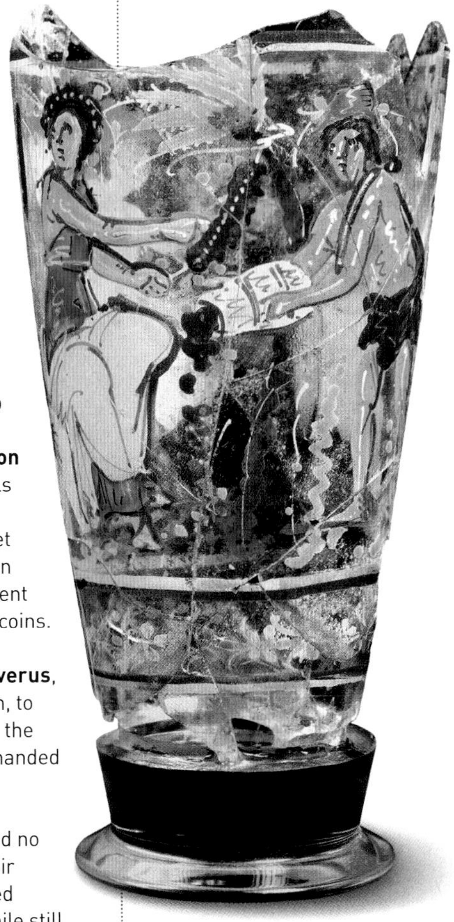

Treasured goblet
This beautiful vase was found in Kapisa (Bagram) near Kabul, which was the Kushan summer capital in the 1st century.

HADRIAN (76–138)

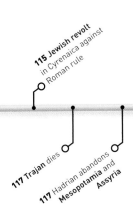

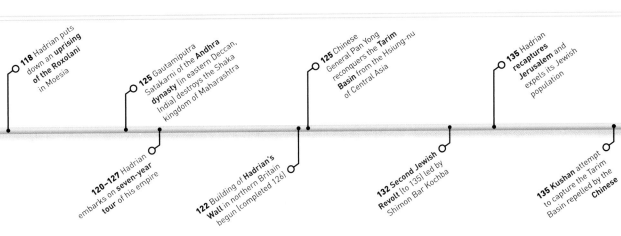

Hadrian came from a Spanish background and was the adopted son of his predecessor, Trajan. He was mocked by some for his grecophile tendencies, and was the first emperor to sport a beard – a Greek fashion. Hadrian was the first emperor to travel widely throughout the Roman empire, giving him first-hand knowledge of the provinces, from Britain to North Africa.

115 Jewish revolt in Cyrenaica against Roman rule

117 Trajan dies

117 Hadrian abandons **Mesopotamia** and **Assyria**

118 Hadrian puts down an **uprising of the Roxolani** in Moesia

120–127 Hadrian embarks on **seven-year tour** of his empire

125 Gautamiputra Satakarni of the **Andhra dynasty** (in eastern Deccan, India) destroys the Shaka kingdom of Maharashtra

122 Building of **Hadrian's Wall** in northern Britain begun (completed 126)

125 Chinese General Pan Yong reconquers the **Tarim Basin** from the Hsiung-nu of Central Asia

132 Second Jewish Revolt (to 135) led by Shimon Bar Kochba

135 Hadrian **recaptures Jerusalem** and expels its Jewish population

135 Kushan attempt to capture the Tarim Basin repelled by the **Chinese**

200 THOUSAND THE TOTAL **POPULATION** OF **TEOTIHUACÁN** AT **ITS PEAK**

The Pyramid of the Sun at Teotihuacán in modern Mexico.

The ruins of Hatra, which was a Parthian-controlled city.

THE CITY OF TEOTIHUACÁN IN THE VALLEY OF MEXICO experienced **massive growth** during the 1st and 2nd centuries, with its population reaching over 80,000 before 200. The city was planned on a grid, with **two huge pyramids** – of the Moon and the Sun – at either end of the main street. The Teotihuacán II phase of the city (0–350) saw the building of the enormous **Temple of Quetzalcoatl** and the acquisition of an empire, with Teotihuacán dominating vast areas of Mexico and overseeing client kingdoms as far south as Guatemala.

Hadrian had adopted **Antoninus Pius** (86–161) as his son and successor, a stop-gap until Antoninus's relative, **Marcus Aurelius** (121–80), was old enough to rule, but Antoninus survived Hadrian by 23 years, and became Roman emperor in 138. He was famed for his moderation and rarely left Rome. Disturbances in **Dacia** (in present-day Romania) around 140 and an uprising in North Africa in 145 did not unduly disturb the empire's calm. Antoninus extended the frontier in both Scotland and Upper Germany, ordering the construction of a new turf barrier around 160km (100 miles) to the north of Hadrian's Wall (see 188–135 BCE) in Britain. This **Antonine Wall** was 63km (35 miles) in length. The Hadrian's Wall garrison was moved north to a new set of forts, but their stay was short – Marcus Aurelius, Antoninus Pius's successor, ordered a **pull-back to Hadrian's Wall** around 161, where the Roman frontier of Britain remained until the 5th century.

As **Christianity** grew, so did the problem of defining a single doctrine. Among the alternative doctrines that sprang up in the 2nd century was **Marcionism**, which taught that the God of Christians was distinct from the Jewish God of the Old Testament and that Jesus Christ did not have a human nature. **Justin Martyr** (*c.*103–165) argued that Christianity was the fulfilment of Jewish prophecy and that Christians were the new chosen people. Justin also wrote to Marcus Aurelius, seeking to explain Christian doctrine.

63 KILOMETRES THE LENGTH OF THE **ANTONINE WALL** IN SCOTLAND

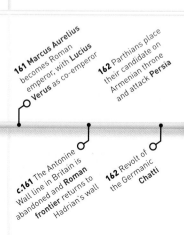

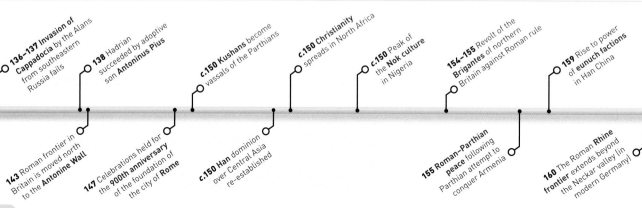

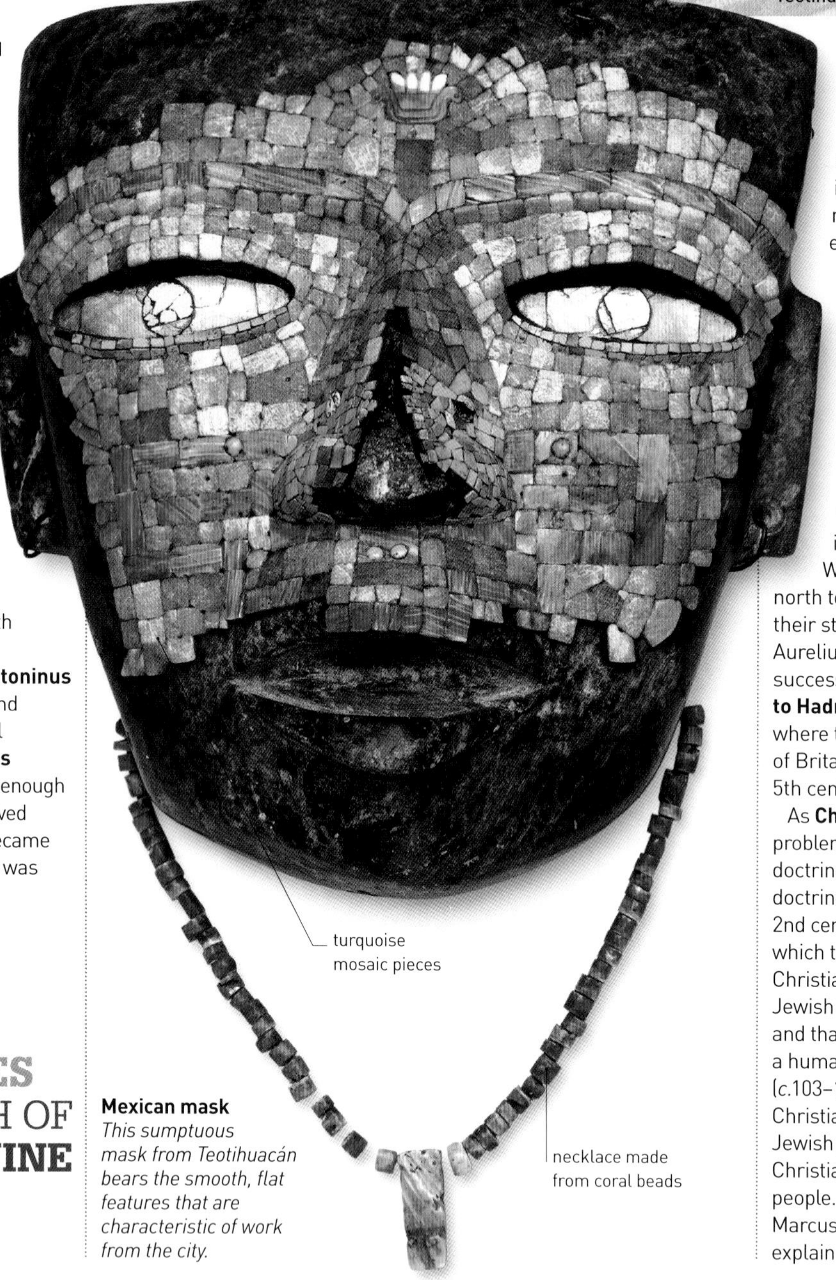

Mexican mask *This sumptuous mask from Teotihuacán bears the smooth, flat features that are characteristic of work from the city.*

MARCUS AURELIUS SUCCEEDED TO THE ROMAN THRONE jointly with **Lucius Verus** in 161. Marcus was the more capable of the two, but it was Lucius who was sent, in 162, to rescue the situation in the east after the governor of Cappadocia was defeated and killed by the Persians following a **disastrous invasion of Armenia**. By 163–164 Lucius had brought Armenia back under Roman control, and renamed its capital Kaine Polis ("New City"). A new pro-Roman king was installed there before the legions moved on, pushing deeper into Persian territory, taking Edessa in Mesopotamia, and reaching the **Parthian capital** of **Ctesiphon** in 165. The Roman general **Avidius Cassius** (*c.*130–175) burnt the Parthian palace and then turned back westward. A swathe of Parthian territory down the Euphrates River was annexed as far east as Dura Europos (in southeastern Syria). However, victory celebrations were short-lived, for the troops brought the **plague** back to Rome and by 167 it had **spread**

> **"** IF IT IS **NOT RIGHT, DO NOT DO IT:** IF IT IS **NOT TRUE, DO NOT SAY IT. "**
>
> **Emperor Marcus Aurelius**, from *Meditations*, 161–180

136–137 Invasion of Cappadocia by the Alans from southeastern Russia fails

138 Hadrian succeeded by adoptive son **Antoninus Pius**

143 Roman frontier in Britain is moved north to the **Antonine Wall**

147 Celebrations held for the **900th anniversary** of the foundation of the city of **Rome**

c.150 Kushans become vassals of the Parthians

c.150 Han dominion over Central Asia re-established

c.150 Christianity spreads in North Africa

c.150 Peak of the **Nok culture** in Nigeria

154–155 Revolt of the **Brigantes** of northern Britain against Roman rule

155 Roman–Parthian peace following Parthian attempt to conquer Armenia

159 Rise to power of **eunuch factions** in Han China

160 The Roman **Rhine frontier** extends beyond the Neckar valley (in modern Germany)

161 Marcus Aurelius becomes Roman emperor, with **Lucius Verus** as co-emperor

c.161 The Antonine Wall line in Britain is abandoned and **Roman frontier** returns to Hadrian's Wall

162 Parthians place their candidate on Armenian throne and attack **Persia**

162 Revolt of the Germanic **Chatti**

A painted stucco of the Moche's most important god, Al Apaec, who is often depicted with the fangs of a snake.

widely throughout the **Mediterranean**.

Barely had the Parthian War ended than the **Marcomannic War** began. In early 167, a group of Germanic warriors from the **Langobardi** and **Obii** tribes crossed the Danube to attack the Roman province of Pannonia. They were pushed back fairly easily, but in spring 168 Marcus Aurelius resolved to visit the region to assess the situation. Two more Germanic tribes, the **Marcomanni** and **Quadi** were threatening to force their way across the frontier unless they were admitted to settle in the empire, but Marcus's presence deterred them. However, the expedition was cut short by the death of Lucius Verus from plague in early 169. Marcus returned to Italy, but was back in Pannonia later in the year to launch a **massive offensive** across the Danube. It was a disaster, with the Romans suffering around 20,000 dead and the Marcomanni and Quadi pouring into Italy, where they laid siege to Aquileia. Far from providing an easy victory for Marcus, the war dragged on for another 10 years.

In **China**, the **eunuch faction** at court had become increasingly powerful and had even engineered the murder of the emperor Shaodi in 125. Under **Emperor Huandi** (146–68) a series of natural disasters weakened the authority of the central government, and the emperor relinquished active control of government to the eunuchs. In 168, an attempt by **Dou Miao**, regent for the 12-year-old emperor **Lingdi** (r.168–89), to have the eunuchs massacred failed – the plot was betrayed and Dou Miao was forced to commit suicide. Several hundred of Dou Miao's supporters were executed and, with its enemies now dead, the eunuch faction was able to exercise power almost unopposed.

Marcus Aurelius
This statue shows Marcus Aurelius adopting a pose of victory, something he claimed but never quite achieved in his Marcomannic Wars.

THE MOCHE CULTURE EMERGED ON THE COAST OF NORTHERN PERU between 100 and 200. From their bases in the Peruvian valleys of Moche, Chicama, and Virú, these people spread to dominate almost the whole northern coastline. A warlike people, they sacrificed those whom they captured to their deities, including **Al Apaec** ("the decapitator"). They were skilled workers in gold and their pottery has an extraordinarily realistic quality.

The **Roman Empire** was in **crisis** in 170 – the Marcomanni and Quadi had occupied parts of northern Italy, and an invasion by the **Iazyges** and **Costobocci** had overun large parts of the Balkans. The Romans trapped the **Marcomanni** as they returned across the Danube and killed many of them. The **Quadi sued for peace later in 171**, but the Marcommani remained recalcitrant, forcing a **new offensive in 172**. The forces of Marcus Aurelius could never quite strike the killer blow, and by 175 the war had reached a **stalemate**.

In May that year, rumours that Marcus Aurelius had died while on campaign prompted a revolt by **Avidius Cassius**, the governor of Syria. Avidius was **declared emperor** in Egypt, and received support in Arabia, as well as in his own province of Syria. Critically, however, he failed to secure the support of **Martius Verus**, the governor of Cappadocia, whom he had fought alongside during the Parthian War.

As Martius's army approached, the loyalty of the usurper's troops wavered, and in July **Avidius Cassius was murdered** by a disaffected centurion, putting an end to his short-lived but dangerous rebellion. There were suggestions that Marcus's wife **Faustina** encouraged Avidius, as she feared for her husband's health and worried her own son Commodus was unfit to rule.

Free from the distraction of Avidius's revolt, Marcus Aurelius returned to the Danube in 177. In the winter of 179–80, the **Roman army** occupied positions deep across the Danube, and it looked as if Marcus might be able to create two new Roman provinces – Marcomannia and Samartia. However, Marcus was old and tired – he died in March 180. His son **Commodus** brought the war to a rapid conclusion, allowing him to return to Rome.

THE GERMANIC TRIBES

The Romans had faced Germanic tribes ever since they had reached the Rhine at the time of Julius Caesar. German groups across the Danube, such as the Quadi and Marcomanni, proved troublesome in the 2nd century, but by the late 3rd century new and more dangerous confederations of Germanic tribes arose, such as the Franks, Alamanns, and Goths, who overran much of the Roman Empire by the mid-5th century.

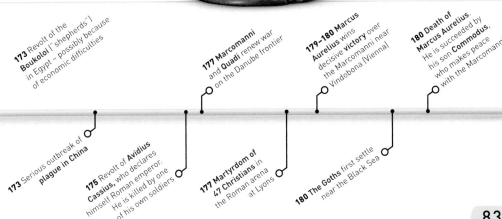

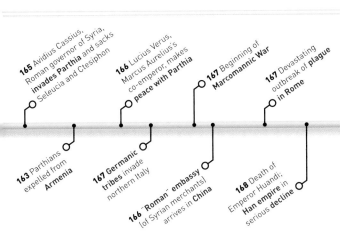

Moche stirrup jar
This jar has a typical Moche "stirrup" attached to the back of it. The realism of the paddling figure is characteristic of the culture's ceramics.

163 Parthians expelled from **Armenia**

165 Avidius Cassius, Roman governor of Syria, **invades Parthia** and sacks Seleucia and Ctesiphon

166 Lucius Verus, Marcus Aurelius's co-emperor, makes **peace with Parthia**

166 "**Roman" embassy** (of Syrian merchants) arrives in **China**

167 Germanic tribes invade northern Italy

167 Beginning of **Marcomannic War**

167 Devastating outbreak of **plague in Rome**

168 Death of Emperor Huandi; **Han empire** in serious **decline**

173 Revolt of the **Boukoloi** ("shepherds") in Egypt – possibly because of economic difficulties

173 Serious outbreak of **plague in China**

175 Revolt of **Avidius Cassius**, who declares himself Roman emperor. He is killed by one of his own soldiers

177 Marcomanni and **Quadi** renew war on the Danube frontier

177 Martyrdom of 47 Christians in the Roman arena at Lyons

179–180 Marcus Aurelius wins decisive **victory** over the Marcomanni near Vindobona (Vienna)

180 The Goths first settle near the Black Sea

180 Death of **Marcus Aurelius**. He is succeeded by his son **Commodus**, who makes peace with the Marcomanni

ANCIENT ROME

THE ROMANS SPREAD A RICH MATERIAL CULTURE THROUGHOUT THEIR VAST EMPIRE

As Roman political control steadily expanded outside Italy, in its wake came the Roman way of life. Roman surveyors laid out new cities, local elites took up Roman practices, and the masses attended gladiatorial spectacles. On a domestic level, Roman fashions in clothing and accessories also spread.

Although many of the territories that the Romans conquered initially resisted, the populations of these provinces, particularly the former ruling classes, gradually adopted many Roman customs. Influential men became Roman citizens, towns were given new public buildings such as baths and courthouses, Roman legionary garrisons were established in strategic places, and new trade routes brought luxury goods from Rome. As a result, similar Roman artefacts have been found across Europe, the Middle East, and North Africa, dating from around the 1st century BCE to the 5th century CE.

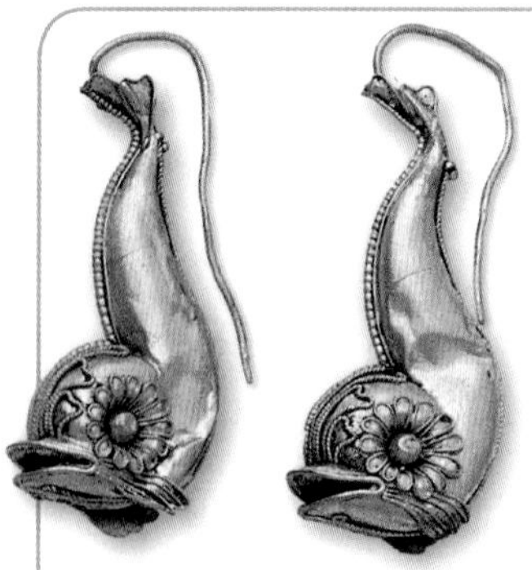

Gold dolphin earrings
Earrings adorned with animal-head motifs were especially popular in the eastern Roman empire. This pair bears a symbol of the sea god Neptune.

Precious necklace
This necklace, made up of gold and red garnets, seems to form the shape of a spectacular fruit tree.

Bone pin
This flat, thin blade or pin is topped by a female head, an ornamental touch for an otherwise humdrum household item.

Plumb line
This bronze weighted plumb line was attached to a groma, an instrument used by the Romans to survey straight lines.

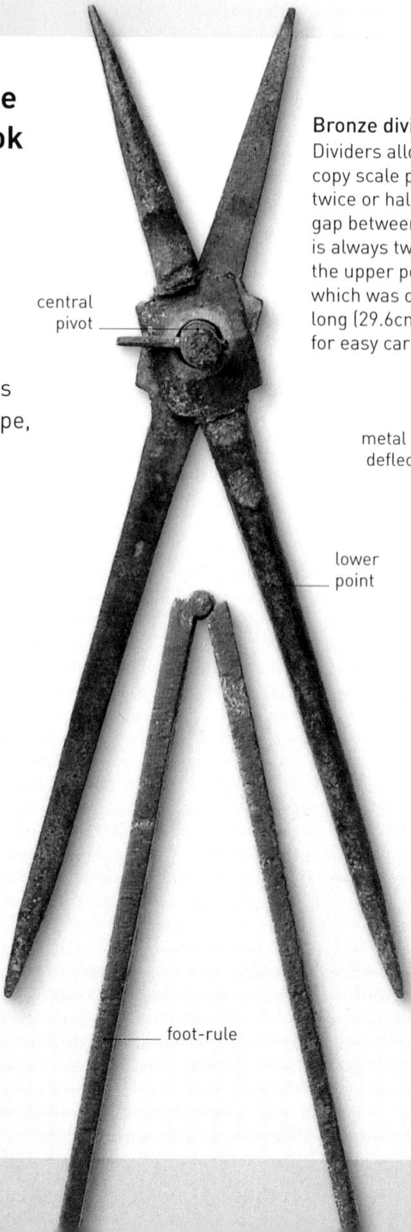

Bronze dividers and foot-rule
Dividers allowed engineers to copy scale plans or models at twice or half their size – the gap between the lower points is always twice that between the upper points. The rule, which was one Roman foot long (29.6cm/11.7in), folded for easy carrying.

Ocean baths
The most important Roman baths were adorned with lavish mosaics, such as this one of Oceanus, the ocean god, from Sabratha in Libya.

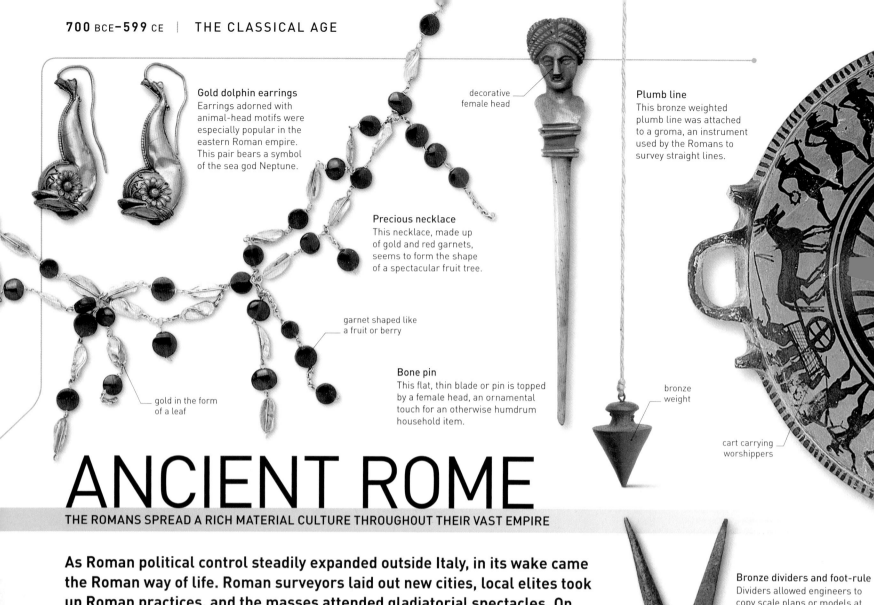

Wooden tablet
This type of tablet, made from very thin wood, was used by the Roman military for everyday letters and record-keeping. This one was found at Vindolanda in England.

Procession bowl
This lekane, a type of shallow dish, is decorated with a scene of half-man, half-goat satyrs in a procession in honour of Bacchus, the god of wine.

Ancient grater
Cheese played an important part in the Roman diet. Graters such as this one were invented to allow cheese to be used as a topping on other foodstuffs.

Amphora
The Romans transported liquid goods such as oil and wine in amphoras, a type of large, double-handled storage jar.

Bathing tools
At the baths, a Roman's skin was oiled and then scraped to remove sweat and dirt. A ring was used to transport the tools.

Short sword
The Roman military sword, or *gladius*, had a short blade – ideal for attacks at close range. It was used by soldiers and some gladiators.

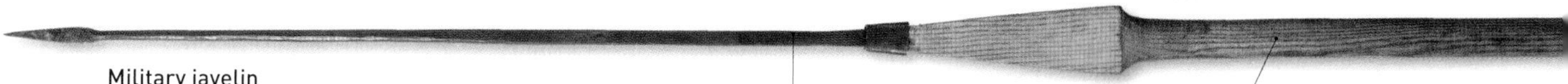

Military javelin
Each Roman legionary carried two of these *pila* (javelins). The javelin's iron head was designed to break off on impact to prevent an opponent throwing it back.

Imperial coins
Coins bearing the head of the current emperor (here Augustus and Claudius) acted as powerful propaganda tools across the empire, showing even the masses an image of their ruler.

Proof of citizenship
Non-citizens who served 25 years in the Roman army were awarded citizenship and given bronze diplomas such as this one to record the grant.

Sling pellets
Roman legionaries normally relied on their swords, but auxiliary light infantry used other weapons to devastating effect, such as these metal sling pellets.

Gladiator helmet
Roman gladiators bore a variety of arms and armour. This sort of helmet was worn by a Thracian, a type of gladiator whose equipment was modelled on that of ancient Thracian warriors.

Bronze gladiator shield
Thracian gladiators – a class of lightly armed gladiator – carried lightweight, round shields such as this one for defence, and a scimitar, with a short, curved blade, to attack their opponents.

181–192

In this engraving by Giovanni Stradano, Emperor Commodus shoots an arrow to subdue a leopard. Fighting in the arena as a gladiator was his great passion.

IN CHINA, INCREASING DISSENT caused by the corruption of the eunuchs at the court of Han Emperor Lindi (r.168–89) and a succession of natural disasters led to the outbreak in 184 of a major insurrection, named the **Yellow Turban revolt** for the colour of its supporters' headgear. Up to 400,000 rebels swept westward towards the capital. Another uprising fuelled by the **Five Pecks of Rice** sect then succeeded in taking over Sichuan in the southwest. Although the Yellow Turbans had been largely crushed by early 185, the **control of the Han emperor was ever weakening**. After Lingdi died in 189, he was replaced by his younger half-brother **Xiandi** (r.189–220) but he never exercised real power. Instead, control of the empire fell to Han general **Cao Cao**, who contended for 30 years with **a series of rival warlords**, notably **Liu Bei** in the southwest and **Sun Quan** in the south.

18

THE AGE AT WHICH **COMMODUS** BECAME **SOLE EMPEROR**

Commodus (r.180–92), Marcus Aurelius's son, was the first Roman emperor to succeed his father for 90 years but he proved to be **a disastrous choice**. In 182, after an assassination attempt on him, apparently organized by his sister Lucilla, Commodus became **increasingly despotic**. Many senators who were implicated in the plot were executed and control of the government fell into the hands of **Tigidius Perennis, the praetorian prefect** (the commander of the imperial bodyguard). There were minor wars in Britain and in Dacia (much of modern Romania), but in 185 Perennis was suspected of a plot to make his own son emperor and was executed by his troops. Commodus increasingly **devoted himself to fighting** in the arena as a **gladiator**, while the imperial chamberlain **Cleander** dominated government and sold public offices to the highest bidder. The man in charge of the grain supply, **Papirius Dionysius**, engineered a shortage that led to Cleander's downfall. This did not result in a more stable government as his replacement only lasted a short time before being murdered. Commodus increasingly identified himself with **Hercules** (the Greek hero) and renamed Rome after himself – *colonia Commodiana*. At the end of 192, the praetorian prefect **Laetus** was convinced that Commodus was planning to have him killed and on **New Year's Day 193** took the initiative and had the emperor **poisoned** and, when that did not work, **strangled**.

193–211

The Severan arch in Leptis Magna (in modern Libya) commemorates a visit by the North African emperor to his home town.

" BE **HARMONIOUS** WITH **EACH OTHER, ENRICH** THE **SOLDIERS, IGNORE** ALL **OTHERS...** "

Septimius Severus, dying words as quoted in Book 77 of Roman historian Dio Cassius's *Roman History*, 211

IN 193, AFTER THE MURDER OF COMMODUS, Helvius Pertinax (126–93), the prefect of the city, was declared emperor but he was murdered after three months. This was followed by rival claimants to the throne engaging in an auction outside the praetorian camp to decide who would be emperor. **Didius Julianus** (133–93) won, but his reign was short, as almost immediately the frontier armies rebelled: that on the Danube proclaimed **Septimius Severus** (*c*.145–211) emperor, while the Syrian legions raised their commander **Pescennius Niger** (*c*.135–94) to the imperial throne. Severus reached Rome first and, after granting the title of Caesar (junior emperor) to **Clodius Albinus**, governor of Britain, he turned east where, in spring 194, his armies defeated Niger at the **Battle of Issus** in Syria. Severus stayed in the east and in 195 attacked the Parthian Empire. But he was forced to return west to deal with Albinus who had revolted, and who was killed near Lugdunum (modern Lyon, France) in 197. Severus then returned to Parthia, this time occupying the capital Ctesiphon in 197. He pushed the line of Roman control towards the Tigris and created the **new province of Mesopotamia**.

Trouble in Britain brought the ageing emperor to the province in 208. A large-scale Roman advance forced the Caledonians and Maetae north of the provincial frontier to come to terms in 209, but they soon broke the peace and a new campaign was launched in 210. Severus was by now very ill, and his son Caracalla took over. In February 211 **Severus died** in Eboracum (modern York, England) and handed succession jointly to sons Caracalla and Geta. After the Scottish war both rushed back to Rome, but their **joint rule was short-lived**: Caracalla had Geta murdered in December 211.

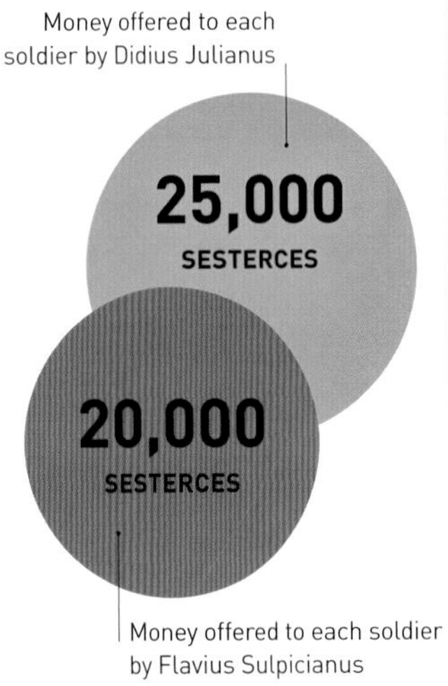

Buying loyalty
The larger bribes offered to the troops by Didius Julianus meant that he won the auction to be emperor.

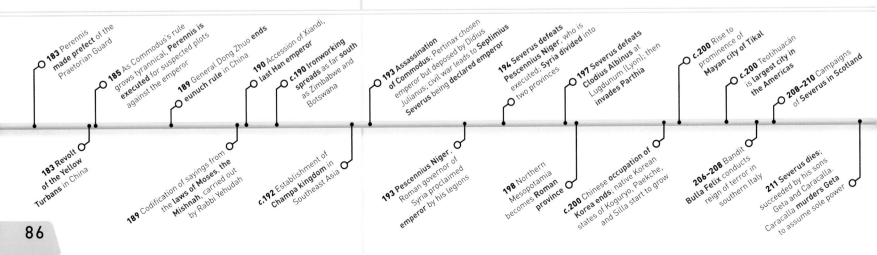

JULIA DOMNA (170–217)

The daughter of a Syrian high priest, Julia Domna married Septimius Severus in 187. A prophecy had predicted that she would wed an emperor and so it turned out. Forceful and intelligent, she failed to mediate between her sons Caracalla and Geta after their father's death and to prevent Geta's murder. When Caracalla was killed she deliberately starved herself to death in protest, a move that rallied support for the remaining Severan family.

- **183** Perennis **made prefect** of the Praetorian Guard
- **183 Revolt of the Yellow Turbans** in China
- **185** As Commodus's rule grows tyrannical, **Perennis is executed** for suspected plots against the emperor
- **189** General Dong Zhuo **ends eunuch rule** in China
- **189** Codification of sayings from the **laws of Moses, the Mishnah**, carried out by Rabbi Yehudah
- **190** Accession of Xiandi, **last Han emperor**
- **c.190 Ironworking spreads** as far **south** as Zimbabwe and Botswana
- **c.192** Establishment of **Champa kingdom** in Southeast Asia
- **193 Assassination of Commodus**; Pertinax chosen emperor but deposed by Didius Julianus; civil war leads to **Septimius Severus** being **declared emperor**
- **193 Pescennius Niger**, Roman governor of Syria proclaimed **emperor** by his legions
- **194 Severus defeats Pescennius Niger**, who is executed; **Syria divided** into two provinces
- **197 Severus defeats Clodius Albinus** at Lugdunum (Lyon); then **invades Parthia**
- **198** Northern Mesopotamia becomes **Roman province**
- **c.200** Chinese **occupation of Korea ends**; native Korean states of Koguryo, Paekche, and Silla start to grow
- **c.200** Rise to prominence of **Mayan city of Tikal**
- **c.200** Teotihuacán **is largest city in the Americas**
- **206–208** Bandit **Bulla Felix** conducts reign of terror in southern Italy
- **208–210** Campaigns **of Severus in Scotland**
- **211 Severus dies**; succeeded by his sons Geta and Caracalla. Caracalla **murders Geta** to assume sole power

212–230

A carving of the Buddha from Sarnath in North India, where a school of Buddhist art flourished under the Kushans.

IN INDIA, THE AREA CONTROLLED BY THE KUSHAN DYNASTY began to shrink after the death of King Kanishka in 140, and particularly severe territorial losses were suffered under Huvishka (r.160–90). Kushan rule finally collapsed under Vasudeva (r.190–225) when Persian invaders swept through northwestern India. Although Kushan kings continued to rule a much-reduced realm for a further century, their influence was purely local and their **heyday was at an end**.

In Rome, Caracalla's government was unpopular. Among his measures was the **Antonine Constitution of 212**, by which citizenship was granted to almost all free males in the empire. After a successful campaign on the Rhine (in 213), Caracalla ventured further afield, arriving in Egypt in 215. For some unknown reason, he became enraged and ordered the **massacre** of the citizens of **Alexandria**. The next year he launched an invasion of Parthia. His praetorian prefect **Opellius Macrinus** came to suspect that Caracalla wanted him dead, so he persuaded a disaffected soldier to murder the emperor. After Caracalla's murder, **the army declared Macrinus emperor**. There was much residual loyalty towards the Severan family, and a revolt broke out in Syria, which aimed to put **Elagabalus** (203–22), grandson of Julia Domna's sister Julia Maesa, on the throne. Macrinus lost support and in June 218 he fled to Cappadocia where he was killed. In 221, Elagabalus **adopted as his heir** his cousin Alexanius. When the two fell out in 222, the army backed Alexianus and Elagabalus was murdered. Alexianus became **Emperor Alexander Severus** aged 13.

In Persia, Parthian rule had been weakened, both by plague and by the effects of successive Roman invasions. In 207, the kingdom had been divided into two when Vologeses VI's brother set himself up as a rival king, **Artabanus V**; and a further Roman invasion in 216 ravaged much of the province of Media. Taking advantage of this disorder, the ruler of the southwestern province of Pars, **Ardashir**, expanded his territory and finally defeated Artabanus V *c.*224. Ardashir I was then declared king (r.224–42) as the **first ruler of the Sasanian dynasty**. Although Persia was temporarily weakened by a civil war, the Sasanians proved to be **much tougher adversaries** to the Romans than the Parthians ever had been.

In China in 220, Cao Cao's son Cao Pi **forced Xiandi to abdicate**. Within two years Cao Pi, Liu Bei, and Sun Quan would each declare himself emperor. The **Han dynasty** and China's unity were at an end.

2,000

THE NUMBER OF **BATHERS** THAT COULD USE THE **BATHS** OF **CARACALLA**

Arch of Caracalla
Originally the arch was topped by a figure of the emperor riding in a chariot. It stands in Volubilis, the main town of Roman Mauretania Tingitana (in modern Morocco).

Bronze diploma
Diplomas were issued to auxiliary soldiers in the Roman army, granting them citizenship. This practice ceased after the Antonine Constitution.

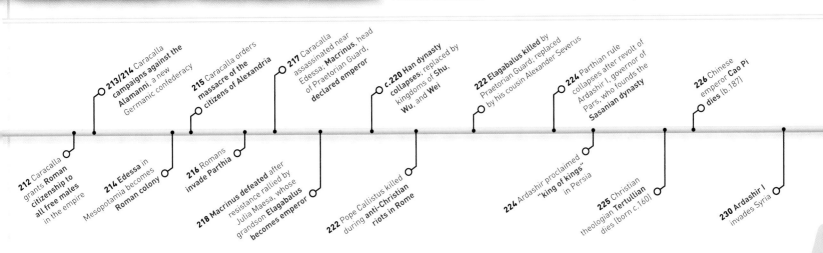

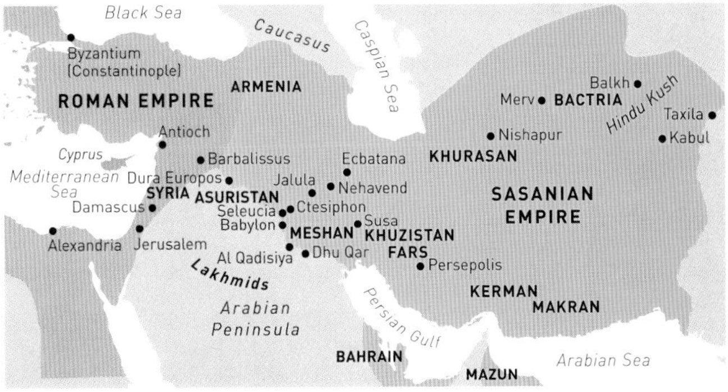

The Sasanian Empire in Persia
After rapidly acquiring the former Parthian Empire, the Sasanians fought a series of wars with the Romans over control of Mesopotamia.

- **212** Caracalla grants **Roman citizenship to all free males** in the empire
- **213/214** Caracalla **campaigns against the Alamanni**, a new Germanic confederacy
- **214 Edessa** in Mesopotamia becomes **Roman colony**
- **215** Caracalla orders **massacre of the citizens of Alexandria**
- **216 Romans invade Parthia**
- **217** Caracalla assassinated near Edessa; **Macrinus**, head of Praetorian Guard, **declared emperor**
- **218 Macrinus defeated** after resistance rallied by Julia Maesa, whose grandson **Elagabalus becomes emperor**
- **c.220 Han dynasty collapses**; replaced by kingdoms of **Shu**, **Wu**, and **Wei**
- **222** Pope Callistus killed during **anti-Christian riots in Rome**
- **222 Elagabalus killed** by Praetorian Guard; replaced by his cousin Alexander Severus
- **224** Parthian rule collapses after revolt of Ardashir I, governor of Pars, who founds the **Sasanian dynasty**
- **224** Ardashir proclaimed **"king of kings"** in Persia
- **225** Christian theologian **Tertullian** dies (born c.160)
- **226** Chinese emperor **Cao Pi dies** (b.187)
- **230 Ardashir I** invades Syria

25 THE NUMBER OF **ROMAN EMPERORS** THAT **RULED** BETWEEN **235** AND **284**

Roman emperor Gordian III succeeded his father and grandfather.

A mural of St Cyprian, Bishop of Carthage at the height of the Decian persecution. He was martyred in 257 during a campaign under Valerian.

IN CHINA, THE FINAL COLLAPSE OF THE HAN DYNASTY IN 220 was followed by 350 years of instability. **The Three Kingdoms** period (220–80) saw China divided into the **Wei** kingdom of the north; (initially under Wei Wendi (r.220–26); the **Shu Han** kingdom in the west whose first ruler was Shu Han Xuande (r.221–23); and the southern **Wu** kingdom under Wu Wudi (r.222–52). Wei Wendi was a capable ruler, but his successors struggled to contain attacks by northern tribesmen.

In 235, the Roman emperor Alexander Severus and his mother Julia Mamaea were **murdered** by mutinous troops, putting an **end to the Severan dynasty**. The uprising's ringleader, **Maximinus Thrax** (r.235–38), an officer from a humble background, was proclaimed emperor, but he spent most of his reign raising funds to reward his troops for their support. This time marks the start of a period of "**military anarchy**" in which Rome had dozens of emperors, most of them short-lived rulers who were raised up by the frontier armies and just as quickly deposed and killed. A rebellion in 238 in North Africa proclaimed the province's elderly governor as **Emperor Gordian I**, but he was quickly and brutally put down. The Senate declared Maximinus deposed and proposed **Pupienus** and **Balbinus** as candidates. Popular sentiment favoured Gordian I's grandson **Gordian III** (r.238–44), so all three briefly shared the throne. Balbinus and Pupienus were killed soon after, leaving Gordian III to rule alone. His six-year reign **briefly restored** some semblance of **stability** to the empire, but he was killed while leading an invasion of Persia in 243–44.

Compounding the Roman Empire's difficulties was the appearance of **barbarian confederacies** among the Germanic peoples of the Rhine and Danube frontiers. Principal among these were the **Alemanni**. In 213, Caracalla campaigned against them; by 260 they were able to **invade Italy** itself.

Art from the Three Kingdoms
High artistic achievements, such as this fine statue, were a feature of the late Han dynasty. Its collapse in 220 did not result in an equivalent decline in China's artistic output.

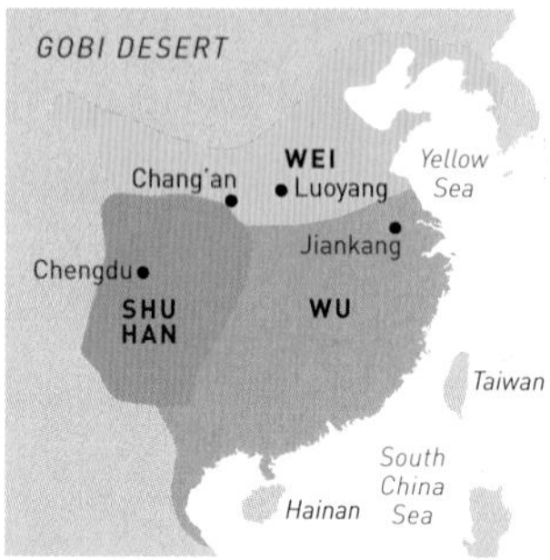

China under the Three Kingdoms
Although the Wei kingdom faced the greatest challenges among the three kingdoms, it would eventually conquer the Wu and the Shu Han.

PERSIA ATTAINED A POSITION OF RENEWED STRENGTH under Shapur I (r.241–72). In 244, he won a decisive battle against Gordian III at Misiche near Ctesiphon. Shortly after, Gordian III was killed and replaced by his army commander Philip (or **Philip "the Arab"**). Philip made peace with Shapur but had to pay a large ransom to escape Sasanian territory. His successors broke the terms of the agreement, so in 256 **Shapur I invaded Syria** and captured the towns of Dura Europos and Antioch. **Valerian**, who by then was emperor (r.253–60), soon retook Antioch. But, in 260, he fell into a trap and was **imprisoned by Shapur**. The Romans were left in disarray and Shapur's armies advanced as far as Iconium (modern Konya, Turkey).

The western part of the Roman Empire also faced increasing pressure. The Romans suffered invasions of Dacia (much of modern Romania) by the **Carpi** people from *c.*214. The Carpi, together with a new group, **the Goths**, took part in a raid across the Danube in 239–40. In 248, Emperor Philip **withdrew an annual tribute** he had been paying the Carpi and the Goths, prompting them to pour into Moesia (modern Bulgaria). Philip sent **Quintus Decius** to deal with the invasion; he was so successful that his troops declared him emperor. Early in 249, Decius marched to Rome and defeated and killed Philip. Hearing of the Roman civil war, the **Goths invaded again**, causing Decius to return to the Balkans in 250. Under their warleader **Cniva**, the

Relief of Shapur I
In this relief, Shapur I triumphs over the Roman emperors Gordian III and Valerian. After Valerian's capture, Shapur is said to have used him as a footstool for mounting his horse.

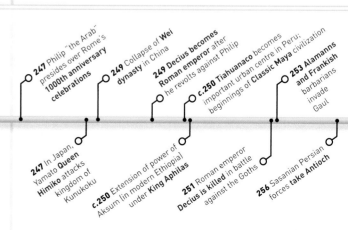

232 Romans **expel Ardashir I** of Persia from Mesopotamia and Cappadocia

235 Start of **"military anarchy" in Rome**; more than 20 Roman emperors in 50 years

235 Serious **Alammanic raids** on the upper Rhine

238 Carpi and Goths cross the Danube and ravage Moesia

238 Gordian I declared emperor but lasts only 22 days; **Gordian III** becomes Roman emperor on his grandfather's death

239 Sasanian Ardashir I captures cities of Carrhae and Nisibis

241 Shapur I becomes ruler of Persia

241 The prophet **Mani** (founder of Manichaeism) begins preaching in Persia

242 Goths **dominate southern Russia**

242 Kushans invade Sasanian province of **Bactria**

244 Gordian III murdered on Persian expedition; **Philip "the Arab"** becomes Roman emperor

247 Philip "the Arab" presides over Rome's **1000th anniversary celebrations**

247 In Japan, Yamato **Queen Himiko** attacks kingdom of Kunukoku

249 Collapse of **Wei dynasty** in China

249 Decius becomes Roman emperor after he revolts against Philip

c.250 Extension of power of Aksum (in modern Ethiopia) under **King Aphilas**

c.250 Tiahuanaco becomes important urban centre in Peru; beginnings of **Classic Maya** civilization

251 Roman emperor **Decius is killed** in battle against the Goths

253 Alamanns and Frankish barbarians invade Gaul

256 Sasanian Persian forces **take Antioch**

261–275

The main colonnade at Palmyra, which grew rich on tariffs paid by merchants who plied the desert route that passed through the Syrian city.

SHAPUR I (d.272)

Shapur's early leadership experience came in a role assisting his father, Ardashir, in mopping up support for the Parthian Arsacid dynasty. Shapur's defeats of Gordian III in 244 and of Valerian in 260 established a temporary Persian dominance in Syria and Mesopotamia. He used the many Roman prisoners captured in 256 at Antioch to build the new town of Veh Antiok Shapur ("Shapur's town, better than Antioch").

Goths ravaged the province of Moesia, laying siege to the main town of Nicopolis (modern Nikopol, Bulgaria). The campaign went badly for the Romans, ending in defeat and Decius's death at the **Battle of Abrittus** in 251.

In Japan, the **Yamato kingdom** emerged on the plain of Nara (in central Japan) around 250. Its rulers were interred in large burial mounds, and its armies conquered most of central Japan. Much of what is known comes from Chinese sources, who name the Queen of Yamato in 238 as **Himiko**.

VALERIAN'S CAPTURE BY THE PERSIANS in 260 proved disastrous for the western part of the Roman Empire as well as the east. Valerian's son **Gallienus** (r.260–68), struggling to contain an invasion of Italy by the Germanic **Iuthungi** had no resources to reinforce the Rhine frontier, which was being breached by **Alemmanic and Frankish raiders**. The Governor of Germania Inferior, **Marcus Postumus**, revolted and killed Gallienus's son Saloninus, who had been left in charge of Gaul and Germany. Postumus **declared himself emperor**, but unlike previous usurpers did not march on Rome, instead setting up a separate **Gallic Empire**; this initially controlled Britain, Spain, parts of western Germany, and Gaul. He established a form of government that mirrored that of the official empire, complete with its own Senate. In 269, Postumus was murdered by his own troops and replaced by his praetorian prefect Victorinus. Gallienus – faced with **Gothic invasions** and the revolt of **Zenobia of Palmyra** in the east – was **never strong enough** to put an end to the Gallic Empire. In 268 he was murdered by the army and replaced by Claudius II Gothicus (r.268–70), who was too busy fighting in the Balkans to deal with Gaul. Only under **Aurelian** (r.270–74) was the Roman Empire strong enough, and by then the Gallic Empire was weakened, with its last ruler, Tetricus (r.270–74), facing splits in the army. In 274, Tetricus was captured near Châlons, and the **Gallic Empire was reabsorbed**.

In the east, a serious **challenge to Roman rule** emerged after 260. The city of **Palmyra** (in Syria) proved Rome's **only reliable ally** against the Sasanian advances of Persia. Its ruler **Septimius Odaenathus** (*c.*220–67) received a number of Roman titles, including *Corrector Totius Orientis* ("Marshal of the entire East"), and invaded the Sasanian Empire in 262 and 266. Odaenathus died in 267; and his wife **Zenobia** (r.267–73) created **an empire of her own**. By 269, her armies had taken Syria and Egypt, and in 271 she declared her son **Vaballathus** emperor. Aurelian marched east and soon rolled back the Palmyrene gains, besieging Palmyra in spring 272. Zenobia was captured while trying to escape, and Palmyra was sacked in 273 when it tried to throw off Roman rule again.

The Gallic Empire
Postumus began the Gallic Empire in control of Gaul, Germany, Britain, and Spain. By its collapse in 274, the last ruler, Tetricus, had lost Spain.

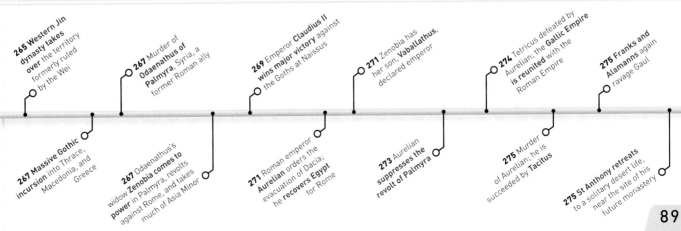

Sepulchral relief from Palmyra
The Palmyrenes buried their dead with exquisite and realistic personal portrayals; the dead were interred in tower tombs outside the city.

In China, **Yuandi** (r.260–64) restored Wei's fortunes by conquering the Shu Han. But soon after he was overthrown by one of his own generals, **Sima Yuan**, who founded the **Western Jin** dynasty and took the title Wudi (r.265–89). His armies crushed and annexed the Wu kingdom in 280, thus **briefly reuniting China**.

> "YOU DEMAND **MY SURRENDER** AS THOUGH YOU WERE **NOT AWARE** THAT **CLEOPATRA** PREFERRED TO **DIE A QUEEN** RATHER **THAN REMAIN ALIVE.**"

Zenobia, Queen of Palmyra, to Aurelian Augustus from *Historia Augusta c.*375–400

257 Decius issues edict **forbidding Christian worship**

258 Martyrdom of **Cyprian**, Bishop of Carthage

260 Shapur I defeats Valerian and takes him prisoner; **Gallienus** declared Roman emperor

260 Breakaway **Gallic Empire established** by Postumus

265 Western Jin dynasty takes over the territory formerly ruled by the Wei

267 Massive Gothic incursion into Thrace, Macedonia, and Greece

267 Murder of **Odaenathus of Palmyra**, Syria, a former Roman ally

267 Odaenathus's widow **Zenobia comes to power** in Palmyra, revolts against Rome, and takes much of Asia Minor

269 Emperor **Claudius II wins major victory** against the Goths at Naissus

271 Roman emperor **Aurelian** orders the evacuation of Dacia; he **recovers Egypt** for Rome

271 Zenobia has her son, **Vaballathus**, declared emperor

273 Aurelian **suppresses the revolt of Palmyra**

274 Tetricus defeated by Aurelian; the **Gallic Empire is reunited** with the Roman Empire

275 Murder of Aurelian; he is succeeded by **Tacitus**

275 Franks and Alamanns again ravage Gaul

275 St Anthony retreats to a solitary desert life, near the site of his future monastery

276–283

> **“ PROBUS** WAS ALMOST A **SECOND HANNIBAL** BECAUSE OF HIS **KNOWLEDGE OF WARFARE... ”**

Aurelius Victor, Roman historian and official, in *De Caesaribus*, *c.*360

IN CHINA, THE FIRST EMPEROR OF THE WESTERN JIN DYNASTY, Wudi (r.265–89), was a strong ruler who secured trade routes to the West and built a bridge over the Yellow River to improve communications. However, the **wars** of the **Three Kingdoms period** (see 231–244) had impoverished the state and as the tax burden rose, many peasants fled to landowners for protection, resulting in the **rise of private armies**.

In the Roman Empire, Emperor Aurelian – who was murdered in 275 – was followed by two short-lived emperors – Tacitus and Florianus – before Probus took power in 276. Within two years, Probus had **defeated the Goths** on the Danube and **pushed back the Franks** from the Rhine. A planned campaign against Persia was frustrated in 281 by the revolt of two usurpers in the West: Bonosus and Proculus. Despite his military successes, in 282 **Probus was murdered by his own troops**, who were resentful at being forced to work on civil engineering projects near Sirmium (in modern Serbia).

Jin sitting bear sculpture
The first half of the Jin dynasty under Wudi gave China a period of comparative peace and stability, which allowed the arts to flourish.

284–300

The Pyramid of the Moon at Teotihuacán (near modern Mexico City) was built some time after 200 at one end of the city's Avenue of the Dead; the Pyramid of the Sun sits at the other end.

IN 284, THE ROMAN ARMY IN ASIA MINOR PROCLAIMED DIOCLES, the former commander of the imperial bodyguard, **Emperor Diocletian** (r.284–305). In 285, he defeated **Carinus** (the then emperor of the Western Empire) and started **a radical reorganization of the empire**, reforming the army, and subdividing provinces. The challenges on the frontier were too great to be faced alone; in 285, he appointed **Maximian** (250–310) **to rule alongside him**, first as Caesar (junior emperor) then as Augustus (senior emperor). Other problems with Britain's break from the empire under **Carausius** in 286, convinced Diocletian that more changes were necessary. In 293, he and Maximian appointed two Caesars: **Constantius Chlorus** (r.293–306) to assist Diocletian in the Western Empire and **Galerius** (r.293–311) to be Maximian's junior in the East. This **tetrarchy** (four emperor system) enjoyed early successes in Britain (296) and in Egypt (298). In 294, Diocletian **reformed the coinage**, reissuing new bronze and silver coins, and in 301 he issued an **Edict on Maximum Prices** to try to curb rising inflation. Unlike his other measures, this one failed.

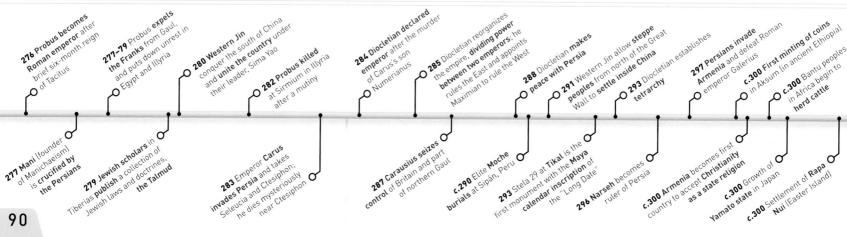

Persian frieze
The Paikuli frieze celebrates the victories of Narseh in Armenia and justifies his deposition of predecessor Vahram III.

After the death of Shapur I in 272 Persia faced **a period of political instability**. In 293, **Narseh** (r.293–302) ascended to the Persian throne. He resolved to recover land in Armenia and Mesopotamia that had been lost to the Romans. He launched a major invasion in 296, **defeating** the Caesar **Galerius** in 297. The next year, however, Galerius smashed Narseh's army in Armenia and captured the Persian ruler's family. Galerius marched as far as Ctesiphon, which he captured in 298. Narseh was forced to make peace (**Treaty of Nisibis**). Persia remained at peace with the Romans for 40 years.

In the Valley of Mexico, the city of **Teotihuacán reached the peak of its power** around 300. Its main street – the Avenue of the Dead – ran between the Pyramid of the Moon and the Ciudadela (which may have been the palace of the ruler) and was lined with the residences of the lords of the city.

30 SQUARE KILOMETRES THE **AREA** OF **TEOTIHUACAN CITY** AT ITS **PEAK**

276 Probus becomes Roman emperor after brief six-month reign of Tacitus

277 Mani (founder of Manichaeism) is **crucified by the Persians**

277–79 Probus **expels the Franks** from Gaul, and puts down unrest in Egypt and Illyria

279 Jewish scholars in Tiberias **publish** a collection of Jewish laws and doctrines, **the Talmud**

280 Western Jin conquer the south of China and **unite the country** under their leader, Sima Yao

282 Probus killed at Sirmium in Illyria after a mutiny

283 Emperor **Carus invades Persia** and takes Seleucia and Ctesiphon; he dies mysteriously near Ctesiphon

284 Diocletian declared emperor after the murder of Carus's son Numerianus

285 Diocletian reorganizes the empire, **dividing power between two emperors**; he rules the East and appoints Maximian to rule the West

287 Carausius seizes control of Britain and part of northern Gaul

288 Diocletian **makes peace with Persia**

c.290 Elite **Moche burials** at Sipán, Peru

291 Western Jin allow **steppe peoples** from north of the Great Wall to **settle inside China**

293 Stela 29 at **Tikal** is the first monument with the **Maya calendar inscription** of the "Long Date"

293 Diocletian establishes **tetrarchy**

296 Narseh becomes ruler of Persia

297 Persians invade Armenia and defeat Roman emperor Galerius

c.300 First minting of coins in Aksum (in ancient Ethiopia)

c.300 Armenia becomes first country to accept **Christianity as a state religion**

c.300 Bantu peoples in Africa begin to **herd cattle**

c.300 Growth of **Yamato state** in Japan

c.300 Settlement of **Rapa Nui** (Easter Island)

This early 16th-century fresco of the Battle of Milvian Bridge is in the Apostolic Palace in the Vatican. Before the battle, the emperor Constantine is said to have seen a Christian monogram in a dream predicting his victory.

SINCE PERSECUTIONS IN THE 250S AND 260S, THE CHRISTIAN COMMUNITY had experienced some 40 years of tranquillity in the Roman Empire. All this changed in 303 when Diocletian issued an **edict** ordering the **destruction of churches** and the handing over and **burning of Christian books**. A sterner edict followed, calling for the arrest of Christian clergy, and one in 304 ordered that all Christians offer a sacrifice to the pagan gods. Devout Christians could not accede to these demands, and many of them were martyred.

In 304, Diocletian fell seriously ill, and in 305 he announced that he and Maximian would abdicate. **Constantius Chlorus** and **Galerius** would take over as Augusti, while the new Caesars were to be **Maximinus** (Galerius's nephew) and **Flavius Severus** (Galerius's army colleague). The new tetrarchy soon unravelled. **Constantius died** in Eboracum (modern York, England) in July 306 and the troops there proclaimed his son **Constantine** the new Augustus. By October, **Maxentius** (r.306–12), the son of Maximian, was crowned emperor in Rome. Severus was killed trying to retake Rome from Maxentius, and Maximian restored himself to the position of Augustus. In 308, the **Conference of Carnuntum** was called to settle the disputes, presided over by Diocletian, who came out of retirement. Constantine accepted a demotion to Caesar in the West, with **Licinius** as Augustus (r.308–24), while **Maximin Daia** became Galerius's Caesar in the East (r.310–13). This new arrangement was no more succesful than the old one.

In 311, **Galerius died** and **Maximin became Augustus** in the East. He ordered **renewed measures against Christians**. Constantine, meanwhile, invaded Italy and in October 312 defeated and killed Maxentius at the **Battle of Milvian Bridge**. Before the battle, Constantine is said to have dreamt of the **Chi-Rho symbol** and ordered his troops to mark it on their shields.

Licinius and Constantine met at Mediolanum (modern Milan) in 313, where they agreed to share power and issued the **Edict of Milan**, which granted toleration to all forms of worship, in effect **legalizing Christianity**. Licinius then turned East and defeated Maximin Daia, securing control over the Eastern provinces. The alliance between Constantine and Licinius broke down in 316; they patched up a peace in 317, and for six years the Roman Empire relapsed into an uneasy calm.

In China, Wudi's successor **Huidi** (r.290–306) was mentally disabled and so a succession of regents contended for imperial control. Huidi's brother **Huaidi** (r.307–12) invited the northern **Xiongnu tribesmen** to help him against the competing Chinese factions, but they took him prisoner. The **last Western Jin emperor Mindi** (r.313–16) saw the Xiongnu sack the capital of Chang'an (modern Xi'an); the Jin moved south, where **Yuandi** (r.317–23) became the **first Eastern Jin emperor** in 317.

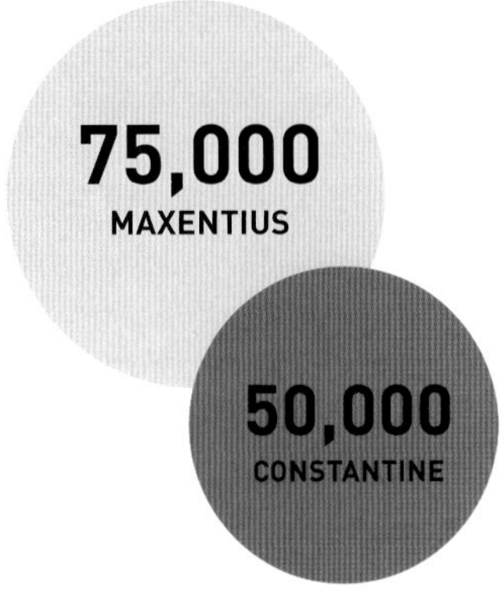

Battle numbers at Milvian Bridge
Maxentius's forces outnumbered those of Constantine, but his army became trapped between Constantine's men and the river.

Palace of Diocletian
Diocletian built the great palace at Split, Croatia, for his retirement after his abdication in 305. Here, he tended his cabbages.

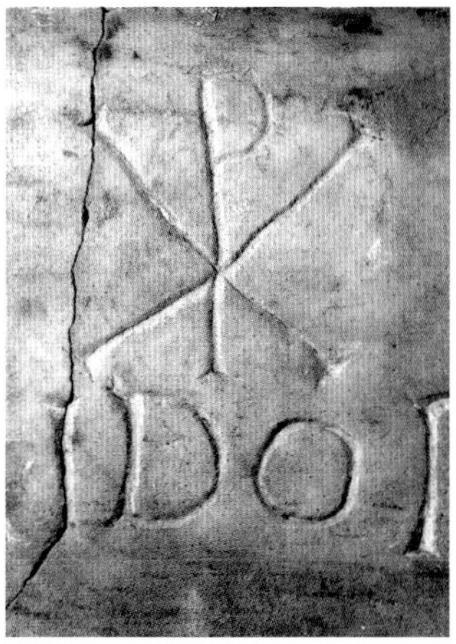

Chi-Rho symbol
The monogram of Chi-Rho, the first two letters of Christ's name in Greek, became an important early symbol of Christianity.

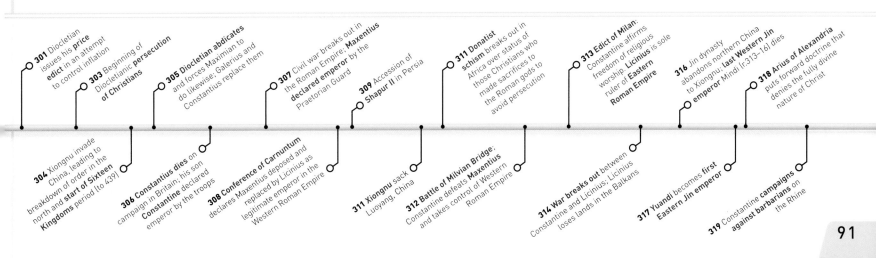

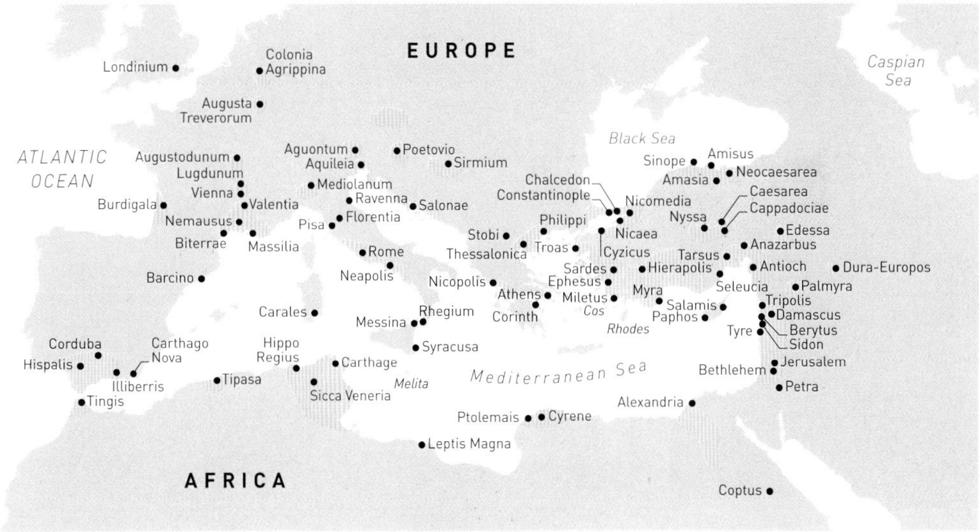

Early spread of Christianity
Christianity spread in the 2nd and 3rd centuries until there were strong Christian communities in Anatolia, southern Gaul, Italy, Egypt, and the province of Africa (Tunisia).

301 Diocletian issues his **price edict** in an attempt to control inflation

303 Beginning of Diocletianic **persecution of Christians**

304 Xiongnu invade China, leading to breakdown of order in the north and **start of Sixteen Kingdoms** period (to 439)

305 Diocletian abdicates and forces Maximian to do likewise; Galerius and Constantius replace them

306 Constantius dies on campaign in Britain; his son **Constantine** declared emperor by the troops

307 Civil war breaks out in the Roman Empire; **Maxentius declared emperor** by the Praetorian Guard

308 Conference of Carnuntum declares Maxentius deposed and replaced by Licinius as legitimate emperor in the Western Roman Empire

309 Accession of **Shapur II** in Persia

311 Xiongnu sack Luoyang, China

311 Donatist schism breaks out in Africa over status of those Christians who made sacrifices to the Roman gods to avoid persecution

312 Battle of Milvian Bridge; Constantine defeats **Maxentius** and takes control of Western Roman Empire

313 Edict of Milan: Constantine affirms freedom of religious worship. **Licinius** is sole ruler of **Eastern Roman Empire**

314 War breaks out between Constantine and Licinius; Licinius loses lands in the Balkans

316 Jin dynasty abandons northern China to Xiongnu; **last Western Jin emperor** Mindi (r.313–16) dies

317 Yuandi becomes **first Eastern Jin emperor**

318 Arius of Alexandria puts forward doctrine that denies the fully divine nature of Christ

319 Constantine **campaigns against barbarians** on the Rhine

320–330

It was largely Eastern Church leaders who gathered at the Council of Nicaea (depicted here) in 325; only eight Western bishops made the journey there.

CHANDRAGUPTA I ASCENDED TO THE THRONE of a small kingdom in the western Ganges Plain in 320. Through an **advantageous marriage** to Princess Kumaradevi of the powerful Liccachevi dynasty and by conquest, he **expanded his realm** to include most of the central Ganges, from Magadha (in southern Bihar) to Prayaga (in Uttar Pradesh). His descendants, the Guptas, ruled northern India for almost 150 years.

The Column of Constantine
The sole surviving monument from the forum that Constantine built for his new city is this column, which sits in central Istanbul today.

Having taken up the **cause of Christianity** in 313, the Roman Emperor Constantine (r.280–337) found that Christians themselves were far from united in **doctrine or organization**. Constantine called a church **council at Nicaea** in western Asia Minor in 325 to establish (and impose) orthodoxy in the face of a division over **Arianism** (the theology of Arius, who held that Jesus Christ was subordinate to God the Father). As well as Constantine, about 300 church leaders attended, and Arius's views were condemned.

14

THE NUMBER OF **DISTRICTS** IN CONSTANTINOPLE

After **defeating Licinius** (r.308–24) in 324, Constantine **founded a new capital** for the Eastern Roman Empire at the ancient city of **Byzantium**, strategically sited between Europe and Asia. He demolished pagan temples and built new churches, such as Hagia Sophia, providing public buildings to rival those of Rome. The city of **Constantinople** (modern Istanbul) was publicly dedicated on 2 April 330. It was the seat of the Eastern Emperors for over 1,000 years.

331–355

> **"** IN OTHER MEN... TASTE FOR **SLAUGHTER** SOMETIMES **LOSES** ITS **FORCE**... IN **CONSTANTIUS** IT BECAME MORE **VIOLENT. "**

Ammianus Marcellinus (d.*c.*330) writing on the character of the Emperor Constantius II in *The Later Roman Empire*

8

THE NUMBER OF **TYPES** OF **PURE-GOLD COINS** ISSUED BY **SAMUDRA-GUPTA**

IN 335, SAMUDRAGUPTA (r.335–75) SUCCEEDED HIS FATHER Chandragupta I as ruler of the Gupta domains in northern India. An inscription he set up in Prayaga survives, recounting a **series of campaigns** he fought in **Uttar Pradesh** and **Mathura**, both of which were annexed to the Gupta kingdom. He also made conquests down the east coast of India, as far as **Madras**, and subdued **West Bengal** as well as parts of **Rajasthan** and the **Punjab**. Various other regions acknowledged his suzerainty, making him the **most powerful Indian ruler** since the Mauryas.

Constantine died in 337, having accepted Christian baptism only on his deathbed. He had made no definite provision for **succession**, leaving his sons to divide the empire between them: **Constantine II** (r.337–40) held Spain, Gaul, and Britain; **Constans** (r.337–50) ruled Italy, and **Constantius II** (r.337–61) governed the Eastern Empire. Their reigns began with a **massacre at Constantinople** in which almost all of their father's other male relatives were killed in order to remove any possible rivals. Constantine II, who was the eldest, tried to assert his seniority, but **died during an invasion of Italy** in 340. Constans then took control of the entire Western Empire, where he was faced with a series of hard-fought campaigns against **Frankish invaders in Gaul**, and problems in **Britain**, which led him to visit the far-flung province (the last undisputed Roman Emperor to do so) in 343.

Disputes between the two surviving brothers, particularly one over the status of **Athanasius, Bishop of Alexandria** (whom Constantius II had exiled, but Constans wanted restored), soured all relations between them. In 350, a senior military officer, **Magnentius**, revolted at Augustodunum in southern Gaul (modern Autun, France) and **Constans was killed**. Distracted by a war against Persia, Constantius II tolerated the upstart initially, but in 351 he moved against him. Since Constantius II had no heir, he promoted his cousin **Gallus** – one of the few survivors of the massacre of 337 – to the rank of Caesar in 351 and left him **in charge in the East**, while he campaigned against Magnentius in the West. Magnentius's army was **defeated at Mursa** (in present-day Croatia); Italy and North Africa were rapidly recovered, and in 353 **Magnentius committed suicide** in Gaul.

For the next seven years **Constantius II ruled the empire alone**, mainly preoccupied with Frankish incursions into Gaul, the revolt of the usurper Silvanus in 355, and **a series of church councils** that sought to resolve doctrinal disputes (Constantius II favoured Arianism over the traditional orthodoxy).

In the end, Gallus proved too ambitious and in 354 he was **deposed and executed**. Constantius II turned instead to Gallus's brother **Julian**, a studious youth with a penchant for pagan philosophy. In 355, after Silvanus's revolt, **Julian was despatched to Gaul** as Caesar, where he proved surprisingly effective at combating Frankish raiders.

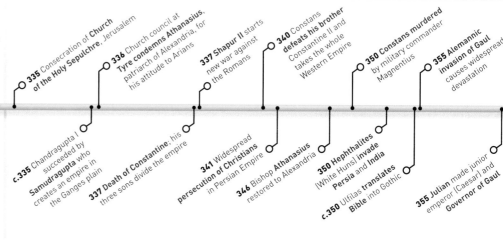

Gold Gupta coin
Many Gupta coins contain images of horses, a possible reference to the ritual horse sacrifice performed by some Gupta rulers.

- **320** Accession of **Aksumite king Ezana**
- **320 Chandragupta I**, founder of the Gupta Empire of India, ascends throne
- **321 Constantine campaigns** in former Roman province of **Dacia**
- **324 Constantine defeats Licinius** to become sole Roman emperor; he founds new capital at **Constantinople**
- **325** Pachomius founds **monastery of Tabenne** in the Egyptian desert
- **325** Constantine summons **Council of Nicaea** to determine orthodox Christian doctrine
- **327** Constantine has his **son Crispus put to death** for plotting
- **329 Saint Peter's basilica** in Rome completed
- **333** Ezana of Aksum **converts to Christianity**
- **335** Consecration of **Church of the Holy Sepulchre**, Jerusalem
- **c.335** Chandragupta I succeeded by **Samudragupta** who creates an empire in the Ganges plain
- **336** Church council at **Tyre condemns Athanasius**, patriarch of Alexandria, for his attitude to Arians
- **337 Shapur II** starts new war against the Romans
- **337 Death of Constantine**; his three sons divide the empire
- **340** Constans **defeats his brother** Constantine II and takes the whole Western Empire
- **341** Widespread **persecution of Christians** in Persian Empire
- **346** Bishop **Athanasius** restored to Alexandria
- **350 Constans murdered** by military commander Magnentius
- **350 Hephthalites** (White Huns) **invade Persia** and **India**
- **c.350** Ulfilas **translates Bible** into Gothic
- **355 Alemannic invasion of Gaul** causes widespread devastation
- **355 Julian** made junior emperor (Caesar) and **Governor of Gaul**

356–360

The acropolis at Tikal, one of the greatest surviving series of ruins in the Mayan world.

IN ETHIOPIA, THE KINGDOM OF AKSUM became one of the earliest states to **embrace Christianity** outside the Roman Empire. The Syrian Christian missionary Frumentius converted the king, Ezana (r.320–60) to Monophysitism (a doctrine emphasizing a single nature of Christ, the divine). A letter from Constantius II to Ezana in 357 has survived, **urging Ezana to shift his allegiance to Arianism** and to replace Frumentius with an Arian bishop – evidence that the Roman emperors took seriously the religious loyalties of their neighbours. Ezana conducted military campaigns beyond his borders; an inscription speaks of expeditions against neighbouring "Gaze, then the Agame, and the Siguene", and it seems his armies may have occupied **Meroë city** (in northern Sudan). Enriched by such conquests and the control of trade from sub-Saharan Africa and Arabia, **Aksum** would **dominate the region** until the 7th century.

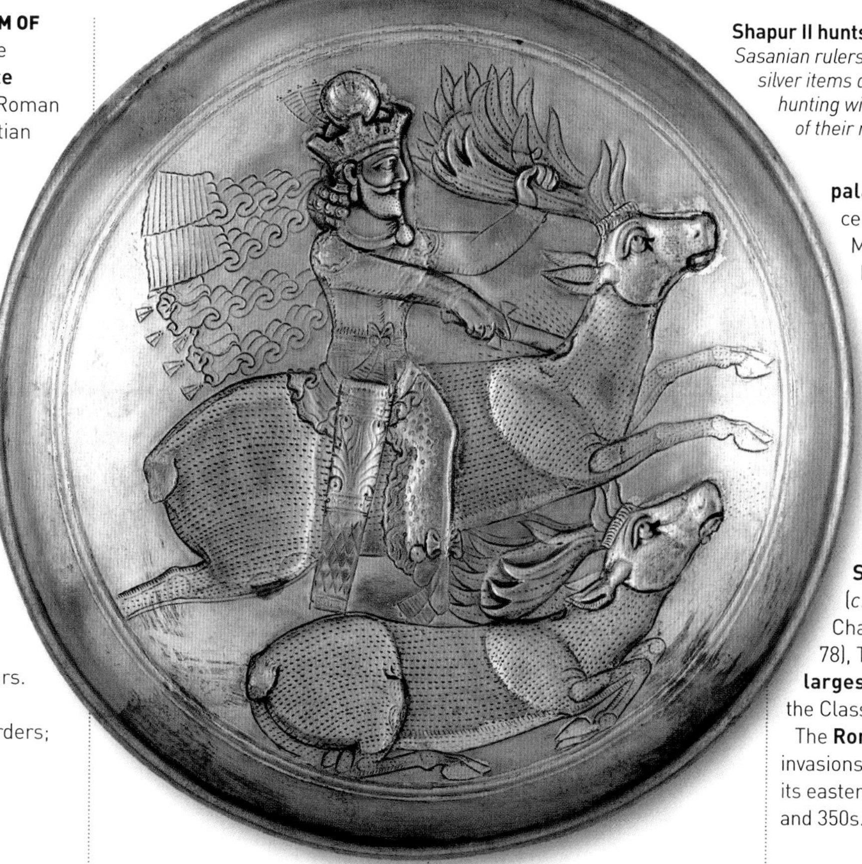

Shapur II hunts a stag
Sasanian rulers commissioned lavish silver items depicting themselves hunting wild beast as a display of their royal power.

16
SQUARE KILOMETRES
THE AREA OF THE CITY OF TIKAL *c.*400

The **pre-Classic Maya kingdoms** of Guatemala and Mexico underwent a collapse some time in 200–300, with populations declining and building activity ceasing. But the region soon recovered, with the emergence of **a new phase** in Maya civilization, the Classic period (300–900), in which a series of **powerful kingdoms emerged**. Their great urban centres, such as those at Tikal (in Guatemala) and Palenque (in Mexico), are characterized by **huge pyramidal temples and palace complexes** set in a central "acropolis". The Mayans developed a **hieroglyphic** form of writing which survives on many of the **stelae** (carved stone slabs) they set up to commemorate important events; in Tikal the first such dated monument is from 292. The first named king of Tikal is **Siyaj Chan K'awiil I** (*c.*305), and by the reign of Chak Tok Ich'aak I (r.360–78), Tikal was by far the **largest and most powerful** of the Classic Maya cities.

The **Roman Empire** faced invasions on both its western and its eastern borders in the 340s and 350s. In the West, **the Franks** began to push across the Rhine, and in the early 350s they overran part of the Rhine frontier, occupying some old Roman fortresses. **Caesar Julian** engaged in a series of **campaigns against the Franks** (356–59) and drove them from most of the territory they had taken.

In the East, **conflict** broke out again between the Romans and the Persians, under **Shapur II** (r.309–79), who took advantage of the political turmoil in the Roman Empire in the 350s. In 359, Shapur II advanced further west and **took the great Roman fortress of Amida** (modern Diyarbakir, Turkey). Other towns were captured and their populations deported to Persia, threatening the Roman position in the East.

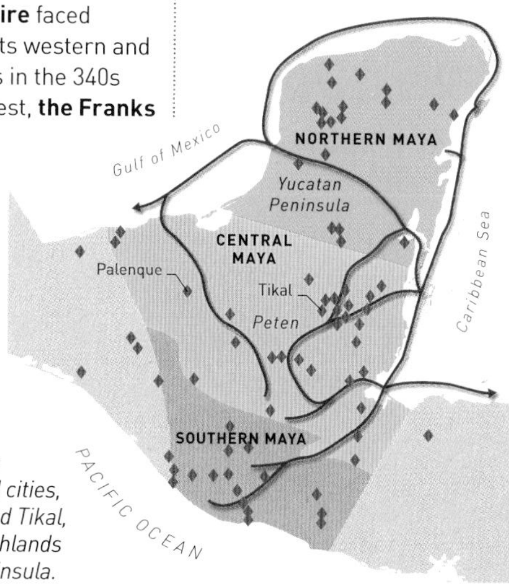

Maya kingdoms
Classic Maya culture originated in lowland cities, such as Uaxactun and Tikal, but spread to the highlands and the Yucatán peninsula.

356 Bishop Athanasius of Alexandria **exiled once more**

356 **St Antony**, leader of monastic movement in Egypt and "Desert Father" **dies** (born c.251)

356–57 Constantius II **issues laws** banning divination and sacrifices, and closing pagan temples

357 Church council at Sirmium issues **pro-Arian creed**

358 Huge earthquake devastates western Asia Minor

358 Constantius II **campaigns** across Danube against **Quadi and Sarmatians**

359 Shapur II invades Syria and captures Amida

359 Church councils at Rimini (of bishops) and at Seleucia in Cilicia agree the **homois formula** – a compromise between Arian and orthodox Nicene Christians

360 Julian's troops declare him **emperor** in Paris

360 Council of Constantinople promulgates pro-Arian creed

Here Emperor Julian is seen in religious debate. He attempted to sow discord among Christians by decreeing the return of those who had been exiled for religious reasons.

IN CHINA, THE EASTERN JIN DYNASTY (317–420) brought comparative stability to the south of the country. Although many of the emperors were short-lived, the bureaucracy in the southern capital of Nanjing functioned efficiently and the period saw a **cultural flowering**. Artists such as Gu Kaizhi (*c*.345–406) painted masterpieces such as the *Admonitions of the Instructress to the Palace Ladies*, as well as producing works on the theory of painting. **Northern China**, on the other hand, was **highly unstable**, divided between the Sixteen Kingdoms, most of them ruled by **nomadic groups**. The Eastern Jin emperors alternated between a defensive stance towards the Sixteen Kingdoms and aggressive campaigns, notably under Mudi (r.345–61) who retook Sichuan and Luoyang. All these gains were lost, however, under Emperor Aidi (r.362–65). In 383, the Eastern Jin (under Xiaouwudi) would be forced to repel a major invasion in the north of the country.

16

THE **NUMBER OF KINGDOMS** IN **CHINA** FROM **304** TO **439**

In the Roman Empire, **Julian** was proclaimed **Augustus** by his troops in 360, so he was a direct challenge to Constantius. The threat from the Persians, who were advancing through Asia Minor, was too great for Constantius to meet immediately. **He died** in November 361 as he was finally marching west to deal with the revolt. Now sole emperor, Julian immediately set about **restoring the role of paganism** in the Roman Empire, trying to establish a kind of pagan orthodoxy and an official pagan hierarchy of priests to counter Christianity's strengths. He reopened pagan temples, and **restored the right to sacrifice**.

In 363, Julian set out on **a campaign against Persia**, planning to punish its leader, Shapur II, for his attacks on the empire in 359–60. He reached Ctesiphon, but was then forced to retreat up the Tigris River. Being short of supplies, the Roman army suffered constant harassment from the Persians and, in one such skirmish, **Julian was killed**. The pagan reaction was over.

On Julian's death the army chose **Jovian** (r.363–64) as emperor, but he ceded key border provinces to Persia, which lost him popularity, and he died (probably murdered) within months. An officer of the imperial bodyguard, **Valentinian** (r.364–75), was then raised to the throne, and he selected his brother **Valens** (r.364–78) to be his **co-ruler**. Valentinian spent much of his reign along the Rhine dealing with Frankish and Alemannic invaders. He died in 375 after suffering some type of fit, brought on by his anger at barbarian Quadi envoys thought to have insulted him. The Western Roman Empire was then subdivided between Valentinian's two sons **Gratian** (r.375–83) and **Valentinian II** (r.375–92). In the Eastern Empire, Valens was forced to spend most of the early 370s in Syria to contain the Persian threat, but growing trouble with barbarians along the Danube later forced him to turn to the Balkans.

JULIAN THE APOSTATE (331–63)

The nephew of Constantine I, Julian was educated as a Christian but *c*.351 became a pagan under the influence of Maximus of Ephesus. When Julian unexpectedly became emperor in 363, he tried to restore paganism in the empire, including banning Christians from teaching literature. He became known by Christian writers as "the Apostate" for his perceived betrayal of Christianity.

Sarmatian dagger
This dagger belonged to the Sarmatians, a tribe of Iranian origin who specialized in horseback fighting, and were defeated by Valentinian I.

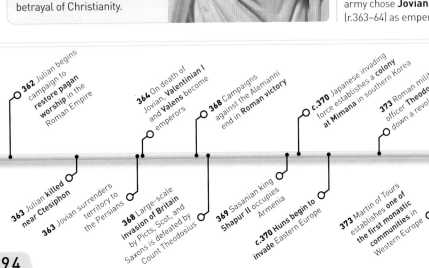

The church of Hagia Eirene in Istanbul was built by Constantine I.

> " ... THE **BARBARIANS,** [ARE] LIKE BEASTS ... **BROKEN LOOSE...** OVER THE **VAST EXTENT...** OF **COUNTRY.** "
>
> **Ammianus Marcellinus**, on the Gothic invasion of the Balkans *c*.390

IN 376, LARGE GROUPS OF GOTHS ARRIVED AT THE DANUBE FRONTIER, pressing to be admitted to the Roman Empire. **The Huns**, a new nomadic group from Central Asia, were at their rear, and the Goths feared being squeezed between them and the imperial frontier. Emperor Valens did not wait for reinforcements before marching out to meet the Gothic army. On 9 August 378, near Adrianople, **the Romans met the Goths**, under Fritigern. Misled by the temporary absence of the Gothic cavalry, Valens attacked but his army was surrounded by the returning barbarian horsemen. Valens was killed and the **Eastern army destroyed,** leaving the Balkans open to the Goths.

Gratian reacted by turning to **Theodosius**, a Spanish military officer, who he appointed as his imperial colleague. For the next three years Theodosius patiently negotiated, bought off some groups, and struck militarily where he could. In 382, the two

- **362** Julian begins campaign to **restore pagan worship** in the Roman Empire
- **363** Julian **killed** near **Ctesiphon**
- **363** Jovian surrenders territory to the Persians
- **364** On death of Jovian, **Valentinian I** and **Valens** become emperors
- **368** Large-scale **invasion of Britain** by Picts, Scot, and Saxons is defeated by Count Theodosius
- **368** Campaigns against the Alemanni end in **Roman victory**
- **369** Sasanian king **Shapur II** occupies Armenia
- **c.370** Japanese invading force establishes a **colony at Mimana** in southern Korea
- **c.370 Huns begin to invade** Eastern Europe
- **373** Roman military officer **Theodosius** puts down a revolt in Morocco
- **373** Martin of Tours establishes **one of the first monastic communities** in Western Europe
- **373 Fu Jian**, ruler of the Former Jin (one of 16 kingdoms) occupies Sichuan, Yunnan, and parts of Guizhou
- **375 Valentinian dies unexpectedly** while negotiating with barbarian Quadi envoys
- **375** Yax Nuun Ayiin becomes **ruler of Tikal**
- **375** Samudragupta dies; Chandragupta II succeeds; the **Gupta Empire now dominates** north and central India
- **376 Fu Jian**, of the Former Jin, **extends control** into Central Asia
- **376 Goths petition Valens** to allow them to settle in the Roman Empire
- **378 Goths defeat the Romans** under Valens at **Adrianople**

St Jerome (*c.*347–420) completed the *Vulgate*, the first definitive translation of the Bible into Latin, *c.*405.

> **“ THE THICKER THE HAY, THE EASIER IT IS MOWED. ”**
>
> **Alaric the Goth,** speaking of his enemies *c.*400

sides agreed a truce, whereby the **Goths** were **allowed to settle** in the empire in return for providing troops for the Roman army.

The **Gupta Empire continued to expand** under Chandragupta II (r.375–415) in northern India. He fought against the Sakas, annexing much of northwestern India. He also made an **astute marriage alliance** that extended his realm to the southwest.

Iron pillar of Delhi
This iron pillar at Qutb complex on the outskirts of Delhi is said to have been erected on the orders of Chandragupta II.

IN CENTRAL AMERICA, THE MAYAN CITY OF TIKAL had reached the peak of its influence in the late 4th century. In 378, a foreign lord called **Siyaj Kak** arrived in the city, possibly from Teotihuacán. His arrival, which may represent a military conquest, led to the **death of Tikal's ruler** Chak Tok Ich'aak and the **destruction of** most of Tikal's **public monuments**. Siyaj Kak installed a new dynasty on the throne of Tikal, possibly drawn from the ruling house of Teotihuacán, with **Yax Nuun Ayiin** ("Curl Snout"; r.379–404) as the first ruler. Monuments depict him in northern Mexican, rather than Mayan, dress. Under his rule, Tikal's direct influence extended some 50 km (30 miles) away.

In the Western Roman Empire, **Gratian** had spent much of his time since the Battle of Adrianople (378) in northern Italy, where he **continued to act against pagans** in Rome, ordering the removal of the Altar of Victory from the Senate House in 382. In 383, he led an army north to face an invasion of Gaul by the Alemanni, but was then faced with **a revolt in Britain,** where the legions declared their commander **Magnus Maximus emperor**. Many of Gratian's commanders defected and in August 383 he was captured and executed by Maximus, who had crossed over to Gaul. **Theodosius,** fearful of trouble with Persia or a Gothic revolt in the Balkans if he moved west, **recognized Maximus** as his colleague. A peace with Persia in 386, however,

St Ambrose
A Roman nobleman by birth, Ambrose was Bishop of Milan from 374 to 397. He exercised a powerful influence over Theodosius I.

freed Theodosius to react when Maximus invaded Italy in 387. In August 388, he marched swiftly into northern Italy, **capturing Maximus** near Aquileia, and having him executed.

As well as campaigning against the Goths and Maximus, Theodosius was preoccupied with the **imposition of Orthodox Christianity**. He moved against the Arians, deposing the Bishop of Constantinople in 380 and calling a council in 381 in the capital, which reaffirmed the anti-Arian decisions of the Council of Nicaea (see 325). He connived in the **destruction of many pagan temples**, including the great temple of Serapis in Alexandria, and in 391 he **forbade all pagan sacrifices** throughout the empire.

IN 392, VALENTINIAN II, WHO HAD CONTINUED TO RULE OVER ITALY, was found hanged. His military commander Arbogast – suspected by some of Valentinian's murder – promptly made **Flavius Eugenius**, a middle-ranking official, emperor. Theodosius refused to recognize Eugenius, and in 393 he **invaded Italy.** To gain support in the Senate – where paganism was still strong – the Christian Eugenius **revoked** all of Theodosius's **anti-pagan laws**. But, in August 394, he was defeated by the Theodosian army at the **River Frigidus** near Aquileia. Theodosius did not enjoy his rule as sole emperor long, dying in January 395. The empire was then divided between his two sons: the older, Arcadius, taking the eastern part and his younger brother, Honorius, taking the western one. Although there was no clear intention to do so, this split marked a permanent division; after 395 no one emperor ruled the whole empire again.

The Goths had taken part on Theodosius's side at the Battle of the River Frigidus and felt they had not been sufficiently rewarded for their losses. In 395, they rose up, led by **Alaric** (r.395–410). Despite an attempt by **Stilicho** (*c.*365–408), the half-Vandal commander of the Western Roman army, to suppress them, the Goths escaped and marauded throughout Greece in 396. Stilicho moved against Alaric again in 397, but once more failed to defeat him. A **brief halt to the Gothic rampage** came after Alaric's appointment by the Eastern Roman government to *magister militum* (a senior general).

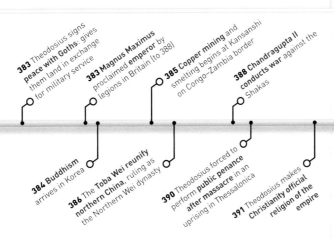

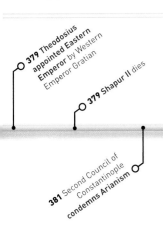

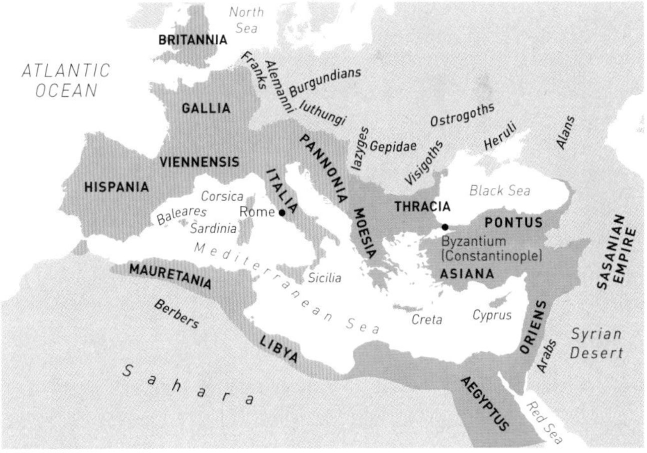

Divided in two
The split of the Roman Empire into Eastern and Western divisions in 395 was permanent. By 476, its Western part would be overrun by barbarians.

KEY
Eastern Roman Empire
Western Roman Empire

379 Theodosius appointed Eastern Emperor by Western Emperor Gratian

379 Shapur II dies

381 Second Council of Constantinople **condemns Arianism**

383 Theodosius signs **peace with Goths**; gives them land in exchange for military service

383 Magnus Maximus proclaimed **emperor** by legions in Britain (to 388)

384 Buddhism arrives in Korea

385 Copper mining and smelting begins at Kansanshi on Congo–Zambia border

386 The **Toba Wei reunify northern China**, ruling as the Northern Wei dynasty

388 Chandragupta II conducts war against the Shakas

390 Theodosius forced to perform **public penance after massacre** in an uprising in Thessalonica

391 Theodosius makes **Christianity official religion of the empire**

392 Emperor **Valentinian II dies** (b.371)

393 The **Yamato of Japan** overrun Silla and Paekche, Korea

394 Theodosius defeats and kills Eugenius, **becoming sole emperor**

395 Theodosius dies; the **empire is divided in two**

396 The half-Vandal general **Stilicho** becomes effective ruler of the Western Empire

397 Gildo begins major **rebellion against Roman emperor Honorius** in North Africa

399 Yazdegird becomes Persian ruler

c.400 Intensive period of **building at Teotihuacán**

400 Revolt of the Goths under Gainas; gains power, but he is soon expelled and killed by the Huns

CLASSICAL TRADE

FLOURISHING TRADE BETWEEN CONTINENTS A WORLD APART

The growth of Roman power in the Mediterranean, the unification of China under the Qin and Han, and the establishment of the Parthian Empire in Iran created three large political blocs, which provided stable conditions under which very long-distance trade routes could flourish.

The expansion of Han power westward in the 2nd century BCE brought the Chinese into contact with new powers they called An-hsi (Persia) and Li-chien (Rome). A Chinese embassy reached the court of Mithridates II of Parthia around 115 BCE. In the wake of diplomats came merchants, carrying the Chinese silk for which both Parthia and Rome had an insatiable appetite. The main Silk Route ran from China through Central Asia, down into Persia and then across Roman-controlled Syria towards the ports of the Mediterranean.

A thriving trade also spanned the Indian Ocean, transporting spices from the East Indies and southern India to ports in Africa and southern Arabia; from here a land route led up through Petra, in present-day Jordan, to Syria. Control of these trade routes was very lucrative, and towns that lay on them were able to exact heavy tolls from merchants, which they used to build spectacular public monuments.

Further west, in the Mediterranean, expensive goods such as fine wine were carried by sea; in general land transportation was expensive, and bulky, low-value products tended to be produced and consumed locally.

13,000
KILOMETRES
THE LENGTH OF THE TRADE ROUTE FROM **CHANG'AN** TO **ROME**

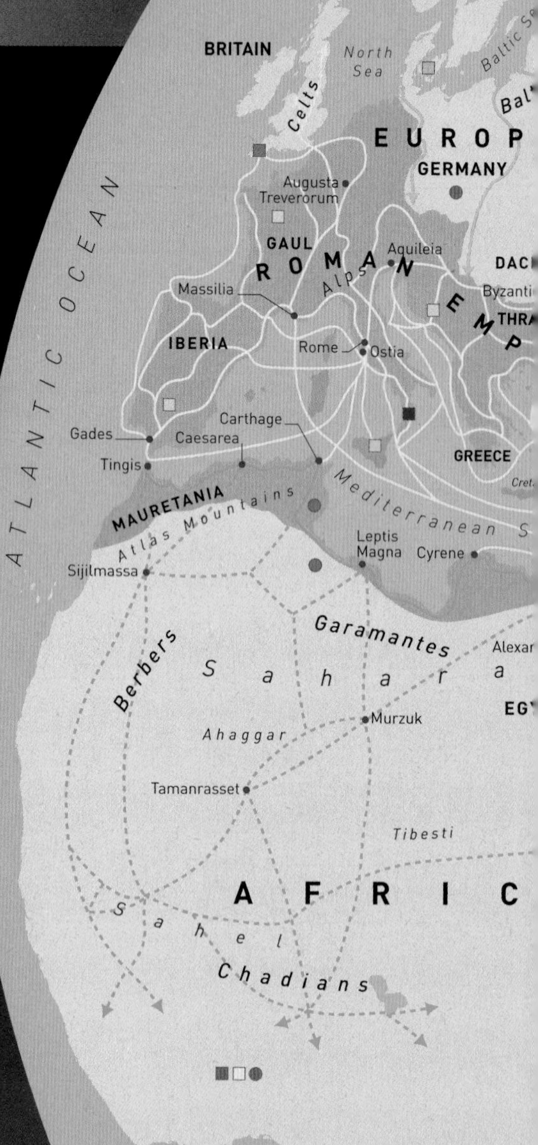

ROMAN TRADE

The expansion of the Roman Empire to cover much of Europe, western Asia, and North Africa created largely peaceful conditions in which both internal and external trade could flourish.

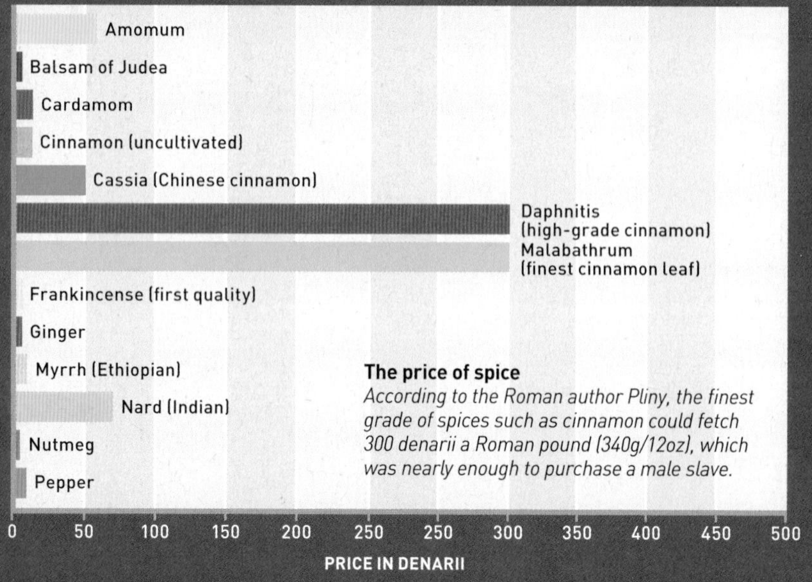

The price of spice
According to the Roman author Pliny, the finest grade of spices such as cinnamon could fetch 300 denarii a Roman pound (340g/12oz), which was nearly enough to purchase a male slave.

Roman imports
The Romans imported huge quantities of raw materials, including luxury goods such as gold and ivory and cheaper goods such as food.

Roman exports
The Romans paid for their imports with precious metal and coins, and exported products such as wine and glassware.

World trade
Trade routes c.1 CE criss-crossed the whole of the classical world. The means of transport used depended on location – Bactrian camels were used in Central Asia, while horses, bullocks, and yaks were used elsewhere. Maritime trade was also extensive – there was an active trading network around the Indian Ocean.

HAN TRADE

The establishment of Chinese control in Central Asia from the late 3rd century BCE opened up a series of routes through Persia to the Mediterranean, which became collectively known as the Silk Route. However, it also involved the Han emperors in continuous and costly defence of their new territories.

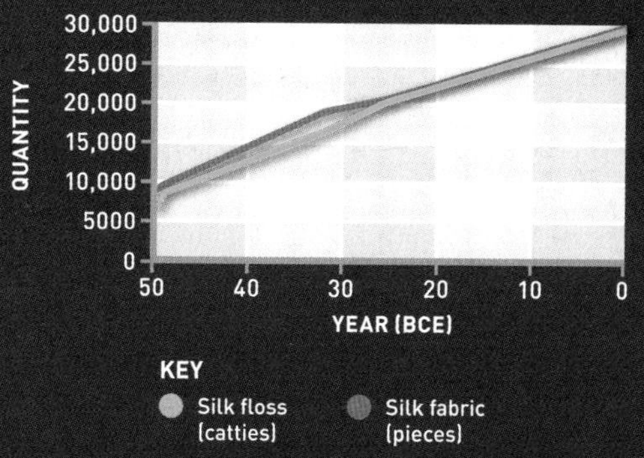

Buying safety
To guarantee security on their frontiers and along trade routes, the Han were forced to pay large bribes in silk to barbarian groups such as the Hsiung-nu.

Han imports
The Han valued spices as much as the Romans did, but they also sent trade expeditions to Ferghana in Central Asia in search of what they called "heavenly horses".

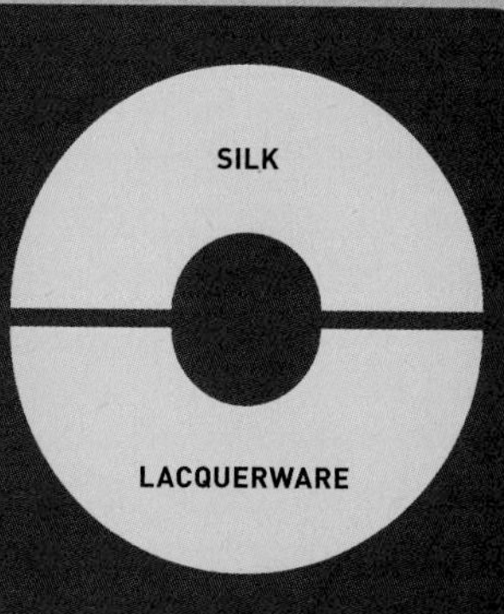

Han exports
Knowledge of silk in China goes back to at least 2600 BCE, but under the Han it became a staple export item, alongside lacquerware.

Around 200 stone heads decorated Tiwanaku's Semi-subterranean temple. They may represent the group that founded the city – their flat head-dresses denote high status.

ALTHOUGH THE WESTERN ROMAN EMPIRE SEEMED RELATIVELY SECURE IN 400, within a decade it had suffered a series of disasters. Gothic raids in 401 and again in 405 ravaged northern Italy. Then on the last day of 406, **hordes of Vandals**, joined by two other barbarian groups, the **Alans** and **Sueves**, crossed the frozen Rhine near Mainz, sacked Treveri (modern Trier, Germany) and Remi (modern Reims, France), and forced their way southwest until they reached the Pyrenees.

Meanwhile, the **armies of Britain** had raised up **a series of usurpers** as emperor from 406. The last of these, **Constantine III** (r.407–11), took most of the remaining Roman troops in Britain and **crossed to Gaul** in spring 407, aiming to seize the throne from the then head of the Western Roman Empire, Honorius. Although he was defeated and captured at Arles in 412, native leaders in Britain had already **expelled the last Roman officials** there in 410 – probably in revenge for their abandonment by Constantine's legion. **Britain** was now **independent from Rome**.

In 408, **Alaric** (r.c.395–410), leader of the **Visigoths**, **invaded Italy** once more. The Roman commander Stilicho persuaded the Senate to **agree to pay Alaric a huge bribe** in exchange for leaving the city, but there seems to have been a coup d'état and Stilicho was overthrown and killed. In 409, Alaric had Attalus, the prefect of Rome, declared emperor in an attempt to seize the initiative, but all negotiations failed. So, on 24 August 410 the **Visigoths entered Rome** and subjected it to a **three-day sack**. The event shook the entire Roman world, but Alaric was unable to secure domination over Italy, as he died later the same year.

In South America, **the city of Tiwanaku**, 25 km (15 miles) south of Lake Titicaca (on the border between modern Peru and Bolivia), **reached its greatest size** in the 5th century, covering an area some 8 sq km (3 sq miles) in extent. Its central area contained a lavish series of **ceremonial buildings and temples**. These included the Semi-subterranean Temple, decorated with stone heads of humans and supernatural beings, and structures such as the massive and beautifully decorated **Gateway of the Sun**. These were erected by a major pre-Columbian culture that **dominated the Altiplano** (flat high plateau) of Peru and Bolivia, and whose influence extended into northern Bolivia.

Visigoths ride on Rome
Alaric's sack of Rome in 410 was particularly shocking, as it was the first time the city had fallen since the Gauls took it in 390 BCE.

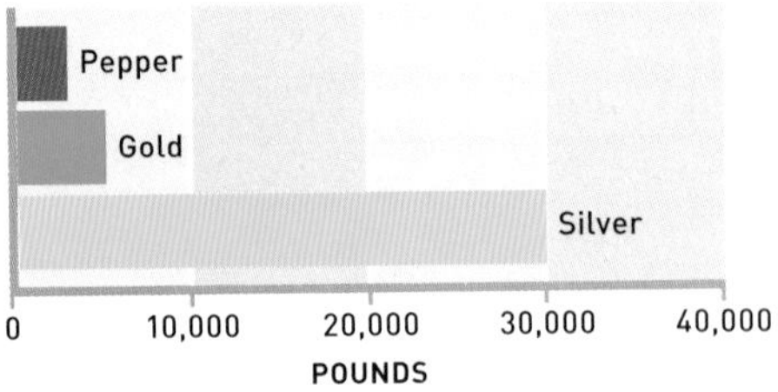

Ransom demands
Alaric initially asked for a huge ransom in return for leaving Rome in 410. Even when he moderated his demands, the Senate refused, and so the city was sacked.

" SO THE **VANDALS,** HAVING **WRESTED LIBYA FROM** THE **ROMANS** IN THIS WAY, MADE IT THEIR OWN... "

Procopius, Byzantine scholar, from *History of the Wars, III iv 1, c.500–550*

THE BARBARIANS WHO HAD INITIALLY CROSSED THE RHINE IN 401 had gone on to sack a number of cities before moving southwest into Aquitania and then crossing the Pyrenees into Spain, where they **occupied large swathes of Roman territory**. In 416–18, the Roman army commander Constantius persuaded the **Visigoths under Wallia** (r.415–18) to invade Spain. There he smashed the Alans and the Siling Vandals, but allowed some of them to settle in southern Spain and left the Asing Vandals and Sueves in possession of northwestern Spain. Wallia was rewarded with official possession of much of southwestern Spain.

On the other side of the Mediterranean in 429, **Boniface**, the Roman Governor of North Africa, revolted against his long-term adversary **Aëtius**, and called on the Siling Vandals for help. The **Vandal king, Gaiseric** (r.428–77), crossed over the Straits of Gibraltar with – it was said – 80,000 of his people and, far from helping Boniface, swiftly occupied most of North Africa. In 435, he made a treaty with the Romans, recognizing his **occupation of Mauretania** (modern Algeria and Morocco). Gaiseric broke this and in 439 his warriors **captured Carthage**, the Roman capital there, and set up an **independent Vandal kingdom**.

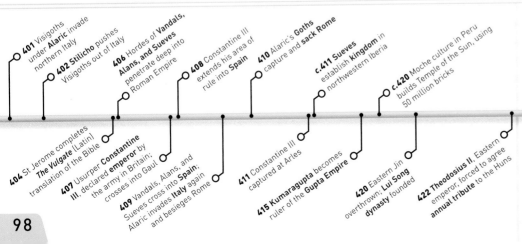

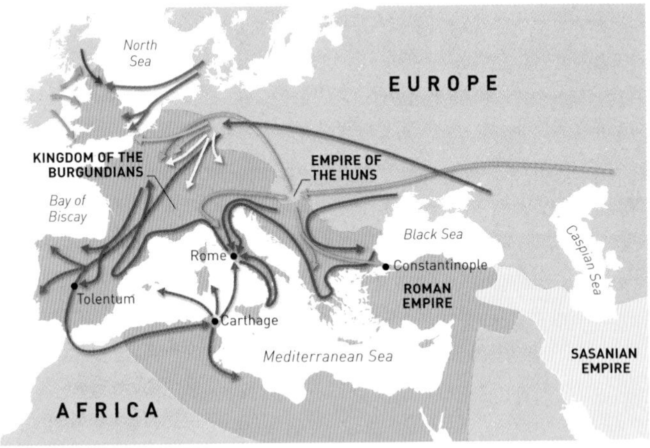

The barbarian invasions
Barbarian groups took more and more Roman territory in the first half of the 5th century, leaving the Western emperors virtually powerless.

KEY
- Roman Empire
- Sasanian Empire
- Huns
- Goths
- Alans
- Vandals, Alans, Sueves
- Burgundians
- Franks
- Jutes, Angles, Saxons
- Irish
- Picts

401 Visigoths under **Alaric** invade northern Italy

402 Stilicho pushes Visigoths out of Italy

404 St Jerome completes ***The Vulgate*** (Latin) translation of the Bible

406 Hordes of **Vandals, Alans, and Sueves** penetrate deep into Roman Empire

407 Usurper **Constantine III**, declared **emperor** by the army in Britain; crosses into Gaul

408 Constantine III extends his area of rule into **Spain**

409 Vandals, Alans, and Sueves cross into **Spain**; Alaric invades **Italy** again and besieges Rome

410 Alaric's **Goths** capture and **sack Rome**

411 Constantine III captured at Arles

c.411 Sueves establish **kingdom** in northwestern Iberia

415 Kumaragupta becomes ruler of the **Gupta Empire**

c.420 Moche culture in Peru builds Temple of the Sun, using 50 million bricks

420 Eastern Jin overthrown; **Lui Song dynasty** founded

422 Theodosius II, Eastern emperor, forced to agree **annual tribute** to the Huns

424 Aëtius invades Italy with Hunnish force intending to support the **usurper John**

425 John defeated; **Valentinian III** becomes emperor in the West

428 Nestorius, Patriarch of Constantinople, **preaches new doctrine** distinguishing Christ's human and divine nature; it is condemned as heretical

429 Vandals cross Strait of Gibraltar into North Africa

429 Bishop Germanus visits Britain on mission to root out Pelagianism

429–31 Struggle between **Boniface** and **Aëtius** for supremacy at Roman court ends in Boniface's death

c.431 Pope Celestine sends **mission to Ireland** under Palladius

433 Attila becomes **king of the Huns**

A colourful Buddhist mural from the Yungang caves, which were begun under the Northern Wei c.450.

THE EASTERN JIN DYNASTY IN CHINA HAD ENDED IN 420, with Gongi's abdication. His successor, Song Wudi (r.420–22), a former fisherman, had risen to become a general and **founded the Liu Song dynasty**. He strengthened the southern kingdom's northern borders against the barbarian tribes, but under his son Wendi (r.424–53), the northerners captured Luoyang in 424, before, some 25 years later **besieging** the Liu Song capital of **Nanking**. Although Song Wudi had strengthened the central bureaucracy, the growing power and wealth of the **Buddhist and Daoist monasteries** weakened the economic basis of the state. Wendi's successors were weak and by 479 the Liu Song were overthrown by the short-lived **Qi dynasty** (479–502).

Meanwhile, in northern China the **Sixteen Kingdoms** had been united under the Toba Wei (a group of Turkic nomads), who founded the **Northern Wei dynasty** (386–534). The Northern Wei ruled over northern China, until its split into two in the early 6th century following a revolt against the imposition of Chinese dress and language on the Wei nomads.

In Europe, the Western Roman Empire continued to lose ground, as barbarians occupied more and more of its territory. In the 420s the **Visigoths under Theoderic** (r.418–51) occupied sections of the Mediterranean shore of Gaul, before they were pushed back southwest in 430. About this time a new group of barbarians, **the Huns**, began to menace the empire. This nomadic group from Central Asia, whose pressure from the rear on the Goths had been indirectly responsible for the crisis of 378 in the Balkans, had since moved further west. In 424, the Roman general **Aëtius recruited a force of Huns** to help him bolster the cause of John, a usurper raised up at Rome after the death of Honorius in 423. Aëtius continued to use the Huns into the late 420s to secure his power base and his appointment as patrician (the most senior post in the late Roman Empire) in 429. **In 435**, he was able to call on them to aid an **attack on the Burgundians** who had raided across the lower Rhine; these were soundly defeated and thereafter confined to a region to the northwest of Italy.

These were all just temporary successes, however, as the **area controlled** by the Western Roman emperors **was diminishing steadily**. The loss of almost all North Africa to the Vandals in 429–39 (and of Sicily in 440), of northern Gaul to the Franks by 450, of southwest Gaul to the Visigoths after 418, and of all save a few isolated outposts in Spain by the 430s meant the remaining strongholds in Italy and southeastern Gaul **could not provide enough tax revenue** to support armies to reconquer the lost provinces. The long reign of **Valentinian III** (r.425–55) in the Western Roman Empire **did not provide any stability** as he ascended to the throne as a child and never asserted himself until the very end, when he had **Aëtius**, the Western Empire's last effective general, **murdered**.

The **barbarians** who settled on the former Roman territories began gradually to **establish kingdoms of their own**, notably the Franks in northern Gaul and the Visigoths in southwest Gaul and Spain. In **Britain**, the situation **was rather different**, since the province had rebelled against Rome rather than being subject to barbarian conquest. In a bygone era, the Roman army might have been expected to reassert its control there, but, with the empire increasingly dependent on barbarian troops fighting under their own commanders, there was virtually no army left to retake it. The Britons were left to their own devices. It seems that some Roman institutions survived for a while; in 429 Bishop Germanus of Auxerre visited the island and found men bearing Roman titles. But **barbarian raiders** – attracted by the weakness of the British defences and the lack of a central political authority to counter them – **came in increasing numbers**. Around 446, the leading men of Britain addressed a desperate letter to Aëtius, appealing for aid. No reply was sent to these "groans of the Britons", and within a few years the **Angle, Saxon, and Jutish raiders** began to occupy parts of the former Roman province.

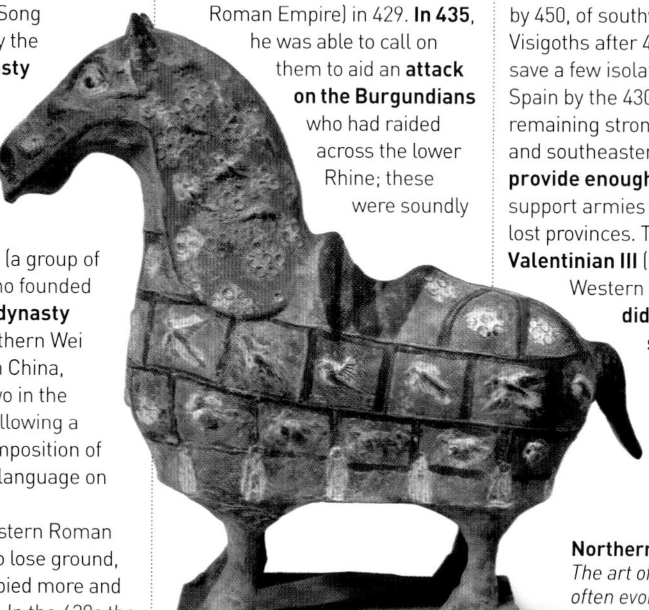

Northern Wei horse
The art of the Northern Wei often evoked their nomadic origins, as in this beautiful terracotta horse.

> “ THE **WORLD** IS **PASSING AWAY... LOSING ITS GRIP,** THE WORLD IS **SHORT OF BREATH.** ”
>
> **St Augustine of Hippo, theologian and philosopher**, from *Sermons 81, 8*

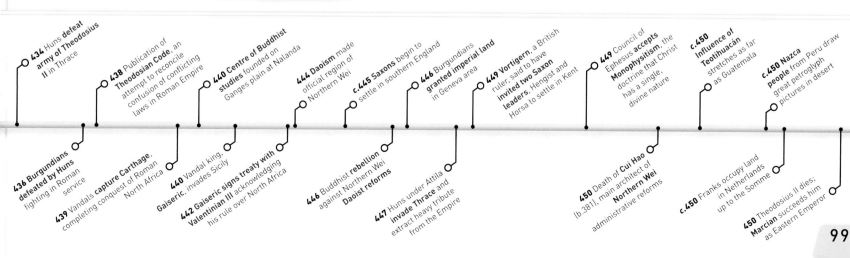

FLAVIUS AËTIUS
(c.395–454)

Born of nobility in Moesia (modern Bulgaria), Aëtius spent time from 408 in the royal court of the Huns. He used these contacts to gain influence and rose to further prominence in the late 420s. The deaths of patricians Felix (in 430) and Boniface (in 433) left him with unrivalled dominance. He shored up the empire's position, and in 451 he scored a notable victory against Attila the Hun. In 454 he was murdered by Valentinian III himself.

- **434** Huns **defeat army of Theodosius II** in Thrace
- **436 Burgundians defeated by Huns** fighting in Roman service
- **438** Publication of **Theodosian Code**, an attempt to reconcile confusion of conflicting laws in Roman Empire
- **439** Vandals **capture Carthage**, completing conquest of Roman North Africa
- **440 Centre of Buddhist studies** founded on Ganges plain at Nalanda
- **440** Vandal king, **Gaiseric**, invades Sicily
- **442 Gaiseric signs treaty with Valentinian III** acknowledging his rule over North Africa
- **444 Daoism** made official region of Northern Wei
- **c.445 Saxons** begin to settle in southern England
- **446** Buddhist **rebellion** against Northern Wei **Daoist reforms**
- **446** Burgundians **granted imperial land** in Geneva area
- **447** Huns under Attila **invade Thrace** and extract heavy tribute from the Empire
- **449 Vortigern**, a British ruler, said to have **invited two Saxon leaders**, Hengist and Horsa to settle in Kent
- **449** Council of Ephesus **accepts Monophysitism**, the doctrine that Christ has a single, divine nature
- **450** Death of **Cui Hao** (b.381), main architect of **Northern Wei** administrative reforms
- **c.450 Influence of Teotihuacán** stretches as far as Guatemala
- **c.450** Franks occupy land in Netherlands up to the Somme
- **c.450 Nazca people** from Peru draw great petroglyph pictures in desert
- **450** Theodosius II dies; **Marcian** succeeds him as Eastern Emperor

In this undated painting Attila the Hun is shown with his army – he is said to have been turned aside from sacking Rome only by the pleas of Pope Leo I.

The baptism of Clovis the first: Clovis's baptism made him an easier diplomatic partner for the eastern Roman Empire than his Arian neighbours.

> **“** [HUNS] **TOOK CAPTIVE** THE **CHURCHES** AND **SLEW** THE **MONKS** AND **MAIDENS. ”**

Callinicus, disciple of Hypatius, from *Life of Saint Hypatius, c.*450

IN JAPAN, THE 5TH CENTURY SAW THE RAPID DEVELOPMENT and expansion of the **Yamato state**. Complex irrigation systems began to appear, and rulers built ever larger burial mounds, such as the 486m (1,600ft) long Nintoku mound. **Ojin** founded a new line of kings, who exercised firmer control over Japan's main islands from a royal centre in the Kawachi-Izumi area. Yamato overseas contacts became more extensive, with ten diplomatic missions visiting China between 421 and 478, and increasing Yamato interference in civil wars between the Korean states of Paekche, Silla, and Koguryo.

The **Sasanian Persian Empire** came under pressure from eastern nomadic groups in the later 5th century. The **Hephthalite Huns** moved into Bactria early in the century, and were a particular threat to the Sasanians, but a famine during the **reign of Peroz (457–84)** caused them to move west again. In 469 Peroz suffered a terrible defeat at the hands of the Hephthalites. He was captured, and only released after leaving his son as a hostage. In 484, Peroz sought revenge in a new campaign against the Hephthalites, but was defeated and killed.

Having demanded, and been refused, the hand in marriage of Honoria, the sister of Roman Emperor Valentinian III in 450, the **Hunnish king Attila** (see 401–450) marched into Gaul. He was defeated near **Châlons** by an army of Romans under Aëtius and Goths under Theodoric.

Pope Leo I
The illustration on this manuscript shows Pope Leo I, an Italian aristocrat, persuading Attila the Hun not to attack Rome.

Clay bear figurine
Clay haniwa figurines have been a feature of rich Japanese burials since the earliest times. The large burial mounds of Yamato rulers contain huge quantities of them.

Undaunted, Attila invaded Italy in 452, but turned back short of Rome. **Attila died** after his wedding feast in 453, and his sons began a civil war that led to the Hunnish empire falling apart.

Following the death of the Roman general Aëtius in 454, real **power in the western Roman Empire** was exercised by a series of barbarian kingmakers, such as **Ricimer**, the leader of the Roman army in Italy. In 457, Ricimer placed **Majorian** on the imperial throne. When Majorian became too independent-minded, Ricimer replaced him with **Libius Severus** (r.461–65), who he later had poisoned. Deprived of effective leadership, the Roman Empire lost more of its Gallic territories to the **Visigoths** and **Franks**.

IN 456, THE VISIGOTHS, encouraged by the western Roman emperor Avitus, had invaded the Iberian Peninsula. The Visigothic king **Theoderic II** (r.453–66) defeated the Suevic ruler **Rechiarius,** who was threatening the Roman province of Tarraconensis, and the remaining Sueves retreated. Theoderic took most of Spain for himself, but left the Romans parts of the east coast. This policy was reversed by his successor **Euric** (r.466–84), who overran the remaining Roman territories in the late 470s. By the time of **Alaric II** (r.484–507) the Visigothic kingdom encompassed almost all of Spain, as well as Aquitaine and Provence in southern Gaul. The situation in Spain was repeated elsewhere in the Roman Empire, and the area of imperial control shrank to little more than Italy. **Anthemius** (r.467–472) tried to recover some ground, but an expeditionary force against Vandal-controlled North Africa in 468 ended in disaster. In Gaul, Euric conquered almost all remaining Roman territory in the south by 475. In 472, Anthemius was overthrown by **Gundobad**, a Burgundian. Gundobad placed **Olybrius** (r.472) and **Glycerius** (r.473–74) on the throne in quick sucession, but, despairing of the empire's frailty, he then left for Burgundy. The last embers of the empire were contested in 475–76, between **Julius Nepos** and **Romulus Augustulus**, the son of **Orestes**, commander of the Roman army. Feeling that the

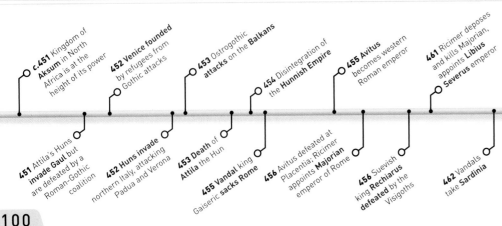

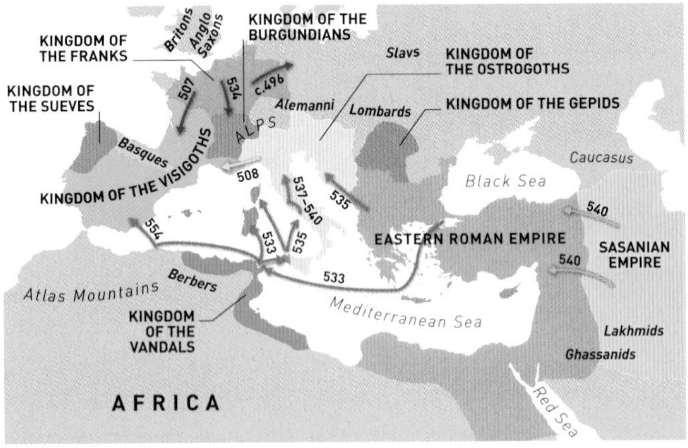

Barbarian kingdoms in Europe *c.*500
By 500, most of the former western Roman Empire was divided between several principal barbarian successor states: the Vandals in North Africa, the Visigoths in Spain and southern Gaul, and the Ostrogoths in Italy.

KEY
- Byzantine reconquests
- Frankish expansion
- Ostrogothic expansion
- Sasanian expansion

c.451 Kingdom of **Aksum** in North Africa is at the height of its power

451 Attila's Huns **invade Gaul** but are defeated by a Roman-Gothic coalition

452 Venice founded by refugees from Gothic attacks

452 Huns invade northern Italy, attacking Padua and Verona

453 Ostrogothic **attacks** on the **Balkans**

453 Death of Attila the Hun

455 Vandal king Gaiseric **sacks Rome**

454 Disintegration of the **Hunnish Empire**

456 Avitus defeated at Placentia; Ricimer appoints **Majorian** emperor of Rome

455 Avitus becomes western Roman emperor

456 Suevish king **Rechiarus defeated** by the Visigoths

461 Ricimer deposes and kills Majorian, appoints **Libius Severus** emperor

462 Vandals take **Sardinia**

467 Gupta empire begins to **collapse**

468 Vandals conquer **Sicily**

472 Zeno becomes eastern **Roman emperor**

473 Julius Nepos proclaims himself western **emperor**

475 Julius Nepos acknowledges rule of Euric, **king of the Visigoths**, in Spain

476 Last Roman emperor in the west deposed

476 Keyhole tomb of **Emperor Nintoku** (d.421) completed

476 Vandal king **Euric conquers** remaining Roman territory in southern Gaul

477 Collapse of the **Liu Song** dynasty

477 Kasyapa comes to power in **Sri Lanka** (to 495)

interests of the Germanic barbarians in the army were being ignored, Orestes's deputy, **Odoacer**, revolted and deposed Romulus in September 476. He did not appoint a new emperor, claiming that he ruled Italy on behalf of the eastern emperor **Zeno** (r.474–91). This marked the end of the Roman Empire in the west after 500 years.

However, in the east the Roman Empire survived. The long reign of **Theodosius II** (408–50) had strengthened its position, and after 400 the eastern empire had not had to face such direct threats from Huns, Goths, Vandals, Alamanns, Burgundians, and Franks as the west. **Marcian** (r.450–57) had consolidated the eastern empire's finances, leaving a surplus of 100,000 pounds of gold at his death. **Leo I** (r.457–74) fended off residual Gothic threats to the Balkans, and even made an attempt to recover North Africa in 468. **Zeno** (474–91) faced the challenge of the new Germanic rulers of Italy, led by Odoacer. He resolved this by commissioning the king of the Ostrogoths, **Theodoric**, to topple Odoacer in 489. By 500, the eastern Roman Empire under **Anastasius** (r.492–518) was in little danger of the implosion that had erased its western counterpart just 25 years earlier.

The western Roman Empire was replaced by a series of **Germanic successor states**. Odoacer ruled as king of Italy, but the legitimacy of his rule was always questionable. In 489, an invasion by Theodoric's Ostrogoths led to a four-year stand-off, with Odoacer blockading himself inside the old imperial capital of Ravenna. After the murder of Odoacer in 493, Theodoric established a regime in which the continuation of Roman administrative practices won the loyalty of the old Roman aristocracy. In 497, the eastern emperor **Anastasius I** recognized Theodoric's right to govern Italy, providing him with a secure base to consolidate his rule and extend it into Gaul.

In northwestern Gaul the Franks had emerged as a threat in the late 4th century, and by the 460s they were carving out a kingdom under **Childeric**. His successor **Clovis** (r.481–511) transformed that kingdom, defeating **Syagrius**, ruler of a Roman enclave around Soissons, and expanding along the Rhine at the expense of the Alamans in the 490s. In 507, he defeated the Visigoths at the **Battle of Vouillé** and drove them out of most of southwestern Gaul. In the late 490s or early 500s, **Clovis converted** to Catholic Christianity, setting him apart from other barbarian rulers who were mostly Arians (members of an alternative Christian church).

In **Britain**, the expulsion of Roman officials had been followed by a period in which petty kingdoms vied for power. These kingdoms were vulnerable to coastal raiders, and, late in the 5th century, groups of Germanic barbarians (**Angles, Saxons, and Jutes**) settled in Britain. The arrival of the Saxons has been dated to 449, when they were invited by the British king Vortigern. Seven years later, they revolted and set up a kingdom in Kent. **Aelle** founded a kingdom in **Sussex** around 477 and **Cerdic,** in **Wessex** (around modern Hampshire), by 495. A British victory at Mons Badonicus around 500 stemmed the Saxon tide, but the respite was short-lived.

Saxon brooch
Anglo-Saxon art in the 5th century valued abstract geometric patterns, as seen on this brooch.

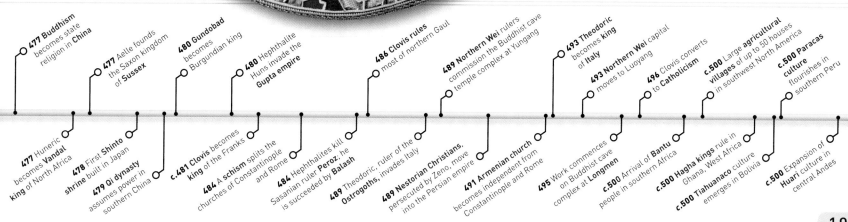

THEODORIC THE GREAT
(454–526)

Son of Thiudmir, a king of the Ostrogoths, Theodoric spent 11 years as a Roman hostage, to guarantee the good behaviour of his father. He returned home to become king of the Ostrogoths in 471, and for the next 17 years alternately allied with and attacked Roman territories in the Balkans. In 493, Theodoric became the first Ostrogothic king of Italy. His rule was generally pro-Roman, and he was buried in this Roman-style mausoleum.

477 Buddhism becomes state religion in **China**

477 Huneric becomes **Vandal king** of North Africa

477 Aelle founds the Saxon kingdom of **Sussex**

478 First **Shinto shrine** built in Japan

479 Qi dynasty assumes power in southern China

480 Gundobad becomes Burgundian king

c.481 Clovis becomes **king** of the Franks

480 Hephthalite Huns invade the **Gupta empire**

484 A **schism** splits the churches of Constantinople and Rome

484 Hephthalites kill Sasanian ruler **Peroz**; he is succeeded by **Balash**

486 Clovis rules most of northern Gaul

489 Theodoric, ruler of the **Ostrogoths**, invades Italy

489 Northern Wei rulers commission the Buddhist cave temple complex at Yungang

489 Nestorian Christians, persecuted by Zeno, move into the Persian empire

491 Armenian church becomes independent from Constantinople and Rome

493 Theodoric becomes **king** of **Italy**

493 Northern Wei capital moves to Luoyang

495 Work commences on Buddhist cave complex at **Longmen**

496 Clovis converts to **Catholicism**

c.500 Arrival of **Bantu** people in southern Africa

c.500 Large **agricultural villages** of up to 50 houses in southwest North America

c.500 Hagha kings rule in Ghana, West Africa

c.500 Tiahuanaco culture emerges in Bolivia

c.500 Paracas culture flourishes in southern Peru

c.500 Expansion of **Huari** culture in central Andes

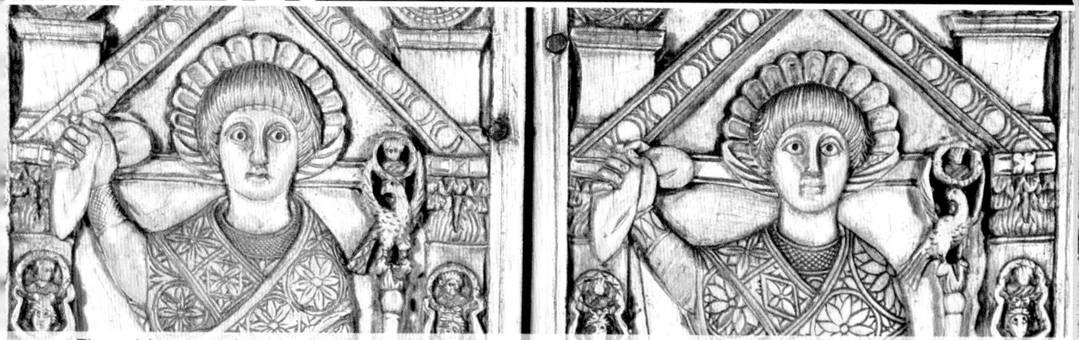

These 6th-century ivory panels show Emperor Anastasius. He amassed a vast financial surplus, which his successors spent on expanding the Eastern Roman Empire.

This 6th-century mosaic, from the curch of San Vitale, Ravenna, Italy, depicts Emperor Justinian with his retinue of officials, guards, and clergy.

IN THE EASTERN ROMAN EMPIRE (generally called the **Byzantine Empire** from about this date), **Anastasius** (r.491–518) faced difficulties in the Balkans, as new groups, including the **Bulgars**, pressed southwards across the Danube between 493 and 502. More serious were **problems on the eastern frontier**, where the **Persians** insisted on Byzantine financial subsidies to pay for the defence of strategic passes in the Caucasus against barbarian incursions. In 502, the **Persian ruler Kavadh** began a war over the issue; the slow Byzantine reaction allowed him to capture Amida as well as several towns in Armenia. Byzantine forces retook Amida in 505, and Kavadh – preoccupied with a Hepthalite invasion in the east – agreed a truce, which lasted until 527.

Anastasius was almost 60 when he **became emperor** in 491, and his place on the throne was only secured by his marriage in 492 to Ariadne, widow of his predecessor **Zeno**. Almost immediately Zeno's brother **Longinus** revolted, and it took six years for Anastasius to subdue Longinus's home area of **Isauria** (in western Asia Minor). Anastasius gained popularity by abolishing the **chrysargyron tax** for traders and craftsmen. Prosperity continued and over his reign his treasury amassed a surplus of 320,000 pounds of gold. He also implemented monetary reforms in 498 and 512 aimed at stabilizing the currency, which had suffered successive debasements in the 5th century. In religious terms Anastasius's reign was less tranquil, as he was a follower of **Monophysite Christianity**, which held that Christ had only a single divine nature and did not combine human and divine in his person. At first, Anastasius supported Zeno's **Henotikon** – an "act of union" issued in 482 that tried to broker a compromise between supporters of the orthodox creed (established at the Council of Chalcedon in 452) and the Monophysites. However, later his attitude became more pro-Monophysite, which led to serious rioting in 512, and the revolt of an army officer, Vitalian, in Thrace in 513. Anastasius left no clear heir, and on his death **Justin** (r.518–27), head of the palace guard, seized the throne. Justin was of humble origins and relied heavily on his nephew **Justinian**. He restored **Chalcedonian Christianity** and developed good relations with the **Ostrogoths** of Italy and the **Vandals** of North Africa. Abroad, his reign was generally peaceful, apart from a minor campaign against Persia in early 527.

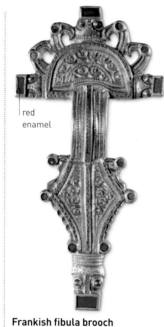

Frankish fibula brooch
Fibula brooches were practical as well as decorative, being used to fasten clothes. This brooch is decorated with the heads of birds.

In Gaul, **Clovis, king of the Franks**, had defeated Syagrius, ruler of a Roman enclave near Soissons, in 486, followed by the Alamanns and the Thuringians in 491. The **Visigothic kingdom** in southwestern Gaul was his next target, and it collapsed after a major Frankish victory at Vouillé in 507. Clovis's marriage to Clotilde, daughter of the Burgundian king Chilperic, led him to convert to **Catholic Christianity** in the 490s, and he maintained cordial relations with the Byzantine emperor Anastasius, who gave him the title of consul *c.*508. Near the end of his reign, Clovis added several previously independent Frankish domains to his kingdom, notably that of the Ripuarian Franks. On his death in 511, Clovis's kingdom was divided among his four sons – Theuderic, Childebert, Chlodomir, and Chlothar. This tradition of subdivision would weaken the **Merovingian dynasty**, as the descendants of Clovis were known. The Merovingians ruled Francia (France) until the 8th century.

THE REIGN OF THE BYZANTINE EMPEROR JUSTINIAN (r.527–65) began with important reforms. In 528, he commissioned a new law code to replace the confusion he had inherited. The new code, the **Codex Justinianus**, came into force in 529 (revised in 534). An enthusiastic builder, Justinian ordered the building of the great church of **Hagia Sophia** in 534. The greatest challenge to his rule came in 532, when rioting among the Blue and Green chariot-racing factions got out of hand and turned into the **Nika Revolt**. The uprising almost caused Justinian to flee Constantinople, and its suppression killed 30,000 rebels.

With his throne secure, Justinian looked abroad. In 533 he sent an army under **Belisarius** to Vandal-controlled North Africa, where **Gelimer** had deposed King Hilderic, a Byzantine ally. On 13 September, Belisarius defeated Gelimer's army at **Ad Decimum**, just outside Carthage, and Vandal resistance collapsed. Carthage was occupied and Gelimer was sent as a captive to Constantinople.

The rapid conquest of the **Vandal kingdom** encouraged Justinian to intervene in Italy. An excuse was provided by the murder in April 535 of his friend **Amalasuintha**, the Ostrogothic queen. Belisarius launched a strike against Italy in 535, landing on Sicily with 7,000 troops. Sicily was secured by the end of 535, and Belisarius moved into southern Italy early in 536. He took Naples after a three-week siege, causing the Ostrogothic king, **Vitigis**, to retreat northwards. On 9 December 536, in a symbolic restoration of the empire's lost provinces, the **Byzantine army occupied Rome**. Rome was soon besieged by Goths. Belisarius finally took the Ostrogothic capital of **Ravenna** in 540. Suspicions that he planned to become emperor led to his recall, encouraging more Ostrogothic resistance.

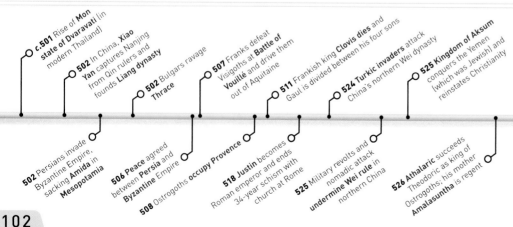

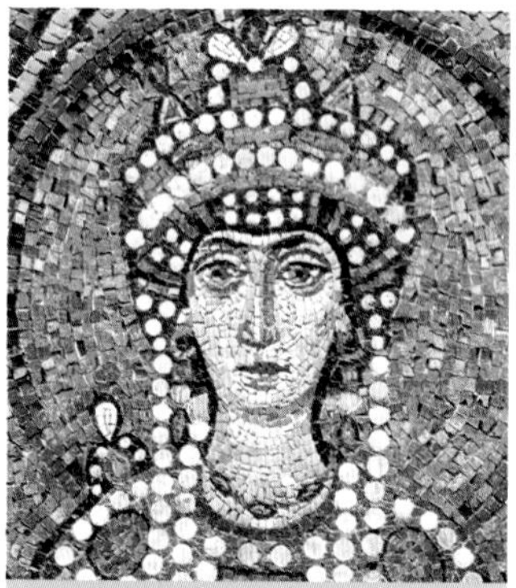

THEODORA (*c.*500–548)

Theodora, who Justinian married in 525, had once been a prostitute and the mistress of Hecebolus, the governor of Libya Pentapolis. After the death of his adoptive mother, Empress Lucipina (who had opposed their relationship), Justinian had the law changed in 524 to allow him to marry Theodora. Theodora became a forceful empress, stiffening Justinian's resolve during the Nika revolt and acting as the protector of Monophysite Christians – she was one herself – during times of persecution.

c.501 Rise of **Mon state of Dvaravati** (in modern Thailand)

502 In China, **Xiao Yan** captures Nanjing from Qin rulers and founds **Liang dynasty**

502 Persians invade Byzantine Empire, sacking **Amida** in **Mesopotamia**

502 Bulgars ravage **Thrace**

506 Peace agreed between **Persia** and **Byzantine** Empire

507 Franks defeat Visigoths at **Battle of Vouillé** and drive them out of Aquitaine

508 Ostrogoths **occupy Provence**

511 Frankish king **Clovis dies** and Gaul is divided between his four sons

518 Justin becomes Roman emperor and ends 34-year schism with church at Rome

524 Turkic invaders attack China's northern Wei dynasty

525 Military revolts and nomadic attack **undermine Wei rule** in northern China

525 Kingdom of Aksum conquers the Yemen (which was Jewish) and reinstates Christianity

526 Athalaric succeeds Theodoric as king of Ostrogoths; his mother **Amalasuntha** is regent

527 Justinian, nephew of Justin, becomes **Byzantine ruler**

529 Issuing of **Justinian's Code**, reforming Roman law

529 Platonic Academy at Athens closed down by Justinian

529 Korean state of **Silla** expands at the expense of states in the southwest

530 Byzantine general **Belisarius** defeats Persians at Dara

531 Khusrau I becomes Sasanian ruler of Persia

531 Justinian tries to enlist **Aksum** as an ally in war against Persia

532 In Constantinople, **Nike Revolt** threatens to overthrow Justinian

532 Peace treaty between Khusrau I and Justinian

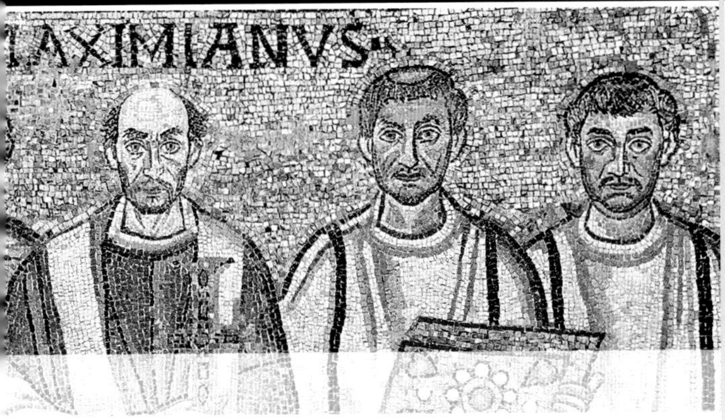

> **“** THE **PLAGUE** FELL **UPON** THE WHOLE **WORLD… NOT A SINGLE MAN** IN THE **WHOLE ROMAN EMPIRE** COULD **ESCAPE… ”**

Procopius, Byzantine scholar, from *Secret History, c.*550

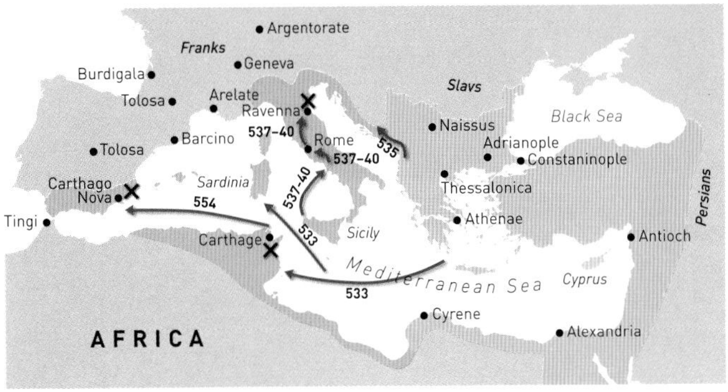

Justinian's reconquests
Vandal Italy fell to Justinian's armies in 533, but it was devastated by the 20-year war needed to take it. An attempted Byzantine reconquest of Spain foundered, capturing only a few coastal areas.

KEY
- Byzantine Empire, 527
- Justinian's reconquests
- → Byzantine campaigns
- ✕ Battle

Persia entered a new period of greatness under **Khusrau I** (r.531–79), who came to the throne at a time when the Mazdakites – a populist religious movement – had caused serious social tensions. Khusrau **reformed the tax system** and established **a new army**, encouraging poorer nobles and their followers to serve by paying salaries. Khusrau **captured Antioch** in 540, forcing Justinian to pay 5,000 pounds of gold to regain it. He attacked again, in 544, but a siege of Edessa failed and so he made a truce. A further Byzantine–Persian war (546–51) resulted in a **50-year peace**.

> **“** TO ME, AND TO MANY OTHERS, **THESE TWO SEEMED NOT** TO BE **HUMAN BEINGS, BUT** VERITABLE **DEMONS… VAMPIRES. ”**

Procopius, Byzantine scholar, on Justinian and Empress Theodora, from *Secret History, c.*550

THE LATTER PART OF JUSTINIAN'S REIGN lacked the achievements of its first half. A serious outbreak of **plague** – probably bubonic plague – began in Egypt in 540 and caused widespread mortalities, robbing the empire of desperately needed manpower. **Tax revenues fell**, further weakening the administration, and **prices rose**, leading to the passing of laws in 544 to reduce inflation. Further outbreaks of plague occurred in the 6th and 7th centuries, sapping the vitality of the Byzantine Empire.

In Italy, the **Ostrogoths** made rapid advances after the departure of **Belisarius**. Their new king, **Totila**, secured the area north of the River Po, and in 542 took control of much of central Italy. Belisarius was recalled to retrieve the sitiation in 544, but Justinian starved him of resources and **Rome fell** in 546. Although the Byzantines retook Rome in 547, it fell once more to Totila in 550. Justinian sent two huge armies under **Artabanes** and **Narses** to finish off the Goths. Artabanes entered Ravenna in June 552, and in July Narses defeated Totila at the **Battle of Busta Gallorum** in the Apennines. Totila later died of his wounds. There was still some Ostrogoth resistance, but the war in Italy was effectively over.

Ostrogothic brooch
This gold and enamel brooch demonstrates the high level of workmanship in the Ostrogothic kingdom of Italy. Its eagle imagery may indicate Roman influence.

- **533–34** Belisarius conquers the **Vandal kingdom** of North Africa
- **534 Burgundian kingdom** absorbed by Franks
- **535 Wei dynasty** splits into eastern and western halves
- **c.535 Nubia** divided into three kingdoms: Nobatia, Alodia, and Mukuria
- **536** Belisarius takes **Rome**
- **537** Rome beseiged by **Ostrogoths**
- **538 Buddhism** reaches Japan
- **c.540** Ethiopian monks **translate the Bible** into their own language
- **540** Byzantines capture **Ravenna**, the Ostrogothic capital
- **540 Bulgars** reach walls of Constantinople
- **542** Outbreak of **plague** in Constantinople kills many thousands
- **543** Nubian kingdom of **Nobatia** converted to Christianity by Coptic missionaries
- **544 Viet kingdom** of Vietnam established
- **546** Ostrogothic king **Totila captures Rome**, which falls again soon after to Belisarius
- **547 Rebellion of Berber tribes** breaks out in North Africa, but is crushed by Byzantine army
- **548** Nanjing sacked as Hou Jing leads rebellion against **Liang dynasty**
- **550** Byzantine general Belisarius replaced by **Narses**; Rome falls again to Ostrogoths
- **c.550** Turkic **Avar** peoples begin to migrate westwards
- **c.550 Khmer** state of **Chenla** throws off suzerainty of Funan
- **c.550** Nubian kingdom of **Alodia** converted to Coptic Christianity

The 13th-century Iona Abbey (pictured) was built on the site of the original monastery founded by St Columba when he arrived on Iona in 563.

MEROVINGIAN FRANCIA (FRANCE) HAD BEEN DIVIDED into separate kingdoms on the death of Clovis in 511 (see 501–526). Despite this, Frankish power continued to grow. By 558, **Chlothar I** (511–61), who ruled the area of Francia around Soissons, had absorbed the Rheims kingdom and the region around Paris after their rulers died. This left Chlothar as the **sole Merovingian ruler of Francia** for three years, until his death in 561. Francia was once again divided, with Charibert I receiving Paris, Guntram getting Orléans, Sigibert Rheims, and Chilperic Soissons. It was not until 613 that the Frankish kingdom was reunited under **Chlothar II** (r.613–29).

Ireland had been converted to Christianity by **Patrick** (d.461) in the mid-5th century and a strong **monastic tradition** took hold there. From the 6th century, Irish monks began conducting missions abroad. In 563, **Columba** (*c.*520–97) set up the **abbey of Iona** on an island off Scotland's western coast. Iona became a centre of Irish-influenced monasticism, which extended into northern England, Scotland, and Francia with the foundation of the monastic centre at Luxeuil in 590.

The **Gupta Empire fell apart** after the reign of Vishnugupta (r.540–50); and northern India split into a number of **regional kingdoms**. A minor branch of the Guptas ruled Magadha, but they were swept aside by the Maukharis of Kanauj. The region fell to the Vardhana king **Harsha**, who established an empire in the early 7th century.

" WHEN **JUSTIN** HAD HEARD THESE EVENTS... HE HAD **NO HEALTHY** OR **SANE THOUGHTS...** HE **FELL INTO** A **MENTAL DISORDER** AND **MADNESS** AND AFTERWARDS HAD **NO UNDERSTANDING OF EVENTS. "**

Evagrius Scholasticus, scholar and aide to Gregory of Antioch, on Justin II's reaction on the fall of Dara to the Persians, from *Ecclesiastical History c.*595

JAPAN'S SOGA FAMILY CAME TO PROMINENCE IN 540, when **Soga no Iname** was made chief minister. **Emperor Bidatsu's death** in 585 led to a succession dispute, from which Iname's grandson **Yomei** emerged successful. The next emperor, **Sushun** (r.586–93), had a Soga mother, reinforcing the family's dominance. When Sushun was assassinated in 593, he was succeeded by Bidatsu's widow **Suiko** (r.593–628), who was another Soga. Suiko's reign saw the start of the **Asuka Enlightenment**, and was a time of great confidence in foreign affairs, state support for Buddhism, and flourishing arts.

In 572, the Byzantine emperor **Justin II** (r.565–78) went to **war with Persia** after he refused to pay a tribute due under the terms of Justinian's 50-year peace deal (see 527–540). In 573, Persia struck back, invading Syria and taking the fortress of Dara. On hearing this, Justin went insane. His wife took power, and had to agree a humiliating peace with Persia.

7 THE NUMBER OF **YEARS** THE **"ENDLESS PEACE"** OF 532 **BETWEEN** THE **BYZANTINE EMPIRE** AND **PERSIA LASTED**

In 567, the **Lombards**, who had settled in the former Roman province of Pannonia (Hungary), destroyed the Gepids and then, under **Alboin** (reign *c.*560–72), moved southwest into Italy, where the Byzantine authorities were too weak to resist them. In 568–69 they **occupied the plain of the Po River** and set up dukes in major cities. By 572, when Pavia fell to them, they had founded duchies as far south as Benevento. Attempted **Byzantine counterattacks** in 575 were a disaster. Under **Agilulf** (r.590–616) the Lombard kingdom consolidated; the Byzantines were limited to small territories around Rome, Naples, and Ravenna.

Under **Khan Bayan** (r.*c.*562–82), the **Avars** – nomadic horsemen from the northern Caucasus – exploited the vacuum left by the departure of the Lombards to **carve out a vast territory** centred around modern Austria. Their conquest of a number of Byzantine towns prompted **Emperor Maurice** (r.582–602) into a successful campaign to dislodge them.

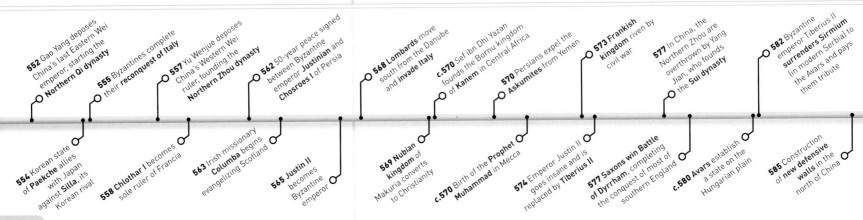

Ajanta cave art
The Ajanta caves, a Buddhist holy site in Maharashtra, India, experienced a second major phase of use during the 6th century.

- **552** Gao Yang deposes China's last Eastern Wei emperor, starting the **Northern Qi dynasty**
- **554** Korean state of **Paekche** allies with Japan against **Silla**, its Korean rival
- **555** Byzantines complete their **reconquest of Italy**
- **557** Yu Wenjue deposes China's Western Wei ruler, founding the **Northern Zhou dynasty**
- **558 Chlothar I** becomes sole ruler of Francia
- **562** 50-year peace signed between Byzantine emperor **Justinian** and **Chosroes I** of Persia
- **563** Irish missionary **Columba** begins evangelizing Scotland
- **565 Justin II** becomes Byzantine emperor
- **568 Lombards** move south from the Danube and **invade Italy**
- **569 Nubian kingdom** of Makuria converts to Christianity
- **c.570** Sef ibn Dhi Yazan founds the Bornu kingdom of **Kanem** in Central Africa
- **c.570** Birth of the **Prophet Muhammad** in Mecca
- **570** Persians expel the **Askumites** from Yemen
- **573 Frankish kingdom** riven by civil war
- **574** Emperor Justin II goes insane and is replaced by **Tiberius II**
- **577** In China, the Northern Zhou are overthrown by Yang Jian, who founds the **Sui dynasty**
- **577 Saxons win Battle of Dyrrham**, completing the conquest of most of southern England
- **c.580 Avars** establish a state on the Hungarian plain
- **582** Byzantine emperor Tiberius II **surrenders Sirmium** (in modern Serbia) to the Avars and pays them tribute
- **585** Construction of **new defensive walls** in the north of China

Painted *c.*581–618, this fresco is from China's Dunhuang caves, in a strategic Silk Road oasis. The caves contain some of the finest examples of Buddhist art.

IN 581, YIANG JIAN, A GENERAL OF THE ZHOU RULERS of northern China, rebelled and took the throne for himself as the emperor **Wendi** (r.581–604). In 589, he invaded southern China. His forces rapidly overcame those of the last Chen emperor, **Hou Zhu**. Wendi was now the country's sole ruler and the first emperor of the **Sui dynasty**; after three centuries of division, **China** was finally **united**. Wendi disarmed private armies and established agricultural colonies along China's frontiers to strengthen central control in remote areas. He implemented a **major land reform** that increased the number of households liable to the land tax from 4 million in 589, to almost 9 million in 606. Wendi also extended the country's canal system to form a "**Grand Canal**" that allowed vessels to travel 2,000km (1,240 miles) from Hangzhuo in the southeast to the northeastern provinces around Beijing, via Luoyang in eastern central China. Austere, strict, and occasionally violent, Wendi seemed to have set the Sui dynasty on firm foundations; in the end, it lasted only 14 years after his death, when it was replaced by the Tang.

“NOT **ANGLES,** BUT **ANGELS.**”

Pope Gregory I, on seeing Anglo-Saxon slaves at a market in Rome

In 582, **Emperor Maurice** succeeded **Tiberius II** (r.578–82) as the Byzantine emperor. He had been commander of the palace guard and then of the war against the Persians from 578. Tiberius's overspending and ineffective campaigns against the Persians, Lombards, and Avars had **emptied the imperial treasury**, leaving Maurice facing an immediate financial crisis. His subsequent economizing led to **mutinies** by the eastern army in 588 and by that of the Balkans in 593. Maurice made his father Paul head of the Senate and his brother-in-law **Philippicus** head of the palace guard; such nepotism further increased his unpopularity.

In 584, Maurice **renewed the war with Persia**, appointing Philippicus to oversee it. The new commander attacked Arzanene, but his campaign was disrupted by the **defection** of **the Ghassanid Arabs** – former allies alienated by the arrest of their king, al-Mundhir. The mutiny of the eastern troops in 588 caused Byzantine efforts to stall further, and in 589 they lost the city of **Martyropolis** (in present-day Turkey) to the Persians. The Byzantines were saved by the outbreak of a civil war in Persia; the involvement of a Byzantine army in the restoration of one Persian claimant, **Chosroes II**, led to the recovery of Martyropolis and Dara in 592.

In the Balkans, the **Slavs** – a non-Germanic people referred to as "Sclaveni" in contemporary sources – seem to have arrived north of the Danube in the early to mid-6th century. When the Avars moved into the region in *c.*559 the Slavs were pushed further south. By the end of the 6th century, Slavic groups had settled as far south as northern Greece, the Dalmatian coast of the Adriatic, and Macedonia, as well as in those areas of Bulgaria, Bohemia, Moravia, Serbia, and Croatia where the great Slav kingdoms of the Middle Ages would later arise.

In 596, **Pope Gregory I** sent a mission to Britain to revive Christianity, following the invasions by **pagan Anglo-Saxons** in the 5th and early 6th centuries. The missionaries set out under **Augustine**, a former prior of a monastery in Rome, and arrived in Kent the following year. Their reception was reasonably warm as Bertha, the wife of the **Kentish king Aethelberht**, was already Christian. After Aethelberht was baptized a Christian, Augustine was able to establish a church in Canterbury. **King Saebert of Essex** and **King Sigebert of East Anglia** – both dependent on Kent – also converted, but the infant English Church would suffer a series of setbacks before the last Anglo-Saxon kingdoms became Christian in the late 7th century.

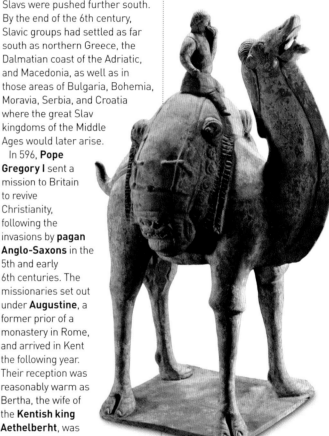

POPE GREGORY I (590–604)

From 572 to 574 Gregory I was prefect of Rome, and only became a monk on his father's death. A man of great ability and energy, he was involved in resistance to the Lombards in Italy in the early part of his papacy, but he maintained good relations with the Merovingians in Francia and the Visigothic rulers of Spain. Relations with the Byzantine emperor Maurice broke down over the use of the title "ecumenical patriarch" by the Bishop of Constantinople, which Gregory viewed as a challenge to his authority.

Sui dynasty figurine
This figure depicting a trader on a camel emphasizes China's continuing concern with commerce along the Silk Road through Central Asia.

589 Visigothic king Recared announces conversion of the country to **Catholicism** at Council of Toledo

589 The western Turks based in Dzungaria, control the **Silk Road**

589 Chosroes II deposed as Persian ruler by a military uprising under Bahram; he flees to Constantinople

589 Yang Jian captures the Yan capital, **reuniting China**

589 Byzantines lose city of **Martyropolis** to the Persians (retaken in 592)

589 Land reform implemented by Sui emperor Wendi in China

590 Slavs begin to move into the **Balkans**

590 Gregory I ("the Great") becomes pope

591 Byzantines restore Chosroes II to the Persian throne

592 Emperor Maurice launches **Byzantine counterattack** against the Slavs in the Balkans

592 Civil war breaks out in China between the pro-Buddhist **Soga** and anti-Buddhist **Mononobe** clans

593 Mutiny of Byzantine army in the Balkans

595 Indian mathematicians use the **decimal system**

597 St Augustine begins mission to convert England to Christianity

598 Byzantines agree treaty with the Lombards, **conceding northern Italy** to them

4

TRADE AND INVENTION 600–1449

In the Medieval period, trade and travel unified the Old World in a single network, with new ideas and inventions emerging even as the political landscape was transformed. Meanwhile, in the New World, great civilizations reached their peak.

600–610

A coin depicting the Eastern Roman emperor Heraclius.

UPHEAVAL IN THE EASTERN ROMAN EMPIRE began when the emperor Maurice (r.582–602) dispatched his armies to the northern Balkans to regain imperial control of the Danube frontier from the Avars (see 568–88). In 602, the army rebelled under officer Phocas and Maurice was killed. **Phocas became emperor** but **Chosroes II** of Sasanian Persia **took advantage** of the eastern empire's weakness, while the Avars invaded from the north. In 610 the son of the military governor of Roman Africa, **Heraclius**, executed Phocas and declared himself emperor.

In 606, in northern India, Harsha (c.590–647) acceded to the thrones of Thanesar and Kannauj, establishing the **last native Indian empire** of ancient times.

> “THE **EMPEROR HARSHA,** NOBLE IN **BIRTH** AND OF WELL-CHOSEN **NAME,** THE SURPASSER OF **ALL THE VICTORIES WON** BY ALL THE KINGS OF ANCIENT TIMES...”

Banabhatta, Indian poet, from *The Deeds of Harsha, c.640*

611–620

A Tang dynasty Mendicant friar, with an unusual travelling companion.

Tang dynasty horse sculpture
Horses were symbols of military prowess, especially warhorses from the western fringes of the empire.

SASANIAN CONQUESTS RESTORED THE PERSIAN EMPIRE at the expense of the **Byzantines** with the falls of Jerusalem in 614 and Egypt in 619. By 618, Constantinople was besieged by the Avars, and their Slavic subjects. In 620, Heraclius bought off the Avars in order to focus on repelling the Persians.

In 613 **Clothar II** (584–629) **reunited the Frankish kingdom**, bringing an end to civil war. His Edict of Paris, issued in 614, introduced reforms to the Merovingian church and state.

In 616–17, rebellions against the despotic rule of Yangdi (r.604–17) caused the collapse of the Sui dynasty in China. A year later military governor **Li Yuan founded the Tang dynasty**, which ruled until 906.

621–630

This 1721 engraving by Austrian architect Johann Fischer von Erlach shows Al-Haram Mosque and Ka'aba in Mecca.

MUHAMMAD FIRST RECEIVED A DIVINE REVELATION IN 610 and began to preach in Mecca from 613; but the start of the Islamic era is traditionally marked by the Hegira or *hijra*, the **flight to Medina**. Hostility from the Meccan authorities forced Muhammad to flee to Medina with his family and followers in 622. In Medina, Muhammad established a political and religious power base. He fought a series of attacks by Meccan forces, with their ultimate surrender in 630 when he took possession of the Ka'aba, the holiest shrine in the Arabian Peninsula. Muhammad's rule was then unchallenged.

Heraclius began to claw back territory ceded to the Persians, starting at the Battle of Issus in 622 and later, in 627, at the Battle of Nineveh. In 628 the **Sasanian and Byzantine Empires** made peace, exhausted by decades of war and unaware of the storm brewing to the south.

In China the emperor's son, **Taizong, consolidated Tang power** by suppressing rebellions across the empire. In 626, Taizong forced his father to step down and inaugurated a golden age of trade, prosperity, and cultural exchange.

MUHAMMAD (570–632)

Born in Mecca, Muhammad ibn Abdallah worked as a merchant and shepherd before growing discontented and retiring to a life of contemplation. In 610, he received the first of a series of divine revelations – these became the Qu'ran. He preached a monotheistic faith based on complete submission to God (Islam). Before his death he unified Arabian tribes within his new religion.

631–640

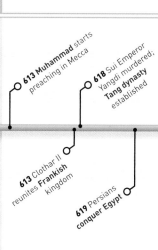

The ruins of the 7th century Byzantine fortresses at Sbeitla, Tunisia.

BY THE TIME OF MUHAMMAD'S DEATH IN 632, the young Muslim community – united by Islam, which transcended traditional rivalries – was ready for expansion. Although Muhammad had left no guidance as to his successor (caliph), four men tied to the prophet by marriage emerged as the Rashidun, or "rightly guided", caliphs. **The first caliph, Abu Bakr** (r. 632–34), suppressed an Arabian rebellion, re-established Islamic dominion over Arabia, and began the conquest of Syria. His successor **Umar** (r.634–44) **became caliph** in 634 and oversaw the conquest of **Syria** and the defeat of the Byzantines at Ajnadayn. By 637, Umar controlled Jerusalem and Damascus, and, in the same year, Arab forces conquered **Persia** (modern Iran and Iraq), occupying the Sasanian capital at Ctesiphon. **Umar established several important practices**: the creation of garrison towns in conquered territory to separate the invading Arabic forces from the locals; the recruitment of soldiers through slavery and tribal

> “THOSE WHO ARE **PATIENT IN ADVERSITY** AND FORGIVE WRONGS ARE THE DOERS OF EXCELLENCE.”

Prophet Muhammad

---

602 Eastern Roman emperor **Maurice** killed; **Phocas** succeeds him

602 Emperor Yangdi orders construction of Grand Canal; completed 610

606 Harsha begins conquest of northern **India**

610 Heraclius becomes Eastern Roman Emperor

613 Muhammad starts preaching in Mecca

613 Clothar II reunites **Frankish** kingdom

618 Sui Emperor Yangdi murdered; **Tang dynasty** established

619 Persians conquer Egypt

622 Battle of Issus, first in a string of **victories for Heraclius** over Persians

624 Northern **China subdued** by Tang

626 Tang Emperor overthrown by his son, **Taizong**

628 Sasanian king Chosroes II "the victorious" deposed and slain by his son

629 Dagobert succeeds Clothar II as king of all the franks

630 Heraclius reaches zenith of his power and fame by marching triumphantly into Jerusalem

630 Xuanxang reaches India on his epic journey to the west

632 Death of the prophet **Muhammad**; start of caliphate

634 Death of caliph **Abu Bakr**; **Umar** becomes second caliph

635 Nestorian Christians reach China

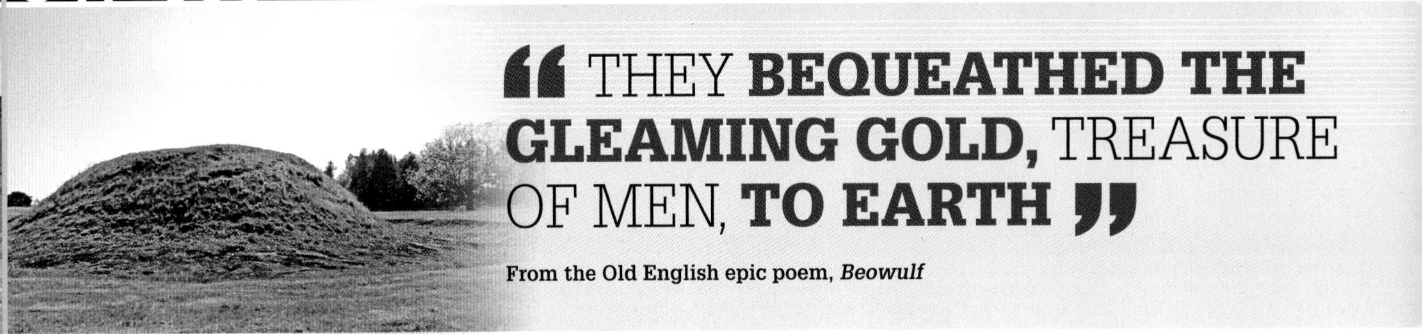

“ THEY **BEQUEATHED THE GLEAMING GOLD,** TREASURE OF MEN, **TO EARTH** ”

From the Old English epic poem, *Beowulf*

One of 20 burial mounds of this type at Sutton Hoo, Suffolk, England, which conceal the graves and funerary treasures of the royal line of East Anglia.

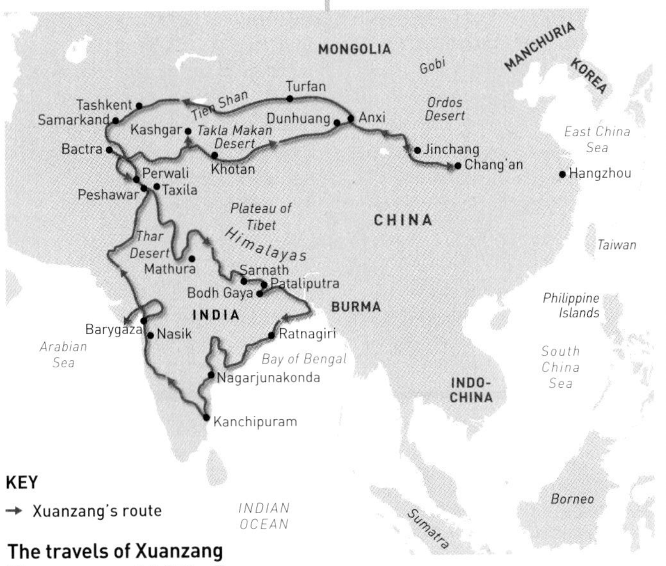

The travels of Xuanzang
The young monk left the Tang capital, Chang'an, in around 630. He crossed Central Asia and reached India in 645.

affiliation – those recruited for fighting were made dependents of tribal members; and a taxation system that favoured Muslims and encouraged conversion but allowed Christians and Jews to follow their religions.

Buddhism became increasingly influential in Tang China; the Buddhist monk **Xuanzang** journeyed far and wide in search of wisdom. His travels became legendary and foresaw the increasing mobility of people and ideas along the **Silk Road**, made possible by the power of the Tang and later the caliphate. Also travelling the Silk Road, **Nestorian Christians** reached **China** from Persia in 635.

ISLAMIC EXPANSION CONTINUED as the Arabs defeated the Persian counterattack at the Battle of Nihavand in 642, **dealing the final blow to the Sasanian Empire**; the last emperor, Yazdgird III, died in 651, and with him died Zoroastrianism, the religion of the empire. Conversion of the population to **Islam** proceeded slowly but steadily over the following centuries. The Arabs met with similar success in Egypt where the Byzantines offered only token resistance. The **fall of Alexandria** came in 642, the same year that the Muslims founded the military settlement of Fustat, which later became Cairo. The following year the marauding Islamic armies conquered Tripolitania in North Africa as their advance continued,

27 METRES

THE LENGTH OF THE SUTTON HOO SHIP

unchecked even by the assassination in 644 of Umar by a Persian slave. His successor, **Uthman**, promulgated the **first written version of the Qu'ran**, which had previously been transmitted orally.

After launching successful expeditions against the Tibetans and Mongolians, but failing to conquer Korea, the **Tang emperor Taizong** (r.626–49) **died** in 649, and his weak-willed son began to cede increasing influence to the **Empress Wu** (624–705). In Japan, the **Fujiwara** clan enacted the **Taika reforms** in 646, bringing all land into imperial ownership and centralizing power following the Chinese model.

In **England**, Christian converts battled pagan kings for control over territory and the religious and cultural direction of the region. In 642, for instance, the Christian king **Oswald of Northumbria**, hitherto one of the most powerful kingdoms, was slain by the pagan king **Penda of Mercia**. The great Anglo-Saxon ship burial at **Sutton Hoo**, Suffolk – filled with marvellously worked artefacts, weapons and treasures – is believed to have once contained the body of an **Anglo Saxon king**. One of the last burials of this type in England, the artefacts comprise a fusion of Christian and non-Christian elements, suggesting transition as **Christianity** gained in popularity and strength.

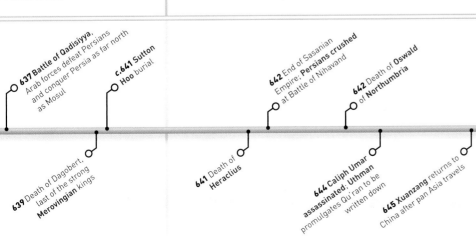

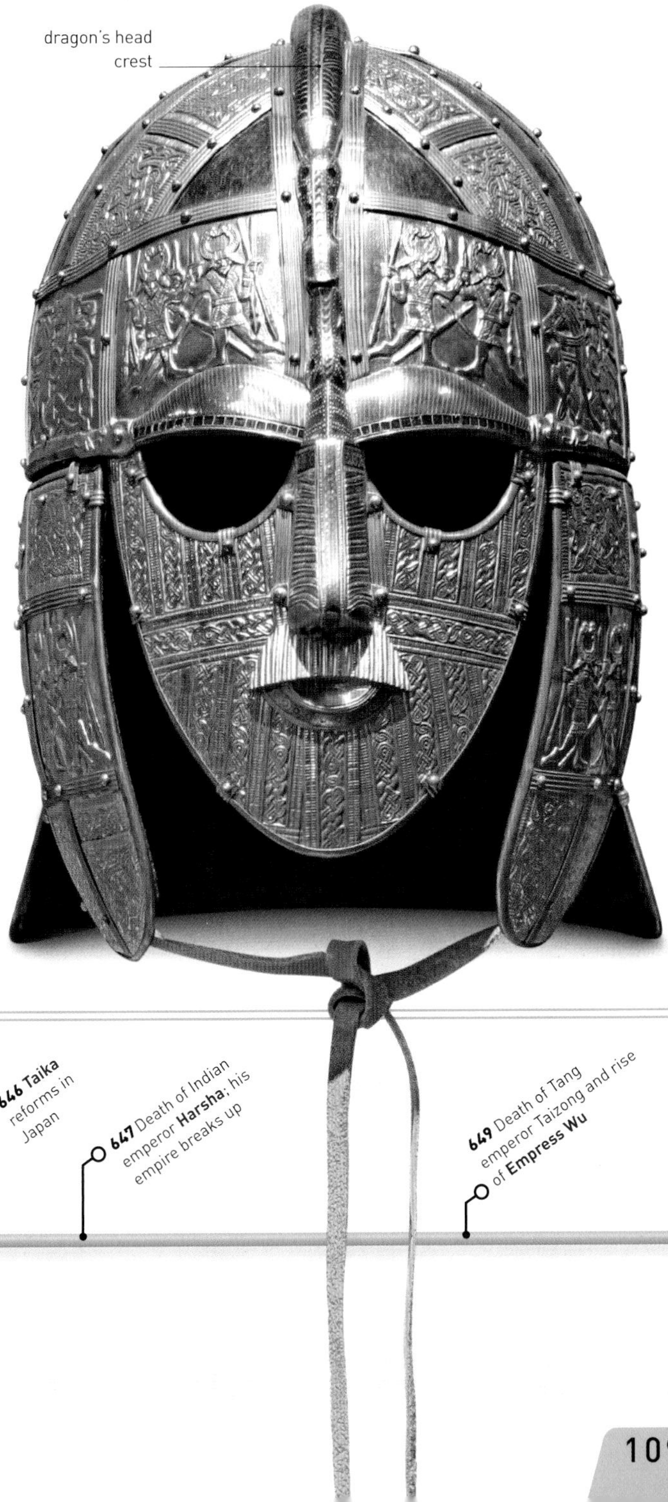

Sutton Hoo helmet
This reconstruction is made from iron with highly-decorated panels of tinned bronze.

637 Battle of Qadisiyya. Arab forces defeat Persians and conquer Persia as far north as Mosul

639 Death of Dagobert, last of the strong **Merovingian** kings

c.641 Sutton Hoo burial

641 Death of **Heraclius**

642 End of Sasanian Empire; **Persians crushed** at Battle of Nihavand

642 Death of **Oswald** of **Northumbria**

644 Caliph Umar assassinated; Uthman promulgates Qu'ran to be written down

645 Xuanzang returns to China after pan Asia travels

646 Taika reforms in Japan

647 Death of Indian emperor **Harsha**; his empire breaks up

649 Death of Tang emperor Taizong and rise of **Empress Wu**

651–670

The weathered landscape of central Anatolia, a Byzantine territory that suffered repeated raids from Arab forces in the 7th century.

THE SPLIT BETWEEN SUNNI AND SHIITE MUSLIMS was the outcome of fierce disagreement over how succession to the caliphate ought to be decided; either by selection (as in the case of the first three caliphs) or by hereditary descent. Caliph Uthman (r. 644–56) had promoted members of his own clan, the **Umayyads**. He was assassinated in 656 by Egyptian soldiers, nursing grievances over their lower status. **Ali Ibn Abi Talib** became the **fourth caliph**. As Muhammad's cousin and son-in-law – next in line by descent – Ali enjoyed unique status in the Islamic world, but he faced many challenges. At the **Battle of the Camel** in 656 Ali overcame a revolt by the prophet's widow A'isha and her allies, opposing his inclusive policies. In 657, the Umayyad emir of Syria, **Mu'awiya**, asserted his claim on the caliphate; Ali was also challenged by the Kharijis, a sect who objected to the application of the hereditary principle. In 661, **Ali was murdered** by a Khariji, opening the way for **Mu'awiya to declare himself caliph**, instituting the Arab Umayyad dynasty. Ali's supporters formed a party of their own, which evolved into a distinctive branch of Islam, **the Shiites**, in opposition to the Sunni.

Emperor Constans II attempted to re-establish **Byzantine claims to Italy** by relocating his court to Rome in 663, but raids deep into Anatolia (modern-day Turkey) by Arab forces led to a collapse in his authority; in 668, he was assassinated and **Constantine IV** took the throne. **Arab incursions** into Anatolia continued and by 670 they had reached the Byzantine capital, Constantinople (modern-day Istanbul), launching the **first siege on the city**, which would last until 677.

The **Unified Silla kingdom** in Korea brought to an end the long Three Kingdoms period, with the help of **Tang China**. In 660 the Tang destroyed the kingdom of Paekche, while in 668 Silla and Tang forces combined to overcome Koguryo, thus bringing all of the Korean Peninsula under Silla control.

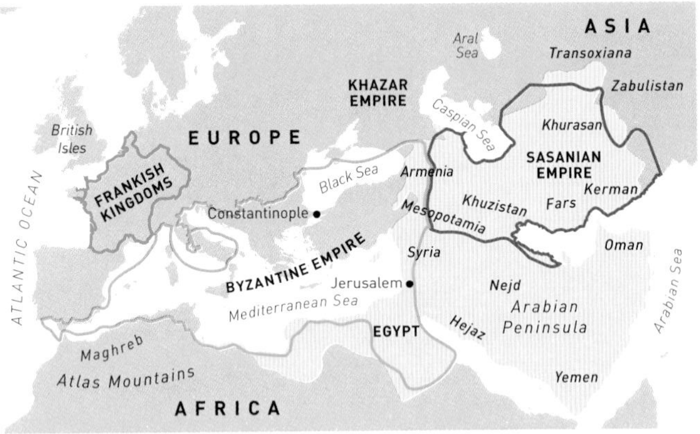

Expansion under the caliphate
The rapid Arab expansion continued throughout the latter half of the 7th century. Islamic armies pushed into Central Asia and North Africa, bringing them within striking distance of Spain.

Stoneware bird
This grey stoneware incense burner dates from the Silla kingdom, which was on the verge of becoming the dominant power during Korea's late Three Kingdoms period.

671–690

A modern-day depiction of the Battle of Karbala; al-Husayn's death is commemorated in the annual Shiite ritual of the ashura.

THE MAYA CITY-STATE OF TIKAL BEGAN ITS RESURGENCE after a century-long period of political and cultural domination by neighbouring city-states known as the Tikal hiatus, which had been marked by an absence of inscriptions in the city's petroglyphic record. An inscription dated to 672 records a military campaign against the **rival city-state of Dos Pilas**, and in the following decades Tikal restored its position among the Maya of the Late Classic period (600–900). The city's rulers engaged in a construction programme to match their political ambitions, **building many impressive structures** including massive pyramids, ball courts, causeways, observatories, and palaces.

The Arab forces besieging the city of Constantinople (see 670) were unable to breach its massive walls and were eventually beaten off with the use of a new **Byzantine secret weapon**– "Greek fire" (see 711–20). Its deployment may also have helped destroy the Arab fleet at the Battle of Syllaeum in 677, forcing **the caliphate to agree a 30-year truce**. The truce bought breathing space for the embattled Byzantine Empire, struggling to hold back the Bulgars, who established the **First Bulgarian Empire** in 681 on conquered Byzantine territory north of the Balkan mountains.

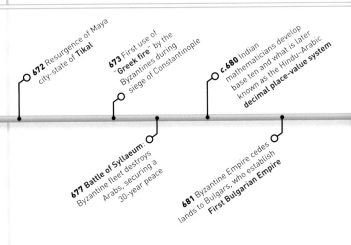

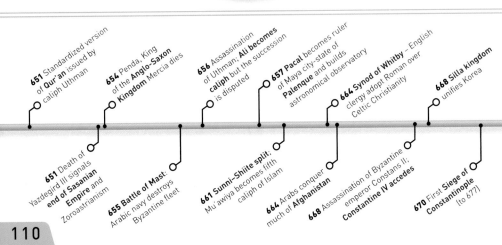

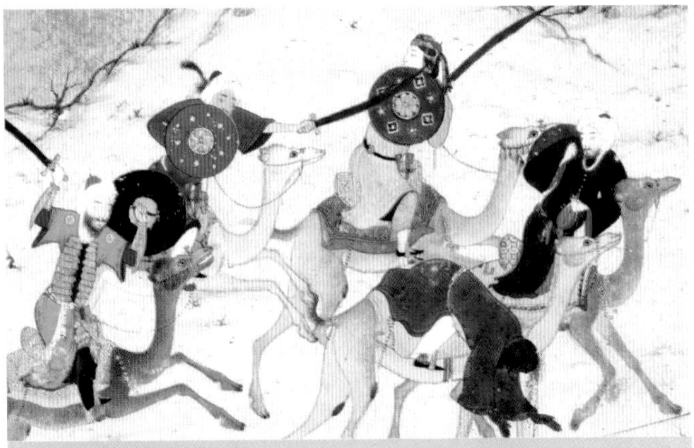

ARAB CONQUESTS

Having consolidated their conquests of Persia and Byzantine North Africa, Arab armies pressed on eastwards and westwards. In Central Asia, Arab forces crossed the Oxus river in 667 and continued to advance to within range of the Silk Road kingdom of Bukhara. In Africa, they crushed the Berber kingdoms, reaching Tangiers in 683.

651 Standardized version of **Qur'an** issued by caliph Uthman

651 Death of Yazdegird III signals **end of Sasanian Empire** and Zoroastrianism

654 Penda, King of the **Anglo-Saxon Kingdom** Mercia dies

655 Battle of Mast: Arabic navy destroys Byzantine fleet

656 Assassination of Uthman; **Ali becomes caliph** but the succession is disputed

657 Pacal becomes ruler of Maya city-state of **Palenque** and builds astronomical observatory

661 Sunni–Shiite split: Mu'awiya becomes fifth caliph of Islam

664 Synod of Whitby – English clergy adopt Roman over Celtic Christianity

664 Arabs conquer much of **Afghanistan**

668 Assassination of Byzantine emperor Constans II; **Constantine IV accedes**

668 Silla kingdom unifies Korea

670 First **Siege of Constantinople** (to 677)

672 Resurgence of Maya city-state of **Tikal**

673 First use of **"Greek fire"** by the Byzantines during siege of Constantinople

677 Battle of Syllaeum: Byzantine fleet destroys Arabs, securing a 30-year peace

c.680 Indian mathematicians develop base ten and what is later known as the Hindu–Arabic **decimal place-value system**

681 Byzantine Empire cedes lands to Bulgars, who establish **First Bulgarian Empire**

Jerusalem's Dome of the Rock – a shrine sacred to all three Abrahamic faiths – has an octagonal floorplan and a massive gold dome.

At the **Battle of Karbala** in 680 the **Shiite leader al-Husayn ibn Ali**, grandson of Muhammad, was surrounded by Umayyad troops, deprived of water for several days, and eventually killed. His death was proclaimed a **martyrdom** by the Shiites, who commemorate it to this day.

In China in 690, the **Empress Wu finally took the throne** in her own name – the only woman in Chinese history to do so – after decades of controlling it through her husband and sons. She even created her own dynasty, **Zhou**, which she headed until 705.

Temple at Tikal
Flanking Tikal's Great Plaza, the 38m (122ft) high Temple II was built during the construction boom of the Late Classic resurgence.

3,000

THE NUMBER OF **MAJOR STONE BUILDINGS** CONSTRUCTED IN TIKAL'S LATE CLASSIC PERIOD

ABD AL-MALIK HAD BECOME CALIPH IN 685, instituting important changes to the way the caliphate was ruled, centralizing government, insisting that all state business was conducted in Arabic, setting up the *barid* (a postal/intelligence gathering service), and issuing, around 697, new coinage: the *dinar* and *dirham*. He also commissioned a great shrine to be built on the Temple Mount in Jerusalem, the **Dome of the Rock** (or Qubbat as-Sakhrah), completed in 692.

The harsh ten-year rule of the **Byzantine emperor Justinian II** had aroused widespread opposition and in 695 he was deposed and had his nose cut off by **Leontius**, who became emperor in his stead. However, in 698, the **loss of Carthage**, the last Byzantine stronghold in North Africa, to the Arabs led to another revolt and Leontius suffered the same fate as his predecessor.

The turn of the century was a time of change and unrest in the Americas. In North America, the spear was superceded by widespread **adoption of the bow and arrow**. In the Valley of Mexico around 700, the great **city-state of Teotihuacán**, which once housed over 100,000 people, **collapsed** bringing six centuries of growth and dominance to an end. Social, economic, and environmental factors were probably to blame.

> **“ I HAVE NOT SEEN THE EQUAL;** NEITHER HAVE I HEARD TELL OF ANYTHING… **THAT COULD RIVAL IN GRACE THIS DOME OF THE ROCK… ”**
>
> **Mukaddasi, Arab geographer**, *c.*10th century

Ancient Teotihuacán mask
This mask was probably tied to a figurine representing a god. The mask would have been decorated with inlays and ear ornaments.

683 Arabs reach Tangiers

690 Empress Wu takes Chinese throne, establishing **Zhou Dynasty** (to 705)

691 Battle of Sebastopolis: Arabs defeat Byzantine emperor **Justinian II** and take Armenia; Justinian massacres defecting Slavs in revenge

692 Dome of the Rock completed

695 Justinian II deposed by **Leontius** and has nose cut off

695 King Jaguar Paw of Maya city-state of Calakmul **captured** and **sacrificed** by forces of Tikal

697 Traditional date of semilegendary first doge of Venice, **Paolo Lucio Anafesto**

698 Arabs conquer and destroy **Carthage**, found Tunis; loss of Carthage causes Leontius to be deposed

c.700 Huare conquer **Moche** in Peru

c.700 Collapse of city of **Teotihuacán** in the Valley of Mexico

c.700 North American Indians adopt **bow and arrow**

701–710

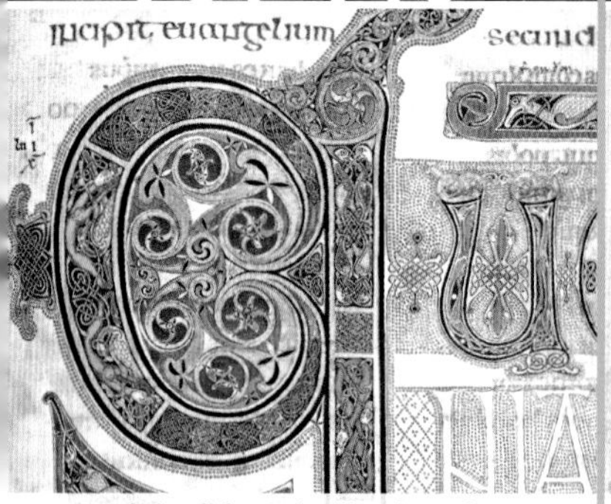

A detail from the illuminated manuscript of the *Lindisfarne Gospels*.

ANGLO-SAXON ART FUSED GERMANIC AND CELTIC ELEMENTS, and, through travellers and Christian pilgrims, it also reflected Roman and Byzantine influences. A product of this unique synthesis was the *Lindisfarne Gospels*, an illuminated manuscript produced *c.*701 at the priory of Lindisfarne, on Holy Island, off the northeast coast of England.

In 705, with the help of Bulgar allies, the deposed emperor **Justinian II returned from exile** (see 690–700), regained the Byzantine throne, and exacted brutal revenge on those who had mutilated him.

By 705, **Zoroastrian refugees** fleeing the Islamic conquest of Persia **established communities in India** and became known as the Parsees. Persian Zoroastrian emigration continued during the following centuries.

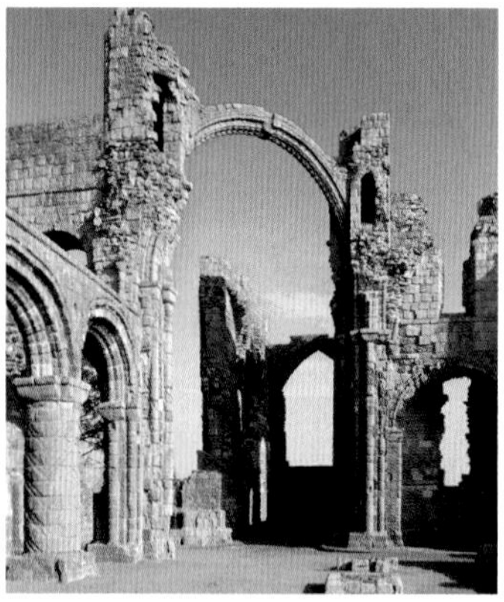

Ruins of Lindisfarne Priory
The Benedictine Priory, built in the 12th century, replaced an earlier church founded by St Aidan in 635.

711–720

Greek fire being deployed, as illustrated in the *Madrid Skylitzes* manuscript from the 12th century, which chronicles the history of the Byzantine Empire.

His favourite concubine
This Tang dynasty scroll shows Xuanzong watching his concubine Yang Guifei mount a horse. The emperor's love for her inspired much drama and poetry.

IN 710, THE VISIGOTHIC KINGDOM OF SPAIN had descended into civil war, presenting a tempting prospect to the Islamic armies now established in North Africa, just a short distance away across the Straits of Gibraltar. In 711, a Muslim army under general **Tariq ibn Ziyad**, landed at Gibraltar. Tariq was a Berber (native of northwestern Africa), or, in the parlance of the times, a Moor, and it was a mixed army of Arabs and Moors that achieved the **conquest of Spain**, known to the Islamic world as **al-Andalus**. According to tradition, Tariq defeated the Visigothic king, Roderick, at the Battle of Guadalete, and by the end of the year most of the Iberian peninsula was under Islamic control. Only the northwest, known as **Asturias, managed to resist the invaders**, with defeat at the Battle of Covadonga in 718 checking the Arab advance. The year 718 is one of the dates traditionally given for the start of the process of Christian reconquest of Spain. Nonetheless, by the end of the decade further expeditions across the Pyrenees, and successful campaigns in Central Asia, had **extended caliphate control** from Provence to the borders of China.

The Arabs did experience some setbacks, however. In 717, yet another incursion into Byzantine lands triggered a change at the head of the empire, bringing **Leo III**, founder of the Isaurian Dynasty, to the throne. Although unable to prevent the Arabs from reaching the walls of the capital and launching the **second siege of Constantinople** (717–18), Leo's energetic command of the defence, and the deployment of the secret weapon **"Greek fire"**, halted Arab advances in the Eastern Mediterranean. Byzantine fleets, wielding Greek fire-spouting siphons, gained control of the seas, and Leo was able to begin restoring the empire.

In 713, the Tang **emperor Xuanzong** came to the throne. His 43-year reign would see **Tang China reach its apogee**, economically and culturally, with the establishment of many schools, patronage of the arts, and a great literary flowering.

GREEK FIRE

The Arab expansion indirectly proved the saviour of the Byzantine Empire, when Kallinikos, a Syrian Greek forced into exile by the Arab invasion, brought to Constantinople the recipe for a secret weapon that came to be known as Greek fire. Now believed to have been a concoction of naphtha, sulphur, quicklime, and nitre – a sort of medieval napalm – this highly flammable mixture was sprayed at enemies from a siphon device that could be fitted to the prow of a Byzantine war galley.

721–730

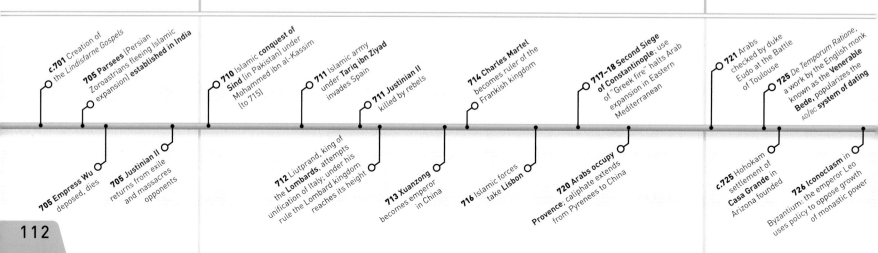

An iconic image of Christ held by Nicephorus, Patriarch of Constantinople

CASA GRANDE FLOURISHED AROUND THE 720s. The success of this settlement of the Hohokam, an ancient people of the Sonoran desert in modern-day Arizona, lay in a watering system that allowed a range of crops to be grown, despite the arid environment. The Hohokam lived here for more than a millennium; they were known as **"canal builders"** because of their sophisticated irrigation technology. Casa Grande was at the **centre of a trade network** that stretched from the **Pacific** coast to Tucson and to the **Gulf of Mexico**. The earliest structures at Casa Grande were probably pit houses; the "great house" that gives the site its name came much later.

In 725, the **Khazars**, a Turkic people of Central Asian origin, **established their capital at Atil**, on the Volga delta at the northwestern corner of the Caspian Sea. From here they **controlled trade routes to all corners of Asia** and built an empire that would control a huge swathe of Eastern Europe and Western Asia for centuries to come.

In Byzantium in 726, the emperor Leo III (see 711–20) instituted **a policy of iconoclasm** (smashing images deemed sacrilegious) in response to the idea that God was punishing Christian Byzantines by their loss of land to the Arabs and Slavs. The controversy encouraged the Roman papacy to assert their independence from Byzantine imperial authority.

c.701 Creation of the *Lindisfarne Gospels*

705 Parsees (Persian Zoroastrians fleeing Islamic expansion) **established in India**

705 Empress Wu deposed, dies

705 Justinian II returns from exile and massacres opponents

710 Islamic **conquest of Sind** (in Pakistan) under Mohammed ibn al-Kassim (to 715)

711 Islamic army under **Tariq ibn Ziyad** invades Spain

711 Justinian II killed by rebels

712 Liutprand, king of the **Lombards**, attempts unification of Italy; under his rule the Lombard kingdom reaches its height

713 Xuanzong becomes emperor in China

714 Charles Martel becomes ruler of the Frankish kingdom

716 Islamic forces take **Lisbon**

717–18 Second Siege of Constantinople; use of "Greek fire" halts Arab expansion in Eastern Mediterranean

720 Arabs occupy Provence; caliphate extends from Pyrenees to China

721 Arabs checked by duke Eudo at the Battle of Toulouse

725 *De Temporum Ratione*, a work by the English monk known as the **Venerable Bede**, popularizes the AD/BC **system of dating**

c.725 Hohokam settlement of **Casa Grande** in Arizona founded

726 Iconoclasm in Byzantium: the emperor Leo uses policy to oppose growth of monastic power

In 1837, artist Steuben depicted the Battle of Tours–Poitiers as a clash over the fate of Christian Europe. In reality Islamic raiders were beaten back in a minor skirmish.

790

PEOPLE PER SQUARE KILOMETRE THE POPULATION DENSITY OF TIKAL

SINCE CONQUERING SPAIN, ISLAMIC FORCES had made regular raids across the Pyrenees, striking deep into modern-day France before retreating to al-Andalus. In 721, an incursion into Aquitaine – a dukedom nominally in vassalage to the Frankish kingdom – had been checked by **Duke Eudo at the Battle of Toulouse**. But in 731, Eudo was unable to halt a fresh invasion of Islamic forces under **Abd al-Rahman I**, emir of al-Andalus. After defeat at the Battle of Arles, Eudo was forced to appeal to **Charles Martel**, the Frankish mayor of the palace, for help. Martel raised an army and met the Islamic forces on the banks of the Loire, between Tours and Poitiers, in 732. He was victorious at the **Battle of Tours–Poitiers**, and subsequent Christian historians would depict this as one of the defining clashes of the age – the moment at which Islamic expansion was checked and Europe preserved for Christianity. Arabic sources record it as a minor skirmish, and in reality its main significance was that it demonstrated the need for the Frankish kingdoms to present a unified defence.

The **Maya city-states** of the Late Classic period reached the **peak of their power** and sophistication in the mid-8th century in Central America. The population of **Tikal**, for instance, swelled to at least 60,000, in a city spread out over 76 sq km (47 sq miles). Mayan rulers built stone temples, palaces, ballcourts, and observatories, and controlled a trade network stretching from California to South America. Yet the height of the city-states' glory sowed the **seeds of downfall**, as the populations overtaxed the surrounding ecology and exceeded their ability to cope with drought. Collapse was just around the corner.

Statue of Chaak, Mayan god
Mayans would have sought help from god of rain and thunder, Chaak, for their crops. Their civilization sat in a region of poor soil and fragile ecology, so rain was vital.

The Great Mosque at Samarra, Iraq, built by the Abbasid Caliphate. Once the largest mosque in the world, the minaret stands at 52m (171ft) tall.

THE FOUNDATION OF THE ABBASID CALIPHATE IN 750 was the culmination of growing tension in the Islamic world. Under the Umayyads (see 651–70) the Arab elite stubbornly maintained their special tax and political status, failing to deal with the growing grievances of the *mawali* (non-Arab Muslims). In 747, revolt broke out in Persian Khorasan, stronghold of the Abbasid clan, who traced their descent back to Muhammad through his uncle, al-Abbas. In 749, **Abu al-Abbas al-Saffah was proclaimed caliph** at Kufa in Iraq, and the following year at the **Battle of the Zab** he defeated Marwan II, the last Umayyad caliph. Marwan fled to Egypt but his head was sent back to Damascus, whereupon al-Saffah instigated a general **massacre of the Umayyad clan** to remove potential opposition.

In 741 **Charles Martel** (see 731–40) **died** and was succeeded by his sons **Pepin the Short** and **Carloman**. In 748, Pepin had a son, Charles, who would go on to unite most of Western Europe under one banner (see 761–90).

Tiwanaku, a pre-Columbian city on the altiplano (high plains) of Bolivia, reached it's height in around 750. Tiwanaku was the centre of a civilization that flourished from the third to tenth centuries (see 951–60). The city itself was probably a **ceremonial and trading centre**; its cultural and economic influence spread far through South America, and it would profoundly affect the development of later civilizations in the Andean region. Tiwanaku thrived in the harsh environment of the Bolivian altiplan thanks to its sophisticated **raised-field agriculture system** and extensive use of **terracing and irrigation**, which enabled it to achieve yields in excess of even modern petrochemical farming (see below), and supported the development of a sophisticated culture. The Tiwanaku people built pyramids, temples, and colossal statues.

Tiwanaku yields
Raised fields combined with irrigation canals enabled Tiwanaku to achieve yields of up to 21 tonnes per hectare, according to experimental reconstructions.

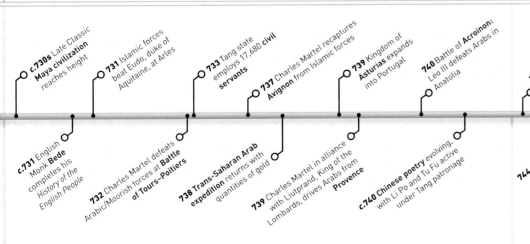

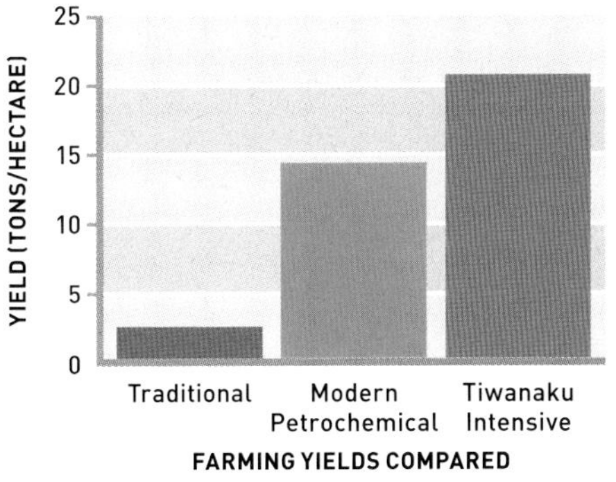

- **c.730s** Late Classic **Maya civilization** reaches height
- **c.731** English Monk **Bede** completes his *History of the English People*
- **731** Islamic forces beat Eudo, duke of Aquitaine, at Arles
- **732** Charles Martel defeats Arabic/Moorish forces at **Battle of Tours–Poitiers**
- **733** Tang state employs 17,680 **civil servants**
- **737** Charles Martel recaptures **Avignon** from Islamic forces
- **738 Trans-Saharan Arab expedition** returns with quantities of gold
- **739** Kingdom of **Asturias** expands into Portugal
- **739** Charles Martel in alliance with Liutprand, King of the Lombards, drives Arabs from **Provence**
- **c.740 Chinese poetry** evolving, with Li Po and Tu Fu active under Tang patronage
- **740** Battle of **Acroinon**: Leo III defeats Arabs in Anatolia
- **741** Death of **Leo III**, Byzantine Emperor
- **741** Death of Charles Martel, succeeded by **Pepin the Short** and **Carloman**
- **744** Assassination of Umayyad Caliph Walid II; Marwan II accedes to caliphate
- **745** Foundation of **Uighur Empire** in Central Asia
- **746** Terrible **plague** afflicts **Byzantine empire**
- **747 Pepin** becomes sole ruler of Frankish kingdoms on his brother's death
- **749 Abu al-Abbas** proclaimed **caliph**
- **750 Battle of the Zab** followed by general massacre of Umayyads
- **c.750** Height of Maya city-state of **Tikal** in Central America, and pre-Inca Andean city-state of **Tiwanaku**

The interior of the Mosque of Cordoba, Spain, shows architecture from the earliest phase of construction during the reign of Abd al-Rahman I.

UNDER THE NEW ABBASID CALIPHS (see 741–50) the Islamic empire continued to grow. Initial success came in 751 against the Chinese in the Silk Route kingdom of Tashkent. The Islamic armies were victorious at the **Battle of Talas River** near Samarkand, which led to the loss of most of Tang China's Central Asian possessions and introduced the Islamic world to **papermaking**. Outlying regions of the caliphate asserted their autonomy. In Spain in 756, one of the last surviving Umayyads, Abd al-Rahman I, declared an independent **Emirate of Cordoba**.

In Europe, the Carolingian Pepin III (*c.*714–68) **deposed the last Merovingian king**, Childeric III. With the pope's support **Pepin was crowned** and was soon able to return the papal favour. When the Lombards conquered Ravenna, the **last Byzantine territory in Italy**, the Lombard king, Aistulf then set his eyes on Rome. Pope Stephen II appealed to Pepin for help, and in 755 and 756 Pepin invaded Italy, seizing Ravenna. It was later claimed by the papacy in a document entitled the **Donation of Pepin**, that Pepin had conceded all former conquered territories in northern Italy to the pope, but this was almost certainly not the case.

Pepin III
Also known as Pepin the Short, Pepin III was the first Carolingian King of the Franks. This carving from his tomb dates to the 13th century.

The two-tier crop rotation system introduced in the 760s divided fields between cultivated and fallow land, then alternated, promoting soil fertility.

THE DEATH OF PEPIN III IN 758, had seen the Frankish kingdom customarily divided between his sons Carloman and Charles (see panel, below).

Meanwhile, the great monastic retreat on the Scottish **isle of Iona** was developing a reputation for piety and scholarship. It is possible that one of the treasures of Celtic Christianity – the **Book of Kells** – was produced by monks in the monastery at Iona. Lavishly decorated and illuminated, this priceless artefact survived the Viking raids (see 791–800), and for safekeeping it was later transferred to a monastery at Kells in Ireland.

The **founding of Baghdad** in 762 signalled the arrival of the first truly Islamic imperial city. Sited near Ctesiphon (the old Sasanian capital), the new city was carefully laid out on a circular plan and was connected to the Tigris and Euphrates rivers by canals. Baghdad became a trading hub that attracted merchants from northern Europe, India, and China.

Charlemagne's European Conquests
Charlemagne inherited land from his father then embarked on war after war, continuing the work of his father and grandfather.

KEY
- Frankish Empire on Charlemagne's accession
- Charlemagne's conquests
- Regions recognizing Charlemagne as overlord

CHARLEMAGNE (748–814)

Athletic and physically impressive, Charlemagne spoke Latin and understood Greek, but never learned to read. His intent was to extend Frankish hegemony, foster a close relationship with the papacy, and reform the Church to ensure divine support for the Frankish Kingdom. This depiction from a 15th century tapestry is testament his enduring legacy.

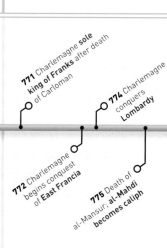

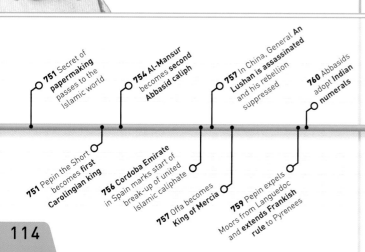

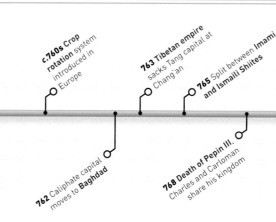

Roland bids farewell to Charlemagne, in this medieval illustration on vellum.

THE DEATH OF CARLOMAN IN 771 meant that Charlemagne became sole ruler of the Franks. The following year he launched a series of bloody campaigns with the aim of bringing the peoples east of the Rhine back under Frankish rule – they had been subject to the authority of the preceding Merovingian Dynasty. At this time the various Saxon tribes were still pagans, and Charlemagne was determined to convert them to Christianity and thus bring them under the hegemony of the Frankish state. From 773–74 he conquered the kingdom of the Lombards, **bringing northern Italy into his empire** and establishing his rule over Venetia, Dalmatia, and Corsica, thus extending his reach down both sides of the Adriatic coast and into the Mediterranean. In the late 770s, he attempted to **project his power into Spain** by taking advantage of infighting among the Muslim rulers. Invited to intervene in local politics by disgruntled emirs, Charlemagne

751 Secret of **papermaking** passes to the Islamic world

751 Pepin the Short becomes **first Carolingian king**

754 Al-Mansur becomes **second Abbasid caliph**

756 Cordoba Emirate in Spain marks start of break-up of united Islamic caliphate

757 Offa becomes **King of Mercia**

757 In China, General **An Lushan is assassinated** and his rebellion suppressed

759 Pepin expels Moors from Languedoc and **extends Frankish rule** to Pyrenees

760 Abbasids adopt **Indian numerals**

c.760s Crop rotation system introduced in Europe

762 Caliphate capital moves to **Baghdad**

763 Tibetan empire sacks Tang capital at Chang'an

765 Split between **Imami and Ismaili Shiites**

768 Death of Pepin III, Charles and Carloman share his kingdom

771 Charlemagne **sole king of Franks** after death of Carloman

772 Charlemagne begins conquest of **East Francia**

774 Charlemagne conquers **Lombardy**

775 Death of al-Mansur; **al-Mahdi becomes caliph**

sent his armies across the Pyrenees but they **failed to take the city of Saragossa** (modern-day Zaragoza in Spain) and were forced to retreat.

This botched expedition inadvertently launched one of the great romances of medieval times, the **legend of Roland**. In 778, Roland, one of Charlemagne's generals, was killed during an attack on the rearguard of the Carolingian armies as they retreated through the Pyrenean valley of **Roncesvalles**. The attack was actually carried out by Basques, but Roland's Breton followers took up the tale and as it spread through France in the following centuries it morphed into a legend with many fictitious elements: Roland became the nephew of an elderly, white-bearded Charlemagne; his attackers the perfidious Saracens; and Roland was Count of the Marches of Brittany. By the 11th century, the **"Song of Roland"** appeared as an early *chanson de geste*; a heroic epic of the age of chivalry.

In Constantinople, the **death of Emperor Leo IV** brought to the throne his infant son, **Constantine VI**. During his minority the empire was under the regency of the **Empress Irene**, his mother.

781–790

Offa's Dyke, which roughly follows the line of the Welsh-English border, was constructed during the reign of Offa of Mercia; stretches are still visible today.

CHARLEMAGNE'S CONQUEST OF WEST SAXONY in 782 comprised a bloody development with the mass execution of 4,500 Saxon prisoners at Werden. This event was appropriated by Nazi historians in the 1930s as a sort of pre-Christian Germanic martyrdom, while others have called into question its details and even occurrence. Meanwhile, concerned about ignorance and illiteracy among clergy, Charlemagne launched a Carolingian cultural renaissance.

In 786, **Haroun al-Rashid** (r.786–809) acceded to the caliphate in Baghdad. Under his rule the Barmakid family gained great power as his viziers (high-ranking advisors) and favourites, while the **intellectual and cultural flowering of the Islamic world** gathered pace. Growing enthusiasm among the rich and powerful for books encouraged scholars to begin translating ancient Greek and Roman texts into Arabic.

In 785, Offa of Mercia (r.757–96), effective overlord of Britain, started constructing the monumental earthwork known as Offa's Dyke, on the border between Wales and Mercia. Originally 27m (89ft) wide and 8m (26ft) high, the purpose of the dyke is unknown, and it probably fell into disuse soon after its completion.

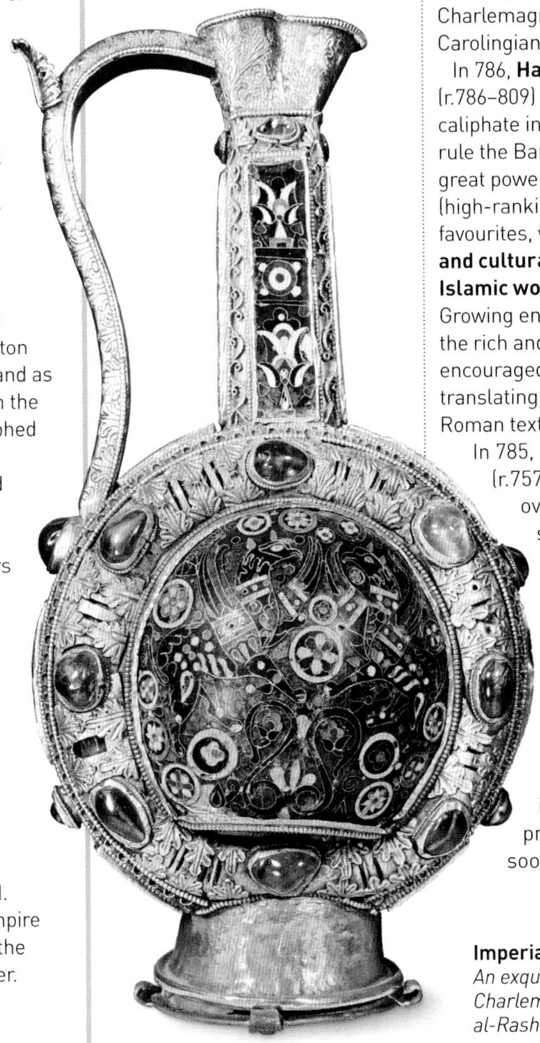

Imperial gift
An exquisite water jug sent to Charlemagne by Haroun al-Rashid, probably c.800.

791–800

The giant Buddha at Leshan in China was begun in 713 and finished 90 years later.

VIKING RAIDS on the shores of the British Isles started in 789 and gathered pace in the 790s with the looting of the rich monasteries of Lindisfarne and Iona. The "Vikings" (possibly from the Old Norse language) originated in Scandanavia.

In Tang China, the **influence of Buddhism continued to grow**, signalled by monuments such as the **Leshan Buddha**, a giant statue of the seated Buddha carved into a bluff next to the confluence of several major rivers.

In Constantinople (modern-day Istanbul), the emperor invited his **mother Irene to become co-ruler** in 792; four years later she had him blinded and declared herself empress. This move spurred the scholar Alcuin of York to suggest that the imperial seat was effectively vacant, and on 25 December 800, **Charlemagne was crowned Emperor of the Romans** by his ally, Pope Leo III. In the same year he received an embassy from Haroun al-Rashid, emblematic of how the focus of power in Europe had shifted.

In 800, the Abbasid caliphs in Baghdad were forced to recognize more or less **complete loss of authority in Africa west of Egypt**. They conceded to the emir of the province of Ifriqiya (modern-day Tunisia and part of Algeria) the right to make his post hereditary. The emir, Ibrahim ibn Aghlab, thus **founded the Aghlabid Dynasty**. This paid tribute to Baghdad and nominally recognized Abbasid authority, but ruled much of North Africa as an independent state.

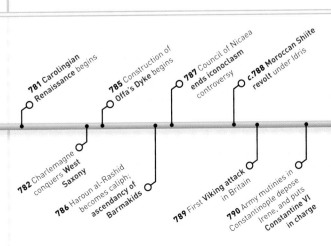

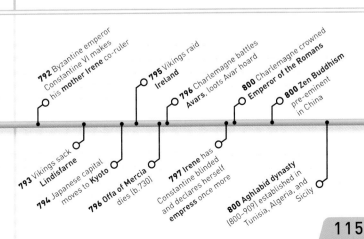

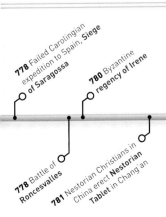

Functional and stylish brooch
Skilfully crafted out of gold, this Viking brooch was not only beautiful but also practical, used to fasten cloaks or other clothing.

> “[CHARLEMAGNE] WAS **LARGE** AND **STRONG** AND OF LOFTY **STATURE**, THOUGH NOT DISPROPORTIONATELY TALL.”
>
> **Einhard**, **Charlemagne's friend and Frankish historian**, *c.*830

778 Failed Carolingian expedition to Spain, **Siege of Saragossa**

778 Battle of **Roncesvalles**

780 Byzantine **regency of Irene**

781 Nestorian Christians in China erect **Nestorian Tablet** in Chang'an

781 Carolingian Renaissance begins

782 Charlemagne conquers **West Saxony**

785 Construction of **Offa's Dyke** begins

786 Haroun al-Rashid becomes caliph; **ascendancy of Barmakids**

787 Council of Nicaea **ends iconoclasm** controversy

c.788 Moroccan Shiite revolt under Idris

789 First **Viking attack** in Britain

790 Army mutinies in Constantinople depose Irene, and puts **Constantine VI in charge**

792 Byzantine emperor Constantine VI makes his **mother Irene** co-ruler

793 Vikings sack **Lindisfarne**

794 Japanese capital moves to **Kyoto**

795 Vikings raid **Ireland**

796 Charlemagne battles **Avars**, loots Avar hoard

796 Offa of Mercia dies (b.730)

797 Irene has Constantine blinded and declares herself **empress** once more

800 Charlemagne crowned **Emperor of the Romans**

800 Zen Buddhism pre-eminent in China

800 Aghlabid dynasty (800–909) established in Tunisia, Algeria, and Sicily

801–810

811–820

821–830

504 THE NUMBER OF **STATUES** AT **BOROBUDUR TEMPLE**

Louis the Pious in a copy of Raban Maur's *Book of the Cross*.

This 14th-century manuscript depicts scholars seated in the House of Wisdom; the Abbasid caliphs recruited scholars of all religions, from Europe to China.

THE TIBETAN EMPIRE EXPANDED in the early part of the 9th century, and extended its control to the Bay of Bengal. Its influence in Central Asia was indicative of **Tang China**'s weakness in the region. Meanwhile, in northern India the **Gurjara-Prathihara dynasty**, which had united the region and held back the advance of Islam, continued to grow in strength with the conquest of Kanauj in modern-day India by **Nagabhata II**, around 801.

The **Temple of Borobudur**, a **Buddhist monument** in central Java, Southeast Asia, was completed in the early 9th century. The colossal structure, which is the largest Buddhist monument in the world, contains over **2 million stone blocks** and is covered in almost 2,000 sqm (21,500 sqft) of carvings. The monument is a three-dimensional *mandala*, or cosmic wheel; walking its path, which is a journey of over 3km (2 miles), re-enacts the journey towards nirvana (englightenment). Its construction was an epic achievement, and a testament to the power of the **Srivijayan Empire** (*c*.760–1402), which had grown rich from the extensive maritime trade of the region.

For much of this era **Srivijayan influence** extended over the Southeast Asian mainland, including the **Mekong basin kingdom** formerly known to the Chinese as Funan. But, in 802, **Jayavarman II**, a vassal ruler whose family had been quietly extending their territory since around 770, was powerful enough to establish an independent **Khmer Empire** and have himself proclaimed *chakravartin*, or "universal ruler". In Sanskrit this translates as "god-king"– the authority of Khmer kings rested on their direct link to the gods, which was reflected in the monuments they would construct at the temple city of Angkor in centuries to come (see 880–90).

Around 801, **Bulan**, the Khan of the Khazar Empire (see 861–70), hosted a debate between the three Abrahamic faiths, and chose **Judaism**.

Jayavarman II
This statue of Jayavarman II from the 12th-century Bayon temple at Angkor Thom, was constructed by his namesake, Jayavarman VII.

CONFLICT BETWEEN THE BYZANTINES AND BULGARS (see 671–90) continued through the early part of the 9th century. Despite Byzantine emperor **Nicephorus I** (r. 802–11) twice sacking the Bulgar capital Pliskas, in 809 and 811, **the Bulgar khan, Krum**, fought back, meeting his foe in battle later in 811. Nicephorus was killed and Krum had his foe's skull lined with silver for use as a drinking cup. Two years later, Krum attempted to besiege the Byzantine capital **Constantinople**, but was unable to breach the walls and so retreated, **devastating Thrace** for good measure.

Charlemagne (see 760–800) died in 814 and his last remaining son, **Louis the Pious** (r. 814–40), acceded to the throne. He had been crowned co-emperor by his father the year before.

ISLAMIC SCIENCE

Thanks to the House of Wisdom and other similar centres of scholarship across the Caliphate, Islamic scholars went far beyond the learning of the ancient Greeks and Romans. Islamic scientists made great advances in fields such as alchemy (proto-chemistry), medicine, toxicology, metallurgy, mathematics, and astronomy. This illustration from *The Book of Knowledge of Ingenious Mechanical Devices* shows an innovative handwashing device.

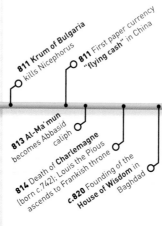

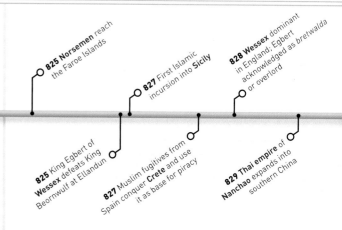

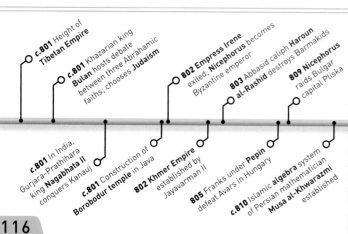

THE HOUSE OF WISDOM, or *Bait al-Hikma*, was an institute devoted to the translation of classical scholarship and the pursuit of learning in **Abbasid Baghdad**. It was the epicentre of the Islamic intellectual renaissance, the heart of the Translation Movement, and the home of great scholars such as **Al-Kharwizmi** (*c*.780–850); algebra takes its name from his great treatise on mathematics of *c*.830, the *Kitab al-Jabir*, or *The Compendious Book on Calculation by Completion and Balancing*.

The House of Wisdom was consolidated *c*.822 by **al-Ma'mun**. After the death of his father **Haroun al-Rashid** (see 791–800), and after a brief struggle, he had succeeded to the Caliphate in 813 and continued the tradition of intellectual patronage, building observatories and gathering the best scholars from around the world. Mimicking the practises of the Abbasid's Persian predecessors – the **Sasanians** – the **Translation Movement** collected manuscripts from other cultures and older traditions, and **translated** them **into Arabic**, thus preserving much ancient scholarship that would otherwise have been lost. Ptolemy's seminal work on cosmology, the *Almagest*, for instance, was translated from Greek into Arabic around 827, and it was only through this translation that European scholars would later be able to access this ancient text.

400 THOUSAND THE NUMBER OF **BOOKS** IN THE **HOUSE OF WISDOM**

Civil strife in the **Carolingian Empire** (800–88) resulted from tension between **Louis the Pious and his sons** over their inheritances. After the death in 819 of his first wife – mother of his sons **Lothair, Pepin**, and **Louis the German** – Louis the Pious had married the ambitious Judith of Bavaria who prevailed on Louis to grant to her son, **Charles the Bald** (823–77), lands that had previously been promised to **Lothair**. In retaliation Lothair,

- **c.801** Height of **Tibetan Empire**
- **c.801** In India, Gurjara-Prathihara king **Nagabhata II** conquers Kanauj
- **c.801** Khazarian king **Bulan** hosts debate between three Abrahamic faiths; chooses **Judaism**
- **c.801** Construction of **Borobudur temple** in Java
- **802 Empress Irene** exiled; **Nicephorus** becomes Byzantine emperor
- **802 Khmer Empire** established by Jayavarman II
- **803** Abbasid caliph **Haroun al-Rashid** destroys Barmakids
- **805** Franks under **Pepin** defeat Avars in Hungary
- **809 Nicephorus** raids Bulgar capital Pliska
- **c.810** Islamic **algebra** system of Persian mathematician **Musa al-Khwarazmi** established
- **811 Krum of Bulgaria** kills Nicephorus
- **811** First paper currency **"flying cash"** in China
- **813 Al-Ma'mun** becomes Abbasid caliph
- **814** Death of **Charlemagne** (born *c*.742); Louis the Pious ascends to Frankish throne
- **c.820** Founding of the **House of Wisdom** in Baghdad
- **825 Norsemen** reach the Faroe Islands
- **825** King Egbert of **Wessex** defeats King Beornwulf at Ellandun
- **827** First Islamic incursion into **Sicily**
- **827** Muslim fugitives from Spain conquer **Crete** and use it as base for piracy
- **828 Wessex** dominant in England; Egbert acknowledged as *bretwalda* or overlord
- **829 Thai empire** of **Nanchao** expands into southern China

Louis' co-emperor since 824, rallied his brothers in revolt against their father. In early 830, **Louis was deposed**, and although Lothair's misrule saw his father restored by the autumn, the older man's authority was compromised and the scene set for worse conflict to come.

Wessex, the Anglo-Saxon kingdom in south and west England, became the **dominant English power** as a result of the victory of King Egbert over King Beornwulf of Mercia at the Battle of Ellandun, Wiltshire, in 825. Egbert was subsequently able to conquer the southeastern counties of England, and by around 828 Wessex was the most powerful state in the land, with Egbert recognized as *bretwalda*, or overlord, of England until his death in 839.

The emergence of **Great Moravia** began around 830, with the establishment of the Principality of Moimir, to the west of the White Carpathians, under the rule of **Moimir I**. Moimir was one of two Slavic polities to establish themselves in the power vacuum left by the collapse of the Avars in 805; the other – to the east of the White Carpathians, in what is now Slovakia – was Nitra, under the rule of **Prince Pribina**. In 833, Moimir would conquer Nitra, setting his principality on the path to becoming the **Great Moravian Empire**.

831–840

The area around Segesta in Sicily, with its Greek ruins, was occupied early on in the Aghlabid invasion of the island.

THE ISLAMIC CONQUEST OF SICILY had begun in 827 with the arrival of an invasion force from Aghlabid in North Africa, sent by the **Emir Ziyadat Allah I** (r. 817–38) to take advantage of **internal divisions** among the **Byzantine** rulers of the island. Hindered by outbreaks of plague, the Islamic forces made little headway until 831 when **Palermo** fell after a year-long siege. The city then became the capital of Islamic Sicily, although total conquest of the island did not happen until 902.

The Field of Lies, in Alsace in 833, was a meeting brokered by the Pope to mediate between the **Frankish rulers**, which resulted in the desertion of Louis the Pious and Charles the Bald by their followers, and their subsequent imprisonment. This was one episode in a series of conflicts that saw the collapse of central authority and increasing Frankish vulnerability to raids from the Norsemen to the north and west, **Bulgars** and **Magyars** to the east, and **Saracen** pirates to the south.

Saracen warriors
"Saracens" was a European term for Muslims, especially those occupying Sicily and raiding Europe.

841–850

The ancient city of Pagan, in Burma, became the capital of a powerful Buddhist state occupying roughly the same area as the current region.

THE TREATY OF VERDUN in 843 marked the definitive division of Charlemagne's empire. After the death of Louis the Pious in 840, his three surviving sons (see 821–30) embroiled themselves in further conflict over land. In 842, Charles the Bald and Louis the German teamed up and swore oaths to impose a settlement on Lothair that saw the **Frankish Empire divided** into regions. These broadly equated to France in the west, Germany in the east, and a middle kingdom that would later become known as *Lotharii regnum*, or Lotharingia (modern Lorraine).

The rise of the **Cholas**, a Tamil dynasty of **southern India**, can be dated to 846, when the Chola king Vijayalaya, captured the city of Tanjore from the **Pandya kingdom**.

The **Capitulary of Meersen** was a proclamation by the West Frankish king Charles the Bald in 847, ordering every free man to choose himself a lord. Charles intended the decree to facilitate the levy of armies, but it was also indicative of the increasing inability of the Frankish rulers to protect their subjects. In place of central authority, the peasants relied on local lords; they gave up freedoms and bound themselves to a feudal aristocracy in return for protection from **Vikings** and other raiders.

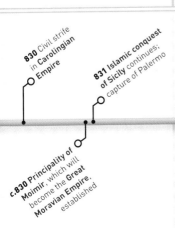

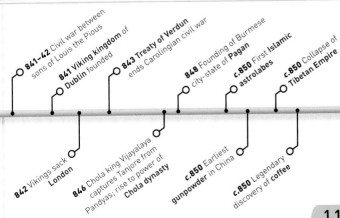

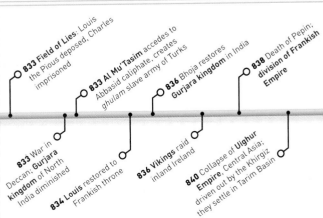

Coffee plant
The coffee bush is native to the mountains of Ethiopia and Yemen, where it was first recorded in use in the mid-15th century.

In around 848, the **Burmese city-state of Pagan** was founded in the Irrawaddy Valley. Indian influence is readily perceivable in the architecture of this part of Southeast Asia due to cultural, religious, and mercantile ties.

The legendary **discovery of coffee** is dated to around 850 when it is said that an Ethiopian goatherd named Kaldi noticed that, after eating some red berries, his goats became extremely lively. He brought a sample to a local Islamic holy man, who, disapproving of intoxicants, threw them on the fire where they roasted and released a delicious aroma.

830 Civil strife in **Carolingian Empire**

c.830 Principality of Moimir, which will become the **Great Moravian Empire**, established

831 Islamic conquest of Sicily continues; capture of Palermo

833 Field of Lies: Louis the Pious deposed, Charles imprisoned

833 War in Deccan; **Gurjara kingdom** of North India diminished

833 Al Mu'Tasim accedes to Abbasid caliphate, creates *ghulam* slave army of Turks

834 Louis restored to Frankish throne

836 Bhoja restores **Gurjara kingdom** in India

836 Vikings raid inland Ireland

838 Death of Pepin; **division of Frankish Empire**

840 Collapse of **Uighur Empire**, Central Asia; driven out by the Khirgiz they settle in Tarim Basin

841–42 Civil war between sons of Louis the Pious

841 Viking kingdom of Dublin founded

842 Vikings sack **London**

843 Treaty of Verdun ends Carolingian civil war

846 Chola king Vijayalaya captures Tanjore from Pandyas; rise to power of **Chola dynasty**

848 Founding of Burmese city-state of **Pagan**

c.850 First **Islamic astrolabes**

c.850 Earliest **gunpowder** in China

c.850 Collapse of **Tibetan Empire**

c.850 Legendary discovery of **coffee**

851–860

Monument in the courtyard of the Maya city of Palenque.

THE DECLINE OF THE CLASSIC MAYA civilization continued as the wave of abandonments that began with **Palenque** at the end of the 9th century spread south and east into the Classic Maya heartland. The last recorded inscriptions at Mayan cities Quiriguá and Copán date to 810 and 822; **at Caracol to 859**; and at Tikal to 889. A combination of **drought, famine, disease**, and social upheaval were probably responsible, as overpopulated cities and their overstretched resources reached a tipping point.

The first recorded use of a **crossbow** was in France in 851. Although slower to reload than a longbow, the crossbow, or *arbalest*, required little training or strength to operate.

The **Fujiwara regency**, assumed by Yoshifusa (*c*.804–72) on the accession of his grandson, the child-emperor Seiwa in 858, marked the Fujiwara clan's domination of Japanese power.

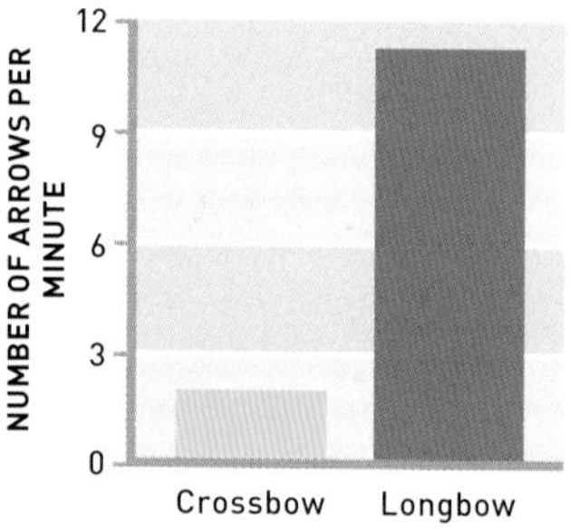

Crossbow vs longbow
Although the longbow could be fired much faster, the crossbow had a greater range and was easy to operate.

861–870

The frontispiece of *The Diamond Sutra*, the earliest known printed work, shows Buddha explaining the sutra (sermon) to an elderly disciple.

KHAZAR EMPIRE

The Caspian Sea is still known in the region as the Khazar Sea for the empire that ruled the area between it and the Black Sea from the 8th to 10th centuries. A contributing cause to the empire's decline may have been a rise of 7m (23 ft) in the sea level.

CYRILLIC SCRIPT WAS INVENTED by the Byzantine missionary later known as **St Cyril** in around 863. Originally named Constantine, Cyril and his brother Methodius were sent to **convert the Slavs** in **Moravia** by Byzantine emperor, Michael III in around 862. Cyril devised a new "Glagolitic" script to **translate the Bible** into Slavic; this later became Cyrillic script.

In 867, Basil, a favourite of Michael III, deposed his master and took the throne as **Basil I**. His reign marked the start of one of the most glorious periods of Byzantine history. Intent on restoring the empire internally and externally, Basil rebuilt the army and navy and revised the legal system.

The **Diamond Sutra** of 868 is the world's oldest surviving printed book. An illustrated Buddhist text, it was found in a cave in Dunhuang, a Silk Road town in northwest China.

Around the mid-9th century, the **Khazars adopted Judaisim** (see 801–10). According to tradition, they chose an **Abrahamic faith** to put them on equal footing with Christianity in the Byzantine Empire and Islam in the Caliphate.

Early Cyrillic script
This wax tablet contains psalms of David, written in the early 11th century. It is believed to be the oldest document written in Cyrillic.

871–880

The landscape of Iceland offered scant welcome, yet Vikings settled here by 874.

ALFRED THE GREAT OF ENGLAND, an educated man who had spent time in Rome with the Pope, acceded to the throne of the Anglo-Saxon kingdom of **Wessex** in 871. During the reign of his elder brother Aethelred I (r.865–71), **Danish Vikings** had invaded Wessex, but Alfred had helped defeat them at the **Battle of Ashdown** in 870. On assuming the kingship, Alfred averted crisis by defeating the Danes at Wilton in southwest England, but another attack in 875 caught him unawares and he was forced to retreat to the Somerset marshes. According to the popular legend, Alfred was here given shelter by a peasant woman who, unaware of his identity, left him to watch some cakes that were cooking on the fire. Preoccupied with the problems of his kingdom, Alfred let the cakes burn. Nonetheless he was able to summon his armies and defeated the Danish king Guthrum at the Battle of Edington in 878, forcing him to conclude the **Peace of Wedmore**, under the terms of which **Guthrum converted to Christianity** and agreed to a division of the country (see 881–90).

The **settlement of Iceland** demonstrated how the **Vikings** were advancing on other fronts. Irish monks had probably already reached the North Atlantic island, and Viking navigators had other clues to its existence, such as the passage of migrating birds. Vikings had already visited the island and even over-wintered there, but the first permanent settlement, according to the medieval Icelandic *Landámabók* (Book of Settlement), was by the Norwegian chieftain Ingolfur Arnarson in around 874. According to legend, he selected the spot for his homestead by throwing his

King Alfred
A statue of King Alfred was erected at his capital, Winchester, in 1901. His sword doubles as a crucifix, emblematic of his militant faith.

c.850s Continued decline of **Classic Maya** civilization

851 Crossbow introduced to France

857 Founding of **kingdom of Navarre** in Spain

857 Plague of **ergot poisoning** in Western Europe from infected cereals

858 Fujiwara regency in Japan; Fujiwara clan cement hold on power

862 Vikings found **Novgorod**

863 Byzantines win victory over Arabs in Anatolia

863 Invention of earliest form of **Cyrillic writing**

866 Bulgars convert to Christianity

866 Vikings capture York, England

867 Accession of **Basil I**, founder of Macedonian dynasty

868 Creation of **Diamond Sutra**, oldest surviving printed book

868 Ahmad ibn-Tulun founds **Tulunid Dynasty** in Egypt

869 Last dated stele at **Tikal** in Mesopotamia

870 Treaty of Meersen divides Frankish lands of the Kingdom of Lothar I

871 Alfred becomes King of Wessex, England

874 Vikings settle **Iceland**

874 Disappearance of **Al-Mahdi**, the Hidden Imam of Twelver Shi'ites

874 Persian literary renaissance begins in Bukhara

874 Peasant revolt against Tang after terrible drought in **China**

875 Catalonia in Spain becomes partially autonomous from Carolingian Empire

878 Battle of Edington in England followed by **Peace of Wedmore**

> **“** WE DISCERN ACROSS THE CENTURIES A **COMMANDING** AND **VERSATILE INTELLIGENCE,** WIELDING WITH EQUAL FORCE THE SWORD OF **WAR** AND OF **JUSTICE. ”**

Winston Churchill, British Politician, on King Alfred, 1956–58

throne pillars overboard and following their drift.

The **Twelfth Imam, al-Mahdi** – believed by some Shi'ites to be the ultimate saviour of humankind – miraculously disappeared in 874. According to some Shi'ites, when the Eleventh Imam, Hasan al-Askari, died in 874, his successor, a seven-year-old boy, went into literal and spiritual hiding, and ever since has been said to be "occulted", or hidden until the day of his **messianic return**.

The **Anglo-Saxon Chronicle**, a unique written record of events from wars and politics to the weather, was kept from around 880 until the mid-12th century. It was indicative of the scholarship that King Alfred fostered, inviting scholars to England and translating major classical works himself.

881–890

The façade of a building known as the Nunnery annex, at Chichen Itza, the leading Maya city-state of the Late or Terminal Classic Period.

SWEDISH VIKINGS, known as the **Varangians or Rus**, used rivers such as the **Volga** and **Dnieper** to push ever further inland from the Baltic, establishing dominion over the **eastern Slavs** of the region. Having **founded the settlement of Novgorod** in 862 and launched audacious raids on Constantinople by navigating rivers all the way to the Black Sea, they now colonized ever further south. In 882, the Rus **prince Oleg** (r. 882–912) defeated his rivals Askold and Dir, **seized** their settlement at **Kiev**, and transferred his capital there from Novgorod. The city would become the capital of **Kievan Rus**, a loose federation of territories, until 1169.

The **Danelaw** – the part of England in which Viking law was upheld – was formalized by the **Treaty of Alfred and Guthrum** in 886, following renewed attacks by Guthrum. Alfred would keep the south, including London, while the area to the north of a line between the Thames and Lea rivers went to the Danish, who would live under their own laws.

In 887, **Charles the Fat** (*c.*839–88), the last Carolingian king to rule both the primary Frankish territories, West and East Francia (modern-day France and Germany), was **deposed**. Charles, already king of the East Franks since 879, had been elected king of the West Franks in 884. However, he was a victim of the declining power and authority of the Carolingian monarchs (see 841–50). Unable or unwilling to meet the Vikings in battle – specifically during their **Siege of Paris** in 885–86 – he was proven incapable of protecting his people. **Odo**, Count of Paris (*c.*860–98), who had led a heroic defence against the Vikings in 885, was elected king of West Francia in 887. From now on, East and West Francia would develop as separate regions.

Slavonic–Viking Jewellery
Viking invaders conquered territories along Russia's waterways, establishing a hybrid culture that mixed Slavonic and Viking styles.

The catastrophic **decline of the Classic Maya city-states** of the southern lowlands continued throughout the 9th century, and **Tikal was abandoned** by around 889. Maya city-states of the north (the area of Mexico's Yucatán Peninsula) now took precedence in what is known as the Late or Terminal Classic Period. Foremost among these civilizations was **Chichen Itza**, which commanded the advantage of *cenotes*, or water holes; of vital importance in this drought-vulnerable region.

891–900

Symeon of Bulgaria, depicted in the centre, had been educated as a monk in Constantinople before returning to take control of the Bulgars in 893.

THE GROWING POWER OF THE BULGAR KHANATE (see 811–20) worried the Byzantine emperor **Leo VI**, who in 895 prompted the **Magyars** to attack the Bulgars. However, this merely provoked the new khan, **Symeon** (r.893–927), to mobilize the Pechenegs – a tribe that had recently arrived on the Dnieper – to invade Magyar lands. The Magyars were forced to migrate west, settling in present-day **Hungary**, from where they launched extensive raids on Frankish territories for years to come. In the summer of 896, Symeon defeated a **Byzantine army** at Bulgarophygon, in modern-day Turkey, forcing the Byzantine emperor to pay tribute. Symeon would rule for another 30 years, vying for the Byzantine throne, only to be thwarted by the impenetrable walls of its capital, **Constantinople**, on numerous occasions.

The **Toltecs** (*c.*800–1000) were probably refugees from the **collapsed Teotihuacan culture** (see 690–700), who settled in the Valley of Mexico, founding a capital at **Tula** *c.*900, and forging a militaristic empire that inspired their descendants, the Aztecs.

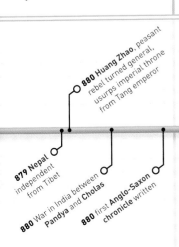

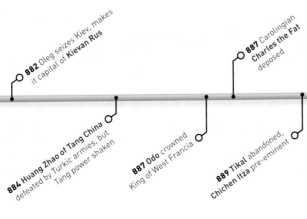

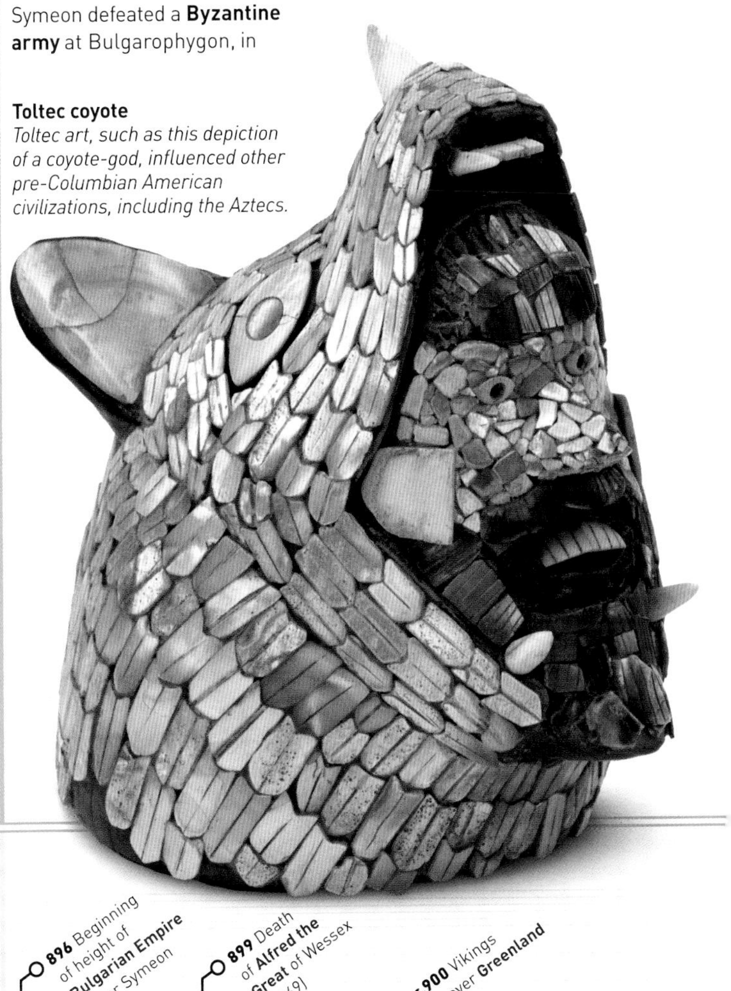

Toltec coyote
Toltec art, such as this depiction of a coyote-god, influenced other pre-Columbian American civilizations, including the Aztecs.

- **879 Nepal** independent from Tibet
- **880** War in India between **Pandya** and **Cholas**
- **880 Huang Zhao**, peasant rebel turned general, usurps imperial throne from Tang emperor
- **880** first **Anglo-Saxon chronicle** written
- **882** Oleg seizes Kiev, makes it capital of **Kievan Rus**
- **884 Huang Zhao of Tang China** defeated by Turkic armies, but Tang power shaken
- **887 Odo** crowned King of West Francia
- **887** Carolingian **Charles the Fat** deposed
- **889 Tikal** abandoned, **Chichen Itza** pre-eminent
- **896** Beginning of height of **Bulgarian Empire** under Symeon
- **899** Death of **Alfred the Great** of Wessex (b.849)
- **c.900** Development of **Toltec** kingdom centred on **Tula** in Valley of Mexico
- **c.900** Vikings discover **Greenland**
- **c.900** earliest versions of *alf-Layla wa-Layla*, "One Thousand and One Nights"

901–910

This stone relief is from the Chinese Five Dynasties and Ten Kingdoms period. Breakdown of central authority in the period led to economic contraction.

TANG CHINA HAD BEEN IN MILITARY DECLINE since defeat by the Arabs at the Battle of Talas River in 751–760, and the **Huang Zhao rebellion** of the 880s signalled the end of the dynasty. **Zhuwen** (*c.*852–912) was a warlord who had originally been part of the Huang Zhao uprising and then instrumental in the rebel defeat. Richly rewarded for his role, he steadily built up his power base until in 904 he was ready to seize control, **executing** the **Tang emperor Zhaozong** and most of his sons, and installing the emperor's 13-year-son on the throne as a puppet ruler. In 907, he took the throne for himself, founding the **Later Liang Dynasty**, but although he controlled the northern heartland of China – the Yellow River Valley region of Huang He – he was unable to prevent the south fragmenting into ten independent kingdoms. The Later Liang Dynasty was short-lived (907–923), with a succession of groups seizing control of the Huang He region and founding dynasties of their own, but proving unable to hold on to power. This period of anarchy, known as the Five Dynasties and Ten Kingdoms, lasted until the establishment of the **Northern Song Dynasty** (see 951–960), and was a time of great hardship. Authority broke down, the economy collapsed, and barter replaced money in many areas. There was extensive flood and famine as flood defences and irrigation works fell into disrepair.

Fatimid era text
Named for Muhammad's daughter, Fatima, the Fatimids proved patrons of learning through their sponsorship of Cairo's al-Azhar school.

To the west and north of the Five Dynasties region, **Shatuo Turks** and **Khitan Mongols** consolidated kingdoms of their own. The Khitans of southern Manchuria established their empire in 905 under the leadership of Yelü Abaoji (872–926). He went on to declare himself emperor in 916, founding the **Liao Dynasty**, which lasted until 1125, including a brief period as one of the Five Dynasties controlling northern China.

In 909, Sa'id ibn-Husayn, an Ismaili Shi'ite, overthrew the **Sunni Aghlabid Dynasty** in Kairouan (modern-day Tunisia), declared himself **al-Mahdi** (the Shi'ite messiah), and **founded the Fatimid Dynasty**, named for the daughter of the prophet Muhammad, from whom he claimed descent.

The **Abbey of Cluny** in Burgundy, founded in 910 by William the Pious, Duke of Aquitaine, became the centre of a **monastic "empire"** in Europe (see panel, above).

Displaced westwards by the Pechenegs (see 891–900), the **Magyars** launched a series of devastating **raids** throughout the decade. In 901, they ravaged Carinthia, in 906 and 907 they wreaked havoc in Moravia, and in 908 they attacked Bavaria, Saxony, and Thuringia. With the Frankish emperor unwilling or unable to help, the East Franks elected regional "dukes" to defend against the incursions.

ABBEY OF CLUNY

William the Pious, who donated the land for the abbey in 910, placed no obligations on its Benedictine monks, so that it was free from secular oversight and answerable only to the Pope. Cluny became the centre of a monastic empire of great power, governing around 10,000 monks. In 1098, Pope Urban II, a former Abbot of Cluny, declared it "the light of the world".

The Five Dynasties
A succession of regimes was unable to consolidate power, leaving warlords to the north and south to set up independent kingdoms. The fractured geopolitical situation is reflected in this map, which shows a tangle of borders and states.

KEY
- Chinese states
- States occupied by non-Chinese peoples

911–920

ABD AL-RAHMAN III BECAME THE NEW UMAYYAD RULER of the **Cordoba emirate** on the death of his grandfather, Abdallah, in 912. His territories had been reduced by rebellions and he quickly set about regaining much of his lost kingdom. During his reign and that of his successors, **Cordoba** reached the peak of its power (see 921–930).

According to traditional sources, **Prince Igor, ruler of Kievan Rus** from 914–945, was the son of the legendary Rurik, who founded **Novgorod** in 862. Under his protection, **Kievan Rus** (see 881–890) became a

Igor I of Kiev
Igor, who ruled from 914 until his death in 945, gestures to his court in this19th-century illustration.

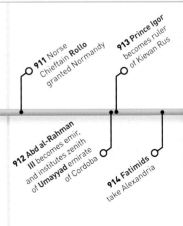

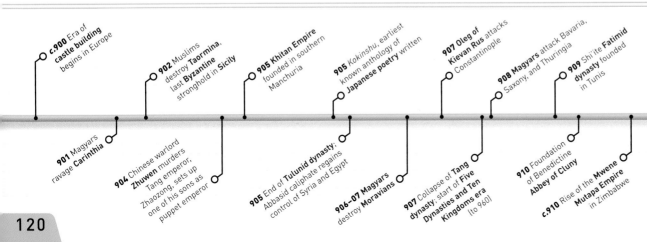

c.900 Era of **castle building** begins in Europe

901 Magyars ravage **Carinthia**

902 Muslims destroy **Taormina**, last **Byzantine** stronghold in **Sicily**

904 Chinese warlord **Zhuwen** murders Tang emperor, Zhaozong, sets up one of his sons as puppet emperor

905 Khitan Empire founded in southern Manchuria

905 End of **Tulunid dynasty**; Abbasid caliphate regains control of Syria and Egypt

905 *Kokinshu*, earliest known anthology of **Japanese poetry** written

906–07 Magyars destroy **Moravians**

907 Oleg of Kievan Rus attacks Constantinople

907 Collapse of **Tang dynasty**; start of **Five Dynasties and Ten Kingdoms era** (to 960)

908 Magyars attack Bavaria, Saxony, and Thuringia

909 Shi'ite **Fatimid dynasty** founded in Tunis

910 Foundation of Benedictine **Abbey of Cluny**

c.910 Rise of the **Mwene Mutapa Empire** in Zimbabwe

911 Norse Chieftain **Rollo** granted Normandy

912 Abd al-Rahman III becomes emir, and institutes zenith of **Umayyad** emirate of Cordoba

913 Prince Igor becomes ruler of Kievan Rus

914 Fatimids take Alexandria

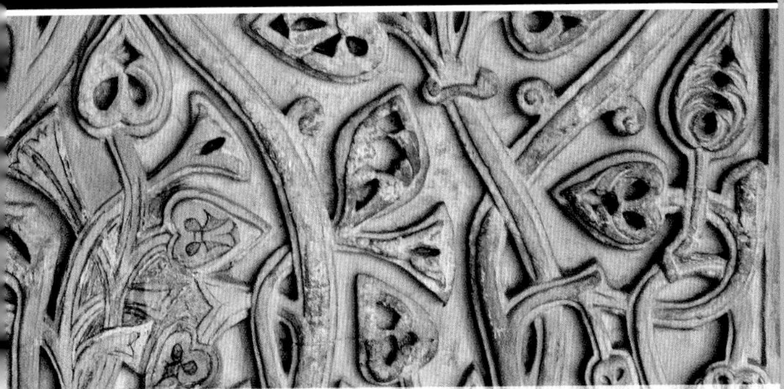

This decorative panel at the Caliph's Palace in Madinat az-Zahra, Spain, was erected by Al-Rahman III in imitation of the Abbasid Caliphs in Baghdad.

Lögberg, or Law Rock, in Iceland is the centre of the oldest parliament.

formidable power in the region, earning the respect of the Byzantines by force of arms during the **Rus-Byzantine war** of 941, and winning lucrative trade concessions from them.

In 911, in recognition of helplessness in the face of constant and devastating **Viking raids** (see 881–890), the West Frankish king, **Charles III**, granted a large area of land guarding the mouth of the River Seine, which consisted of a large part of what later became Normandy, to the Norse chieftain, **Rollo**, also known as Hrolf, on the condition that he became a Christian. Charles' grip on the crown was tenuous; the authority of the Carolingian monarchs had declined precipitously, with local counts ruling what were effectively independent fiefs that owed only nominal authority to the king (see 841–850). A powerful faction of West Frankish magnates had elected **Count Odo** of Paris to the kingship in 887, so Charles spent much of his reign engaged in civil war with Odo and his descendants.

One of the tribal dukes who came to power with the impotence of the Carolingians in the face of the Magyar threat, **Henry I,** was elected king of the East Franks in 919, founding the **Saxon Dynasty**. The last Carolingian monarch of the East Frankish kingdom, Louis the Child, died in 911, after which Conrad, duke of Franconia, was elected as king. On his death he nominated his strongest rival, Henry, as successor.

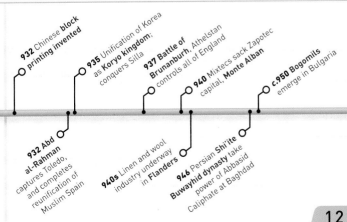

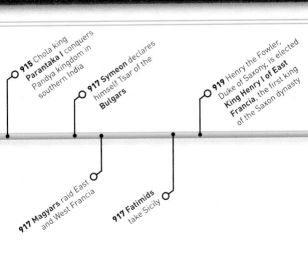

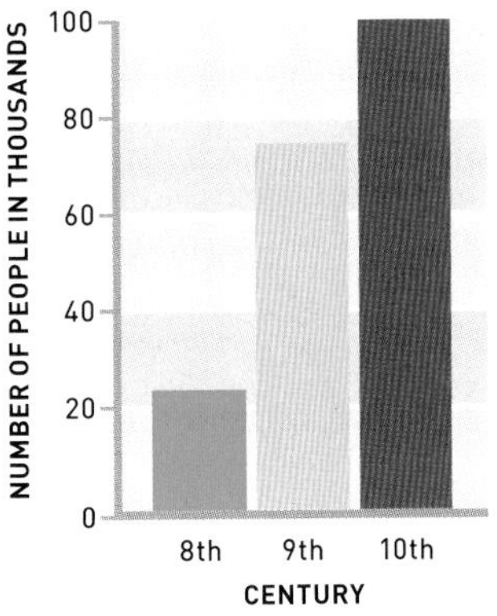

Cordoba's population growth
This estimate shows how Cordoba grew rapidly from a small town to become one of the world's biggest medieval cities.

THE WANING AUTHORITY OF THE ABBASIDS IN BAGHDAD prompted Abd al-Rahman III to declare himself the true caliph in 929, thus amending his kingdom, from emirate to **caliphate**. During the 10th century, his capital, Cordoba, became the largest and most developed city in Western Europe.

In 930, **Icelanders** started meeting to decide on justice and legislation at an outdoor assembly on the plains of **Thingvellir**. All free men who had not been outlawed could attend the **Althing**, making it the **oldest representative assembly** in the world.

During what archaeologists call the **Pueblo II phase**, the Pueblo peoples of Chaco Canyon, North America, were thriving. They built immense structures called "great houses", some with up to 700 rooms.

> **"** IN THIS YEAR, **KING AETHELSTAN,** LORD OF WARRIORS, RING-GIVER TO MEN... WON ETERNAL GLORY, IN BATTLE WITH SWORD EDGES, **AROUND BRUNABURH "**
>
> **Unknown author,** from the Old English poem, *The Battle of Brunaburh,* 937

IN 932, THE UMMAYAD CALIPH ABD AL-RAHMAN III (see 911–920) captured Toledo, bringing all of Muslim Spain back under one banner. Al-Rahman also waged a successful war against the Christian kingdoms of **Leon** and **Navarre** on his northern borders, forcing them to acknowledge his overlordship. In general, Jews and Christians enjoyed tolerance under the caliphate, though they remained second-class citizens, making issues such as tax status a driving force behind conversion.

The **Silla kingdom** (see 651–670) was conquered by the **Koryo kingdom** in 935, completing the reunification of **Korea** under the Koryo leader Wang Kon, who now became **King T'aejo** (r.918–943). Wang Kon had acceded to power in the Three Kingdoms state of Koguryo in 918, renaming it and leading it in successful military ventures against the Kingdom of Paekche, who were conquered in 934, and the Silla. During his reign, T'aejo consolidated power by incorporating Silla nobility into his new ruling bureaucracy.

In one of the bloodiest battles ever fought on British soil, the Anglo-Saxon king Athelstan (*c.*893–939) crushed an alliance of forces in 937, cementing his control of Britain and his kingship of a the now unified **Anglo-Saxon** realm of England. Alarmed by the prospect of Anglo-Saxon expansionism, the king of Alba (in modern-day Scotland) had joined forces with the Vikings and other northern British realms to counter the threat. The results were immortalized in an Old English poem recorded in the Anglo-Saxon Chronicle (see 871–880), which reported that five kings and seven earls died on the battlefield, alongside "unnumber'd crowds" of soldiers. Victory confined the Welsh and Scottish to their borders, halted Viking expansionism, and helped create **England** as a nation.

In 946, the Persian Shi'ite **Buwayhids** took Baghdad and forced the caliph to recognize Ahmad ibn-Buwayh as supreme commander. Although **Abbasid caliphs** remained in place until 1258, they were mere figureheads; real power now passed to Buwayhid sultans who ruled from their capital in **Shiraz**, Persia.

Henry I (see 911–920) was one of the tribal dukes who came to power in the face of Magyar threat to the Carolingians. Known as Henry the Fowler, he enlarged the kingdom and inflicted the first great defeat that the Magyars (see 901–910) had experienced since beginning their raids into Europe, at the **Battle of Riade** in 933. Henry was powerful enough to ensure that on his death the succession would be hereditary, and the election of 936 was a formality, acknowledging his son, **Otto**, as the new king. Otto's coronation ceremony in 962 consciously emulated that of **Charlemagne** (see 761–770), and he was crowned at Aachen, the old imperial capital.

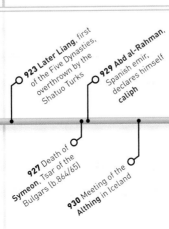

915 Chola king **Parantaka I** conquers Pandya kingdom in southern India

917 Magyars raid East and West Francia

917 Symeon declares himself Tsar of the **Bulgars**

917 Fatimids take Sicily

919 Henry the Fowler, Duke of Saxony, is elected **King Henry I of East Francia**, the first king of the Saxon dynasty

923 Later Liang, first of the Five Dynasties, overthrown by the Shatuo Turks

927 Death of **Symeon**, Tsar of the Bulgars (b.864/65)

929 Abd al-Rahman, Spanish emir, declares himself **caliph**

930 Meeting of the **Althing** in Iceland

932 Chinese **block printing invented**

932 Abd al-Rahman captures Toledo, and completes reunification of Muslim Spain

935 Unification of Korea as **Koryo kingdom**; conquers Silla

937 Battle of Brunanburh, Athelstan controls all of England

940s Linen and wool industry underway in **Flanders**

940 Mixtecs sack Zapotec capital, **Monte Alban**

946 Persian **Shi'ite Buwayhid dynasty** take power of Abbasid Caliphate at Baghdad

***c*.950 Bogomils** emerge in Bulgaria

Statue of Frey
The Vikings worshipped Frey, the Norse god of fertility. This statue from Sweden shows Frey holding his beard – a symbol of growth and virility.

Thor's hammer pendant
Thor's hammer – a symbol of power and virility – was a common theme for jewellery. Thor was the Norse god of thunder.

gold beading and wire work

Gold arm ring
Decorated with patterns made by stamping, beading, and minute engraving, this arm ring from Räbylille in Denmark has crosses and tree motifs.

sword indicates that rider is a warrior

Silver figure of horseman
This stylized metal figure from Sweden probably represents a warrior on horseback. The Vikings were fine horsemen, but they preferred to travel by ship.

THE VIKINGS

THE ARTISTRY AND SKILL OF VIKING ARTISANS BELIES THEIR REPUTATION AS SAVAGES

Between the 8th and 11th centuries, the Viking world spanned Europe, from the Pontic Steppes in the south and east to the shores of North America in the west and north. This realm was tied together by a culture of arts and crafts.

The unifying motifs of Viking art and crafts were elaborate ornamentation, interlacing patterns, and stylized animals. The material culture of the Vikings was mostly utilitarian yet finely crafted. Common, ceremonial, and military objects were ornamented heavily. Techniques such as etching, engraving, and inlaying and the use of metal beading helped to create patterns of interweaving tendrils, "gripping beasts", and stylized limbs.

ends of ring are in shape of cat heads

Silver brooch/pin
This gold-coated silver brooch or cloak pin from Sweden is highlighted with niello, a black metallic compound.

buckle plate for securing baldric

baldric (sling-like shoulder strap)

double-edged blade

Sword
Swords were rare and extremely valuable for the Vikings. This sword could be easily drawn out from its sheath and wielded with one hand.

Wooden shield
Shields were made from spruce, fir, pine, or linden wood with iron handles behind an iron boss. They were painted with bright colours and often had intricate designs.

colours signified intent or allegiance

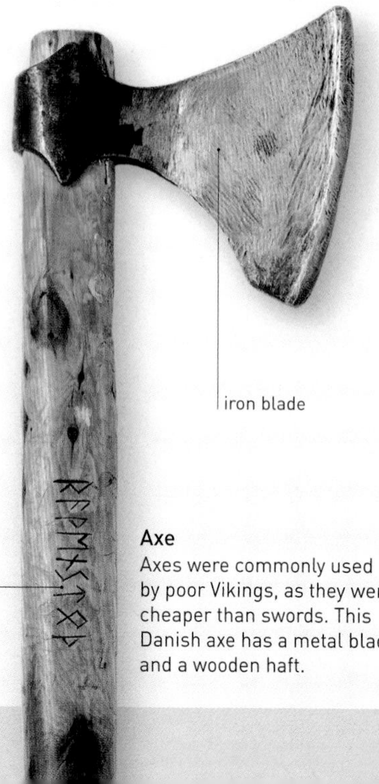

iron blade

stout wooden haft with runic inscription

Axe
Axes were commonly used by poor Vikings, as they were cheaper than swords. This Danish axe has a metal blade and a wooden haft.

Buckle plate
This metal plate was fixed to a Viking's leather belt so that it could be buckled. It has two sections, one for each end of the belt.

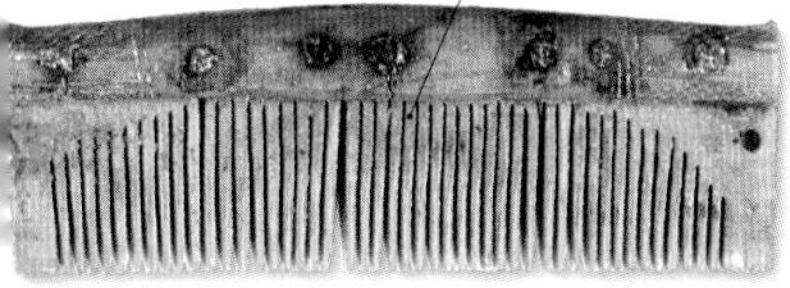

Hair comb
A typical Viking grooming kit included a comb, tweezers, and scoops for cleaning ears. This wooden comb has a handle secured with iron rivets.

Brooch
This box brooch (top view), from Martens on the Swedish island of Gotland, is decorated with four squatting human figures in gold.

Gilded weather vane
Weather vanes were originally mounted on the prows of ships and later on the tops of churches. This gilded weather vane was found in Sweden.

Helmet
Made from iron plates welded together over a leather cap, this Norwegian helmet has an attached face guard, complete with nose protector.

Early Danish coins
Originally, the Vikings used looted coins, hack silver (chunks), and barter in place of their own money. King Harald Bluetooth started mass minting of coins in 975.

Trading weights
Found in Sweden, these brass-coated iron weights were used to measure quantities of goods and the value of hack silver.

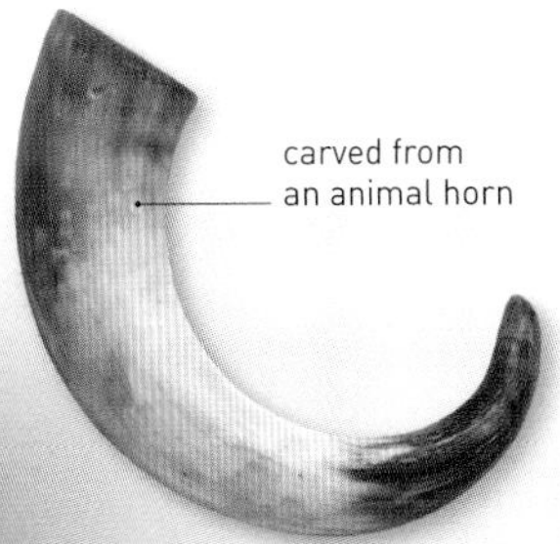

Drinking horn
Vikings believed they would use drinking horns like this in Valhalla, the heaven for warriors, if they died in battle. This drinking vessel was used in feasting.

Sledge
This oak-and-beech sledge is from a ship burial at Oseberg in Norway. It has finely carved runners and animal heads on each corner post of the box.

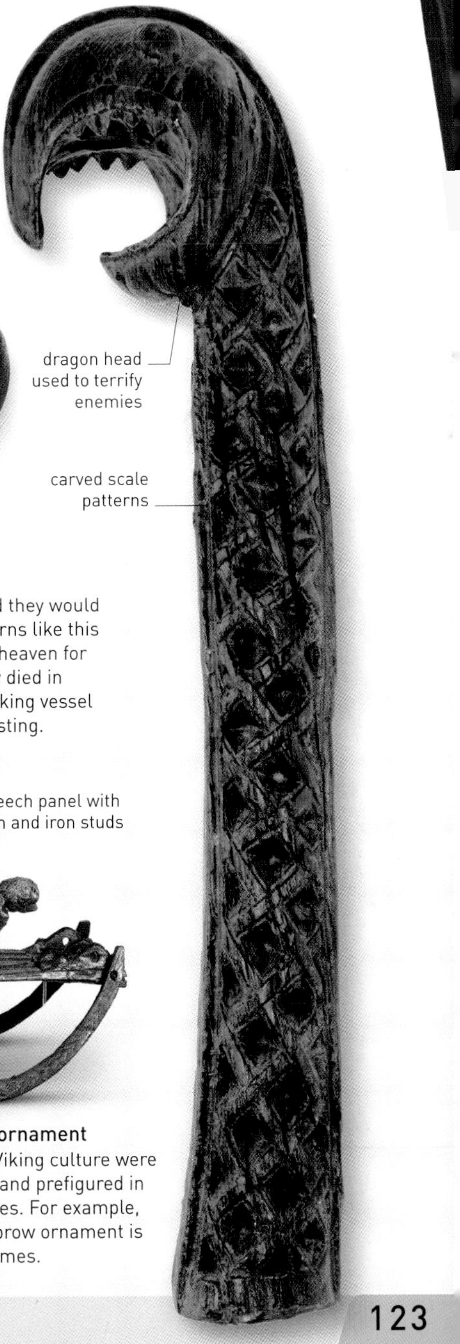

Ship's prow ornament
Elements of Viking culture were derived from and prefigured in earlier cultures. For example, this wooden prow ornament is from Saxon times.

951–960

This detail from the "Gateway of the Sun", a great stone doorway at Tiwanaku, is carved with a figure known as the Staff God.

THE PRE-INCA, ANDEAN CIVILIZATION OF TIWANAKU declined precipitously in the second half of the 10th century. Sophisticated agricultural and irrigation techniques (see 741–50) had allowed Tiwanaku to support a **population** of up to 60,000 people, with up to **1.4 million** in the wider region, according to some estimates. A **prolonged drought** is believed to have been responsible for its **decline** and archaeological evidence suggests that the main city was abandoned as citizens retreated to smaller, rural settlements, and returned to a pre-urban lifestyle.

The **establishment of the Song dynasty** in China brought an end to the anarchy and warfare of the Five Dynasties and Ten Kingdoms era (see 901–10). Known as the **Northern Song** in its early stages because the capital was at Kaifeng in northern China, the dynasty was founded by **Zhao Kuangyin** (r.960–76), who was a general under the Late Zhou, the last of the Five Dynasties. He dealt with the threat from external states such as the Khitan Liao (see 901–10), the Tangut kingdom of Xia Xia, a confederation of Tibetan tribes, and conquered several of the Ten Kingdoms to the south. Zhao used the civil service examination system to assert control over the military, and centralize power.

Emperor Otto I, "the Great" (912–73), defeated the **Magyars** at the **Battle of Lechfeld** in 955. Since being displaced by **Byzantine–Bulgar conflict** (see 891–900), the Magyars had raided Frankish territories, reaching as far west as Aquitaine in 951. The son of Henry I (see 911–20), Otto vigorously asserted royal authority from his coronation in 936, gaining control of all the East Frankish duchies. His powerful army **ended the Magyar menace** and also defeated the **Wends** – tribes on the eastern border engaged in a long struggle to resist Frankish **colonization and Christianization**.

Bronze Mirror
This intricately decorated mirror from the Song dynasty illustrates the artistic sophistication of China in this period.

961–970

This detail from the imperial crown of Otto I shows the biblical figure, King Solomon, holding a scroll.

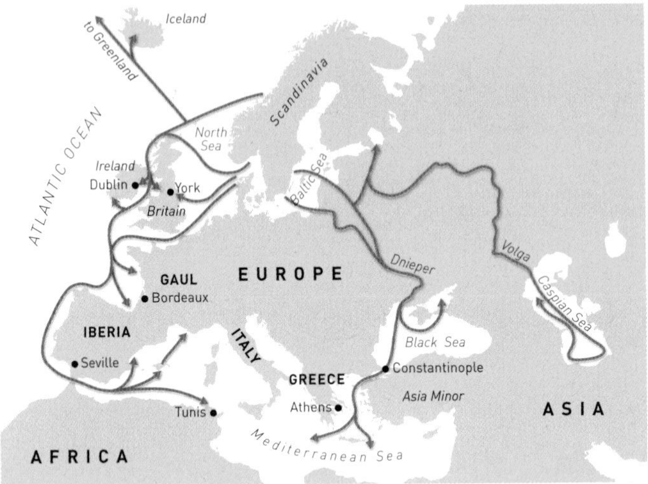

Viking sea routes
By the late 10th century, Viking seafarers had penetrated to every corner of Europe and beyond, reaching as far as Greenland in the north.

KEY
→ Viking expansionist exploration 8–10th centuries

THE POPE'S IMPERIAL CORONATION OF OTTO I as emperor in 962, revived the **Carolingian Roman Empire** in the West. In 961, Otto made an expedition to Italy in response to a plea for protection from Pope John XII, and in Pavia he had assumed the Italian crown. The following year he went to **Rome** to receive the imperial crown and assert his authority over the fractious papacy. His son was crowned co-emperor as Otto II in 967.

In 965, **King of Denmark, Harald Bluetooth**, converted to Christianity, and the **religion** spread rapidly through the Nordic region. Denmark had been forced to accept missionaries as the consequence of defeat by the East Frankish king, Henry I, in 933. Further afield, Vikings continued to prosper as they penetrated into all parts of Europe.

The **death of** Byzantine emperor **Constantine VII** in 963 brought his infant son **Basil II** (958–1025) to the throne. In practice, authority was assumed by the general **Nicephorus Phocas**. As **Nicephorus II** (r.963–969), he continued the restoration of the empire that had begun with the reconquest of Crete in 961, regaining Cyprus and Cilicia in 965, subduing the Bulgars in 966–69, and invading northern Syria in 969. That same year he was assassinated by his nephew, **John Tzimisces**.

971–980

" A RECKLESS MAN BY NATURE [WHO]... ATTEMPTED UNUSUAL DEEDS "

Leo the Deacon on John Tzimisces, late 10th century

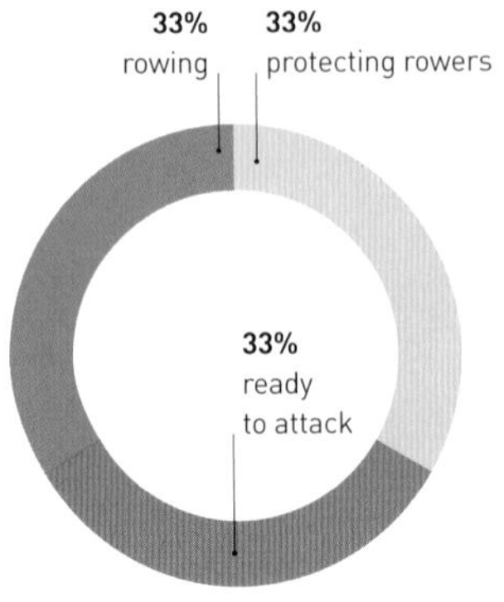

Longboat crew in battle
By keeping part of the crew at the oars Viking raiding parties maintained an aggressive posture without sacrificing mobility.

DURING HIS SHORT REIGN, JOHN TZIMISCES, nephew of Nicephorus II (see 961–70), won a string of victories. Having fought off a revolt by general Bardas Phocas in 971, Tzimisces crushed a campaign by the **Kievan Rus** leader, Sviatoslav, and **conquered Bulgaria** as far as the Danube. In 972, he campaigned in the East, taking Edessa, Damascus, and Beirut, reaching the gates of Jerusalem in 976. He died suddenly that year.

In 980, the **Vikings** started **raiding** England again, though they suffered a reverse in Ireland, where Malachy II forced Viking Dublin to pay tribute.

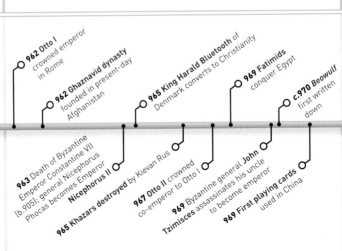

- **c.950** Abandonment of **Tiwanaku**
- **951** Emperor **Otto I** of East Francia invades Italy
- **951 Magyars** raid as far west as Aquitaine
- **954** Construction of **Hindu Lakshmana temple** at Khajuraho in central India
- **955 Battle of Lechfeld**; Otto I defeats Magyars, who cease raiding and settle in Hungary
- **957** Byzantine general **Nicephorus Phocas** takes the city of Hadath, continuing Byzantine advance in Syria
- **958** Byzantine **victory at Raban** in Syria
- **960** Founding of **Northern Song dynasty, China**
- **962 Otto I** crowned emperor in Rome
- **962 Ghaznavid dynasty** founded in present-day Afghanistan
- **963** Death of Byzantine Emperor Constantine VII (b.905); general Nicephorus Phocas becomes Emperor **Nicephorus II**
- **965 King Harald Bluetooth** of Denmark converts to Christianity
- **965 Khazars destroyed** by Kievan Rus
- **967 Otto II** crowned co-emperor to Otto I
- **969** Byzantine general **John Tzimisces** assassinates his uncle to become emperor
- **969 Fatimids** conquer Egypt
- **969 First playing cards** used in China
- **c.970 Beowulf** first written down
- **972 Bulgar Khanate** annexed by Byzantine Empire
- **973** Death of **Otto I** (b.912)
- **973** Taila II overthrows the Rashtrakuta dynasty of central India, establishing the **Chalukya dynasty**
- **975** Beginnings of Hungarian state under **Duke Geisa**, who converts to Roman Catholicism
- **980 Vizier Al-Mansur** becomes true power in **Cordoba** after death of al-Hakam II

Venice's modern splendour is the result of control of the lucrative trade routes between Europe, the Byzantine Empire, and the East in the 10th century.

IN 981, THE ISLAMIC FORCES OF CORDOBA defeated the Christian kingdom of **Leon** in Spain, under the leadership of **Al-Mansur**. "Al-Mansur" was the honorific title taken by Muhammad ibn Abi' Amir, the powerful and energetic vizier who was the true power behind the **Umayyad** throne (see 911–20). He campaigned successfully against Leon, Navarre, and Catalonia, making their kings subordinate to the caliphate, and extended Umayyad control to Africa via campaigns in **Mauretania** (modern-day Morocco and part of Algeria).

In 986, the Viking explorer, **Eric the Red**, led a party of Icelandic colonists to the shores of the bleak landmass he misleadingly named "Greenland" in the hope of attracting settlers. He succeeded in recruiting 24 boatloads of men, women, and children willing to entrust their lives to Viking longboats, and brave the perilous crossing. Only 14 ships arrived, but they quickly established a thriving colony that may have eventually numbered around 5,000 people.

Otto II, the emperor and king of East Francia, died of malaria in 983 after an expedition to southern Italy. Although his infant son, **Otto III** (r.983–1001), managed to hold on to the crown thanks to the strong regency of his mother, Theophano, the East Franks were also faced with an uprising among the **Wends**, the forcibly converted Slavic tribes on the eastern border. The Wends restored their pagan religion and resisted Frankish colonization for nearly two centuries.

In 987, **Toltec** forces conquered the Yucatán Maya and made **Chichen Itza** the **capital** of a Toltec–Maya state. According to the early Mayan chronicle *Chilam Balam*, Chichen Itza was conquered by Toltecs led by Kukulcan, the Mayan name for the Toltec god Quetzlcoatl or "the feathered serpent" – possibly the exiled Toltec king, Topiltzin. Despite the record in the chronicle, however, archaeological findings suggest that the city collapsed around this time.

By the end of the 10th century, the mercantile powers of **Venice** and **Genoa** were beginning to dominate the Adriatic and Tyhrrenian seas respectively. Venice, in particular, enjoyed lucrative trade links with the Byzantine Empire.

Al-Mansur
This 17th century oil painting depicts Al Mansur, or Almanzor to his Christian subordinates. Al Mansur means "the Victorious".

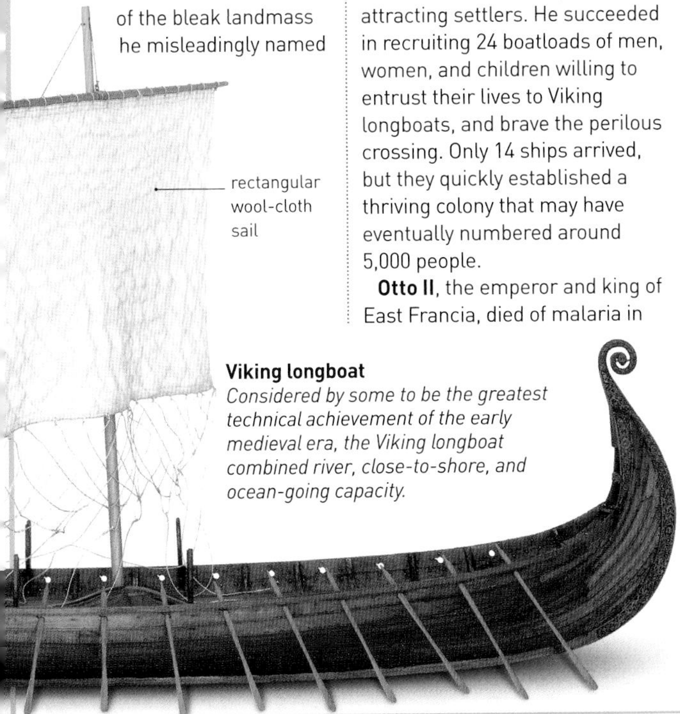

Viking longboat
Considered by some to be the greatest technical achievement of the early medieval era, the Viking longboat combined river, close-to-shore, and ocean-going capacity.

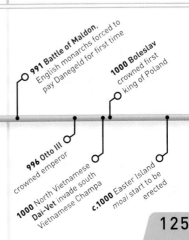

TOLTECS

The Toltecs, who ruled a state centred on Tula in modern-day Mexico, were notable for their aggressive militarism, which changed society in Central America, paving the way for militaristic states such as the Aztec. The term "Toltec" came to mean "city-dweller" or "civilized person", but its literal meaning is "reed person" – signifying an inhabitant of Tollan ("Place of the Reeds", the city now known as Tula). Toltec art and architecture, characterized by monumental masonry and giant statues, was greatly influential in the region.

10,000 KILOGRAMS THE **WEIGHT** IN SILVER OF THE **DANEGELD** IN 991

IN 991, A FORCE OF ANGLO-SAXON WARRIORS made a stand against a much larger army of Vikings at the **Battle of Maldon** in East Anglia, England. They were slaughtered. The English king, **Aethelred II, "the Unready"** (r.978–1016), was forced to pay a tribute known as the **Danegeld**, to buy off further incursions.

Byzantine emperor **Basil II** launched the first of a long series of **campaigns against** his greatest enemy, the **Bulgarian tsar** Samuel, in 996. Basil had won major victories in Syria the year before, but it took him nearly 20 years to finally defeat the Bulgarians.

From around 1000, the inhabitants of **Easter Island**, or **Rapa Nui** – an island in the Pacific Ocean – began to carve monumental statues known as *moai*. Thought to represent ancestors and to channel *mana* – spiritual energy – the cult of *moai* consumed the Easter Islanders to the point where they may have fatally compromised their environment – setting them on the path to ecological disaster.

981 Al-Mansur subjugates Leon, Spain

981 Annam repulses the Northern Song

982 Dai Viet Kingdom destroys Champa capital

983 Death of **Otto II** (b.955)

983 Fatimids control Palestine, Syria

983 Great Wend Rebellion against East Francian expansion

984 Oldest surviving **astrolabe** made in Isfahan

986 Norse settlement of **Greenland**

987 Capetian dynasty founded in France by Hugh Capet

987 Toltec Kukulcan conquers Yucatán Maya and makes Chichen Itza his capital

988 Al-Mansur overruns Leon

988 Byzantine emperor Basil II defeats rebel general Bardas Phocas with help of **"Varangians"** (Russian Vikings) sent by Prince Vladimir of Kievan Rus

c.990 Italian trading city-states **Genoa and Venice** flourish

991 Battle of Maldon, English monarchs forced to pay Danegeld for first time

996 Otto III crowned emperor

1000 North Vietnamese **Dai-Viet** invade south Vietnamese Champa

1000 Boleslav crowned first king of Poland

c.1000 Easter Island *moai* start to be erected

1001 – 1010

These ruins at Pueblo Bonito in Chaco Canyon, reveal one of more than a dozen Great Houses constructed by the Anasazi.

AROUND 1000, THE ANCIENT PUEBLO CIVILIZATION centred on Chaco Canyon in southwest North America reached its climax. The **Anasazi** used sophisticated dryland agriculture and hydrology to thrive in the arid environment, and controlled trade routes that extended as far as the Pacific coast of present-day California and the Valley of Mexico. They achieved **impressive feats of architecture**, most notably the construction of Great Houses such as Pueblo Bonito, one of 13 such buildings in Chaco Canyon. Pueblo Bonito was six stories high and comprised more than 600 rooms. It probably functioned as a ceremonial centre, storage depot, and elite residence. Well-maintained roads – some with stone kerbs – connected Chaco Canyon to thousands of smaller Anasazi settlements across the region. The canyon itself may have been home to as many as 10,000 people, and this set the Anasazi on a collision course with the fragile ecology of the region (see 1161–65).

Mahmud of Ghazni (c.971–1030) was a Muslim intent on **spreading the faith into India**. In 1001, at Peshawar, he defeated Jaipal, raja of Punjab, who then committed suicide.

Probably the **first European to set foot on North America**, Leif Ericson landed in a place he called **Vinland** in around 1002. Shortly after this discovery, Greenlanders under Thorfinn Karlsefni tried to **establish a colony**, spending three winters there. The remains of settlements at L' Anse aux Meadows, in northern Newfoundland, attest to Viking presence in North America.

LEIF ERICSON (970–1020)

Leif was the son of Eric the Red, founder of the Greenland colony (see 981–990). Stories differ on the exact details of his discovery of North America. According to one account, he was returning from a visit to Norway in 1002, where he had been converted to Christianity, and was blown off course, landing at the place he called Vinland because of the grapes growing there. Another account suggests that he aimed for a land sighted to the west by an Icelandic trader.

1011 – 1020

One of the greatest but cruellest Byzantine emperors, Basil II became emperor in 976. Aged 20, he ruled for nearly 50 years.

MURASAKI SHIKIBU (LADY MURASAKI) wrote the novel *Genji Monogatari* (*The Tale of Genji*) in instalments between 1011 and 1021. It is regarded as the **first Japanese novel**, and possibly the first psychological novel in world literature.

In 1014, **Brian Boru, High King of Ireland** and self-styled Emperor of the Gael, defeated a coalition of Dublin Vikings and Celtic Leinstermen at Clontarf, in Ireland. Although the Norse kingdom was crushed and Viking incursions into Ireland halted, Brian Boru was killed in the battle and his **dream of a united Irish kingdom** fell apart thereafter.

In 1014, at the culmination of an 18-year war (see 991–1000), the **Byzantine emperor Basil II** defeated the armies of the Bulgarian tsar at Belasita. Earning the name Bulgaroktonos (Bulgar Slayer), he put out the eyes of 15,000 captured warriors before sending them home. Basil's arch-enemy, Samuel the Bulgarian, was said to have died of shock. By the end of the decade the Bulgarians finally submitted to **Byzantine annexation**.

Lady Murasaki
A scene from a 16th century hanging scroll depicts author Lady Murasaki. Of noble birth, she chronicled the affairs of the Heian court.

The bloody Battle of Clontarf
Fought between the largest armies yet assembled in Ireland, the Battle of Clontarf was a bloody affair. Up to 4,000 Gaels and up to 6,000 Norse and their allies were killed.

1021 – 1030

The Brihadishvara temple was built by the Cholas in their capital Tanjore.

IN 1025, THE CHOLA KING RAJENDRA CHOLADEVRA launched an audacious naval expedition against the maritime empire of Srivijaya in Sumatra, also sacking the Pegu kingdom in Burma. Rajendra had inherited a strong kingdom from his father, Rajaraja I, who had conquered Sri Lanka and instituted a programme of **Hindu temple building** centred on the Chola capital of Tanjore. Under Rajendra, the Cholas expanded their kingdom to include Bengal, and shattered the power of Srivijaya, securing control of the **lucrative Indian-Chinese trade routes**.

Cnut (also known as Canute) was the son of Sven Forkbeard, king of Denmark and Norway, who had **invaded England** and driven the Anglo-Saxon king, Aethelred II, into exile in Normandy in 1013. After staging his own successful invasion in 1015, Cnut was accepted as overlord of all England in 1016, and went on to expand his empire. By 1030, it included Norway, Denmark, and the Faroe, Shetland, and Orkney islands.

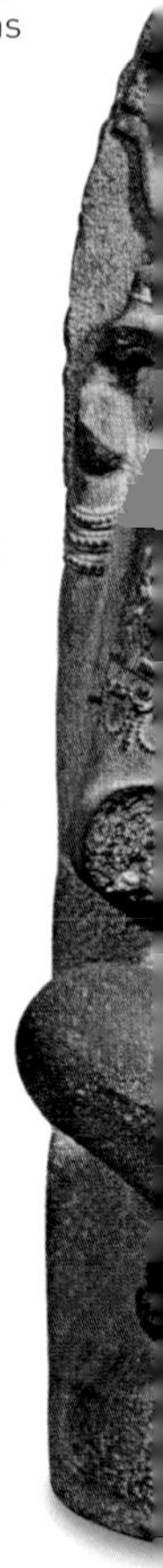

Chola sculpture of Shiva
The Cholas were staunch Hindus and enthusiastic temple builders. Shiva, one of the major Hindu deities, is depicted here as a young and handsome man.

c.1000 Height of **Chaco Canyon Anasazi**

c.1000 Great age of **Chinese ceramics** begins

1001 Mahmud of Ghazni conquers Punjab

1001 Stephen becomes the first king of **Hungary**

1002 Leif Ericson discovers Vinland

1002 Death of **Otto III**; Henry II claims German crown

1003 Brian Boru becomes High King of **Ireland**

1003 Byzantine emperor **Basil II** defeats the Bulgarian tsar Samuel

1009 Completion of **Siva temple** in Tanjore

1009 Mahmud of Ghazni conquers Ghur in Afghanistan

1010 Founding of **Ly Dynasty** of Vietnamese kingdom of Dai-co-viet

1010 Khitans ravage Korea

c.1010 Persian poet **Firdausi** completes *Shah-nama* (*The Book of Kings*)

1013 Boleslaw the Brave of Poland pays homage to Henry II (the **Peace of Merseberg**)

1013 Sven Forkbeard of Denmark conquers England

1014 Battle of Clontarf breaks Viking dominion in Ireland

1014 Henry II crowned Emperor

1014 Cnut becomes ing of England

1014 Basil II blinds Bulgarian army

1016 Cnut establishes overlordship over all England

1016 Norman adventurers active in southern Italy

1018 Rajendra Chola conquers Sri Lanka

1018 Celibacy introduced for Roman Catholic priests

1019 Jaroslav defeats his brother to become Grand Duke of Kievan Rus

1021 St Vitus' Dance epidemic, affecting the nervous system, sweeps Europe

1022 Suppression of the **Bogomil heresy**; Roman Catholic Church begins practice of burning heretics

1022 Avicenna's *Book of Healing* written

1024 Boleslaw the Brave crowned king of Poland, dies the following year

A wise and capable king, Cnut managed conciliation between his Danish and Anglo-Saxon subjects. He collected Danegeld (Danish tax) to pay for a standing navy and army – an important innovation.

1031 – 1040

The Seljuks are shown here battling the Byzantines, having already conquered Persia.

IN 1037, THE SELJUKS, UNDER CHAGRI BEG AND HIS BROTHER TUGHRIL BEG, invaded Khurasan in Persia. In 1040, they crushed the Ghaznavids at the Battle of Dandanqan, winning control of eastern Persia, the first step on the road to creating a **new Islamic empire**. The Seljuks were Oghuz Turks, originally nomads from Central Asia who had converted to Islam and moved to Transoxiana where they served as mercenaries in the region, before turning their attentions to Khurasan.

In 1031, 40 lesser dynasties were founded on the shattered remnants of the **Cordoba caliphate**, in Spain. Known as the Muluk al-Tawa'if ("Party Kings"), these short-lived dynasties took control of different provinces of Cordoba after the strife that brought down the Umayyads following the **execution of Abd al-Rahman Sanchol**, son of al-Mansur, in 1009. He was the last capable leader of the caliphate but his attempt to move out from behind the throne and take the crown led to his downfall.

Subsequently, the Berber faction nominated their own candidate for caliph and **Cordoba descended into civil war for 22 years**. In 1031, the death of Hisham III, the last Umayyad caliph, who had already lost control of several provinces, led to the final break up of the caliphate, with the **Abbadids** seizing Seville, the **Jahwarids** taking Cordoba and the **Hudids** seizing Saragossa. With the **Islamic state in disarray** the Christian kingdoms to the north were encouraged to expand southwards.

Sancho III of Navarre, who had conquered Castile and was overlord of Christian Spain, died in 1035, and his kingdoms were divided between his two sons. **Ferdinand inherited Castile**, and in 1037 he killed his brother-in-law, the king of Leon and made himself emperor there in 1039. He went on to conquer Navarre and impose serfdom on parts of Muslim Spain and Portugal.

King and Emperor
Ferdinand I was the first ruler of Castile to call himself king. He added the title of emperor after his conquest of Leon.

1041 – 1050

Between 1041 and 1048, Bi Sheng invented the first moveable type printing system, using clay letters held in wax within an iron frame.

BANTU IS A FAMILY OF LANGUAGES that originated in the Bantu homeland (now southern Nigeria and northwestern Cameroon). Bantu-speaking people spread from here to the east and south and Bantu became the **dominant language family in sub-Saharan Africa**, although whether this indicates conquest, colonization, or simply cultural influence is less clear. The Bantu expansion started in the Late Stone Age, accelerating as the Bantu speakers acquired iron technology and cattle-husbandry skills. By the mid-11th century, Bantu tribes had become **sophisticated pastoralists**, able to sustain high population densities and complex social and economic networks. This in turn led to the emergence of chiefdoms, and Bantu speakers dominated Central and southern Africa.

In 1044, Anawrata seized power in the **Pagan kingdom in Burma**. His military prowess and skilful use of Hinayana Buddhism as a cultural and political driver made Pagan the centre of Burmese politics, culture, and religion. He developed Burmese as a written language, instituted a programme of building, and forged trade and cultural links to India and China.

In China, sometime between 1041 and 1048, the commoner Bi (or Pi) Sheng invented the **first moveable type system**. Block printing had been in use in China for centuries, and since the Later Tang dynasty (923–36) had been used for most book production, but Bi Sheng introduced the innovation of using **tiny clay blocks** – one for each character. The characters were moulded on the ends of thin rods of wet clay, which were fired to harden them. Unlike wood, this clay type did not distort when wet and could be used over and over again.

KEY
■ Bantu homeland 2000 BCE
→ Spread of Bantu

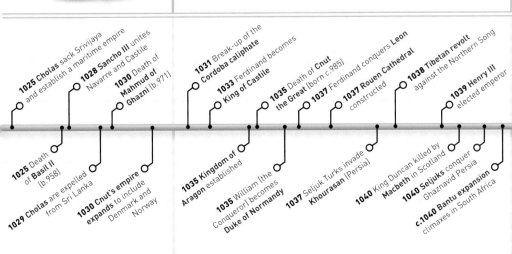

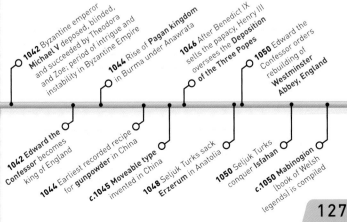

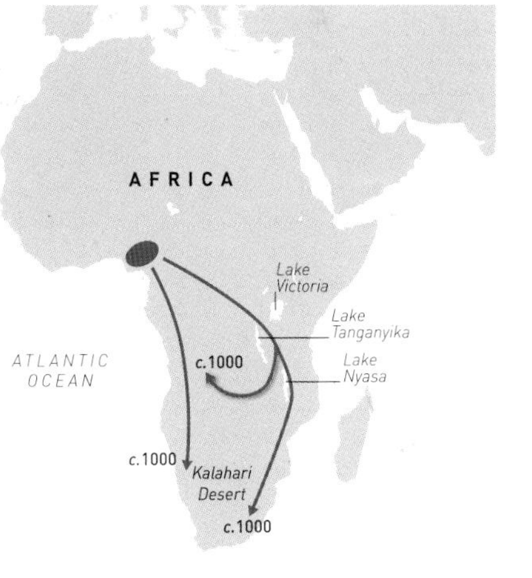

Bantu expansion
From their homeland in the border region of southern Nigeria and northwestern Cameroon, Bantu speaking people spread east and south, through the tropical forest, eventually spreading to all parts of central and southern Africa.

- **1025 Cholas** sack Srivijaya and establish a maritime empire
- **1025** Death of **Basil II** (b.958)
- **1028 Sancho III** unites Navarre and Castile
- **1029 Cholas** are expelled from Sri Lanka
- **1030** Death of **Mahmud of Ghazni** (b.971)
- **1030 Cnut's empire expands** to include Denmark and Norway
- **1031** Break-up of the **Cordoba caliphate**
- **1033** Ferdinand becomes **King of Castile**
- **1035 Kingdom of Aragon** established
- **1035** Death of **Cnut the Great** (born c.985)
- **1035** William (the Conqueror) becomes **Duke of Normandy**
- **1037** Ferdinand conquers **Leon**
- **1037 Rouen Cathedral** constructed
- **1037** Seljuk Turks invade **Khourasan** (Persia)
- **1038 Tibetan revolt** against the Northern Song
- **1039 Henry III** elected emperor
- **1040** King Duncan killed by **Macbeth** in Scotland
- **1040 Seljuks** conquer Ghaznavid Persia
- **c.1040 Bantu expansion** climaxes in South Africa
- **1042** Byzantine emperor **Michael V** deposed, blinded, and succeeded by Theodora and Zoe; period of intrigue and instability in Byzantine Empire
- **1042 Edward the Confessor** becomes king of England
- **1044** Earliest recorded recipe for **gunpowder** in China
- **1044** Rise of **Pagan kingdom** in Burma under Anawrata
- **c.1045 Moveable type** invented in China
- **1046** After Benedict IX sells the papacy, Henry III oversees the **Deposition of the Three Popes**
- **1048** Seljuk Turks sack **Erzerum** in Anatolia
- **1050** Edward the Confessor orders rebuilding of **Westminster Abbey, England**
- **1050** Seljuk Turks conquer **Isfahan**
- **c.1050 Mabinogion** (book of Welsh legends) is compiled

1051–60

Labanga Mosque in Ghana is possibly the oldest mosque in sub-Saharan Africa. Ghana was Islamicized by the Almoravids in the 11th century.

IN MOROCCO, IN 1054, A FIREBRAND CLERIC NAMED IBN YASIN inspired the unification of Saharan tribal groups.The confederation – known as the **Almoravids**, from the Arabic "al-Murabitun" ("people of the frontier garrisons") – **built an empire** that would eventually encompass much of northwestern Africa and Muslim Spain (see 1081–90). In 1056, the Almoravids began the **Islamic conquest of West Africa**, where a number of powerful states had arisen, including that of Ghana.

Yoruba was the name given by outsiders to a group of **city-states in Nigeria** that shared a common language and culture. The oldest and most prestigious Yoruba kingdom was **Ife**, where a **sophisticated urban culture** was well established by the mid-11th century. Ife was the spiritual and mythical centre of the Yoruba, but its poor location meant that it never exerted wide-ranging military or political control over the other Yoruba states. Ife is most famous for its artistic achievements, most notably **terracotta and bronze heads**.

In 1059, Pope Nicholas II recognized **Robert Guiscard** the Norman as Duke of **Apulia** and **Calabria**, and Count of **Sicily** – territories under Byzantine and Arab control – legitimizing his attempts to conquer them.

Ife bronze head
This head probably dates from the 14th century, but it represents an artistic tradition stretching back to the 11th century that was at least as sophisticated as any in contemporary Europe.

1061–70

In this detail from the Bayeux Tapestry, completed in 1080, William the Conqueror exhorts his troops to prepare themselves for battle.

IN 1066, AT THE BATTLE OF HASTINGS, William Duke of Normandy (*c.*1028–87) defeated Harold Godwinson (*c.*1022–66), the last Anglo-Saxon king of England. England had fallen into the Norman orbit earlier, with **Edward the Confessor** spending his youth in exile at the Norman court while Cnut (see 1021–30) ruled England. William claimed that Edward had promised him the English crown, but when Edward died, in 1066, **Harold was elected king**. He marched north to defeat a Norse invasion, before dashing south to Hastings to face William, where **he was killed and his army shattered**. William the Conqueror quickly took southeast England, then the southwest, and suppressed a great uprising in the north in 1069.

Under their leader **Tughril Beg**, the Seljuks had occupied Baghdad and **ended the Buwayhid dynasty** (see 931–50), retaining the Abbasid caliph as a figurehead but giving him the title of sultan. Tughril Beg died in 1063; his successor Alp Arslan **extended Seljuk dominion** into Anatolia, Armenia, and Syria.

2:1 **Battle of Hastings**
Anglo-Saxon casualties outnumbered Norman losses by two-to-one, thanks in part to their forced march from the north, and the advanced Norman tactics.

1071–80

INVESTITURE CONTROVERSY

Which was greater: secular or religious authority? This was the question at the heart of the Investiture Controversy. This 12th-century manuscript illumination shows Henry IV requesting mediation from Matilda of Tuscany and Hugh of Cluny. Matilda was one of the most powerful women of the Middle Ages. It was her stronghold of Canossa where Henry made his penitence.

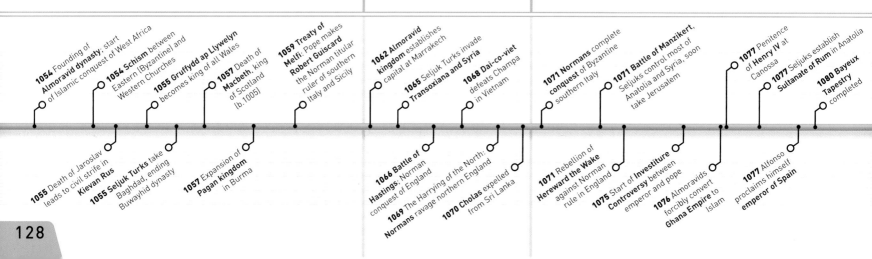

SINCE CHARLEMAGNE'S CORONATION BY THE POPE (see 791–800), the Western emperors had considered it their divine right to appoint – or invest – bishops. Emperors had derived great income and power through their **dispensation of religious offices**, and Emperor Henry III (1017–56) had gone further still, in 1046, insisting that it was the **emperor's right** to appoint the pope. **Pope Gregory VII** represented the opposite view; he held that only popes had the right to invest clerics. In 1075, at the Lent synod, Gregory issued a decree forbidding lay investiture. The emperor, **Henry IV** (1050–1106), who was fighting to reduce the power of German prelates, defied the decree. In 1076, Gregory **excommunicated** him, absolving his subjects of their oaths of loyalty and triggering a **rebellion by Saxon nobles against the king**. In 1077, Henry IV crossed the Alps in the dead of winter and appeared at Canossa, dressed as a penitent, to submit to the pope (see panel, above). He was absolved but controversy quickly flared up again, with a rival, **Rudolf of Swabia**, being elected to the German (formerly East Frankish) throne. In 1080, Henry had a rival pope elected, while Gregory allied himself with **Roger Guiscard**, Count of Sicily, against the imperial camp.

In 1071, the **Seljuks crushed the Byzantine army** at Manzikert, capturing and ransoming Emperor Romanus IV and going on to conquer Anatolia (present-day Turkey). This began its transformation into a **Muslim Turkish region**. In 1077, the Seljuks established the **Sultanate of Rum** there, while other conquests brought them Syria and Jerusalem.

1054 Founding of **Almoravid dynasty**; start of Islamic conquest of West Africa

1054 Schism between Eastern (Byzantine) and Western Churches

1055 Death of Jaroslav leads to civil strife in **Kievan Rus**

1055 Gruffydd ap Llywelyn becomes king of all Wales

1055 Seljuk Turks take Baghdad, ending Buwayhid dynasty

1057 Death of **Macbeth**, king of Scotland (b.1005)

1057 Expansion of **Pagan kingdom** in Burma

1059 Treaty of Melfi: Pope makes **Robert Guiscard** the Norman titular ruler of southern Italy and Sicily

1062 Almoravid kingdom establishes capital at Marrakech

1065 Seljuk Turks invade **Transoxiana and Syria**

1066 Battle of Hastings; Norman conquest of England

1068 Dai-co-viet defeats Champa in Vietnam

1069 The Harrying of the North: **Normans** ravage northern England

1070 Cholas expelled from Sri Lanka

1071 Normans complete **conquest** of Byzantine southern Italy

1071 Battle of Manzikert, Seljuks control most of Anatolia and Syria, soon take Jerusalem

1071 Rebellion of **Hereward the Wake** against Norman rule in England

1075 Start of **Investiture Controversy** between emperor and pope

1076 Almoravids forcibly convert **Ghana Empire** to Islam

1077 Penitence of **Henry IV** at Canossa

1077 Seljuks establish **Sultanate of Rum** in Anatolia

1077 Alfonso proclaims himself **emperor of Spain**

1080 Bayeux Tapestry completed

1081–90

Hassan-i Sabbah leads initiations at Alamut, in an illustration from Marco Polo's 13th-century *Travels*.

IN 1090, A GROUP OF ISMAILI SHI'ITES BECAME INVOLVED IN A DISPUTE over the Fatimid succession in Cairo (see 901–10). Under the leadership of the charismatic **Hassan-i Sabbah**, this group recognized the claims of an infant called Nizar, and were therefore known as **Nizari Ismailis**. Forced to flee Cairo, Hassan led the Nizaris to his homeland in Persia where they captured a fortress known as **Alamut** in the mountainous region of Kazvin and made it the base of a de facto **Nizari kingdom**. Thus was born the group later known as the **Assassins** – a name derived from the word "hashashins", a label applied by their enemies who claimed they used intoxicants such as hashish to brainwash devotees into blind obedience.

Alarmed by the advances of **Alfonso VI of Castile**, the **Abbadids** (see 1031) summoned the **Almoravids** from North Africa to defend against the Christian threat. Defeating Alfonso at Zallaka in 1086, they annexed most of Islamic Spain.

In 1085, **William the Conqueror** (see 1061) commissioned a survey of his new kingdom – known as the **Domesday Book** – probably to regulate military service and assess taxation opportunities.

13 THOUSAND
THE NUMBER OF PLACES LISTED IN THE **DOMESDAY BOOK**

The Domesday Book
Nicknamed "Domesday" in reflection of the trepidation that the great undertaking inspired in the native English, William's survey actually comprised two manuscripts; the Great and Little Domesday.

1091–1100

❝ LET SUCH AS ARE GOING TO FIGHT FOR CHRISTIANITY PUT THE FORM OF THE CROSS UPON THEIR GARMENTS THAT THEY MAY OUTWARDLY DEMONSTRATE THEIR DEVOTION TO THEIR INWARD FAITH. ❞

Pope Urban II, 1095

IN 1092, CHINESE POLYMATH SU SUNG DESIGNED AND CONSTRUCTED A COSMIC ENGINE. This mechanical astronomical clock was 9m (30ft) high, and was water-driven with an armillary sphere, which showed the position of celestial objects.

In 1094, a Castilian who had served both Christian and Islamic Masters, Rodrigo Diaz de Vivar, known by the Moors as **El Cid** ("the lord"), captured Valencia in eastern Spain and established himself as ruler.

At the **Council of Clermont** in 1095, Pope Urban, a French Cluniac (see 910), preached to an assembly of mainly Frankish clerics and nobles about Muslim "defilement" of the Holy Land, urging his audience to take up arms in a **holy war**. Urban had been entreated by the Byzantines for help against the Seljuks, and saw a way to channel the energies of European nobility away from constant in-fighting and towards a **Christian expansion** that would benefit the papacy. Fired by religious zeal and spurred by the promise of remission of sins, together with the prospect of winning booty, land, and control of the lucrative trade with the Orient, many nobles of France (formerly West Francia) and Lorraine joined, or "took the cross".

Other nations were either in conflict with the papacy or indifferent, so the **First Crusade** was a largely French affair. Taking advantage of disarray in the Muslim world, three groups of Crusaders under Godfrey and Baldwin of Bouillon, Count Raymond of Toulouse, and the Norman Bohemond of Otranto, took the Seljuk Rum capital of **Nicaea** in 1097, conquered **Edessa** in the same year, captured **Antioch** in 1098, and marched on **Jerusalem** in 1099. Godfrey was elected king of Jerusalem but took the title **Defender of the Holy Sepulchre**; his brother, Baldwin became king the following year. Under the overlordship of the King of Jerusalem, the Crusaders established **four principal states**: the kingdom of Jerusalem, which thrived on trade mediated by the Italian trading powers; the county of Tripoli, set up by Raymond; the county of Edessa, established by Baldwin; and the principality of Antioch, set up by Bohemund.

Battle of the Crusades
This manuscript illustration shows Crusader knights joining battle with Saracens – the generic term used by Europeans to refer to their Muslim foes. Around 30,000 knights took part in the First Crusade.

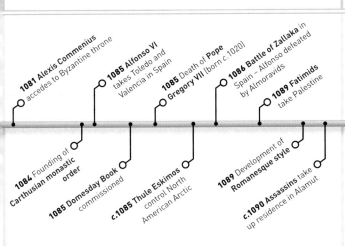

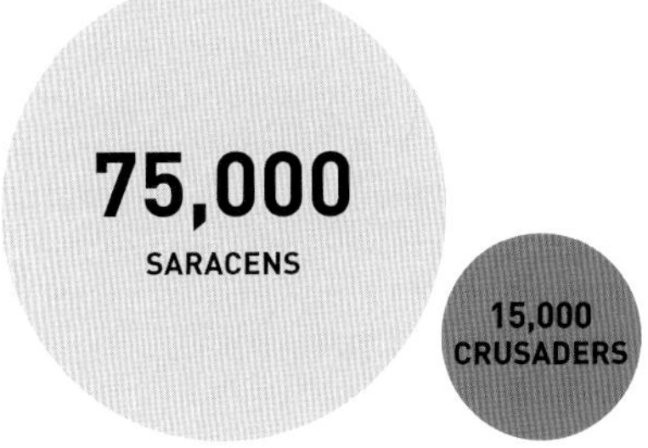

The Siege of Antioch
Islamic forces at the Siege of Antioch outnumbered the Crusaders considerably. In fact Antioch fell only when a traitor opened a gate to a party of knights led by Bohemond of Otranto.

- **1081 Alexis Commenius** accedes to Byzantine throne
- **1084** Founding of **Carthusian monastic order**
- **1085 Alfonso VI** takes Toledo and Valencia in Spain
- **1085 Domesday Book** commissioned
- **1085** Death of **Pope Gregory VII** (born c.1020)
- **c.1085 Thule Eskimos** control North American Arctic
- **1086 Battle of Zallaka** in Spain – Alfonso defeated by Almoravids
- **1089 Fatimids** take Palestine
- **1089** Development of **Romanesque style**
- **c.1090 Assassins** take up residence in Alamut
- **1092** Normans complete conquest of **Sicily**
- **1092** Su Sung builds **Cosmic Engine mechanical clock** in Peking
- **1092** Death of **Seljuk** sultan **Malik Shah**; Seljuk Empire begins to break up
- **1094 El Cid** takes Valencia
- **1095** Pope Urban proclaims **First Crusade**
- **1096** Construction of **Basilica San Marco**, Venice
- **1097** Crusaders sack **Constantinople**
- **1098 Antioch** falls to Crusaders after year-long siege
- **1098** Founding of the **Cistercian order**
- **1098 Council of Bari**: attempt to reunify Eastern and Western Churches
- **1099** Crusaders take Jerusalem: **end of the First Crusade**
- **1099 Knights Hospitaller** established
- **1099** Death of **El Cid** (b.1043)
- **1100 Baldwin I** becomes first king of Jerusalem
- **1100** William II killed in hunting accident, **Henry I** becomes king of England
- **1100** Euclid translated from Arabic into Latin by **Adelard of Bath**

1101–05

An illustration from Edward Fitzgerald's translation of the *Rubaiyat*; of the 600 verses, only around 120 are thought to have been written by Khayyam himself.

SOMETIME AROUND THE START OF THE 12TH CENTURY, OMAR KHAYYAM (1048–1131), an astronomer and mathematician in the service of the **Seljuk sultans**, composed a series of four-line poems, or "roba'iyat", which became famous thanks to the translation made by **Edward Fitzgerald** in 1859. Khayyam's career reflected the Seljuk era. At **Samarkand**, in the early 1070s, he was able to pursue his **mathematical studies** thanks to patronage from a local jurist, and under the strong Seljuk sultan **Malik Shah** (r.1072–92), Khayyam was invited to **Isfahan** in 1073 to **set up an observatory** and lead a team of top scholars. In this period he made many **mathematical and astronomical breakthroughs**, including an unprecedented accurate measurement of **the length of the year** to 12 decimal places. Although he is now most famous for the ***Rubaiyat***, it is not certain that Khayyam wrote most or any of the verses involved, and he was little regarded as a poet in his own time. Much of the current reputation of the work derives from the very free translation by Edward Fitzgerald.

The success of the **First Crusade** (see 1091–1100) owed much to the disarray of the Islamic regimes it had dispossessed. The **Fatimid Caliphate** in Cairo was rich but decadent; the **Abbasids** in Baghdad were little more than figureheads; the **Seljuk Turks** had failed to forge a unified empire, and instead warlords and tribal groups had set up a patchwork of competing states such as **Rum**, **Danishmend**, and **Damascus**. Throughout the early 12th century, the Crusaders battled constantly against these foes. In 1101, **Raymond IV of Toulouse** (*c.*1042–1105) led a new Crusader army from **Constantinople** against the Sultanate of Rum, taking **Ankara** in June, only to be destroyed by Danishmend Turks in August. **Baldwin I of Jerusalem** (*c.*1058–1118) steadily improved his access to the Mediterranean by taking a series of coastal cities from the **Fatimids**, defeating them at **Jaffa** in 1102, **Acre** in 1104, and **Ramleh** in 1105, although Raymond died in an attempt to take **Tripoli** in 1105.

Baldwin of Bourcq
This coin features Baldwin of Bourcq, cousin of Baldwin I who he succeeded as count of Edessa, then as king of Jerusalem (see 1118).

1106–10

Monumental ruins in the city of Great Zimbabwe, capital of the Mwene Mutapa Empire. After it seized control of the gold trade, the empire grew rich.

NOTED FOR ITS FINE ARTS AND CRAFTS and construction of **monumental temple mounds**, the post-Moche culture, known as the **Sicán** or **Lambayeque** on the northern coast of Peru, reached its height in the early 11th century. But a prolonged drought, followed by catastrophic flooding, led to **cultural and political collapse**. In the early 12th century, the state recovered from the convulsions of the 11th century and rebuilt around a new capital at **Túcume**. New temples were built and the capital flourished until its conquest by the **Chimú** (see 1375), by which time there were 26 mounds and accompanying enclosures.

In central southern Africa, in what is now Zimbabwe, the **Mwene Mutapa Empire**, also known as **Great Zimbabwe** after its monumental capital, emerged as the most significant regional power. A kingdom of the **Shona** peoples that emerged around 900, Mwene Mutapa was initially based on cattle herding, but from around 1100 it took control of the lucrative **trade routes** linking the gold, iron, and ivory production centres of the interior to the **Arab trading kingdoms** on the east coast, which offered luxury goods from Asia.

Ceremonial knife
This gold knife is from the Middle Sicán culture in Peru. The early 1100s mark the threshold between the Middle and Late Sicán cultures.

1111–15

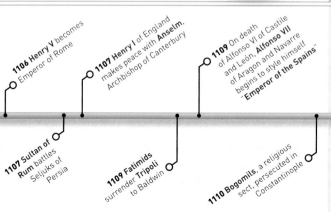

The 12th-century Cathedral of St Nicholas at Novgorod, Russia.

THE 12TH CENTURY SAW AN EXPLOSION OF CATHEDRAL BUILDING all over Europe, as population growth, increased wealth, and architectural **advances** combined with religious zeal, **civic pride**, and the personal ambition of potentates. The development of the **Romanesque and Gothic styles** was given expression in the great cathedrals, but each region developed its own, distinctive idiom. In **Novgorod**, for instance, the **Cathedral of St Nicholas** (started in 1113) was given domed cupolas.

The **Investiture Controversy** between the papacy and the Western emperors rumbled on (see 1071–80). **Henry IV**'s failure to reconcile with the papacy had helped bring about his downfall; concerned that the ongoing dispute was undermining royal authority, his own family had conspired against him, and he was imprisoned. His successor, **Henry V** (1086–1125) launched a powerful expedition to **Italy** to force an **imperial coronation**. Under duress (he was a prisoner of Henry at the time), **Pope Paschal II** offered major concessions on the investiture issue in the **Treaty of Sutri**, but he repudiated them the following year and the issue remained unsettled (see 1122).

- **c.1100** Apogee of the **Mwene Mutapa Empire**, also known as Great Zimbabwe
- **c.1100** Omar Khayyam composes the *Rubaiyat*
- **1101 Raymond IV of Toulouse** invades Sultanate of Rum but is defeated by Danishmend Turks
- **c.1102 Baldwin I**, king of Jerusalem, defeats Fatimids at Jaffa
- **c.1105** Baldwin I defeats **Fatimids** at Ramleh
- **1105** Construction of the **Ananda Temple** in Burma
- **1106 Henry V** becomes Emperor of Rome
- **1107 Sultan of Rum** battles Seljuks of Persia
- **1107 Henry I** of England makes peace with **Anselm**, Archbishop of Canterbury
- **1109 Fatimids** surrender **Tripoli** to Baldwin
- **1109** On death of Alfonso VI of Castile and León, **Alfonso VII** of Aragon and Navarre begins to style himself **"Emperor of the Spains"**
- **1110 Bogomils**, a religious sect, persecuted in Constantinople
- **1111** Imperial coronation of **Henry V** in Rome
- **1112** Start of reign of **Alaungsithu**; Burmese kingdom of **Pagan** reaches height
- **1115 Raymond Berengar III**, count of Barcelona, expels **Moors** from Balearics
- **1115 Matilda of Tuscany** dies (b.1046); **Florence** becomes a self-governing commune

1116–20

1121–25

Stained glass window of a Templar Knight in Warwickshire, England.

Guelph and Ghibelline forces join battle in Italy. These factions, based on the German Welf and Hohenstaufen dynasties, would come to dominate Italian politics.

> “IN THIS **RELIGIOUS ORDER** HAS **FLOURISHED** AND IS **REVITALIZED** THE **ORDER** OF KNIGHTHOOD.”

From *The Primitive Rule of the Knights Templar*

In **Jerusalem**, in 1119, a group of knights, led by the French Hugues de Payens (*c.*1070–1136), formed an order to **protect pilgrims** travelling along the dangerous road from Jaffa, on the coast, to the holy city. The new king of Jerusalem, **Baldwin II** (cousin of Baldwin I and his successor as count of Edessa), assigned them quarters in part of the **Temple Mount** compound, next to the site where the **Temple of Solomon** had once stood. Accordingly, they called themselves the Poor Fellow Soldiers of Christ and of the Temple of Solomon – also known as the **Knights Templar**.

Bologna University was the first in the western world. It was founded in 1119 (or possibly earlier, depending on the source). Institutions such as Bologna University were the incubators for the philosophical school of thought known as **Scholasticism** (see panel, right).

IN 1121, MOHAMMAD IB-TUMART, A BERBER LEADER from the Atlas Mountains, was hailed as the **al-Mahdi** (the Muslim messiah – see 874) and led his forces, known as the **Almohads**, in a **campaign of conquest** against Almoravid territories in Africa.

A synod at the German town of **Worms**, in 1122, presided by a papal legate drew up a concordat (agreement) ending the **Investiture Controversy** – though not the imperial–papal rivalry. A compromise was agreed along the lines already adopted between **Henry I of England** and **Anselm** (see 1107), under which the emperor would be involved in investiture but not control it. Essentially it was a **victory for the papacy**.

In 1123, **Frankish forces** from Jerusalem **defeated a Fatimid army** at Ibelin, while off the coast at Ascalon (Ashkelon), Venetian ships destroyed the Fatimid fleet. This marked the start of the dominance of **Italian maritime power** in the Mediterranean.

Emperor Henry V died in 1125, with no male heir, and an election was held to choose his successor. The closest heir was **Conrad of Swabia** (1122–90), of the house of **Hohenstaufen** (allied to the Salian dynasty and their anti-papal policies), but the powerful archbishops of Mainz and Cologne angled for the election of a candidate more friendly to the Church. **Lothair of Saxony** (1075–1137), of the house of Welf, was chosen and became **Emperor Lothair II** (III in some sources). Immediately he was plunged into a bitter **civil war** with the Hohenstaufens, and the two opposing sides became entrenched as pro-papal and pro-imperial factions known as the **Guelphs** and **Ghibellines** respectively. They would plague relations between and within the **city-states of northern Italy** into the 14th century – long after they had ceased to dominate German power politics – as they became associated with class struggles and **reactionary versus reforming parties**.

The work of **Aristotle** (384–322 BCE) had survived in Byzantium and among the Arabs, but Western Europeans only had access to a translation by the philosopher **Boethius** of one treatise on logic. This began to change in the early 12th century, as the conquest of Islamic areas such as **Toledo** and **Sicily** gave Christian scholars access to Arabic works. Increasing exposure to the works of Aristotle led medieval scholars to consider him the "**master of those who know**" and the chief authority on matters of reason.

In 1125, the French king **Louis VI** (1081–1137) successfully rallied French nobles to repel an **English–German invasion**. This proved to be a milestone in the French monarchy's attempts to assert its authority, and thus in the emergence of **France as a nation-state**.

SCHOLASTICISM

The school of thought known as Scholasticism – because it was taught by the scholastics, or school masters – developed as the dominant philosophy of learning in medieval Europe, hand in hand with the emergence of the universities. Scholasticism was an approach to learning that used a method of formal discussion and debating. It became the intellectual basis for medieval religious and philosophical dogma.

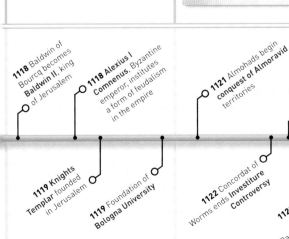

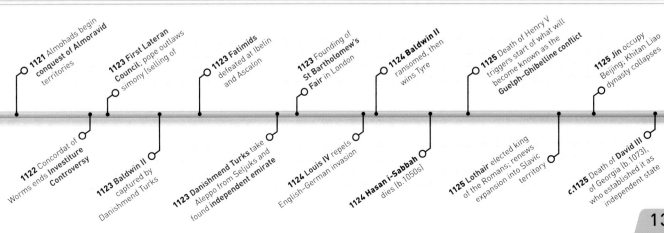

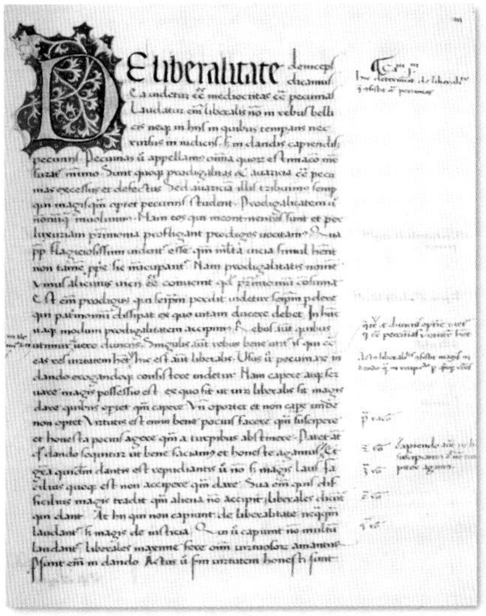

De liberalitate

Aristotle in translation
A page from a translation of Aristotle's Nicomachean Ethics, *written on vellum – a writing material made from calf skin, which is more durable than papyrus or paper.*

25 PER CENT THE APPROXIMATE **PROPORTION** OF **ARISTOTLE'S WORK SURVIVING** TODAY

1118 Baldwin of Bourcq becomes **Baldwin II**, king of Jerusalem

1118 Alexius I Comnenus, Byzantine emperor, institutes a form of feudalism in the empire

1119 Knights Templar founded in Jerusalem

1119 Foundation of **Bologna University**

1121 Almohads begin **conquest of Almoravid** territories

1122 Concordat of Worms ends **Investiture Controversy**

1123 First Lateran Council, pope outlaws simony (selling of

1123 Baldwin II captured by Danishmend Turks

1123 Fatimids defeated at Ibelin and Ascalon

1123 Danishmend Turks take Aleppo from Seljuks and found **independent emirate**

1123 Founding of **St Bartholomew's Fair** in London

1124 Louis IV repels English–German invasion

1124 Baldwin II ransomed, then wins Tyre

1124 Hasan i-Sabbah dies (b.1050s)

1125 Death of Henry V triggers start of what will become known as the **Guelph–Ghibelline conflict**

1125 Lothair elected king of the Romans; renews expansion into Slavic territory

1125 Jin occupy Beijing; Khitan Liao dynasty collapses

c.1125 Death of **David III** of Georgia (b.1073), who established it as independent state

1126–30

A mosaic shows Roger II being symbolically crowned by Christ.

IN 1126, THE JIN – the Jurchen dynasty established by Aguda (see 1115) in Manchuria – turned on their erstwhile Chinese allies, **overrunning northern China** and seizing the Northern Song capital at **Kaifeng**. The Jin took control of northern China and moved the capital to Beijing. This marked the **end of the Northern Song**. However, a Song prince, **Gaozong**, escaped to the south and established the **Southern Song** dynasty in Hangzhou in 1127.

The death of **Pope Honorius**, in 1130, resulted in the election of two rival popes, **Innocent II** and **Anacletus II**. During this papal schism, **Roger II**, count of Sicily, recognized Anacletus as pope – his reward was the throne of Sicily.

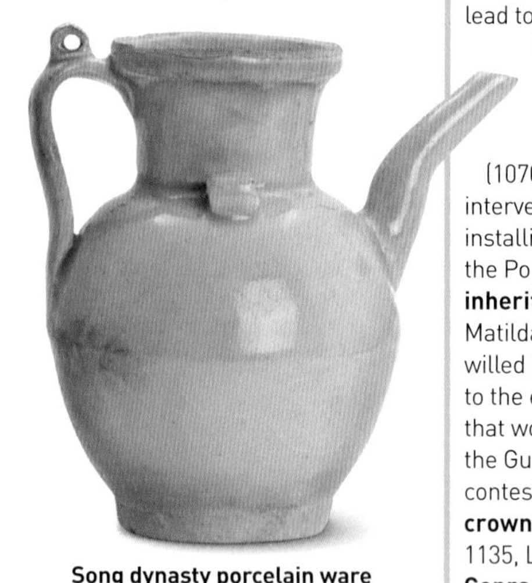

Song dynasty porcelain ware
The Qingbai ("blue-white") glaze on this ewer is characteristic of Song dynasty porcelain from southeastern China, where the dynasty survived the Jin invasion.

1131–35

St Alban's Chronicle, shows Matilda of England holding a charter.

THE DEATH OF HENRY I, IN 1135, PITCHED ENGLAND INTO DYNASTIC STRIFE. His only male heir died in 1120 while crossing the English Channel, and although Henry had made his nobles swear allegiance to his daughter, the **Empress Matilda** (1102–67), she had spent little time in England and her second husband, **Geoffrey of Anjou**, was unpopular with the English nobles. Among those who had sworn fealty to Matilda was Henry's nephew and ward **Stephen of Blois** (r.1135–54). On his uncle's death he immediately went to London, secured the support of most of the nobles and the Church, and **had himself proclaimed king**. However, Matilda refused to renounce her claim, and their contest would lead to a period of warfare and breakdown of central authority known as the **Anarchy** (see 1136–40).

In 1133, **Lothair II** (1070–1137) went to Italy to intervene in the **papal schism**, installing **Innocent II**. In return, the Pope confirmed the **Matildine inheritance** (the vast estates of Matilda of Tuscany, which she had willed first to the papacy and then to the emperor, sparking a dispute that would become tied up with the Guelph versus Ghibelline contest – (see 1121–25) and **crowned Lothair as emperor**. In 1135, Lothair pacified his rivals, **Conrad of Hohenstaufen** and his brother **Frederick of Swabia**, apparently securing the German crown for his son-in-law **Henry the Proud**, of the House of Welf.

1136–40

An illustration from a 15th-century copy of the *History of the Kings of Britain*, by Geoffrey of Monmouth, shows Brutus the Trojan setting sail for Britain.

IN 1137, LOTHAIR DIED SUDDENLY while returning from a successful campaign in Italy against **Roger of Sicily**. Lothair's plans to concentrate German territories in the hands of the **Welf clan**, and create a stable inheritance for his son-in-law, evaporated when the election of 1138 chose the Waiblinger **Conrad of Hohenstaufen** (1135–95). The Waiblingers were descended from the dukes of Franconia; the name was later corrupted by the Italians into "Ghibelline". Conrad set about reversing the grants of Lothair, taking Saxony away from the Welfs, which promptly sparked renewed civil war.

In 1139, Matilda entered England to reclaim her crown from the usurper Stephen of Blois. Stephen had failed to strengthen his position since taking the crown, alienating many of his nobles, on one hand, and powerful clerics, on the other. He particularly blundered by arresting his chief minister Roger, Bishop of Salisbury. At a stroke, he lost many of his ablest administrators, and was henceforth unable to rein in the depredations of barons and other landowners, who became laws unto themselves. The country deteriorated into a state of anarchy famously lamented by the author of the Peterborough Chronicle, who wrote that under Stephen's reign the English "suffered nineteen long winters... when Christ and all his saints slept".

Sometime around 1140, the Welsh cleric **Geoffrey of Monmouth** (*c.*1100–55) wrote the *History of the Kings of Britain*, an important example of early Anglo-Norman literature that introduced the legend of **King Arthur** to a European audience.

Legendary castle
Tintagel, Cornwall, where the ruins of a 13th-century castle still stand, is featured in the Arthurian legends created by Geoffrey of Monmouth.

1141–45

A scene from the Siege of Damascus, a battle of the Second Crusade.

IN 1141, JOHN OF SEVILLE TRANSLATED FROM THE ARABIC the *Epitome of the Whole of Astrology*, while in 1142 **Adelard of Bath** translated an Arabic version of Euclid's *Elements of Geometry*, one of the founding texts of mathematics. This **transmission of learning**, ancient and contemporary, via Arabic into Latin, was a key contributor to the emergence of an **intellectual renaissance** in Europe, and beyond that to the scientific achievements of the **Early Modern period** (1500–1800).

In an attempt to end the **civil war** that was convulsing Germany, an 1142 meeting, or diet, at Frankfurt confirmed the Welf **Henry the Lion** (1129–95) as **Duke of Saxony** (which he had already taken by force). Henry engaged in a vigorous renewal of **German expansion** to the east, where his

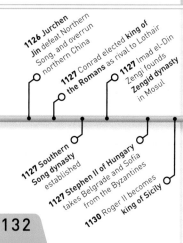

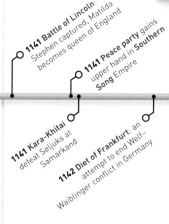

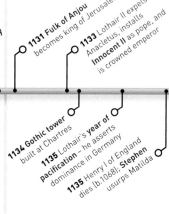

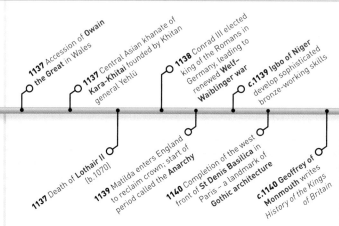

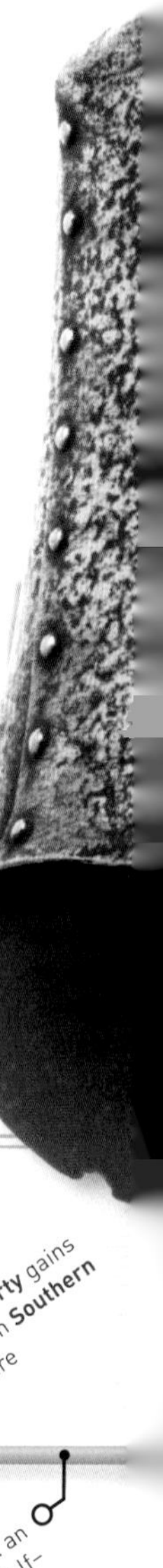

Pot helm helmet
This type of helmet was typical of those worn by Crusader knights. Made of steel, the pot helm helmet completely covered the head save for two small eyeslits.

- **1126 Jurchen Jin** defeat Northern Song, and overrun northern China
- **1127 Southern Song dynasty** established
- **1127** Conrad elected **king of the Romans** as rival to Lothair
- **1127** Imad el-Din Zengi founds **Zengid dynasty** in Mosul
- **1127 Stephen II of Hungary** takes Belgrade and Sofia from the Byzantines
- **1130** Roger II becomes **king of Sicily**
- **1131 Fulk of Anjou** becomes king of Jerusalem
- **1133** Lothair II expels Anacletus, installs **Innocent II** as pope, and is crowned emperor
- **1134 Gothic tower** built at Chartres
- **1135** Lothair's **year of pacification** – he asserts dominance in Germany
- **1135** Henry I of England dies (b.1068); **Stephen** usurps Matilda
- **1137** Accession of **Owain the Great** in Wales
- **1137** Central Asian khanate of **Kara-Khitai** founded by Khitan general Yehlü
- **1137** Death of **Lothair II** (b.1070)
- **1138** Conrad III elected king of the Romans in Germany, leading to renewed **Welf–Waiblinger war**
- **c.1139 Igbo of Niger** develop sophisticated bronze-working skills
- **1139** Matilda enters England to reclaim crown; start of period called the **Anarchy**
- **1140** Completion of the west front of **St Denis Basilica** in Paris – a landmark of **Gothic architecture**
- **c.1140 Geoffrey of Monmouth** writes *History of the Kings of Britain*
- **1141 Battle of Lincoln**: Stephen captured, Matilda becomes queen of England
- **1141 Peace party** gains upper hand in **Southern Song** Empire
- **1141 Kara-Khitai** defeat Seljuks at Samarkand
- **1142 Diet of Frankfurt**: an attempt to end Welf–Waiblinger conflict in Germany

1146–50

Angkor Wat, in Cambodia, was built during the reign of Suryavarman II. It covers nearly 200 hectares (500 acres) and the central tower is 42m (138ft) high.

“ THOSE WHO ARE OF GOD… **STRIVE** TO **OPPOSE** THE MULTITUDE OF THE **INFIDELS,** WHO **REJOICE** IN A VICTORY GAINED OVER US, AND **DEFEND THE ORIENTAL CHURCH** FREED FROM THEIR **TYRANNY** BY SO GREAT AN OUTPOURING OF THE **BLOOD OF YOUR FATHERS…** **”**

Pope Eugenius III, from Papal bull calling for the Second Crusade, 1145

campaigns against the heathen **Slavs** were given the status of Crusades.

In 1144, the atabeg (governor) of Mosul, **Imad el-Din Zengi** (1085–1146), founder of the **Zengid dynasty**, took advantage of feuding between the Crusader principalities to seize the Crusader county of Edessa. Fulk, king of Jerusalem, had died in 1143 and his successor **Baldwin III** (1130–63) was only a child, under the regency of his mother **Melisende**. She did not have the authority to settle a dispute between Antioch and Edessa, and Imad el-Din besieged Edessa until it fell to him. **The loss of Edessa** caused alarm and outrage in Europe, and provided the trigger for the **Second Crusade** (see 1146–50).

In 1145, Eugenius III issued a call-to-arms in the form of a Papal bull.

IN 1146, THE INFLUENTIAL CISTERCIAN MONK, BERNARD OF CLAIRVAUX (1090–1153), egged on by Pope Eugenius III, preached a new Crusade to liberate Edessa from the clutches of the Zengids; **Conrad III of Germany** (1093–1152) and **Louis VII of France** (1120–80) "took the cross". But the expedition was a **disastrous** affair, except for incidental success in Portugal achieved by a contingent of English and Flemish Crusaders who helped Afonso-Henriques, Count of Portugal, take Lisbon from the **Moors** in 1147. Conrad and Louis took different routes to the Holy Land, their armies meeting equally disastrous fates as they struggled through Anatolia. In 1148, forced to hitch a lift on a Byzantine ship, having lost his army at the **Battle of Dorylaeum**, Conrad met up with Louis. Rather than pitch their depleted forces against the powerful Zengids, they decided instead to launch an attack on Damascus, the only Muslim state that was friendly to the Crusader kingdoms. Hampered by **lack of supplies** and threatened by the Zengid leader Nur al-Din, successor to Imad el-Din, the **Siege of Damascus** also **failed**. The Second Crusade broke up having failed to achieve anything beyond a damaging fallout. Louis was cuckolded by one of his generals, eventually leading to a divorce from his wife, **Eleanor of Aquitaine** (*c.*1122–04), and the loss of her territories (see 1151–55). The **Byzantines** were forced to step in where the Crusade had failed, occupying western Edessa, but **Roger of Sicily** took advantage of Byzantine distraction to invade and plunder Greece in 1147. The disasters of the Second Crusade marked the beginning of the **decline** of the **Frankish Crusader kingdoms**.

In 1147, the **Almohads** under **Abd al-Mu'min** (1094–1163) completed the conquest of Almoravid Morocco, taking **Marrakech**, before invading **Moorish Spain** (although it took them until 1172 to subjugate all the Islamic kingdoms).

Suryavarman II (*c.*1113–50) was the most warlike **Khmer king**, although most of his foreign adventures were unsuccessful. He launched attacks against the **Dai Vet** of northern Vietnam and made repeated attempts to subjugate the **Champa**. More significant was his building programme, the zenith of which was the **temple of Angkor Wat**. This vast complex includes five towers symbolizing holy mountains, and masses of elaborate carvings.

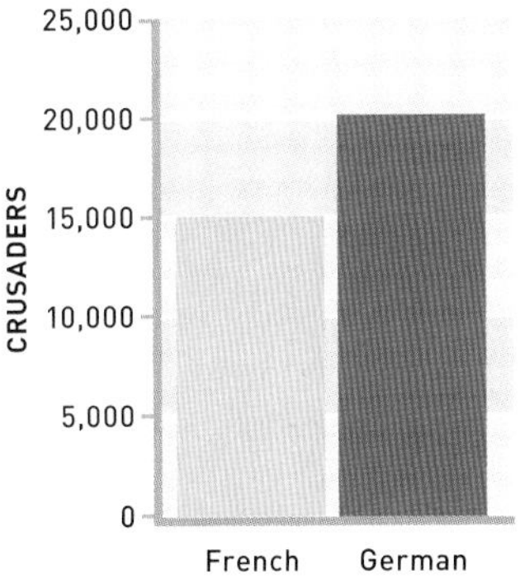

French and German Crusaders
The German force outnumbered the French contingent during the Second Crusade. Neither army achieved any success: defeat in Anatolia preceded failure at Damascus.

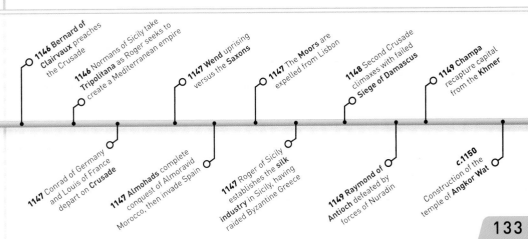

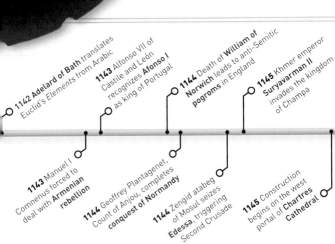

Koutoubia Mosque in Morocco
The Koutoubia ("booksellers") Mosque, built by the Almohads, reflects the mercantile success of Almohad Marrakech, where book, cloth, and other souqs flourished.

200
HECTARES
THE **AREA** OF **ANGKOR WAT**

1142 Adelard of Bath translates Euclid's *Elements* from Arabic

1143 Manuel I Comnenus forced to deal with **Armenian rebellion**

1143 Alfonso VII of Castile and León recognizes **Afonso I** as king of Portugal

1144 Geoffrey Plantagenet, Count of Anjou, completes **conquest of Normandy**

1144 Death of **William of Norwich** leads to anti-Semitic **pogroms** in England

1144 Zengid atabeg of Mosul seizes **Edessa**, triggering Second Crusade

1145 Khmer emperor **Suryavarman II** invades the kingdom of Champa

1145 Construction begins on the west portal of **Chartres Cathedral**

1146 Bernard of Clairvaux preaches the Crusade

1146 Normans of Sicily take **Tripolitana** as Roger seeks to create a Mediterranean empire

1147 Conrad of Germany and Louis of France depart on **Crusade**

1147 Wend uprising versus the **Saxons**

1147 Almohads complete conquest of Almoravid Morocco, then invade Spain

1147 The **Moors** are expelled from Lisbon

1147 Roger of Sicily establishes the **silk industry** in Sicily, having raided Byzantine Greece

1148 Second Crusade climaxes with failed **Siege of Damascus**

1149 Raymond of Antioch defeated by forces of Nuradin

1149 Champa recapture capital from the **Khmer**

c.1150 Construction of the temple of **Angkor Wat**

Persian ceramic and gold leaf ewer
1200–1399 • IRAN
It was prohibited to make drinking vessels from gold and silver, as these were considered indulgent, so Islamic craftsmen became expert in alternatives such as ceramic, which was then richly decorated.

Bronze vase
18TH CENTURY • CHINA
Although this bronze vase from China displays a text from the Qu'ran in Arabic, it nonetheless shows clear Chinese influence.

Star-shaped tile
1267 • IRAN
Though distinctively Islamic in its use of lustre (a ceramic technology mimicking gilding) and arabesques (stylized foliage), this tile shows Mongol influence with the inclusion of dog-like animals.

THE ISLAMIC WORLD

TECHNOLOGICAL INNOVATION AND RELIGIOUS INSPIRATION COMBINE TO CREATE A UNIQUE HERITAGE OF ARTS AND CRAFTS

Islamic arts and crafts were shaped by religious restrictions, cultural heritage acquired through conquest, and the elaboration of unique features, notably the use of ornamentation and colour, and inclusion of Arabic script.

Through its rapid conquest of a huge empire, the Islamic caliphate was exposed to a diverse mix of cultural styles and heritages; Islamic art reflects these while maintaining a high degree of homogeneity due to religious uniformity. Restrictions imposed by Islam, such as prohibitions on representative art and on the use of gold and silver, generated creative responses, especially stylized abstract designs, elaborate ornamentation, strong use of colour, and the use of Arabic script and Qu'ranic quotations.

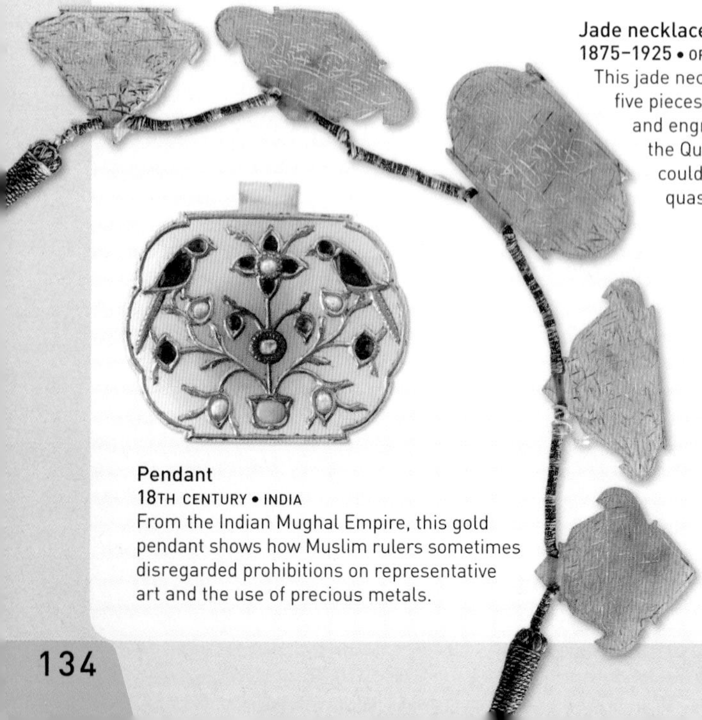

Jade necklace
1875–1925 • ORIGIN UNKNOWN
This jade necklace is made from five pieces, all different in shape and engraved with verses from the Qu'ran. Such artefacts could serve as amulets with quasi-magical powers.

Surgical scissors and scalpel
10TH CENTURY • ORIGIN UNKNOWN
Islamic physicians made huge advances in medicine and surgery, including devising a range of surgical instruments such as the *mibda* (scalpel) and *miqass* (scissors).

Khanjar
19TH CENTURY • INDIA
Although from India, this curved, double-edged dagger is actually a traditional Omani blade. It is decorated with ornate foliage, a typical Islamic motif.

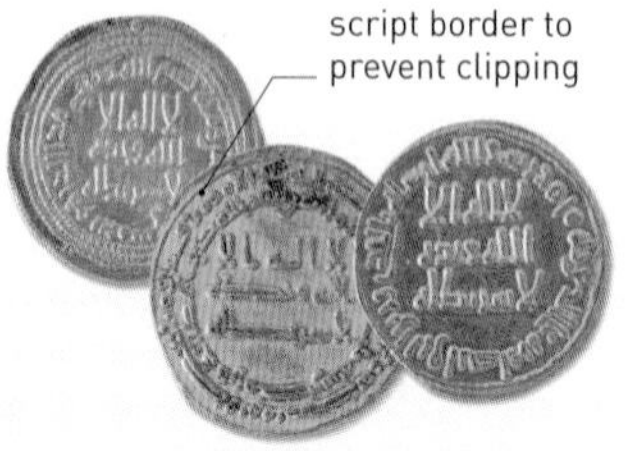

Coins
720–910 • SYRIA/EGYPT
Coins from the Ummayad and Abbadis caliphates, minted in Damascus and Cairo, bear Arabic text in place of pictures of heads of state.

Pendant
18TH CENTURY • INDIA
From the Indian Mughal Empire, this gold pendant shows how Muslim rulers sometimes disregarded prohibitions on representative art and the use of precious metals.

Ornate gilded Shi'ite alam
17TH CENTURY • IRAN
This alam, or standard, made of brass and gold, symbolically recalls the Shi'ite standard planted at the Battle of Kerbala in 680.

owl
000–1199 • IRAN/IRAQ
he bold colours of this simple bowl are ypically Islamic, as is the interlacing cord esign. The lace of highlighted detail lends meditative quality to the design.

Feline incense burner
11–12TH CENTURIES • IRAN/AFGHANISTAN
Burners like this, in the shape of a big cat, were used in the courts of Medieval Islamic kings – lions and cheetahs symbolized power. The head tilts to allow insertion of charcoal.

Candlestick
15TH CENTURY • MAMLUK EGYPT
To circumvent the prohibition on precious metals, Islamic metalworkers became adept at combining baser metals like brass with silver and gold inlay.

Qibla compass
DATE AND ORIGIN UNKNOWN
This ornamental compass was used to indicate the direction, *qibla*, of Mecca, so that worshippers could orient themselves properly for prayer.

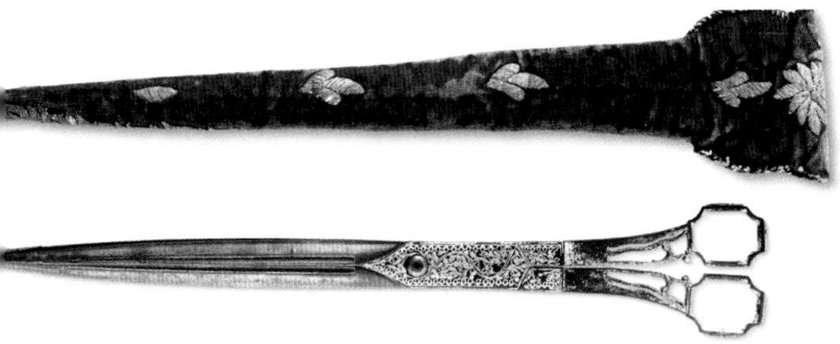

Calligraphy scissors
1700–99 • IRAN
These scissors were used for shaping pens and brushes. The blades are inlaid with gold, a variety of damascening known as *koftgari*.

Islamic lamp
DATE AND ORIGIN UNKNOWN
This hourglass-shaped lamp bares a design of Arabic script on the side, which is picked out in vibrant blue, a ceramic dye perfected by Islamic craftsmen.

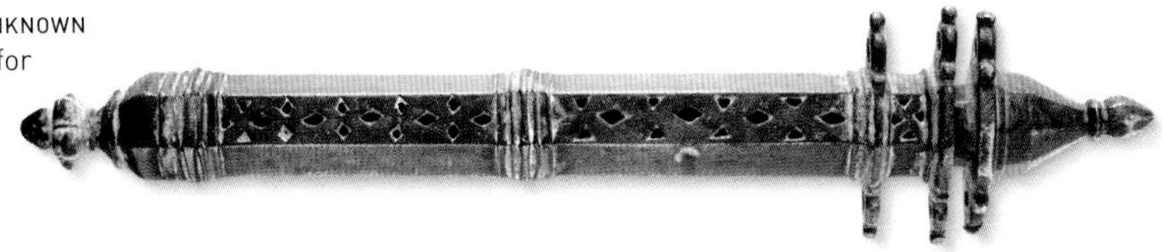

en case
1700–1899 • ORIGIN UNKNOWN
This hexagonal case for carrying pens bares geometric shapes, a typical feature of slamic design.

Illuminated Divan
1800–99 • INDIA
A Divan, or Diwan, is a collection or anthology of poems, inspired by ancient Persian poetry models. This illuminated Divan of the Persian poet Hafez from 19th-century India has typical Kashmiri painted lacquer covers.

1151–55

Monks Mound, the largest mound at Cahokia, is over 30m (100ft) high. It has been estimated that it took 15 million baskets of earth to make it.

THE CITY OF CAHOKIA SPRANG UP AT THE CLIMAX of the Mississippian (or Cahokian) culture of the American Bottom (an area of the Mississippi River Valley). Around the mid-12th century they constructed more than **100 mounds**, including one with a base that is larger than that of the Great Pyramid at Giza, along with a huge landscaped plaza that may be the **biggest earthen city square in the world**. The most remarkable feature of Cahokia is the speed with which it came into existence. Until around 1050, **Mississippians** lived in small villages and had never built on anything approaching this scale. By the 1150s the city may have covered **493 hectares (4,000 acres)** and been home to **30,000 people**. Its cultural and economic influence spread across the **Midwest**, from the present Canadian border to the Gulf Coast. Perhaps because urban living was so exceptional for the Mississippians, Cahokia would **decline rapidly**, within around a century, with a return to low-density farming communities.

In 1152, **Conrad III** (b.1093), king of the Romans, died and his nephew **Frederick of Swabia**, known as **Barbarossa** (see panel, below) was elected as successor. Of combined Welf and Waiblinger parentage (see 1131–35), he brought relative peace to Germany. His coronation as **emperor** in Rome was delayed because the city was in the grip of a **revolutionary commune** led by radical reformer **Arnold of Brescia** (1090–1155). Frederick allied with the papacy against Arnold and Norman Sicily, making his first expedition to Italy in 1154. The following year, in the face of Roman hostility, he was crowned by the new pope, **Adrian IV** (1100–59), but had to retreat to Germany, abandoning Adrian, who was forced to ally himself with **the Normans**.

FREDERICK BARBAROSSA (1122–90)

Energetic and ambitious, Frederick I was determined to make Germany the dominant state in Europe, and to reassert authority over all the imperial lands in Italy. Aware of the historic context of his office, he desired to restore the imperial crown to Roman-era glory, and began to style his realm the Holy Roman Empire. In Germany, he pacified rebels and expanded royal lands.

1156–60

The University of Bologna was originally a school for jurists.

WITH ORIGINS DATING BACK TO PERHAPS 1088, BOLOGNA CLAIMS to be the **oldest university** in the Western world (see 1116–20) – in the sense of an institution specifically designated as a ***universitas***, as opposed to a *studium generale*, as centres for teaching had previously been known. In 1158, the emperor **Frederick I** (1122–90), on the advice of scholars who may have been **Bologna alumni**, granted the university a charter, firmly establishing the institution as an **independent centre of scholarship**. Early universities tended to specialize in one field of study, and Bologna was **dedicated to law**.

In 1159, **Alexander III** (*c.*1100–81) was chosen as pope, although his election was opposed by the emperor, **Frederick I**. Frederick had once again invaded Italy, this time intent on assuming his full imperial inheritance. With the aid of the **League of Pavia** (Bresci, Parma, and others), he had subdued Milan and its associated cities, but at the **Diet of Roncaglia**, in 1158, he had gone too far. Harking back to the Roman era, Frederick insisted that ancient law gave him the right to appoint an **imperial podestà** (local governor) to rule each city. Milan was pushed into revolt, and other cities joined them in forming a **Lombard League** under the auspices of the papacy. Alexander III would earn the title "**the Great**" for leading this anti-imperial rebellion.

1161–65

The Hassan Tower in Rabat, Morocco, is all that was built of what was intended to be an Almohad super-mosque.

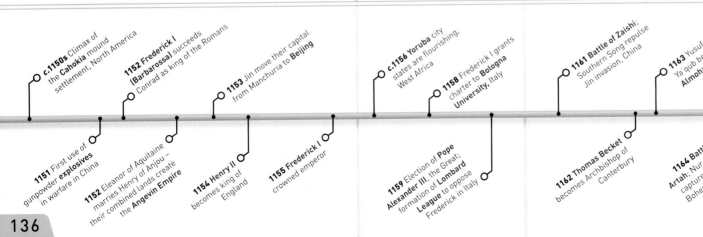

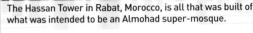

The Bodhisattva Guanyin
This 12th-century Chinese statue depicts the Buddhist deity Guanyin, who protects those in danger – perhaps accounting for his popularity.

IN 1161, THE SOUTHERN SONG REPULSED AN INCURSION by the northern Jin (see 1126–30), securing their kingdom from invasion. A peace treaty of 1165 recognized an uneasy truce between the two powers.

The **Almohad** caliph **Abd al-Mu'min** died in 1163, having destroyed the **Almoravids** and extended Almohad rule from Morocco to Tunisia (the province of Ifriqiya). He made his office **hereditary**, and his son **Yusuf abn Ya'qub** (1135–84) succeeded him. He would spend most of his reign battling **internal opposition**, although he was also noted for military success in **Muslim Spain** and for his patronage of the arts.

In 1164, the Zengid emir **Nur al-Din** (1118–74) defeated the Crusader princes at **Artah**. Throughout the 1160s, Nur al-Din contested with the Crusader kingdoms, particularly as they vied for control of the **ailing Fatimid** kingdom in **Egypt**, led by the vizier **Shawar**. **Amalric**, who had become king of Jerusalem in 1162, was the first to occupy Egypt, but **Zengid success** at Artah forced him to march north, leaving the way clear for Nur al-Din's general Shirkuh and his nephew **Saladin** to invade Egypt (see 1167).

Around the mid-12th century, the dense urban culture of the ancient **Pueblo peoples** at **Chaco Canyon** in North America collapsed, probably because their marginal system of agriculture had overtaxed the **fragile dryland ecology**, leaving them vulnerable to drought. Dating of timbers from the Chaco Canyon pueblos show that the youngest timbers date from around the 1160s – in other words, there was no construction after this. Other Pueblo, or **Anasazi**, sites show evidence from this period of fortification, destruction, and even cannibalism, but there is also evidence of orderly abandonment, presumably by people moving to new sites.

- **c.1150s** Climax of the **Cahokia** mound settlement, North America
- **1151** First use of gunpowder **explosives** in warfare in China
- **1152 Frederick I (Barbarossa)** succeeds Conrad as king of the Romans
- **1152** Eleanor of Aquitaine marries Henry of Anjou – their combined lands create the **Angevin Empire**
- **1153** Jin move their capital from Manchuria to **Beijing**
- **1154 Henry II** becomes king of England
- **1155 Frederick I** crowned emperor
- **c.1156 Yoruba** city states are flourishing, West Africa
- **1158** Frederick I grants charter to **Bologna University**, Italy
- **1159** Election of **Pope Alexander III**, the Great; formation of **Lombard League** to oppose Frederick in Italy
- **1161 Battle of Zaishi**; Southern Song repulse Jin invasion, China
- **1162 Thomas Becket** becomes Archbishop of Canterbury
- **1163** Yusuf abn Ya'qub becomes **Almohad** caliph
- **1164 Battle of Artah**; Nur al-Din captures Prince Bohemond III of Antioch
- **1164 Constitutions of Clarendon** issued by Henry II of England to curb the power of papal authority
- **c.1165** Collapse of **Chaco Canyon** Pueblo culture

"WILL NO ONE RID ME OF THIS TURBULENT PRIEST?"

Attributed to **Henry II**, 1170

The murder of Thomas Becket is depicted in stained glass at Canterbury Cathedral. Canonized in 1173 , Becket became one of the most popular English saints.

IN 1170, THOMAS BECKET, ARCHBISHOP OF CANTERBURY, was murdered in Canterbury Cathedral, England, by four knights of the court of **Henry II** (r.1154–89). Although he swore that he had not ordered the crime, and was absolved of responsibility by **Pope Alexander** in 1172, Henry's famous outburst (see above) had prompted the action of the knights. The context for this outrage was an ongoing dispute over the extent of ecclesiastical versus royal jurisdiction. During the anarchy of **Stephen's reign** (see 1136–40), clerical courts had encroached on areas previously under royal jurisdiction. Following Stephen's death, **Henry Plantagenet** came to the throne. He controlled England alongside the territories of Anjou, Normandy, and Aquitaine – known as the **Angevin Empire** – and set about instituting a badly needed reorganization of his new kingdom. **Taxation reforms**, for instance, replaced the Danegeld with new levies, but it was the **judicial reform** that brought him into conflict with his friend and chancellor **Thomas Becket**. Becket had already been forced into exile after being found guilty of violating the **Constitutions of Clarendon** (see 1164). On his return he vexed Henry by **excommunicating** royally favoured bishops.

At its height, in the late 12th century, the commercial **empire of Srivijaya**, based in Sumatra, controlled much of the **Malay Archipelago**. Its authority extended to colonies around the East Indies and as far as **Sri Lanka** and **Taiwan**. Srivijayan power was based almost exclusively on its **maritime prowess**. By securing the seas in the region against piracy they enabled and directed **trade** between China, India, and the Islamic world, but imposition of heavy duties and taxes stoked resentment and, eventually, revolt.

Frederick I's fourth expedition to Italy, beginning in 1166, prompted the renewal of the **Lombard League** (see 1156–60) and the construction of the mighty fortress town **Alessandria**, named for the pope. With this citadel guarding the mountain passes, **Italy became virtually independent** of imperial authority.

Votive tablet
This votive tablet from the trading empire of Srivijaya is engraved with Buddhist figures. The ruling Sailendras were ardent Buddhists.

Muhammad of Ghur, travelling by elephant, leads his army in the Islamic conquest of India.

THE GHURIDS WERE A DYNASTY FOUNDED IN 1151 by Ala-ud-Din Husayn, who conquered much of **Ghaznavid Afghanistan** and founded a new state based at **Ghur** in western Afghanistan. In 1173, **Ghiyas-ud-Din** became emir, making his brother Mu'izz-du-Din, better known as **Muhammad of Ghur**, co-emir. Together the brothers brought most of Afghanistan under their control, and in 1175 Muhammad launched the **Islamic invasion** of northern India.

The Spanish rabbi **Benjamin of Tudela** (1130–73) was the **first recorded European** to have approached the borders of **China**, in an epic journey he made from 1159 to 1173. His account, *The Travels of Benjamin of Tudela*, recounts many exotic legends, including **Noah's Ark** resting on Mount Ararat.

In the medieval period, the city of **Pisa**, in Tuscany, became the centre of a thriving **city-state**. Its cathedral was constructed in the 11th century, but in 1173 work began on a separate **bell tower**. Even during construction the foundations sank and the tower **began to slant**. Eventually it came to lean 4.5m (15ft) from the perpendicular.

During the 1170s, a new **religious movement** emerged in Lyons. Also known as the Poor Men of Lyons and the Vaudois, the **Waldenses** were led by Peter Waldes (c.1140–1218), a rich merchant who gave away his property and began to preach a radical creed of **gospel simplicity** that rejected many of the teachings of Catholicism. Despite initial blessing by **Pope Alexander III**, the Waldensians' refusal to abide by his injunction against preaching led to their **denunciation as heretics** in 1179 and a long history of persecution (see 1206–10).

In 1174, the Zengid emir **Nur al-Din** died. His nephew **Saladin**, who had already assumed control of **Egypt**, quickly marched north to secure **Syria**, and was duly recognized as **sultan** of Egypt and Syria by the caliph in Baghdad, founding the **Ayyubid dynasty**.

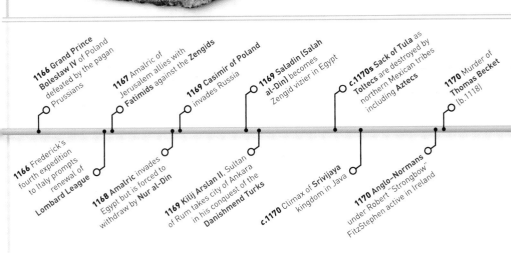

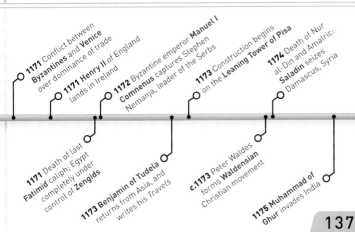

Leaning Tower of Pisa
Pisa's famous leaning tower is 54.5m (179ft) tall and 17.5m (57ft) in diameter at the base.

1166 Grand Prince Boleslaw IV of Poland defeated by the pagan Prussians

1166 Frederick's fourth expedition to Italy prompts renewal of **Lombard League**

1167 Amalric of Jerusalem allies with **Fatimids** against the **Zengids**

1168 Amalric invades Egypt but is forced to withdraw by **Nur al-Din**

1169 Casimir of Poland invades Russia

1169 Kilij Arslan II, Sultan of Rum takes city of Ankara in his conquest of the **Danishmend Turks**

1169 Saladin (Salah al-Din) becomes Zengid vizier in Egypt

c.1170 Climax of **Srivijaya** kingdom in Java

c.1170s Sack of Tula as **Toltecs** are destroyed by northern Mexican tribes including **Aztecs**

1170 Anglo-Normans under Robert "Strongbow" FitzStephen active in Ireland

1170 Murder of **Thomas Becket** (b.1118)

1171 Conflict between **Byzantines** and **Venice** over dominance of trade

1171 Death of last **Fatimid** caliph; Egypt completely under control of **Zengids**

1171 Henry II of England lands in Ireland

1172 Byzantine emperor **Manuel I Comnenus** captures Stephen Nemanja, leader of the Serbs

1173 Benjamin of Tudela returns from Asia, and writes his Travels

1173 Construction begins on the **Leaning Tower of Pisa**

c.1173 Peter Waldes forms **Waldensian** Christian movement

1174 Death of Nur al-Din and Amalric; **Saladin** seizes Damascus, Syria

1175 Muhammad of Ghur invades India

1176–80

This depiction of the Battle of Yashima during the Gempei wars illustrates a heavily armed Minamoto discovering the terrified mother of Emperor Taira.

EMPEROR FREDERICK BARBARROSA'S FIFTH EXPEDITION TO ITALY in 1176 (see also 1151–55) ended in disaster for the imperial forces when his army was crushed at the **Battle of Legnano**. The battle marked one of the earliest occasions in the medieval era when cavalry were defeated by infantry. This had class implications as knights on horses generally belonged to the feudal aristocracy, while footmen with pikes represented freemen of the rising bourgeoisie. In 1177, Frederick was forced to concede the **Peace of Venice** with the pope; a prelude to the more comprehensive Peace of Constance in 1183 (see 1181–85).

Now reconciled with the emperor, **Pope Alexander III** was able to call an ecumenical council at the Lateran Palace in Rome, in 1179. The council decreed that **papal elections** would be solely in the hands of the cardinals, and that a two-thirds majority was needed to elect a pope. It was hoped that this would draw a line under years of contention between papal candidates elected by the anti-imperial party and **"anti-popes"** – persons selected by the emperor to oppose the legitimately elected or sitting pope.

In 1176, the army of **Byzantine emperor** Manuel Commenus was destroyed by the Turks of the **Sultanate of Rum** (see 1100–05) at the **Battle of Myriocephalum**. The Byzantines were never again able to send land forces to help the Crusaders.

The **Gempei Wars** (1180–85) in Japan marked the **end of Taira domination** of Japan (see 641–650), and the start of the **Minamoto shogunate**. Civil wars in 1156 and 1159 had left control of Japan in the hands of Taira no Kiyomori (*c.*1118–81), who quickly assumed a similar level of power to the **Fujiwara clan** (see 851–860). Not only did he act as prime minister, but he also married his daughters to the imperial family, enabling him to place his infant grandson on the throne as emperor in 1180. But his excessive lust for power and perceived corruption alienated his provincial supporters, and in the same year there was an uprising by the **Minamoto clan** against Taira rule, which grew into the five-year-long Gempei Wars.

Pope Alexander III
This 14th-century fresco shows Pope Alexander III presenting a sword to the Venetian Doge for use against the emperor, Frederick Barbarossa.

COAL AND IRON IN MEDIEVAL EUROPE

Growing populations, new agricultural implements, and constant military activity increased the demand for iron in the Middle Ages. Charcoal was still the main source of power for iron forges, but deforestation caused wood shortages. As a consequence, demand for coal increased in and scavenging for sea coal was increasingly supplemented by mining. The first record of a coal mine comes from Escomb near Durham, in northern England in 1183.

1181–85

> **SALADIN'S** HOPE HAD AN EASY PASSAGE, HIS **PATHS** WERE **FRAGRANT,** HIS **GIFTS POURED OUT, ...** HIS **POWER** WAS **MANIFEST,** HIS **AUTHORITY SUPREME.**

Imad al Din, Secretary to Saladin, from *Lightning of Syria*, *c.*1200

BY THE 1180S, THE CRUSADER KINGDOMS OF OUTREMER ("beyond the sea", as they were known in Europe) were in an increasingly precarious position. Europe was deaf to entreaties for **Crusader reinforcements**, and the Christian Byzantines were preoccupied with other matters, such as war with Norman Sicily. Meanwhile, their Muslim opponents were gathering under the leadership of **Saladin**, or Salah al-Din, (*c.*1137–93) the sultan of Egypt and Syria. By 1183, he had suppressed Christian rebels at Edessa and Aleppo, and with both sides reeling from the effects of a drought, had brokered a peace treaty with the leper **king of Jerusalem, Baldwin IV** (*c.*1161–85). The uneasy peace was shattered, however, by the actions of Reynald of Châtillon, an adventurer from the Second Crusade, who persistently raided unarmed caravans of Islamic pilgrims, and sponsored a pirate fleet that pillaged the Red Sea.

Saladin mobilized his army, intent on punishing Reynald, but his progress was checked by **Frankish fortresses** and another prolonged **famine**. In 1185, Baldwin died and his sickly infant nephew inherited the crown as **Baldwin V** (1177–86).

In 1183, the peace between Emperor Frederick Barbarossa and his Italian foes was ratified as the Peace of Constance, but although imperial authority over Italy was recognized, the **Lombard** cities were granted effective autonomy.

The **Battle of Dannoura** of 1185 marked the climax of the **Gempei Wars**. Warrior Minamoto Yoshitsune, younger brother of Yoritomo, the founder of the shogunate, destroyed the Taira in the naval battle.

Saladin, sultan of Egypt and Syria
Saladin escapes from battle on a camel in this 18th-century engraving. He was renowned as a generous and principled leader.

1176 Byzantine army defeated by Turks at **Battle of Myriocephalum**

1176 Battle of Legnano between Frederick Barbarossa and the Lombard League

1177 Kingdom of Champa sacks Khmer city of Angkor

1177 Peace of Venice between Frederick Barbarossa and the pope

1179 Third Lateran Council held in Rome

1180 Philip II Augustus (r.1180–1223) becomes **king of France**

1180 Gempei Wars in Japan (to 1185)

1181 Accession of **Jayavarman VII** of Khmer (reigned until 1215)

1183 Saladin mobilizes his **army** against Reynald of Châtillon

1183 Peace of Constance between Frederick Barbarossa and Lombard League

1184 Diet of Mainz; leads to Third Crusade

1185 The Taira defeated at **Battle of Dannoura** in Japan

1185 Second Bulgarian Empire is founded (to 1396)

1186–90

The Horns of Hattin, an extinct volcano crowned with two rocky outcrops, was the site of the Battle of Hattin in 1187.

ON 4TH JULY 1187, THE CRUSADER ARMY WAS DEFEATED by the forces of Saladin. The Crusader forces were led by the new king of Jerusalem, **Guy of Lusignan**, who had seized power on the death of the infant Baldwin V in 1186. Baldwin's regents had negotiated another truce with Saladin, but once again, Reynald of Châtillon had broken it, raiding a caravan of pilgrims and provoking **Saladin** into a final campaign to sweep the Holy Land clear of the Christian principalities. Goaded by Reynald, King Guy led a combined force of Crusader knights, **Templars**, Hospitallers, and English mercenaries (see 1116–20) across a waterless plateau in the blazing heat to take up a position on the **Horns of Hattin**, an extinct volcano. Between them and Lake Tiberias – the main source of fresh water for the thirst-crazed knights – lay the well-rested and provisioned army of Saladin. Using raiding tactics, Saladin drove the Crusaders into desperate confusion, surrounding and capturing them all. More than 200 Templars and Hospitallers were executed, while Saladin personally beheaded Reynald. King Guy was later released, but, with his army annihilated, it was easy for Saladin to cow many of the remaining Crusader strongholds into surrender. He took **Acre** in July and **Jerusalem** in October. Tyre, Antioch, Tripoli, and a few castles were all that remained of the Crusader kingdoms.

The Crusader kingdom of Outremer had been pleading for European assistance for years and the **fall of Jerusalem** in 1187 finally prompted Pope Gregory VIII to preach a **new Crusade**. The dispatch of Anglo-French forces was delayed by disputes between Henry II of England and Philip II of France, and then by the death of Henry and the accession of Richard I in 1189. Richard I and Philip II finally set out in late 1190. Frederick Barbarossa had already set out overland in 1189, but was drowned en route the following year.

3:2 **Battle of Hattin**
Saladin's troops outnumbered the Crusaders by 30,000 to 20,000, yet his success was owed to his tactics and the Christians' desperate thirst.

Samurai armour
This beautifully presented Japanese armour dates from the 19th century, though the first samurai warriors fought with similar armour in the 12th century.

1191–1200

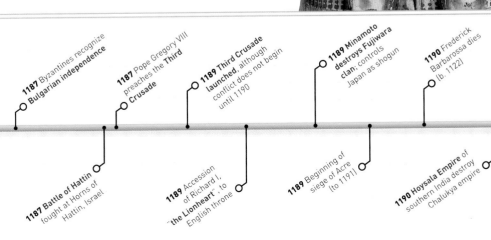

King Richard I of England, also known as Richard the Lionheart, is shown leading Crusaders into battle.

THE THIRD CRUSADE was hampered by infighting among the European factions of the Crusaders of Outremer, and although **Richard the Lionheart** won most of his battles, he was unable to achieve his sworn aim of "liberating" Jerusalem. The Crusade had already got off to a bad start (see 1186–90), and there were further delays en route when, in 1191, Richard stopped to conquer Byzantine **Cyprus**. He sold the island to the Templars, who would later pass it on to the diminished Crusader kingdoms, where it became one of the main supports for continuing Christian presence in the **Holy Land**.

On finally arriving in Palestine, Richard joined Philip II of France in the **siege of Acre**, which was actually a double siege – King Guy had laid siege to the city on his release from captivity (see 1186–90), but Saladin had then encircled his forces. Acre was taken by the Crusaders in July and much of the population was massacred. Philip II returned to France, but Richard I had sworn to liberate Jerusalem, and marched along the coast, retaking towns and defeating Saladin at Arsuf in September. Although he would go on to clear Muslim forces from the rest of the coastal strip, and camp within sight of Jerusalem, Richard realized he did not have the forces needed to take and hold the holy city. With continued infighting among the Crusader barons, the murder of Conrad of Montferrat by **Assassins** (see 1081–90) soon after being made king, reinforcements arriving for Saladin, and bad news from England – where his brother John was scheming to seize the crown – Richard was forced to conclude a peace treaty with Saladin in 1192. **Outremer** would henceforth be confined to a 145km (90 mile) coastal strip, from Tyre to Jaffa, along with Antioch and Tripoli.

In 1192, **Minamoto Yoritomo** (see 1181–85) awarded himself the title Seii tai-shogun ("barbarian-subduing great general"). Since the end of the Gempei Wars, Yoritomo had dispatched all challengers, including his brother Yoshitsune. As undisputed military dictator, his *bakufu*, or administration, at Kamakura now supplanted the imperial court. Japan would be ruled by **shoguns** – military dictators - for centuries to come.

In 1192, the **Ghurids of Persia** defeated a Hindu rebellion at the Battle of Taraori near Thanesar in India. The following year, Delhi was taken and Muhammad of Ghur founded the **Sultanate of Delhi**.

CRUSADER ARMOUR

27kg THE WEIGHT OF **ARMOUR**

1.5kg THE WEIGHT OF A **SWORD**

0.4kg THE WEIGHT OF A **MACE**

- **1187** Byzantines recognize **Bulgarian independence**
- **1187 Battle of Hattin** fought at Horns of Hattin, Israel
- **1187** Pope Gregory VIII preaches the **Third Crusade**
- **1189** Accession of Richard I, **"the Lionheart"**, to English throne
- **1189 Third Crusade launched**, although conflict does not begin until 1190
- **1189 Minamoto destroys Fujiwara clan**; controls Japan as shogun
- **1189** Beginning of siege of Acre (to 1191)
- **1190** Frederick Barbarossa dies (b. 1122)
- **1190 Hoysala Empire** of southern India destroy Chalukya empire
- **1192 Battle of Tararori**; Ghurids crush Hindu confederacy
- **June 1192 Treaty of Ramla** signed between Richard I and Saladin
- **1198 Innocent III** elected pope

A Persian painting shows Temujin, later known as Genghis Khan, battling the Tartars. The Tartar tribes fought constantly with the Mongols.

POPE INNOCENT III HAD PROCLAIMED A NEW CRUSADE in 1199, intent on restoring papal supervision to the crusading movement, and hoping to reunite the Greek and Latin churches to fulfil his vision of a **single Christian dominion** under the papacy. In 1201, envoys met Enrico Dandolo, Doge of Venice, to arrange passage to Egypt for the **Fourth Crusade**. Under the **Peace of Venice** (see 1176–80), the Venetians agreed to transport 33,500 men and 4,500 horses for a payment of 85,000 marks. In addition, they would supply 50 war galleys in return for half of the Crusaders' conquests.

When the Crusaders gathered in Venice in 1202, it transpired there were too few of them, and they could not pay the agreed bill. Instead, they agreed to help Venice by taking Zara in Dalmatia – a rich source of wood for Venetian galleys. Pope Innocent protested, but worse was to come. In 1204, the Crusaders arrived in **Constantinople**, where relations with the Byzantines quickly soured; the city was taken for the first time in its history, and was brutally sacked. A new **Latin Empire of the East** was proclaimed under a new emperor, Baldwin of Flanders, while Venice was awarded nearly half the city, numerous Mediterranean islands, and other territories. Although the Byzantine emperors relocated to **Byzantine Nicaea**, the Fourth Crusade marked the end of the Byzantine Empire as a true power, which discredited the Crusading movement and helped the Turks.

In the late 12th century, the Mongolian and Turkic nomads of the steppes were fearsome but disunited. Temujin (*c*.1162–1227), who later became known as **Genghis Khan**, was a minor leader who became a *nokhor* (companion) to Toghril, Khan of the Kereits, the dominant tribe in Central **Mongolia**. Through ability and charisma, he rose to become a great general, crushing the neighbouring **Tartar** tribes in 1202, but inciting resentment among other Kereits so that in 1203 he clashed with Toghril himself. He emerged from this confrontation as the dominant leader among the Mongol tribes.

Jayavarman VII
This bronze statue of King Jayavarman VII, in Mahayana Buddhist style, portrays a serene and contemplative king.

Jayavarman VII (*c*.1125–1220) had returned from exile to claim the **Khmer** crown in 1181. He avenged the destruction of the capital by deposing the Champa king in 1191, suppressed a revolt in the west, restored Angkor, and finally gained ascendancy over the Champa kingdom. Jayavarman made **Mahayana Buddhism** the state religion and taxed the resources of the kingdom to build great temples, as well as hospitals, shrines, roads, and bridges. One of his temples, Preah Khan, was served by 98,000 retainers.

In around 1200, the **Chimú** state, centred on their capital at Chan Chan in the **Moche valley** in Peru, began to expand. Their power rested on their mastery of intensive agriculture techniques and elaborate irrigation. At Chan Chan, Chimú leaders built citadels, or palaces, high-walled buildings with audience chambers and storage depots. It is believed that each new Chimú ruler was obliged to build and fund his own citadel, which drove the expansion of the empire.

In 1202, the **mathematician** Leonardo of Pisa, better known as **Fibonacci** (*c*.1177–1250), produced the most influential book in European mathematics to date, the *Liber Abaci*, or *Book of Calculation*. Based on Arabic mathematics, it introduced Europe to Hindu numerals (0–9) and to the word *zephirum*, a Latinized version of an Arabic word that, in the Venetian dialect, became zero in algebra, addition, and the **Fibonacci Sequence**.

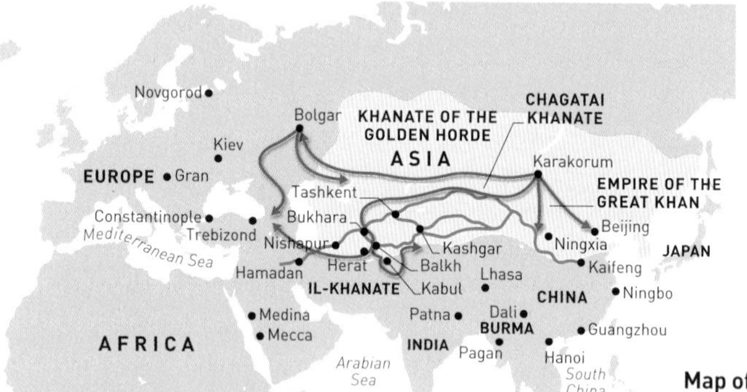

Map of Genghis Khan's empire
Temujin would go on to unite the Mongol tribes and conquer a huge empire. His successors would extend it still further.

Peterhouse college, Cambridge was founded 75 years after the university.

BY 1206, TEMUJIN HAD UNITED ALL THE TRIBES OF MONGOLIA into the *Khamag Mongol Ulus* "the All Mongol State", reorganizing tribal society into an army grouped on a decimal system. At the Mongolian capital of Karakorum, he took the title Chinggis Khan or "ruler of the world". The name is now most commonly spelled, "Genghis".

In 1208, Pope Innocent III proclaimed a **crusade against heretics** in the south of France – the **Albigensians** (Cathars based around Albi) and **Waldenses** (see 1171–75). Their teachings challenged the worldliness of the established church, while their anticlericalism attracted nobles keen to appropriate church lands; the Cathars, for instance, were under the protection of Raymond of Toulouse, who ruled much of southern France. The pope's declaration gave license for the French king, Philip II (1165–1223), to allow his northern lords to wreak havoc in areas outside of

> **"KILL THEM ALL, GOD WILL KNOW HIS OWN."**
>
> **Abbot Arnaud Amaury,** on the Albigensian Crusade

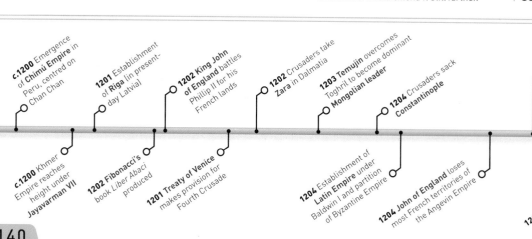

c.1200 Emergence of **Chimú Empire** in Peru, centred on Chan Chan

c.1200 Khmer Empire reaches height under **Jayavarman VII**

1201 Establishment of **Riga** (in present-day Latvia)

1202 Fibonacci's book *Liber Abaci* produced

1202 King John of England battles Phillip II for his French lands

1201 Treaty of Venice makes provision for Fourth Crusade

1202 Crusaders take **Zara** in Dalmatia

1203 Temujin overcomes Toghril to become dominant **Mongolian leader**

1204 Establishment of **Latin Empire** under Baldwin I and partition of Byzantine Empire

1204 Crusaders sack **Constantinople**

1204 John of England loses most French territories of the Angevin Empire

1205 Second Bulgarian Empire defeats Latin Empire and captures Baldwin I

1205 Hojo Yoshitoki becomes regent of Kamakura shogunate, inaugurating period of Hojo rule in Japan

1206 Temujin takes title **Genghis Khan** and begins conquest of Asia

1206 Qutb-ud-din Aibak, Sultan of Delhi, founds dynasty of slave kings, India

1209 Pope Innocent III proclaims **Albigensian Crusade** in Languedoc, France

1209 Massacre of Beziers, Languedoc, by Crusaders

1211–15

This 19th-century oil painting depicts the Battle of Las Navas de Tolosa, said to have been the decisive battle of the Reconquista.

1216–20

A detail from the south gate of the great Khmer city of Angkor Thom.

1221–25

> **“ I AM THE PUNISHMENT OF GOD... ”**
>
> **Genghis Khan, Mongolian warlord**

PERSECUTION OF THE CATHARS

Although only 200 Cathars lived in the town of Beziers in Languedoc, Crusaders massacred the entire population in 1209. Asked how the attackers should distinguish between Catholics and heretics, crusade leader Abbot Amaury is reputed to have given his famous order to "kill them all". In its pursuit of Cathars, the papacy would eventually create the Inquisition (see 1231–35).

his control, preparing the way for an expansion of royal power.

In 1209, **Cambridge University was founded** by scholars who had relocated from Oxford. By 1226, they had aquired some formal organization.

PETER II OF ARAGON (1178–1213) AND ALFONSO VIII OF CASTILE (1155–1214) defeated the **Almohads** (see 1146–50) at the **Battle of Las Navas de Tolosa** in 1212. Alfonso had earlier been crushingly defeated by the Almohads in 1195 but had fought off invasions by the other **Christian Spanish kingdoms** and rebuilt his army. After this decisive victory, the Almohads were soon expelled from Spain, leaving only local Muslim dynasties that could not stand up to the Christian advance. Accordingly, this battle is traditionally said to be a decisive point in the Christian reconquest or "**reconquista**" of Moorish Spain (see 1241–45).

Having lost most of his lands in France, **King John of England** (1166–1216) joined in alliance with Emperor Otto IV (1178–1215) and others, but they were crushed at the **Battle of Bouvines** in Flanders in 1214 by Philip II of France and the rival German emperor, Frederick II. This ended Anglo-Norman hopes of regaining French territories. King John's barons were forced to concentrate on England, where they had cause for discontent. Thanks to a dispute with the pope, the king had been briefly **excommunicated**. More importantly, he was taxing the barons heavily and invalidating the law when it suited him. The **barons revolted** and after a brief civil war, John was forced to sign the Articles of the Barons, known in history as the Great Charter or **Magna Carta**. Although this mainly concerned the rights of barons, in stating that the king was not above the law, it was an important milestone for human rights. King John immediately disowned the charter and war broke out once more, this time with added French involvement. Retreating from a French invasion force in 1216, the king lost his baggage train – and royal treasure – while crossing the Wash in Lincolnshire, England, and died soon after. His infant son, Henry III (1207–72) came to the throne.

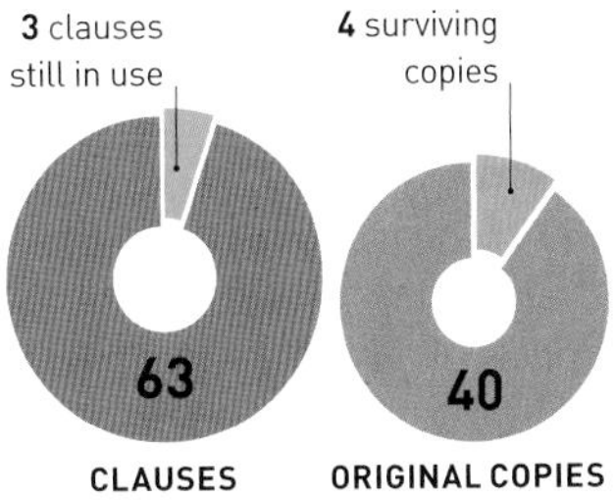

The Magna Carta
Of the 63 clauses contained in the original Magna Carta, only three survive as laws today. Numerous copies were made, to be distributed around England; four survive.

8
METRES
THE HEIGHT OF THE WALLS OF ANGKOR THOM

JAYAVARMAN VII DIED IN AROUND 1220, having seen his greatest creation take shape. At Angkor, in modern-day Cambodia he had created a new city, Angkor Thom, centred on the great state temple of Bayon. The temple comprises towers decorated with huge, sculpted faces; the identities of these are disputed, although they may include Jayavarman himself.

Having conquered most of Central Asia and northern China, Genghis Khan's empire (see 1201–05) now bordered the Khwarazm Empire of Persia.

Mongolian dagger
The Mongolians had a deservedly fearsome reputation. After archers had decimated the enemy, fighters with hand weapons would close in.

DOMINGO DE GUZMAN, A CASTILIAN CLERIC DIED IN 1221. In 1203, he had gone to Rome to ask permission to do missionary work with the Tartars (see 1201–10), but was sent to France to preach to the **Cathars of Languedoc** instead. By adopting absolute poverty, he was able to **challenge the Cathars** and make some headway, although ultimately his failure to "correct" the heretics led to the Albigensian Crusade (see 1206–10). However, like Francis of Assisi (see 1226–30), he had created a new kind of monastic order – the Dominicans – adapted to the new urban culture. The **Dominicans** and **Franciscans** were mendicant friars, mainly recruited from the middle classes, living off charity rather than farming, and devoted to preaching and charity in towns and cities.

A largely ineffective affair, the **Fifth Crusade** was the fruit of Pope Innocent's determination to reboot the Crusading movement. Targeting Egypt, the Crusaders took that but then lost Damietta, and failed to account for the Nile floods, which foiled their advance on Cairo. They high-handedly rejected a treaty offered by the sultan that would have given them Jerusalem, and left Egypt in 1221 having accomplished nothing.

1209 Founding of **Cambridge University**, England

1209 Francis of Assisi establishes **Franciscans**, Catholic religious order

1209 Otto IV elected Emperor

1210 Hindu rebellions against Sultanate of Delhi, India

1211 Genghis Khan conquers Kara-Khitai, Central Asia and invades Jin China

1211 Civil strife in Germany as **Frederick II** elected rival emperor to Otto IV

1212 Battle of Las Navas de Tolosa, Spain

1214 Philip II and Frederick II defeat anti-Capetian alliance at **Battle of Bouvines**, France

1215 Magna Carta signed following civil war in England

1215 Fourth Lateran Council calls halt to Albigensian Crusade and calls for a Fifth Crusade to Egypt

1215 Genghis Khan takes Beijing, China

1216 Death of **King John of England** (b.1166)

1218 Genghis Khan invades **Khwarazmid Empire**, Western Asia

1218 Death of **Jayavarman VII** (b.1125)

1219 Shokyu War in Japan

1220 Khmer Empire withdraws from Champa, Southeast Asia

1221 Fifth Crusade ends with loss of Damietta and retreat

1221 Death of **St Dominic** (b.1170) founder of the Dominicans

1221 Genghis Khan sacks **Samarkand**

1221 Toltecs expelled from **Chichen Itza**, Mexico

1222 Icelandic scholar **Snorri Sturlson** writes *Edda*, a book of Nordic mythology

1226–30

This 13th-century painting by Giotto di Bonodore shows St Francis of Assisi preaching to the birds.

1,000,000

THE NUMBER OF **PEOPLE KILLED** DURING THE **ALBIGENSIAN CRUSADE**

THE RENEWAL OF THE ALBIGENSIAN CRUSADE (see 1206–10) in 1226 was in spite of the Pope declaring an "official" end to the Crusade at the Fourth Lateran Council of 1215. In reality, the battle for the south of France descended into vicious guerrilla warfare. Renewal of the Crusade was followed eventually by the submission of Raymond VII, Count of Toulouse – the Cathars' protector. Under the **Treaty of Meaux** (also known as the Peace of Paris) of 1229, the town of Toulouse was ceded to the **Capetian dynasty** – the ruling house of France from 987 to 1328.

Crusader coin
A rare Crusader coin from the Kingdom of Jerusalem illustrates the effects of intermingling policy: the inscription is written in Arabic.

Meanwhile, **Emperor Frederick II of Germany** realized that peace with the Muslims was better than unwinnable military adventures. In 1229, he concluded a treaty with the sultan of Egypt that **restored Jerusalem** and some surrounding land to the Christians. The **Sixth Crusade** thus passed without bloodshed, although Frederick was roundly condemned for this achievment.

A former soldier, **Francis of Assisi** had founded the **Franciscan order** in 1209 (see 1221–25). In 1224, he received the stigmata (the wounds of Christ), and he was canonized just two years after his death in 1226.

Cathar stronghold
The Cathar castle of Peyrepertuse in the Pyrenees was located in a strategic defensive position on the French–Spanish border.

1231–35

This 14th-century image shows Pope Gregory IX receiving a list of heretics.

IN 1231, POPE GREGORY IX established the **Papal Inquisition**, a campaign by the church against heresy. Prior to 1231, the investigation of heresy had been the responsibility of bishops but it now became the preserve of specialist **inquisitors**, mostly drawn from the Dominican and Franciscan orders (see 1221–25). In 1233, the Dominicans were charged with bringing the Inquisition to Languedoc in France, where the **Cathar** heresy clung on despite the military defeat of the Count of Toulouse (see 1226–30).

Mongolian expansion continued, though Genghis Khan (see 1201–05) had died in 1227 while suppressing a rebellion in Xia Xia in China. He was succeeded by his second son, **Ogodei** (*c.*1186–1241), who was still more ambitious. Ogodei sent armies to the east and west, leading the final assault on the Chinese **Jin Empire** (see 1126–30), which was conquered by 1234. The **Southern Song** had aided the Mongol advance, but when they tried to seize Kaifeng in northern China in 1235, the Mongols turned on them.

In 1235, **Sundiata, king of the Keita**, a Mande people from sub-Saharan Mali, defeated the Susu king Sumnaguru at the **Battle of Kirina**. The Susu had destroyed the old Ghana Empire (*c.*830–1235), and Sundiata now built a new Mande empire on the ruins of Ghana.

1236–40

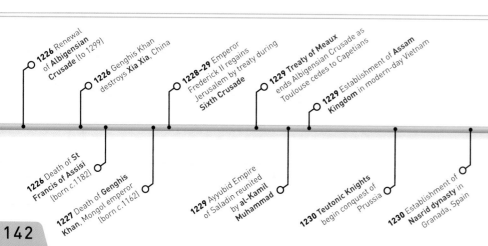

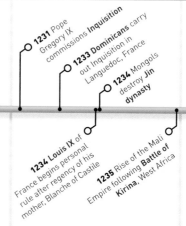

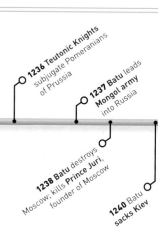

Steppe landscape; little changed since the days of the Mongol Empire.

ON HIS DEATH, GENGHIS KHAN had informally **divided his empire** between four of his sons. Given authority over the west, **Batu Khan** (*c.*1207–55) established the Kipchak Khanate, also known as the **Golden Horde Khanate**. In the winter of 1237, when the frozen rivers allowed his cavalry to cross, Batu **invaded Russia**. Over the next four years, his armies conquered the Russian principalities and blazed a trail of destruction deep into Central Europe. Under the overlordship of Ogodei (see 1231–35), the expanding reach of the Mongol Empire had important implications for pan-Eurasian trade. The ***Pax Mongolica*** or "Mongol Peace" achieved in the lands under Mongolian control made the perilous passage across Central Asia and the silk road increasingly viable, enabling the **first direct contact** between **Europeans and the Chinese** since Roman times in around 1240.

By 1236, the **Teutonic Knights** – a military order formed in 1198 by German merchants serving at the Hospital of St Mary of the Teutons in Jerusalem – had completed the subjugation of the **Pomeranians**, a pagan tribe in Prussia. Under their grand master, **Hermann von Salza** (*c.*1179–1239), the knights established numerous strongholds, and in 1237, they merged with the Livonian Brothers of the Sword and advanced into **Livonia** (present-day Estonia and Latvia).

1226 Renewal of **Albigensian Crusade** (to 1299)

1226 Genghis Khan destroys **Xia Xia**, China

1226 Death of **St Francis of Assisi** (born c.1182)

1227 Death of **Genghis Khan**, Mongol emperor (born c.1162)

1228–29 Emperor Frederick II regains Jerusalem by treaty during **Sixth Crusade**

1229 Treaty of Meaux ends Albigensian Crusade as Toulouse cedes to Capetians

1229 Ayyubid Empire of Saladin reunited by **al-Kamil Muhammad**

1229 Establishment of **Assam Kingdom** in modern-day Vietnam

1230 Teutonic Knights begin conquest of Prussia

1230 Establishment of **Nasrid dynasty** in Granada, Spain

1231 Pope Gregory IX commissions **Inquisition**

1233 Dominicans carry out Inquisition in Languedoc, France

1234 Louis IX of France begins personal rule after regency of his mother, Blanche of Castile

1234 Mongols destroy **Jin dynasty**

1235 Rise of the Mali Empire following **Battle of Kirina**, West Africa

1236 Teutonic Knights subjugate Pomeranians of Prussia

1237 Batu leads **Mongol army** into Russia

1238 Batu destroys Moscow; kills **Prince Juri**, founder of Moscow

1240 Batu **sacks Kiev**

1241–45

This miniature from the *Annalistic Code* of the 16th century depicts the "Battle of the Ice", fought on the frozen waters of Lake Peipus, Novgorod.

IN 1241, THE GERMAN TRADING TOWNS OF LUBECK AND HAMBURG formed an alliance to protect the **Baltic trade routes**. This was the first act in the formation of the **Hanseatic League** (from the medieval Latin *hansa*, meaning a group or association). Lübeck quickly became the centre of expanding German trade in the Baltic region, which extended along the Russian rivers as far as **Novgorod,** and linked to the European trading centres of **England and Flanders**.

In 1242, the efforts of the **Teutonic Knights** (see 1236–40) to extend their Livonian territories eastward and launch the conversion of the Russians from the Greek to the Roman church were checked by defeat at the **Battle of Lake Peipus**. Led by **Alexander Nevski**, prince of Novgorod, the Russians checked the knights' progress and Lake Peipus thereafter served as the eastern limit of Livonia.

In a series of stunning victories in Eastern and Central Europe, the **Mongol armies** destroyed all opposition. Early in 1241, an army of horsemen crossed the frozen River Vistula into Poland, sacking Kracow and defeating an alliance of **Poles, Silesians, and Teutonic Knights** at Leignitz in April. Just three days later, another force under **Batu** (see 1236–40) overwhelmed the Hungarian army in their camp at Mohi. By December, Batu was destroying Pest, the largest city in Hungary. The Mongols had reached the gates of Vienna when, in 1242, the news reached them that Ogodei, the Great Khan, had died. As was traditional, Batu withdrew his forces back to Karakorum, the Mongol capital, for the **election of a new leader.** Elsewhere, Mongol forces had penetrated the Indian subcontinent, sacking Lahore in 1241.

In 1244, **Jerusalem**, which had been under partial Christian control since Frederick II's treaty with the sultan of Egypt (see 1226–30), was **lost to medieval Christians** for the final time. The Egyptian sultan, Ayyub, was engaged in a contest with the Syrian branch of the **Ayyubids** (see 1171–75) at Damascus, which had allied itself with the Christian Crusader kingdoms. In 1244, Ayyub's forces overran Jerusalem and **expelled the Christians**.

Medieval trade
A manuscript illumination of the port of Hamburg, a founder member of the Hanseatic League, which had its roots in an alliance of 1241 with Lübeck.

RECONQUISTA

The notion of the *Reconquista* – the Christian reconquest of Islamic Spain – as a single, continuous project, is a myth, first created by clerical propagandists in the 14th century. In practice, the advance of the Christian kingdoms was by degrees, driven by the need for land, and facilitated by Muslim dissention and advances in military technology.

1246–50

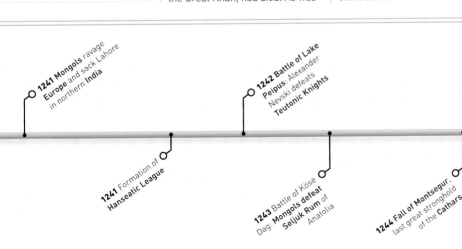

In this 16th-century painting, Ferdinand III, King of Castile and Lon, accepts the surrender of the city of Seville from the Moors in 1248.

IN 1247, FERDINAND III OF CASTILE AND LEON (*c.*1199–1252) laid siege to the Moorish city of Seville. It fell to him in 1248, and with it the **last Moorish kingdom in Spain** – with the exception of Granada. Here, Mohammad ibn-Yusuf ibn Nasr had established the **Nasrid dynasty** in 1230. By 1238, the Nasrids had begun to reconstruct an old fortress, the **Alhambra**, which would become one of the wonders of world architecture by the mid-14th century (see 1350–55). In 1246, the emir of Granada agreed to become Ferdinand's vassal, but the last relic of Moorish al-Andalus would resist Christian pressure until 1492 (see 1490–92).

Louis IX of France (1214–70) was much respected throughout Europe and had a reputation for justice. Under his reign, royal control was extended to the Mediterranean, and the previously autonomous realms of Languedoc and Provence would become part of **French Capetian** territories. In 1244, Louis "took the cross", embarking on a crusade in 1248. Theobald of Navarre had launched a crusade in 1239, but it was so unsuccessful that it is not usually recognized as an ordinate crusade; Louis' crusade of 1248 is accounted the **Seventh**, the last Crusade of this magnitude ever undertaken. Louis landed in Egypt and took Damietta without opposition, but in 1250 his army was **destroyed by the Egyptians** at Fariskur and he was taken captive. His mother, Blanche of Castile, raised a large ransom to buy his freedom.

The **Mamluks** (or Mamelukes) of Egypt were slave soldiers captured from Turkic and Circassian tribes (of the Pontic–Caspian steppes), who formed the main component of the Ayyubid army. Eventually they became strong enough to take power for themselves, **murdering Turan Shah**, the last Ayyubid sultan of Egypt, in 1250. At first the Mamluk commander Izz-ad-Din Aybak used the sultan's widow as a puppet ruler, but he soon married her and founded the **Mamluk dynasty**, the first slave dynasty to hold power in its own name.

THE CRUSADES

1096–99 **FIRST** CRUSADE
1145–49 **SECOND** CRUSADE
1189–92 **THIRD** CRUSADE
1202–04 **FOURTH** CRUSADE
1213–21 **FIFTH** CRUSADE
1228–29 **SIXTH** CRUSADE
1248–54 **SEVENTH** CRUSADE

1241 Mongols ravage **Europe** and sack Lahore in northern **India**

1241 Formation of **Hanseatic League**

1242 Battle of Lake Peipus: Alexander Nevski defeats **Teutonic Knights**

1243 Battle of Köse Dag: **Mongols defeat Seljuk Rum** of Anatolia

1244 Fall of Montsegur, last great stronghold of the **Cathars**

1246 Provence becomes part of Capetian France

1248 Cologne cathedral burns down; reconstructed in **gothic style**

1248 Ferdinand III completes conquest of al-Andalus, apart from Granada, with successful **siege of Seville**

1248 Seventh Crusade: Louis IX of France lands in Egypt

1249 Franciscan friar **Roger Bacon** records recipe for **gunpowder**

1250 Mamluk dynasty founded in Egypt

Lip ornament
AZTEC/MIXTEC
This eagle-shaped lip plug, or labret, would have been worn by a member of the Aztec elite. The Mixtec, a conquered tribe, made most Aztec gold jewellery.

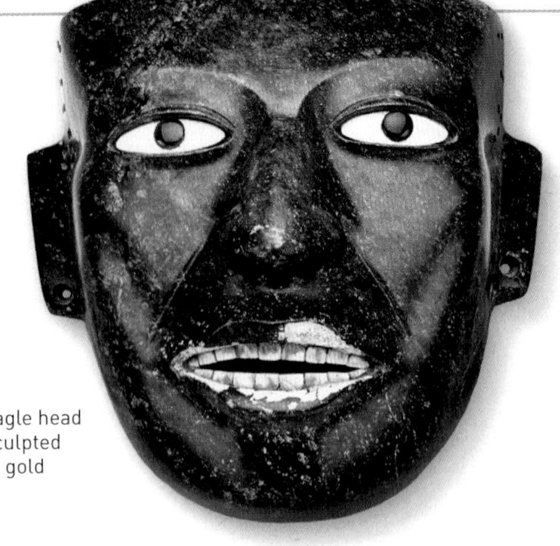

Human mask
AZTEC
Found at the Great Temple of the Aztecs in their capital Tenochtitlan (now Mexico City), this greenstone mask was a votive offering.

Warrior effigy pot
MOCHE
This pot from the Moche culture of the north coast of Peru shows a warrior in a head-dress grasping a club. Constant warfare was a way of life.

THE AZTECS, INCAS, AND MAYA

THE EXTRAORDINARY ARTISTIC TRADITIONS OF PRE-COLUMBIAN AMERICA THAT SPANNED MILLENNIA

Obsidian knife
AZTEC
Long-bladed, razor-sharp obsidian knives such as this one were used by warriors and in the gory human sacrifices practised by the Aztecs.

The Incas, Aztecs, and Maya were advanced civilizations with sophisticated arts and crafts and highly developed graphic systems. The artefacts they created dazzled the medieval European invaders and still fascinate today.

The art and culture of the pre-Columbian civilizations of Mesoamerica and the Andes represent the height of ancient traditions stretching back to the 4th millennium BCE. The conquistadors had a devastating effect on these cultures, but the artefacts that survive are a testament to their rich heritage. Much of Incan culture came from client states, such as the Moche, while the Aztecs and Mayans derived theirs from older cultures, such as the Olmecs.

Maquahuitl
AZTEC
Lacking iron or steel, pre-Columbian Americans used obsidian (volcanic glass) to form cutting edges. The *maquahuitl* – a wooden club fringed with obsidian blades – was a common Aztec weapon.

Sun stone
AZTEC
This sun stone, or calendar stone, is the largest Aztec sculpture ever found. It represents the Aztecs' mythical history of the universe. The Sun, believed to have been formed in the most recent era of creation, is at the centre.

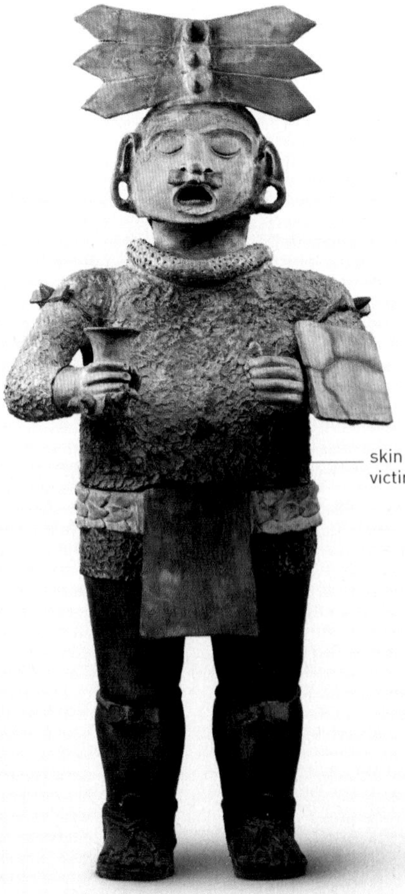

Xipe Totec, god of the springtime
AZTEC
The name of this grisly god translates as "our flayed lord"; he is depicted wearing the skin of a sacrificial victim, denoting the spring renewal of the Earth's "skin".

Priceless heart
AZTEC
The heart was considered the most precious organ that could be offered to the gods, and this replica was carved in jade, which the Aztecs regarded as their most valuable substance.

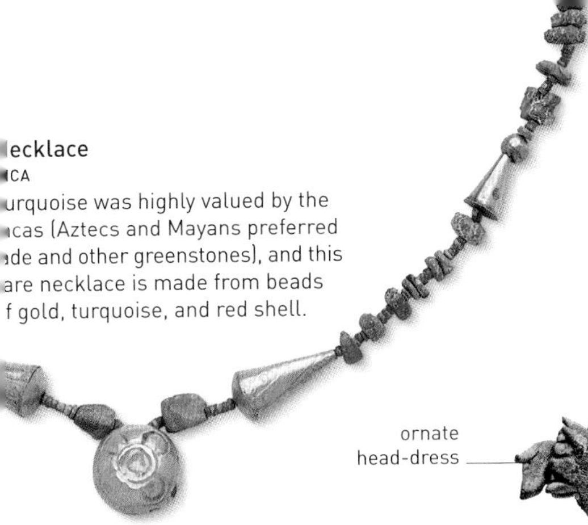

ecklace
ICA
urquoise was highly valued by the
icas (Aztecs and Mayans preferred
ide and other greenstones), and this
are necklace is made from beads
f gold, turquoise, and red shell.

Decorative plate
MAYA
This plate from the Yucatan Maya shows hunting scenes – in the centre, a hunter drapes a deer he has caught across his head and shoulders, while around the edges other hunters wear deer masks.

Jaina figurine
MAYA
This pottery figure from the island of Jaina shows a powerful man dressed in all his finery, with a heavy bead necklace, massive head-dress, and ear plugs.

Tomb figurine
INCA
This cast gold figurine representing an Inca god made up part of the grave goods interred in the tomb of a high-status individual.

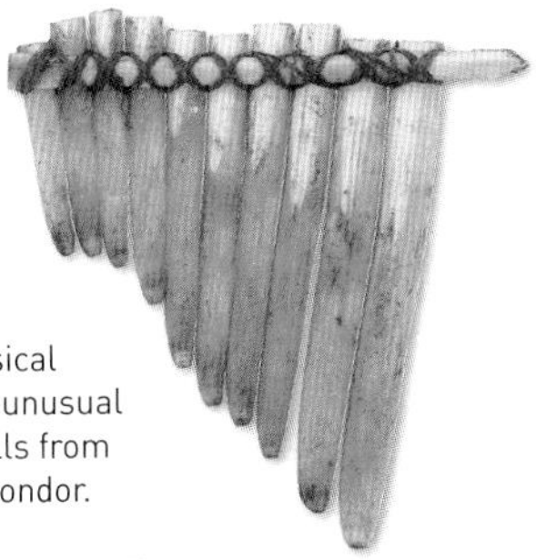

Panpipes
INCA
Known in Europe as the syrinx, the panpipes were among the most common Inca musical instruments. This unusual set is made of quills from the feathers of a condor.

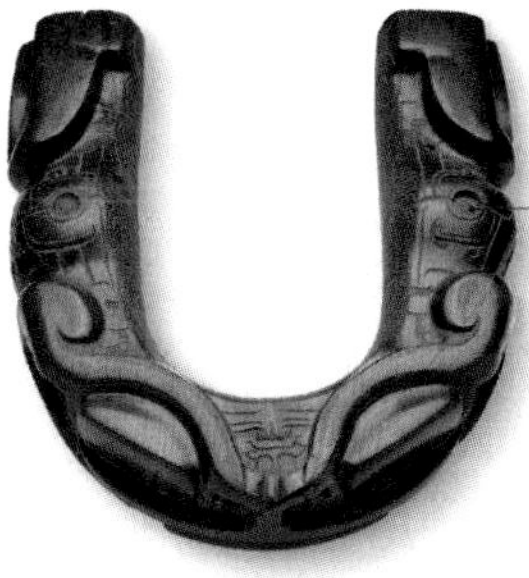

Greenstone yoke
MAYA
Yokes were worn as protective belts in the sacred ball game *ulama*, played by most Mesoamerican cultures. This ornate yoke was probably a ceremonial replica.

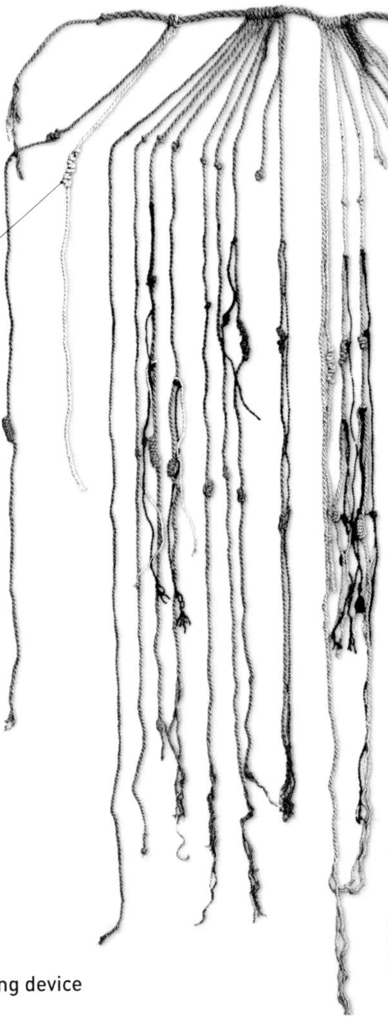

Counting device
INCA
This *quipu*, or counting device, was a versatile accounting tool that helped the Incas keep track of the tribute and population of their empire – data was recorded in lengths of string and knots.

Codex Tro-Cortesianus
MAYA
One of only four surviving Mayan codices, this one records instructions for divination (predicting the future) and priestly rituals. Sheets of bark paper were coated in gesso (chalky paste) to form a writing surface.

1251–55

Although not as sophisticated as Mayan hieroglyphs, Aztec pictographs such as the one shown could express simple concepts.

BY THE MID-13TH CENTURY, THE MEXICA TRIBE – better known today as the **Aztecs** – were established in the Valley of Mexico. Aztec legend suggests that they migrated from the ancestral homeland of *Aztlan* in the early 12th century. Settling at Chapultepec, near Lake Texcoco, Mexico, in around 1250, they were soon **expelled by the Tepanecs**, one of the tribal confederations competing for dominance in the wake of the **Toltec collapse** in the early 12th century.

Although the **Mongols** had conquered most of the Russian principalities (see 1236–40), and the **Golden Horde Khanate** had claimed authority over **Russia**, surprisingly little changed for the Russians. In return for tribute and military service, the Russian princes were left in power and the Russian Church was not interfered with. **Alexander Nevski** (*c.*1220–63), the prince of Novgorod who had led the Russians to victory against the **Teutonic Knights** in 1242, became the dominant Russian noble, appointed Grand Duke of Vladimir after his brother was driven out by the Mongols.

Under the support of the new **Great Khan**, Mongke (r.1251–59), his brothers Kublai and Hulagu renewed the **Mongol expansion**.

In 1253, Hulagu led a huge army into Western Asia to conquer the **Great Seljuk sultanate** (see 1031–40), while Kublai launched campaigns against the **Southern Song** and the **Kingdom of Nanchao** in China.

Prince of Novgorod
This statue depicts Russian leader, Alexander Nevski, whose name derives from the Russian victory at the Battle of the River Neva.

1256–60

This illustration of Mongols battling the Seljuks is from a chronicle by Rashid al-Din, a Muslim minister in the service of the Il-Khanate.

HULAGU KHAN (SEE 1251–1255) CONTINUED HIS CAMPAIGN AGAINST THE SELJUKS and other Islamic powers. In 1256, he crushed the **Order of the Assassins** (see 1081–90), taking their stronghold at Alamut in Persia. In 1258, he sacked Baghdad and **executed the Abbasid Caliph** – the figurehead of Islam – in just one of countless atrocities committed by Mongol invaders who massacred hundreds of thousands of Muslims during their campaigns. In 1259, Hulagu penetrated deep into Syria, but as with Batu's campaign in Europe 18 years earlier (see 1241–45), his progress was halted by news of the **death of the Great Khan**, and he withdrew his armies while he returned to the Mongolian capital to help select a new leader.

Taking advantage of Hulagu's withdrawal, the **Mamluk** general **al-Zahir Baybars** marched north and struck at the Mongol garrisons in Syria. At the **Battle of Ayn Jalut** in Palestine, General Baybars **defeated the Mongols** and expelled them from Palestine and Syria. On his return to Egypt he murdered the sultan and took his place. Distracted by dynastic struggles, and later by a protracted inter-khanate war, Hulagu was not able to regain his Syrian conquests and the westward expansion of the Mongol Empire was halted. **Hulagu's conquests**, which encompassed Iran, Iraq, most of Anatolia, Armenia, Azerbaijan, and Georgia, became the **Il-Khanate**, or Ilkhanate. Meanwhile, the Mamluks gave refuge to a **fugitive Abbasid prince**, setting him up in Cairo as the **new caliph**. Recognized as guardians of the Islamic faith, the **Mamluks** were formally made **sultans of Egypt, Syria,** and the **Levant**.

Alfonso X of Castile (r.1252–1284) won the nickname "the Wise" thanks to his learning, patronage of the arts and Castilian literature, sponsorship of natural philosophy, and judicial reforms. He oversaw the final expulsion of the **Almohads** (see 1121–25) from Spain in 1257.

KUBLAI KHAN (1215–94)

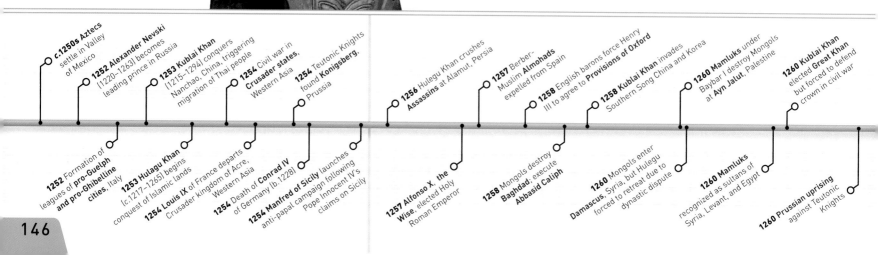

The grandson of Genghis Khan, Kublai spent eight years campaigning in southern China before succeeding his brother Mongke as Great Khan in 1260. His own kingdom, the Great Khanate, encompassed Mongolia and China, where he founded the Yuan dynasty, moved the capital to Shangdu, and did much to foster trade and international links.

> **"** HAD I BEEN PRESENT **AT THE CREATION, I WOULD HAVE GIVEN** SOME USEFUL **HINTS FOR** THE BETTER **ORDERING OF** THE **UNIVERSE. "**
>
> **Alfonso X, the Wise,** on the Ptolemaic system

- **c.1250s Aztecs** settle in Valley of Mexico
- **1252 Alexander Nevski** (1220–1263) becomes leading prince in Russia
- **1252** Formation of leagues of **pro-Guelph and pro-Ghibelline cities**, Italy
- **1253 Kublai Khan** (1215–1294) conquers Nanchao, China, triggering migration of Thai people
- **1253 Hulagu Khan** (c.1217–1265) begins conquest of Islamic lands
- **1254** Civil war in **Crusader states**, Western Asia
- **1254 Louis IX** of France departs Crusader kingdom of Acre, Western Asia
- **1254** Teutonic Knights found **Konigsberg**, Prussia
- **1254** Death of **Conrad IV** of Germany (b.1228)
- **1254 Manfred of Sicily** launches anti-papal campaign following Pope Innocent IV's claims on Sicily
- **1256** Hulegu Khan crushes **Assassins** at Alamut, Persia
- **1257 Alfonso X, the Wise**, elected Holy Roman Emperor
- **1257** Berber-Muslim **Almohads** expelled from Spain
- **1258** English barons force Henry III to agree to **Provisions of Oxford**
- **1258** Mongols destroy **Baghdad**; execute **Abbasid Caliph**
- **1258 Kublai Khan** invades Southern Song China and Korea
- **1260 Mamluks** under Baybar I destroy Mongols at **Ayn Jalut**, Palestine
- **1260** Mongols enter **Damascus**, Syria, but Hulegu forced to retreat due to dynastic dispute
- **1260 Mamluks** recognized as sultans of Syria, Levant, and Egypt
- **1260 Kublai Khan** elected **Great Khan** but forced to defend crown in civil war
- **1260 Prussian uprising** against Teutonic Knights

1261–65

This example of Mamluk architecture from the height of the sultanate adorns the entrance to the mausoleum of Qalawun in Cairo, Egypt.

ITALIAN NOBLEMAN AND LATER DOMINICAN MONK, THOMAS AQUINAS (1225–74) became one of the most important philosophers in the history of Western thought. Renowned for his work in **uniting faith and reason**, Aquinas's period of greatest productivity occurred between 1258 and 1273, when he penned his two best-known works, the *Summa contra Gentiles* and the *Summa Theologiae*.

In 1261, Michael VIII Paleologus (r.1259–61), the Byzantine emperor of Nicaea, concluded the **Treaty of Nymphaeum** with the Genoese, agreeing to cede them all the trading privileges once enjoyed by the Venetians (see 981–990). He had already secured an alliance with the Bulgarians, and was now poised to achieve his dream of re-taking Constantinople from the **Latin Empire** (Constantinople and environs, captured from the Byzantines during the fourth crusade), and reconstituting the Byzantine Greek Empire. In July 1261, a Byzantine army took advantage of the absence of the Venetian fleet to cross the Bosporus strait and take Constantinople. The Latin emperor, Baldwin II fled, and the **Paleologus Empire** was established.

Paleologus would campaign tirelessly to restore lost Byzantine lands.

The **Second Baron's War** in England between 1264 and 1267 was brought about by a combination of newly kindled national consciousness and resentment at foreign interference. **Henry III** of England (r.1216–72) had introduced many foreign officers into government and taxed the English heavily to fund overseas adventures and papal extortion. Rebels led by **Simon de Montfort**, Earl of Leicester, captured the king at Lewes in 1265 and summoned the first European parliament that included elected representatives.

Meanwhile, the **Mamluks** began a push to rid the Holy Land of the Crusader kingdoms once and for all.

Thomas Aquinas
This 15th-century altarpiece depicts Thomas Aquinas, whose philosophy still underpins Catholic dogma.

1266–71

Geneta Mariam church in Ethiopia, built during the Solomonid era.

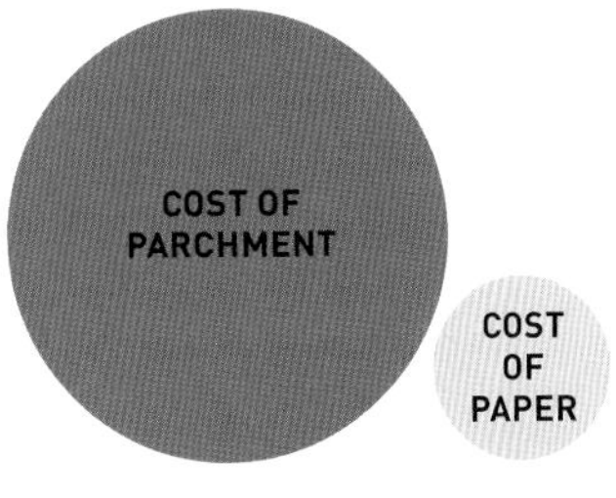

Cost of paper versus parchment
After paper-making technology was introduced to Italy, the cost of vegetable-based paper fell to 1/6 of the cost of animal-based parchment.

THE SOLOMONID DYNASTY IN ETHOPIA was founded in 1270 by Yekuno Amlak, displacing the previous Zagwe dynasty, and claiming to have restored the legitimate line of the ancient Christian kings of Aksum. Amlak claimed descent from the biblical Solomon, via the possibly Ethiopian Queen of Sheba.

The town of **Fabriano** in Italy lies close to the Adriatic port of Ancona, which was notable in the 13th century for trade with the Muslim world. This is probably how paper manufacture became established there in the 1270s. Use of animal gelatin in place of more degradable vegetable gel made Fabriano paper more durable, and the town became the principal paper manufacturing site in Europe.

In 1270, Louis IX of France made another attempt at crusading, but on the request of Charles of Anjou, **the Eighth Crusade** was diverted to Tunis where disease killed Louis and his army.

1272–75

Former stronghold of the Knights Hospitaller, Krak des Chevaliers or "fortress of the knights" in Syria was taken by the Mamluks and fortified further.

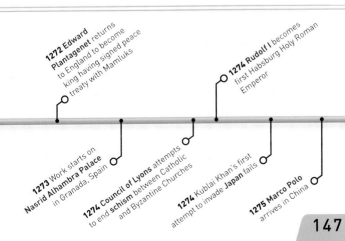

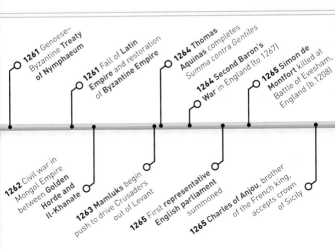

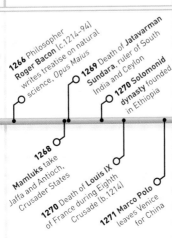

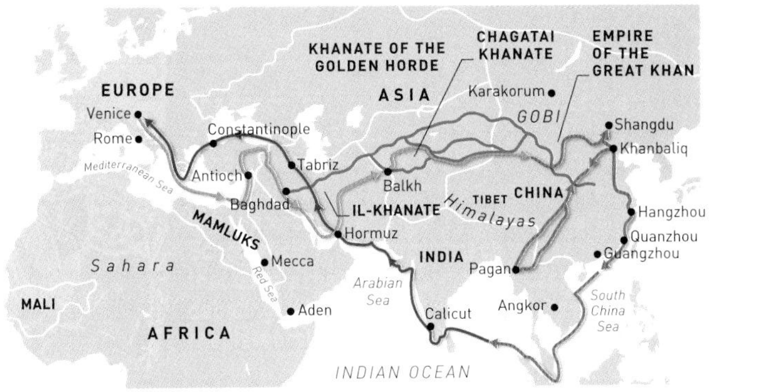

Travels of Marco Polo
To reach China, Marco Polo travelled through Anatolia, Iran, and Afghanistan. On his return, he sailed to Hormuz in Persia via Sumatra.

IN 1271,THE VENETIAN MERCHANT AND EXPLORER, MARCO POLO (*c.* 1254–1324), travelled to China. Arriving at Kublai Khan's court in 1275, the Great Khan employed Marco Polo in various capacities. In 1292, he escorted a Mongol princess to Persia, returning to Italy three years later and writing a **travel memoir** while a prisoner of the Genoese. Polo's memoir, *The Travels* – known by Italians as *Il Milione*, because of the belief that it contains a million lies – is a fascinating portrait of the Mongolian Empire at its height. The *Pax Mongolica* (see 1236–40) allowed freedom of movement through lands under the authority of **Il-khanate**, and it was said that a virgin with a pot of gold on her head could pass unmolested from Constantinople (modern-day Istanbul) to Beijing.

In 1272, **Edward Plantagenet** (r.1272–1307), heir apparent to the English throne, returned from the **Holy Land**, having forced the **Mamluks** to conclude a 10-year truce in his attempts to destroy Acre, one of the last remaining Crusader footholds in Outremer. The Mamluks had already taken the apparently impregnable **Krak des Chevaliers** from the Knights Hospitaller in 1271.

22
PER CENT THE **WORLD LAND AREA** COVERED BY THE **MONGOL EMPIRE** AT ITS HEIGHT

1261 Genoese–Byzantine **Treaty of Nymphaeum**

1261 Fall of **Latin Empire** and restoration of **Byzantine Empire**

1262 Civil war in Mongol Empire between **Golden Horde** and **Il-Khanate**

1263 Mamluks begin push to drive Crusaders out of Levant

1264 Thomas Aquinas completes *Summa contra Gentiles*

1264 Second Baron's War in England (to 1267)

1265 First **representative English parliament** summoned

1265 Simon de Montfort killed at Battle of Evesham, England (b.1208)

1265 Charles of Anjou, brother of the French king, accepts crown of Sicily

1266 Philosopher **Roger Bacon** (c.1214–94) writes treatise on natural science, *Opus Maius*

1268 Mamluks take Jaffa and Antioch, Crusader States

1269 Death of **Jatavarman Sundara**, ruler of South India and Ceylon

1270 Death of **Louis IX** of France during Eighth Crusade (b.1214)

1270 Solomonid dynasty founded in Ethiopia

1271 Marco Polo leaves Venice for China

1272 Edward Plantagenet returns to England to become king having signed peace treaty with Mamluks

1273 Work starts on **Nasrid Alhambra Palace** in Granada, Spain

1274 Council of Lyons attempts to end **schism** between Catholic and Byzantine Churches

1274 Rudolf I becomes first Habsburg Holy Roman Emperor

1274 Kublai Khan's first attempt to invade **Japan** fails

1275 Marco Polo arrives in China

1276–85

Statues adorn the Meenakshi Temple at Madurai, in India. Originally constructed by Kulasekhara Pandya, the temple was destroyed by Muslim invaders and later rebuilt.

IN SOUTHERN INDIA, KING KULASEKHARA I (r.1268–1308) expanded the empire of the **Pandyas** to its greatest extent. The Pandyas were an ancient **Tamil** people of the far south, who contended for supremacy over the centuries with neighbouring kingdoms such as the **Cholas** and the island of **Ceylon** (Sri Lanka). Under **Sundara** (r.1251–68) the Pandya empire had expanded dramatically and reduced some neighbouring states to vassalage. His son **Kulasekhara** went on to conquer Kerala, Kongu, and Ceylon, and in 1279 he defeated the last **Chola** king, **Rajendra III**, and annexed his territories. The greatness of the Pandya court was attested to by Venetian merchant, **Marco Polo**, who would pass through in 1293, but the empire was short-lived, breaking up in the early 14th century due to family quarrels and **Muslim invasions**.

By the late 13th century, the **Maori** had settled in **New Zealand** – with the exception of Antarctica, the last land mass to be colonized by humans. Dating the Maori colonization is contentious. According to estimates based on Maori traditions, the first **Polynesians** visited the islands in the early 10th century, and waves of colonization climaxed with the arrival of the **Great Fleet** of ocean-going canoes in 1350. Archaeological findings tell a slightly different story. However, it seems likely that Polynesians, probably from **Tahiti**, arrived in New Zealand around 1280, dividing the territory between **hapu** (clans). Hapu that traced a common ancestry formed **iwi** (tribes), some of which could trace their lineage back to a single **waka houra** (ocean-going canoe).

Having conquered Korea and most of China, **Kublai Khan** (1215–94) set his sights on **Japan**, sending embassies demanding submission as early as 1268. Under the bold leadership of the **Hojo regency**, the Japanese refused to be cowed. After a failed invasion attempt in 1274, Kublai sent **150,000 men** in two huge fleets in 1281, but the Japanese held off the invading armada until a great typhoon, known in Japan as the **kamikaze** ("divine wind"), devastated the Mongol fleet.

MAORI CARVING

Maori culture is noted for its tradition of arts and crafts; chief among these is Te Toi Whakairo (carving). Master craftsmen were believed to channel the voices of the spirits and ancestors, and intricately carved posts and lintels adorning structures around the marae (sacred space) and waka (canoes) were believed to accumulate and pass on mana (spiritual power).

Divine wind
An engraving shows the destruction of the Mongol fleet by the kamikaze ("divine wind") in 1281.

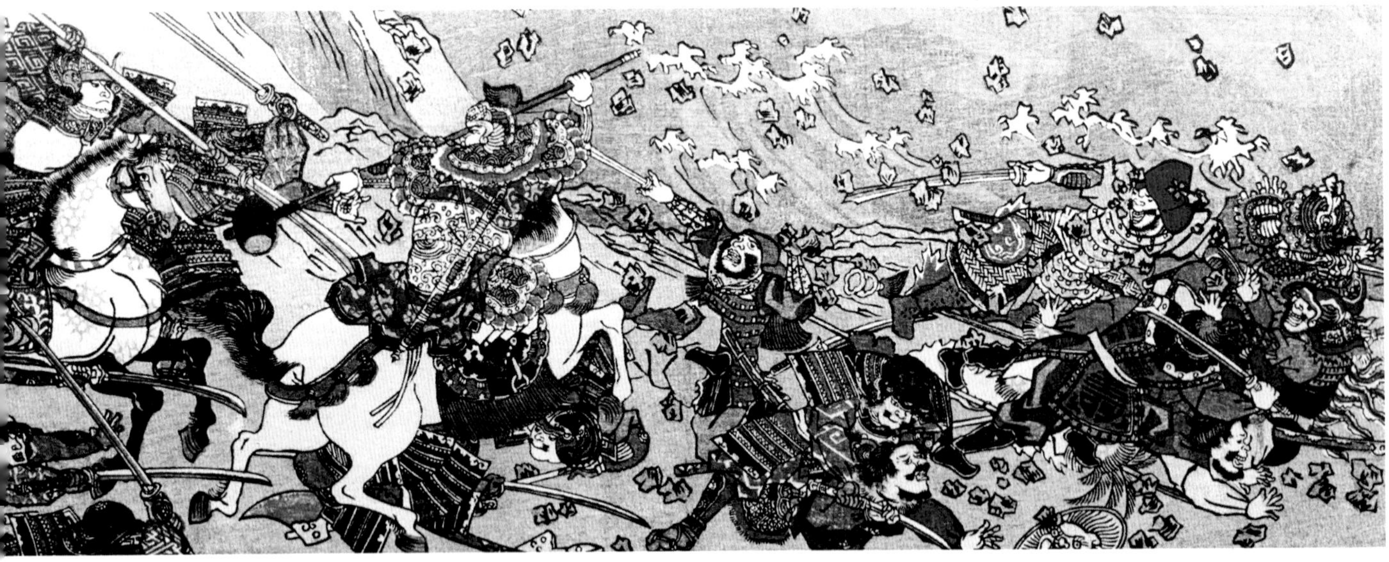

1286–90

Guglielmo Berardi da Narbona was killed at the Battle of Campaldino.

IN THE 1280S, A TRIBE OF TURKOMAN NOMADIC HORSEMEN and raiders based in northwestern Anatolia, known as the **Ottomans**, elected **Osman** (1258–1354) as their chieftain. At this time, the political map of Anatolia was fractured: the Mongol onslaught had broken up Seljuk Rum and replaced it with many small principalities, while also driving waves of Muslim refugees into the region. Meanwhile, the **Byzantine Empire** had been successively **reduced** and broken up by Seljuk and Latin encroachment. Osman was able to lead his tribe in a **territorial expansion**, rapidly conquering Byzantine territory.

Florence, like many other Italian cities, had developed into a largely **autonomous republic** or commune. It was typically easier for the German emperors – the notional feudal overlords – to grant cities powers of self-government than try to control them directly. Since the mid-13th century, Florence had see-sawed violently between **Guelph** and **Ghibelline** regimes (see 1221–25). This **Guelph–Ghibelline** conflict had gripped the Italian city-states, providing a vehicle for the expression of local **class tensions** as well as national and international politics. When one faction gained the upper hand in a city, the other was typically expelled. In the 1280s, the Guelphs had the upper hand, and Guelph partisans exiled from Arezzo encouraged them to take up arms against the rival city. The Florentines defeated Arezzo at the

1276 Treaty of Vienna; Rudolf I of Germany makes Vienna the capital of **Hapsburg lands**

1278 Otto Visconti comes to power in Milan

1279 Formation of the **Guelph Tuscan League**

1279 Kulasekhara of Pandya defeats the last Chola king

1279 Kublai Khan completes the **conquest of Southern Song** by destroying their fleet at Macau

c.1280 Maori colonization of New Zealand

c.1280s Osman elected chieftain by Turkoman tribesmen; **Ottoman dynasty** founded

1281 Battle of Homs; Mamluks defeat Mongol–Knights Hospitaller alliance

1281 Under the influence of Charles of Anjou, **Pope Martin IV** renounces the union of Byzantine and Roman churches

1281 Kamikaze (typhoon) destroys Kublai Khan's Japanese invasion fleet

1282 Sicilian Vespers Revolt against Angevin rule; Sicily is offered to **Peter III of Aragon**

1284 Genoese fleet defeats Angevin navy off Naples, and destroys the **Pisan fleet** off Meloria

1284 Venice issues regulations regarding **spectacles** – possibly invented there in 1280

1285 Having completed the conquest of Prussia, **Teutonic Knights** begin an assault on Lithuania

1286 Kublai Khan's army defeated by **Dai Viet**; he abandons plans to invade Japan

c.1286 Compilation of the **Zohar** (a collection of Jewish Kabbalah literature)

1287 Kublai Khan's army destroys **Pagan Empire** (present-day Burma)

1287 The Genoese defeat Venetian fleet off **Acre**

Battle of Campaldino, heralding the start of a period of **Florentine dominance** in Tuscany. Among those battling on the Florentine side was the poet **Dante Alighieri** (see 1311–17).

The line of Slave Kings of Delhi came to an end in 1290 with the seizure of power by **Firuz** of the **Khalji Turks** – a tribe living in Afghanistan – thus founding the **Khalji dynasty**. Firuz is best remembered for releasing into Bengal **1,000 Thugs** or Thuggees, cult followers of the goddess Kali devoted to **murder and robbery** in her name.

Ornate Mughal screen
This screen from the main gateway of the Qutb complex in Delhi was built by the Khalji sultan Ala-ud-din, murderer and successor of Firuz.

1291–95

The Eleanor Cross at Geddington, Northamptonshire, England, features an ogee arch, marking a milestone for the English Gothic style.

IN 1291, AFTER A DESPERATE SIX-WEEK SIEGE, the **Mamluks** took Acre, the last major Crusader stronghold in **Palestine**, and a few months later they took Beirut, the last remnant of the Crusader kingdom known as **Outremer** (see 1181–85). After nearly 200 years, Christian presence in the Holy Land was extinguished, and the Mamluks **plundered the region** to deter future Crusades.

To limit the risk of disastrous fires, **Venice** moved its **glass-making industry** to the island of Murano in 1291. Venetian glass makers were the only ones in Europe to master the art of producing **clear glass**. Their expertise in working with glass had earlier born fruit in the invention of **spectacles** (see 1284).

Edward I of England (r.1272–1307) had married **Eleanor of Castile** in 1254. Though unpopular with the English, she and Edward enjoyed a happy marriage, and he was devastated when she died in 1290. The following year he ordered the erection of 12 so-called **Eleanor crosses** to mark the passage of her funeral cortege to London.

The contest for **mastery of the Mediterranean** between **Genoa** and **Venice** continued, with a Genoese fleet defeating the Venetians off **Laiazzo** in 1294. The following year, Genoa put together a **huge fleet**, with the aim of landing a killer blow. However, despite a formal challenge being made, it was not engaged. Developments in Venetian shipbuilding, however, were underway. Capable of carrying more cargo and a larger crew, the construction of the first of the great galleys in 1294 heralded a distinct advantage for the Venetians.

Murano glass
This Murano glass vessel dates to around 1330. As well as increasing fire safety, concentrating the glass industry on an island helped to regulate it and guard its secrets.

165

THE NUMBER OF **GALLEYS** IN THE 1295 FLEET OF **GENOA**

1296–1300

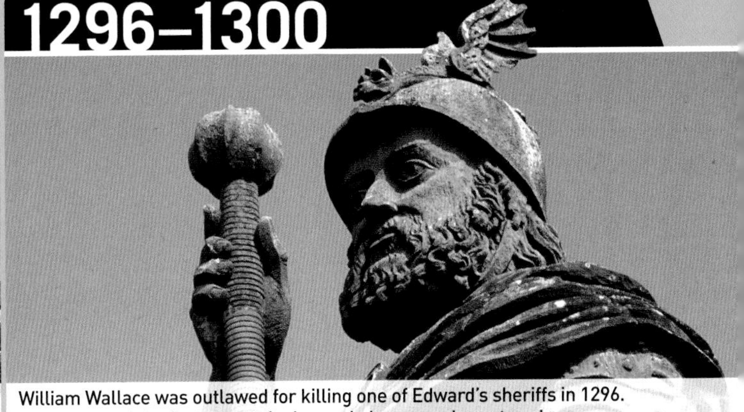

William Wallace was outlawed for killing one of Edward's sheriffs in 1296. He was one of the first men to be hanged, drawn, and quartered.

THE EXTINCTION OF THE CANMORE DYNASTY, followed by dissent among the Scottish nobles, had allowed **Edward I** to exercise increasing dominance over the Scots, and in 1292 he awarded the crown to **John Baliol**. However, in 1295, Baliol made an alliance with England's enemy, **France**. The following year Edward launched a campaign to **subdue the Scots**, defeating them at Dunbar, and taking the **Stone of Destiny** – the Scottish coronation stone – back to London. In 1297, the Scottish nationalist **William Wallace** (c.1272–1305) led a revolt against English dominance, overcoming a larger English army at **Stirling Bridge**, but he was defeated at **Falkirk** in 1298 and forced into years of guerrilla warfare and overseas fundraising.

1:4 **Battle of Stirling Bridge**
Under William Wallace, an estimated 2,500 Scots defeated a much larger force of English soldiers (numbering up to 10,000) at the Battle of Stirling Bridge.

The **Genoese–Venetian naval conflict** continued, with battles in the Black Sea and the Greek islands. At the **Battle of Curzola**, in 1298, the Genoese fleet inflicted a **disastrous defeat** on the Venetians, destroying all but a few of their ships and killing up to 7,000 men.

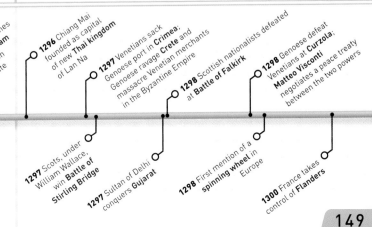

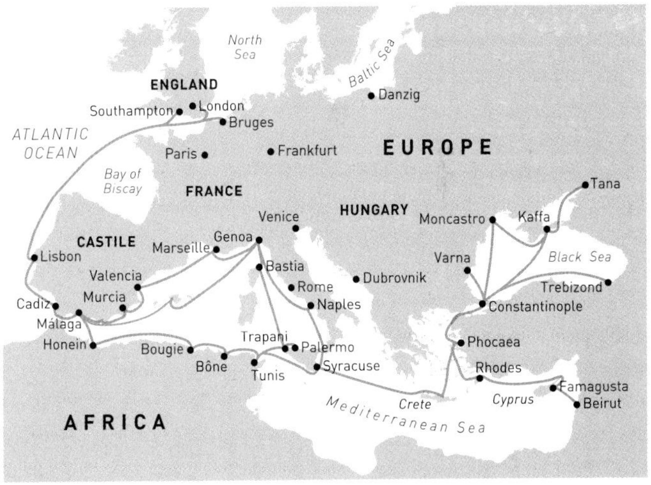

Genoese trade routes
The Genoese opened a lucrative trade route to the North Sea, and competed with Venice to dominate trade with the Byzantines and the East.

KEY
— Trade routes

1287 Mongol invasion of Punjab halted at **Lahore**

1289 Battle of **Campaldino**; Florence is dominant in Tuscany

1289 **Mamluks** take Tripoli

1290 Firuz founds the **Khalji dynasty** of the Sultanate of Delhi

1291 Mamluks take **Acre**; end of Crusader kingdoms in Palestine

1291 Edward I builds **Eleanor crosses** in England

1291 Venetian glass industry moves to **Murano**

1292 Edward of England nominates **John Balliol** as king of Scotland in face of Scottish opposition

1292 Marco Polo travels to **Java** with Kublai Khan's fleet

1294 **Kublai Khan** dies (b.1215)

1295 **Marco Polo** returns to Italy, and is captured by the Genoese

1295 Ghazan becomes Ilkhan, makes **Islam** the state religion of the Ilkhanate

1295 **Genoese** build massive fleet

1296 Chiang Mai founded as capital of new **Thai kingdom** of Lan Na

1297 Scots, under William Wallace, win **Battle of Stirling Bridge**

1297 Venetians sack Genoese port in **Crimea**; Genoese ravage **Crete** and massacre Venetian merchants in the Byzantine Empire

1297 Sultan of Delhi conquers **Gujarat**

1298 Scottish nationalists defeated at **Battle of Falkirk**

1298 First mention of a **spinning wheel** in Europe

1298 Genoese defeat Venetians at **Curzola**; **Matteo Visconti** negotiates a peace treaty between the two powers

1300 France takes control of **Flanders**

Domenico di Michelino's painting *The Comedy Illuminating Florence*, depicts Dante, the city of Florence, and scenes from the *Divine Comedy*.

ALTHOUGH THE GHIBELLINES HAD BEEN EXPELLED FROM FLORENCE (see 1286–90), factionalism still plagued the city, with a drawn-out **power struggle** between the old aristocratic nobility, the new mercantile nobles, and the powerful guilds. The **Guelph** faction split into Black (extreme) and White (moderate) parties. In 1301, the Whites expelled the Blacks, only for them to return when **Charles, count of Valois**, entered the city. The following year the Black Guelphs sentenced the Whites to death or exile – among them the poet **Dante Alighieri** (see panel, right).

In 1301, **Pope Boniface VIII** (*c.*1235–1303) supposedly issued a bull asserting **papal supremacy** over France. In fact, the bull was a forgery, put out by the French king **Philip IV the Fair** (r.1285–1314) to stir up animosity against the pope. Philip "responded" by calling one of the first **Estates General** – including representatives of the towns and clergy – and received their backing. Boniface **excommunicated** Philip and Philip called for the Pope to face **criminal charges**. In 1303, agents acting for Philip forced their way into the papal apartments in Anagni and **arrested the Pope**, who died soon after. Facing tumultuous conditions in Italy, in 1303 the cardinals elected the archbishop of Bordeaux as **Pope Clement V**. Although hoping to establish himself in Italy when the violence subsided, Clement remained in southern France, finally settling in **Avignon** in 1309, then owned by the king of Naples. This temporary arrangement for the papacy would last until 1378.

Palais des Papes
Situated on a rocky outcrop, the papal palace in Avignon is one of the largest and most important medieval Gothic buildings in Europe.

" LET EVIL SWIFTLY BEFALL THOSE WHO HAVE WRONGLY CONDEMNED US – GOD WILL AVENGE US. "

Jacques de Molay, the Grand Master of the Knights Templar, cursing King Philip and Pope Clement V, 1314

The torture of Jacques de Molay, Grand Master of the Knights Templar.

FROM THEIR HUMBLE BEGINNINGS, WHEN THEY HAD BEEN SO POOR that two knights sometimes had to share a horse, the **Knights Templar** had risen to dizzying heights. With the backing of Cistercian abbot **Bernard of Clairvaux** (1090–1153), and subsequently the Pope, they had won exemption from secular jurisdiction and taxation, and thrived as donations of land and money poured in. By the 13th century they had become **de facto bankers** to much of Europe, able to direct a large fleet and maintain the primary **Crusader army** in Outremer. Templar knights rose to prominence all over Europe, especially in England, where the **Master of the Temple** was the first baron of the realm. In the early 13th century, then **Master William Marshal** ruled the country as regent for the young king **Henry III** (1207–72). However, after the **fall of Outremer**, the Templars were struggling to stay afloat, and presented an easy target for their enemy, **Philip IV of France**. Philip coveted the Templar lands and cooked up charges of **heresy** in which to indict them. On 13 October 1307, Philip's officials simultaneously **arrested every Templar in France**. They were accused of a **variety of crimes**, including sexual and occult outrages and worshipping an idol. The **use of torture** obtained lurid confessions, and over the next few years around **60 Templars were executed**. Elsewhere in Europe, some arrests were made, but there was much less appetite for condemning the order. At the **Council of Vienne** (1311–12), Philip forced Pope Clement to **dissolve the Templars**, and in 1314 the last Grand Master, Jacques de Molay, was burned at the stake.

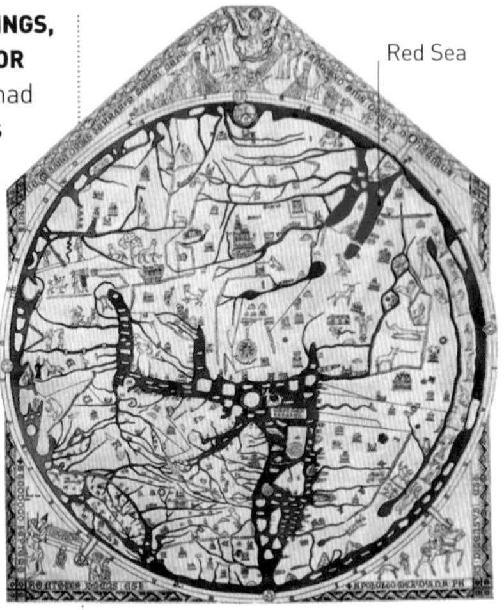

Hereford Mappa Mundi
The world is shown as a disc, with Jerusalem at the centre. Trade and pilgrimage routes are illustrated, together with places of interest.

Hereford, in England, was an important centre for the **wool trade** – one of the main sources of wealth in medieval England. Foreign buyers flocked to the country to buy wool for export to the **textile industries** of Flanders and Italy, and the wool trade was described as "**the jewel in the realm**". The wealth of places such as Hereford was expressed in the magnificence of their **cathedrals** and the richness of their accessories. At Hereford Cathedral a huge **Mappa Mundi** (map of the world) was created in around 1300 (its creation is variously dated to 1285 and 1314) and used as an altarpiece; it is the largest mappa mundi in existence. Such maps encapsulated the medieval world view on the eve of the **Age of Discovery**.

At the Battle of Bannockburn in 1314, **Robert the Bruce**, king of Scotland (r.1306–29), finally expelled the English from Scotland.

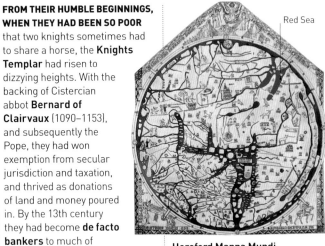

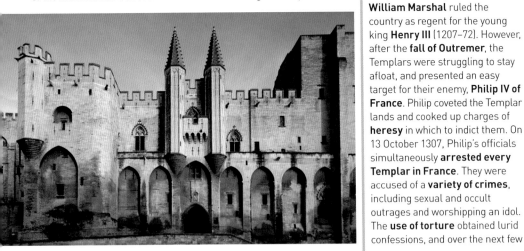

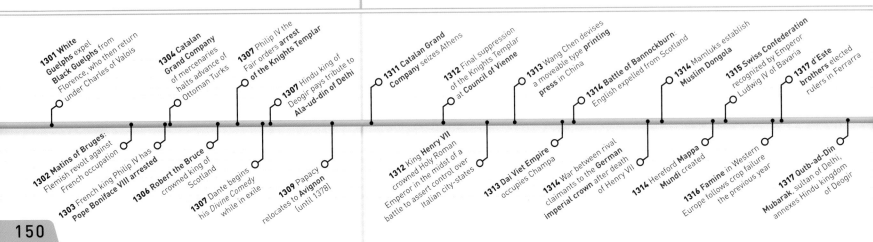

DANTE ALIGHIERI
(1265–1321)

Dante is the greatest Italian poet to have lived and one of the most important writers in European literature. He is best known for his epic poem the *Divine Comedy*, and for his tragic love for Beatrice, who married another and died young. Exiled from his native Florence for political reasons, Dante spent much of his life travelling from one city to another. He died in Ravenna in 1321.

- **1301 White Guelphs** expel **Black Guelphs** from Florence, who then return under Charles of Valois
- **1302 Matins of Bruges**: Flemish revolt against French occupation
- **1303** French king Philip IV has **Pope Boniface VIII arrested**
- **1304 Catalan Grand Company** of mercenaries halts advance of Ottoman Turks
- **1306 Robert the Bruce** crowned king of Scotland
- **1307** Philip IV the Fair orders **arrest of the Knights Templar**
- **1307** Dante begins his *Divine Comedy* while in exile
- **1307** Hindu king of Deogir pays tribute to **Ala-ud-din of Delhi**
- **1309** Papacy relocates to **Avignon** (until 1378)
- **1311 Catalan Grand Company** seizes Athens
- **1312** King **Henry VII** crowned Holy Roman Emperor in the midst of a battle to assert control over Italian city-states
- **1312** Final suppression of the Knights Templar at **Council of Vienne**
- **1313** Wang Chen devises a moveable type **printing press** in China
- **1313 Dai Viet Empire** occupies Champa
- **1314 Battle of Bannockburn**: English expelled from Scotland
- **1314** War between rival claimants to the **German imperial crown** after death of Henry VII
- **1314** Mamluks establish **Muslim Dongola**
- **1314** Hereford **Mappa Mundi** created
- **1315 Swiss Confederation** recognized by Emperor Ludwig IV of Bavaria
- **1316 Famine** in Western Europe follows crop failure the previous year
- **1317 d'Este brothers** elected rulers in Ferrarra
- **1317 Qutb-ad-Din Mubarak**, sultan of Delhi, annexes Hindu kingdom of Deogir

1318–25

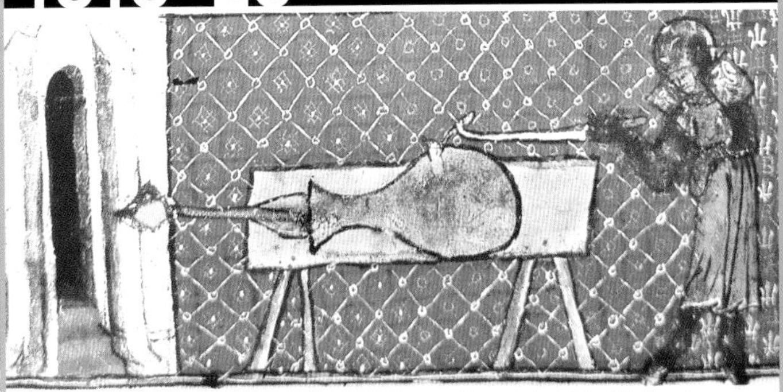

The earliest European illustration of a cannon, from a book by Walter de Milemete, presented to the future Edward III of England in 1326.

GUNPOWDER WAS SLOWLY BUT STEADILY CHANGING THE FACE OF WARFARE. Arabs and Moors had probably gained knowledge of gunpowder from the **Chinese**, using cannons in Spain as early as 1284. The **Mamluks** are believed to have used **handguns** at Ain Jalut, while the Mongols acquired the technology on conquering China. Europeans probably picked it up from **Spain** and contact with the **Mongols**. The first record of cannons forged from iron comes from Metz in 1324; later that year an English fortress in Gascony was bombarded for a month.

The **Mali Empire** of West Africa reached its height under **Mansa Musa** (r.1312–37), extending from the Atlantic to Nigeria, and from the Sahara to the rainforest. His great wealth was based on **Mali's gold**, and when he travelled on pilgrimage to Mecca in 1324–25, he dispensed so much gold on his passage through **Cairo** that he destabilized the economy. On his return, he employed an Andalusian architect to build a new palace at **Timbuktu**, which became a centre for **Islamic scholarship**. Mali was later visited by the Moroccan scholar **Ibn Battuta** (*c.*1304–69), who first set out on his travels in 1325.

25

THE **PERCENTAGE** OF **TIMBUKTU'S POPULATION** AT **SANKORE UNIVERSITY**

The travels of Ibn Battuta
Ibn Battuta's first journey was the Hajj (pilgrimage) to Mecca. He made seven further journeys, visiting almost every corner of the Muslim world.

1326–39

The gilded bronze doors on the Baptistry in Florence, sculpted and cast by Andrea Pisano, took six years to make after he won the commission in 1329.

FLORENCE IN THE 1320S AND 1330S WAS HOME TO ARTISTS including **Giotto di Bondone** (*c.*1267–1337) and **Andrea Pisano** (*c.*1290–1349) – both seen as forerunners of the Italian Renaissance (see pp.208–09). Giotto painted naturalistic frescoes on the walls of the **Basilica of Santa Croce** in around 1325, and in 1334 was put in charge of the construction of the **Duomo** (cathedral). Greatly influenced by Giotto, Pisano won a commission to craft a set of **bronze doors for the Baptistry of Florence**, finishing them in 1336.

The **Tughluk dynasty** of the Delhi sultanate had expanded the reach of the **Muslim** state, reducing neighbouring **Hindu kingdoms** to vassal status, and repelling a series of **Mongol incursions**. In 1325, **Muhammad Tughluk** (*c.*1300–51) murdered his father and took the throne, quickly establishing a reputation for cruelty. In 1327, he transferred the capital from Delhi to **Daulatabad** for defensive reasons, forcing the entire population to relocate. In 1336, a revolt led by **Harihara I** and his brother **Bukka** of the **Sangama dynasty** in the south, led to the establishment of the last great Hindu empire in India, centred on the city of **Vijayanagar**.

Edward II of England invested power in favourites, especially **Piers Gaveston** (murdered by resentful barons in 1312) and the **Despenser family**. He also alienated his wife, **Isabella of France**, who was sent to France in 1325 to arrange the marriage of their son. While there, she became the lover of **Roger Mortimer**, and when they returned, in 1326, they led a **revolt against the king**. The Despensers were hanged, Edward was **forced to abdicate** in favour of his teenage son, and **Roger and Isabella ruled as regents**. Eight months later, Edward II was horribly murdered. The regents ceded Gascony to France and acknowledged **Robert the Bruce** as king of an independent Scotland. In 1330, **Edward III** (r.1327–77) had Mortimer hanged and began his own rule. Rising **tension with France** was exacerbated by Edward's embargo on wool exports to **Flanders**, which **triggered a revolt** there against French domination. In 1337, Philip VI of France declared Edward's French territories forfeit, while Edward claimed the French crown, triggering the start of the **Hundred Years War**.

> **" THE FIRST KING** AFTER THE CONQUEST WHO WAS **NOT A MAN OF BUSINESS. "**
>
> **William Stubbs, English historian,** describing Edward II, 1875

Vijayanagar sculpture
Lord Hanuman, the Hindu monkey god, is shown carved on a rock surface in Vijayanagar, the heart of the last great Hindu empire.

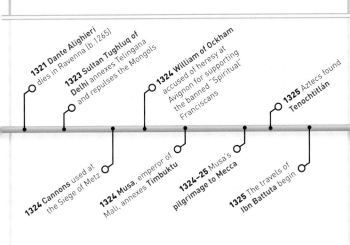

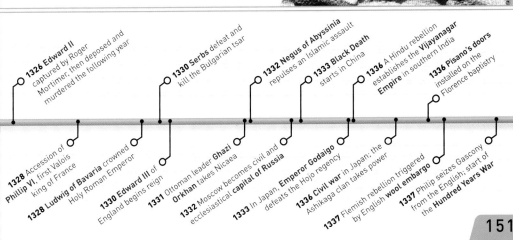

1321 Dante Alighieri dies in Ravenna (b.1265)

1323 Sultan Tughluq of Delhi annexes Telingana and repulses the Mongols

1324 Cannons used at the Siege of Metz

1324 William of Ockham accused of heresy at Avignon for supporting the banned "Spiritual" Franciscans

1324 Musa, emperor of Mali, annexes **Timbuktu**

1324–25 Musa's **pilgrimage to Mecca**

1325 Aztecs found **Tenochtitlán**

1325 The travels of **Ibn Battuta** begin

1326 Edward II captured by Roger Mortimer, then deposed and murdered the following year

1328 Accession of **Phillip VI**, first Valois king of France

1328 Ludwig of Bavaria crowned Holy Roman Emperor

1330 Serbs defeat and kill the Bulgarian tsar

1330 Edward III of England begins reign

1331 Ottoman leader **Ghazi Orkhan** takes Nicaea

1332 Negus of Abyssinia repulses an Islamic assault

1332 Moscow becomes civil and ecclesiastical **capital of Russia**

1333 Black Death starts in China

1333 In Japan, **Emperor Godaigo** defeats the Hojo regency

1336 A Hindu rebellion establishes the **Vijayanagar Empire** in southern India

1336 Civil war in Japan; the Ashikaga clan takes power

1336 Pisano's doors installed on the Florence baptistry

1337 Flemish rebellion triggered by English **wool embargo**

1337 Philip seizes Gascony from the English; start of the **Hundred Years War**

1340–44

The Strait of Gibraltar, where Marinid forces destroyed the Castilian fleet.

THE BATTLE OF RIO SALADO IS CONSIDERED, BY SOME, to be the defining battle of the **Reconquista**, ending forever the threat of **Islamic incursion** into the Iberian Peninsula from Africa. The **Marinid dynasty** of Morocco, which had overthrown the **Almohads** in the mid-13th century, gathered a vast force and destroyed the Castilian fleet in the **Strait of Gibraltar**. The Marinids then marched inland to the River Salado where they were defeated by the Christian kings **Alfonso XI of Castile** (r.1312–50) and **Afonso IV of Portugal** (r.1325–57).

800,000
THE AMOUNT IN FLORINS **OWED** BY **EDWARD III**

To finance his expensive war in France, **Edward III** of England (r.1327–77) had taken out **huge loans** from Florentine bankers, especially the **Peruzzi family**. When the money ran out, Edward renounced his loan in 1342. With the king of Naples also defaulting on loans, the Peruzzi were bankrupted, throwing **Florence** into **economic chaos**. Walter de Brienne, the mercenary duke of Athens, was called in to take power in Florence but, eventually, a **mercantile oligarchy** took over.

1345–49

An illustration from Froissart's *Chronicle*, of 1346, depicts the Battle of Crecy, at which the English used mobile artillery for the first time.

HAVING GAINED MASTERY OF THE ENGLISH CHANNEL at the naval battle of **Sluys** in 1340, **Edward III** was free to invade France. He landed in **Normandy** in 1346 and took **Caen**, but retreated in the face of a huge French army. At bay, on the borders of the **forest of Crecy**, Edward took up a defensive position and inflicted a **crushing defeat** on the forces of Philip VI. This was largely thanks to the indiscipline and arrogance of the **French knights** and the effectiveness of the **Welsh** and **English longbowmen**. At the cost of a handful of casualties, **the English killed tens of thousands**, including the kings of Bohemia and Majorca, the duke of Lorraine, the count of Flanders, the count of Blois, eight other counts, and three archbishops. The English use of **combined aristocratic and yeoman forces** had produced a powerful new form of army. They would go on to **besiege Calais**, which fell in 1347, after a protracted siege.

Also in 1347, the **Black Death** arrived in Europe. It is thought to have been carried initially by Genoans returning from the **Crimea**, where they had been exposed to it by infected Mongols. Transmitted by **fleas that were carried by rats**, the plague was spread by ship to the principal ports, and then to every corner of Europe and Western Asia. A large proportion of the population died.

THE BLACK DEATH

The effects of the Black Death are best recorded in Europe, where it had profound consequences. It depopulated the land, depressed the economy, checked intellectual and artistic progress, changed the social order, contributed to the end of feudalism, and triggered a wave of anti-Semitic pogroms on Jews, who were blamed for the pestilence, forcing many to migrate to Eastern Europe.

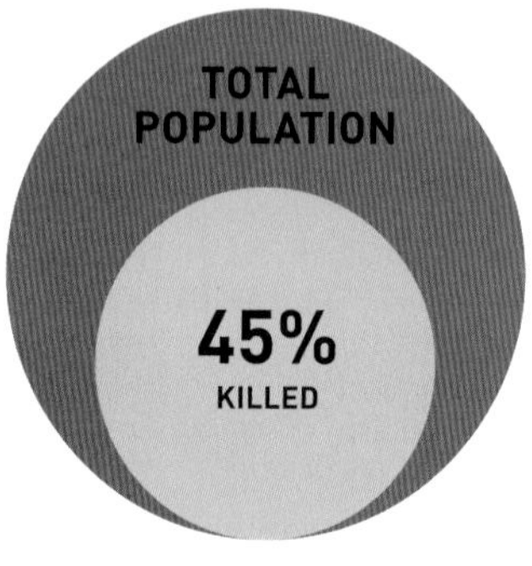

Plague deaths
It is estimated that up to 45 per cent of the total population of Europe was killed by the various waves of the Black Death plague.

1350–55

“ WHATEVER THE WORLD **FINDS PLEASING,** IS BUT A **BRIEF DREAM.”**

Petrarch, Florentine scholar and poet, from *Canzoniere number 1* (*c.*1352)

THE PAPACY WAS REFORMING ITS BUREAUCRACY and improving its finances under the Avignon popes. In 1348, **Clement VI** (1291–1352) bought **Avignon** from Joanne of Naples and work continued on its papal palace. **Scholars and artists** were attracted to the papal city, briefly among them the Florentine **Francesco Petrarch** (1304–74), who had been crowned **poet laureate** in Rome in 1341. In 1351, Petrarch started to arrange his poems in **sonnet** form. He was also a scholar, whose translation and popularization of **Classical literature** contributed to the emergence of **humanism**, a new school of philosophy that would help to trigger the **Renaissance**.

In 1354, the Nasrid king of Granada, **Yusuf I**, was murdered by his son **Mohammed V** (1338–91) who took the throne. Under Mohammed, the **Alhambra** – the fortress-palace of Granada – was further developed, becoming a **treasure of Islamic architecture**.

The **Ottomans** were invited to **Gallipoli**, on the Dardanelles (the straits separating Asia from Europe), by John Cantacuzenus (*c.*1292–1383), claimant to the **Byzantine throne**, to help in his attempt to gain power. Led by Orhan, the **Turkish dynasty** soon seized the peninsula, securing themselves a foothold in Europe.

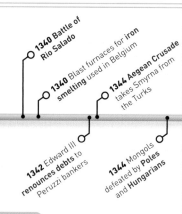

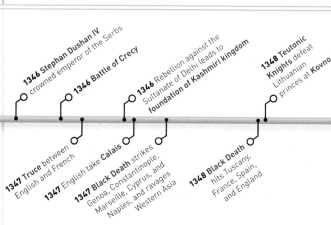

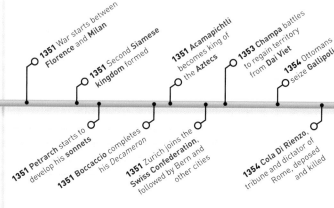

Architectural jewel
The Court of the Lions is at the heart of the Alhambra palace, built by Mohammed V as the winter residence of the royal family.

- **1340 Battle of Rio Salado**
- **1340** Blast furnaces for **iron smelting** used in Belgium
- **1342** Edward III **renounces debts** to Peruzzi bankers
- **1344 Aegean Crusade** takes Smyrna from the Turks
- **1344** Mongols defeated by **Poles** and **Hungarians**
- **1346 Stephan Dushan IV** crowned emperor of the Serbs
- **1346 Battle of Crecy**
- **1346** Rebellion against the Sultanate of Delhi leads to **foundation of Kashmiri kingdom**
- **1347 Truce** between English and French
- **1347** English take **Calais**
- **1347 Black Death** strikes Genoa, Constantinople, Marseille, Cyprus, and Naples, and ravages Western Asia
- **1348 Teutonic Knights** defeat Lithuanian princes at **Kovno**
- **1348 Black Death** hits Tuscany, France, Spain, and England
- **1351** War starts between **Florence** and **Milan**
- **1351** Second **Siamese kingdom** formed
- **1351 Petrarch** starts to develop his **sonnets**
- **1351 Boccaccio** completes his *Decameron*
- **1351 Acamapichtli** becomes king of the **Aztecs**
- **1351** Zurich joins the **Swiss Confederation**, followed by Bern and other cities
- **1353 Champa** battles to regain territory from **Dai Viet**
- **1354** Ottomans seize **Gallipoli**
- **1354 Cola Di Rienzo**, tribune and dictator of Rome, deposed and killed

To many people, Petrarch is known as the "father of humanism".

This mural features Timur Leng, who rose from humble beginnings to found the Timurid dynasty after outmatching the conquests of Genghis Khan.

Constructed of brick and timber, the Bell Tower of Xi'an, was built during the early Ming dynasty, in the reign of Zhu Yuanzhang, the first Ming emperor.

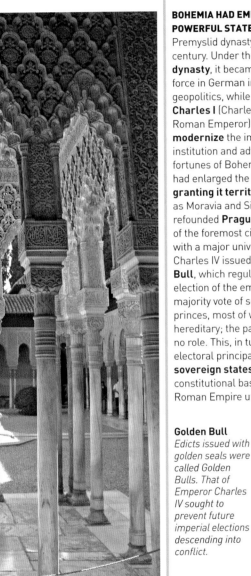

BOHEMIA HAD EMERGED AS A POWERFUL STATE under the Premyslid dynasty in the 13th century. Under the **Luxembourg dynasty**, it became the central force in German imperial geopolitics, while its ruler **Charles I** (Charles IV as Holy Roman Emperor) sought to **modernize** the imperial institution and advance the fortunes of Bohemia. In 1348, he had enlarged the kingdom by **granting it territories** such as Moravia and Silesia, and refounded **Prague** to become one of the foremost cities in Europe, with a major university. In 1356, Charles IV issued the **Golden Bull**, which regularized the election of the emperor to a majority vote of seven electoral princes, most of which were hereditary; the papacy would have no role. This, in turn, allowed the electoral principalities to develop **sovereign states**, and set the constitutional basis of the Holy Roman Empire until its final dissolution in 1806. The Bull established Bohemia as first among the electors and guaranteed its independence.

Timur Leng (1336–1405) – also known as Tamerlane – rose from modest beginnings to become leader of a **Turkic-Mongol Chagatai tribe** in Transoxiana, Central Asia, in around 1362. Despite having a limp, and the fact that he was not of **Chinggid descent** (directly descended from Genghis Khan – only Chinggids could become khans), he was destined to become one of the **greatest conquerors** in history.

Edward of Woodstock, eldest son of Edward III, also known as the **Black Prince** (1330–76), had won his spurs at the **Battle of Crécy** aged just 16. He went on to become one of the most effective English commanders. When **hostilities renewed** between England and France in 1355, he invaded France, winning a great victory near **Poitiers** in 1356, in which he captured **King John of France**.

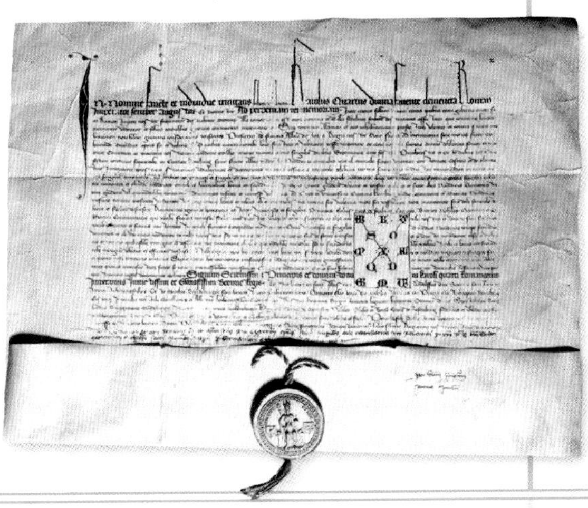

Golden Bull
Edicts issued with golden seals were called Golden Bulls. That of Emperor Charles IV sought to prevent future imperial elections descending into conflict.

EDWARD, THE BLACK PRINCE, HAD BEEN MADE PRINCE OF GASCONY AND AQUITAINE in 1362, moving to Bordeaux and becoming a major player in continental affairs. In 1367, he intervened in a **dynastic dispute in Castile**, where French ally Henry of Trastamara (1334–79) had deposed English ally Pedro I, thereby **placing control of the Castilian navy in the French camp**. Edward defeated Henry at **Nájera** but was forced to withdraw owing to illness. Subsequently, Henry regained the Castilian throne. In 1372 – after **Charles V of France** (r.1364–80) had fomented a **Gascon rebellion**, restarting the **Hundred Years War** – the Castilian navy proved instrumental in defeating an English fleet at **La Rochelle**.

China was reunited by conquest from the south, as a native rebellion drove out the **Mongol Yuan dynasty**. In 1368, rebels under **Zhu Yuanzhang** (1328–98) – a former peasant turned Buddhist monk then general – struck north from their base in Nanjing, **displacing the Yuan from Beijing**. Taking the imperial name **Hongwu**, Yuanzhang established the **Ming dynasty**, setting up a strong, centralized, government, in which the position of emperor was strengthened, but so was access to the bureaucracy. In 1372, he passed an edict attempting to ban maritime trade and thus **limit contact with foreigners**.

276

THE SPAN, IN YEARS, OF THE **MING DYNASTY**

Under **Murad I** (r.1362–89), the Ottoman Turks extended their control deep into the **Balkans**. In 1371, Murad defeated an alliance of Serbs, Byzantines, and Bulgars, and held control over much of Thrace, Macedonia, Bulgaria, and Serbia. He also created the **Janissaries**, a slave-warrior corps that became the mainstay of Ottoman armies.

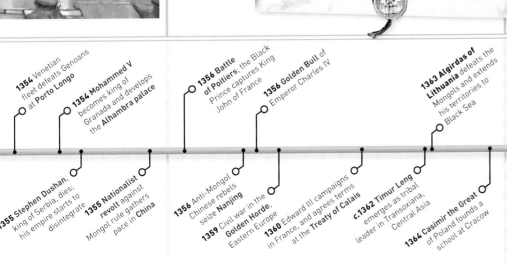

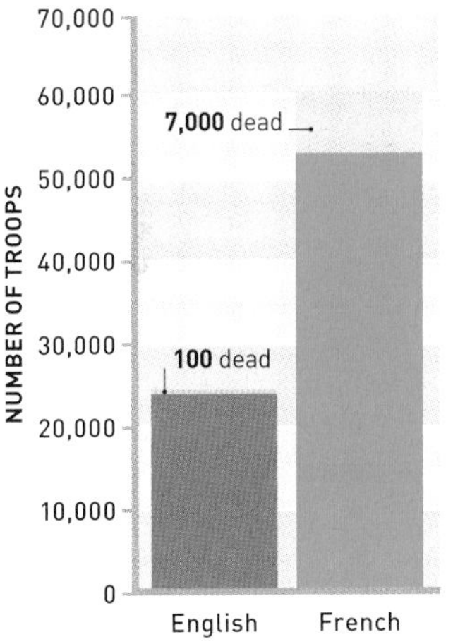

Battle of Nájera
Outnumbered by almost three to one, the English-Gascon army defeated the French-Castilian forces with the loss of only around 100 men.

1354 Venetian fleet defeats Genoans at **Porto Longo**

1354 Mohammed V becomes king of Granada and develops the **Alhambra palace**

1355 Stephen Dushan, king of Serbia, dies; his empire starts to disintegrate

1355 Nationalist revolt against Mongol rule gathers pace in **China**

1356 Battle of Poitiers; the Black Prince captures King John of France

1356 Anti-Mongol Chinese rebels seize **Nanjing**

1356 Golden Bull of Emperor Charles IV

1359 Civil war in the **Golden Horde**, Eastern Europe

1360 Edward III campaigns in France, and agrees terms at the **Treaty of Calais**

c.1362 Timur Leng emerges as tribal leader in Transoxiana, Central Asia

1363 Algirdas of Lithuania defeats the Mongols and extends his territories to Black Sea

1364 Casimir the Great of Poland founds a school at Cracow

1367 Battle of Nájera

1368 Zhu Yuanzhang expels Yuan dynasty and founds **Ming dynasty**

1368 Tibet regains **independence** following Yuan collapse

1369 Timur Leng conquers Samarkand

1369 Hundred Years War restarts

1369 Hanseatic League at peak of its power

1371 Battle of Chernomen

1372 French are victorious in naval battle of **La Rochelle**, and recover Poitiers

THE STORY OF PRINTING

A REVOLUTION IN HUMAN COMMUNICATION CHANGES THE WORLD FOREVER

By making it possible to communicate and disseminate information at a speed and scale previously unthinkable, printing wrought changes that are still unfolding today, from triggering religious mania, to scientific and political revolutions – even changing language itself.

Printing is the impression of marks on a medium – most commonly ink on paper. The earliest writing, cuneiform, was a form of printing composed of indentations made by a stylus in clay. Printing, in the modern sense of the word, first arose in 8th-century China with the development of block printing. Blocks of wood carved into bas-relief were used as stamps to reproduce multiple copies of a single text, complete with images, such as the *Diamond Sutra*, the earliest dateable printed book (see 861–70).

MECHANICAL PRINTING

Block printing was laborious and slow, as each block was specific to one page. Moveable type was a major advance (see panel, opposite), first achieved in eastern Asia but perfected by German printer Johannes Gutenberg (see 1454–55). His printing press was so advanced that, except for refinements such as new typefaces and mechanization of the presses and paper handling, the basic process remained unchanged until the 19th century.

In the 1880s, the development of linotype allowed a typesetter to compose lines of type using a keyboard, rather than by hand. Stereotyping made it possible to duplicate complete pages for multiple printing. In the 20th century, filmsetting enabled rapid photographic creation of printing plates. By the end of the century, computers allowed every aspect of printing, from typesetting and graphics to inking and drying, to be done on one machine.

> “HE WHO FIRST **SHORTENED** THE **LABOUR** OF COPYISTS **BY** DEVICE OF **MOVEABLE TYPES** WAS … **CREATING** A WHOLE NEW **DEMOCRATIC WORLD;** HE HAD **INVENTED** THE **ART OF PRINTING.**”

Thomas Carlyle, Scottish essayist and historian, 1759–1881

c.2291–2254 BCE
Sumerian cuneiform
Stamping cuneiform inscriptions, rather than drawing them by hand, is introduced. Stamps are pressed into soft clay bricks, which are then fired.

Sumerian cuneiform

8th century
Block printing
Printing using carved wooden blocks and ink is known as xylography; the earliest surviving xylographic fragment is a Buddhist *dharani* scroll from Korea.

Japanese *dharani* scroll

868
Block printed book
The earliest dated book (entire manuscript) is the *Diamond Sutra*, a Buddhist text found in a cave in Dunhuang, China.

The *Diamond Sutra*

c.1275–1313
Moveable type
Invented in China in the 11th century, moveable type is refined by Wang Shen, who uses over 60,000 wooden types in his treatise.

1377
Moveable metal type
The first metal moveable type is cast in bronze in Korea and is used to produce the *Jikji Simche Yojeol*, a Buddhist scripture.

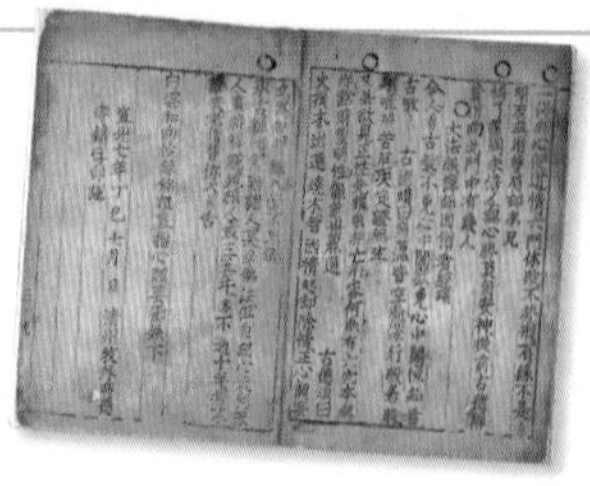

Early Korean book

c.1455–56
The printing press
Gutenberg prints the first book in Europe – the Gutenberg or 42-line *Bible* (because of the number of lines on each page).

Gutenberg's printing press

1790s–1820s
Metal presses
The all-metal Columbian printing press is the first to replace the screw with levers and weights.

Columbian metal press

Gutenberg's press
Gutenberg created a screw press for pressing inked type, set on a wooden frame, against a sheet of paper. This was a dramatic improvement on the traditional method of taking impressions by means of rubbing.

MOVEABLE TYPE

The key technology in the printing revolution was moveable type, in which each character in a script had a corresponding single, small block, or type, allowing lines of type to be assembled, and then reordered for different texts. The first book, printed by moveable type cast in bronze, was published in Korea in the late 14th century. Gutenberg improved upon this technology by developing a technique that enabled rapid, precision casting of metal type.

Letterpress printing with moveable type

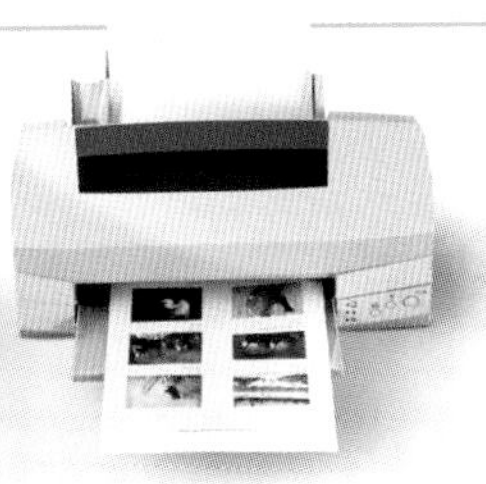

Laser printer

Late 20th century–present
Desktop printing
The laser printer offers technology that would once have filled an entire workshop.

1886
Linotype
A linotype machine allows a typesetter to make up entire lines of type, using a typewriter-like keyboard, rather than hand-compositing letter-by-letter.

Linotype typesetter

1903
Offset printing
In offset printing, the inked image is transferred (or offset) from the printing plate to the paper via a rubber sheet, achieving smooth, precise transfer and reducing wear on the plate.

Early photocopier

1949
Photocopying
Developed by American Chester Carlson at the Xerox Corporation in the US, the photocopier uses electrostatic distribution of powder ink or toner, rather than wet ink, to create an exact copy.

1373–80

A 16th-century painting captures the triumphant return of the Doge to Venice after victory over the Genoese.

THE WAR OF CHIOGGIA, BETWEEN VENICE AND GENOA, was triggered by the continuing contest for control of the **trade routes through the Dardanelles**, along which flowed the lucrative trade of the **Byzantine Empire** and the **Silk Road** beyond it. In 1376, the Byzantine emperor **John V Palaeologus** (r.1341–76) granted to Venice the Aegean island of **Tenedos**, key to the Dardanelles. Meanwhile, his son and rival **Andronicus IV** (1348–85) granted it to Genoa. In the ensuing war, the Genoans defeated the Venetians at **Pola** and, in 1379, seized **Chioggia** in Italy and **blockaded Venice**. Under Vittorio Pisano, the Venetians counter-blockaded the Genoese fleet, starving it into submission. **Genoese maritime power was broken** and Venice now controlled the Levantine trade.

> **“ NOTHING GREAT** IS EVER ACHIEVED WITHOUT **MUCH ENDURING. ”**
>
> **St Catherine of Siena,** (1347–80)

In 1376, Dominican mystic and miracle worker **Catherine of Siena** travelled to Avignon to convince **Gregory XI** (*c*.1336–78) to return the papacy to Rome. A few months later, Gregory went to Rome to attempt to restore order in the Papal States, and died soon after. The **Roman mob** pressured the conclave of cardinals to choose an **Italian pope**, and **Urban VI** (*c*.1318–89) was duly elected. French cardinals, meanwhile, elected **Robert of Geneva** (1342–94) as **anti-pope Clement VII**. The French king, Charles V, threw his weight behind Clement, while **Richard II of England** allied with the Holy Roman Emperor Charles IV in supporting the Roman candidate. Thus began the **Western, or Great Schism**, which saw rival popes installed in Rome and Avignon until 1417.

Executioner of Cesena
The anti-pope Clement VII was known as the "executioner of Cesena" for his brutal suppression of a rebellion in the Papal States while acting as a papal legate.

1381–85

An illustration from Froissart's Chronicle depicts the Peasants' Revolt, the first great popular rebellion in English history, led by Wat Tyler, who was executed by the mayor of London.

THE BLACK DEATH AND SUBSEQUENT LABOUR SHORTAGES contributed to rising social tension in England. Around 1362, for instance, the poor country priest William Langland had written *Piers Plowman*, a poem in English sympathizing with the plight of the poor peasant. Churchman and scholar **John Wycliffe** (or Wiclif) had caused a stir with writings that prefigured **Protestantism**, and a popular Biblical egalitarian sect, known as the **Lollards**, partially inspired by Wycliffe, was winning widespread support. In 1377, the so-called **Bad Parliament**, dominated by the king's son **John of Gaunt**, earl of Lancaster and soon-to-be regent to his infant nephew **Richard II** (1367–1400), introduced a **poll tax**; subsequent parliaments extended it, causing **widespread grievance**. In 1381, attempts to reintroduce serfdom triggered the **Peasants' Revolt**, which saw peasants rising against landlords, burning manors, and destroying records. Up to 100,000 men, under **Jack Straw** and **Wat Tyler**, marched on London and seized the Tower, burning the palace of John of Gaunt and **killing Archbishop Sudbury**, who was blamed for the poll taxes. Richard II cleverly appeased the rebels; Tyler was executed and **the revolt was brutally suppressed**.

Japanese **Noh drama** developed in the 14th century, mainly under the aegis of Kanami Kiyotsugo (1333–84) and his son Zeami Motokiyo (1363–1443), who wrote hundreds of Noh plays and developed the highly stylized and symbolic performances.

Castilian influence in Portugal in the 1380s threatened the independence of the kingdom and sparked **resentment among the Portuguese**. An uprising triggered by a nun resulted in **Joäo** (1358–1453), illegitimate son of Pedro I, seizing control of the country. In 1384, **John I of Castile** (1358–90) invaded Portugal, but Joäo was elected king by the Portuguese parliament and, with English help, defeated Castile at the **Battle of Aljubarrota**, in 1385. In doing so, he freed Portugal from Castilian influence and, after marrying the daughter of John of Gaunt, founded the **Anglo-Portuguese Avis dynasty**.

In 1384, **Philip the Bold of Burgundy** inherited the county of Flanders, adding to his extensive territories. France, ruled by the young and mentally ill **Charles VI**, was now dominated by rivalry between the houses of **Burgundy** and **Orléans**.

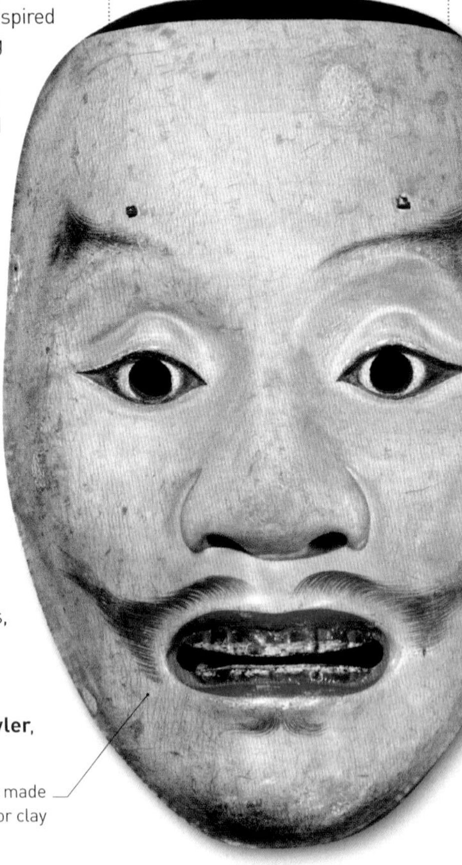

mask usually made of wood or clay

Noh mask
In Noh drama, which involves music, singing, speech, and mime, masks are used by the principal character, and by female and elderly characters.

1373 John Hawkwood's **White Company** mercenaries defeat the Milanese

1375 Mamluks invade Armenia

1377 Edward III dies (b.1312); **Richard II** is crowned king of England

1377 Papacy returns to Rome

1378 Schism of rival popes at Rome and Avignon

1378 Ayutthaya (present-day Thailand) subjugates Sukhothai

1378 War of Chioggia begins (to 1381); Venice ends Genoan supremacy

1380 Russians under **Dmitri III of Moscow** defeat the Golden Horde at Kulikovo

1380 Timur Leng begins to overrun Persia

1381 The **Peasants' Revolt** in England

1382 Golden Horde sacks Moscow and reasserts control over Russia

1382 Ming take complete control of China and **expel** the **Mongols**

1382 Timur Leng conquers Khorasan

1384 John Wycliffe dies; rise of **Lollards**

1384 Kanami Kiyotsugo, dramatist who shaped development of Noh theatre in Japan, dies

1384 Philip the Bold of Burgundy becomes count of Flanders

1385 Ottomans take Sofia

1385 Battle of Aljubarrota establishes Portuguese independence

1386–90

Travelling pilgrims are shown in an illustration from the *Canterbury Tales*. This unfinished poem by Geoffrey Chaucer, 17,000 lines long, vividly illustrates the medieval world view on social, religious, and moral matters.

JAGIELLO OF LITHUANIA (C.1362–1434), THE LAST PAGAN RULER in Europe, was crowned king of Poland and converted to Christianity in 1386. Marriage to **Jadwiga of Poland** united the two kingdoms, and brought Lithuania into the Catholic Church, although pagan traditions lingered on.

Timur Leng (see 1356–65) completed his **conquest of Persia** in 1386 and raided deep into the Caucasus, sacking **Tbilisi** in Georgia and capturing the Georgian king. However, when the army of the **Golden Horde** attacked his Central Asian territories, in 1387, he was forced to turn back and meet them. It took another nine years for him to destroy the threat.

Geoffrey Chaucer (*c.*1340–1400) was a soldier, scholar, writer, diplomat, government official, and Member of Parliament. He was instrumental in the development of **Middle English** – a combination of Old English and French influences. His greatest work, the ***Canterbury Tales***, partially modelled on Italian author Giovanni Boccaccio's *Decameron*, tells the story of pilgrims on the road to the shrine of **Thomas Becket** (see 1170); it was begun in 1387.

At the **Battle of Kosovo**, in 1389, the Ottomans defeated the Serbs and Bosnians, **smashing the Serbian empire** and absorbing most of its territories. The Ottoman leader, Murad, was killed in the battle but his son **Bayezid the Thunderbolt** (1360–1403) took over. News of Murad's death prompted the **Ottoman vassals** in Europe and Anatolia to **revolt**, but Bayezid swiftly reduced most of them, bringing their territories under **direct Ottoman rule**. The Ottomans now controlled most of Anatolia and the Balkans south of the Danube. Bayezid introduced the **devshirme** – the levy of Christian children who were converted to Islam and used in the administration and **Janissary** corps.

CHRISTIANIZATION OF EUROPE

In Europe, the medieval period saw the vigorous advance of Christianity until it encompassed the entire region (with just a few exceptions). The spectacular success in converting Europe posed extreme challenges to the Church, as it struggled to reconcile temporal and spiritual power. Internal forces would continue to revolutionize the religion.

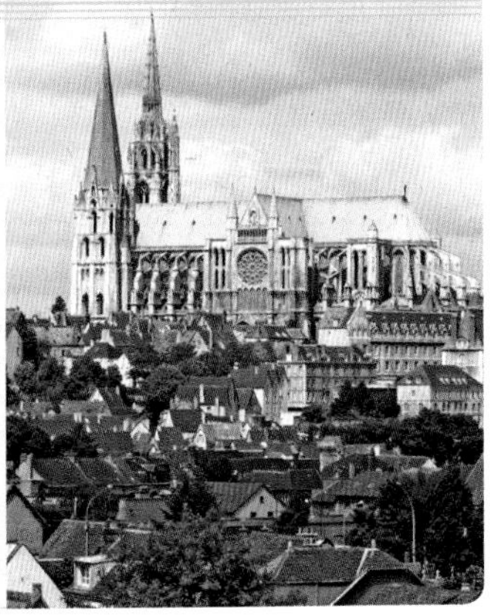

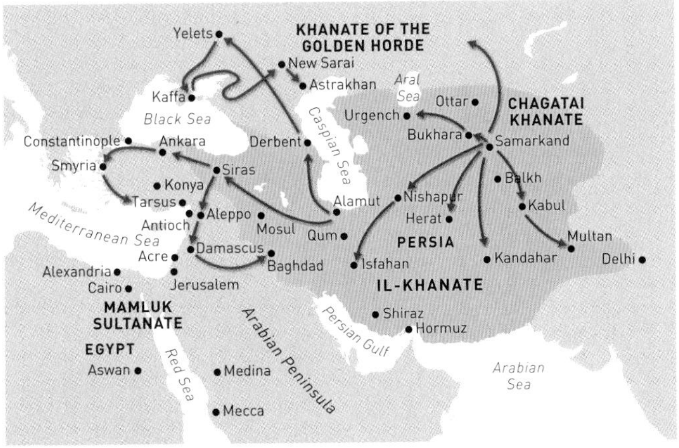

The Timurid Empire
Established by Timur Leng, the Timurid Empire eventually reached a greater extent even than that of Genghis Khan, but it would not long survive Timur's death.

KEY
→ Campaigns of Timur
Extent of Timur's empire

1391–1400

A miniature from the Topkapi Museum in Istanbul, shows the Battle of Nicopolis, at which the Ottomans destroyed a crusading army.

THE START OF THE MING DYNASTY IN CHINA TRIGGERED CHANGE IN KOREA, which was considered a client state by the Ming. The **Koryo empire** had supported the new Chinese dynasty, but this did not prevent the Ming from threatening to invade. In 1388, **Yi Songgye** (1335–1408), a leading general who favoured the Chinese, seized power in Korea. In 1392, as **King Taejo**, he founded the **Yi dynasty**, also known as the Choson (or Joseon), a name taken from an ancient Korean kingdom. Taejo restructured his government on the Chinese model, and instituted **wide-ranging land reforms** to redistribute estates from the hands of the oligarchy, replacing them with a new class of technocrats known as the yangban. **Neo-Confucianism** was adopted as the state religion, and a new capital was founded at **Hanseong** (Seoul). The Yi dynasty lasted until 1910.

In **Japan**, the union of the northern and southern imperial courts in 1392 brought to an end the **Yoshino period** (also known as the Period of Northern and Southern Courts). During this period, the line of the emperor **Godaigo** – driven out of the capital, Kyoto, by the Ashikaga shogun Takauji, in 1336 – had maintained a **rival court** in the mountainous Yoshino region south of Nara. Japan was wracked by **civil war** until the shogun **Ashikaga Yoshimitsu** (1358–1408) negotiated a reunification and brought Ashikaga power to its apogee.

The **Nicopolis Crusade** of 1396 – intended to roll back the Ottoman advance in the Balkans – saw a Franco-Hungarian expedition led by **Sigismund of Hungary** humiliatingly crushed at the Bulgarian town of Nicopolis on the Danube. A huge army, featuring volunteers from most of the **Christian states**, proved ill-disciplined. The failure of this adventure proved that Christian Europe had to look to its defence.

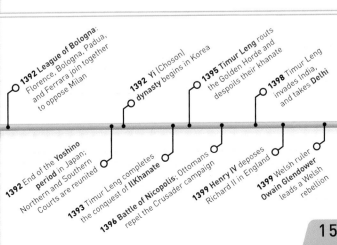

Gyeongbokgung Palace
This colossal palace, built by King Taejo (Yi Songgye) in 1395, is also known as the "Palace of Shining Happiness" and the "Palace Greatly Blessed by Heaven".

1386 Jagiello of Lithuania, the last pagan ruler in Europe, crowned king of Poland and converts to Christianity

1386 Timur Leng completes the conquest of Persia and sacks Georgia

1387 English writer Geoffrey **Chaucer** begins to write the *Canterbury Tales*

1387 War between Timur Leng and the **Golden Horde**

1388 Milan, under **Gian Galeazzo Visconti**, adds Padua to other conquests in northern Italy

1388 John Wycliffe's English translation of the **Bible** published; a later version is known as the Lollard's Bible

1389 Wenceslas IV, king of Bohemia and Holy Roman Emperor, puts in to effect a **general peace** in Germany

1389 Battle of Kosovo; Serbian empire absorbed by Ottomans

1392 League of Bologna: Florence, Bologna, Padua, and Ferrara join together to oppose Milan

1392 End of the **Yoshino period** in Japan; Northern and Southern Courts are reunited

1392 Yi (Choson) **dynasty** begins in Korea

1393 Timur Leng completes the conquest of **IlKhanate**

1395 Timur Leng routs the Golden Horde and despoils their khanate

1396 Battle of Nicopolis; Ottomans repel the Crusader campaign

1398 Timur Leng invades India, and takes **Delhi**

1399 Henry IV deposes Richard II in England

1399 Welsh ruler **Owain Glendower** leads a Welsh rebellion

The wall of skulls at the Templo Mayor archaeological site in Mexico City is made from skulls carved in stone, covered with stucco; the Aztecs practised human sacrifice at the vast temples in the centre of Tenochtitlan.

FOUNDED BY THE AZTECS IN 1325, the city of **Tenochtitlan** – existing on the apparently unpromising site of a marshy island in a partially brackish lake – reached its height at the beginning of the 15th century. Tenochtitlan means "Place of the Fruit of the Cactus" – a reference to the vision that supposedly informed the choice of location. In this vision, the tossed heart of a conquered enemy landed on the island where an eagle wrestled with a snake on a cactus growing out of a rock – as depicted on the present-day Mexican flag. The **Aztecs** drained the island, reclaiming surrounding land, and joined the land together with causeways. Meanwhile, they expanded their political territory through marriages, alliances, and conquest. After a flood, Tenochtitlan was laid out on a grid pattern, with quarters arranged around a **central sacred district**, regarded as the centre of the world. A huge population of up to 200,000 was supported by **intensive agriculture** and extensive **networks of trade** and tribute.

The African **Songhay kingdom** was centred on the trading metropolis of Gao, in the Niger Bend area of **West Africa**. Gao had long been a prosperous city thanks to interregional and trans-Saharan trade with the Islamic world, especially in salt, gold, slaves, and ivory. In the mid-13th century, because of the allure of its riches, it became an eastern province of the **Mali Empire** (see 1231–35). However, in the early 15th century, Mali declined and Gao won its independence, beginning the growth of a Songhay Empire that would eclipse the other two largest empires of the late Iron Age in West Africa – Ghana and Mali.

In 1398, **Timur Leng** (see 1356–65) had invaded northern India and destroyed the **Delhi sultanate** with astonishing speed and terrifying cruelty. Marching 260km (160 miles) in two days, he captured and massacred 100,000 fugitives outside Delhi before sacking the city, supposedly building a huge pyramid from the skulls of his victims. In 1401, Timur massacred the population of Baghdad and launched an invasion of Syria. He then moved against the **Ottomans** (see 1286–90), occupying Anatolia and restoring the old Turkoman principalities.

Songhay gold coin
This coin from the Songhay Empire is from the Songhay city of Gao; rich and powerful, the city provided the basis for building the empire.

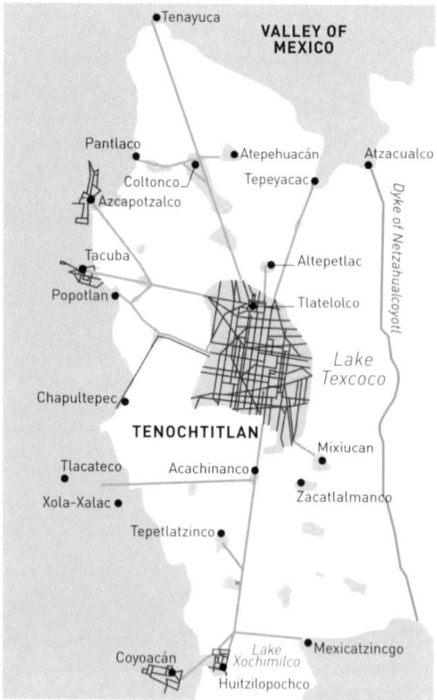

Map of Tenochtitlan
Causeways connected Tenochtitlan to other settlements on the lake and the mainland. The city and its emperor dominated the Valley of Mexico.

KEY
- street
- aqueduct
- causeway
- dyke

“ WE HAVE SET EYES ON... REGIONS... FAR AWAY... ”

Zheng He, Chinese explorer

HAVING CONQUERED AS FAR AS RUSSIA in the East, **Timur Leng** (see 1386–90) set his sights on the greatest empire – **China**. In 1405, he embarked on a campaign, but died en route to China and was buried at his capital, Samarkand. Despite his possibly exaggerated reputation for cruelty, Timur was a devout Muslim and a **patron of the arts** and architecture. His enormous empire did not long survive him, quickly breaking down into a Timurid state ruled by his son Shah Rukh (1377–1447), which soon fragmented further.

In 1404, John the Fearless (1371–1419) became **duke of Burgundy**, leading opposition to the regency of Louis, duke of Orleans (1372–1407), brother of the mad king, Charles VI of France (1368–1422). In 1407, John ordered the assassination of Louis, triggering **civil war** between the Burgundians and the Armagnacs (named for the count of Armagnac, the father-in-law of Charles, the new duke of Orleans). The **Burgundians**, who favoured peace with the English, were popular in Paris and the north, while the **Armagnacs**, who were anti-English and pro-war, had the support of Queen Isabeau of Bavaria, the great nobles, and the south of the country.

In 1404, **Zheng He**, (1371–1435) – a Muslim captured from Yunnan in China as a boy, castrated, and pressed into military service – was named grand, or high-ranking, eunuch at the imperial court. The following year he led the first of seven epic voyages of discovery.

Wladyslaw II Jagiello of Poland prepare for the Battle of Tannenberg.

THE RELENTLESS ADVANCE OF THE ORDER OF TEUTONIC KNIGHTS (see 1236–40) had brought Prussia and much of the Baltic coast under their control, cutting Poland off from the sea. The union of Poland and Lithuania under King Wladyslaw II Jagiello (*c.*1362–1434) posed a new threat to the Order, and the **Great Northern War** ensued. At the **Battle of Tannenberg** in 1410 – one of the greatest cavalry confrontations of the age – a huge Polish–Lithuanian army of up to 16,500, including Bohemian mercenaries, Russians, and even Tatars (Turkic Mongols), defeated

c.1400s Height of Aztec city of **Tenochtitlan**

c.1400s Expansion of West African **Songhay Empire**

1401 Timur (1336–1405) massacres population of Baghdad

1402 Italian architect **Lorenzo Ghiberti** commissioned to design doors of **Florence Baptistry**

1402 Battle of Ankara; **Timur captures Ottoman sultan**

1403 Malay ruler Parmesvara establishes **Sultanate of Malacca**

1405 Break up of Visconti domains; **Venice seizes** Padua, Verona, and Vincenza

1405 Death of Timur (b.1336); **fragmentation of Timurid Empire**

1405 First voyage of explorer **Zheng He**

1407 Civil war in France pits Armagnacs against Burgundians

1409 Donatello di Niccolò di Betto Bardi completes his masterpiece, *David*

1409 Council of Pisa results in three papal claimants

the forces of the Teutonic Knights who were around 11,000 strong. The Order was crushed, but Jagiello was unable to keep the powerful Polish nobles in order and thus could not press home his advantage. The **Peace of Thorn**, concluded the following year, failed to secure Polish access to the Baltic and enabled the Teutonic Knights to regain some of their advantage.

Andrei Rublev (*c.*1370–1430) was a Russian monk and painter, based at the St Sergius monastery of the Holy Trinity in Moscow. He worked during a period of monastic revival in Russia, when the Eastern Orthodox Church offered comfort in the face of internecine war and the hated **Mongol Yoke** – the tribute and service exacted by the Golden Horde. Though inspired by the great icon painter Theophanes the Greek, Rublev was celebrated for pioneering a new, more serene and symmetrical style.

The Holy Trinity
This detail from Andrei Rublev's greatest icon, painted around 1410, shows the three angels who visited Abraham. Each angel represents a different aspect of the Trinity.

1411–15

This later depiction of the Battle of Agincourt shows cavalry engaged in conflict; around 10,000 French troops were killed or captured.

IN 1413, HENRY IV OF ENGLAND DIED and his son, Henry V (1386–1422), came to the throne. In 1415, Henry concluded an alliance with Burgundy and reasserted the **English claim to the French crown** as a pretext for renewing the **Hundred Years War** (see panel, right). In October, Henry inflicted a terrible defeat on a far superior French force at **Agincourt**, taking the Duke of Orleans prisoner, and going on to conquer Normandy.

> **"** ...THE LIVING **FELL ON** TOP OF THE **DEAD,** AND OTHERS **FALLING ON** TOP OF **THE LIVING** WERE KILLED AS WELL. **"**
>
> From ***Gesta Henrici Quinti***, *c.*1416

During **Chinese explorer Zheng He's** fourth and greatest expedition in 1413, he visited Calicut in India, and reached Hormuz on the Persian Gulf, sending ships to explore down the African coast as far as Malindi in Kenya. The fleet included 63 ships of up to 80m (260ft) long.

In 1414, anti-pope **John XXIII** – one of three men claiming to be pope – was expelled from Rome by King Ladislas of Naples. John sought refuge with the emperor, **Sigismund**, who forced him to convene a general council – the **Council of Constance** – to resolve the split in the Catholic Church known as the **Great Schism** (see 1373–80). In 1415, the Council deposed the existing claimants, and condemned the Bohemian priest, religious reformer, and philosopher **Jan Huss**, who was executed the same year.

THE HUNDRED YEARS WAR

The series of conflicts from 1337 to 1453, later known as the Hundred Years War, was triggered by a combination of factors: tensions over the status of the duchy of Guienne, which belonged to the kings of England but owed sovereignty to the French crown; English claims to that crown, based on descent from the Capetians; anxieties of influence on both sides; and the need of English kings to use foreign adventures to shore up support at home. There should have been little contest between France, the most powerful nation in Europe, and smaller, poorer England, but the English used new tactics and weapons, especially the longbow, to devastating effect. The war drained resources on both sides, but also forged a new degree of national identity for both countries.

1416–20

This illustration from the Chronicle of Ulrich von Richental shows the papal electors taking their leave from Emperor Sigismund at the Council of Constance.

THE COUNCIL OF CONSTANCE ENDED THE GREAT SCHISM in 1417 by trying and deposing the last anti-pope, Benedict XIII, and electing Martin V (*c.*1348–1431) as the sole true pope.

The burning at the stake of Bohemian religious reformer **Jan Huss** (see 1411–15), and the death of Wenceslaus IV of Bohemia (1361–1419), sparked a **Hussite uprising** in Bohemia. This combined a religious tussle between the papacy and anti-papists, with a nationalist struggle between Czechs (Bohemians and Moravians) and Germans. The Hussites made up of moderate (Utraquist) and extreme (Taborite) factions, united to face a crusading alliance led by Wenceslaus' brother, the emperor Sigismund. The Hussites defeated the alliance outside Prague.

In 1411, **peace** was concluded between **Portugal and Castile** (see 1381–85). Portugal now began to look outwards, winning a foothold on the north coast of Africa at Ceuta in 1415. Explorer **Henry the Navigator** (1394–1460) distinguished himself in the expedition; his visit to Africa sparked an interest in exploration, and he may have set up the first school of navigation in Europe at Sagres, in Portugal (see 1434).

45
THE **NUMBER** OF **SESSIONS** HELD AT THE 42-MONTH-LONG **COUNCIL** OF **CONSTANCE**

1410 Polish-Lithuanian forces defeat Teutonic Knights at **Battle of Tannenburg**

1410 Death of **Kanajejdi, king of Kano**, present-day Nigeria

1410 Anti-pope John XXIII makes **Medici Bank in Florence** the papal bank

1411 Peace of Thorn ends conflict between Teutonic Knights and Polish-Lithuanian forces

1413 Henry IV of England dies (b.1366)

1413 Battle of Jamurlu in Serbia

1413 Accession of **Henry V** of England

1413 Fourth and greatest expedition of **Zheng He**

1414 Khizr Khan (r.1414–21) establishes **Sayyid dynasty** in Delhi

1415 Battle of Agincourt fought between French and English

1415 Portugal conquers **Ceuta** in Africa

1416 Nobleman **Amadeus VII** named duke of Savoy; **annexes Piedmont**, Italy

1417 Council of Constance ends **Great Schism**

1417 Ming emperor Yongle (1360–1424) fixes **Confucian canon**, reinstitutes civil service exam system

1419 Henry the Navigator (1394–1460) possibly sets up school of navigation in Portugal

1420 Hussite Wars: Hussites under Jan Zizka defeat anti-Hussite crusade

1421–22

Fillipo Maria Visconti of Milan sits in state; having assassinated his brother to become duke of Milan, he restored Visconti hegemony over northern Italy.

SULTAN MEHMED I (1382–1421) had successfully **restored the Ottoman state** after the Timurid invasion (see 1401–03), although his navy had come off worse in a conflict with the **Venetians** at the **Battle of Galipoli** in 1416, forcing the Ottomans to recognize Venetian claims in Albania. In 1421, Mehmed died and his son, **Murad II** (1404–51) became sultan. Domestically, he restored the *devshirme* practice of training Christian slaves for key roles in government; externally, he pursued a policy of renewed expansion, beginning with the first **Ottoman siege of Constantinople**. The siege was unsuccessful and Mehmed was distracted by an uprising led by the Sufi theologian and preacher, Sheikh Bedreddin – it was suppressed, and the sheikh was executed.

Sultan Murad II
Murad defended and extended the Ottoman Empire, and was also a patron of poetry and learning, making his court a cultural centre.

The **Visconti family** had ruled **Milan** since Archbishop Otto Visconti rose to power in 1277; their domain had spread to encompass much of northern Italy, reaching its height under **Gian Galeazzo** (1351–1402), sole ruler from 1385. He had made marriage alliances with the chief monarchs of Europe; was made hereditary duke in 1395; mastered Verona, Vicenza, Padua, Pisa, Siena, Assisi, and Perugia between 1386 and 1400; and threatened Florence until his death in 1402. Strife between his sons Gian Maria and Filippo Maria saw this empire disintegrate, but when Filippo had Gian assassinated in 1412, he set about restoring it, **regaining Genoa** in 1421. The Visconti patronized the arts and scholarship, helping to drive the **Renaissance** (see pp. 208–09).

The French had suffered great losses at **Agincourt** (see 1411–15), and in 1420, at the prompting of the pro-English **Burgundians**, Charles VI of France had accepted the **Treaty of Troyes** and acknowledged Henry V of England as his heir and immediate regent. The agreement ceded all the conquered lands up to the Loire to the English and declared the dauphin, Charles, to be illegitimate. The **English** now **controlled northern France**. In 1422, both Henry and Charles died, and under the terms of the Treaty, the infant Henry VI was acclaimed king of both England and France. The dauphin, based at Bourges, refused to accept this, and the **Hundred Years War** (see 1411–15) continued.

1423–25

The Doge's Palace, seat of the doge of Venice, is a masterpiece of 14th-century Gothic architecture, overlain with 15th, 16th, and 17th century additions.

IN THE 1420S, THE CULTURAL MOVEMENT known later as the Italian or **High Renaissance** gathered pace, particularly in the field of **painting and the visual arts**. In 1424, the sculptor Lorenzo Ghiberti (1378–1455) completed the gilded bronze doors for the **Florence Baptistry** that he had been commissioned to make in 1403; the following year he was commissioned for a further set. Working at the same time as Ghiberti were a host of other artists, including Brunelleschi, Jacopo della Quercia, Masaccio, Donatello, Gentile da Fabriano, Jan van Eyck, and many more.

Although **Florence** was the heart of the Renaissance in the 15th century, the other great Italian power centres of Milan, Rome, and Venice also fostered artistic and architectural achievement. In Venice, the **Doge's Palace**, which had been evolving since its origins in the 9th century, embodied many of the architectural highpoints of the previous six centuries. The current building began to take shape around 1340; work on the side overlooking the Piazzetta did not begin until 1424, under doge Francesco Foscari (1373–1457).

In 1424, Timur's descendant, Ulugh Beg (1394–1449) – astronomer and future Mongol leader – built a great **observatory** in Samarkand. It was equipped with a 40m (130ft) sextant, and Ulugh and his team of scholars catalogued over a thousand stars.

The Tribute Money
Tommaso di Ser Giovanni di Simone Masaccio died aged just 27, but created some of the most influential artworks of the Renaissance.

1426–30

Joan of Arc here leads troops into battle, wielding a crossbow.

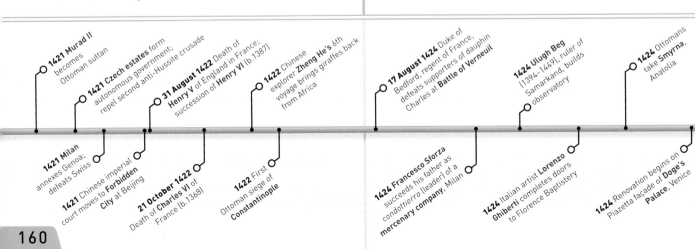

Bodkin point
This type of arrowhead is an uncomplicated, squared, metal spike, extensively used during the wars of the Middle Ages.

THE DAUGHTER OF A FARMER, JOAN OF ARC (1412–31) was 16 when in 1429 voices in her head commanded her to bear aid to the French dauphin (see 1421–22). The English under John, duke of Bedford (1389–1435), had made further gains against the forces of

1421 Murad II becomes Ottoman sultan

1421 Czech estates form autonomous government; repel second anti-Hussite crusade

1421 Milan annexes Genoa; defeats Swiss

1421 Chinese imperial court moves to **Forbidden City** at Beijing

31 August 1422 Death of **Henry V** of England in France; succession of **Henry VI** (b.1387)

21 October 1422 Death of **Charles VI** of France (b.1368)

1422 Chinese explorer **Zheng He's** 6th voyage brings giraffes back from Africa

1422 First Ottoman siege of **Constantinople**

17 August 1424 Duke of Bedford, regent of France, defeats supporters of dauphin Charles at **Battle of Verneuil**

1424 Francesco Sforza succeeds his father as condottierro (leader) of a **mercenary company**, Milan

1424 Ulugh Beg (1394–1449), ruler of Samarkand, builds observatory

1424 Italian artist **Lorenzo Ghiberti** completes doors to Florence Baptistery

1424 Ottomans take **Smyrna**, Anatolia

1424 Renovation begins on Piazzetta façade of **Doge's Palace**, Venice

1426 Hussites under **Procopius the Great** (c.1380–1434) defeat third anti-Hussite crusade

1427 Portuguese discover the **Azores**, North Atlantic

1427 Venetian forces take **Bergamo** from Milan, northern Italy

1428 Le dynasty in Vietnam wins independence from China

May 1429 Joan of Arc relieves **siege of Orleans**

1431–33

The Arnolfini Marriage by Jan van Eyck is noted for its detailed interior.

1434

> **WE READ** THAT WE OUGHT TO **FORGIVE OUR ENEMIES;** BUT **WE DO NOT READ** THAT WE OUGHT TO **FORGIVE OUR FRIENDS.**
>
> Cosimo de Medici

Painting of the first Medici ruler of Florence, Cosimo.

the dauphin and were **besieging Orleans**, while the dauphin had still not managed to secure his coronation. Joan succeeded in obtaining an interview with him at Chinon, won him over, and was provided with troops and the title *chef de guerre* ("war leader"). She successfully relieved Orleans, going on to **defeat the English** twice more, and stood next to the dauphin at his coronation as Charles VII at Reims in 1429. Joan failed to take Paris, however, and the following year, she was **captured** by the Burgundians, who ransomed her to their English allies (see 1431–33).

In 1428, Le Loi, leader of Vietnamese resistance to the Chinese occupation, expelled the Chinese and founded the **Le dynasty of Dai Viet**. On admitting Chinese authority, his dynasty was recognized by the Ming.

FROM 1431 TO 1433, ZHENG HE (see 1404–07) made a seventh and final expedition, returning to the **Persian Gulf**. Despite this last trip, China's period of exploration had come to an end with the death of **Emperor Yongle** in 1424, after which the **Ming dynasty** returned to its isolationist policy. Surrendering the lead in exploration to Portugal and the Europeans would have profound consequences for the Chinese, and world history.

SHIP LENGTHS

22m COLUMBUS'S SHIP

134m ZHENG HE'S SHIP

Not all the great Renaissance painters were Italian; **Jan van Eyck** (*c.*1390–1441) was Flemish. Celebrated for his mastery of realism and his perfection of oil painting, van Eyck produced some of his greatest masterpieces in the 1430s. In 1432, he and his brother Hubert completed their largest surviving work, the altarpiece of St Bavo's Cathedral in Ghent, Belgium. Later that year, in London, van Eyck painted the *Portrait of an Unknown Man* and the *Man with the Red Turban;* possibly a self-portrait.

In 1431, **Joan of Arc** was turned over by the English to the French ecclesiastical authorities for trial. She was found guilty of heresy, and was **burned at the stake** in Rouen.

SINCE THE 1380S, FLORENCE HAD BEEN DOMINATED by the **Albizzi** family, who extended the city's control of Tuscany. The attempts of Visconti Milan (see 1421–22) to gain control over all of Tuscany forced Florence into a ruinously expensive war, although alliance with Venice saw **Milan defeated**. A leader of the peace party was wool merchant and banker Giovanni de Medici, possibly the richest man in Europe. After his death in 1429 and a disastrous war with Lucca in Tuscany, the Albizzi succeeded in having Giovanni's son, Cosimo de Medici banished from Florence in 1433, but new elections saw him recalled the following year, marking the start of **Medici domination** of the city. Cosimo combined business acumen with political shrewdness, winning popular support for his policies.

All attempts by **anti-Hussite forces** under the emperor Sigismund to dislodge the Hussites and regain control of the **Czech territories** had failed (see 1416–20). The superior organization and tactics of the Hussites, first under Jan Zizka and after his death in 1424 under **Andrew Prokops**, made them militarily powerful. In 1430, they invaded Germany and raided as far as Franconia. Negotiations with the ecumenical **Council of Basel** in 1413 led to the Compact of Prague, or *Compactacta*, under which moderate Hussites (the Utraquists) agreed to go back to the Catholic Church. The extreme anti-papist Taborites rejected the Compact, and civil war broke out between the factions, which represented different classes as well as religious ideals. In 1434, at the **Battle of Lipany** the upper-class Utraquists vanquished the Taborites, killing Prokops.

The rising power of the Sukhothai kingdom of Thailand had increasingly threatened the **Khmer Empire** (see 1201–05) through the 14th century. Repeated **Thai raids**, particularly an incursion in 1431, may have helped trigger the 1434 **abandonment of Angkor** (see 1146–50) and the transfer of the Khmer capital to Phnom Penh, further south, although it is also possible that the new location offered better connections for foreign trade.

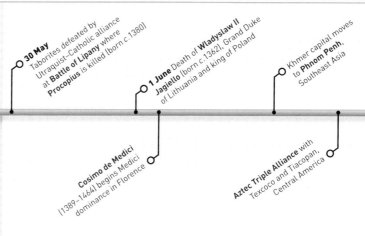

The Windrose
The Windrose mosaic at Sagres in Portugal – possibly a sundial – was commissioned by Portuguese navigator, Prince Henry.

Sponsored by Prince **Henry the Navigator** (see 1416–20), Portuguese explorers pushing out into the Atlantic had discovered the islands of **Madeira** and the **Azores**. Henry personally oversaw the colonization of these Atlantic outposts, successfully establishing them as centres of agricultural production and forward bases for **Portuguese exploration**. Henry's next target was to round Cape Bojador on the coast of West Africa, the furthest limit of Portuguese exploration; contemporary European sailors' lore viewed the seas beyond as a dangerous and terrifying otherworld. **Cape Bojador** was finally rounded by Gil Eannes in 1434. The experiences of his sailors on these voyages of discovery convinced Henry that the traditional barca ships in use were unsuitable, and he worked with shipwrights to design a new type of vessel, **the caravel**. This was smaller, lighter, and swifter, with a shallow draft for near-shore operations and more space for stores to allow the ships to stay at sea for longer.

- **17 July 1429** Coronation of dauphin as **Charles VII** of France
- **23 May 1430** Capture of **Joan of Arc** by the Burgundians
- **1430** Ottomans take **Salonika** in Greece from Venice, demonstrating their naval power
- **c.1430 Full plate armour** introduced for European knights
- **30 May 1431 Joan of Arc** burned at stake (b.1412)
- **1431** Khmer capital moved from **Angkor** after Thai raid, Southeast Asia
- **1432** Flemish artist **Jan van Eyck** completes the *Adoration of the Mystic Lamb*
- **1433** Tuaregs conquer **Timbuktu**, Mali Empire
- **1433 Compacts of Prague** end Hussite wars
- **1433** Zheng He's last voyage and subsequent **isolation of China**
- **30 May** Taborites defeated by Utraquist-Catholic alliance at **Battle of Lipany** where **Procopius** is killed (born c.1380)
- **Cosimo de Medici** (1389–1464) begins Medici dominance in Florence
- **1 June** Death of **Wladyslaw II Jagiello** (born c.1362), Grand Duke of Lithuania and king of Poland
- Khmer capital moves to **Phnom Penh**, Southeast Asia
- **Aztec Triple Alliance** with Texcoco and Tiacopan, Central America
- Portuguese explorers round **Cape Bojador**, West Africa
- **Zara Ya'qub** (1399–1468) becomes king of **Ethiopia**

1435–37

This manuscript illustration shows Charles VII entering Paris in triumph.

> **“** THE **KINGDOM OF FRANCE...** WILL BE THUS **RULED BY** KING **CHARLES VII...** HE WILL ENTER PARIS IN GOOD COMPANY. **”**
>
> Joan of Arc, Christian visionary

THOUGH ALLIED WITH THE ENGLISH OCCUPATION OF FRANCE, the Burgundians (see 1404–07) were increasingly concerned at English gains. With the **Treaty of Arras**, the Burgundians and the French king, Charles VII, made peace but the English, unwilling to accept the terms, withdrew from negotiations. The following year, the French alliance took Paris from English control.

The 1430s saw increasing **tension** between the **papacy** and the **conciliar movement**, which held that the Church ought to be governed by a Church council, rather than an individual pope. Pope Eugenius IV summoned a **General Council at Basel** in 1431, but it was dominated by **anti-papal sentiment** and, in 1437, he tried to transfer the Council to Ferrara, where it would be more amenable to his influence. Most of the delegates refused to leave Basel, resulting in **two concurrent councils**.

1438–40

Founded by King Henry VI of England, construction of Eton college was halted when the king was deposed during the War of the Roses.

IN 1438, PACHACUTEC (C.1438–1472) BECAME THE NINTH INCA KING, or *Sapa Inca*. His reign heralded the beginning of a great expansion of the Inca realm, which had been confined to the immediate area around **Cuzco** since its foundation (see 1201–1205). It began with invasion by the rival Chancas, who besieged Cuzco, and were completely defeated. **Inca expansion** was facilitated by the sophisticated nature of most of the kingdoms and tribes they conquered; tight-knit, centralized administration focused on the emperor; a genius for organization and record-keeping (despite having no writing); and an imperial road-building programme rivalled only by the Roman Empire.

In 1440, the young king of England founded a new college at Eton. The King’s College of Our Lady of Eton near Windsor, now known as **Eton College**, was intended to be part of a large foundation including a massive church, an almshouse, and 70 scholars who were to receive free education before going on to King’s College, Cambridge.

Inca expansion
The Inca Empire had expanded greatly between 1400 and the end of Pachacutec’s reign. It would triple in size by the 16th century.

With the **Ottomans** (see 1286–90) occupying territories on all sides of the tiny **remnants of the Byzantine Empire**, and threatening Constantinople itself, the embattled Byzantine emperor John VIII Palaeologus (see 1448–49) arrived in Europe to plead for help from the **Council of Ferrara** in 1438.

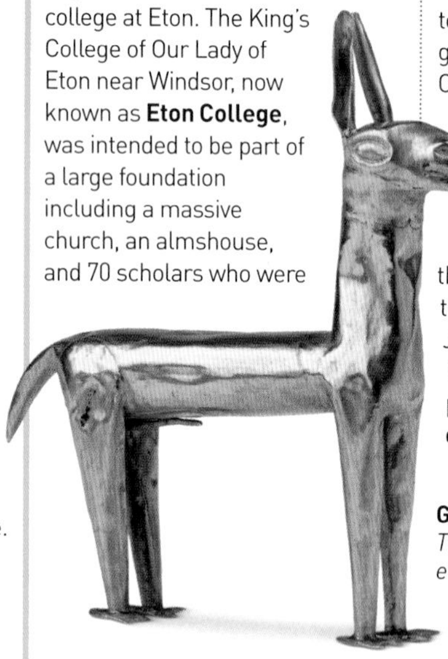

Gold llama statuette
The Inca were so rich in gold that emperor Atahualpa was able to offer a ransom of 750 tonnes of it when captured by conquistadors in 1532.

1441–44

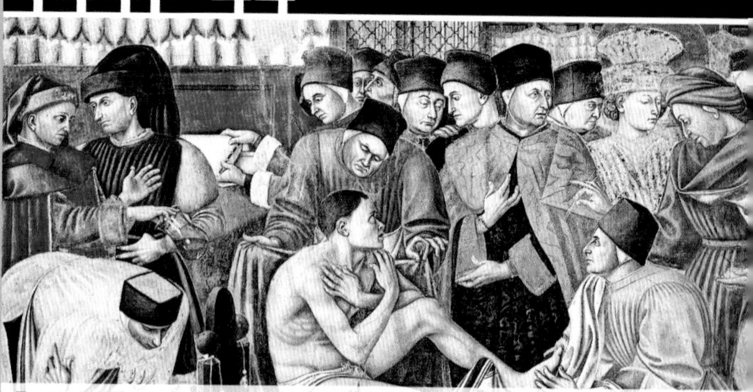

Fresco by Domenico di Bartolo, (*c.*1410-1461), of the Sienese school, from Siena’s hospital of Santa Maria della Scala.

MACHU PICCHU (meaning “Old Peak” in Quechua, the language of the Incas) is a mountaintop citadel about 70km (43 miles) northwest of Cuzco. Construction probably began in the 1440s, under the auspices of **Pachacutec**. The maximum population of Machu Picchu was possibly only around 1,000, and it is thought that it served as a ceremonial centre, as well as being an impregnable stronghold for the Inca elite in case of attack.

Resistance to **Ottoman occupation of the Balkans** increased, and in 1443, a crusading army defeated the Ottomans at Nis, in Bulgaria. The Ottoman sultan, Murad II (see 1421–22), was forced out of retirement to take over from his son, Mehmed II, to whom he had attempted to entrust his crown. At Adrianople, Murad made a 10-year truce with Albanian military leader Hunyadi Skandebeg and other resistors of Ottoman advance. However, with the pope **preaching crusade**, the resistors were absolved of their oaths of peace and they launched a new attack. Led by Hunyadi and Wladyslaw III of Poland and Hungary (1424–1444), the crusading army – the last major

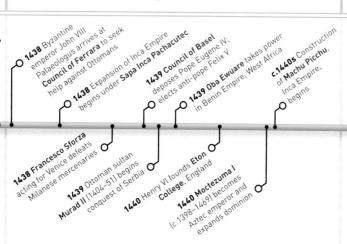

Machu Picchu
High above the Urubamba Valley in the Peruvian Andes, on an inaccessible ridge, lies Machu Picchu, sacred citadel of the Inca kings.

1435 Treaty of Arras; alliance of Burgundians with Charles VII of France against English

1436 Completion of Italian architect **Filippo Brunelleschi’s** Duomo, Florence

9 December 1437 Death of Emperor **Sigismund** (b.1368)

1437 Civil war in **Scotland**

1437 Moors retake **Ceuta**, North Africa

1438 Byzantine emperor John VIII Palaeologus arrives at **Council of Ferrara** to seek help against Ottomans

1438 Expansion of Inca Empire begins under **Sapa Inca Pachacutec**

1438 Francesco Sforza acting for Venice defeats Milanese mercenaries

1439 Council of Basel deposes Pope Eugene IV; elects anti-pope Felix V

1439 Ottoman sultan **Murad II** (1404–51) begins conquest of Serbia

1439 Oba Ewuare takes power in Benin Empire, West Africa

1440 Henry VI founds **Eton College**, England

1440 Moctezuma I (c.1398–1469) becomes Aztec emperor and expands dominion

c.1440s Construction of **Machu Picchu**, Inca Empire, begins

1441 Francesco Sforza negotiates **Treaty of Cavriana** between Venice and Milan

1441 Mayan city of **Mayapán** destroyed in revolt, Central America

1442 Death of **Alexander I the Great** (b.1386), who reunited Georgia

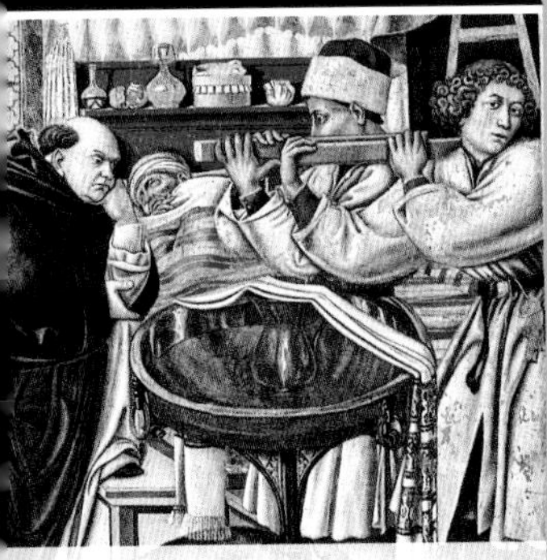

2:1 **Battle of Varna**
The Hungarian-led crusader army, with a strength of 30,000, suffered heavy losses at the hands of the Ottoman troops, who numbered 60,000.

attempt to expel the Ottomans from the Balkans and relieve Constantinople – was decisively crushed by Murad at the **Battle of Varna**. Wladyslaw disappeared in the battle and was presumed dead, despite rumours of his miraculous survival.

1445–47

The rocky north coast between Paul and Ribeira Grande in Santa Antao in the Cape Verde islands.

HENRY THE NAVIGATOR'S EXPENSIVE PROJECT to open up the coast of Africa (see 1434) was met with scepticism at home in Portugal, until in 1441, one of his ships returned with **gold dust and slaves**, prompting an acceleration of activity. Between 1444 and 1446, around 35 of Henry's vessels sailed for the **West African coast**. In 1445, sailing in one of Henry's new caravels, explorer **Dinis Dias** sighted the mouth of the Senegal River, which offered a trade route deep into the African interior, and rounded **Cape Verde**, the westernmost point of Africa. Dias returned the following year as part of a fleet of caravels intending to plant the Portuguese flag and explore what Henry believed might be the western branch of the Nile, while another of Henry's captains, Nuño Tristão, sighted the Gambia River.

The marriage of **Margaret of Anjou** (*c.*1430–82) to Henry VI of England in 1445 was negotiated by William de la Pole, chief advisor to the king and power behind the throne, whose aim was to stop the war in France (see 1435–37). At first, the match and the bride were popular in England, but in 1448, the territory of Maine in northern France was lost to Charles VII and the queen was blamed for her influence over the weak king. Margaret would survive this, however, and become an important player in the **Wars of the Roses** (see 1454–55).

The death of **Filippo Maria Visconti** in 1447 signalled the end of the Visconti ducal line of Milan (see 1421–22). There were multiple claimants to the ducal throne, and eager to avoid domination by a foreigner, the Milanese powers immediately constituted the *Aurea Repubblica Ambrosiana* of Milan, or the **Ambrosian Republic**, but they faced insurmountable obstacles. Riven by internal dissension and unwilling to lose control of the other cities controlled by Milan, they were soon forced to turn military control over to a *condotierre*, or mercenary soldier-leader - the powerful Muzio Attendolo, nicknamed *Sforza* meaning "exert" or "force".

In the mid-15th century, the Shona kingdom of **Mwene Mutapa**, also known as Great Zimbabwe (see 1106–10), was nearing the end of its glory days. By this time, the riches of the gold fields had funded construction of the Great Enclosure, an elliptical space enclosed by a giant wall 244m (800ft) around, and up to 11m (36ft) high in places, built from almost a million granite blocks.

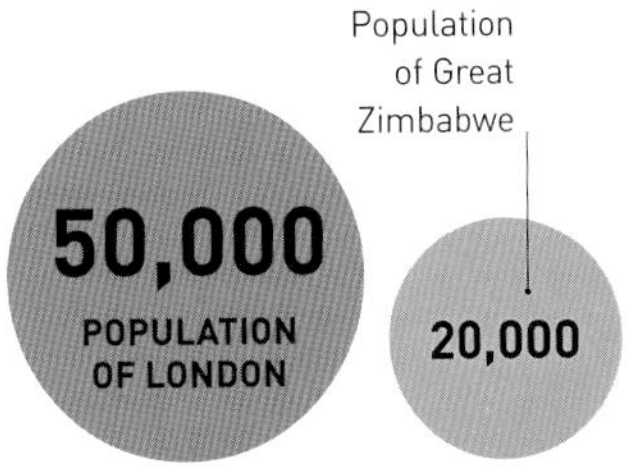

Golden age of Great Zimbabwe
In the mid-15th century, the population of Great Zimbabwe was just under half the size of the population of London.

1448–49

Illustration from a Muromachi period manuscript, the arts flourished in Japan under Ashikaga patronage.

IN 1449, ASHIKAGA YOSHIMASA (1435–90) BECAME SHOGUN, or military dictator, of Japan. Although his reign marked a cultural highpoint of the Ashikaga, or Muromachi period (1336–1573) it was also a period of increasing civil strife. Repeated famines triggered constant uprisings, while the Ashikaga practice of issuing *tokuseirei* or "acts of grace" to cancel debts, damaged the economy. Despite this, Yoshimasa presided over a cultural flowering at his Higashiyama estate.

The new pope, Nicholas V, elected in 1447, was intent on bringing an end to the schism caused by his predecessor's clash with the **Council of Basel** (see 1435–37), and on restoring peace to Italy and achieving harmonious relations with other rulers. At the **Concordat of Vienna** in 1448, he made concessions to Emperor Frederick III and the other German princes, who in return abandoned the Council of Basel and recognized some papal powers. The following year, the Council of Basel finally disbanded and the anti-pope, Felix V, abdicated in return for a cardinalship. This marked the final **victory of the papacy** over the conciliar movement.

Following the death of Byzantine emperor John VIII, his brother Constantine XI Palaeologus (see panel, right) acceded to the throne in Constantinople – he would be the **last Byzantine emperor**. The Ottomans had defeated another of Jan Hunyadi's crusades to clear them from the Balkans at the second Battle of Kosovo in 1448, regaining control of Albania. It was clear that there would be no European rescue for the embattled Byzantines. The Ottomans were closing in on Constantinople.

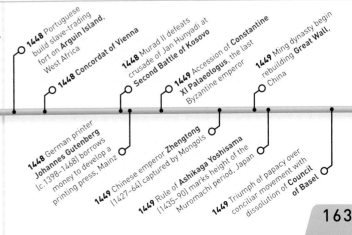

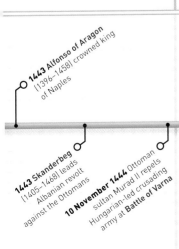

PALAEOLOGUS
(1404–53)

Constantine XI Palaeologus succeeded to the remnants of a once-great empire, left without the resources to defend itself. He was the last emperor of Byzantium, a state that had lasted throughout the medieval period, providing a unique bridge between east and west, ancient and modern. He died on the walls of Constantinople, having done everything in his power to secure its defence.

1443 Alfonso of Aragon (1396–1458) crowned king of Naples

1443 Skanderbeg (1405–1468) leads Albanian revolt against the Ottomans

10 November 1444 Ottoman sultan Murad II repels Hungarian-led crusading army at **Battle of Varna**

23 April 1445 Marriage of **Margaret of Anjou** to Henry VI of England

1445 Portuguese explorer **Dinis Dias** rounds Cape Verde, West Africa

1445 Zara Ya'qub of Ethiopia (1399–1468) defeats sultanate of Ifat and kills sultan of Adal, Somalia

c.1445 Last golden age of **Great Zimbabwe**

1446 Death of **Deva Raya II** (b.1424) who had expanded Vijayanagar Empire, India, to greatest extent

1447 Ambrosian Republic founded in Milan

1447 Casimir IV (1427–92) reunites Lithuania and Poland

1448 Portuguese build slave-trading fort on **Arguin Island**, West Africa

1448 Concordat of Vienna

1448 Murad II defeats crusade of Jan Hunyadi at **Second Battle of Kosovo**

1448 German printer **Johannes Gutenberg** (c.1398–1468) borrows money to develop a printing press, Mainz

1449 Accession of **Constantine XI Palaeologus**, the last Byzantine emperor

1449 Chinese emperor **Zhengtong** (1427–64) captured by Mongols

1449 Ming dynasty begin rebuilding **Great Wall**, China

1449 Rule of **Ashikaga Yoshisama** (1435–90) marks height of the Muromachi period, Japan

1449 Triumph of papacy over conciliar movement with dissolution of **Council of Basel**

5

REFORMATION AND EXPLORATION

1450–1749

The 16th and 17th centuries were determined by new horizons, as new lands were explored and new ideas formulated. Religious reform and conflict, global exploration, and a scientific revolution laid the grounds of a new understanding

1450–52

A detail from Ghiberti's *Doors of Paradise* for Florence Cathedral's Baptistry. The second pair of doors he completed, they show scenes from the Old Testament.

THE GREAT ZIMBABWE CIVILIZATION of southeast Africa (see 1106–10) was in decline by the mid-15th century. This coincided with the rise of the **Mutapa Empire** in the fertile, copper-rich uplands between the Zambezi and Limpopo rivers in present-day Zimbabwe and Mozambique. Sustained by lucrative trade in copper, cattle, ivory, slaves, and gold with Muslim coastal settlements, the Mutapa Empire remained the dominant regional power for more than a century, when repeated Portuguese attempts to infiltrate it finally succeeded (see 1629).

On the Indian subcontinent, the **Delhi sultanate** had fractured into competing regional powers in the aftermath of Timur's invasion of 1398. But in 1451, the new **Afghan Lodi dynasty** reasserted the sultanate's former dominance in the region, which lasted until it was ousted by the Mughal Babur in 1526.

In Europe, Florentine goldsmith **Lorenzo Ghiberti** completed his second set of bronze doors for the Baptistry in Florence in 1452. The first door, begun in 1403, took him 21 years; the second, 27 years. In the same year, **Leon Battista Alberti** published *De Re Aedificatoria*, (*Ten Books of Architecture*). Both works were masterpieces in their fields and exemplified the self-confidence and intellectual daring of the Florentine Renaissance.

> **“ NO ART**, HOWEVER MINOR, **DEMANDS** LESS THAN **TOTAL DEDICATION. ”**
>
> **Leon Battista Alberti**, Italian polymath (1404–72)

Mosque pavilion in Mehrauli
The remains of a mosque in Mehrauli, Delhi, built during the reign of the Lodi dynasty (1451–1526), who were the last rulers of the Delhi sultanate.

1453

This 16th-century fresco depicts the siege of Constantinople, which began on 2 April 1453 and ended when the Ottomans took the city on 29 May.

English defeat at Castillon
The Battle of Castillon decisively ended the hopes of England's French Plantagenet kings to pursue their claim to the French throne.

THE HUNDRED YEARS WAR, a grimly drawn-out period of Anglo–French conflict (see 1411–15), ended with absolute French triumph in 1453. Any hopes England's French Plantagenet kings had of asserting their rights to the French throne came to a final halt at **Castillon** outside Bordeaux. Two years earlier, Bordeaux, which had been in English hands for 300 years, had fallen to the French. This prompted a last, desperate attempt by the English to reassert themselves against the forces of the French king, Charles VII, which were massing in strength in the southwest of France. **Bordeaux was recaptured** by the English, but an attempt in July to relieve the English stronghold of Castillon, which was besieged by a large French force, was a calamitous failure. In the first major European conflict to be decided by artillery, the English lost 4,000 men; the French, scarcely 100. Three months later, in October, Bordeaux itself fell again to the French. This brought to an **end the Hundred Years War** and left **Calais** on the Channel coast as the only remaining English possession in France. For the English, defeat provoked the first of a series of descents into madness by the country's hapless king, Henry VI. For the French, victory brought closer the goal of a properly united kingdom under a single monarch.

In **Western Asia** and on the borders of Christendom, **Constantinople**, capital of the beleaguered **Byzantine Empire**, remained the centre of Orthodox Christian civilization. But it faced an imminent threat from the Muslim Ottoman Empire. This threat materialized when the **Ottoman sultan, Mehmed II** ("The Conqueror"), who believed that only relentless conquest would guarantee continued Ottoman supremacy, mustered an army of 80,000 to attack Constantinople; the defenders of the city could call on fewer than 7,000 troops. In addition, Mehmed had the most formidable artillery in the world. The ancient, crumbling walls of the city were no match for destructive force on this scale, and the city fell to the Ottomans in May 1453.

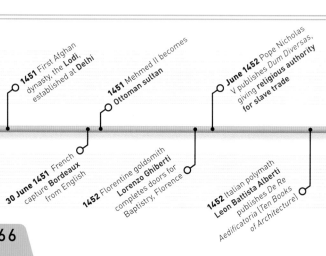

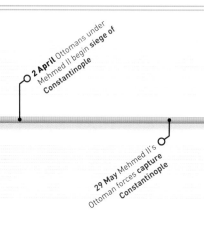

1:12 **Siege of Constantinople**
Mehmed led 80,000 men against only 7,000 defenders during the siege of Constantinople, a disparity that made the city's fall almost inevitable.

Conscious of their destiny as world conquerors in need of a suitably imposing capital, the Ottomans were careful to preserve the city after they had taken it: they needed it as a symbol of their own, newly gained grandeur. Its imposing Christian buildings were pressed into service for Muslim worship, and the city itself remained a symbol of **Ottoman military might** for more than 450 years. The Ottoman conquest of Constantinople – now renamed Istanbul – was the clearest possible signal that the Turkish Ottomans were the most dynamic military and political force in the region, and that they were an unmistakable threat, not only to what remained of Christian claims in Western Asia but also to Europe as a whole.

1451 First Afghan dynasty, the **Lodi**, established at **Delhi**

30 June 1451 French capture **Bordeaux** from English

1451 Mehmed II becomes **Ottoman sultan**

1452 Florentine goldsmith **Lorenzo Ghiberti** completes doors for Baptistry, Florence

June 1452 Pope Nicholas V publishes *Dum Diversas*, giving **religious authority for slave trade**

1452 Italian polymath **Leon Battista Alberti** publishes *De Re Aedificatoria* (*Ten Books of Architecture*)

2 April Ottomans under Mehmed II begin **siege of Constantinople**

29 May Mehmed II's Ottoman forces **capture Constantinople**

17 July France defeats English forces in **Battle of Castillon**

19 October France recaptures Bordeaux from the English, **ending the Hundred Years War**

“IT IS A PRESS, CERTAINLY, BUT A PRESS **FROM WHICH SHALL FLOW** IN **INEXHAUSTIBLE STREAMS…THROUGH IT, GOD** WILL **SPREAD HIS WORD.”**

Johannes Gutenberg, German inventor and printer (c.1398–1468)

A Turkish miniature painting showing Mehmed II's forces attacking Belgrade, which they tried unsuccessfully to take from Hungary in 1456.

THE COMPETING AMBITIONS OF ITALY'S CITY-STATES, which had led to almost a century of war, was ended by the **Treaty of Lodi** in 1454. Milan, Venice, Florence, the Papal States, and Naples were the signatories. The treaty had been given additional impetus by the fall of Constantinople to the Ottomans a year earlier, when it became clear there was a need to present a united Christian front.

In 1454 or 1455, **Johannes Gutenberg** produced the first major book to be printed with a movable type **printing press**: the Gutenberg Bible. His method of printing meant that thousands of copies of books could be made relatively easily. The result was an explosion in the **spread of ideas and knowledge**, above all because works appeared in vernacular languages rather than exclusively in Latin and Greek.

In England, on 22 May 1455, armies belonging to the Duke of Somerset and Duke of York clashed in the Battle of St Albans, the opening conflict of the **Wars of the Roses**. These were a series of civil wars between the **rival Plantagenet houses** of York and Lancaster, both of which had claims to the throne. **Henry VI**, a Lancastrian, was on the throne at the outbreak of the wars, but with the victory and accession of **Edward IV** in 1461, the conflict seemed to have been won by the Yorkists. The wars continued until 1485, when Henry Tudor seized the throne (see 1483–85).

By the mid-15th century, **Prussia** (conquered by the Teutonic Knights two centuries earlier) had become resentful of its lowly status within the Baltic territories of the Teutonic Order. In 1454 the Prussian Estates revolted, and asked for Polish military support, beginning what was to become the **Thirteen Years War** against the Teutonic Knights. The war ended in 1466 with the division of Prussia into two territories: one in the east still controlled by the Order, and so-called Royal Prussia, now a vassal state of the kings of Poland.

King Henry VI
This anonymous portrait is of King Henry VI, reputedly a peaceful, pious man who suffered from prolonged bouts of severe mental illness.

Gutenberg Bible
Johannes Gutenberg produced only 180 copies of his Gutenberg Bible, but it marked the start of the age of the printed book.

OTTOMAN EXPANSION CONTINUED IN THE BALKANS AND GREECE as Mehmed II pressed ahead in his determination to conquer the world for Islam. Mehmed attempted to take **Belgrade** in 1456 but was repulsed by Hungary. However, by 1459 the rest of **Serbia** was under Ottoman control. Simultaneously, the Ottomans conquered the Peloponnese in southern Greece, with Athens falling in 1456. Over the next two decades, Ottoman control of the Balkans was consolidated with the conquest of **Bosnia** and **Herzegovina**, and in the Aegean, remaining Christian-held islands – which were chiefly Venetian and Genoan – were clearly under threat.

In 1458, **Matthias Corvinus**, second son of Janos Hunyadi, the man who had led the successful defence of Belgrade against Mehmed II's Ottoman troops in 1456, was elected **king of Hungary.** His reign promised much: not only to draw the Hungarians into the wider European Renaissance, but also to increase the reach and prestige of his country.

Corvinus was permanently distracted by the need to defend Hungary against further Ottoman incursions, but he had **territorial ambitions** to the west. He was successful in substantially expanding Hungarian territory at the expense of **Bohemia**, against whose Hussite ruler, George of Podebrady (r.1458–71), he obtained papal sanction in 1468 to lead a crusade. During the crusade, Corvinus gained control of **Moravia**, **Silesia**, and **Lusatia**. However, in the longer run his actions destabilized both Hungary and Bohemia, and brought him into conflict with the Holy Roman Emperor, Frederick III. His actions also sparked suspicion among Hungary's nobles, who feared that their own positions would be undermined.

Despite these initial territorial gains engineered by Corvinus, the net result was that most of Hungary fell victim to **Ottoman conquest** in 1526, and Bohemia and the remaining part of Hungary came under direct **Habsburg control**.

- **9 April 1454 Treaty of Lodi** signed in Lombardy, Italy
- **1454 Thirteen Years War begins** between Poland and Teutonic Order
- **1454/55** German printer Johannes Gutenberg publishes the **Gutenberg Bible**
- **18 February 1455** Italian painter **Fra Angelico dies** (b.1395)
- **8 April 1455 Calixtus III becomes pope**, succeeding Nicholas V
- **22 May 1455** Rival claimants to English throne clash in **Battle of St Albans**, starting the Wars of the Roses
- **1 December 1455** Florentine goldsmith **Lorenzo Ghiberti dies** (b.1378)
- **21–22 July 1456** Hungary defeats Ottomans at **Battle of Belgrade**
- **20 August 1456 Vlad III** ("the Impaler") becomes **king of Romania**; his brutality gives rise to the legend of Dracula
- **20 January 1458 Matthias Corvinus** becomes **king of Hungary** at age of 14
- **1458** Ottomans take **Athens**
- **1459** Ottomans annex **Serbia**

1461–65

Tsar Ivan III, "Ivan the Great", declared Moscow free of Tartar domination by tearing up the deed (money demand) of Tartar Khan.

APTLY NAMED "THE SPIDER KING" Louis XI acceded the French throne in July 1461 marking a critical point in the evolution of the French state. The medieval monarchs of France, whatever their nominal power, were **heavily limited in their influence**. They exercised direct rule over only a limited area, chiefly in the north and centre, with the rest of the country controlled by a series of mostly hostile magnates, of whom the **Duke of Burgundy** (Charles the Bold) in 1461 was the most obviously threatening (see 1472–76). By the end of the Hundred Years War in 1453, France was effectively also bankrupt. Yet by 1481, Louis had not only seen off the last of the dukes of Burgundy, bringing **Artois, Picardy, and Burgundy** itself under his rule, but by a combination of inheritance and clever diplomacy had added **Roussillon, Cerdagne, Maine, Provence, and Anjou**. This extension of centralizing, **royal authority** was a crucial step in the subsequent emergence of a unified, much more powerful French state. In reality, relations between the French monarchy and its most powerful subjects would remain fraught well into the 17th century. As elsewhere, it proved necessary both to assert authority and to negotiate with provincial and noble elites. This dual process, central to the making of **early modern France**, led to friction and tension long after the reign of Louis XI.

Louis XI
Crowned king of France in 1461, Louis XI extended his rule over an increasing numbers of territories during his 22-year reign.

Expansion on an even more dramatic scale also marked developments in **Muscovy** – the Grand Duchy of Moscow – with the accession of **Ivan III "the Great"** in **March 1462**. The collapse of Mongol rule over the 14th and 15th centuries, and the fall of **Constantinople** (now Istanbul) in 1453, had opened the way for Muscovy not merely to assert leadership of the Orthodox world, but to defy any last Mongol attempts at overlordship. In the process, it sparked a burst of expansion that characterized **Russia** well into the 19th century.

The most notable of these extensions under Ivan was in the vast **Novgorod Territory**, which although sparsely populated, economically marginal, and imperfectly known, was rich in natural resources. In 1478, Ivan simply annexed it.

However much it may have increased the stability and prosperity of China, the **Ming dynasty** faced a series of substantial internal threats to its authority as well as continuing conflict with the **Mongols** to the north. If most revolts were the product of famine, a number were also the result of the increasingly autocratic and rigid nature of **Ming rule**. In every case, they were harshly suppressed. In 1464, the same year that the 16-year-old **Emperor Chenghua** came to the throne, such a revolt broke out among the native **Miao and Yao people** in the provinces of Huguang and then Guangxi in south-central China. The revolt took two years to put down. In addition to the **160,000 troops** stationed in the south, a further 30,000 were sent to the two provinces. No accurate estimate of the death toll is possible. The revolt flared up again in 1467 and, on a larger scale, in 1475.

1466–69

Malbork Castle was the headquarters of the Teutonic Knights. It was Europe's largest medieval brick-built castle and is in what is now Poland.

THE THIRTEEN YEARS WAR between Poland–Lithuania and the **Teutonic Knights** – a military order founded in Palestine – ended with the **Second Treaty of Torun** in 1466. The Teutonic Knights, powerful since the early 13th century (see 1236–40), were obliged to cede much of the western half of their territory to **Prussia**, and, in return for Polish–Lithuania aid in the war, this territory became the property of the Polish crown.

The underlying political fragility of **Japan** and the relative impotence of the **Ashikaga shoguns**, rulers of Japan since 1333, was made starkly clear by the **11-year Onin War**, which broke out in 1467. It left Japan devastated and led to more than a century of turbulence – the *Sengoku jidai* or **Warring States Period** – as a series of regional magnates or *daimyo* attempted to eradicate their rivals. The war began as a succession dispute over who would replace the elderly and retiring **Ashikaga Yoshimasa** as shogun, the Hosokawa clan supporting the claims of Yoshimasa's brother, the Yamana clan those of his

> **"THE CAPITAL** WHICH WE BELIEVED WOULD **FLOURISH** FOR **TEN THOUSAND** YEARS HAS NOW BECOME A **LAIR FOR THE WOLVES."**
>
> **Onin Ki,** late 15th–mid 16th century account of the Onin War

Samurai sword
This 15th-century katana, *with its scabbard, is typical of those used in the Onin war. It could deliver a sweeping cut in a single movement.*

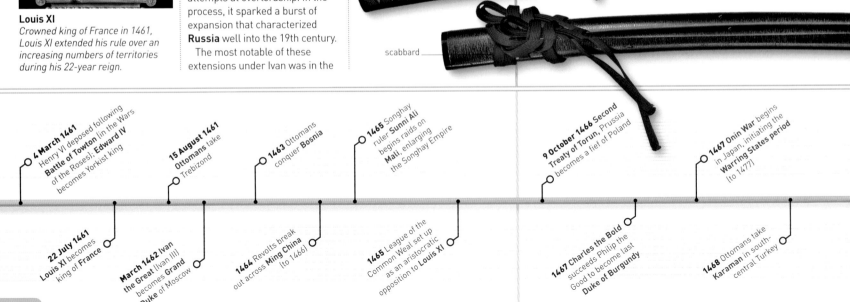

4 March 1461 Henry VI deposed following **Battle of Towton** (in the Wars of the Roses); **Edward IV** becomes Yorkist king

22 July 1461 Louis XI becomes king of **France**

15 August 1461 **Ottomans** take Trebizond

March 1462 Ivan the Great (Ivan III) becomes **Grand Duke** of Moscow

1463 Ottomans conquer **Bosnia**

1464 Revolts break out across **Ming China** (to 1466)

1465 Songhay ruler **Sunni Ali** begins raids on **Mali**, enlarging the Songhay Empire

1465 League of the Common Weal set up as an aristocratic opposition to **Louis XI**

9 October 1466 Second Treaty of Torun, Prussia becomes a fief of Poland

1467 Charles the Bold succeeds Philip the Good to become last **Duke of Burgundy**

1467 Onin War begins in Japan, initiating the **Warring States period** (to 1477)

1468 Ottomans take **Karaman** in south-central Turkey

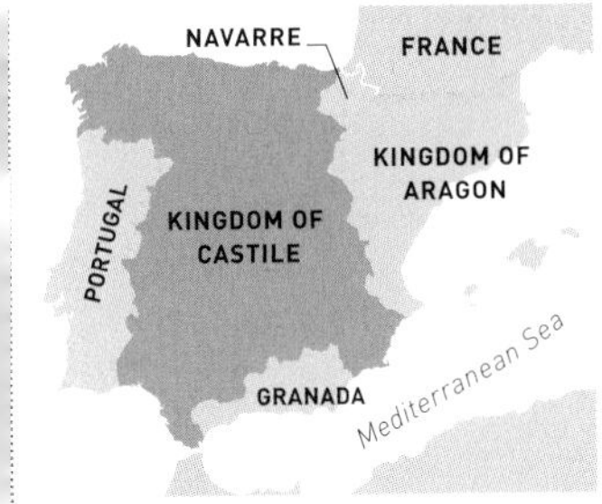

Castile and Aragon
The two kingdoms of Aragon and Castile became a composite monarchy through the marriage of Ferdinand and Isabella in 1469.

infant son. In the process, not only was **Kyoto**, the imperial capital, **entirely destroyed**, the Hosokawa and Yamana themselves became victims of the conflict, their power and status swept away as the increasingly brutal fighting continued.

The marriage in 1469 of **Isabella**, heir to the **Castilian throne** (which she inherited in 1474) and **Ferdinand**, heir to that of **Aragon** (which he inherited in 1479), led directly to the emergence of a **unified, unbendingly Christian Spain**. This resulted in the development of Spain as the most powerful state in early 16th-century Europe. Isabella was 17 years old when she married Ferdinand. In choosing to marry him, she risked the wrath of her older half-brother Henry IV who perceived her as a threat to his own power. But the marriage, in the Spanish city of Valladolid, was the beginning of an important phase of Spanish history. Within eight years Ferdinand and Isabella – *Los Reyes Católicos*, the Catholic Monarchs – were jointly ruling Castile and Aragon, although the kingdoms were not formally unified. Administratively, politically, and financially, they remained separate and, as such, were consistently bedevilled by competing priorities and rivalries.

Even at the height of Spanish power in the 16th and early 17th centuries, no Spanish monarch was able to resolve the problem satisfactorily. Nonetheless, Spain's potential to emerge as the dominant force in Renaissance Europe was unmistakable under Ferdinand and Isabella. It was a position that the tirelessly hard-headed Isabella and the politically astute Ferdinand were well placed to exploit.

“ THE **LANDLOCKED SEA** IS GREEK OR **ROMAN,** THE **BOUNDLESS SEA** IS **PORTUGUESE.** ”

Fernando Pessoa, Portuguese poet and writer, 1885–1935

BY ABOUT 1470, PORTUGUESE exploration of the **west coast of Africa** had reached as far as modern-day Sierra Leone. It had been a hesitant process, limited by ship-types, principally galleys and cogs, that were unsuited to long-range exploration. Its goals were uncertain beyond a general hope to trace the **trans-Saharan gold trade** to its source and to exploit the **West African slave trade**. The death in 1460 of **Prince Henry, "the Navigator"**, the early champion of Portuguese exploration (see 1434), had made further progress unlikely. However, in 1469 Portuguese **king Afonso V** agreed – in exchange for an annual fee – to allow a Lisbon merchant, **Fernão Gomes**, to continue to push Portuguese efforts south along the West African coast. The results were spectacular. Within five years Gomes had explored a further 3,200km (2,000 miles) of coastline. Not only was Portugal able to lay claim to a series of what would prove immensely **lucrative trading stations** (see 1480–82) on the West African coast, Gomes opened the way to the Portuguese penetration of the South Atlantic.

4,000 KILOMETRES THE **EXTENT** OF THE **INCA EMPIRE**

The **Inca Empire**, more short-lived even than its Aztec neighbour to the north, was formed in a surge of conquest after 1438 from its **Andean heartlands** in central Peru. **Tupac Yupanqui** (Topa Inca), **who came to the Inca throne in 1471**, had been made **head of the Inca armies** in 1463 and had already substantially enlarged Inca control to the north, well into modern-day Ecuador.The empire extended about 4,000km (2,500 miles). Topa Inca's principal contribution to **Inca expansion** came with his conquest from about 1470 of the Peruvian kingdom of **Chimor**.

In southeast Asia, the kingdom of **Champa** (in modern-day Vietnam) had existed since the 7th century. But in **1471 it was effectively destroyed** by Viet troops who laid waste the Champa capital, Vijaya. What remained of the kingdom would henceforth be a vassal state of the Vietnamese.

Inca ruler
This 18th-century painting shows Tupac Yupanqui (Topa Inca), the fifth Inca of the Hanan dynasty.

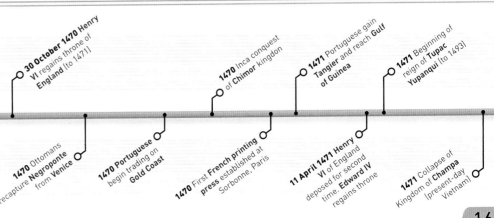

Portuguese explorers
Fernão Gomes (right) continued the age of exploration began by Henry the Navigator (left) as depicted in the Monument to the Discoveries, Lisbon.

19 October 1469 Marriage of Ferdinand and Isabella unites **Castile and Aragon**

1469 Axayacatl assumes control of **Aztec empire** (to 1481)

1469 Lorenzo de Medici takes control of **Florence** beginning a period rich in culture and intellectual thought

1470 Ottomans recapture **Negroponte** from **Venice**

30 October 1470 Henry VI regains throne of **England** (to 1471)

1470 Portuguese begin trading on **Gold Coast**

1470 Inca conquest of **Chimor** kingdom

1470 First **French printing press** established at Sorbonne, Paris

1471 Portuguese gain **Tangier** and reach **Gulf of Guinea**

11 April 1471 Henry VI of England deposed for second time. **Edward IV** regains throne

1471 Beginning of reign of **Tupac Yupanqui** (to 1493)

1471 Collapse of Kingdom of **Champa** (present-day Vietnam)

A carving of what would become the central Aztec deity Quetzalcoatl in Teotihuacán located near present-day Mexico City.

The Battle of Nancy left thousands dead, including Charles the Bold.

FOLLOWING THE OTTOMAN CONQUEST of Constantinople in 1453, its conqueror, **Mehmed II**, set out not merely to extend Ottoman rule in the Balkans, but to reassert it in Anatolia, where Ottoman strength had been significantly reduced in the wake of Timur's early 15th-century invasion (see 1401–03). It was now most obviously opposed in the region by a Turcoman people, the **White Sheep Turcomans,** under the rule of **Uzun Hasan**. They had been actively, if not particularly successfully, wooed by various Christian powers, notably Venice, in an attempt to enlist them in Christian struggles against Ottoman expansion. The result of Uzun Hasan's efforts was a comprehensive defeat in 1473 at the **Battle of Otlukbeli**, the light cavalry of the Turcoman forces swept aside by the Ottomans' overwhelming firepower.

By the mid-1470s, the territories of Burgundy were at their height. Their heartlands were the **Duchy and County of Burgundy**, awarded to the first duke of Burgundy, Philip the Bold, brother of King **Charles V of France**, in 1363. In 1369, with his marriage to Margaret, the countess of Flanders, Philip also acquired **Flanders and Artois** – in effect a significant portion of modern-day **Belgium**. To this constellation of territories, Philip's grandson, **Philip the Good**, then added parts of northeast France and much of modern Holland. These holdings, however imposing, were still far from being a single, continuous territory. Furthermore, as many of them were within the **Holy Roman Empire**, these were at least theoretically subject to the Holy Roman Emperor, just as Burgundy's French lands were nominally subject to the king of France. But their size and, crucially, the fact that they held many of the richest of the burgeoning trading centres of the **Low Countries** made the Burgundians a formidable power. Philip the Good's heir, **Charles the Bold,** inherited this state within states in 1467 and determined not just to make it a continuous territory – which by 1472 he had succeeded in doing through an audacious combination of purchase and conquest – but to assert its independence as a separate kingdom. The Burgundians were inevitably opposed by the infinitely more calculating French king, Louis XI. In little more than four months in1476, they suffered two calamitous defeats by **Swiss mercenary armies** in the pay of Louis – at Grandson and at Morat in modern northwest Switzerland.

The rigidly hierarchical **Aztec Empire** (1428–1521) became a formidable military force, imposing itself with brutal finality on its neighbours in **central Mexico** from **Tenochtitlan**, its capital. **Axayacatl**, who came to the Aztec throne in 1469, added substantially to the empire, mainly with the conquest of the state of **Tlatelolco in 1473**.

Expansion of Burgundy
This map shows the territories held by Charles the Bold, who pursued an aggressive expansionist policy. The duchies of Bar and Lorraine gave Charles an almost continuous stretch of land by 1475.

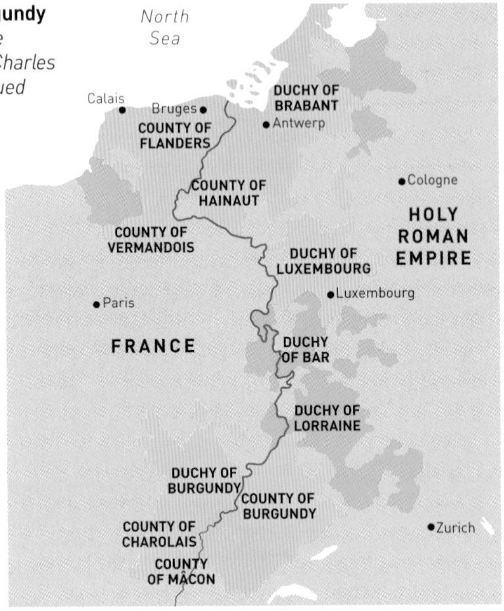

KEY
- Territories held 1467
- Territories added by 1475
- — Border of Holy Roman Empire

Ottoman drums
The Janissaries of the Ottoman army parade with the drums that were used to urge the soldiers into battle.

IN JANUARY 1477, CHARLES THE BOLD'S Burgundian forces confronted the Swiss again, at **Nancy** in Lorraine. They were comprehensively routed and the body of the duke was discovered face down in a frozen pond. While **Louis XI** (see 1461) seized the Burgundians' French territories, those in the Low Countries passed to the Habsburgs with the marriage of Charles's only child, Margaret, to the future Holy Roman Emperor, Maximilian I.

William Caxton (c.1420–92) was an English merchant whose continental travels introduced him to printing. He established the **first printing press in England in 1476**, printing the first book a year later. He published 87 books, many also translated by him.

Caxton's printing press
The first printing press in England, established by William Caxton in Westminster, London, produced its first book in 1477.

1472 Portuguese discover island of **Fernando Po** off West African coast

1472 First publication of the *Etymologies* of Bishop Isidore of Seville, first **Christian encyclopedia**

1473 Aztecs defeat and annex **Tlatelolco**

1473 Venetians destroy **Smyrna** and take **Cyprus**

11 August 1473 Ottomans defeat **Turkomans at Battle of Otlukbeli**

1474 Territories of **Novgorod** incorporated into the **Grand Duchy of Muscovy**

1474 Austrian **Habsburgs** forced to recognize independence of **Swiss League**

1474 Treaty of Utrecht grants **Hanseatic League** major trading advantages in England

1475 Burgundian expansion at its height under **Charles the Bold**

2 March 1476 Swiss defeat **Burgundians** at **Grandson**, Switzerland

1476 Incas conquer south coast of **Peru**

22 June 1476 Swiss defeat Burgundians at **Morat**, Switzerland

5 January 1477 Burgundians defeated at **Battle of Nancy**; death of **Charles the Bold** (b.1433)

1477 Louis XI of France initiates Royal Postal Service to speed royal communications

Built in 1482 as São Jorge da Mina, Elmina Castle was one of the first Portuguese trading forts on the west coast of Africa (now Ghana).

> “ IT IS **NOT NECESSARY TO HOPE** IN ORDER **TO UNDERTAKE, NOR** TO **SUCCEED** IN ORDER **TO PERSEVERE.** ”

Charles the Bold, Duke of Burgundy (1433–77)

The Ottomans continued their expansion with the **Treaty of Constantinople** of 1479, which ended the intermittent Ottoman–Venetian war that had begun in 1463. It confirmed the **Ottomans as a naval power** of growing importance. It also brought with it Ottoman control of the Greek island **Negroponte (Euobea)** and of Lemnos in the north Aegean. **Venice** remained a major power in much of the region but it was anxious not to jeopardize its lucrative Ottoman trading links.

The accession of **Isabella I** to the throne of Castile in 1474 was challenged by her step-niece, **Joan, wife of King Afonso V of Portugal**, in part to disrupt Castilian claims in the exploration of the West African coast. At its heart was a dispute as to which country could lay claim to the Atlantic island groups – the Canaries, the Azores, and Madeira – successively colonized by Spain and Portugal since the early 15th century. The outcome was the 1479 **Treaty of Alcáçovas**, which confirmed Castile's claims to the Canaries and Portugal's claims to the Azores and Madeira, as well as Portuguese rights in West Africa.

87

THE NUMBER OF **BOOKS PUBLISHED** BY **CAXTON'S PRESS**

BY ABOUT 1440, THREE SEPARATE MOSSI KINGDOMS had become established in West Africa, roughly in present-day Burkina Faso. These were Tengkodogo, Yatenga, and Wogodogo. Making use of formidable cavalry, from about 1480 they exploited the **gradual decline of Mali** in the face of **Songhay expansion** by raiding deep into Mali territories. They would remain an important presence until colonization by France some 400 years later.

The year 1482 saw two crucial developments in the continuing **Portuguese exploration** and settlement of **West Africa**. The first was the construction of **São Jorge da Mina**, now called Elmina Castle, on what was later known as the **Gold Coast** and is today **Ghana**. It was a strongly fortified trading post, built on royal authority and the first permanent European settlement in sub-Saharan Africa, designed to secure a Portuguese monopoly of the **West African gold trade**. It proved immensely lucrative. By the early 16th century, 680 kg (1,500 lb) of gold a year were passing through Elmina.

The second development was a further series of voyages, led by **Diogo Cão**, southwards along the West African coast. The voyages were sponsored by the new king of Portugal, **John II, who came to the throne in 1481** and who committed his country to a deliberately aggressive policy of Portuguese expansion. On **Cão's first voyage**, in 1482, he reached – and claimed for Portugal – the mouth of the Congo. On his second voyage, in 1484–86, he penetrated almost a further **1,600 km (1,000 miles) south** to Walvis Bay (now in Namibia), once again imperiously claiming the coast in the name of the **Portuguese throne**. Both voyages were epics of tenacity, made in the face of consistently unfavourable winds and currents. This was a discouraging discovery. Where sailing conditions around **West Africa to the Gulf of Guinea** were generally benign, aided by northeast trade winds and the Guinea Current, to the south they were much more arduous. Cão's achievement was impressive, but it emphasized that if a practical route existed to the Indian Ocean and the East, it would be left to later Portuguese navigators – notably **Bartolomeu Dias** in 1487 – to pioneer the new route, deep into the **South Atlantic**.

Cão's cross
Portuguese explorer Diogo Cão marked his discoveries of the west coast of Africa with a series of imposing stone crosses.

THE SPANISH INQUISITION

Founded by Ferdinand and Isabella in 1478, the aim of the Inquisition was to impose an overarching Christian Catholic identity on all Spanish territories. Tribunals were held in which heretics – which at this time meant Jews and those who had converted to Christianity from Judaism – were punished and expelled. After the fall of Granada in 1492, it was also applied to Muslims. The Inquisition was finally disbanded in 1820.

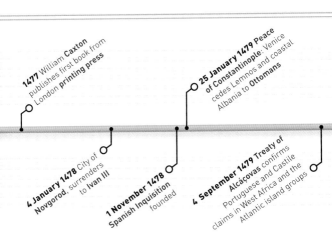

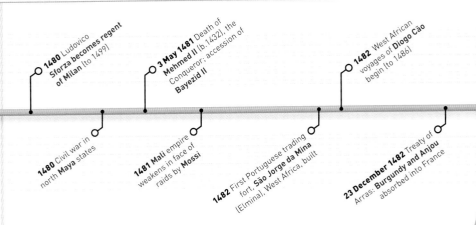

1477 William **Caxton** publishes first book from London **printing press**

4 January 1478 City of **Novgorod** surrenders to **Ivan III**

1 November 1478 Spanish Inquisition founded

25 January 1479 Peace of Constantinople: Venice cedes Lemnos and coastal Albania to **Ottomans**

4 September 1479 Treaty of Alcáçovas confirms Portuguese and Castile claims in West Africa and the Atlantic island groups

1480 Ludovico **Sforza becomes regent of Milan** (to 1499)

1480 Civil war in north **Maya** states

3 May 1481 Death of **Mehmed II** (b.1432), the Conqueror; accession of **Bayezid II**

1481 Mali empire weakens in face of raids by **Mossi**

1482 First Portuguese trading fort, **São Jorge da Mina** (Elmina), West Africa, built

1482 West African voyages of **Diogo Cão** begin (to 1486)

23 December 1482 Treaty of Arras: **Burgundy and Anjou** absorbed into France

VOYAGES OF EXPLORATION

SETTING SAIL AROUND THE GLOBE IN THE AGE OF DICOVERY

Christopher Columbus's voyage across the Atlantic in 1492 sparked an unprecedented opening-up of the world – first by the Portuguese and Spanish, then by the Dutch, English, and French. By 1700, European explorers and colonizers had established themselves globally.

European explorers were motivated by glory, Christian zeal, and – above all – gold, spices, and slaves. The goal was the East, source of legendary riches. With overland routes blocked by Muslim states, maritime routes offered the prospect of outflanking them. By 1488, the Portuguese had rounded southern Africa. Ten years later they reached India and, by 1512, the Spice Islands. There, they were later challenged by the Dutch.

The Spanish went west. Theirs was a more dramatic discovery: an unknown continent, America. By the 1550s, they had conquered two empires – the Aztecs and the Incas – and created a huge New World empire. By 1522, they had also completed the first circumnavigation of the globe. English and French efforts were directed initially at finding a way around North America. Though futile, this paved the way for two further European empires there.

> “I AND MY COMPANIONS SUFFER FROM A **DISEASE** OF THE **HEART** WHICH CAN BE **CURED** ONLY BY **GOLD.**”

Hernán Cortés, Spanish explorer, on his quest to defeat the Aztecs, 1519

Major European voyages
This map shows the date and routes taken by the first European voyages of discovery and exploration: the earliest Christopher Columbus in 1492, through to Francis Drake in 1577–80. Ships sailed for months at a time to cross the vast oceans, often with crude systems for navigation.

1:13 **Survival ratio of Magellan's circumnavigation**
Magellan left Spain in September 1519 with 237 men. Just 18 men made it back three years later. Magellan himself was killed in the Philippines, in April 1521.

Ships commanded by Magellan
Five ships set sail on Magellan's cicumnavigation . Two were wrecked, one abandoned, and one deserted. Only Victoria returned.

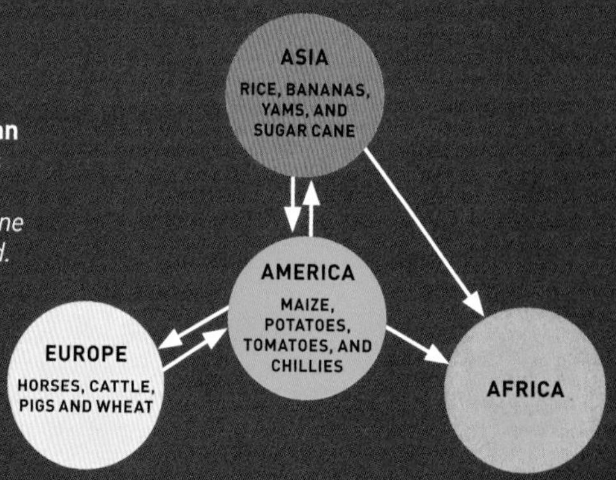

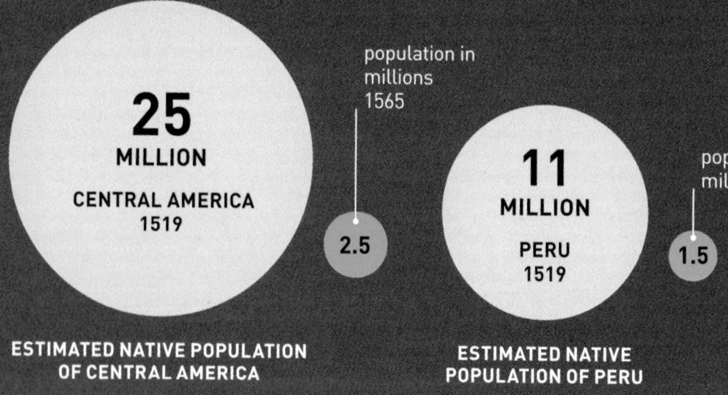

Effect on populations
The Spanish conquests had a devastating impact on native populations. African slaves were taken over to replace them.

Biological exchange
New foods – and new diseases – passed between Europe and the New World as a direct result of the voyages of discovery. The results were at times beneficial; at others, fatal.

COST AND IMPACT

European maritime exploration was made possible by better ship types and navigation. But journeys were still arduous, and many ships simply disappeared. The fate of Magellan's fleet in 1519–22 reflected these risks.

Relations with native peoples also proved fraught and almost invariably ended violently. Europeans generally saw natives as a resource to be exploited and Christianized. But the startling death tolls in the New World were more the result of the dislocation of settled ways of life and of imported European diseases than of deliberate policy. The sudden intermingling of previously separate worlds had a dramatic impact in both directions, with crops and animal types introduced to new environments.

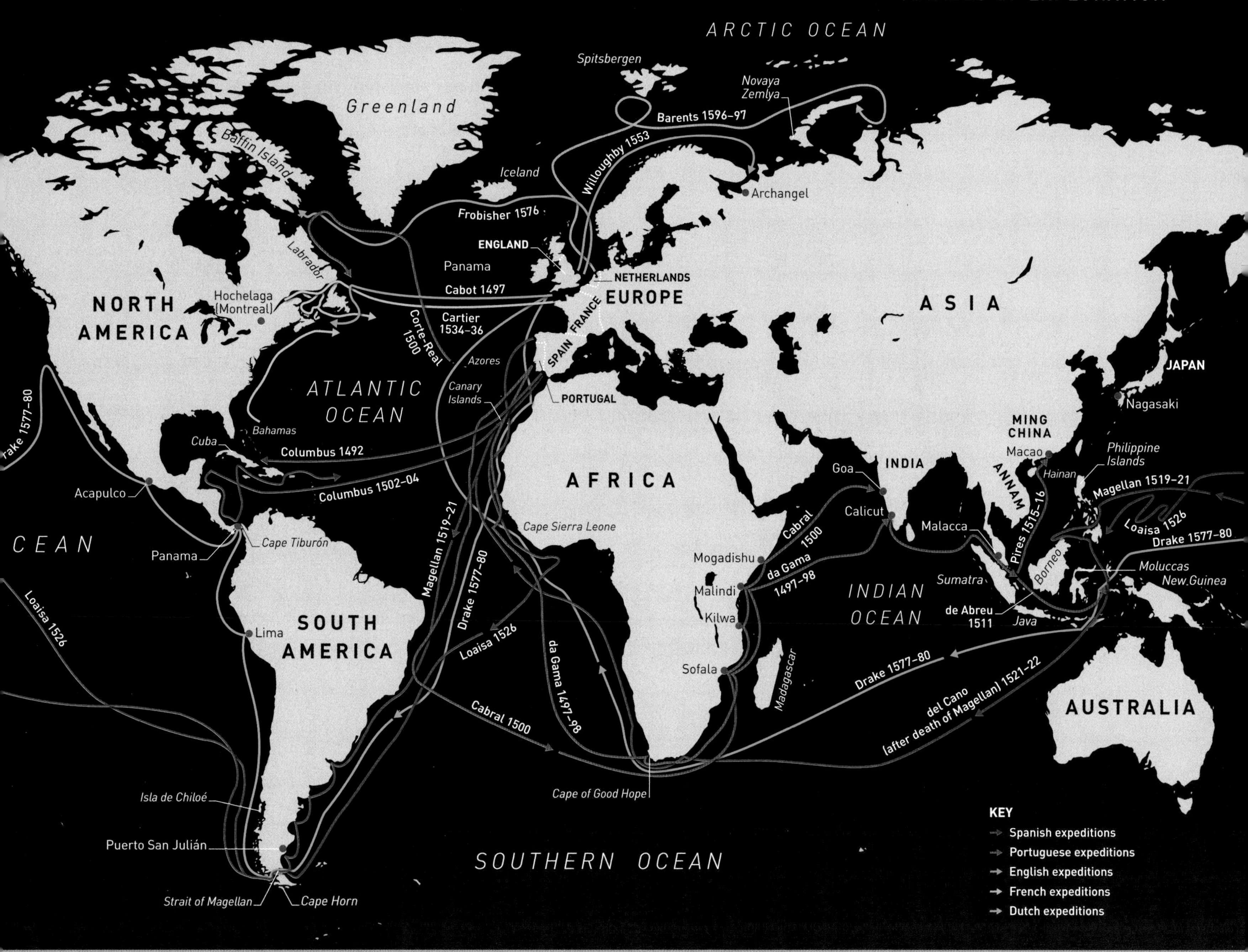

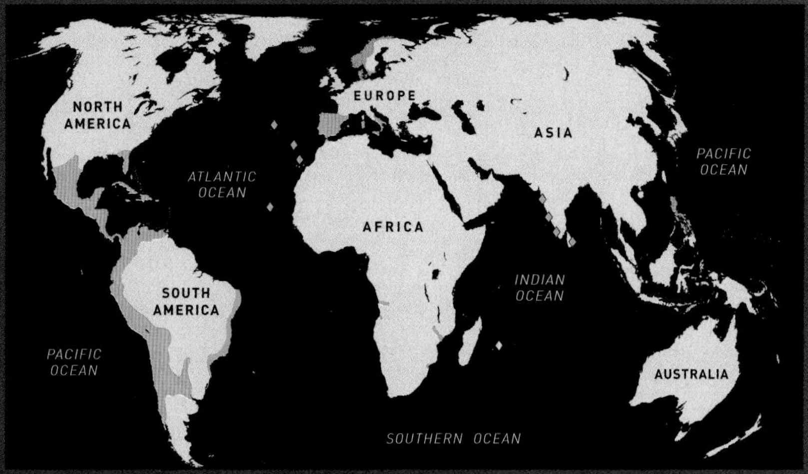

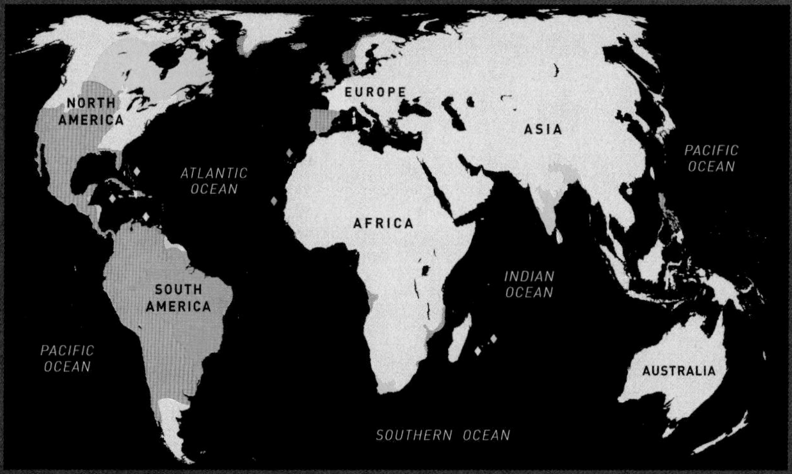

1600 Spain took the lead in exploring and claiming new lands, especially in Central and South America. By 1600, Spain also had claims on the Philippine Islands. Portugal claimed only a handful of coastal trading posts in Africa, India, and the Spice Islands, along with a strip of Brazilian coast.

KEY

- ◇ Spain and possessions
- ◇ Portugal and possessions
- England and possessions
- Denmark and possessions
- ◇ Dutch (United Provinces) possessions

1800 European expansion continued in the 17th and 18th centuries, with massive areas of the world claimed by Europe by 1800. Britain, in particular, despite losing its American colonies, was gaining ground – in Canada, in southern Africa, and above all, in India.

KEY

- ◇ Britain and possessions
- ◇ France and possessions
- ◇ Denmark and possessions
- ◇ Spain and possessions
- ◇ Portugal and possessions
- ◇ The Netherlands and possessions

Most of what remains of the Great Wall of China was rebuilt during the Ming dynasty. Dotted with fortifications it extends over 6,400km (4,000 miles).

IN 1483, THE WARS OF THE ROSES flared up again (see 1454–55). Fought between Lancastrians and Yorkists – rival **Plantagenet** claimants to the English throne – it had appeared to have been settled for good in 1471. In 1470, the **Yorkist Edward IV**, who had seized the throne from the hapless **Lancastrian Henry VI** in 1461, had been forced from it by a group of vengeful magnates. In 1471, with **Burgundian support** from Charles the Bold (see 1472–76), Edward retook the throne. Henry was murdered, probably on Edward's orders.

Edward, now grossly corpulent, died in 1483. Instantly, the conflict reignited, albeit in a different form. The problem was that the new king, **Edward V**, was only 12 and that his mother's family, the **Woodvilles**, saw the boy-king as an obvious opportunity to proclaim themselves regents – in effect, to seize the throne themselves, undoing Edward IV's legacy. This at least was the view of the dead king's most consistent champion, his brother the **Duke of Gloucester**, who was competent, intelligent, and loyal. Gloucester characteristically pre-empted the Woodvilles by seizing the throne himself, as **Richard III**, executing the leading Woodvilles, and **imprisoning Edward V** with his younger brother in the **Tower of London** where both were then murdered. If no definitive proof has ever been offered that Richard III was responsible for the deaths of his nephews, the overwhelming probability is that **he ordered their killings**; his hold on the throne was too shaky to permit any rivals to survive if he could eliminate them. Richard III was vilified in later Tudor propaganda. But given the turbulent treachery of late-medieval England, Richard's actions seem fairly rational. Sooner or later the Woodvilles would have sought an excuse for his death.

THE RENAISSANCE

The Renaissance (literally "rebirth") grew out of the Italian Middle Ages and marked a re-evaluation of European thought. At its heart was a reinterpretation of Europe's Classical past. It gave rise, first in Florence (left), to an artistic and architectural revolution, and later, to a scientific one. Its early impact was fitful but eventually spread to most of Europe in the following 200 years.

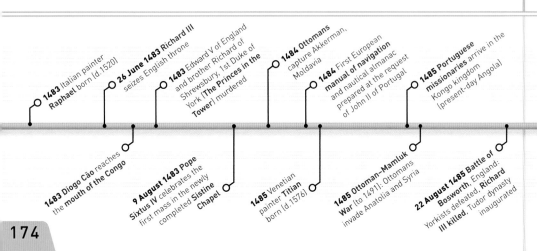

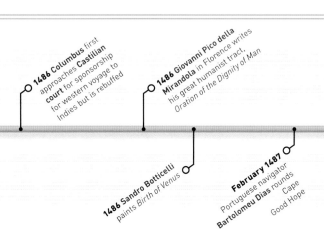

5:8 **Battle of Bosworth** *Henry's Tudor army of 5,000 troops overcame Richard III's much larger force, which was undermined by poor leadership.*

But there was a further **Lancastrian claimant, Henry Tudor** (1457–1509). His right to the throne was tenuous at best, but critically he had the support of the French king, **Charles VIII** (r.1483–98). In August 1485, Henry led an invasion from France. By the end of the month, Richard was dead, killed at the **Battle of Bosworth**, his superiority in numbers undone by the ineptitude of many of his commanders. Henry Tudor, in turn, crowned on the field of the battle, had become **Henry VII**. The Tudor monarch's seizure of the throne might easily have provoked yet another round in this destabilizing infighting. But Henry VII would prove among the most pragmatic, capable, and far-sighted of kings. Under the Tudors, England was significantly strengthened, its magnates tamed, and its government comprehensively overhauled.

FOLLOWING ON FROM EARLIER PORTUGUESE VOYAGES (see 1470–71), two further expeditions were despatched in 1487 to investigate routes to and across the Indian Ocean. **Pêro da Covilhã** was charged with investigating the East African coast as well as the Indian Ocean. From Aden, reached via the Red Sea, he sailed to Calicut in India, as far south as Sofala in **East Africa** and north to the Strait of Hormuz in the Persian Gulf, reporting favourably on all these routes in 1492. The second expedition, under **Bartolomeu Dias**, was specifically charged with finding a navigable passage around the presumed southern tip of Africa. In January 1488, rather than simply following the African coast southwards as Cão and others before him had done, at around 27°S (several hundred miles short of the tip of south Africa) he headed southwest, away from the coast. By any measure, that was remarkably daring. Miles from land, he picked up the westerlies that blow in the South Atlantic and was carried almost 500km (300 miles) to the east of the **Cape of Good Hope** on the tip of southern Africa. Dias's voyage provided a better understanding of the wind systems that linked the Atlantic and Indian Oceans, and proved vital in calculating the route to the Cape of Good Hope and beyond. Later, **Vasco da Gama** and **Pedro Cabral** exploited this knowledge in their own voyages.

Human sacrifice is a feature common to many early societies.

20,000

THE ESTIMATED NUMBER OF **PEOPLE SACRIFICED** AT THE **INAUGURATION** OF THE **TENOCHTITLAN** PYRAMID

- **1483** Italian painter **Raphael** born (d.1520)
- **26 June 1483 Richard III** seizes English throne
- **1483 Diogo Cão** reaches the **mouth of the Congo**
- **1483** Edward V of England and brother Richard of Shrewsbury, 1st Duke of York (**The Princes in the Tower**) murdered
- **9 August 1483 Pope Sixtus IV** celebrates the first mass in the newly completed **Sistine Chapel**
- **1484 Ottomans** capture Akkerman, Moldavia
- **1484** First European **manual of navigation** and nautical almanac prepared at the request of John II of Portugal
- **1485** Venetian painter **Titian** born (d.1576)
- **1485 Portuguese missionaries** arrive in the Kongo kingdom (present-day Angola)
- **1485 Ottoman–Mamluk War** (to 1491): Ottomans invade Anatolia and Syria
- **22 August 1485 Battle of Bosworth**, England: Yorkists defeated, **Richard III killed**, Tudor dynasty inaugurated
- **1486 Columbus** first approaches **Castilian court** for sponsorship for western voyage to Indies but is rebuffed
- **1486 Giovanni Pico della Mirandola** in Florence writes his great humanist tract, *Oration of the Dignity of Man*
- **1486 Sandro Botticelli** paints *Birth of Venus*
- **February 1487** Portuguese navigator **Bartolomeu Dias** rounds Cape Good Hope

This 19th-century painting shows the Fall of Granada in 1492, which ended 780 years of Muslim rule in Spain.

None is known to have practised it with the vigour of the **Aztecs**, however – or on the same gargantuan scale. It is estimated that the Aztecs ritually sacrificed upwards of **20,000 victims a year** – slaves, enemies captured in battle, and people simply offered in tribute. The aim was to placate their gods, above all the god of war, **Huitzilopochtil**, whose daily battles with the sun could be sustained only by blood. In 1487, on the opening of the **new great temple** in the Aztec capital, **Tenochtitlán**, up to 20,000 people were ritually executed, their hearts sliced from their bodies, in a single ceremony that may have lasted anything from 4 to 20 days.

In China, the **Ming dynasty** (1368–1644) continued the ambitious rebuilding of the 6,400-km (4,000-mile) long **Great Wall**. First built in 200 BCE, the wall had presented a symbol of superiority as well as a barrier to incursions from barbarians in the north. Under the Ming, its mountainous eastern length was built mostly of brick and stone, its western, desert-like length of clay and earth, often reinforced with wood. It stood on average 8m (25ft) high and 5.5m (18ft) wide and was studded with 25,000 towers and upwards of 15,000 garrisons – a monumental feat of construction.

Tenochtitlán
This mural of the 16th-century Aztec capital imagined by 20th-century Mexican artist Diego Rivera shows the city's massive scale.

Mamluk helmet
This 15th-century iron Mamluk helmet, as worn by Mamluk soldiers, is decorated with inlaid silver calligraphy.

THE OTTOMAN–MAMLUK peace treaty of May 1491 ended a war that had begun in 1485 for control of the Western Asia and Red Sea trade routes. Neither side gained much but the war exhausted the Mamluks financially, making their subsequent conquest by the Ottomans in 1516–17 inevitable.

By 1490, **Vladislas II** (1456–1516) ruled over a vast kingdom, including **Poland–Lithuania, Bohemia, and Hungary**, whose crown he accepted in 1490. Despite the size of these territories, they had little influence on Europe as a whole. Poland–Lithuania – vast, desolate, and impoverished – was on the margins of Europe. Hungary and Bohemia, although more sophisticated, remained not just separate kingdoms but uneasy rivals. The potential of these sprawling lands would never be realized.

On 2 January 1492, Spanish monarchs **Ferdinand and Isabella** (see 1469) presided over the **fall of the Kingdom of Granada**, marking the end of a 10-year campaign to claim the last Moorish territory in Iberia. It was the end of a process begun in the 8th century – the **Christian reconquest** or **reconquista**. It underlined Spain's determination to project itself as an aggressively expansionist Christian power.

In 1492, the Spanish crown finally decided to back **Christopher Columbus's** first Atlantic crossing. Columbus had made a series of extravagant claims about the rewards his voyage to the Indies (Asia) would generate. Spain was anxious to match the spoils flowing to Portugal from its West African ventures. It also needed to replace the lost revenues from "crusading" taxes, previously paid before the fall of Granada. Success depended on Columbus's undoubted navigational ability and on his insistence that Asia lay much further to the east than conventionally believed. On his arrival in the **New World** on 12 October, somewhere in the **Bahamas**, he immediately despatched emissaries to the "Chinese" court. Columbus's self-belief blinded him to the reality of what he had discovered.

> “**SAILED** THIS DAY **NINETEEN LEAGUES…** (COUNTED) LESS THAN THE TRUE NUMBER, THAT THE **CREW** MIGHT NOT BE **DISMAYED** IF THE **VOYAGE** SHOULD PROVE **LONG.**”
>
> **Christopher Columbus**, 1492

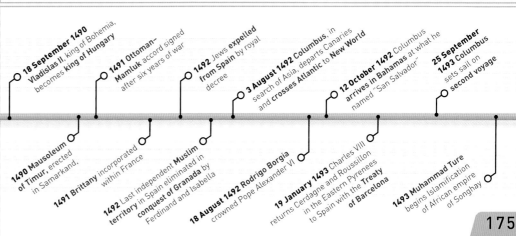

CHRISTOPHER COLUMBUS
(c.1451–1506)

Born in Genoa, Italy, Christopher Columbus made four transatlantic voyages believing that the riches of the East could be reached by sailing west from Spain. His first journey (1492–93) was followed by others in 1493–96, 1498–1500, and 1502–04. He was the first European to sight South America, in 1498, and charted most of the Caribbean. He died still certain he had reached Asia.

- **1487 Pêro da Covilhã** sails through Red Sea on voyage to India (to 1489)
- **1487** Great pyramid inaugurated at **Tenochtitlán**
- **1488** First major uprising of **Ikko Buddhists** in Japan
- **1489** Approximate date of **Songhay raids** into **Mossi** territory
- **1489 Venetians purchase Cyprus**, ending Frankish rule
- **18 September 1490 Vladislas II**, king of Bohemia, becomes **king of Hungary**
- **1490 Mausoleum of Timur**, erected in Samarkand
- **1491 Ottoman–Mamluk** accord signed after six years of war
- **1491 Brittany** incorporated within France
- **1492** Jews **expelled from Spain** by royal decree
- **1492** Last independent **Muslim territory** in Spain eliminated in **conquest of Granada** by Ferdinand and Isabella
- **3 August 1492 Columbus**, in search of Asia, departs Canaries and **crosses Atlantic** to **New World**
- **18 August 1492 Rodrigo Borgia** crowned Pope Alexander VI
- **12 October 1492** Columbus **arrives in Bahamas** at what he named "San Salvador"
- **19 January 1493** Charles VIII returns Cerdagne and Roussillon in the Eastern Pyrenees to Spain with the **Treaty of Barcelona**
- **25 September 1493 Columbus** sets sail on **second voyage**
- **1493 Muhammad Ture** begins Islamification of African empire of Songhay

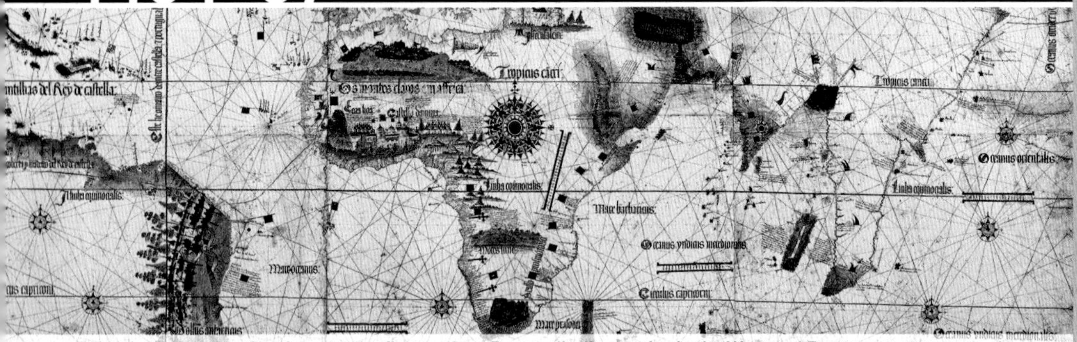

This map by Alberto Cantino was the first to show Portugal's discoveries in the West and East and the division between Spanish and Portuguese territories agreed at Tordesillas.

IN 1494, POPE ALEXANDER VI drew up the **Treaty of Tordesillas**, which effectively divided up existing and future New World discoveries between **Spain and Portugal**. It drew a north–south line 370 leagues (about 2,000km or 1,350 miles) west of the Cape Verde Islands. Land to the west was assigned to Spain; that to the east, to Portugal.

The political crisis provoked in Florence by the **death of Lorenzo ("the Magnificent") de Medici** in 1492 was expoited by a Dominican monk, **Girolamo Savonarola**, who imposed on the city a "Christian and religious republic". In 1494, he denounced tyrants and instituted the **Bonfire of the Vanities**: the destruction of idolatrous goods. He was overthrown, tortured, and executed four years later.

The **Italian Wars**, nominally sparked by the desire of Charles VIII of France (1470–98) to **assert a claim** to the kingdom of Naples, saw an intermittent **65-year struggle** between France and Spain for control of Italy. Its opening salvo, which ended in 1499, was both destructive and inconclusive. The first phase ended with the **Battle of Fornovo**, fought near Parma in July 1495. However, having made his triumphant way to Naples to claim its throne, Charles VIII found his former Italian allies, notably Milan, had joined forces with Venice, the papacy, and the Holy Roman Empire to oppose him in a **Holy League**, ending his dreams of Italian conquest.

LEONARDO DA VINCI
(1452–1519)

Born in Italy, Leonardo was a self-taught polymath – a painter, sculptor, inventor, and scientific enquirer – whose restless genius drove him to embrace a limitless range of projects, but to complete almost none. Among his masterpieces are *Mona Lisa* and *The Last Supper*. He died in France in the service of Francois I.

By about 1496, an outbreak of what was commonly called the **French pox** (so-named as it was first recorded among French troops there) occurred in Italy. It was syphilis. By the middle of the 16th century, about **one million people** had contracted the disease – probably from a more virulent strain brought by **sailors returning from the New World**.

From about 1490, **Genoese mariner** John Cabot had lobbied Portugal and Spain to sponsor a westward voyage to Asia across the Atlantic, but was rebuffed. He turned his attentions to England, basing himself in Bristol. An early voyage failed, but in May 1497 – with royal backing – he set out again. He **reached northern Newfoundland**, then sailed south along 650km (400 miles) of coast. He returned to England certain he had reached China. The following year, he led a much larger expedition. All but one of its five ships were lost, Cabot with them. But his initial success prompted five further voyages to **Newfoundland** from 1501 to 1505, which confirmed the new discoveries were clearly not Asian. Despite these disappointments, the English ventures were important in proving the existence of a hitherto unsuspected continent – **North America** – and in staking a claim to later English primacy in its exploration and settlement.

1,000,000

THE APPROXIMATE NUMBER OF **EUROPEANS** WHO **CONTRACTED SYPHILIS** IN 50 YEARS **FROM 1496**

This 20th-century painting depicts King Manuel I of Portugal blessing Vasco da Gama and his expedition as they get ready to set sail from Lisbon.

THE SOUTHWARD PROBING ALONG the African coast by the Portuguese in the 15th century had reached a climax when **Bartolomeu Dias** rounded the tip of Africa in 1488. In May 1498, **Vasco da Gama** consolidated this achievement when he continued into the Indian Ocean and reached Calicut in southwest India. A practical **route to the East had been discovered**. Da Gama's crossing of the Indian Ocean – criss-crossed by Arab and other trade routes since the 9th century – depended on local Muslim knowledge. His route to the Indian Ocean, on the other hand, was new. Where previous Portuguese mariners had hugged the African coast, da Gama made a vast sweep **westwards into the South Atlantic**. It was not only the longest ocean crossing yet made,

Battle of Zonchio
This woodcut depicts ships in the first battle of the Ottoman–Venetian War. It was the first time cannons had been used in a naval battle.

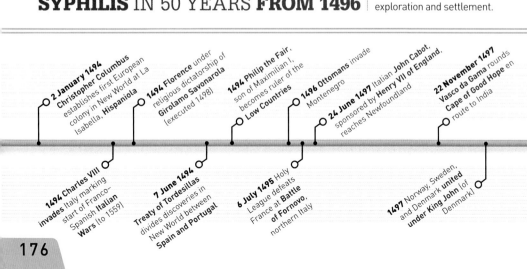

2 January 1494 Christopher Columbus establishes first European colony in New World at La Isabella, **Hispaniola**

1494 Charles VIII invades Italy marking start of Franco-Spanish **Italian Wars** (to 1559)

1494 Florence under religious dictatorship of **Girolamo Savonarola** (executed 1498)

7 June 1494 Treaty of Tordesillas divides discoveries in New World between **Spain and Portugal**

1494 Philip the Fair, son of Maximilian I, becomes ruler of the **Low Countries**

6 July 1495 Holy League defeats France at **Battle of Fornovo**, northern Italy

1496 Ottomans invade Montenegro

24 June 1497 Italian **John Cabot**, sponsored by **Henry VII of England**, reaches Newfoundland

22 November 1497 Vasco da Gama rounds **Cape of Good Hope** en route to India

1497 Norway, Sweden, and Denmark **united under King John** (of Denmark)

1498 Leonardo da Vinci completes The Last Supper

20 May 1499 Vasco da Gama reaches **Calicut, India**

12–25 August 1499 Venetian fleet defeated by Ottoman navy at **Battle of Zonchio**

1499 France seizes **Milan**

22 September 1499 Treaty of Basle confirm independence of **Swiss Confederation**

This scene from a fresco in Chehel Stun Palace in Isfahan, Iran, depicts Safavid Emperor Shah Ismail I in battle against Uzbek warriors.

it initiated the route used throughout the "Age of Sail" (see pp.172–73).

The ongoing **Ottoman naval threat** to Christendom was underlined by the Venetian–Ottoman War of 1499–1503. Both sides enjoyed profitable trade links. But Venetian sea-power represented an obstacle to Ottoman designs in the **eastern Mediterranean**. The Venetian defeat at the **Battle of Zonchio** in August 1499 made Ottoman naval power strikingly clear.

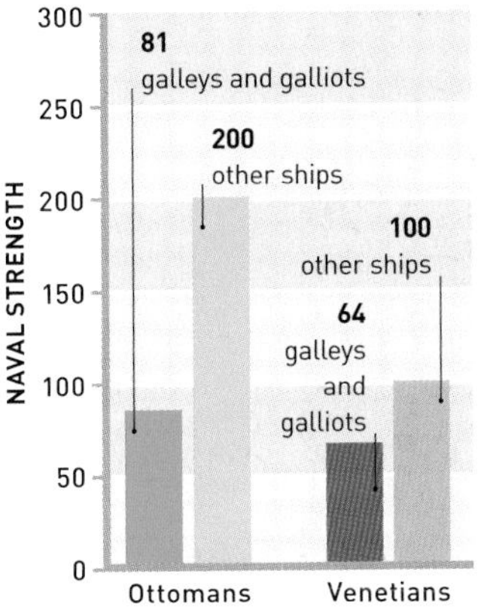

Zonchio ship numbers
The disparity in numbers between the Ottoman and Venetian fleets was compounded by the refusal of some Venetian commanders to fight at all.

A further round in the **Franco–Spanish struggle** for mastery of Italy was launched in 1499, when Louis XII of France (1462–1515) seized Milan. He then allied with Ferdinand of Aragon (1452–1516), agreeing to divide Naples between them. With Naples secured, Louis and Ferdinand fell out. Twice defeated by his former ally, **Louis reluctantly made peace** in 1504.

The burst of **European exploration** sparked by Columbus continued in 1500 when a **Spanish expedition** under Vicente Pinzón and a **Portuguese enterprise** under Pedro Alvares Cabral bound for India made the coast of **Brazil**. Cabral's sighting of this new land would prove important in establishing Portuguese claims to Brazil. Of greater significance was the growing realization that this was indeed a **New World**.

THE YEAR 1501 IS CONSIDERED the date the **Safavid Empire was founded**. With the Ottoman Empire to the west and the Mughal Empire to the east, it formed one of a bloc of sophisticated, centralized, **highly cultured Muslim empires** that dominated West Asia in the 16th and 17th centuries. It began in a burst of conquest launched by **Shah Ismail I** whose troops surged westwards across Persia, putting an end to the political vacuum and in-fighting that had followed the death of Timur (see 1386–90) in 1405. Proclaiming himself Shah of Persia, Ismail I was a Shi'ite Muslim and vigorously promoted his faith as the official state religion. Checked to the west by the military might of the Ottomans, the Safavids increasingly turned their focus to the east. In the process the Safavid capital was moved eastwards, finally ending at Isfahan.

Safavid Empire
From modest beginnings on the Caspian Sea, by 1501 the Safavid Empire extended to occupy a swathe of Western Asia.

The introduction of African slaves by European settlers to the New World began in 1502, hardly 10 years after Columbus's first Atlantic crossing. In part, this was a response to the **alarming death rates** of the native populations, who had been similarly enslaved. The Portuguese rapidly followed suit. This initial phase of the trade, known as the **First Atlantic system**, lasted until around 1580.

The **spread of Islam** in East Africa was reinforced by the establishment in 1504 of the **Funj Sultanate of Sennar** in the north of Sudan, at the expense of the previous Christian rulers of Sennar. The sultanate rapidly established itself as a major power in the region, threatening both Ethiopia and the Ottomans in Egypt.

In Europe, the **role of Florence** in the early years of the High Renaissance (see pp.204–205) was highlighted by **two remarkable works**: Michelangelo's statue of *David*, which he completed in 1504; and Leonardo's painting *Mona Lisa*, completed sometime around 1505–07.

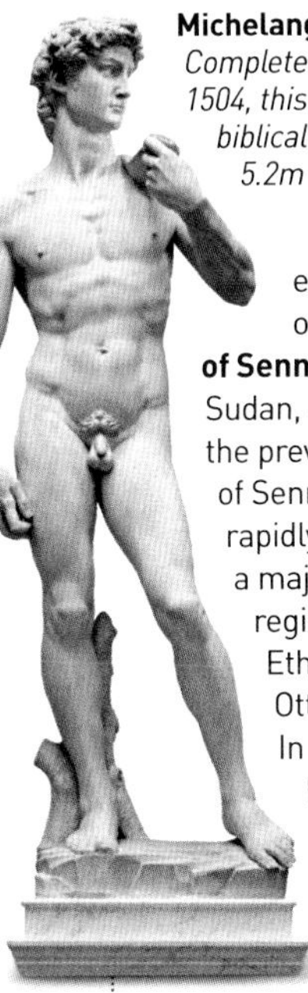

Michelangelo's *David*
Completed by Michelangelo in 1504, this giant marble statue of biblical hero David *stands at 5.2m (17ft) tall.*

> **"...ANYONE WHO HAS SEEN MICHELANGELO'S *DAVID* HAS NO NEED TO SEE ANYTHING ELSE BY ANY OTHER SCULPTOR..."**
>
> **Giorgio Vasari, Italian author,** from *Lives of the Artists*, 1568

- **1499 Venetian–Ottoman War** begins (to 1503)
- **22 April 1500** Portuguese explorer **Pedro Alvares Cabral** sights **Brazil**
- **April 1500** French defeat forces of Ludovio Sforza, Duke of Milan, at **Novara**, Milan
- **c.1500 First Inuit settlement** of Arctic
- **1500 Vicente Yáñez Pinzón** discovers mouth of **Amazon river**
- **1501** Accession of Shah Ismail I **establishes Safavid dynasty**, Persia
- **1502** Introduction of **African slaves** to Caribbean by Spanish
- **1502** German **Peter Henlein** makes first **pocket watch**
- **1502** Safavid ruler **Shah Ismail I** executes Sunni dissenters
- **1502 Donato Bramante,** one of the greatest **architects of the Renaissance**, completes Tempietto (the "Little Chapel"), Rome
- **1502 Alberto Cantino** produces **first map** to show discoveries in the New World, India, and divisions of the Treaty of Tordesillas
- **1 November 1503 Giuliano delle Rovere** becomes Pope Julius II, beginning a period of remarkable **artistic patronage** in Rome
- **April 1503** Spanish army routs French forces at **Cerignola**, Italy
- **1503 Moscow** becomes **politically independent**
- **1504 Michelangelo** completes statue of *David*
- **1504 Muslim Funj** rulers defeat Christian rulers of **Sennar** between the Blue and White Nile

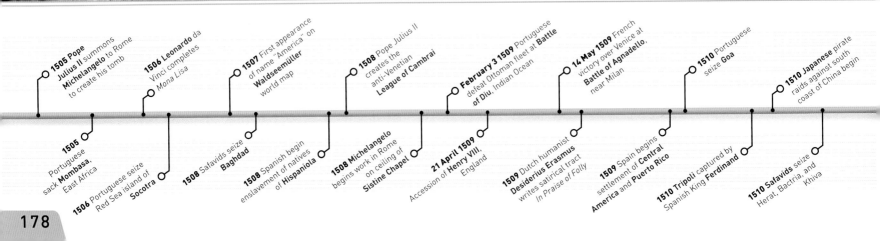

“THE TRUE WORK OF ART IS BUT A SHADOW OF THE DIVINE PERFECTION.”

Michelangelo Buonarroti, Italian artist (1475–1564)

MICHELANGELO BUONARROTI (1475–1564) was one of the defining figures of the High Renaissance (see pp.204–05). In 1505, he was invited to Rome by Pope Julius II to begin work on a monumental tomb, an association that would last for 40 years. In 1508, he began work painting a fresco on the Sistine Chapel ceiling, which he completed 4 years later.

The pace of **Portuguese expansion** across the Indian Ocean in the early 16th century was remarkable. From 1505, the Portuguese established themselves in a string of ports along the **East African coast**. The goal was simple and ruthlessly pursued – the domination of the lucrative spice trade with India and East Asia. A key player in this campaign was **Afonso de Albuquerque**, who in 1509 became viceroy of the fledgling Portuguese colony in India. By 1510, he had secured **Goa** as the principal Portuguese base in India; by 1511, he had overseen the foundation of the first Portuguese settlement in Southeast Asia, **Malacca**. He also sponsored the first Portuguese voyage to the Spice Islands, the **Moluccas**, which were reached in 1512 by **Francisco Serrão**, who had sailed in company with **Antonio de Abreu** and **Francisco Rodrigues**.

Sistine ceiling
Commissioned by Pope Julius II, the ceiling of the Sistine Chapel in the Vatican is one of the masterworks of Michelangelo. It depicts scenes from the Old Testament.

- **1505 Pope Julius II** summons **Michelangelo** to Rome to create his tomb
- **1505** Portuguese sack **Mombasa**, East Africa
- **1506 Leonardo** da Vinci completes *Mona Lisa*
- **1506** Portuguese seize Red Sea island of **Socotra**
- **1507** First appearance of name "America" on **Waldseemüller** world map
- **1508** Safavids seize **Baghdad**
- **1508** Spanish begin enslavement of natives of **Hispaniola**
- **1508** Pope Julius II creates the anti-Venetian **League of Cambrai**
- **1508 Michelangelo** begins work in Rome on ceiling of **Sistine Chapel**
- **February 3 1509** Portuguese defeat Ottoman fleet at **Battle of Diu**, Indian Ocean
- **21 April 1509** Accession of **Henry VIII**, England
- **14 May 1509** French victory over Venice at **Battle of Agnadello**, near Milan
- **1509** Dutch humanist **Desiderius Erasmus** writes satirical tract *In Praise of Folly*
- **1509** Spain begins settlement of **Central America** and **Puerto Rico**
- **1510** Portuguese seize **Goa**
- **1510 Tripoli** captured by Spanish King **Ferdinand**
- **1510 Japanese** pirate raids against south coast of China begin
- **1510 Safavids** seize Herat, Bactria, and Khiva

Depiction of the Battle of Agnadello, one of the major battles of the Italian Wars, from the tomb of Louis XII and Anne of Brittany, France.

This detail shows the coronation of Ottoman Sultan Selim I. The empire almost trebled during his nine-year reign.

Where the latter two were forced to turn back in the Banda Sea, Serrão was able to continue to the Moluccas using native craft.

However initially unpromising, it was a measure of the excitement sparked by **Columbus's Atlantic crossings** (see 1492) that within 20 years a variety of **Spanish expeditions** had explored and mapped almost the whole of the **Caribbean**. This included, in 1508–09, the **Yucatán Peninsula** on the east coast of Mexico, a discovery that led directly to the conquest of Mexico by **Hernan Cortés** (see 1519). The European conquest of the New World was driven largely by greed and effected principally by violence. It nonetheless laid claim to a Christian imperative, given **papal sanction** as early as 1452, by which "saracens, pagans, and any other unbelievers" could be enslaved. It was a view explosively challenged in 1511 in a sermon by a Spanish Dominican friar,

> “ ARE THEY **NOT MEN?** DO THEY **NOT HAVE** RATIONAL **SOULS?** ”
>
> **Antonio de Montesinos, Dominican friar,** delivering a sermon to Spanish colonists, Hispaniola, 4 December 1511

Antonio de Montesinos, in which, to predictable outrage, he denounced the "cruelty and tyranny" of the settlers.

Similarly aggressive Spanish and Portuguese attempts at colonization in **Morocco**, where both seized coastal strongholds in the 15th and early 16th centuries, partly helped the rise of a new Moroccan dynasty after 1511 – the **Sa'dis** – who filled the political vacuum created by the crumbling of Marinid rule in the 1480s.

The **Venetian Republic** was diplomatically isolated and opposed by almost every major Western European power when Pope Julius II established the **League of Cambrai** in 1508. The Republic was quickly plunged into crisis by its defeat in May 1509 by Louis XII's French army at the **Battle of Agnadello,** one of the major battles of the **Italian Wars** (1494–1559). The following year Julius II allied himself with Venice against France, anxious that Venetian territorial designs in northern Italy had been replaced by identical French ambitions. This shuffling of alliances was typical of the period. It was given a further twist with the formation in 1511 of a new **Holy League**, including England, now directed against France. One outcome of this was a subsequent Franco–Venetian alliance.

Hemmed in to the west by the **Ottomans** and threatened to the south by the Portuguese, the **Safavids** were nonetheless successful in confronting the loose **Uzbek confederation** of peoples of Central Asia to their north. In December 1510, with victory over the Uzbeks outside the city of Merv, substantial territories, including Herat, Bactria, and Kandahar, came under **Safavid** rule.

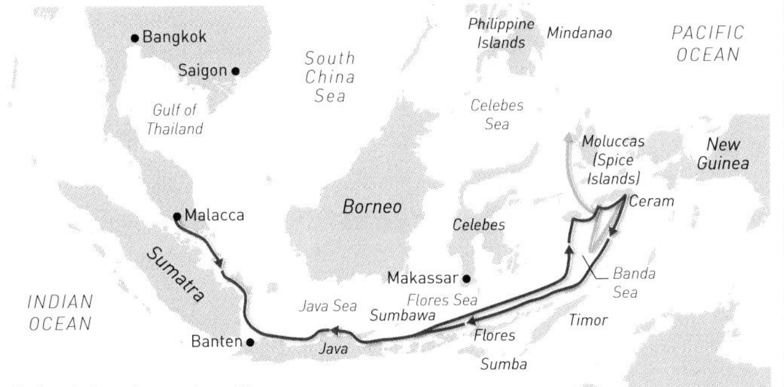

Spice Islands exploration
Portuguese explorer Francisco Serrao successfully reached the Moluccas (Spice Islands) after others had turned back.

NO LESS SIGNIFICANT than the Spanish exploration of the Caribbean in the immediate aftermath of Columbus's 1492 crossing was the discovery by **Juan Ponce de León** in April 1513 of the "island" of Florida. It was the first Spanish contact with the mainland of North America and the basis for subsequent Spanish claims to the region. In attempting to circumnavigate his island, Ponce de León made a further discovery almost as important in the age of sail as Columbus's discovery of the wind systems of the central Atlantic – the **Gulf Stream**.

Niccolò Machiavelli was a diplomat in Florence when, in 1513, he wrote the first modern handbook of political science, *The Prince* (published in 1532). Its central theme – that the exercise of political power requires violence and deceit – earned it lasting notoriety. It offers advice about the most effective means of ruling: essentially a pragmatic determination to use all means to hand.

Ottoman territorial expansion was renewed after the civil war of 1509–12 which saw **Selim I** emerge as sultan at the expense of both his father, Bayezid II, who was forced to abdicate, and Selim's older brother, Ahmed, who was killed in battle. Selim initiated this burst of growth – directed south and east against fellow Muslims rather than north against Christian Europe – in 1514 when the Safavids, vastly outnumbered and with no answer to the Ottoman artillery, were overpowered at the Battle of Caldiran. His Eastern flank secured, Selim swept into **Syria** and **Mamluk Egypt**, which instantly crumbled.

Selim I not only dramatically increased Ottoman territories but, in securing almost all the Muslim holy places of the Near East, added substantially to Ottoman prestige (see pp.230–31).

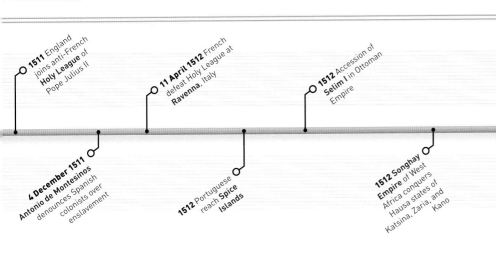

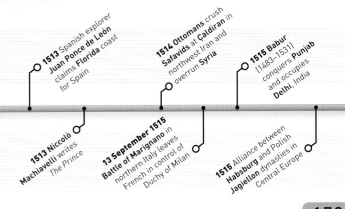

NICCOLO MACHIAVELLI
(1469–1527)

Philosopher and writer, Niccolò Machiavelli was a functionary in Florence, where he witnessed the power of aggressive rulers at first hand, including, in 1502–03, that of the pope's illegitimate son, the ruthless Cesare Borgia. He completed several diplomatic missions, but in 1513 was arrested and tortured. He wrote *The Prince* in the same year. He died aged of 58, impoverished, before his book enjoyed its later notoriety.

1511 England joins anti-French **Holy League** of Pope Julius II

4 December 1511 Antonio de Montesinos denounces Spanish colonists over enslavement

11 April 1512 French defeat Holy League at **Ravenna**, Italy

1512 Portuguese reach **Spice Islands**

1512 Accession of **Selim I** in Ottoman Empire

1512 Songhay Empire of West Africa conquers Hausa states of Katsina, Zaria, and Kano

1513 Spanish explorer **Juan Ponce de León** claims **Florida** coast for Spain

1513 Niccolò Machiavelli writes *The Prince*

1514 Ottomans crush **Safavids** at **Çaldiran** in northwest Iran and overrun **Syria**

13 September 1515 Battle of Marignano in northern Italy leaves French in control of Duchy of Milan

1515 Babur (1483–1531) conquers **Punjab** and occupies **Delhi**, India

1515 Alliance between **Habsburg** and Polish **Jagiellon** dynasties in Central Europe

> **“** WHY DOES NOT THE **POPE... BUILD... ST PETER’S** WITH HIS **OWN MONEY,** RATHER **THAN WITH** THE **MONEY... OF POOR BELIEVERS. ”**
>
> **Martin Luther, German priest,** from *95 Theses*, 1517

THE OTTOMAN CONQUESTS IN THE MIDDLE EAST under **Selim I** – who in 1517 also brought Algeria into the Ottoman orbit – meant that the Ottoman Turkish state was now emphatically an **empire**. It was also rapidly developing as a major naval power. Control of Egypt both consolidated the Ottoman presence in the eastern Mediterranean and, crucially, gave them access to the Red Sea. Already effectively masters of the overland trade routes with the East, the Ottomans were now poised to dominate the lucrative "**route of spices**". In doing so, they found themselves in direct conflict with the Portuguese, who had been actively probing the Red Sea since 1513. The stage was set for another round of conflict between the Muslim world and the Christian West.

In October 1517, the priest and professor of theology **Martin Luther** (1483–1546) nailed his *95 Theses* to the door of All Saints Church in Wittenberg, Saxony, as part of what was a growing protest movement against religious practices and corruption in the Catholic Church. In 1521, after being excommunicated by the pope, his opposition to the Church hardened. The ready response to Luther's teachings and the influence of the printing press (see pp.154–55) in disseminating his ideas resulted in a major force for religious change known as the **Reformation**.

The arrival of a **Portuguese fleet** under Tomé Pires in **Canton, China**, in August 1517 was the climax of a campaign to open up trading routes across the Indian Ocean, begun when Vasco da Gama rounded the Cape of Good Hope in 1498. However, the early results of these encounters were not promising as the Chinese regarded the newcomers as **uncouth barbarians**. A Portuguese trade mission to Peking in 1520 was treated with similar scorn.

THE REFORMATION

The Reformation – the religious revolt against the Catholic Church instigated by Martin Luther (right) – tore the Western Church apart. Politics intruded from the start as the revolt spread across Europe. The consequence was a legacy of violent religious division and confrontation between Catholics and Protestants that led to a permanent divide in European Christendom.

The fall of Tenochtitlan on 13 August 1521 was the result not just of Spanish ferocity but of a 20,000-strong native army recruited by Hernán Cortés.

THE ELECTION OF CHARLES V AS HOLY ROMAN EMPEROR in 1519 appeared pivotal. Charles (1500–58) was already the ruler of several territories across Europe: in Italy, Austria, the Low Countries, and in Spain. Now, as Holy Roman Emperor, his status appeared unassailable. For the earnest Charles, the imperatives were clear – to preside over a prosperous, pan-European Catholic entity which, properly mobilized, would then **rout the Ottoman menace**. The reality was painfully different. The size of his territories made effective control impossible. Few of his subjects were prepared to surrender traditional "liberties" to a distant, foreign ruler; almost none was prepared to finance him; and religious differences persistently intruded. Simultaneously, the prospect of Habsburg domination alarmed every other major European power, above all France. The result was a **reign of near permanent warfare** and dutiful hopes consistently frustrated.

Emperor Charles V
Few rulers were more dutiful than Charles V or as conscious of their divine destiny. However, his best efforts consistently proved in vain.

The daring, ruthlessness, and single-mindedness **Spain** brought to overseas adventuring paid dividends with **Hernán Cortés's** march on Tenochitlan, capital of the Mexican **Aztec Empire**. Beginning in 1519, in less than five years the Spanish force, aided by Tlaxaclan warriors, had subjugated an entire nation. A minor noble and self-financing adventurer, Cortés brought about Spanish domination of Central America.

A further milestone in the cementing of Spain's global role was marked in 1519 – the launch of the **first circumnavigation of the globe**. The expedition leader, **Ferdinand Magellan** (b.1480) was a Portuguese nobleman who, despite his nationality, succeeded in persuading Charles V to bankroll his scheme to reach the Spice Islands in the Pacific by sailing

> **“ HE KNEW BETTER** THAN ANY OTHER THE **TRUE ART** OF **NAVIGATION. ”**
>
> **Antonio Pigafetta, Italian navigator,** on Ferdinand Magellan, 1521

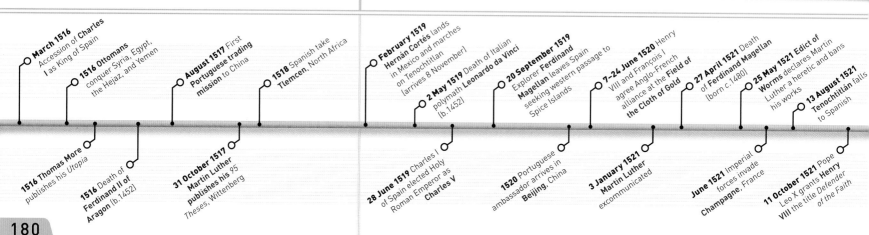

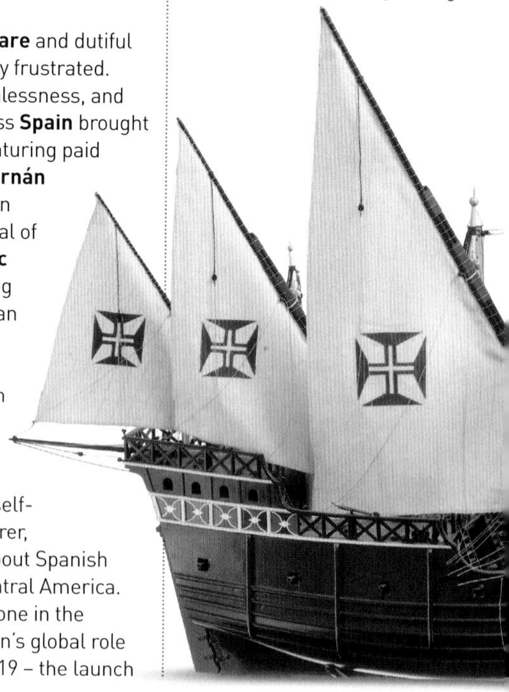

- **March 1516** Accession of **Charles I** as King of Spain
- **1516 Ottomans** conquer Syria, Egypt, the Hejaz, and Yemen
- **1516 Thomas More** publishes his *Utopia*
- **1516** Death of **Ferdinand II of Aragon** (b.1452)
- **August 1517** First **Portuguese trading mission** to China
- **31 October 1517 Martin Luther publishes his** *95 Theses*, Wittenberg
- **1518** Spanish take **Tlemcen,** North Africa
- **February 1519 Hernán Cortés** lands in Mexico and marches on Tenochtitlan (arrives 8 November)
- **2 May 1519** Death of Italian polymath **Leonardo da Vinci** (b.1452)
- **28 June 1519** Charles I of Spain elected Holy Roman Emperor as **Charles V**
- **20 September 1519** Explorer **Ferdinand Magellan** leaves Spain seeking western passage to Spice Islands
- **1520** Portuguese ambassador arrives in **Beijing**, China
- **7–24 June 1520** Henry VIII and François I agree Anglo-French alliance at the **Field of the Cloth of Gold**
- **3 January 1521 Martin Luther** excommunicated
- **27 April 1521** Death of **Ferdinand Magellan** (born c.1480)
- **25 May 1521 Edict of Worms** declares Martin Luther a heretic and bans his works
- **June 1521** Imperial forces invade **Champagne**, France
- **13 August 1521 Tenochtitlán** falls to Spanish
- **11 October 1521** Pope Leo X grants **Henry VIII** the title *Defender of the Faith*

1523–25

At Pavia in 1525, the French army's siege lines were broken by a Spanish relief army, then the soldiers were cut to pieces by pikemen and gunfire.

west. Five ships set out; one returned, three years later, and without Magellan, who had been killed by islanders in 1521. It was, nonetheless, perhaps the most remarkable enterprise of the age of sail, an epic which for the first time revealed the immensity of the Pacific.

1521 saw another round in the **Italian wars** (1494–1559), this time sparked by French fears of a Habsburg-dominated Europe after the election of Charles V as Holy Roman Emperor. France and, at least initially, Venice joined forces to oppose Charles, England, and the papacy. For the French, the war was as unsatisfactory as its predecessors, culminating in a series of defeats.

Portuguese caravel
Magellan's flagship Trinidad *was a caravel like this Portuguese vessel. Typically less than 30m (100ft) long, they were sturdily seaworthy ships.*

THE BELIEF THAT THE LANDS IN THE WEST discovered by European explorers from Columbus onwards were unknown Asian coasts, rather than a new continent, proved tenacious. It was likewise widely held that a **navigable passage to the East** through these landmasses must exist. It was only the voyages between 1524 and 1528 from Florida to Nova Scotia by **Giovanni da Verrazano** (1485–1528), a Florentine in the service of François I of France, that revealed the existence of a **continuous coastline**. Yet Verrazano persisted in the belief that the Pacific was within reach.

The **German Peasants' War** of 1524–25 was a sharp reminder of the way that the language of Protestant reformation could be appropriated by groups who usually lacked a voice in politics. The revolts were attempts by huge numbers of the politically disenfranchised in Germany and in Austria, by no means all of them peasants, to end what they saw as abuses against them – chiefly taxes and labour services – by the Church and the nobility. At the war's height in the spring of 1525, perhaps 300,000 people had gathered in a variety of loose groupings and hastily assembled armies. The **uprising was savagely repressed**, with thousands killed. Luther and other leaders of the "official" Reformation vehemently denied any connection with the rebels, and the revolt provoked a brutal clampdown on forms of Protestant religious radicalism, such as **Anabaptism**, which were considered to challenge both social hierarchy and Protestant authority.

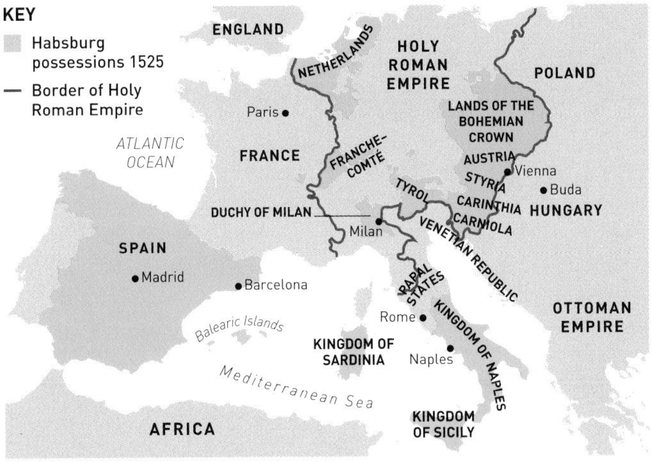

Habsburg Empire under Charles V
The very size of Charles V's empire made it effectively ungovernable. Whatever its potential power, it was riven by religious and political strife.

The **Battle of Pavia** in 1525 saw **François I captured** and shipped to Madrid, where he was obliged to surrender all claim to Italy. But it was an agreement the French king had no intention of honouring.

100,000

THE NUMBER OF **REBELS KILLED IN** THE **POPULAR UPRISING** IN **GERMANY**

8:1 **Battle of Pavia**
The French Army was virtually wiped out at Pavia on 24 February 1525, with 8,000 casualties compared to 1,000 Imperial casualties.

1526

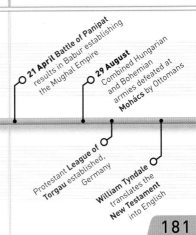

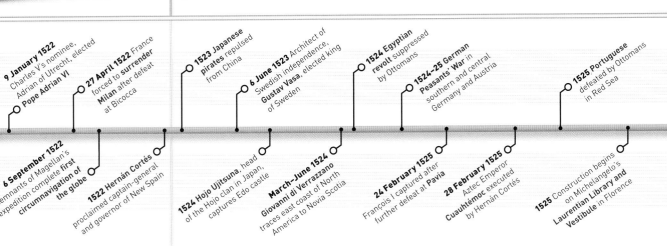

Babur's Mughal empire could only be created – and sustained – by force.

> IF THERE IS A **PARADISE ON EARTH**, IT IS THIS, IT IS THIS, IT IS THIS.

Inscription on Babur's tomb 1530

IN HIS STRUGGLES AGAINST CHARLES V (see 1521), François I had solicited the help of the Ottomans in 1525, in the process initiating a **Franco–Ottoman alliance** that lasted 250 years. The alliance also provided the Ottomans with further justification to renew their conflict with Hungary and, in August 1526, they obliterated a combined Hungarian–Bohemian force at Mohács.

In 1526, the **Mughal Empire** was founded in northern India. It was the creation of **Babur** (1483–1530), a descendant of Genghis Khan (see 1201–05). Babur hailed from Ferghana in central Asia, from where he had been expelled. In 1522, however, he captured Kandahar, an important staging point on the road to India and, in 1526, defeated the Afghan Sultan of Delhi, Ibrahim Lodi, and declared himself emperor. At its height at the beginning of the 18th century, the Mughal empire (Mughal is Persian for Mongol) covered almost the entire subcontinent. It was a byword for sophisticated and courtly life, fattened by trade and conquest, and, though Islamic, tolerant of other religions.

9 January 1522 Charles V's nominee, Adrian of Utrecht, elected **Pope Adrian VI**

27 April 1522 France forced to **surrender Milan** after defeat at Bicocca

6 September 1522 Remnants of Magellan's expedition complete **first circumnavigation of the globe**

1522 Hernán Cortés proclaimed captain-general and governor of New Spain

1523 Japanese pirates repulsed from China

6 June 1523 Architect of Swedish independence, **Gustav Vasa**, elected king of Sweden

1524 Hojo Ujitsuna, head of the Hojo clan in Japan, captures Edo castle

March–June 1524 Giovanni di Verrazzano traces east coast of North America to Novia Scotia

1524 Egyptian revolt suppressed by Ottomans

1524–25 German Peasants' War in southern and central Germany and Austria

24 February 1525 François I captured after further defeat at **Pavia**

28 February 1525 Aztec Emperor **Cuauhtémoc** executed by Hernán Cortés

1525 Portuguese defeated by Ottomans in Red Sea

1525 Construction begins on Michelangelo's **Laurentian Library and Vestibule** in Florence

21 April Battle of Panipat results in Babur establishing the Mughal Empire

29 August Combined Hungarian and Bohemian armies defeated at **Mohács** by Ottomans

Protestant **League of Torgau** established, Germany

William Tyndale translates the **New Testament** into English

THE STORY OF ASTRONOMY

ONE OF THE OLDEST SCIENCES, ASTRONOMY MAY HOLD THE KEY TO THE ORIGIN OF EVERYTHING

Newton's telescope (front view)

The development of astronomy has been influenced by two key factors: the invention of the telescope, which revealed previously undetectable celestial objects, and advances in mathematics, physics, chemistry, and computing, which have been crucial to explaining astronomical observations.

Early astronomy was closely linked to mythology, religion, and prognostication. Celestial observations were used to measure time, devise calendars, set the dates of religious festivals, and for astrological prediction. For millennia, it was believed that the Earth was the centre of the cosmos. However, this did not fully explain the observed movements of the Moon, Sun, and planets.

MODERN ASTRONOMY

In 1543, Nicolaus Copernicus published his heliocentric model, which put the Sun at the centre of the cosmos and is widely considered to mark the birth of modern astronomy. Then, after 1609, the newly invented telescope revealed a host of new astronomical objects. The 17th century also saw the establishment of the laws of planetary motion by Johannes Kepler, and an explanation of the gravitational force controlling that movement by Isaac Newton. In the 19th century, the distance to the Sun and nearby stars was accurately measured, spectroscopy was introduced, and advances in theoretical physics provided explanations for problems such as how stars generate their energy (by nuclear reactions in their cores). Prior to 1920, many thought the Universe consisted of only our own Milky Way Galaxy. However, Edwin Hubble measured the speed at which distant nebulae were receding, and it was realized that these nebulae were independent galaxies. Not only were the galaxies moving away, but the speed they were moving away increased with distance, implying that the Universe had a beginning, when everything was close together. It was proposed that the expansion had been caused by a massive explosion – the Big Bang. Findings from modern space astronomy have supported the Big Bang theory, but it has also been discovered that much of the Universe consists of dark matter and dark energy, the nature and origin of which are still unknown.

Persian astrolabe
Astrolabes show a representation of the night sky and were used until the 17th century to estimate time and for navigation.

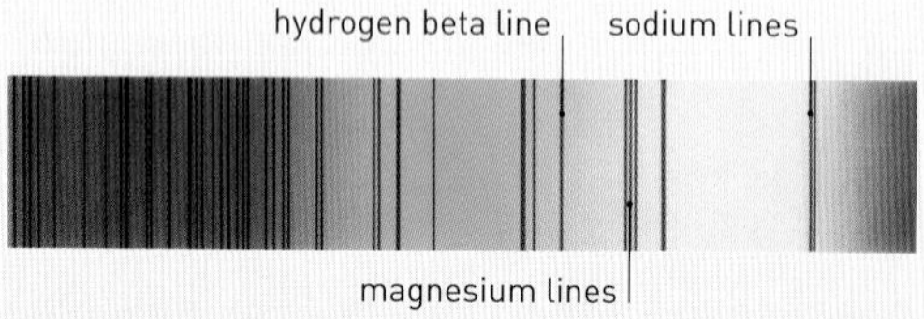

THE ELECTROMAGNETIC SPECTRUM

Stars and other astronomical objects emit light and other forms of electromagnetic energy, such as X-rays and radio waves. Using spectroscopy, these electromagnetic emissions can be broken up into a spectrum of colours. A star's spectrum is crossed by dark absorption lines, each corresponding to a different chemical element. By investigating the intensity of these lines, a star's chemical composition can be discovered. Further study can also establish its temperature, relative velocity, and the pressure and density of its atmosphere.

2000 BCE
Solar and lunar calendars
The Babylonians produce the first calendar by integrating the 365.25 days of the solar year with the 29.53 days of the lunar month. Similar calendars are used in ancient Egypt.

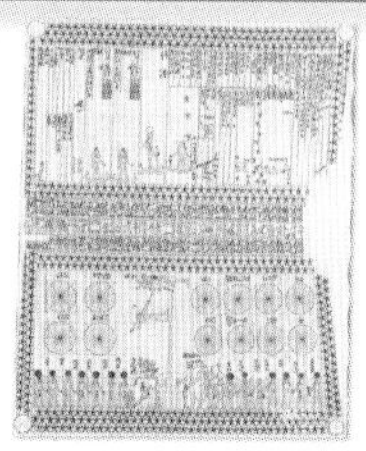
Zodiac of Senenmut

Babylonian boundary stone

c.1400 BCE
Deities and the Zodiac
The ancient Egyptians produce the earliest known representation of the Zodiac, in which stars, planets, and associated deities appear. Zodiacs also appear in Babylonian artefacts.

c.90–168 CE
Ptolemy's Universe
Greek polymath Claudius Ptolemy proposes that the Earth is the centre of the cosmos, a view that prevailed until the 16th century.

Ptolemy's constellations

1420
Ulugh Beg
The Persian Ulugh Beg builds an observatory in Samarkand. He measures the tilt of Earth's axis to 1/100th of a degree.

Ulugh Beg observatory

1543
The Sun-centred Universe
Nicolaus Copernicus suggests the Earth orbits the Sun and not vice versa. This demotes the Earth to being just one of the six known planets.

The Copernican Solar System

1608/1668
The first telescopes
German-born Dutch lensmaker Hans Lippershey makes the first refracting telescope in 1608. English scientist Isaac Newton makes the first reflecting telescope in 1668.

Newton's telescope

3CM THE DIAMETER OF THE **OBJECTIVE MIRROR** IN NEWTON'S TELESCOPE. TELESCOPES USED BY **MODERN ASTRONOMERS** HAVE MIRRORS UP TO **1,040CM IN DIAMETER**.

Newton's telescope
Isaac Newton made his first reflecting telescope in 1668. Shortly afterwards, he made a second model (shown here), which stands about 20cm (8in) high. Newton's telescope was the first to use a primary mirror rather than a lens to collect light. A secondary mirror then reflects the light through a magnifying eyepiece for viewing.

1780s
William Herschel
Herschel discovers Uranus (1781) using a home-made telescope. He makes over 400 more, including a 1.26m reflector.

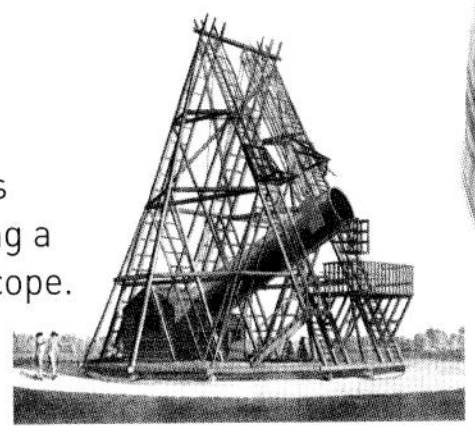
Herschel's 1.26m telescope

Hubble Space Telescope

1990–present
Space telescopes
Telescopes are put into space near Earth or orbit around it, from where they probe the sky in a range of wavelengths.

1920s
Edwin Hubble
Using the US's 2.5m Hooker telescope, Hubble shows that the Universe has more than 100 billion galaxies, and that it is expanding.

The Hooker telescope

1930s
Radio telescopes
A new branch of astronomy – radio astronomy – begins when early radio telescopes detect radio waves from the Sun and distant galaxies.

Grote Reber's radio telescope

1960s–present
Exploring other worlds
Spacecraft are used to explore the Solar System. They fly past, orbit, and land on planets, moons, asteroids, and comets.

Mars rover

1527–31

The Sack of Rome in 1527 shocked Europe and devastated the Church. Although it also deeply embarrassed Charles V, it meant his dominance in Italy was confirmed.

THE MOST SHOCKING EVENT OF THE ITALIAN WARS was the **Sack of Rome** in 1527 by Charles V's Imperial troops. It also highlighted the contradictions facing Charles V as he struggled to impose order on his vast territories. As Holy Roman Emperor, Charles V was the natural ally of the Catholic Church just as he was the natural enemy of Lutheranism (see 1517). Yet not only was Charles now at war with the papacy's Holy League – assembled to challenge his dominance in Italy – some of the troops who laid waste to Rome when his army ran out of control in protest at their unpaid wages were openly sympathetic to the reformist doctrines of Luther. But, while Pope Clement VII cowered in the Castel San' Angelo as churches and palaces were ransacked and nuns raped and priests murdered, it was clear that Charles's control of Italy was now absolute.

Following their victory at Mohács in 1526 and the conquest of much of Hungary in 1529, the **Ottomans** feared the Habsburgs would try to recapture the lost territories and so laid siege to **Vienna**. It proved too ambitious a task even for the formidable Ottoman army, for the weather proved as arduous a foe as the Austrians. A second attempt on the city in 1532 also failed.

After his victory at Panipat in 1526, **Babur** consolidated his hold over north India the following year, defeating a Rajput army under Rana Sanga at the **Battle of Khanwa**. The final establishment of Mughal power came in 1529 with the destruction of an Afghan army at Ghagra.

In 1531, the **Schmalkadic League** was formed. This was a military alliance, made originally between the Lutheran rulers of Hesse and Saxony in northern Germany, under which each promised to aid the other if Charles V attempted, by force, to re-impose Catholicism. It rapidly expanded to include other German Protestant states and gained the support of Charles's external enemies, the Ottomans and France. It was also an opportunity for each territory to enrich itself by taking over church property.

Siege of Vienna
The Ottoman siege of Vienna in 1529 failed because of the bad weather – bitter autumn rains and early snow – and over-extended supply lines.

SULEIMAN I (1494–1566)

The 46-year rule of Suleiman was marked by a succession of victories in the Balkans, the Middle East, and North Africa that left the Ottomans as the most dynamic and dominant presence in the western hemisphere. He is known as "Suleiman the Magnificent" in the West and as *Kanuri*, "The Lawgiver", in the Islamic world, and his reign saw a flowering of Ottoman art and culture.

1532

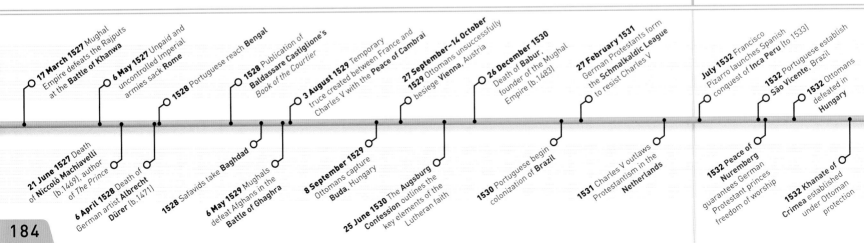

Atahualpa, the last Inca emperor, leads his army at Caxamalca.

SPANISH EXPLORATION AND CONQUEST IN THE NEW WORLD, so decisively reinforced by the subjection of Mexico in 1521, was continued on an even more spectacular scale with the takeover of the Peruvian **Inca Empire** by **Francisco Pizarro** (1476–1541) in 1532. In little more than a year, a force of 188 Spaniards defeated a highly organized state of five million. Like Cortés's invasion of Mexico, its success depended on internal divisions within the Inca Empire, and a combination of religious zeal, greed, and superior military means – steel, guns, and armour against the Incas' weapons of sharpened stones and padded cotton armour – the whole driven by Pizarro, a man of huge ambition.

On the other side of the continent, further European penetration of South America was also taking place, albeit on a far smaller scale. In 1532, Portugal established its first permanent settlement in **Brazil**, at São Vicente. This was the nucleus of what by the end of the century would be a huge colonial enterprise based on slavery and sugar plantations.

In 1532, hostilities between Germany's Schmalkaldic League and Emperor Charles V ceased with the signing of a **treaty at Nuremberg**. The concessions made to the Protestants by Charles, which, most importantly, included freedom of worship, were welcomed by Martin Luther and enabled German Protestants to spread throughout the country in the following decade.

17 March 1527 Mughal Empire defeats the Rajputs at the **Battle of Khanwa**

21 June 1527 Death of **Niccolò Machiavelli** (b.1469), author of *The Prince*

6 May 1527 Unpaid and uncontrolled Imperial armies sack **Rome**

6 April 1528 Death of German artist **Albrecht Dürer** (b.1471)

1528 Portuguese reach **Bengal**

1528 Safavids take **Baghdad**

1528 Publication of **Baldassare Castiglione's** *Book of the Courtier*

6 May 1529 Mughals defeat Afghans in the **Battle of Ghaghra**

3 August 1529 Temporary truce created between France and Charles V with the **Peace of Cambrai**

8 September 1529 Ottomans capture **Buda**, Hungary

27 September–14 October 1529 Ottomans unsuccessfully besiege **Vienna**, Austria

25 June 1530 The **Augsburg Confession** outlines the key elements of the Lutheran faith

26 December 1530 Death of **Babur**, founder of the Mughal Empire (b.1483)

1530 Portuguese begin colonization of **Brazil**

27 February 1531 German Protestants form the **Schmalkaldic League** to resist Charles V

1531 Charles V outlaws Protestantism in the **Netherlands**

July 1532 Francisco Pizarro launches Spanish conquest of **Inca Peru** (to 1533)

1532 Peace of Nuremberg guarantees German Protestant princes freedom of worship

1532 Portuguese establish **São Vicente**, Brazil

1532 Ottomans defeated in **Hungary**

1532 Khanate of Crimea established under Ottoman protection

1533–34

> **“…THE SCANDAL OF CHRISTENDOM AND A DISGRACE TO YOU.”**
>
> **Catherine of Aragon** to Henry VIII about Anne Boleyn, 1533

1535–37

Charles V's seizure of Tunis in June 1935 was almost the only unequivocal success of his reign. Briefly, the prospect of a resurgent Christendom loomed.

HENRY VIII OF ENGLAND had been awarded the title *Fidei Defensor* – Defender of the Faith – by Pope Leo X in 1521 in recognition of his vehement defence of the Catholic Church against Protestant attacks. Henry would remain a devout Catholic to the end of his life, opposed to all attempts to reform Catholic practice. And yet by 1533 he had been excommunicated from the Roman Church. The following year, he completed the rupture, establishing a national church, wholly independent from Rome, with himself as its "supreme head". The reasons for this improbable split were simple. Initially, Henry wanted a **divorce** from his ageing Spanish wife, **Catherine of Aragon**, who after 24 years of marriage had yet to give birth to a son. Henry had convinced himself this was divine punishment for marrying his brother's widow – in 1501, Catherine had married Henry's elder brother Arthur, who died the following year; Henry and Catherine married in 1509. The pope, under pressure from Catherine's nephew, Charles V, refused to grant a divorce. Henry's response, formulated over several years, was in effect to become his own pope, able to authorize his own divorce. Prompted in addition by the knowledge that, as elsewhere in Europe, any ruler asserting control of the Church in his own country would necessarily increase his own authority, in 1534 the **Church of England** was brought into being under the Act of Supremacy. In pursuit of Henry's personal interests, **Roman Catholicism was abolished**.

HAVING BROKEN WITH ROME, it followed that all the structures of the Catholic Church in England should be taken over by the state. This was not just a question of wanting to eradicate papal authority in England. The Catholic Church in England was immensely wealthy, and this was money that Henry VIII, permanently strapped for cash, was determined to have. In 1535, the king's secretary, **Thomas Cromwell** (*c.*1485–1540), took charge of the two-part **dissolution of the country's monasteries**. Starting in 1536 and culminating with all the great monasteries in 1539, the dissolution involved systematic vandalism and saw the greatest transfer of land ownership in England since the Norman Conquest in 1066. Every one of the 560 monasteries in England was suppressed, yielding the crown an additional income of around £200,000 *per annum*. However, within years the money was gone, squandered by the king.

Henry VIII's divorce from Catherine of Aragon in 1533 had been necessary to allow him to marry **Anne Boleyn**. When she, too, failed to produce a son, Henry had her executed on **charges of adultery** in 1536. In the same year, tensions at the pace and extent of religious change, and the sincere concerns of many that the break with Rome signalled larger changes in the fabric of the traditional Church, had reached boiling point in the North of England. The **Pilgrimage of Grace** saw the largest uprisings in England since the Peasants Revolt in 1381. Those involved had shown little or no dissatisfaction with the Catholic church and were unprepared to see centuries of settled faith discarded. Faced with protest on this scale, the king conceded to the movement's demands. But when the crisis was over, he had the rebellion's leaders executed.

Distracted by events in Europe, Charles V was rarely able to pursue his goal of driving the Ottomans back to their Turkish heartlands. In 1535, however, he achieved a rare success with the **conquest of Tunis** in North Africa. It proved to be a costly victory, provoking an Ottoman raid on Majorca that captured 6,000 Christians and encouraged the French monarch to co-operate more closely with the Ottomans.

While it never achieved the notoriety of its Spanish equivalent (see 1480), the **Portuguese Inquisition**, founded in 1536, was nonetheless vigorous in rooting out heresy in Portugal and, from 1560, in its colonies, such as Goa. Its chief target was Jews, many originally Spanish, who were forcibly converted to Catholicism.

THE JESUIT ORDER

The initial Catholic response to the Reformation was hesitant and uncoordinated, and was led by a series of individuals rather than the Church itself. The Jesuits, the Society of Jesus, were established in 1534 by a Basque nobleman, Ignatius of Loyola. Loyola's goal was to produce a new generation of highly educated priests to spread a new militantly Catholic faith. Given papal sanction in 1540, the Jesuits spearheaded the Catholic revival.

Anne Boleyn
Henry VIII married Anne Boleyn in secret in January 1533, four months before he divorced Catherine of Aragon. She was crowned in June.

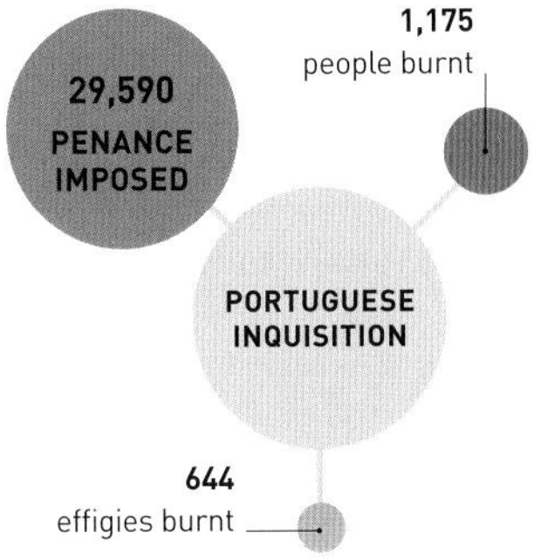

Portuguese Inquisition
Between 1540 and 1794, tribunals held in Lisbon, Porto, Coimbra, and Evora led to the death by burning of 1,175 people, most of them Jews.

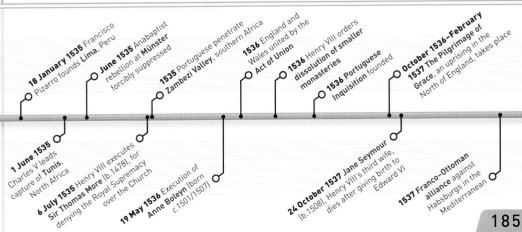

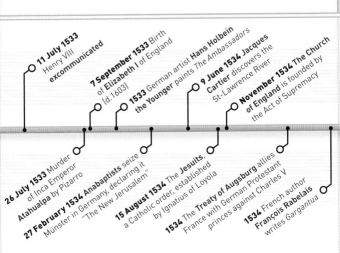

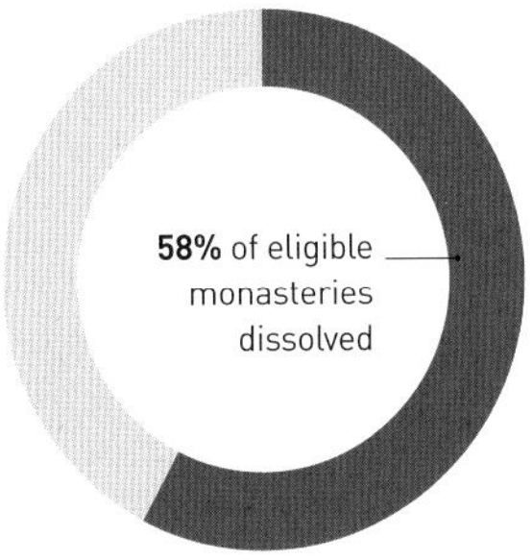

Dissolution of monasteries
Under the Dissolution of Lesser Monasteries Act *of 1536, 243 of the 419 eligible monasteries were suppressed or dissolved.*

- **11 July 1533** Henry VIII **excommunicated**
- **26 July 1533** Murder of Inca Emperor **Atahualpa** by Pizarro
- **7 September 1533** Birth **of Elizabeth I** of England (d.1603)
- **1533** German artist **Hans Holbein the Younger** paints *The Ambassadors*
- **27 February 1534 Anabaptists** seize Münster in Germany, declaring it "The New Jerusalem"
- **9 June 1534 Jacques Cartier** discovers the St-Lawrence River
- **15 August 1534** The **Jesuits**, a Catholic order, established by Ignatius of Loyola
- **November 1534 The Church of England** is founded by the Act of Supremacy
- **1534** The **Treaty of Augsburg** allies France with German Protestant princes against Charles V
- **1534** French author **François Rabelais** writes *Gargantua*
- **18 January 1535** Francisco Pizarro founds **Lima**, Peru
- **1 June 1535** Charles V leads capture **of Tunis,** North Africa
- **June 1535** Anabaptist rebellion at **Münster** forcibly suppressed
- **6 July 1535** Henry VIII executes **Sir Thomas More** (b.1478), for denying the Royal Supremacy over the Church
- **1535** Portuguese penetrate **Zambezi Valley**, southern Africa
- **19 May 1536** Execution of **Anne Boleyn** (born *c.*1501/1507)
- **1536** England and Wales united by the **Act of Union**
- **1536** Henry VIII orders **dissolution of smaller monasteries**
- **1536 Portuguese Inquisition** founded
- **October 1536–February 1537 The Pilgrimage of Grace**, an uprising in the North of England, takes place
- **24 October 1537 Jane Seymour** (b.1508), Henry VIII's third wife, dies after giving birth to Edward VI
- **1537 Franco-Ottoman alliance** against Habsburgs in the Mediterranean

This illustration from the *Vallard Atlas* of 1547 depicts Jacques Cartier and members of the abortive French–Canadian colony of 1541–42.

“ I AM INCLINED TO BELIEVE THAT **THIS IS THE LAND GOD GAVE TO CAIN.** ”

Jacques Cartier, French explorer, about Canada, 1536

THE BATTLE OF PREVEZA, fought off western Greece in September 1538, further underlined the reach of Ottoman naval power. It pitched the Ottomans against a combined Papal, Venetian, Genoese, and Spanish fleet brought together by Pope Paul III. The **Ottoman victory** highlighted the difficulty the Christians faced in welding together disparate, uneasily allied forces.

In August 1539, **Ghent**, the birthplace of Charles V, **rose in revolt** against him. The issue was tax, demanded by Charles to finance his Italian wars. It revealed the difficulties faced by Charles V in imposing authority over autonomous cities determined to guard their "liberties" by refusing to pay a distant ruler for an equally distant campaign. Charles personally oversaw the suppression of the revolt and the city's notables were forced to parade barefoot. The underlying tension, however, remained.

Despite concerted efforts, the **Spanish exploration of North America** in the 16th century proved discouraging. The myths that drove it – a waterway linking the Atlantic and Pacific, the "Seven Cities of Gold" – proved to be just that. The reality was vast territories that proved hostile and unrewarding. Nonetheless, from 1539, **Hernando de Soto** led a four-year expedition across much of the southern territories of today's US. Similarly, in 1540–42, **Francisco Vázquez de Coronado** headed a still larger force north from Mexico, penetrating as far as Kansas. And in 1542–43, **Juan Rodríguez Cabrillo** led a fleet north along the unknown Pacific coast, discovering San Diego harbour. But none of these ventures would be followed up until the end of the century.

French attempts at settlement in North America, promoted in part by nervousness of being beaten to it by Spain (just as Spain was anxious not to be outflanked by France), proved no more fruitful. Initial efforts had been made in 1534 and then in 1535–36 by **Jacques Cartier** (1491–1557), in the course of which the Gulf of St Lawrence and then the St Lawrence River in present-day **Canada** were reached and claimed for France. In 1541, by now thoroughly alarmed by Spanish intentions, a more substantial French expedition was sent to Canada with the explicit goal of establishing a permanent settlement. It was led by Jean-Francois de la Rocque de Roberval, with Cartier his deputy, and was a dismal failure. Cartier returned, unauthorized, to France in 1542 with "gold and diamonds" that proved worthless. Roberval abandoned the colony the following year after a winter of near starvation. French efforts in North America would not be renewed for half a century.

A consequence of the Catholic response to the Reformation was the missionary work undertaken between 1541 and 1552 by **Francis Xavier** (1506–52), a co-founder of the **Jesuits** in 1534. Conceived on an heroic scale, its aim was to spread Christianity to East Asia. Xavier travelled via Mozambique to Goa, then to the Spice Islands between 1545 and 1547, and then to Canton and Japan before returning to China, where he died in 1552. His Christian conversions are said to have been exceeded only by St Paul.

Battle of Préveza
Despite the size of the Christian fleet at the Battle of Préveza in September 1538, it proved no match for the Ottoman fleet led by Khair ed-Din (Barbarossa).

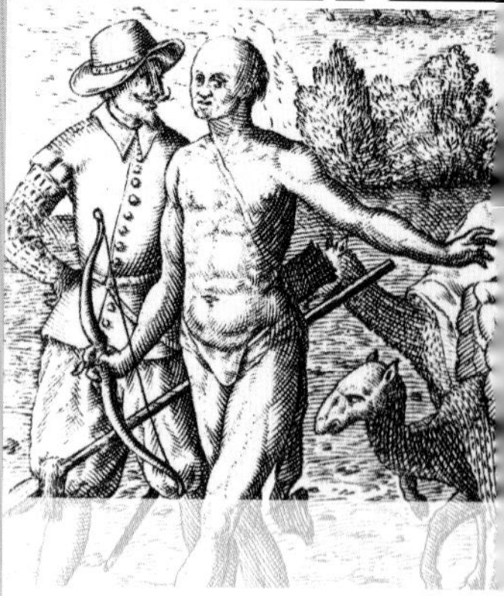

THE FIRST CONTACT BETWEEN EUROPE AND JAPAN WAS IN 1543. According to the Portuguese writer and explorer **Fernão Mendes Pinto**, it occurred on the island of Tanegashima, to the south of the main Japanese archipelago. Not only did the Portuguese introduce firearms to Japan, but they became intermediaries between China and Japan, whose merchants had been forbidden to trade with the Chinese as a result of persistent raids by Japanese pirates.

In 1543, the Polish mathematician **Nicolaus Copernicus** (1473–1543) published *On the Revolution of the Heavenly Bodies*. It was based not on Copernicus's own observations of the heavens so much as on those of Greek and Arab astronomers. Nonetheless, he was able to demonstrate that these much older observations were more readily explained by the **Earth orbiting the Sun** rather

Copernicus's Universe
This painting by Andreas Cellarius from 1660 shows "The system of the entire created Universe according to Copernicus".

28 September 1538 Ottomans win **Battle of Préveza**

1538 Portuguese subjugation of **Yemen and Aden**

August 1539 Revolt in **Ghent** suppressed by Charles V

1539 Hernando de Soto explores southern North America (to 1543)

6 January 1540 Henry VIII marries **Anne of Cleves** (1515–57), his fourth wife

28 July 1540 Execution of **Thomas Cromwell** (born c.1485), Henry VIII's chief minister

28 July 1540 Henry VIII marries **Catherine Howard**, his fifth wife

27 September 1540 Papal authority granted to the **Jesuits**

1540 Mughal expansion temporarily halted by **Afghans**

1540 Portuguese trade links established with **Cochin China** (present-day Vietnam)

1540 Pedro de Valdivia crosses the Atacama Desert, Peru, extending Spanish conquests to the south

1540 Francisco Vásquez de Coronado explores southwest North America (to 1542)

7 April 1541 Jesuit mission to the Far East led by **Francis Xavier** departs from Portugal

26 June 1541 Assassination of Spanish conquistador **Francisco Pizarro** (born c.1471/1476)

1541 Jacques Cartier founds **Charlesbourg-Royal**, French colony in Canada (abandoned 1543)

1541 Southern part of **Hungary** made an Ottoman province

13 February 1542 Catherine Howard executed (born c.1520–25)

6 May 1542 Francis Xavier arrives in Goa

26 August 1542 Spaniard **Francisco de Orellana** completes first navigation of entire Amazon River

28 September 1542 Portuguese explorer **Juan Rodríquez Cabrillo** lands at present-day San Diego while exploring the Californian coast

Natives and llamas were pressed into service to transport silver from Potosí, Bolivia. The sprawling shanty town became the largest in the New World.

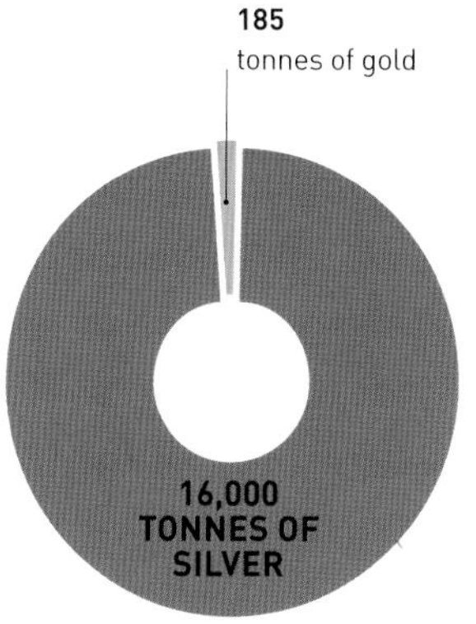

Gold and silver shipped to Seville
The silver mountain at Potosí meant it dominated the exports of precious metals shipped to Spain from Chile and Mexico from 1503 to1660.

than the other way round. It took others, notably the Danish astronomer Tycho Brahe in the 1570s, to show by direct observation that Copernicus was right. But a major breach in the geocentric universe theory had been made.

Also published in 1543 was Vesalius's *On the Fabric of the Human Body*. Like Copernicus, **Andreas Vesalius** (1514–64) looked to ancient Greek learning. Unlike him, he made his own direct observations, based on dissections of human bodies. If any moment can be pinpointed as initiating a **scientific revolution** in the West – the belief the world is best understood by empirical observation – it was perhaps this.

Ever since the formation of the Protestant **Schmalkaldic League** in 1531, Charles V had been forced to skirt its threat to his authority as Holy Roman Emperor. Persistently distracted by the French and the Ottomans, he had had little option but to appease the league (see 1532) and only in 1546, with France temporarily sidelined after the **Treaty of Crépy** of 1544, did he feel able to confront it directly. The result, decided at the **Battle of Mühlberg** in April 1547, was an overwhelming military success for Charles. The longer-term consequences were mixed.

In 1545, Spanish colonists discovered at **Potosí**, in present-day Bolivia, the biggest single concentration of silver ever found – in effect an entire mountain of silver. Together with silver found in northern Mexico, it would prove to be the motor of the cash-hungry Spanish Empire, for it was New World silver from Potosí that drove Spanish trade with China just as it financed Spain's attempts at European dominance.

In the same year, at Trent in the Italian Alps, the Catholic Church set out to challenge the Protestant Reformation by reforming and remodelling itself. The **Council of Trent** aimed to eradicate corruption, make the Church's teachings more coherent, and to project itself as a dynamic and competitive religious force. It gave rise to a series of **new Catholic orders** and met twice more, between 1551–52 and 1559–63.

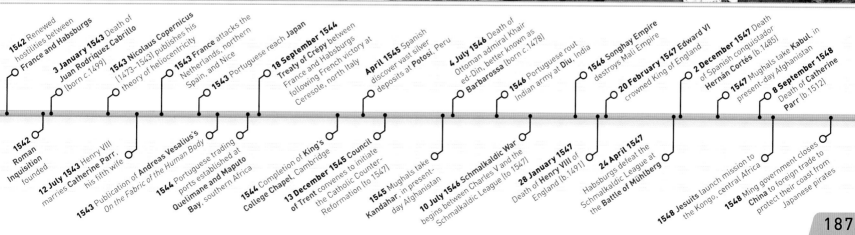

The Portuguese arrive in Japan
Portuguese merchants display some of their wares to the intrigue of the locals on their arrival on Japanese shores in 1543.

1542 Renewed hostilities between **France and Habsburgs**

1542 **Roman Inquisition** founded

3 January 1543 Death of **Juan Rodríguez Cabrillo** (born c.1499)

1543 Nicolaus Copernicus (1473–1543) publishes his theory of heliocentricity

12 July 1543 Henry VIII marries **Catherine Parr**, his fifth wife

1543 France attacks the Netherlands, northern Spain, and Nice

1543 Portuguese reach **Japan**

1543 Publication of **Andreas Vesalius's** *On the Fabric of the Human Body*

1544 Portuguese trading ports established at **Quelimane and Maputo Bay**, southern Africa

18 September 1544 Treaty of Crépy between France and Habsburgs following French victory at Ceresole, north Italy

1544 Completion of **King's College Chapel**, Cambridge

April 1545 Spanish discover vast silver deposits at **Potosí**, Peru

13 December 1545 Council of Trent convenes to initiate the Catholic Counter-Reformation (to 1547)

1545 Mughals take **Kandahar**, in present-day Afghanistan

4 July 1546 Death of Ottoman admiral Khair ed-Din, better known as **Barbarossa** (born c.1478)

10 July 1546 Schmalkaldic War begins between Charles V and the Schmalkaldic League (to 1547)

1546 Portuguese rout Indian army at **Diu**, India

1546 Songhay Empire destroys Mali Empire

28 January 1547 Death of **Henry VIII** of England (b.1491)

20 February 1547 Edward VI crowned King of England

24 April 1547 Habsburgs defeat the Schmalkaldic League at the **Battle of Mühlberg**

2 December 1547 Death of Spanish conquistador **Hernán Cortés** (b.1485)

1547 Mughals take **Kabul**, in present-day Afghanistan

1548 Jesuits launch mission to the Kongo, central Africa

8 September 1548 Death of **Catherine Parr** (b.1512)

1548 Ming government closes **China** to foreign trade to protect their coast from Japanese pirates

1549–51

> **"ART OWES** ITS **ORIGIN TO NATURE...** THIS BEAUTIFUL CREATION... **SUPPLIED** THE **FIRST MODEL,** WHILE THE **ORIGINAL TEACHER WAS** THAT **DIVINE INTELLIGENCE..."**
>
> **Giorgio Vasari**, from *Lives of the Most Excellent Italian Painters...* 1550

THE ACCESSION OF THE NINE-YEAR-OLD EDWARD VI (1537–53) to the English throne in 1547 marked a violent break with his father's religious settlement. Henry VIII's Church of England (see 1534) was Protestant only in its rejection of papal authority. Edward VI, guided by the actively Protestant **Lord Protector, the Duke of Somerset**, acting head of the government, and **Thomas Cranmer** (1489–1556), the Archbishop of Canterbury, introduced a new, vehemently Protestant church, given legal force in 1549 by the **Act of Uniformity**. Many of the outward forms of **Catholic worship**, including bell-ringing, were **forbidden**. It was reinforced by the publication of Cranmer's *Book of Common Prayer* – its use was compulsory.

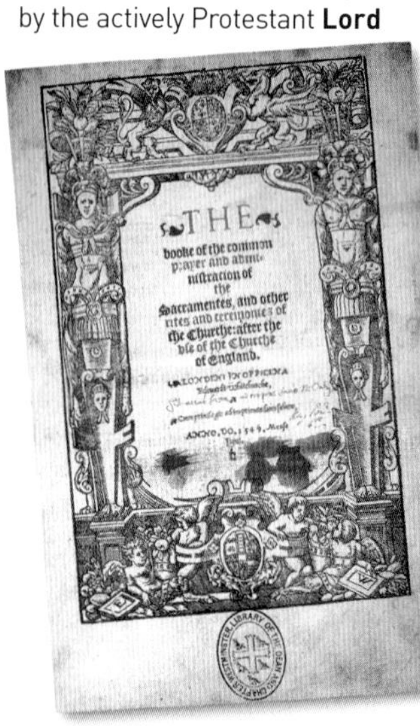

Book of Common Prayer
The Book of Common Prayer made English the language of the English Church for the first time. It also provoked bitter protests and uprisings.

When the first **Portuguese Governor-General**, Tomé de Sousa, arrived in **Brazil** in 1549 he was accompanied by five Jesuits, sent at the express wish of the Portuguese king, João III, and led by Manuel de Nóbrega (1517–70). The **Jesuits** (see 1533–34), in other words, were central to the Portuguese colonization of Brazil from the beginning. Nóbrega not only celebrated the first mass in Brazil, at Salvador, first capital of the new colony, he established the **first Jesuit College in the New World**. He and his companions proved energetic missionaries, establishing **schools** and **chapels** and, importantly, concentrating their efforts among the natives' children. He was a consistent champion of the Indians in the face of routine brutality by the Portuguese colonizers.

Throughout the 16th century, the **North African coast** was one of the key battlegrounds between the Christian West, chiefly Spain, and the Ottomans for control of the Mediterranean. Spain needed to eradicate the devastating raids by **Barbary pirates** – actively encouraged by the Ottomans – that permanently threatened to disrupt Habsburg communications with its Italian lands. The **fall of Tripoli** to the Ottomans in 1551, with some assistance from French ships, was a striking blow to Habsburg strategic hopes, just as it marked a significant **victory for the Turks**. The city withstood repeated efforts to retake it.

1552–54

The only surviving child of Henry VIII and Catherine of Aragon, Mary I was the first queen of England to rule in her own right.

IN 1552, THE LAST CHAPTER of the 60-plus years of the **Italian Wars** (see 1505–12) was opened. It saw France allied with the Ottomans in the Mediterranean, and with a series of German Protestant princes, notably Maurice of Saxony, in Germany. England would make a late and disastrous contribution to the Spanish cause in 1557. This came about because Henry VIII's daughter, **Mary**, became queen in 1553 and **married** Charles V's son, the future **Philip II of Spain**, in 1554. That the ruler of an England that had been Protestant since 1534 should be married to the son of the most militantly Catholic ruler in Europe is easily explained. Where her brother, Edward VI, had been aggressively Protestant (see 1549–51), **Mary I was no less aggressively Catholic**, determined on the full restoration of Catholic – and papal – supremacy. In the space of less than a year, England was wrenched from one religious extreme to another. From 1555, she began the systematic **persecution** of leading **Protestant** figures, 283 of whom she had **burned alive** – hence her later demonization as **Bloody Mary**.

Burned at the stake
Michael Servetus died in Geneva, a copy of his book chained to his leg, uttering the words: "Jesus, Son of the Eternal God, have mercy on me."

4:1 **Heretics put to death**
During her five-year rule, Mary I had 283 Protestants burnt at the stake for heresy – 227 of them were men and 56 were women.

The execution in Geneva in October 1553 of the Spanish theologian and radical **humanist**, **Michael Servetus**, burned at the stake at the express command of the French religious reformer **John Calvin** (1509–64), marked a critical moment in the **Reformation** (see 1516–18). Servetus was a keen exponent, guilty in Calvin's view of "execrable blasphemies" because he rejected Calvin's belief in predestination – that all events are "willed by God", with eternal salvation available only to those who submit to God's will (largely as defined by Calvin). What was significant about the death of Servetus was that for the first time it made plain that Protestantism was every bit as intolerant of heresy as Catholicism. The implications were bleakly ominous.

1555–56

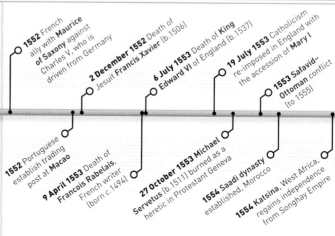

This copper engraving depicts the Peace of Augsburg of 1555.

THE FINAL PHASE OF THE ITALIAN WARS made plain that Charles V could never impose himself militarily on those of his nominal subjects within the Holy Roman Empire who had embraced Protestantism. Charles accordingly, and reluctantly, allowed his brother Archduke Ferdinand, Holy Roman Emperor designate, to negotiate a compromise, the **Peace of Augsburg**, agreed in September 1555. At its heart was a formula – *cuius regio eius religio* ("whose realm, his religion") – that allowed each ruler to **impose his own religion** on his territory. Tolerance of this sort suggested a major breakthrough. But the choice was between Catholicism and Lutheranism only – Calvinism (see 1552–54) was not included.

The accession of the 14-year-old **Akbar** to the **Mughal throne** in 1556 marked a decisive moment in the dynasty's fortunes. His father, Humayun, had seen a substantial erosion of Mughal power in the face of Afghan and Hindu advances. Having fought off a determined Hindu attempt on his throne at the **Second Battle of Panipat** in November 1556, Akbar presided over an enormous expansion of Mughal power.

The claims of **Russia's tsars** to be the sole legitimate heirs of Rome and, therefore, the only guardians of Christianity led naturally to a belief that the expansion of Russia by conquest was not just desirable but inevitable. Under **Ivan IV**, known as **"the Terrible"** (1530–84), such ambitious assertions were

March 1549 Salvador da Bahia established as Brazil's first colonial capital

27 July 1549 Jesuit **Francis Xavier** arrives in Japan

1549 First Book of Common Prayer published in England

1549 Jesuits begin mission to Brazil

1550 Helsinki founded by King Gustav I of Sweden

1550 Magdeburg, centre of Protestant opposition, **besieged** by Charles V

1550 Publication of Georgio Vasari's *Lives of the Most Excellent Italian Painters, Sculptors and Architects*

21 April 1551 Death of Japanese warlord **Oda Nobuhide** (b.1510)

1551 Ottomans recapture **Tripoli**

1552 French ally with **Maurice of Saxony** against Charles V, who is driven from Germany

1552 Portuguese establish trading post at **Macao**

2 December 1552 Death of Jesuit **Francis Xavier** (b.1506)

9 April 1553 Death of **Francois Rabelais,** French writer (born c.1494)

6 July 1553 Death of **King Edward VI** of England (b.1537)

19 July 1553 Catholicism re-imposed in England with the accession of **Mary I**

27 October 1553 Michael Servetus (b.1511) burned as a heretic in Protestant Geneva

1553 Safavid–Ottoman conflict (to 1555)

1554 Saadi dynasty established, Morocco

1554 Katsina, West Africa, regains independence from Songhay Empire

23 January 1555 Shaanxi earthquake in northwest China kills estimated 830,000

12 July 1555 Creation of the **Jewish Ghetto** in Rome by order of Pope Paul IV

25 September 1555 Lutheran princes guaranteed freedom of religion at **Peace of Augsburg**

25 October 1555 Charles V progressively **abdicates** (to 1558)

This oil painting shows Henri II of France and Philip II of Spain meeting at Cateau-Cambrésis on 3 April 1559 to sign the peace treaty. In reality, it was signed by their ambassadors.

Akbar the Great in procession
During the 46-year reign of Akbar, Mughal India enjoyed expansion of territory, prosperity, religious tolerance, and cultural richness.

significantly boosted. Although his efforts in the west were thwarted by Lithuanian arms, those to the south were strikingly successful. He had already conquered the Khanate of Kazan in 1552. In 1556, he achieved an even more notable breakthrough, destroying the enfeebled Khanate of Astrakhan.

Russia now found itself not only in control of the **trade routes to Central Asia**, it was also poised to sweep eastwards across Siberia.

THE TENSE RELATIONS BETWEEN the Portuguese, who had been attempting to establish trading posts in China since 1513, and the **Chinese**, always suspicious of Portuguese intentions, had thawed during the 1540s to the point that by 1552 China agreed to allow **Portugal a trading post in Macau** on the south coast of China. It was the key foothold the Portuguese had been seeking. By 1557, this temporary settlement had become permanent. It would, in turn, prove a crucial link in the Portuguese, later Spanish, global trading system. Macau remained Portuguese until 1999.

In 1557, **Mary I of England** (see 1552–54) was persuaded by her husband Philip II to join Spain in its renewed **war with France**. This proved disastrous, leading directly to the **loss of Calais to the French** in January 1558; Calais had been English since 1360 and was the country's last foothold in continental Europe. Mary had been unable to have children and when she died in November 1558, she was succeeded by her Protestant half-sister Elizabeth I, the daughter of Anne Boleyn.

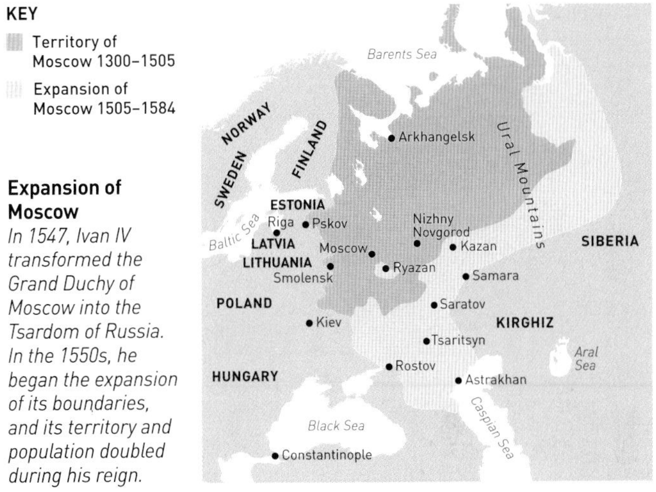

Expansion of Moscow
In 1547, Ivan IV transformed the Grand Duchy of Moscow into the Tsardom of Russia. In the 1550s, he began the expansion of its boundaries, and its territory and population doubled during his reign.

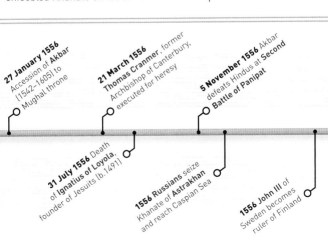

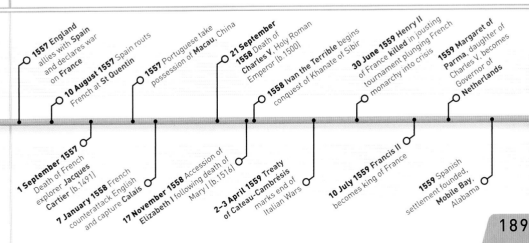

Capture of Calais
This enamel plaque by French artist Leonard Limosin celebrates the capture of Calais by French forces led by Francis, Duke of Guise on 7 January 1558.

The **Treaty of Cateau-Cambrésis** of April 1559 marked the definitive **end of the Italian Wars**. It proved a short-lived success. Habsburg Spain was the clear victor, its dominance in Italy absolute (at the expense of the papacy as much as of France). For its part, France kept Calais as well as Metz, Toul, and Verdun. By the terms of the treaty, Philip II was tacitly making plain that the military and financial contributions of the Netherlands to the conflict had been principally to advance Spain's Italian goals. Future conflict in the Spanish Netherlands was more or less guaranteed. A less predictable consequence was the **death of the French king, Henry II** (b.1519) three months later in a tournament held to celebrate the treaty. The succession of boy-kings that followed led France to 40 years of bitter civil war (see 1572).

In 1558, **Tsar Ivan IV** continued his policy of **Russian expansion** with the beginning of the settlement of the Khanate of Sibir (western Siberia). Ivan's conquest of Kazan in 1552 had opened up the way to the Urals and Siberia to the east. Colonization was led by rich merchants, such as the Stroganovs, who had been granted estates and tax privileges by Ivan in the lands they took. Protected by Cossacks, **large-scale migration** into Siberia followed in the 1570s, establishing trade links with local tribes. The Khanate of Sibir was eventually conquered in 1582, greatly increasing the size of Russia.

27 January 1556 Accession of **Akbar** (1542–1605) to Mughal throne

31 July 1556 Death of **Ignatius of Loyola**, founder of Jesuits (b.1491)

21 March 1556 **Thomas Cranmer**, former Archbishop of Canterbury, executed for heresy

1556 Russians seize Khanate of **Astrakhan** and reach Caspian Sea

5 November 1556 Akbar defeats Hindus at **Second Battle of Panipat**

1556 John III of Sweden becomes ruler of Finland

1557 England allies with **Spain** and declares war on **France**

1 September 1557 Death of French explorer **Jacques Cartier** (b.1491)

10 August 1557 Spain routs French at **St Quentin**

7 January 1558 French counterattack English and capture **Calais**

1557 Portuguese take possession of **Macau**, China

17 November 1558 Accession of **Elizabeth I** following death of Mary I (b.1516)

21 September 1558 Death of **Charles V**, Holy Roman Emperor (b.1500)

1558 Ivan the Terrible begins conquest of Khanate of Sibir

2–3 April 1559 Treaty of Cateau-Cambrésis marks end of Italian Wars

30 June 1559 Henry II of France **killed** in jousting tournament plunging French monarchy into crisis

10 July 1559 Francis II becomes king of France

1559 Margaret of Parma, daughter of Charles V, becomes Governor of **Netherlands**

1559 Spanish settlement founded, **Mobile Bay**, Alabama

Lacquer inro
1750–1799
Inros were small boxes hung from the belt and secured by a netsuke. This lacquer and gold example is decorated with scenes around Kyoto.

Wrestler's netsuke
1800–1850
In the Edo period much ingenuity went into the designs of carved toggles called netsuke. This example, depicting a snail on a mushroom, is made of boxwood.

Tea jar
17th century
This formerly lidded jar is Agano stoneware. Its shape, black body, and blue glaze imitate wares imported from China for the tea ceremony.

Porcelain tea bowl
1700–1750
Used as a delicate cup, this example of blue-and-white Arita ware, decorated with figures, imitates a design of the Chinese Kangxi dynasty period (1662–1722).

Imari charger
Edo period
Vast quantities of Imari porcelain, named after its principal port of distribution, have featured this charger's palette, dominated by blue, pink, and orange shades.

EDO PERIOD

JAPANESE ARTS FLOURISHED UNDER THE TOKUGAWA SHOGUNS' RULE

The Edo period (1603–1868) was one of peace. The merchant class grew wealthier and better educated, and began to enjoy arts that were previously the preserve of the landowning elites and the samurai warrior class.

Japanese craftsmen were inspired by the culture of *ukiyo* (Floating World), itself inspired by the Buddhist idea that all is illusion. In Edo Japan *ukiyo* became associated with fleeting pleasures – from dallying with courtesans to attending kabuki dance dramas. Craftsmen strove for an aesthetic of otherworldly elegance. Surrounded by beauty, their clients set about their pursuits, from writing to prayer, as though they too were part of the illusory Floating World.

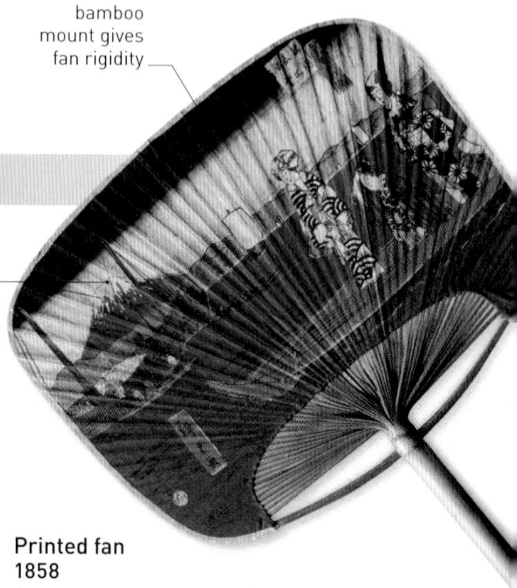

Printed fan
1858
This late Edo artefact is made of split bamboo and paper. On each side is a different silkscreen-printed scene by Hiroshige II (1826–69).

Wooden Buddha figure
18th century
Buddhism lay at the heart of Tokugawa ideas of a coherent society. This small figure was kept as a reminder of Buddha.

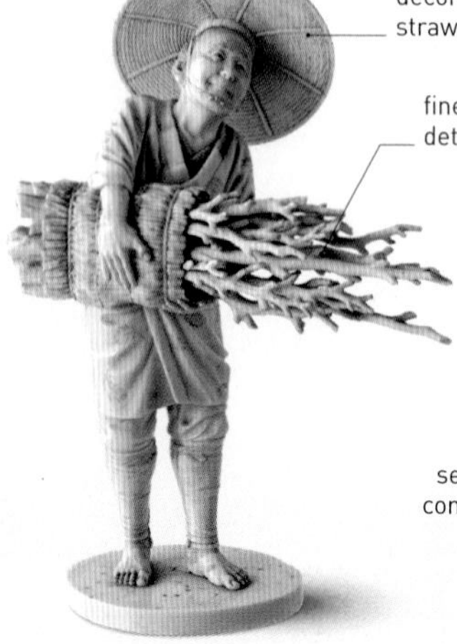

Ivory figure
18th century
This delicately carved ivory figure of an old woman carrying a bundle of faggots carries the inscription of Gyokusen.

Brass lantern
18th century
Intended for exterior use, probably at an entrance approach, this monumental brass lantern disassembles into five parts.

Folding screen
Edo period
Sliding panels (*fusuma*) and folding screens served as movable interior walls in Edo Japan.

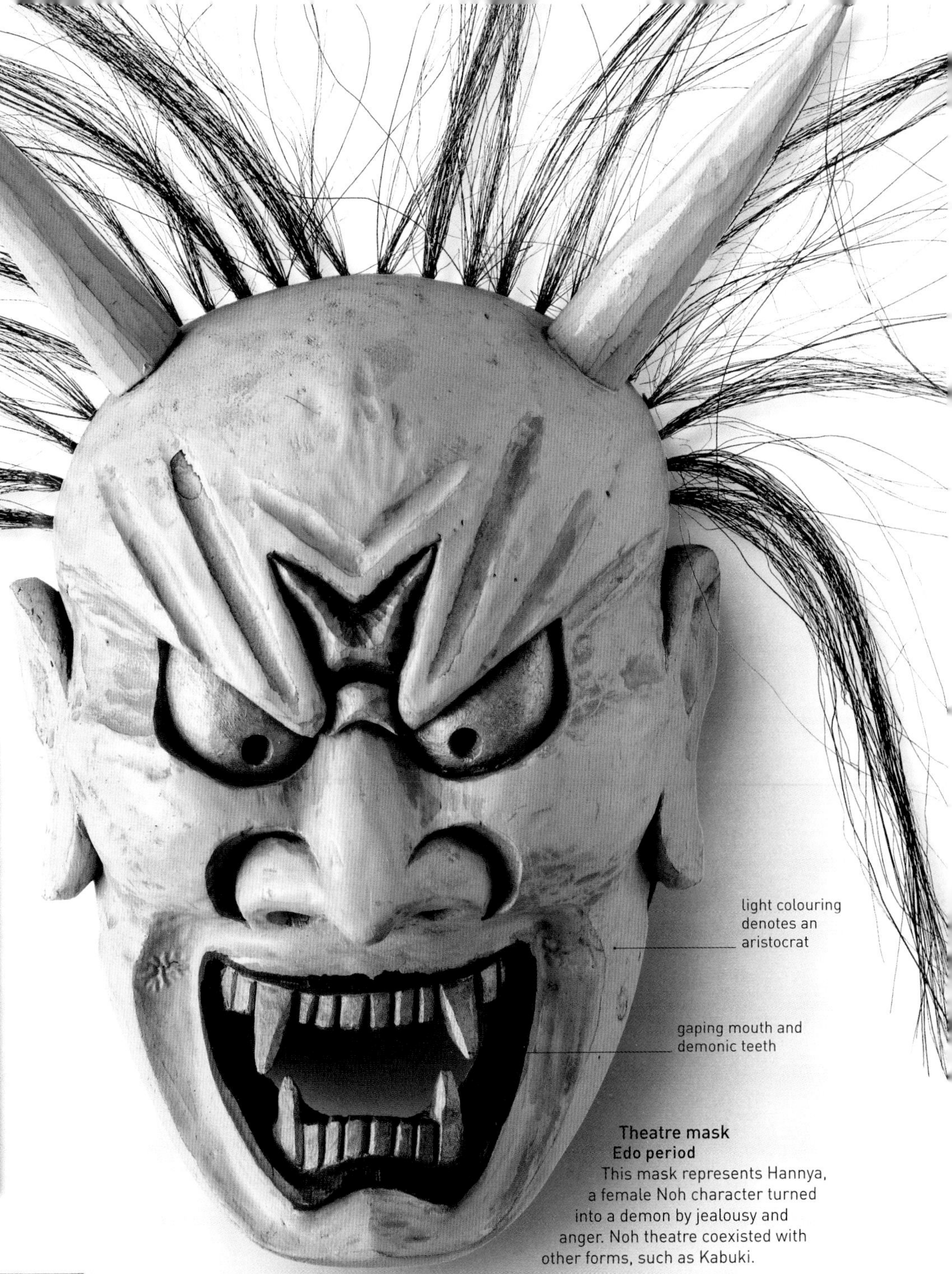

Theatre mask
Edo period
This mask represents Hannya, a female Noh character turned into a demon by jealousy and anger. Noh theatre coexisted with other forms, such as Kabuki.

Brocade picture
18th century
Entitled *Truth-Sincerity*, this is one of the *nishiki-e* (brocade pictures) of Suzuki Harunobu (*c.*1725–70), made by superimposing printings of woodblocks inked with a range of colours.

Writing tools
1800–1899
Calligraphy was widely practised by the well-to-do as a leisure pursuit. The compartments of this box contain brushes and other paraphernalia of the art.

Bound woodblock prints
1779
A monochrome print consists of a single impression from a carved woodblock. Some later examples were hand-coloured, in anticipation of colour printing.

“ WITHOUT DESTRUCTION,
THERE IS **NO CREATION...**
THERE IS **NO CHANGE. ”**

Oda Nobunaga (1534–82)

Oda Nobunaga ruthlessly broke the military power of Japan's leading regional warlords in a drive for control that eventually united Japan.

BY ABOUT 1560, ODA NOBUNAGA, LEADER OF THE ODA CLAN in central Japan, was emerging as the greatest of the country's regional warlords, or *daimyo*. Since the calamitous Onin War, which began in 1466, **Japan had been effectively ungovernable** – the *daimyo* brutally vying for supremacy. The arrival of the Portuguese in the mid-15th century, bringing with them firearms, added to the chaos – the Japanese proved to be ready students of the possibilities of Western-style artillery bombardments (see 1574–77).

From 1561, the substantial **Baltic territories** of the **Livonian Order** (see 1236–40), which had already lost East Prussia in 1525 when the Teutonic Grand Master, Albrecht von Hohenzollern, converted to Protestantism, were **progressively dismembered** by Russia, Sweden, Poland, and Denmark. Originally a Crusading (that is, Christian) frontier entity, Livonia was a victim in part of the Reformation, but more of Polish–Russian rivalries – neither willing to see the other strengthened in the region at its own expense.

Few conflicts were more destablizing than the **French Wars of Religion**, which began in 1562 and dragged on until 1598. There were, technically, eight separate wars; in reality, it was a single, long-drawn-out struggle. On one level, it was a purely religious conflict – was France to be Catholic or Protestant? Inevitably, this meant that the principal **Catholic and Protestant rulers of Europe** were periodically **dragged into the conflict**, neither the pope nor Philip II of Spain wanting a Protestant triumph any more than the Protestant rulers wanted a Catholic one. Yet it was also a matter of determining who exercised authority in France – the crown or the nobles, whether **Catholic or Huguenot**. The French Protestants were known as Huguenots, from the Swiss–German *Eidgenossen* or "oath companions". The Catholics were in the majority, but the Huguenots were exceptionally well organized. Both parties had powerful aristocratic leaders for whom the struggle was also political. A royal minority always brought political instability in its wake (see 1557–59), but from 1560 it was compounded by three successive kings who had very limited ability to manage the nobles. As none produced an heir and civil war intensified, what was at stake by the end was not just the country's religious destiny but royal authority itself.

Massacre of Huguenots
The killing of 80 Huguenots at Vassy in northeast France in March 1562 was the spark that began the French Wars of Religion.

44 THE NUMBER OF **KNIGHTS WHO** SERVED AS **GRAND MASTER** OF THE **LIVONIAN ORDER**

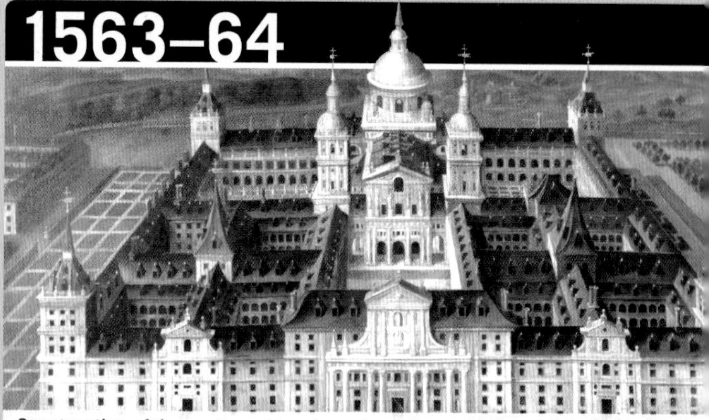

Construction of the austere yet vast royal residence, El Escorial, began in 1563. It was intended to underline the piety as well as the majesty of Spain's rulers.

IN 1563, SWEDEN AND DENMARK CLASHED FOR SUPREMACY in the Baltic. The **first modern naval war ensued** – that is, with sailing ships, rather than galleys (as was still common in the Mediterranean), heavily armed with cannon. Both countries were competing for control of the maritime invasion routes, the Danes supported by the semi-independent German city of Lübeck. **Seven major naval battles** were fought between 1563 and 1570, by which point both sides were effectively bankrupt. As other countries would discover, custom-built **men-of-war** may have been the most formidably **powerful weapons of the period** but the ships were prodigiously expensive. The war ended with no territorial gain for either side.

Escaping persecution at home, in 1564 a group of **Huguenot settlers** established a **colony in Florida** on the banks of the St John's River on the site of what today is Jacksonville. Called **Fort Caroline**, it was the **first French colony** in what would become the US. It lasted little more than a year before it was **destroyed by a Spanish force** determined not to allow French settlers, especially Protestant ones, to encroach on a territory where they enjoyed superiority. All the settlers and the relieving force, bar a number of women and children, were killed. In revenge, in 1568, a **French force destroyed a Spanish colony, Fort Matanzas**, built after the destruction of Fort Caroline.

Battle of Oland
The Danes were victorious at the Battle of Oland on 30–31 May 1564, during which the Swedes lost their new royal flagship, Mars.

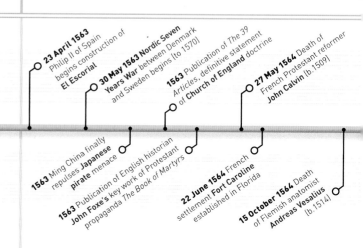

19 April 1560 Death of German reformer **Philipp Melanchthon** (b.1497)

5 December 1560 Death of Francis II (b.1544); his mother **Catherine de Medici** becomes Regent of France

6 December 1560 Charles IX (1550–74) becomes king of France

1560 Foundations laid for the eventual unification of Japan under **Oda Nobunaga** (1534–82)

1560 Portuguese begin **sugarcane cultivation** in Brazil

1560 Diplomat Jean Nicot (1530–1600) introduces **tobacco** from New World to French court

1561 Collapse of Livonian Order and subsequent partition of **Livonia**

1561 Completion of **St Basil's Cathedral**, Moscow

1 March 1562 Massacre at Vassy marks start of **French Wars of Religion** (to 1598)

1562 Ottomans occupy **Transylvania**

c.1562 Flemish artist **Peter Breugel the Elder** (c.1525–69) paints *The Triumph of Death*

23 April 1563 Philip II of Spain begins construction of **El Escorial**

1563 Ming China finally repulses **Japanese pirate** menace

30 May 1563 Nordic Seven Years War between Denmark and Sweden begins (to 1570)

1563 Publication of English historian **John Foxe's** key work of Protestant propaganda *The Book of Martyrs*

1563 Publication of *The 39 Articles*, definitive statement of **Church of England** doctrine

22 June 1564 French settlement **Fort Caroline** established in Florida

27 May 1564 Death of French Protestant reformer **John Calvin** (b.1509)

15 October 1564 Death of Flemish anatomist **Andreas Vesalius** (b.1514)

1565–67

Breugel's *Massacre of the Innocents* notionally has a Biblical subject, but in reality it is a commentary on Spanish brutality during the Dutch Revolt.

IN ESTABLISHING HIS OWN BRAND of divinely sanctioned Orthodox absolutism, **Ivan IV** (see panel, right) never had to contend with the substantial vested interests – mercantile, aristocratic, or clerical – that frustrated his counterparts in Western Europe. His principal opponents were the Cossacks – free-ranging frontiersmen – and the boyars, the hereditary nobility.

Spanish settlement
St Augustine in Florida, founded by Spain in August 1565, is the oldest continuously inhabited European settlement in North America.

The **Cossacks were co-opted as allies** by the obvious strategy of bribing them, while, from 1565, the **boyars were dispossessed**, and in most cases slaughtered. Their former estates now became Ivan's "private domain", the *oprichina* – a vast area of central Russia parcelled out among a new nobility, the *dvoriane*, loyal to the tsar.

The key **maritime challenge confronting Spain** after its conquests in Mexico and Peru (see 1532) was to link them with the Philippines and the Spice Islands on the western extremity of the Pacific, which, in 1564, Spain determined to colonize. A westward route across the Pacific had been pioneered in 1527, but no return route was known. Between June and October 1565, Spanish navigator **Andrés de Urdaneta** made the critical breakthrough, sailing far to the north to find favourable winds in the **longest non-stop voyage yet made** – 18,700km (11,600 miles). It completed a **vital trade network**.

In much the same way that religious conflict and power politics in the French Wars of Religion produced a savage conflict, so the **Dutch Revolt** – which began in 1566 and lasted until 1648 – was the product of a toxic mix of religious intolerance and a drive for political domination. In 1566, **Philip II of Spain, Catholic ruler of the Netherlands**, asserted: "I do not propose nor desire to be the ruler of heretics." Given that there was considerable support for a growing **Protestant** minority in the **Netherlands**, his divine obligation to eradicate these heresies was inescapable. But there was a further complication. The Netherlands, whether Protestant or Catholic, had no desire to submit to Philip's rule given that this would mean surrendering its own "liberties" – its right to govern itself even while acknowledging Philip as its overall ruler. More particularly, it saw no reason why it should be forced to pay taxes to finance the Spanish king's campaigns elsewhere. While this was a problem that could never be resolved peacefully, even by the standards of the period, the resulting conflict was shocking in its violence (see 1572–73).

IVAN THE TERRIBLE
(1530–84)

Though capable of bouts of remorse – as when, in 1581, he killed his eldest son and heir by staving in his head with a staff – Ivan IV applied a ruthless brutality to his rule. Hence Ivan "the Terrible". One key consequence was that vast numbers fled Russia during his reign from 1547 to 1584, depopulating the country to the point that serfdom (bonded peasantry) was the only means of retaining an agricultural workforce.

- **13 February 1565** Spanish colonization of **Philippines** begins with settlement on Cebu
- **28 August 1565** Spanish establish **St Augustine**, Florida
- **June–October 1565 Andrés de Urdaneta** (1498–1568) pioneers return route across northern Pacific to New World
- **1565 Malta** successfully resists siege to halt Ottoman advance in western Mediterranean
- **1565 Ivan the Terrible** begins reign of terror, Russia
- **1565** Venetian artist **Tintoretto** (1518–1594) paints *Scenes from the Life of Christ*
- **19 June 1566** Birth of **James IV of Scotland/James I of England** (d.1625)
- **c.6 September 1566** Death of **Suleiman the Magnificent**, Sultan of the Ottoman Empire (b.1494)
- **2 July 1566** Death of French seer **Nostradamus** (b.1503)
- **1567** Spanish troops dispatched to **Netherlands**
- **1566 Dutch Revolt** begins (to 1648)
- **1567 Second French War of Religion** (to 1568)

1568–69

A priest blesses two soldiers in the Northern Rising of 1569, the last sustained attempt by Catholics in England to protest against the Reformation.

IN 1568, OMURA SUMIDATA, a Japanese *daimyo* who in 1563 had converted to Christianity, gave permission for Portuguese traders and missionaries to establish a port at a fishing village at the southern tip of Japan – **Nagasaki**. Until the suppression of Christianity in Japan in 1614, Nagasaki, effectively a Jesuit colony, was not only almost entirely Catholic – or "kirishitan" – it was Portugal's most important trading centre in East Asia.

The most urgent task facing **Akbar** in his consolidation of Mughal power in India (see 1555–56) was the defeat of the **Hindu Rajputs of the northwest**. This was a decade-long campaign, which climaxed in 1569 with the fall of the fortresses of Mewar and Ranthambore. Having secured the submission of the principal Rajput rulers, Akbar married a series of Hindu princesses (he had 36 wives in all), tying his defeated enemies to him in matrimonial alliances.

In 1659, the failure of **Sigismund II**, last of the Jagiellonian rulers of the Grand Duchy of Lithuania and of Poland, to produce an heir led to a formal union between the two states. This new **Polish–Lithuanian Commonwealth** became the **largest territorial state in Europe**. The move was prompted by Sigismund's desire to ensure that his dynasty's territories were preserved, and the need to protect Lithuania from the Ottomans and the Russians. The nobles of both territories quarrelled over the new constitutional arrangement, anxious it should not be to their disadvantage. For the **Poles**, the clinching factor was the **transfer to them of immense territories**, among them the **Ukraine**.

The **Northern Rising** of November 1569 was the **most serious threat to Elizabeth I's pragmatic Protestantism**. Led by the Catholic earls of Westmorland and Northumberland, it swept across northern England before being **savagely repressed**.

In 1569, the Flemish cartographer **Gerardus Mercator** (1512–94) devised a **world map** that for the first time showed the true compass bearing of every landmass. The **Mercator projection** remains the most familiar map of the world.

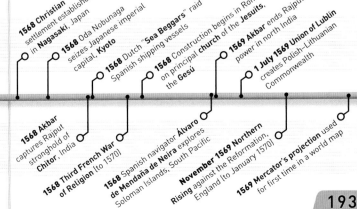

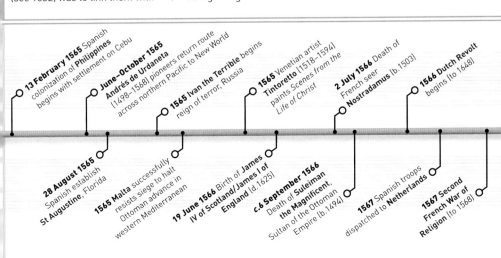

Gerardus Mercator
Mercator was an engraver and a mathematician as well as a skilled cartographer. He devised his world map of 1569 for marine navigation.

- **1568 Christian** settlement established in **Nagasaki**, Japan
- **1568 Akbar** captures Rajput stronghold of **Chitor**, India
- **1568** Oda Nobunaga seizes Japanese imperial capital, **Kyoto**
- **1568 Third French War of Religion** (to 1570)
- **1568** Dutch **"Sea Beggars"** raid Spanish shipping vessels
- **1568** Spanish navigator **Álvaro de Mendaña de Neira** explores Soloman Islands, South Pacific
- **1568** Construction begins in Rome on principal **church** of the **Jesuits**, the **Gesù**
- **November 1569 Northern Rising** against the Reformation, England (to January 1570)
- **1569 Akbar** ends Rajput power in north India
- **1 July 1569 Union of Lublin** creates Polish–Lithuanian Commonwealth
- **1569 Mercator's projection** used for first time in a world map

1570–71

“ BEAUTY WILL **RESULT FROM** THE **FORM AND** THE **CORRESPONDENCE OF** THE **WHOLE... ”**

Andrea Palladio, from *Four Books of Architecture*, 1570

Andrea Palladio, the most influential architect of the later Renaissance.

THE MANILA GALLEON was one of the most distinctive elements of Spain's **New World trading system**. From the 1570s, three galleons (two after 1593) made an annual round-trip between Acapulco in Mexico and Manila in the Philippines. In return for New World silver, Spain imported silks, spices, porcelain, lacquer ware, and ivory. It is estimated that by 1600 the value of a single cargo of these ships – the largest in the world – exceeded the entire annual revenue of the English crown.

In 1571, the **Portuguese** attempted to **colonize Angola**, but the Kimbundu people proved impossible to subdue, the soil of the coast was too poor to cultivate, and the salt trade could not be wrested from African control. They did establish trading forts at Luanda and Benguela in 1575 and 1587, boosting their slave trade.

The **Battle of Lepanto**, fought off the coast of western Greece in October 1571, was the last major engagement between galleys – with 208 Christian galleys against 251 Ottoman. The Christian fleet, commanded by **Don Juan of Austria**, illegitimate son of Charles V, triumphed, largely through its artillery. Although the Christians failed in the wider goal to retake Cyprus, the threat of Ottoman expansion in the western Mediterranean was ended.

Battle of Lepanto
An estimated 20,000 Ottomans and 7,500 Christians died at the Battle of Lepanto. The ramming tactics of the Ottoman galleys proved ineffective.

1572–73

In the background of this painting of the St Bartholomew's Day Massacre by the Huguenot François Dubois, Catherine de Medici inspects a pile of corpses.

DESPITE THE SPANISH CONQUEST of **Inca Peru** (see 1532), a remnant Inca state was set up in the Upper Amazon in 1539 under a minor Inca noble, Manco Inca Yupanqui, in a small settlement, Vilcabamba. From here, he and his descendants waged an intermittent, generally ineffective campaign against the Spanish. In 1572, Vilcabamba was overrun and **the last Inca leader, Túpac Amaru, was executed**.

In 1566, a delegation of Dutch nobles appeared before **Margaret of Parma** (1522–86), half-sister of Philip II and governor-general of the Netherlands, objecting to Philip's drive against heresy in the Netherlands. They were referred to contemptuously by one of Margaret's counsellors as *"gueux"* – "beggars". The name was enthusiastically taken up by the protesting Dutch, particularly the **Sea Beggars**, privateers (or pirates) whose raids on Spanish shipping from 1568 significantly hampered Spain's military efforts. The Sea Beggars depended to a considerable extent on support from England, discreetly doing what it could to disrupt the Spanish. But in the spring of 1572, **Elizabeth I** (see 1586–89), anxious not to offend Spain too obviously, closed English harbours to them. In response, in a more or less desperate gamble, on 1 April 1572 the Sea Beggars seized Brill in Holland. Within three months they had **taken practically every town in Zeeland and Holland**, purging them of royalists and Catholics. **William of Orange** (1533–84), politically and military the most significant figure in the Revolt, agreed to take command of them. Rebellion had turned to open war.

The **massacre of Huguenots** in Paris on 24 August 1572, St Bartholomew's Day, was the worst atrocity of the **French Wars of Religion**. It stemmed from an attempt to resolve the wars by a marriage. Henry of Navarre, a leading Huguenot close to the succession of the French throne, was to wed Marguerite of Valois, sister of the young French king, Charles IX. This was largely brokered by the king's mother, **Catherine de Medici** (see panel, right) who, as fearful for her son's throne as she was alarmed by growing Huguenot power, had nonetheless persistently sought to bring the warring factions to terms. In this over-heated atmosphere, Catholics and Huguenots descended on Paris for the marriage. However, there was a **plot to assassinate** the Huguenot's dominant figure, **Gaspard de Coligny**. Who was behind it remains uncertain. In

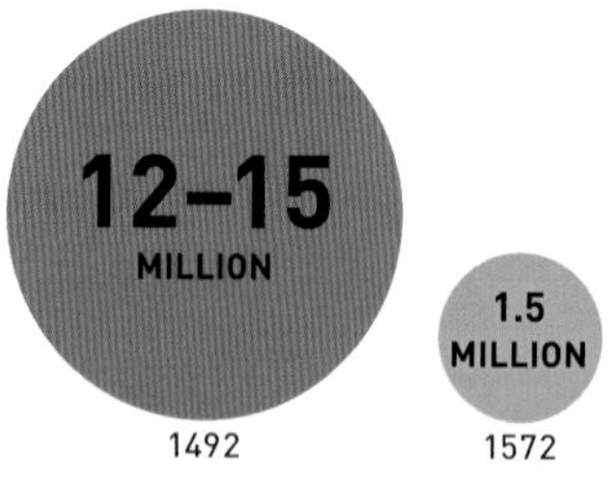

Inca population
The European conquest of the Incas was devastating. Imported European diseases rather than deliberate genocide was the chief culprit.

20 May 1570 Flemish cartographer **Abraham Ortelius** issues the first modern atlas, *Theatre of the World*

8 August 1570 Peace of St Germain ends the Third French War of Religion

1570 Cyprus taken by Ottomans

1570 Portuguese trading mission to **Nagasaki**, Japan

1570 First official shipment, via Manila, of **Spanish silver** from South and Central America reaches China

1570 Publication in Italy of *Four Books of Architecture* by **Andrea Palladio**

13 February 1571 Death of Italian artist **Benvenuto Cellini** (b.1500)

May 1571 Crimean army led by Devlet I Giray starts **Great Fire of Moscow**

7 October 1571 Ottomans defeated by combined Christian fleet at **Battle of Lepanto**

1571 Portuguese colony founded in **Angola**

1571 Oda Nobunaga destroys rebellious Ikko sect near Nara, Japan

1 April 1572 Sea Beggars revive opposition to the Spanish in the Netherlands

1572 Final collapse of Inca resistance to Spanish rule with fall of **Vilcabamba**

24 August 1572 St Bartholomew's Day **Massacre**, Paris

1572 Portuguese epic poem *Os Lusiadas* written by **Luís de Camões**

1572 Mughals overrun **Gujerat**, India

11 February 1573 Duke of Anjou leads Catholic siege of Huguenot **La Rochelle** (to 6 July)

13 July 1573 Spanish capture **Haarlem**, Netherlands after seven-month siege

July 1573 Edict of Boulogne limits Huguenot worship to La Rochelle, Montauban, and Nîmes

1574–77

“ SOVEREIGNTY IS THE **ABSOLUTE** AND PERPETUAL **POWER OF** A **COMMONWEALTH...** THE **HIGHEST POWER** OF **COMMAND... ”**

Jean Bodin, French political philosopher, 1576

1578–79

Hopelessly outnumbered, the Portuguese were in effect exterminated at the Battle of Alcácer Quibir. Portugal lost not only its king but most of its nobles.

CATHERINE DE MEDICI
(1519–89)

The Italian-born Catherine married Henry II of France in 1533. On his death in 1559, she became monarch in all but name as France fell into turmoil with her first two sons Francis II and Charles IX proving too young and inexperienced, and Henry III facing a deteriorating political situation. Her goal to preserve the Valois monarchy proved a spectacular failure.

any case, the plot failed – Coligny, though wounded, survived – but the mood in Paris became explosive. Catherine may then have persuaded the king that a Huguenot takeover was in the offing and could be forestalled only by killing all the principal Huguenots in the city. Equally, the subsequent bloodletting may have been spontaneous. At all events, not only was Coligny murdered, but **more than 3,000 Huguenots were killed**. Across France, 20,000 may have died in the following weeks.

THE NORTH AFRICAN COAST of the western Mediterranean was a key focus of **Ottoman–Christian rivalry**, with Spain, in particular, seeking to prevent Muslim raids on its shipping. Yet, gradually, the handful of North African cities in Spanish hands were lost – Algiers in 1529, Tripoli in 1551, and Bugia in 1555. By 1574, only Tunis remained. Its final fall in August 1574 to an overwhelming Ottoman fleet marked the **end of Habsburg ambitions in North Africa**, which from now was to remain firmly within the Ottoman orbit.

The **Battle of Nagashino**, fought in June 1575 between the forces of **Takeda Katsuyori** (1546–82) and an alliance led by the warlord **Oda Nobunaga** (see 1560–62), marked a decisive moment in the evolution of warfare in Japan – the first effective use of firearms. The arquebus muskets introduced by the Portuguese in the 1540s had been eagerly imitated by the Japanese despite being very slow to load. Nobunaga's solution was to have three guns for each man firing them, supported by teams of loaders. The result was a near continuous fire against which the Takeda clan's conventional cavalry and infantry were helpless.

Selimiye Mosque
Built by Mimar Sinan for Selim II in Edirne and completed in 1575, this mosque is the supreme statement of Ottoman Islamic architecture.

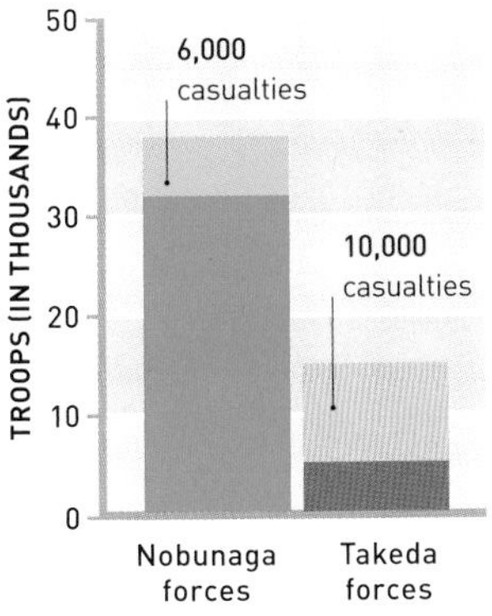

Battle of Nagashino
Nobunaga's men outnumbered the Takeda troops by more than 2:1, but it was Nobunaga's skilful use of firearms that won the day for them.

Spain's efforts to suppress the **Dutch Revolt** (see 1572–73) foundered in 1575. Unable to levy taxes in the Netherlands, Philip II could not pay his troops and they mutinied, looting and murdering indiscriminately. Philip's authority in the Netherlands disintegrated. The vacuum was filled by the Dutch themselves – Catholics and royalists as well as the rebellious Protestants. Their agreement was sealed by the **Pacification of Ghent**, signed in November 1576.

JUST AS PHILIP II'S ATTEMPTS TO REASSERT HIS AUTHORITY over the heretical Netherlands were derailed by his simultaneous need to confront the Ottomans in the Mediterranean, so the Ottomans' attempts to confront the heretical Safavids in Persia were distracted by their conflicts with Spain. The pause in the conflict after the fall of Tunis in 1574, confirmed by a peace treaty in 1580, freed both states to pursue their goals elsewhere. The benefits for the **Ottomans** were immediate – a **string of conquests in Georgia and Azerbaijan** that, by the fall of Tabriz in 1585, saw both incorporated within their empire.

In August 1578, the king of Portugal, Sebastian, was killed at the **Battle of Alcácer Quibir** in northern Morocco. The battle had two consequences. One was to confirm **Ahmad al-Mansur** (1549–1603) as the new sultan of an Ottoman-backed **Morocco**. The other was a **succession crisis in Portugal**. Sebastian's heir was his 66-year-old great-uncle, Henry, a cardinal. He died, childless, 17 months later. Among the claimants to the throne was Philip II (see 1580).

After the Pacification of Ghent (see 1576), Philip II was forced to agree not just to pull out his troops but to restore traditional privileges across the provinces. But, on the question of religion, he remained adamant – Catholicism must be restored everywhere. The violence flared again. Philip's envoy, Don Juan, stormed the city of Namur; in retaliation, Calvinist dissenters established themselves in cities across the south. In January 1579, the Catholic nobility of the south reaffirmed their loyalty to Philip, forming the **Union of Arras**. The northern provinces formed the **Union of Utrecht**. To the miseries of the Netherlands were added the horrors of civil war.

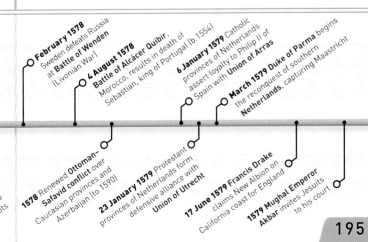

Chichak helmet
The Ottoman rawhide helmet with copper gilt was so effective it was widely imitated in Europe in the 17th century.

- **27 August 1573** **Muromachi shogunate** submits to Odo Nobunaga, Japan
- **1573** Slavery legalized in **Brazil**
- **1573** Massive peasant revolts in **Croatia and Slovenia** crushed by local nobility
- **27 June 1574** Death of **Giorgio Vasari**, Italian painter and writer (b.1511)
- **1574** Dutch force Spanish to abandon siege of **Leiden**
- **28 June 1575 Battle of Nagashino**, Japan
- **1575** Spanish agree to withdraw troops from the Netherlands at **Breda conference**
- **1575** Completion of the **Selimiye Mosque,** Erdine, Anatolia
- **8 November 1576** Dutch unite to call for the withdrawal of Spanish troops at **Pacification of Ghent**
- **27 August 1576** Death of **Titian**, Italian painter (born c.1488/1490)
- **1576** Mughals overrun **Bengal**
- **17 September 1577** **Peace of Bergerac** signed in France between Henry III and the Huguenots
- **February 1578** Sweden defeats Russia at **Battle of Wenden** (Livonian War)
- **4 August 1578** **Battle of Alcácer Quibir**, Morocco, results in death of Sebastian, king of Portugal (b.1554)
- **1578** Renewed **Ottoman–Safavid conflict** over Caucasian provinces and Azerbaijan (to 1590)
- **6 January 1579** Catholic provinces of Netherlands assert loyalty to Philip II of Spain with **Union of Arras**
- **23 January 1579** Protestant provinces of Netherlands form defensive alliance with **Union of Utrecht**
- **March 1579 Duke of Parma** begins the reconquest of southern **Netherlands**, capturing Maastricht
- **17 June 1579 Francis Drake** claims New Albion on California coast for England
- **1579 Mughal Emperor Akbar** invites Jesuits to his court

Resistance to Philip II's claim on the Portuguese crown in 1580 was weak – while an army advanced on Lisbon, the Spanish fleet assaulted it from the sea.

THE PUBLICATION IN DRESDEN of the *Book of Concord* in 1580 was a pivotal moment in the development of **Lutheranism** (see 1516–18). While reaffirming the supreme importance of the Holy Scriptures – the Bible – it set out a strict interpretation of them "as the unanimous consensus and exposition of our Christian faith". It remains the basis of Lutheran beliefs today.

Philip II of Spain's claim to the **Portuguese crown** after the throne became vacant (see 1578–79) was made good in August 1580 by a combination of military force and bribery.

> NOTHING IS SO **FIRMLY BELIEVED** AS **THAT WHICH LEAST IS KNOWN.**
>
> **Michel de Montaigne, French Renaissance writer,** *Essais Book I*

In July 1581, the northern provinces of the Netherlands – the **United Provinces** – declared their independence by the **Act of Abjuration**, renouncing their oaths of loyalty to Philip II. With the Spanish king now technically deposed, a new throne, that of the Netherlands, was created and accepted by the **Duke of Anjou** (1555–84), brother of Henry III of France. The south remained broadly loyal to Philip, but the Act's assertion that a **legal king could be legally overthrown** would have significant consequences.

Francis, Duke of Anjou
Foreign support – English or French – was essential to defeat the Spanish, so the Dutch Protestants made the Duke of Anjou their ruler in 1581.

The impact of the **Single Whip Reform**, or "simple rule", in 1581 in **Ming China** was immense. The reform meant that not only would all taxes be based on property – itself recorded in a universal census – but they would be **paid in silver**. It was introduced to simplify China's tax system and to avoid problems of inflation created by a paper currency and debased coinage. It was made possible by the inflow of Spanish and Japanese silver. The new tax system created even greater demand for bullion, raised the price of silver still further, and in the long term contributed to destabilizing the entire Ming economy.

Toyotomi Hideyoshi's victory at Shizugatake in May 1583 was typical of his ruthless deployment of overwhelming force against his enemies.

THE RITUAL SUICIDE OF ODA NOBUNAGA (see 1560–62) in 1582 brought to power his most able general, **Toyotomi Hideyoshi** (*c.*1536/37–98). Within a decade, he had succeeded in **unifying almost the whole of Japan** under his rule. It was a remarkable achievement for one born a peasant. All non-samurai were disarmed to ensure that commoners could not challenge his authority, while his reorganization of the tax system and redistribution of land guaranteed the revenues needed to complete his conquests.

On 24 February 1582, **Pope Gregory XIII** (1502–85) decreed a **revision to the Julian Calendar**, introduced in 46 BCE, which underestimated the length of every year by 11 minutes. By the late 16th century, the Julian date was 10 days adrift from the actual date, meaning that the spring equinox, from which the date of Easter was calculated, fell on 11 March rather than 21 March. Thus, for doctrinal reasons, the pope's modest adjustment was made. The change was introduced in October – Thursday 4th being followed by Friday 15th – but only in Spain, Portugal, Italy, and Poland-Lithuania. The rest of Europe, especially Protestant Europe, scenting a popish plot, was much slower to follow suit.

Songhay Empire
The death of Askia Daud in 1582 followed by the Moroccan invasion (see 1591) were key factors in the Songhay Empire's decline.

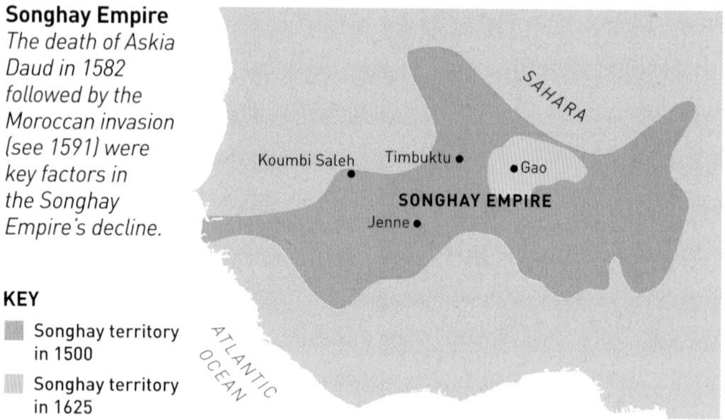

Sir Francis Drake (1540–96) became the first English captain to circumnavigate the globe in 1577–80, renewing English interest in the New World. **Sir Humphrey Gilbert** had already voyaged to **Newfoundland** in 1578–79. In 1583, he returned, with Elizabeth I's backing, and claimed it for England. In 1584, again with royal approval, **Sir Walter Raleigh** (*c.*1552–1618) sent an expedition to found the **Virginia Colony**, named for the "Virgin Queen". It was established the following year at Roanoke Island, today in North Carolina, but, by 1590, it had disappeared.

The **surrender of Antwerp** on 17 August 1585 to the Duke of Parma was not merely a striking **military triumph for Spain**, it brought the city's commercial pre-eminence to an abrupt end.

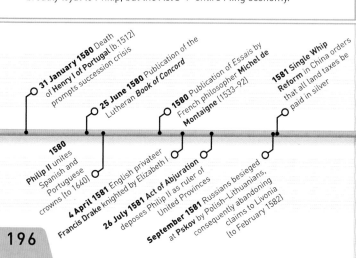

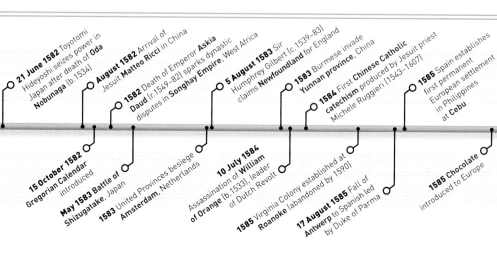

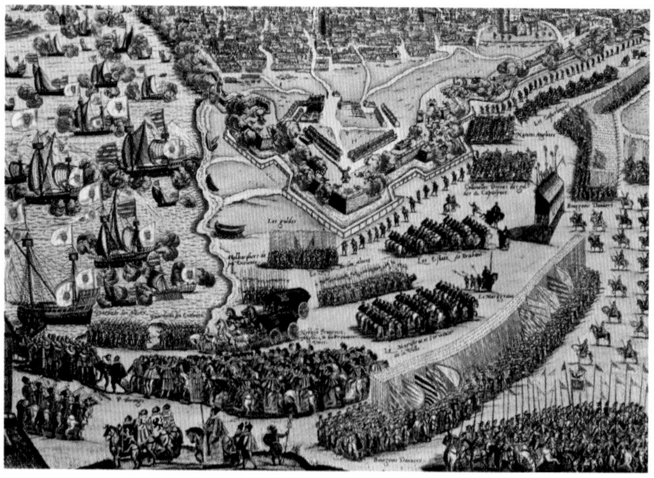

Siege of Antwerp
The 13-month siege reduced the city's population from 100,000 to 40,000, but it returned the southern Netherlands to Spanish control.

31 January 1580 Death of **Henry I of Portugal** (b.1512) prompts succession crisis

25 June 1580 Publication of the Lutheran ***Book of Concord***

1580 Philip II unites Spanish and Portuguese crowns (to 1640)

1580 Publication of *Essais* by French philosopher **Michel de Montaigne** (1533–92)

4 April 1581 English privateer **Francis Drake** knighted by Elizabeth I

26 July 1581 Act of Abjuration deposes Philip II as ruler of United Provinces

September 1581 Russians besieged at **Pskov** by Polish-Lithuanians, consequently abandoning claims to Livonia (to February 1582)

1581 Single Whip Reform in China orders that all land taxes be paid in silver

21 June 1582 Toyotomi Hideyoshi seizes power in Japan after death of **Oda Nobunaga** (b.1534)

August 1582 Arrival of Jesuit **Matteo Ricci** in China

15 October 1582 Gregorian Calendar introduced

1582 Death of Emperor **Askia Daud** (r.1549–82) sparks dynastic disputes in **Songhay Empire**, West Africa

May 1583 Battle of Shizugatake, Japan

1583 United Provinces besiege **Amsterdam**, Netherlands

5 August 1583 Sir Humphrey Gilbert (c.1539–83) claims **Newfoundland** for England

1583 Burmese invade **Yunnan province**, China

10 July 1584 Assassination of **William of Orange** (b.1533), leader of Dutch Revolt

1584 First **Chinese Catholic catechism** produced by Jesuit priest Michele Ruggieri (1543–1607)

1585 Virginia Colony established at **Roanoke** (abandoned by 1590)

17 August 1585 Fall of **Antwerp** to Spanish led by Duke of Parma

1585 Spain establishes first permanent European settlement in Philippines at **Cebu**

1585 Chocolate introduced to Europe

1586–87

After keeping her in custody for 19 years, Elizabeth I finally had Mary, Queen of Scots tried and executed for treason in February 1587.

ENGLAND'S INTERVENTION IN THE DUTCH REVOLT (see 1572–73) was characterized by the Battle of Zutphen in September 1586 – it was a comprehensive defeat of the combined Anglo-Dutch forces by the Spanish. **Elizabeth I** had better luck with her attempts to destabilize Spain. In a series of plundering voyages to the Caribbean, **Drake** had highlighted how Spain's lucrative New World trade could be disrupted. In April 1587, Elizabeth despatched him on a mission to Spain with a goal of further raiding and destruction. Characteristically, she almost immediately changed her mind but her message recalling Drake never reached him. It was a spectacular success – Spanish and Portuguese vessels and ports were attacked with audacious abandon. The highlight was a **three-day assault on Cadiz** in southern Spain, in which 23 Spanish ships were sunk (according to Spanish sources; Drake claimed 33) and four were captured. The raid delayed Philip II's Armada by over a year.

Plots and rebellions plagued Elizabeth's reign and she had her Catholic cousin, **Mary, Queen of Scots**, executed in 1587 as a dangerous claimant to her throne.

Christianity in Japan thrived when first introduced by the Portuguese in the mid-16th century. By about 1580, there were an estimated 130,000 Japanese Christians, most in and around Nagasaki. For **Toyotomi Hideyoshi** (see 1582–85) they represented an organized and armed force around which opposition to him could be rallied. A prime motive for the conversion of many warlords had been that it would make it easier for them to obtain gunpowder as its trade was still largely controlled by the Portuguese. At the same time, Hideyoshi was anxious not to jeopardize the trading links the Portuguese had established. His response was typically hard-headed – trade was still to be encouraged but Christianity would be banned. In July 1587, a **Purge Directive Order to the Jesuits** was issued. In addition, Nagasaki was brought under his direct rule. Though the Order was not fully enforced for a decade or more, Christianity in Japan would in future be forced underground.

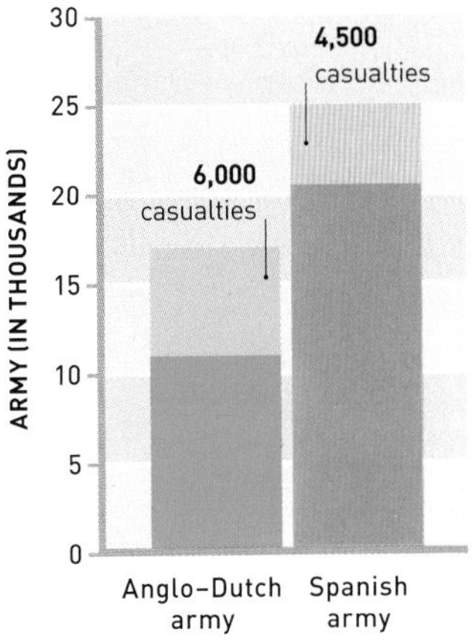

Battle of Zutphen
The Anglo-Dutch forces suffered huge losses in the Battle of Zutphen in 1586, which resulted in the city being handed over to the Spanish.

1588–89

> **"** I HAVE THE **BODY** BUT **OF** A WEAK AND **FEEBLE WOMAN,** BUT I HAVE THE **HEART AND STOMACH OF** A **KING... "**
>
> **Elizabeth I, Queen of England,** addressing the troops at Tilbury, 19 August 1588

THE SPANISH ARMADA was Philip II's most obvious military gamble – a massive deployment of Spanish naval might meant first to overthrow England, then to crush the Protestant provinces of the Netherlands. It failed entirely. It showed how outright military success was elusive, and that logistical difficulties confronted any long-range military operation. Launched on 30 May 1588, the Armada was the victim of English seamanship, of lengthening lines of supply, and of the weather – the gale-wracked Spanish fleet was forced home in disarray. Spanish hopes of exterminating Protestant heresies were decisively checked.

Spanish Armada
Severe storms and the English fleet caused heavy losses to the Armada, which numbered around 150 ships when it left Lisbon.

ELIZABETH I (1533–1603)

Elizabeth faced many problems on her accession to the English throne in 1558 – religious division, economic hardship, and threats from Scotland, France, and Spain. She overcame them with a combination of guile and intelligence and presided over a reinvention of England as a defiantly self-confident Protestant nation.

The death in 1589 of Henry III of France, stabbed by a Dominican monk, brought **Henry of Navarre** (1533–1610) to the throne and plunged France into crisis. Henry IV's claims to the crown were clear, yet he was a Protestant. To the powerful Catholic League of France, and to Philip II in Spain, **the prospect of a Protestant king of France was unthinkable**. Henry IV's eventual acclamation as king came only in 1593, after a series of debilitating wars, when he – conveniently – converted to Catholicism.

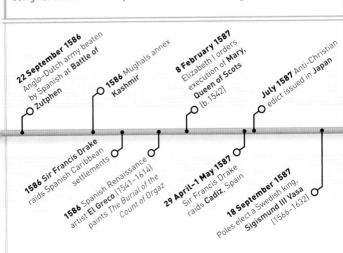

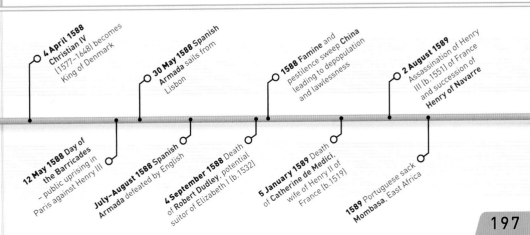

22 September 1586 Anglo-Dutch army beaten by Spanish at **Battle of Zutphen**

1586 Sir Francis Drake raids Spanish Caribbean settlements

1586 Mughals annex **Kashmir**

1586 Spanish Renaissance artist **El Greco** (1541–1614) paints *The Burial of the Count of Orgaz*

8 February 1587 Elizabeth I orders execution of **Mary, Queen of Scots** (b.1542)

29 April–1 May 1587 Sir Francis Drake raids **Cadiz**, Spain

July 1587 Anti-Christian edict issued in **Japan**

18 September 1587 Poles elect a Swedish king, **Sigismund III Vasa** (1566–1632)

4 April 1588 **Christian IV** (1577–1648) becomes King of Denmark

12 May 1588 **Day of the Barricades** – public uprising in Paris against Henry III

30 May 1588 **Spanish Armada** sails from Lisbon

July–August 1588 Spanish **Armada** defeated by English

1588 **Famine** and pestilence sweep **China** leading to depopulation and lawlessness

4 September 1588 Death of **Robert Dudley**, potential suitor of Elizabeth I (b.1532)

5 January 1589 Death of **Catherine de Medici**, wife of Henry II of France (b.1519)

2 August 1589 Assassination of Henry III (b.1551) of France and succession of **Henry of Navarre**

1589 Portuguese sack **Mombasa**, East Africa

Dastana forearm guard
DATE UNKNOWN
Forearm guards (*dastanas*) were worn by Mughal warriors to shield limbs from glancing blows. The hinged plate also protected the inner arm surface.

Metal turban helmet
DATE UNKNOWN
The warriors of early Mughal armies wore lightweight but effective turban helmets with nose and neck guards to deflect enemy arrows and blades.

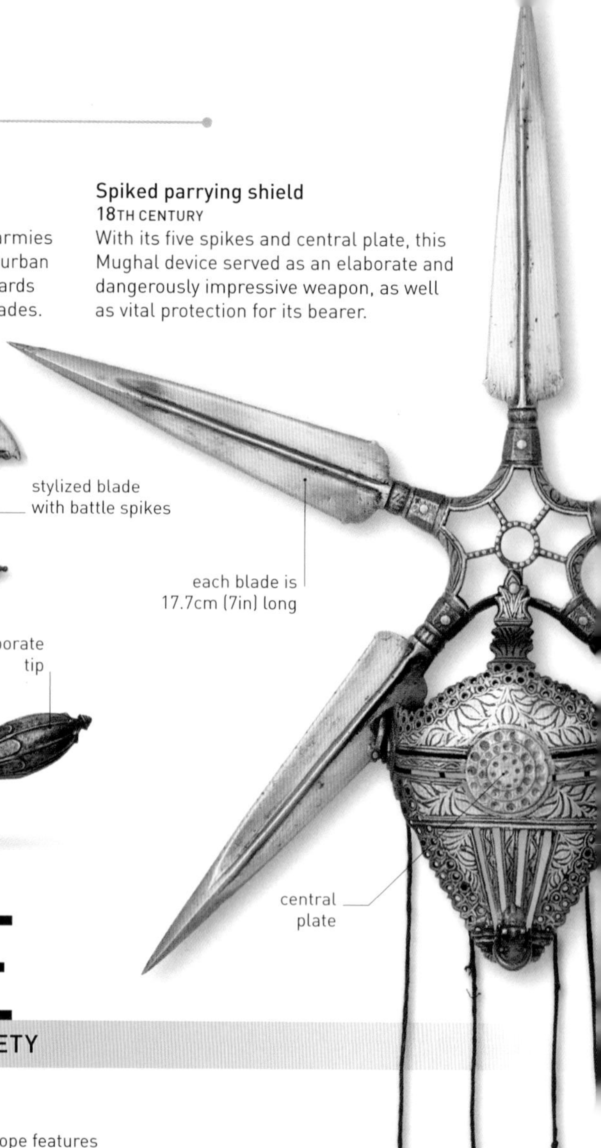

Spiked parrying shield
18TH CENTURY
With its five spikes and central plate, this Mughal device served as an elaborate and dangerously impressive weapon, as well as vital protection for its bearer.

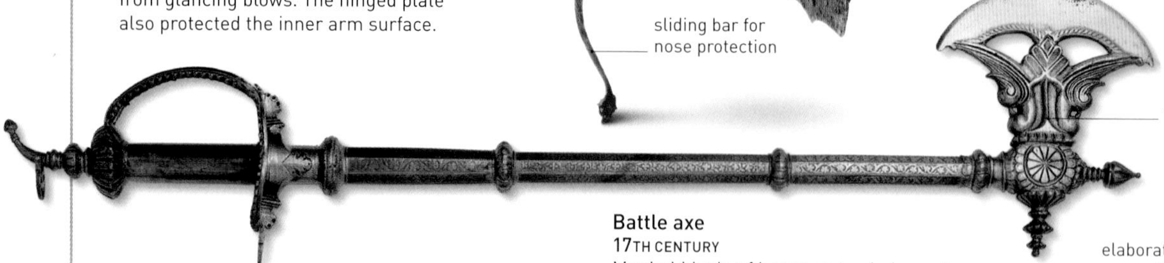

Battle axe
17TH CENTURY
Mughal ideals of beauty extended even to weapons, such as this ornate but formidable calvaryman's axe from India's Deccan region.

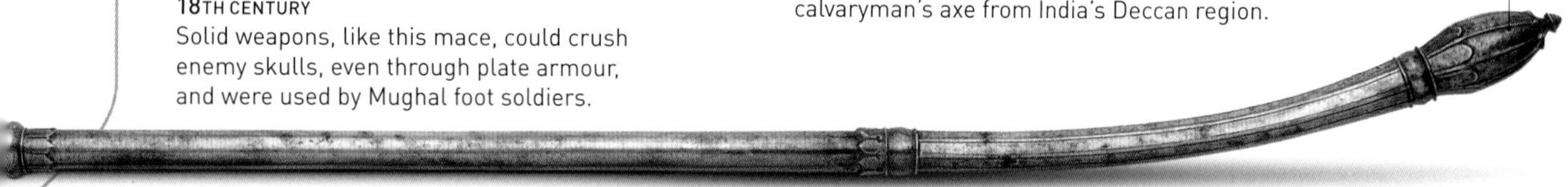

Iron mace
18TH CENTURY
Solid weapons, like this mace, could crush enemy skulls, even through plate armour, and were used by Mughal foot soldiers.

MUGHAL EMPIRE

OUT OF A POWER STRUGGLE EMERGED AN ADVANCED, WEALTHY, AND INTEGRATED SOCIETY

For over two centuries (1526–1761), Mughal rulers dominated most of India. Through military might and administrative prowess, they integrated Hindus and Muslims into a rich culture of imperial splendour.

With their roots in Mongol and Turkish cultures, seven generations of Mughal kings, beginning with Babur (r.1526–30), blended Persian and Islamic military and artistic influences into India's indigenous Hindu culture. The result was one of the most impressive medieval empires, which, at its height (1556–1707), commanded vast wealth, assimilated Hindus into its ruling elite, expanded education, and provided patronage in the arts and literature.

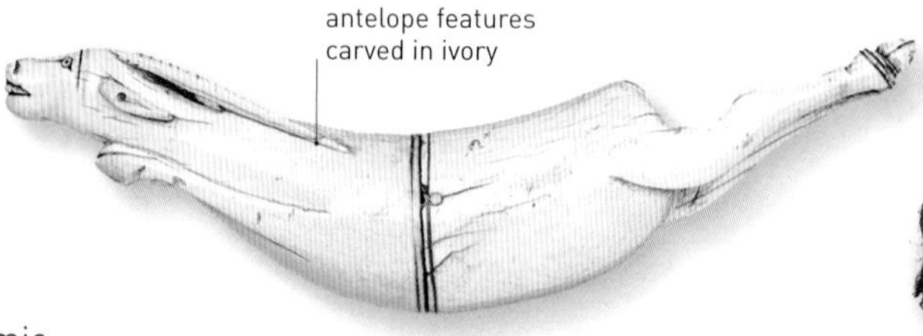

Ivory priming powder horn
DATE UNKNOWN
Ivory carving had an ancient history in India, and it became equally revered in Mughal courts. This powder horn, used on hunts, has an antelope shape.

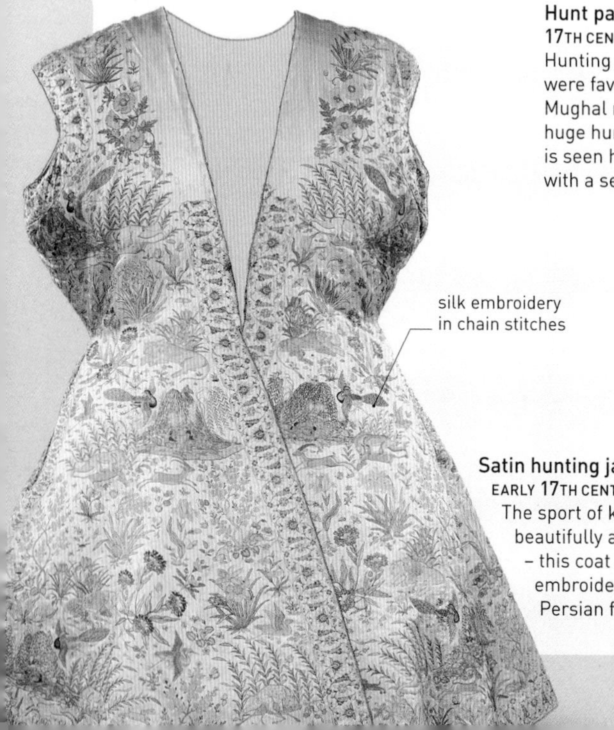

Satin hunting jacket
EARLY 17TH CENTURY
The sport of kings required beautifully adorned clothing – this coat is lavishly embroidered with typically Persian floral patterns.

Hunt painting
17TH CENTURY
Hunting and horsemanship were favourite pastimes of Mughal rulers, who created huge hunting parks. A prince is seen here on horseback with a servant and hound.

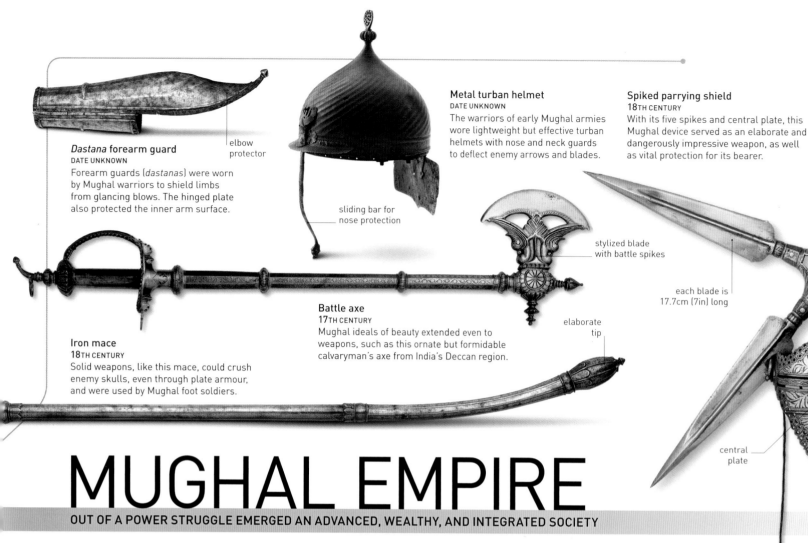

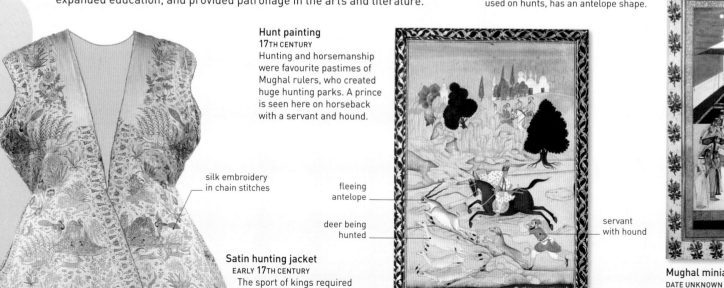

Mughal miniature
DATE UNKNOWN
Arts and architecture flourished under the patronage of Mughal kings such as Akbar (r.1542–1605). Miniature painting, introduced as manuscript illustration, was most prized.

Sarpech
DATE UNKNOWN
The extraordinary wealth of the Mughals was evident in their love of jewelled objects. This *sarpech*, made of gold, emeralds, diamonds, rubies, and a pearl, adorned a royal turban.

Hansli necklace
18TH CENTURY
Cast in gold and heavily encrusted with precious stones, this rigid torque or necklace was known as a *hansli*, because it was designed to rest on the wearer's collarbone – or *hansli* in Urdu.

Talisman
DATE UNKNOWN
Mughal craftsmen were famed for the intricacy of their work. This talisman, or *tabeez*, is decorated with verses from the Qur'an.

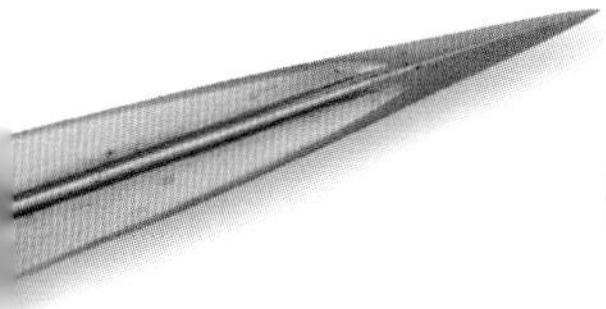

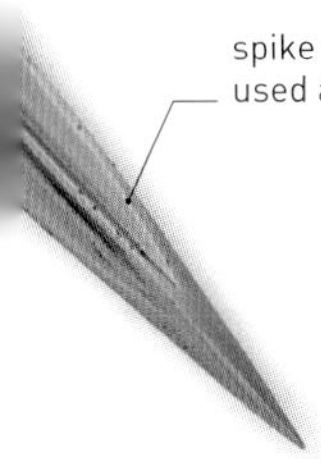

Mortar and pestle
17TH CENTURY
Jade could only be worked using diamond dust, so it was highly prized in Mughal society. This mortar and pestle was carved from one block.

Bowl inlaid with jade
18TH CENTURY
Parchîn kârî, or inlay, reached its peak during the reign of Jahan (1628–58). This bowl is inlaid with jade and precious stones.

Enamelled gold wine goblet
17TH CENTURY
Records of Mughal courtly life describe kings sipping their wine from enamelled gold or silver goblets, and dozens of dishes served on gold and silver plates.

Mughal court painting
17TH CENTURY
The splendour of the Mughal court is clear from this painting of the emperor Jahan (r.1628–58) among his nobles, grouped in strict hierarchical order around the throne.

Hookahs
18TH CENTURY
The Mughals brought the Persian tradition of hookah-smoking to India. Both men and women used hookahs, in which tobacco smoke is cooled with water.

1590–91

An estimated 40,000–50,000 people died in Paris in 1590 until the Spanish army led by the Duke of Parma broke the four-month siege in September.

BY 1590, TOYOTOMI HIDEYOSHI (see 1582–87) had effectively completed the **unification of Japan**, and the distinctive character of the regime that was to dominate the country for over 250 years was established. Though it was not the capital, from 1590 Hideyoshi based himself at **Edo**, where the feudal nobility, now entirely subservient to him, were required to spend every other year. It proved a highly effective means of preventing rebellion. This elaborate social structure was largely supported by the peasantry, who had to pay heavy taxes.

Attempting to impose himself on France as king, **Henry of Navarre** (see 1588–89) **besieged Paris** in May 1590. The siege was broken in September by Spanish troops under the Duke of Parma.

In 1591, the **Sultan of Morocco, Ahmad al-Mansur**, (see 1578–79), launched an invasion of the troubled **Songhay Empire** (see 1582–85). Al-Mansur's goal was the **trans-Saharan gold trade**. The invasion involved a perilous four-month crossing of the Sahara by a fighting force of 4,000 men sustained by 8,000 camels. In March 1592, a Songhay army over 40,000 strong was routed at the **Battle of Tondibi** by the Moroccans' vastly superior firepower, which included numerous arquebuses and eight English cannons.

Castle complex
Himeji, or "White Egret", Castle is one of 200 massive castles built on the orders of Toyotomi Hideyoshi to ensure his power across Japan.

1592

£500,000

THE **GREATEST** EVER **PRIZE** TAKEN **BY ENGLISH PRIVATEERS,** FROM THE **MADRE DE DEUS**

Rialto Bridge
The Rialto Bridge over the Grand Canal in Venice was completed in 1592. It was the fifth bridge built at the site, the first to be of stone.

THE SEVEN YEAR WAR began in the spring of 1592 when **Japanese forces** mounted a sustained **invasion of Korea**. Partly an attempt by Toyotomi Hideyoshi to unite the Japanese in a common cause, it was more particularly the fulfilment of his predecessor Oda Nobunaga's ambitious goal of a **conquest of Ming China** itself. The campaign met with mixed results. Japanese land victories in Korea were matched by Korean naval victories – the heavily armed and protected Korean turtle ships proving decisive against Japan's progressively weakened fleets. **Chinese intervention** late in the year tipped the balance against Japan. By the spring of 1593, the Japanese were forced to sue for peace. By the middle of the year, they had begun to pull out. In 1597, the ageing Hideyoshi renewed the campaign, sending larger forces. The result was a **further defeat for Japan** in 1598, but the savage fighting **devastated Korea**. Though the war did not formally end until 1608, by 1599 it was effectively over. Paradoxically, it was Japan that benefitted most. The defeat had a significant influence on its subsequent, if never absolute, isolation from the wider world. Korea, by contrast, took years to recover, while the immense cost of the war to Ming China not only provoked riots against the extra taxes levied but weakened its military capacity on its vulnerable northeastern frontier.

From 1592, **Akbar** (see 1555–56) launched a further round of conquests that saw the **Mughal Empire's frontiers** reach their greatest extent during his reign. In the east, Orissa was annexed. In 1594, Baluchistan and the coastal strip of Makran on the Safavid Persian border were conquered. And in 1596, the **key Afghan city of Kandahar**, lost by Akbar's father Humayan, was retaken.

1593–94

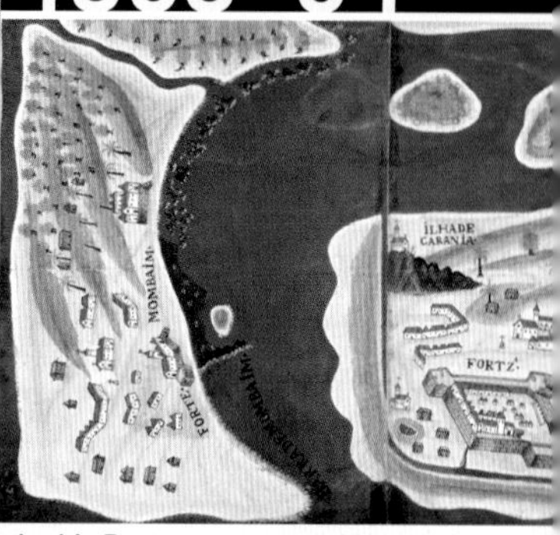
In this Portuguese map of Mombasa, Fort Jesus is depicted bottom right.

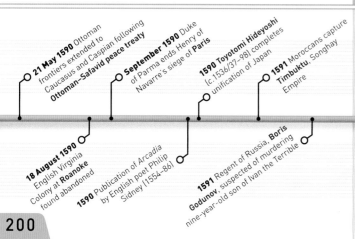

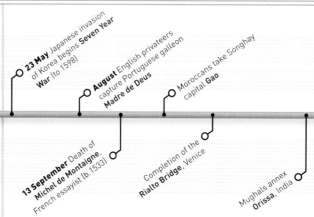

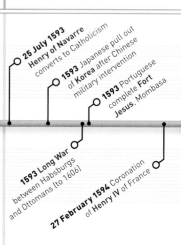

THE OTTOMAN–HABSBURG FRONTIER, generally stable after the renewed Ottoman attempt on Vienna in 1529, was a key focus of Ottoman–Christian conflict. It came centre-stage again in 1593 with the **Long War**. A series of inconclusive campaigns followed in Hungary and the Balkans, with the nominal Ottoman vassals of Transylvania, Wallachia, and Moldavia supporting the Habsburgs. The net result of the eventual peace settlement – the **Treaty of Zsitvatorok** of 1606 – was to leave the frontier in a state of simmering uncertainty.

On 10 June 1594, in the Spanish settlement of St-Augustine in Florida, Father Diego Escobar de Zambrana baptized Maria, daughter of Juan Jimenez de la Cueva and Maria Melendez. The event was recorded in the oldest public document in what would become the US and is the first authentic record of a **child born to European settlers** there.

Fort Jesus in Mombasa, East Africa was built at the command of Philip II and completed in 1593. It proved to be crucial to Portuguese endeavours in the Indian Ocean throughout the 17th century.

> **“ PARIS** IS WORTH A **MASS. ”**
>
> Henry IV of France, 1593

21 May 1590 Ottoman frontiers extended to Caucasus and Caspian following **Ottoman-Safavid peace treaty**

18 August 1590 English Virginia Colony at **Roanoke** found abandoned

September 1590 Duke of Parma ends Henry of Navarre's siege of **Paris**

1590 Publication of Arcadia by English poet Philip Sidney (1554–86)

1590 Toyotomi Hideyoshi (c.1536/37–98) completes unification of Japan

1591 Moroccans capture **Timbuktu**, Songhay Empire

1591 Regent of Russia, **Boris Godunov**, suspected of murdering nine-year-old son of Ivan the Terrible

23 May Japanese invasion of Korea begins **Seven Year War** (to 1598)

August English privateers capture Portuguese galleon **Madre de Deus**

13 September Death of **Michel de Montaigne**, French essayist (b.1533)

Moroccans take Songhay capital **Gao**

Completion of the **Rialto Bridge**, Venice

Mughals annex **Orissa**, India

25 July 1593 Henry of Navarre converts to Catholicism

1593 Japanese pull out **of Korea** after Chinese military intervention

1593 Long War between Habsburgs and Ottomans (to 1606)

1593 Portuguese complete **Fort Jesus**, Mombasa

27 February 1594 Coronation of **Henry IV** of France

Despite the perils of the venture, all four Dutch ships that set out for the East Indies in 1595 made it back safely to Amsterdam in 1599 along with their cargo.

THE FINAL CONVULSIONS OF THE FRENCH WARS OF RELIGION (1562–98) were played out after 1595. **Henry IV** (see 1588–89), by his conversion to Catholicism in 1593, succeeded in winning broad acceptance as king. Yet his conversion aroused the suspicions of the **Huguenots** – fearful he now intended to turn against them – and did nothing to appease the ambitions of the leaders of the **Catholic League**, whose goal was not merely the extermination of Protestantism in France but the seizure of the throne. Henry's response, in January 1595, was to **declare war on Spain**. His aim was both to eradicate the Catholic League, supported by Spain, while demonstrating to the Huguenots that, Catholic or not, he was no puppet of the Spanish monarchy. An early French victory in June 1595 against a combined Spanish–Catholic League force in Burgundy was followed the following spring by a renewed Spanish offensive that saw the capture of Calais and Amiens. The inevitable sieges by Henry followed, and the capitulation of Amiens in September 1597 marked his final triumph.

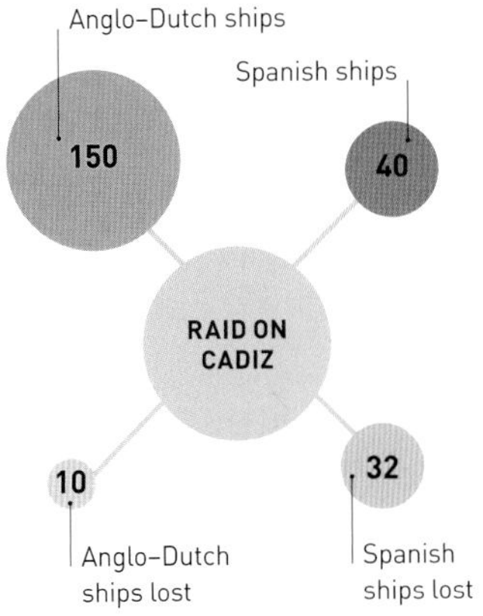

Raid on Cadiz
The Spanish lost 80 per cent of the fleet anchored at Cadiz. They set many of their ships on fire to deny the Anglo–Dutch raiders their prize.

Until the beginning of the Dutch Revolt in 1566, the Netherlands largely dominated the **lucrative maritime trade** between Spain and Portugal and northern Europe – it was Dutch ships that carried spices and other New World goods from Iberia to the north. Thereafter, forbidden to trade with Iberian ports and conscious of the failings of Spain's maritime reach highlighted by the Armada, the **Dutch determined to break into the spice trade**. In 1595, four Dutch ships under Cornelius van Houten accordingly sailed for the East Indies. The crews endured scurvy and repeated clashes with local rulers and the Portuguese, and Van Houten was killed in Sumatra. When, in 1599, the beleaguered fleet returned to Amsterdam, it brought with it an apparently meagre quantity of spices, yet this was enough to secure a huge profit. The stage for Dutch domination of the East India trade was set (see 1602–03).

Anglo–Dutch fleet attacks Cadiz
Nominally a joint Anglo–Dutch operation, in reality, of the 150 ships in the fleet that attacked Cadiz in 1596, 130 were English.

One of **England's few successes** in its participation in the Dutch Revolt was a **raid on Cadiz** in southern Spain in July 1596. Much like Drake's raid in 1587, it caused enormous devastation, with most of the city destroyed, and contributed to the bankruptcy of the Spanish crown in 1597.

This ceiling fresco at Chehel Sotoun Palace in Isfahan, Iran, shows Shah Abbas I, seated on the right, playing host to Vali Muhammad Khan of Bukara.

ALTHOUGH THE BANNING OF CHRISTIANITY IN JAPAN had been enforced only partially since 1587, in December 1596, certain that Spain and Portugal were using Christian penetration as a prelude to conquest, Toyotomi ordered the **deaths of 26 Christians** – six Franciscan missionaries and 20 Japanese. On 5 February 1597 in Nagasaki, they were strapped to crosses and speared to death. The significance of their deaths was less that Christianity would not be tolerated in Japan, more that any challenge to the central authority would not be allowed.

The uneasy compromise brokered by Henry IV in France after 1597 was symbolized by the **Edict of Nantes** of April 1598. Under it, Protestants in France were granted the right to organize a quasi-independent state within France. Not only could they practise their religion freely – other than in Paris – the Crown guaranteed their security, paying them to garrison their towns. Nothing if not pragmatic – and effective enough in the short term in **ending the French Wars of Religion** – inevitably it satisfied no one. The Huguenots still felt themselves unequally treated compared to the Catholics, while the latter were horrified that the Huguenots should be tolerated at all, let alone protected.

The accession in 1587 of the 16-year-old **Abbas I** as the **shah of Safavid Persia** rejuvenated its fortunes. Under his father Shah Mohammed, Persia had been in a state of near civil war created by rival factions within the Qizilbash army and had lost substantial territories to the Ottomans and Uzbeks. Abbas set about a **major reform of his rebellious army**, drafting in new troops, principally from the Caucasus, who were directly loyal to him. He rearmed them with muskets supplied by an English diplomat, Sir Anthony Shirley, who was negotiating an Anglo–Persian anti-Ottoman treaty. Between April and August 1598, Abbas launched a **major campaign against the Uzbeks**, driving them from the northwest of Persia.

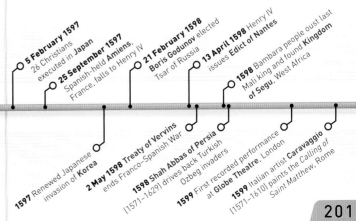

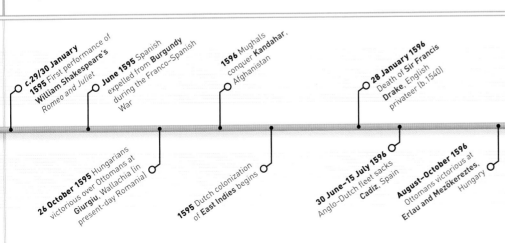

WILLIAM SHAKESPEARE
(1564–1616)

William Shakespeare exerted more influence on English literature and European drama than any other writer. The son of a Stratford-upon-Avon wool dealer, he was an actor turned author, and wrote at least 37 plays and 154 sonnets. He is believed to have written the tragedy *Hamlet* around 1599–1602. He also excelled at comedy.

c.29/30 January 1595 First performance of **William Shakespeare's** *Romeo and Juliet*

June 1595 Spanish expelled from **Burgundy** during the Franco-Spanish War

26 October 1595 Hungarians victorious over Ottomans at **Giurgiu**, Wallachia (in present-day Romania)

1596 Mughals conquer **Kandahar**, Afghanistan

1595 Dutch colonization of **East Indies** begins

28 January 1596 Death of **Sir Francis Drake**, English privateer (b.1540)

30 June–15 July 1596 Anglo–Dutch fleet sacks **Cadiz**, Spain

August–October 1596 Ottomans victorious at **Erlau and Mezőkeresztes**, Hungary

5 February 1597 26 Christians executed in **Japan**

25 September 1597 Spanish-held **Amiens**, France, falls to Henry IV

1597 Renewed Japanese invasion of **Korea**

21 February 1598 **Boris Godunov** elected Tsar of Russia

13 April 1598 Henry IV issues **Edict of Nantes**

2 May 1598 Treaty of Vervins ends Franco–Spanish War

1598 Bambara people oust last Mali king and found **Kingdom of Segu**, West Africa

1598 Shah Abbas of Persia (1571–1629) drives back Turkish Ozbeg invaders

1599 First recorded performance at **Globe Theatre**, London

1599 Italian artist **Caravaggio** (1571–1610) paints the *Calling of Saint Matthew*, Rome

1600–01

The English East India Company began trading with Surat, a key centre of Indian Ocean trade, in 1608. By 1615, it had ousted the Portuguese.

BY ABOUT 1600, THE POLYNESIAN PEOPLES OF NEW ZEALAND, the Maori, had become progressively better established in their new lands (see 1276–85). Although theirs was still a Stone Age society – and would remain so until the arrival of Europeans and the introduction of metal – it was one remarkably well adapted to the new environment. Known as the **Classic Maori phase**, the culture was distinguished by elaborate wood carving, precisely patterned bone tools and weapons, and substantial earthwork settlements.

The establishment, with royal approval, on 31 December 1600 of the **English East India Company** was a clear statement of English intent that Spain and Portugal could not expect exclusive domination of trade with East Asia. That said, from the start the East India Company was a speculative venture at best. It depended not merely on an uncertain ability to reach these distant lands but, once there, to present itself – militarily and diplomatically – as a credible alternative to its European rivals. It called for a combination of seamanship, commercial intuition, and force – the last a permanent necessity. Eventually, it would establish itself almost as an arm of the English, later the British, state. But it was never intended as a means of conquest or colonization – **enrichment for its shareholders was its sole goal**. Ironically, its penetration of these new markets coincided with that of another latecomer, the Dutch. European domination for the riches of the East Indies would be contested not between England and Iberia but between England and the Dutch.

Maori weapon
The wahaika, a short wooden club held by a dog-skin thong looped around the thumb and wrist, was used for close combat.

30
CUBIC KM
THE **VOLUME** OF **MATERIAL EJECTED** FROM **HUAYNAPUTINA VOLCANO,** PERU

1602–03

Tokugawa Ieyasu was 60 years old when he received the title of shogun from Emperor Go-Yōzei. He remained the effective ruler of Japan until his death.

FOR AROUND 100 YEARS, THE DUTCH EAST INDIA COMPANY, established in 1602 and exact equivalent of its English rival, was the **most successful commercial venture in the world**. Its navigators not only outflanked the Portuguese in the Indian Ocean – pioneering new routes deep into the Southern Ocean as a means of access to the East Indies – but, having reached their lucrative goals, they exploited them with a single-mindedness that left their predecessors floundering. In 1602, the Dutch had laid claim to Guiana in South America. More importantly, by 1605 they had ousted the Portuguese from the Moluccas (Spice Islands). The foundations of a Dutch East Asian trading empire had been laid.

When **James I** (1566–1625) became **King of England** in 1603 on the death of Elizabeth I, he had already been **King of Scotland**, as James VI, for 36 years. Although they remained two quite clearly separate countries, sharing only a common monarch, James did manage to drive through the repeal of mutually hostile laws. Otherwise, the closest he came to the union he sought was an Anglo-Scots flag, the **Union Jack**, known for his preferred French name, Jacques.

On the very same day as James's accession, **Tokugawa Ieyasu** (1543–1616) became **shogun** of the Tokugawa shogunate of **Japan**. He presided over a rigidly stratified, inward-looking society that endured for 250 years.

French exploration in the New World was resumed by **Samuel de Champlain** in 1603. Over the following 12 years, he made a series of pioneering journeys along the St Lawrence River towards the Great Lakes. In 1605, he also established a short-lived French colony, Port Royal, in Novia Scotia and, in 1608, a **permanent French base at Québec**. Though partly motivated by a search for a river passage to the Pacific, Champlain recognized that this rugged land was valuable in itself, above all for its **furs**. He subsequently sponsored a series of westward explorations beyond the Great Lakes, championing the potential of *Nouvelle France*.

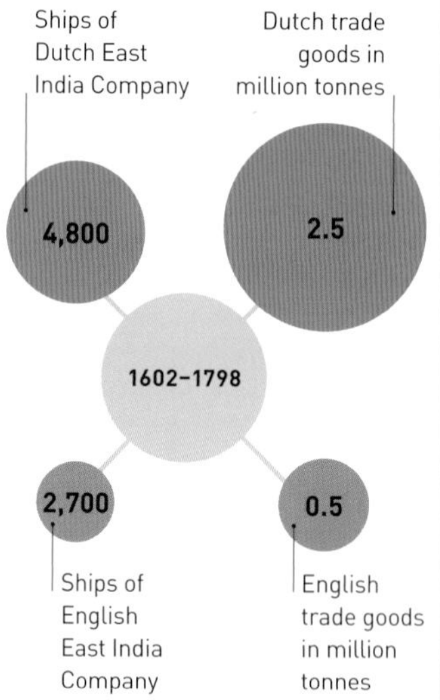

Trade in East Asia
The Dutch East India Company was five times as successful as its English equivalent throughout the 17th and 18th centuries.

1604–05

Guy Fawkes (third from the right) and his fellow Catholic conspirators.

> “THE **SPANISH ASSAILED** THE UNASSAILABLE; THE **DUTCH DEFENDED** THE INDEFENSIBLE.”

Anonymous, Siege of Ostend

WHEN SPANISH FORCES UNDER GENERAL SPINOLA TOOK OSTEND from a combined Anglo–Dutch force on 16 September 1604, it **ended a siege** that had lasted three years, two months, and 17 days. Even by the standards of 17th-century Europe – a century that saw only four years of peace – it was an extraordinarily brutal business. Siege warfare developed in response to artillery, to which the medieval castle, with high, thin walls, was vulnerable. Instead, fortifications became lower, thicker, and very much larger. So much so that many fortified towns were beyond the range of contemporary guns, and a blockade was the only practical means of taking them.

The **death of Tsar Boris Godunov** in 1605 brought to a head a **political crisis** rapidly engulfing Russia, one heightened by a terrible **famine** that between 1601–03 killed two million people – **a third of the population**. Hoping to exploit Russia's divisions to its own advantage, and supported by disaffected Russian nobles, an unofficial **Polish–Lithuanian force** had already

19 February 1600 Huaynaputina volcano, Peru, erupts, killing around 1,500 people

c.1600 Classic Maori phase in New Zealand

31 December 1600 East India Company established, England

c.1600 Hausa city-states of West Africa flourish

c.1600 Statue-building culture of **Easter Island** begins to decline

1601 Russian famine (to 1603) heralds "Time of Troubles"

24 October 1601 Death of **Tycho Brahe**, Danish astronomer (b.1546)

1601 Deccan kingdoms absorbed by Mughals, India

20 March 1602 Dutch East India Company established

1602 Dutch colony established, **Guiana**

15 March 1603 French explorer **Samuel de Champlain** (1567–1635) arrives in Canada

24 March 1603 Union of English and Scottish crowns with accession of **James I** of England following death of Elizabeth I (b.1533)

24 March 1603 Tokugawa Ieyasu proclaimed shogun of Japan

August 1603 Internal conflict in Morocco following death of **Ahmad al-Mansur** (b.1549)

1603 Scientific institute **Accademia dei Lincei** founded, Rome

1603 Renewed **Safavid–Ottoman conflict** (to 1619)

18 August 1604 Treaty of London signed, concluding the Anglo–Spanish War

1604 Posthumous publication of *Dr Faustus* by English dramatist **Christopher Marlowe** (1564–93)

16 September 1604 Ostend in the United Provinces falls to Spanish

A reconstruction of Jamestown, the first permanent English settlement in North America, established in 1607 on the James River in what is now Virginia.

invaded the country, its aim in part to claim Orthodox Russia for the Catholic church. With Godunov's death, the interlopers placed on the Russian throne a man claiming to be Ivan the Terrible's youngest son. After less than a year, this False Dimitri was overthrown by **Vasili IV** (1552–1612), who slaughtered the Poles in Moscow, perhaps 2,000. Seeking to strengthen himself against continuing Polish agitation, in 1609 Vasili allied with Sweden, provoking an official Polish declaration of war against Russia. The following year, the **Poles had taken Moscow** and their king, **Sigismund III**, asserted his own right to the Russian throne. Alarmed at the prospect of Poland–Lithuania taking over Russia, the **Swedes invaded and captured Novgorod**. In 1612, **Russia was saved** when a patriotic rising under Prince Pozharsky forced the Poles out of Moscow and elected the **first Romanov tsar, Mikhail** (1596–1645). Though unable to oust the Swedes, Russia came to terms with Sweden in 1617 at the cost of giving up its access to the Baltic. In 1619, the **Polish–Russian conflict was ended** by Russia ceding substantial territories on its western border.

In Strasbourg in 1605, **Johann Carolus** (1575–1634) published what is generally acknowledged as **the world's first newspaper**, *Relation aller Fürnemmen und gedenckwürdigen Historien* – "Collection of all Distinguished and Commemorable News". Carolus already produced a hand-written news-sheet. He realized, however, that a printed version, sold more cheaply and to a wider audience, would be more profitable. By 1617, there were a further four German newspapers.

The hopes of James I of England for religious toleration were dashed with the discovery on 5 November 1605 of a **Catholic plot to blow up the Houses of Parliament**. It is possible that the plotters were encouraged by Robert Cecil, chief minister of James I, in order to stoke anti-Catholic opinion.

First newspaper on sale
The appearance of the Relation *in Europe in 1605 was early evidence of a growing demand for information in a fast-changing world.*

> **“** THE **FIFTEENTH** DAY OF **JUNE, WE** HAD **BUILT** AND **FINISHED OUR FORT… THIS COUNTRY** IS A **FRUITFUL SOIL, BEARING** MANY GOODLY AND **FRUITFUL TREES… ”**
>
> George Percy, English colonist, from *Jamestown Narratives*

IN DECEMBER 1605, PORTUGUESE NAVIGATOR Pedro Fernández de Quiros received royal approval for a second voyage across the Pacific **in search of the presumed southern continent**, *Terra Australis Incognita*. After sailing through the Tuamotu Archipelago in February 1606, he reached the New Hebrides in May, but was swept out to sea by the trade winds and forced to return to New Spain. The expedition had a second ship, under the command of **Luis Váez de Torres**. Continuing to the west, he discovered the strait that bears his name between **New Guinea** and **Australia**, sighting the continent in the process. In the event, his discoveries, meticulously noted but never published, would not be followed up by Spain. It was left to the Dutch to confirm the existence of Australia.

On 4 May 1607, the **first permanent English settlement** was established in **North America**. **Jamestown**, in present-day Virginia, was a highly speculative venture, financed by the London Company (later the Virginia Company). It was intended partly to forestall Spanish, French, and Dutch attempts at settlement, and more particularly to locate a sea passage to East Asia, as well as to prospect for gold and other precious metals. Its early years were unpromising. The site, chosen principally because it was easily defended, was swampy, malarial, and had little arable land. The colonists succumbed to disease and starvation, and relations with the **Powhatan Indians** were tense as well. It was only in 1612, when the **first tobacco crop** was exported, that the colony looked to have any prospects of survival.

Torres Strait Islanders mask
The sea-faring Torres Strait Islanders had a range of masks for ritual occasions, many of the most elaborate made from turtle shells.

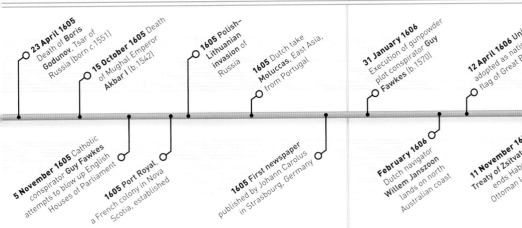

- **23 April 1605** Death of **Boris Godunov**, Tsar of Russia (born c.1551)
- **5 November 1605** Catholic conspirator **Guy Fawkes** attempts to blow up English Houses of Parliament
- **15 October 1605** Death of Mughal Emperor **Akbar I** (b.1542)
- **1605 Port Royal**, a French colony in Nova Scotia, established
- **1605 Polish–Lithuanian invasion** of Russia
- **1605** Dutch take **Moluccas**, East Asia, from Portugal
- **1605 First newspaper** published by Johann Carolus in Strasbourg, Germany
- **31 January 1606** Execution of gunpowder plot conspirator **Guy Fawkes** (b.1570)
- **February 1606** Dutch navigator **Willem Janszoon** lands on north Australian coast
- **12 April 1606 Union Jack** adopted as national maritime flag of Great Britain
- **19 May 1606 Vasili IV** becomes Tsar of Russia
- **11 November 1606 Treaty of Zsitvatorok** ends Habsburg–Ottoman Long War
- **26 December 1606 William Shakespeare's** play *King Lear* first performed
- **1606** Spanish navigator **Luis Váez de Torres** explores strait between New Guinea and Australia
- **14 May 1607 Jamestown**, Virginia, becomes first permanent English settlement in North America
- **1607** Mughal emperor **Jahangir** sends envoy to Portuguese in Goa, India

Processional cross
15th century • ITALY
The wealth of the Italian Catholic Church is expressed by this cross, made of gold, silver, and enamel, and paraded on religious holidays.

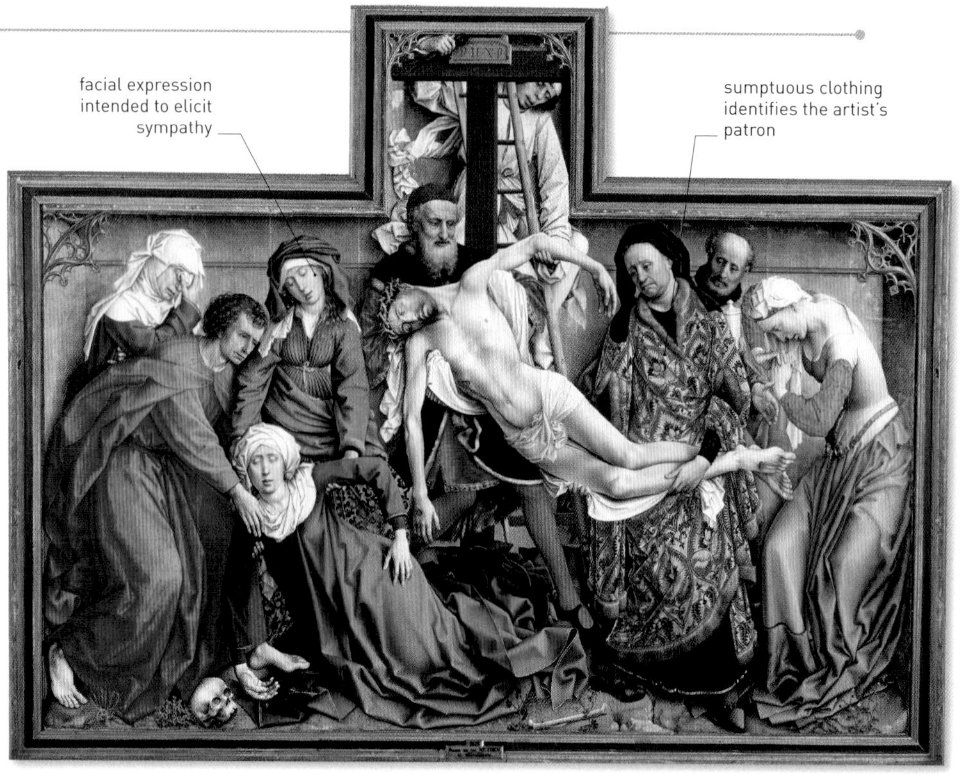

The Descent from the Cross
*c.*1435 • NETHERLANDS
This painting by Rogier van der Weyden (*c.*1399–1464) exemplifies Flemish assimilation of the Renaissance move towards idealization of faces and figures.

Venetian gold ducat
16th century • ITALY
This gold coin depicts the Doge of Venice (right) receiving the city's banner from a dominating St. Mark the Evangelist.

THE RENAISSANCE

A REBIRTH OF EUROPEAN CULTURE INSPIRED BY ANCIENT GREECE AND ROME

A thousand years after the Roman Empire's collapse, scholars in Florence, Italy, arrived at a renewed understanding of the art, architecture, and literature of the classical period, sparking a cultural revolution.

In the 14th century, trade among European states increased and Florence, as a banking and commercial centre – eventually under Medici control – developed a class of wealthy, educated individuals who became patrons of artists and thinkers. If Florence stood initially at the forefront of these artistic and intellectual developments, by the 16th century, the lead had passed to Papal Rome and Venice.

Figure of Moses
*c.*1515 • ITALY
Sculpted by Michelangelo (1475–1564) for the tomb of Pope Julius II, this statue now stands in the Church of San Pietro in Vincoli, Rome.

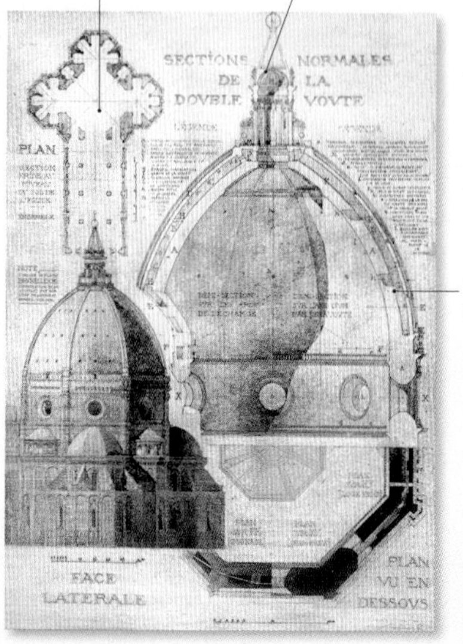

Florence Cathedral's dome
15th century • ITALY
The octagonal cathedral dome by Filippo Brunelleschi (1377–1446) consists of three parts, with the innermost visible from inside the building, as shown by this 19th-century engraving.

Mona Lisa
1503–06 • ITALY
Also known as *La Gioconda*, this enigmatic painting by Leonardo da Vinci (1452–1519) is the most famous Renaissance work and the world's best-known painting.

Medici ceramic
15th century • ITALY
This tin-glazed majolica plate, emblazoned with the Medici coat of arms, suggests the wealth and prestige of the Medici dynasty in Florence.

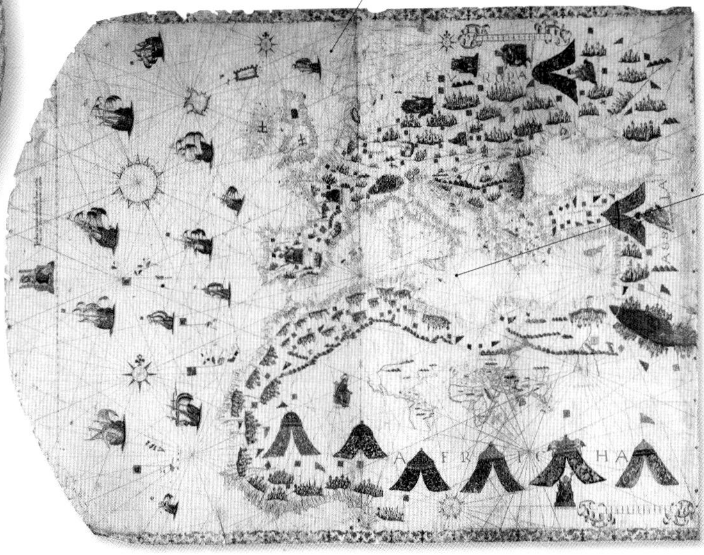

Mappa Mundi
1502 • SPAIN
Venice's wealth derived from its dominance of world trade routes. This map shows the Mediterranean and its adjacent seas, which Venetian ships regularly visited to distribute goods that were carried to the west by overland trade routes.

The Birth of Venus
*c.*1486 • ITALY
This masterly painting of the early Renaissance by Botticelli (*c.*1445–1510) refers directly to the Renaissance desire to appropriate and update ancient Roman ideals of beauty.

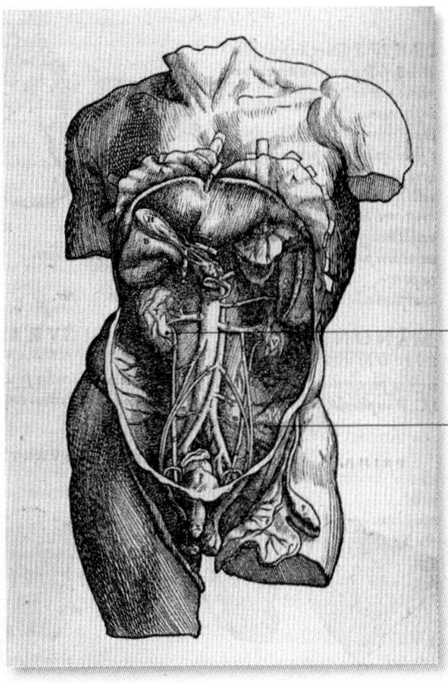

Organs in the abdominal cavity
*c.*1453 • ITALY
From *De humani corporis fabrica* by Andreas Vesalius (1514–64), this anatomical diagram typifies the Renaissance determination to expand scientific knowledge.

The Ambassadors
1533 • GERMANY
A highly detailed painting with complex symbolism, this portrait of two young French diplomats by Hans Holbein the Younger (*c.*1497–1543) includes much evidence of their lives and accomplishments as cultured men of the Renaissance.

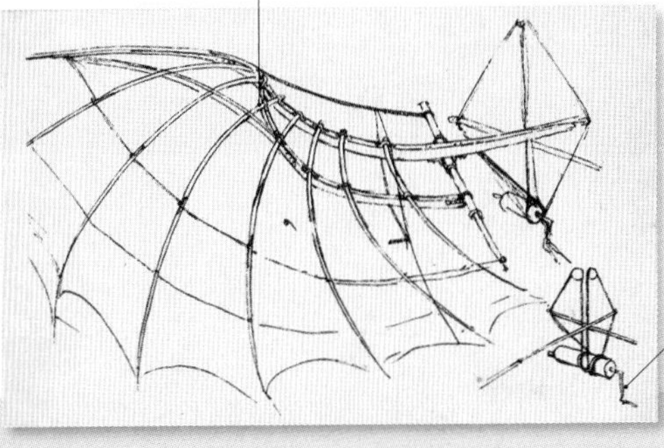

Hand-powered wing
*c.*1490 • ITALY
Leonardo da Vinci produced several proposals for human-powered flying machines, including this sketch for a hand-cranked wing from his 12-volume *Codex Atlanticus*.

1608–09

“SO LONG AS THE MOTHER, **IGNORANCE, LIVES,** IT IS **NOT SAFE FOR SCIENCE,** THE OFFSPRING, **TO DIVULGE** THE **HIDDEN CAUSE** OF THINGS.”

Johannes Kepler, German astronomer

ON 2 OCTOBER 1608, HANS LIPPERSHEY (1570–1619), a lens-maker in Zeeland in the Dutch Netherlands, applied for a patent for a device for "seeing things far away as if they were nearby". This was soon known as a **telescope**. Lippershey's device was crude, only magnifying by three times, and was soon exceeded by others. But it was still a milestone in the development of scientific observation in 17th-century Europe.

Since 1606, the Dutch had been trying to broker a truce with Spain to halt the ongoing wars of the **Dutch Revolt**. Forty years of war had left both sides spent, yet each feared the other would use a ceasefire to regroup – as each intended to do. Despite this, in April 1609, a **12-year truce** was agreed.

In 1526, Charles V had decreed that all Muslims in Spain convert to Catholicism. The resulting minority **Morisco** population remained on the margins of Spanish society – valued for their cheap labour, but suspected for their religious affiliation. In 1609, Philip III agreed to **expel** them from Spain entirely. The decision caused whole communities to be summarily expelled and their possessions forfeited. It also created economic dislocation in many parts of the country as a valuable source of labour disappeared. Muslim resentment toward Spain predictably increased.

In 1609, the Dutch East India Company had sent **Henry Hudson** to investigate North America's east coast. He explored the Hudson River to present-day Albany, claiming the region for the Dutch.

Hudson River
New York state's river is named for Englishman Henry Hudson, who explored the river's course.

1610

A copper engraving depicts the assassination of Henry IV, King of France, in Paris. Henry IV had survived 18 previous attempts on his life.

THE ASSASSINATION OF HENRY IV in Paris on 14 May 1610, stabbed by a one-time monk and teacher, Francois Ravaillac, promised a reawakening of the brutal religious divisions Henry had worked so hard – and killed so many – to avoid. The reality was quite the opposite. Not only was Henry's nine-year-old son immediately accepted as the new monarch, **Louis XIII**, but the threat of renewed conflict between France and Spain was averted. Both had been sparring for control of the duchy of Jülich-Cleves in Germany, threatening a renewed pan-European religious conflict. With Henry's death, both could now legitimately retire with no loss of face. Henry IV, first of the Bourbon kings, was among the most remarkable of France's kings: his **reconstruction** of the pestilential medieval shambles of Paris echoed his far-sighted reconstruction of France itself.

Less than a year after Hans Lippershey's claim to have invented a telescope, **Galileo** (see panel, right), working from no more than descriptions of Lippershey's device, had devised his own. It took him, he claimed, less than one day to put together. It was 10 times more powerful. It was with this basic instrument that, in January 1610, Galileo began to observe the "three fixed stars", invisible to the naked eye, that were next to the planet Jupiter. They were, he realized, **orbiting** the planet. This was a discovery that challenged the accepted notion of how heavenly bodies could orbit only one fixed point in the skies: the Earth. This explosive revelation was reinforced later the same year when Galileo began a systematic series of observations of the planet Venus. Its phases – crescent, partial, and full – could be explained only if it, too, was orbiting another body, the **Sun**. Observations made possible by the telescope were poised to revolutionize humanity's understanding of its relationship with a vast, impersonal universe.

GALILEO (1564–1642)

Galileo Galilei, born in Pisa, was an Italian scientist who, despite obstruction from religious orthodoxy, revealed an entirely new, scientific understanding of the world. The Church regarded his revelations as heresy but, reluctant to condemn the scientific pioneer outright, did its best to accommodate him. Heretic or not, Galileo died with his reputation not just growing but assured.

1611

This painting shows the Battle of Kalmar on the Baltic Sea.

IN 1604, KING JAMES I OF ENGLAND authorized a new English translation of the **Bible**. Since the Reformation there had been two previous English translations: the *Great Bible* of 1539 and the *Bishops' Bible* of 1568. However, it was felt that both contained minor **inaccuracies** and neither fully reflected the doctrinal authority and structure of the **Church of England**. The new translation, published in 1611 as *The Holy Bible*, was the work of 47 scholars under the direction of the Archbishop of Canterbury, Richard Bancroft. Though accepted relatively slowly by the Anglicans, by the 18th century it was widely regarded by all English-speaking Protestant churches as the **definitive** English-language Bible. It was only when the revised edition was issued in the late 18th century that it became commonly referred

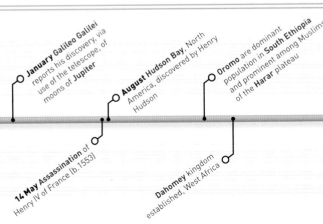

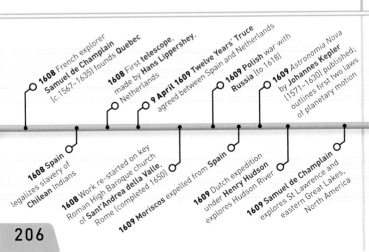

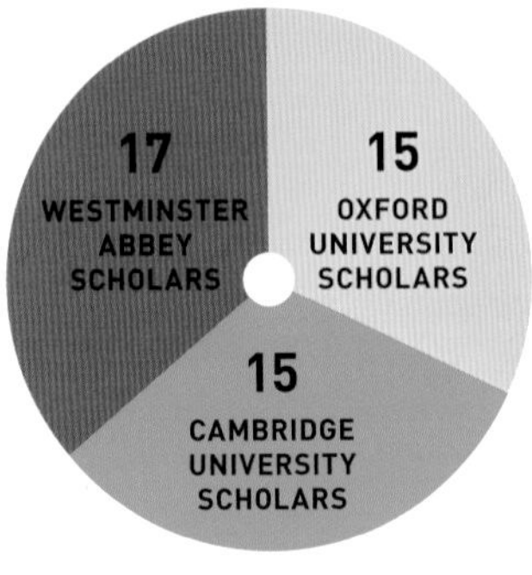

King James Bible
Several scholars from each institution translated the Bible *from Greek, Hebrew, and Latin into English in 1604–08.*

- **1608** French explorer **Samuel de Champlain** (c.1567–1635) founds **Quebec**
- **1608 Spain** legalizes slavery of **Chilean Indians**
- **1608** First **telescope**, made by **Hans Lippershey**, Netherlands
- **1608** Work re-started on key Roman High Baroque church of **Sant'Andrea della Valle**, Rome (completed 1650)
- **9 April 1609 Twelve Years' Truce** agreed between Spain and Netherlands
- **1609 Moriscos** expelled from **Spain**
- **1609 Polish** war with **Russia** (to 1618)
- **1609** Dutch expedition under **Henry Hudson** explores Hudson River
- **1609** *Astronomia Nova* by **Johannes Kepler** (1571–1630) published; outlines first two laws of planetary motion
- **1609 Samuel de Champlain** explores St Lawrence and eastern Great Lakes, North America
- **January Galileo Galilei** reports his discovery, via use of the telescope, of moons of **Jupiter**
- **14 May Assassination** of Henry IV of France (b.1553)
- **August Hudson Bay**, North America, discovered by Henry Hudson
- **Dahomey** kingdom established, West Africa
- **Oromo** are dominant population in **South Ethiopia** and prominent among Muslims of the **Harar** plateau
- **Poles** occupy **Moscow** after Swedish invasion of Russia
- **English** trading post established at **Masulipatam**, East India

Tully Castle in County Fermanagh, Northern Ireland, was built in 1619 for Sir John Hume, a Scottish "planter", or settler.

The title page of Don Quixote, part one of which was published in 1605, and part two in 1615. It remains a cornerstone of European literature.

to as the "King James Bible". And it was only in the early 19th century that it came to be known as the Authorized Version.

In June 1611, English explorer **Henry Hudson**, then in the pay of a group of English merchants, was abandoned by his crew after spending an arduous winter on the southern shore of the great bay in **northwest Canada** that bears his name. He was never seen again. Hudson was searching for a northwest passage to Asia. Just as Magellan had discovered a route to the Pacific around the tip of South America, so it was believed that a comparable **northern passage** must exist. The search for it had sparked one of the most heroically futile episodes in global exploration, a series of mostly English endeavours from 1576 that revealed only unnavigable, ice-choked, dead-ends.

Control of **the Sound** – the narrow waterway between **Denmark** and **Sweden** at the mouth of the Baltic – was a central preoccupation in the continuing Scandinavian struggle for supremacy in the Baltic. In 1611, Sweden, determined to end Denmark's stranglehold on this vital waterway, began what became known as the **Kalmar War**. The result, in 1613, was inconclusive, the Dutch and England in particular supporting the Swedes once a Danish victory threatened. Future conflict was, in effect, merely postponed.

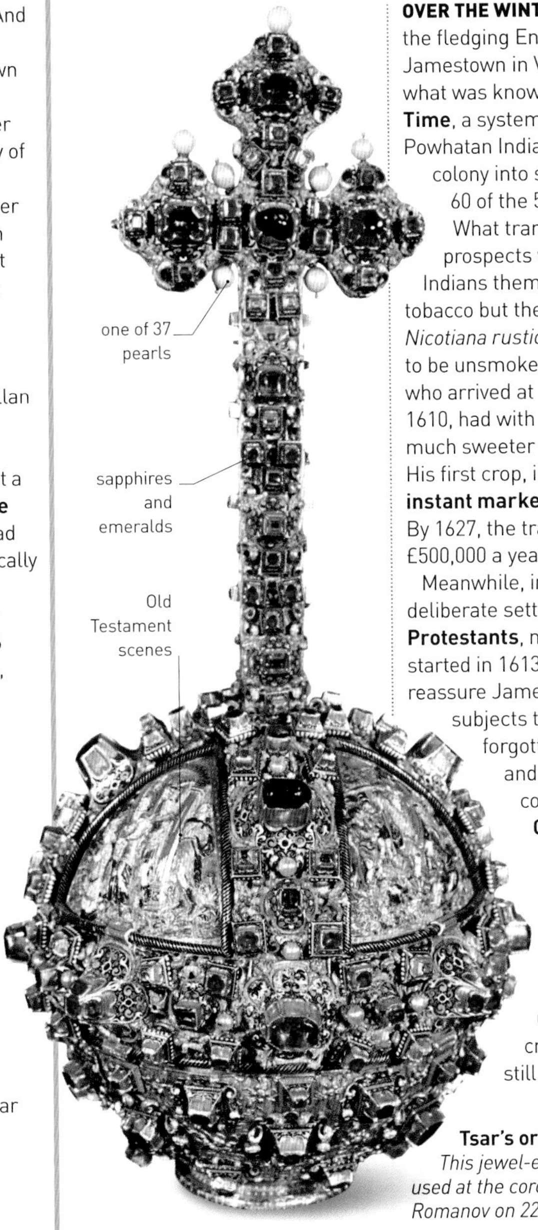

Tsar's orb
This jewel-encrusted orb was used at the coronation of Mikhail Romanov on 22 July 1613.

OVER THE WINTER OF 1609–10, the fledging English colony at Jamestown in Virginia endured what was known as the **Starving Time**, a systematic attempt by the Powhatan Indians to starve the colony into submission. All but 60 of the 500 colonists died. What transformed its prospects was **tobacco**. The Indians themselves cultivated tobacco but the native strain, *Nicotiana rustica*, was so harsh as to be unsmokeable. John Rolfe, who arrived at Jamestown in 1610, had with him seeds of the much sweeter *Nicotiana tabacum*. His first crop, in 1612, found an **instant market** in London. By 1627, the trade was worth £500,000 a year.

Meanwhile, in **Ireland** the deliberate settlement of **Protestants**, many from Scotland, started in 1613. It was intended to reassure James I's Scottish subjects that he had not forgotten their interests and to "pacify" and convert the rebellious **Catholic** population of Ireland. Its results were generally only to inflame religious passions and, by creating a Catholic underclass, to create tensions that still slumber today.

100,000
THE ESTIMATED NUMBER OF **EUNUCHS** EMPLOYED **BY** THE **MING DYNASTY** IN CHINA

IN STARK CONTRAST TO ENGLAND, where parliamentary authority would progressively increase throughout the 17th century, the influence of **France**'s legislative assembly, the **Estates-General** withered almost entirely. During the crises of the French Wars of Religion and their aftermath, the Estates-General met regularly, if ineffectually: six times between 1560 and 1614. But it would not meet again until 1789, by which point France would be on the verge of revolution.

By 1615, China was grappling with financial crisis and social breakdown. There were **tensions** in the **Chinese government** over conflict between the scholars of the Donglin Academy (literally, "the Eastern Grove Academy") in eastern China, and the court eunuchs – particularly the notoriously capricious and cruel Wei Zhongxian. With the semi-retirement of the Wanli emperor, Wei Zhongxian had assumed personal control of the government. The Donglin scholars, adherents of the moral imperatives of Confucianism, objected to the self-glorification and extravagance of the eunuchs. By 1624, Wei Zhongxian had ensured the execution of the leading Donglin academics.

Meanwhile, the **Dutch** started to settle **North America**. In 1615, the Dutch cemented their 1609 claim to the region of present-day Albany by building Fort Nassau at the same site. In 1625, they would build a further settlement at the mouth of the Hudson River, **New Amsterdam**. Dutch colonial settlement would, however, dwindle by the end of the 17th century.

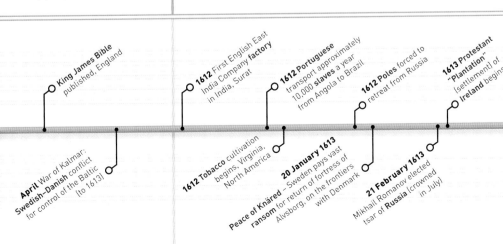

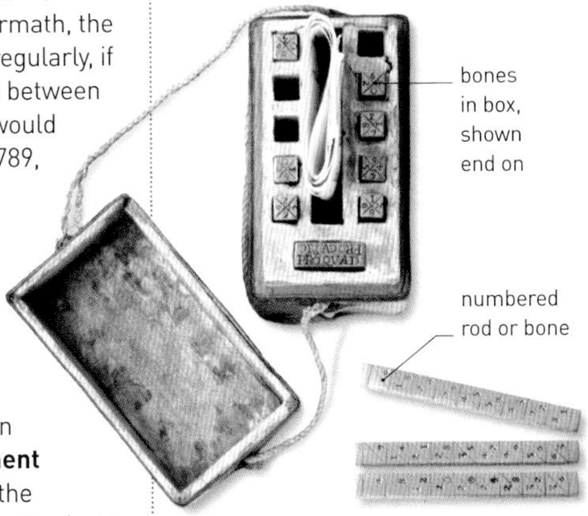

Napier's Bones
This is an abacus created by John Napier around 1615, which used numbered rods in order to simplify multiplication.

King James Bible published, England

April War of Kalmar: **Swedish–Danish** conflict for control of the Baltic (to 1613)

1612 First English East India Company **factory** in India, Surat

1612 **Portuguese** transport approximately 10,000 **slaves** a year from Angola to Brazil

1612 Tobacco cultivation begins, Virginia, North America

1612 Poles forced to retreat from Russia

20 January 1613 **Peace of Knäred** – Sweden pays vast **ransom** for return of fortress of Alvsborg, on the frontiers with Denmark

21 February 1613 Mikhail Romanov elected tsar of **Russia** (crowned in July)

1613 Protestant "Plantation" (settlement) of **Ireland** begins

1614 Scottish mathematician **John Napier** (1550–1617) publishes logarithmic tables

1614 Last meeting of the **French Estates-General** before 1789 Revolution

1614 Romanovs defeat **Cossacks** at Rostokino

1614 Christianity formally prohibited in **Japan**

1615 England sends first European ambassador to **Mughal** court

1615 Samuel de Champlain reaches Lake Huron, one of the **Great Lakes** in North America

1615 Internal conflict in **China** between **Donglin** party and corrupt **eunuch** party (to 1627)

1615 Publication of final part of ***Don Quixote de la Mancha***, by Miguel de Cervantes, Spain

1616–17

> **“** I HOPE IT WILL BE **HARD FOR** THE **RUSSIANS** TO **JUMP ACROSS** THAT **CREEK. ”**

Gustavus Adolphus, king of Sweden, Treaty of Stolbovo, 1617

THE SEEDS OF THE LATER FALL of China's Ming dynasty (see 1644) were sown in 1616 when Manchu tribal leader, Nurhaci (1559–1626), **pronounced himself Great Jin**, establishing the Qing dynasty.

20,000
THE NUMBER OF **BLUE CEILING TILES** THAT GIVE THE **BLUE MOSQUE** ITS NAME

Since 1599, he had united other Manchu tribes in the **Eight Banners military system**. War with the Ming followed in 1618.

Although the Magellan Strait, linking **the Atlantic and Pacific** in southern South America, had been discovered in 1519, it was difficult to navigate. In 1616, a **Dutch expedition** under Jakob le Maire and Willem Schouten found a new route through open water to the south, naming its southernmost island, **Cape Horn**.

One of **Islam's finest buildings** was completed after seven years in 1616. The Sultan Ahmed Mosque, in Constantinople (now Istanbul), is **known as the Blue Mosque** because of the many ceramic tiles of its interior.

Gorée Island, to the south of Africa's Cape Verde, was purchased by the Dutch from its Portuguese owners in 1617. They turned it into a **major slave trading base**, a role continued by the French, who took it in 1677.

The 1617 **Treaty of Stolbovo** ended the war between Russia and Sweden that had lasted seven years. It drew a new, more **secure boundary for Sweden** that made use of lakes Ladoga and Peipus.

Dutch slave base
This coloured engraving shows the fort at Gorée Island when it was controlled by the Dutch. It proved a highly profitable venture for them.

1618

An illustration depicts the defenestration of two regents by Protestants in Prague Castle, Bohemia, an event that sparked the Thirty Years War.

> **“** THIS IS A **SHARP MEDICINE,** BUT IT IS A **PHYSICIAN FOR ALL DISEASES** AND **MISERIES. ”**

Sir Walter Raleigh, last words before execution, 29 October 1618

ON 23 MAY 1618, THE PROTESTANT Count Thurn had the two regents of the Catholic king of Bohemia, and future Holy Roman Emperor, Ferdinand II (1578–1637), thrown from an upper window of Prague Castle, in Bohemia. The **Defenestration of Prague** sparked the brutal **Thirty Years War**. It was mostly confined to Germany, which by 1648 was a scene of wholesale destruction and slaughter. Initially a religious conflict, **Ferdinand's quest to erase Protestantism** from all his dominions became a Europe-wide fight for supremacy involving, at different points, every major European power.

On 29 October 1618, the English soldier and explorer **Sir Walter Raleigh** (1552–1618) was **executed by beheading** at the Tower of London. He had been one of the early English colonizers of Virginia, North America, but his failure to find the legendary South American **city of El Dorado**, as well as his attacking a Spanish settlement against the expressed wishes of King James I, had sealed his fate.

English privateers (state-sponsored raiders) had bought and sold **African slaves** since the late 16th century, but in 1618 England's involvement in the Atlantic slave trade became deeper when the **first slave shipment to its North American colonies** arrived from West Africa at Jamestown, Virginia.

EARLY SLAVE TRADE

Although it was in the 18th century that the Atlantic slave trade reached its peak, in the early 17th century it was developing rapidly. Slaves were transported from a series of slave forts on the west coast of Africa to the burgeoning European colonial lands of the New World. Male slaves were branded with irons (pictured) on the Atlantic Ocean crossing, in which about 25 per cent died.

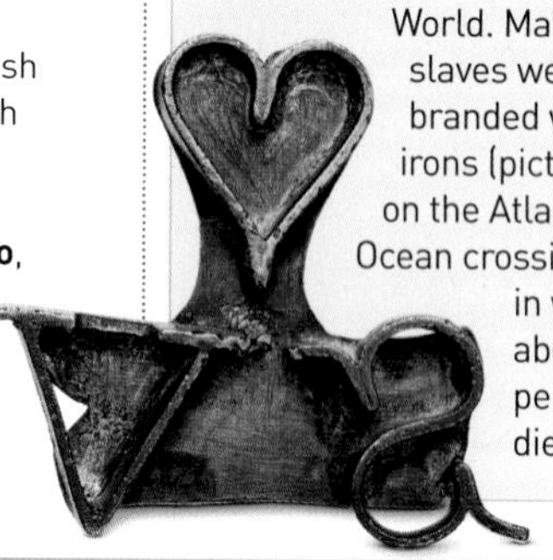

1619–20

The work of the English philosopher Fr Bacon was to have a lasting impact.

THE DUTCH, IN AGGRESSIVELY SEEKING to supplant the Portuguese in the **East Indies**, had first attempted to establish a **trading post in Java** in 1596. From 1602, they also had to contend with English efforts to infiltrate themselves in the East Indies. In 1619, the **Dutch struck back** decisively, ousting the English and their Javanese allies, and establishing themselves in Jayakarta, which they **renamed Batavia**. It would become not merely the **capital of the Dutch East Indies** but the focal point of the Dutch colonial empire, dismembered only by its conquest by Japan in 1942.

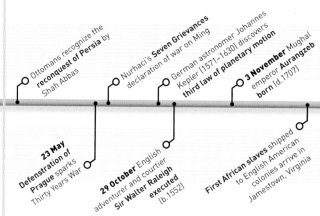

- **1616** Manchu leader **Nurhaci declares himself Great Jin** (khan) of China
- **January 1616** Dutch discover route around **Cape Horn**
- **23 April 1616** English playwright **William Shakespeare** dies (b.1564)
- **23 April 1616** Spanish writer **Miguel de Cervantes** dies (b.1547)
- **1616 Blue Mosque**, in Constantinople, completed
- **1617 Gorée Island**, south of Cape Verde, Africa, becomes a **Dutch possession**
- **27 February 1617** Treaty of Stolbovo **ends Ingrian War** between Sweden and Russia
- **21 March 1617** Algonquian Indian princess **Pocahontas dies** (b.c.1595)
- Ottomans recognize the **reconquest of Persia** by Shah Abbas
- **23 May Defenestration of Prague** sparks Thirty Years War
- Nurhaci's **Seven Grievances** declaration of war on Ming
- German astronomer Johannes Kepler (1571–1630) discovers **third law of planetary motion**
- **29 October** English adventurer and courtier **Sir Walter Raleigh executed** (b.1552)
- **3 November** Mughal emperor **Aurangzeb born** (d.1707)
- **First African slaves** shipped to English American colonies arrive in Jamestown, Virginia
- **March 1619 Qing defeat Ming** at Battle of Sarhu
- **6 March 1619** French poet **Cyrano de Bergerac born** (d.1655)
- **30 May 1619 Dutch found Batavia**, Java
- **1619 Treaty of Deulino** ends Polish–Russian War
- **8 May 1619 Synod of Dort**, Netherlands, endorses hardline Calvinist theology

“ MANY WILL TRAVEL AND KNOWLEDGE WILL BE INCREASED. ”

Francis Bacon, English philosopher, from *Novum Organum*, 1620

American Indians of the Powhatan attack a farm in the English colony of Virginia in 1622, massacring all of its inhabitants.

Novum Organum, one of the **great books of philosophy**, was written by English philosopher and scientist Francis Bacon (1561–1626) in 1620. It was a major work in the development of scientific method.

The initial phase of the Thirty Years War climaxed in the **Battle of White Mountain** in November 1620, when the forces of Holy Roman Emperor Ferdinand II **decisively routed** those of the Calvinist Frederick V (1596–1632), ruler of what was called the Palatinate, in southwest Germany. **Ferdinand's victory** over Frederick had almost exactly the opposite effect from that he might have expected. It galvanized Protestant opposition to him, importantly including Denmark.

The founding of Jamestown in 1607 as the first permanent **English colony** in the New World was overshadowed by the arrival near modern Boston in November 1620 of the ***Mayflower***. The 102 passengers on board were **Puritan pilgrims**, Protestant self-exiles staking all on a new life in a new world.

Battle of White Mountain
This major engagement – a Catholic victory – took place near Prague, and ended the first, or Bohemian, period in the Thirty Years War.

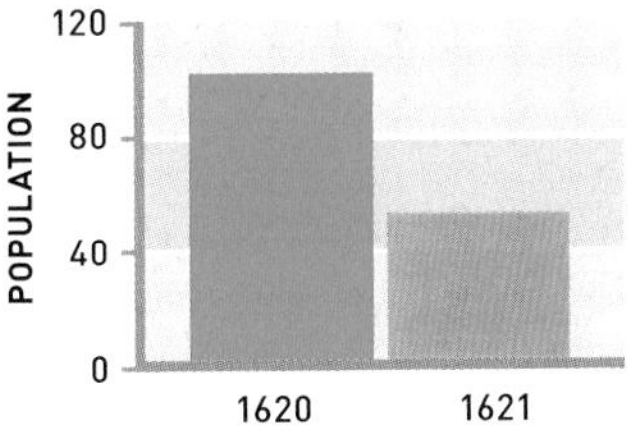

Population of Plymouth
The population of Plymouth Colony dropped dramatically in the first, difficult year of its founding.

THE PURITAN PILGRIMS of the *Mayflower* had arrived in the New World in 1620 not only late in the year, with the New England winter settling in, but in the wrong place: their original goal was the Hudson River, several hundred kilometres to the south. Their **early survival** at what they named Plymouth Colony was almost entirely a **matter of luck**, a harsh winter survived largely through American Indian aid. Thereafter, they scraped a **desperate existence**, dependent on uncertain reinforcement from England and their own, meagre efforts.

The **expiration in 1621 of the Twelve-Year Truce** between Spain and the Dutch Republic in 1609 was, perhaps predictably, the signal for a further round of **Spanish–Dutch conflict**. Both sides had increased their armies and navies in expectation of a resumption of the war. In addition, Dutch financial if not military help to Frederick V – now in exile in the Dutch Republic after his crushing defeat at White Mountain the year before – provided an obvious motive for **renewed Spanish hostility**. Yet the subsequent fighting was less an attempt by Spain at the reconquest of the Dutch so much as an **effort to destabilize them politically and economically** by attempts to ban Dutch mercantile activities and to blockade their principal ports. The Spanish were successful in besieging Jülich and Steenbergen in 1622 but an attempted siege of Bergen-op-Zoom had to be abandoned at huge cost.

The **Banda Islands**, in the East Indies, were the only known **sources of nutmeg and mace**, spices that commanded a huge premium in Europe. They were accordingly the focus of bitter, often **violent rivalry**, first between the Portuguese and the Dutch, and by the early 17th century between the English and the Dutch. In 1621, having ousted the English from the islands, the Dutch, actively encouraged by the Governor-General of the East Indies, Jan Pieterszoon Coen, set about the **extermination of the islanders**. It is estimated that of a population of 15,000, all but 1,000 were killed or expelled.

On 22 March 1622, the **Powhatan American Indians** in what was now the English colony of Virginia, **killed 347 of the settlers** – men, women, and children – approximately 25 per cent of the total number of colonists. As early as 1610, **tensions** between the settlers and the American Indians had flared into **open conflict**. By 1622, the Indians, realizing that when the settlers claimed to want peaceful relations with the Powhatan they meant it exclusively on their own terms, rose against them. The predictable consequence was a **violent English backlash**, which by the middle of the century had all but **eliminated the Powhatan** American Indians.

Determined to end the **power of the Janissaries** – the elite military group that formed the household troops and bodyguard of the Ottoman sultan – Osman II (1604–22) had made a dangerous enemy for himself since becoming sultan in 1618. His attempts to assert himself as an independent ruler provoked a **Jannissary uprising** that saw him imprisoned in his own palace. On 20 May 1622, the 17-year-old **sultan was murdered**, probably strangled, by one of his captors.

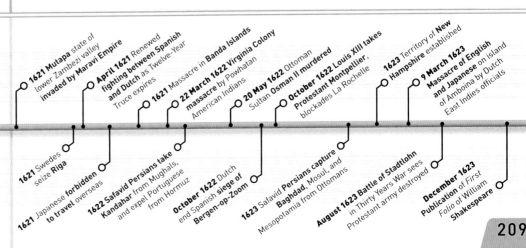

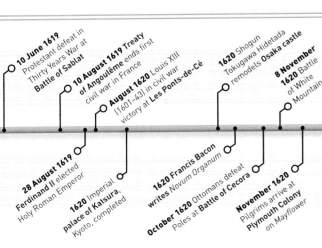

Sultan Osman II
This equestrian portrait of gouache on paper shows the Ottoman sultan Osman II. His short, but brave, reign ended in violent tragedy.

- **10 June 1619** Protestant defeat in Thirty Years War at **Battle of Sablat**
- **10 August 1619 Treaty of Angoulême** ends first civil war in France
- **28 August 1619 Ferdinand II** elected Holy Roman Emperor
- **August 1620** Louis XIII (1601–43) in civil war victory at **Les Ponts-de-Cé**
- **1620** Imperial **palace of Katsura**, Kyoto, completed
- **1620** Shogun Tokugawa Hidetada remodels **Osaka castle**
- **1620 Francis Bacon writes** *Novum Organum*
- **October 1620** Ottomans defeat Poles at **Battle of Cecora**
- **8 November 1620** Battle of White Mountain
- **November 1620** Pilgrims arrive at **Plymouth Colony** on *Mayflower*
- **1621 Mutapa** state of lower Zambezi valley **invaded by Maravi Empire**
- **1621** Swedes seize **Riga**
- **April 1621** Renewed **fighting between Spanish and Dutch** as Twelve-Year Truce expires
- **1621** Japanese **forbidden to travel** overseas
- **1621** Massacre in **Banda Islands**
- **22 March 1622 Virginia Colony massacre** by Powhatan American Indians
- **1622 Safavid Persians take Kandahar** from Mughals, and expel Portuguese from Hormuz
- **20 May 1622** Ottoman Sultan **Osman II murdered**
- **October 1622** Dutch end Spanish **siege of Bergen-op-Zoom**
- **October 1622 Louis XIII takes Protestant Montpellier**, blockades La Rochelle
- **1623** Safavid **Persians capture Baghdad**, Mosul, and Mesopotamia from Ottomans
- **1623** Territory of **New Hampshire** established
- **9 March 1623 Massacre of English and Japanese** on island of Amboina by Dutch East Indies officials
- **August 1623 Battle of Stadtlohn** in Thirty Years War sees Protestant army destroyed
- **December 1623 Publication** of *First Folio* of William **Shakespeare**

1624–25

“ WAR IS ONE OF THE SCOURGES WITH WHICH IT HAS PLEASED GOD TO AFFLICT MEN. ”

Cardinal Richelieu, chief minister of France, 1620s

IN AUGUST 1624, CARDINAL RICHELIEU (1585–1642) became chief minister to the king of France, 23-year-old Louis XIII (1601–43). Richelieu claimed that his goals were "to destroy the military power of the Habsburgs, to humble the great nobles [of France], and to raise the prestige of the **House of Bourbon** in Europe." It was ambitious, and involved alliances with groups that had little commitment to his programme. Eventually, the price of confronting enemies abroad and Protestants at home would be popular revolt in France against the financial and military burdens imposed by him. It would also lead to rebellion by the elites that culminated in the civil war of the Fronde (see 1648–49). His political **astuteness and manipulation of faction**, however, prevented political breakdown, and by his death, France was making progress against her Habsburg enemies. Richelieu also knew that Huguenot military power at home (see 1597–98) was a permanent threat to France's stability, but that the persecution of Protestant worship would lead to last-ditch resistance at home and imperil France's alliances with foreign Protestant powers, on which its **anti-Habsburg strategy** rested.

In 1625, the already tangled conflicts of the unfolding **Thirty Years War** became more complex still. With the Twelve-Year Truce over, Spain squeezed the Dutch, **taking Breda after an 11-month siege**, while France, whose policy was now being directed by the hawkish Richelieu, became covertly involved in supporting an **anti-Habsburg struggle in northern Italy**. This was an attempt by Richelieu to sever the Spanish Road, the tenuous but vital link between Habsburg Italy and the Netherlands. At almost precisely the same moment, Christian IV of Denmark (1577–1648) entered the war, in part seeking to **bolster the Protestant cause**, but more particularly to forestall Swedish ambitions to control northern Germany and the Baltic. In August 1626, his army was **defeated at the Battle of Lutter** (see right) by a Bavarian Catholic army led by Count Tilly and in alliance with the Habsburg emperor. It seemed for the moment that French scheming and Dutch fighting could not prevent a comprehensive victory for the Habsburgs.

The Surrender of Breda
Justin von Nassau is shown surrendering Breda in 1625 to Ambrosio Spinola, the Spanish commander, after an 11-month-long siege. Breda was retaken in 1637.

1626–27

This illustration shows Peter Minuit purchasing the island of Manhattan from the local American Indians, most likely the Lenape people, in 1626.

ONE OF THE MOST FAMOUS EVER TRANSACTIONS occurred on 26 May 1626 when **Peter Minuit**, director-general of the Dutch West India Company's New Netherlands settlement, **bought Manhattan island** – site of Fort Amsterdam since 1625 – from its American Indian inhabitants. The fee was 60 Dutch guilders, estimated since to be around $24. Neither side felt the deal to be overly unreasonable.

The **Thirty Years War** was a **brutal watershed** in 17th-century Europe, but its cruelty was not merely a grim consequence of battle. Always strapped for money, armies took funding into their own hands and **imposed taxes directly** on the peasants and the towns. Faced by the collection of overly heavy taxes by soldiers, peasants and poor townspeople became even more **vulnerable to fluctuations in food supply** through bad harvests, military activity, and looting. Across much of Europe, but notably in France, the Austrian Habsburg lands, and Spanish southern Italy, **peasant revolts and urban riots** threatened to take whole areas out of the control of government. With the onset of the Little Ice Age in the mid-17th century (see 1645), the problem multiplied.

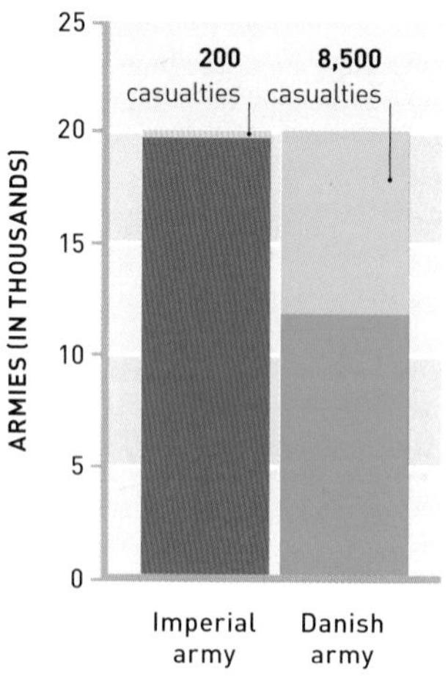

Battle of Lutter
In 1626, a Danish army, with a huge loss of about 8,500 men, failed to hold ground against a similar-sized Holy Roman Empire force.

BAROQUE ARCHITECTURE

Gathering pace in the early 17th century, the Roman High Baroque was a strong Catholic response to the Protestant Reformation, and reasserted classical Renaissance architecture. Its church building, in particular St Peter's Basilica in Rome (pictured), sought to advertise and glorify the Catholic Church, and produced numerous new and grandiose buildings.

- **January 1624** Safavid Persians **recapture Baghdad** after 90 years of Ottoman rule
- **1624** Dutch **trading post established** in Taiwan
- **May 1624** Bahia, Brazil, **seized by Dutch** from Portugal
- **June 1624** Dutch **settlers arrive in New Amsterdam**
- **12 August 1624 Cardinal Richelieu** becomes chief minister of France
- **1624 First English Caribbean settlement** at St Christopher
- **1624** Gian Lorenzo Bernini (1598–1680) completes statue of *David*
- **1625** In China, Manchus establish **capital at Mukden**
- **27 March 1625 James I** of England dies (b.1566)
- **5 June 1625** Breda, in the Netherlands, **surrenders to Habsburgs**
- **1625 Dutch seize San Juan**, Puerto Rico, from Spain
- **c.1625** Queen Nzinga (c.1583–1663) becomes **queen of Ndongo and Matamba**, southwest Africa
- **1626** German **harvest fails**
- **24 May 1626 Dutch acquire Manhattan** from American Indians
- **27 August 1626** Danes routed by Habsburgs at **Battle of Lutter**
- **30 September 1626** Manchu leader **Nurhaci dies** (b.1559)
- **18 November 1626** Consecration of **St Peter's Basilica**, Rome
- **1627 Company of New France** established for trade and settlement in North America
- **1627** Manchu **invasion of Korea**
- **1627 Auroch**, ancestor of domestic cattle, **becomes extinct**; last one killed in Poland

This 17th-century ink and watercolour miniature of Shah Jahan shows the fifth Mughal emperor with a holy nimbus around his turbaned head.

Siege of La Rochelle
Chief minister of France, Cardinal Richelieu, inspects the formidable sea wall defences of La Rochelle, during the siege of 1628.

AFTER MORE THAN A YEAR, THE SIEGE OF LA ROCHELLE, the strongest Protestant enclave in France, ended in October 1628 with **defeat for the Huguenots**. The siege was Richelieu's response to lingering hopes of Huguenot opposition to the French Crown, and was designed to both crush Huguenot resistance and dismantle its still formidable military. Though Richelieu acknowledged their right to religious toleration, he made sure they could mount **no further threat to the Crown**.

The publication in 1628 of *On the Motion of the Heart and Blood*, by royal physician **William Harvey** (1578–1657), marked one of the major discoveries of the 17th century. It **explained** both the circulation of the blood and the **functioning of the heart**, by using observation and experimentation.

One of the great leaders of India's Mughal Empire, **Shah Jahan** (1592–1666), was **crowned emperor in 1628**. His 30-year reign would be a **golden age for Mughal India**, hugely increasing the size of its territory as well as initiating a great flowering of Mughal architecture and culture.

In the 17th century, rulers across Europe embraced the idea of **strong central authority** as the only guarantee of stability. In England, for Charles I (1600–49), absolute monarchy was legitimized by his conviction that he had been divinely sanctioned by God to rule. In 1629, irritated by its checks on his authority, **he dismissed Parliament**, provoking a **growing resentment** among those seeking to share power at what were seen as attempts to impose illegal taxes.

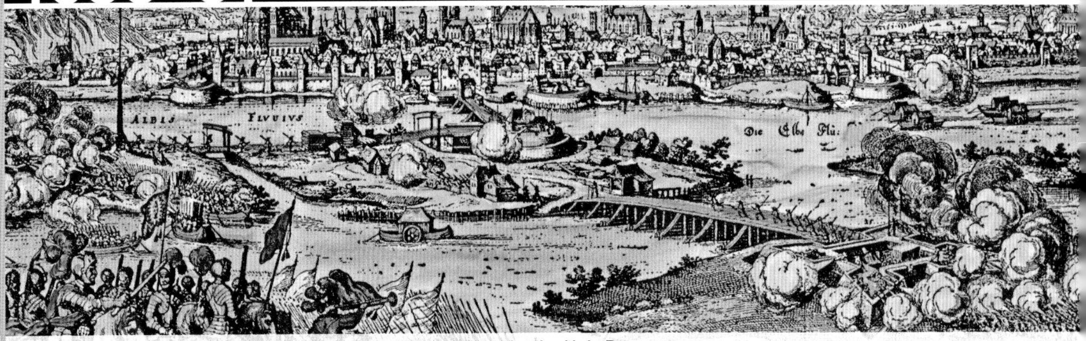

A hand-coloured woodcut depicting the siege of Magdeburg by the Holy Roman Empire. The city was later burned and 20,000 people massacred.

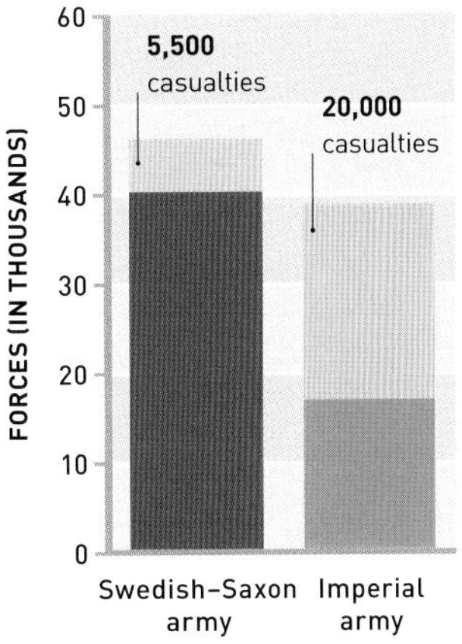

Battle of Breitenfeld
At Breitenfeld in 1631, a strong Swedish-Saxon army inflicted huge numbers of casualties on an army of the Holy Roman Empire.

THE ENTRY OF SWEDEN INTO THE THIRTY YEARS WAR in 1630 added a new dimension to the conflict. It was still essentially a religious war – one that the Catholic Holy Roman Emperor Ferdinand II was clearly winning. Exploiting this, Sweden's Lutheran king, **Gustavus Adolphus** (1594–1632), presented himself as the **saviour of the Lutheran princes** of north Germany. Yet he was potentially as much a threat to them as to Ferdinand. Having spent the previous 19 years fighting the Russians, Poles, and Danes for control of the Baltic, he now **hoped to dominate its German coast** too. His intervention might have led to nothing, however, had Imperial troops besieging the Lutheran stronghold of Magdeburg in 1631 not then **massacred the population**. This provoked outrage among the Lutheran princes. With their political support, in addition to substantial French funding, Gustavus Adolphus inflicted a **crushing defeat** over an Imperial army at **Breitenfeld**, near Leipzig, in September 1631. At this stage, his army marching triumphantly south, Gustavus Adolphus seems to have conceived a vision of an empire that included both Sweden and Germany. Yet the events of the following year would destroy this hope (see 1632).

On a day in November 1630, forever known as the **Day of Dupes**, the enemies of Cardinal Richelieu attempted to overthrow him. They demanded Louis XIII replace Richelieu with **Marie de Medici** (1575–1642), the mother of the king, and when he retired to ponder his decison they believed they had been successful. Yet **powerful friends saved Cardinal Richelieu**, and the king's mother was exiled to Compiègne.

Queen of France
Portrait of Marie de Medici, the second wife of King Henry IV of France, who attempted to displace Cardinal Richelieu in 1630.

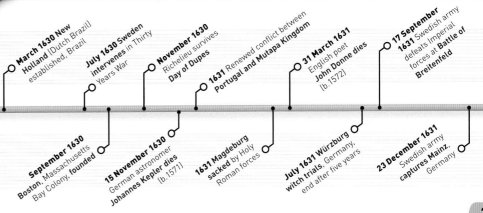

Swedish field cannon
This cannon was used by the army of Gustavus Adolphus. The barrel has a calibre (diameter) of 7cm (2¾in), and weighs 200kg (440lb).

900
THE APPROXIMATE NUMBER OF **PEOPLE BURNT AT THE STAKE** AFTER THE WÜRZBURG **WITCH TRIALS**

25 January 1628 Shah Jahan crowned emperor of Mughal Empire

1628 English physician **William Harvey** publishes key work on circulation of blood

10 August 1628 Swedish flagship *Vasa* **sinks** on maiden voyage, Stockholm

10 March 1629 Charles I of England **dissolves Parliament**

28 October 1628 Siege of La Rochelle ends

25 September 1629 Treaty of Altmark ends Polish-Sweden War

1629 North Italian Plague breaks out (to 1631)

1629 Mutapa Kingdom, East Africa, defeated by Portugal

March 1630 New Holland (Dutch Brazil) established, Brazil

July 1630 Sweden intervenes in Thirty Years War

September 1630 Boston, Massachusetts Bay Colony, **founded**

November 1630 Richelieu survives **Day of Dupes**

15 November 1630 German astronomer **Johannes Kepler dies** (b.1571)

1631 Renewed conflict between **Portugal and Mutapa Kingdom**

1631 Magdeburg sacked by Holy Roman forces

31 March 1631 English poet **John Donne dies** (b.1572)

July 1631 Würzburg witch trials, Germany, end after five years

17 September 1631 Swedish army defeats Imperial forces at **Battle of Breitenfeld**

23 December 1631 Swedish army **captures Mainz**, Germany

An oil painting depicting the trial of Galileo shows the Italian physicist and astronomer sitting before the assembled ranks of the Inquisition, in Rome.

The assassination of Field Marshal Albrecht Wallenstein took place at the Pachelbel House, at Eger, Bohemia. He was awoken and killed by his own men.

2,000,000

THE NUMBER OF **PEOPLE** WHO **DIED IN** THE **DECCAN FAMINE, 1630–32**

ANXIOUS TO MAKE GOOD ITS LOSSES TO POLAND–LITHUANIA under the Treaty of Deulino of 1619, and exploiting the death of the Polish king, Sigismund III Vasa, **Russia besieged Smolensk** in October 1632. Polish forces were unable to attempt a lifting of the siege for almost a year. Their **ultimate defeat of the Russians** in 1634, however, was absolute.

Sweden's success of the previous year in the Thirty Years War continued with a **defeat of the Imperial armies** in April 1632 at the Battle of Rain, in Bavaria. A minor triumph in November at the **Battle of Lützen**, near Leipzig, might then have confirmed Swedish territorial ambitions in Germany had **King Gustavus Adolphus** not been **killed in the battle**. At a stroke, the impetus went out of the Protestant campaign. **Habsburg supremacy** seemed to have been assured.

In 1633, Italian astronomer **Galileo Galilei** (1564–1642) was called before the **Roman Inquisition** of the Catholic Church. His crime was to support the heliocentric view of the Solar System that placed the Sun, and not the Earth, at its centre. He was **found guilty of heresy**, forced to recant, and spent the rest of his life under house arrest.

Under Japan's **Tokugawa shogunate**, a policy of *kaikin* ("sea restriction") was declared in 1633. **Contact** with the outside world was **strictly controlled**, though trade with Korea and China was allowed, and the Dutch kept a trading post. The idea was to prevent possible territorial incursions into Japan. It remained official policy until 1853.

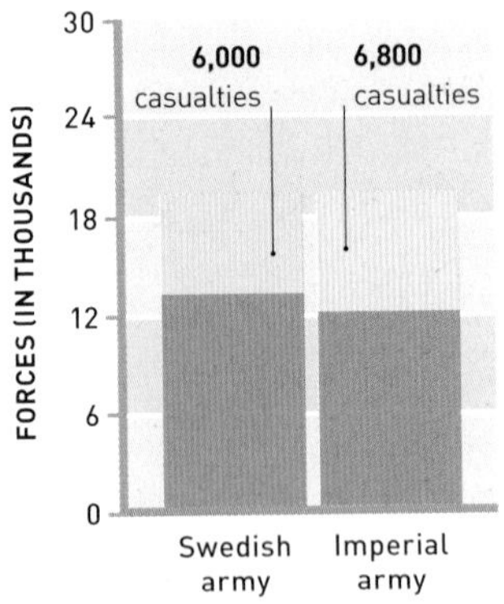

Battle of Lützen
Similar-sized forces suffered similar casualties at the Battle of Lützen. Critically, though, the Swedes lost their leader, Gustavus Adolphus.

THE DEFEAT AT LÜTZEN WAS one of the last times that **Albrecht Wallenstein** (1583–1634) led an Imperial army. Although generally successful, he was distrusted by almost everyone and was believed to be negotiating a separate peace. He was charged with treason by Holy Roman Emperor Ferdinand II, but in February 1634 was **murdered by some of his own officers**, with the tacit approval of Ferdinand. Yet, with the Swedes having failed to follow up their victory at Lützen, the initiative returned to the Imperial forces, who crushed the Swedes at the **Battle of Nördlingen** in November 1634. The subsequent Treaty of Prague, in 1635, made clear the extent of the **Habsburg triumph and the Swedish defeat**. Germany's Protestant princes now backed Ferdinand II. It provoked the final and most brutal phase of the Thirty Years War, and direct **French intervention**.

As in the 16th century, France feared Habsburg encirclement. Up to now, it had sought to secure itself by financing those states most likely to defeat the Habsburg forces, Sweden above all. With the Swedes on the verge of pulling out of Germany, the French now took the field themselves. As Franco-Swedish armies **progressively ravaged Germany**, the Swedes gradually reversing their previous losses, so Germany was devastated. The **fighting spilled into France** when, in 1636, a Spanish army invaded the northeast, briefly threatening Paris, and again, in 1637, when Spain launched an attack on Languedoc in the south. In 1639, France retaliated by invading Catalonia in the northeast of Spain. In this wave of violence, all the **participants** were by now effectively **bankrupt**. It was Spain that suffered the most, with attempts at raising revenue provoking bitter resentment, even in Spain itself. In 1640, outright revolt against the Spanish Crown broke out in Catalonia and Portugal, both **uprisings openly encouraged by France**. In the

Battle of Nördlingen
Fought in southern Germany, this battle resulted in a crushing victory for the Habsburgs – but it was not a conclusive end to the war.

April 1632 Swedish **crossing of River Rain** destroys Bavarian army, an ally of the Habsburgs

1632 Mughal emperor Shah Jahan **destroys Hindu temples**

1632 Russians **besiege Smolensk**

16 November 1632 Battle of Lützen; Swedish king, Gustavus Adolphus, killed

1632 Fasilides becomes **emperor of Ethiopia**

June 1633 Galileo condemned by Catholic Inquisition

1632 Deccan Famine, India, ends after two years

1633 Shogun Tokugawa Iemitsu (1604–51) **begins isolation of Japan**

24 February 1634 Commander of the Imperial armies **Albrecht Wallenstein** assassinated (b.1583)

1634 English **trading post opens at Canton**, China

1 March 1634 Poles and Cossacks **lift siege of Smolensk**

11 October 1634 Burchardi Flood drowns up to 12,000 on German–Denmark North Sea coast

6 September 1634 Battle of Nördlingen sees Habsburgs defeat Swedes

1634 Dutch capture Caribbean **island of Curaçao**

1634 English colony of **Maryland established**, in North America

1635 Ottomans capture Yerevan, Armenia, from Safavid Persians

1635 First meeting of **Académie Française**

1635 Treaty of Prague confirms Habsburg triumph in Germany

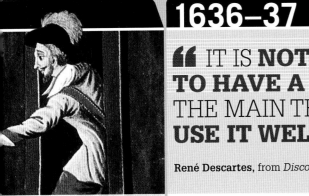

1636–37

> **“ IT IS NOT ENOUGH TO HAVE A GOOD MIND;** THE MAIN THING IS TO **USE IT WELL. ”**
>
> **René Descartes,** from *Discours de la Méthode,* 1637

1638–39

This engraving depicts the Ottoman sultan, Murad IV, sitting on a horse. His reign restored internal authority and brought secure borders with Persia.

same year, there was no Spanish New World treasure fleet. By now, the original causes of the Thirty Years War had been superseded. **Habsburg weakness**, in Spain as much as in Germany, **was increasingly apparent**.

When not conspiring against his enemies, chief minister **Cardinal Richelieu** schemed to promote French prestige, or *gloire*. He championed colonial expansion, and **promoted French arts and learning**. Among his lasting achievements was the **Académie Française**, set up in 1635. Part of a pan-European move toward officially sanctioned institutes of learning, it was also **designed to consolidate** what France saw as one of its chief claims to *gloire*: **its language**. The Académie's 40 members continue to pronounce on language usage today.

In 1635, the system of *sankin kotai* ("alternate attendance"), **introduced to Japan** by Toyotomi Hideyoshi in the 1590s, was made compulsory. The daimyo (feudal lords) were forced to spend every other year at the shogun's court at Edo to participate in lavish rituals. The cost of such submission, plus the time spent at court, **made rebellion less likely**. When they returned to their estates, which they held from the shogun, each daimyo's wife and heir remained behind. **Exacting demands were enforced** as to dress, types of weapons carried, soldier numbers accompanying each daimyo, and the contributions – military and financial – the daimyo were expected to provide.

Gondar Castle
Part of the Fasil Ghebbi, founded by Fasilides, in Ethiopia, this 17th-century castle shows Arab, Nubian, and Baroque design influences.

ETHIOPIAN EMPEROR since 1632, **Fasilides** (*c.*1603–67) founded a permanent imperial **capital at Gondar** in 1636. The buildings he constructed there included the Fasil Ghebbi, a fortress complex that became **home to Ethiopia's emperors** until the 18th century.

An early **speculative bubble burst** in February 1637, when the Dutch price of tulip bulbs peaked and then suddenly nosedived, allegedly ruining many investors. A luxury item, they were seen as a safe haven for investment in an uncertain time. Although **Tulip Mania** prices are difficult to be certain about, and have been disputed, anecdotal evidence suggests significant highs.

One of the founders of modern philosophy, French writer **René Descartes** (1596–1650), an advocate of rationalism, produced *Discours de la Méthode* in 1637. It was one of the most influential works of Western philosophy.

A major new **encyclopedia**, *The Exploitation of the Works of Nature*, by minor provincial bureaucrat, **Song Yingxing**, was published in China in May 1637. Its wide range of information regarding Chinese technology distinguished it from earlier traditions, and provided an obvious and extensive resource.

1,000 PER CENT

THE **RELATIVE PRICE OF TULIP BULBS** COMPARED TO THE **ANNUAL INCOME** OF A SKILLED DUTCH **CRAFTSMAN**

THE INTERMITTENT CONFLICT between the Ottoman Empire and the Safavid Persian Empire, which had begun in 1623, climaxed in 1638. **Baghdad fell to the Ottomans** under Sultan Murad IV (1612–40), the last Ottoman ruler to lead his troops in battle. This was followed in 1639 by the **Treaty of Qasr-i-Shirin**, which definitively settled the long-disputed Ottoman–Safavid border, largely to the benefit of the Ottomans. It granted the whole of **Mesopotamia** (modern Iraq) to the Ottomans, while handing the city of Yerevan (in present-day Armenia) to the Safavid Persians.

The problems that would eventually lead to the execution of **Charles I** of England in 1649 stemmed from the king's high-handed conviction that he could always impose himself on his kingdoms. This was not exclusively a matter of royal versus parliamentary authority. A significant element of **religious controversy** was involved, too. In 1637, Charles, encouraged by William Laud, the archbishop of Canterbury, had made the use of the **Church of England**'s *Book of Common Prayer* compulsory in Scotland. Both Charles and Laud cordially despised the **Calvinist Scottish Kirk** (Church). For their part, Scotland's Kirk elders, much like their Puritan counterparts in England, considered any attempt to **impose Anglican religious uniformity** little better than papism. Their virulent protests in the following year, known as the **Great Covenant**, were followed in 1639 by the **invasion of England** by a "Covenanter" army **from Scotland**. The king's options were narrowing.

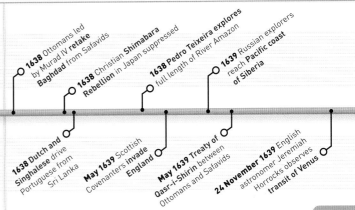

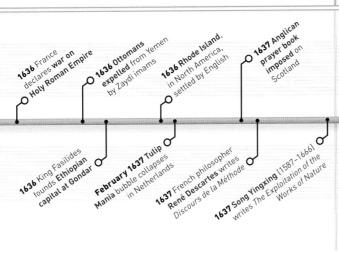

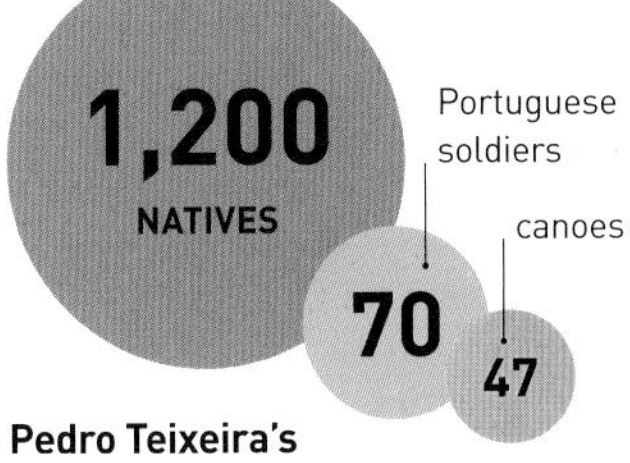

Pedro Teixeira's Amazon expedition
Teixeira's expedition was immense and expensive. Of some political interest, it was financed by the governor of Maranhão, in Brazil.

In 1638, **Portuguese explorer Pedro Teixeira** (d.1641) achieved a remarkable double first in becoming the first person to make the **return journey of the entire length of the River Amazon**, reaching Belém, at the river's mouth, more than two years after he had set out. The previous year Teixeira had been the first person to make the journey upstream, a venture partly inspired by the need to know how far east **Spanish colonists** had advanced beyond the Andes and into the Amazon Basin.

On 24 November 1639, English astronomer **Jeremiah Horrocks** (1618–41) became the first person to both predict and observe a **transit of Venus**. This rare event sees Venus pass directly between the Sun and the Earth. Observing the transit provided information vital to calculating the distance from the Earth to the Sun.

- **1635** *Sankin kotai* system **introduced in Japan**
- **1635** English colony of **Connecticut established**, in North America
- **April 1635 France** declares war on Habsburg Spain
- **25 December 1635** French explorer **Samuel de Champlain dies** (b.c.1567)
- **1636** France declares **war on Holy Roman Empire**
- **1636** King Fasilides founds **Ethiopian capital at Gondar**
- **1636 Ottomans expelled** from Yemen by Zaydi imams
- **February 1637 Tulip Mania** bubble collapses in Netherlands
- **1636 Rhode Island**, in North America, settled by English
- **1637** French philosopher **René Descartes** writes *Discours de la Méthode*
- **1637 Anglican prayer book imposed** on Scotland
- **1637 Song Yingxing** (1587–1666) writes *The Exploitation of the Works of Nature*
- **1638** Ottomans led by Murad IV **retake Baghdad** from Safavids
- **1638 Dutch and Singhalese** drive Portuguese from Sri Lanka
- **1638** Christian **Shimabara Rebellion** in Japan suppressed
- **May 1639** Scottish Covenanters **invade England**
- **1638 Pedro Teixeira explores** full length of River Amazon
- **May 1639 Treaty of Qasr-i-Shirin** between Ottomans and Safavids
- **1639** Russian explorers reach **Pacific coast of Siberia**
- **24 November 1639** English astronomer Jeremiah Horrocks observes **transit of Venus**

An illustration of Malacca, which was taken from the Portuguese by the Dutch in 1641. An earlier attack by the Dutch in 1605 had failed.

FOLLOWING A SCOTTISH INVASION OF ENGLAND IN 1639, in April 1640 Charles I (1600–49) **recalled the parliament** he had dismissed 11 years earlier. He needed approval to raise taxes for an army. Determined not to submit to its lists of grievances, he dismissed it, but a second invasion in August forced a recall. In December 1641, Parliament presented a **Grand Remonstrance**, an accusation of royal abuses of power. The king responded, in January 1642, with an attempt to arrest his parliamentary opponents. By August, the **country was at war**.

Life dancing to music
Poussin's A Dance to the Music of Time *shows four dancing figures representing poverty, labour, wealth, and pleasure in a perpetual cycle.*

By 1640, French painter **Nicolas Poussin** (1594–1665) completed *A Dance to the Music of Time*, **a key work of the era**. Poussin stressed clarity and order rather than the emotion and colour of the then dominant Baroque style.

From 1641, a devastating plague struck China, further **weakening a Ming China** threatened by both the Manchu military to the north and increasingly lawless bands of peasants roaming the country, victims of repeated famines. An almost complete **breakdown of central control** in China followed.

Continuing Dutch encroachment on the territory and trade of the Portuguese in Asia saw the **capture of the key trading base of Malacca** in 1641. It would prove a valuable cornerstone of the vast Dutch Empire in the East Indies.

A depiction of the Battle of Rocroi, fought on 19 May 1643. It resulted in the crushing victory of a French army over a Spanish force.

THE COURSE, NOT TO MENTION THE CAUSES, of the **English Civil War** that began in August 1642 was never clear cut. It pitted a **king bent on absolutism** against a Parliament determined not so much to overthrow the monarchy as to reassert its claim to **shared sovereignty in the government** of the kingdom. As the opening battles were fought, Charles I proved himself a surprisingly obstinate and able war leader. However, he was soon to become undone, not just by his compulsive deviousness but by the fact that he found himself confronting increasingly assertive and better organized Parliamentarian forces. These would be largely dominated by the formidably imposing figure of **Oliver Cromwell** (1599–1658), a Puritan, East-Anglian country squire and Member of Parliament. The war's significance, at least in English terms, was to be that Parliament could claim greater legitimacy than that of any king: in short, that **Parliament could restrain a king**, divinely sanctioned or not, held to have broken his trust with his people.

Eleven years after the village of Breitenfeld, in Saxony, had seen King Gustavus Adolphus of Sweden defeat a Holy Roman Empire army (see 1631), the **Second Battle of Breitenfeld** in October 1642 saw another decisive victory for Sweden in the Thirty Years War. Sweden was subsequently free to occupy Leipzig and the rest of Saxony, further **strengthening Protestantism** in Central Europe, and making the Catholics of the Holy Roman Empire more amenable to negotiation.

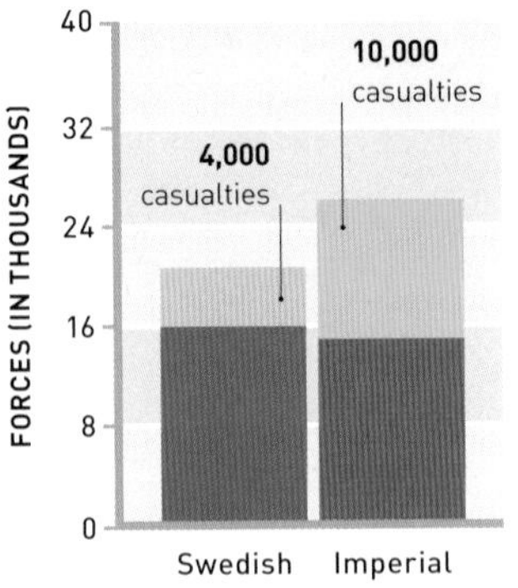

Second Battle of Breitenfeld
The imperial army of the Holy Roman Empire suffered heavy losses at the hands of the Swedish army at Breitenfeld, in Saxony.

The overwhelming French defeat of Spain at the **Battle of Rocroi** in northeast France in May 1643 put to an end to hopes of a Spanish triumph against either of the Dutch Republic or France in the Thirty Years War. **Spain was already on the defensive** against both countries. Rocroi marked the end of its dreams of European imperial dominance. The Spanish army in Flanders was destroyed, **losing almost all its most experienced infantry** in the battle. Combined with its internal struggles against the Catalonians and the Portuguese, and its chronic shortage of money, Spain risked permanent eclipse. In the short term, defeat reduced the threat from the Dutch, who were anxious that they had potentially swopped the prospect of Spanish domination for that of control by the French. In the longer term, **Spanish decline seemed inevitable**.

In 1643, Italian physicist and mathematician **Evangelista Torricelli** (1608–47) made a major contribution to scientific method in Europe with his **invention of the mercury barometer**. He had not intended to make this invention, but while working on a water pump for the Duke of Tuscany, and substituting the much heavier mercury for water, he realized that the rising and falling of a column of mercury in a tube sealed at one end was due to **changes in atmospheric pressure**.

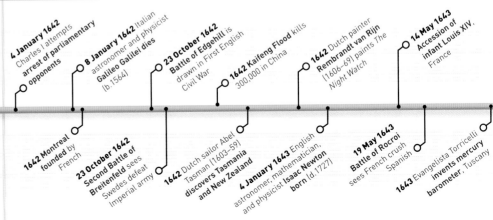

Torricelli's barometer
In this engraving, Torricelli demonstrates the existence of atmospheric pressure through the use of mercury-filled tubes.

April 1640 Short Parliament, in England, called by Charles I

1640 Nicolas Poussin completes *A Dance to the Music of Time*

May 1640 Catalan revolt against Castilian military impositions breaks out

December 1640 End of Iberian Union; John IV proclaimed king of Portugal

November 1640 Long Parliament called, ending Charles I's personal rule

1641 Revolts begin against Ming rule in China; **plague sweeps through China**

1641 Dutch take Portuguese possession of **Malacca**

22 November 1641 Grand Remonstrance of English Parliament

4 January 1642 Charles I attempts **arrest of parliamentary opponents**

1642 Montreal founded by French

8 January 1642 Italian astronomer and physicist **Galileo Galilei dies** (b.1564)

23 October 1642 Second Battle of Breitenfeld sees Swedes defeat Imperial army

23 October 1642 Battle of Edgehill is drawn in First English Civil War

1642 Dutch sailor Abel Tasman (1603–59) **discovers Tasmania and New Zealand**

1642 Kaifeng Flood kills 300,000 in China

4 January 1643 English astronomer, mathematician, and physicist **Isaac Newton born** (d.1727)

1642 Dutch painter **Rembrandt van Rijn** (1606–69) paints *The Night Watch*

19 May 1643 Battle of Rocroi sees French crush Spanish

14 May 1643 Accession of infant Louis XIV, France

1643 Evangelista Torricelli **invents mercury barometer**, Tuscany

> “ WE STUDY THE GLORY OF GOD, AND THE **HONOUR** AND **LIBERTY** OF **PARLIAMENT, FOR WHICH WE… FIGHT,** WITHOUT SEEKING OUR OWN INTERESTS… ”

Oliver Cromwell, English Parliamentarian general, Battle of Marston Moor, 1644

ON 24 APRIL 1644, AS A REBEL MING ARMY under Li Zicheng prepared to take Beijing, the **Chongzhen Emperor**, the last Ming ruler, **committed suicide**. In February, Li had proclaimed the Shun dynasty, but it was not to last long. In May, the Manchus, allying with a remnant Ming force, crushed Li's army at the Battle of Shanhai Pass. By the autumn, the **first Manchu Qing emperor** of China, the six-year-old Shunzhi Emperor (1638–61), had been installed in Beijing. Ming resistance in the south continued until 1681. The Qing themselves ruled until their collapse in 1911.

In the **English Civil War**, the Battle of Marston Moor in July 1644 saw a **decisive victory for Parliament**. The following summer, at Naseby in June 1645, ultimate victory was virtually guaranteed when the main army of Charles I was annihilated by Parliament's newly formed **New Model Army**. Led by Oliver Cromwell and Sir Thomas Fairfax, the New Model Army brought a greater professionalism and mobility into the conflict, and emphasized the ultimately superior resources of the Parliamentary cause.

Potala Palace in Tibet
The Potala Palace, seen atop the Marpo Ri hill in this view from the south, rises more than 300m (1,000ft) above the valley floor.

From about 1645, the northern hemisphere saw **crop failures** brought about by abnormally cold winters. The result was **famine** on a massive scale, leading to both war and the collapse of state structures across the globe. These **climatic changes**, known since 1976 as the Maunder Minimum, were the result of reduced sunspot activity, the direct consequence of which was the **Little Ice Age** in which global temperatures fell by several degrees.

In 1645, the 5th Dalai Lama, Lozang Gyatso (1617–82), began the construction of the **modern Potala Palace**, in Lhasa, Tibet. Construction finally ended in 1694, and it remained the seat of the Dalai Lama up to 1959.

GROWTH OF QING EMPIRE

Having secured control of China proper in 1644, the Qing Empire continued to expand throughout the 17th and 18th centuries, provoked in part by the threat of Russian, British, and French moves into Asia. Only some areas of the vast empire were governed directly by the Manchu or settled by the Chinese. Much was secured, at huge expense, through military garrisons.

Carisbrooke Castle, on the Isle of Wight, England, was where Charles I was imprisoned for 14 months, from 1647, after his defeat in the English Civil War.

POWER IN THE EARLY YEARS OF THE QING DYNASTY was exercised by the child-emperor's uncle, **Prince Dorgon** (1612–50). A distinctive feature of the Qing was their hair, shaved at the front, plaited into a pigtail at the back, and known as a "queue". Dorgon now made this **compulsory for all male Han Chinese** (the Queue Order). Clashing with Confucian contention that hair, as a gift from your parents, should never be cut, to wear a Manchu pigtail was seen as a mark of servility, as Dorgon intended. **Thousands** who refused to adopt it **were put to death**.

On 26 May 1647, the **Massachusetts Bay Colony banned Jesuit priests** from the colony. Founded as a staunchly Puritan enclave, the colonists loathed the Jesuits as a sinister manifestation of popery. Also, increasingly alarmed by the French Jesuit missionaries in Canada, who had converted many Huron and Algonquin American Indians, they were determined that a movement **"subversive to society"** should have no place in the new colony.

After escaping Parliament's siege of Oxford in April 1646, King **Charles I surrendered** to a Scottish army. The next year they delivered him to Parliament. He was **imprisoned at Carisbrooke Castle**, on the Isle of White. From there, he continued to try to bargain with the various parties, but his secret negotiations with the Scottish Presbyterians to invade England led to a **renewal of the civil war**.

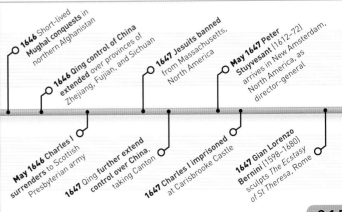

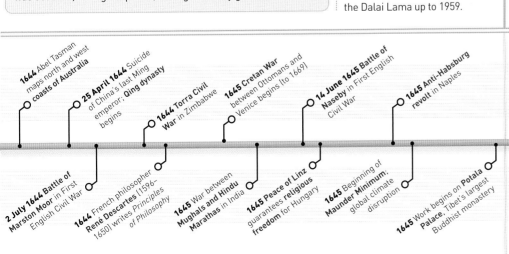

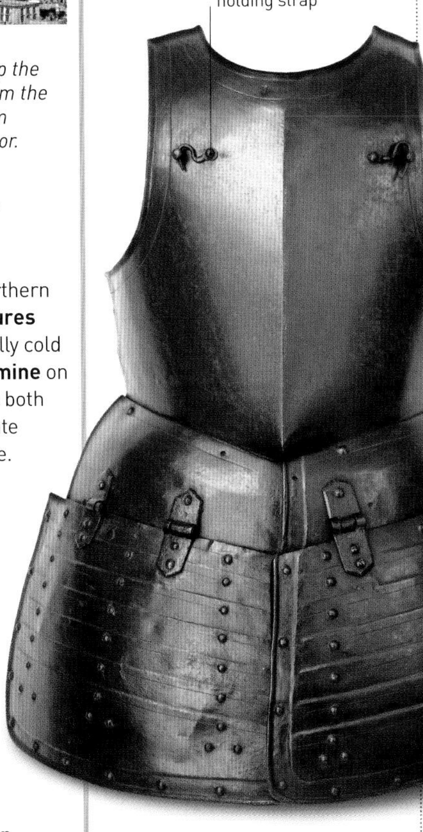

English Civil War armour
Metal breastplates with appended tassets (to protect the legs and lower body) were used by foot soldiers on both sides during the civil war.

- **1644** Abel Tasman maps north and west **coasts of Australia**
- **2 July 1644 Battle of Marston Moor** in First English Civil War
- **25 April 1644** Suicide of China's last Ming emperor; **Qing dynasty** begins
- **1644** French philosopher **René Descartes** (1596–1650) writes *Principles of Philosophy*
- **1644 Torra Civil War** in Zimbabwe
- **1645** War between **Mughals and Hindu Marathas** in India
- **1645 Cretan War** between Ottomans and Venice begins (to 1669)
- **1645 Peace of Linz** guarantees **religious freedom** for Hungary
- **14 June 1645 Battle of Naseby** in First English Civil War
- **1645** Beginning of **Maunder Minimum**; global climate disruption
- **1645 Anti-Habsburg revolt** in Naples
- **1645** Work begins on **Potala Palace**, Tibet's largest Buddhist monastery
- **1646** Short-lived **Mughal conquests** in northern Afghanistan
- **May 1646 Charles I surrenders** to Scottish Presbyterian army
- **1646 Qing control of China extended** over provinces of Zhejiang, Fujian, and Sichuan
- **1647** Qing **further extend control over China**, taking Canton
- **1647 Jesuits banned** from Massachusetts, North America
- **1647 Charles I imprisoned** at Carisbrooke Castle
- **May 1647 Peter Stuyvesant** (1612–72) arrives in New Amsterdam, North America, as director-general
- **1647 Gian Lorenzo Bernini** (1598–1680) sculpts *The Ecstasy of St Theresa*, Rome

THE STORY OF ARMS AND ARMOUR

FROM STICKS AND STONES TO A DEADLY ART FORM

Whether for hunting or sport, conflict or contests of skill, hand-held arms have played a crucial role in human existence and advancement. The first weapons developed out of survival tools: found objects, such as stones, were used to bludgeon prey, or to fend off predatory animals or rival humans.

As prehistoric man's skills advanced, simple clubs and stone hand-axes gave way to carefully crafted wooden spears used to hunt animals or impale fish. Even more effective weapons married wooden shafts with razor-sharp flint blades to form axes, daggers, spears, and arrowheads. Soft, easily worked metals such as copper replaced flint, followed by stronger, sharper, and longer Bronze and Iron Age swords, daggers, javelins, and battle-axes. Until the advent of firearms, the history of hand-held weapons is one of variations on a theme, culminating in the sophisticated forging processes of Japan's samurai swords, which at their height in the 14th–16th centuries, wrapped super-sharp steel around a flexible iron core.

SHIELDS

Like arms and body armour, shields – a type of "accessory armour" – could be functional, decorative, or both. During the medieval period in Europe, when knights held high status in society, shields were often embellished with elaborate scenes of courtly devotion or prowess in battle. Decoration like this was thought to bring added protection to the bearer.

15th-century Flemish shield

THE DEVELOPMENT OF ARMOUR

Early "armour" consisted of padding: thick layers of cloth with a stiff leather "helmet" to protect the head. Plated helmets, breastplates, and wooden shields were used by classical Greek and Roman armies, but elsewhere, ordinary soldiers relied on padding, leather, and luck – a situation that changed little in Europe until chain mail was perfected in 11th-century France. Full suits of armour were costly, so they were also used as status symbols.

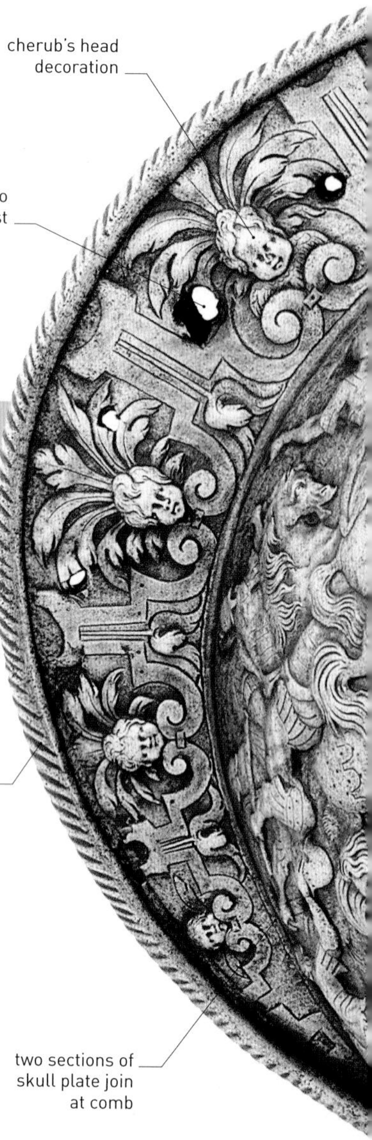

French 16th-century embossed helmet
Armour reached its greatest decorative heights during the Renaissance. Suits and helmets were embossed and etched, gilded or silvered, particularly for tournaments – and to show the owner's wealth and status.

750,000–50,000 BCE
Flint cutting edges
Razor-sharp flint daggers, spears, and axes are used for both hunting and warfare.

Flint dagger

450,000–400,000 BCE
Wooden weapons
Easily worked and readily available, wood is shaped into spears for hunting or defence.

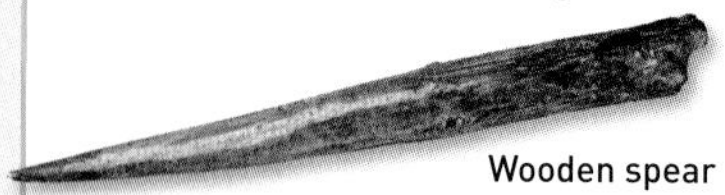

Wooden spear

5500–3300 BCE
Flint arrowheads
The wooden bow combined with arrowheads made from sharpened flint prove a deadly combination, allowing users to strike their victims from a safe distance.

3700–2300 BCE
Metal weapons
Metalworking gives rise to sophisticated and effective blades in the Bronze and Iron Ages.

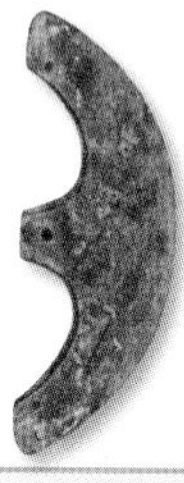

Bronze axe

2500 BCE
Helmets
The first part of the body to be protected is the head. Early armies use plated helmets, but most soldiers rely on leather caps.

Attic helmet

c.1400 BCE
Suit armour develops
Plated body armour is an early invention, but it is expensive and not always practical for movement in battle.

Mycenaean armour

6th–mid-5th centuries BCE
The crossbow
Crossbows can be cocked well in advance of firing – providing one of the earliest "loaded" weapons.

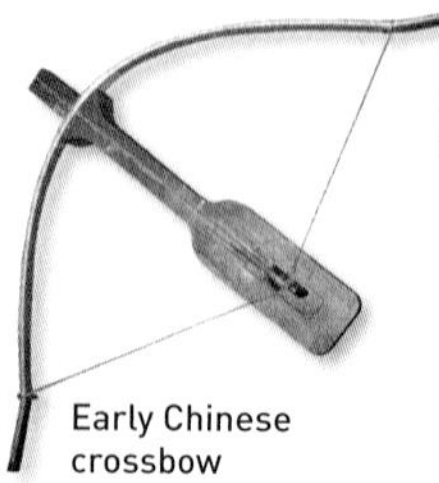

Early Chinese crossbow

3rd–4th centuries
Steel blades
Adding carbon to iron produces steel, which allows bladed weapons to be mass-produced. Blades also become stronger and longer.

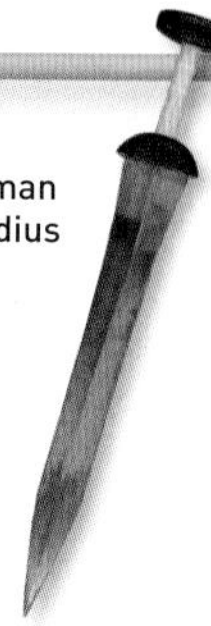

Roman gladius

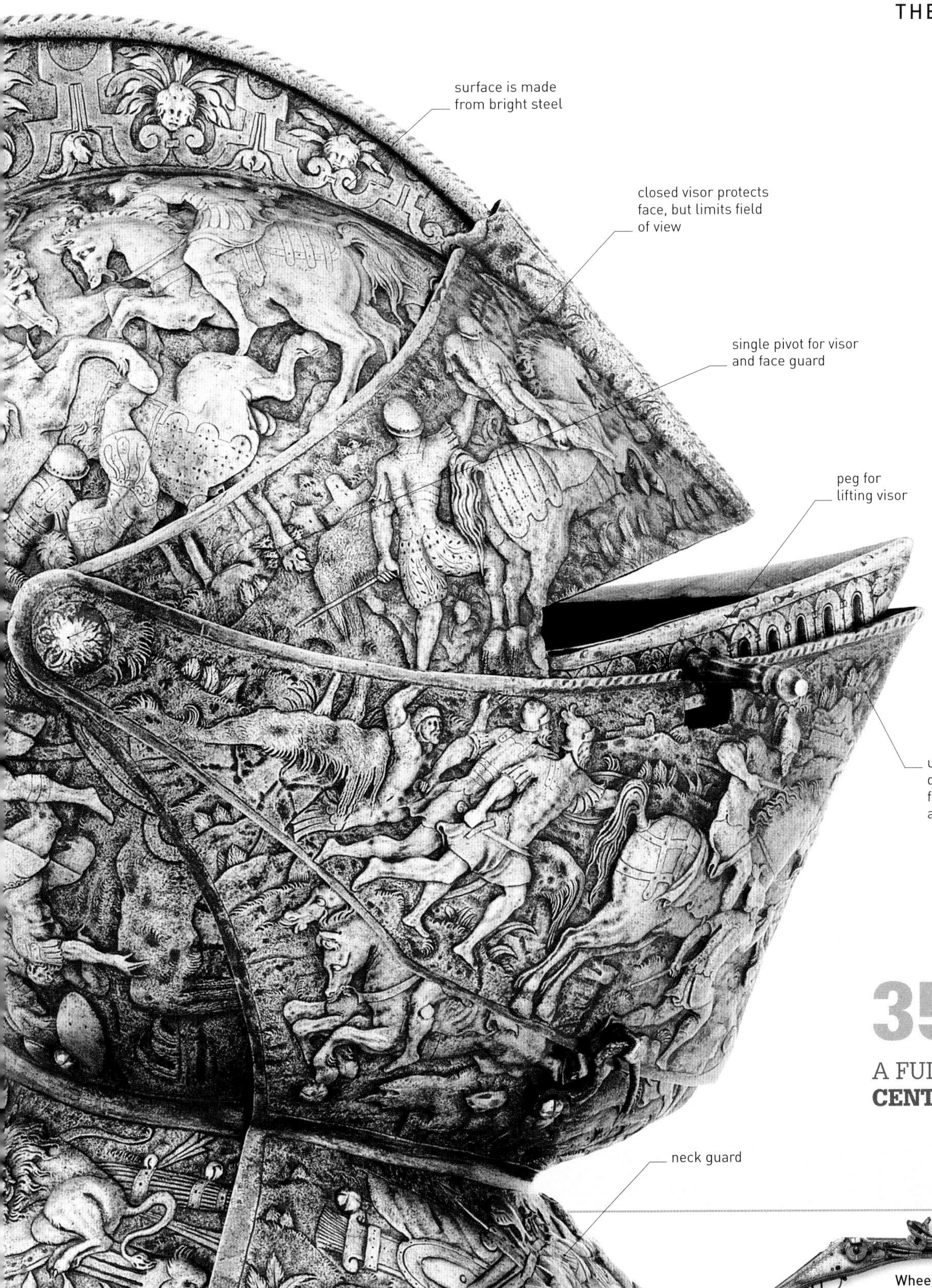

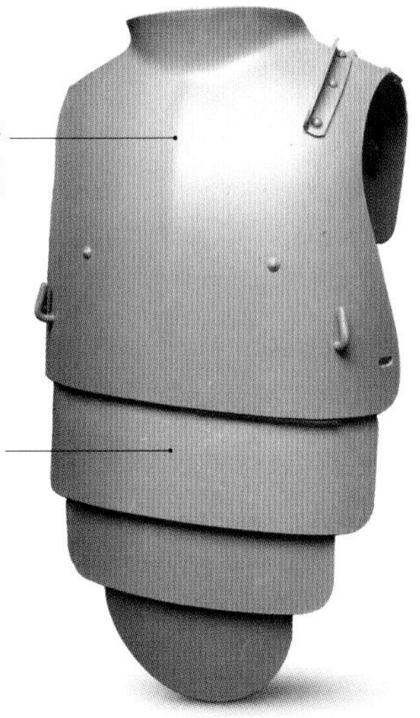

The return of armour
During World War I, body armour was revived. German machine gunners wore suits like this one when firing from exposed places.

35kg THE APPROXIMATE WEIGHT OF A FULL SUIT OF EUROPEAN **16TH-CENTURY TOURNAMENT ARMOUR**

Chain mail

11th century
Mail perfected
Lighter and less bulky than armour plate, chain mail worn over a gambeson (padded jacket) saves lives.

1100 onwards
Swords improve
The cross-guard is added to protect the hand, and marks the first big change to sword design since Roman times. Refined edges mean swords can now cut and stab.

15th century
First suits of full plate armour develop
Suits of armour provide the best protection. Gloves now have jointed fingers, while shoulder plates bring freer movement and less exposure.

Wheel-lock pistol

15th–17th centuries
Firearms developed
With the invention of guns, body armour shrinks back to the cuirass (breastplate), to allow for drawing of pistols.

19th century
Automatic-loading firearms
The advent of the revolver, with its rotating cylinder, meant that multiple shots could be fired before reloading.

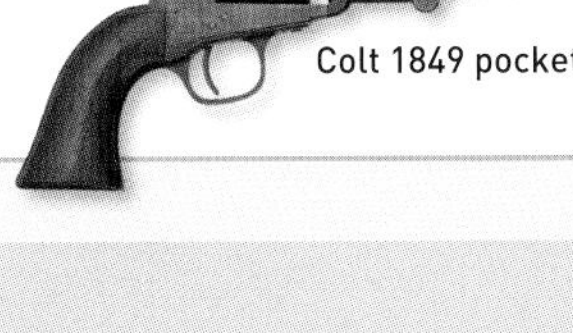
Colt 1849 pocket pistol

1939–1945
Flak jackets
Based on the same design as the cuirass, World War II flak jackets stop shrapnel, but not bullets.

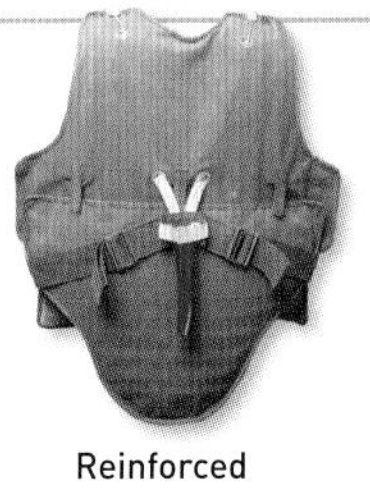
Reinforced flak jacket

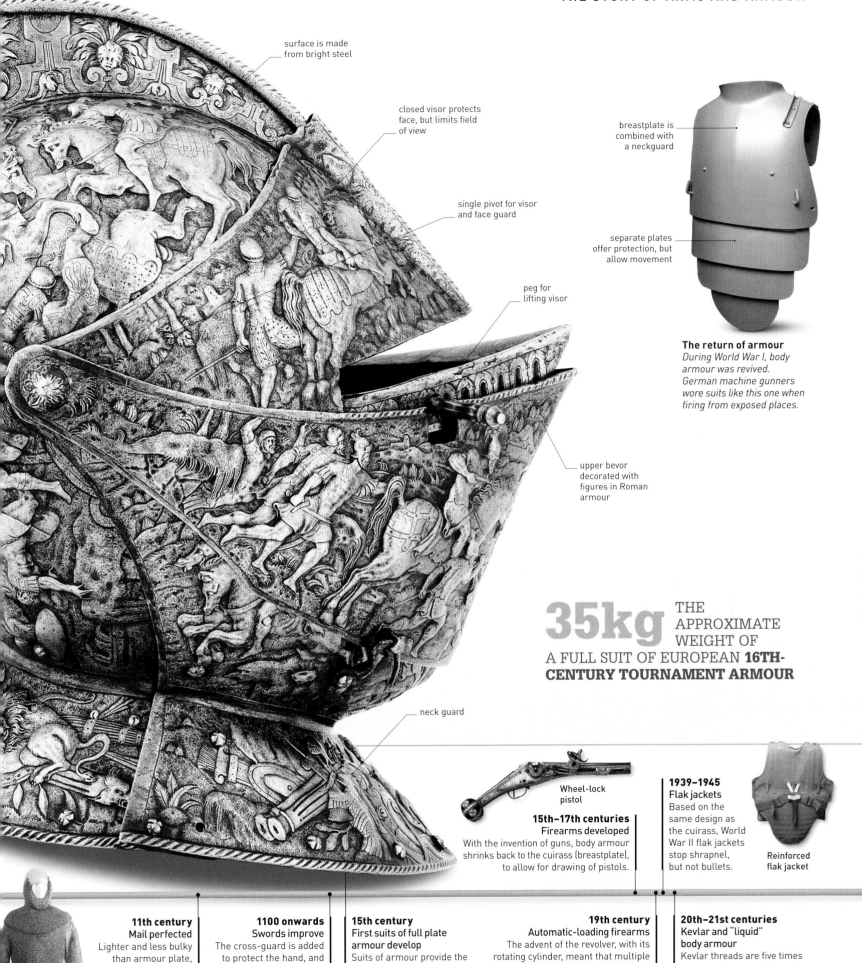

20th–21st centuries
Kevlar and "liquid" body armour
Kevlar threads are five times stronger than steel. Soaked in shear thickening fluid (STF), it can withstand bullet penetration.

1648

Cannon and gunners are seen in this 17th-century painting commemorating the actions of the royalist forces in defeating the Fronde uprising in France.

THE DEATH OF LOUIS XIII in May 1643 had brought to the French throne the **four-year old Louis XIV**, under the regency of his mother, Anne of Austria (in direct defiance of Louis XIII's will). Whatever France's successes in the Thirty Years War (see 1635) and its emerging supremacy over Spain, the country was not only **strapped for cash**, it had to confront continuing **peasant uprisings** brought about by harvest failures and punitive **demands for tax**. In addition, those nobles that Cardinal Richelieu (see 1624) had excluded from government were invited back to counter those supporters of Richelieu who were hostile to Anne and her new chief minister, Cardinal Mazarin (1602–61). Bungled attempts to manage factional rivalries while maintaining a costly war were to lead to government breakdown in 1648 with the **Fronde** – initially a parliamentary protest, but later an **aristocratic uprising**. Four years of turmoil followed: Paris was taken, the royal family fled, and Mazarin was twice forced into exile. When it fizzled out in 1652, the way lay open to a better management of aristocratic loyalties that was to come with the personal rule of Louis XIV from 1661.

> “ DO YOU NOT KNOW, MY SON, **WITH** WHAT **LITTLE WISDOM THE WORLD IS GOVERNED?** ”
>
> **Axel Oxenstierna, Swedish chancellor,** Westphalia, 1648

In October 1648, after four years of negotiations, the **Thirty Years War** in Germany was brought to a close with a series of treaties collectively known as the **Treaty of Westphalia**. France was still at war with Spain (as it would be until 1659), but Germany's horrors at least had been ended. France secured rather vaguely defined gains on its eastern border; Sweden was confirmed in its possession of Pomerania on the Baltic coast, as well as receiving a huge cash payment from the **Holy Roman Emperor**, Ferdinand III, to withdraw its troops. Among the German states, **Brandenburg–Prussia** gained the most.

Crucially, Spain also recognized the independence of the Dutch Republic, and Germany's local rulers were given the right to make **alliances with foreign powers**, in effect confirming them as sovereign states. The authority of the Holy Roman Emperor appeared **fatally undermined**.

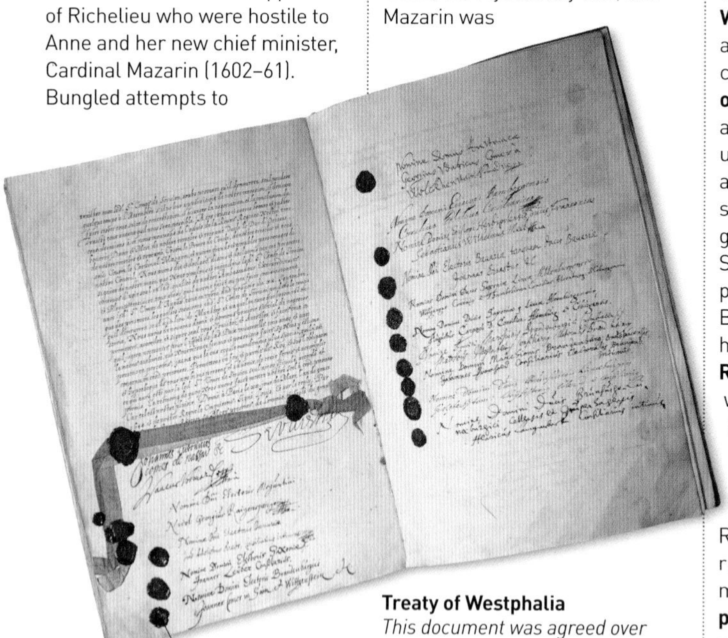

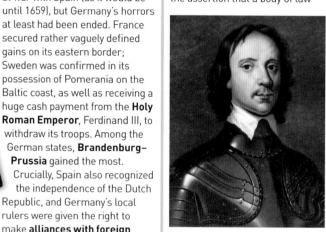

Treaty of Westphalia
This document was agreed over several months and signed by the Holy Roman Emperor and the king of France, ending 30 years of war.

1649–50

This depiction of the execution of King Charles I of England outside the Banqueting House, in London, was painted by English artist John Weesop.

ON 30 JANUARY 1649, Charles I of England was beheaded. He remains the only **king of England** to have been **legally executed**. His conviction by the High Court of Justice as "tyrant, traitor, and murderer" was carried by a vote of 68 to 67. Throughout his trial, Charles consistently rejected any idea that any court could legally try a king. "I would know by what power I am called hither... Remember I am your King, your lawful King." In reality, there is little doubt that since the triumph of the parliamentary New Model Army, **dominated by Oliver Cromwell**, his death became a possible outcome to the crisis. The awkward question was whether one form of tyranny was being swapped for another. Nonetheless, what counted was the assertion that a body of law separate from the person of the king existed that no one, legal ruler or not, could disregard: **Parliament, not the king, was the law's rightful custodian.**

Oliver Cromwell
This portrait of Oliver Cromwell, the chief instigator of the trial and execution of the king, was painted by English artist Robert Walker.

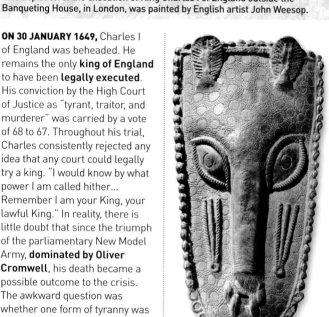

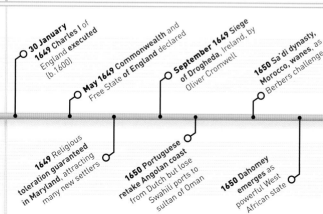

Dahomey panther mask
This bronze pendant in the shape of a stylized head of a panther, dating from 17th-century Dahomey, shows the country's cultural sophistication.

At the end of the 1640s, the **Kingdom of Dahomey** began to emerge as a **powerful force** under King Wegbeja (d.1685). After uniting the lands of the Aja and the Fon, he introduced new laws, **reformed government** and bureaucracy, and initiated a religion and culture that would characterize this **West African state** for more than two centuries.

- **January Khmelnytsky Uprising** (to 1651): Ukrainian Cossacks seek independence from Poland–Lithuania
- **17 January** Long Parliament breaks off negotiations with Charles I, leading to **Second English Civil War**
- **30 January Eighty Years War** between Dutch and Spanish ends
- **The Fronde**, a French aristocratic rebellion against Cardinal Mazarin, begins (to 1652)
- **24 October Treaty of Westphalia** ends Thirty Years War in Germany
- Mughals **transfer imperial court** to Shahjahanabad (Delhi)
- **April Portuguese defeat Dutch army** in Brazil
- **Ottomans besiege** Venetian-held **Crete**
- Russian **serfs lose rights**; anti-tax risings in Moscow
- Russian explorer Semyon Dezhnev (1605–72) **discovers Bering Strait**
- **12 September** Battle of Stirling fought during **Scottish Civil War**
- **11 December Pride's Purge** expels majority from England's Long Parliament, **creating Rump Parliament**
- **30 January 1649 Charles I** of England **executed** (b.1600)
- **May 1649 Commonwealth** and Free State of England declared
- **1649** Religious **toleration guaranteed in Maryland**, attracting many new settlers
- **September 1649 Siege of Drogheda**, Ireland, by Oliver Cromwell
- **1650 Portuguese retake Angolan coast** from Dutch but lose Swahili ports to sultan of Oman
- **1650** Sa'di **dynasty**, Morocco, **wanes**, as Berbers challenge
- **1650 Dahomey emerges** as powerful West African state

> **“ IT IS NOT WISDOM BUT AUTHORITY THAT MAKES A LAW. ”**

Thomas Hobbes, English philosopher, from *Leviathan*, 1651

The Coronation of Louis XIV, a tapestry from a painting by Charles Le Brun, court artist to Louis XIV, shows the young Louis about to receive his crown.

CHARLES I'S EXECUTION did not mark the final collapse of the royalist cause in England. A rump army, much of it Scottish, was still active. The royalists had an obvious **figure to rally round**, Charles's elder son, also called Charles. Yet his **defeat at Worcester** in September 1651 marked the final battle of the English Civil War, and saw Charles forced into a nine-year exile.

One of the foundations of **Western political philosophy** appeared in 1651 when Thomas Hobbes (1588–1679) published *Leviathan*. It argued for the **absolutism of a sovereign authority**. Though recognizing the liberty of the individual, Hobbes believed that anarchy could only be averted through a strong central government. It was an early example of **social contract theory** (individuals in society are united by mutual consent) and was profoundly influential.

In 1648, the **Khmelnytsky Uprising** saw a Cossack revolt against the rule of the Polish–Lithuanian Commonwealth in the Ukraine, which had been awarded to Poland under the Treaty of Lublin of 1589. The uprising climaxed in 1651 with the **Battle of Berestechko**, the largest single battle of the 17th century. The result was a victory of sorts for the Polish–Lithuanians. However, the ultimate effect of the struggle was a **weakening of the Commonwealth**, which was already wracked by numerous internal disputes among its querulous nobles.

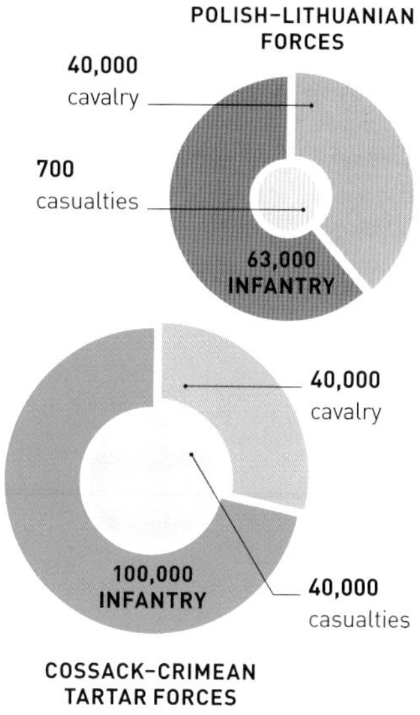

Battle of Berestechko, 1651
The Cossack–Crimean Tartar forces suffered 40,000 casualties at Berestechko, far more than their Polish–Lithuanian adversaries.

The first of three **wars between England and the Netherlands** began in 1652 (two followed in 1665–67 and 1672–74). All were naval wars fought for command of the sea and **ship-borne commerce**. For the Dutch, a small nation with few natural resources, but still the leading mercantile power of Europe, they assumed vast importance. For the English, they marked the **emergence of a new bullish confidence**. England's eventual victory signalled the decline of Dutch commercial pre-eminence, and launched a new **Anglo-French rivalry** for commercial and colonial supremacy.

ONE OF THE WORLD'S ICONIC structures, the **Taj Mahal**, in Agra, India, was completed in 1653 after 19 years. A mausoleum built by Mughal emperor Shah Jahan (1592–1666) **in memory of his third wife, Mumtaz Mahal**, it combined Indian, Persian, and Islamic styles of architecture.

In December 1653, **Oliver Cromwell** was made **Lord Protector of England**. Various types of government for the new republic had previously been tried, including military rule, while **parliaments were formed and dissolved**, generally by the irascible Cromwell, with great rapidity. Cromwell resisted the idea that he be made king. In the end, after his death in September 1658, it appeared desirable and inevitable that the vacuum could be filled only by the restoration of the actual king-in-waiting, the future Charles II.

Weakened by its struggle with the Cossacks during the Khmelnytsky Uprising, the partial **dismemberment of the Polish–Lithuanian Commonwealth** by neighbours eager for territorial gains became inevitable. The **resulting devastation** – its population almost halved, its economy all but destroyed – is known as The Deluge. Not only did Poland endure a Russian invasion in June 1654, in what became known as the **Thirteen Years War**, the following year Sweden, too, invaded the country. The most enduring consequence of this calamitous period was not merely **Poland's loss of the Ukraine** to Russia under the Treaty of Andrusovo in 1667; rather, that Orthodox Russia was immensely boosted, and its tsars' claims to rule "all the Russias" made tangible.

On 7 June 1654, the 15-year-old **Louis XIV was crowned king of France**. Since acceding to the throne when aged four, first his mother and then Cardinal Mazarin acted as regent. His subsequent reign, of 72 years and 110 days, remains one of history's longest.

Taj Mahal
This view of the white domed marble of the Taj Mahal, in India, has made it one of the most recognizable and admired buildings in the world.

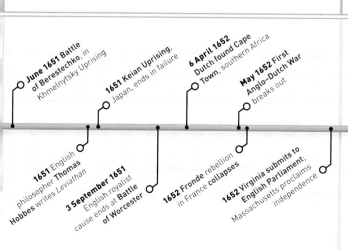

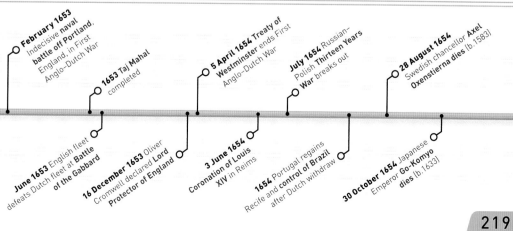

- **June 1651 Battle of Berestechko**, in Khmelnytsky Uprising
- **1651** English philosopher **Thomas Hobbes** writes *Leviathan*
- **1651 Keian Uprising**, Japan, ends in failure
- **3 September 1651** English royalist cause ends at **Battle of Worcester**
- **6 April 1652 Dutch found Cape Town**, southern Africa
- **1652 Fronde** rebellion in France **collapses**
- **May 1652 First Anglo-Dutch War** breaks out
- **1652 Virginia submits to English Parliament**; Massachusetts proclaims independence
- **February 1653** Indecisive naval **battle off Portland**, England, in First Anglo-Dutch War
- **June 1653** English fleet defeats Dutch fleet at **Battle of the Gabbard**
- **1653 Taj Mahal** completed
- **16 December 1653** Oliver Cromwell declared **Lord Protector of England**
- **5 April 1654 Treaty of Westminster** ends First Anglo-Dutch War
- **3 June 1654 Coronation of Louis XIV** in Reims
- **July 1654** Russian–Polish **Thirteen Years War** breaks out
- **1654** Portugal regains **Recife and control of Brazil** after Dutch withdraw
- **28 August 1654** Swedish chancellor **Axel Oxenstierna dies** (b.1583)
- **30 October 1654** Japanese Emperor **Go-Komyo dies** (b.1633)

1655–56

This engraving on wood depicts Brandenburg forces storming Polish positions at the Battle of Warsaw in 1656 during the First Northern War.

12,000,000

SQUARE KILOMETRES

THE APPROXIMATE **SIZE OF** THE **EMPIRE** CLAIMED BY **PORTUGAL**

FEARFUL OF RUSSIAN DOMINATION OF THE BALTIC, Sweden entered the Thirteen Years War between Russia and Poland–Lithuania in 1655, thus creating the **First Northern War**. Other countries were sucked in and alliances changed. In 1656, the Polish capital Warsaw was taken by a Swedish–Brandenburg force, further **undermining the Polish–Lithuanian state**.

One of the **greatest paintings in Western culture** was created in 1656 when Spanish artist Diego Velázquez (1599–1660) painted *Las Meninas*, an enigmatic work that has been hugely influential.

A renewed phase of **Ottoman** confidence began when Köprülü Mehmed (1575–1661) became **grand vizier** in 1656, Sultan Mehmed IV handing him control of the empire. He ruthlessly stamped out opposition and embarked on a series of military campaigns – completed after his death in 1661 – that saw the **empire at its greatest extent**.

Las Meninas

Diego Velázquez's painting of Margarita, the daughter of Philip IV of Spain, and her entourage, is known for its complex composition.

1657

A manuscript showing Ottoman troops on the island of Lemnos.

ON 2 MARCH 1657, the **Great Fire of Meireki** began in Edo (Tokyo). In two days, fed by relentless winds, it destroyed almost 70 per cent of the city, consuming the paper and wooden buildings and **killing around 100,000** people.

Although an offshoot of the First Northern War, the **Swedish–Danish Wars** of 1657–58 and 1658–60 developed into a largely separate conflict over control of the Baltic when, in June 1657, Denmark joined the coalition confronting Sweden in Poland. Sweden had made consistent **gains at Denmark's expense** since the mid-16th century; the prize, control of The Sound – the strategically and economically vital entrance to the Baltic – still under Danish control in 1657. In the winter of 1657–58, Charles X of Sweden (1622–60) outflanked the Danes, marching his troops into Denmark and then, in February, across the frozen Baltic to Copenhagen itself. The **Treaty of Roskilde** in 1658 confirmed Sweden's territorial dominance. The second war, if less favourable to Sweden, still underlined **Sweden's Baltic superiority**.

With the Ottoman Empire now re-invigorated by Grand Vizier Köprülü Mehmed, in late 1657 its fleet **captured the Aegean islands of Lemnos and Tenedos** from the Venetians. The islands, which dominated the approaches to the Dardanelles, had been used by the Venetians to **blockade Constantinople**, the Ottoman capital. The Venetians would not pose such a threat again.

1658–59

IN JUNE 1658, AURANGZEB (1618–1707), or Alamgir ("Conqueror of the World") as he called himself, was **crowned Mughal emperor**. It ended two years of in-fighting between him and his brothers for their father, Shah Jahan's, throne – this despite Shah Jahan still being alive. All three **brothers were subsequently executed** (two by Aurangzeb). His reign would prove paradoxical. Mughal India was still immensely rich and powerful. Under Aurangzeb, a devout Muslim, it reached it **greatest territorial extent** (see p.234). Yet the near continuous warfare of his 49-year reign, in which immense

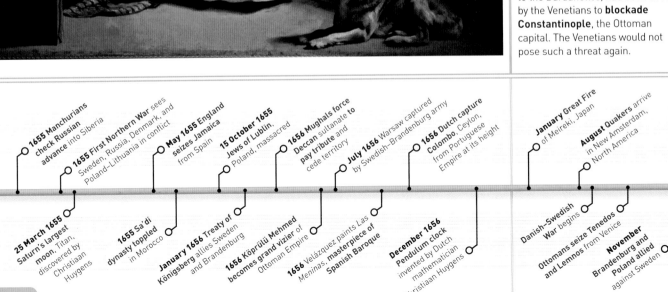

Conqueror of the World

This portrait of the Mughal emperor, Aurangzeb I, seen here with his courtiers, is attributed to the Indian artist Bhawani Das.

- **1655 Manchurians check Russian advance** into Siberia
- **25 March 1655 Saturn's largest moon**, Titan, discovered by Christiaan Huygens
- **1655 First Northern War** sees Sweden, Russia, Denmark, and Poland–Lithuania in conflict
- **May 1655 England seizes Jamaica** from Spain
- **1655 Sa'di dynasty toppled** in Morocco
- **15 October 1655 Jews of Lublin**, Poland, massacred
- **January 1656 Treaty of Königsberg** allies Sweden and Brandenburg
- **1656 Köprülü Mehmed becomes grand vizier** of Ottoman Empire
- **1656 Mughals force Deccan** sultanate to **pay tribute** and cede territory
- **1656** Velázquez paints *Las Meninas*, **masterpiece of Spanish Baroque**
- **July 1656** Warsaw captured by Swedish–Brandenburg army
- **1656 Dutch capture Colombo**, Ceylon, from Portuguese Empire at its height
- **December 1656 Pendulum clock** invented by Dutch mathematician Christiaan Huygens
- **January Great Fire** of Meireki, Japan
- **Danish–Swedish War** begins
- **August Quakers** arrive in New Amsterdam, North America
- **Ottomans seize Tenedos and Lemnos** from Venice
- **November Brandenburg and Poland allied** against Sweden
- **26 February 1658 Treaty of Roskilde**, Sweden gains southern Scandinavian peninsula from Denmark
- **1658** Dutch complete **capture of Ceylon** from Portugal
- **1658 Aurangzeb** proclaims himself Mughal emperor
- **June 1658 Battle of the Dunes** sees Anglo-French force defeat Spanish; Dunkirk ceded to England (to 1662)

The Peace of the Pyrenees in 1659 saw Louis XIV of France (centre left) meet Philip IV of Spain to ratify the treaty that ended Franco-Spanish conflict.

“ THE TRUTH IS, **I DO INDULGE** MYSELF A LITTLE THE MORE **IN PLEASURE,** KNOWING THAT **THIS IS THE PROPER AGE** OF MY LIFE **TO DO IT. ”**

Samuel Pepys, English diarist, diary entry, 1660

Swedish Empire
The Swedish Empire reached its peak in 1658 in the reign of Charles X, following the Treaty of Roskilde. However, the need to defend its new territories forced it into a series of unsustainably expensive wars.

LOUIS XIV (1638–1715)

Louis XIV, known as *Le Roi Soleil* (Sun King), had a greater impact on France than any other monarch. Determined to be the absolute ruler of his nobles and his country, he centralized the state, fought numerous wars, and also encouraged culture. By his later reign, France had expanded its territory and was the leading nation in Europe, much admired and imitated.

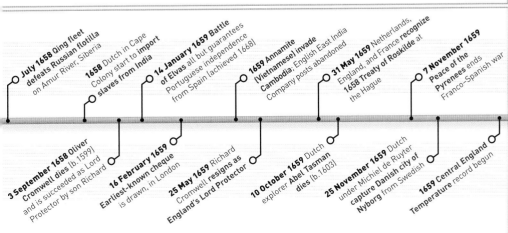

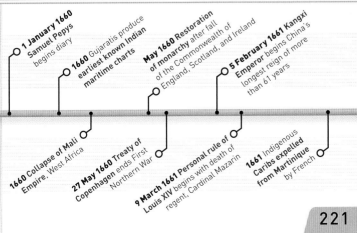

campaigns were launched against the Sikhs and the Marathas, **exhausted the country's treasuries** and highlighted the internal flaws of his vast empire. By his death in 1707, it was visibly in decline.

Near Dunkirk, in northeastern France, on 14 June 1658 a combined Anglo-French force defeated the Spanish. This was the last decisive conflict of the **Franco-Spanish War** that had begun in 1635, and as such the last battle of the Thirty Years War. It was also the last confrontation of the **Anglo-Spanish War** that had begun in 1654. For the French, the imperative, as ever, was dominance in Europe; for the English, to steal whatever advantage, commercial or territorial, they could over Spain, hence the **pragmatic alliance** between Oliver Cromwell's Puritan England with Louis XIV's Catholic France.

The year 1659 marked the start of one of the most remarkable developments of the **scientific revolution** in Europe with the beginning of what is now known as the **Central England Temperature**, or CET, record. It was a scientific experiment on an unprecedented scale, an attempt to measure temperatures almost nationally, in reality within a triangle bounded in the north by Manchester, the east by London, and in the west by Bristol. Today, it constitutes the oldest continuous **measurement of temperatures** in the world. It had a precedent of sorts in 1657 in Italy, the Accademia del Cimento (Academy of Experiment) in Florence instituting what has been called the "world's first weather observation network". If Europe's scientific revolution depended on **accurate observation** and measurement, the CET was a crucial forerunner.

The **Peace of the Pyrenees** in November 1659 ended the enduring Franco-Spanish conflict in Europe. France was now **Europe's major power**, and Spain, its New World revenues diminishing, its internal tensions multiplying, and its support from Austria curtailed, was slowly subsiding. The change roused those states able to confront an assertive France to do just that, putting France on a collision course with the other **emerging powers in Europe**: England, the Dutch, and Habsburg Austria.

£400
THE **VALUE** OF THE **EARLIEST-KNOWN CHEQUE**

"I... BLESSED GOD... IT WAS THE LORD'S DOING." With these words diarist John Evelyn recorded the overwhelming reception accorded Charles II (1630–85) in London in May 1660 on his **restoration as king of England**. By any measure, Charles's restoration was a triumphant vindication of the principles of kingship, as well as of the contradictory limitations of Oliver Cromwell's republican experiment. Charles II swept back to his throne on a wave of popular sentiment. Worldly, knowing, and, at heart, lazy, Charles was always **ready to compromise** with his parliamentary opponents. His charm was legendary. That said, his weakness for pleasure-seeking combined with his instinctive sympathy for Catholicism, especially when funded by Louis XIV in France, highlighted a **still unresolved political crisis**. Charles, by turns vengeful and forgiving, never resolved this dilemma. It was left to his successor, the rather less shrewd James II, to provoke the crisis that would later definitively propel England into a **unique parliamentary revolution** (see 1688).

The famous **English diarist Samuel Pepys** (1633–1703) began putting his daily thoughts on paper in 1660. Pepys was a high-ranking naval official, and his diary, which he kept until 1669 but was not published until the 19th century, provided one of the most valuable sources of information on **life during the English Restoration**.

The death of Cardinal Mazarin (see 1648) in 1661 began the **personal rule of the 22-year-old Louis XIV**. He would remain on the French throne for a further 53 years. A childhood in which France was divided made him aware of the need to develop a style of personal assertiveness and grandeur. This was to impress on the French elites that they were part of his great project for French glory and **pre-eminence in Europe**. United under a ruler who recognized their privileges and status, French nobles and officials supported a series of wars to assert this position. However, these wars would bring France to the brink of disaster and pauperize most of its population. Yet the **cultural impact** of Louis' rule remained; no other European country would approach France in the second half of the 17th century for such a projection of national pre-eminence.

July 1658 Qing fleet defeats Russian flotilla on Amur River, Siberia

1658 Dutch in Cape Colony start to **import slaves from India**

3 September 1658 Oliver Cromwell dies (b.1599) and is succeeded as Lord Protector by son Richard

14 January 1659 Battle of Elvas all but guarantees Portuguese independence from Spain (achieved 1668)

16 February 1659 Earliest-known cheque is drawn, in London

1659 Annamite (Vietnamese) invade Cambodia; English East India Company posts abandoned

25 May 1659 Richard Cromwell **resigns as England's Lord Protector**

31 May 1659 Netherlands, England, and France **recognize 1658 Treaty of Roskilde** at the Hague

10 October 1659 Dutch explorer **Abel Tasman dies** (b.1603)

7 November 1659 Peace of the Pyrenees ends Franco-Spanish war

25 November 1659 Dutch under Michiel de Ruyter **capture Danish city of Nyborg** from Swedish

1659 Central England Temperature record begun

1660 Collapse of Mali Empire, West Africa

1 January 1660 Samuel Pepys begins diary

1660 Gujaratis produce **earliest known Indian maritime charts**

27 May 1660 Treaty of Copenhagen ends First Northern War

May 1660 Restoration of monarchy after fall of the Commonwealth of England, Scotland, and Ireland

9 March 1661 Personal rule of Louis XIV begins with death of regent, Cardinal Mazarin

5 February 1661 Kangxi Emperor begins China's longest reign of more than 61 years

1661 Indigenous **Caribs expelled from Martinique** by French

1662–63

A 1635 view of Fort Zeelandia, in Tainan, present-day Taiwan.

FOR ALMOST FOUR DECADES the **Dutch East India Company** had controlled western **Formosa** (Taiwan), with its trading base Fort Zeelandia at its heart. Hostile to this alien presence, the Chinese Ming dynasty besieged the fort, which was inadequately supplied by water, and captured it in February 1662. The **Dutch** were forced to **abandon Formosa**.

The **pace of scientific investigation** in the 17th century led Europe's scientists to share ideas, and then to form bodies devoted to a better understanding of science. In 1662, the **Royal Society**, the world's oldest such scientific body, was founded in London. That it had royal approval showed how both the practical application of **science** and the pursuit of **pure knowledge** had become of interest to the state.

5 MILLION
THE **PRICE** IN LIVRES FOR WHICH **FRANCE BOUGHT DUNKIRK**

1664

The people of New Amsterdam plead with its director-general, Peter Stuyvesant, not to resist the English warships gathering in the harbour.

NUMEROUS ENGLISH RAIDS on Dutch shipping and trading posts in this year were the result of an **English desire to win** as much Dutch trade as possible. The most successful of these took place on 27 August, when a small English fleet arrived at **New Amsterdam**, the capital of the Dutch North American colony of New Netherland, and demanded its surrender. Director-general Peter Stuyvesant eventually complied. By March 1665, the Second Anglo–Dutch War broke out.

The **Austro–Turkish War** that broke out in 1663 reached a climax in August 1664, when an Ottoman army, intent on capturing Vienna, was defeated by a Habsburg force at **St Gotthard, Hungary**. Although the Ottomans gained favourable peace terms, their **invasion was curtailed**.

Alarmed at English and Dutch domination of trade with Asia, in 1664 the **French East India Company** was established, with royal patronage. It was lavishly funded, but it resulted only in the settlement of the island of Réunion in the Indian Ocean and a **handful of trading posts** in India.

> “ONE IS EASILY **FOOLED BY** THAT **WHICH ONE LOVES.**”
>
> **Molière, from *Tartuffe, 1664***

Battle of St Gotthard
This woodcut, based on a drawing by Adolf Ehrhardt, shows an attack by the Habsburg cavalry in the defeat of the Ottomans at St Gotthard.

1665

This representation of London's Great Plague shows, in the centre foreground, the Angel of Death holding an hourglass and a spear.

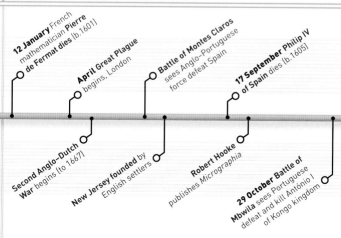

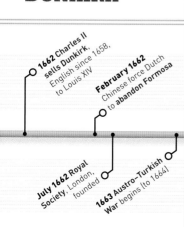

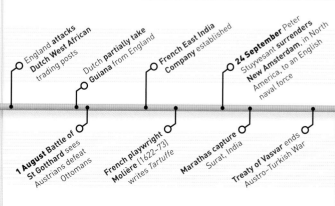

Hooke's findings
This page from Robert Hooke's 1665 publication, Micrographia, *shows a detailed illustration of an ant. Hooke had drawn the ant after viewing it under his microscope, which is shown here.*

THE PUBLICATION IN THIS YEAR OF *Micrographia*, by English natural philosopher and polymath Robert Hooke (1635–1703), was the first work **under the patronage of the Royal Society**. It was not merely the first time that those other than a closed circle of specialists had been made aware of the remarkable world revealed by **microscopes**. His drawings of an ant, louse, and flea, lovingly detailed and precisely executed, sparked particular astonishment at the complexity of this hitherto **unsuspected micro-world**. It was, according to diarist Samuel Pepys, "the most ingenious book that I ever read in my life". Of greater significance was that Hooke was the **first to use the term "cell"** for the smallest unit of a living organism, the term derived from the fact those cells Hooke observed reminded him of a monk's cell.

The year 1665 also saw the last outbreak of **bubonic plague in England**. The disease was concentrated mostly in London, where, at its height in September, 7,000 a week were dying. In the 18 months the **plague ravaged the city**, 100,000 people died.

- **1662 Charles II sells Dunkirk**, English since 1658, to Louis XIV
- **February 1662** Chinese force Dutch to **abandon Formosa**
- **July 1662 Royal Society**, London, founded
- **1663 Austro–Turkish War** begins (to 1664)
- England **attacks Dutch West African** trading posts
- **1 August Battle of St Gotthard** sees Austrians defeat Ottomans
- Dutch **partially take Guiana** from England
- **French playwright Molière** (1622–73) writes Tartuffe
- **French East India Company** established
- **Marathas capture** Surat, India
- **24 September** Peter Stuyvesant **surrenders New Amsterdam**, in North America, to an English naval force
- **Treaty of Vasvar** ends Austro–Turkish War
- **12 January** French mathematician **Pierre de Fermat dies** (b.1601)
- **Second Anglo–Dutch War** begins (to 1667)
- **April Great Plague** begins, London
- **New Jersey founded** by English settlers
- **Battle of Montes Claros** sees Anglo–Portuguese force defeat Spain
- **Robert Hooke** publishes Micrographia
- **17 September Philip IV of Spain** dies (b.1605)
- **29 October Battle of Mbwila** sees Portuguese defeat and kill António I of Kongo kingdom

1666

In 1666, a major fire swept through the central parts of London, consuming thousands of houses and wiping away centuries of history.

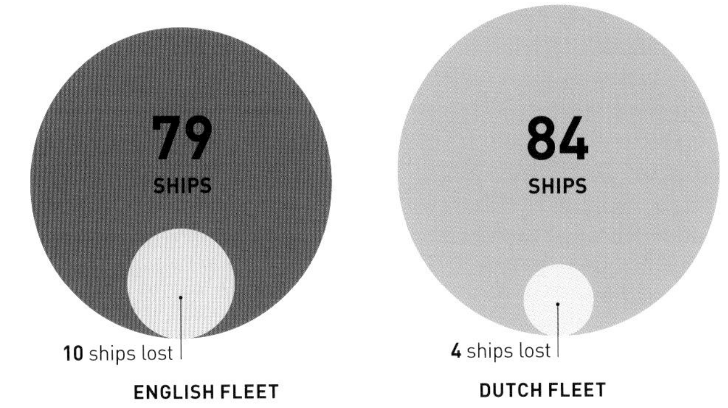

Four Days Battle
In one of the longest naval engagements ever, the Four Days Battle, fought in June 1666 during the Second Anglo-Dutch War, saw the Dutch inflict a defeat on the English.

THE BIGGEST ENGAGEMENT OF THE SECOND ANGLO-DUTCH WAR, which had begun in 1665, the **Four Days Battle** was an English attempt to destroy the Dutch fleet before it could grow to challenge them. However, the **English** suffered such **losses** that it handed the initiative to the Dutch. Disaster then followed for England in June 1667 after a daring **Dutch raid** on the River Medway, in the Thames estuary. With discontent at home, England brought the war to a halt.

As the Great Plague ended, a new **disaster overtook London**, the **Great Fire**, which burned from 2 to 5 September. London was still a medieval city, filthy and unplanned, with no great spaces and few public buildings of note. The City, which was the commercial heart, was especially overcrowded and unsanitary. It was here the fire began. Although the risk of fire was well known, no effective precautions were taken. Though **drought and a heat wave** had made the city especially vulnerable, a crucial added factor was a strong easterly wind. The result was that the **whole of the City was destroyed**, including the medieval St Paul's Cathedral, 87 other churches, and upwards of 13,000 houses. The official death toll of six has long been disputed.

Not to be outdone by the founding of the Royal Society of London (see 1662), in December 1666 Louis XIV gave his blessing to the creation of the **French Academy of Sciences**, which in 1699 became the Royal Academy of Sciences and was installed in the Louvre Palace, in Paris. Today, it is part of the *Institut de France*. It was at the heart of a **drive for verifiable scientific knowledge**. As an arm of the state it was also interested in discoveries that could enrich its country, such as in agriculture and armaments.

1667

> **"THE MIND** IS ITS OWN PLACE AND IN ITSELF, **CAN MAKE** A **HEAVEN OF HELL,** A **HELL OF HEAVEN."**

John Milton, English poet, from *Paradise Lost*, 1667

THE TREATY OF ANDRUSOVO in January 1667 ended the Polish-Lithuanian Commonwealth's calamitous war with Russia that had begun in 1654. It also climaxed The Deluge – its **dramatic decline** above all **in the face of Russian expansion**. Russia, granted Smolensk and present-day Belarus, could for the first time claim to have **unified the Slavic peoples of the region**.

The completion in 1667 of the **Piazza San Pietro**, by Gian Lorenzo Bernini (1598–1680), saw the high point of urban planning in Baroque Rome. Many of Rome's public spaces were ambitiously rebuilt by a series of architects to make them deliberately imposing, and worthy to be at the centre of the Catholic Church.

The **War of Devolution** began in May 1667 as a result of Louis XIV's continuing **claims to the Spanish Netherlands**. It saw France take some Habsburg cities in Flanders, as well as Franche-Comté to its east. However, a Triple Aliance of England, Sweden, and the Dutch Republic forced the isolated Louis to return most of his gains by the 1668 **Treaty of Aix-la-Chapelle**.

80,000
THE NUMBER OF **PEOPLE KILLED IN** THE **SAMAKHI EARTHQUAKE** IN AZERBAIJAN

In 1667, the **epic poem** *Paradise Lost*, by English poet John Milton (1608–74), gave the English language one of its **greatest literary achievements**. It told the Christian story of man's fall from grace in the Garden of Eden.

Siege of Lille
Louis XIV directs French forces at Lille during the War of Devolution. Its capture provided one of France's few gains from a frustrating conflict.

1668

A woodcut portrait of the admiral and privateer Henry Morgan.

THE PORTUGUESE TRADING POST AT BOMBAY (Mumbai) had **passed to the English Crown** in 1662 as part of the dowry of Catherine of Braganza, Charles II's Portuguese wife. In 1668, the king leased it to the **East India Company** for an annual rent of £10, making it the Company's third trading post in India after those at Surat and Madras. With Bombay Castle completed in 1675, from 1687 it became the focus of all the Company's trading in India, resisting attempts to storm it by the Mughals and the Dutch.

In 1668, the **Welsh privateer** (state-sponsored raider) **Henry Morgan**, famous for his attacks on Spanish settlements in the Caribbean, succeeded in one of the **most daring assaults ever** when his ships captured the well-protected **Spanish trading city of Porto Bello**, in Panama. It won him both great wealth and further English support for his buccaneering endeavours.

Just as Philip II's seizure of the Portuguese crown in 1580 was a sign of Spanish power, so its **recognition of Portuguese independence in 1668** under the Treaty of Lisbon, which confirmed the House of Braganza as rulers of Portugal, was evidence of its decline. From 1640, Portugal had been in open revolt against Spain, and in June 1665 at the **Battle of Montes Claros** a combined Anglo-Portuguese force inflicted a crushing defeat on them. Close to bankruptcy, and sure of further French hostility, the Spanish had little option but to concede.

- **22 January** Mughal emperor **Shah Jahan dies** (b.1592)
- **Sultan Moulay al-Rashid** (1631–72), founder of Moroccan Alaouite dynasty, **captures Fes**
- **June Four Days Battle** sees Dutch naval victory over English
- **September Great Fire of London**
- **26 August** Dutch painter **Frans Hals dies** (b.1580)
- **22 December French Academy of Sciences** (Académie des Sciences) founded
- **Mughals expel Portuguese** from Chittagong, Bengal
- **26 December** 10th Sikh Guru **Gobind Singh born** (d.1708)
- **20 January Treaty of Andrusovo** between Russia and Polish–Lithuanian Commonwealth
- **June** Dutch **Raid on Medway** destroys English fleet
- **24 May War of Devolution** begins in Europe
- **August Lille besieged** in War of Devolution
- **31 July Treaty of Breda** ends Second Anglo-Dutch War
- **25 November Samakhi earthquake**, Azerbaijan
- **18 October** Emperor **Fasilides of Ethiopia dies** (b.1603)
- **John Milton** publishes *Paradise Lost*
- Completion of **Piazza San Pietro**, Rome
- English East India Company **gains Bombay**
- **Treaty of Lisbon**; Portugal independent from Spain
- **May Treaty of Aix-la-Chapelle** ends War of Devolution
- **July** Privateer Henry Morgan **captures Porto Bello**, Panama

1669

The Badshahi Mosque, Lahore, was commissioned by Aurangzeb.

ONE OF THE REASONS GIVEN FOR THE DISINTEGRATION of the Mughal Empire after the death of **Aurangzeb** in 1707 has been his supposed religious **persecution of Hindus** and other minorities. Where his predessor Akbar I had pursued an active policy of religious toleration as the most effective means of controlling his Hindu vassals, Aurangzeb – himself a Sunni Muslim – was said to have **systematically destroyed Hindu temples**. In addition, he banned the use of music, central to Hindu practice, issuing a decree, perhaps in 1669, to this effect. He also had drawn up an **exhaustive digest of Muslim law**, the *Fatawa-e-Alamgri*, said to have been rigorously imposed. All these claims are disputed, however. In fact, the number of Hindu temples said to have been destroyed varies improbably from 80 to 60,000. That Aurangzeb was **strongly anti-Christian**, though, seems certain to have been true.

£100 MILLION
THE **ANNUAL REVENUE** RAISED BY **AURANGZEB'S EXCHEQUER**

1670

“ COME QUICKLY, I AM DRINKING THE STARS. ”

Attributed to Dom Pérignon, while tasting champagne, 1670

Cossack leader
Stepan Razin, the Cossack leader who rose up against the nobility and the tsar's bureaucracy, is seen here on the River Volga, South Russia.

IN MAY 1670, THE HUDSON'S BAY COMPANY WAS FORMED under British royal charter on the initiative of two French fur trackers, Pierre-Esprit Radisson and Médard de Groseilliers. They had learned that **the best furs** came from the **Cree territory** to the north of Lake Superior. Easier to reach via Hudson Bay rather than via the rivers and lakes to the south, they proposed a base there. Rebuffed in France, they **solicited support in England**. The Hudson's Bay Company would become one of the great commercial enterprises of England, the **basis of its claim to Canada**, and source of regional rivalry with France.

The claim that in 1670 **Dom Pérignon** (1638–1715), a monk at the Benedictine Abbey of Hautvillers, in Champagne in northeast France, **invented the sparkling wine** of that name, is largely discounted today. In fact, he was devoted to **eliminating the bubbles** such wines produced, as the pressure they built up in the bottles tended to explode them. But as cellar master of the Abbey, he did make a major contribution to the **production of white wines**, by using grapes otherwise used in red wine. It was not until the early 18th century that the **taste for sparkling wines**, in England and France, grew rapidly.

A **Cossack uprising** in South Russia in 1670 was **brutally suppressed** by the tsar, and its leader Stepan Razin executed the following year. An attempt to protect Cossack independence against the **centralized Russian state** had become a revolt by a disaffected peasantry that saw several cities sacked and looted.

1671–72

Portuguese glazed tiles decorate the São Miguel Fortress in Luanda, a key military strongpoint in the colonization of Angola in the later 17th century.

IN 1671, PORTUGAL ENDED THE INDEPENDENCE of the kingdom of Ndongo, in what is today Angola. A Portuguese colony had largely **dominated the Ndongo** since the 16th century, but a rebellion by their king, Philip, in 1671, saw **Portuguese troops capture the capital** and take control of its entire territory.

Just as fears of Spanish dominance in Europe had allied France, England, and the Dutch Republic, so French dominance after 1659 saw **anti-French alliances** throw Spain and the Dutch Republic together. Spain opposed Louis XIV's claim to the Spanish Netherlands by marriage, while the Dutch preferred a weak Spain as a neighbour to a strong France. The War of Devolution of 1667–68 had seen French gains, and then losses, in the Spanish Netherlands, but in 1672 Louis, allied with England and Sweden, tried again in the **Franco–Dutch War**. The war ended with the Dutch granting New Amsterdam to England, while the French – although their conquest of the Dutch Republic failed – gained the former Burgundian territory of the Franche-Comté and a string of border territories in the Spanish Netherlands. Yet the peace proved a brief pause in Louis' attempts to expand and safeguard France.

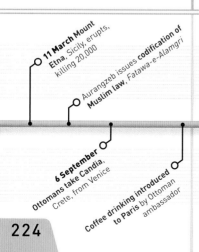

FUR TRADE

A valuable natural asset of North America was fur. It drove the French westwards into Canada and saw the English establish the Hudson's Bay Company (see 1670). It also led to Anglo–French conflict there. While the French would accompany the American Indians on fur-trapping expeditions, the English, and the Dutch (pictured) before them, usually took delivery of furs from the Indians at their trading posts. All depended on Indian aid, while the Indians became dependent on European weapons and tools.

11 March Mount Etna, Sicily, erupts, killing 20,000

Aurangzeb issues **codification of Muslim law**, *Fatawa-e-Alamgri*

6 September Ottomans take Candia, Crete, from Venice

Coffee drinking introduced to Paris by Ottoman ambassador

Cossack anti-Polish uprising in Ukraine suppressed

Colony of **South Carolina** established, North America

2 May Hudson's Bay Company established

1 June Secret Treaty of Dover signed between England and France

Date claimed for **discovery of champagne** by Dom Pérignon

Privateer **Henry Morgan captures Panama**

Mali capital Niani sacked by Bambara of Segou Empire

First French settlers arrive in what is now Senegal

1671 Ndongo defeated by Portugal and cede territory to Portuguese colony in Angola

1671 Spain allies with Dutch Republic against France

April 1671 Battle of Saraighat sees Mughal defeated by Ahom kingdom

16 June 1671 Execution of Cossack leader Stepan Razin (b.1630)

1671 German mathematician Gottfried Leibniz builds **first calculator**

30 December 1671 French Royal Academy of Architecture founded

1672 English Royal African Company established

12 March 1672 Third Anglo–Dutch War begins (to 1674)

Marquette and Jolliet descend the Mississippi River with their guides.

Ceremonial entrance of the Qing emperor, Kangxi, to Beijing. Kangxi oversaw the complete suppression of the Three Feudatories revolt.

Frederick William I leads his troops at the Battle of Fehrbellin.

Leibniz mechanical calculator
One of the first calculating machines, developed by Gottfried Leibniz, this device multiplies by making repeated additions.

In 1671, German mathematician **Gottfried Leibniz** (1646–1716) demonstrated one of the **world's first mechanical calculators**. It was the first such machine that could perform all four of the basic arithmetic functions. Leibniz went on to further refine his calculating machines, thus providing the basis of the modern calculator.

Repeated **Cossack and Crimean Tartar revolts** against the weakened Polish–Lithuanian Commonwealth in 1672 drew their Ottoman allies into a four-year **Polish–Ottoman War**. Polish resistance under Jan III Sobieski (1629–96) was greatly undermined by grudging support from the Polish parliament, the Sejm, and was hardly equal to the progressively larger armies of the Ottomans. The result was the **loss of what little prestige Poland could still claim** as well as most of its Ukrainian territories.

THE EXTENSIVE WATERWAYS OF North America provided a ready-made means of exploring its interior. In 1673, **French–Canadian explorer** Louis Jolliet and French Jesuit Jacques Marquette **travelled down the Mississippi River** to within 600km (370 miles) of the Gulf of Mexico. They turned back for fear of arousing Spanish hostility but discovered the Missouri and Ohio rivers, as well as confirming that the river led to the Gulf and not the Pacific. **English exploration** inland from their scattered coastal settlements was much more hesitant, rarely co-ordinated, and additionally blocked by the **Appalachian mountain chain**. It almost always depended on native assistance. For example, it was after spending a year with a group of Tomahitan Indians in present-day Georgia that Gabriel Arthur travelled with them **across the Cumberland Gap**, unwittingly discovering what in the 18th century would be the principal route to Kentucky and the west.

3,200 KILOMETRES, THE LENGTH OF THE APPALACHIAN MOUNTAINS

FOLLOWING THEIR TAKEOVER OF CHINA WITH THE COLLAPSE of the Ming dynasty in 1644, the Qing co-opted some of the more **powerful Ming generals**, making them regional governors and allowing them considerable latitude in their rule over what became almost independent territories. It was felt that if they **enriched themselves** – as they did on a prodigious scale – the less likely it was that they would revolt. The risk was that their progressively greater revenues would be matched by greater **pretensions to rule China**. In 1674, the **Revolt of the Three Feudatories** broke out across southern China in those provinces controlled by the three most prominent rebels, Wu Sangui, Shang Kexi Gungdong, and Geng Jingzhong, joined by lesser Ming governors. Led by the Kangxi Emperor (1654–1722), the Qing response, with its **superior military**, was successful, albeit not until 1681. With the rebels as wary of each other as they were of the Qing, they rarely co-operated, **allowing the Qing to pick them off** one by one. Those rebels who did not commit suicide were executed.

After freeing the Hindu Maratha from the Sultan of Bijapur, **Shivaji** (1630–80) was crowned Maratha king in 1674, establishing the **Maratha Empire** (see p.242) that would later defeat the Mughals to dominate India until the early 19th century.

Statue of Shivaji
This bronze statue of Shivaji on horseback in Maharashtra, India, commemorates his leadership of the Maratha campaign for self-rule.

IN 1675, MUGHAL EMPEROR AURANGZEB ORDERED THE EXECUTION of Tegh Bahadur, ninth guru of the Sikhs, after he had refused to convert to Islam. It brought to the Sikh throne his nine-year-old son, **Gobind Singh** (1666–1708). It would be several years later that, under Singh's leadership, the Sikhs would pose a growing **military threat to Mughal rule**, and contribute significantly to its collapse. However, the pattern of **religious opposition to the Mughals** was already well established in many parts of India, most obviously in the Western Ghats, where Shivaji had declared the Maratha Empire.

On 18 June 1675, a combined Prussian and Brandenburg army, led by Frederick William I, Elector of Brandenburg (1620–88), met and **defeated a Swedish army**, led by Count von Wrangel, near **Fehrbellin**, in Brandenburg. This relatively insignificant battle in the **Scanian War**, itself a by-product of the Franco–Dutch War, nonetheless marked a crucial moment in Sweden's long struggle to impose itself as the dominant Baltic power. Defeat at the hands of an otherwise relatively minor German state **dealt the Swedes a lasting blow**. Swedish pretensions to great power status were revealed as precarious at best.

- **April 1672 Franco-Dutch War** begins with invasion of Dutch Republic (to 1678)
- **7 June 1672 Battle of Solebay** in Third Anglo-Dutch War is inconclusive
- **4 July 1672** William III of Orange appointed **Stadtholder of Holland**
- **18 October 1672 Treaty of Buczacz** between Ottoman Empire and Polish-Lithuania Commonwealth
- **17 February** French writer and actor **Molière dies** (b.1622)
- **May** Jolliet and Marquette begin **exploration of Mississippi River**
- English explorer Gabriel Arthur **crosses Appalachians**
- **Battles of Schooneveld** between English and Dutch fleets
- **Revolt of the Three Feudatories** breaks out in China
- **19 February Treaty of Westminster** ends Third Anglo-Dutch War
- **21 May Jan III Sobieski** elected king of Polish-Lithuanian Commonwealth
- **6 June** Shivaji declares Hindu **Maratha Empire**
- Pondicherry, south India, becomes base of **French East India Company**
- **11 August Battle of Seneffe** sees French defeat Dutch-Spanish-Austrian army
- **8 November** English poet **John Milton dies** (b.1608)
- **10 November New Netherland** (including New Amsterdam), in North America, ceded to England
- Sikh leader, **Tegh Bahadur**, executed by Mughals
- **18 June Battle of Fehrbellin** sees Brandenburg and Prussia defeat Sweden
- **Development of haiku** poetry, Japan
- **War** between **English** colonists and **Algonquian** American Indian **tribes**

1676–78

Horseshoe Falls, on the Canadian side of Niagara Falls, is about 800m (2,600ft) wide. Europeans first discovered this natural wonder in 1677.

IN FRANCE, LOUIS XIV'S principal architectural endeavours concentrated on his **immense palace at Versailles**, just outside Paris. Louis was also determined to continue the transformation of the French capital, begun by his grandfather Henry IV at the start of the 17th century. Henry's intent had been to lift the city from medieval slum to a **capital worthy of the first power of Europe** – a city to rival Rome for its imposing public buildings and commanding spaces. The Louvre Palace, predictably, was significantly enlarged and remodelled, notably the east wing, whose stately façade encapsulated the **French taste for Classicism** at its most austere and precise. But the building that most memorably reflects Louis's contribution to Paris is **Les Invalides**, or more properly *L'Hôtel National des Invalides*. Part hospital, part retirement home for French soldiers, it was completed in 1676. Designed by Libéral Bruant (1635–97), Les Invalides was conceived on an grand scale, with vast formal gardens sweeping up to its immense façade and 15 courtyards clustered behind. Its most memorable feature, the **lavish** royal chapel *L'Église du Dôme*, was added slightly later. Placed at the southern end of the complex, it was designed with a vast dome and spire, with details picked out in gold.

Louis XIV's reign marked one of the most **fertile periods of French literature**. The year 1677 saw the first performance of *Phèdre*, the greatest tragedy of French dramatist **Jean Racine** (1639–99). Dramatists such as Racine, Pierre Corneille (1606–84), and **Molière** (1622–73) thrived under royal patronage, captivating court audiences in different ways. Corneille and Racine reflected courtly concerns through their use of formal verse, classical themes, and emphasis on honour, virtue, and renunciation, while Molière's racy dramas mocked the social pretensions of the bourgeoisie. As a result of this rich and growing theatrical tradition, the **Comédie-Française** was established in Paris under royal patronage. This official state theatre aimed to showcase the glories of the French stage and French culture as widely as possible.

European explorers began to realize the **immensity of North America** as the 17th century progressed. The extraordinary variety and natural beauty of its landscape also continued to amaze. The **discovery of Niagara Falls** in 1677, a waterfall hugely larger than any in Europe, with over 170,000 cu m (6,000,000 cu ft) of water thundering over it every minute, provoked wonder in the Old World. There is doubt as to which European can claim to have seen the falls first. However, the French Franciscan missionary Louis Hennepin (1626–1701), exploring at the request of King Louis XIV, is generally credited with their discovery, in 1677.

Religious work

This is the frontispiece from the third edition of John Bunyan's The Pilgrim's Progress, *a hugely influential work in the 17th century.*

One of **literature's most significant religious works** was published in February 1678. *The Pilgrim's Progress* was written by English writer and Christian preacher **John Bunyan** (1628–88), who completed much of the work while imprisoned in Bedford Gaol. It was published in two parts (the second part appeared in 1684) and is an **allegorical tale** of an everyman's journey from this world to heaven. *The Pilgrim's Progress* has become one of the most translated books in history.

Les Invalides, Paris

These sumptuous buildings now contain museums and monuments relating to France's military history, and a hospital for war veterans.

1679–81

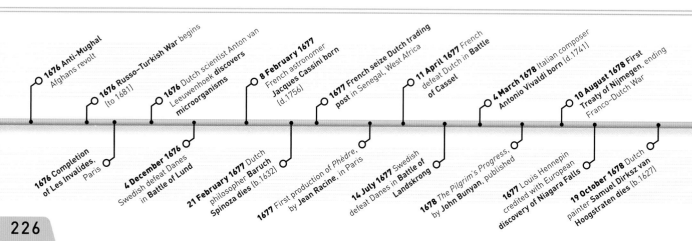

A 19th-century image of the Asante, wh[o] dominated West Africa from the 1680s.

IN 1679, THE ENGLISH PARLIAMENT passed the **Habeas Corpus Act**. Like Magna Carta (see 1215), it represented a cornerstone of English liberty. It is the legal assertion that **no one may be unlawfully detained**. The law was passed for pragmatic reasons rather than as a liberal **principle of justice**. Its aim was to prevent James, Duke of York, the Catholic brother and heir of Charles II, from arresting his Protestant opponents without legal justification, as Charles's chief minister, the Earl of Clarendon, had begun to do. The underlying principle of the Act, which is incorporated into the **American Constitution**, remains fundamental to most Anglo-Saxon legal systems as an **ultimate guarantee of individual liberty**. However, in reality the law is hardly ever invoked.

> **"** YOU MAY **HOLD THE BODY,** SUBJECT TO EXAMINATION. **"**
>
> **English writ of Habeas Corpus,** 1679

In August 1680, the **Pueblo people** of the colony of New Mexico **rose against the Spanish occupiers** and drove them from the area for 12 years. Spanish claims to New Mexico, though dating back to Francisco Coronado's expeditions of the

- **1676 Anti-Mughal** Afghans revolt
- **1676 Russo–Turkish War** begins (to 1681)
- **1676 Completion of Les Invalides,** Paris
- **1676** Dutch scientist Anton van Leeuwenhoek **discovers microorganisms**
- **4 December 1676** Swedish defeat Danes in **Battle of Lund**
- **8 February 1677** French astronomer **Jacques Cassini born** (d.1756)
- **21 February 1677** Dutch philosopher **Baruch Spinoza dies** (b.1632)
- **1677 French seize Dutch trading post** in Senegal, West Africa
- **1677** First production of *Phèdre*, by **Jean Racine**, in Paris
- **11 April 1677** French defeat Dutch in **Battle of Cassel**
- **14 July 1677** Swedish defeat Danes in **Battle of Landskrona**
- **4 March 1678** Italian composer **Antonio Vivaldi born** (d.1741)
- **1678** *The Pilgrim's Progress*, by **John Bunyan**, published
- **10 August 1678 First Treaty of Nijmegen**, ending Franco–Dutch War
- **1677** Louis Hennepin credited with European **discovery of Niagara Falls**
- **19 October 1678** Dutch painter **Samuel Dirksz van Hoogstraten dies** (b.1627)
- **1679** Renewed **Mughal–Rajput conflict** (to 1709)
- **27 May 1679 Habeas Corpus**, cornerstone of English liberty, becomes law
- **1679** Colony of **New Hampshire** established
- **December 1679 Second Treaty of Nijmegen** ending Franco–Dutch War

“ HE THAT DOES GOOD FOR GOOD’S SAKE **SEEKS NEITHER PARADISE NOR REWARD, BUT** HE **IS SURE OF BOTH** IN THE END. **”**

William Penn, English Quaker, establishing Philadelphia, 1682

mid-16th century, had never amounted to much more than statements of priority and Christian pre-eminence over the region. New Mexico was seen as a land of marginal value as it was **remote and arid**. The Pueblo revolt was provoked partly by drought and by the suffering such natural events inevitably brought in their wake, but more particularly by Spain’s determination to **crush local religious practices** – Pueblo shamen were consistently accused of witchcraft and executed. When the Spanish returned in 1692, they did so in overwhelming numbers.

The **Asante kingdom**, founded in about 1680, was formed from the Akan, who dominated West Africa. The most prominent group of the Akan was the Oyoko. Using diplomacy and warfare, the **Oyoko consolidated the Akan** tribes in the 1670s, uniting them against the threat of the neighbouring Denkyira, who they eventually conquered in 1701 at the Battle of Feyiase (in modern Ghana).

Few projects revealed the determination of Louis XIV’s France to extend itself than the construction of the **Canal du Midi**, a navigable inland waterway that stretched between the Mediterranean Sea and the Atlantic Ocean. Its construction was necessary because it would replace a perilous and indirect sea-passage with a simple canal route. The technical problems, no less than the cost, were daunting. The main problem was how to ensure a sufficient supply of water to the highest parts of the canal. It was easily the most complex engineering problem undertaken by any 17th-century European state, calling for labour on a massive scale, and used entirely untried engineering solutions. When **completed in 1681**, the Canal du Midi stretched a distance of 240km (149 miles).

PUEBLO POTTERY

The Pueblo of southwest North America, so called by the Spanish for their *pueblos*, or villages, were famed for their sophisticated and elaborate pottery. It is characterized by a light background on which are painted stylized animals and repeated abstract patterns in ochre, black, and grey colouring.

Penn in America
This detail from a painting shows English Quaker William Penn’s meeting with American Indians in what is now the state of Delaware.

THE 1682 CORONATION OF nine-year-old **Peter the Great** (1672–1725) as tsar of Russia brought to a close this vast nation’s vague, imperial influence as a semi-power on the margins of Europe. Peter’s childhood was scarred by revolt, and it left him determined to punish his internal enemies and reshape **Russia as a western European power**. In a life of compulsive energy, he built a new capital, **St Petersburg**, and ruthlessly imposed himself on his boyars (nobles). His version of Versailles, recreated on the edge of the Baltic, did not amount to much more than a statement of intent, but by the end of his reign **Russia** was a massive power-in-waiting, **looming over Europe**.

In 1682, nine years after Jolliet and Marquette had ventured down the **Mississippi**, confirming that these territories contained neither easily exploited wealthy natives nor obvious sources of gold, **Robert de La Salle** (1643–87), a veteran of North American exploration, determined to follow the river to its mouth. With his party of 19 American Indians, he reached it on 9 April 1682, and **proclaimed the river** and its hinterlands a **French possession**, **Louisiana**, named after the French king. This formed the basis of a French claim to a vast swathe of North America. Yet a follow-up expedition by sea in 1684 failed to find the river and saw three of its four ships wrecked. La Salle was murdered by the remainder of his party.

In 1682, **William Penn** (1644–1718), an English Quaker and philosopher who had been granted land in North America belonging to James, Duke of York, founded the settlement that would grow into the city of **Philadelphia, Pennsylvania**. Penn promised religious freedom and material wealth to all those Europeans who settled there.

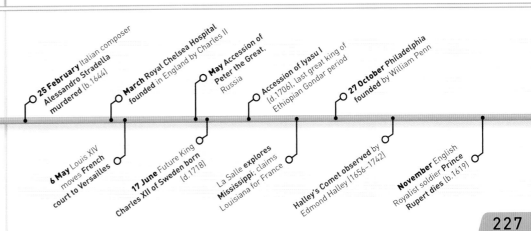

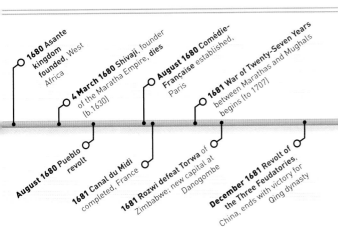

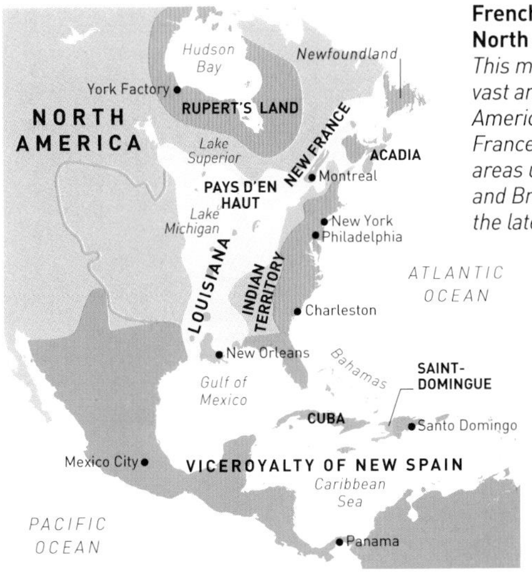

French claims to North America
This map depicts the vast areas of North America claimed by France, as well as the areas under Spanish and British control in the late 17th century.

1680 Asante kingdom founded, West Africa

4 March 1680 Shivaji, founder of the Maratha Empire, **dies** (b.1630)

August 1680 Pueblo revolt

August 1680 Comédie-Française established, Paris

1681 Canal du Midi completed, France

1681 War of Twenty-Seven Years between Marathas and Mughals begins (to 1707)

1681 Rozwi defeat Torwa of Zimbabwe; new capital at Danogombe

December 1681 Revolt of the Three Feudatories, China, ends with victory for Qing dynasty

25 February Italian composer **Alessandro Stradella murdered** (b.1644)

March Royal Chelsea Hospital founded in England by Charles II

6 May Louis XIV moves **French court to Versailles**

May Accession of Peter the Great, Russia

17 June Future King **Charles XII of Sweden born** (d.1718)

Accession of Iyasu I (d.1706), last great king of Ethiopian Gondar period

La Salle **explores Mississippi**; claims Louisiana for France

27 October Philadelphia founded by William Penn

Halley’s Comet observed by Edmond Halley (1656–1742)

November English Royalist soldier **Prince Rupert dies** (b.1619)

1683–84

The Battle of Kahlenberg saw a Polish–Imperial army lift the Ottoman Empire's two-month siege of Vienna.

ON 14 JULY 1683, AN OTTOMAN army **besieged Vienna**. As with the previous Ottoman attempt on the city in 1529, this was a direct assault on the Christian West. In the event, the siege failed just as it had in 1529. But whereas 1529 had been the climax of a series of conquests that had seen the Ottomans sweep across Hungary, the 1683 Ottoman assault was a **frantic final attempt to regain former glories** in the face of internal weakness. Confronted with renewed resistance, the **siege was broken** in September **at Kahlenberg** by a combined Imperial–Polish force led by the Polish king, Jan III Sobieski. The **collapse of Ottoman rule in Hungary** followed, with a Holy League of the Holy Roman Empire, Poland, and Venice, formed in 1684 under papal authority, driving them south across the Balkans.

Taiwan's Tunging kingdom, a supporter of China's ousted Ming, had supported military **assaults against the Qing** since 1661. By 1683, negotiations towards a settlement had led nowhere and so the Kangxi Emperor (1654–1722) launched the Qing's military might, securing a huge **naval and land victory** over the Tunging at the **Battle of Penghu**, resulting in their kingdom becoming part of the Qing empire.

The climatic changes of the Maunder Minimum, which had begun in 1645 as a result of reduced sunspot activity, had by the 1680s initiated a particularly cold period of the **Little Ice Age** across the world, and global temperatures had fallen by several degrees. Amid its **many bitter winters**, that of 1683–84 was considered by many to be the worst. The Little Ice Age only ended in the 19th century.

Dissatisfied with the Treaty of Nijmegen in 1679, Louis XIV strove to **extend France's frontiers** at the expense of the German states and the Spanish Netherlands with bids to **occupy territory** in Flanders and the Rhineland – the latter crucial in controlling trade on the Rhine. Using bluster, threat, and bogus legal claims, he gained Alsace, Luxembourg, and key forts in Flanders, consolidated by the **Treaty of Ratisbon** in 1684 at the end of the brief War of the Reunions of 1683–84. Now at the peak of his power, Louis was **determined to impose himself** on Europe, but succeeded only in uniting Protestant and Catholic Europe alike against him.

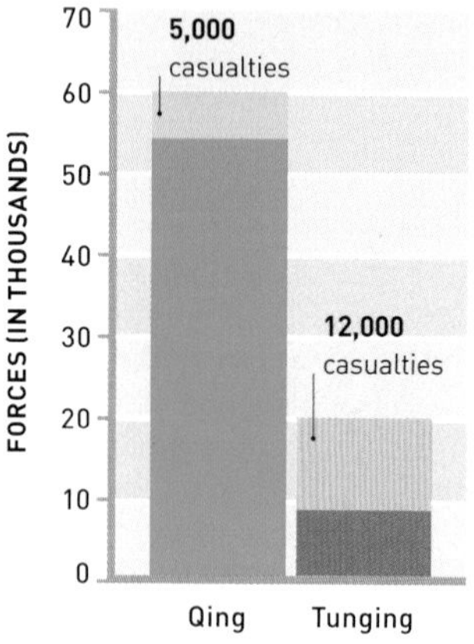

Battle of Penghu
So seriously did the Qing take the Tunging threat that it sent a huge land and naval force, including more than 200 ships, to guarantee victory.

Thames Frost Fair, 1683–84
Frost fairs were a regular feature on the River Thames, in London, during the winters of the Little Ice Age, with tents and coaches on the ice.

1685–86

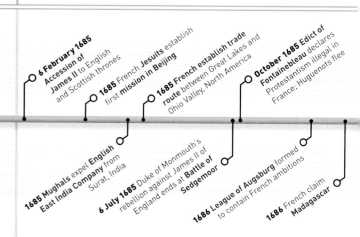

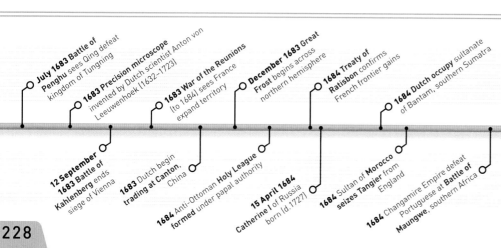

This 19th-century illustration shows Friedrich Wilhelm I, elector of Brandenburg, welcoming French Protestant Huguenots to Berlin in 1685.

THE EDICT OF NANTES, AGREED by Henry IV in 1598, was essential to ending the French Wars of Religion. Of necessity, it was a compromise, and it saw France's substantial **Protestant Huguenot minority granted religious toleration** in return for accepting Henry as king. In October 1685, with the **Edict of Fontainebleau**, Louis XIV **revoked it**. His decision was entirely logical. There was practically no European state that permitted religious toleration. Louis's absolutism clearly demanded nothing less than an **officially sanctioned state religion**, and that religion was Roman Catholicism. In every other respect, however, it was a disaster for France. The **huge numbers of Huguenots who fled the country** were among the most industrious in France, and they were eagerly embraced by those countries to which they emigrated, chiefly England, the Dutch Republic, and Prussia. Simultaneously, so naked an act of aggression was this against France's Protestants – the policy was imposed with consistent brutality – that it aroused not just the **indignation of Protestant Europe** but reinforced its alarmed perception that Louis XIV's France had to be opposed at all costs.

The consequence of Louis XIV's obvious designs on Europe was the establishment in 1686 of the anti-French **League of Augsburg**, subsequently known as the **Grand Alliance**. The League was created initially by the newly confident Holy Roman Emperor, Leopold I (1640–1705) – vanquisher of the Ottomans – and urged on by William III of Orange (1650–1792), ruler of the Dutch Republic. In time, every western European state bar Switzerland was **ranged against France**.

In 1685, the ageing **James II** (1633–1701), younger son of Charles I and younger brother of Charles II, **brought a curious incompetence** to a brief occupation of the English and Scottish thrones. **Determined to reimpose Catholicism** on a now Protestant, parliamentary nation, in less than three years he would overturn the delicately cynical political settlement of Charles II.

900,000

THE NUMBER OF **HUGUENOTS** IT WAS **CLAIMED FLED FRANCE AFTER** LOUIS XIV ISSUED **THE EDICT OF FONTAINEBLEAU**

July 1683 Battle of Penghu sees Qing defeat kingdom of Tungning

1683 Precision microscope invented by Dutch scientist Anton von Leeuwenhoek (1632–1723)

12 September 1683 Battle of Kahlenberg ends siege of Vienna

1683 War of the Reunions (to 1684) sees France expand territory

1683 Dutch begin **trading at Canton**, China

December 1683 Great Frost begins across northern hemisphere

1684 Anti-Ottoman **Holy League formed** under papal authority

1684 Treaty of Ratisbon confirms French frontier gains

15 April 1684 Catherine I of Russia born (d.1727)

1684 Dutch occupy sultanate of Bantam, southern Sumatra

1684 Sultan of **Morocco seizes Tangier** from England

1684 Changamire Empire defeat Portuguese at **Battle of Maungwe**, southern Africa

6 February 1685 Accession of James II to English and Scottish thrones

1685 French **Jesuits** establish first **mission in Beijing**

1685 Mughals expel **English East India Company** from Surat, India

1685 French establish trade route between Great Lakes and Ohio Valley, North America

6 July 1685 Duke of Monmouth's rebellion against James II of England ends at **Battle of Sedgemoor**

October 1685 Edict of Fontainebleau declares Protestantism illegal in France; Huguenots flee

1686 League of Augsburg formed to contain French ambitions

1686 French claim **Madagascar**

1687–88

This Dutch painting shows William III's fleet departing the Netherlands for England at the start of the Glorious Revolution of 1688.

IN OCTOBER 1688, DESPITE A LACK of finances, Louis XIV's forces devastated the Rhineland Palatinate, in Germany, provoking the **Nine Years War**. His goal was to force Leopold I to recognize French rule over the frontier territories previously annexed, as well as create a devastated strip of land that would be difficult for armies to cross to attack France. The next month, **William III of Orange landed in England** with an army of 15,000. These two events provoked a kind of volcanic eruption in European political history. Whereas Louis's invasion, almost immediately bogged down in winter mud, eventually led to **an eclipse of French power** in the face of a Europe united in opposition to him (see 1685–86), within three months William III had become not just the joint monarch of England (with his wife, Mary) but the leader of the **pan-European, anti-French Protestant alliance**. At stake was a fundamental clash over the nature of legitimate rule.

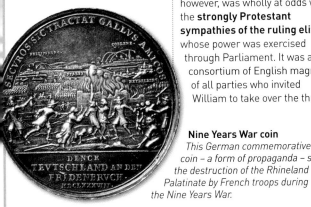

ISAAC NEWTON (1642–1727)

In 1687, the English physicist Isaac Newton published the universal law of gravitation, one of the most remarkable of all scientific discoveries. It explained what holds the universe together: that all heavenly bodies exert a force called gravitas, or weight. Newton's work would dominate science's views on the physical universe for almost 300 years.

If Louis XIV's apparently absolute monarchy seemed the pattern by which modern princes could most effectively exercise power, the **accession of William III** to the English and Scottish thrones made plain a radical alternative: that Parliament was the ultimate arbiter of who should rule. No one had disputed the right of William's ousted predecessor, James II, to the English throne. His clumsily active promotion of Catholicism, however, was wholly at odds with the **strongly Protestant sympathies of the ruling elite**, whose power was exercised through Parliament. It was a consortium of English magnates of all parties who invited William to take over the throne of England in what was, legal inventions aside, a direct deposition of a reigning monarch. The consequence, known as the **Glorious Revolution of 1688**, was a triumph of Parliamentary authority, and England would be immeasurably strengthened.

However, for Louis XIV the **result of the Nine Years War**, which would be mainly fought around France's borders, but also in Ireland, North America, and India, would not be the one he had intended. Although **France** had fought well, it was **crippled by economic woes**, and eventually welcomed a settlement with the Grand Alliance, which too was **financially exhausted**. By 1697, although Louis would retain Alsace, he would have to return the province of Lorraine and all his gains on the east bank of the Rhine, as well as accept William as king of England and a string of Dutch fortresses along his border with the Spanish Netherlands.

Nine Years War coin
This German commemorative coin – a form of propaganda – shows the destruction of the Rhineland Palatinate by French troops during the Nine Years War.

1689

" I HAVE **CONQUERED AN EMPIRE BUT** I HAVE **NOT** BEEN ABLE TO **CONQUER MYSELF.** "

Peter I (the Great), tsar of Russia, reflecting on his rule, 1672–1725

WHEN CONFRONTED WITH THE INVASION OF WILLIAM III IN 1688, James II of England abandoned an army he sent to confront William and **fled to Louis XIV's France**. Charles II had been happy to be financed by Louis XIV, but he had disguised the fact. James II now actively reveled in French backing. In March 1689, he **landed with a French-financed army in Ireland**, and attracting substantial Catholic support briefly threatened the new Dutch Protestant settlement. However, William's victory in 1690 at the Battle of the Boyne saw James back in France three days later. Henceforward, the Stuart Jacobite claim to its thrones in Britain (see 1715 and 1745) would complicate French diplomacy, and seem unlikely to change political reality.

In **New York**, the Glorious Revolution produced a short-lived echo when German Calvinist **Jacob Leisler overthrew the royal governor** in May 1689 in the name of William III. An English force arrived to compel Leisler to surrender in January 1691, and he was executed for treason.

Since 1682, a young **Peter I** (1672–1725) had ruled Russia jointly with his disabled half-brother Ivan V, but the real power had been his **sister and regent, Sophia**. The power struggle came to a climax in 1689 when, gaining the support of the Streltsy royal guardsmen, he overthrew Sophia, forcing her into a convent and leaving him and Ivan as co-tsars.

Leisler's Rebellion
Leisler is shown swearing-in volunteers to support his overthrow of the governor of New York. He captured Fort James, Manhattan, briefly renaming it Fort William.

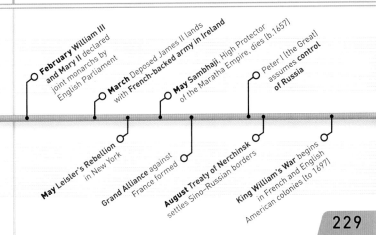

- **19 March 1687** French explorer **Robert Cavelier de La Salle murdered** on Mississippi expedition
- **July 1687** Isaac Newton's *Principia* **explains gravity**
- **4 April 1687** Declaration of Indulgence briefly brings **religious toleration** to England
- **September 1687** Venetians **attack Ottomans** in Dalmatia and Greece
- **12 August 1687** Battle of Mohács sees Holy League defeat Ottomans in Hungary
- **1688** Genroku Era, Japan; flowering of kabuki theatre
- **December 1687** French Huguenots settle in Dutch **Cape Colony**, Africa
- **November 1688** William III of Orange arrives in England
- **November 1688** Nine Years War begins (to 1697)
- **1688** Lloyds coffee house (venue of Lloyds insurance) opens, London
- **December 1688** In England, **Glorious Revolution** sees James II deposed
- **1688** Holy League captures Belgrade from Ottomans
- **February** William III and Mary II declared joint monarchs by English Parliament
- **May** Leisler's Rebellion in New York
- **March** Deposed James II lands **with French-backed army in Ireland**
- Grand Alliance against France formed
- **May** Sambhaji, High Protector of the Maratha Empire, dies (b.1657)
- **August** Treaty of Nerchinsk settles Sino-Russian borders
- Peter I (the Great) assumes **control of Russia**
- King William's War begins in French and English American colonies (to 1697)

THE RISE AND FALL OF THE OTTOMAN EMPIRE

AN ENDURING POWER THAT DOMINATED IN EUROPE AND THE MIDDLE EAST FOR NEARLY 500 YEARS

The long decline of the Ottoman Empire in the 19th century disguised the fact that for 450 years after its emergence in about 1300, it was not just one of the most dynamic and sophisticated polities in the world, but also one of the largest. It dwarfed its European and Middle Eastern rivals.

At its height, towards the end of the 17th century, the Ottoman Empire stretched from the gates of Vienna to the Indian Ocean, and from the Crimea to Algiers. Though the Mongol leader Timur had checked Ottoman ambitions in the early 15th century, once Murad I took the throne in 1413, the expansion programme was vigorously renewed. His son, Mehmed II (r.1451–81), extended Ottoman rule across the Balkans and seized Constantinople (Istanbul) in a blaze of conquest. Under Selim I (r.1512–20), the Safavids were contained at Caldiran and much of the Middle East and North Africa was conquered. Suleiman the Magnificent (r.1520–66) expanded Ottoman territories deep into Hungary and almost as far as the Atlantic. Faced with such potency, the Christian West could do little. Enormously rich, technologically advanced, and buoyed by its leadership of the Muslim world, Ottoman power seemed irresistible. The empire's decline after the failure of the siege of Vienna in 1683 was the result less of internal weakness than of the growing strength of its European opponents.

FORMIDABLE OPPONENTS

The Ottoman state began as a small frontier principality preying on Christian Byzantium. Under a succession of 14th-century warrior-sultans, a series of rapid conquests were launched, notably at Kosovo in 1389, when a combined Christian–Balkan force was defeated. Bayezid I (r.1389–1402) exploited this victory by annexing Bulgaria and invading Hungary. Ottoman success was based on a highly trained army. The most feared troops, the janissaries, were recruited from the conquered peoples of the Balkans, converted to Islam. In addition, Ottoman artillery in the 15th and 16th centuries was among the most destructive in the world.

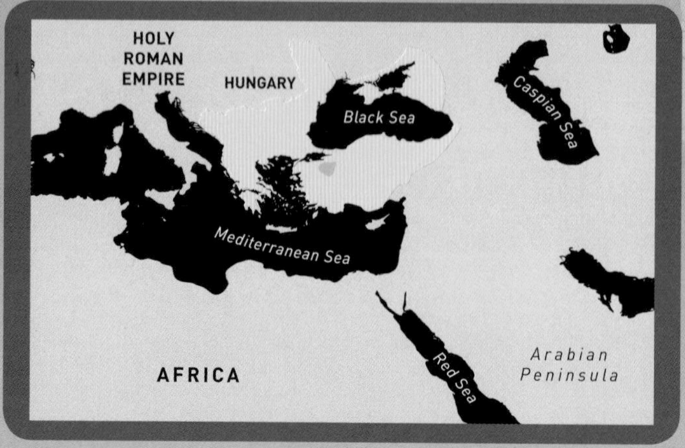

1481 From a small nucleus in *c.*1300, the Ottomans went on to conquer a vast area, covering much of Anatolia and the area around the Black Sea by 1481.

KEY
- Empire at 1300
- Empire at 1481

Size of the Ottoman Empire
By the turn of the 20th century the Ottoman Empire had shrunk to a third of the size it been three centuries earlier. Modern Turkey is a fraction of that.

16th-century Empire
At its peak, the Ottoman Empire was not just a land power – its navy dominated the eastern Mediterranean and the maritime routes with the Indian Ocean. It challenged not merely European but its Middle Eastern rivals, too: Mamluk Egypt, conquered in 1517, and Safavid Persia, an equally dynamic and sophisticated state.

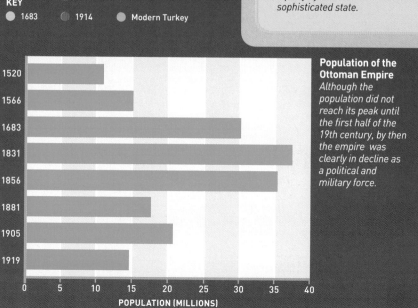

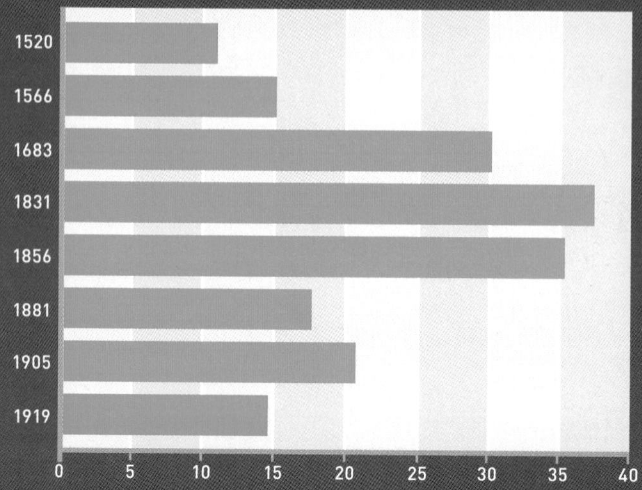

Population of the Ottoman Empire
Although the population did not reach its peak until the first half of the 19th century, by then the empire was clearly in decline as a political and military force.

“ THE PRESENT TERROR OF THE WORLD. ”

Attributed to a European ambassador *c.*1600

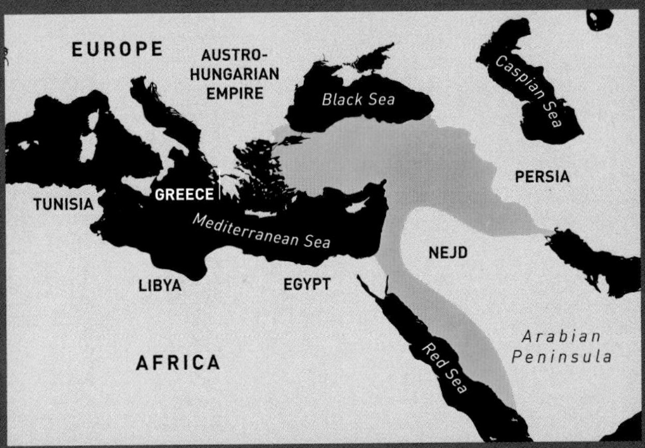

1913 Ottoman power had dwindled. Greece, Serbia, Romania, and Montenegro were now independent, and other European powers had taken over North Africa and the Black Sea.

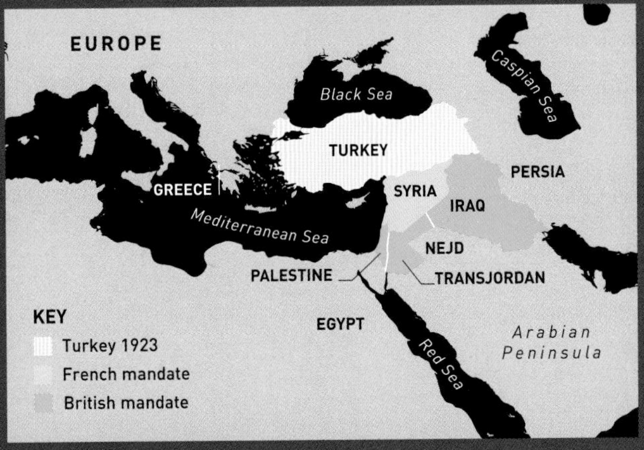

1923 The Ottomans' remaining Arab territories were divided between Britain and France. Turkey was reduced to its Anatolian heartlands, sparking nationalist conflict with Greece and Armenia.

1690

Fort William, shown here in the 1700s, was built after the English East India Company moved its main Bengal trading station to Calcutta in 1690.

THE ENGLISH EAST INDIA COMPANY had been a presence in Bengal since the early 17th century. **Seeking greater security for their trade**, a new base, **Fort William**, named after William III, was established in 1690 in what is now Calcutta. The fort, continually enlarged and improved, would be critical to the later British dominance in India.

In 1690, **English philosopher John Locke** (1632–1704) wrote *An Essay Concerning Human Understanding*. It marked Locke as a **key thinker** in the Western philosophical tradition, above all for his assertion that knowledge of the world came through experience of it, and that the basis of this understanding was reasoned, empirical (based on observation) thought. Reinforcing many of his established ideas about property rights, religious toleration, and monarchy, it also ensured his influence in debates about **liberty and reason** in 18th-century France and America.

Philosopher John Locke
John Locke contended that there is a contract between monarch and people under which the monarch can be overthrown if he abuses it.

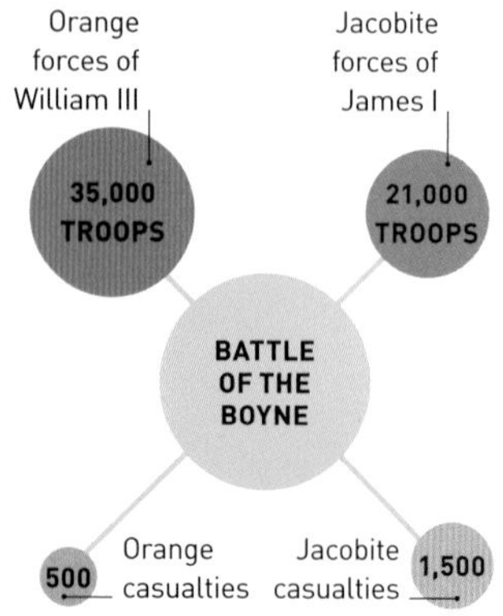

Battle of the Boyne, Ireland
The Orange army of William III inflicted a decisive defeat on the Jacobites of James II, giving the lie to William's "bloodless revolution".

The **turnip**, a basic root crop of the agricultural revolution of the 17th century, was **first cultivated in England in about 1690**. The Dutch, to make best use of their limited lands, had already discovered that **crop rotation** (arable crops alternated with root crops rather than leaving fields fallow) not only improved fertility but provided food for sheep whose manure furthered productivity.

On 12 July 1690, William III's victory over the deposed Catholic James II at the **Battle of the Boyne**, in Ireland, was decisive in maintaining the **Protestant supremacy** that had been established there by the Glorious Revolution of 1688. In Ireland, brutal **sectarian violence** would continue for centuries.

1691–92

This woodcut, taken from the title page of a pamphlet, shows the devastation of Port Royal, Jamaica, by both an earthquake and a tsunami in June 1692.

> **"** THE **EUROPEANS ARE** VERY **QUIET;** THEY **DO NOT EXCITE ANY DISTURBANCES...** THEY **DO NO HARM** TO ANYONE, THEY **COMMIT NO CRIMES... "**

Kangxi, Chinese Qing emperor, announces the Edict of Toleration, 1692

ALTHOUGH THE NINE YEARS WAR had quickly settled in 1688 into a stalemate on land that would last to 1697, at sea the Grand Alliance enjoyed a clear superiority over France. The six-day **Battle of La Hogue** from May to June 1692 saw much of the French fleet either beached or destroyed by fireships. It **ended hopes of a French invasion of England**.

At 11:43am on 7 June 1692, a catastrophic **earthquake struck Port Royal**, capital of the English colony of Jamaica, and one of the most important ports in the Caribbean, as well as a legendary base for pirates. **Most of the city sank beneath the sea**. With the subsequent tsunami and outbreaks of disease, the death toll was about 5,000.

In **Salem**, Massachusetts, in late 1691, young girls started having fits and hallucinations, citing demonic possession. This led to claims of witchcraft, which by 1692 had reached the point of hysteria. On 10 June, an elderly widow, Bridget Bishop, was **hanged as a witch**, and by September a further 18 people had been executed on the same charge, and one man crushed to death. Trials for witchcraft were no longer common in England by this time, and the **mass hysteria** of Salem remains hard to explain.

Jesuit missionaries had been in East Asia since the 16th century. In contrast to Japan (see 1597–99), in China they were **valued by a succession of emperors**, not least for their knowledge of western science. They made many converts, and in 1692 the Kangxi Emperor issued an **edict of toleration of Christianity**.

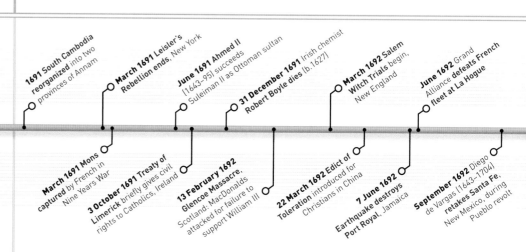

Salem Witch Trial
The trial of George Jacobs was one of many in a Puritan community riven by petty jealousies, where none disputed the existence of Satan.

- Aya kingdom of Whydah, West Africa, **principal supplier of slaves** for Atlantic trade
- Chinese **Qing repel Zunghar** invasion, Outer Mongolia
- **Fort William** established in Calcutta, India
- **10 July Battle of Beachy Head** sees French defeat Anglo-Dutch navy
- **12 July Battle of the Boyne** sees William III defeat James II
- **John Locke publishes** *An Essay Concerning Human Understanding*
- Approximate date for **introduction of turnip** into England
- **Belgrade recaptured** by Ottomans from Austrians
- **1691 South Cambodia reorganized** into two provinces of Annam
- **March 1691 Leisler's Rebellion ends**, New York
- **March 1691 Mons captured** by French in Nine Years War
- **June 1691 Ahmed II** (1643–95) succeeds Suleiman II as Ottoman sultan
- **3 October 1691 Treaty of Limerick** briefly gives civil rights to Catholics, Ireland
- **31 December 1691** Irish chemist **Robert Boyle dies** (b.1627)
- **13 February 1692 Glencoe Massacre**, Scotland: MacDonalds attacked for failure to support William III
- **March 1692 Salem Witch Trials** begin, New England
- **22 March 1692 Edict of Toleration** introduced for Christians in China
- **7 June 1692 Earthquake destroys Port Royal**, Jamaica
- **June 1692** Grand Alliance **defeats French fleet at La Hogue**
- **September 1692** Diego de Vargas (1643–1704) **retakes Santa Fe**, New Mexico, during Pueblo revolt

1693

The summit vent of Mount Etna, an active volcano on the east coast of Sicily, in Italy, has witnessed many destructive eruptions, not least in 1693.

IF SOUTHERN EUROPE had been spared the worst of the Little Ice Age (see 1683–84), the eruption on 11 January 1693 of **Mount Etna**, in Sicily, proved a cruel reminder of the power of nature. The eruption **set off an earthquake** that **devastated Sicily** and large areas of southern Italy and Malta. About 60,000 were killed in Sicily alone, and thousands of square kilometres became uninhabitable due to lava flows and tsunamis.

For several years after the summer of 1693, a series of **famines swept western Europe**. In France alone, about two million died. These were among the most calamitous **consequences of the Little Ice Age**, with bitter winters giving way to dismal, rain-soaked summers, and stunted crops rotting in sodden fields. Even in years of relative plenty, the vast **majority of Europe's peasants**, themselves the overwhelming majority of the continent's population, enjoyed a subsistence existence at best, with root vegetables, bread, and porridge as their staple diet. When the crops failed, they starved. In the face of these near Biblical visitations of mass misery, there seemed to be no answer. Almost entirely dependent on the food surpluses generated by its heavily taxed peasant population, even as obviously powerful a state as late-17th-century France could do little more than suffer and acccept its unavoidable fate.

Dodo
The flightless dodo stood about 1m (3ft 3in) in height and weighed about 20kg (44lb). It had a long, hooked bill, greyish or brownish plumage on a fat body, and very small wings.

In 1598, on the **isolated island of Mauritius**, in the Indian Ocean, the Dutch admiral Wybrand van Warwijck described a bird he called a "walghvogel". Later Dutch settlers there called it a "dodaars", which was a reference to what they saw as the knot of tails at its rear. Portuguese sailors that visited the island called it a "doudo", meaning "fool" or "crazy". By perhaps 1693, the **dodo, a flightless bird**, which was related to the pigeon, had **become extinct**. The dodo is the first animal whose extinction can be exactly ascribed to man, victim of its trusting nature, the destruction of its woodland habitats, and the introduction of cats, rats, pigs, and dogs who hunted it to its destruction.

1694–96

The forces of the Grand Alliance, led by William III of England, gather outside Namur, where a French garrison is besieged. The siege lasted two months.

IN JULY 1694, ENGLAND FOUND A NOVEL SOLUTION to the problem of a lack of funds that had plagued the combatants of the Nine Years War. The **Bank of England** served both Crown and government, and was closely modelled on the Bank of Amsterdam, founded in 1609. A private venture (until 1931), it **immediately loaned the government** £1.2 million – raised by its investors in 12 days – at an annual interest rate of 8 per cent and for an annual service charge of £4,000, in return for the right to print bank notes. It also **created a National Debt**, but at the same time allowed England not merely to finance its own part in the war but to finance its allies. The bank was possibly the most significant factor in Britain's subsequent emergence on the world stage.

European colonialism in the 17th and 18th centuries had the simple goal of money. In the New World, the Spanish had conquered two rich civilizations and found a vast silver mine. The **Portuguese in Brazil** had found only native peoples and tropical jungles; sugar cane plantations worked by slave labour were the source of its marginal profits. Then, in **Minas Gerais**, in the southeast, **gold was found** in 1695. It transformed colonial Brazil, as did the later discovery of diamonds in the same region. Vast, lawless towns appeared, chiefly Ouro Preto ("Black Gold") and Diamantia, and the region's **population exploded**, from scattered handfuls to 320,000 (half of them slaves). A result was the near collapse of the sugar cane industry, stripped of most of its workforce.

One of the few moments of significance in the Nine Years War took place in September 1695, when the **Grand Alliance retook the city of Namur** after three years in French hands. The loss of the most important fortress in the Netherlands further weakened an already defensive French position.

In 1696, **China** began an **eastward expansion** that by the end of the 18th century would see it **almost double in size**. It was provoked by the invasion of Khalkha (Outer Mongolia) by the nomadic Zunghar people of Central Asia in 1690, who were anxious to forestall a possible Chinese takeover of the region. The **invasion failed**, sparking only a confused series of campaigns under the Zunghar ruler, Galdan, as well as a civil war. In 1696, the Kangxi Emperor led a Khalkha-Chinese army across the Gobi Desert into Mongolia and crushed the Zunghar. **Outer Mongolia** was **incorporated within the Chinese empire** the following year.

Russia fought two campaigns in 1695–96 to capture the **Ottoman-held fortress port of Azov**. The port was key to Russia as it blocked access to the Black Sea, a factor that had contributed to the failure of its Crimean campaigns against the Ottomans in 1687–89. Finally, Peter I (the Great), now the sole tsar of Russia since the death of his disabled half-brother, Ivan, attacked Azov with a combined land and naval force, capturing the city in July 1696. A lesson learned was that Russia needed a navy, and it embarked on a massive shipbuilding programme.

Battle of Azov
In this painting by Robert Kerr Porter, Peter the Great is seen personally leading his galley fleet during the capture of Azov in 1696.

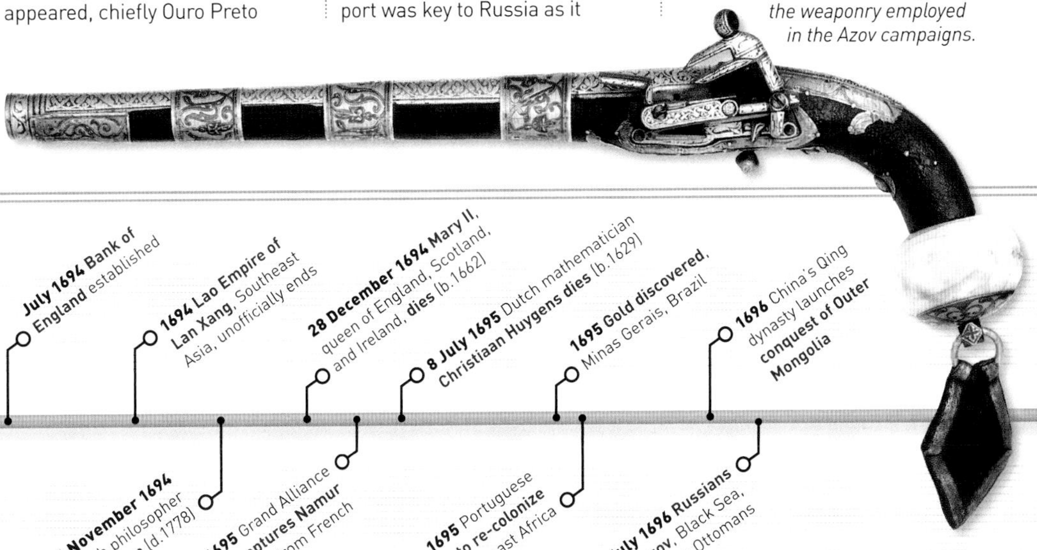

Caucasian pistol
This ornately fashioned pistol with a long barrel and a short, gently curved handle was typical of the weaponry employed in the Azov campaigns.

11 January Eruption of Mount Etna, Sicily

Great Famine begins in Europe; millions die

Grand Alliance defeated by French, at Neerwinden, Flanders

Diego de Vargas completes **re-conquest of New Mexico** for Spain

Portuguese expelled from Zimbabwe

October French capture Charleroi in Nine Years War

Kingston, Jamaica, founded

Approximate date of **extinction of dodo**, Mauritius

July 1694 Bank of England established

21 November 1694 French philosopher **Voltaire born** (d.1778)

1694 Lao Empire of Lan Xang, Southeast Asia, unofficially ends

28 December 1694 Mary II, queen of England, Scotland, and Ireland, **dies** (b.1662)

1695 Grand Alliance **recaptures Namur** from French

8 July 1695 Dutch mathematician **Christiaan Huygens dies** (b.1629)

1695 Portuguese **attempt to re-colonize** southeast Africa

1695 Gold discovered, Minas Gerais, Brazil

July 1696 Russians take Azov, Black Sea, from Ottomans

1696 China's Qing dynasty launches **conquest of Outer Mongolia**

1697–99

“ THE **GREATEST COMFORTS** AND **LASTING PEACE** ARE **OBTAINED,** WHEN ONE **ERADICATES SELFISHNESS FROM WITHIN.** ”

Guru Gobind Singh, 10th Sikh Master, 1697

THE NINE YEARS WAR THAT HAD SEEN FRANCE TAKE ON the Grand Alliance of England, the Holy Roman Empire, Spain, and the Dutch Republic was **ended by the Treaty of Ryswick** in 1697. It established that all territory taken since 1679 was to be returned.

The Ottoman defeat at the Siege of Vienna in 1683 marked not just the beginning of a protracted Ottoman decline, but the **emergence of Habsburg Austria** as a European power to challenge France, England, and the Dutch Republic. After 1683, Austrian Imperial armies pursued the retreating Ottomans south across the Balkans, a process that climaxed at the **Battle of Zenta**, in Serbia in September 1697. Under the Italo-French general Eugene of Savoy (1663–1736), who was rapidly emerging as one of the foremost commanders in Europe, an Imperial army surprised the Ottomans as they attempted to cross the River Tisa. There they massacred them, with about 10,000 Ottomans drowned, and a further 20,000 killed in battle. The **Treaty of Karlowitz** in 1699 confirmed the Austrian gains, including the gradual absorption of Hungary by the Austrian crown.

Treaty of Ryswick
The treaty was signed at the palace of Huis ter Nieuwburg, the country house of William of Orange, in Ryswick, in the Dutch Republic.

In July 1698, English military engineer **Thomas Savery** (1650–1715) **registered a patent** for “a new invention for raiseing of water... of great use and advantage for drayning mines.” Basic forms of steam power had existed since the 1st century CE, but none of these had ever been translated into working machines. Savery’s **steam engine was basic**, prone to violent explosions, and unable to pump water more than 10m (33ft) below it, meaning that in mines it had to be installed, dangerously, underground. It was only in 1721 when Thomas Newcomen (1664–1729), working with Savery, produced his **atmospheric engine**, that a viable commercial use was found. Yet, the real potential of steam as **an engine of industrialization** would not be realized until the invention by the Scot, James Watt (1736–1819), in 1769, of a separate condenser, and then only with the backing of English businessman Matthew Boulton (see pp.274–75).

MUGHAL EMPIRE

The crushing of a Sikh revolt in the Punjab in 1699 saw the Mughal Empire at its zenith. From its Afghan heartlands, it had grown under Akbar, taking all but the tip of India’s subcontinent by the end of the 17th century. The harsh rule of Aurangzeb saw many revolts, and the later rise of the Marathas (see 1720) left the Mughals as puppets.

KEY
- Akbar’s domains, 1556
- Additional areas held by Mughals at Akbar’s death, 1605
- Additional areas acquired up to the death of Aurangzeb, 1707

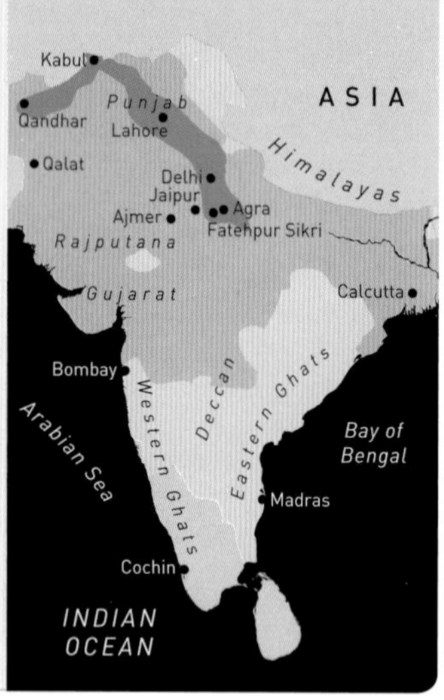

1700

An engraving depicting 16-year-old Philip, duke of Anjou, being recognized as Philip V, king of Spain, on 2 October 1700.

THE DEATH IN 1700 OF CHARLES II, the childless king of Spain, caused a major crisis when he nominated Philip of Anjou (1683–1746), the grandson of Louis XIV of France, as his successor. Charles hoped that French power would preserve the **Spanish Empire** if **ruled by a Bourbon**. Louis accepted the vast increase in family prestige and French influence, but **opposition** to the succession and its increase in French power **grew hugely**.

The accession in 1697 of the 15-year-old Charles XII (1682–1718) to the throne of Sweden was the signal for **Sweden’s Baltic rivals**, Denmark, Saxony, Poland, and, increasingly, Russia, to attempt to end Swedish pre-eminence. In fact, in the conflict that followed, the **Great Northern War** of 1700–21, Charles, “the Swedish Meteor”, would prove himself a general of genius. In the four months from August 1700, he successively defeated the Danes and then, over on the other side of the Baltic, at Narva, **annihilated a Russian army** four times the size of his own. The following July, he inflicted a similarly crushing defeat on a combined Polish–Saxon force at Klissow in Poland. With **Sweden never more dominant**, Charles’s bold campaigning, whatever the odds against him, had apparently been wholly vindicated.

From about 1700, a **major development in European culture** began to take shape: a musical tradition, part courtly, part church-based, known as the **High Baroque**. It evolved from later Renaissance music, above all in Italy, but developed to reach a new level of polyphonic tonal and **instrumental complexity**. It was characterized by both new and more elaborated musical forms: the concerto, fugue, oratorio, prelude, cantata, and opera. It was made possible by **new forms of existing instruments**: the organ, harpsichord, and, above all, violin. It depended also on **composers of genius**, such as Johann Sebastian Bach (1685–1750) and George Handel (1685–1759), and on a more extensive world of courtly and private patronage of them.

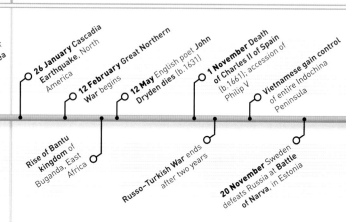

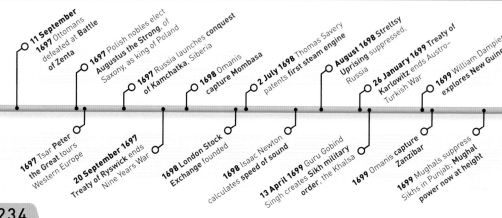

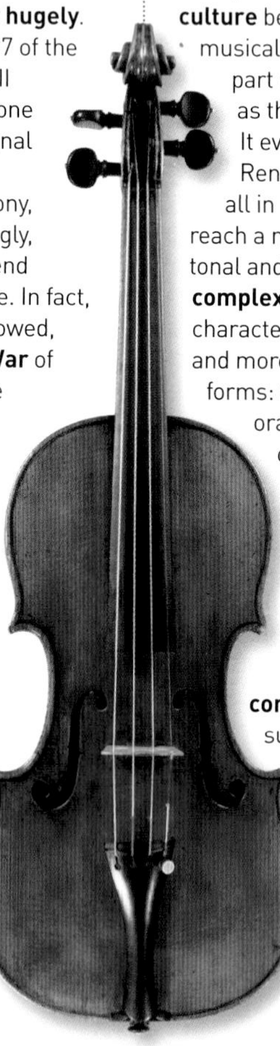

Stradivarius violin
The Stradivarius violin, made by Italian Antonio Stradivari, entered a golden age in 1700. These violins were larger than earlier models.

11 September 1697 Ottomans defeated at **Battle of Zenta**

1697 Polish nobles elect **Augustus the Strong**, of Saxony, as king of Poland

1697 Tsar **Peter the Great** tours Western Europe

1697 Russia launches **conquest of Kamchatka**, Siberia

20 September 1697 Treaty of Ryswick ends Nine Years War

1698 Omanis **capture Mombasa**

1698 London Stock Exchange founded

2 July 1698 Thomas Savery patents **first steam engine**

1698 Isaac Newton calculates **speed of sound**

August 1698 Streltsy Uprising suppressed, Russia

26 January 1699 Treaty of Karlowitz ends Austro-Turkish War

13 April 1699 Guru Gobind Singh creates **Sikh military order**, the Khalsa

1699 William Dampier **explores New Guinea**

1699 Omanis **capture Zanzibar**

1699 Mughals suppress Sikhs in Punjab; **Mughal power now at height**

26 January Cascadia Earthquake, North America

12 February Great Northern War begins

Rise of Bantu kingdom of Buganda, East Africa

12 May English poet **John Dryden dies** (b.1631)

1 November Death of Charles II of Spain (b.1661); accession of Philip V

Russo-Turkish War ends after two years

Vietnamese gain control of entire Indochina Peninsula

20 November Sweden defeats Russia at **Battle of Narva**, in Estonia

Jethro Tull's seed drill is shown here being operated manually. It sowed seeds in rows, performing work that previously required several labourers.

A REVOLUTION IN AGRICULTURE BEGAN IN 1701 when English agriculturalist **Jethro Tull** (1674–1741) created the horse-drawn **seed drill** (see pp.250–51). A major time- and labour-saving device, it sowed great numbers of seeds in neat rows. Although not taken up at once, it later proved popular with large landowners and would lay the basis of modern **productive agriculture**.

No sooner had the Nine Years War ended than Europe's powers found themselves in another lengthy and costly war. The surprise choice of Philip, duke of Anjou, as King Philip V of Spain (see 1700), hugely **disturbed the European balance of power**, and Louis XIV did nothing to discourage fears of a Franco-Spanish military alliance. He took over military duties in Philip's lands, moving troops into the Spanish Netherlands to defend them from the English and the Dutch. With renewed confidence in France's European status, Louis then **recognized James III**, son of the exiled James II (1633–1701), as king of England. With England and the Dutch Republic **backing Austria's claims** to the Spanish throne – in the form of their candidate, Archduke Charles of Austria – armed opposition to France was now guaranteed. The **War of the Spanish Succession** that began in 1701 saw a Grand Alliance oppose the unification of the French and Spanish thrones. It would last until 1713–14 and redraw the map of the continent and the world.

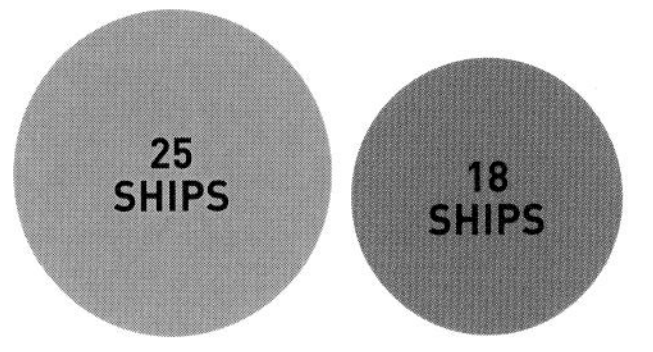

Battle of Vigo Bay, October 1702
In an early encounter in the War of the Spanish Succession, 25 ships of an Anglo-Dutch fleet defeated a Franco-Spanish fleet at Vigo Bay.

Freelance **Samurai warriors known as ronin** emerged from the Japanese civil wars of the 14th and 15th centuries. In 1651, they engaged in rebellion and continued to **instigate dissent** into the 18th century. In 1701, a respected lord, Asano Nugatory, was forced to commit suicide after assaulting an official who had insulted him. In revenge, 47 of his samurai became ronin and murdered the official, an act normally punished by execution. But because Confucianism taught that it is honourable to avenge a lord's death, they were allowed to commit suicide in turn.

The **kingdom of Prussia** – later the forerunner of the German state – **was proclaimed in 1701** when Frederick I, duke of Prussia and elector of Brandenburg, was crowned the first "king in Prussia", in Konigsberg Castle.

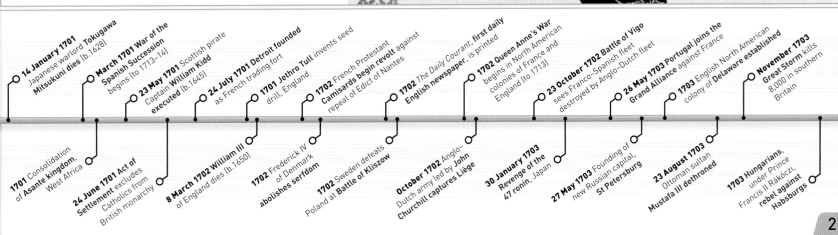

Revenge of the 47 ronin
This colour woodcut is one of a series on the 47 ronin uprising, the most famous incident of the samurai code of honour, bushido.

14 January 1701 Japanese warlord Tokugawa **Mitsukuni dies** (b.1628)

March 1701 War of the Spanish Succession begins (to 1713–14)

1701 Consolidation of **Asante kingdom,** West Africa

23 May 1701 Scottish pirate Captain **William Kidd executed** (b.1645)

24 June 1701 Act of Settlement excludes Catholics from British monarchy

24 July 1701 Detroit founded as French trading fort

1701 Jethro Tull invents seed drill, England

8 March 1702 William III of England dies (b.1650)

1702 French Protestant **Camisards begin revolt** against repeal of Edict of Nantes

1702 Frederick IV of Denmark **abolishes serfdom**

1702 *The Daily Courant*, **first daily English newspaper**, is printed

1702 Sweden defeats Poland at **Battle of Kliszow**

1702 Queen Anne's War begins in North American colonies of France and England (to 1713)

October 1702 Anglo-Dutch army led by **John Churchill captures Liège**

23 October 1702 Battle of Vigo sees Franco-Spanish fleet destroyed by Anglo-Dutch fleet

30 January 1703 Revenge of the 47 ronin, Japan

26 May 1703 Portugal joins the Grand Alliance against France

27 May 1703 Founding of new Russian capital, **St Petersburg**

1703 English North American colony of **Delaware established**

23 August 1703 Ottoman sultan **Mustafa III dethroned**

November 1703 Great Storm kills 8,000 in southern Britain

1703 Hungarians, under Prince Francis II Rákóczi, **rebel against Habsburgs**

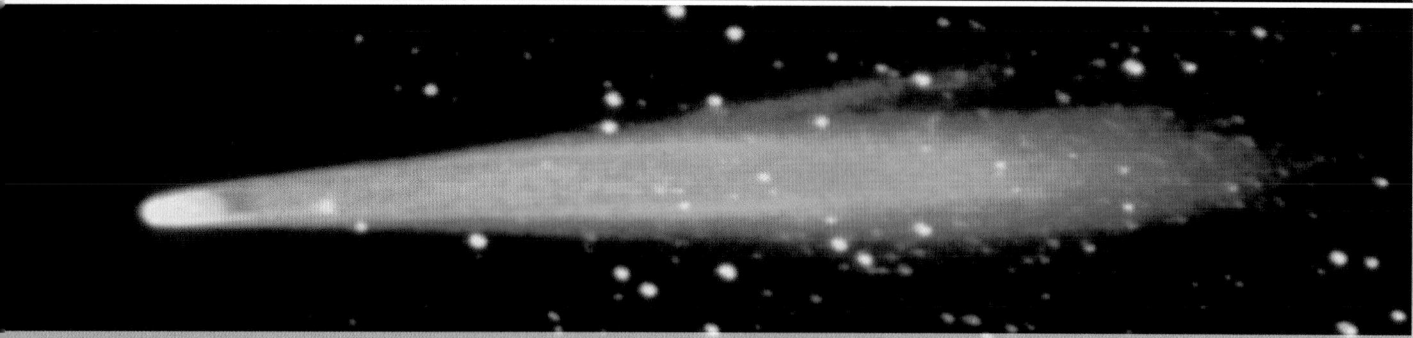

This modern photograph shows Halley's Comet, named after the British astronomer Edmond Halley, who was the first to determine that the comet returned periodically, every 76 years.

This picture depicts the Mughal emperor Aurangzeb hunting nilgai.

THE BATTLE OF BLENHEIM, fought in 1704 near the village of Blindheim on the Danube in Bavaria, Germany, ended in victory for the Duke of Marlborough and the Grand Alliance (see 1701), and turned the **War of the Spanish Succession** in favour of the Grand Alliance. The battle halted a Franco–Bavarian march on Vienna, and Bavaria played no further part in the war.

Meanwhile, the **Gibraltar peninsula** on the Spanish mainland was seized by a combined Dutch–English force in 1704; Gibraltar was ceded perpetually to Britain in 1713.

Victor of Blenheim
The Duke of Marlborough (in red) sits astride his horse in this tapestry, now hanging in his eventual home, Blenheim Palace, England.

300

THE NUMBER OF **POCUMTUCKS AMONG** THE **RAIDERS** AT **DEERFIELD**

In Tunisia to the southeast, the **Husaynid dynasty** was established in 1705 when Al-Husayn ibn 'Ali (1669–1740) was recognized by the Ottoman sultan as governor of the province. The Husaynid dynasty lasted until Tunisia gained independence in 1957.

In North America, **Deerfield, Massachusetts**, was the scene in 1704 of a massacre of English colonists by a combined force of French-Canadians and American Indians. Also in 1704, ***The Boston News-Letter***, North America's first continuously published newspaper, appeared, largely funded by the British government.

In 1706, the most decisive event in the War of the Spanish Succession occurred in North Italy, where the Duke of Savoy, allied with Austria and Britain, was defending his territory against French invasion and siege of the capital, Turin. The French were crushed when the Duke of Savoy and Prince Eugene broke through French lines and routed the army, driving them out of North Italy.

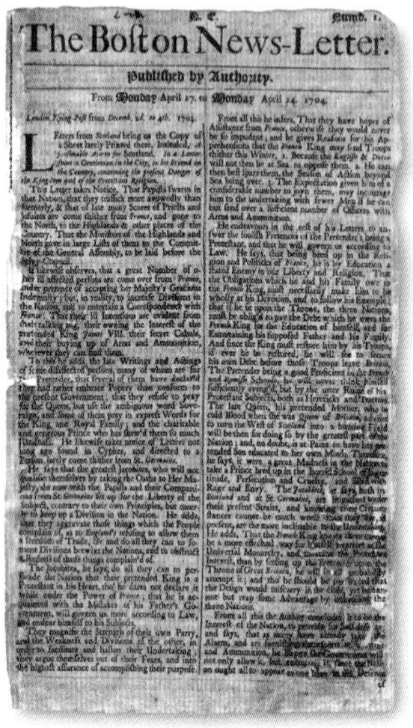

The Boston News-Letter.
Published by Authority.
From Monday April 17. to Monday April 24. 1704.

News from home
Published weekly, The Boston News-Letter *provided English colonists in America with news of England's political events and wars.*

Also in 1706, Spanish conquistador **Juan de Uribarri** claimed southeastern Colorado, an area populated by warring American Indian tribes, and joined it to **Spanish New Mexico**.

In England, the **first steam engine** using moving parts was built in 1704 by **Thomas Newcomen** (1663–1729) and Thomas Savery (see 1698). The first working Newcomen engine was installed to pump water from a mine in Staffordshire in 1712.

Edmond Halley (1656–1742), English mathematician and astronomer, published *A Synopsis of the Astronomy of Comets* in 1705, in which he described the parabolic orbits of 24 comets. He proved that three sightings, many decades apart, were of a single comet – the comet that is now known as Halley's Comet – and determined that this comet returns to the Solar System every 76 years.

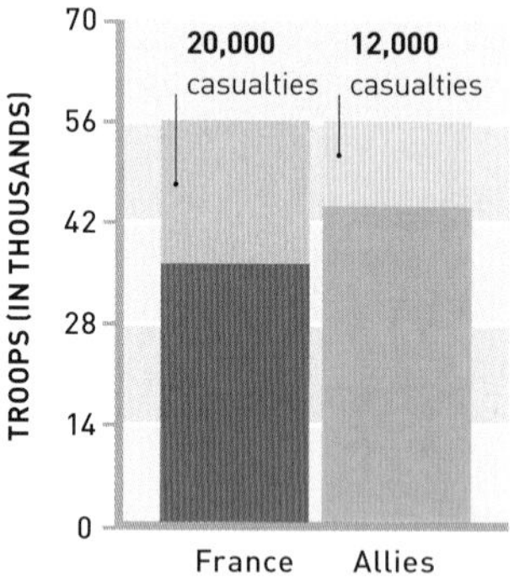

Battle of Blenheim losses
About 112,000 troops took part in the Battle of Blenheim, with 20,000 French casualties but almost half as many from Britain and its allies.

THE DEATH IN 1707 OF AURANGZEB, sixth Mughal emperor of India (b.1618), marked the start of the decline of the Mughal Empire. Aurangzeb's successors squandered the dynasty's fortunes while losing control of regional governors, who went on to built their own empires. Aurangzeb, disturbed by the growing power of the **Sikh Guru Gobind Singh**, had

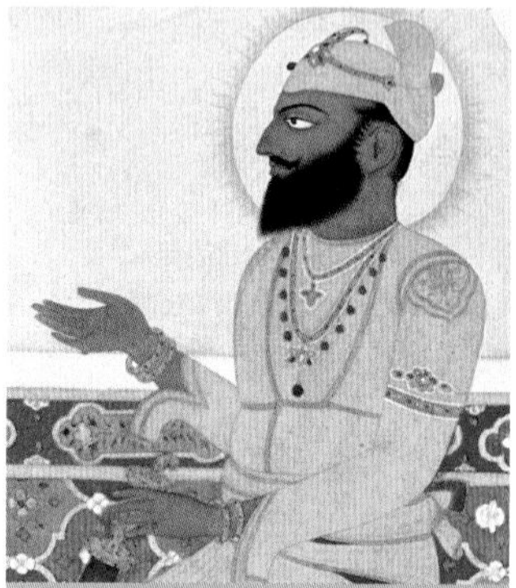

GURU GOBIND SINGH
(1666–1708)

The tenth and last guru of Sikhism, Gobind Singh was a powerful figure in Indian history. In 1699 he transformed Sikhism by creating the Khalsa (Pure), a community of the faith that trained as warriors; now the Khalsa embraces all Sikhs. Aurangzeb considered coming to terms with Gobind Singh, but the rajas of the Sivalik Hills remained hostile, and Gobind Singh was assassinated in 1708.

- **29 February 1704** English colonists in Massachusetts massacred and **Deerfield sacked**
- **13 August 1704** Grand Alliance and Franco-Bavarian troops fight **Battle of Blenheim**
- **1704** British inventors Thomas Newcomen and Thomas Savery build **first steam engine** with moving parts
- **1705** British astronomer **Edmond Halley** publishes *A Synopsis of the Astronomy of Comets*
- **November 1705** Capitol building completed in **Williamsburg**, capital of English colony of **Virginia**
- **17 January 1706** A future Founding Father of the US, **Benjamin Franklin**, is born (d.1790)
- **7 September 1706** French defeated by Austrian and Savoyard forces in **Battle of Turin**
- **1706** Southeastern **Colorado** claimed by Spanish New Mexico
- **17 March 1707** Mughal Emperor **Aurangzeb dies** (b.1618)
- **25th April 1707** Defeat of Grand Alliance at **Almanza, Spain**
- **1 May 1707** Acts of Union come into effect, uniting **Scotland** and **England**

In a detail of a painting by Ignace Jacques Parrocel, Prince Eugene of Savoy's troops are shown confronting the French at the Battle of Malplaquet.

Aurangzeb's reign
Emperor Aurangzeb reigned for 48 years, from 1658 until his death in 1707, but for 27 of those years he was at war with the Marathas.

summoned him, but died before they could meet. Gobind Singh became friends with the new emperor, Bahadur Shah (r.1707–12), but was assassinated in 1708 on the orders of a rival leader, Nawab Wazir Khan.

Far from India, the kingdom of **England** and the kingdom of **Scotland** were formally unified as Great Britain by the **Acts of Union** of 1707. Henceforth, both were ruled by a single monarch and by a parliament based in London.

Britain, still embroiled in the War of the Spanish Succession, joined Dutch forces to seize **Minorca** and **Sicily** from France in 1708; both were used as military bases. Also in 1708, British settlers lost control of the Canadian east coast after a defeat by the French at **St John's, Newfoundland**.

THE BATTLE OF MALPLAQUET in 1709 was the bloodiest of the **War of the Spanish Succession** (see 1701) and, indeed, the entire 18th century. Grand Alliance forces under the Duke of Marlborough attacked the French at Malplaquet, France, southwest of the French-held fortress of **Mons**, which lay over the present-day Belgian border. In gaining possession of the battlefield, the Allies suffered more than 21,000 casualties, twice as many as the French, but the French retreated in good order and remained a future threat.

Meanwhile, in the **Great Northern War** (1700–21) between Russia and its western neighbours (see 1700), Charles XII of Sweden had been leading forces in a march on Russia. The Swedish army of 17,000 men attacked the fort of **Poltava** in the Ukraine in July 1709. The Swedes were faced by Peter the Great's army of 80,000, which eventually ran them from the battlefield. Charles, exiled in Moldavia, persuaded the **Ottoman Empire** to go to war with Russia in 1710, but Peter the Great (1672–1725) agreed terms in 1711.

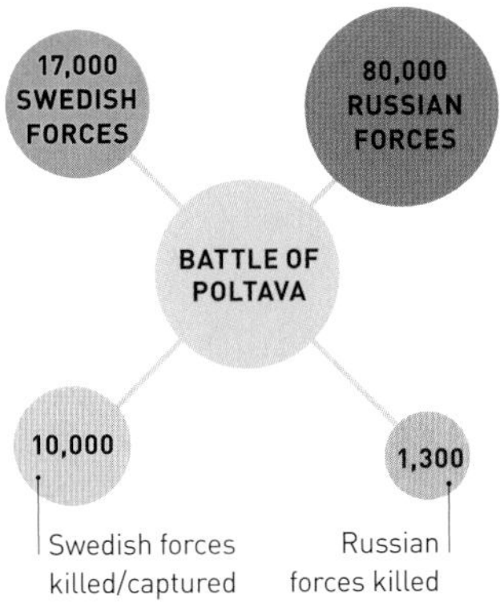

Forces in the Battle of Poltava
In the Battle of Poltava, 60 per cent of the Swedish troops were killed or captured, while less than 2 per cent of the Russian troops were killed.

In 1709, the Persian Safavid rulers of southwestern **Afghanistan** were overwhelmed by an **uprising** organized by **Mirwais Khan Hotak** (1673–1715), a tribal chief of the Ghilzai Pashtuns and founder of the Hotaki dynasty (which lasted from 1709 to 1738). Furious at Safavid cruelty and attempts to force them to convert from Sunni to Shia Islam, the Afghans assassinated their Safavid governor, Gurgin Khan, and massacred many Persians.

In Britain, revolution of an industrial kind was in the making. In 1709, **Abraham Darby** (1678–1717), a Quaker ironmaster who was **smelting iron** using charcoal, was the first to produce high-quality pig iron using **coke**. His new process freed iron smelting from its dependence on wood supplies, and coke – processed from coal – was much more plentiful. In 1710, it was Germany's turn to transform an industry. In that year, the **Meissen** factory, near Dresden, produced the first successful **European porcelain**.

North of Germany, **Denmark** was taking an interest in the Great Northern War between Sweden and Russia. Denmark had lost the provinces of **Scania**, **Halland**, and **Blekinge** to Sweden in 1700 but still had hopes of seizing them back. Assuming Sweden to be weakened by the Battle of Poltava, Denmark found pretexts to declare war on 18 October 1709. In November, a large Danish invasion force landed in Sweden virtually unopposed. However, by February 1710 Sweden had managed to amass 16,000 men, and this force defeated the Danes in the **Battle of Helsingborg**. Denmark lost 7,500 men in the battle and thereafter abandoned hope of regaining its former possessions.

In 1710, French settlers of the Canadian east coast region of **Arcadia** (now Nova Scotia) endured a third, and this time successful, British attempt to seize **Port Royal**. The victory secured Britain their first French colonial possession and helped to obstruct French colonization of Canada for years to come.

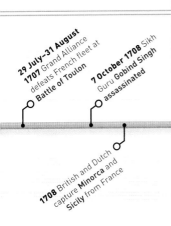

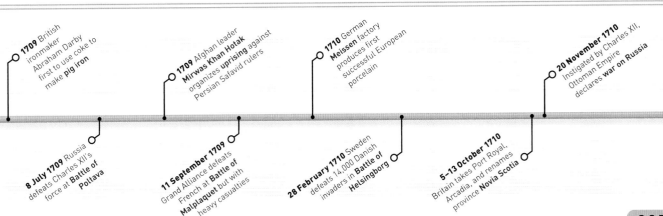

German chinoiserie
This 18th-century Meissen porcelain vase has mouldings picked out in gold leaf. Its form and decorative motifs were inspired by imported Chinese porcelain.

- **29 July–31 August 1707** Grand Alliance defeats French fleet at **Battle of Toulon**
- **1708** British and Dutch capture **Minorca** and **Sicily** from France
- **7 October 1708** Sikh Guru **Gobind Singh assassinated**
- **1709** British ironmaker Abraham Darby first to use coke to make **pig iron**
- **8 July 1709** Russia defeats Charles XII's force at **Battle of Poltava**
- **1709** Afghan leader **Mirwas Khan Hotak** organizes **uprising** against Persian Safavid rulers
- **11 September 1709** Grand Alliance defeats French at **Battle of Malplaquet** but with heavy casualties
- **1710** German **Meissen** factory produces first successful European porcelain
- **28 February 1710** Sweden defeats 14,000 Danish invaders in **Battle of Helsingborg**
- **5–13 October 1710** Britain takes Port Royal, Arcadia, and renames province **Novia Scotia**
- **20 November 1710** Instigated by Charles XII, Ottoman Empire declares **war on Russia**

THE STORY OF NAVIGATION

THE QUEST TO EXPLORE AND MAP THE WORLD'S OCEANS AND CONTINENTS

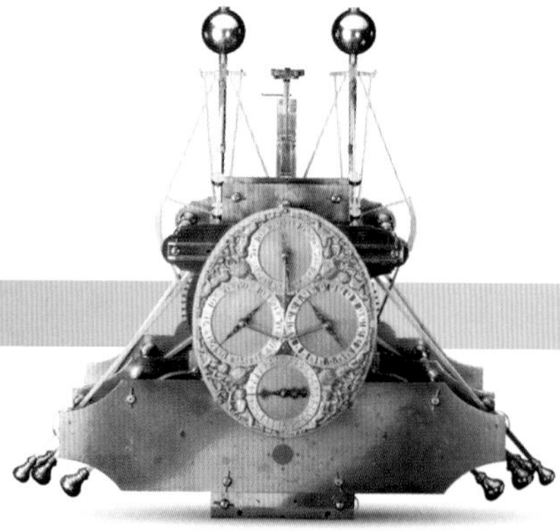

H1 chronometer

Perhaps the most surprising fact in the history of navigation is that, until the 18th century, it was impossible for explorers and mariners to determine their position accurately. Today, thanks to developments in navigational technology, it is possible to pinpoint locations to within a few metres.

The earliest sailors had no means of accurate navigation other than by sight, relying on landmarks along coastlines, judging distances and directions from the positions of the Sun, Moon, and stars, and using simple sounding devices, such as weighted lines, to keep ships from running aground. The invention of instruments such as the magnetic compass, astrolabe, and sextant enabled direction and latitude to be gauged reasonably accurately (by measuring the angle of the Sun or a star above the horizon) but the problem remained of how to determine longitude.

John Harrison
English clockmaker John Harrison was the first to make accurate timepieces that enabled longitude to be calculated with precision.

ACCURATE NAVIGATION

Calculating longitude depends on comparing local time with "universal" time (the time at an agreed location, which is now Greenwich, England). Each hour's difference equates to 15 degrees' difference in longitude. Calculating longitude therefore relies on accurate timepieces, which did not exist until John Harrison developed his chronometer in the 18th century. The next major advances in navigation did not come until the 20th century, with the advent of the gyroscopic compass, radar, and, from the 1990s, of the global positioning system.

LATITUDE AND LONGITUDE

LATITUDE
Latitude lines (parallels) run horizontally on a map and are measured in degrees north or south of the equator. Each degree is about 111km (69 miles) apart.

latitude line

LONGITUDE
Longitude lines (meridians) run vertically on a map and are measured in degrees east or west of Greenwich, England. They meet at the poles and are furthest apart at the equator.

longitude line

> **"** ONE OF THE MOST **EXQUISITE MOVEMENTS** EVER MADE. **"**
>
> **William Hogarth, English artist,** on Harrison's H1 chronometer, from *Analysis of Beauty*, 1753

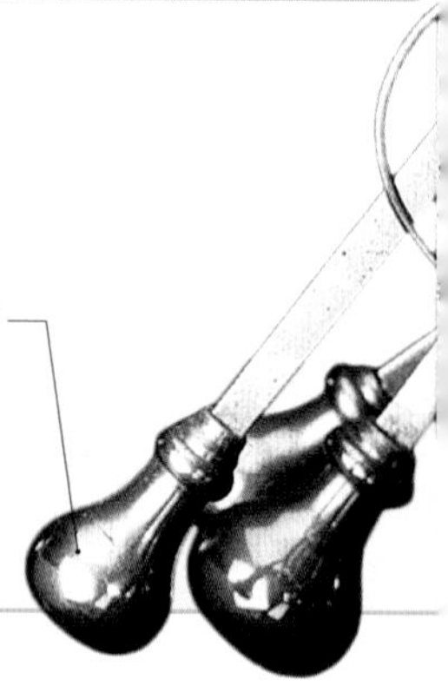

winding handle

3000–1500 BCE
Early sounding
Ancient Egyptians use sounding reeds to measure water depth and gauge their position from coastal landmarks.

12th-dynasty sailing boat

c.150
Ptolemy's maps
A Roman based in Egypt, Ptolemy creates maps using a grid system that influenced navigational maps until the 17th century.

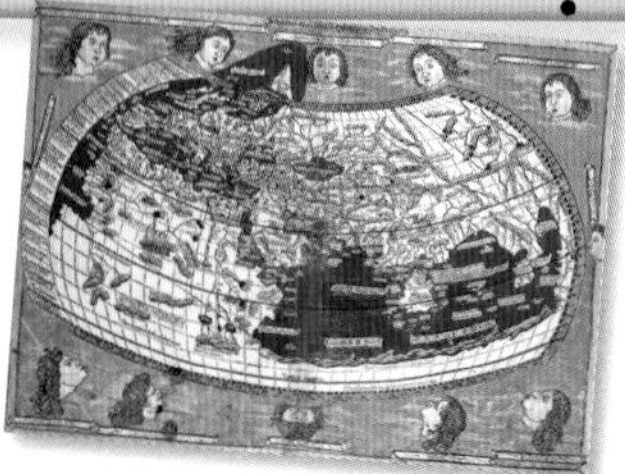

Ptolemy's map

11th century
Dead reckoning
Sand clocks are used for dead reckoning: measuring the time travelled and speed to estimate a vessel's position.

Sand clock

c.1100
The compass
Chinese sailors are the first to use a magnetic compass (which uses a magnetized needle to show the direction of north and south) for navigation.

Mariner's compass

1300–1500
Navigational charts
Portolan charts of the Mediterranean and European coastlines allow sailors to navigate from port to port using compass bearings.

Portolan chart

c.1480
The astrolabe
Sailors start to use astrolabes to estimate latitude by measuring the angle of the Sun or a particular star above the horizon.

Mariner's astrolabe

Harrison's H1 chronometer
John Harrison's first "sea clock" was the H1, which he made to solve the longitude problem – how to measure time accurately enough at sea to calculate longitude. However, the H1 was impractically large, a problem Harrison solved in 1759 with his H4 chronometer.

1735–59
The chronometer
John Harrison makes the first marine chronometer (the H1) in 1735. He then makes improved versions, culminating in the H4 in 1759.

1907
Gyroscopic compass
American Elmer Sperry invents the gyroscopic compass, a major advance for accurate navigation because it always points to true north and is not subject to deviation.

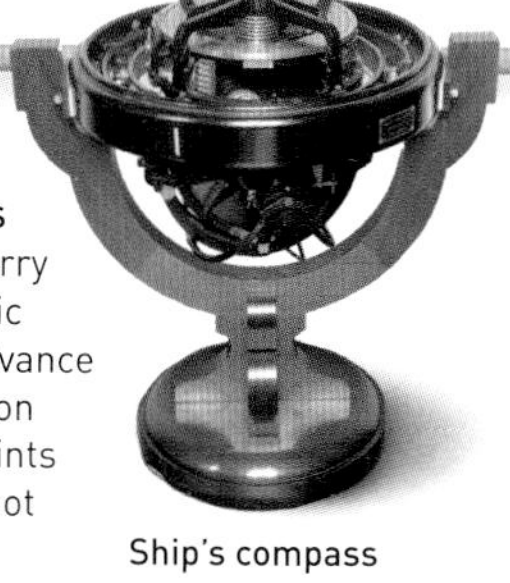
Ship's compass

1930s–40s
Radar
The invention of radar makes it possible to determine an object's position even when it cannot be seen.

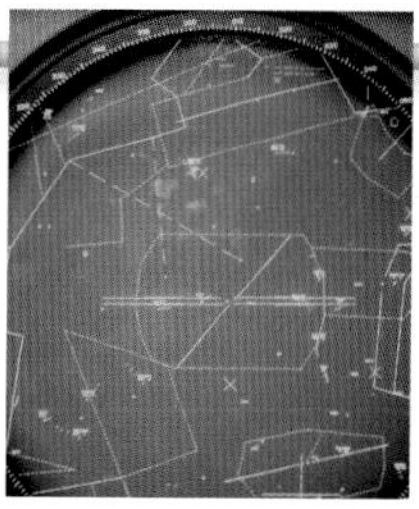
Radarscope

Late 20th century
Global positioning systems
The introduction of satellite-based GPS makes it possible to pinpoint locations and navigate to within a few metres.

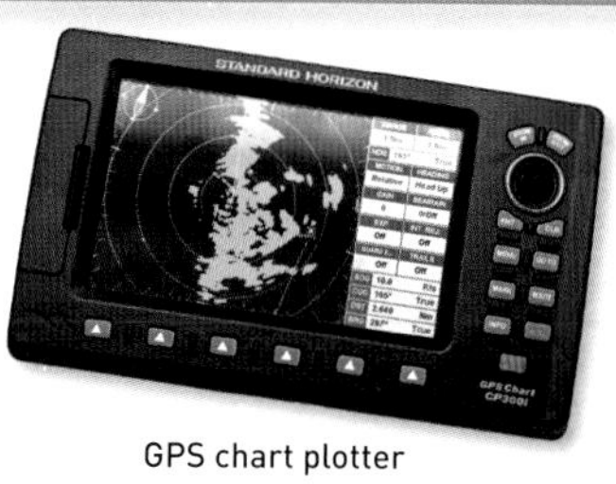
GPS chart plotter

On completion, St Paul's Cathedral dominated the north bank of the River Thames. It remained the tallest building in London until 1962.

IN AN EXTENSION OF THE WAR OF THE SPANISH SUCCESSION (see 1701–03) in South America, a squadron of French ships attacked Portuguese-held **Rio de Janeiro**, incapacitated Portuguese ships in the harbour, and only spared the city's defences from destruction on payment of a ransom. French morale, which had been at a low since their withdrawal from the Battle of Malplaquet (see 1709), was raised by this proof that French long-range naval power had not been extinguished.

In North America, the **Tuscarora War** began in **North Carolina** between Tuscarora American Indians and settlers from Britain, Germany, and the Netherlands. The settlers and northern Tuscarora American Indians began to kidnap the Tuscarora in the south, sell them into slavery, and appropriate their lands. The southern Tuscarora retaliated in September with widespread attacks on settlements in which hundreds of settlers were killed.

In Asia, the Persian Safavid rulers of western **Afghanistan** moved to counter the uprising organized by Mirwais Khan Hotak (see 1709–10), but the Safavid army and its leader, Khosru Khan, were annihilated, and **Afghan independence** was secured.

In December 1711, **St Paul's Cathedral**, London's most iconic building, was completed. Designed by Christopher Wren, it was the fourth church to occupy its site; its predecessor was badly damaged in the Great Fire of London in 1666. The building had the **first triple dome** in the world: a light, timber-framed outer dome, supported by a hidden brick cone, and inside it, the inner dome that is visible from the interior.

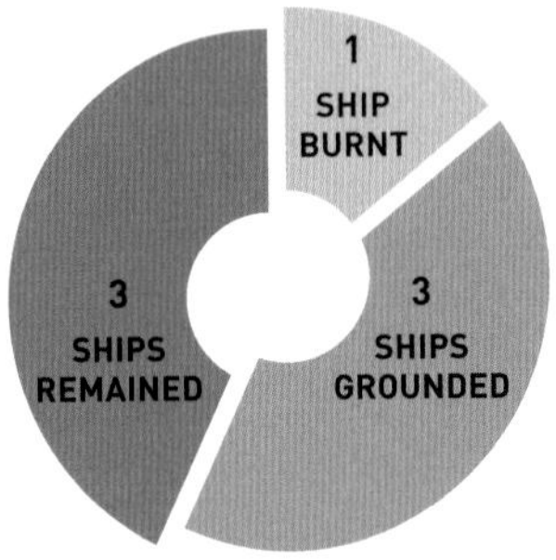

Losses at Rio de Janeiro
Caught unawares by a French naval attack in Rio de Janeiro harbour, Portuguese ships tried to escape. Three drifted aground, and one was destroyed by its crew.

Attack on Rio de Janeiro
French corsair René Duguay-Trouin's ships enter Rio de Janeiro harbour to salvage French honour – and profit at the same time.

“ RIGHT IS RIGHT, EVEN IF EVERYONE IS AGAINST IT; AND WRONG IS WRONG, EVEN IF EVERYONE IS FOR IT. ”

William Penn, founder of Pennsylvania, 1681

An end to war
This painting from the French royal almanac for 1714 shows signatories of the Treaty of Utrecht, which ended the War of the Spanish Succession.

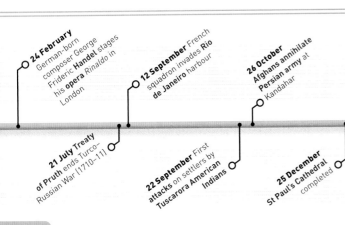

1:9 **Smallpox epidemic**
In the South African Cape, smallpox ravaged the native Khoisan population, killing nine people for every one survivor.

ON 7 JUNE 1712, PENNSYLVANIA, under moral pressure from its Quaker population, freed all the slaves in the state, an early step in the abolition of slavery. However, Queen Anne reversed the decision in the following year. Quaker state-founder and slaver trader William Penn (1644–1718) was not himself an opponent of slavery.

In **South Africa's Cape** region, Dutch sailors infected with **smallpox** inadvertently caused a catastrophic decimation of the native **Khoisan people** in 1713. The disease rapidly spread from laundrywomen infected by the sailors' dirty linen to the wider population because none had immunity or medicine. The epidemic killed 90 per cent

24 February German-born composer George Frideric **Handel** stages his **opera** *Rinaldo* in London

21 July Treaty of Pruth ends Turco-Russian War (1710–11)

12 September French squadron invades **Rio de Janeiro** harbour

22 September First **attacks** on settlers by **Tuscarora American Indians**

26 October Afghans annihilate Persian army at Kandahar

25 December St Paul's Cathedral completed

1712 Pennsylvania prohibits importation of **slaves**

1713 Britain begins supplying slaves to Spanish colonies after Spain signs **Asiento Agreement**

13 February 1713 Dutch sailors inadvertently introduce **smallpox** to **Khoisan people** of South Africa's Cape

11 April 1713 Final document of **Treaty of Utrecht** signed

13 July 1713 Treaty of Portsmouth ends Queen Anne's War (began 1702) in America

27 July 1714 Russian navy defeats the Swedes in **Battle of Gangut**

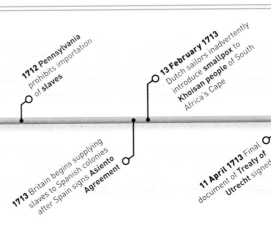

William Penn, English Quaker leader and colonialist.

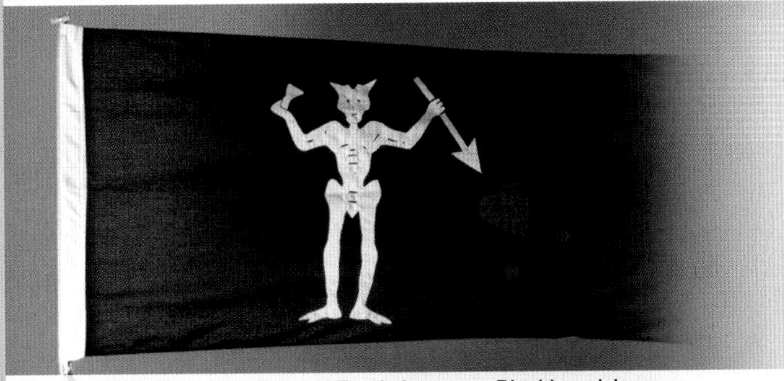

The flag of English pirate Edward Teach, known as Blackbeard, became notorious in the Caribbean between 1717 and his death in 1718.

> **"** ...SUCH **A FIGURE,** THAT **IMAGINATION CANNOT FORM** AN **IDEA** OF A **FURY** FROM **HELL,** TO LOOK MORE **FRIGHTFUL. "**
>
> **Captain Charles Johnson** describing Edward Teach, from *A General History of the Robberies and Murders of the most notorious Pyrates*, 1724

of the southwest Cape's Khoi. Survivors fleeing inland were killed by neighbouring tribes to limit the disease's spread.

In 1713, the **Treaty of Utrecht** was signed; together with the **Treaty of Rastatt** in 1714, it was to **end the War of the Spanish Succession**. Underlying the Utrecht Treaty (actually a series of treaties) was the principle of maintaining the balance of power between France, Spain, and their neighbours, so that no state could dominate Europe. The lines of succession of the two countries were separated, so no Spaniard could claim the French throne, and vice versa. Savoy gained Sicily, Austria received the Spanish Netherlands, and Britain was ceded Newfoundland, Nova Scotia, and Gibraltar. In addition, the **Asiento Agreement** gave Britain a 30-year contract to supply slaves and goods to Spanish colonies.

In Britain, after the death of Queen Anne in 1714, **George I** (1660–1727) became the **first monarch** of the German **House of Hanover** to rule Great Britain and Ireland. The Hanoverian succession in 1714 ended the reign of the House of Stuart, which had ruled Scotland from 1371, and Great Britain and Ireland since 1603.

In 1714, the **Ottomans declared war on the Venetian Republic**. The final conflict between the two powers, the war ended in 1718 with an **Ottoman victory** and Venice's loss of the Peloponnese, its major possession in Greece.

THE STATE OF WAR BETWEEN THE MAJOR EUROPEAN POWERS in the late 17th and early 18th centuries created a profound sense of **lawlessness**. This was most marked in regions where desperate efforts were being made to seize colonial power. With the standing navies at war, some of the work of policing the new colonies fell to **privateers**. For many it was only a short step to becoming outright **pirates**. One of the most notorious, Edward Teach, known as **Blackbeard** (*c*.1680–1718), became a target for the authorities after he took charge of his own ship in November 1717. He was finally murdered in November 1718.

In **North America**, the signing of the Treaty of Utrecht (see 1713) had failed to bring an end to the hostilities between the European colonizing powers, and, in turn, these were struggling to dominate competing American Indian tribes. In 1716, in an attempt to block French expansion westwards from Louisiana, the **Spanish entered east Texas**; they established several missions and, in 1718, the town of San Antonio. While the latter became the target of raids by Apache American Indians, the Spanish successfully encouraged the Yamasee and other tribes in their attacks on hundreds of British settlers in South Carolina, a conflict known as the **Yamasee War** (1715–17).

> **"** NO CHINESE CATHOLICS ARE **ALLOWED TO WORSHIP ANCESTORS** IN THEIR FAMILIAL TEMPLES. **"**
>
> **Pope Clement XI**, Papal bull, 1715

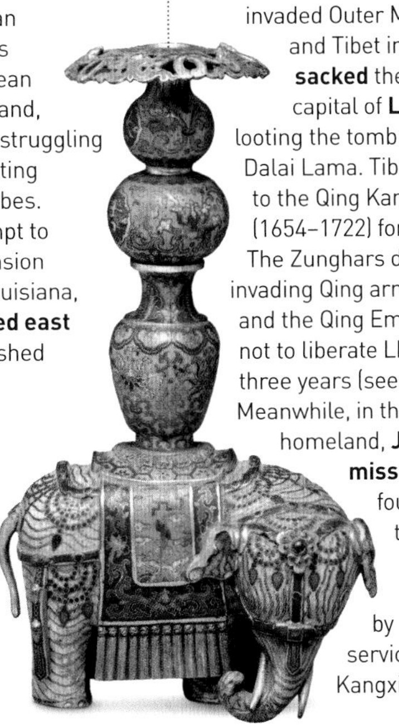

Qing cloisonné
This ornamental elephant with two miniature vases exemplifies the sophistication that cloisonné enamel work reached during the Qing dynasty period.

In Asia, **Zunghar Mongols** invaded Outer Mongolia and Tibet in 1717, and **sacked** the Tibetan capital of **Lhasa**, looting the tomb of the fifth Dalai Lama. Tibet appealed to the Qing Kangxi emperor (1654–1722) for assistance. The Zunghars defeated an invading Qing army in 1718, and the Qing Empire was not to liberate Lhasa for three years (see 1720). Meanwhile, in the Chinese homeland, **Jesuit missionaries** found themselves under threat. Impressed by their services, the Kangxi emperor had ensured their protection with an Edict of Toleration (see 1692). However, in 1715 Pope Clement XI issued a Papal bull condemning Chinese ancestor worship. In retaliation, the Kangxi emperor was to repeal his edict in 1721, officially forbidding Christian missions in China.

In Europe, King **Louis XIV** of France **died in 1715**, leaving the infant Louis XV as his heir. Ignoring the terms of the Treaty of Utrecht, King Philip V of Spain claimed the throne of France if the infant were to die. In 1717, a **Triple Alliance** was signed by the Dutch Republic, France, and Great Britain with a view to compel Philip to abandon his expansionist ambitions. Austria's joining of the alliance in the following year turned this into a Quadruple Alliance against Spain (see 1718–19).

In Britain, the Hanoverian succession (see 1714) had provoked anger among Jacobites – supporters of the deposed Stuart king James VII of Scotland and II of England – and in 1715 this erupted into the **First Jacobite Rebellion**. Over-estimating the support they could count on in England, about 4,000 men (mainly Scottish) marched towards London but were defeated in November by Hanoverian forces at the **Battle of Preston**. While his lieutenants countered the threat to his reign in the north, life for Hanoverian king George I in London was seemingly unaffected: there were several performances for the king and members of the court of *Water Music* by the German Baroque composer **George Frideric Handel** (1685–1759), who had made his home in London in 1712.

BAROQUE MUSIC

A style of European music that began around 1600 and lasted until about 1750, baroque developed from the masses and madrigals of the Renaissance. It had a stronger emphasis on counterpoint and rhythm, greater expression of emotion, and gave greater importance to the solo voice and instrumental solos. It also established opera, with Monteverdi and Cavalli being early practitioners. Notable baroque composers include Peri and Allegri (early baroque); Lully, Pachelbel, and Purcell (middle); and Bach, Handel, Telemann, and Vivaldi (late baroque).

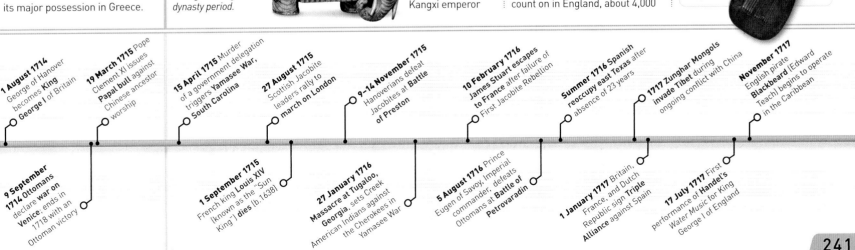

BAROQUE LUTE

- **1 August 1714** George of Hanover becomes **King George I** of Britain
- **9 September 1714 Ottomans** declare **war on Venice**; ends in 1718 with an Ottoman victory
- **19 March 1715** Pope Clement XI issues **Papal bull** against Chinese ancestor worship
- **15 April 1715** Murder of a government delegation triggers **Yamasee War, South Carolina**
- **27 August 1715** Scottish Jacobite leaders rally to **march on London**
- **1 September 1715** French king **Louis XIV** (known as the "Sun King") **dies** (b.1638)
- **9–14 November 1715** Hanoverians defeat Jacobites at **Battle of Preston**
- **27 January 1716 Massacre at Tugaloo, Georgia**, sets Creek American Indians against the Cherokees in Yamasee War
- **10 February 1716 James Stuart escapes to France** after failure of First Jacobite Rebellion
- **5 August 1716** Prince Eugen of Savoy, Imperial commander, defeats Ottomans at **Battle of Petrovaradin**
- **Summer 1716 Spanish reoccupy east Texas** after absence of 23 years
- **1717 Zunghar Mongols invade Tibet** during ongoing conflict with China
- **1 January 1717** Britain, France, and Dutch Republic sign **Triple Alliance** against Spain
- **17 July 1717** First performance of **Handel's** *Water Music* for King George I of England
- **November 1717** English pirate **Blackbeard** (Edward Teach) begins to operate in the Caribbean

Admiral Sir George Byng's British fleet sail into the Straits of Messina prior to the Battle of Cape Passaro, in a painting by Richard Vale.

THE TREATY OF UTRECHT (see 1713) had ceded Sardinia and Sicily to Savoy, but the treaty was ignored by King Philip V of Spain (1683–1746), who sailed to capture the islands in 1717. Set against Philip was the **Triple Alliance** (see 1717) of Britain, France, and the Dutch Republic, which Austria joined on 2 August 1718, expanding it into the **Quadruple Alliance**. On 21 July, Austria – under Holy Roman Emperor Charles VI (1685–1740) – had signed the **Treaty of Passarowitz**, ending the Austro-Turkish War (1716–18). This freed Charles's forces to turn their attention to Spain, and the **War of the Quadruple Alliance** was declared on 17 December 1718.

Previously, the Triple Alliance had set an ultimatum for the withdrawal of Philip's invasion force. The British fleet, led by Sir George Byng, clashed with the Spanish invasion fleet – which had not been informed of the ultimatum – in the **Battle of Cape Passaro** on 11 August 1718. The larger Spanish warships were captured, while the smaller ships escaped. Later that year, an Austrian army landed at Messina, Sicily, to oust the Spanish garrison, but was defeated on 15 October in the first **Battle of Milazzo**.

In 1719 there were further attempts by the **Quadruple Alliance**, now joined by **Savoy**, to curb Spain. France invaded the Spanish **Basque Country** and then **Catalonia**, but disease forced both forces to withdraw. The Austrians attacked in **Sicily** and eventually the Spanish occupiers capitulated, their supplies having been blocked by the British navy. In another example of Spain's vulnerability from the sea, the British captured the port of **Vigo** in October.

War casualties

In the War of the Quadruple Alliance, 28,350 men were killed or wounded, including more than 2,000 from Sardinia, which was invaded by Spain.

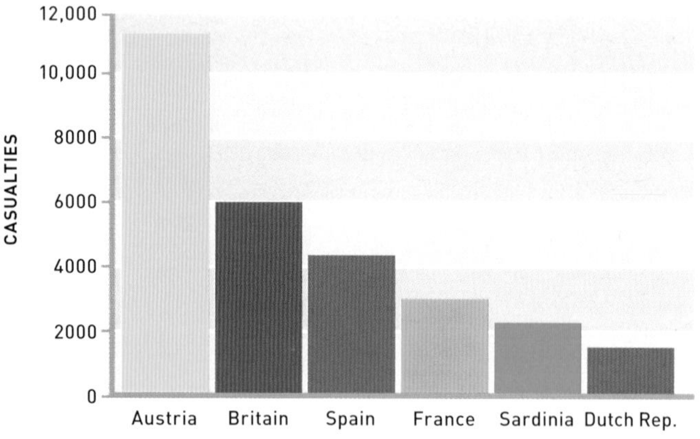

This detail of a map by Willem Blau (*c.*1650) shows the position of British-controlled Honduras, lying on the east coast of the Yucatán peninsula.

THE BRITISH COLONY IN HONDURAS (now Belize), the only British possession in Central America before it gained full independence in 1981, was established on the eastern coast of the Yucatán peninsula by **British buccaneers**. By the turn of the 18th century the colony had begun to exploit the region's logwood (*Haematoxylum campechianum*), which yielded an important dye used for textiles and paper. In 1720, **slaves** – many from Jamaica and others direct from Africa – were first imported to this area of the so-called Mosquito Coast to expand logging operations on the Belize River.

The year 1720 saw the end of the War of the Quadruple Alliance (see 1718) with the signing of the **Treaty of the Hague**. Philip agreed to abandon his claims to Sicily and Sardinia, which came under the control of Austria and the Duchy of Savoy respectively, with the duke being titled king of Sardinia. In North America, the French returned **Pensacola** in Florida to King Philip V, along with places they had occupied in the north of Spain, receiving trade advantages in exchange. The treaty also confirmed **Texas** was a Spanish possession.

Meanwhile, the **Maratha**, a sub-ethnic group inhabiting the Maharashtra region of western India, began a major expansion of the empire that it had re-established in 1674. The catalyst for the expansion, which began in 1720, was the death in 1719 of Balaji Vishwanath (b.1680) and the succession of his son **Bajirao** (1700–40), who was only 20 years old at the time but already a charismatic and dynamic leader. Recognizing the weakness of the grip that the **Mughal Empire**, based in Delhi, had on the states around him, Bajirao's army struck out into Hindustan. The campaign was successful and gained Bajirao great credit at home. This helped him negotiate peace treaties with Mughal authorities in the Deccan. With the security of the Maratha homeland assured, Bajirao began further expansions in 1728, when he also moved his capital from Satara to **Pune**.

Far to the northeast, the **Zunghar Mongols** had taken possession of **Tibet** (see 1717). In 1720, a force of Qing and Tibetan warriors drove the Zunghars from Tibet. The Zunghars had killed the sixth Dalai Lama, claiming he was an impostor. The Qing force brought with it a replacement, Kelzang Gyatso, who was made the **seventh Dalai Lama**. Tibet became a tribute-paying protectorate of Qing China, and the Tibetan region of Kham was annexed to China's Sichuan province. However, disputes over who should govern under the Qing emperor resulted in **harsh suppressions** by the Chinese in the years that followed.

Maratha expansion

The Maratha expanded their empire to the north, south, and east. Such was their reputation that they were able to raise taxes even beyond areas of their direct administration.

KEY
Maratha Empire
→ Maratha campaigns

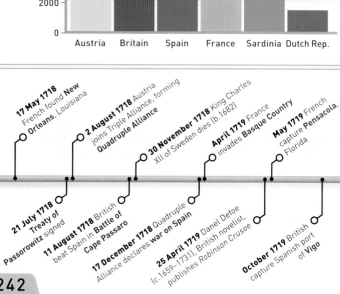

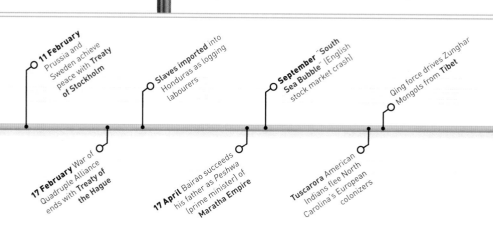

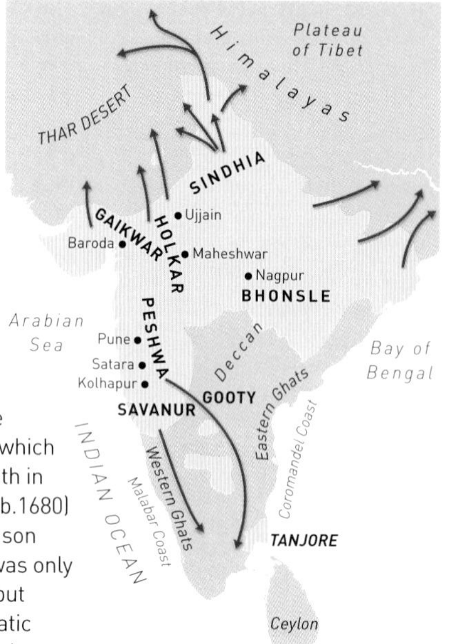

Maratha mace

The head of 118 spikes and a quadrangular top spike on this Maratha mace testify to its fearsome effectiveness as a weapon.

17 May 1718 French found **New Orleans**, Louisiana

21 July 1718 **Treaty of Passorowitz** signed

2 August 1718 Austria joins Triple Alliance, forming **Quadruple Alliance**

11 August 1718 British beat Spain in **Battle of Cape Passaro**

30 November 1718 King Charles XII of Sweden dies (b.1682)

17 December 1718 Quadruple Alliance declares **war on Spain**

April 1719 France invades **Basque Country**

25 April 1719 Danel Defoe (c.1659–1731), British novelist, publishes *Robinson Crusoe*

May 1719 French capture **Pensacola**, Florida

October 1719 British capture Spanish port of **Vigo**

11 February Prussia and Sweden achieve peace with **Treaty of Stockholm**

17 February War of Quadruple Alliance ends with **Treaty of the Hague**

Slaves imported into Honduras as logging labourers

17 April Bairao succeeds his father as Peshwa (prime minister) of **Maratha Empire**

September "**South Sea Bubble**" (English stock market crash)

Tuscarora American Indians flee North Carolina's European colonizers

Qing force drives Zunghar Mongols from **Tibet**

1721–22

Brilliant polychromatic decoration characterizes this detail of a rectangular Persian dish made in the 18th century during the Safavid dynasty.

THE GREAT NORTHERN WAR (1700–21) between Sweden and Russia was brought to an end by the conclusion of the **Treaty of Nystad**. In 1719, Russia had successfully challenged Sweden's supremacy in the Baltic by attacking cities on the Swedish east coast. An alliance of the British and Swedes in 1719 then gave Sweden British navy protection that discouraged further raids. The Nystad Treaty restored Finland to Sweden, but former Swedish **Baltic territories** in Estonia and elsewhere went to Russia. Sweden was irrevocably diminished by the terms of the treaty, while Russia, with its new Baltic ports, now dominated Eastern Europe.

In one of the landmark moments of Dutch exploration, Jakob Roggeveen (1659–1729) set out in 1721 to find **Terra Australis**, the mysterious southern continent earlier mapped in part by Spaniard Juan Fernández and Dutchman Abel Tasman, among others. A former employee of the Dutch East Indies Company but now sponsored by its West Indies counterpart, Roggeveen and his three ships sailed to the Falkland Islands, Chile, and the Juan Fernández Islands. While crossing the South Pacific Ocean the following year, the three ships chanced upon **Easter Island** (now Rapa Nui), so-named because it was discovered on Easter Sunday. Roggeveen also discovered the **Society Islands** and **Samoa** before returning home.

In 1722, the declining **Safavid dynasty** of Persia was deposed by **independent Afghans** to the east. Mahmud Hotaki (*c.*1697–1725), son of Mirwais Khan Hotak (see 1709), brought an army to the Safavid capital of Isfahan, sacked the city, and proclaimed himself **shah of Persia**. It was not until 1729, and the defeat of the Hotaki dynasty by Afsharid Persians who were descended from the Mongols at the **Battle of Damghan,** that the Afghans were finally forced back to Kandahar.

Deified ancestors
Moai were erected by clans on Easter Island to watch over their fields. This group, at Ahu Akivi, is the furthest inland.

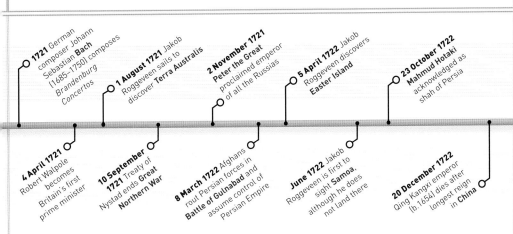

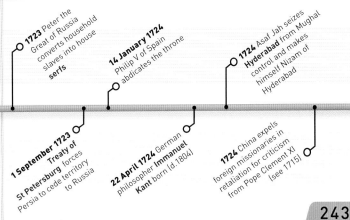

1723–24

> **SLAVES WHO ARE DISABLED** FROM WORKING …SHALL BE…**PROVIDED FOR** BY THEIR MASTERS.

From the Louisiana *Code Noir*, 1724

EUROPEAN SUCCESS in procuring slaves in West Africa for transporting to the new colonies depended on the enthusiastic co-operation of certain tribes. In **Dahomey**, in what is now the Republic of Benin, King Agadja (r.1708–40) presided over a culture of enslavement and human sacrifice. His conquest of neighbouring Allada in 1723 provided a ready source of **captives for sale**, and by 1724 Dahomey had become the Europeans' principal source of slave labour.

In 1724, the ***Code Noir***, King Louis XIV of France's extensive definition of the conditions of slavery, was introduced in the French territory of Louisiana, North America. The code was partly intended to give slaves basic protection from their masters – all were to be given food and clothes, for example – but it also legitimized **cruel punishments**: runaway slaves were to be branded, their ears cut off, and, after a second offence, crippled by having their hamstrings cut.

Also in 1724, the disintegrating Mughal Empire saw the **Indian state of Oudh** gain independence under Saadat Ali Khan (*c.*1680–1739). He founded the Moghul **Awadh dynasty**, which ruled until its power was seized by the British in the early 19th century.

1721 German composer Johann Sebastian **Bach** (1685–1750) composes *Brandenburg Concertos*

4 April 1721 Robert Walpole becomes Britain's first prime minister

1 August 1721 Jakob Roggeveen sails to discover **Terra Australis**

10 September 1721 Treaty of Nystad ends **Great Northern War**

2 November 1721 Peter the Great proclaimed emperor of all the Russias

8 March 1722 Afghans rout Persian forces in **Battle of Gulnabad** and assume control of Persian Empire

5 April 1722 Jakob Roggeveen discovers **Easter Island**

June 1722 Jakob Roggeveen is first to sight **Samoa**, although he does not land there

23 October 1722 Mahmud Hotaki acknowledged as shah of Persia

20 December 1722 Qing Kangxi emperor (b.1654) dies after longest reign in **China**

1723 Peter the Great of Russia converts household slaves into house **serfs**

1 September 1723 Treaty of St Petersburg forces Persia to cede territory to Russia

14 January 1724 Philip V of Spain abdicates the throne

22 April 1724 German philosopher **Immanuel Kant** born (d.1804)

1724 Asaf Jah seizes **Hyderabad** from Mughal control and makes himself Nizam of Hyderabad

1724 China expels foreign missionaries in retaliation for criticism from Pope Clement XI (see 1715)

Peter the Great's Academy of Sciences in St Petersburg, founded in 1725, was rehoused in this building of 1783–85 on the River Neva.

" YOU ARE NOW **TRAVELLING INTO** THE **PARADISE OF THE SCHOLARS. "**

Caspar Wolff, German scientist, praising the Academy of Sciences in a letter to mathematician Leonhard Euler, *c.*1779

The Shinto gate (*torii*) at the entrance to the Itsukushima Shrine, Japan.

THE TREATY OF THE HAGUE (see 1720) did not end rivalries between the major European powers. In 1725, Austria signed the **Treaty of Vienna** with Spain, gaining trading advantages in the colonies for its Imperial Ostend Company; in exchange, Austria abandoned all claims to the Spanish throne and also promised to help Spain recapture Gibraltar. In 1726, Britain embarked on an attempt to blockade Spanish treasure ships at Porto Bello, Panama, but withdrew without success in 1727 after severe losses from disease.

Emboldened by its promise of Austrian support, which was negated by a secret pact made between Britain and Austria, **Spain besieged Gibraltar** in 1727, an act that precipitated the **Anglo-Spanish War**. The four-month siege failed, costing Spain 1,400 men to British casualties of 300. The war ended with the Treaty of Seville in 1729.

In Russia, the **St Petersburg Academy of Sciences** was founded in 1725 by Peter the Great (1672–1725). The most eminent scholars of all disciplines were invited to work there – for example, German embryologist Caspar Wolff (1733–94) offered Swiss mathematician Leonhard Euler a 200-rouble salary as an enticement, which he accepted.

CATHERINE I (1684–1727)

The orphaned daughter of Lithuanian peasants, the future wife of Peter the Great was born Marta Skowrońska. She was secretly married to Peter in 1707, and she reigned as Russia's first female monarch from his death until her own. In her reign, she was supported by the Supreme Privy Council, which wanted to deny power to the aristocracy.

Coffee in Brazil
This 19th-century woodcut shows a Brazilian coffee plantation. From small beginnings in 1727, Brazil grew into the world's largest coffee producer.

To the southeast, the Afghan shah of Persia, Mahmud Hotaki (see 1721–22), died in 1725. He was succeeded by his cousin, Ashraf Khan (d.1730), who may have murdered him. By then, **Persian lands** were being encroached upon by **Ottoman forces**, who were linked to the previous regime by an **Ottoman–Safavid alliance**. However, Ashraf Khan defeated the Ottomans in a battle near Isfahan at Kermanshah, and peace was eventually declared at Hamadan, Persia, in 1727.

Satirical novel
Clergyman and writer Jonathan Swift (1667–1745) first published Gulliver's Travels *in 1726. This edition of the satire on humanity was published in the 1860s.*

Also in 1727, the **Treaty of Kyakhta** was signed by **Imperial Russia** and the **Chinese Qing Empire**; it remained the basis of relations between the two until the mid-19th century. Mongolia's northern border was mapped and agreed, and routes established for trade in furs and tea.

The late 1720s saw the start of **coffee-growing** in the Caribbean and South America. Seedlings were first brought to Martinique around 1720, and in 1727 the king of Portugal sent to French Guinea for seeds. His envoy, Francisco de Mello Palheta, persuaded the French governor's wife to provide seeds and seedlings, and these enabled the Portuguese to start a coffee industry in Brazil.

THE RUSSIAN EMPEROR PETER THE GREAT was determined to discover the full **extent of his lands to the east**. A Danish seaman, Vitus Bering (1681–1741), was commissioned to follow the Siberian coast northwards from the Kamchatka Peninsula, and in 1728 **Bering** sailed into the narrow **strait**, now named after him, that **separates Siberia and Alaska**. By sailing further north, Bering established that Siberia reaches its eastward limit at the strait. Bering suspected that there must be land further east, but it was only during a second voyage, in 1741, that he first saw the coast of Alaska across the strait.

On the Indian subcontinent, the **Maratha** people, after nearly a decade of consolidating their power under Bajirao (see 1720), struck out into the Deccan region surrounding their homeland. In 1728, in the **Battle of Palkhed**, they confronted rival prince Asaf Jah I of Hyderabad (also known as Nizam-ul-Mulk) who had been laying claim to Maratha leadership and who was refusing to pay them *chauth* (a tribute tax). In a strategic masterstroke, the Marathas cornered the nizam's army in a waterless zone, where it refused to fight. In consequence, the nizam abandoned his leadership claim and payment of *chauth* was resumed.

The year 1729 was a pivotal point in **trading** relations **between China and the West** because the Qing Yongzheng Emperor banned almost all

28 January 1725 Peter the Great dies (b.1672). Catherine I continues work of founding his Academy of Sciences

22 April 1725 Afghan-born **Shah Mahmud Hotaki of Persia dies** or is murdered (born c.1697)

30 April 1725 Austria and Spain sign **Treaty of Vienna**

1726 Vast **Chinese encyclopedia** *Gujin Tushu Jicheng* **printed using movable type**

11 February 1727 Spain begins **siege of Gibraltar** (to 12 June)

1727 Portuguese introduce **coffee** to **Brazil**

23 August 1727 Russia and China sign **Treaty of Kyakhta** in Mongolian border town

18 November 1727 Foundation stone laid of new city of **Jaipur**, India

28 February 1728 Maratha defeat Asaf Jah I, ruler of Hyderabad, in **Battle of Palkhed**

18 May 1728 Peter II crowned **tsar of Russia**, succeeding Catherine I

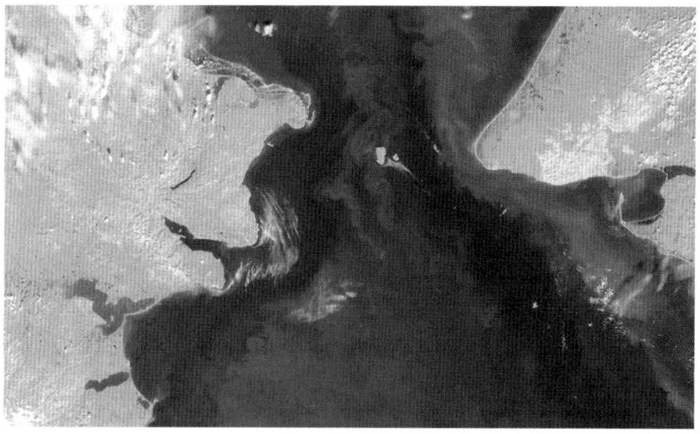

Bering Strait
This satellite image shows the Bering Strait, a 96-km (56-mile) stretch of water that separates Asia and North America.

importation of **opium**. Chinese goods were in high demand in Europe, but the Chinese were unimpressed by European goods and accepted payment only in silver – which Britain, in particular, had to obtain at exorbitant cost. In the early 18th century, British traders had begun to trade Indian opium for Chinese goods, and there was soon a growing number of **addicted Chinese** that greatly reduced Europe's silver requirement. European opium smugglers remained a major problem for China into the 19th century.

Also in 1729, after more than a decade of mistreatment, **Natchez American Indians killed** more than 200 French **settlers at Fort Rosalie**, Mississippi. However, by 1731 the French, assisted by the Choctaw people, were to retaliate by enslaving a large number of Natchez for work on Caribbean plantations.

The short-lived **Ottoman Tulip Period** (1718–30) was ended by a rebellion against unpopular measures led by a janissary (soldier), **Patrona Halil**, that caused Sultan Ahmed III to be supplanted by Mahmud I. The Tulip Period was one of stability in the Ottoman Empire and was marked by increased interest in Western ways. Just as Western Europe had been fascinated by tulips in the 17th century, the Ottoman court became equally obsessed. Ottoman **architecture and art were invigorated**, but high prices for tulips and tulip bulbs distorted the economy. The instatement of Mahmud I in 1730 brought an end to the Tulip Period, but **Halil was strangled** in front of the sultan in 1731 for overreaching himself.

In **Japan**, whose population had been ruled by the Tokugawa shogunate since 1603, there was a resurgence of the **Shinto religion.** Beginning around 1730, it was fuelled by the writings of scholars such as Kada no Azunamaro (1669–1736) and Kamo no Mabuchi (1697–1769). The Shinto scholars rejected Chinese and Buddhist influences and sought to identify a purely **Japanese spiritual identity**. Shintoism was reinstated as the national religion of Japan more than a century later in 1868.

Meanwhile, the Arabian state of **Oman** was expanding its dominions in Africa. The Portuguese-held Kenyan city of **Mombasa** and the island of Pemba had been captured by the Omanis in 1698, and by 1730 they had driven the Portuguese from the Kenyan and Tanzanian coasts and gained control of the island of **Zanzibar** (now part of Tanzania).

In **West Africa**, Islamic Fulbe, or Fulani, people began to unify into larger communities in what is now known as the **Fulbe Revolution**. The first such state was Bondu, in Guinea, formed in the late 17th century. Then came Futa Jallon (centred in Guinea but sprawling over neighbouring territories), where the Islamic Fulbe took power from the existing leaders and non-Islamic Fulbe people. A **confederation of provinces** was formally created in 1735 with its capital at Timbo, Guinea. Other areas that were profoundly affected by the Fulbe Jihad – as the seizure of power was termed – included the formerly declining **Bornu Empire** (in present-day Nigeria), the fortunes of which underwent a significant revival.

In 1731, formerly independent **Dahomey** in West Africa finally accepted the suzerainty of the **Yoruba Oyo Empire** (present-day Nigeria). The Yoruba had invaded and defeated them after a protracted and bitterly fought campaign in 1728, but resistance in Dahomey did not end until 1748.

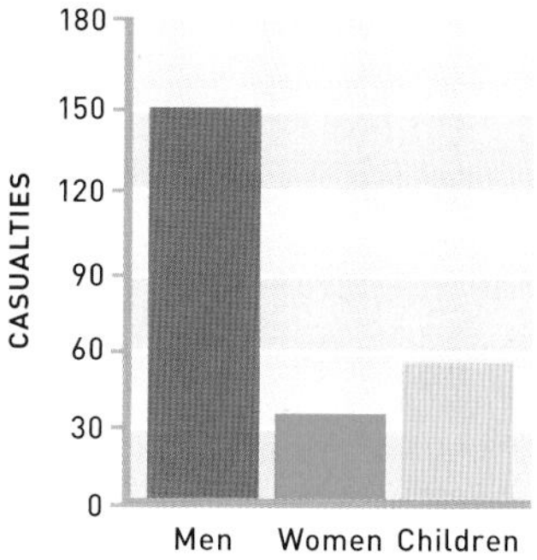

Massacre at Fort Rosalie
On 28 November 1729, Natchez American Indians killed 242 settlers at Fort Rosalie, Mississippi, in retaliation for years of mistreatment.

> **"...IN LESS THAN TWO HOURS** THEY **MASSACRED** MORE THAN **200** OF THE **FRENCH."**
>
> **Father le Petit, missionary,** in a letter to Father D'Avaugour, Procurator of the Missions in North America, 1730

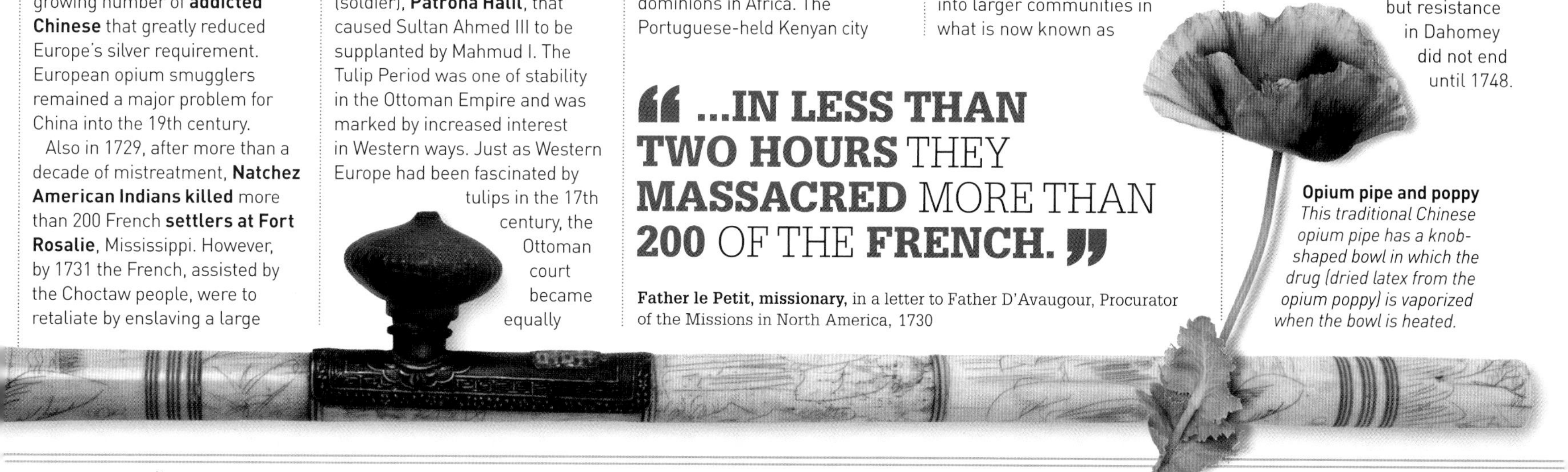

Opium pipe and poppy
This traditional Chinese opium pipe has a knob-shaped bowl in which the drug (dried latex from the opium poppy) is vaporized when the bowl is heated.

14 August 1728 Danish explorer Vitus Bering discovers **Bering Strait** is eastward limit of Siberia

20–23 October 1728 More than a quarter of **Copenhagen**, Denmark, **destroyed by fire**

1728 Nigerian **Oyo Empire** invades **Dahomey**

1729 Persians under Nader Shah defeat occupying Afghans in **Battle of Damghan**

21 April 1729 Catherine II (the Great) of Russia born (d.1796)

30 July 1729 City of **Baltimore**, Maryland, **founded**

9 November 1729 Britain, France, Spain, and Dutch Republic sign **Treaty of Seville**

28 November 1729 Natchez American **Indians kill settlers at Fort Rosalie**, Mississippi

1729 Qing emperor bans sale and smoking of **opium in China**

29 January 1730 Anna of Russia becomes **tsarina** on death of Peter II (b.1715) from smallpox

September 1730 Patrona Halil leads rebellion that topples Ottoman emperor Ahmed III

20 September 1730 Mahmud I succeeds Ahmed III as Ottoman emperor

16 March 1731 Austria, Britain, Dutch Republic, and Spain sign **Treaty of Vienna**

1731 Dahomey accepts suzerainty of Nigerian Oyo Empire

"Tavern Scene" is one of the eight paintings of British artist William Hogarth's *A Rake's Progress* (1732–33), which depicts the downfall of a rich merchant's feckless heir.

OBSESSED WITH CREATING a strong, independent state, Frederick William I (r.1713–40), the "Soldier King" of **Prussia**, instituted **compulsory military service**: every young man had to serve in the military for three months of each year. In this way, the Prussian army became the fourth-largest in Europe, with 60,000 soldiers, despite having the twelfth-largest population.

In America, the state of **Georgia** was founded in 1732, becoming the last of the Thirteen Colonies established by Britain on the Atlantic coast. Named after Britain's King George II, the new state was intended to strengthen the British presence in the south. The first settlers began to arrive in 1733 and included many released from debtors' prisons.

> " WHERE SOME **STATES** HAVE AN **ARMY,** THE **PRUSSIAN ARMY** HAS A **STATE.** "
>
> **Voltaire, French thinker** (1694–1778)

Also in 1733, Danish seaman Vitus Bering (1681–1741), after whom the Bering Strait is named (see 1728), began the **Great Northern Exploration**. Empress Anna of Russia (1693–1740) had authorized a large expedition involving 3,000 people in three separate groups: one group was to map northern Siberia; the second, to explore north of Japan; and Bering's group, to determine what lay east of the strait. It was not until June 1741, just months before his death in December, that Bering first caught sight of Mount St Elias on the **Alaskan mainland**. In the same month, his second ship sent men ashore on Alaska's Prince of Wales Island.

Meanwhile, during the **Kyoho era** (July 1716 to April 1736) in Japan, **famine** had struck. In 1732, swarms of locusts attacked the crops, especially rice, of agricultural communities around the inland sea. Heavy rains then destroyed winter crops of wheat and barley, and insects decimated the following year's rice crop. The worst-affected area was the north of Kyushu Island, where around 15,000 people died. In cities such as Edo (present-day Tokyo) and Osaka, the cost of rice rose seven-fold, and in 1733 rice shops were attacked during **food riots**.

In 1733, Poland's King Augustus II died. Stanislaw Leszczyński was made king when 12,000 Polish nobles voted for him in the Sejm election. However, 3,000 nobles who voted for Augustus III used the backing of Russia and Austria to install Augustus as king in 1734. What began as a civil war developed into the **War of the Polish Succession** (1733–38) as the Bourbons (France and Spain), the Habsburgs (Austria), Prussia, Saxony, and Russia campaigned outside Poland to seize territories lost after the War of the Spanish Succession (see 1701). Only with the **Treaty of Vienna** in 1738 did Stanislaw give up his legal claim.

British culture in this period came to be dominated by **radical humanism**, a conviction that human identity, ethics, and knowledge need not be based on a belief in God. Alexander Pope (1688–1744) wrote in his poem *An Essay on Man* (1734), "Know then thyself, presume not God to scan / The proper study of Mankind is Man." Secular humanism spread to the arts, with artists such as William Hogarth (1697–1764) bringing sharp **social criticism and satire** to their depictions of humanity.

Another British development was the patenting in 1733 of a **flying-shuttle loom** by John Kay (1704–80). The loom had a wheeled, thread-carrying shuttle, which greatly increased the rate at which fabrics could be made. Kay's new loom **threatened the livelihood of weavers**, who attempted to get the loom banned. However, they were unsuccessful, and Kay's invention was adopted widely.

Prussian blue
The conscripted army of Prussian king Frederick William I wore dark blue coats with red linings and red and white facings.

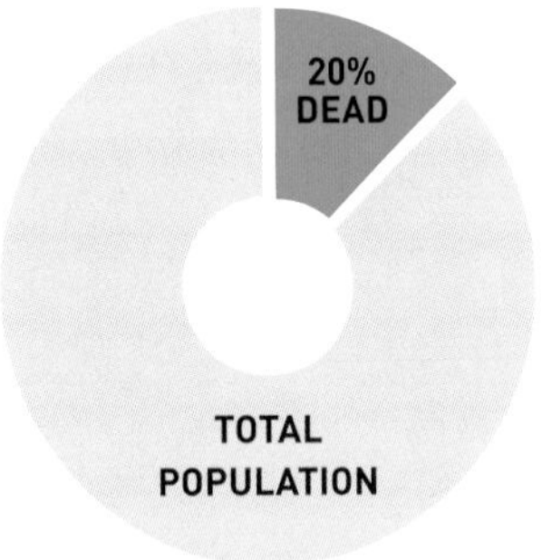

Kyoho famine in Japan
In the Fukuoka Domain, northern Kyushu, about 20 per cent of the population died during the 1733 famine of the Kyoho era.

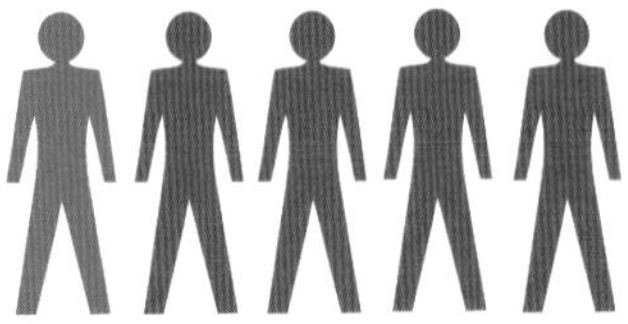

1:4 **Polish election, 1733**
Stanislaw Leszczyński gained 12,000 votes and temporarily became king of Poland. Augustus III gained only 3,000 votes but succeeded him in 1734.

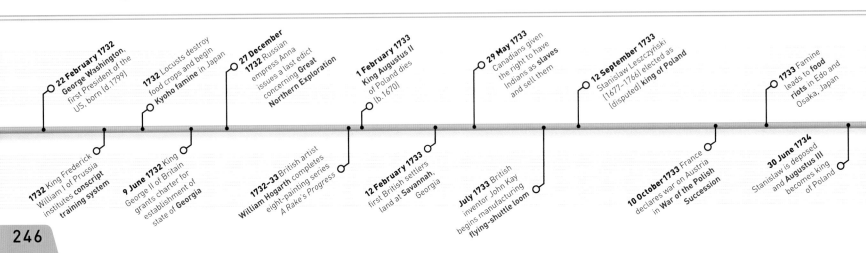

VOLTAIRE (1694–1778)

Born François-Marie Arouet in Paris, Voltaire was a prolific writer, historian, and philosopher of the French Enlightenment (see 1763), who disseminated his radical humanist ideas in works that ranged from essays and historical works to poems, plays, and novels. His ideas – on social reform and civil liberties, for example – often met with hostility, forcing him to flee several times, but they had a major influence on thinkers of the French and American revolutions.

22 February 1732 **George Washington**, first President of the US, born (d.1799)

1732 King Frederick William I of Prussia institutes **conscript training system**

1732 Locusts destroy food crops and begin **Kyoho famine** in Japan

9 June 1732 King George II of Britain grants charter for establishment of state of **Georgia**

27 December 1732 Russian empress Anna issues a last edict concerning **Great Northern Exploration**

1732–33 British artist **William Hogarth** completes eight-painting series *A Rake's Progress*

1 February 1733 **King Augustus II** of Poland dies (b.1670)

12 February 1733 First British settlers land at **Savannah**, Georgia

29 May 1733 Canadians given the right to have Indians as **slaves** and sell them

July 1733 British inventor John Kay begins manufacturing **flying-shuttle loom**

12 September 1733 Stanislaw Leszczyński (1677–1766) elected as (disputed) **king of Poland**

10 October 1733 France declares war on Austria in **War of the Polish Succession**

1733 Famine leads to **food riots** in Edo and Osaka, Japan

30 June 1734 Stanislaw is deposed and **Augustus III** becomes king of Poland

An illustration depicting sugar processing in the Caribbean from *Histoire des Antilles* by French clergyman and plantation owner Jean-Baptiste Labat.

CHARLES MARIE DE LA CONDAMINE (1701–74), French explorer, scientist, and mathematician, joined an expedition to Peru in 1735. After falling out with his colleagues, he continued alone to Quito, Ecuador, from where he travelled down the **Amazon** to Cayenne, thereby making the first scientific exploration of the river. Returning to Paris in 1744, he published the journal of his travels and discoveries in 1751. When in **Ecuador**, La Condamine was the first European to encounter **rubber** – the Mayans had been making flexible rubber for centuries – and in 1736 he introduced the product to Europe when he sent sheets of processed rubber to Paris.

By the early 18th century, the Portuguese, Spanish, British, French, and Dutch had **slave-worked sugar plantations** in Brazil and throughout the Caribbean. In 1735, the French East India Company began to develop plantations on the islands of **Ile-de-France** and **Bourbon** (now Mauritius and Réunion). Soon to follow was the first **sugar refinery** on Mauritius, built at Ville Bague in the north.

In North America, pressure from expanding British colonies forced the French to strengthen their claim to **Indiana** by establishing a **permanent settlement**. In 1732, a trading fort had been erected at the site of present-day Vincennes, but in 1735 the traders were joined by a wave of agricultural workers. **Vincennes** quickly grew, becoming not only the foremost French trading post in Indiana but also the dominant **centre of French culture** in the region.

Meanwhile, the year 1736 marked the **end of Safavid rule** in Persia. Persian military leader **Nader Shah** (1698–1747) had become more powerful than the Safavids he served (Tahmasp II until 1732, and Tahmasp's young son, Abbas III). When Nader proposed himself as **shah**, few stood against him. He was crowned in 1736. In 1737, Nader moved against Persia's former Afghan overlords by occupying southern **Afghanistan**. When Tahmasp and Abbas were murdered in 1740, the Safavid dynasty was extinguished.

The **Russo-Austrian-Turkish War** (1735–39) signalled that no treaty could easily end the War of the Polish Succession (see 1733). In addition, Russia, joined by Austria in 1737, intended to seize the **Crimea** and gain access to the Black Sea, at the same time ending raids by Crimean **Tartars**. One Russian army captured part of the Crimea in 1736, but was forced by disease to retreat. Another army recovered **Azov** from the Ottomans in Romania and advanced to **Jassy** (Iași), Moldavia. In 1737, renewed Russian gains in the Crimea were reversed due to a lack of supplies.

By 1737, the **Maratha Empire** in India (see 1728) was enjoying its greatest **expansion** to the north, at the expense of the Mughal Empire. Peshwa (prime minister) **Bajirao I** (r.1721–40) masterminded this expansion, but almost as powerful as the Peshwa were Maratha chieftains called Sardars – among them Gaekwads of Baroda, Shindes of Gwalior, and Holkars of Indore – who established their own kingdoms in the captured lands.

In 1737, Swedish taxonomist and botanist **Carl Linnaeus** (1707–78) published *Genera Plantarum*, later partnered by *Species Plantarum* (1753). Together with his earlier *Systema Naturae* (1735), these works laid the foundation for the system of biological classification still used today.

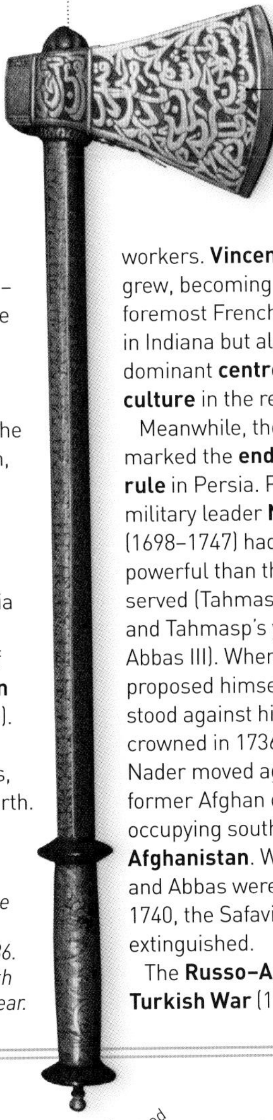

Weapon of conquest
This finely decorated battle axe belonged to Nader, who was crowned shah of Persia in 1736. He led the Persians to war with Afghanistan in the following year.

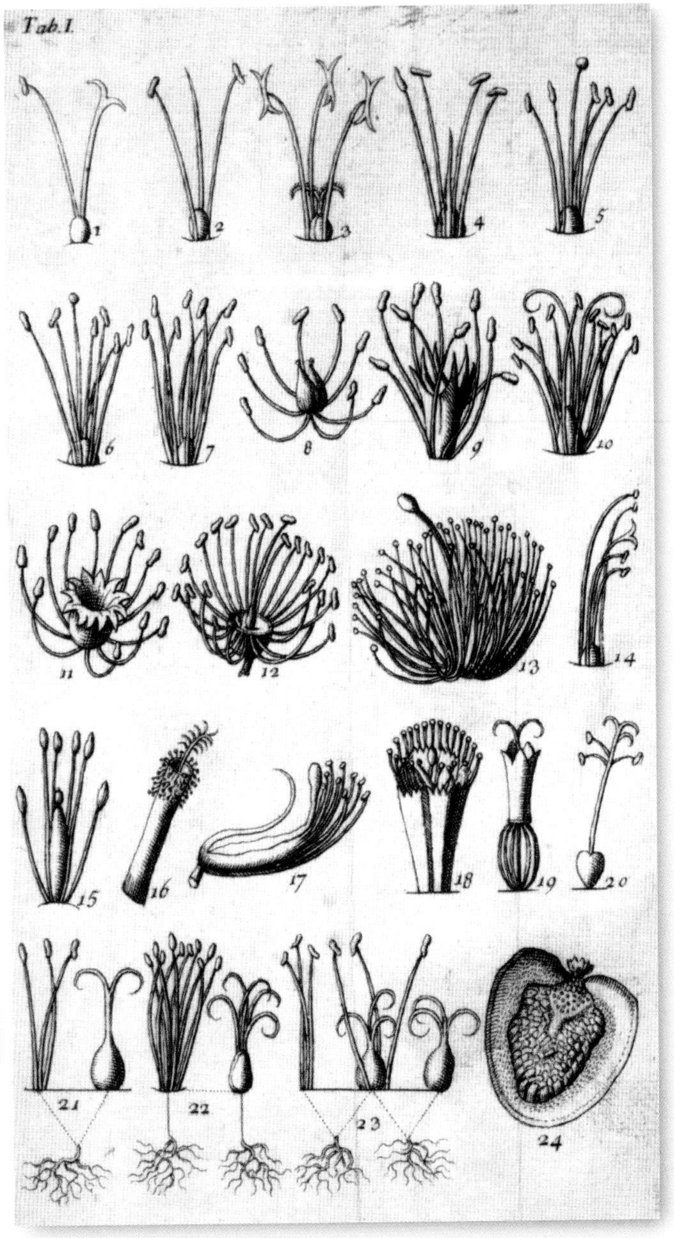

Plant anatomy
Carl Linnaeus's Genera Plantarum *classified plants by their sex organs – the numbers of stamens and pistils in their flowers.*

1735 Carl **Linnaeus** publishes first edition of *Systema Naturae*

April 1735 French explorer La Condamine embarks on expedition to **Peru**

1735 Vincennes, Indiana, is established on Wabash River

3 October 1735 Signing of **Preliminary Peace** ends fighting in War of the Polish Succession

8 October 1735 Qianlong succeeds Yongzheng as Qing **emperor of China**

8 March 1736 Nader Shah, founder of Afsharid dynasty, crowned **shah of Persia**

19 June 1736 Russian army seizes **Azov**, Romania, from Ottomans

1736 La Condamine sends first samples of **processed rubber** to Europe

30 June 1737 Russian army storms Ottoman fortress of **Ochakov**, Romania

July 1737 Austria joins Russia in its **war with the Ottomans** but suffers several defeats

July 1737 Russian army defeats army of **Crimean khan** but withdraws due to lack of supplies

1737 Carl **Linnaeus** publishes first edition of *Genera Plantarum*

The ruins of the old Kandahar citadel, Afghanistan, lie on the hilltop behind the 12th-century arch. In the Persian siege, Hussein Hotaki took refuge in the citadel but surrendered after it was bombarded by Nader Shah.

THE AFGHAN HOTAKI DYNASTY had been expelled from Persia in1729 by Nader Shah (1698–1747), and he was also determined to eliminate the remaining threat posed by the Afghan **Ghilzai** people. Having occupied southern Afghanistan in 1737, he besieged the Hotaki stronghold of **Kandahar** in 1738. Nader Shah exiled Hussein, last of the Hotakis, destroyed the towns of Kandahar and Qalat-i-Ghilzai, and finally **crushed the hopes of the Ghilzais** by backing the rise of the rival Afghan **Durrani** people. Afghanistan was then part of the Mughal Empire, centred in Delhi, but the Mughal governor had been powerless to stop Nader Shah's **Persian force**, which swept through Kabul and **crossed the Indus** in December 1738. After defeating the forces of Mughal Muhammad Shah in the **Battle of Karnal** in February 1939, around 110km (68 miles) from Delhi, Nader Shah entered the city victorious on 9 March 1739. The Mughal treasury was empty but the shah **seized the emperor's personal jewels**, including the famous Koh-i-Noor and Darya-e-Noor diamonds.

8:1 **Battle of Karnal**
Trying to prevent Nader Shah's Persian invading army from reaching Delhi, the Mughals lost 20,000 men while the Persians lost only 2,500.

Also in 1739, the **Austro-Turkish War** (1737–39) was ended by the Treaty of Belgrade. In the same year, the Treaty of Niš brought the **Russo-Turkish War** (1735–39) to a conclusion. Both these treaties confirmed Austria's loss of northern Serbia and Belgrade to the Ottomans, obliging Russia to abandon hopes of capturing the Crimea, although the Russians were allowed to build an unfortified port at Azov and trade on the Black Sea.

Hostilities broke out once again between **Britain** and **Spain** in 1739. Britain had been awarded limited rights to trade slaves and goods in the Spanish colonies (see 1713), but increasingly, the Spanish were seizing British cargoes. In 1731, Spanish coastguards had severed the ear of a British captain, Robert Jenkins, and in 1739 the case led to a war, which was later dubbed the **War of Jenkins' Ear** by the Scottish historian Thomas Carlyle. Britain began to attack Spanish possessions in the New World, such as the Spanish naval base of Porto Bello in Panama. Following the **Battle of Porto Bello**, the British took possession of the settlement in November 1739. The Viceroyalty of New Spain, first established in the early 16th century, responded by increasing its defences around the Caribbean coast.

Administration of empire
The Viceroyalty of New Spain, centred on the Caribbean and Gulf of Mexico was the first of four created to govern Spanish New World territories.

In **North America**, French colonists were maintaining their drive to **push westwards** into Spanish territories. A priority was to identify a route to **link the Mississippi Basin** with Spanish **Colorado** and **Santa Fe**. In 1739, two French brothers, **Pierre and Paul Mallet, opened up a route** by negotiating the Missouri and Platte rivers, travelling southwards to the Arkansas River, from where a local man guided them to Santa Fe. Despite the continuing existence of a buffer state of warring American Indian tribes, a link between the French and Spanish settlements was established.

Battle of Porto Bello
Fought in 1739, in the early stages of the War of Jenkins' Ear, the Battle of Porto Bello resulted in the British seizing the settlement from Spain.

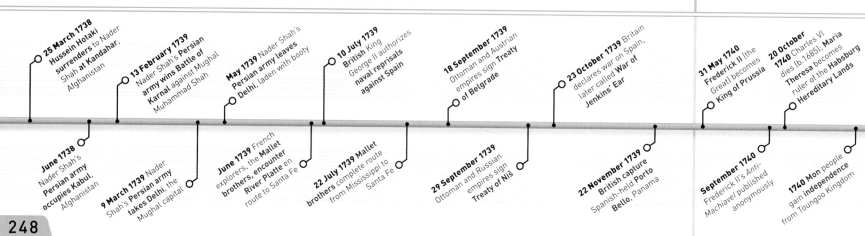

Frederick II (left) converses with the Marquis d'Argens near Sanssouci.

WITH THE DEATH OF KING FREDERICK WILLIAM I OF PRUSSIA in 1740, his son, Frederick II (1712–86), ascended to the throne. In his youth, Frederick II had been fond of music, poetry, and philosophy. He studied the works of Niccolò Machiavelli (see 1513) in preparation for kingship, and in 1739 wrote a refutation of the Renaissance Florentine's ideas, *Anti-Machiavel*, which he published anonymously in 1740. His rule was characterized by modernization, tolerance, and patronage of the arts. Yet he became known as **Frederick the Great** for the political and military feats by which he first expanded the borders of Prussia (until 1701 known as Brandenburg–Prussia) far beyond their historical limits, then defended these acquisitions against massive coalitions of powerful enemies. Frederick II's first opportunity to expand Prussia's frontiers arrived quickly after his accession. The Habsburg emperor, Charles VI, died in 1740 and was succeeded by his daughter, Maria Theresa (1717–80), who was to rule Austria's hereditary domains with her husband, Francis Stephen, as Holy Roman Emperor. Immediately Prussia and France challenged the arrangement. Most of Europe took sides in what became the **War of the Austrian Succession** (1740–48), with Britain, the Dutch Republic, Sardinia, and Saxony supporting the queen. Frederick, claiming inheritance of **Silesia** – parts of present-day Poland, Germany,

25 March 1738 **Hussein Hotaki surrenders** to Nader Shah at **Kandahar**, Afghanistan

June 1738 Nader Shah's **Persian army occupies Kabul**, Afghanistan

13 February 1739 Nader Shah's **Persian army wins Battle of Karnal** against Mughal Muhammad Shah

9 March 1739 Nader Shah's **Persian army takes Delhi**, the Mughal capital

May 1739 Nader Shah's **Persian army leaves Delhi**, laden with booty

June 1739 French explorers, the **Mallet brothers, encounter River Platte** en route to Santa Fe

10 July 1739 **British** King George II authorizes **naval reprisals against Spain**

22 July 1739 **Mallet brothers** complete route from Mississippi to Santa Fe

18 September 1739 Ottoman and Austrian empires sign **Treaty of Belgrade**

29 September 1739 Ottoman and Russian empires sign **Treaty of Niš**

23 October 1739 Britain declares war on Spain, later called **War of Jenkins' Ear**

22 November 1739 **British capture** Spanish-held **Porto Bello**, Panama

31 May 1740 **Frederick II** (the Great) becomes **King of Prussia**

September 1740 Frederick II's *Anti-Machiavel* published anonymously

20 October 1740 Charles VI dies (b.1685); **Maria Theresa** becomes ruler of the **Habsburg Hereditary Lands**

1740 **Mon** people gain **independence** from Toungoo Kingdom

“ …TOWARDS THE NORTH, FROM THERE SHONE **FREDERICK, THE POLE STAR, AROUND WHOM** GERMANY, EUROPE, EVEN **THE WORLD SEEMED TO TURN. ”**

Johann Wolfgang von Goethe, German writer (1749–1832), on Frederick the Great

Poppelsdorf Castle, Germany, exemplifies Rococo style, which became popular during the 18th century, particularly in France, Germany, Bohemia, and Austria.

and the Czech Republic – seized the territory from Habsburg, Austria, and made it a Prussian province. It was later incorporated into the German Empire, in 1871.

In Asia, the Mon kingdom centred in **Pegu**, Burma (Myanmar), rebelled in 1740 against the northern Burmese **Toungoo kingdom** that had first subjugated it in 1539. After the rebellion, a Burmese monk with Toungoo royal heritage was made king of Pegu. The independent kingdom lasted until 1757.

Also in 1740, a major expansion of the **Lunda kingdom** of Central Africa began when a party exploring to the west established the kingdom of **Kazembe**. For the next hundred years, an aggressive policy of annexation increased Kazembe's size to cover most of Katanga in the present-day Democratic Republic of the Congo.

Meanwhile, the War of the Austrian Succession was having repercussions in the north. Sweden, still bridling at losing its **Baltic territories** after the Great Northern War (see 1721–22), deployed troops on the Russian border and declared the **Russo–Swedish War** (1741–43). The threat to St Petersburg pushed forward a planned coup d'état in Russia, but the new tsarina, Elizabeth Petrovna (1709–62), continued with the war rather than cede the Baltic territories to Sweden, as had been promised.

In Ulster (Northern Ireland), **emigration to North America** increased dramatically. Those leaving included many members of the **Scottish Presbyterian Church**, most of whom were descendents of families who had colonized the Irish north in the 17th century. Ireland's English overlords distrusted the Scottish–Irish colony, which supported Scottish interests. Presbyterian ministers were **fined or incarcerated**, and economic activities of the Scottish Presbyterians were curtailed, causing poverty and famine. In the early 18th century, this discrimination worsened; they were forced to pay tithes in support of the Church of England and excluded from important office. A severe **famine** in 1741–42 resulted in about 12,000 annually leaving for the New World. These **Scottish–Irish emigrants**, resentful of their treatment by the English, later gave fierce support to the cause of American independence from Britain in the 1770s and 1780s.

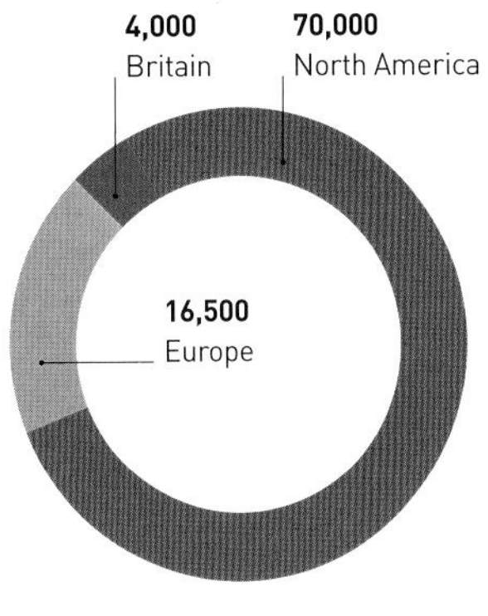

The Ulster diaspora
Between 1680 and 1750, 70,000 Scottish–Irish emigrants left Ulster for North America, 4,000 moved to Britain, and 16,500 left for Europe.

Growth of Brandenburg-Prussia
In the late 17th and 18th centuries, successive leaders enhanced the power and territory of Brandenburg–Prussia through military and political means.

KEY
Brandenburg 1648
Acquisitions 1648–1786

THE OPPORTUNISTIC SEIZING OF SILESIA by Frederick II of Prussia (see 1740–41) proved a successful gambit. The Austrian army had challenged the Prussians but had been defeated in the Battle of Mollwitz in 1741. In 1742, Maria Theresa of Austria and the victorious Prussians signed the **Treaty of Berlin**, by which a large part of Silesia was ceded to Prussia. The treaty brought an **end to the First Silesian War** (1740–42), though the wider European conflict known as the War of the Austrian Succession continued until 1748.

In 1742, Swedish astronomer **Anders Celsius** (1701–44) developed the Celsius, or centigrade, **thermometer**. Celsius actually set the melting point of ice at 100 degrees and the boiling point of water at zero degrees, an arrangement that was reversed in 1744 by Swedish botanist Carl Linnaeus (1707–78).

In **Spanish Peru**, a new leader of the native people, **Juan Santos Atahualpa**, a Jesuit-educated man claiming to be a direct descendant of the murdered Inca king Atahualpa (1497–1533), began a **rebellion in Quisopango** in 1742. The Spanish mounted a military campaign against him in 1742, and again in 1743, 1746, and 1750, but never defeated him in his home territory in the Andes.

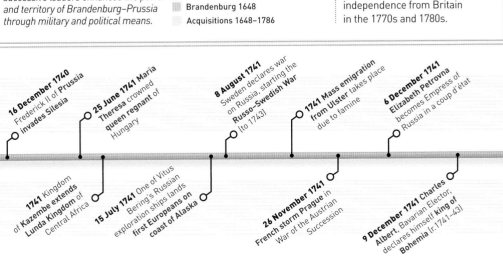

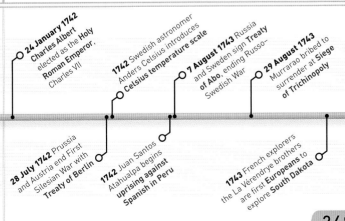

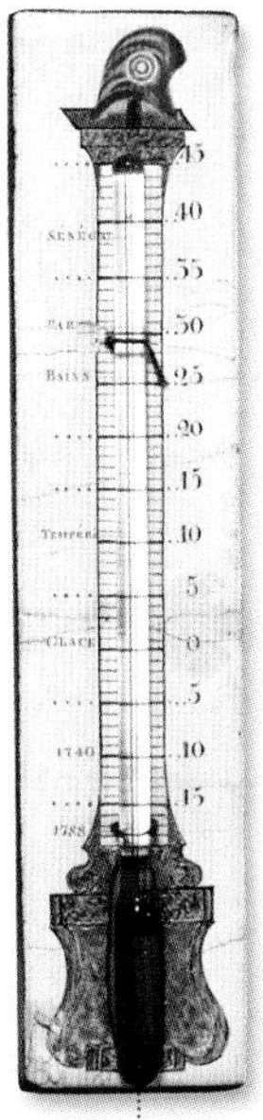

Celsius thermometer
This 18th-century French instrument, intended for measuring outdoor temperatures, features Celsius's scale, with a range of –15 to +45 degrees.

In India, the **struggle** for power continued between the **Maratha** people (see 1720) and the **nizam of Hyderabad**, the semi-independent representative of the Mughal Empire. The Marathas seized **Trichinopoly**, leaving Murrarao Ghorpade as governor of the town, and refused to pay tribute to the nizam. In 1743, the nizam, determined to regain control of the area, had 80,000 men besiege the town. Defeated, Murrarao accepted payment to change allegiance.

The Russo–Swedish War (1741–43) was ended by the **Treaty of Abo** in 1743. Intent on reducing the Swedish threat to St Petersburg, Russia had occupied **Finland**, and the treaty moved the Swedish border north. Most of Finland was returned to the Swedes, who in exchange accepted **Adolf-Frederick of Holstein-Gotthorp** (1710–1771), a client of Empress Elizabeth of Russia, as heir to the Swedish throne.

In North America, **South Dakota** was first **explored by Europeans** in 1743, when the French de La Vérendrye brothers returned west after being the first Europeans to see the **Rockies** during their attempt to reach the Pacific.

16 December 1740 Frederick II of **Prussia invades Silesia**

1741 Kingdom of **Kazembe extends Lunda Kingdom** of Central Africa

25 June 1741 Maria Theresa crowned **queen regnant** of Hungary

15 July 1741 One of Vitus Bering's Russian exploration ships lands **first Europeans on coast of Alaska**

8 August 1741 Sweden declares war on Russia, starting the **Russo–Swedish War** (to 1743)

1741 Mass emigration from Ulster takes place due to famine

26 November 1741 French storm **Prague** in War of the Austrian Succession

6 December 1741 Elizabeth Petrovna becomes Empress of Russia in a coup d'état

9 December 1741 Charles Albert, Bavarian Elector, declares himself **king of Bohemia** (r.1741–43)

24 January 1742 Charles Albert elected as the **Holy Roman Emperor**, Charles VII

28 July 1742 Prussia and Austria end First Silesian War with **Treaty of Berlin**

1742 Swedish astronomer Anders Celsius introduces **Celsius temperature scale**

1742 Juan Santos Atahualpa begins **uprising against Spanish in Peru**

7 August 1743 Russia and Sweden sign **Treaty of Abo**, ending Russo–Swedish War

29 August 1743 Murrarao bribed to surrender at **Siege of Trichinopoly**

1743 French explorers the La Vérendrye brothers are first **Europeans** to explore **South Dakota**

THE STORY OF AGRICULTURE

FROM HUNTER-GATHERERS AND DOMESTICATION TO CULTIVATION AND GENETIC MANIPULATION

No other activity has made a greater impact on both human society and the environment than agriculture. Its discovery and use first allowed small, previously nomadic, hunter-gathering societies to settle in one place, transform the landscape, form communities, and establish civilizations.

Most archaeologists agree that the earliest plants were domesticated in the Fertile Crescent region of the Middle East around 10,000 BCE. While the fig is thought to be the first truly cultivated food, emmer wheat, barley, lentils, chickpeas, and flax were also common early crops. The first animals to be domesticated were sheep and goats, followed by small breeds of cattle.

On the other side of the world, in what is now South and Central America, squash and maize were being planted, joined by beans; these three plants became known as the "Three Sisters" crops and represented an early knowledge of nutrition: planting them together not only retained soil nutrients but provided essential vitamin and minerals needed for human health.

TOOLS OF THE TRADE

Neolithic farmers used digging sticks – long, flat blades with rounded points – to scrape shallow depressions in the earth, into which they dropped seeds. They also cleared areas of woodland using axes as well as fire to make space for crops and animal enclosures. However, sophisticated farming techniques such as irrigation and large-scale monocropping were practised in Sumeria as early as 5000 BCE, while in Egypt, farmers made use of ploughs and sickles, and boasted a range of crops and livestock.

The light scratch plough used by Mediterranean countries dominated farming in Europe until the Middle Ages, when the heavy horse-drawn plough and a three-field system of crop rotation revolutionized agriculture and greatly increased food supplies. Voyages to Asia and the discovery of the New World in the 15th century had a profound impact on agriculture worldwide, as crops and animals were exchanged between Europe, Asia, and the Americas. This changed agriculture on a scale not seen again until engine-driven farm machinery and mass-production techniques, including the use of chemical fertilizers and pesticides, became the norm in the 20th century.

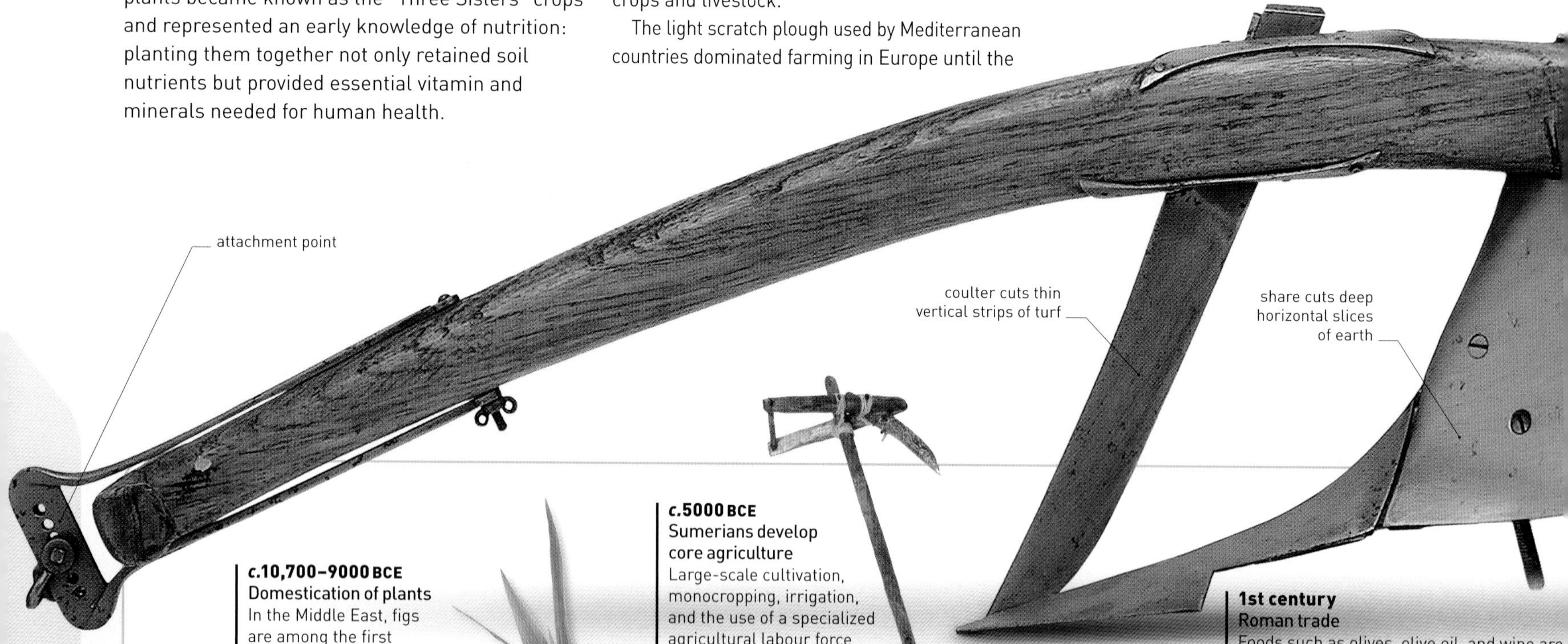

Green figs

c.10,700–9000 BCE
Domestication of plants
In the Middle East, figs are among the first crops to be cultivated actively by man.

c.8000–2000 BCE
The Three Sisters
The planting together of squash, teosinte (a primitive form of maize), and beans in the Americas shows a knowledge of companion planting techniques.

Teosinte corn cob

c.5000 BCE
Sumerians develop core agriculture
Large-scale cultivation, monocropping, irrigation, and the use of a specialized agricultural labour force allows the Sumerian culture to flourish and expand.

Sumerian plough

2500–1500 BCE
Egypt cultivates the Nile
The Egyptians use a sophisticated system of planting and harvesting crops that is dependent on the annual flooding of the Nile Delta.

Egyptian harvest

1st century
Roman trade
Foods such as olives, olive oil, and wine are traded across the Roman Empire, where agriculture is an important business.

Roman millstone

Small's wooden plough
Scottish inventor James Small was a major contributor to the development of the plough. In the mid-1700s, he significantly redesigned the single-furrow horse plough and remodelled the mouldboard, which was now made of iron, making it stronger and more efficient at turning soil.

1950
3,400,000

1907
600

US 20th-century tractor usage
Tractors became more widespread as their design improved. They became smaller and mass production made them more affordable.

THE AGRICULTURAL REVOLUTION

From the end of the 16th century in Europe, landowners began to take a more scientific approach to farming. This entailed following such practices as crop rotation to ensure soil fertility was not depleted, using more efficient machinery such as improved ploughs, and cross-breeding livestock to avoid genetic weaknesses. While the success of these practices resulted in more food, it came at a cost: the need for farm labourers was greatly reduced, and land enclosures dispossessed many peasants who had nowhere to go.

1050–1300
The Middle Ages
The heavy plough, pulled first by teams of oxen then draught horses, changes the shape of fields, gives bigger yields, and greatly improves the way medieval Europe feeds itself.

Wooden plough

1492
Columbian exchange
Columbus's discovery of the New World results in an unprecedented cultural exchange of animals and plants, including tobacco and maize.

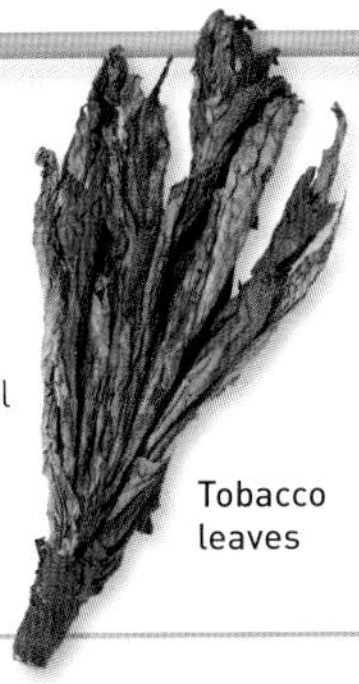
Tobacco leaves

Late 18th century
The cast-iron plough
The invention of first a cast-iron mouldboard, then a cast-iron ploughshare greatly improves ploughing efficiency in both Old and New World agriculture.

1800–40
The mechanical reaper
Although still horse-drawn, the mechanical reaper is the first step in the mechanization of farming, harvesting crops in much less time than could be achieved by hand.

McCormick's reaping machine

1890s–early 1900s
Gasoline-powered vehicles
The internal-combustion engine-powered agricultural tractor signals the end of horse-drawn farming. By World War I, tractors become common parts of farm machinery in the US.

The Ivel tractor

1970s
Move to sustainability
In a countermovement to the high-impact and environmentally damaging chemical practices of the mid-20th century, green and sustainable practices begin to be developed.

2000–present
Urban farming
As world populations rise, the search for new ways to feed more people increases. Vertical hydroponic farms in urban spaces have proved successful.

This 18th-century, hand-coloured copperplate engraving shows disciplined ranks of red-coated Hanoverian troops falling upon Jacobite Highlanders at the Battle of Culloden, the last battle of the Jacobite uprising.

THE EAST AFRICAN PORT OF MOMBASA was used in the 18th century for trade in gold, ivory, and slaves. Mombasa was held for 200 years by the Portuguese, until a native rebellion drove them out in 1729. The **Arabs of Oman** took over, and in 1744, with a new dynasty installed in Oman, the new governor of Mombasa seized power there from the Omanis. He was killed by Omani assassins in 1745, but his brother, 'Ali ibn Athman (r.1746–55) stirred up a rebellion and the assassins were executed. 'Ali ibn Athman proclaimed himself **Sultan of Mombasa**, thereby securing the port's independence from Oman.

Meanwhile, Prussia's war with Austria (see 1740) continued. In the **Second Silesian War** (1744–45), the Austrians tried to regain Silesia but the Prussians eventually defeated the forces of Empress Maria Theresa in 1745 in the battles of **Hohenfriedberg**, Soor, and Kesselsdorf. Maria Theresa finally recognized Frederick II's sovereignty in Silesia by signing the **Treaty of Dresden** at the end of the year; in return, Prussia recognized her husband, Francis, as Holy Roman Emperor. This left only France prosecuting the War of the Austrian Succession (1740–48).

9,000 AUSTRIANS AND SAXONS

5,000 PRUSSIANS

Losses at Hohenfriedberg
In this battle the victorious Prussians had significantly fewer casualties than the Austrians and their allies from Saxony.

In 1744, France attempted a major **invasion of Britain** in support of Prince Charles Edward Stuart (1720–88) – grandson of the deposed Stuart King James II and the "**Young Pretender**" to the Hanoverian throne of Britain. But the invasion foundered due to terrible weather. In 1745, **"Bonnie Prince Charlie"**, as Charles became known, crossed to Scotland and rallied the **Jacobite chiefs** of several Scottish Highland clans to march on England. The Scots defeated a Hanoverian force in the **Battle of Prestonpans** and eventually reached Derby but then retreated, having gained little support from the English or the French. Military successes followed on their return to Scotland, but in 1746 the Scottish force was overcome by a Hanoverian force at the **Battle of Culloden**. The hounding and killing of fleeing and wounded Highlanders earned the Hanoverian commander, William Augustus, Duke of Cumberland, notoriety as the "**Butcher of Culloden**". The battle ended the Second Jacobite Rebellion and wiped out Jacobite hopes of regaining power in Britain.

Deadly Coehorn mortar
The Hanoverian army at Culloden had six short-barrelled Coehorn mortars; easily portable, they were deadly weapons on the battlefield.

In 1745, an English farmer began experiments in selective animal breeding that were to revolutionize **animal husbandry**. The principle of mating animals with desired traits was already known, but the methods developed by farmer **Robert Bakewell** were better than earlier ones. His work resulted in the New Leicester breed of sheep and New Longhorn cattle breed, both of which are still widely influential in animal breeding today.

In Japan, the hold of the **Tokugawa dynasty** on power was weakening. In 1745, Tokugawa Ieshige (1712–61) was elected as shogun. The retiring shogun's eldest son, was poor in health, defective in speech, and had little interest in government affairs, but his father demanded his succession as primogeniture dictated. Natural **disasters and famine** characterized his reign, and as the power of the mercantile class grew, his own authority declined, the result of poor decisions and **delegation of power** to subordinates.

Meanwhile, France was still at war with Austria and its allies. In 1746 a French force, authorized by Governor-General Joseph Francois Dupleix (1697–1763), took the British-held Indian port of **Madras**. In 1747, Dupleix followed this with an **attack on Fort St David**, the strongly fortified British headquarters in southern India, 160km (100 miles) south of Madras, but this time he was unsuccessful. However, the French remained in occupation of Madras until the **Treaty of Aix-la-Chapelle** (see 1748) returned the port to the British in exchange for Louisbourg in Nova Scotia.

In China, during the reign of the Qianlong Emperor (r.1736–99), **Christians** were subjected to renewed **persecution** from 1746 to 1748 as a matter of **imperial policy**. In 1715, Pope Clement XII had criticized idolatrous elements in Chinese religious practices, and the Qianlong Emperor realized that Chinese Christians felt greater **loyalty to foreign powers** than to him. As a result,

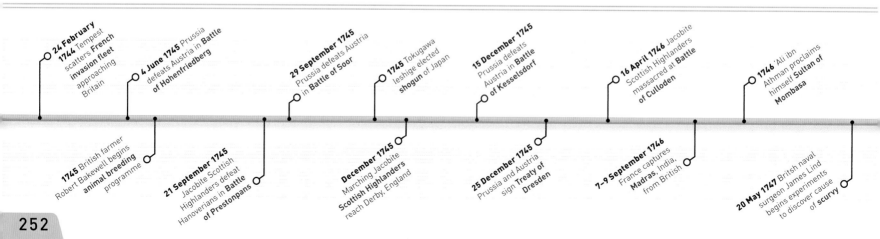

Selectively bred sheep
This 1842 engraving depicts a New Leicester ram, a breed developed by Robert Bakewell's new breeding methods at his Leicestershire farm.

24 February 1744 Tempest scatters French **invasion fleet** approaching Britain

1745 British farmer Robert Bakewell begins **animal breeding** programme

4 June 1745 Prussia defeats Austria in **Battle of Hohenfriedberg**

21 September 1745 Jacobite Scottish Highlanders defeat Hanoverians in **Battle of Prestonpans**

29 September 1745 Prussia defeats Austria in **Battle of Soor**

1745 Tokugawa Ieshige elected **shogun** of Japan

December 1745 Marching Jacobite **Scottish Highlanders** reach Derby, England

15 December 1745 Prussia defeats Austria in **Battle of Kesselsdorf**

25 December 1745 Prussia and Austria sign **Treaty of Dresden**

16 April 1746 Jacobite Scottish Highlanders massacred at **Battle of Culloden**

7–9 September 1746 France captures **Madras**, India, from British

1746 'Ali ibn Athman proclaims himself **Sultan of Mombasa**

20 May 1747 British naval surgeon James Lind begins experiments to discover cause of **scurvy**

A firework display on the River Thames on 15 May 1749, organized by the Duke of Richmond to celebrate the signing of the Treaty of Aix-la-Chapelle.

“ THE MOST SUDDEN AND VISIBLE **GOOD EFFECTS** WERE…FROM **ORANGES** AND **LEMONS.** ”

James Lind, British surgeon, from ***Treatise of the Scurvy,*** 1753

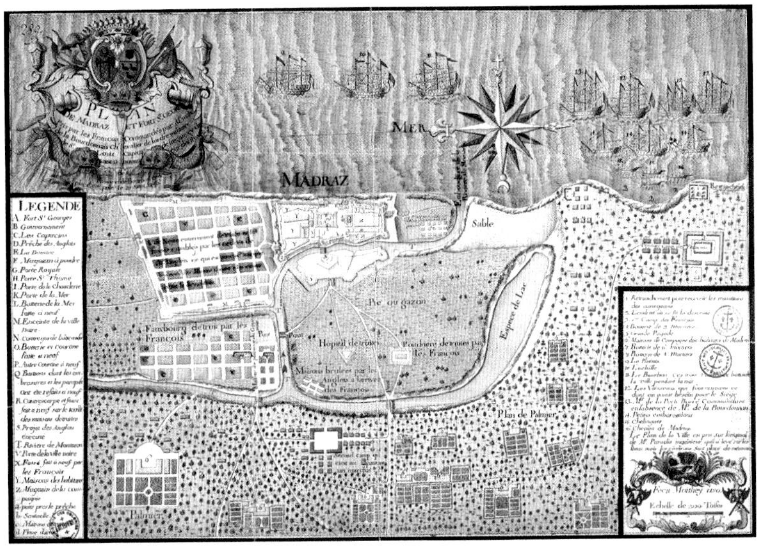

Map of Madras
This 1750 engraving depicts the Indian port of Madras, together with its British Fort of St George, both captured by a French naval expedition in 1746.

evangelization was banned, and Chinese Christians were forced to go into hiding. Wherever missionaries were discovered flouting the law by preaching, the persecution of Christians was intensified.

Another scientific breakthrough in 1745 was the **Leyden jar**, probably the most important 18th-century development in the understanding of **electricity**.

Early capacitor
The Leyden jar could store electric charge, which was created by an electrostatic generator and conducted into the jar through its metal rod.

Invented by the Dutch scientist Pieter van Musschenbroek of the University of Leiden, this device, an early type of **capacitor**, demonstrated that electricity could be stored. From this developed the idea of a battery, originally a group of Leyden jars combined to generate a more powerful electric charge.

In 1747, the powerful Persian overlord **Nader Shah** (b.1688), who had become paranoid and mercilessly cruel, was **murdered** by his bodyguards. A grand assembly at Kandahar in Afghanistan, recognizing the resulting weakness of the Persian Empire, elected Nader's Afghan lieutenant, **Ahmad Khan Abdali,** (also known as Ahmad Shah Durrani, 1722–73) as head and founder of the **modern state of Afghanistan**. Abdali was to unify the country under his rule and develop a large empire, including parts of present-day Iran, Pakistan, and India.

In West Africa, the **Yoruba** people, occupying territory from eastern present-day Benin to southern Nigeria, invaded the **Kingdom of Dahomey** in 1747. The kingdom was rich from trade in slaves and commodities such as palm oil, and was forced to pay tribute to the **Yoruba Empire of Oyo**, an arrangement that lasted until 1818.

1747 also saw a development that was to improve the lives of **sailors**. In a pioneering study, James Lind, a surgeon of the Royal Navy, proved that **scurvy**, a sometimes fatal disease common during long voyages, could be treated by eating **citrus fruit**. However, only in 1795 did the Royal Navy begin to use lemon juice to prevent and treat scurvy.

THE WAR OF THE AUSTRIAN SUCCESSION (see 1740) was concluded by the signing of the **Treaty of Aix-la-Chapelle** (present-day Aachen) in 1748. Prussia's conquest of Silesia was recognized, France regained some of its colonies in exchange for withdrawing from the Netherlands, and Britain's **Asiento** contract with Spain (see 1713) was renewed.

Nader Shah's lucrative **sacking of Delhi** (see 1739) became the incentive for a second attack, this time on the **Punjab** by Ahmad Khan Abdali (see 1747). His army of 12,000 horsemen was met in the **Battle of Manupur** by a defensive Mughal force of 60,000. Abdali's Afghans held their own until 1,000 of them were killed by an exploding gunpowder store; devastated, they fled. Meanwhile, a rising power in the south was the **Kingdom of Mysore** under the control of Hyder Ali (1720–82), father of the famous Tipu Sultan (1750–99). Under Hyder Ali, the Mysore Empire **seized territory** from the Marathas, Hyderabad, and neighbouring kingdoms.

In **North America**, the British presence in Nova Scotia was consolidated with the establishment of **Halifax** in 1749; the area capital was transferred there from Annapolis Royal. In violation of a previous treaty, Lieutenant General **Edward Cornwallis** (1713–76) arrived with transport ships containing **2,500 settlers**, sparking a war in which the French and native Mi'kmaq kept the British settlement constantly under attack.

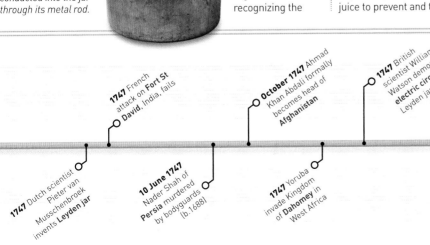

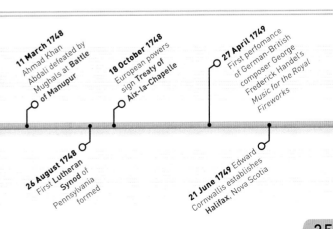

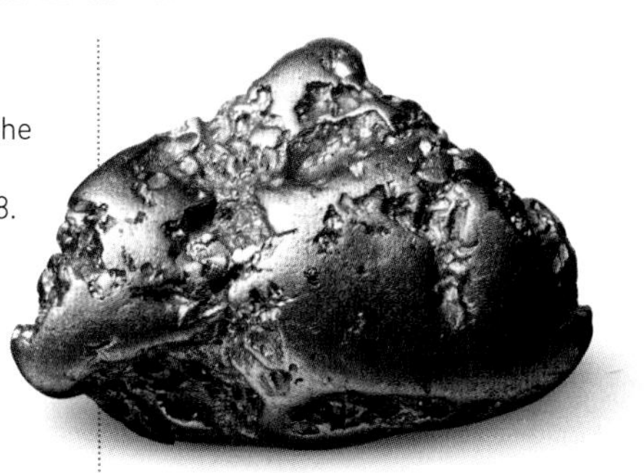

Unrefined platinum ore
Platinum was discovered in South America by Spanish conquerors. The name is derived from the Spanish term platina, *meaning "little silver".*

In Pennsylvania, the **first Lutheran Synod** was founded in 1748 by Henry Melchior Mühlenburg (1711–87). German Lutherans had first arrived in Pennsylvania in 1683, but it was the creation of the Synod that **unified the Lutheran community**.

South America's gold and silver had long been valued in Europe, but it was not until 1748, with a report from Spanish explorer Antonio de Ulloa (1716–95), that the value of **South America's platinum** was realized. A dense, corrosion-resistant metal, it was mined in the Cordillera Occidental of **Colombia** and in central **Peru**.

Another Spaniard, Giacobbo Rodríguez Pereire (1715–80), made history in 1749 when he took a pupil to the Paris Academy of Sciences to demonstrate his new **sign language** for deaf-mutes in which the sign alphabet required the use of only one hand.

1747 Dutch scientist Pieter van Musschenbroek invents **Leyden jar**

1747 French attack on **Fort St David**, India, fails

10 June 1747 Nader Shah of **Persia** murdered by bodyguards (b.1688)

October 1747 Ahmad Khan Abdali formally becomes head of **Afghanistan**

1747 Yoruba invade Kingdom of **Dahomey** in West Africa

1747 British scientist William Watson demonstrates **electric circuit** using Leyden jar

11 March 1748 Ahmad Khan Abdali defeated by Mughals at **Battle of Manupur**

26 August 1748 First **Lutheran Synod** of Pennsylvania formed

18 October 1748 European powers sign **Treaty of Aix-la-Chapelle**

27 April 1749 First performance of German-British composer George Frederick Handel's *Music for the Royal Fireworks*

21 June 1749 Edward Cornwallis establishes **Halifax**, Nova Scotia

6

THE AGE OF REVOLUTION

1750–1913

Often dramatic, war-torn, and violent, this period was also a time of remarkable technological advances in medicine, communication, and transportation – ushering in the beginnings of the modern world.

1750

José I of Portugal's coat of arms on the ceiling of Coimbra University.

THE COLONIAL BOUNDARY BETWEEN SPAIN AND PORTUGAL in the New World was settled by the **Treaty of Madrid**, signed on 13 January, which significantly amended the **Treaty of Tordesillas** (1494). The previous agreement stipulated that the Portuguese empire extend no further than 370 leagues west of the Azores (around 46 degrees west), but the new treaty took into account the extent of Portuguese settlement in Brazil. Spain hoped that by allowing Portugal some concessions it would discourage any further Portuguese territorial expansion in the region.

MARQUIS OF POMBAL
(1699–1782)

The Marquis of Pombal was a controversial political figure, appointed prime minister of Portugal in 1750, the year José I (1714–77) took the throne. His 27 years in power saw economic and social reform, and the expulsion of the Jesuits.

1751

A detail from engraver William Hogarth's 1751 work *Gin Lane* depicts the public drunkenness and social problems caused by cheap gin.

17

THE NUMBER OF **VOLUMES** OF THE ENCYCLOPÉDIE PUBLISHED BETWEEN 1751 AND 1765

ENGLAND WAS EXPERIENCING AN ALCOHOL CRISIS, fuelled by the popularity of cheap gin, as illustrated by the darkly satirical engraving *Gin Lane* by **William Hogarth** (1697–1764), issued in 1751. Gin production had been refined over the previous 50 years, and the spirit proved hugely popular – by the year Hogarth's print was completed, the British were drinking more than two gallons of gin per capita a year. Public outcry over the social effects of gin led to the Gin Act of 1751, which attempted to limit the amount that could be bought.

In France, intellectuals led by the writer and philosopher **Denis Diderot** (1713–84) began the publication of the *Encyclopédie, ou dictionnaire raisonné des sciences, des arts et des métiers*. Known as the **Encyclopédie**, it became one of the defining works of the **Enlightenment** (see 1763). Many influential French thinkers – such as **Montesquieu** (1689–1755), **Jean-Jacques Rousseau** (1712–78), and **Voltaire** (1694–1778) – contributed to tens of thousands of articles in the work, which attempted to catalogue the depths of human knowledge in science, philosophy, politics, and religion. With its emphasis on reason, the volumes were banned in some countries, such as Spain, where the **Catholic Inquisition** objected to its content.

Halfway across the world, China was extending its power in the **Dzungaria and Tarim basin** by fighting the Mongolian tribes for control to this key part of the steppes. The basin's importance lay in its proximity to the **Silk Road** (see pages 100–01), the vital trade route between China and the West.

ROCOCO

This 18th-century painting on the ceiling of a Bavarian church exemplifies the work of the Rococo movement that dominated European decorative arts, architecture, painting, and sculpture. Rococo evolved out of Baroque (see 1626), but its details and flourishes were even more ornate and often playful. The period is often associated with French design during the reigns of Louis XV (r.1715–54) and Louis XVI (r.1774–92).

1752

This Buddha statue is in the Sulamani Pahto temple in Bagan, Burma, which was built in 1181 but contains images and frescos from the Konbaung period.

BURMA (MYANMAR) HAD LONG BEEN DIVIDED among warring factions until a chief, **Alaungpaya** (1714–60), began to unite the country through a series of military victories, and established the **Konbaung dynasty**. Not only did he have to bring disparate groups together, he faced the challenge of troops from Britain and France, who were eager to gain territory in Burma and who were willing to arm Alaungpaya's enemies. But for the next seven years, Alaungpaya resisted both threats, and British and French troops were driven out. Under successive kings, the unified kingdom continued to become stronger, and over the following decades it went so far as to make incursions into Siam (Thailand).

In Britain, the public went to bed on 2 September and woke up on 14 September. The government had made the decision to change from the **Julian calendar** to the **Gregorian** one, joining the other western European countries that had made the change hundreds of years before. This calendar was introduced in 1582 by Pope Gregory XIII, who chose to make the change when it became clear that the old Julian calendar put around 11 extra days between vernal equinoxes, making the celebration of Easter arrive earlier each year.

In British North America, scientific discoveries were making their own leap forward. Inventor, politician, and diplomat **Benjamin Franklin** (1706–90) invented the **lightning conductor**. Before the advent of Franklin's lightning rod, buildings were often destroyed by fires started by lightning. Franklin thought there was a relationship between lightning and **electricity** and was said to have flown a kite in a lightning storm to prove his theory. The rod, developed after this experiment, attracts lightning, which is conducted into the ground, bypassing the building and keeping it safe from a lightning strike.

> “ ENERGY AND PERSISTENCE **CONQUER ALL THINGS.** ”
>
> **Attributed to Benjamin Franklin, American inventor, politician, and diplomat**

13 January Treaty of Madrid signed

José I ascends to Portuguese throne, and the **Marquis de Pombal** becomes his prime minister

The Sino-Tibetan War follows Tibetan anger and subsequent murder of Chinese people in Tibet

12 September Britain captures **Arcot**, a turning point against the French in India in **Second Carnatic War**

Denis Diderot begins publication of *l'Encyclopédie*

William Hogarth's *Gin Lane* is completed

Benjamin Franklin invents the lightning rod

11 February First hospital in the present-day US opened, in Pennsylvania

August The **Liberty Bell**, symbol of American independence, arrives in Philadelphia from foundry in London

September Britain adopts **Gregorian** calendar

1753

Based on the work of the botanist Carl Linnaeus, this botanical drawing of blackberries is by J. Miller.

BY THE TIME SIR HANS SLOANE (1660–1753), an Irish-born physician and collector, died, he had amassed 71,000 different objects, ranging from samples of flora and fauna from all over the world, to books and manuscripts about a wide range of subjects. Like other intellectuals and scientists across Europe, he was part of wider Enlightenment intellectual currents, and he had realized the scholarly value of his collection, which he bequeathed to Britain. In exchange, he wanted a payment of £20,000 to his estate – well below the value of the collection. The English Parliament approved the deal and passed an act establishing the **British Museum**. Parts of the collection were put on public display a few years later.

Sloane's contemporaries across Europe were engaged in collecting and other scientific pursuits. In the same year, Swedish botanist **Carl Linnaeus** (1707–78) published his *Species Plantarum*, which classified more than 7,000 species of plants by putting each genus into a class and order, a system that is still used today.

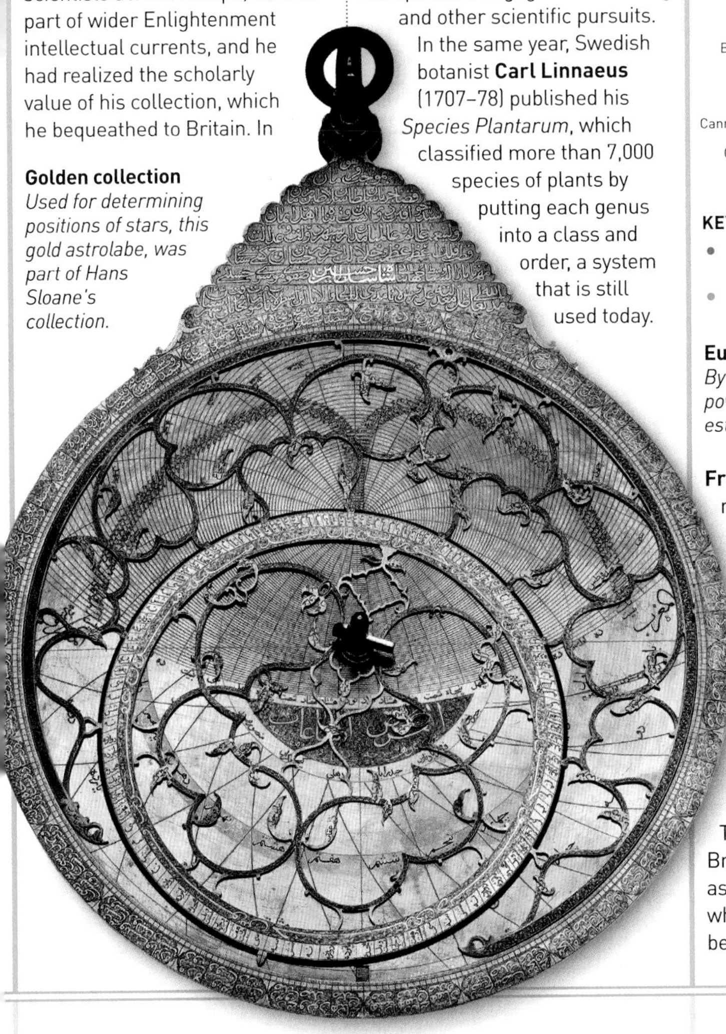

Golden collection
Used for determining positions of stars, this gold astrolabe, was part of Hans Sloane's collection.

1754

This scene shows troops mounted on elephants during the Carnatic War.

THE SECOND CARNATIC WAR (1749–54) and the **French and Indian War** (1754–63) were both precursors to the larger **Seven Years War** (1756–63). However, the theatre of these Anglo-French disputes was not Europe. The

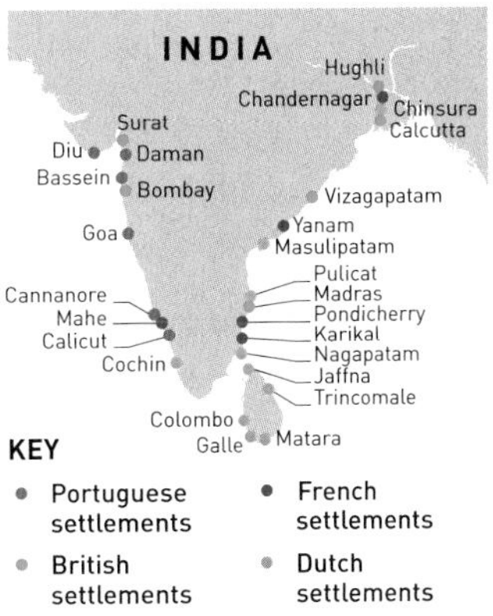

Europe in India
By the mid-18th century, European powers held territories and established settlements in India.

French and Indian War ranged from Virginia in the south to Nova Scotia in the north of North America.

Battles of the **Second Carnatic War** took place in South India. The **Treaty of Pondicherry** temporarily halted tensions between France and Britain, whose troops were technically employed by corporations – the **East India companies**. The treaty recognized the British-backed Mohammad Ali as the new **Nawab of Carnatic**, which had been a key factor behind the dispute.

1755

A painting depicts the desperate search for survivors in Lisbon after the city was heavily damaged by an earthquake in November.

> “I AM NOT SO **LOST IN LEXICOGRAPHY** AS TO FORGET THAT **WORDS** ARE THE DAUGHTERS OF EARTH.”

Samuel Johnson, English writer, from the preface of his *Dictionary of the English Language*, 1755

AN EARTHQUAKE KILLED TENS OF THOUSANDS OF PEOPLE in Lisbon, Portugal, when it shook the city on the morning of 1 November. It was later estimated by historians to have measured 9 on the Richter scale, while estimates of the number of deaths range from 10,000 to 100,000 in a population of 200,000. The earthquake also triggered a tsunami that destroyed settlements further south in the Algarve region. The disaster had a profound effect across Europe – **Voltaire** (1694–1778) was inspired to write his *Poème sur le désastre de Lisbonne* about the event, and German philosopher Immanuel Kant (1724–1804) wrote a series of essays about it. The **Marquis of Pombal** (see panel, left) immediately took action, making sure fires were put out and the dead were quickly buried. He then began the rebuilding of the city, including the construction of buildings meant to withstand another earthquake.

Earlier in the year, in England, the writer **Samuel Johnson** (1709–84) had completed the commission he had received for a ***Dictionary of the English Language*** from a syndicate of London printers. It took him eight years and six assistants to finish it. Although it was not the first English dictionary, it quickly became the most celebrated and authoritative. Some of its more notorious definitions include "patron: commonly a wretch who supports with insolence, and is paid with flattery" and "oats: a grain, which in England is generally given to horses, but in Scotland supports the people".

English by definition
This is the front cover of the first edition of Samuel Johnson's Dictionary of the English Language.

- **March** Sweden adopts **Gregorian calendar**
- **5 April** Founding charter of **British Museum** is enacted
- **Carl Linnaeus** publishes his *Species Plantarum*
- The **French and Indian War** between Britain and France and its Indian allies begins
- **Treaty of Pondicherry** ends Second Carnatic war
- Scottish chemist and physicist **Joseph Black (1728–99)** discovers **carbon dioxide**
- The British drive French settlers out of **Acadia** (now part of Canada)
- **15 April Samuel Johnson** publishes his ground-breaking English-language dictionary
- **1 November** Violent **earthquake** devastates **Lisbon**

1756

This detail taken from an engraving by Paul Revere depicts the British capture of the French fort in Louisbourg, Nova Scotia. The fort was built to protect France's interests in the region and became a target for the British when war was declared in 1756. The town was attacked by land and sea, falling to the British in 1758.

THE SEVEN YEARS WAR (1756–63) was fought in theatres from India to North America to Europe, making it a truly global conflict. Its roots, however, were European. The earlier **War of Austrian Succession** (see 1740) left many territorial issues unresolved. **The Treaty of Aix-la-Chapelle** (1748) did not settle the dispute between **Prussia** and **Austria** over the province of **Silesia**, located in southeast Prussia and bordering Austria. At the same time, **British** and **French** tensions continued to simmer. Because of complicated alliances, these situations escalated into what became known as the Seven Years War.

By 1756, some key incidents had made the battle lines clear. In April, **France invaded Minorca** in the Mediterranean, which Britain had taken from Spain in 1708. The French sent 15,000 troops to the island, where the British had only around 2,500. Britain formally declared war on France. The conflict brought in the **Electorate of Hanover**, in northwest Germany, which was willing to send the British extra troops.

Prussia's **Frederick II** (1712–86), meanwhile, was increasingly suspicious of the alliance between **France and Russia**. In May, his troops entered the **Electorate of Saxony**, between Prussia and Russia. They outnumbered those in Saxony by more than 3:1, but Austria's leader, **Maria Theresa** (1717–80), was quick to send more troops. The war had begun.

Britain and Prussia formed an alliance against France, Russia, Austria, Sweden, Saxony, and eventually Spain. But each country was also pursuing its own interests: Britain wanted France out of **India** and **North America**; Austria and Prussia both wanted Silesia. Russia wanted to curb Frederick II's growing powers and assist Austria and France.

The European conflict had been preceded by skirmishes in colonial territories: the British and French had been fighting in North America, as well as in India. **Anglo–French tensions** had spilled over into disputes with local rulers in India, leading to an infamous incident – the **Black Hole of Calcutta**. The **Nawab of Bengal, Siraj-ud-Dawlah** (1733–57), who France supported, attacked the British in Calcutta and imprisoned many of them in a small cell in Fort William. Estimates of the captives range from 60 to 150. Overnight, between 40 and 123 of them died due to overcrowding and heat.

FREDERICK II (1712–86)

Known as "Frederick the Great", the Prussian King Frederick II ruled for 46 years. With his interest in culture and philosophy, Frederick's reign was marked by a liberal spirit. But it was his military prowess that earned Frederick II his reputation, as he transformed the small kingdom of Prussia into a European power.

Men at arms

The sizes of the armies involved in the Seven Years War are shown here. Although some of the important battles were at sea, most of the fighting was done by army soldiers.

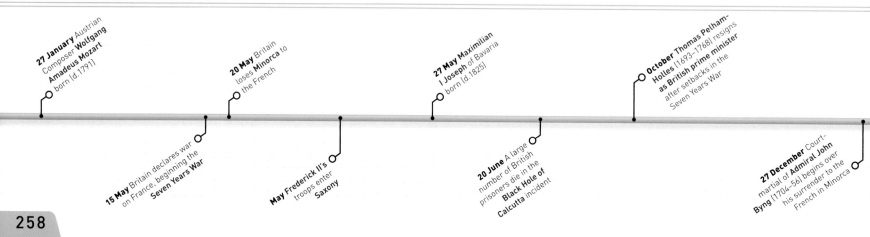

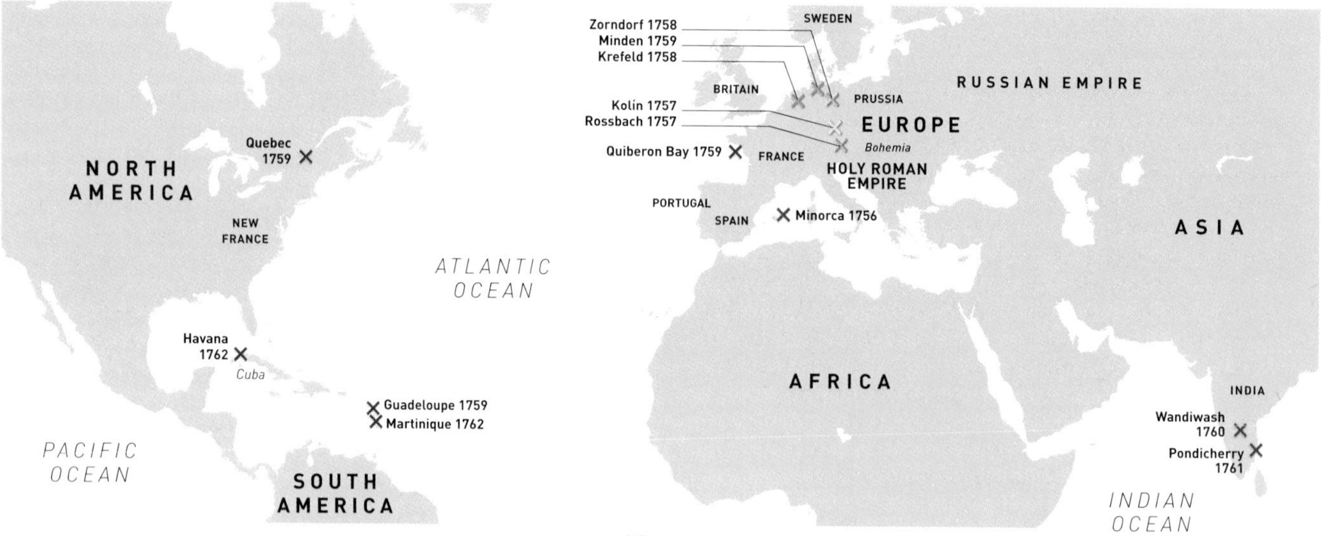

The Seven Years War

The battlefields of this conflict spanned the globe, stretching from Canada to India to Europe, making it the first global war. The coloured crosses show the victors in the key battles.

27 January Austrian Composer **Wolfgang Amadeus Mozart** born (d.1791)

15 May Britain declares war on France, beginning the **Seven Years War**

20 May Britain loses **Minorca** to the French

May Frederick II's troops enter **Saxony**

27 May Maximilian I Joseph of Bavaria born (d.1825)

20 June A large number of British prisoners die in the **Black Hole of Calcutta** incident

October Thomas Pelham-Holles (1693–1768) resigns **as British prime minister** after setbacks in the Seven Years War

27 December Court-martial of **Admiral John Byng** (1704–56) begins over his surrender to the French in Minorca

1757

Barbary pirates in an engagement with the Venetian navy.

THE BRITISH-PRUSSIAN ALLIANCE (see 1756) received a number of boosts during 1757. **Robert Clive** (1725–74) recovered Calcutta for the East India Company (see 1600) and Britain by defeating the Nawab of Bengal at the **Battle of Plassey**. The Holy Roman Emperor **Francis I** – who was married to Austria's Maria Theresa – officially declared war on Prussia. **King Frederick II** then attacked Bohemia, though he was defeated by Austrian troops. Although Prussia defeated Austro-French forces in Rossbach in November, they lost to Austrian troops in Leuthan in December.

In Morocco, **Muhammad III** (*c.*1710–90) brought stability to the country as sultan after 30 years of unrest. Muhammad was known for curbing the power of the **Barbary pirates**, who raided towns across the Mediterranean.

Robert Clive
Calcutta was recaptured for the British by Major General Robert Clive at the Battle of Plassey. The victory secured Clive's control over Bengal.

1758

Frederick II leads his soldiers to victory at the Battle of Zorndorf.

AS THE SEVEN YEARS WAR CONTINUED, the British won key victories over France by taking **Fort Duquesne** and **Louisbourg** in North America and **Pondicherry** in India (see map, opposite), and by claiming **Senegal** in West Africa. In Europe, Britain and Prussia defeated the French near the banks of the Rhine at **Krefeld** in June and Russia at the battle of **Zorndorf**, on Prussian soil, in August.

Meanwhile, in India, warfare was breaking out on a different front – between Afghans and Marathas. Territorial disputes were behind the **Afghan–Maratha War** (which continued until 1861). After the death of **Nader Shah** (1688–1747), his Persian empire began to disintegrate and Afghanistan emerged independent under the rule of **Ahmad Shah Durrani** (*c.*1722–73) who wanted to gain control of the nearby territories of the **Punjab** and the **Upper Ganges**. Durrani had sacked the Mughal city of **Delhi** the previous year. The neighbouring Marathas, who felt they should rule over the territory, then went to war against the Afghans.

In the **Arabian Peninsula**, significant – though not violent – political change was taking place as the chieftains of the **Utub** confederation elected **Sabah bin Jaber (Sabah I)** (*c.*1652–1762) emir of an emerging territory that would soon become known as **Kuwait**. His family, the al-Sabah dynasty, continues to rule Kuwait to the present day.

1759

Spain's new king, Charles III, would rule for nearly 30 years. Luis Paret y Alcázar (1746–99) depicts palace life in his painting *Charles III Eating Before his Court*.

> “ ALL IS FOR THE BEST IN THE **BEST OF ALL** POSSIBLE WORLDS. ”
>
> **Voltaire, French writer,** from *Candide*, 1759

FOR THE BRITISH THE SEVEN YEARS WAR reached a turning point. They took the French West Indian island of **Guadeloupe** in May, Canadian territory in July, and Quebec in September. They also defeated French naval forces off Portugal at **Lagos Bay** in August and at **Quiberon Bay**, in the west of France, in November. Anglo-Prussian troops defeated the French at the **Battle of Minden** in Germany in early August, although less than two weeks later Prussia faced a humiliating surrender at **Kunersdorf**, in Germany, followed in November by further defeat by the Austrians in the **Battle of Maxen** in Saxony.

In Spain, the throne was taken by the Bourbon **Charles III** (1716–88), who would become known for his reforming zeal.

Portugal, meanwhile, had grown suspicious of the activities of the Catholic **Jesuit** order (see 1533), expelling them from its territories.

Cultural developments included the publication by the Frenchman **François Marie Arouet de Voltaire** of *Candide*, a satire about mindless optimism.

ABOLITIONISM

The image of a kneeling slave and the inscription "Am I not a man and a brother?" became a famous symbol of the British abolitionist movement and was later adopted by the American Anti-Slavery Society, founded in 1833. The seal was made by Josiah Wedgwood for the Society for Effecting the Abolition of the Slave Trade. After decades of pressure, the British slave trade ended in 1807. Abolitionist groups were also established in other countries involved in slavery, such as the French *Société des Amis des Noirs.*

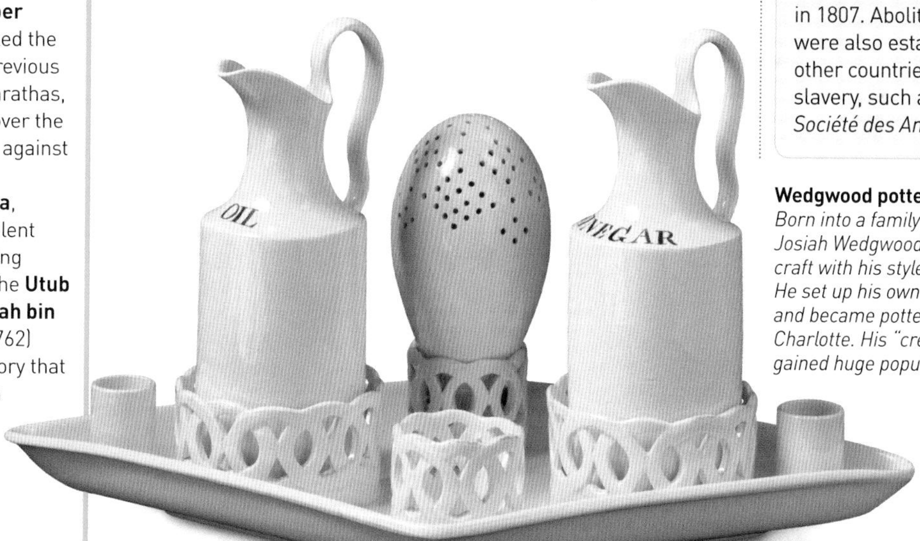

Wedgwood pottery
Born into a family of English potters, Josiah Wedgwood transformed his craft with his style and technique. He set up his own business in 1759 and became potter to Queen Charlotte. His "creamware" dishes gained huge popularity.

23 June Lord Clive (1725–74) recovers Calcutta and Bengal

Mustafa III (1717–74) becomes sultan of the **Ottoman Empire**

The Holy Roman Empire (Austria) declares war on Prussia

Afghanistan's **Ahmad Shah Durrani** (c.1724–73) sacks Delhi

Afghan–Maratha war begins over disputed territorial claims

25 August Prussia defeats Russia at **Battle of Zorndorf**

Sabah bin Jaber (1718–62) is elected emir by Utub confederation

British defeat **French** at Fort Duquense in American colonies and Gorée, Senegal, West Africa

French writer and philosopher **Voltaire** (1694–1778) publishes *Candide*

May Britain captures **Guadeloupe** from France

1 August Anglo-Prussian forces defeat France at the **Battle of Minden**

12 August Prussia defeated by Austrian and Prussian forces at the **Battle of Kunersdorf**

August Charles III (1716–88) takes the **Spanish throne**

13 September Britain captures **Quebec** from France

English potter **Josiah Wedgwood** (1730–95) sets up his own business

The Royal Botanic Gardens ("Physick Gardens") at Kew formally established

12 November Austria defeats Prussia at the **Battle of Maxen**

Jesuits are **expelled** from Portuguese territories

1760

A caricature of George III and his wife Queen Charlotte. King George III was born in Britain, which he ruled for nearly 60 years.

WHEN GEORGE III (1738–1820) TOOK THE THRONE OF ENGLAND in 1760, he was the first king from the German royal dynasty, the Hanoverians, to be born in Britain. Unlike his German-speaking grandfather, **George II** (1683–1760), English was his first language. The crown skipped a generation owing to the death of George's father, Frederick Lewis (1707–51). Before his death, he left instructions for the 12-year-old George to separate the Electorate of Hanover from England and reduce the national debt, when he took the throne.

After the death of his father, George fell under the influence of **John Stuart, Third Earl of Bute** (1713–92), who was his tutor and adviser. During the early years of George III's reign, Bute held much sway. This was especially evident in the souring of relations with **William Pitt, the Elder** (1708–78) and the Newcastle–Pitt coalition, which governed Britain during the height of the **Seven Years War** (see 1756). Most significant in this period is George III's desire to have the war come to an end, as well as have Britain distance itself from Prussia. These wishes were made manifest when Bute became prime minster in 1762.

While George III was embroiled in British and European politics, his dominions in the **Caribbean** had undergone a transformation. No longer were they imperial outposts, but wealthy sugar colonies. However, these riches depended on the use of thousands of **African slaves** to work on the plantations. The population of British America had reached two million by 1760, and of this more than 300,000 were slaves. Similarly, the slave population in France's Caribbean colonies would reach 379,000 by the end of the decade. In the Spanish sugar islands, however, Cuba had fewer than 40,000 slaves, but its sugar boom would come later.

The British island of **Jamaica** had become a large sugar producer and seen a rapid rise in the importation of slaves, many of whom ran away or rebelled. A rebellion took place on Easter Sunday in 1760, when a **revolt led by a slave** named Tacky began in St Mary's parish. It spread from there, and some 30,000 slaves participated before it was suppressed the following year.

Meanwhile, in **Qing China**, the **ongoing revolts** in the northwest frontier by **Mongol tribes**, which started around 1755, had finally been supressed. The conflict had begun after the Mongols refused to pay the annual tribute the Chinese government had demanded – indeed, the Mongols went so far as to kill the Chinese revenue collectors. However, China was eventually able to overpower the Mongols and bring thier territory under their dominion by 1760.

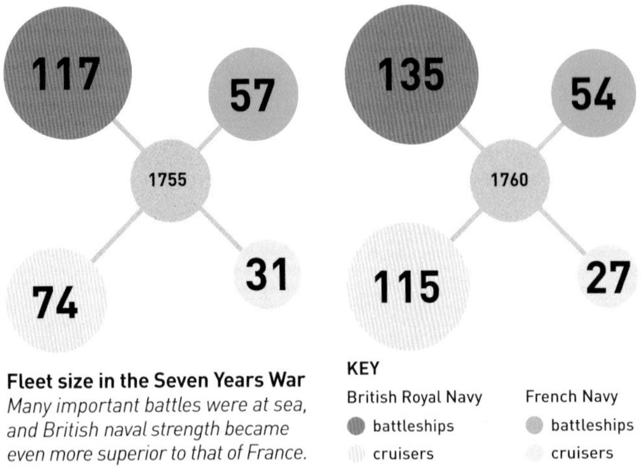

Fleet size in the Seven Years War
Many important battles were at sea, and British naval strength became even more superior to that of France.

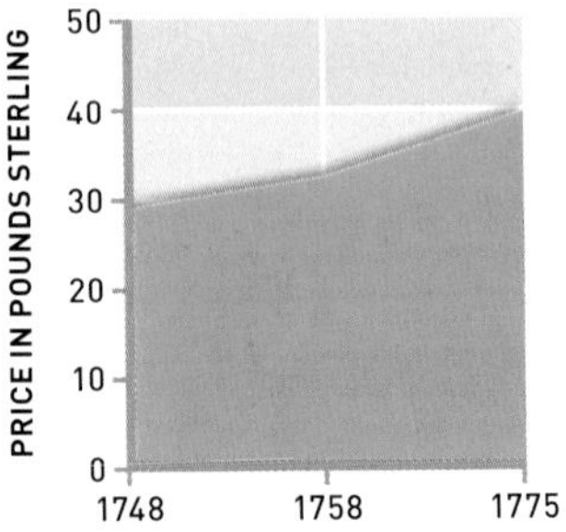

Price of a male slave
As British Caribbean colonies began to increase sugar production, they had to bring in more African slaves as labour, as did the French.

1761

Hyder Ali, the ruler of the Indian kingdom of Mysore, who became an enemy of British East India Company troops.

AS THE SEVEN YEARS WAR INTENSIFIED within Europe, it also reached a climax in the colonial possessions. The British effectively destroyed French power in India when they seized **Pondicherry** (see map, below). The port had been settled by the French East India Company in 1674 and had become one of France's main bases of operations for trade as well as ongoing fights against the British East India Company. This victory followed another one against the French the previous year in **Wandiwash**, in southeast India.

At the same time in India, the fighting between **Afghans and Marathas** (see 1758) came to a head in the battle of **Panipat**, in the north of the territory, on 14 January. The battle was bloody, with high casualty rates – some 75,000 Marathas were killed and 30,000 captured. However, Ahmad Shah Durrani, who led the Afghans, was forced by his troops to return to the throne in Afghanistan. This outcome meant that the Marathas and British began to divide the former Mughal territory among themselves. The war contributed to the weakening of the Maratha Confederacy and the further decentralization of its power, leading to the break-up of its kingdoms and subsequent battles over territory with Britain.

Further south, in **Mysore**, another future enemy of Britain, **Hyder Ali** (1720–82), was building up his army and consolidating his power base in order to take control of the territory.

Halfway across the world, British and French troops were fighting in the **Caribbean**. The British used the island of Guadeloupe, which they had captured two years earlier (see map, 1756), as a base from which to take Dominica from the French. The following year they stormed Martinique.

To complicate matters further, **Spain** had entered the conflict, and Britain's naval fleet was making preparations to attack Spanish ships. However, the attack plans would go beyond naval skirmishes, as British troops managed to not only invade and occupy the Cuban port of **Havana** the following year, they also used ships stationed in India to mount a similar attack on **Manila**, the capital of the Spanish colony of the Philippines.

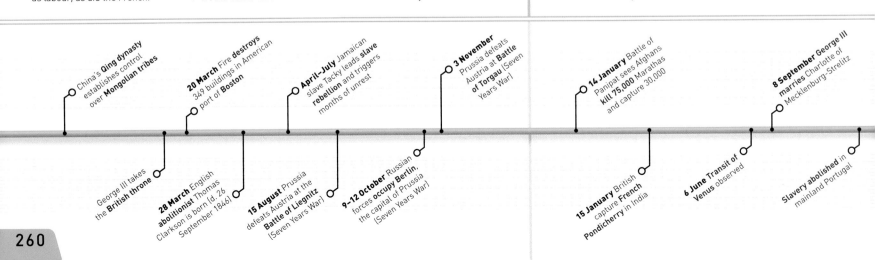

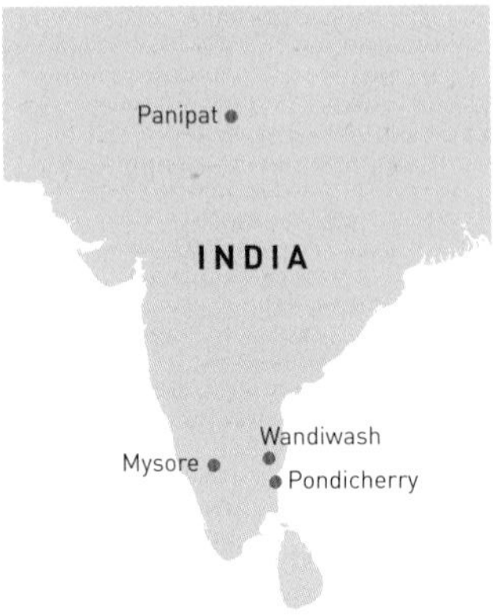

Conflicts in India
India was the site of important battles in 1761, not only for Britain and France, but also in the fight between Marathas and Afghans.

- China's **Qing dynasty** establishes control over **Mongolian tribes**
- George III takes the **British throne**
- **20 March** Fire **destroys** 349 buildings in American port of **Boston**
- **28 March** English **abolitionist** Thomas Clarkson is born (d. 26 September 1846)
- **April–July** Jamaican slave Tacky leads **slave rebellion** and triggers months of unrest
- **15 August** Prussia defeats Austria at the **Battle of Liegnitz** (Seven Years War)
- **9–12 October** Russian forces **occupy Berlin**, the capital of Prussia (Seven Years War)
- **3 November** Prussia defeats Austria at **Battle of Torgau** (Seven Years War)
- **14 January** Battle of Panipat sees Afghans **kill 75,000** Marathas and capture 30,000
- **15 January** British capture **French Pondicherry** in India
- **6 June Transit of Venus** observed
- **8 September George III marries** Charlotte of Mecklenburg-Strelitz
- **Slavery abolished** in mainland Portugal

1762

> **"** I SHALL BE AN **AUTOCRAT, THAT'S MY TRADE;** AND THE GOOD LORD WILL **FORGIVE ME, THAT'S HIS. "**

Attributed to **Catherine the Great, Empress of Russia**

RUSSIA SAW THE ARRIVAL OF TWO RULERS over the course of 1762, first with the ascension of **Peter III** (1728–62) and later **Catherine II** (1729–96), who became known as Catherine the Great. When Peter III became emperor, he made clear his support of Prussia in the Seven Years War and then pulled Russia out of the conflict. His views were deeply unpopular with ministers and the public. A conspiracy against him was quickly organized, leading to his arrest. His wife, Catherine, was installed as empress of Russia. Peter III was imprisoned, where he died in dubious circumstances. Catherine the Great's reign was marked by **Russian aggression and territorial expansion**. She introduced wide-ranging reforms in agriculture, industry, and education. She also relaxed Russia's censorship laws and was known for her love of literature and particular fondness for French philosophers and writers – including Voltaire, with whom she corresponded for 15 years.

As the Seven Years War continued, **Spain** became further drawn into events as the British occupied its key Caribbean port of Havana. In addition to this, Britain was able to use troops in India to occupy Manila, in the Philippines, which was also a Spanish colony. At the same time, **Spain and France** entered a secret agreement known as the **Treaty of Fontainebleau**. Under the terms of the treaty, Spain received France's Louisiana territory in

Catherine the Great
The German-born empress of Russia, who reigned from 1762 until 1796, oversaw the territorial expansion of her adopted country.

North Ameria, which stretched west of the Mississippi River. The treaty was partly to thank Spanish Bourbons for their support of French forces, and also to get rid of a potential drain on resources. Spain also benefited from the deal because it would block British expansion towards Spanish territory, especially nearby Mexico.

In France, the philosopher and writer **Jean-Jacques Rousseau** (1712–78) published his influential treatise, *The Social Contract* (*Du Contrat Social*) in which he examined the relationship between governments and the governed, and the question of freedom in the face of political authority. It was immediately banned by French authorities.

1763

A print of a fireworks display in London celebrating the Peace of Paris, which ended the Seven Years War.

OUT OF MONEY AND EXHAUSTED, THE EUROPEAN POWERS fighting the Seven Years War **brought the conflict to a close** with the Treaty of Paris (also known as the Peace of Paris) and the Treaty of Hubertusburg. The cost had been enormous – the lives of hundreds of thousands of soldiers, and mountains of money. Britain saw its national debt rise from £75m to £133m; Prussia raised taxes and debased the taler three times. For Austria it cost 392m gulden (the original estimate had been 28m) and French national debt rose from 1,360m livres in 1753 to 2,350m livres in 1764.

The **Treaty of Paris** involved Britain, France, and Spain. The French faced the largest losses: they ceded to Britain their territories in present-day Canada, with the exception of the islands of St Pierre and Miquelon; their territories in present-day USA east of the Mississippi River; the Caribbean islands of Grenada, Dominica, St Vincent and the Grenadines, and Tobago; Minorca in the Mediterranean; and Senegal in West Africa. They also formalized their cessation of the **Louisiana territory** to Spain. In exchange, Britain returned to France the valuable Caribbean sugar islands of Martinique and Guadeloupe; Belle Island, off the coast of Brittany; and the slave-trading island of Gorée in West Africa. France also regained its Indian factories, but they were not allowed to fortify them. The Spanish were forced to give their Florida territory to Britain, but in exchange British troops left Havana and Manilla. In Europe, France agreed to evacuate German territories.

Under the **Treaty of Hubertusburg**, the borders of 1756 were reinstated, so Austria retreated from Silesia and Prussia left Saxony, and Europe reverted to its former boundaries.

In the Ohio River valley territory, Pontiac (1720–69), a chief of the **Ottawa people**, was angered by the deal, which would put the land under British rule. In what became known as **Pontiac's Rebellion,** he led attacks against settlements, a situation that lasted until a deal between the Ottawa and British was reached in 1766.

ENLIGHTENMENT IN EUROPE

The Enlightenment was a time of questioning many established beliefs in Europe – a change in ideas reflected in the writings and other cultural output from around the mid-18th century. It is also marked by scientific curiosity and advancement. This painting by Luke Howard (1772–1864) shows a fascination with weather that led him to classify and name many cloud types.

1764

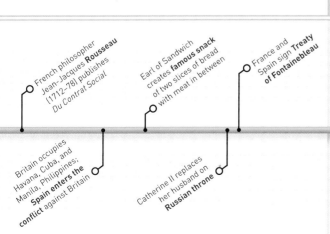

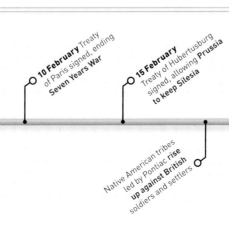

Wolfgang Amadeus Mozart, aged 8, around the time he visited Britain.

IN AN ATTEMPT TO FILL THE COFFERS DEPLETED BY WAR, the British government brought in the **Sugar Act**, which clamped down on tax avoidance on imported molasses in North America, a move that angered traders and colonists.

At this time, the musical prodigy **Wolfgang Amadeus Mozart** (1756–91) was on a three-year tour of Europe wth his family. He visited Munich, Brussels, Paris, and London where his father Leopold presented him to play at the royal courts. While in London he met the German composer **Johann Christian Bach** (1735–82), who became an important musical mentor.

French philosopher Jean-Jacques **Rousseau** (1712–78) publishes *Du Contrat Social*

Britain occupies Havana, Cuba, and Manila, Philippines; **Spain enters the conflict** against Britain

Earl of Sandwich creates **famous snack** of two slices of bread with meat in between

Catherine II replaces her husband on **Russian throne**

France and Spain sign **Treaty of Fontainebleau**

10 February Treaty of Paris signed, ending **Seven Years War**

15 February Treaty of Hubertusburg signed, allowing **Prussia to keep Silesia**

Native American tribes led by Pontiac **rise up against British** soldiers and settlers

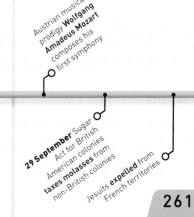

Austrian musical prodigy **Wolfgang Amadeus Mozart** composes his first symphony

29 September Sugar Act for British American colonies **taxes molasses** from non-British colonies

Jesuits **expelled** from French territories

EUROPEAN NATION STATES

PLANNING PEACE FOR A CONTINENT AT WAR

Europe at the dawn of the 19th century bore little resemblance to the peaceful political unit of co-operative countries that it has become in the 21st century. Indeed, prior to 1815, the power balances and political alliances were constantly shifting, leading to near-continual confrontation.

The Napoleonic Wars had seen Europe in a cycle of almost constant conflict for more than a decade and left Europe in a state of imbalance. To address the questions of how to reorganize the war-ravaged continent, a congress was called at Vienna in 1814. Decisions were made on what to do with the new states that Napoleon had created, such as the Grand Duchy of Warsaw (see map below), and the regions of Germany, Italy, and the Low Countries that had been annexed to France. The peacemakers aimed to avoid a repetition of the conflicts that had torn Europe apart and a spirit of conservatism and restoration prevailed – though not all deposed rulers were restored, and not all possessions lost in the Napoleonic Wars were regained.

The national boundaries resulting from the Treaty of Vienna in 1815 stayed in place for more than four decades. Fear of revolution led to a desire among Europe's statesmen to maintain the status quo. Although there were threats from liberal and nationalist elements, the Vienna system survived and disputes were largely settled by diplomacy.

1815 The Congress of Vienna's reorganization of Europe led to the creation of the German Confederation. The growth of liberalism and nationalism in Europe saw uprisings across the continent but the Vienna system held firm until the revolutions of 1848.

KEY
- Threat to Vienna system
- Internal frontiers 1815
- German confederation

NAPOLEONIC EMPIRE

When Napoleon became First Consul of France in 1799, he soon made clear his imperial ambitions by crowning himself emperor of France in 1804 and mounting military campaigns throughout Europe.

1812 Since coming to power in 1799, Napoleon had managed to dramatically extend France's power in Europe, controlling the Low Countries, parts of Germany and Italy, Spain, and Poland, though his attempts to encroach on Russia were met with a humiliating defeat in 1812.

KEY
- French territory ruled directly from Paris 1812
- Dependent state 1812

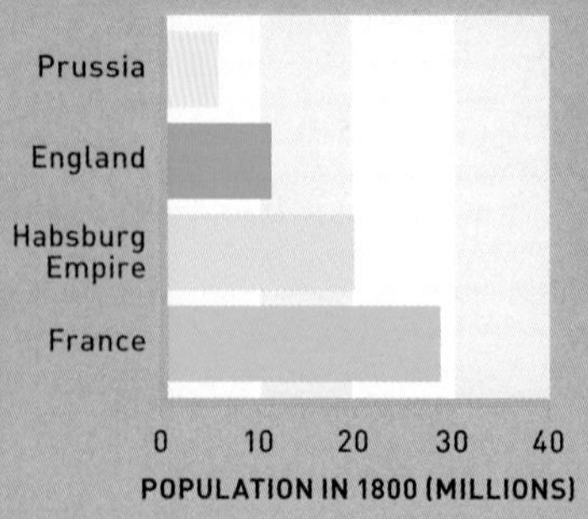

Population chart
At the beginning of Napoleon's rule, France had a far larger population than the surrounding states. This chart shows population figures c.1800.

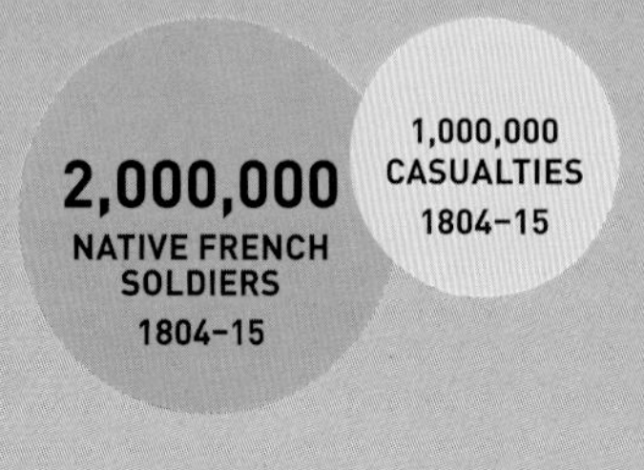

French forces
Over the course of the Napoleonic Wars, soldiers from all over the French Empire fought, and died, in Napoleon's army. At its height, it comprised nearly 600,000 men.

200
THE NUMBER OF **STATES REPRESENTED** AT THE **VIENNA CONGRESS**

A RETURN TO WAR

Many of the ongoing tensions between countries that arose in the 19th century gained momentum in the 20th. The assassination of the Austrian archduke Franz Ferdinand by Serbian nationalists in 1914 sparked World War I, a global conflict that would reshape Europe.

1914 The Vienna system was swept away by the wave of nationalism that crossed Europe from the mid-19th century. Countries such as Italy and Germany were unified by the time Europe sat on the brink of war in 1914. However, at Versailles in 1919, the map would be redrawn yet again.

KEY

- German Empire
- Austro-Hungarian Empire
- Russian Empire
- Netherlands
- France
- United Kingdom
- Norway
- Spain
- Switzerland
- Sweden
- Belgium
- Montenegro
- Portugal
- Romania
- Italy
- Greece
- Ottoman Empire
- Albania
- Luxembourg
- Denmark
- Serbia
- Bulgaria

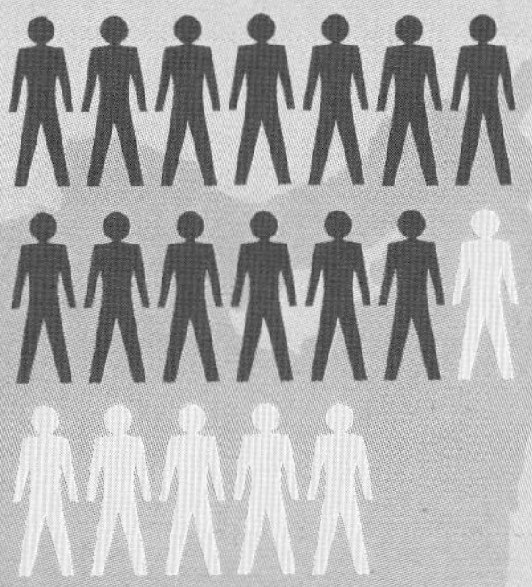

13:6 **Rival populations** *The population of the Allied countries at the outset of World War I was more than double the population of the Central Powers.*

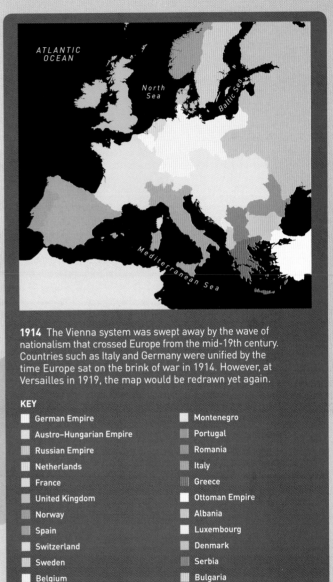

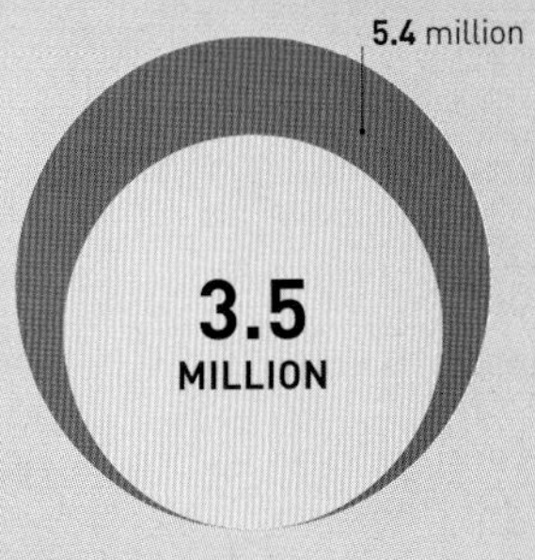

KEY

- Allied Powers: Russia, France, Britain, Belgium, and Serbia
- Germany and Austria–Hungary

Troop numbers
The Allied Powers had far greater forces to mobilize in 1914, than the armies of the Central Powers.

> “ ANY **PLAN** CONCEIVED IN MODERATION **MUST FAIL WHEN THE CIRCUMSTANCES** ARE SET IN THE EXTREMES. ”

Prince Klemens von Metternich (1773–1859), Austrian foreign minister

1765

A cartoon about the Stamp Act shows the Treasury Secretary, George Grenville, with a child's coffin bearing the words "Miss Ame-Stamp, born in 1765, died 1766".

THIS YEAR WOULD BE ONE OF GROWING DISCONTENT with colonial rule within British and Spanish colonies in the Americas. In May, the residents of the Andean city of **Quito** (in today's Ecuador) protested against the imposition of a new system of tax administration aimed at increasing revenues for Spain's depleted Treasury. The rioters drove out the royal officials, installing in their place a government that controlled the city until troops arrived a year later to reestablish royal control.

Further to the north, Britain's American colonists were growing angry at similar revenue-raising exercises. Following the unpopular Sugar Act (see 1764) was the **Stamp Act**. This piece of legislation stipulated that all American colonists would have to pay a **tax on every piece of printed paper** they used. This meant that products from legal documents to newspapers and playing cards would carry the duty. The colonists feared the tax represented a form of press censorship. They also resented the tax's introduction, not so much because of the cost, but because the Crown was beginning to look at internal American commerce and not just external trade for additional revenue, something not done before. In addition, Britain was imposing taxes without the consent of the colonists, who responded with **protests**, and the act was repealed the following year.

Meanwhile, in Lancashire, England, a weaver and carpenter named James Hargreaves (1720–78) had completed work on an invention known as the **spinning jenny**. The device was an improvement on the spinning wheel because it could power multiple spindles. Hargreaves supposedly came up with the idea for the device after observing a spinning wheel lying overturned on the ground. He realised that by creating a machine that was horizontal, more spindles could be added. The spinning jenny enabled cloth production to increase by eightfold, and other inventors continued to modify Hargreave's design to make the machine even more efficient.

In Germany, **Joseph II** (1741–90) became Holy Roman Emperor and also co-ruler of the Habsburg family lands with his mother Maria Theresa until her death in 1780. Joseph later began a programme of reform that included the emancipation of serfs and improvement of the education system, a reflection of the Enlightenment works he read. He was considered to be an "enlightened despot".

> “ IF OUR **TRADE** BE **TAXED,** WHY NOT OUR **LANDS,** OR **PRODUCE,** IN SHORT, EVERYTHING **WE POSSESS?...** ”
>
> **Samuel Adams, American politician,** on the Sugar Act, 1764

Dawn of the machine age
A woman working at a spinning jenny in an early 19th-century mill. James Hargreaves' invention revolutionized cloth production.

1766

Jacobites toast Charles Stuart – "Bonnie Prince Charlie" – in Edinburgh. Many of his supporters were Scottish.

JAMES FRANCIS EDWARD STUART DIED IN 1766 at the Palazzo Muti in Rome, having failed in his mission to be **restored to the British thrones** as James III. His birth in 1688 had initiated the Glorious Revolution, forcing his father James II (1633–1701) to take his family to France to live in exile. At the heart of the matter was the Stuart faith: **Catholicism**. After the royal family had fled, the English Parliament passed the Act of Settlement of 1689, barring any Roman Catholics from succession to the throne. The Stuarts, however, had many supporters in England, Scotland, and Ireland. They were known as Jacobites after "Jacobus", the Latin for James.

Several attempts were made to return James III, or the "Old Pretender" as he became known, to the throne, the most notable being the risings of 1715 and 1745. All proved unsuccessful. Over the course of the Old Pretender's exile his son, **Charles Edward Stuart** (1720–88) – known as "Bonnie Prince Charlie" or the "Young Pretender" – also took up his father's fight, but to little avail. Charles never recovered from his defeat at the Battle of Culloden (the last clash of the 1745 rising – see 1744–47) though he made later efforts to secure support from France and the Holy Roman Empire for further uprisings. By the time the **Old Pretender died** and Charles became the official claimant to the Stuart throne, the battle that had consumed both their lives had been lost, though admiration for the cause continued.

Bonnie Prince Charlie's star and garter
The star and garter worn by Charles Stuart indicated he was the son of a legitimate sovereign. It was awarded while the family was in exile.

In Denmark, **Christian VII** (1749–1808) **became king** shortly before his seventeenth birthday. Later that year, he married Caroline Matilda, one of the sisters of Britain's George III. His reign was marked by his **mental instability** and **debauchery**. During his early days of rule, the German doctor **Johann Freidrich Struensee** (1737–72) infiltrated the court and exercised much influence over the weak king, eventually enacting policy and having an affair with the queen. Struensee was finally arrested and executed. The later years of Christian's reign were in name only, and from 1784 his son, Frederick VI (1768–1839), acted as regent.

Stamp Act for British American colonies meet with protests

18 May A serious **fire in Quebec** destroys one-quarter of the city

22 May Riots in **Quito** start over imposition of a new tax system

Mughal emperor grants *diwani* (right to collect revenue) to **Bengal**, establishing British control of the territory

18 August Josef II (1741–90) becomes Holy Roman Emperor

December Burmese-China War (to 1769) begins when **China invades Burma** after Burmese troops enter Chinese territory

14 January Christian VII (1749–1808) becomes **king of Denmark**

January First Mysore War (to 1769) in India between the **East India Company** and **Hyder Ali**

17 March Stamp Act repealed in British American colonies followed by **Declaratory Act** asserting British authority

30 July William Pitt "The Elder" (1708–78) becomes British prime minister (to 1768)

1767

A depiction of the Jesuits being expelled from the kingdom of Spain.

Jesuit settlements in the New World
The Society of Jesus was instrumental in the settlement of territory in the Americas and by 1767 had extensive missions.

LIKE THE PORTUGUESE NEARLY A DECADE EARLIER, the Spanish Crown grew concerned about the **Jesuits** and the order's activities in the American colonies. One of the underlying causes for concern had been Jesuit resistance to paying **tithes** to the Crown, and this reluctance was symptomatic of longer-running struggles between the order and the king. At issue was the Jesuits' **growing influence and wealth** in Spanish America through their schools, extensive landholding, and agricultural success. Claiming he was "moved by weighty reasons", Charles III decided to expel the Jesuits from his realm. This enabled the Crown to confiscate valuable Jesuit land and property. Thousands of the order's members fled to the Papal States and Corsica.

1768

Captain James Cook and his crew at the watering place in the Bay of Good Success, Tierra del Fuego.

CAPTAIN JAMES COOK (1728–79) made his name in the Royal Navy with his excellent navigational skills and cartography of Canadian waters during the Seven Years War (1756–63). These accomplishments paved the way for his next assignment – an expedition to the South Pacific. The mission was organized by the Royal Society, with the Admiralty providing the ship. The *Endeavour* set off from Plymouth on 25 August and arrived in Tahiti – via Madeira, Rio de Janeiro, and Cape Horn – on 13 April 1769. Cook then headed further south encountering the island later known as **New Zealand**. He eventually sailed from there to the unknown eastern coast of Australia where he landed in what became known as **Botany Bay**. The *Endeavour* returned to England in 1771 and Captain Cook's expedition was hailed a success.

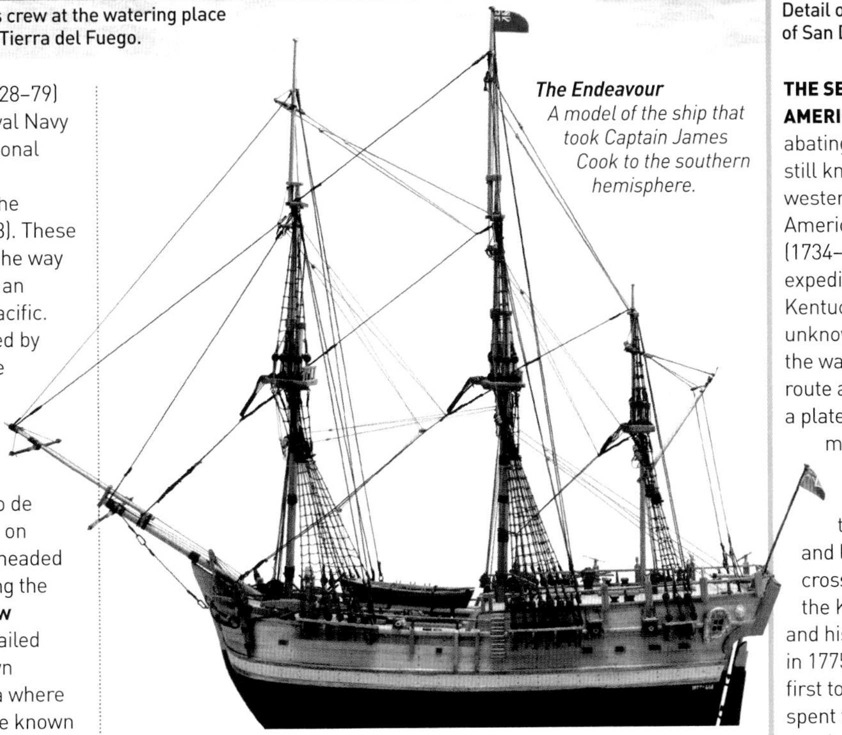

The Endeavour
A model of the ship that took Captain James Cook to the southern hemisphere.

96
THE NUMBER OF **CREW** AND **CIVILIANS** WHO SET OFF **WITH CAPTAIN COOK**

As Cook was sailing the Pacific, other changes were afoot in Britain. Reflecting the growing desire for knowledge (the Enlightenment), the first volume of the **Encyclopaedia Britannica**, was published in Edinburgh. It was "compiled upon a new plan in which the different Sciences and Arts are digested into distinct Treatises or Systems". It soon sold out and by 1771 a three-volume set was completed.

Meanwhile, in London, former soldier **Philip Astley** (1742–1814) opened a riding school in 1768 called **Halfpenny Hatch** based in Lambeth, where he performed tricks on horseback in a ring. He added musicians, acrobats, and clowns to provide entertainment during the interludes, and the **modern circus was born**.

In Russia, events had taken a serious turn. Tensions with the Ottoman Empire had pushed the two into the **Russo-Turkish War** of 1768–74. The root cause was Catherine the Great's refusal to comply with the treaty ending the previous war with the Ottomans (1736–39), as well as her interventions in Poland. The Ottomans declared war after Russia sacked a Turkish town.

Further east, **Prithvi Narayan Shah** (1723–75) brought together kingdoms in the Kathmandu Valley to create the kingdom of **Nepal**.

1769

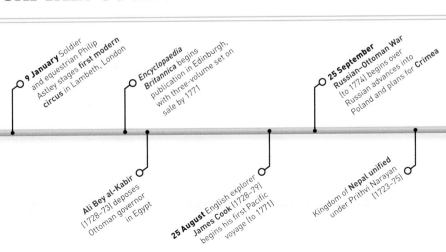

Detail of the bell tower at the Mission of San Diego de Alcalá in California.

THE SETTLEMENT OF NORTH AMERICA showed no sign of abating, though its inhabitants still knew very little about the vast western territory. In 1769, an American named **Daniel Boone** (1734–1820) set off for a hunting expedition in present-day Kentucky, an area virtually unknown to white settlers. Along the way he worked out a better route along the Cumberland Gap, a plateau in the Appalachian mountains. This became part of the Wilderness Road, a trail blazed by Boone and the Transylvania Company, and later used by settlers to cross the mountains and reach the Kentucky territory. Boone and his family moved to Kentucky in 1775 and established one of the first towns, Boonesborough. He spent the rest of his life working as a hunter and explorer.

The **Spanish**, too, were looking to expand their territory in North America. They had claimed a region in present-day southern California that **Charles III** was eager to populate with Spanish settlers after rumours that Russia was planning to move into the area. To this end he sent Franciscan friars to establish missions in the region. Spanish Franciscan **Junípero Serra** (1713–84) began work on a series of missions throughout Spain's California territory. The first one, established in 1769, was **San Diego de Alcalá**, and over the course of the next 54 years a chain of 20 further missions was built along the California coast.

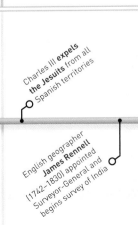

- Charles III **expels the Jesuits** from all Spanish territories
- English geographer **James Rennell** (1742–1830) appointed Surveyor-General and begins survey of India
- **9 January** Soldier and equestrian Philip Astley stages **first modern circus** in Lambeth, London
- ***Encyclopaedia Britannica*** begins publication in Edinburgh, with three-volume set on sale by 1771
- **Ali Bey al-Kabir** (1728–73) deposes Ottoman governor in Egypt
- **25 August** English explorer **James Cook** (1728–79) begins his first Pacific voyage (to 1771)
- **25 September Russian–Ottoman War** (to 1774) begins over Russian advances into Poland and plans for **Crimea**
- Kingdom of **Nepal unified** under Prithvi Narayan (1723–75)
- Former English wig-maker **Richard Arkwright** (1732–92) invents **water-powered spinning frame**
- Scottish inventor **James Watt** (1736–1819) patents **steam engine**
- **French East India Company** dissolves

1770

An engraving depicting the violence of the Boston Massacre.

AFTER THE FAILURE OF THE STAMP ACT (see 1765) the British government was still left with the question of how to raise money in the colonies. The answer came in a series of acts formulated by the Chancellor of the Exchequer, **Charles Townshend** (1725–67). The legislation included duties on paint, paper, glass, lead, and tea imported to the American colonies, as well as a reorganization of customs to cut down on smuggling. In addition, another act suspended the New York legislature because it refused to comply with the **Quartering Act**, which demanded that colonial assemblies provide basic necessities for British soldiers in the territories. On 5 March, a group of dock workers began to harass some British soldiers on patrol near a customs house in Boston, and a crowd formed. More soldiers arrived and opened fire on the colonists – the majority of whom were unarmed – killing five and wounding a further six. This episode became known as the **Boston Massacre** and fuelled resentment between Britain and its American colonies.

In Europe, the Dauphin of France, the future **Louis XVI** (1754–93), married the daughter of Maria Theresa of Austria, **Marie Antoinette**. They were aged 15 and 14 respectively at the time.

Marie Antoinette miniature
A cameo of Marie Antoinette, who would become one of the most infamous queens of France.

14

THE AGE AT WHICH **MARIE ANTOINETTE** MARRIED LOUIS XVI

1771

The Cromford Mill set up by Richard Arkwright in Derbyshire.

THE BIRTH OF THE INDUSTRIAL REVOLUTION came a step closer when Englishman **Richard Arkwright** (1732–92) worked with clockmaker John Kay to develop a **spinning frame**. By 1771 they had decided to use a waterwheel to power it – hence the name "**water frame**" and built a factory – Cromford Mill – in northern England, making this the first **water-powered textile mill**. The venture was a success and the textile factories became profitable, leading Arkwright to open a series of factories in Engand and Scotland.

Arkwright's inventions are considered an important part of the **Industrial Revolution**, which transformed Britain from an agricultural economy to a manufacturing one. The mills saw the development of the **mass-production** factory system which would be adopted all over the world.

INDUSTRIAL REVOLUTION

The Industrial Revolution was an economic transformation that took place in Europe during the late 18th and early 19th centuries, changing rural, agrarian economies to ones based on manufactured goods, which were often made in cities. This transformation began in England, and was facilitated by the arrival of inventions such as the spinning jenny (see 1765) and the use of steam power (see 1775), which led to the growth of industries such as textiles in cities like Manchester. New technologies soon spread throughout Europe, and other countries such as France, Germany, and Belgium were seeing similar economic shifts as agricultural workers left the countryside for jobs in growing urban centres, or to work in the coal mines that powered the urban factories.

1772

A engraving showing the assassination of Gustavus III of Sweden (bottom), whose constitution and reforms angered the nobility and led to his death.

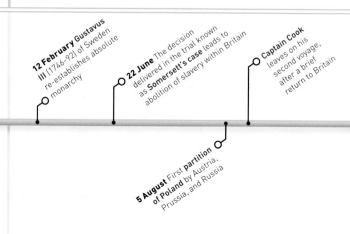

Partition of Poland
Russia, Austria, and Prussia recieved parts of Poland in the first partition.

POLAND FACED the first of three **partitions** of its territory. This resulted from **Russia's defeats of the Ottoman Turks** in the Russo-Turkish War (see 1768), which had alarmed **Austria** and **Prussia.** Frederick II aimed to shift Russian expansion from Turkish territory to the Polish–Lithuanian Union, which was weakened by civil war. On 5 August, Russia, Prussia, and Austria signed a **treaty** – ratified by the Polish legislature (Sejm) – depriving Poland of a third of its land, of which all three powers took a share.

In Sweden, **Gustavus III** (1746–92) took the throne, though the monarchy had been weakened by a government faction wishing to limit the Crown's power. In response, Gustavus staged a coup and issued a new constitution. He introduced judicial reforms and strengthened Sweden's navy. However, he was unpopular with the nobility, of whom he was critical, and was denounced for his expenditure of public funds. He was assassinated in 1792.

In England, a legal case was mounted over a slave, **James Somersett**, who had been brought from Jamaica to England in 1771 and was due to be sent back. The Lord Chief Justice, Lord Mansfield, ruled Somersett must be freed. This set a precedent that people could not be taken out of England against their will.

- **5 March** Five colonists killed in **Boston Massacre** anti-British riots
- **19 April** Marriage of France's **Louis XVI** (1754–93) to **Marie Antoinette** (1755–93)
- **29 April Captain Cook** arrives at Botany Bay, Australia
- Belgian inventor **John-Joseph Merlin** (1735–1803) develops forerunner of modern **wheelchair**
- **5–7 July** Russians beat Turks at naval **Battle of Chesma**
- **12 July** English carpenter and weaver **James Hargreaves** (1720–78) patents the **spinning jenny**, which he invented in 1765
- **Richard Arkwright** sets up the first **water-powered mill** in Derbyshire, England
- **17 October Mozart** premiers his opera, *Ascanio in Alba*, aged 15
- **12 February Gustavus III** (1746–92) of Sweden re-establishes absolute monarchy
- **22 June** The decision delivered in the trial known as **Somersett's case** leads to abolition of slavery within Britain
- **5 August** First **partition of Poland** by Austria, Prussia, and Russia
- **Captain Cook** leaves on his second voyage, after a brief return to Britain

1773

This painting by Vasily Perov shows Cossack leader, Emelyan Pugachev, holding court and passing judgement on his enemies.

BRITAIN'S AMERICAN COLONISTS were becoming increasingly agitated by the number of restrictions being placed on them – even if some had unexpected benefits, such as a reduction in the price of tea. Indeed, because of the **Tea Act of 1773**, which allowed direct exportation from India to North America, as well as having it taxed at source rather than upon arrival, American colonists would pay less than anyone in Britain for their tea. However, there were many colonial merchants who dealt in smuggled tea and so faced ruin if legal tea became cheaper than their contraband goods. They put pressure on East India ships to not dock in American ports. The *Dartmouth*, however, proceeded to anchor in Boston. On 16 December, angry traders took 342 chests of tea worth £10,000 from the *Dartmouth* and tipped it into the city's harbour. This was heralded as a key moment of resistance to British governance.

Russia also was experiencing unrest, led by a Cossack called **Emelyan Pugachev** (1742–75). Pugachev served in the Seven Years War, though he deserted in 1762. He travelled around Russia, claiming to be the deposed emperor Peter III, and promising to abolish serfdom. Through his travels he managed to rally about 25,000 willing troops. Despite early victories against Catherine the Great's army, his troops were eventually overpowered. He was executed on 10 January 1775.

The Ottoman Empire was facing upheaval in Egypt. **Ali Bey al-Kabir** (1728–73) had been Egypt's de facto ruler, but in 1769 he deposed the Ottoman governor of Egypt and tried to make the country independent. He also sent troops into the territories of Palestine and Syria, but by 1773 he was defeated by Ottoman forces and died from his wounds while in prison in Cairo.

On his ship in the South Atlantic, Captain James Cook crossed the **Antarctic Circle**. He had set out on another mission the year before, in a ship called the *Resolution*, determined to explore the vast and unknown areas of the southern hemisphere.

Boston Tea Party
Merchants dump chests of tea worth £10,000 from an East India Company ship into Boston harbour.

1774

The funeral procession of Louis XV (1710–74), whose nickname had been "the well-beloved". Louis XV ruled France for almost 60 years.

IN THE AMERICAN COLONIES, representatives from each of the 13 colonies except Georgia met in Philadelphia to discuss what to do about a slew of legislation that became known as the **Intolerable Acts**. These acts were issued in retaliation for the dumping of tea in Boston harbour (see 1773) and growing American rebellion. They stipulated that Boston harbour must be closed to all but British ships; that the colonists must house British troops if necessary; that British officials would not be tried for crimes in the colonies but in Britain instead, allowing them to act with impunity; and self-government in Boston was to be stopped. Also included was the **Quebec Act**, which enlarged the boundaries of the Canadian province, permitted a degree of self-rule through a governor and appointed councillors, guaranteed religious freedom for the many Catholic settlers, and allowed the continuation of French civil law in conjunction with British criminal law. This act added insult to injury for many American settlers. They objected to the expansion of Quebec into territory they believed was theirs, and many were suspicious of the type of government that had been installed there. The **Continental Congress** – a group of delegates drawn from each of the thirteen colonies – decided to take action, and agreed to boycott British goods and trade, sending a strong message to the English king, George III.

Louis XVI
The king of France, Louis XVI, wearing his coronation robes. He came to power aged just 17.

In France, **Louis XVI** became the king at the age of 17 after the death of his grandfather, Louis XV.

Meanwhile, fighting between **Russia** and the **Ottoman Empire** came to an end. They signed the **Treaty of Kuchuk Kainarji** in July, which granted Russia the right of free navigation in the Black Sea and recognized the Crimean Peninsula as independent, meaning **Crimea** was free from Ottoman rule. The region soon aligned itself with Russia.

The Ottomans faced further disruption with the death in October of Sultan **Mustafa III** (1717–74), succeeded by his brother, **Abdul Hamid I** (r.1774–89). When Mustafa became ruler, the empire was already in decline, as earlier economic growth had faltered. The situation was exacerbated by the costly and disastrous war with Russia.

Warren Hastings (1732–1818) becomes Governor-General of **Bengal** until 1785

Captain Cook crosses the Antarctic Circle and circumnavigates the continent

Serf risings in Russia, led by Emelyan Ivanovich **Pugachev** (1726–75)

16 December Boston Tea Party: British North American colonists dump tea into Boston harbour in protest

Abd-ul-Hamid I (1725–89) becomes Ottoman sultan

Louis XVI is crowned King of France

21 July Russia and the Ottoman Empire sign the **Treaty of Kuchuk-Kainarji** giving Russia control of much of the Black Sea coastline

Quebec Act grants more religious freedom to Catholics in North America, reinstates French civil law, and expands Quebec

Intolerable Acts authorize punitive measures against the 13 colonies

The opening shots of war between the British troops (in red) and the American colonial militia (in the foreground) on Lexington Common in Massachusetts, by English artist William Barnes Wollen (1857–1936).

> **"** LET **JUSTICE** BE DONE THOUGH THE **HEAVENS** SHOULD **FALL. "**
>
> **John Adams, American statesman,** 5th December 1777

THE ANGRY RECEPTION GIVEN TO LEGISLATION and discontent over the issue of **"taxation without representation"** in the 13 American colonies had begun to worry British officials and they feared an armed rebellion. On 18 April, General Thomas Gage (1721–87), who was also Governor of Massachusetts, sent British soldiers (known as "redcoats") to seize the guns and ammunition being stored by the colonists in the town of Concord, just outside of Boston. Aware that the British might execute such a plan, the colonists had set up a system of alerts should any event come to pass. Once news was received of the planned raid on Concord, Boston engraver **Paul Revere** (1735–1818) set off from the city that night to warn fellow organizers that British troops were on the march. Minutemen (militia who were ready to fight "at a minute's notice") grabbed their guns and waited for the arrival of the redcoats.

On the morning of 19 April the "shot heard around the world" was fired and battle ensued between colonists and British troops in **Lexington** and nearby **Concord**. The **American War of Independence** – or the **American Revolution** – had begun.

Fighting continued through the summer. Colonial forces, under the command of **General George Washington** (1732–99) captured key points near **Lake Champlain**, but the British defeated them at the **Battle of Bunker Hill** on 17 June, despite losing half their troops in the process.

Within the colonies the war was divisive. Not all colonists were willing to fight against Britain and soon people were divided into **patriots** and **loyalists**. Some 20 per cent of the population of the 13 colonies were estimated to have supported the Crown. Within this number were **American Indians** and **slaves**. In the case of the former, some tribes felt compelled to side with the British because they were valued trading partners. Many also thought their interests, such as territorial boundaries, stood a better chance of being protected by Britain. For slaves, the incentive to side with the British Crown was the possibility of **emancipation** – they had been told they would be freed if they fought for the king. Some residents, such as the **Quakers**, opposed warfare. Many others simply wanted to avoid participation in either side of the conflict.

Halfway across the world, British East India Company troops were embroiled in the domestic troubles of the Marathas (see 1758). The **First Anglo-Maratha War** (1775–82) was the result of the East India Company's intervention into the Maratha Confederacy, a union of five clans that came to power after the collapse of the kingdom of Maharashtra. This war left many issues unresolved and tensions would rise again between the British and Marathas, leading to two further wars (see 1803).

In Britain, Scottish inventor and engineer **James Watt** (1736–1819) had struck up a business partnership with Matthew Boulton (1728–1809), who owned an engineering works. Watt had improved the **Newcomen steam engine**, which had been around since the turn of the century. He developed a separate condensing chamber for the engine which meant it lost less steam and was more efficient. In partnership with Boulton, Watt began to manufacture these engines in 1775. At this point steam engines were used mostly to pump water from mines, but Watt saw more potential uses for steam and continued working on engines for the rest of his life. His inventions allowed later engineers to revolutionize transport and he effectively laid the foundations of modern industry.

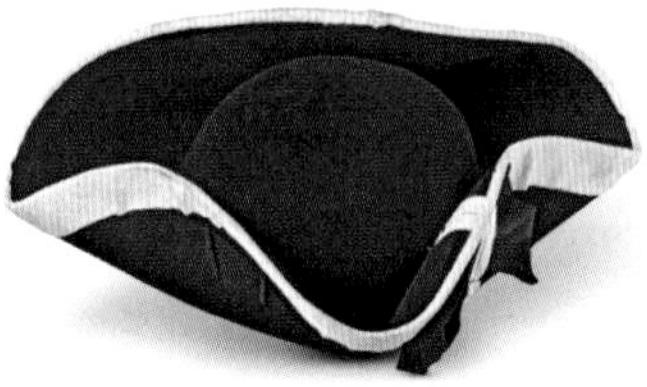

Continental soldier's hat
This style of tricorne was worn by American colonists fighting for the Continental army.

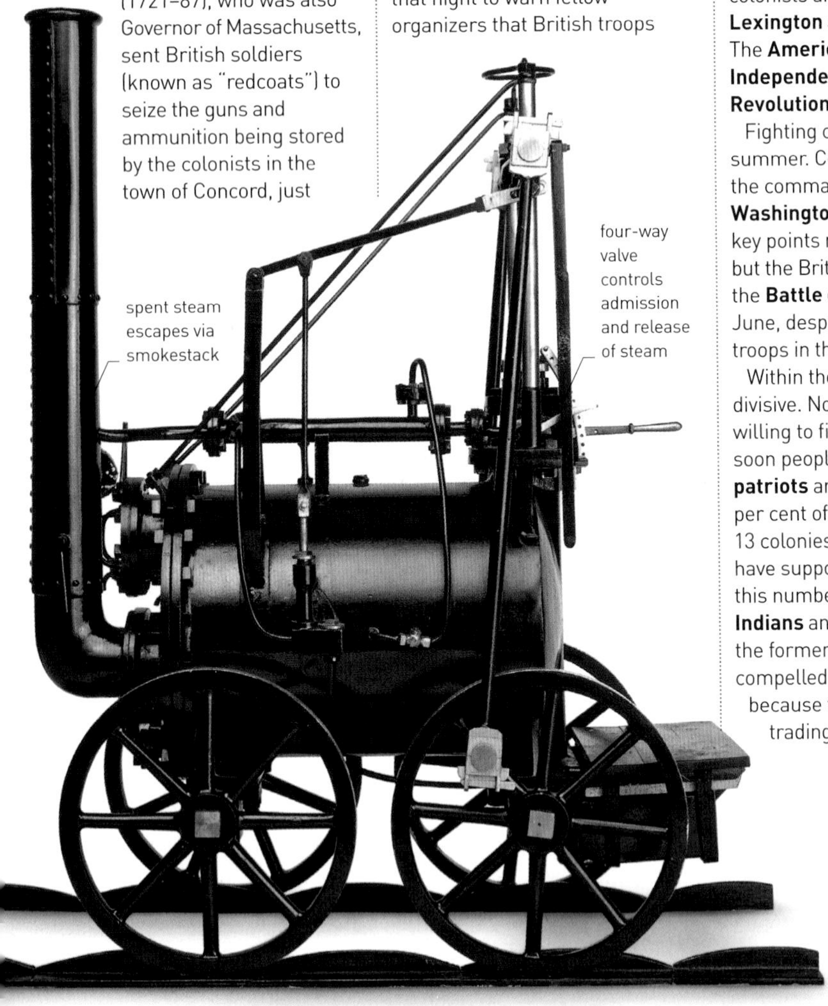

Steam power
James Watt's work on steam engines allowed for the development of steam-powered trains.

THOMAS PAINE

Thomas Paine (1737–1809) was born in Norfolk, England. He emigrated to America and advocated independence. He returned to England and wrote *Rights of Man*, defending the French Revolution, which cemented his reputation as a radical propagandist.

15 February Pope Pius VI succeeds Pope Clement XIV

19 April American War of Independence begins with battles in Lexington and Concord

30 July Captain Cook lands at Portsmouth, ending his second voyage

7 November Freedom is promised to male slaves who fight for the British in the American War of Independence

First Maratha War (to 1782) between the Maratha Confederacy and British East India Company

James Watt patents his steam engine

1776

Ecstatic colonists tear down a statue of King George III in New York in celebration of the signing of the Declaration of Independence.

" WE HOLD THESE TRUTHS TO BE SELF-EVIDENT THAT ALL MEN ARE **CREATED EQUAL;** THAT THEY ARE ENDOWED BY THEIR CREATOR WITH CERTAIN **INALIENABLE RIGHTS;** THAT AMONG THESE ARE **LIFE, LIBERTY** AND THE **PURSUIT OF HAPPINESS. "**

US Declaration of Independence, 4 July 1776

AS THE WAR FOR AMERICAN INDEPENDENCE WAS GAINING MOMENTUM, on 4 July the **First** Continental Congress issued a **Declaration of Independence**, formally announcing the separation of the North American colonies from British rule and calling this collective the **United States**. The document outlined reasons for the decision to separate from Britain while asserting certain natural rights. The ideas put forth in this declaration – that all men were created equal and had the right to "life, liberty and the pursuit of happiness" – would not, however, apply to everyone. Enslaved Africans – some of whom had been fighting on the Americans' side – were excluded.

The year 1776 also witnessed the publication of many influential works. In January, the writer and radical thinker **Thomas Paine** (see panel, opposite), who had been living only a short time in Philadelphia, issued a pamphlet entitled *Common Sense*, calling for American independence and the establishment of a republican government. The pamphlet, initially published anonymously, was hugely influential both nationally and internationally and had a significant role in furthering the cause. In Britain, Scottish philosopher **Adam Smith** (1723–90) published *An Enquiry into the the Nature and Causes of the Wealth of Nations,* which outlined the advantages of a system of free trade, changing the way politicians and the public thought about economic expansion.

Also in this year, the first volume of *The History of the Decline and Fall of the Roman Empire* by English historian **Edward Gibbon** (1737–94) was published. The work struck a chord and was a success. It was also noteworthy for Gibbon's methodology, which was objective and meticulous in his use of reference material, making it the yardstick for future historians. A further five volumes were published over the following decade.

1777

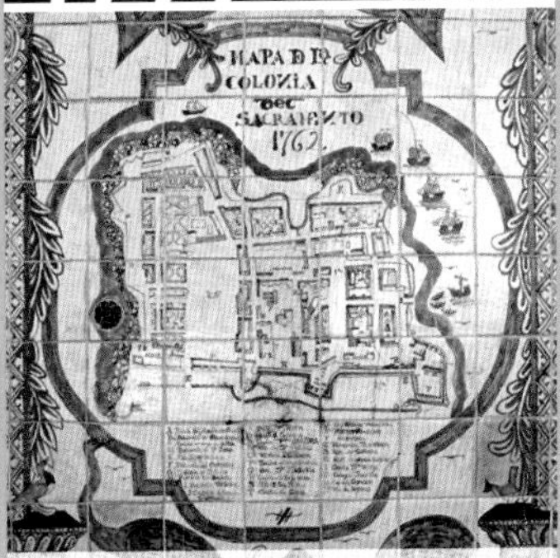

A colonial map of the city Colonia del Sacramento in Uruguay.

IN BAVARIA, there was unrest over the succession to the throne. Elector **Maximilian III Joseph** (1727–77), last of the Wittelsbach line, died, and **Charles Theodore** (1724–99), Elector Palatine was crowned. Charles had no legitimate heir but several bastards for whom he sought land. He signed a treaty with Joseph II of Austria to cede Lower Bavaria to Austria in exchange for part of the Austrian Netherlands. This angered Frederick II of Prussia and in 1778, the **War of the Bavarian Succession** broke out, ending in 1779.

Spain and Portugal finally settled ongoing disputes in the **Río de la Plata** region with the **First Treaty of San Ildefonso**. Spain ceded territory in the Amazon basin in return for control over the Banda Oriental (in present-day Uruguay).

Charles Theodor
The Elector Palatine, Charles Theodore, had no legitimate heirs though several illegitimate ones. He proved an unpopular king.

1778

A view of the opulent interior of La Scala opera house in Milan.

Clubs used against Cook
Traditional Hawaiian clubs like these may have been used in the attack that caused James Cook's death.

WITH TWO SUCCESSFUL VOYAGES TO HIS NAME, Captain James Cook (see 1773) set out for a third in 1776, this time to search for the **Northwest Passage**, a fabled Arctic shortcut that was supposed to connect the Atlantic and Pacific Oceans. By 1778 he had made the first European contact with the **Hawaiian islands**. He continued on to the Arctic circle, but failed to find the passage. He later sailed back to Hawaii, where a dispute over a missing boat led to his being killed by Hawaiians in 1779.

In **Milan**, a grand opera house was opened – **La Scala**. It was founded under the patronage of Maria Theresa of Austria (the city was under Austrian rule) to replace a theatre that had been destroyed in a fire. The new theatre was built on the site of the church of Santa Maria alla Scala and financed by wealthy patrons. It opened on 3 August with a performance of *L'Europa riconosciuta*, an **opera** by Antonio Salieri (1750–1825).

1779

A Xhosa family, from a painting by French naturalist Pierre Sonnerat.

THE RELOCATION OF THE BOERS (Dutch-speaking settlers) to remote regions hundred of kilometres north of Cape Town was causing problems for the **Xhosa** people. These tribes had settled in the territory long before the Boers' arrival. Both groups were cattle farmers and competed for rich pasture land for their herds.

Attempts were made to establish a border between the **Fish and Sundays River**, though both groups violated any agreement. Tension turned to violence, with the Xhosa raiding Boer cattle and murdering some herdsmen, possibly in retaliation for the death of a tribesman. The Boers then attacked and captured more than 5,000 head of cattle.

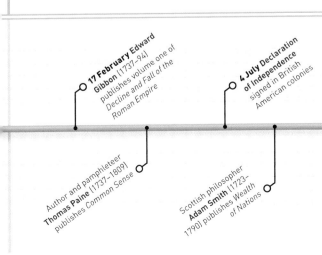

Boer house
Dutch settlers in South Africa moved away from Cape Town, deep into rural areas where they raised livestock.

These skirmishes, amounting to the first **Xhosa War**, did not resolve the root cause of the dispute – access to grazing lands and water. Intermittent battle continued for almost a century.

17 February Edward Gibbon (1737–94) publishes volume one of *Decline and Fall of the Roman Empire*

Author and pamphleteer **Thomas Paine** (1737–1809) publishes *Common Sense*

4 July Declaration of Independence signed in British American colonies

Scottish philosopher **Adam Smith** (1723–1790) publishes *Wealth of Nations*

1 October Treaty of San Ildefonso confirms Spanish possession of Uruguay and Portuguese control of Amazon land

War of Bavarian Succession between Prussia and Austria (to 1779)

6 February France formally enters **American Revolutionary War** against Britain

Knight v. Wedderburn case rules that slavery laws do not apply in Scotland

14 February Captain Cook is killed on his third voyage while in the Hawaiian islands

Xhosa Wars against British and Boer settlers (to 1879)

A mural from Daria Daulat Bagh, the summer palace belonging to Tipu Sultan, ruler of the southwestern Indian kingdom of Mysore from 1782–99.

AS BRITAIN'S EAST INDIA COMPANY attempted to extend its reach outside of Bengal, it often met resistance from Indian princely states. This was especially true of the southwestern kingdom of Mysore, which was under the rule of the powerful **Haidar Ali Khan** (1722–82). Disputes over territory and had led to the First Mysore War (1767–69), which was soon followed by the **Second Mysore War** (1780–84). The fighting did not completely settle the conflict between them, which continued until 1799.

Unrest in India was not the only military preoccupation for Britain, which was now fighting on many fronts. In addition to the ongoing war in North America, dispute broke out with the Dutch. The **Fourth Anglo–Dutch War** (1780–84), which saw no actual fighting, was a direct consequence of the conflict in America. The Dutch were supplying arms to the rebelling colonists, and a dispute erupted over Britain's seizure of Dutch ships. The Dutch maintained Britain should respect their neutrality, but the British did not agree.

The North American colonists were not alone in their struggle, as their southern neighbours in Peru took up arms in the **Túpac Amaru revolt** (1780–82), which was prompted by dissatisfaction with the Spanish colonial regime. Some 75,000 Indians and Creoles (those born in Peru but of Spanish descent) rose up in protest at their treatment. The leader Túpac Amaru II (see box, below) was captured and killed in 1781, but it took another year and 60,000 Spanish troops to quell the unrest.

In Africa, the kingdom of **Buganda**, located on the northern shore of Lake Ukerewe (Lake Victoria), emerged as a regional power as it expanded its territory. Around the same time, the **Masai**, who occupied the southeastern side of the lake, were also becoming a significant presence in the region and were moving further south and east – helped by their large, organized warrior class.

TUPAC AMARU II (*c.*1742–81)

Born José Gabriel Condorcanqui in Cuzco, Peru, around 1742, Túpac Amaru II re-named himself after the last Inca leader, who ruled the Incan Empire from 1545–1572. Of *mestizo* (Indian and Spanish) heritage, he fought against the colonial regime to gain better conditions for the indigenous population of Peru.

Lord Cornwallis, left, surrenders his sword to George Washington, right, after the British defeat at the Battle of Yorktown.

THE ONGOING WAR between Britain and North American colonists took a decisive turn at the battle of **Yorktown**, Virginia, on 19 October. The **Continental Army** had received a boost from French support the previous year, and the **Comte de Rochambeau** (1725–1807) led troops alongside the American **General George Washington** (1732–99). Their combined force of ground soldiers meant that when rebel forces took their positions on 28 September **General Charles Cornwallis** (1738–1805) was outnumbered by more than two to one, and his hoped-for reinforcements failed to arrive in time. That, along with a French naval blockade, meant Cornwallis had no option but to surrender. Although this was the last major battle of the **War of Independence**, official recognition of American independence would not come until later.

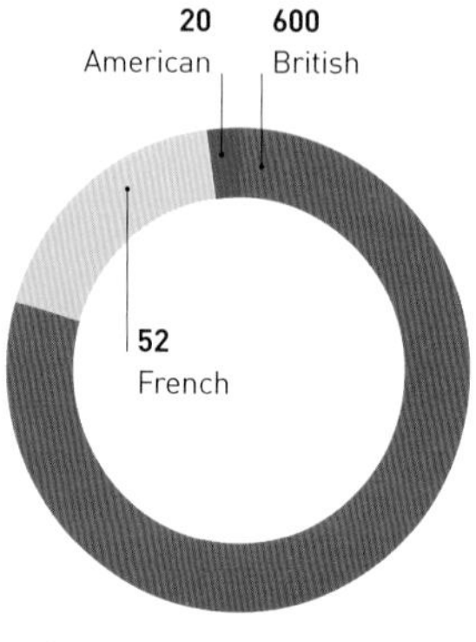

Deaths at the Battle of Yorktown
Yorktown took a high toll on British troops and proved decisive in the quest to end British rule in America.

The politics of the American colonies was changing. The **Articles of Confederation** had been ratified earlier in the year, on 1 March. The process of ratification had started in 1777 under the **Second Continental Congress**. The agreement set up a "firm league of friendship" for what were to be known as the **United States of America**, while outlining what the responsibilities of the central government would be. The document would eventually be replaced with the US Constitution (see 1787).

In Europe, tensions between the Dutch and British led to a convoy of British ships setting off from India on 9 August with orders to destroy Dutch settlements in **Sumatra**. When the British arrived, the small Dutch population in the outposts surrendered immediately and all the Dutch factories and warehouses in **Padang** were turned over to the British crown.

Meanwhile, colonial subjects in the **Viceroyalty of New Granada** – which comprised present-day Colombia, Venezuela, Panama, and Ecuador – were discontent with the Spanish regime. They revolted over mounting taxes on tobacco and alcohol in what became known as the **Comunero Rebellion**. Plans to march on Bogotá were abandoned after a deal was reached over taxes but the Spanish viceroy then attacked the *comuneros* and killed two of their leaders.

Revolution of an intellectual kind was taking place in Prussia with the publication of the *Critique of Pure Reason* by the philosopher **Immanuel Kant** (1724–1804). His work challenged existing notions about the nature of knowledge.

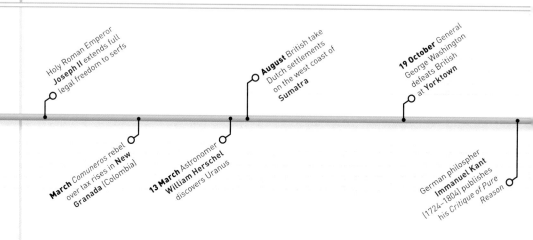

American riflemen
This cartoon depicts an American rifleman as worn out and badly equipped. However, these soldiers defeated British regular troops.

> **"SCIENCE IS** ORGANIZED **KNOWLEDGE. WISDOM IS** ORGANIZED **LIFE."**
>
> **Immanuel Kant, German philosopher,** from *Critique of Pure Reason*, 1781

Second **Anglo–Mysore War** triggered over the Nawab of Arcot's debt payments (to 1784)

Túpac Amaru leads indigenous rebellion in Peru (to 1781)

Buganda emerges as major power in Central Africa

English language *Bengal Gazette* first published

British declare war on the Dutch (to 1784) for supplying French and Spanish arms to American troops

Holy Roman Emperor **Joseph II** extends full legal freedom to serfs

March *Comuneros* rebel over tax rises in **New Granada** (Colombia)

13 March Astronomer **William Herschel** discovers Uranus

August British take Dutch settlements on the west coast of **Sumatra**

19 October General George Washington defeats British at **Yorktown**

German philosopher **Immanuel Kant** (1724–1804) publishes his *Critique of Pure Reason*

1782

Chakri Mahaprasad Hall in Bangkok was built under Rama I.

WHILE THE VICTORIOUS FORMER COLONIES OF NORTH AMERICA entered into complicated and protracted negotiations with Britain over their official recognition and their future, **Ireland** found that it was also in a position to receive a **new political settlement** from the British government. The Declaratory Act of 1720 and Poynings' Law of 1494 were repealed. These laws had been designed to place Ireland under the rule of the English Parliament. With many of the restrictions in these Acts lifted, Ireland was able to establish some degree of **legislative independence**. Despite the new freedoms, however, political participation was only open to **Protestants**, and the unrest this arrangement eventually prompted in the largely Catholic territory meant that self-rule had a short life span.

In **Siam (Thailand)**, a new ruling dynasty was established – the **Chakri** – after a power struggle following the demise of the previous ruler, **King Taksin**, who had left no heir. The Chakri remains Thailand's ruling house. It was established by **Rama I** (1737–1809), who had been the chief commander in the army and had won loyal support fighting against the Burmese. Rama I spent much of his reign on the **reconstruction of Siam** after years of warfare, building extensively, including a royal palace and Buddhist temples, though he remained a strong military leader, and repelled five further invasions from Burma.

1783

This bronze frieze depicts the signing of the Treaty of Paris in 1783, in which Britain recognized the independence of its former American colonies.

NEARLY TWO YEARS AFTER THE SURRENDER at Yorktown, the **Treaty of Paris**, which formally ended the **American War of Independence**, was finally signed on 3 September between Britain and its former American colony, calling for them to "forget all past misunderstanding and differences". The document gave formal recognition to the United States and established the boundaries of the 13 states that it comprised. Although the settlement saw the establishment of the United States, there was still a significant European presence, with Spain holding large territories to the west.

A further treaty was signed between Britain, France, and Spain, in which Britain surrendered **Tobago** and **Senegal** to France and agreed to Spain retaining **Minorca** – which it had regained the year before – and its territories in **Florida**.

In a small village called Annonay, in the southeast of France, two brothers were about to make aviation history. On 4 June, **Joseph** (1740–1810) and **Etienne Montgolfier** (1745–99) had the first public trial of a **hot air balloon** officially recorded. Only a couple of months later, and after some design modifications, they gave a demonstration of their balloon in front of Louis XVI and Marie Antoinette at Versailles. In the 19 September flight – one of several flights made in 1783 – they put a sheep, a duck, and a rooster in the balloon's basket to see how the animals would fare at a high altitude. The first manned free flight, when the balloon was not tethered to the ground, took place on 21 November of the same year.

KEY
Western Territory
United States

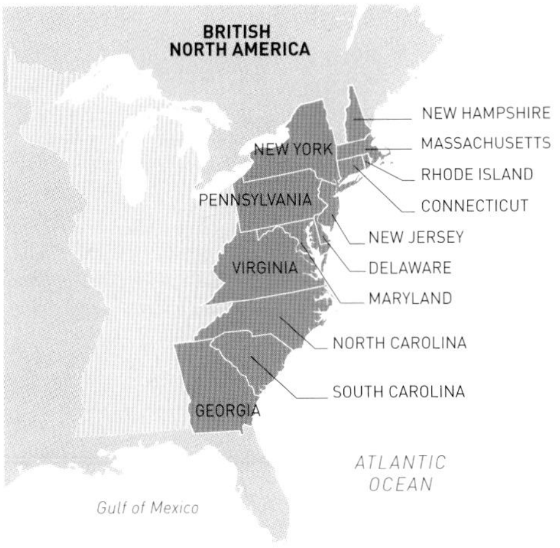

States of the Union
This map shows the 13 original United States as recognized by the Treaty of Paris. US borders were extended to the Mississippi River under the treaty.

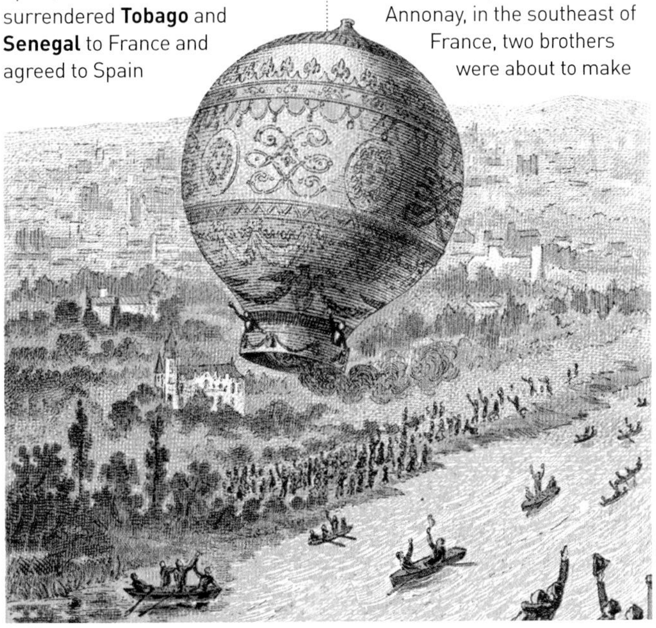

Balloon ride
This engraving shows a later Montgolfier balloon, named Le Flesselles, *ascending over Lyon with seven passengers, on 19 January 1784. One of those onboard was Joseph Montgolfier.*

1784

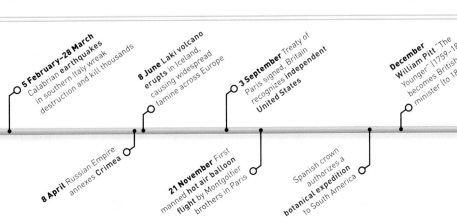

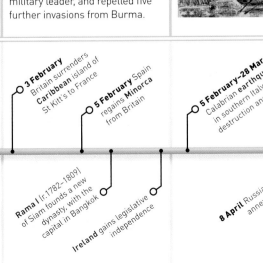

A cartoon depicts the political implications of the India Act.

BECAUSE THE BRITISH PRESENCE IN INDIA had evolved through the East India Company (EIC), the 18th century saw a growing tension between the EIC and the British government. The **India Act 1773** had already brought the company under tighter control, but its demands for government money to cover the cost of its many battles had prompted further action. The **India Act 1784**, which was ushered in under the government of British prime minister **William Pitt the Younger** (1759–1806), placed the EIC under even more scrutiny by establishing a Board of Control to look after civil, military, and financial affairs, which would include members of the British government. The Act also stipulated that trade and territorial rule were to be two separate activities. Legislation that followed in the 19th century went even further, abolishing the EIC's monopoly and opening up trade, as well as allowing the settlement of Christian missionaries in the region.

> "EVERY **RUPEE** OF **PROFIT MADE** BY AN **ENGLISHMAN** IS **LOST** FOR EVER TO **INDIA**."
>
> **Edmund Burke, British politician,** on the East India Company, 1783

3 February Britain surrenders Caribbean island of St Kitt's to France

5 February Spain regains **Minorca** from Britain

Rama I (r.1782–1809) of Siam founds a new dynasty, with the capital in Bangkok

Ireland gains legislative independence

5 February–28 March Calabrian **earthquakes** in southern Italy wreak destruction and kill thousands

8 April Russian Empire annexes **Crimea**

8 June Laki volcano erupts in Iceland, causing widespread famine across Europe

3 September Treaty of Paris signed; Britain recognizes **independent United States**

21 November First manned **hot air balloon flight** by Montgolfier brothers in Paris

Spanish crown authorizes a **botanical expedition** to South America

December William Pitt "The Younger" (1759–1806) becomes British prime minister (to 1801)

Pitt's **India Act** puts more government control on East India Company

British **Loyalist settlement** founded at New Brunswick, Canada

13 December Samuel Johnson, English poet and essayist, dies (b.1709)

1785

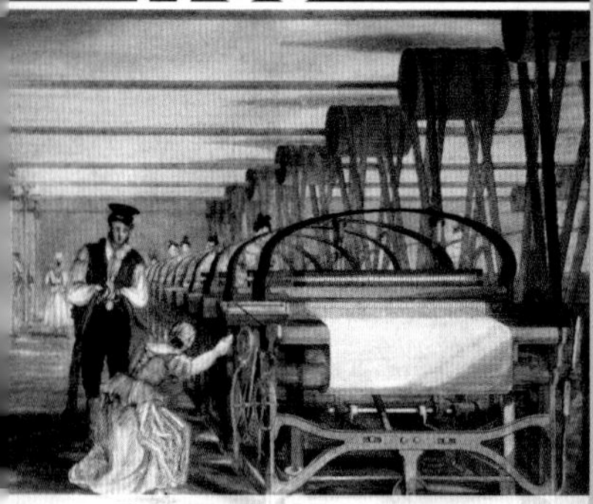

The power loom transformed the textile industry.

IN 1784, EDMUND CARTWRIGHT (1743–1823), an English clergyman, paid a visit to a cotton-spinning mill established by Richard Arkwright (see 1771). What he saw inspired him to invent similar machines to weave textiles. By 1785 he had patented his first **power loom**. Cartwright's loom became an integral part of the textile industry in Britain. The design was later improved by the American businessman **Francis Cabot Lowell**, who had seen the looms in operation on a visit to Britain, and its use was widespread on both sides of the Atlantic after 1820.

In Burma, the Konbaung dynasty's **King Bodawpaya** (1745–1819) had captured the coastal kingdom of Arakan the previous year. Bolstered by this victory, he decided to move to the east and invade the kingdom of Siam (Thailand), but was defeated.

Round-the-world expedition
Jean-François de Galaup, the comte de Lapérouse, was sent by Louis XVI on an expedition to map out the uncharted waters of the Pacific.

1786

Frederick II of Prussia was feared and admired throughout Europe for his military prowess.

First steamboat
John Fitch managed to take steam-engine technology and apply it to boats. However, commercial success was some way off.

THE US WAS EXPERIENCING AN ERA OF TECHNOLOGICAL innovation. In Philadelphia, Pennsylvania, inventor **John Fitch** (1743–1798) had set up the Steamboat Company with the aim of designing a steam-powered boat. Fitch found success ahead of his rivals in August 1787 when the **Perseverance** successfully sailed on the Delaware River. By 1790, a fledgling steamer service was running between Philadelphia and Trenton, New Jersey, but Fitch struggled as he had trouble attracting investors. It would take the more advanced boat designs and superior business acumen of **Robert Fulton** (1765–1815) before steamboat travel became a viable commercial enterprise.

Shipping still had its perils and **pirate** raids were common. US merchants wishing to trade in the Mediterranean markets risked attack and the **Barbary corsairs** were particularly feared. On 23 July, the US signed a treaty with Morocco which assured safe passage for US ships in exchange for trading on equal terms.

In Europe, Prussia mourned the death of **Frederick II**. He had turned **Prussia** into a formidable power, and reshaped Europe's political balance.

> **“** AN **EDUCATED PEOPLE** CAN BE **EASILY GOVERNED. ”**
>
> Attributed to Frederick II, king of Prussia

1787

This 19th-century engraving depicts the coastal settlement of Sierra Leone, West Africa.

AFTER THE RULING IN THE SOMERSETT CASE (see 1772), which established that slaves who arrived in Britain were free, many slaves were abandoned by their masters and the "**black poor**" of London were left with no means of support. Abolitionist Granville Sharp (1735–1813) arranged for a free settlement to be established in **Sierra Leone**, West Africa. The ship *Nautilus* returned some 400 former slaves to Africa. These initial settlers were later joined by slaves from **Nova Scotia,** Canada, who had fought for the British in the American War of Independence. At the same time, West Africa was still rife with other European slavers.

In the US, there was a growing call for a stronger central government and, from May to September, the **Constitutional Convention** met, ostensibly in order to amend the Articles of Confederation (see 1781). But instead, the delegates drew up a new system of government. They created a **bicameral legislature** in which all states would be equally represented in the Senate and proportionally based on population in the House of Representatives.

In Russia, designs on Ottoman territory led to the **Russo–Turkish War**, lasting until 1792.

Slave settlement
Sierra Leone is located on the west coast of Africa. Previously a trading post for slavery it became a place of settlement for freed slaves.

US CONSTITUTION

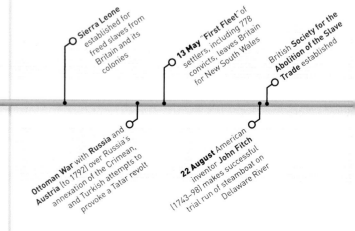

The US Constitution is the oldest written constitution in the world still in use. It was adopted on 17 September 1787 and has been amended 27 times to deal with issues such as freedom of speech. George Washington (left) led the Constitutional Convention and became the first US president in 1789. During his presidency, the first ten amendments, known as the Bill of Rights, was ratified.

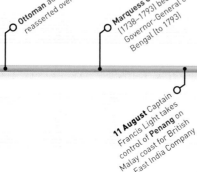

- **Edmund Cartwright** revolutionizes weaving with invention of the power loom
- **Lapérouse** sets off on his voyage to **map the Pacific**
- Burma's King Bodawpaya (1745–1819) invades Siam, triggering **Siamese–Burmese War** (to 1792)
- **Ottoman** authority reasserted over Egypt
- **Marquess Cornwallis** (1738–1793) becomes Governor-General of Bengal (to 1793)
- **11 August** Captain Francis Light takes control of **Penang** on Malay coast for British East India Company
- **17 August Frederick II**, king of Prussia dies
- **Sierra Leone** established for freed slaves from Britain and its colonies
- **Ottoman War** with **Russia** and **Austria** (to 1792) over Russia's annexation of the Crimean, and Turkish attempts to provoke a Tatar revolt
- **13 May** "**First Fleet**" of settlers, including 778 convicts, leaves Britain for New South Wales
- **22 August** American inventor **John Fitch** (1743–98) makes successful trial run of steamboat on Delaware River
- British **Society for the Abolition of the Slave Trade** established

35 MILLION PESOS

THE AMOUNT OF **MONEY SPAIN RECEIVED ANNUALLY** FROM ITS **COLONIES** AT THE TIME OF **CHARLES III'S DEATH**

A portrait of Charles IV (centre right) and his family by Spanish painter Francisco Goya (1746–1828).

AFTER ALMOST 30 YEARS ON THE SPANISH THRONE, the "enlightened despot" Charles III died, and his son, **Charles IV** (1748–1819), inherited the crown. Unlike his father, Charles IV was not a strong leader. His wife, **Maria Luisa** of Parma (1751–1819), and her political protégé **Manuel de Godoy** (1767–1851), who eventually became prime minister, ran the country and the empire, leading it into disaster. This period was marked by **constant warfare with France**, culminating in an occupation in 1808 when Charles was forced to abdicate (see 1808).

In France, as in Britain, there was growing public support for the **abolition** of slavery. The Committee for the Abolition of the Slave Trade had been established in Britain in May 1787 with the aim of ending the slave trade. Shortly afterward, in February 1788, a group of Parisian men met to set up the **Société des Amis des Noirs** (Society of the Friends of the Blacks), which called not only for the abolition of the slave trade and slavery, but also urged equality for people of mixed race, the treatment of whom was a growing issue in the French Caribbean sugar colonies.

First Fleet
Despite its reputation, only about half of those on the First Fleet were convicts. The remainder included marines, crew, and their families.

Arrival in Port Jackson
Colonists arrive in the bay that would later become Sydney, Australia. Native women are shown watching them on the shore.

Meanwhile, in Sweden, **Gustav III** was trying to realize his imperial ambitions by declaring war against Russia without the approval of parliament. He hoped to capture **Finnish** territory while the **Russians** were occupied with their **war against Turkey**. Gustav's efforts failed initially due to a conspiracy by aristocrats and officers angry at the expansion of the Crown's power at the expense of the **Riksdag** (parliament) and the nobility. Officers attempted to negotiate with Catherine the Great of Russia without Gustav's prior knowledge. **Denmark** later joined the **Russo-Swedish War** (to1790) as an ally of Russia, and laid siege to the key port of Gothenburg, in the southwest of Sweden.

In the neighbouring Habsburg Empire, the **Magyar** (Hungarian) nobles were unhappy about Joseph II's reforms (see 1765), in particular the introduction of German as the official language of government and secondary education. Joseph was also planning to restructure the land tax system, and had already abolished serfdom. By the time of his death in 1790, the Magyars were on the brink of a rebellion, and even appealed to Prussia to support them. However, their discontent did not escalate to armed conflict due to the intervention of Leopold II (1747–92), who succeeded his brother and promised to rescind the previous reforms. He swore to treat Hungary as an independent kingdom and allow for it to be administered under its own laws.

In Britain, Royal Navy Captain Arthur Phillip (1738–1814) had set sail on 13 May 1787 with 11 ships full of convicts destined for settlement at **Botany Bay** in Australia. Captain James Cook (see 1768) had first come across the bay in1770, and the British government was eager to settle the territory. At the same time, the shipping of convicts to Australia presented a way of relieving Britain's overcrowded prisons. Known as the **First Fleet**, these ships carried more than 1,400 people, with convicts making up 778 passengers. The fleet arrived in Botany Bay in 1788, but Phillip soon decided the site was not suitable for permanent settlement and the colony moved further inland to Port Jackson, which would later become known as **Sydney**. Although the early days of settlement were difficult, a stream of ships continued to bring felons, and less than 50 years later there were nearly 60,000 settlers in Australia.

18 January Captain Arthur Phillip's ship, *HMS Sirius*, arrives at **Botany Bay, Australia**.

26 January First Fleet sails from Botany Bay and lands in what will become **Sydney, Australia**.

February 9 Austria enters **Russo-Turkish War** (1787–1792)

Governor-General of India, **Warren Hastings'** trial starts over allegations of crimes committed in India

Sweden at war with **Russia** and **Denmark** (to 1790) triggered by Sweden's invasion of Russian Finland

24 July Governor-General Lord Dorchester divides **Canada** into five districts

Magyar revolt (to 1790) against Josef II in Holy Roman Empire

French abolitionists set up the **Société des amis des Noirs**

14 December Charles IV (1748–1819) takes Spanish throne

Beam engine
The engine developed by Thomas Newcomen and improved by James Watt works by the beam at the top rocking back and forth, which transfers power from a piston that moves up and down in a cylinder.

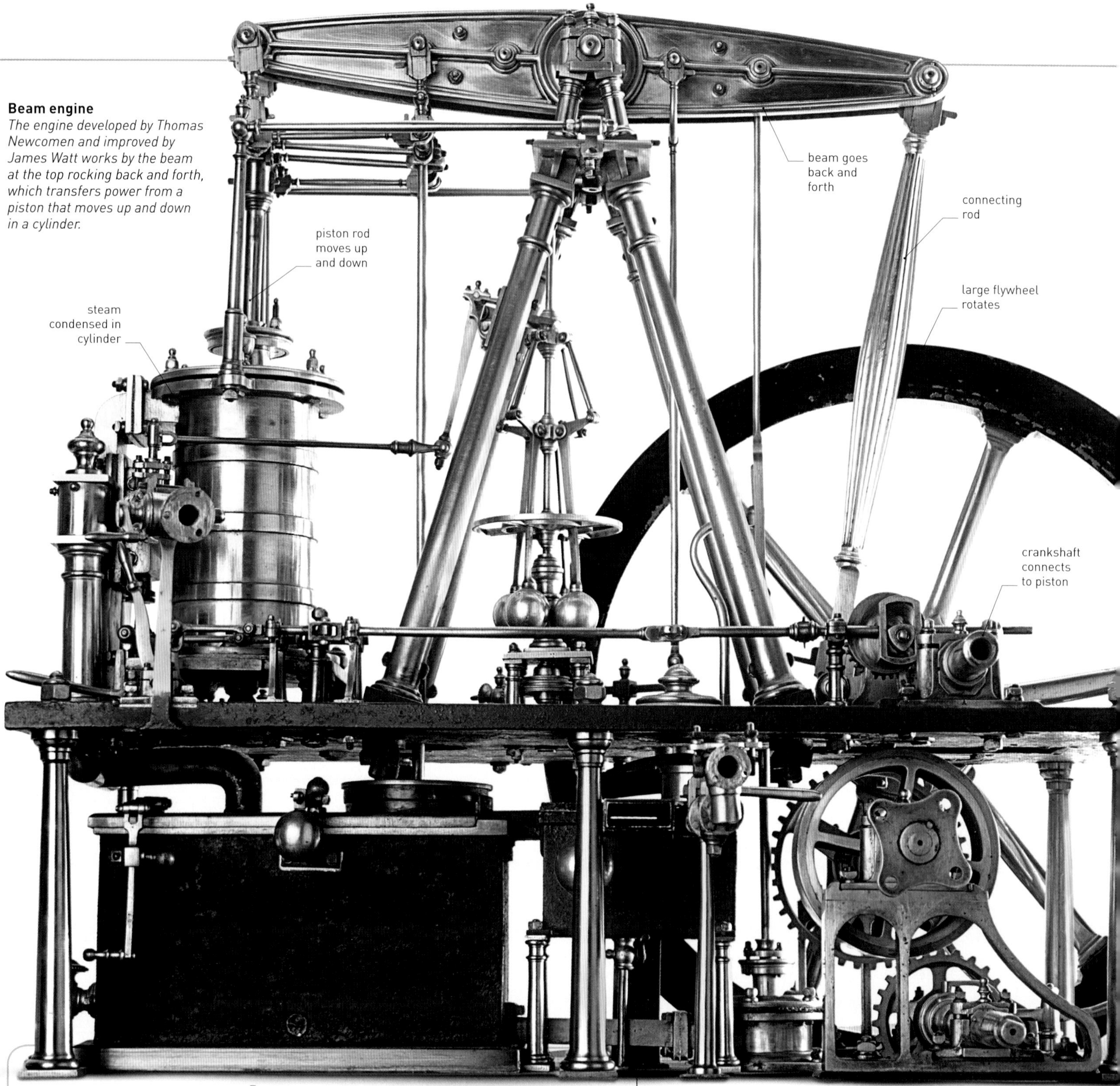

1st century CE
Hero's engine
The Greek scientist Hero describes an aeolipile, which has a rotating ball that is spun by jets of steam.

The Hero engine

1679
The first boiler
French inventor Denis Papin designs a device that can convert liquid to vapour, making it the first pressure cooker.

Papin's steam digester

1698
The high-pressure steam engine
In England, Thomas Savery uses steam power to create "The Miner's Friend" to pump water out of coal mines, though it was not a success.

1712
Newcomen's engine
Thomas Savery joins forces with Thomas Newcomen and they create the much-improved atmospheric steam pumping engine.

Newcomen's atmospheric engine

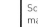

1765
James Watt's engine
Scottish inventor James Watt makes improvements to the Newcomen engine by adding a condenser, and develops an engine that rotates a shaft instead of pumping.

1769–70
The steam car
In France, Nicholas Cugot invents a road vehicle that can run on steam by converting it into piston action and rotary motion.

1801–04
Trevithick's engine
English mine engineer Richard Trevithick develops a smaller, lighter steam engine and puts it on wheels, creating a "road locomotive".

1802–07
The steamboat
In the US, Robert Fulton applies steam power to a passenger boat, and it proves a success in sailing against currents.

THE STORY OF STEAM POWER

HOW WATER VAPOUR WAS UTILIZED TO DRIVE THE INDUSTRIAL REVOLUTION

Although the power of steam was not harnessed until the 17th century, scientists had understood its potential for hundreds of years. As far back as the 1st century CE, the Greek scientist, Hero of Alexandria, had discussed a device – the aeolipile – that illustrated the possibilities of water vapour.

The aeolipile worked by heating water in a mounted sphere that had two bent nozzles. When steam was released through the nozzles, the sphere would rotate. Although it had no practical use at the time, this was the first indication of experiments with steam power. More dramatic developments took place in the 17th century, when the first boiler was invented. Although it was little more than a pressure cooker, from this point onwards, a steady stream of innovations followed.

POWERING INDUSTRY

By the 18th century, engineers had realized how steam-powered devices could be used to pump water out of mines – an important issue in light of the growing demand for coal in Europe during the Industrial Revolution. Scientists soon realized that steam could also be used to power engines. Thomas Newcomen had invented a steam engine in 1712, but it was the improvements made by James Watt that made the device more efficient. Watt's key innovation consisted of condensing steam, so that the engine did not need to heat and cool the cylinder, making it far more efficient. Soon, steam power was being used to fuel ships and locomotives, enabling them to travel farther and faster. By the 19th century, it was being used to produce electricity, something that continues to the present day, using much of the technology developed over the preceding centuries.

Richard Trevithick
As well as developing the world's first steam railway locomotive, the English engineer Richard Trevithick also adapted his high-pressure engine for use in iron mills and steam-powered barges.

> “IN THE WHOLE HISTORY OF **TECHNOLOGY** IT WOULD BE DIFFICULT TO FIND **A GREATER SINGLE ADVANCE** THAN THIS.”

L.T.C. Rolt, English writer and engineer, *Thomas Newcomen: The Prehistory of Steam*, 1963

1819
Crossing the Atlantic
The US vessel *Savannah* becomes the first ship to cross the Atlantic using steam power as well as sails. The era of sails ends soon after.

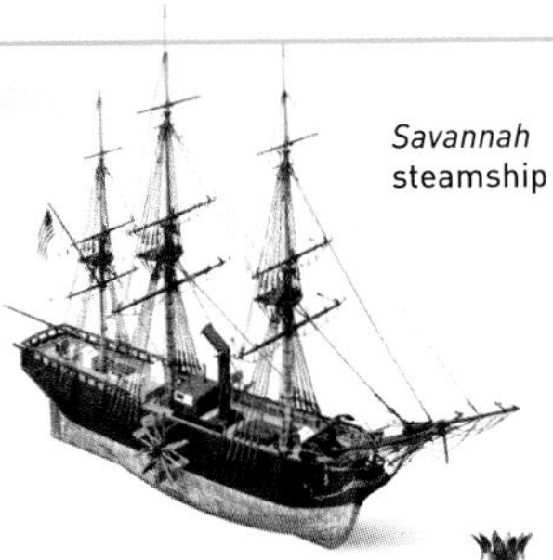

Savannah steamship

1829
Stephenson's "Rocket"
English engineer George Stephenson applies steam power to locomotives, and his "Rocket" becomes a commercial success.

Stephenson's "Rocket"

1867
The water-tube boiler
In the US, George Babcock and Stephen Wilcox invent the water-tube boiler, in which water circulates in tubes. It is used to make electricity in 1882.

Babcock and Wilcox steam boiler

1884–97
The steam turbine
Sir Charles Algernon Parsons develops a steam turbine generator, which produces huge amounts of electricity. It is used to power large ships, such as the *Titanic*.

The *Titanic* powered by Parson's steam turbine

Early 20th century
Geothermal power
Scientists in Lardarello, Italy, discover "geothermal", or "dry steam", energy and build the first power station of its kind in 1911.

Geothermal power station

20th century
Steam turbines and nuclear power
Controlled nuclear chain reactions create heat in reactors, which boils water to produce steam and drive a steam turbine in order to produce electricity.

Representatives of France's "Third Estate" – the people – swore the "Tennis Court Oath" not to separate until they had established a constitution in France.

“LIBERTÉ, EGALITÉ, FRATERNITÉ!”

"Liberty, Equality, Fraternity!"
Rallying cry of the French Revolution, 1789

BY 1789 FRANCE'S LOUIS XVI was facing multiple crises: he was bankrupt from endless warfare, there was popular unrest, and the failure of the 1788 grain crop meant riots over bread. The decision was made to summon the **Estates-General**, France's representative assembly. It had not met since 1614, so between January and April elections were held to select deputies. The Estates-General was composed of three "estates" or orders: the

The three estates
These figures (from left to right) symbolize each of the estates representing France: the nobility, the people, and the clergy.

First Estate (the clergy); the Second Estate (the nobility); and the **Third Estate – the people**. The assembly met at Versailles on 5 May. The immediate issue was how much voting power to give the Third Estate; the First and Second Estates wanted voting to be by estate rather than a vote per head, so that they would not be outnumbered by the public's representatives. By 17 June the frustrated Third Estate declared themselves a **National Assembly** and decided to proceed without the nobles and clergy. This prompted officials to lock them out of their usual meeting place, so they occupied Louis XVI's indoor tennis court and swore an oath on 20 June to remain united until they produced a constitution for France, a pledge that became known as the **Tennis Court Oath**. All but one of the 577 deputies signed; Joseph Martin Dauch from Castelnaudary refused to endorse it because it was not sanctioned by the king.

Louis XVI felt he had no option but to give in to the demands of the Third Estate and urged the nobility and clergy to join what, by 9 July, was named the **National Constituent Assembly** (though it continued to be called the National Assembly).

A few days later, Paris was awash with rumours, including that troops were on their way into the city to disperse the National Assembly. In response, on the afternoon of 14 July, some 600 people armed with weapons seized from the Hôtel des Invalides attacked the **Bastille**, a medieval fortress used as a prison. The Bastille held only seven prisoners at the time of the attack, but it symbolized the despotism of the monarchy and contained ammunition the people wanted to seize. The uprising, in which a whole garrison and 98 attackers died, became a defining moment of the **French Revolution**, which was now underway.

600

THE NUMBER OF **PEOPLE** WHO **STORMED** THE **BASTILLE**

Storming of the Bastille
The crowd of around 600 people that gathered outside the prison calling for its surrender was peaceful at first, but violence soon broke out.

During late July and early August, rumours spread throughout the French countryside, which was already in a state of unrest due to grain shortages. There were fears of bandits sweeping the land and stories of crops being burned. During this period, known as the **Great Fear**, panic set in among many peasants, who armed themselves and attacked nobles and their châteaux.

By 4 August the National Constituent Assembly sought to control the situation and so they decreed the **abolition of feudalism** and the tithe. This was followed on 26 August by the publication of the ***Declaration of the Rights of Man and of the Citizen***, which proclaimed that "men are **born free** and **remain free** and equal in rights" and that "the source of all sovereignty lies essentially in the Nation".

Throughout this period of upheaval, uncensored newspapers reported events and **political clubs** formed where people could voice their opinions. Despite the onslaught of new freedoms and monumental social reform, the Revolution was in its infancy – France's future was far from clear.

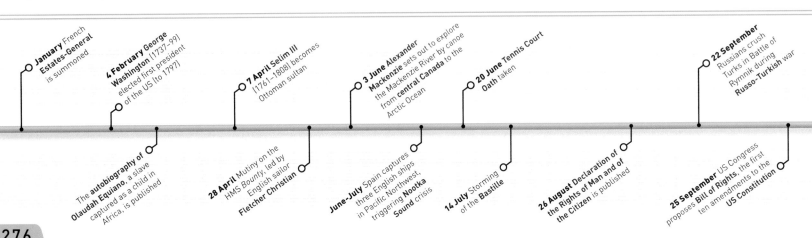

January French **Estates-General** is summoned

4 February George Washington (1737–99) elected first president of the US (to 1797)

The **autobiography of Olaudah Equiano**, a slave captured as a child in Africa, is published

7 April Selim III (1761–1808) becomes Ottoman sultan

28 April Mutiny on the *HMS Bounty*, led by English sailor **Fletcher Christian**

3 June Alexander Mackenzie sets out to explore the Mackenzie River by canoe from **central Canada** to the Arctic Ocean

June–July Spain captures three English ships in Pacific Northwest, triggering **Nootka Sound** crisis

20 June Tennis Court Oath taken

14 July Storming of the **Bastille**

26 August Declaration of the Rights of Man and of the Citizen is published

22 September Russians crush Turks in Battle of Rymnik during **Russo-Turkish** war

25 September US Congress proposes **Bill of Rights**, the first ten amendments to the **US Constitution**

1790

General Josiah Harmar met with defeat when he mounted a campaign against a coalition of American Indians in the Northwest Territory, US.

NEWS OF THE EVENTS IN PARIS spread to French colonies. As the National Assembly knew, **slavery** did not sit well with the ideas espoused in the *Declaration of the Rights of Man*. Neither did the inequity that **free people of colour** faced in France and its empire.

Part of the French empire was Saint-Domingue (Haiti), half of the the island of Hispaniola – the other half of the island, Santo Domingo (Dominican Republic), belonged to Spain. In 1790 two wealthy mixed-race planters from Saint-Domingue, **Vincent Ogé** (1750–91) and **Julien Raimond** (1744–1801) were in Paris, where they argued that because they were property owners, they ought to be given full rights. Ogé was frustrated by the Assembly's failure to confront white planters on this issue and continued his protest back in Saint-Domingue. He led a **revolt** of some 200 supporters in the town of Grande-Rivière. It was quickly suppressed, and Ogé fled to Santo Domingo.

Throughout 1790 the National Assembly continued working on a **constitution**, pushing through the official ban on the nobility and suppressing the **religious orders**.

Revolutionary cartoon
This illustration shows a version of the French Revolutionary emblem issuing the famous call for liberty, equality and fraternity or death.

In the US, General Josiah Harmar (1753–1813) had been ambushed by a coalition of American Indians. The attack near the Maumee River (Ohio) in the **Northwest Territory** was led by **Chief Little Turtle** (1752–1812). Harmar was ordered to lead an expedition against the Indians, but his force of 1,100 militiamen and 320 troops was forced to **retreat**.

> “ MEN ARE BORN AND REMAIN **FREE** AND **IN EQUAL RIGHTS. SOCIAL DISTINCTIONS** MAY BE FOUNDED ONLY UPON THE **GENERAL GOOD.** ”
>
> Article 1, *Declaration of the Rights of Man and of the Citizen*, 1789

1791

Plantations go up in flames in Le Cap in the north of Saint-Domingue (Haiti) during the slave rebellion.

IN JANUARY, VINCENT OGÉ and **Jean-Baptiste Chavannes** (*c.*1748–1791), who had helped Ogé organize the 1790 revolt, were in hiding in the Spanish colony, Santo Domingo. They were, however, returned by the Spanish to Saint-Domingue where their bones were broken on a wheel and their **heads placed on stakes**. This was met with outrage in France, and by May political rights were granted to free people of colour, if born of two free parents.

Slaves in Saint-Domingue had also been hearing a mixture of news and rumours about events in Paris and begun to hope they would see abolition. In the end, they decided not to wait for France to grant it to them.

One hot August evening, a slave leader named **Dutty Boukman** (?–1791) gathered slaves at a religious voodoo ceremony in Bois-Caïman and told them to "listen to the voice of liberty that speaks in all of us". A week later Boukman and his followers launched a **massive revolt** in the north of the island. They attacked estates, killed slave owners, destroyed tools, and torched cane fields. They had numbers on their side: the slave population in Saint-Domingue was more than 15 times the population of whites. Unlike previous revolts, this one would prove **unstoppable**.

In France, Louis XVI and his family had tried to **flee** to the royalist stronghold of Montmédy on the eastern border. They reached **Varennes**, in the northeast of the country, before being stopped and forcibly returned to Paris. After this failed attempt at escape, Louis lost all credibility as a monarch.

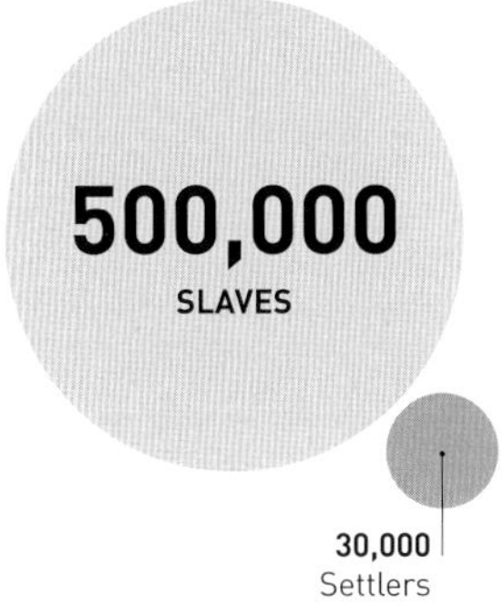

Slaves vs settlers
The high number of slaves imported to Saint-Domingue to work in the sugar industry became a liability when they launched a rebellion.

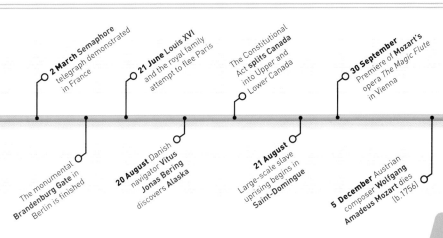

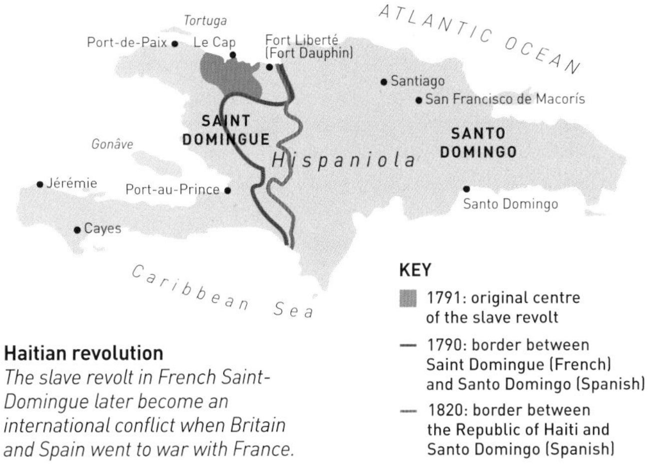

Haitian revolution
The slave revolt in French Saint-Domingue later become an international conflict when Britain and Spain went to war with France.

VOODOO AND SAINT-DOMINGUE

Haitian Voodoo (or Voudou) is a religion that was born out of slavery. It draws on a range of African traditions, especially those of Benin, the former home of many slaves. It also incorporates Catholicism, the religion forced on the slaves by their captors, and may also have links to the practices of the indigenous Arawak people. The Catholic practices slaves adopted enabled them to disguise their true religion from their masters, with Catholic saints standing in for *Loa* (spirits) worshipped in Voodoo. This new system of belief allowed slaves to form their own identity and also provided a way of organizing resistance, as in Saint-Domingue.

- **Leopold II** (1746–92) becomes emperor of the Holy Roman Empire
- **Third Anglo-Mysore War** (to 1792) leads to the defeat of Tipu Sultan (1750–99)
- **14 August Russo-Swedish War** ends with Treaty of Värälä
- **October** Vincent Ogé and Jean-Baptiste Chavannes lead first **revolt** in France's **Saint-Domingue**
- **2 March Semaphore** telegraph demonstrated in France
- The monumental **Brandenburg Gate** in Berlin is finished
- **21 June Louis XVI** and the royal family attempt to flee Paris
- **20 August** Danish navigator **Vitus Jonas Bering** discovers **Alaska**
- The Constitutional Act **splits Canada** into Upper and Lower Canada
- **21 August** Large-scale slave uprising begins in **Saint-Domingue**
- **30 September** Premiere of **Mozart's** opera *The Magic Flute* in Vienna
- **5 December** Austrian composer **Wolfgang Amadeus Mozart** dies (b.1756)

1792

A detail from the painting *Battle of Valmy*, by French artist Emile-Jean-Horace Vernet, shows Prussia's defeat by France.

EVENTS IN FRANCE TOOK A DRAMATIC TURN on 20 April 1792 when the National Assembly declared war on the Holy Roman Empire, perceiving it as a threat. Emperor Leopold II had signed the **Declaration of Pilnitz** with Frederick William II of Prussia, swearing to defend Louis XVI and destroy Paris should anything befall him. Provoked by the French call to war, Austrian and Prussian troops set off for France.

News of this enraged the French people, who thought they had been betrayed by their king and the aristocracy, and on 10 August a group of revolutionaries found **Louis XVI** when they stormed the **Tuileries Palace**. The king and the rest of the royal family were **jailed in the Temple** prison.

By early September, fears that royalist prisoners were organizing a counter-revolutionary plot were growing, and on 2 September an armed group of Parisians attacked and killed some prisoners who were being transferred to a different jail. This set off a wave of action, known as the **September Massacres**, in which angry mobs in Paris and elsewhere took suspects from prison and executed them. Around **1,200** people were killed in five days.

The war began with setbacks for France, but by 20 September, the French successfully held off the Prussians at the **Battle of Valmy**, in north-eastern France, then attacked the Austrian Netherlands winning a victory at **Jemappes** in what is now Belgium. In Paris, a new ruling body, the **National Convention**, met and the following day abolished the constitutional monarchy in favour of establishing a **republic**.

MARY WOLLSTONECRAFT (1759–97)

Mary Wollstonecraft was an English writer and early advocate for women's rights. Deeply influenced by events in France and subsequent debates in Britain, she published, *A Vindication on the Rights of Woman*, in 1792. The work, calling for the education system to allow girls the same advantages as boys, was controversial. It would be many years before any changes were enacted, but the book has endured as a work of early feminist philosophy.

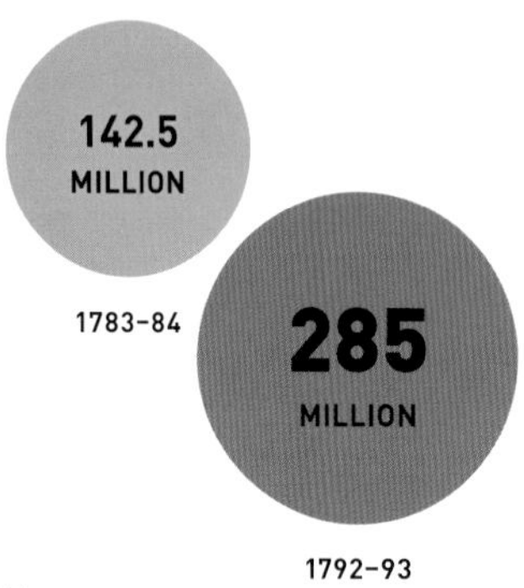

Tea export
The British public's taste for tea became evident, as the pounds of tea the East India Company exported from China doubled.

By this point the rest of Europe was concerned about events within France and its boldness beyond its borders, so Holland, Spain, Austria, Prussia, and Russia established the **First Coalition**, with Britain joining in 1793. They fought against France throughout the following six years during the **War of the First Coalition**.

Meanwhile, halfway across the world, the East India Company had found that supplying the British with **Chinese tea** – for which they were paying China in opium produced in Bengal – was proving a profitable trade. Exports doubled in a decade as the hot drink became popular in Britain and North America. Conducting business with China, however, was complicated for the Company. It was only allowed commercial access through one port, **Canton** (Guangzhou), as the Chinese kept strict controls on the entry of foreigners to the rest of the country.

1793

This image shows the execution of Louis XVI by guillotine in the Place de la Révolution, Paris. His wife Marie Antionette was executed a few months later.

ON 18 JANUARY, THE NATIONAL CONVENTION OF FRANCE condemned Louis XVI to death. On 21 January he was taken to the Place de la Révolution, Paris, where he was guillotined. His wife, **Marie Antoinette**, remained in prison until October, when she appeared before a Revolutionary tribunal. She met the same fate as her husband on 16 October.

Marie Antoinette's death occurred during the **Reign of Terror**, which was the result of a decree on 5 September that made "terror" the means of governance. A couple of weeks later the **Law of Suspects** was passed, which established **Revolutionary Tribunals**. Anyone suspected of being an enemy of the Revolution was tried and if deemed guilty received a death sentence. The activities of hundreds of thousands of people were monitored, and many were arrested. The **Committee of Public Safety**, led by **Maximilien**

Eli Whitney's cotton gin
This machine separated cotton seeds from the plant's fibre more quickly than if done by hand, which increased cotton production greatly.

16 March Attempted assassination of **Gustavus III** of Sweden, who dies from his wounds on 29 March (b.1746)

20 April War of the First Coalition (to 1797): France declares war on Holy Roman Empire, Prussia, and Piedmont

English writer **Mary Wollstonecraft** (1759–1797) publishes *A Vindication of the Rights of Woman*

25 April French national anthem, **La Marseillaise,** composed by Claude-Joseph Rouget de Lisle

September Léger-Félicité Sonthonax arrives in Saint-Domingue to quell slave rebellion

21 September France abolishes monarchy and declares itself a republic

Denmark abolishes the slave trade

21 January Louis XVI is executed

23 January Second partition of **Poland**

February Second Nootka Convention signed by **Britain** and **Spain**

France declares war on Britain, the Dutch Republic, and Spain; Britain enters fighting in **Saint-Domingue**

“ MY **PEOPLE, I DIE INNOCENT!** ”

Louis XVI of France, before his execution

This detail from a fresco depicts the battle of Raclawice on 4 April 1794, when Polish troops led by General Tadeusz Kosciuszko defeated the Russians.

Robespierre (1758–94), was, in effect, in control of the government. Members of the same political club as Robespierre – the **Jacobins** – also become involved in the surveillance of potential suspects.

In **Saint-Domingue (Haiti)**, fighting on the island was complicated by the arrival of **British troops**. Prompted by the French declaration of war in 1792, Britain hoped to seize control of the island and add it to their other Caribbean sugar islands, such as Jamaica. The struggle lasted for five years.

In the US, **Eli Whitney** (1765–1825) perfected a machine called the **cotton gin**, which he patented the following year. Many planters wanted to diversify into the cotton trade, but the long-staple variety of cotton grown – which yields long, silky fibres – could only be cultivated near the coast. Heavily seeded **short-staple** cotton – producing shorter fibres – was the only other option, but removing the seeds was a laborious and time-consuming task. Whitney's machine, however, combed cotton very quickly, and it led to the development of the cotton industry in the American South.

Back in Europe, **Poland** faced a **second partition**, this time with Prussia and Russia taking some 300,000 sq km (115,000 square miles), leaving Poland a fraction of its former size. Poland ceded eastern provinces from Livonia to Moldavia to Russia, while Prussia was given Great Poland, Torun, and the port city of Gdansk.

17,000

THE NUMBER OF **PEOPLE EXECUTED** DURING **“THE TERROR”**

Britain and Spain averted a war over the **Nootka Sound** in the Pacific, north west of the American territory, by signing the Second Nootka Sound Convention. Another agreement was signed the following year in which Spain capitulated to British demands. The diplomatic stand-off – which eventually involved the European allies of both sides – had started in 1789 when Spain seized three British ships sailing nearby. This escalated into a battle of words over who had **the right to settle** in that territory.

In China, East India Company officer George Macartney (1737–1806) had arrived in Beijing (Peking) in 1792 with a party of 94 people and a range of British goods. He was finally presented to the emperor Quinlong (1735–99) in September 1793. The British government and the East India Company were eager to expand trade between Britain and China, but Qing officials were not interested and they refused to negotiate a treaty.

THE REIGN OF TERROR in France eliminated the enemies of the Committee of Public Safety on the left and right by 1794. However, the committee felt the need to go further and suspended a suspect's right to public trial and legal assistance, with juries instructed to issue either acquittal or death. This measure was passed in June, but little more than a month later a revolt in the National Convention ended the reign of Robespierre. Known as the **Thermidorian Reaction**, this refers to 9 Thermidor Year II (27 July 1794), the date in the French Revolutionary Calendar. This change to the calendar system began in 1792 and lasted until 1806. The calendar began on the year of the anniversary of the proclamation of the Republic (21 September, also the autumn equinox). Each month was 30 days long, divided into "decades" of 10 days.

Maximilien Robespierre
The head of the Committee of Public Safety tried to eliminate his enemies, but he ended up dying on the guillotine.

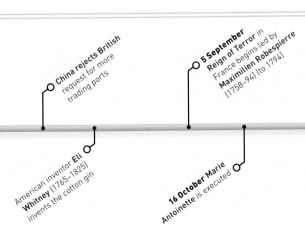

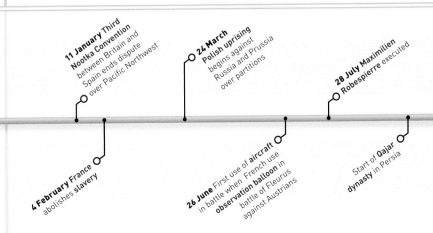

Revolutionary coin
The French king Louis XVI was replaced on the country's coinage by the figure of Hercules, flanked by Liberty and Equality.

On 27 July, Robespierre was arrested and he and another 100 supporters faced the same **guillotine** used on their enemies.

This was a turning point in the French Revolution, as the National Convention asserted its strength, but the Terror had exacted a high price – some 17,000 people were officially executed and hundreds of thousands arrested.

In Saint-Domingue, the former slave turned military leader, General **Toussaint Louverture**, was persuaded to leave the Spanish and join French Commissioner **Léger-Félicité Sonthonax** (1763–1813) to lead French Republican troops – though he later broke with the French (see 1803). Sonthonax was posted to Saint-Domingue in 1792 to keep the island under control after the slave rebellion, and to enforce the National Convention's ruling that free people of colour were to have equality. However, France's declaration of war against Britain had complicated the situation, and Spain and Britain fought alongside the former slaves. This prompted Sonthonax to look to existing slaves as possible troops. In 1793 he promised slaves in the north of the island **freedom** if they fought for the French cause, and by that August he decreed the **abolition of slavery**, ratified by the National Convention on 4 February 1794.

Meanwhile, in **Poland**, anger had mounted over the devastating partition the previous year, and patriots organized the **Polish Rebellion of 1794**. Despite an initial victory in Russian-held Warsaw, the Poles were crushed by Russia's forces.

“ I WAS **BORN** A **SLAVE,** BUT **NATURE GAVE** ME A **SOUL OF** A **FREE MAN...** ”

Toussaint Louverture, former slave and military leader

China rejects British request for more trading ports

American inventor **Eli Whitney** (1765–1825) invents the cotton gin

5 September Reign of Terror in France begins led by **Maximilien Robespierre** (1758–94) (to 1794)

16 October Marie Antoinette is executed

11 January Third Nootka Convention between Britain and Spain ends dispute over Pacific Northwest

4 February France abolishes **slavery**

24 March Polish uprising begins against Russia and Prussia over partitions

26 June First use of **aircraft** in battle when French use **observation balloon** in battle of Fleurus against Austrians

28 July Maximilien Robespierre executed

Start of **Qajar dynasty** in Persia

1795

A view of the island of Penang, north of the Dutch settlement of Malacca. The Strait of Malacca remains a key trade route linking Europe and Africa to China.

THE SECOND PARTITION OF POLAND had sparked an uprising in 1794 led by Polish officer Tadeusz Kościuszko (1746–1817) . After eight months of fighting, a Prussian–Russian alliance defeated the Poles, and the **Third Partition** of 1795 occurred. This saw the remaining Polish territory divided among Russia, Prussia, and Austria. After this final partition, Poland ceased to exist.

Elsewhere in Europe, the War of the First Coalition was drawing to a close, negotiated partially with three treaties under the **Peace of Basel**. These agreements gave German lands west of the River Rhine to France, and ended Franco–Spanish fighting around the Pyrenees mountains through Spain's cessation of Santo Domingo to France. This meant the French now had control of the whole island of Hispaniola, although the fighting that had begun in Saint-Domingue showed few signs of abating.

In **Jamaica**, the peace that had been established in 1739 between the British and former runaway slaves, known as **maroons** (from the Spanish word for runaways, *cimarrón*) ended. Maroons had initially invaded and raided colonists but, on signing a treaty that granted them land and autonomy, had largely desisted. However, in 1795, an incident in which the British severely whipped two maroons for stealing pigs, triggered a revolt. Fearful that the island could follow the example of Saint-Domingue, the governor brought in troops to suppress it. Upon surrender, some maroons were shipped to **Nova Scotia**.

Further afield, the Dutch-controlled **Cape of Good Hope** in South Africa and the port of **Malacca** in the Strait of Malacca, which connects the Indian and Pacific Oceans, were seized by the British.

300,000
THE NUMBER OF **NEWSPAPERS SOLD EACH DAY** IN **REVOLUTIONARY FRANCE** AROUND **1795**

Maroon colony, Jamaica
This engraving shows a maroon settlement in Jamaica. Maroons were former runaway slaves who had established their own autonomy.

1796

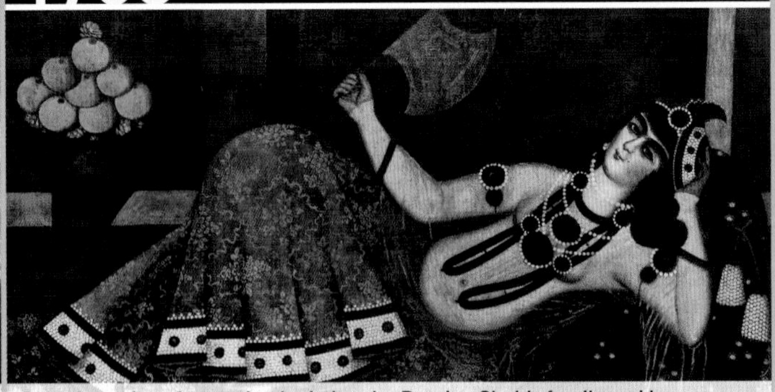

One of a series of portraits depicting the Persian Shah's family and harem. It was commissioned by Fat'h Ali Shah, the second Qajar ruler.

OVER A YEAR AFTER SETTING OUT to find the River Niger, **Mungo Park** (1771–1806), a Scottish surgeon and explorer, finally located it. He had been sent on the expedition by the Association for Promoting the Discovery of the Interior Parts of Africa, in order to "ascertain the course" of this large African river. He embarked from the River Gambia in 1795, and on 20 July, after prolonged illness and four months spent captive, he reached Ségou (in present-day Mali), which lies on the river.

The first documented inoculation was completed by British physician **Edward Jenner** (1749–1823) on 14 May. In an attempt to prevent the deadly **smallpox** virus, which had killed thousands across Europe, Jenner experimented by using **cowpox**, a similar but less lethal virus often contracted by milking infected animals. His experiment entailed inoculating eight-year-old James Phipps with cowpox taken from Sarah Nelmes, a dairymaid. The early success of this experiment led to the development of the **modern vaccine**.

In Europe, French army commander **Napoleon Bonaparte** (see panel, right) took charge of the French army in northern Italy in March. He was given orders to seize Lombardy, and went on to win many victories over the Austrian army, subsequently forcing Austria into peace negotiations. The result was the **Treaty of Campo Formio**, signed the following year, in which Austria recognized the French puppet state, the Cisalpine Republic, and ceded the Austrian Netherlands (Belgium) to France.

In **Persia**, a new dynasty – the **Qajar** – was established. The leader, **Agha Mohammad Khan** (1742–97), had spent the past decade attempting to unite disparate factions in the region, eventually asserting his authority over territory as far as Georgia in the Caucasus mountains. He declared himself shah (king) in 1796, but died the next year. His family continued to rule until 1925.

Further east, China was in the throes of a rebellion. The **White Lotus**, a secret Buddhist sect, sought to overthrow their **Manchu** rulers and restore the previous ruling dynasty, the **Ming**. The White Lotus attracted much support, but ultimately failed after eight years of fighting.

1797

A painting of Marquis Wellesley viewing an elephant fight.

A PERIOD OF AGGRESSIVE EXPANSION of Britain's territorial claims in Bengal began when Irish nobleman Richard Wellesley (1760–1842) was appointed **Governor-General of Bengal** in 1797. He left for Calcutta in November and set about increasing British territory through both military and diplomatic channels.

During his term as governor (1797–1805) some of the most powerful rulers in India were defeated – including Tipu Sultan, who was known as the Tiger of Mysore (see 1761 and 1799). This period also saw efforts to professionalize the East India Company. These included setting up a **college** in order to teach junior clerks subjects such as Indian languages, though some of these measures were considered controversial at the time.

NAPOLEON BONAPARTE (1769–1821)

Napoleon Bonaparte was born in Corsica and educated in France, where he became an army officer in 1785. His successful campaign in Italy (1796–97) was followed by further military and political victories. In 1804, he was declared emperor and led France on to more battles, though with diminishing success, draining the nation's resources and ultimately leading to his downfall. He died in exile on the remote island of St Helena, in the South Atlantic.

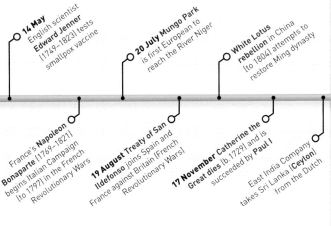

- **19 January** French conquer the Dutch and establish the **Batavian Republic** (until 1806)
- Third partition of **Poland**
- **August Second Maroon War** in Jamaica between runaway slave community and the British
- War of the First Coalition ends with **Peace of Basel** treaties
- **16 September** Dutch territory in the **Cape of Good Hope** seized by the British
- **14 May** English scientist **Edward Jenner** (1749–1823) tests smallpox vaccine
- France's **Napoleon Bonaparte** (1769–1821) begins Italian Campaign (to 1797) in the French Revolutionary Wars
- **20 July Mungo Park** is first European to reach the River Niger
- **19 August Treaty of San Ildefonso** joins Spain and France against Britain (French Revolutionary Wars)
- **White Lotus rebellion** in China (to 1804) attempts to restore Ming dynasty
- **17 November Catherine the Great dies** (b.1729) and is succeeded by **Paul I**
- East India Company takes Sri Lanka (**Ceylon**) from the Dutch
- **31 January** German composer **Franz Schubert** born (d.1828)
- **4 March John Adams** becomes second US president
- **16 November Frederick William III** (1770–1840) becomes king of Prussia (to 1840)

1798

This painting shows the destruction of the French flagship, *L'Orient*, during the Battle of the Nile, Egypt, where Britain's Royal Navy destroyed France's fleet.

DESPITE THE TERMINATION OF the War of the First Coalition in 1795, France still considered Britain an enemy. The French mooted the idea of a possible **invasion** but it was ultimately rejected due to Britain's superior **sea power** and naval defences. Seeking a way to get around the Royal Navy – as well as disrupt valuable trade – Napoleon proposed to attack the British on the colonial front in India, via **Egypt**, which he also hoped to conquer. Setting off from France, he took **35,000 troops**, capturing the Mediterranean island of Malta along the way. Upon reaching Alexandria in July, Napoleon quickly defeated **Mameluke** troops at the **Battle of the Pyramids**. However, on 1 August, French forces were completely destroyed by the British navy, under the command of **Horatio Nelson** (1758–1805) at the **Battle of the Nile**. Napoleon and his troops were left stranded in Egypt, but the defeat and humiliation did little to hamper the French commander's imperial ambitions.

10–25 THOUSAND
ESTIMATED NUMBER OF **IRISH DEAD AFTER** THE **REBELLION**

In 1796, the British had taken advantage of warfare in Europe to wrest the island of **Sri Lanka** from Dutch control, meeting with very little resistance. The British named the island off India's coast **Ceylon**, and ran its administration from Madras. By 1798, the British had begun to realize the strategic importance of the island and **Frederick North** (1766–1827) was sent there as the colony's first governor. Not all of Ceylon was under British control, however. The kingdom of **Kandy**, whose subjects occupied the interior of the island, remained independent. Their autonomy would become a cause for concern for British governors in Ceylon.

At the same time, in **Ireland**, resentment at British rule had turned to rebellion, led by nationalists called the **Society of United Irishmen**. Headed by Theobald Wolfe Tone (1763–98) and James Napier Tandy (1740–1803), the group had made numerous attempts to enlist the support of Revolutionary France, but the British, learning of these plots, had forced the rebels to change their plans. They decided to rise up, although lacking French reinforcements, and managed to seize control of **County Wexford.** A French expeditionary force sent to assist them was intercepted by British troops and the revolt soon collapsed. Tone committed suicide while awaiting his execution.

Irish Revolt
Protestant prisoners, suspected of being loyal to British rule, were executed by Irish nationalists in Wexford during the revolt.

1799

“ THE REVOLUTION IS OVER. I AM THE REVOLUTION. ”

Napoleon Bonaparte, 1799

ONCE NAPOLEON BONAPARTE had returned to France from Egypt, he began to focus on his political future, and was soon plotting a **coup d'état** that involved dissolving the Directory, the body that had been governing the country since 1795. The outcome of the **18 Brumaire Coup** of 9 November was that the Directory was replaced with the Consulate, and Napoleon took charge of France as **First Consul**.

While in Egypt, French soldiers had unearthed an object that transformed the understanding of the ancient world. A block of black **granite** inscribed with strange writing. It was named the **Rosetta Stone** after the town where it was found. It fell into British possession by 1801, although it took years of study before anyone was able to **translate** it. Eventually scholars established a relationship between the three scripts on the stone: **hieroglyphics**, demotic script (Egyptian handwriting used in everyday life), and Greek. It became clear that this discovery would permit the transcription of hieroglyphics, a type of communication not used since the 4th century CE. Deciphering the stone provided a window into Egyptian antiquity.

In India, soldiers for the East India Company emerged victorious from a violent battle with the fearsome **Tipu Sultan** (1750–99), the ruler of **Mysore**. Tipu had made alliances with French troops in India, and on this pretext the British Governor-General Richard Wellesley (see 1797) authorized the **Fourth Mysore War**, intent on driving out the French and annexing the territory. Tipu was killed in battle, and the East India Company took half of his territory.

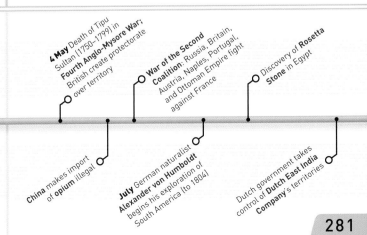

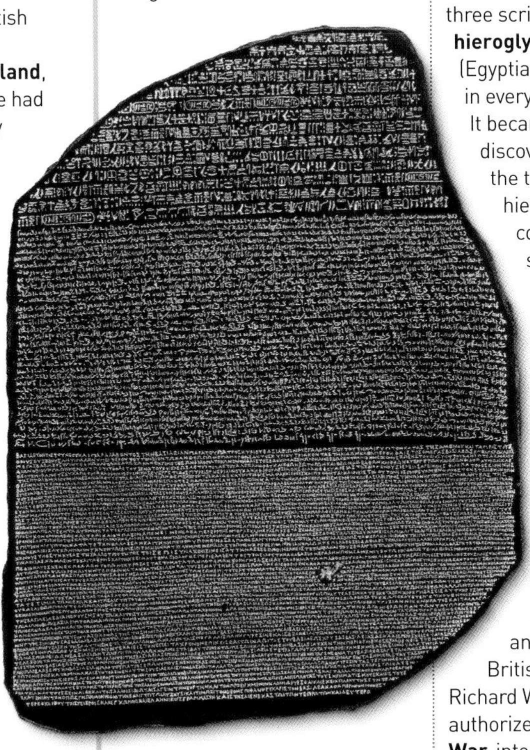

The Rosetta Stone
The translations between three different scripts on this large piece of granite unlocked the world of hieroglyphics and ancient Egypt.

Lord Mornington, later Marquis of Wellesley (1760–1842), takes up post of Governor-General of Bengal (to 1805)

24 May First fighting of **Rebellion in Ireland** against British rule

1 July Napoleon invades and occupies **Egypt** (to 1801)

14 July First **federal direct tax** law passed in the US, introducing tax on property

21 July Napoleon defeats Mameluke troops at the **Battle of the Pyramids**

1 August Napoleon defeated by British at **Battle of Nile**

English economist **Thomas Malthus** (1766–1834) publishes *Essay on the Principle of Population*

4 May Death of Tipu Sultan (1750–1799) in **Fourth Anglo-Mysore War;** British create protectorate over territory

China makes import of **opium** illegal

War of the Second Coalition: Russia, Britain, Austria, Naples, Portugal, and Ottoman Empire fight against France

July German naturalist **Alexander von Humboldt** begins his exploration of South America (to 1804)

Discovery of **Rosetta Stone** in Egypt

Dutch government takes control of **Dutch East India Company**'s territories

THE STORY OF MEDICINE

ANCIENT BELIEFS GIVE WAY TO SCIENTIFIC ADVANCES, TRANSFORMING HUMAN HEALTH

The understanding of the human body and disease made important advances during the 18th and 19th centuries, laying the foundation for modern medical care. Ancient practices, such as bloodletting to cure illness, were replaced with ones that were borne of a more rigorous scientific approach.

People have attempted to treat disease since prehistoric times, but until the 18th century medicine was based largely on superstition, natural remedies, and unscientific practices and theories, such as the theory that the body had four fluids (humours) that needed to be in balance for health. There had been progress in anatomy and surgery, but, overall, medicine remained primitive.

THE DEVELOPMENT OF MODERN MEDICINE

In the 18th century, medicine started to become more scientifically rigorous, and significant advances were made, such as the development of a vaccine for smallpox in 1796. The 19th century saw the establishment of the germ theory of disease, the introduction of antiseptic techniques and anaesthetics, and the use of X-rays to image the body. Around 1900, pharmacology began to make great progress, with the invention of aspirin in 1897 and the first synthetic antibacterial drug in 1908. During the 20th century, more vaccines and drugs were developed, such as antibiotics and anticancer drugs. Surgical techniques also became more sophisticated; successful organ transplants were performed, and keyhole surgery became routine. In diagnosis, scanning techniques were invented, and screening became widely used. From the late 20th century, genetics also began to have a significant impact on medicine as genetic causes of diseases were discovered and genetic testing was developed.

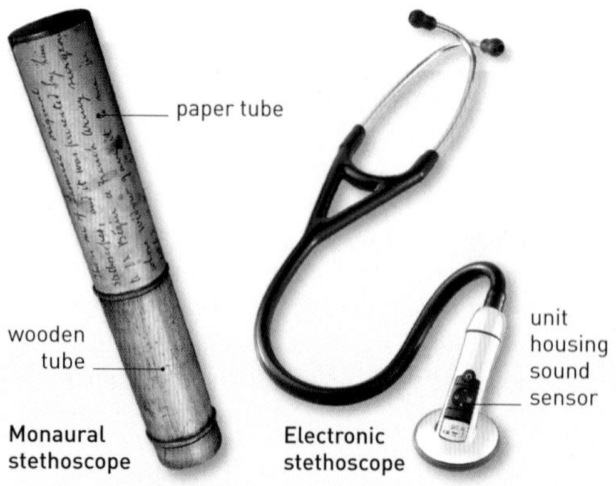

THE STETHOSCOPE

The stethoscope was invented in 1816 by French physician René Laennec, who used a simple tube (a monaural stethoscope) to listen to a woman's chest. In 1851, British physician Arthur Leared invented the binaural stethoscope, with an earpiece for each ear, and, in the 1940s, the Americans Maurice Rappaport and Howard Sprague developed the modern acoustic stethoscope, which has two "bells", one for listening to the heart, the other for listening to the lungs. The latest development is the electronic stethoscope, which uses an electronic sound sensor and amplifier.

> “ THE **DEVIATION OF MAN** FROM THE STATE IN WHICH HE WAS ORIGINALLY PLACED BY **NATURE** SEEMS TO HAVE PROVED TO HIM **A PROLIFIC SOURCE OF DISEASES.** ”

Edward Jenner, English surgeon, *An Inquiry into the Causes and Effects of the Variolae Vaccinae, or Cow-Pox*, 1798

c.5100–4900 BCE
Neolithic trepanation
Trepanation, which involves drilling holes in the skull, is used as far back as the Neolithic period to treat a variety of health problems.

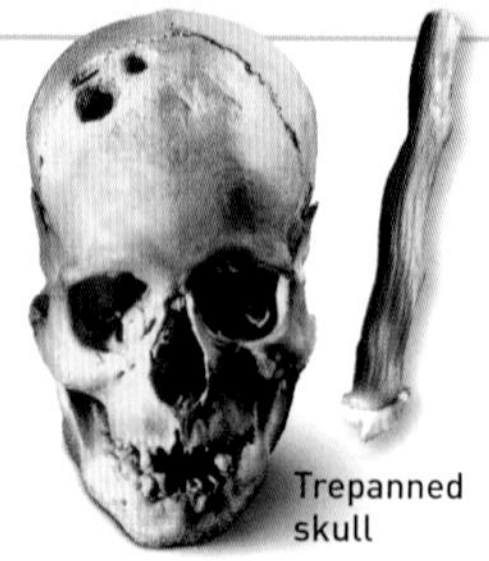
Trepanned skull

c.1550–700 BCE
Ancient Egyptian surgery
Medical, especially surgical, knowledge advances due to the practice of mummification, which gives doctors greater insight into anatomy.

Egyptian knives and curettes

c.420 BCE
Hippocrates develops diagnostics
Hippocrates, the Greek physician considered to be the father of modern medicine, moves health away from religion and into the realm of science.

c.1000–1300
Arab medical advances
The Arab world adds to medical progress with the development of pharmacists, who work with plants and use them to find new cures.

Arabic medical manuscript

1543
Andreas Vesalius
The Brussels-born surgeon writes his influential anatomical work, with accurate diagrams of human anatomy based on many dissections and operations.

De Humani Corporis Fabrica

1796
Vaccination
British scientist Edward Jenner develops a vaccine for smallpox. It was the first vaccine created for any disease, and his work saves countless lives.

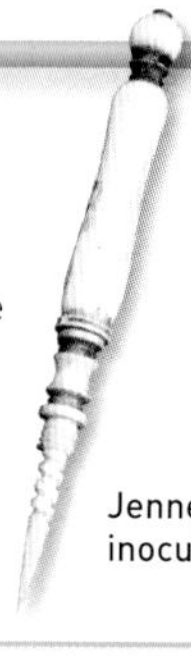
Jenner's inoculation point

1818
First blood transfusion
British obstetrician James Blundell performs the first successful human-to-human blood transfusion, using a syringe to transfer blood between the patients.

Antiseptic machine
Patented by British surgeon Anthony Bell in 1879, this device was used to make the air in operating theatres free of disease-causing microorganisms. Using a clockwork-powered fan, the machine blows antiseptic powder and carbolic acid into the air.

1865–67
Antisepsis
British surgeon Joseph Lister pioneers antiseptic surgery by using a solution of carbolic acid to kill infectious organisms during operations.

1881
Blood pressure measurement
Samuel von Basch invents a non-invasive way of measuring blood pressure using a bulb connected to an anaeroid manometer.

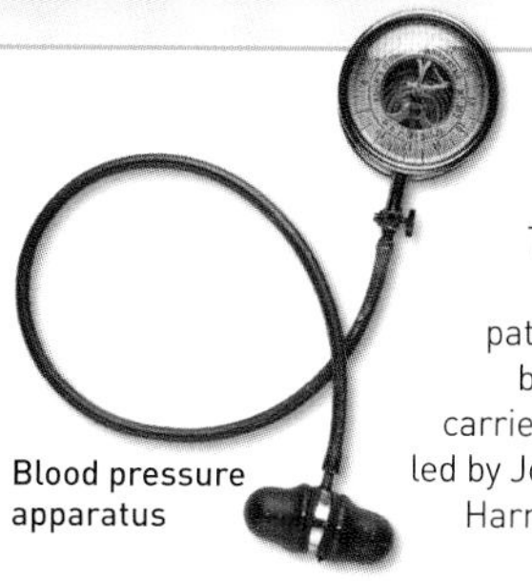
Blood pressure apparatus

1954
Organ transplant
The first successful organ transplant between living patients (a kidney transplant between identical twins) is carried out in Boston by a team led by Joseph Murray, J. Hartwell Harrison, and John P. Merrill.

Late 20th century
Keyhole surgery
Laparoscopic (keyhole) surgery becomes widely used after the first laparoscopic appendix removal using a microchip camera is performed in 1981.

21st century
Robotic surgery
Developments in robotics allow for more precise, less invasive surgery, with quicker healing and less pain for the patient.

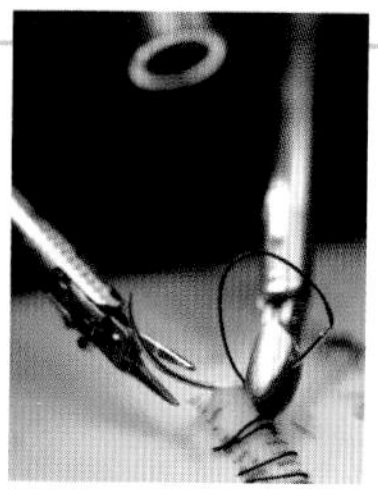
Robotic suturing

1846–47
Practical anaesthesia
In 1846, US dentist Henry Morgan publicly uses ether for anaesthesia. In 1847, Scottish doctor James Simpson uses chloroform.

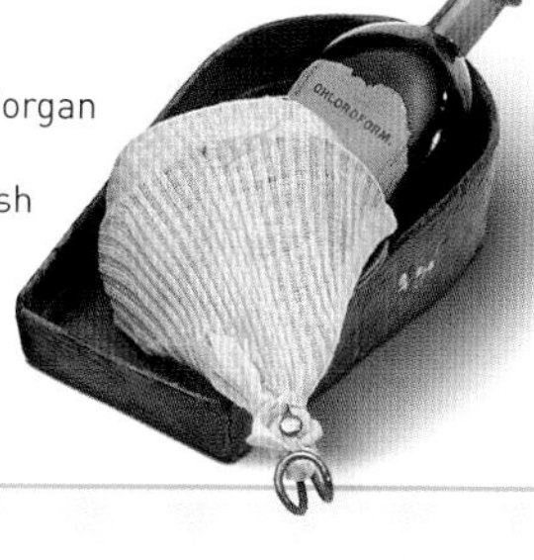
Chloroform inhaler

1901
Blood types identified
US scientist Karl Landsteiner publishes his discovery of the four main human blood groups (A, B, AB, O), which allows for more successful transfusions.

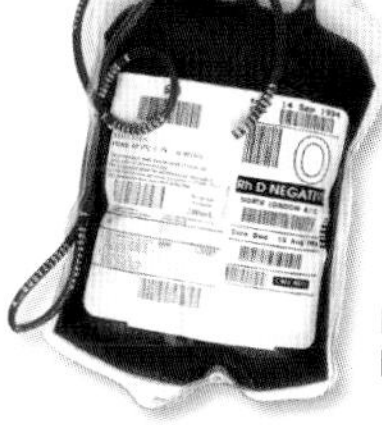
Blood bag

1971 and 1977
CT and MRI scans
British scientist Godfrey Hounsfield invents the first commercial CT scanner in 1971. The first MRI scan of a human is carried out in 1977.

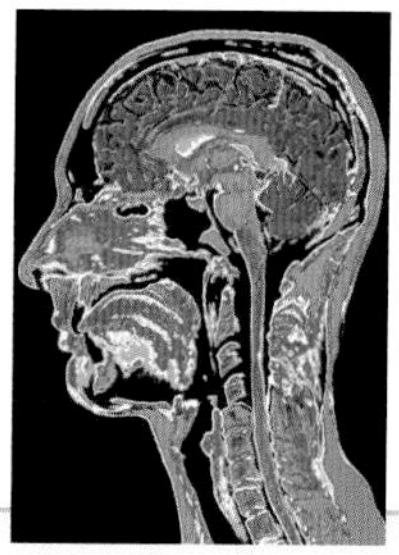
MRI scan

1800

The Battle of Marengo was a victory for France over Austria.

AS A NEW CENTURY BEGAN, unrest in Europe continued. Despite previous treaties, French military action increased in aggression. Mistrust of France prompted the formation of the **Second Coalition** in 1798; by 1799, it comprised Austria, Britain, Russia, Portugal, Naples, and the Ottoman Empire. On 14 June, Napoleon scored a significant victory against Austria in the **Battle of Marengo**, the result of which was French control of northern Italy.

Spain, meanwhile, had done little to develop its Louisiana territory in North America, lacking the resources to settle it. So when Napoleon put pressure on Charles IV to return Louisiana, the Spanish monarch obliged. Under the terms of the secret **Treaty of San Ildefonso**, Napoleon agreed not to give the land to a third power.

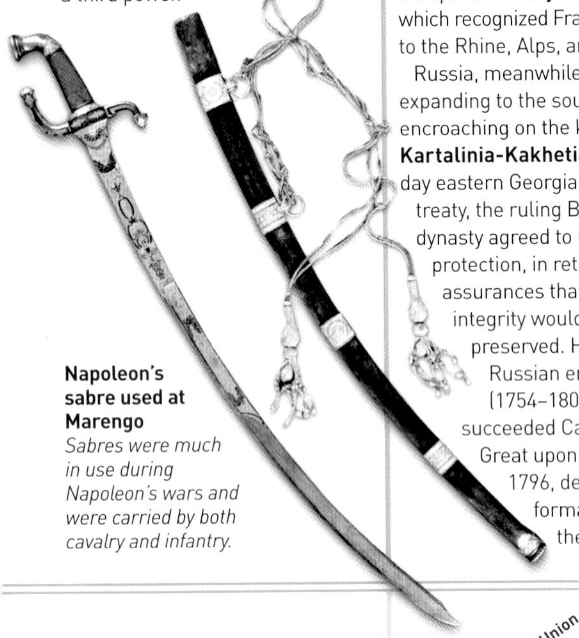

Napoleon's sabre used at Marengo
Sabres were much in use during Napoleon's wars and were carried by both cavalry and infantry.

1801

An engraving depicting peace celebrations in Milan, Italy, after the Treaty of Lunéville, in which Austria was forced to recognize France's growing borders.

IN THE AFTERMATH OF THE IRISH REBELLION (see 1798), British prime minister William Pitt the Younger concluded that the solution to the "Irish question" was a political union. In 1800 a bill outlining these plans was presented to the Irish parliament. After much controversy, the bill was passed. The **Act of Union**, also approved by the British Government, came into effect on 1 January 1801. It saw the Irish parliament closed down and representation moved to London, where 32 Irish peers were put in the House of Lords and 100 MPs in the House of Commons. Pitt had hoped the move would allow the granting of concessions to Catholics, but the bill maintained a ban on their holding public office.

In Europe, Austria's defeat at Marengo in 1800 forced them to accept the **Treaty of Lunéville**, which recognized France's frontiers to the Rhine, Alps, and Pyrenees.

Russia, meanwhile, was expanding to the south, encroaching on the kingdoms of **Kartalinia-Kakhetia** (present-day eastern Georgia). In a 1783 treaty, the ruling Bagratid dynasty agreed to Russian protection, in return for assurances that its territorial integrity would be preserved. However, Russian emperor **Paul I** (1754–1801), who had succeeded Catherine the Great upon her death in 1796, decided to formally annex the territory.

THOMAS JEFFERSON
(1743–1826)

Virginia-born planter and slave-owner Thomas Jefferson was a leading republican and one of the primary authors of the United State's Declaration of Independence. He remained politically powerful all through his life, serving as vice-president (1797–1801) and president (1801–09). Yet for all the influence of his writings on issues like liberty, he did not free his own slaves during his lifetime.

In Vienna, composer **Ludwig van Beethoven** (1770–1827) finished composing his Piano Sonata 14 in C-sharp Minor Op. 27 No 2, known as the "***Moonlight Sonata***", which became one of his most famous works and is thought to be dedicated to his pupil, the Countess Giulietta Gucciardi, who did not return his affections.

The United States saw the election of **Thomas Jefferson** (see panel, above) as the country's third president.

1802

The mausoleum of emperor and Nguyen dynasty founder, Gia Long.

AFTER 30 YEARS OF CIVIL WAR, Vietnam was united under the leadership of **Nguyen Phuc Anh** (1762–1820), a powerful general who, with the help of French mercenaries, was able to defeat the rival Trinh family. Nguyen Anh declared himself emperor, taking the name **Gia Long**, and re-established the Nguyen family as the ruling dynasty.

Ongoing warfare in Europe and further afield came to an end with the **Treaty of Amiens.** Signatories included Britain, France, Spain, and the Netherlands (which was known as the Batavian Republic from 1795 until 1806).

Under the terms of the treaty, Britain kept the colonies of **Trinidad**, which had been taken from Spain, and **Ceylon**, which had been captured from the Dutch. **Egypt** was restored to the Ottoman Empire, and France agreed to relinquish **Malta**. This state of affairs was short-lived.

France and Britain at the table
A political cartoon of Britain's William Pitt and France's Napoleon Bonaparte carving up the globe around the Peace of Amiens.

1803

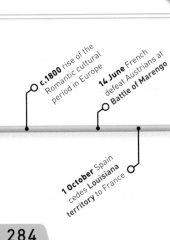

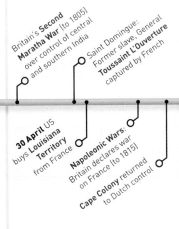

Jean-Jacques Dessalines who fought for Haitian independence.

IN SAINT-DOMINGUE (HAITI), THE ONGOING WAR TOOK A DECISIVE turn with the capture and exile of **General Toussaint Louverture** in 1803. He had joined the French Republican cause ten years earlier (see 1793) and drove out the remaining British forces on the island, before taking up the title of **governor** in 1801. Napoleon was, however, displeased with Louverture's successes and was infuriated when he defied orders, riding into Santo Domingo – then under French control – and freeing the slaves. In 1802, Napoleon **reinstated slavery** and sent 25,000 troops to reclaim the island. After months of fighting Louverture was invited to negotiate a settlement. He was then seized and exiled. The battle for abolition then fell to his deputy **Jean-Jacques Dessalines**.

With most of Napoleon's troops in Saint-Domingue killed on the battlefield or ravaged by **yellow fever**, Dessalines' men drove out the remaining soldiers. French reinforcements were held up by a British **blockade** of French ports as part of the ongoing war, and France abandoned the island.

The cost of fighting in Haiti had put further strain on France's troubled finances and it occurred to Napoleon that he could raise revenue by selling the large and mostly undeveloped land controlled by France in North America. The US had become interested in the Louisiana territory, especially the port of **New Orleans** as more people

c.1800 rise of the Romantic cultural period in Europe

14 June French defeat Austrians at **Battle of Marengo**

1 October Spain cedes **Louisiana territory** to France

1 January Act of Union, uniting Britain and Ireland as Great Britain, takes effect

9 February Treaty of Lunéville signed between Austria and France

16 February British prime minister **Pitt the Younger** resigns

4 March Thomas Jefferson (1743–1826) takes office as US president (to 1809)

German composer **Ludwig van Beethoven** (1770–1827) completes his *Moonlight Sonata*

27 March Treaty of Amiens signed by Britain, France, and Spain

Gia Long (Nguyen Phuc Anh, 1762–1820) proclaimed emperor of united Annam (Vietnam)

Britain's **Second Maratha War** (to 1805) over control of central and southern India

Saint Domingue: Former slave, General **Toussaint L'Ouverture** captured by French

30 April US buys **Louisiana Territory** from France

Napoleonic Wars: Britain declares war on France (to 1815)

Cape Colony returned to Dutch control

> **“ FREEDOM OR DEATH! ”**

Inscription from Haiti's Act of Independence and on Haitian flag

KEY

Territory gained by US from France in 1803

→ Onward route of Lewis and Clark

Territory gained by the US

The massive Louisiana territory almost doubled the size of the US. The following year, it was extended south to New Orleans.

settling further west came to depend on trade along the Mississippi River. On 2 May a deal, the **Louisiana Purchase**, was signed in which the United States bought the territory stretching from the Gulf of Mexico to the Rocky Mountains – an area of 2,147,000 square kilometres (829,000 square miles). The price agreed was $15,000,000, but, including interest, the total paid was closer to $27,000,000.

Napoleon faced further challenges in Europe as Britain declared war on France, beginning the **Napoleonic Wars**. Meanwhile, British East India Company troops were waging another war involving the internal politics of the Maratha Confederacy, the **Second Maratha War** (to 1805). The Company's attempt to gain control of the territory in India only laid the ground for further conflict.

1804

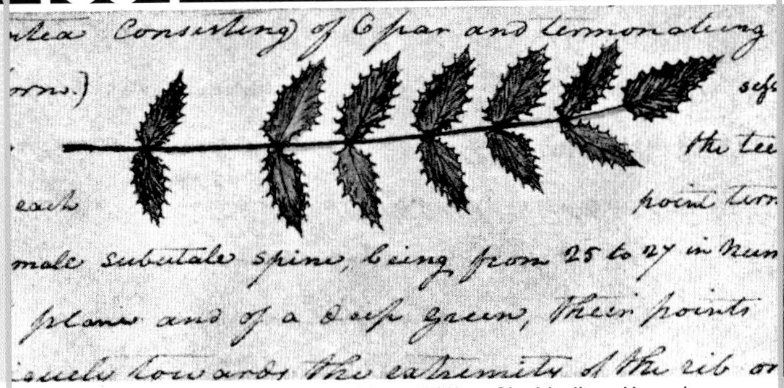

A sketch of an evergreen shrub leaf from William Clark's diary. He and Meriwether Lewis spent years exploring the vast Louisiana territory.

AFTER FINALLY DRIVING THE FRENCH OUT of Saint-Domingue, Jean-Jacques Dessalines declared the independence of the **new republic of Haiti** on 1 January 1804. The name was based partly on the original indigenous name for the island. It was the first – and only – former slave colony to throw off colonial rule and slavery. Despite this, its birth was met with a wary reception – some in the slave-owning US did not want Haiti setting an example to the southern states, a concern shared by Britain, whose slave colony of Jamaica was also in close proximity.

The defeat in the Caribbean did little to weaken Napoleon's stranglehold on power in Europe. In 1804 he made France a **hereditary empire**, ostensibly to ward off any assassination attempts, but also to showcase his own might. The coronation ceremony on 2 December was remarkable as Napoleon was not crowned by Pope Pius VII (1742–1823) who officated, but placed the crown on his own head, crowning himself **Napoleon I**. In this year he also made sweeping reforms to the legal system in France and French territories, known as the Napoleonic Code (see panel, right).

In the US, two explorers – **Meriwether Lewis** (1774–1809) and **William Clark** (1770–1838) – set off on an expedition through the newly acquired Louisiana Territory (see map, left). They were under instructions from President Thomas Jefferson to find the River Missouri, establish relations with the indigenous people of the region, and find the fabled **Northwest Passage**. They made detailed maps and recorded the flora and fauna of the region. The two explorers finally returned to St Louis in 1806.

In West Africa, **Usman dan Fodio** (1754–1817), a Muslim scholar and teacher, began a four-year **jihad** (holy war) that resulted in the creation of the **Sokoto Caliphate** in 1808 and the **Fulani empire** in Hausaland (in present-day northern Nigeria).

NAPOLEONIC CODE

One of Napoleon Bonaparte's most far-reaching reforms was to codify French law. Enacted in 1804, the Napoleonic Code (*Code Napoléon*) was a civil code created with the intention of breaking from the institutions of the past. Based on reason, it was also heavily influenced by Roman law, and declared all men equal, ending any hereditary nobility. Women fared less well, as they were put under male control.

The laws also dealt with issues such as property rights, marriage, and civil rights. The Napoleonic Code was disseminated throughout French-controlled territory in Europe and beyond, making it highly influential – an adapted version is still in force in the Dominican Republic today.

It was also later adopted by some of the new Latin American republics, including Bolivia and Chile.

1805

This painting shows the aftermath of the Battle of Trafalgar, in which France and Spain suffered heavy losses at the hands of Britain's Royal Navy.

FRANCE'S DEFEAT IN THE CARIBBEAN at Saint-Domingue was soon overshadowed by victory against Russia and Austria, which had been pulled back into war. Napoleon had also declared himself the king of Italy, then comprising Venice and northern Italian kingdoms. This act provoked the formation of a **Third Coalition** against France, with Britain, Austria, Russia, and Sweden as members. Deciding against an invasion of Britain, Bonaparte sent forces to **Ulm**, Bavaria (25 September–20 October), where he was victorious. However, the day after the Battle of Ulm ended, France suffered a humiliating naval defeat at the hands of the British in the **Battle of Trafalgar**, under the command of Napoleon's old enemy, Horatio Nelson (see 1798). The battle, fought near Cape Trafalgar, between Cadiz, Spain, and the Strait of Gibraltar, saw the meeting of 18 French and 15 Spanish ships against 27 British vessels. Britain was victorious, capturing or destroying 18 ships, but Nelson, fatally wounded in action, died before the end of the battle. Napoleon decided to change tactics and turned to Europe, occupying Vienna and defeating Russia and Austria at the **Battle of Austerliz** on 2 December.

In Egypt, the Macedonian-born soldier **Muhammad Ali** (1769–1849) was named viceroy, or pasha, to the Ottoman sultan. Ali had arrived in Egypt in 1801 as part of a regiment sent to drive out the French.

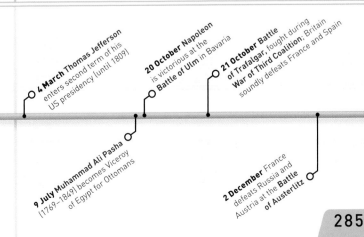

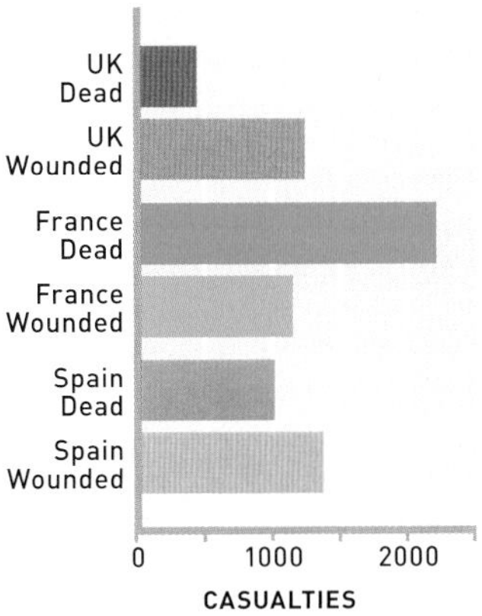

Casualties of Trafalgar

This sea battle saw heavy losses for France and Spain, though British Admiral Horatio Nelson was among the dead.

Mecca falls to Wahhibis, challenging Ottoman control

New elements Rhodium, Palladium, Osmium, Iridium, and Cerium **discovered**

November 18 Saint Domingue: Former slaves led by **Jean-Jacques Dessalines** defeat French army at Battle of Vertières

1 January Republic of Haiti **established** after French defeat in Saint-Domingue

14 February First Serbian uprising against Ottoman Empire (to 1813) over demands for autonomy

18 May Napoleon declared emperor of the French; introduces **legal code**

Russian war with **Persia** (to 1813) over Russia's annexation of Georgia and Karabakh

Pitt the Younger returns as British prime minister until 1806

4 March Thomas Jefferson enters second term of his US presidency (until 1809)

9 July Muhammad Ali Pasha (1769–1849) becomes Viceroy of Egypt for Ottomans

20 October Napoleon is victorious at the **Battle of Ulm** in Bavaria

21 October Battle of Trafalgar, fought during **War of Third Coalition**; Britain soundly defeats France and Spain

2 December France defeats Russia and Austria at the **Battle of Austerlitz**

1806

Napoleon after his victory at the Battle of Jena in Saxony.

PRUSSIA SUFFERED A DEVASTATING defeat against France at the **Battle of Jena** on 14 October. Fought in Jena and Auserstädt in Saxony (southeast Germany), 122,000 French troops and 114,000 Prussians met in combat. As a result, Frederick William III (1770–1840) decided that internal reform in Prussia was necessary in order to bolster the country's flagging fortunes. Among the numerous measures taken, **serfdom** was abolished. Although the transition later proved profitable for agriculture, it took years to implement the changes.

In addition to his other conquests, Napoleon wanted control of the **Holy Roman Empire**, which would expand his territory in Germany. Emperor Francis II (1768–1835) was in no position to challenge France and **abdicated**, officially ending the empire, of which France took possession.

In the Middle East, the Islamic holy pilgrimage site of **Mecca** was invaded by members of the Arabian **Saudi** dynasty who practiced a strict version of the religion known as **Wahhabi**. In 1805, they had captured **Medina**, which, like Mecca, was under the control of the Ottoman Empire. They also made incursions into the Arabian Peninsula, sacking the city of **Karbala**, in Iraq (also under Ottoman rule), and extending their influence south to **Yemen**, a cause for concern among Ottoman officials.

1807

> **“** YOU MAY **CHOOSE TO LOOK THE OTHER WAY** BUT YOU CAN NEVER SAY AGAIN THAT **YOU DID NOT KNOW. ”**

William Wilberforce, to the English parliament prior to the vote on the Abolition Bill, 1789

Elite force
A Janissary, left, in Cairo. Initially the bodyguards of the sultan, the Jannissaries became the elite troops of the Ottoman Empire army.

THE LONG BATTLE LED BY English abolitionist and politician **William Wilberforce** (1759–1833) – and the thousands of members of the British public who supported his campaign – finally came to fruition in 1807 as the bill to **abolish the slave trade** was passed with an overwhelming majority. The legislation, however, only ended the trade in Britain. It did not end the practice of slavery.

Russia, alongside Prussia, had re-entered the hostilities against France with the **Battle of Eylau** (7–8 February) in eastern Prussia. The battle was inconclusive and resulted in a stalemate, with both sides losing more than 20,000 troops. After a decisive Russian defeat at the later **Battle of Friedland**, Russia signed one of the **Treaties of Tilsit** on 7 July, while Prussia signed the other on 9 July. Under the terms of the treaties, France and Russia formed an alliance, while the territories of Austria and Prussia were significantly reduced.

In the Ottoman Empire, auxiliary troops called **Yamaks** erupted into a revolt over attempts to introduce European-style reforms to the military. They were soon joined by the elite **Janissary** soldiers. The unrest culminated in the assassination of Selim III (1761–1808).

1808

Francisco Goya's painting *The Third of May* depicts the French troops' execution of Spanish insurgents involved in the Madrid uprising.

ALREADY IN CONTROL OF MOST of western and central Europe, Napoleon now turned towards the Iberian Peninsula. Enraged by the Portuguese refusal to back a French boycott against Britain, he sent troops into Portugal via northern Spain. The presence of French troops, as well as previous unpopular concessions to France, provoked the Spanish people to rise up, calling for the abdication of their monarch, **Charles IV**, in favour of his son, **Ferdinand VII** (1784–1833). Ferdinand took the throne, but it was to be very short-lived.

Lured to Bayonne, France, by Napoleon's offer to mediate, Ferdinand VII was forced to abdicate. As Charles VII had already abdicated, Napoleon was now able to declare his brother, Joseph Bonaparte (1768–1844), the new king of Spain, triggering the **Peninsular War**. When news of these events reached Spain's colonies, there were furious outbursts. In Santo Domingo, loyalists mounted the **War of Reconquest** (to 1809), driving out the occupying French troops, and declaring the island once more under Spanish control.

1809

LONG-STANDING ENEMIES, Spain and Britain now fought alongside each other as they united against France. British troops met early defeat at the **Battle of La Coruña**, northwest Spain, fighting French troops under Napoleon's direct command. Britain was subsequently victorious at the **Battle of Talavera** (27–28 July), southwest of Madrid, under the leadership of Arthur Wellesley (1769–1852), later known as the **Duke of Wellington**.

The Spaniards, while fighting the French, had also been establishing provincial bodies, called **juntas**, in order to organize their resistance. The central junta in Spain had also issued a decree declaring the American territories to be more than just colonies, but still a part of the monarchy. Across the Atlantic it was obvious that there was a crisis of **legitimacy** in Spanish rule – without a king, with whom did allegiance lie? While debates about this were under way, similar American juntas were set up, and it soon it became clear that not all the colonies would stay on the path of loyalty to the Crown.

Pistol from Peninsular War
Flintlock pistols were widely used in this period. The term "guerrilla" also arose, named for Spanish tactics.

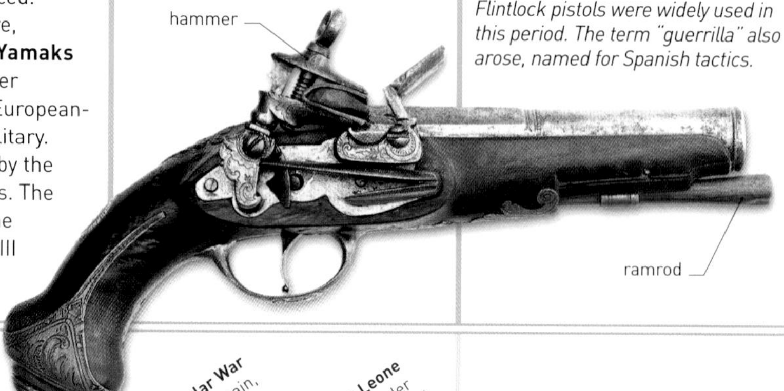

- French urge **Ottomans** to declare war on Russia; fighting lasts until 1812
- British take **Cape Colony** from the Dutch again to prevent French control
- **6 August** Formal abolition of **Holy Roman Empire**
- **14 October** Napoleon defeats Prussians at twin of **Jena** and **Auerstädt** battles
- **7–8 February** Napoleon defeats Russia at **Battle of Eylau**
- **Janissary revolt** leads to deposition of Ottoman leader **Selim III**, replaced by **Mustapha IV** (1779–1808)
- **25 March** Britain **abolishes the slave trade** in all its territories
- **14 June** Russians defeated by France at **Battle of Friedland**
- British fail to take **Buenos Aires** during attempt to seize colonies of Spain, the ally of France
- **November** Portuguese royal family flees to **Brazil** after France invades **Portugal**
- **Peninsular War** (to 1814): Spain, Portugal, and Britain against France
- **6 June** **Joseph** (1768–1844), Napoleon's brother, is placed on the Spanish throne
- **Sierra Leone** comes under British control
- **16 January** **Peninsular War**: British defeated at La Coruña, Spain
- **8 February** **Austria** declares war on France
- **17 September** Sweden cedes Finland to Russia under the **Treaty of Hamina**

1810

A mural by José Clemente Orozco (1883–1949) depicting Miguel Hidalgo, whose anti-colonial document sparked the Mexican War of Independence.

Latin America on the eve of independence
Spain and Portugal still controlled the majority of Central and South America during the early days of the Peninsular War.

USING THE EXISTING POLITICAL CHAOS as an opportunity for reform, Spanish politicians called a congress, known as a **Cortes**, on 24 September in the port of Cadiz. Deputies numbered 104, with 30 representing the colonial territories, although more arrived later. The Cortes declared itself the source of national sovereignty and began to draw up a constitution, though Spaniards were divided as to the extent they wished the government to be restructured. There was also the question of how much political **representation** to allow overseas territories. The colonies represented a population far greater than Spain's, meaning they could, in theory, dominate the Cortes. The peninsular politicians wished to avoid this, yet needed the colonies' continued support.

Some members of the public in the colonies began taking matters into their own hands. In Dolores, Mexico, a parish priest named **Miguel Hidalgo y Costilla** (1753–1811) distributed a document calling for the end of Spanish rule, while advocating racial equality and land redistribution, an act known as the ***Grito de Dolores*** (Cry of Dolores). Thousands responded to his call and set off for Mexico City, where they were put down by loyalist troops the following year. But Hidalgo's actions had sparked the Mexican struggle for freedom.

In other Spanish colonies, similar upheavals took place. The viceroyalty of **New Granada** also declared its independence on 20 July, and there had been uprisings in Quito and Buenos Aires.

Meanwhile, on the **Hawaiian islands** in the Pacific Ocean, **King Kamehameha I** (1758–1819) became the first ruler of a united Hawaii, helping the islands withstand European incursions.

1811

A caricature compares the Luddites to mobs of the French Revolution.

ON 5 JULY, THE SOUTH AMERICAN TERRITORY of Venezuela joined New Granada (see map, left) and Mexico in declaring independence from Spain. One of the rebels involved in the deliberations for independence, **Simón Bolívar** (see panel, below), had recently returned from England, where he had tried to elicit British support for their cause, but he was unsuccessful.

Bolívar's trip was confined to London, but had he travelled further north, he would have seen rebels of another kind: the group known as the **Luddites,** who were attacking textile mills in the industrial north of England. The Luddites aimed to destroy the new machinery in the mills. They feared the machines would eventually **replace** them, thereby forcing them into unemployment and poverty.

SIMON BOLIVAR (1783–1830)

Simón Bolívar was born in Caracas to a wealthy family. He was sent to Europe at 16, where he was inspired by the writings of Enlightenment thinkers on the issue of liberty. Soon after returning to South America in 1807, he became involved in independence conspiracies. Later known as *El Libertador*, he led much of northern South America to independence from Spain. He also ruled Gran Colombia, but the political union ultimately failed.

1812

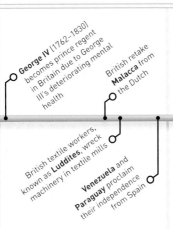

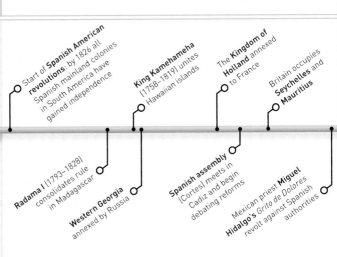

When Napoleon Bonaparte's troops arrived in Moscow, they found the city ablaze, as portrayed by this painting by Jean-Charles Langlois (1789–1870).

RUSSIA, LIKE PORTUGAL, DECIDED to resist Napoleon's **Continental System**, measures intended to damage the economy of Britain. Russia had withdrawn from it in 1810, and Napoleon resolved to mount an invasion in retaliation. He sent more than **500,000 troops** to Russia in June and won early victories at the battles of **Smolensk** on 17 August and **Borodino** on 7 September, arriving with his forces in Moscow on 14 September. There they found the city gutted, and its inhabitants gone. Russian troops held off any further advance, and as the brutal Russian winter set in, Napoleon's troops began to falter. The **Grand Armée** was running short on food and many soldiers, unaccustomed to such extreme cold, died. Napoleon had no other option but to make a humiliating **retreat** in December. Only around 30,000 French soldiers survived.

In North America, merchants prospered in their trade with France, claiming to be a neutral party in the dispute between the British and the French. Britain refused to recognize this **neutrality** and began to seize American ships, often capturing the American sailors and pressing them into service with the British Royal Navy. This triggered the **War of 1812** (to 1814), which also included battles on the mainland where Britain persuaded American Indians loyal to the Crown to attack settlements in the Northwest Territory.

In Spain, the Cortes had finally produced a **constitution**. It limited the power of the monarchy – although Ferdinand VII was still in exile – and did not provide any special representation in the Cortes for the nobility or the clergy. Its liberal ideas provoked an angry reaction among some supporters of the Crown and Church, and triggered a long-running fight between liberals and conservatives, which would continue for decades.

In Egypt, Muhammad Ali was ordered on a campaign to re-establish Ottoman rule in the holy city of **Mecca**, and drive out the Wahhabis, who had seized much of Arabia. His troops took Medina in 1812, and Jeddah and Mecca the following year.

- Start of **Spanish American revolutions**; by 1826 all Spanish mainland colonies in South America have gained independence
- **Radama I** (1793–1828) consolidates rule in Madagascar
- **King Kamehameha** (1758–1819) unites Hawaiian islands
- **Western Georgia** annexed by Russia
- **Spanish assembly** (Cortes) meets in Cádiz and begin debating reforms
- The **Kingdom of Holland** annexed to France
- Britain occupies **Seychelles** and **Mauritius**
- Mexican priest **Miguel Hidalgo's** *Grito de Dolores* revolt against Spanish authorities
- **George IV** (1762–1830) becomes prince regent in Britain due to George III's deteriorating mental health
- British textile workers, known as **Luddites**, wreck machinery in textile mills
- British retake **Malacca** from the Dutch
- **Venezuela** and **Paraguay** proclaim their independence from Spain
- **19 March** Spanish national assembly in Cádiz unveils a **democratic constitution**
- **Napoleon's** Russian campaign (to 1814)
- Usman dan Fodio (1754–1815) establishes the **Sokoto Caliphate** in Nigeria
- **War of 1812** between US and Britain, triggered by the seizure of American ships (to 1814)

1813

> **" THE BULLET THAT WILL KILL ME IS NOT YET CAST. "**
>
> **Napoleon Bonaparte, statement at Montereau,** 17 February 1814

NAPOLEON BONAPARTE, AFTER HIS HUMILIATING RETREAT IN Russia (see 1812), began to experience the rapid decline of his military might. This was driven home by the decisive defeat at the **Battle of Leipzig** (also known as the Battle of the Nations) fought from 16–19 October. France had nearly 185,000 troops, but the allies outnumbered them with more than 300,000 soldiers from Austria, Russia, Prussia, and Sweden. Even after this loss Napoleon still refused to sign a peace deal that would put France's boundary back to the River Rhine and the Alps.

While Russia was caught up in the Napoleonic conflict, it was also entangled with territorial deals further east; Russia and Persia signed the **Treaty of Gulistan**, in which Russia was given a large area of Persian Caucasus territory. The deal brought to an end the **Russo–Persian War** (1804–13), which had been triggered by Russia's annexation of Georgia and the **Karabakh** (a region in present-day Azerbaijan). The territories, which had been a dominion of Persia, had appealed to Persia's shah for help in resisting Russia.

In **Venezuela**, Simón Bolívar (see 1811) had won an important victory against the Spanish and captured **Caracas**, though Spain's forces would later defeat him, forcing him into exile for two years. During this period he went to Jamaica and Haiti to regroup and enlist further support before returning to Venezuela in 1816.

1814

An engraving of a palanquin (litter) being carried in Mauritius.

ALLIED TROOPS PURSUED Napoleon to Paris, where he was captured. He abdicated on 6 April and was exiled to the island of Elba, off the Tuscan coast of Italy. To replace him, **Louis XVIII** (1755–1824) – brother of the beheaded Louis XVI – was placed on the French throne. Afterwards, the European powers convened the **Congress of Vienna** (September 1814 to June 1815). Part of the resulting settlement gave Prussia two-fifths of Saxony; set up a German Confederation; and allowed Britain to retain France's Indian Ocean islands of **Mauritius** and the **Seychelles**, which it had captured.

1815

A painting depicts the 17th-century Temple of Tooth, located in the kingdom of Kandy, where one of Buddha's teeth is preserved.

ALTHOUGH HE WAS EXILED FROM FRANCE, Napoleon rallied enough supporters to help him mount his return, and he entered Paris on 20 March – just 11 months after his forced departure. Louis XVIII fled, and what became known as the "**Hundred Days**" began. Once he had an army assembled, Napoleon mounted attacks against his enemies, defeating Prussia at **Ligny** (in present-day Belgium) on 16 June. He fared much worse two days later at the **Battle of Waterloo**, against British troops led by the Duke of Wellington, who had brought the Peninsular War (see 1808) to an end the previous year. Napoleon had been on the verge of victory, but the arrival of Prussian reinforcements secured his defeat. Napoleon was forced to abdicate once again, but this time he was to be exiled much further away – the island of **St Helena**, a British outpost in the South Atlantic, where he died in 1821.

At the same time, Britain's troops in **Ceylon** (Sri Lanka) had taken control of the kingdom of **Kandy**, which meant the entire island was under British rule.

Battle of Waterloo
This clash was the definitive defeat of Napoleon Bonaparte, after which he was forced to abdicate and go into exile.

1816

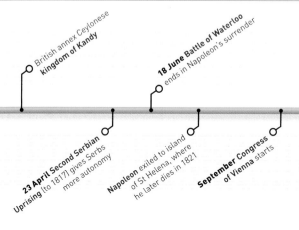

A native inhabitant in Alaska, territory which Russia had claimed.

A RUSSIAN ORTHODOX PRIEST, Father Sokoloff, was sent to **Sitka**, in the Alaska territory, to build a church in the town as part of Russia's bid to colonize the region. Alaska had lingered as an outpost but settlements began to grow as trade in sea otter furs flourished.

In southern Africa, **Shaka** (*c.*1787–1828), a fierce warrior, took over the rule of the **Zulus**. He reorganized the army, leading his tribe to military victory, and incorporated conquered tribes into the Zulu nation.

- **Charter Act** ends East India Company monopoly and allows missionaries to enter India
- Egyptian forces recapture **Jeddah** and **Mecca** from Wahhabis
- **19 October Napoleon** defeated by Allies at **Leipzig** (Battle of the Nations)
- **Simón Bolívar** leads invasion of **Venezuela** and is proclaimed "El Libertador" (The Liberator)
- **14 January Treaty of Kiel:** Denmark gives Sweden Norway in exchange for Pomerania
- **6 April Napoleon** abdicates; exiled to island of Elba, returning less than a year later
- **11 April Louis XVIII** (1755–1824) regains French throne (to 1824)
- **30 May Treaty of Paris** signed
- **War in Nepal** between East India Company troops and Gurkhas over annexation of villages (to 1816)
- **11 December Ferdinand VII** (1784–1833) is returned to Spanish throne; scraps liberal reforms
- British annex Ceylonese **kingdom of Kandy**
- **23 April Second Serbian Uprising** (to 1817) gives Serbs more autonomy
- **Napoleon** exiled to island of St Helena, where he later dies in 1821
- **18 June Battle of Waterloo** ends in Napoleon's surrender
- **September Congress of Vienna** starts
- **United Provinces of the Rio de la Plata** set up as independent states in South America
- **9 July Argentina** gains independence from Spain
- **27 August Bombardment of Algiers** by Anglo-Dutch allies seeking release of Christian slaves
- **Shaka** (*c.*1787–1828) becomes Zulu king
- **Java** returns to **Dutch rule** after a period of British control

1817

1818

1819

Argentine general José de San Martín with his horse and officers.

> **“ LET US BE FREE.** THE REST MATTERS NOT! ”
>
> **José de San Martín,** revolutionary leader

A depiction of the Peterloo Massacre in which a peaceful political protest in Manchester, England, was attacked by armed cavalrymen.

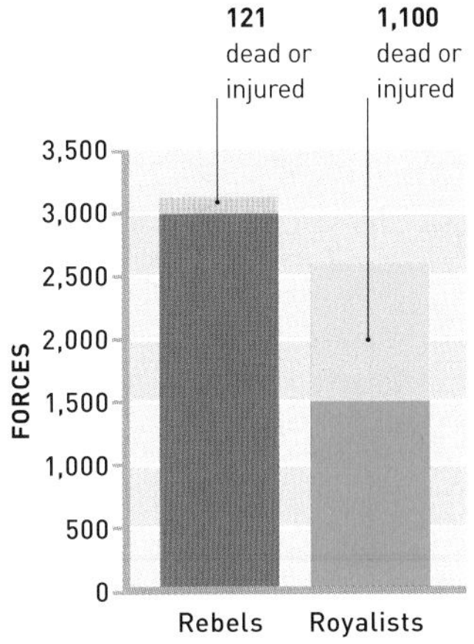

Battle of Chacabuco
A bold risk by rebel leader José de San Martín resulted in a highly successful ambush against the Spanish, who sustained heavy losses.

THE FIGHT AGAINST SPANISH rule took a decisive turn when Argentine-born General **José de San Martín** (1778–1850) led around 3,000 troops from Argentina into Chile through treacherous passages in the **Andes** mountains, and launched a surprise attack on royalist forces on 12 February – the **Battle of Chacabuco**. He then moved on to take Santiago. He refused the offer of governorship of Chile, passing it instead to fellow soldier **Bernardo O'Higgins** (*c.*1776–1842), who became the territory's "supreme director".

Serbia had also been fighting once more for independence, after being invaded by the Turks in 1813. The **Second Serbian Uprising** was successful, and most of their former rights were regained by 1817.

THE BATTLE IN ARABIA, ongoing since 1811 between Egypt and the Wahhabi sect of Islam, drew to a close in 1818. Egyptian forces led by Muhammad Ali recaptured the holy cities of Mecca and Medina. **Wahhabi** power had spread quickly, and from their Arabian base they had secured control of Mecca, Medina, and Jedda. Syria was under threat when Muhammad Ali received his orders to defeat the Wahhabi and return the cities to Ottoman rule. A final siege of the capital **Diriyah** (in present-day Saudi Arabia) put a temporary end to Wahhabi ambitions.

In South America, the effort led by José de San Martín at the Battle of Maipú on 5 April secured **independence for Chile** when loyalist troops suffered a crushing defeat. With a small naval fleet of seven ships under the command of British mercenary Lord Thomas Cochrane, the rebels also managed to break the Spanish hold on the coastline.

In Paris, German inventor Baron Karl von Drais de Sauerbrun was impressing crowds with a display of his **draisienne**, a two-wheeled machine that was the precursor to the modern **bicycle**. Made of wood and propelled by pushing the feet along the ground, rather than by pedals, it was known in German as the **Laufmaschine**, or "running machine". While testing the design the previous year, he had managed to ride it 14 km (9 miles). The idea was soon picked up and modified by other inventors, including Briton **Denis Johnson** (*c.*1759–1833), a coachmaker by training, who designed a "pedestrian curricle", later known as a **dandy horse**.

In England, **Mary Shelley** (1797–1851), the daughter of writer Mary Wollstonecraft (see 1792) and wife of poet Percy Bysshe Shelley (1792–1822), published the novel *Frankenstein; or, The Modern Prometheus*. The novel concerns a scientist who artificially creates another human being, and the consequences they both suffer. The work was an instant success, and is considered a classic work of **Gothic** literature as well as one of the earliest examples of science fiction.

Mary Shelley
The English novelist Mary Shelley published her first novel, Frankenstein, *in 1818, and it remains a literary classic today.*

ON 16 AUGUST, A POLITICAL RALLY of around 60,000 people on St Peter's Field in Manchester, England, turned from a protest about high food prices and lack of popular suffrage into the **Peterloo Massacre**. Magistrates, concerned about the size of the crowd, ordered the Yeomanry (voluntary cavalry officers) to arrest the speakers, but they **attacked** the crowd when they refused to make way. A regiment, the 15th Hussars, was then sent in, and an estimated 15 people were killed and more than 500 injured.

Upon his return from exile, Venezuelan general **Simón Bolívar**, had begun to make considerable headway against royalist forces. In 1819, he led his troops from Venezuela over the Andes to launch an attack. The Spanish were defeated at the **Battle of Boyacá** on 7 August and Bolívar marched south to Santa Fé de Bogotá, which secured the independence of **New Granada**. Bolívar was named the president of the new Republic of Colombia.

In a bid to challenge Dutch dominance of trade routes between China and India (see 1795) the British East India Company sought a new base in the Malay peninsula. **Stamford Raffles** arrived in **Singapore**, which was then part of the Riau-Johor empire. He negotiated a deal with the local ruler and founded a port.

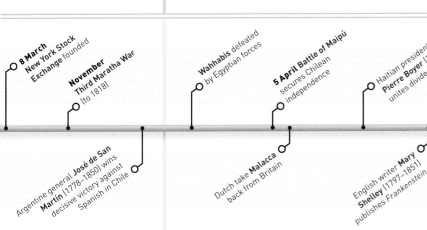

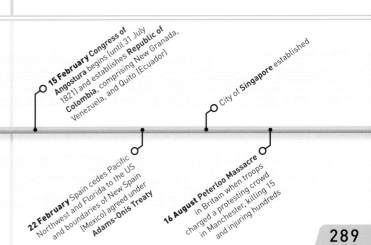

THE EAST INDIA COMPANIES

The East India Companies monopolized trade between Europe and Southeast Asia, India, and the Far East from the early 17th century. However, the French Compagnie Française des Indes Orientales ceased trading at the time of the French Revolution (see 1789). The charter for the Dutch Vereenigde Oost-Indische Compagnie was revoked in 1799 when the government took control of it. Sweden's Svenska Ostindiska Companiet folded in 1813, while Britain's East India Company (above) traded until 1874.

- **8 March** New York Stock Exchange founded
- **November** Third Maratha War (to 1818)
- Argentine general **José de San Martín** (1778–1850) wins decisive victory against Spanish in Chile
- **Wahhabis** defeated by Egyptian forces
- **5 April Battle of Maipú** secures Chilean independence
- Dutch take **Malacca** back from Britain
- Haitian president **Jean Pierre Boyer** (1776–1850) unites divided island
- English writer **Mary Shelley** (1797–1851) publishes *Frankenstein*
- **15 February Congress of Angostura** begins (until 31 July 1821) and establishes **Republic of Colombia**, comprising New Granada, Venezuela, and Quito (Ecuador)
- **22 February** Spain cedes Pacific Northwest and Florida to the US and boundaries of New Spain (Mexico) agreed under **Adams-Onís Treaty**
- City of **Singapore** established
- **16 August Peterloo Massacre** in Britain when troops charged a protesting crowd in Manchester, killing 15 and injuring hundreds

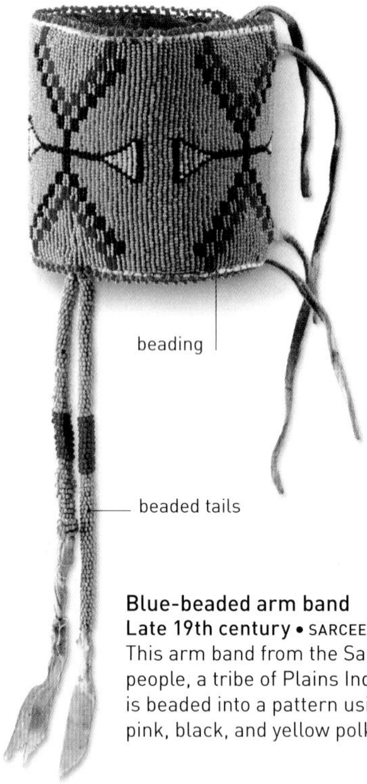

Blue-beaded arm band
Late 19th century • SARCEE
This arm band from the Sarcee people, a tribe of Plains Indians, is beaded into a pattern using blue, pink, black, and yellow polka dots.

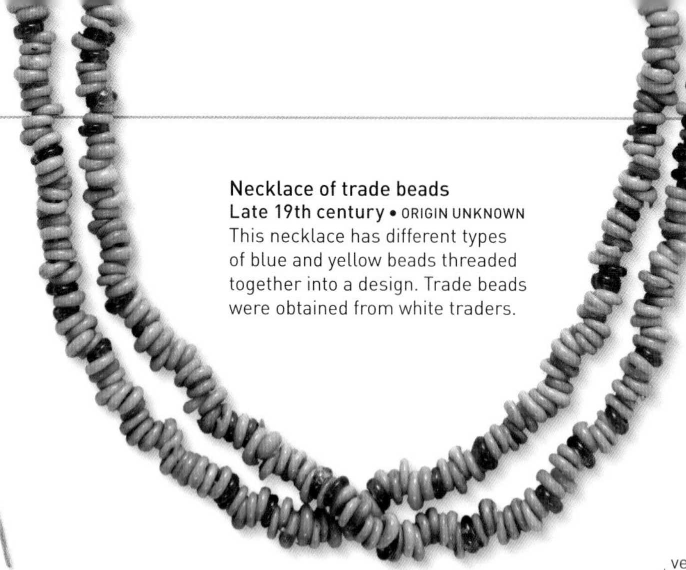

Necklace of trade beads
Late 19th century • ORIGIN UNKNOWN
This necklace has different types of blue and yellow beads threaded together into a design. Trade beads were obtained from white traders.

Glenary hat
*c.*1860 • IROQUOIS
Made of black velvet, this Iroquois hat has intricate beadwork and a floral pattern woven around the bottom.

Chieftain's headdress
*c.*1930 • ARAPAHO
This headdress of Yellow Calf, the last chief of the Arapaho, has been made with feathers and decorated fur. It was worn close to the head.

AMERICAN INDIANS

ARTEFACTS FROM THE DIVERSE TRIBES WHO LIVE THROUGHOUT NORTH AMERICA

For thousands of years, millions of aboriginal people lived in North America, but their world was shattered and their population declined drastically when the Europeans arrived, bringing new diseases and weapons.

European explorers encountered diverse cultures in the North American continent, ranging from the Arctic world of the Aleut, Innu, and Inuit to the hot, dry home of the Hopi in the southwest. Trade was one way Europeans exerted their influence on native populations, and tribes such as the Sioux, Blackfoot, Sarcee, and Arapaho in the Great Plains, and the Iroquois and Mohawk of the Great Lakes were soon in regular contact with the European settlers.

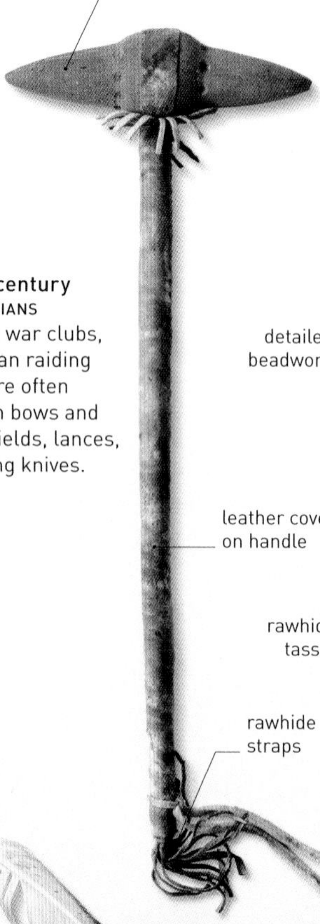

War club
Late 19th century
• PLAINS INDIANS
Apart from war clubs, Plains Indian raiding parties were often armed with bows and arrows, shields, lances, and scalping knives.

Pipe bag
Late 19th century • SIOUX
American Indians smoked tobacco in pipes. The tobacco was believed to have special powers and was used to please spirits

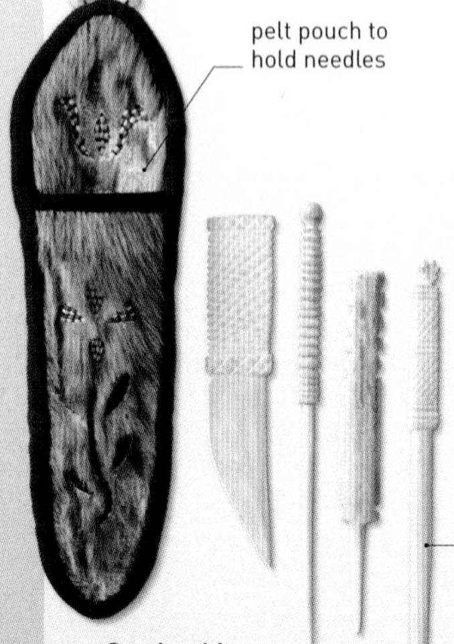

Sewing kit
*c.*1880 • INNU AND INUIT
This sewing kit consists of tools made by carving bones and a pouch made from seal skin and animal fur.

Hide working tool
*c.*1890 • ALEUT
Skinning and butchering was usually a woman's task. This hide working tool scrapes the hides of sea otters and whales hunted by the Aleut.

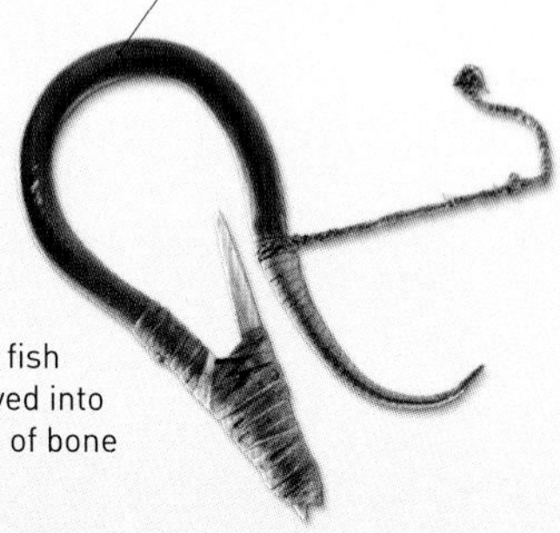

Fish hook
19th century • ALEUT
Wood, bone, and fibre have been used in this fish hook. The wood is carved into a U-shape, with points of bone at both the ends.

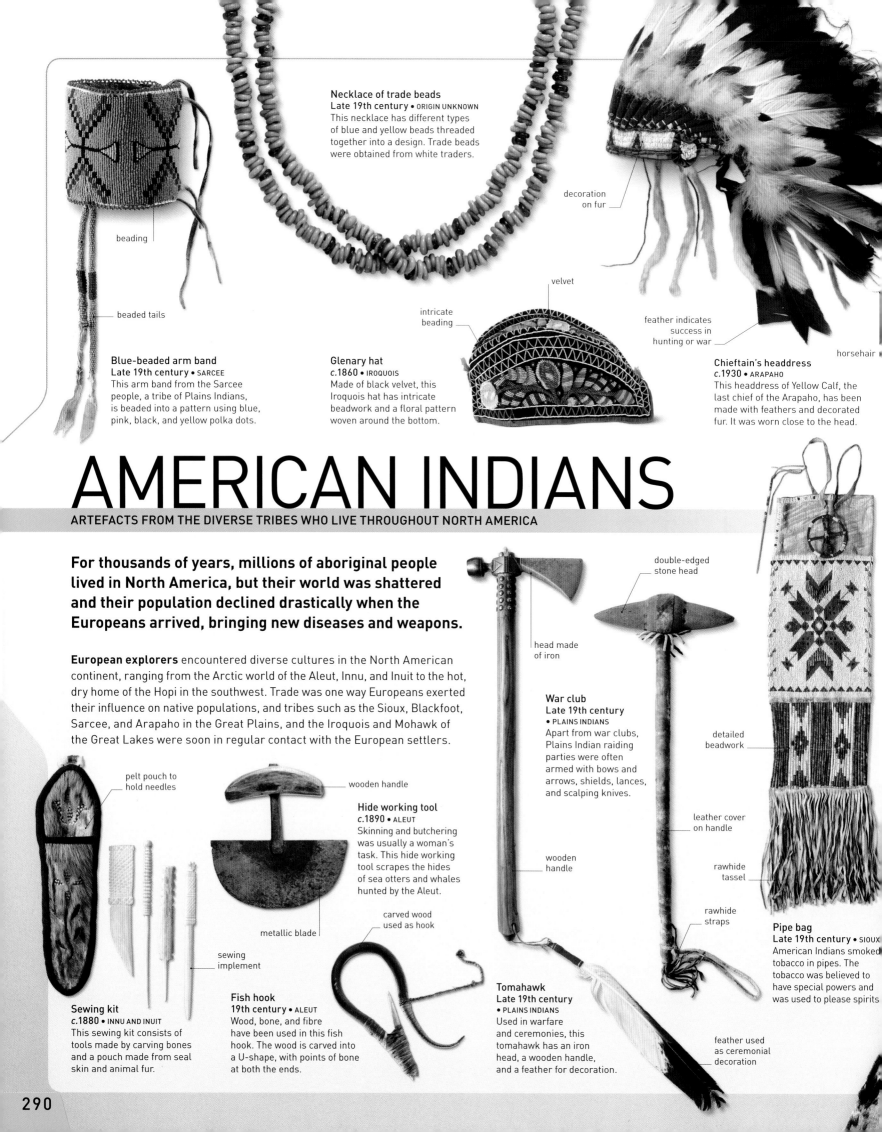

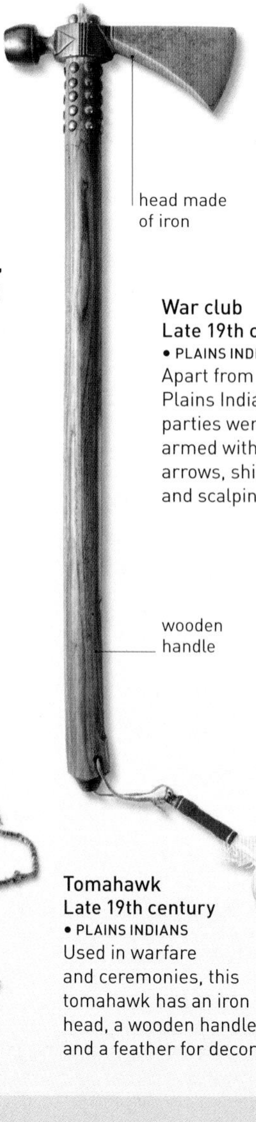

Tomahawk
Late 19th century
• PLAINS INDIANS
Used in warfare and ceremonies, this tomahawk has an iron head, a wooden handle, and a feather for decoration.

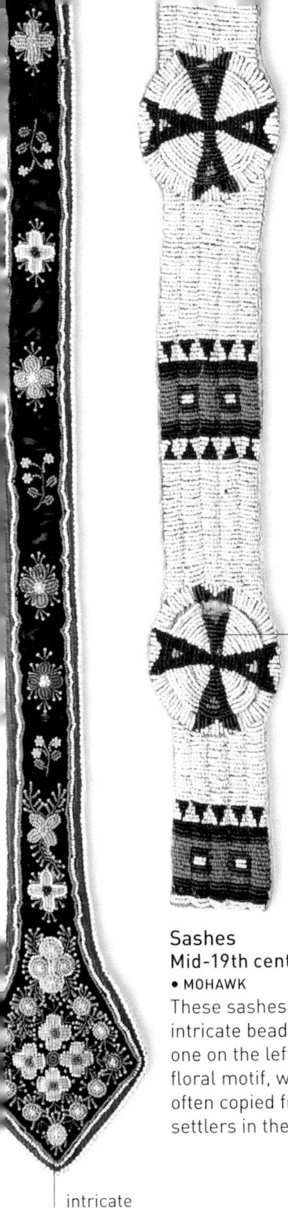

Sashes
Mid-19th century • MOHAWK
These sashes display intricate beadwork. The one on the left has a floral motif, which was often copied from white settlers in the area.

Jacket
c.1890 • SIOUX
This jacket has been made with buckskin and decorated with beads, which were brought in by white traders.

Beaded moccasins
Late 19th century • SIOUX
Leather moccasins with decorative beading were worn by Sioux hunters and traders. The sole extends over the toes.

Wooden bears
Early 20th century • INUIT
These wooden polar bears were made by the Inuit people who live in the Arctic and subarctic regions of North America.

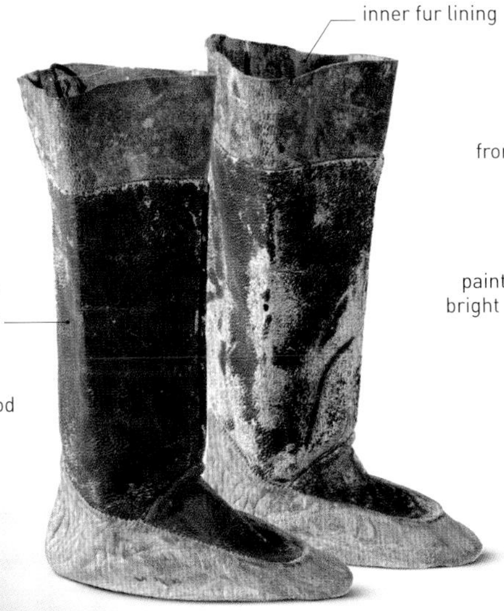

Mukluks
Early 20th century • INUIT
These boots for children have seal or reindeer skin on the outside and fur on the inner lining.

Kachina figure
20th century • HOPI
Hopi kachina figures of this type were used to teach children about the world of spirits.

Winter coat
Late 19th century • INNU
Anoraks were winter coats, typically loose at the bottom to allow the wearer to draw in cold air if ventilation was needed.

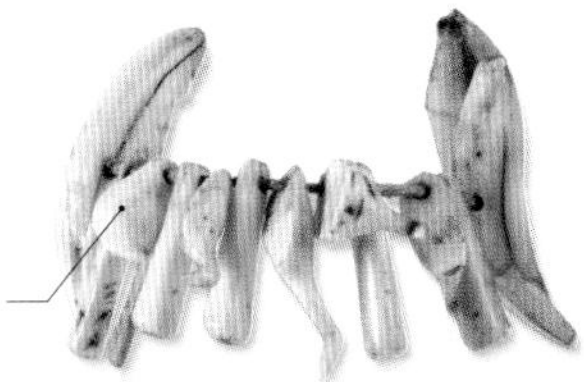

Carved and pierced teeth
19th century • INUIT
Used by shamans – or medicine men – in their practices, these teeth, some shaped into birds, are strung together along a ring.

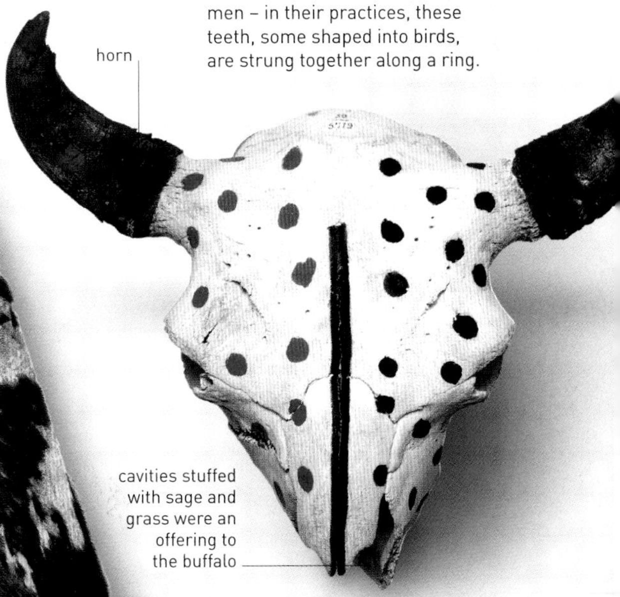

Buffalo skull
19th century • BLACKFOOT
Used in the Sun Dance ritual of the Plains Indians, this Blackfoot buffalo skull has horns and is decorated with polka dots.

1820

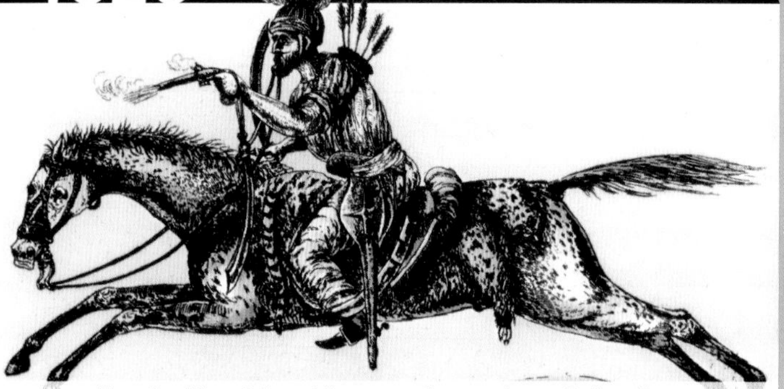

Egyptian Mameluke soldiers were former slaves. By invading Sudan, Egypt hoped to add Sudanese captives to their ranks.

AS THE UNITED STATES began the settlement of western territories, the issue of **slavery** could not be ignored. Most of the northern states had abolished the practice, but the southern states had become increasingly dependent on slave labour. When the Missouri territory petitioned for statehood in 1817, it caused a political crisis over whether the federal government had the right to restrict slavery in this territory. The solution was the **Missouri Compromise**, which allowed slavery in Missouri, but not in any new state north of 36°30' latitude.

Much of Europe, meanwhile, was convulsed by political unrest, with **revolts** in the Italian states, Portugal, France, and the Low Countries. In **Spain**, Ferdinand VII had returned to the throne in 1814, rejecting the new constitution (see 1812) and arresting liberal leaders. Following public unrest, Ferdinand was forced to accept the 1812 Constitution, marking the start of the **Trienio Liberal** – three years of a liberal regime (1820–23). In 1823, France's Louis XVIII – who had been restored to the throne (see 1815) – sent in troops to "free" Ferdinand. These soldiers toppled the liberal regime, and returned Ferdinand to power.

Egypt invaded its southern neighbour, **Sudan**. Pasha Muhammad Ali wanted Sudanese gold and slaves for his army. By 1821, Sudan had fallen and the Egyptian Empire extended down the Nile to what is now Uganda.

Slave population
Although the slave population was small in Missouri, the question of permitting slavery in the state caused a political crisis in the US.

> **“** ....THIS **MOMENTOUS QUESTION,** LIKE A **FIRE BELL** IN THE NIGHT, AWAKENED AND FILLED ME WITH **TERROR. ”**

Thomas Jefferson, third president of the US, on the implications of the Missouri Compromise in a letter to John Holmes, 22 April 1820

1821

A woodcut illustrates the battle for independence in Mexico.

IN GREECE, A FIGHT FOR INDEPENDENCE FROM THE TURKS began. Resentful at years of living under oppression, people from across Greek society – including the **Orthodox Church** – began to plot their liberation. Some rebel groups had been organizing through secret patriotic societies such as the **Philikí Etaireía** (Society of Friends). These organizations involved people living on the islands, but also had significant support from the large **Greek diaspora**.

At the same time, rebels in the **Americas** were able to take advantage of Spain's internal crisis and weakness to make the final **push for independence**. **Mexico** managed to secure its liberation after Mexican royalists, upon hearing the news of events in Spain (see 1820), decided that self-rule was the only way to **avoid a liberal regime** as had happened in Spain. On 24 August, a treaty was signed recognizing Mexican independence, and on 19 May the former royalist Agustín de Iturbide (1783–1824) crowned himself emperor **Augustín I**.

Further south, the **Congress of Cúcuta** was formed and formally established **Gran Colombia**, consisting of present-day Colombia, Panama, Venezuela, and Ecuador. **Simón Bolívar** was named president and Bogotá was made the capital.

In Peru, **José de San Martín** led his troops into Lima and declared **Peru independent**, though fighting to secure its freedom continued.

1822

A depiction of the coronation of Pedro I as emperor of Brazil. Pedro, the son of the king of Portugal, had declared the colony's independence.

THE RELATIONSHIP BETWEEN PORTUGAL AND BRAZIL had been fundamentally affected when the Portuguese court, fleeing Napoleon, arrived in Brazil in 1808. After **John VI** (1769–1826) returned to Portugal in 1821, he left his son, **Dom Pedro**, (1798–1834) in charge of the kingdom of Brazil, as Prince Regent. Dom Pedro, frustrated by the attempt of the Portuguese Cortes to reduce Brazil to its pre-1808 colonial status, issued his ***Grito de Ipiranga*** (Cry of Ipiranga) declaring Brazil's independence, and crowning himself Emperor Pedro I.

Even the loyalist **Santo Domingo**, on the island of Hispaniola, was swept up in the revolutionary spirit of the time, declaring **independence** in 1821, though it failed to realize a plan to join Gran Colombia. Santo Domingo's neighbour, **Haiti** (previously Saint Domingue), grew concerned that France or Britain might sneak through the now poorly guarded ports in Santo Domingo and launch an attack to recolonize and **re-enslave** the island. With this pretext – and the fact that slavery still persisted in Santo Domingo – Haiti's president, **Jean-Pierre Boyer** (in office 1818–50) arrived in Santo Domingo with his forces. The provisional government turned control over to Boyer, who united both sides of the island under Haitian rule.

The issue of slavery remained contentious in the US, and there arose the additional question of how to treat **freed slaves**. The American Colonization Society, founded in 1816, advocated they be returned to Africa. The society secured agreements with local rulers in West Africa, near **Cape Mesurado**, establishing a settlement that would become known as **Liberia**.

12 THOUSAND THE NUMBER OF **FREED SLAVES RELOCATED** TO LIBERIA FROM 1822–1862

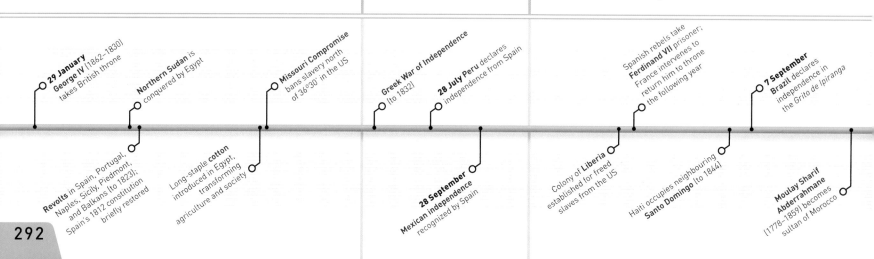

Liberia
Located on the West Coast of Africa, alongside slaving ports, a colony for freed slaves was established by the American Colonization Society.

29 January **George IV** (1862–1830) takes British throne

Revolts in Spain, Portugal, Naples, Sicily, Piedmont, and Balkans (to 1823); Spain's 1812 constitution briefly restored

Northern Sudan is conquered by Egypt

Long-staple **cotton** introduced in Egypt, transforming agriculture and society

Missouri Compromise bans slavery north of 36°30' in the US

Greek War of Independence (to 1832)

28 July Peru declares independence from Spain

28 September **Mexican independence** recognized by Spain

Colony of **Liberia** established for freed slaves from the US

Spanish rebels take **Ferdinand VII** prisoner; France intervenes to return him to throne the following year

Haiti occupies neighbouring **Santo Domingo** (to 1844)

7 September **Brazil** declares independence in the *Grito de Ipiranga*

Moulay Sharif Abderrahmane (1778–1859) becomes sultan of Morocco

1823

The Alaungpaya dynasty's invasion of northern India led to Britain declaring war and eventually capturing the coastal city of Rangoon, pictured.

IN HIS ANNUAL MESSAGE TO THE US Congress on 2 December, President James Monroe (see panel, below) outlined a new diplomatic policy: the **Monroe Doctrine**. Concerned about the possibility of European incursion into the new republics of Latin America, Monroe attempted to **set boundaries** between Europe and the Americas. The doctrine stated that the US would not interfere in the internal affairs or wars of European powers, nor in any colonies in the Americas, but likewise declared the western hemisphere now closed to any further European attempts at **colonization.** Interference with territories in the Americas would now be viewed as hostile acts against the US.

Earlier in the year, another republic had joined the Americas: the **United Provinces of Central America**, which was composed of Guatemala, El Salvador, Nicaragua, Honduras, and Costa Rica. They had achieved independence from Spain in 1821, but were joined to the empire of Mexico. The local leaders decided to break away and establish a federal republic, with the capital in **Guatemala City**.

The **Alaungpaya Dynasty** of Burma (present-day Myanmar, see 1752), had been making incursions into the northern Indian state of **Assam**, bringing them into contact with the British, who were occupying the region. In an effort to protect their interests in India, Britain launched the **First Anglo–Burmese War** the following year (1824–26). This resulted in the British capture of much of the territory of Burma, including **Rangoon**, which was taken in 1825.

US ISOLATIONISM

James Monroe (1758–1831, see right) was the fifth president of the United States, serving from 1817–25. His time in office was a period during which the US began to emerge as a serious global power. This period was known as the "era of good feelings", and was marked by significant economic growth and general public optimism. With its aversion to interference in other nations' affairs set out in the Monroe Doctrine, the US began to pursue a policy of isolationism.

1824

This print depicts the Ottoman siege of Missolonghi, where the Greeks had established a provisional government during their war for independence.

Lord Byron
The Romantic poet Lord Byron was inspired by the Greek struggle for independence from the Ottoman Empire, and went to Greece to fight.

AS THE FIGHT FOR GREEK INDEPENDENCE INTENSIFIED, it attracted the public's attention across Europe, especially among writers and artists. One such person was the English **Romantic** poet **Lord Byron** (1788–1824), famed for his poem *Don Juan*. Byron had arrived in Greece the previous year to help fight in the struggle. However, while he was abroad he contracted a serious illness and died on 19 April in **Missolonghi**.

In Peru, a decisive victory at the **Battle of Ayacucho**, 9 December, meant the end of Spanish rule, though to the north, in the territory known as **Upper Peru**, loyalist forces were still holding out against rebel troops, in one of the last bastions of fighting.

1825

THE TERRITORY OF UPPER PERU received a much-needed boost with the arrival of Simón Bolívar (see 1811) and **Antonio José de Sucre** (1785–1830), whose troops helped to defeat the Spanish. Bolívar wanted this territory to **unite** with the rest of Peru, but Sucre had already agreed with the rebel leaders that it would become a separate **republic**. In honour of Bolívar's help the rebels named the new nation **Bolivia**, and they invited Sucre to be its first president, which he accepted. With the creation of Bolivia, all the former Spanish colonies – with the exception of Cuba, Puerto Rico, and the Philippines – had become independent nations.

In England, there was great excitement over the opening, on 27 September, of the **Stockton to Darlington** railway line, in the industrial north of the country. Technological innovations in the use of steam (see 1775 and 1786) to power engines had led to the development of railway **locomotives**, such as the one designed by English inventor **John Blenkinsop** in 1812. **George Stephenson** (1781–1848), a colliery mechanic, improved on that design and caught the attention of a group of investors wishing to link the towns of Stockton and Darlington. Darlington was in the middle of a **coal mining** region and the Pennine mountains made transportation difficult. The 40-km (25-mile) line opened the way for further railroad development.

Crowd puller
The opening of the Stockton to Darlington rail line marked the first time that a locomotive was used to pull a passenger train.

10 January Edward Jenner, smallpox vaccine pioneer, dies (b.1749)

United Provinces of Central America declare their independence (Guatemala, Honduras, Nicaragua, Costa Rica)

10 September Simón Bolívar named president of **Peru**

2 December New diplomatic policy by US, the **Monroe doctrine**, posits **non-intervention** by US and Europe in the Americas

19 April Poet **Lord Byron** dies in Missolonghi, Greece (b.1788)

First Anglo-Burmese War (to 1826) over Burma's occupation of territory in northeast India

Dutch cede **Malacca** to British

9 December Battle of Ayacucho in Peru is a decisive victory over Spain

4 March John Quincy Adams becomes sixth US president

Javanese revolts against Dutch rule (to 1830)

20 June Bourbon **Charles X** crowned King of France

6 August Bolivia gains independence from Spain

27 September Opening of the **Stockton–Darlington Railway** in Britain marks start of passenger rail travel using locomotives

26 October Erie canal opens in New York state, linking Lake Erie and the Hudson River

1826

1827

1828

1829

1830

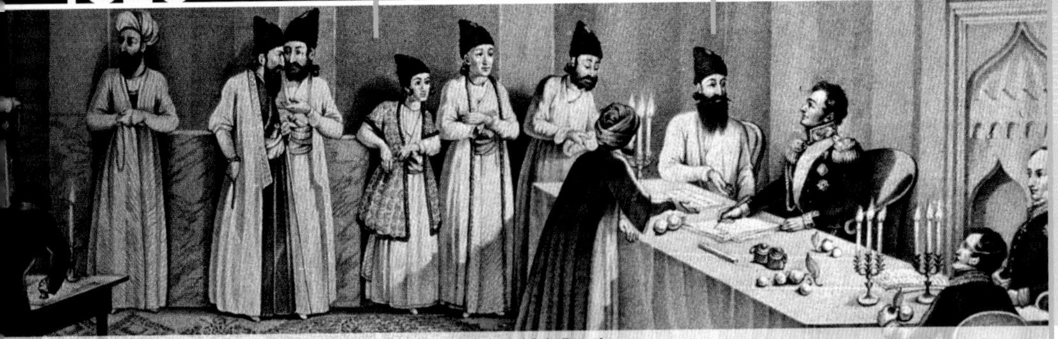

The signing ceremony at the Treaty of Turkmanchai, in which Persia returned contested land in the Caucasus region to Russia.

29 KILOMETRES PER HOUR THE TOP SPEED OF THE **FIRST US STEAM LOCOMOTIVE**

A depiction of the uprising that led to the Belgian independence.

TENSIONS BETWEEN RUSSIA AND Persia restarted (see 1813) over the Caucasus region, with the Persians attempting to take back the territory of **Georgia** in 1825. However, a crushing defeat at the **Battle of Ganja** on 26 September 1826 halted the Persian advance. Russian troops then marched into Persia, eventually taking Tehran, leaving the Persians no option but to accept **defeat**. They negotiated the **Treaty of Turkmanchai**, which put the Russian border at the Aras River, returning the Caucasus territory to Russia.

In **Hawaii**, US missionaries had started to settle on the islands and America had become one of the kingdom's largest trading partners. The US was looking to protect its growing interests thereby formalizing trade arrangements in the face of possible European competition, so it convinced the regency government of **King Kamehameha III** (1813–54) to sign the **Hawaii–United States Treaty** of 1826. The treaty stipulated that there would be peaceful and friendly political and trading relations between the two.

In France, inventor **Joseph-Nicéphore Niépce** (1765–1833) took the world's first **photograph**, known as *View from the Window at Le Gras*, which was of a barnyard in France. His technique involved making an eight-hour exposure onto a pewter plate using a **camera obscura**, which was a dark box with a tiny hole – a forerunner of the modern camera.

AS GREECE'S BATTLE AGAINST the Ottoman Empire continued, neighbouring powers began to call for an end to the conflict. Britain, France, and Russia joined together to sign the **Treaty of London** on 6 July, which demanded the establishment of an independent Greek state. The Ottomans refused, confident they had the land and sea power to defeat the Greeks.

By autumn, the Ottoman resources were put to the test as a Turkish–Egyptian fleet went up against a naval force comprising British, French, and Russian ships at the **Battle of Navarino** on 20 October. The Russo–European ships sunk three-quarters of the Ottoman fleet, and this humiliating defeat led to the eventual withdrawal of Turkish troops from Greece, which won independence in 1832.

A one-sided battle
A Turkish warship burns fiercely at the Battle of Navarino, in which the Ottoman fleet was devastated but not a single allied ship was lost.

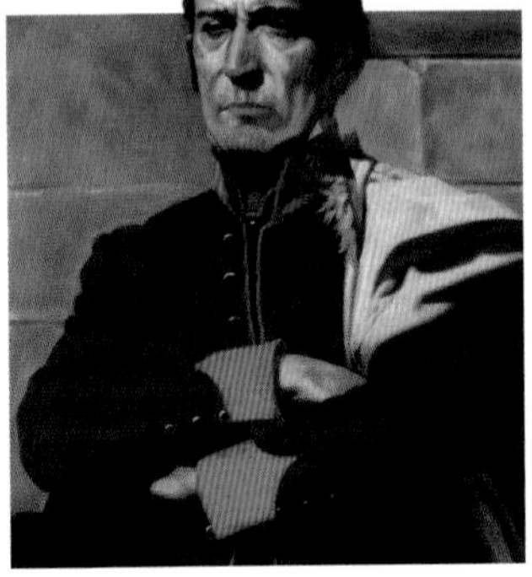

José Gervasio Artigas
Artigas was the father of the Uruguayan independence movement, but had been in exile for several years when it was finally liberated.

THE TREATY OF MONTEVIDEO RECOGNIZED the independence of Uruguay in August 1828. The area, then known as the **Banda Oriental**, was disputed between Brazil and Argentina. It had been under Spanish control but during the wars of independence in South America, under the leadership of **José Gervasio Artigas** (1764–1850), the territory established its independence from Spain and Argentina in 1815. However, the following year, **Brazil invaded** and occupied it. This led to a further war, led by **Juan Antonio Lavalleja** (1784–1853) and his group known as the "**thirty-three immortals**". Lavalleja, with Argentinian support, defeated Brazilian troops and founded an independent Uruguay.

Territorial disputes were also behind another conflict between the **Ottoman Empire** and **Russia**, with the Russians capturing **Vidin** and **Varna** (in present-day Bulgaria).

DEBATE OVER IRELAND HAD intensified after the Act of Union (see 1801). **Daniel O'Connell**, a Catholic lawyer, called for England to repeal its **anti-Catholic laws**, arguing that it could not claim to be representing the people of Ireland. In addition, he staged mass meetings about the issue of **Catholic emancipation**. In 1828, O'Connell stood for parliament and won, though he was not allowed to sit in government because of his Catholicism. His victory, however, attracted the attention of the British prime minister, Arthur Wellesley, the **Duke of Wellington** (see 1815), who was Irish though not Catholic. He oversaw the **Catholic Relief Act 1829**, which allowed Catholics in Ireland and England to take seats in Parliament and hold public office.

Elsewhere in England, inventor George Stephenson (see 1825) unveiled a new locomotive engine, known as the ***Rocket***, which could reach speeds of about 58km (36 miles) per hour. He had entered the **Liverpool and Manchester Railway** competition for best new engine. The *Rocket* was the clear victor.

This year also saw progress of the railway in the US, with the first American-built steam locomotive, **Tom Thumb**. In 1830, a race was staged against a horse-drawn cart to prove the **superiority of steam power**. Although the horse won on this occasion due to a techinal fault with the train, the point was made and the owners of the **Baltimore and Ohio Railroad** agreed to switch to steam trains.

EUROPE HAD SCARCELY RECOVERED from the unrest of the previous decade (see 1820) when France was convulsed by the **July Revolution**, an insurrection that forced the abdication of Charles X (r.1824–30), who was replaced by **Louis-Philippe**, duke of Orléans (r.1830–48). The rebellion had been triggered by Charles's attempt to enforce repressive ordinances, such as suspending the freedom of the press and modifying electoral law so many people lost their right to vote.

Louis-Philippe's succession to the throne signalled the arrival of power for the **bourgeoisie**, who were his chief support, rather than the aristocracy, and he remained in power until 1848.

Around the same time, **revolts** were taking place in the Italian and German kingdoms; in the Netherlands; and in Russia, as the **Polish** living under Russian rule rose up against the tsar.

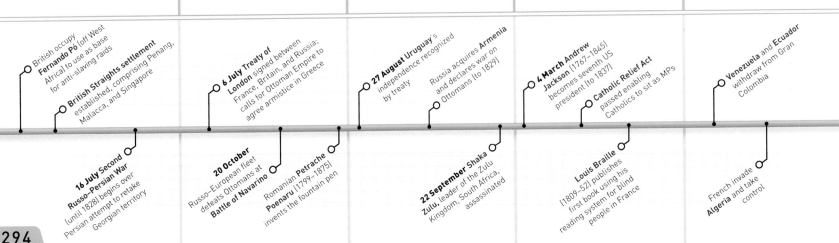

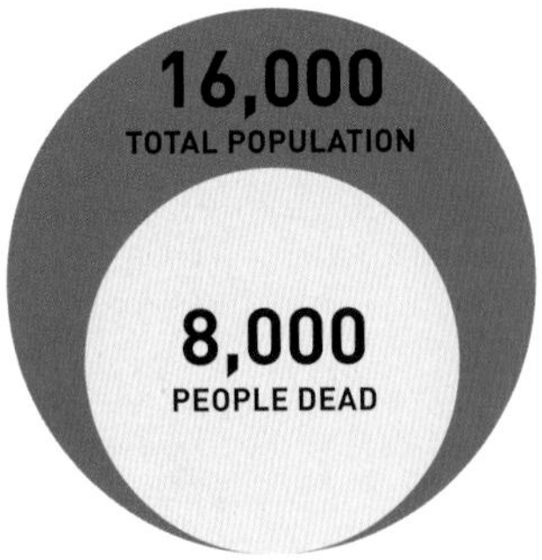

Cherokee deaths on Trail of Tears
Thousands of American Indians were forcibly relocated from the southeast of the US, travelling a route later called the Trail of Tears.

- British occupy **Fernando Pó** (off West Africa) to use as base for anti-slaving raids
- **British Straights settlement** established, comprising Penang, Malacca, and Singapore
- **16 July Second Russo–Persian War** (until 1828) begins over Persian attempt to retake Georgian territory
- **6 July Treaty of London** signed between France, Britain, and Russia; calls for Ottoman Empire to agree armistice in Greece
- **20 October** Russo–European fleet defeats Ottomans at **Battle of Navarino**
- Romanian **Petrache Poenaru** (1799–1875) invents the fountain pen
- **27 August Uruguay**'s independence recognized by treaty
- Russia acquires **Armenia** and declares war on Ottomans (to 1829)
- **22 September Shaka Zulu**, leader of the Zulu Kingdom, South Africa, assassinated
- **4 March Andrew Jackson** (1767–1845) becomes seventh US president (to 1837)
- **Catholic Relief Act** passed enabling Catholics to sit as MPs
- **Louis Braille** (1809–52) publishes first book using his reading system for blind people in France
- **Venezuela** and **Ecuador** withdraw from Gran Colombia
- French invade **Algeria** and take control

> **“ NO MINISTER** EVER STOOD, OR **COULD STAND,** AGAINST **PUBLIC OPINION. ”**

Robert Peel, British politician, on the Reform Act, 1834

Also during this period, French troops arrived in **Algiers**, with the intention of taking control. A few years earlier, in 1827, the provincial Ottoman ruler, or dey, Husayn (r.1818–38), had struck a French consul with a fly whisk, giving the French a pretext for war. The source of the tension was an unpaid debt between France and the dey. During a French blockade of Algiers, matters escalated. By 5 July, the French had raised their flag over the kasbah in Algiers and this marked the start of French control over this North African territory.

In **South America**, political alliances were also fragile. Before his death in 1830, Simón Bolívar (see 1811) had witnessed the secession of **Venezuela and Ecuador** from Gran Colombia, which ended his dream of **political unity** among the new republics.

Further north, more settlers in the US were making their way west, and this was known as the **era of the wagon train**. Settlers, travelling in groups of horse-drawn wagons carrying all of their possessions, headed out to unknown territory to set up farms and settle the land.

Meanwhile, to facilitate settlement in the east, the US government passed the **Indian Removal Act** in 1830. This stripped American Indians of legal rights, and forced them to leave their desirable territory in the southeast of the country and relocate to sparsely populated land west of the Mississippi. The moves resulted in many deaths.

Liberty leading the people
This famous painting by French artist Eugène Delacroix (1798–1863) was inspired by the July Revolution, and depicts "Liberty" as a woman.

THE KINGDOM OF THE NETHERLANDS was caught up in the turmoil across Europe. The Congress of Vienna (see 1815) had forced the Belgian territories, which had been under French control, to unite with the Dutch, thereby creating a buffer between Russia and France. This move proved unpopular and tensions grew over the intervening years.

By August 1830, inspired by events in France, the **Belgian Revolution** had begun. The result was a clear break from the kingdom of the Netherlands. Later that year a **constitution** was issued, which created a constitutional monarchy and a parliamentary system. On 20 January 1831, the new state of **Belgium** was officially recognized by Britain and France, though not the Netherlands. The Belgians were forced to choose a monarch with no direct connection to other major European powers. They finally elected Leopold of Saxe-Coburg-Saalfeld – the uncle of Britain's Queen Victoria – and he ruled as **Leopold I** until 1865.

The same year, Syria was annexed by Egypt until 1840, when the latter was finally forced to return the region to the Ottomans.

The English Reform Act
A cartoon shows the reformers' attack on the "Old Rotten Tree", which symbolizes the corrupt "rotten" boroughs. They wanted a fairer distribution of parliamentary seats.

BRITAIN ALSO SAW UPHEAVAL AND SOCIAL CHANGE in the 1830s. There had been growing public discontent over the outdated voting system (see 1819). A bill was drafted, aimed at transferring votes and redistributing seats from small "rotten" boroughs controlled by the nobility to the more populous industrial towns. The first **Reform Bill**, failed to be passed in parliament. This caused serious riots in many cities, as well as a political crisis with the prime minister, **Charles Grey** (1764–1845), who threatened to step down over the matter. The bill finally became law on 4 June 1832. This legislation allowed more middle-class men the vote, but the working class and women were still excluded.

- **7 February** Belgian constitution recognized; **Belgium** declares independence
- **26 May** US Congress passes **Indian Removal Act**
- **26 June William IV** (1765–1837) ascends to the British throne
- First wave of **rebellion** and social unrest in Europe calling for liberal political reforms
- **9 August Louis Philippe** (1773–1850) declared king of France after revolution in Paris
- **25 August** Start of the **Belgian Revolution** (to 1831)
- **29 November Polish uprising** against Russia
- Egypt occupies **Syria** (to 1840)
- First official Ottoman newspaper ***Takvim-i Vekayi*** begins publication
- **21 August Nat Turner slave rebellion** in US, leaving more than 50 white people in Virginia dead
- **4 June** British parliament passes the **Reform Act**, which makes significant changes to the electoral system
- Russia annexes **Duchy of Warsaw**
- **30 August Treaty of London** creates an **independent kingdom of Greece** and installs a monarchy.

1833–34

This engraving shows children working in an English mill. The size of the first cotton spinning machines meant they were best operated by children.

48 THE MAXIMUM **HOURS** PER WEEK **CHILDREN AGED 9–12** COULD **WORK** IN ENGLISH **MILLS**

IN BRITAIN, INDUSTRIAL development and urban growth progressed rapidly. Laws were introduced to address exploitation of labour and the growing cost of providing for the poor. The **1833 Factory Act** appointed inspectors to monitor factories and limited the hours that children could work.

In England, local parishes provided some relief for the elderly, ill, and impoverished. Out of this grew a system of **workhouses,** aiming to give employment to the able-bodied. The **Poor Law Amendment Act of 1834** stipulated that the poor could only receive assistance if they went to workhouses, which were to be built in every parish. Conditions in the workhouses were deliberately harsh and the legislation immediately proved unpopular.

In China, British merchants were granted permission to **engage in trade** after legislation ended the East India Company's monopoly. Although there had been private traders in Canton before the act, now more were allowed to sell their wares and export Chinese goods, such as **tea**, the imports of which rose 40 per cent after the beginning of free trade.

In 1832, **Egypt invaded Syria**. Muhammad Ali, the pasha, was angered by a failed promise from the Ottoman sultan to give him the territory. Ali took Gaza and Jerusalem in the **First Turko–Egyptian War**, and by 1833 the Ottoman government begged Russia for help, and 18,000 troops were sent to Constantinople. Britain and France got involved, demanding a settlement, in which Egypt was given Syria, and Russia withdrew.

Commemorative coin
The Slave Emancipation Act outlawed the buying or selling of people, set free young children, and compensated planters in most of the British Empire.

1835

A Galápagos cactus finch, one of the species noted by Charles Darwin.

IN THE PACIFIC OCEAN, almost a thousand kilometres from the coastline of South America, English naturalist **Charles Darwin** (1809–82) took extensive notes on the nature of the **Galápagos Islands**. Darwin had accepted a post on a scientific voyage aboard the *Beagle*, which left England on 27 December 1831, arriving in the Galápagos in September 1835 (see also 1839). It was in the Galápagos where Darwin first noticed the difference in the species of wildlife on the island compared with mainland South America. This discovery laid the foundation for his later scientific work on the **evolution** of different species (see 1859).

In Britain, the **National Colonisation Society** had been set up to facilitate the settlement in Australia of people who were not convicts. Founder **Edward Gibbon Wakefield** (1796–1862) – who had served time in prison – came up with a scheme for populating colonies based on the sale of land and a tax on the price, which would pay for the transportation to the colony. A fleet set off for **South Australia**, where the city of Melbourne was established in 1835, and Adelaide a year later.

> “ IT SEEMS TO BE **A LITTLE WORLD** WITHIN **ITSELF.** ”
>
> **Charles Darwin**, from *Journal of Researches*, September 1835

1836

The Alamo, the site of a key battle for Texan independence.

AS SETTLERS IN THE US MOVED WEST, many decided to live in the Texas territory, which was part of Mexico. However, Mexican authorities wanted tighter control over this large territory and the settlers rebelled in October 1835, launching the **Texas War of Independence**. The following March, after months of unrest, General Antonio López de Santa Anna (1794–1876) marched into Texas with 5,000 Mexican troops. Although massively outnumbered, the rebels managed to hold them off during a battle at a San Antonio fortress, called the Alamo. The rebels were eventually defeated but the Alamo proved a rallying point for Texans bent on revenge. Soon after, General **Samuel Houston** (1793–1863) led a Texan army with the battle cry "Remember the Alamo!" and beat Santa Anna at the **Battle of Jacinto** on 21 April, forcing Mexico to recognize the new republic of Texas.

Battle of the Alamo
Texans were vastly outnumbered by Mexican forces in the battle fought between 23 February and 6 March and there were very few survivors.

1837

A painting of Queen Victoria's coronation in Westminster Abbey.

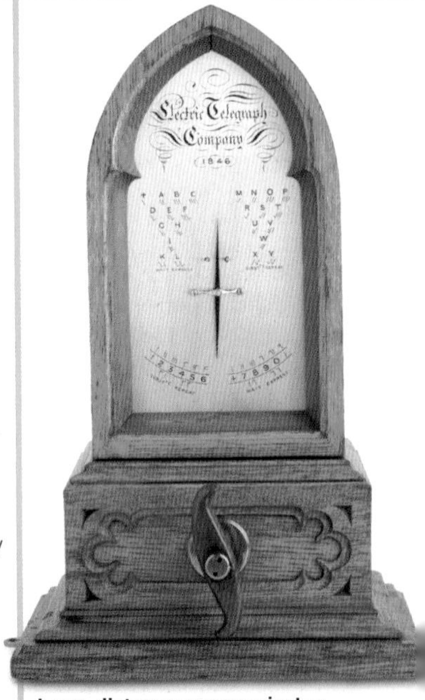

Long-distance communicator
This is a single-needle electric telegraph machine, which later developed into double-needle and four-needle instruments.

EXPERIMENTS had been taking place for decades over the question of how to transmit electric current through wires. In 1837, two British inventors, **William Fothergill Cooke** and **Charles Wheatstone**, made a breakthrough and secured a patent for an **electric telegraph** device that allowed for communication through wires and had **needles that could point to specific letters and numbers**. At the same time in the US, **Samuel Morse** received a patent on an electromagnetic transmitter that could transfer

---

1833 Slave Emancipation Act abolishes slavery in British Empire; not in force until 1838

1833 Factory Act in Britain prohibits employment of children under age of nine

1833 Isabella II (1830–1904) takes Spanish throne, with Maria Christina (1806–78) as regent

1833 First Turko–Egyptian War ends; Egypt retains Syria, which it had invaded in 1831

1834 Poor Law Amendment Act passed in Britain calling for the poor to support themselves

1834 First Carlist War in Spain over succession to the throne (to 1839)

1834 British East India Company's monopoly on trade to China abolished

5 May First railway in continental Europe opens in Belgium

1 December Danish author **Hans Christian Andersen** publishes first book of fairy tales

30 August Founding of the town of **Melbourne** in Australia

2 March Texans rebel against Mexican rule and declare their territory a republic

6 March Defeat of Texans at Battle of the **Alamo**

Spain recognizes **independence of Mexico**

24 October A. Phillips patents the **match**

26 December Colony of **South Australia** officially proclaimed

Death of **Muhammad Bello,** whose kingdom of Sokoto (northern Nigeria) reached a population of around 10 million

Charles Wheatstone and **William Cooke** patent the telegraph in Britain; **Samuel Morse** in US

4 March Martin van Buren becomes third US president

> **“ HE’LL HAVE US GOING TO THE MOON YET. ”**

Great Western Railway director, on Isambard Kingdom Brunel

The East India Company’s steamer, *Nemesis*, attacks Chinese war junks in Anson’s Bay, at the mouth of the Pearl River, China, during the First Opium War.

information using dots and dashes. Morse’s telegraph was far simpler than the Cooke Wheatstone design, and soon became the standard instrument worldwide, revolutionizing the global movement of information.

When Britain’s King William IV died on 20 June, he had no surviving legitimate heir, so the crown passed to **Victoria**, his niece (see panel, below). She was the daughter of Edward, Duke of Kent, and granddaughter of George III. Her reign was viewed as a time of growing prosperity, technological innovation, and colonial expansion.

In **Japan**, **Tokugawa Ieyoshi** (1793–1853) became shogun. At the time of his rule, Japan was experiencing social and economic decline. He introduced measures known as the **Tempo Reforms**, restricting migration to urban areas and instigating price controls, but they failed.

QUEEN VICTORIA (1819–1901)

Ruling for 63 years and 216 days, Queen Victoria remains the longest-reigning monarch of Britain. In 1840, she married her cousin, Albert of Saxe-Coburg and Gotha (1819–1861). She adored him and they had nine children together. The Victorian era contrasted sharply with the excesses of previous Hanoverian rulers, and Victoria’s domestic life was held up as the model for families in this period.

Brunel’s *Great Western*
The Great Western *steamship shown off the west coast of England. The sails helped to propel the ship and keep it on an even keel.*

TRANSPORTATION TECHNOLOGY was rapidly changing. Along with the expansion in rail transport, travel by sea was also being revolutionized by many innovations. The power of steam was finally harnessed in an efficient way that allowed for much quicker sea crossings (see 1786). On 8 April 1838, the **Great Western** left Bristol for its maiden transatlantic voyage, and arrived in New York 15 days later; the paddle-wheeled steamship had cut the voyage time in half and arrived with fuel to spare. The ship had been designed by leading British civil engineer **Isambard Kingdom Brunel** (1806–59), who had also been involved in other engineering projects, including the Great Western Railway. The idea for the steamship started as a suggestion by Brunel to Great Western Railway directors that the train line could be extended to New York by way of a regular transatlantic service. Soon after, the **Great Western Steamship Company** was set up to facilitate the construction of the ship.

In the Americas, **Guatemala**, **Honduras**, and **Nicaragua** became independent nations.

WHILE BRITISH TRADE IN CHINA CONTINUED TO EXPAND, so too did the Chinese opium problem. Decades earlier, the East India Company had started exporting the drug, produced from **poppies** grown in Bengal, to China in order to trade it for tea, which it then sent to Britain. Despite numerous attempts to ban the importation of the substance, British ships continued to import it. On 30 March 1839, one frustrated Chinese commissioner ordered British warehouses and ships in Canton to be destroyed. Britain sent warships in retaliation, attacking China’s coastline in the **First Opium War**.

Meanwhile, tensions between Egypt and the Ottoman sultan erupted again in the **Second Turko–Egyptian War**. This time it was triggered by an Ottoman attempt to invade Syria, which it had previously ceded to Egypt (see 1833).

At the same time, British political meddling in Afghanistan triggered the **First Afghan War** (to 1842). Worried about Russia’s growing influence over the Afghan emir, **Dost Muhammad Khan** (1793-1863), Britain attempted to replace him with an emir more sympathetic to British interests in northern India, including the protection of overland trade routes through the region.

In England, naturalist Charles Darwin (see 1835) published an account of the diary he kept while on the ***Beagle***. The journey had taken Darwin around the world. He had set off from Plymouth in 1831 for the Cape Verde Islands, then Brazil, Argentina, Uruguay, and Tierra del Fuego. He then sailed north along the Pacific Coast of South America, stopping at the Galápagos Islands, before going onward to Tahiti, New Zealand, Australia, Mauritius, and finally back to England, arriving in October 1836. Darwin’s account helped make his name in science.

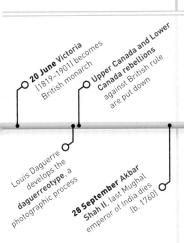

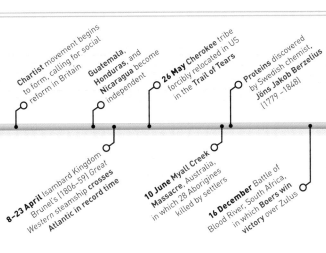

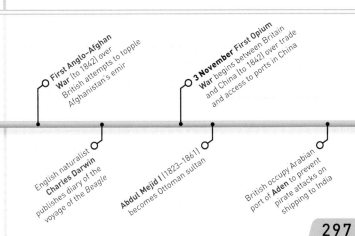

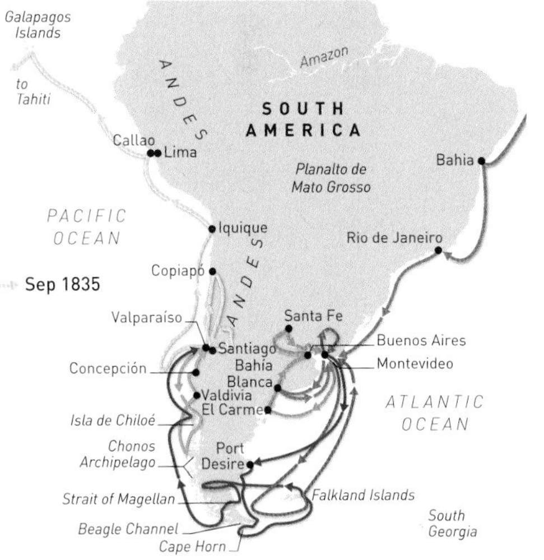

Darwin’s *Beagle* voyages
Charles Darwin’s five-year voyage (1831–36) on the Beagle, *a warship carrying ten cannons, led him to consider scientific evidence in new ways.*

20 June Victoria (1819–1901) becomes British monarch

Louis Daguerre develops the **daguerreotype**, a photographic process

Upper Canada and Lower Canada rebellions against British rule are put down

28 September Akbar Shah II, last Mughal emperor of India dies (b. 1760)

Chartist movement begins to form, calling for social reform in Britain

8–23 April Isambard Kingdom Brunel’s (1806–59) *Great Western* steamship **crosses Atlantic in record time**

Guatemala, Honduras, and **Nicaragua** become independent

26 May Cherokee tribe forcibly relocated in US in the **Trail of Tears**

10 June Myall Creek Massacre, Australia, in which 28 Aborigines killed by settlers

Proteins discovered by Swedish chemist, **Jöns Jakob Berzelius** (1779 –1848)

16 December Battle of Blood River, South Africa, in which **Boers win victory** over Zulus

First Anglo–Afghan War (to 1842) over British attempts to topple Afghanistan’s emir

English naturalist **Charles Darwin** publishes diary of the voyage of the *Beagle*

Abdul Mejid I (1823–1861) becomes Ottoman sultan

3 November First Opium War begins between Britain and China (to 1842) over trade and access to ports in China

British occupy Arabian port of **Aden** to prevent pirate attacks on shipping to India

THE STORY OF ELECTRICITY

HARNESSING THE FORCE THAT BUILT THE MODERN WORLD

When Thales, a mathematician and philosopher in ancient Greece, experimented with a piece of amber – known as "elektron" in Greek – little could he have known that his initial observations would still hold a significant place in science more than 2,000 years later.

What Thales noticed was that if he rubbed a piece of amber against fur it would attract bits of dust and feathers lying nearby – although he did not know it, he had stumbled on what we know today as static electricity. Over the following centuries, scientists all over the world experimented with this form of electricity, as well as magnets and magnetism. By the 17th and 18th centuries, technological leaps had been made, though the connection between electricity and magnets would not be clear until the 19th century (see panel, right).

POWER TO THE PEOPLE

As the 1800s progressed, understanding about electricity rapidly increased, and new innovations were rolled out in quick succession. By the dawn of the 20th century, many of the technologies were in place that are still with us today – such as batteries and light bulbs – though they have since been further adapted and refined. Nowadays, the scientific challenge is to find ways of generating electricity that do not cause pollution.

Wimshurst machine
The English inventor James Wimshurst developed a device that could generate static electricity and store it in a vessel called a Leyden jar. For many years, scientists studying electricity used Wimshurst machines to produce electric charge.

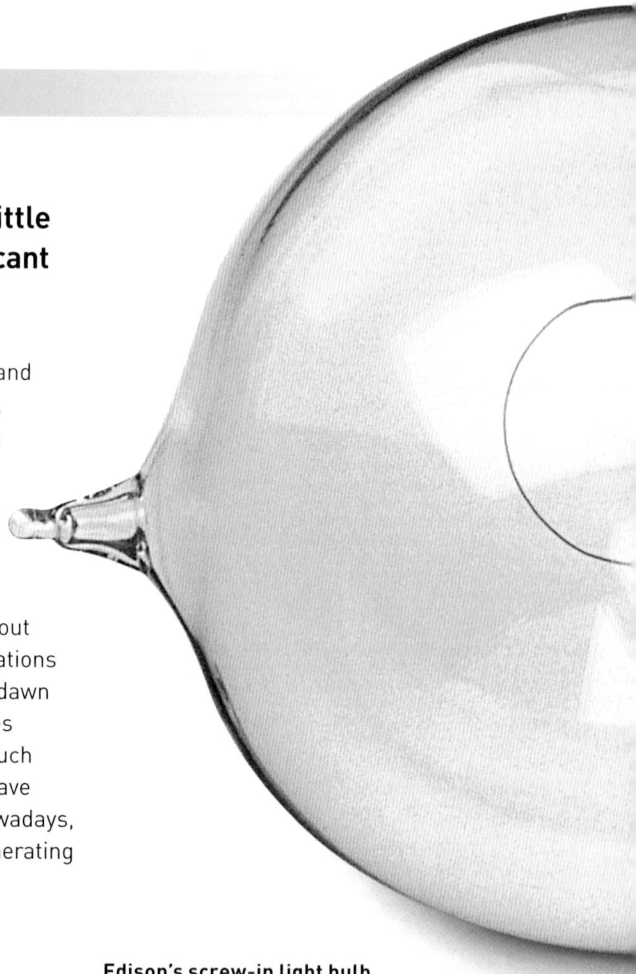

Edison's screw-in light bulb
Although US inventor Thomas Edison is often credited with inventing the light bulb, what he really did was improve an existing idea (see below). He spent years working out a way – using incandescent bulbs – to make electric lighting practical and safe for public use.

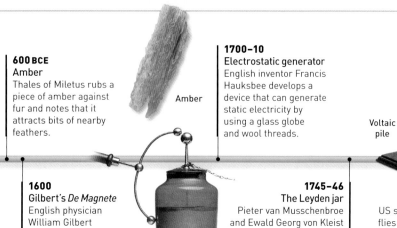

600 BCE
Amber
Thales of Miletus rubs a piece of amber against fur and notes that it attracts bits of nearby feathers.

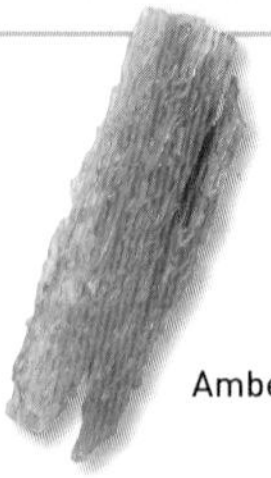

Amber

1600
Gilbert's *De Magnete*
English physician William Gilbert publishes his famous work on magnetism.

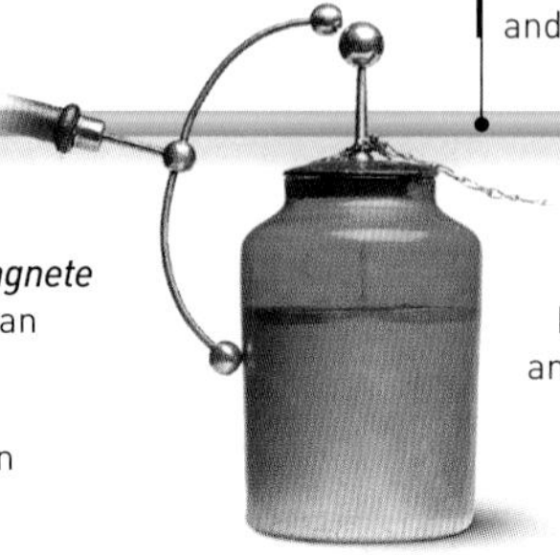

Leyden Jar

1700–10
Electrostatic generator
English inventor Francis Hauksbee develops a device that can generate static electricity by using a glass globe and wool threads.

1745–46
The Leyden jar
Pieter van Musschenbroe and Ewald Georg von Kleist independently invent a device that allows static electricity to be stored.

1752
Lightning conductor
US scientist Benjamin Franklin flies a kite during a storm, with a key tied to the string, and proves that lightning is a form of electricity.

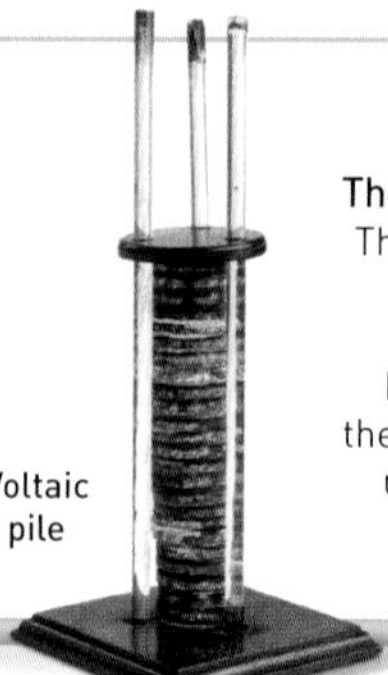

Voltaic pile

1799–1800
The first voltaic pile
The Italian inventor Alessandro Volta creates the first battery, known as the voltaic pile – the unit "volt" is later named after him.

1820
Electromagnetism discovered
Danish physicist Hans Christian Ørsted notices that a magnet is affected by a nearby wire connected to a battery, and discovers the relationship between magnets and electricity.

1820s–30s
Faraday experiments
English scientist Michael Faraday further illustrates the relationship between electricity and magnetism with his induction ring.

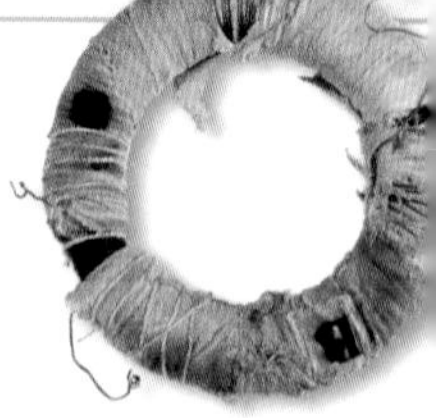

Faraday's induction ring

“ GENIUS IS ONLY ONE PER CENT INSPIRATION, AND NINETY-NINE PER CENT PERSPIRATION. ”

Thomas Edison, US inventor, *c.*1903

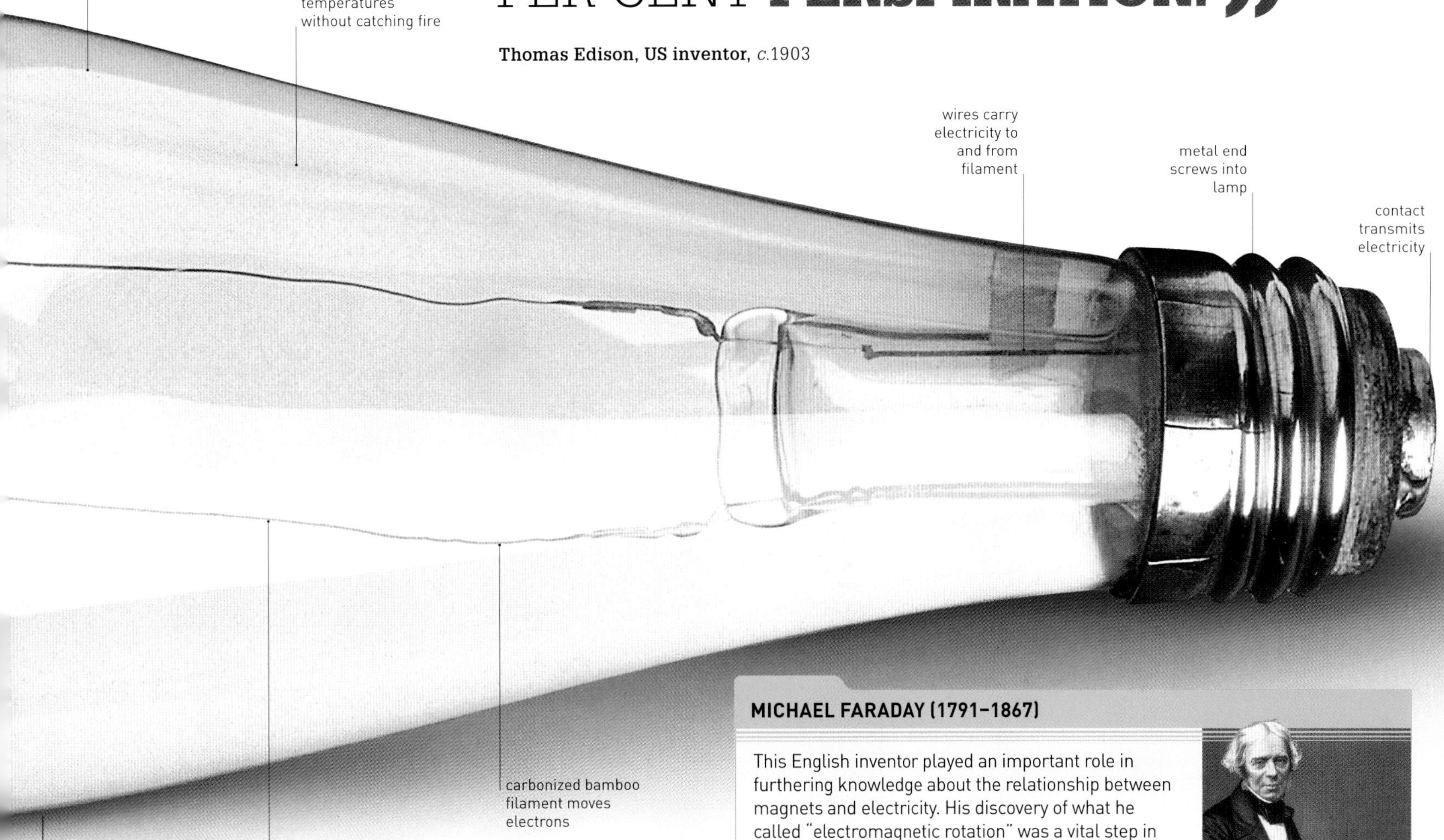

MICHAEL FARADAY (1791–1867)

This English inventor played an important role in furthering knowledge about the relationship between magnets and electricity. His discovery of what he called “electromagnetic rotation” was a vital step in the development of what would become the electric motor. Faraday worked out that the interaction between electricity and a magnet would lead to the constant rotation of current, something he tested using a wire carrying electricity, a magnet, and a bowl of mercury.

1825
The electromagnet
This device, built by Joseph Henry, uses two metal plates, which are put in acid in order to form a voltaic cell.

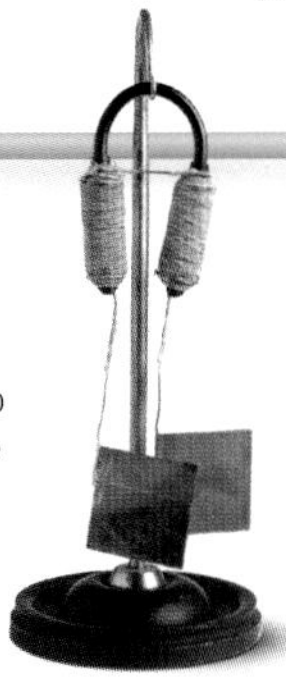

Henry's electromagnet

1878–79
The electric light bulb
British inventor Joseph Swan creates an incandescent “electric lamp”. The idea is improved by US scientist Thomas Edison, and the light bulb is born.

1881
The world's first public electric lighting
The English town of Godalming, Surrey, brings to a close the era of the gas lamp when it wires its streets with electric lighting.

Hoover Dam

1882
Hydroelectric power
Scientists begin to realize that the force of water can generate electricity, and build dams and hydroelectric power plants to harness this energy.

Tesla coil

1883–84
The Tesla coil
Serbian-American inventor Nikola Tesla develops a coil that can transmit electricity over long distances – it is a crucial discovery that aids the spread of electricity.

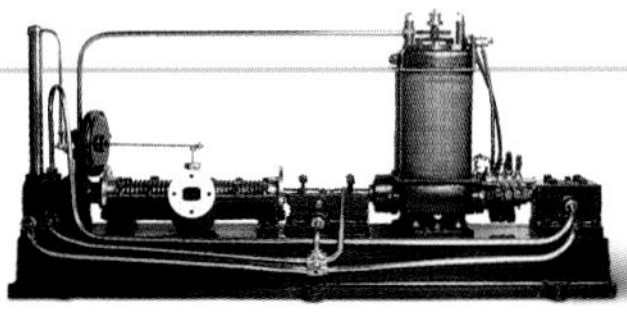

Steam turbine

1884
Electricity from steam
Like liquid water, steam is also harnessed for electricity by devices like the turbine, created by Charles Patton.

1950s
Nuclear power
Scientists discover that atoms can be used – in controlled nuclear reactions – as a source of energy to heat water, which then generates electricity. By 1951, the first nuclear power plant is built in Arco, Idaho, in the US.

Early 21st century
Sustainable electricity
Growing worries about pollution caused by the older ways of generating energy lead to the development of “green” technology, such as wind turbines.

Wind turbines

1840

Horse and coach at a London station leaving to deliver mail. The development of stagecoaches meant post could be delivered all over Britain.

EUROPEAN SETTLEMENT OF New Zealand had gradually increased over the previous decade, and included the introduction of many missions. Settlers traded with the **Maori** who were already living on the island – exchanging European muskets for Maori crops and livestock. This had led to an arms race between rival tribes in the Maori **Musket Wars** (1820–35).

The British wanted to establish a colony and the **New Zealand Company** was set up, selling land for settlement (see 1835). A ship of settlers left for New Zealand in 1839. All involved were aware of potential hostility from the Maori. In 1840, William Hobson (1792–1842), lieutenant-governor of New Zealand, approached Maori chiefs with the **Treaty of Waitangi**. This offered protection by the British in exchange for ceding sovereignty.

Tamati Waka Nene
Nene was a warrior and chieftain of the Maori Ngatihoa tribe in the early 19th century. He spoke out in favour of the Treaty of Waitangi.

The Maori would keep their land on the basis that if they sold it only the British Crown could buy it. There was much opposition to the treaty but some Maori chiefs believed that the British presence would bring stability to the country. On 21 May sovereignty was proclaimed over the territory.

In Britain, the **postal system** was reformed. Improved transport meant that mail could be delivered all over the country, but costs rose as postage was paid for on receipt, based on distance travelled. A "**penny post**" system was proposed, whereby any letter could be sent anywhere in the country for a penny, and postage would be pre-paid using stamps. These measures came into force in 1840 and was the first system of its kind in the world.

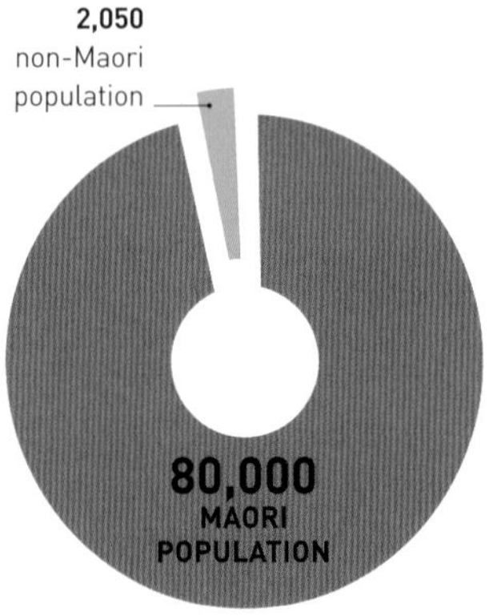

New Zealand's population in 1840
The European population was still very small at the end of 1840, though the Treaty of Waitangi opened the way for further settlement.

1841

The port of Hong Kong was key to Britain's trade in the East.

AS CHINESE AND BRITISH TROOPS continued to fight in the **Opium War**, Britain's ships sailed up the Pearl River, capturing forts around Canton, followed by the ports of Amoy and Ningpo. The British also occupied the key port of Hong Kong. A preliminary agreement to end the war, drafted in January and known as the **Convention of Chuenpee**, ceded Hong Kong to the British, but the document was written amid continued hostilities and was never ratified.

Egypt and the Turks, meanwhile, ended their second **war over Syria** (see 1839), with Egyptian troops withdrawing from Syria.

1842

An illustration depicting a caravan of African slaves. The slave trade remained prevalent in many parts of the world despite a growing effort to eradicate it.

THE OPIUM WAR between Britain and China finally came to an end after British troops took further territory, reaching Nanking in August. Chinese officials sued for peace, resulting in the **Treaty of Nanking** on 29 August. China was forced to pay an indemnity of $20 million to the British and officially cede Hong Kong. It was also made to open the ports of Canton, Amoy, Foochow, Ningpo, and Shanghai to British trade. These cities became known as "**treaty ports**".

Industrialization and the **mining** industry resulted in many children finding themselves in dirty and dangerous working conditions. In Britain, social reformer Anthony Ashley Cooper, seventh earl of Shaftesbury (1801–85), became a driving force for the **Mines Act of 1842**, prohibiting children under ten and women from working in mines. In the US, the state of Massachusetts passed legislation to **limit a child's work day** to ten hours. Belgium's King Leopold I also tried to regulate child and female labour conditions, but his plans were rejected.

The **slave trade** and the practice of slavery still persisted in many countries. France had brought slavery back to its colonies (see 1803), and while Spain had signed a treaty over abolition in 1817 with the British, who had abolished the slave trade in 1807, it was not enforced for decades. Likewise, **Portugal's** 1818 treaty with Britain and subsequent treaties were not honoured, nor was slavery abolished in its colonies. However, in 1842, a further treaty allowed British ships to attack Portuguese slave ships off East Africa. The Portuguese colony of **Mozambique** was a huge slave port, with 15,000 slaves a year taken from 1820 to 1830.

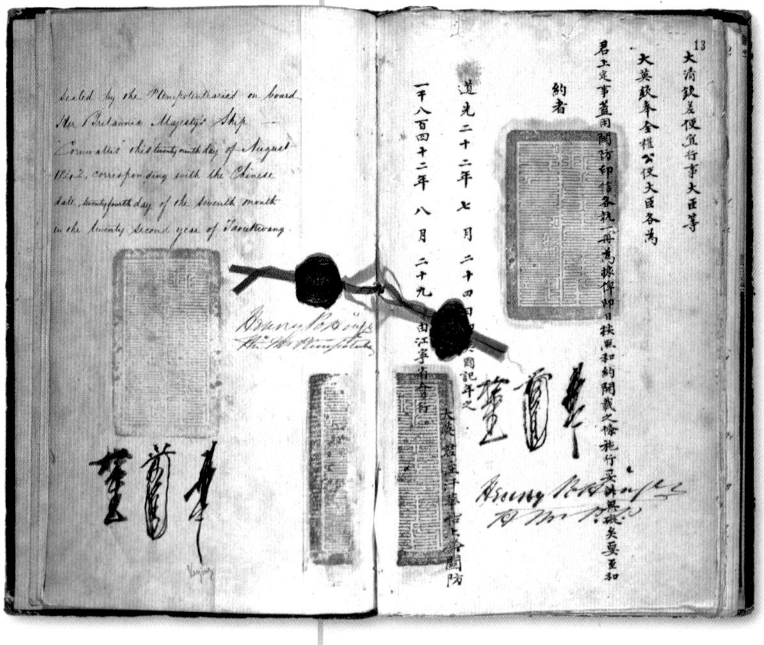

Treaty of Nanking
This treaty ended the three-year Opium War, gave Britain control of Hong Kong, and opened up five "treaty ports" to traders.

6 February Britain takes over **New Zealand** under Treaty of Waitangi between Maori chiefs and British Crown

1 May World's first postage stamp issued in Britain – the **Penny Black**

4 June Frederick William IV (1795–1861) takes Prussian throne

15 July Convention of London: European powers and Ottoman Empire try to check power of Egypt's Mohammad Ali who threatens Ottoman Empire

4 April US President **William Henry Harrison** dies in office

26 July Britain occupies **Hong Kong**

7 February Battle of Debre Tabor, Ethiopia; Ras Ali Alula, Regent of Emperor of Ethiopia, defeats warlord Wube Haile Maryam of Semien

30 March Anesthesia used for first time in an operation

9 August US–Canada border agreed by **Webster-Ashburton Treaty**

29 August Treaty of Nanking cedes Hong Kong to British, opening five ports to foreign trade

Mines Act prohibits the underground work of women and young children in Britain

1843

A portrait of Abdul Rahman. His father, Faisal, revived Saudi fortunes.

THE OTTOMAN DESTRUCTION OF the first Saudi state (see 1818), established by the Wahhabi movement and **Saud** family, did not prevent the founding of a second Saudi state in 1824. After initial upheavals, **Faisal al-Saud**, second leader of the second state, resumed his rule in 1843, and led the state successfully until 1865.

In South Africa, after a series of victories against the Zulu people, Boer settlers (see 1880) established the **Republic of Natal** in the southeast of the country. The territory was annexed by the British in 1843. Many Boers decided to move further north to what later became the Transvaal and the Orange Free State, joining the emigration of Boers from the Cape Colony, in a move known as the **Great Trek**.

12,000 THE NUMBER OF BOERS WHO MIGRATED FROM THE CAPE COLONY

Despite the treaty between the Maori and the British in New Zealand (see 1840), the issue of illegal land sales caused increased tensions, culminating in the **Wairau Massacre** on 17 June, in which a chief's wife and 22 Europeans were killed.

1844

“WHAT HATH GOD WROUGHT?”

Samuel Morse, American artist and inventor, in his telegraph message

With the backing of the US Congress, Samuel Morse managed to have wires built that could transmit messages.

Friedrich Engels
The Prussian philosopher wrote about the condition of the working classes in England. His work with Karl Marx made him famous.

FRIEDERICH ENGELS (1820–95) was the son of a prosperous businessman who owned textile mills in Prussia and a cotton mill in England. He went to work at the family firm in Manchester in 1841, but he lived a double life. In his spare time he met workers and studied the economic conditions of people in England, and the result of his work was a book, ***The Condition of the Working Class in England in 1844***, in which Engels described working-class life. Around this time he also began a lifelong friendship with fellow writer and philosopher, **Karl Marx** (1818–83), and the two went on to publish hugely influential works about capitalism and communism.

In the Caribbean, a group of conspirators known as **La Trinitaria**, led by Juan Pablo Duarte (1813–76), launched their fight for the independence of the Spanish-speaking side of the island of Hispaniola (see 1822). With neighbouring Haiti distracted by its own civil war, Duarte and his fellow rebels were able to eject the Haitians and declared the new **Dominican Republic** independent from Haiti on 27 February.

Meanwhile, Samuel Morse (see 1837) had managed to get funding from the US government to build the first **telegraph line** in the US from Baltimore to Washington. The line was completed in 1844. In his first public demonstration of the telegraph that year he sent a message which famously read "What hath God wrought?"

Glass and iron
The Palm House at the Royal Botanical Gardens, Kew, UK, was built in 1844, constructed with plate glass and iron. It was the first large-scale structure to be made using wrought iron.

1845

A painting depicts sufferers of the Irish famine. One million died when the potato crop failed over successive years, while millions more left the island for ever.

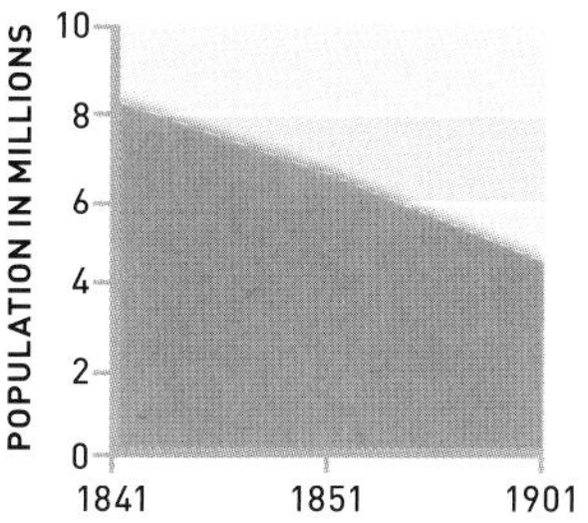

Population decline in Ireland
Partly due to famine deaths, but mostly due to massive emigration to escape deprivation, Ireland's population had halved by the 1900s.

SUCCESSIVE FAILURES OF THE potato crop in Ireland triggered a famine that lasted five years and left more than one million people dead. The crop failure, due to **late blight** (see panel, right), was particularly devastating because for millions of the rural poor, the **potato** was their staple food. The British government's response was limited. Rather than intervene directly, it directed landlords to shoulder the burden. However, as many small tenant farmers had no crops to sell, rents went unpaid and landlords ran their tenants off the land. Landowners soon were unable or unwilling to provide local poor relief. To compound matters, many larger farms continued to export grain, meat, and other foods to Britain as there was no market for them in Ireland, given that there was little extra money available for the purchase of such goods. The fact that these foods were not given to the millions who were starving in Ireland, served to further strain relations between the Irish people and the British government. Many Irish decided to **emigrate** and more than two million people left for Britain, Canada, and the US, contributing to the decline in population from 8 million to 6.5 million between 1841 to 1851.

On the other side of the Atlantic, the Republic of **Texas** had been trying unsuccessfully to join the US since 1836. When it became clear that Britain had a stake in keeping Texas independent, to halt US westward expansion, the suit was finally approved in December.

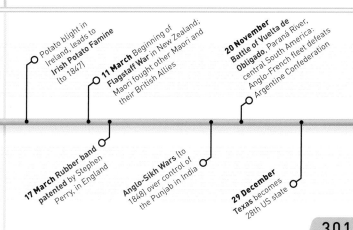

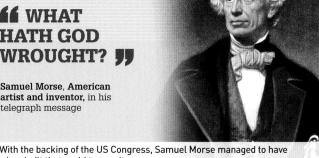

POTATO BLIGHT

The blight responsible for the failure of Ireland's potato crop was *Phytophthora infestans*, a mould that caused rot within two weeks. Blight spreads quickly when humidity stays above 75 per cent and temperatures above 10°C (50°F) for two full days; both factors were present during the summer of 1845. By autumn the crop was lost and people abandoned the land.

17 June First New Zealand War (Land Wars) (to 1847) begins with **Wairu Massacre**

Fortunes of Saud family restored by **Faisal bin Turki** al-Saud (1785–1865)

27 February Santo Domingo wins independence from Haiti and becomes **Dominican Republic**

German political theorist and author **Friedrich Engels** (1820–95) publishes *The Condition of the Working Class in England*

1 May Hong Kong Police Force, first Asian police force, formed

24 May American inventor **Samuel Morse** (1791–1872) sends first telegraph message

24 June Charles Goodyear patents **vulcanized rubber** in the US

Potato blight in Ireland, leads to **Irish Potato Famine** (to 1847)

17 March Rubber band patented by Stephen Perry, in England

11 March Beginning of **Flagstaff War** in New Zealand; Maori fought other Maori and their British Allies

Anglo-Sikh Wars (to 1848) over control of the Punjab in India

20 November Battle of Vuelta de Obligado, Paraná River, central South America: Anglo-French fleet defeats Argentine Confederation

29 December Texas becomes 28th US state

1846

1847

1848

The Battle of Palo Alto, the first battle of the Mexican War, fought near Brownsville, Texas. The war was triggered by a boundary dispute.

A poster from 1848, showing the Parisian public facing the municipal guards during the February revolution against the government.

DIPLOMATIC RELATIONS BETWEEN MEXICO AND THE US became strained after Texas became the 28th state (see 1845). The **Mexican** government did not want to accept this annexation and refuted the US claim that the new state's southern border was at the Rio Grande, stating it lay further north, at the River Nueces. A diplomatic mission was sent to Mexico City in 1845 to settle the matter, as well as to attempt the purchase of the New Mexico and California territories, but these efforts were met with a snub. The following year, on 25 April, Mexican troops crossed the Rio Grande and attacked soldiers stationed there. The US President, **James K. Polk** (1795–1849) declared war, and fighting lasted until Mexico surrendered in 1847.

The US also faced **boundary** disputes with the British, over the Oregon Territory, which lay between 42°N and 54°40' N. The US claim for land as far north as 54°40' N gave rise to Polk's campaign slogan of "Fifty-four Forty or Fight!". However, under the 1846 **Treaty of Oregon** the boundary was set at 49°N.

In Britain, the control of the import and export of grains – known as the **Corn Laws** – had been the source of controversy for decades. Poor harvests, blockades, and disruption to supplies during wartime had led to fluctuating wheat prices. Legislation to protect domestic agriculture by limiting the **import** of cheap grain and fix prices had proved unpopular and led to the establishment of the **Anti-Corn Law League** in 1839. The League argued that the laws impeded prosperity as restrictions on grain imports caused a price increase and a consequent rise in the cost of wages. The control of exports also limited the external market for British goods. A combination of pressure from the League and the failure of the potato crop in Ireland (see 1845) led to the repeal of the laws.

In **Japan**, there was international pressure for the **isolationist nation** to open up its ports to foreign trade. The Dutch, who were the only Europeans allowed limited access to trade in Japan, sent a mission in 1844 urging the country's rulers to open up trade. This was followed by the French and British requesting trading rights. In 1846, a US delegation arrived and was also sent away empty-handed, but the US would soon try again in its quest for access to Japanese ports (see 1853).

> **" FIFTY-FOUR FORTY** OR **FIGHT! "**
>
> **William Allen, Governor of Ohio,** during his election campaign

Rebellion of Abd al-Qadir
Although the Algerian troops were hugely outnumbered by the French, Abd al-Qadir made effective use of guerilla tactics.

IN THE YEARS FOLLOWING FRANCE'S ATTACK and colonization of **Algiers** (see 1830), the French faced much resistance from Algerians, including emir **Abd al-Qadir al-Jaza'iri** (1807–1883). He gained the support of Algerian tribes who aided him in his fight against the French. After a series of defeats, he was forced to **surrender** in 1847. He was taken prisoner, but was later freed.

In Germany, a **telegraph** line connecting Frankfurt to Berlin was installed by a firm owned by **Werner Siemens** (1816–92), who had developed a technique for seamless insulation of copper wire.

Meanwhile, English author, **Emily Brontë** (1818–48), published *Wuthering Heights*. Though not met with much critical acclaim it later became one of the most influential literary examples of the **Romanticism** movement.

FRIEDRICH ENGELS AND KARL MARX (see 1844) joined a revolutionary group of Germans known as the League of the Just who soon changed their name to the **Communist League**. Engels and Marx were charged with developing a programme of action for the group, and the result was a pamphlet which became known as the ***Communist Manifesto***. This called for the overthrow of the bourgeoisie, with the cry of "working men of all countries, unite". Marx believed the gulf between rich and poor in Europe meant conditions were ripe for a socialist revolution.

In February, only a couple of weeks after the manifesto's publication, the streets of **Paris** erupted into revolution. Although it was dramatic and violent, it was not a socialist insurrection. **France** had been suffering an economic depression and a minister named **François Guizot** had come to symbolize the government's inability to alleviate the situation. The monarchy fared little better as the king, Louis-Philippe (see 1830), was also very unpopular with the public. Fighting broke out on 22 February and quickly became violent, with soldiers opening fire on the

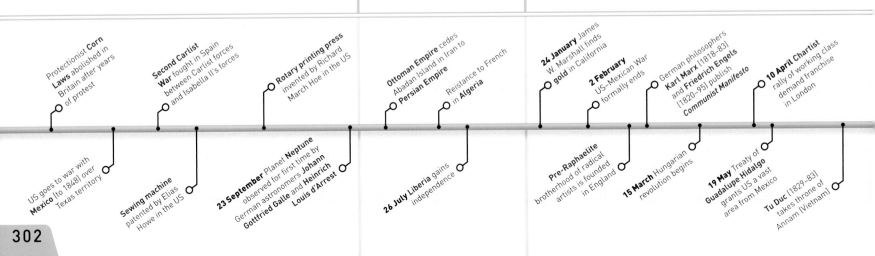

Europe in revolt
Republican uprisings in 1848 saw an end to the monarchy in France, although revolutionaries in other countries were less successful in their aims.

Protectionist **Corn Laws** abolished in Britain after years of protest

US goes to war with **Mexico** (to 1848) over Texas territory

Second Carlist War fought in Spain between Carlist forces and Isabella II's forces

Sewing machine patented by Elias Howe in the US

Rotary printing press invented by Richard March Hoe in the US

23 September Planet **Neptune** observed for first time by German astronomers **Johann Gottfried Galle** and **Heinrich Louis d'Arrest**

Ottoman Empire cedes Abadan Island in Iran to **Persian Empire**

Resistance to French in **Algeria**

26 July Liberia gains independence

24 January James W. Marshall finds **gold** in California

2 February US–Mexican War formally ends

Pre-Raphaelite brotherhood of radical artists is founded in England

German philosophers **Karl Marx** (1818–83) and **Friedrich Engels** (1820–95) publish ***Communist Manifesto***

15 March Hungarian revolution begins

10 April Chartist rally of working class demand franchise in London

19 May Treaty of **Guadalupe Hidalgo** grants US a vast area from Mexico

Tu Duc (1829–83) takes throne of Annam (Vietnam)

Merchant ships crowd the bay at San Francisco during the gold rush years, when tens of thousands of fortune-seekers arrived in California.

COMMUNISM

With the publication of the *Communist Manifesto* Marx and Engels laid the foundation of a political movement that sought to share the means of production, such as land or factories, equally among the public. Communists aimed to create a classless and stateless society, as well as abolish the capitalist trappings of private property and wage labour.

crowds.The following day, Guizot was forced out of office and Louis-Philippe abdicated from the throne. A provisional government was set up and the **Second Republic** established, eventually producing a constitution and extending the vote. However, internal power struggles led to a workers' rebellion in June. By the end of the year, another Bonaparte was in power – this time Napoleon's nephew, **Prince Louis-Napoleon Bonaparte**, (1808–73), who had been elected president.

This unrest was not limited to France. The rebellions had started in Sicily in January, and spread from there. There were a number of factors involved: high food prices, economic depression, **nationalist movements**, desire for **constitutional reforms**, and frustration with monarchies. The revolutions varied in intensity and success. In some places, they amounted to large-scale protests, such as the **Chartists'** demonstrations for changes to the voting system in Britain, or the call for institutional reforms in Belgium and the Netherlands.

It was in France, the Austrian Empire, Germany, and the Italian states where the real agitation lay. In the **Kingdom of the Two Sicilies** (see map, left), the king was forced to grant a constitution. **Germany** saw street fighting in Berlin in March, with the king of Prussia promising to grant Germany a constitution. **Austria**, too, saw fighting break out in Vienna, and a new government was appointed, while many of its territories, such as **Hungary**, called for more autonomy. In broad terms, however, the events of 1848 **ended in failure** and further social repression.

> " ...**DISGRACED** BY THE **STINK OF REVOLUTION,** BAKED OF DIRT AND MUD. "
>
> **Frederick William IV of Prussia**, on the Crown after the 1848 Revolution

WITH THE END OF THE WAR BETWEEN THE US AND MEXICO in 1847, the US gained – through the Treaty of Guadalupe Hidalgo (1848) – a vast area of land that included **California**. The following year, a carpenter named James Wilson Marshall noticed shiny metal nuggets in a river near present-day Sacramento, which he soon realized were **gold**. News of this discovery spread throughout the country – aided by President James K. Polk's announcement – and by 1849 the **rush** had begun. That year some 40,000 people arrived in San Francisco by boat and another 40,000 by wagon train from around the US and other countries. Most of the prospectors ended up empty-handed but many stayed in California, making the West Coast a booming region in the mid-19th century.

In **southern Africa**, a British explorer and missionary named **David Livingstone** (1813–73) had finally reached a lake in the interior that he had heard about – known today as **Lake Ngami**. He had been living in South Africa since 1841 and had been travelling extensively in the region. In order to find this body of water, Livingstone had to cross the **Kalahari Desert**, where he also encountered the River Botlette, which he thought could be "the key to the Interior".

In **India**, the past four years had seen two wars between the British East India Company troops and the Sikhs in the northwest. The **First Sikh War** (1845–46) had been triggered by the death of their ruler Ranjit Singh (1781–1839). Previously, the Company considered Singh's force of 100,000 Khalsa warriors far too powerful to confront. But after his death, British troops moved in and took areas near the border, seizing the city of **Lahore** by 1845. A treaty between the two forced the Sikhs to give up even more territory. A revolt against the British in 1848 triggered the **Second Sikh War**, and by 1849 the Punjab region had been annexed by the British.

Yemen, at the foot of the Arabian Peninsula, was fighting against imperial advances from the **Ottoman Empire**, which was trying to reassert its authority in the Tihama region, on the **Red Sea**. In the south of the country, the British East India Company had already taken control of the **port of Aden** a decade earlier in order to set up a coaling station for British ships en route to India.

Livingstone's compass
The magnetic compass used by David Livingstone, who spent much of his time as a missionary exploring Africa's interior.

PRE-RAPHAELITES

Three young artists frustrated with the state of British painting at the Royal Academy, where they were students, decided to create a movement to bring a moral seriousness into art – in contrast to the pomposity and frivolity they perceived in Victorian art. Known as the Pre-Raphaelite Brotherhood, Dante Gabriel Rossetti, William Holman Hunt, and John Everett Millais painted religious and romantic subjects with realist clarity, although their work was also symbolic.

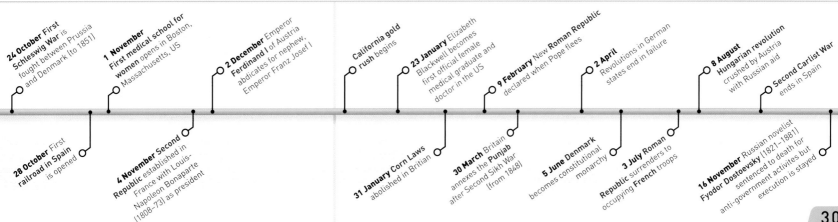

24 October First Schleswig War is fought between Prussia and Denmark (to 1851)

28 October First **railroad in Spain** is opened

1 November First medical school for women opens in Boston, Massachusetts, US

4 November Second Republic established in France with Louis-Napoleon Bonaparte (1808–73) as president

2 December Emperor **Ferdinand I** of Austria abdicates for nephew, Emperor Franz Josef I

California gold rush begins

23 January Elizabeth Blackwell becomes first official female medical graduate and doctor in the US

31 January Corn Laws abolished in Britian

9 February New **Roman Republic** declared when Pope flees

30 March Britain annexes the **Punjab** after Second Sikh War (from 1848)

2 April Revolutions in German states end in failure

5 June Denmark becomes constitutional monarchy

3 July Roman Republic surrenders to occupying **French** troops

8 August Hungarian revolution crushed by Austria with Russian aid

Second Carlist War ends in Spain

16 November Russian novelist **Fyodor Dostoevsky** (1821–1881) sentenced to death for anti-government activites but execution is stayed

1850

A depiction of one of the many bloody battles during the Taiping Rebellion.

IN THE SAME WAY CHINA HAD TRIED TO KEEP European ships from its ports, it had also tried to drive out Christian missionaries thereby limiting the influence of **Christianity**. Despite this, by the mid-19th century some 200,000 Chinese had been **converted**, and thousands more were familiar with the religion.

In 1850, officials sent troops to disband a religious society whose beliefs were loosely based on **Protestant** ideas. This sect was led by **Hong Xiuquan** (1814–64) who, believing himself to be the younger brother of Jesus Christ, launched a revolt that became the **Taiping Rebellion**. Drawn by his call to share property, many starving peasants joined the ranks and fighting went on for 14 years, claiming millions of lives.

20 MILLION THE NUMBER OF **PEOPLE KILLED** OVER THE COURSE OF THE **TAIPING REBELLION**

1851

A hand-coloured lithograph shows the Crystal Palace at the Great Exhibition of 1851 in London's Hyde Park. Some six million people visited it in six months.

> “IT IS A WONDERFUL PLACE – **VAST, STRANGE, NEW,** AND **IMPOSSIBLE TO DESCRIBE.**”
>
> **Charlotte Brontë, English novelist,** on her visit to the Great Exhibition

IN LONDON, THE WORLD WAS ON DISPLAY. An exhibition had been organized, billed as the "Great Exhibition of the Works of Industry of all Nations". The **Great Exhibition**, as it became known, was housed in the Crystal Palace, an exhibition hall made of glass and iron built for the occasion. Some six million people pored over the 100,000 exhibitions between 1 May and 31 October. Of the 14,000 participating exhibitioners, almost half were from overseas. An enormous variety of agricultural and manufactured items were on display, ranging from the **Koh-i-Noor diamond** from India to tapestries from Persia, and British engineering equipment.

In the same year as this global event, a **telegraph cable** was laid across the English Channel, facilitating rapid international communication.

Britain by this point had seen a large **population** boom and become more **urbanized** as agricultural workers moved to the cities to work in the growing number of factories (see 1771). Detailed censuses showed that the population of London had surged from about one million in 1801 to over two million by 1851.

In **Australia**, the discovery of gold in Victoria and New South Wales the same year prompted a **gold rush** that tripled the country's population over the next ten years.

In Siam (Thailand), **King Mongkut** (1804–68) began his rule. His reign saw increased relations with the West. During this period, he employed an English governess, **Anna Leonowens** (1831–1915), whose memoirs inspired the 20th-century musical *The King and I*.

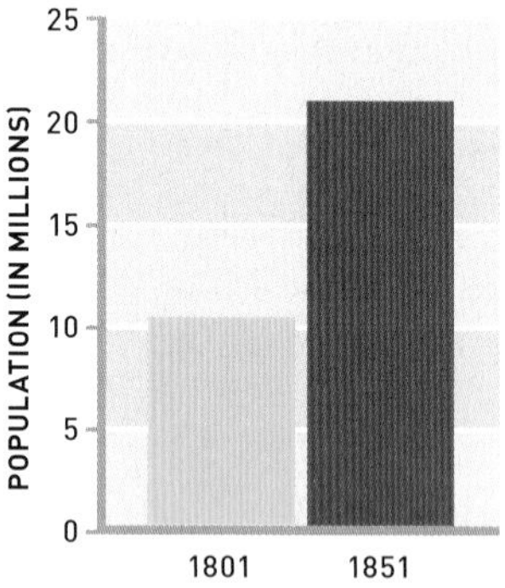

Rise in Britain's population
The population of England, Scotland, and Wales almost doubled in fifty years, from 10.6 million in 1801 to almost 21 million by 1851.

1852

The Royal Navy played a significant role in the Anglo–Burmese War.

HOSTILITIES HAD ONCE AGAIN flared up between British troops and the Burmese. After making extensive territorial gains in the last war against **Burma** (see 1823), Britain was eager to control more of the area. Wider control would create an overland coastal connection from Calcutta in Britain's Indian territory to the British port in Singapore. The East India Company also wanted access to the **teak forests** in Burma. In 1852, the British seized a ship belonging to Burma's king, and this was enough to start the **Second Anglo–Burmese War.** Lasting only a few months, British troops were able to take southern territory, ousting the reigning king, Pagan Min (1811–80), and installing his brother, Mindon Min (1814–78), who was willing to accept British control of the southern portion of the kingdom.

In **West Africa**, in present-day Senegal, Muslim Tukulor chief **Umar Tall** (1797–1864) capitalized on unrest between the Dinguiraye and Bambara people to wage a jihad (holy war) on part of upper **Senegal**, taking control of the territory. His empire would eventually stretch to **Timbuktu** in present-day Mali. His rule was a time of further entrenchment of Islam in West Africa.

In South Africa, the British acknowledged the independence of the **Transvaal** after refusing to accept the previous Boer Republic of Natal (see 1843). This was followed two years later with a similar acceptance of the settlers' new **Orange Free State**.

1853

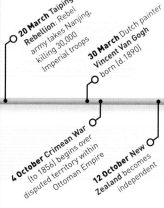

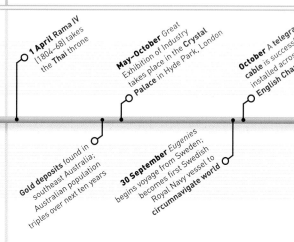

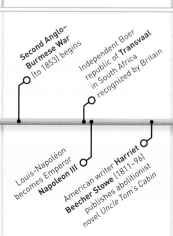

Commodore Matthew Perry brought Japan a railway carriage as a gift.

US COMMODORE MATTHEW PERRY (1794–1858) had been charged with opening up trade with the secluded **Japan**. Japan had been under international pressure to open up its ports to foreign merchants for years. The Dutch, who were the only Europeans allowed very limited **access to trade** in Japan, sent a mission in 1844, urging the country's rulers to allow in more ships. This was followed by French and British requests for trading rights. A delegation from the US arrived and was also sent away empty-handed (see 1846). However, the US government was eager to secure trading rights in East Asia and so sent Perry to further negotiate. He arrived on 8 July and refused to leave until he had delivered his letters. The Japanese relented after a few days and took his papers, which requested a trade treaty. They eventually consented to the terms, and the **Treaty of Kanagawa** was concluded the following year.

As **China** was contending with the Taiping Rebellion (see 1850), another uprising broke out in the central and eastern provinces. The rebels were composed of many outlaws, as well as peasants from famine-stricken areas. With the government otherwise engaged, the rebels were able to form armies and begin the **Nien Rebellion**. Over the course of the next 15 years they gained control of much of northern China, though they were eventually defeated.

- **Taiping Rebellion** leads to civil war in China (to 1864)
- **16 December** First **settlers** for Christchurch arrive in **New Zealand**
- **1 April Rama IV** (1804–68) takes the **Thai** throne
- **Gold deposits** found in southeast Australia; Australian population triples over next ten years
- **May–October** Great Exhibition of Industry takes place in the **Crystal Palace** in Hyde Park, London
- **30 September** Eugenies begins voyage from Sweden; becomes first Swedish Royal Navy vessel to **circumnavigate world**
- **October** A **telegraph cable** is successfully installed across **English Channel**
- **Second Anglo–Burmese War** (to 1853) begins
- Louis-Napoléon becomes Emperor **Napoleon III**
- Independent Boer republic of **Transvaal** in South Africa recognized by Britain
- American writer **Harriet Beecher Stowe** (1811–96) publishes abolitionist novel *Uncle Tom's Cabin*
- **20 March Taiping Rebellion**: Rebel army takes Nanjing, killing 30,000 Imperial troops
- **4 October Crimean War** (to 1856) begins over disputed territory within Ottoman Empire
- **30 March** Dutch painter **Vincent Van Gogh** born (d.1890)
- **12 October New Zealand** becomes independent

1854

“ MEN, REMEMBER THERE IS NO RETREAT FROM HERE. YOU MUST DIE WHERE YOU STAND. ”

Colin Campbell, Commander of the Highland Brigade, at the Battle of Balaclava, 25 October 1854

THE TENSIONS THAT HAD BEEN mounting between **Russia** and the **Ottoman Empire** in the previous year spilled over into a war. Britain and France joined the fight from October. The conflict was fuelled by the decision of Tsar Nicholas I (1796–1855) to declare the right to protect **Orthodox Christians** living under Ottoman rule. When this claim was rejected by the Ottomans, Nicholas sent troops into Moldavia and Wallachia, and the Ottoman Empire declared war. By March 1854, Britain and France had also declared war on Russia, and in September they landed troops in Russia's **Crimea** territory and began a siege of **Sevastopol**. In October, a brigade of British troops at the **Battle of Balaclava** misinterpreted orders, charging down a valley instead of up it, allowing Russians to bombard the 673 soldiers on all sides. Had it not been for French intervention, the casualty rate would have been higher than 40 per cent. This incident was memorialized in the poem by Lord Alfred Tennyson, *The Charge of the Light Brigade*.

Austria threatened to enter the war against Russia in 1856 and a preliminary peace was arranged on 1 February, followed by the 30 March **Treaty of Paris**.

The Crimean War was the first conflict to be covered by newspapers, which were taking advantage of the new telegraphic and photographic technology. The war also established the reputation of the **"Lady with the Lamp"**, British nurse Florence Nightingale (1820–1910), whose reforms to field hospitals caused a dramatic reduction in deaths from disease during wartime. She helped promote nursing as a respectable career for women.

The Crimean War
Brigadier Scarlett leads the British Heavy Brigade uphill at Balaclava, on 25 October 1854 against the Russians during the Crimean war.

1855

A painting of King Mongkut of Siam, who was also known as Rama IV.

MISSIONARY DAVID LIVINGSTONE was exploring the interior of Africa (see 1849) on his second expedition. He was convinced a trade route to the sea existed, and sailed up the **Zambezi River** in November 1853 to find it. Two years later, he and his party came across a gigantic waterfall, known as **Mosi-oa-Tunya**, "the Smoke that Thunders". He was the first European to see the falls and renamed them **Victoria Falls**.

To the East, in Siam (Thailand), King Mongkut (see 1851), known for his interest in the West, signed commercial agreements with Britain and the US in an effort to open up **Siamese** trade.

1856

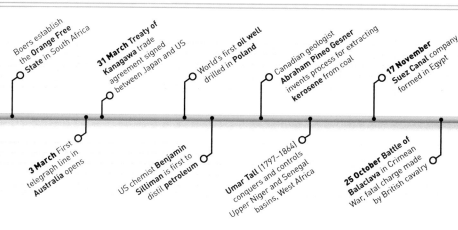

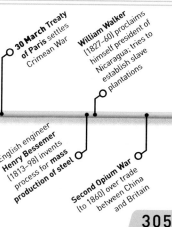

US filibusterer William Walker surrenders to Costa Rican troops.

IN NICARAGUA, US-BORN WILLIAM WALKER (1824–60), who had arrived in the country in 1855 with 58 men, declared himself **president**. He was initially invited by Francisco Castellón (1815–55), who had been trying to organize a liberal revolt. This was a period of **filibustering**: attempts by privately funded mercenaries to take over small countries and annex them to the US. Walker intended to establish Nicaragua as a **slave state**; southern US states wanted to enlarge slave-holding territory as abolitionism grew. Walker was eventually captured by invading Costa Rican forces and later shot.

- Boers establish the **Orange Free State** in South Africa
- **3 March** First telegraph line in **Australia** opens
- **31 March Treaty of Kanagawa** trade agreement signed between Japan and US
- World's first **oil well** drilled in **Poland**
- US chemist **Benjamin Silliman** is first to distil **petroleum**
- Canadian geologist **Abraham Pineo Gesner** invents process for extracting **kerosene** from coal
- **Umar Tall** (1797–1864) conquers and controls Upper Niger and Senegal basins, West Africa
- **17 November Suez Canal** company formed in Egypt
- **25 October Battle of Balaclava** in Crimean War, fatal charge made by British cavalry
- **11 February Kassa Hailu** crowned Tewodros II, emperor of Ethiopia
- **David Livingstone is** first European to see **"Victoria Falls"**, as he renames them
- Start of **British trade with Siam**
- **17 March** Taiping army of 350,000 invades **Anhui**, eastern China, during **Taiping Rebellion**
- **30 March Treaty of Paris** settles Crimean War
- English engineer **Henry Bessemer** (1813–98) invents process for **mass production of steel**
- **William Walker** (1827–60) proclaims himself president of Nicaragua; tries to establish slave plantations
- **Second Opium War** (to 1860) over trade between China and Britain

English painter Thomas Jones Barker's *The Relief of Lucknow* completed in 1859, depicts British forces defending this colonial city after the end of a prolonged siege during the Sepoy Rebellion.

IN 1857, A RUMOUR SPREAD THROUGH THE INDIAN TROOPS – known as **sepoys** – in the Bengal Army stationed at Meerut, Northern India. Their new rifle cartridges were reputed to be greased with pork and beef fat. The cartridges were for a new type of rifle, the **Enfield**, and to load them the ends of the paper cartridges needed to be bitten off. For Hindu and Muslim soldiers, allowing beef or pork fat in their mouths went against their respective religions beliefs. Added to this rumour were various other grievances, together with a growing suspicion that the British were also trying to undermine Indian culture and traditions. The soldiers refused to use the cartridges, and the subsequent row that broke out between Indian troops and British commanders sparked the revolt known as the **Sepoy Rebellion** (also known as the **Indian Mutiny**).

The unrest lasted for more than a year as the mutineers were joined by peasants angry at their exploitative landlords, as well as those who resented the recent British annexation of the north Indian region of Oudh. The rebels managed to capture Delhi and "restore" an ageing Mughal emperor, **Bahadur Shah II** (1775–1862), to power, while killing the British in Delhi and the nearby cities of Kanpur and Lucknow. The retaliation by the British army was similarly brutal, and they recaptured Delhi in September and Lucknow the following March. The revolt was suppressed by June 1858.

This conflict was the culmination of frustration with the East India Company's rule as well as creeping **westernization** as Britain annexed more territories and sent out more officials. The uprising provoked deep concern in Britain, and the East India Company was stripped of its power to control India. The Company by this point was hated throughout India, and the British government thought it could no longer be relied on to keep stability (see panel, 1858). The Mutiny had shown the level of Indian discontent and anger, which would continue to grow under British rule, while at the same time helping to fuel the independence movement.

In additon to the conflict in India, British troops had returned to battle in **China**. Britain demanded greater freedom of trade in China in the wake of the Treaty of Nanjing (see 1842), but the Chinese resisted. In 1856, the British sent an expedition with the French to attack China's ports, culminating in the **Second Opium War**. Anglo-French forces attacked Canton in 1857. By the following year, the **Treaties of Tianjin** were negotiated between China, Britain, and France, as well as with Russia and the US. These agreements called for China to open more ports and to legalize opium importation. In addition, foreign diplomats were given the right to live in **Peking**. The Chinese refused to ratify these agreements until 1860.

In the US, the **abolitionist** cause suffered a serious setback when a Supreme Court ruling in the case Dred Scott v. John F.A. Sandford declared slavery to be **legal** in all US territories. The case was brought by **Dred Scott**. He was taken by his owner, John Emerson, from the slave state of Missouri (see 1820) to the "free" Wisconsin territory, later returning to Missouri. Scott, with the aid of abolitionists, filed a lawsuit claiming the move from slave to free state had broken his chain of servitude. The case reached the Supreme Court in 1857 where the justices voted against freeing Scott on the grounds that he was not entitled to rights as a **US citizen**, including the right to sue in a court of law. The judges also declared the Missouri Compromise (see 1820) unconstitutional because Congress could not deprive citizens of their property. It was up to the states to decide to ban slavery, and there was nothing to stop new territories becoming slave states.

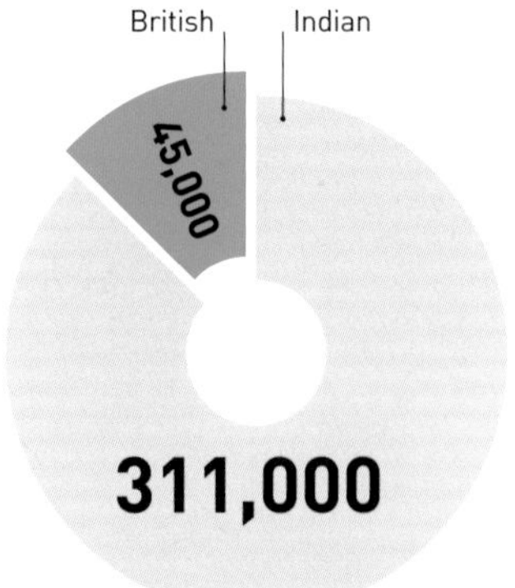

British–Indian army in 1857
A much larger proportion of Indians than British served in the army, making an uprising involving the Indian troops a serious threat.

> **"** A **FREE NEGRO** OF THE AFRICAN RACE…**IS NOT** A **'CITIZEN' WITHIN** THE MEANING OF THE **CONSTITUTION OF THE UNITED STATES. "**
>
> **Chief Justice Roger Taney** in the Dred Scott v. Sandford case, April 1854

Dred Scott
A slave in the US, Dred Scott sued his owner for his freedom. The case went to the US Supreme Court where his emancipation was denied.

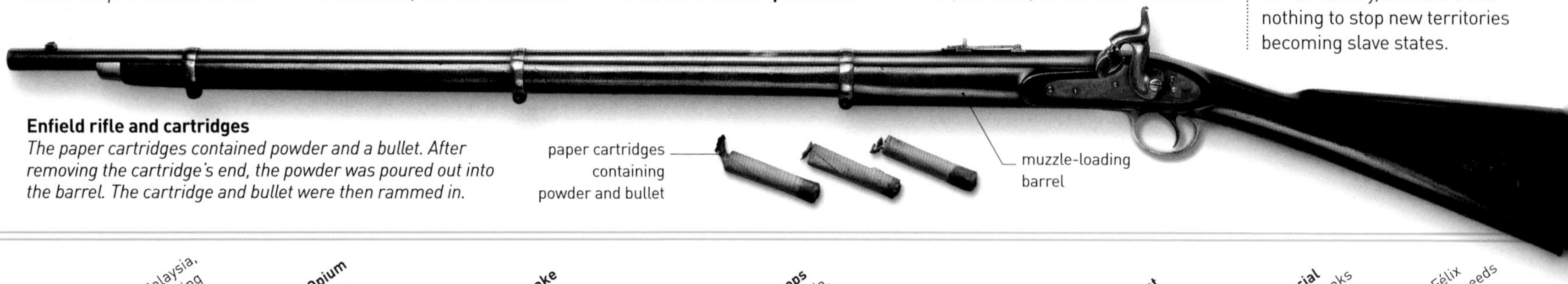

Enfield rifle and cartridges
The paper cartridges contained powder and a bullet. After removing the cartridge's end, the powder was poured out into the barrel. The cartridge and bullet were then rammed in.

- **Kuala Lumpur**, Malaysia, is founded as tin-mining settlement
- **3 March Second Opium War** declared in China by France and Britain
- **6 March** In US, slave **Dred Scott** sues unsuccessfully for freedom in landmark case heightening tensions over abolition
- **21 March Earthquake** in Tokyo, **Japan**, kills over 100,000
- **23 March** First safety **passenger elevator** installed in New York by inventor **Elisha Otis**
- **10 May Sepoy troops rebel** in northern India, unleashing uprisings against the British
- **11 May** Indian rebels capture Delhi during **Sepoy Rebellion**
- **15 July** Second **massacre at Kanpur** by Indian rebels
- **13 October Financial panic** in **New York**; banks close until 12 December
- **1 November** Area of present-day **Pakistan** becomes part of Indian Empire
- **30 November** Félix María **Zuloaga** succeeds Ignacio Comonfort as president of Mexico

1858

A contemporary oil painting illustrates the 1860 Battle of Guadalajara during the Mexican Reform War between liberals and conservatives.

AFTER MEXICO'S DEFEAT BY THE US (see 1846), many Mexicans were in favour of reform, including the middle-class liberal **Benito Juárez** (1806–72). Installed in the government as justice minister, Juárez and other liberals, including president **Ignacio Comonfort** (1812–63), drafted a new constitution curbing military and ecclesiastical privileges, such as the allocation of special courts for civil trials, and some landholding rights. The constitution, which also prohibited slavery and called for a democracy in Mexico, went into effect in 1857.

However, the Catholic Church and the military refused to accept these reforms, and the antagonism turned into the **War of the Reform** (1857–60). With the conservatives in charge of the military, the liberals found themselves pushed out of Mexico City, and were eventually forced to make a new capital at the port of **Veracruz** in 1858. The US decided to intervene in the conflict, recognizing the liberal government at Veracruz in 1859 and sending them much-needed arms. This aided the rebels in their retaliation, and they managed to defeat conservative forces. Juárez returned to Mexico City on 1 January 1861 as president, taking control of the whole country, and he once again put the constitution into effect.

France, meanwhile, was embroiled in battles not only in China, but in other kingdoms in East and Southeast Asia where the French sought a foothold in trade. France was concerned about the rise of Siamese power, as well as the continuing attacks on French missionaries in Vietnam. By the end of 1858, a Franco-Spanish expedition had seized the city of Da Nang in Vietnam, starting the **Cochinchina Campaign**. In 1859, the coalition captured the key port of **Saigon**, where a garrison of 1,000 troops later faced a year-long siege from 1860 to 1861. The war finally ended in a settlement with Vietnam's king, **Tu Duc** (1829–83), in 1863, in which three provinces were ceded to France.

RISE OF THE RAJ

With the end of the East India Company's administration in 1857, India was governed directly from London by the Viceroy. This was brought about on 1 November 1858 by governor-general Charles John Canning (1856–62) who became the first Viceroy of India. The period, known as the Raj, lasted until Indian independence in 1947.

1859–60

US Marines under the command of Colonel Robert E. Lee smash the armoury door at Harper's Ferry, behind which John Brown and his men were besieged.

> "...THE CRIMES OF THIS **GUILTY** LAND WILL NEVER BE PURGED BUT WITH **BLOOD!**"
>
> **John Brown, American abolitionist,** before his execution, 2 December 1859

EUROPE IN SOUTHEAST ASIA

Throughout the 19th century European powers vied for control of the profitable trade routes from China through Southeast Asia. Goods such as spices were imported to Europe from colonies in Asia, while textiles were exported. The opening of the Suez Canal in 1869 made trade between Europe and Asia quicker and cheaper.

CONSTRUCTION WORK HAD FINALLY BEGUN ON A CANAL that would link the Mediterranean Sea and the Red Sea. It would cut voyages between Europe and Asia by thousands of miles by allowing ships to avoid sailing around the Cape of Good Hope. In 1854, French official **Ferdinand de Lesseps** (1805–94) managed to obtain permission from the khedive (viceroy) of Egypt, Said Pasha (1822–63), to construct a canal at Suez. In 1856, the Suez Canal Company (*Compagnie universelle du canal maritime de Suez*) was set up and given the right to run the canal for 99 years after its completion.

In the US, abolitionist **John Brown** (1800–59) attacked a federal armoury in **Harpers Ferry, Virginia** on the night of 16 October. He also took more than 60 slave owners hostage, hoping that the slaves of these people would join his cause. They were attacked by the local militia and the rebellion was finally ended by federal troops, led by Colonel Robert E. Lee. Of the 22 men who participated in the raid, 10 were killed, including Brown's two sons. Brown himself was later hanged.

Meanwhile, in England, naturalist **Charles Darwin** (see 1835, 1839) cemented his reputation with the publication of *On the Origin of Species by Means of Natural Selection*. The work explained the process of **evolution** and he set out his ideas about species adaptation and the survival of the fittest.

In the US, Abraham Lincoln (1809–65) won the race for presidency as the candidate for the newly formed **Republican** party, which had been established to curtail the power of existing slave states and stop the creation of new ones. The Democrats had split and fielded two candidates.

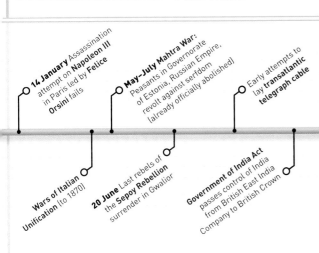

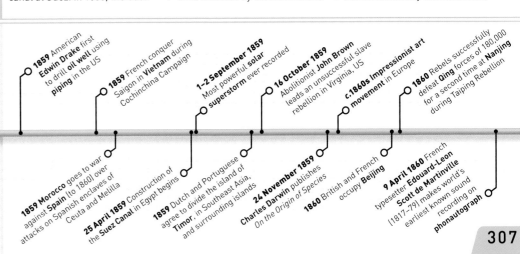

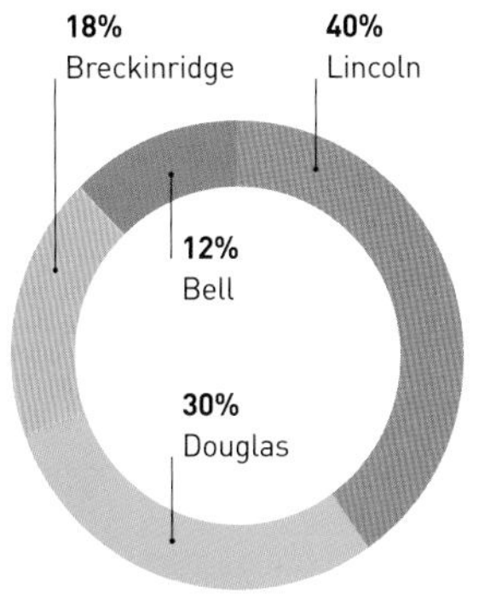

A clear majority
The Democratic candidates, Douglas and Breckinridge, combined had more of the popular vote, but Lincoln won the necessary electoral votes.

14 January Assassination attempt on **Napoleon III** in Paris led by **Felice Orsini** fails

Wars of Italian Unification (to 1870)

May–July Mahtra War: Peasants in Governorate of Estonia, Russian Empire, revolt against serfdom (already officially abolished)

20 June Last rebels of the **Sepoy Rebellion** surrender in Gwalior

Early attempts to lay **transatlantic telegraph cable**

Government of India Act passes control of India from British East India Company to British Crown

1859 American **Edwin Drake** first to drill **oil well** using **piping** in the US

1859 French conquer Saigon in **Vietnam** during Cochinchina Campaign

1859 Morocco goes to war against **Spain** (to 1860) over attacks on Spanish enclaves of Ceuta and Melilla

25 April 1859 Construction of the **Suez Canal** in Egypt begins

1–2 September 1859 Most powerful **solar superstorm** ever recorded

1859 Dutch and Portuguese agree to divide the island of **Timor**, in Southeast Asia, and surrounding islands

16 October 1859 Abolitionist **John Brown** leads an unsuccessful slave rebellion in Virginia, US

24 November 1859 Charles Darwin publishes *On the Origin of Species*

c.1860s Impressionist art movement in Europe

1860 British and French occupy **Beijing**

1860 Rebels successfully defeat **Qing** forces of 180,000 for a second time at **Nanjing** during Taiping Rebellion

9 April 1860 French typesetter **Edouard-Leon Scott de Martinville** (1817–79) makes world's earliest known sound recording on **phonautograph**

The Confederate battery at Fort Moultrie firing on Fort Sumter in Charleston harbour on 12 April 1861. The attack triggered the Civil War which devastated the US.

THE SPLIT IN THE US DEMOCRATIC PARTY ahead of the 1860 election precipitated a much larger, more dangerous fracture that came in 1861 – the **secession** of Southern states to a confederacy. Many northerners, President Lincoln included, initially thought that slavery might just die out if it were not allowed in any new territories. But a gradual approach was not possible as abolitionism kept growing, with more of the public supporting it over the 1850s.

The US was economically divided, which intensified the debate over slavery. The South was mostly rural, and slave labour was used to grow cotton, tobacco, and rice. The more urban Northern states, in contrast, had a high population of immigrant workers.

Lincoln's presidential victory proved the last straw for southern slave owners, and by December 1860 South Carolina had seceded from the Union. Over the next few months, it was followed by Georgia, Alabama, Louisiana, Mississippi, Texas, and Florida. These states formed the **Confederacy**, and elected Jefferson Davis (1808–89) as their president. They were soon joined by Virginia, Arkansas, Tennessee, and North Carolina in the spring, though the slave-holding states of Kentucky, Missouri, Maryland, and Delaware did not secede. One of the underlying causes of secession, besides slavery, was the issue of the **states' rights** versus that of **federal** government. South Carolina and the other Confederate states argued that states held the right to own slaves and to leave the Union.

The situation grew increasingly tense. The continued presence of Union forces at **Fort Sumter**, in the harbour of Charleston, South Carolina, made many people there feel that their new sovereignty was being compromised. So, at 4:30am on 12 April, Brigadier-General P.G.T. Beauregard gave the order to fire on the soldiers stationed there. These would be the **opening shots** of the **American Civil War**.

Meanwhile, the second Italian War of Independence, which began in 1859 and was part of the wider struggle for unification of the **Italian states**, was coming to a close. France and Piedmont–Sardinia had formed an alliance to drive out Austrian rule in Italy, which they achieved through a series of victories in 1859. But during negotiations of the **Peace of Zurich**, Napoleon III of France allowed Austria to retain Venetia (mostly Venice), causing uproar among supporters of Italian independence. In the south, **Giuseppe Garibaldi** (1807–82), an Italian military commander, attacked the Kingdom of Two Sicilies, seizing Palermo in 1860. With most of the Italian kingdoms in a degree of upheaval, **Victor Emmanuel II** (1820–78) of Piedmont–Sardinia was declared "king of Italy". The struggle was not yet over, however, as France occupied Rome while Venice was under Austrian rule. Garibaldi's attempt to liberate the Papal States (Rome) in 1862 at the Battle of Aspromonte on 29 August ended in defeat, leaving the project of unification still incomplete.

In Russia, **serfdom** was abolished in wide-reaching changes by Russian emperor **Alexander II** (1818–81) who, after defeat in the Crimean War (see 1854), wanted to reform the country, starting with labour. He set out the **Edict of Emancipation** in 1861, despite opposition from landowners. Earlier attempts to abolish serfdom had been made around 1818, but with little success. Some 10 million people were freed on 19 February, and were promised their own land.

Union cap
Forage cap, with regiment badge, as worn by northern Union soldiers during the Civil War. Confederate soldiers wore the colour grey.

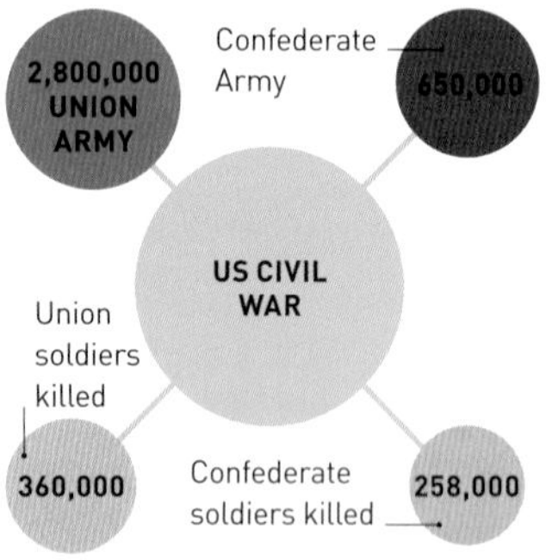

Costly civil war
The conflict between the North's federal government and 11 Southern states was brutal and bloody with a high rate of casualties and deaths.

Alexander II
Alexander was the emperor of Russia from 1855–81. He freed the serfs, and reformed the judicial and education systems.

SOUTHERN CONFEDERACY

The Southern Confederacy equated to a new nation, and as such, needed a flag. The national flag of the Confederacy, known as the "Stars and Bars", closely resembled the northern states' Union flag. To avoid confusion on the battlefield, a new battle flag (right) was adopted, first by the Army of Northern Virginia, and later, by all Southern forces.

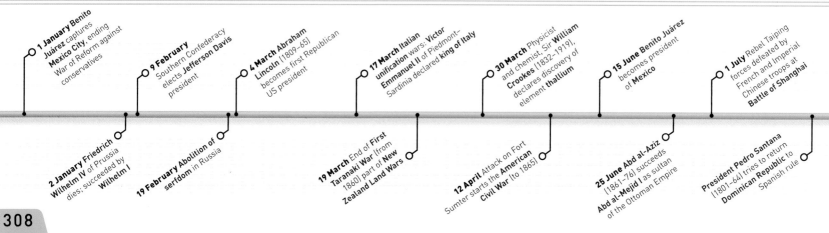

> IT IS BETTER TO **ABOLISH SERFDOM FROM ABOVE THAN** TO **WAIT FOR IT TO ABOLISH ITSELF** FROM BELOW.
>
> **Tsar Alexander II of Russia**

1 January Benito Juárez captures **Mexico City**, ending War of Reform against conservatives

2 January Friedrich Wilhelm IV of Prussia dies; succeeded by **Wilhelm I**

9 February Southern Confederacy elects **Jefferson Davis** president

19 February Abolition of serfdom in Russia

4 March Abraham Lincoln (1809–65) becomes first Republican US president

17 March Italian unification wars: **Victor Emmanuel II** of Piedmont–Sardinia declared **king of Italy**

19 March End of **First Taranaki War** (from 1860) part of **New Zealand Land Wars**

30 March Physicist and chemist, Sir **William Crookes** (1832–1919), declares discovery of element **thallium**

12 April Attack on Fort Sumter starts the **American Civil War** (to 1865)

15 June Benito Juárez becomes president of **Mexico**

25 June Abd al-Aziz (1861–76) succeeds **Abd al-Mejid I** as sultan of the Ottoman Empire

1 July Rebel Taiping forces defeated by French and Imperial Chinese troops at **Battle of Shanghai**

President Pedro Santana (1801–64) tries to return **Dominican Republic** to Spanish rule

1862

“ POLITICS IS THE ART OF THE POSSIBLE. ”

Otto von Bismarck in a remark to Meyer von Waldeck, 11 August 1867

IN MEXICO, AN EXPEDITION OF British, French, and Spanish forces arrived to collect payment on the money they were owed. After the War of the Reform (see 1858) President Benito Juárez had declared in 1861 that he was placing a **moratorium** on the payment of interest **on foreign debt** for two years. The lending countries disputed his decision, and soon resorted to **armed conflict**. France sent in troops, which faced a defeat early on, but reinforcements eventually reached Mexico City. Napoleon III saw an opportunity to establish an empire in Mexico.

Further north, in the **American Civil War**, Union troops attempted, but failed, to capture the Confederate capital, Richmond, by advancing up the peninsula east of **Yorktown**. This was followed by the **Second Battle of Bull Run** (28–30 August, see p.310), which saw 70,000 Union troops defeated by 55,000 Confederates. A few weeks later, on 17 September, one of the bloodiest battles of the war took place at **Antietam**, in Maryland, where Union troops suffered around 12,000 casualties and the Confederates around 11,000. Further west, Union troops under General **Ulysses S. Grant** (1822–85) won a crucial victory at the **Battle of Shiloh**, Tennessee.

In Japan, the **Tokugawa** regime had become increasingly suspicious of foreigners (see 1853), taking measures that included the passing of **anti-foreigner acts** and efforts to expel people. This precipitated attacks on ships from the US, Britain, France, and Holland. In retaliation, in 1863 the US fired on two Japanese ships and French warships fired on – and subsequently burnt down – a small village. The following year, France, Britain, the Netherlands, and the US sailed into the **Straits of Shimonosekei** and destroyed Japanese batteries along its coast. They eventually secured a treaty giving them free passage and the right to trade.

OTTO VON BISMARCK (1815–98)

One of Prussia's most influential leaders, Otto von Bismarck came into power as prime minister in 1862 and he masterminded the unification of Germany (see 1871). Bismarck built up the army and also tried to develop a German national identity; he fought against the Catholic Church and tried to stem the growth of socialism.

1863

Workers hurry to catch their morning train at the Gower Street station on the Metropolitan (underground) railway in London.

30 THOUSAND THE NUMBER OF PASSENGERS ON THE FIRST DAY OF THE METROPOLITAN LINE

THE SITUATION IN MEXICO became more complex as conservative Mexicans, still angry about their defeat in the War of the Reform (see 1858), capitalized on the fighting between French and Mexican troops (see 1862) and conspired with **Napoleon III** to overthrow the government. As a result, Austrian archduke Ferdinand Maximilian Joseph (1832–67) was invited to become **emperor** of Mexico. He accepted, thinking that he had been voted in by the people, and became **Maximilian I** the following year.

In the US, Abraham Lincoln tried to persuade Confederate states to return to the Union by giving them the option of abolishing slavery gradually, rather than immediately. Not one state took up his offer, so on 1 January, he followed through with his plan and issued the **Emancipation Proclamation**, abolishing slavery in the South.

On the battlefields, Union troops were making serious gains in the south, as General Grant captured the Mississippi port of Vicksburg in July, giving Union forces control over key parts of the Mississippi River. The Union Navy, meanwhile, had captured the port of **New Orleans**, and occupation of the city followed. Further north, Confederate defeat at the **Battle of Gettysburg**, Pennsylvania, from 1–3 July, had marked a turning point in the war.

In Britain, Londoners were thrilled by the opening of the **Metropolitan Railway**, which ran underground, from Farringdon Street to Paddington. This was the first part of what would eventually become the **London Underground**, also known as the Tube. Other train companies soon followed suit.

Emancipation proclamation
Abraham Lincoln reads the Emancipation Proclamation before his cabinet members. The decree abolished slavery in the South.

1864

Prussia and Denmark went to war over Schleswig and Holstein.

IN THE ONGOING AMERICAN CIVIL WAR, President Lincoln made General Grant commander-in-chief of the Union forces. A few months later, Union general **William T. Sherman** (1820–91), began his “march to the sea”. Sherman pursued a “scorched earth” policy, destroying railway lines and setting towns on fire from Atlanta to Savannah, on the coast of Georgia.

Relations between **Denmark** and **Prussia**, part of the German Confederation, had soured. A brief war was the result of a revolt by the Germans in the duchies of **Schleswig** and **Holstein**, who were living under Danish rule. Prussian troops occupied the territory and by 1 August, Denmark gave up rights to the duchies, which were to be placed under joint Austrian and Prussian rule – a situation that would become a future source of conflict (see 1866).

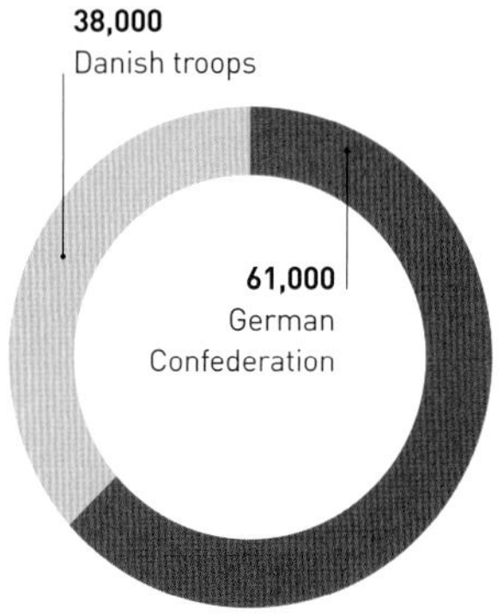

The Prussian–Danish War
The war began when Prussian forces crossed the border into Schleswig, and Denmark was forced to relinquish control of the duchy.

9 March First battle between two **ironclad warships**, the USS *Monitor* and USS *Virginia*

Umar Tall conquers Massina in present-day Mali, West Africa

British annex **Lagos**

6–7 April Confederate defeat at **Battle of Shiloh**

France, Britain, and Spain launch expeditions to **Mexico** starting **French intervention**

28–30 August Second Battle of Bull Run (American Civil War)

17 September Battle of Antietam; costly battle ending in strategic victory for Union

23 September Otto von Bismarck takes office as prime minister of Prussia

1 January Abraham Lincoln signs **Emancipation Proclamation** freeing slaves in the US

10 January World's first **underground railway** opens in London

22 January January Uprising begins against Russian rule in former Polish–Lithuanian Commonwealth

26 May Beginning of **Siege of Vicksburg** (American Civil War)

1–3 July Battle of Gettysburg; largest battle of American Civil War

French protectorate established in **Cambodia**

1 February Danish–Prussian War begins (to 30 October); part of Wars of German Unification (to 1870)

10 April Maximilian I of Austria (1832–67) crowned Mexican emperor

Umar Tall killed attempting to suppress Fulani rebellion, West Africa

November–December General Sherman's **“march to the sea”** in American Civil War

ORIGINS OF THE CIVIL WAR

As the US expanded, the issue of which states would be allowed to have slaves became the central political focus between North and South. By 1860, the 18 free states of the North and the 15 slave states were on the brink of war.

KEY

- Free states
- Slave states
- Free territories
- Territories where slavery legal

1820: THE MISSOURI COMPROMISE

Slavery became a more pressing political issue as the US began to settle its western territories. When the Missouri territory petitioned to become a state in 1817, its slavery status prompted a political crisis. The outcome was the Missouri Compromise, which allowed slavery in Missouri but not in any new state north of 36°30′ latitude.

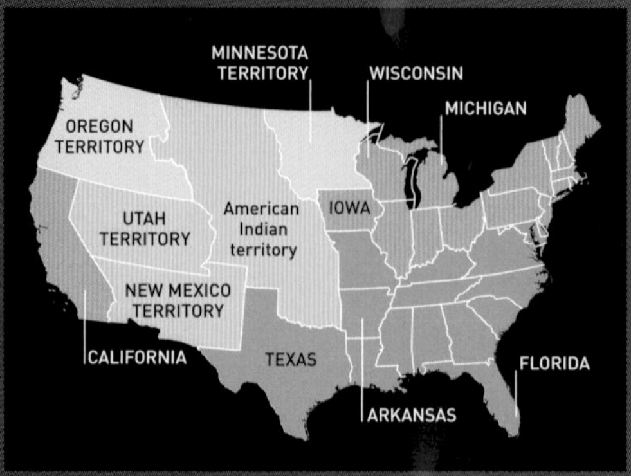

KEY

- Free states
- Slave states
- Free territories
- Territories where slavery legal

1850: A NEW COMPROMISE

Thirty years after the Missouri Compromise, the debate over slavery intensified as the US extended further west. Senator Henry Clay organized a series of bills that were considered a compromise. California was to be admitted as a free state but the controversial Fugitive Slave Act, which penalized officials who did not arrest alleged runaway slaves, was also passed, angering abolitionists.

1861: CIVIL WAR

The bombardment of Fort Sumter in South Carolina triggered a ferocious conflict that would consume the whole country for four brutal, bloody years, until the Confederacy had no choice but to surrender.

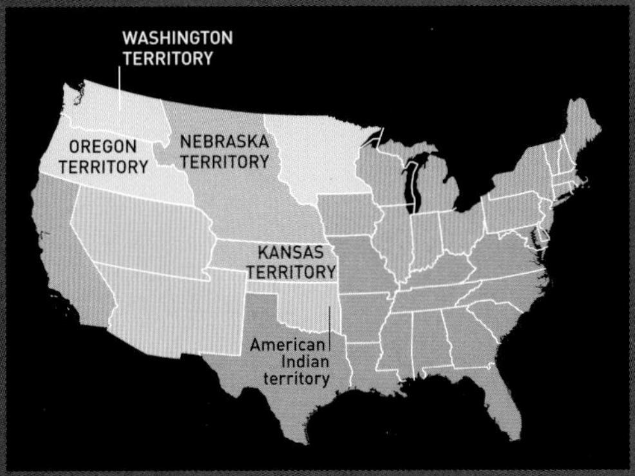

1854: THE KANSAS–NEBRASKA ACT
One of the compromise acts in 1850 was to allow the Utah and New Mexico territories to reach a decision on slavery when they became states. The Kansas–Nebraska Act applied this principle for people in those states, allowing them to vote on the issue. This act also controversially repealed the Missouri Compromise, causing further anger in the North.

KEY
- Free states
- Free territories
- Slave states
- Territories where slavery legal
- Territories newly opened to slavery 1854
- Area not subject to standard territorial laws

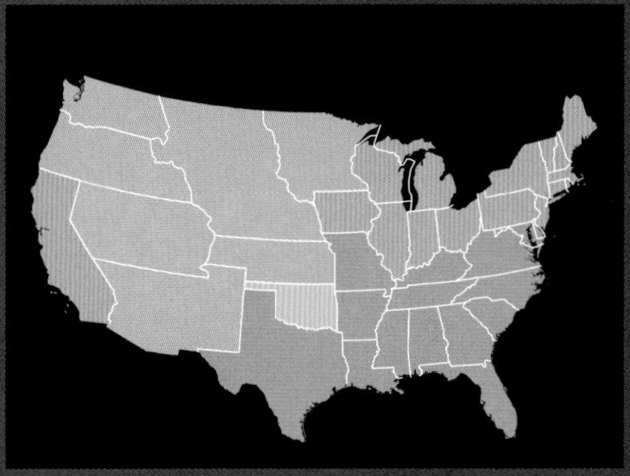

1857: THE DRED SCOTT DECISION
The growing abolitionist cause received a setback when the Supreme Court ruled in the case of Dred Scott v John F.A. Sandford (see 1857) that slavery was legal in all the territories. The judges also declared that the Missouri Compromise was unconstitutional. They argued that it was up to states to decide to ban slavery, but that territories were not states.

KEY
- Free states
- Slave states
- Territories opened to slavery
- Area not subject to standard territorial laws

AMERICAN CIVIL WAR

THE CONFLICT THAT TORE THE UNITED STATES APART

The shells fired at Fort Sumter, South Carolina, in 1861 not only ripped the country in two, but began a deadly conflict that would pit families against each other, with brother fighting brother on the battlefield, as the Confederacy of Southern states took up arms in defence of slavery.

The issue was not only ideological, but also economic. Southerners felt that their rural, agrarian livelihood was under direct threat from the policies of the federal government. And for the industrial and urban North and President Abraham Lincoln, the question was about more than freedom for slaves. Without the 15 slave states what would the future hold for the Union? The war cost billions and destroyed the Southern economy. The Union navy blockaded ports causing prices in the South to rocket; the price of a cup coffee in a restaurant in Richmond, Virginia, reached around $5 by 1864. By the time the South conceded defeat and surrendered in 1865, both sides had been heavily battered – but the country emerged united.

The war was also significant because it was the harbinger of modern warfare. Infrastructure developments, such as railways, and technological innovations in armaments like breech-loading rifles had changed the nature of battle, and led to a much higher number of casualties.

OVER THE COURSE OF THE CIVIL WAR, THE UNION PROVIDED SOLDIERS WITH

1 **BILLION** ROUNDS OF **AMMUNITION**

100 **MILLION** POUNDS OF **COFFEE**

10 **MILLION** PAIRS OF **TROUSERS**

1 **MILLION** **HORSES** AND **MULES**

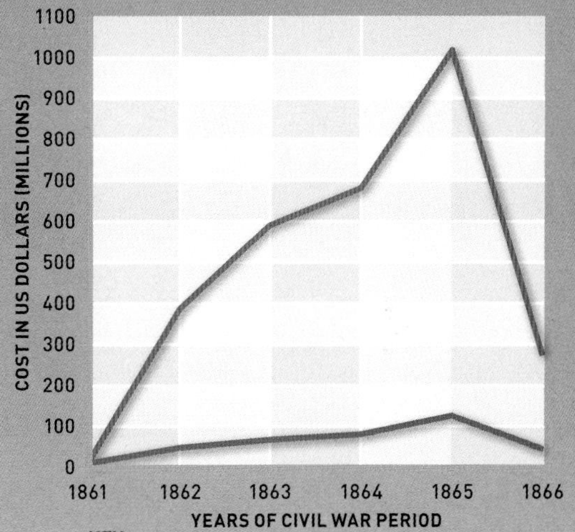

KEY
- Union army expenditure
- Union navy expenditure

Cost of the war
Billions were spent fighting the Civil War, with the army and navy costing the Union millions during this period. The estimated cost to the Confederacy, including the emancipation of the slaves, was around $2.1 billion, inflicting serious damage to the Southern economy.

Populations
The industrial North had a much larger population than the mostly agrarian Southern states.

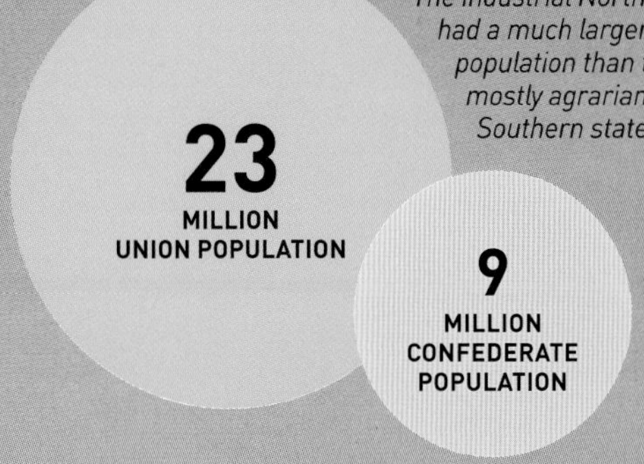

$1,200
THE COST OF **A BARREL OF FLOUR** IN VIRGINIA BY 1865

1:3 **Outnumbered**
Despite the South being significantly outnumbered, the fighting continued for four years, leaving some 600,000 dead.

The War of the Triple Alliance devastated Paraguay. This painting by Cándido López depicts the arrival of the Allied Army at Itapiru, Paraguay.

THE AMERICAN CIVIL WAR DREW TO A CLOSE. By the spring, Union troops had captured the Confederate capital of Richmond, and after several other defeats, Confederate general **Robert E. Lee** (1807–70) saw no other option but to **surrender** on 9 April, signalling the end to the bloodiest conflict the US had seen. The war had left the US intact, but more than 600,000 men had been killed and half a million wounded. The new peace was soon marred: only a few days after the Union's victory, President Lincoln attended Ford's Theatre in Washington DC. There, Confederate **John Wilkes Booth** crept into the state box and shot him. Lincoln died the following morning on 15 April.

The American Civil War was over, but the situation in **Mexico** remained complicated. US troops were deployed there as the US government under Andrew Johnson (1808–75) objected to French intervention in Mexican affairs (see 1863).

Further south, a war had erupted between **Paraguay** and its neighbours Uruguay, Brazil, and Argentina. Brazil invaded Uruguay in 1864 to assist in the overthrow of the ruling party. In response, the president of Paraguay, Francisco Solano López (1827–70), declared war on Brazil, and shortly after, on Argentina. Uruguay aligned itself with Brazil and the **War of the Triple Alliance** (also Paraguayan War) began. López was killed in battle on 1 March 1870, and a peace treaty was negotiated. The war devastated Paraguay, reducing the population of 525,000 to 221,000.

In **Jamaica**, a group of peasants who had been denied government land for planting stormed the courthouse in **Morant Bay** during a meeting of the parish council, and 19 white people died in the altercation. In retaliation, governor **Edward Eyre** led a ruthless attack on the black community, declaring martial law, and killing hundreds of people while imprisoning hundreds more. When news of this reached Britain there was a public outcry and Eyre was recalled to England.

Forces in War of Triple Alliance
Although Paraguay had the far larger force at first, it was untrained and without a chain of command as leader López made all decisions.

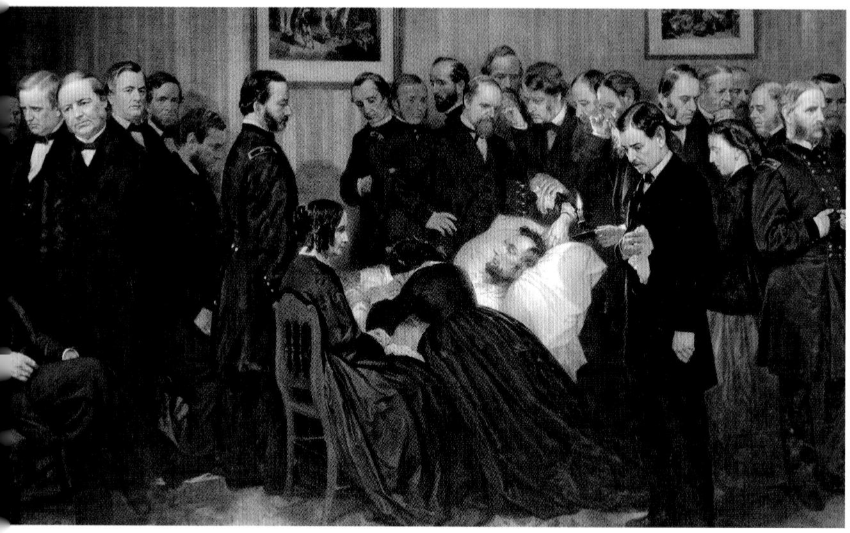

Lincoln's death
This painting by Alonzo Chappel depicts the death of Abraham Lincoln, 16th President of the United States.

IN 1866, PERU DECLARED WAR ON SPAIN, JOINED BY CHILE. The cause of the war dated back to the Talambo Affair in 1862, when Spanish immigrants were attacked by Peruvian workers on the Talambo estate in northern **Peru**. Spain's demand for compensation was ignored, so it seized the **Chincha Islands** off the coast of Peru in 1864. These were valuable as a source of **guano**, used as fertilizer. Spain demanded 3 million pesos in exchange for the islands in 1865.

Peru's General Mariano Ignacio Prado declared war on Spain in January 1866. Chile, fearful of a renewed Spanish presence in South America, joined Peru. They tried to close their ports, but Spain managed to bombard **Valparaiso** in Chile on 31 March and **Callao** in Peru on 2 May before a ceasefire the following week. This was the last attempt by Spain to recapture South American territory.

Battle of Callao
A detail of a painting shows Peruvian troops defending the fortified port of Callao, Peru, while being bombarded by the Spanish navy.

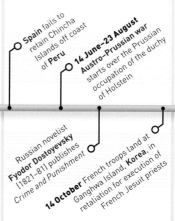

French painter Edouard Manet's *The execution of Maximilian I.*

“ A **SPECTRE** IS **HAUNTING EUROPE;** THE SPECTRE **OF COMMUNISM. ”**

Karl Marx, from the *Communist Manifesto*, 1848

FRANCE'S ATTEMPT TO GAIN CONTROL OF MEXICO (see 1863) seemed doomed with the arrival of US reinforcements. France abandoned Mexico's emperor, Maximilian I, who had been installed at their behest as well as that of Mexican monarchists. He was captured by liberal forces, court-martialled, and executed on 19 June. Benito Juárez then returned to his post as president.

Further north, the size of the US received a huge boost with the **purchase of** the vast **Alaska** territory from Russia. For the price of $7.2 million, the US received 1,717,856 sq km (663,268 sq miles) of territory.

In Europe, Karl Marx (see panel, right) had published the first of three volumes in what would become one of his most influential works, ***Das Kapital***. The book, through an examination of the capitalist system, tried to address larger economic and historical questions about the nature of class and social relations.

In **Prussia**, tensions with Austria had led to the **Seven Weeks War** the previous year. Under the resulting Treaty of

War of the Triple Alliance (to 1870) between Paraguay and an alliance of Argentina, Brazil, and Uruguay

9 April Confederate General Robert E. Lee **surrenders** to General Ulysses S. Grant, effectively **ending American Civil War**

14 April Assassination of Abraham **Lincoln** (b.1809)

23 June Last significant rebel army in American Civil War surrenders in Oklahoma Territory

31 July First narrow gauge mainline railway in the world opens at Grandchester, Queensland, **Australia**

16 August Dominican Republic regains **independence** from Spain

11 October Paul Bogle leads the **Morant Bay Rebellion** in Jamaica

10 December Léopold II becomes king of **Belgium**

Spain fails to retain Chincha Islands off coast of **Peru**

14 June–23 August Austro-Prussian war starts over the Prussian occupation of the duchy of Holstein

Russian novelist **Fyodor Dostoyevsky** (1821–81) publishes *Crime and Punishment*

14 October French troops land at Ganghwa Island, **Korea**, in retaliation for execution of French Jesuit priests

11 January Benito Juárez (1807–72) becomes president of **Mexico**

30 January Emperor Kōmei dies; Crown Prince **Mutsuhito** becomes emperor of **Japan**

Dual monarchy of **Austria-Hungary** established

Karl Marx publishes first part of *Das Kapital*

KARL MARX (1818–83)

Karl Marx was a German philosopher, political economist, historian, political theorist, sociologist, and communist revolutionary, whose ideas played a significant role in the development of modern communism and socialism – theories collectively known as Marxism. His critique of capitalism, *Das Kapital*, remains influential today.

Prague, Prussia received Schleswig-Holstein, Hanover, Hesse-Kassel, Nassau, and Frankfurt, allowing it to organize the **North German Confederation**. The king of Prussia, **William I** (1797–1888) was at its helm, backed by Prime Minister **Otto von Bismarck** (see 1862). Austria also gave up control of the Venetia (Venice), allowing the region to be unified with Italy.

1868

This painting shows battleships in the Ten Years War (1868–78), which was part of the long-running struggle for Cuba's independence from Spain.

WITH THE FALL IN 1868 OF THE TOKUGAWA SHOGUNATE in Japan and the rise of the emperor Meiji Tenno (1852–1912) the island reversed its policy of isolationism and began a programme of Westernization, with the aim of being able to stand up to the Western powers that were demanding access to Japan (see 1853). This period, known as the **Meiji Restoration**, was a time of long-lasting fundamental social reforms, such as the ending of feudalism, formation of a national army, and implementation of tax systems, with a constitutional government being convened by 1890. There was a boom in infrastructure modernization throughout this period, with the arrival of railroads and the telegraph.

In **Cuba**, discontent with the Spanish regime had been growing. When Queen Isabella II (1830–1904) was deposed by a military rebellion in Spain, Cubans seeking independence took the opportunity to launch a war against the Spanish rulers on their island. Led by Carlos Manuel de Céspedes, this uprising, known as ***El Grito de Yara*** (The Cry of Yara), resulted in The Ten Years War (1868–78), a campaign of guerilla warfare that ended in failure for the Cuban rebels.

In the same year, there was also an uprising against Spanish rule in Puerto Rico. The Lares uprising, or *El Grito de Lares*, was shortlived and, like the Cuban uprising, also ended in failure.

In **South Africa**, British control was spreading. Boer settlers had moved away from the Cape Colony, taking land from local tribes, including the neighbouring Basutoland. Sotho leader **Moshoeshoe I** (*c.*1786–1870) asked Britain for help against further incursions into **Sotho territory**, and the result was that the kingdom was annexed to the British Crown in 1868, becoming a protectorate. On Moshoeshoe's death in 1870, it was made part of the Cape Colony region without consulting the Sotho people.

Meiji vase
A Japanese Satsuma cabinet vase from the Meiji period. Art was well supported by the Japanese government during this period.

1869

> **“** ...REJOICE THAT I HAVE **LIVED TO SEE THIS DAY,** WHEN THE **COLORED PEOPLE... HAVE EQUAL PRIVILEGES** WITH THE MOST FAVORED. **”**
>
> **Thomas Garrett, American abolitionist,** on the passing of the 15th Amendment

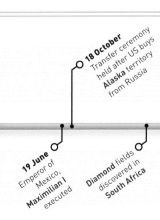

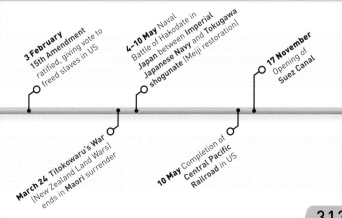

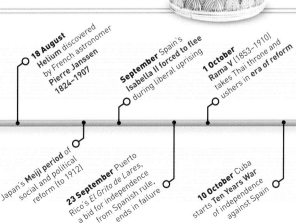

Grand opening
The opening of the Suez Canal, Port Said, Egypt. The project took a decade to complete but its impact on global trade was immediate.

AS RECONSTRUCTION CONTINUED in the war-torn southern US, Congress enacted an amendment to the Constitution – ratified by the states in February 1869 – that extended the right to vote to all black men, whether they had been enslaved or not. The **Fifteenth Amendment** declared that "the rights of the citizens of the United States to vote shall not be denied or abridged by the United States or by any State on account of race, color, or previous condition of servitude".

Meanwhile, westward expansion in the US continued to grow, aided by the arrival of railways. By 1869, the **first transcontinental railway** had been completed by the Central Pacific Railroad. The project was supported by government bonds. Part of the track was started from Sacramento, California, heading east and joining with existing lines in Promontory, Utah, on 10 May 1869. Much of the work on this stretch of railway was done by more than 10,000 Chinese immigrant labourers. The construction of this line allowed rapid coast-to-coast travel in the US, further facilitating western settlement.

Another feat of engineering also opened around the same time – the **Suez Canal** (see 1859). After a decade of construction, this canal linked the Mediterranean and Red seas, and provided a much quicker passage to the Indian Ocean.

In South Africa, **diamonds** had been discovered in the **Northern Cape province** in 1866, and soon a rush was on between the Boers, British, and native people to mine them. The British swiftly stepped in to annex the territory while **thousands of prospectors** arrived to try their luck.

19 June Emperor of Mexico, **Maximilian I** executed

18 October Transfer ceremony held after US buys **Alaska territory** from Russia

Diamond fields discovered in **South Africa**

18 August **Helium** discovered by French astronomer **Pierre Janssen** 1824–1907

Japan's **Meiji period** of social and political reform (to 1912)

September Spain's **Isabella II forced to flee** during liberal uprising

23 September Puerto Rico's *El Grito de Lares*, a bid for independence from Spanish rule, ends in failure

1 October **Rama V** (1853–1910) takes Thai throne and ushers in **era of reform**

10 October Cuba starts **Ten Years War** of independence against Spain

3 February **15th Amendment** ratified, giving vote to freed slaves in US

March 24 **Titokowaru's War** (New Zealand Land Wars) ends in **Maori** surrender

4–10 May Naval Battle of Hakodate in Japan between **Imperial Japanese Navy** and **Tokugawa shogunate** (Meiji restoration)

10 May Completion of **Central Pacific Railroad** in US

17 November Opening of **Suez Canal**

This 19th-century painting depicts Prussian hussars firing up at a French observation balloon during the Franco–Prussian War in 1870.

> **“** THE **ARMY** IS THE **TRUE NOBILITY OF** OUR **COUNTRY. ”**
>
> Napoleon III, Emperor of the French

PRUSSIA'S VICTORY IN THE SEVEN WEEKS WAR (see 1867) gave the impetus to further pursue plans for German unification, this time by bringing the southern German states into the union. Attempts had also been made to place Prince **Leopold of Hohenzollern-Sigmaringen** (1835–1905) on the Spanish throne, left vacant after Queen Isabella II's deposition in 1868 (see panel, 1872). Intense French diplomatic pressure from Napoleon III prevented this. Otto von Bismarck, the Prussian prime minister, however, wished to provoke France into war. To these ends he published the **Ems telegram** (as it was later known), editing it to appear as though insults had been exchanged between King Wilhelm I of Prussia and the French Ambassador. France declared war on Prussia on 19 July. Prussia was victorious at the battles of **Gravelotte** on 18 August, and **Sedan** on 1 September, where an ill Napoleon **surrendered** to German forces and was taken prisoner. While Napoleon was held captive, a provisional government for national defence was set up in Bordeaux where it was decided to depose him and establish the **Third Republic**. By mid-September, the Prussians had besieged Paris. The city was forced to surrender in early 1871 after severe food shortages. By March, an armistice had been agreed and Germany was given the regions of **Alsace** and **Lorraine**.

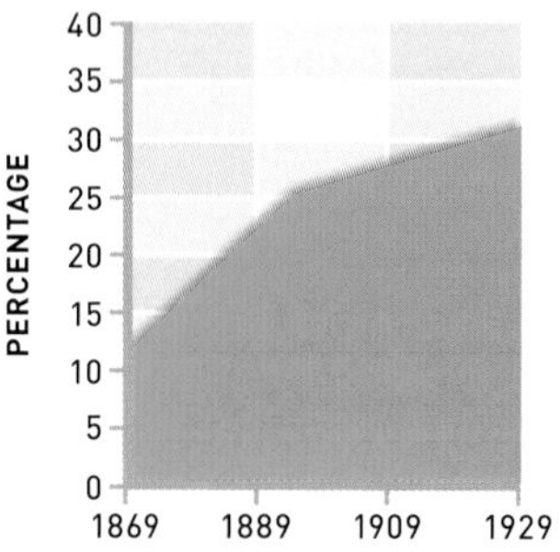

Immigration in Argentina
This graphic shows the steady rise in the percentage of Spanish and Italian immigrants who arrived in Argentina between 1869 and 1929.

Meanwhile, a steady stream of **immigrants** escaping poverty and war in Europe flowed to the Americas. In the US, the **population** hit 40 million and by the end of the century it would nearly double to 76 million. Likewise, in **Argentina** the 1870 population of 1.8 million would reach 8 million by 1914, with many immigrants from Italy and Spain – both places that had been seriously affected by years of warfare.

Siege of Paris
The siege resulted in the capture of the city by Prussian forces, leading to a humiliating French defeat in the Franco–Prussian War.

Men at their battery during the war between the Third Republic and the Paris Commune that erupted at the end of the Franco-Prussian war.

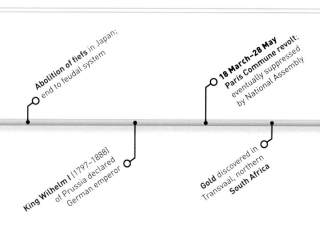

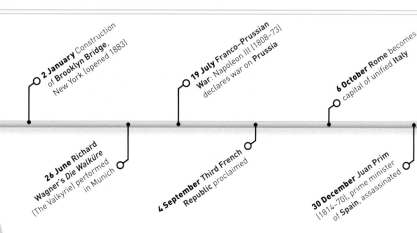

German unification
This map shows the newly unified German Empire, which was organized after Prussia's victory in the Franco–Prussian War.

KEY
- Prussian gains by 1866
- other states in North German Confederation 1867
- other German states 1866
- Austro-Hungarian empire 1867
- → Prussian invasion of France in Franco-Prussian War of 1870–71
- — boundary of German Empire 1871

ITALIAN TROOPS HAD ENTERED ROME the previous September and in October a **plebiscite**, or referendum, made Rome the capital of the united Italy – which became official by 1871. The pope, however, was not pleased with his settlement offer and **excommunicated** Italian king Victor Emmanuel II, entrenching himself in the Vatican while Rome developed as the new capital. The tension between the Vatican and the Italian government would not be resolved until the 20th century.

While France and Prussia were negotiating the end of the Franco–Prussian war in 1871, angry Parisians had risen up over the surrender and established the radical **Paris Commune**. A council of citizens – including republicans, Jacobins, socialists, and anarchists – governed Paris for over two months. The retaliation of the National Assembly, which had relocated to Versailles, was swift. Troops were sent to Paris and 20,000 people were killed.

Following victory against France, Wilhelm I of Prussia declared himself **Emperor of Germany** and named Bismarck (see 1862) as **Chancellor**.

In South Africa, a diamond rush (see 1869) in the Northern Cape was followed by the discovery of **gold** in the **Transvaal** region. This sparked the arrival of thousands of prospectors to the region.

2 January Construction of **Brooklyn Bridge**, New York (opened 1883)

26 June Richard Wagner's *Die Walküre* (The Valkyrie) performed in Munich

19 July Franco–Prussian War: Napoleon III (1808–73) declares war on **Prussia**

4 September Third French Republic proclaimed

6 October Rome becomes capital of unified **Italy**

30 December Juan Prim (1814–70), prime minister of **Spain**, assassinated

Abolition of fiefs in Japan; end to feudal system

King Wilhelm I (1797–1888) of Prussia declared German emperor

18 March–28 May Paris Commune revolt; eventually suppressed by National Assembly

Gold discovered in Transvaal, northern **South Africa**

1872

A portrait of the US women's suffragist leader Susan B. Anthony, who brought her campaign to public attention by illegally voting in 1872.

100 DOLLARS

THE **FINE** IMPOSED **ON SUSAN B. ANTHONY FOR VOTING**

IN THE AFRICAN KINGDOM OF ETHIOPIA, **Yohannes IV** (1831–89) was crowned emperor. He was considered a strong ruler, staving off the increasing incursions from Europeans as well as from African neighbours. By the end of the following decade, Ethiopia had defeated **invasions** by Egyptian forces, as well as Italian forces.

In the US, pressure was growing for women to be given the **right to vote**. One of the leading advocates was **Susan B. Anthony** (1820–1906), who, during the 1872 presidential election, marched up to the polling station in Rochester, New York and cast her vote in defiance of the law. She was arrested and fined. Although she refused to pay the fine, the court case did not continue and Anthony carried on with her crusade.

Meanwhile, in New York, Captain Benjamin Briggs set out to cross the Atlantic on the ship ***Mary Celeste*** on 7 November. By 4 December, the crew of the *Dei Gratia* spotted the *Mary Celeste* drifting around the coast of Portugal completely **deserted**. The lifeboat was missing and the ship had drifted some 1,110 km (700 miles) from the last point entered in the log. Its crew was never seen again, and the **maritime mystery** was never solved.

In France, physicist Louis Ducos du Hauron had been working on creating a **colour photograph** using a three-colour principle. He patented his process in 1868 and went on to produce some of the earliest colour photographs.

CARLIST WARS IN SPAIN

The 19th century in Spain was dominated by the Carlist Wars. These civil wars began in 1834, triggered by the death of Ferdinand VII. The conservative Carlists did not want the king's daughter, Isabella (1830–1904), to take the throne, but rather Ferdinand's brother, Don Carlos (1788–1855). After three wars, the dispute was resolved in 1876 with the accession of Isabella's son Alfonso XII (1857–85) to the throne, who drove some 10,000 Carlists out of Spain.

1873

> **" THE MAIN THING IS TO MAKE HISTORY, NOT TO WRITE IT. "**
>
> **Otto von Bismarck, 19th-century German statesman**

Royal Canadian Mounted Police
"Mounties", as they became known, wearing their distinctive uniforms at an annual sports event at Regina, Saskatchewan, Canada.

EAGER TO PROTECT GERMANY'S GROWING POWER, Bismarck proposed the **Three Emperors' League**, an alliance between Germany, the Austro-Hungarian Empire, and Russia, with the purposeful exclusion of France. Formed in 1873, the league lasted for three years, was later re-established in secret in 1881 and renewed in 1884, and finally collapsed in 1887. At issue were the continued conflicts of interest between Austria–Hungary and Russia in the Balkan territory.

In the Caribbean, the island of **Puerto Rico** finally abolished slavery. Although the slave trade had been suppressed earlier, the practice had continued on the island and in neighbouring Cuba. Both were still under Spanish control. The end of slavery was announced in May 1873, although an **apprenticeship** system was put in place, extending slave conditions for some until 1876.

In **Canada**, the North West Mounted Rifles was formed to enforce the law on a national and local level. The force was charged with policing the largely rural provinces of the huge Canadian territory. The initial few hundred officers had some 800,000 sq km (300,000 sq miles) under their jurisdiction. But the US was uncomfortable with the idea of armed troops patrolling the border, so the force's name was changed to the North West Mounted Police – though later the name would be altered again to the **Royal Canadian Mounted Police**, which is still in use, along with the famous abbreviation of "Mounties".

1874

A depiction of Garnet Wolseley's reception among the Asante people.

IN MARCH, BRITISH ARMY OFFICER CHARLES GEORGE GORDON (1833–85) arrived in the province of **Equatoria**, in the south of Egyptian-occupied Sudan. He was to take control of the territory but under the auspices of the khedive (viceroy) of **Egypt**. Gordon was tasked with establishing way stations up the White Nile and to attempt to suppress the ongoing **slave trade**. He mapped parts of the Nile and set up outposts along the river as far as Uganda. He became governor-general of Sudan in 1877.

Meanwhile, in West Africa, a British expedition led by **Sir Garnet Wolseley** (1833–1913) defeated the **Asante Empire** (present-day Ghana) and asserted control over the southern part of their territory, known as the **Gold Coast**.

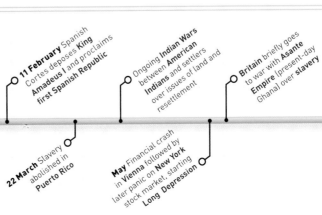

Charles George Gordon
A British general and colonial administrator, Gordon was invited by Egypt's khedive to govern part of Egypt's Sudan territory.

- **12 January Yohannas IV** (1831–89) of Ethiopia crowned king
- French physicist **Louis Ducos du Hauron** (1837–1920) pioneers **colour photography**
- **1 March** World's **first national park** created at Yellowstone, US
- **April Third Carlist War** (to 1876) starts in **Spain**
- **18 November** American suffragette **Susan B. Anthony arrested for voting** in a US election
- **4 December Mary Celeste** ship found abandoned at sea
- **11 February** Spanish Cortes deposes **King Amadeus I** and proclaims **first Spanish Republic**
- **22 March** Slavery abolished in **Puerto Rico**
- Ongoing **Indian Wars** between **American Indians** and settlers over issues of land and resettlement
- **May** Financial crash in **Vienna** followed by later panic on **New York** stock market, starting **Long Depression**
- **Britain** briefly goes to war with **Asante Empire** (present-day Ghana) over **slavery**
- The **Sudan** comes under British administration
- British win **Second Asante War** (1873–74) and assert control over **Gold Coast**
- **15 April** First exhibition by group of painters who became known as **Impressionists**

Elm chair
*c.*1850
This Ming-style elmwood chair has a shaped crest rail and curved back splat with openwork cartouches above a beaded apron.

Elm cabinet
*c.*1860
The doors of this black lacquered elm cabinet of rectangular outline are painted with a colourful decoration that includes birds and flowering trees.

Jade brush holder
*c.*18th century
The detail of this jade brush holder contains the figure of Taoist philosopher Lao Tzu. The ancient Taoist practices were popular in the Ming period but fell out of favour with Qing rulers.

Soapstone Lohan
1600–1799
This statue shows a Lohan, a human who achieved enlightenment through meditation on the teaching of Buddha. Buddhism flourished during the Qing period.

THE QING DYNASTY

OBJECTS FROM THE EMPIRE THAT RULED CHINA FOR MORE THAN TWO CENTURIES

The Qing dynasty was established after the last Ming emperor was overthrown in 1644. Rule was instituted by Manchu chieftains and the Qing period of rule lasted until 1911. It was a time in which China witnessed a trebling in the population to around 450 million.

Although the Manchus were seen as outsiders by the Chinese, they maintained their rule for so long by continuing to use the existing form of government from the Ming dynasty (1368–1644). This continuity spilled over into the arts and crafts as well, and much of the work produced in the Qing years was heavily influenced by Ming designs, especially porcelain.

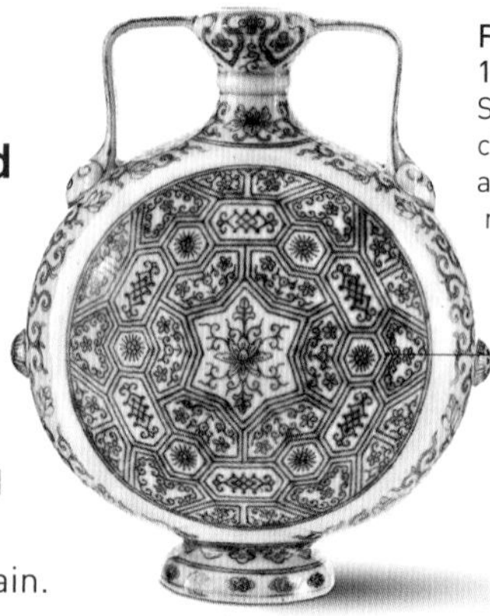

Flask
1736–95
Supported on a spreading circular foot, this flask has a short, contracted neck and right-angle handles. The sides have bands of exotic blooms.

Axe head
19th century
Made from chalcedony, this translucent green and red axe head has a flat, curved cutting edge. Carved in relief is a Taotie mask and sleeping silkworms.

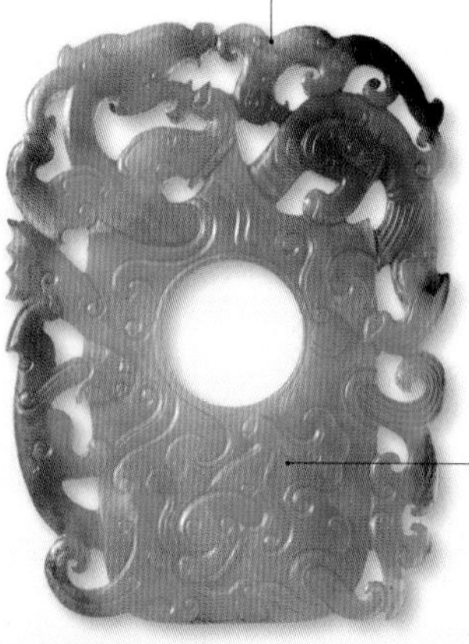

Belt hook
19th century
This jade belt hook has a Taoist design, shaped as two dragons and a bat laid on the outside, a phoenix on one side, and a silkworm pattern on the reverse.

Covered box
1736–95
The top of this peach-shaped covered box (the fruit is a symbol of long life) shows a *chun* (spring) character enclosing, in the centre, Shou Lao, the god of longevity, with a dragon on either side.

Pewter tea caddy
18th century
This tea caddy is constructed from pewter. Its simple design is embellished with floral and calligraphic engravings.

Blue tea set
1850–99
Part of a set of two, this porcelain bowl with lid and saucer is decorated with famille rose enamel colours on a blue background.

Brass wedding bowl
18th century
This brass wedding bowl is part of a set of two. This one is lined with silver – the other has a gilt silver interior – and the base has an engraved design.

Sancai teapot
1662–1772
This teapot is sancai porcelain and has a rectangular shape, with raised panels on each side illustrating the four seasons.

Portable set of eating implements
1736–95
The contents of this travelling set of eating implements include two pairs of chopsticks, a knife, a pair of forks, and an ivory pick.

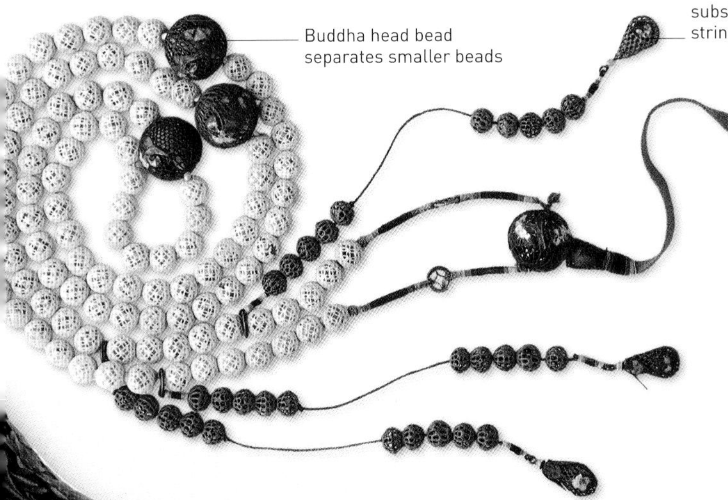

Ivory necklace for civil servant
1900s
These beads are made of painted ceramic and gold leaf. The larger beads, called Buddha heads, divide up the smaller beads into groups of 27. There are also subsidiary strands of 10 blue beads.

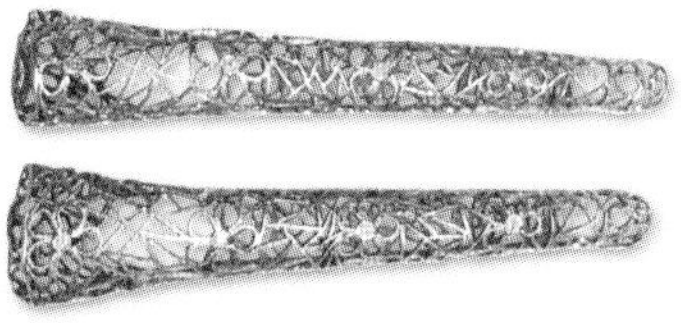

Golden nail guards
*c.*19th century
These elaborate nail guards have gold openwork with a "cracked ice" pattern. The device was designed to protect the nail of the little finger.

Xian seal
19th century
This oval Xian seal has an incised inscription on each of the long sides. The base reads "Living by the Golden Tower".

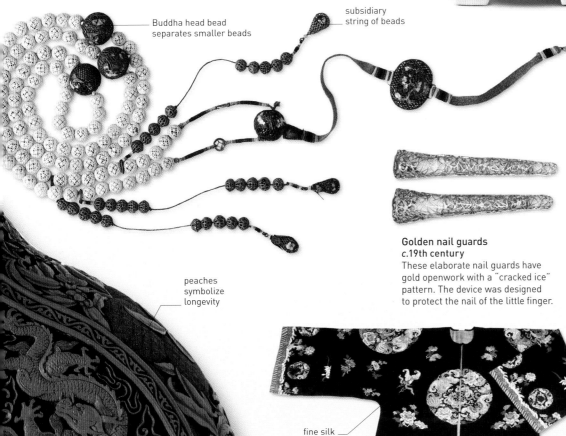

Silk robe
*c.*19th century
This woman's black silk robe has a pattern of flowers woven into the fabric. The design also includes a springtime scene involving flowers and butterflies.

Pair of bowed shoes
1800–1900
These bowed shoes with a pointed head and high heel were used for outdoor activities for a woman with bound feet. The sides have an intricate embroidered decoration of birds and flowers.

A painting entitled *The Victor* by Russian war artist Vasily Vereshchagin (1842–1904) depicts Turks celebrating a victory during the Russo–Turkish War. Hostilities between Russia and the Ottoman Empire were long-running and the two had gone to battle many times over the previous two centuries.

THE RIFT BETWEEN THE OTTOMAN EMPIRE AND ITS SUBJECTS IN Bosnia and Herzegovina grew wider as **Christian** inhabitants of the two territories **rebelled** against Ottoman rule, requesting aid from neighbouring **Serbia**, which had a much higher degree of autonomy. Buoyed by Russian promises of support and inspired by the nationalism sweeping through the region, Serbia too declared war on the Ottoman Empire on 30 June 1876; **Montenegro** followed suit the next day, leading the weakening empire into another destabilizing conflict. Montenegro was initially successful, with a victory in Herzegovina, but Russian support in Serbia did not materialize and the Turks won the battle of Aleksinac on 9 August 1876. This forced the Serbs to appeal to other nations for help.

In other parts of the Ottoman world, **Egypt** continued to make incursions into **Ethiopia**, leading its king, Yohannes IV (see 1872), to declare war on the Egyptians. The conflict arose because Ismail Pasha (1830–95), the khedive (viceroy) of Egypt, wanted to put settlements on strategic points along the **Red Sea** coastline in Ethiopian territory (present-day Eritrea). By 1875 Egypt had succeeding in occupying many coastal towns, as well as the inland city of Harar. The fighting lasted until 1877, by which time Ethiopia had managed to defeat two Egyptian campaigns.

ANGER AND UNREST HAD BEEN growing among American Indians in the US, many of whom had been forced off their land. This issue often resulted in armed conflict with US troops. One of the most infamous confrontations was the **Battle of Little Bighorn** where, on 25 June, Lieutenant Colonel George A. Custer (1839–76) and his men were killed by a coalition of Eastern **Sioux** and Northern **Cheyenne** Indians. Around the same time, US forces were fighting the **Apache** people, who lived near the border with Mexico. They too were angered by attempts to move them on to a reservation, and attacked white settlements. This conflict continued for another decade until their leader, **Geronimo** (1829–1909), surrendered in 1886.

> “ THE NATION THAT **SECURES CONTROL OF** THE **AIR WILL** ULTIMATELY **CONTROL** THE **WORLD.** ”
>
> **Alexander Graham Bell, Scottish inventor**

Elsewhere in the US, a Scottish-born inventor named **Alexander Graham Bell** (1847–1922) patented his device for "transmitting vocal or other sounds telegraphically" – **the first telephone**. This development would change for ever the way the world communicated.

In Mexico, former soldier **Porfirio Díaz** (see panel, right) tried to launch a revolt against president Sebastián Lerdo de Tejada. His attempt in early 1876 failed and he fled to the US. He returned in November and defeated the government's troops. In May 1877 he was elected president and controlled Mexico for decades.

Explorer **Henry Morton Stanley** (1841–1904), meanwhile, was trying to follow the uncharted Lualaba River in the **Congo** to establish which river it joined. Stanley's African exploits were already famous; he had been previously sent by a US newspaper to find fellow explorer David Livingstone (see 1855) and in 1871, on the shores of Lake Tanganyika, he had supposedly uttered the celebrated words "Doctor Livingstone, I presume?".

PORFIRIO DIAZ
(1830–1915)

Mexican general, politician, and president, Porfirio Díaz was of mixed European and indigenous descent. From a humble background, he made a name for himself in the military. After he was elected president, he shored up his support and created a political machine that kept him in power and the opposition divided and suppressed, leaving him to control politics in Mexico for more than 30 years.

Early telephone
This early example of a telephone – known as a box telephone – has a trumpet-like mouthpiece and it transmitted sound through the use of an electromagnet.

IN CHINA, FAMINE SPREAD through the northern provinces. A drought the previous year affecting the **Yellow River** – a vital source of water – was compounded by a lack of rain in 1877 and the arrival of locusts. When the rains returned towards the end of the following year, some 9 to 13 million people had died in a region of 108 million.

In South Africa, the discovery of **gold** (see 1871) had exacerbated tensions between the Boer settlers and the British, who by this point governed much of the country. By 1877 the British managed to **annex the Transvaal**. However, the Afrikaners rebelled against this move and regained their independence a few years later (see 1881).

Famine in China
An illustration in a French magazine shows the state of poverty during the famine years in China, when millions died in the northern region.

- Revolts in **Balkans** over Ottoman rule
- **3 March** French composer **Georges Bizet's** (1838–75) opera **Carmen** debuts in Paris
- Asia's first **stock exchange** opens in present-day **Mumbai**
- **7 September Egyptian invasion** of Ethiopia defeated
- **7 March** Scottish inventor **Alexander Graham Bell** (1847–1922) patents telephone in US
- **16 April Bulgarian** uprising in **Ottoman Empire**; leads to Bulgaria's independence in 1878
- **1 May Queen Victoria** takes title Empress of India
- **25–26 June Battle of Little Bighorn**: American Indian alliance wipes out US force of 250 soldiers
- **July Serbia and Montenegro** declare war on their Ottoman rulers
- Japan forces **Korea** to sign unequal treaty, opening ports to Japanese ships
- **31 August Murat V** of Ottoman Empire succeeded by **Abdul Hamid II**
- **31 October Cyclone** kills 200,000 in **India**
- **28 November** Start of dictatorship by **Porfirio Díaz** in **Mexico**
- **Russia** declares war on **Ottoman Empire** (to 1878) over Ottoman control of Serbia
- **6 May Chief Crazy Horse** (c.1840–1877) of Oglala Sioux surrenders to US army; later killed in custody
- **Great North China Famine** (until 1879)
- **Romania** declares independence from Ottoman Europe

1878

Vasily Vereshchagin's *Mass for the Dead (The Defeated)* shows the aftermath of a Russian defeat during the Russo–Turkish War of 1877–78.

RUSSIA DECIDED TO ONCE AGAIN DECLARE WAR on the Ottoman Empire on 24 April 1877, in an attempt to aid the Serbians in their fight against the Ottomans (see 1875). Russia was aided by Romania (the united Moldavia and Wallachia). The **Russo–Turkish War of 1877–78** included a five-month siege of the Ottoman Bulgarian town of Plevna, which eventually fell to Russian forces. Russia also managed to take some key fortresses and a truce was called. A settlement was reached on 3 March 1878, known as the **Treaty of San Stefano**, which gave Serbia, Romania, and Montenegro their independence, while Bulgaria was granted some autonomy and put under Russian authority.

However, European powers were not satisfied with this settlement as there were many competing interests. **Prussia** backed Great Britain's desire to curb Russian expansion into Bulgaria – which at this point reached the Aegean sea – by refusing to let Russia extend naval power in the Mediterranean. **Austria-Hungary** wanted to continue occupation of Bosnia and Herzegovina to keep its regional influence intact and stem growing Slav nationalism.

Meanwhile, Britain had signed the **Cyprus Convention** with Turkey. This deal would allow British administration of the island while it remained under Ottoman sovereignty. This allowed Britain to establish a presence and a naval base in the eastern part of the Mediterranean, with the aim of blocking further Russian incursions into the region.

Away from the European diplomatic bargaining table, the British were once again caught up in warfare with Afghans. The **Second Afghan War** (to 1880) was ignited when British agents learned of negotiations between Afghan leader Sher Ali Khan (1825–79) and Russia. This was compounded by Sher Ali's refusal to receive a British delegation. In November 1878, British forces invaded the region. Sher Ali turned to Russia for support, but was told to make peace with Britain. Sher Ali died the next year and his son, Mohammad Yaqub Khan (1849–1923), signed a **treaty** ceding the **Khyber Pass** to the British. Soon after, a British envoy was murdered and British troops returned to take Kabul. Yaqub was forced to flee. He was succeeded by Abdur Rahman Khan (c.1844–1901), who ended the conflict and supported British interests.

Afghan fighters
A photograph of Afghan soldiers holding hand-crafted rifles, at Jalalabad, Afghanistan, during the second Anglo–Afghan conflict.

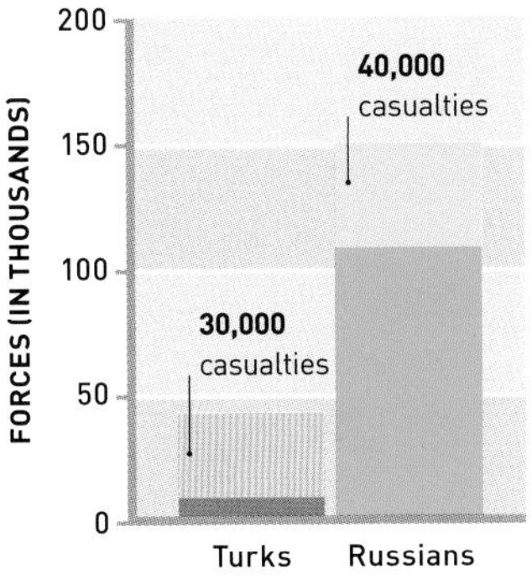

Siege of Plevna
Although the Russians eventually overcame the Turks, the small Turkish force heroically held up the Russian advance into Bulgaria.

1879

This oil painting shows the defence of Rorke's Drift on 22 January, where a handful of British soldiers faced an attack by of 4,000 Zulu soldiers.

IN SOUTH AMERICA, PERU, BOLIVIA, AND CHILE began a dispute over who had control over the **Atacama Desert** region, running along the Peru–Chile border. In the previous decade the valuable mineral **sodium nitrate** had been discovered there. Initially Chilean companies went into the desert to extract the mineral and issues over territorial control soon arose. Chile and Bolivia at first agreed that the 24th parallel was their boundary. But Bolivia, dissatisfied with the deal, entered into a secret agreement with Peru to defend its interests in the desert. Bolivia later seized the property of Chilean companies, prompting Chile's president to send in troops. Chile formally declared **war on Bolivia and Peru** on 5 April. The war of the Pacific took place on land and sea, and was not resolved until 1883, with Chile keeping control of the mineral-rich Antofagasta region.

In South Africa, British forces came up against the Zulu nation in the **Anglo–Zulu War**. The British wanted to expand into Zulu territory, but this was met with resistance by King Cetshwayo (1826–84) who organized some 60,000 warriors. The British established a depot at **Rorke's Drift**, which was later attacked by Zulus after their victory in Isandlwana. The Zulus were successfully repelled after 550 warriors were shot by the handful of British troops stationed at the depot. After seven months of conflict, the British managed a final victory over the Zulus in the Battle of Ulundi on 4 July, and took control of their territory.

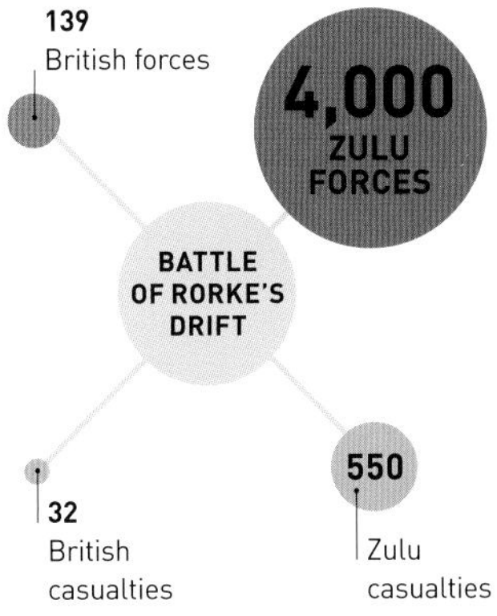

Battle of Rorke's Drift
Although the Zulus had some rifles, these were put to little effective use, and superior British firepower won out despite overwhelming numbers.

Sunken ship in War of the Pacific
This scene from the Battle of Iquique, during the War of the Pacific, shows Chilean and Peruvian ships. The dispute also included Bolivia.

- **2 February** Greece declares war on **Ottoman Empire**
- **3 March Treaty of San Stefano** gives Montenegro, Serbia, and Romania independence
- **24 April Russia** declares war on **Ottoman Empire**
- US inventor **Thomas Edison** (1847–1931) sets up **Edison Electric Light Company**
- **June–July Congress of Berlin** meets to discuss the Balkans
- **21 November Second Anglo–Afghan War** (to 1880) over Afghanistan's talks with Russia
- **11 January Anglo–Zulu War** begins
- **14 January War of the Pacific** (to 1883) begins: Chile declares war on Bolivia and Peru
- **22 January Battle of Isandlwana; Zulu** troops massacre **British** troops
- **3 February** First **electric streetlight** in Britain
- **4 July Anglo–Zulu War** ends with British victory at **Battle of Ulundi**
- **31 December Thomas Edison** gives first public demonstration of **incandescent light bulb** in Menlo Park, New Jersey, US

1880

West Indian labourers cutting a channel during the first – and failed – attempt to construct a canal in Panama connecting the Atlantic and Pacific oceans.

BUOYED BY THE SUCCESS OF THE SUEZ CANAL (see 1869), Ferdinand de Lesseps (see 1859) began to draw up plans for a waterway connecting the Atlantic and Pacific oceans through the isthmus of **Panama**. However, the project got off to a difficult start the following year in 1881. There were disagreements over the canal's plans, the machinery did not function well in the terrain, and many workers died of disease in the tropical heat.

Meanwhile, the development of commercial **refrigeration** began to alter the relationship between consumers and producers. Cheese and meats could now be exported long distances. On 2 February, the first shipment of frozen meat to survive the journey intact arrived in London from Australia. The following years saw a boom in **shipments** of meats and other agricultural goods from Australia, New Zealand, and Argentina to Europe.

Around the same time, the problem of creating a safe means of artificial light was solved by the US inventor **Thomas Edison** (1847–1931). He had perfected existing designs on **lightbulbs** of the day (see pp.298–99) by preventing them from overheating and making them much safer to use. Almost as soon as he had patented the design, lighting systems began to spring up on the streets, in businesses and hotels, and in homes.

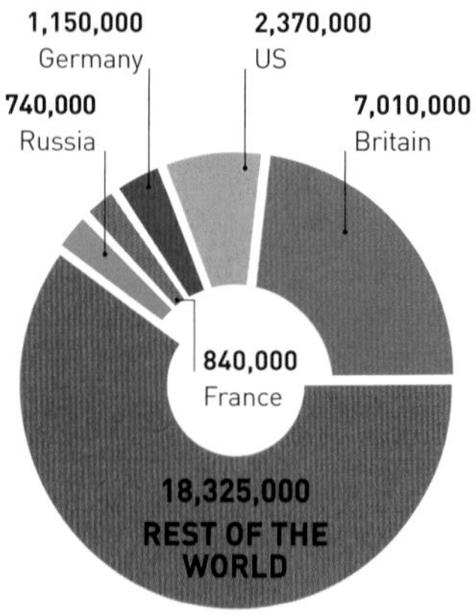

Shipping tonnage 1881
This chart shows total goods shipped by country in vessels over 100 tonnes. Refrigeration sparked a rise in food transport and the use of vast ships.

THE BOERS

The Boers ("farmers" in Dutch) in South Africa were settlers of Dutch, French Huguenot, and German descent that left the Cape Province in search of autonomy further north. They spoke Afrikaans, a language that evolved from Dutch. The earliest settlers arrived in the Cape of Good Hope after the Dutch East India Company established a port in 1652. The Boers had a strong ethnic identity and clashed often with the Zulus and the British.

1881

> **"** THE **DOOR** THAT **NOBODY ELSE WILL GO IN** AT, **SEEMS ALWAYS** TO SWING **OPEN** WIDELY **FOR** ME. **"**

Clara Barton, American humanitarian

Clara Barton was the founder of the American Red Cross organization.

IN SOUTH AFRICA, TENSIONS BETWEEN BOER SETTLERS (see panel, above) and the British over the annexation of the Transvaal (see 1877) had tipped into violence. Boers had established the **South African Republic** in the Transvaal area and begun to use arms to support their claim, starting the First Anglo-Boer War in 1880. British troops suffered a defeat at the hands of the Boer settlers in the battle at Majuba Hill on 27 February 1881, bringing the dispute to an end by March. The **Convention of Pretoria** treaty granted the South African Republic independence over its affairs, although Britain was allowed to maintain an unclear "suzerainty" over it. This did little to rectify the situation, and the simmering resentment between the British and Boers would erupt again before the end of the century (see 1899).

France, meanwhile, was attempting to extend its influence in North Africa. With Algeria under its control, it looked to the neighbouring Ottoman territory of **Tunisia**. The past 50 years had seen Tunisian rulers caught in between Ottoman demands and European creditors, especially after the government went bankrupt in 1869, after which a British, French, and Italian financial commission was imposed on the territory. France decided to send in 36,000 troops in 1881, under the pretext that Tunisians had been moving into Algerian territory. Under the **Treaty of Bardo** that same year, Tunisia became a **French protectorate**. French military occupied the territory and a French minister was installed to liaise with the Tunisian bey (ruler), who now only had limited control.

In **Russia**, there was an outbreak of anti-Jewish violence culminating in **pogroms** in the south of the country, including Kiev, which continued until 1884. This was triggered by the **assassination** of the reformist **Alexander II** (1818–81) who was killed by a group known as People's Will. False rumours circulated that Jewish people were responsible and that the government was going to instruct the public to take their revenge on Jews. The violent attacks caused many Jewish people to emigrate to Western Europe, the US, and Palestine.

In the US, teacher and nurse **Clara Barton** (1821–1912) organized the American Red Cross, a part of the growing International Red Cross relief organization that had been founded in 1863.

Meanwhile, in New Mexico, sheriff **Pat Garrett** (1850–1908) captured one of the United States' most notorious outlaws, **Billy the Kid** (c.1859–81) on 30 April. Born William H. Bonney Jr., Billy the Kid became an infamous gunfighter, and was rumoured to have killed at least 27 men by the age of 21. After his arrest he was jailed and sentenced to death, but he escaped until Garrett tracked him down and shot him dead on 14 July.

Garrett's gun
A replica of the holster that held Pat Garrett's gun around the time he captured Billy the Kid.

- Census puts **US population** at 50 million
- **2 May** First shipment of **frozen meat** from Melbourne, **Australia** to **Britain**
- **29 June Tahiti** cedes to **France**
- **22 July Abdur Rahman Khan** becomes emir of **Afghanistan**
- **20 December First Anglo-Boer War** (to 1881) over annexation of the **South African Republic** (Transvaal region)
- **16 January** Russia attacks **Turkmen Fort** in **Turkmenistan** which later becomes part of **Russia**
- **13 March Alexander II** of Russia **assassinated** by bomb, triggering **anti-semitic** violence
- **21 May** US nurse **Clara Barton** sets up the **American Red Cross**
- **French** protectorate established in **Tunisia**
- **20 July** Indian Wars: **Chief Sitting Bull** surrenders **Sioux** people to **US troops**
- **23 July Boundary** treaty between **Chile** and **Argentina** establishes exact border between them
- **3 August** Official end to **First Anglo-Boer War** with Pretoria Convention treaty; **South African Republic** in Transvaal re-established

1882

This illustration shows the bombardment of Alexandria – a sea battle won by the British, who succeeded in destroying the port's fortified batteries.

OVER THE COURSE OF THE PREVIOUS FEW YEARS, the power of French and British interests had grown substantially in Egypt. This led to increasing European interference in Egyptian affairs – something that was considered legitimate because of the financial debt Egypt owed to Britain and France. By 1882, Egypt was bankrupt and the khedive (viceroy) was scarcely able to hold on to his own authority. Ismail Pasha (1830–95) had been deposed by the Ottoman sultan in 1879 – under pressure from Britain and France – in favour of his son, Muhammad Tawfiq Pasha (1852–92). This **Dual Control** by the French and British persisted while there was growing internal nationalist unrest.

Britain was fearful of what a nationalist uprising might mean for the Suez Canal, in which it had a substantial interest. So British forces decided to mount an attack to stifle any further action; the Royal Navy bombarded the forts of **Alexandria** on 11 July 1882. Egypt was then placed under military occupation, becoming a British protectorate.

Further south, in **Sudan**, British troops were continuing to fight the **Sudanese War** (1881–99) against the followers of the powerful **Muhammad Ahmad bin Abd Allah** (1844–85) who had declared a holy war after taking the title Mahdi. His mission was to restore justice to the world, believing it was soon going to end.

In Europe, an **anti-French union** was being formed, known as the **Triple Alliance**. It consisted of Germany, Austria–Hungary, and Italy. The first two members had signed previous unions (see 1873), which included Russia. Italy joined after disputing France's territorial claims in North Africa.

Meanwhile, in France, scientist **Louis Pasteur** (1822–95) – well known for his development in 1863 of the **pasteurization** process which reduced harmful germs in food and drink – had turned his attention to vaccines (see 1796). He investigated anthrax, a bacterial disease that had killed many sheep in Europe and also affected humans. By 1881, he had conducted successful large-scale experiments with animals, and vaccines were produced.

1883–84

A hand-coloured woodcut showing the island of Krakatoa, Indonesia, before its destruction, when its volcano erupted in 1883.

BRITISH TROOPS SUFFERED EARLY DEFEATS IN THE WAR IN SUDAN at the hands of the **Mahdi** revolutionary army (see 1882). At the beginning of the year on 26 January, Ahmad and the Mahdi troops captured the city of El Obeid, situated in the centre of the territory. Mahdi troops continued their march towards **Khartoum**, which had earlier been placed under British administration by the Egyptian khedive (see 1874), capturing the city after a siege of nine months.

Meanwhile, France had seized more of the territory around the **Niger River** (Niger) and became involved in conflict on the island of Madagascar off the coast of East Africa in a bid to protect French territory. In 1883, France invaded the island in the **Franco–Hova War** against the Hova people – the largest Malagasy group on the island – and bombarded the coastal towns of Majunga and Tamatave from the sea. In 1885, they reached a settlement allowing the French occupation at Diégo-Suarez in the north. However, tensions continued and the French sent in 15,000 troops in 1885, landing at Majunga and capturing the capital.

Triggered by the ongoing **Berlin Conference on Africa** (see 1885) Germany claimed territory in southwest Africa (Namibia), Togoland (Togo), Cameroon, and part of the island of Zanzibar off the coast of Tanzania, East Africa. **Italy** took control of Eritrean coastal towns along the Red Sea, though made no further inroads into **Ethiopian** territory.

In the **Pacific**, Britain and Germany divided up more territories. By the 1870s, Britain had established settlements along the coast of the eastern half of **New Guinea** (present-day Papua New Guinea), annexing it by 1884. Germany took control of the northeast part of the island.

Brooklyn Bridge

The Great East River Suspension Bridge in New York City was built between 1870 and 1883. It stretches 1825m (5,988ft) across its span.

20 March Britain enters **Liberia** demanding land is ceded to British **Sierra Leone**

11 June Urabi revolt against khedive and European powers in **Egypt**

20 May Triple Alliance formed between Germany, Austria-Hungary, and Italy

11 July British occupy **Egypt**

20 August Pyotr Ilyich **Tchaikovsky's** *1812 Overture* debuts in Moscow

July Boers create Republic of **Stellaland** in present-day North West Province, **South Africa**

1 September Kimberley, South Africa, becomes first town in Africa to be **lit by electricity**

1883 Start of French conquest of **Madagascar**; France takes **Niger** occupying Agadez (to 1904)

20 October 1883 War of Pacific; Peru leaves conflict after Treaty of Ancon with **Chile**

26 August 1883 Volcano Krakatoa erupts and kills around 40,000, destroys island of Krakatoa, and causes tsunamis; explosion heard 5,000km (3,000 miles) away

1884 British inventor **Hiram Maxim** (1840–1916) invents Maxim gun, **first self-powered machine gun**

13 March 1884 Siege of Khartoum, Sudan, by Mahdi troops begins (to 26 January 1885)

5 July 1884 Germany claims **Cameroon**

1884 Coup in Korea staged with Japan's aid, put down with aid of China

1884 Berlin Conference on African Affairs (to 1885) leads to **"Scramble for Africa"**

1884 Germany acquires **Togo** and **Cameroon**

October 1884 Greenwich Meridian designated as Prime Meridian at international conference

December 1884 Porfirio Díaz returns as president of **Mexico**

1885

A village in the valley of the River Congo in Africa in the 1800s. Congolese territory was put under the control of the Belgian king, Leopold II, in 1885.

AS SOME OF THE NATIONS IN EUROPE became more powerful – especially the new nations of Germany and Italy – they were eager to participate in the growing European colonization of overseas territories, notably in Africa. To this end, the **Berlin Conference on Africa** was held from 15 November 1884 until 26 February 1885. Later known as the meeting that triggered the "**Scramble for Africa**", competing powers jostled for territory – though no African leaders were even consulted, much less invited. The meeting was initiated by Portugal in the interests of protecting its claim to part of the **Congo** estuary. This claim would, however, be rejected and the river basin was declared neutral in order to protect trade in the region. A group of European investors were given part of the Congo region, which was put under the control of Belgium's King Leopold II (1835–1909), and named the **Congo Free State**.

> **" BESIDE LEOPOLD,** NERO, CALIGULA, ATTILA, TORQUEMADA, GENGHIS KHAN AND SUCH **KILLERS OF MEN ARE** MERE **AMATEURS. "**
>
> **Mark Twain, American author,** on Leopold II's regime in the Congo

Meanwhile, in Germany, engineer **Gottlieb Daimler** (1834–1900) patented a high-speed internal-combustion engine. Daimler and partner Wilhelm Maybach (1846–1929) conducted further research with the engine, placing it on bicycles and carriages. Around the same time fellow German **Karl Benz** (1844–1929) had also been experimenting with engines. He came up with the idea for the Benz car, and in 1885 assembled the **first automobile** in the world. He set up Benz & Co, which would later merge with Daimler to make **Mercedes-Benz** cars.

In **India**, a growing political awareness and the burgeoning nationalist movement led to the establishment of the **Indian National Congress**, which held its first meeting in December.

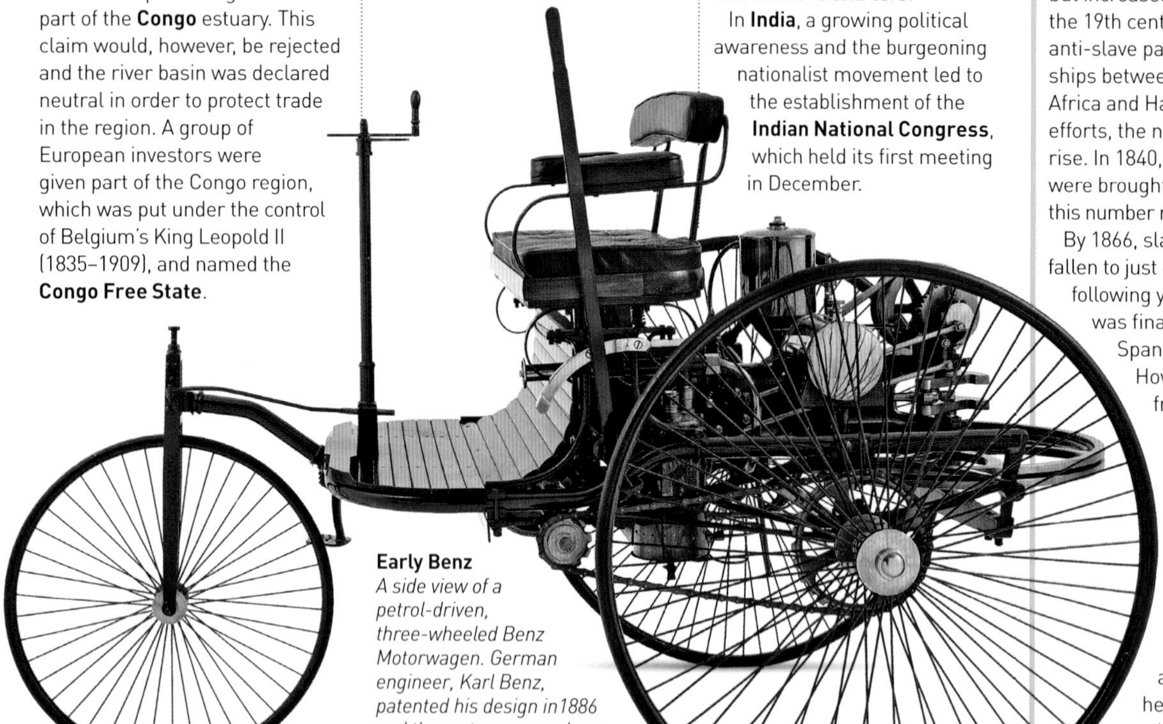

Early Benz
A side view of a petrol-driven, three-wheeled Benz Motorwagen. German engineer, Karl Benz, patented his design in1886 and the motor car was born.

4 January First successful **appendectomy** performed

31 March Bechuanaland (present-day Botswana) becomes British protectorate

Tanganyika becomes German protectorate

Indian political party, **Indian National Congress**, meets for first time

Germany annexes **Marshall Islands**, Pacific Ocean

Belgium's **Leopold II** (1835–1909) establishes **Congo Free State**

Serbia defeated in war with **Bulgaria**

One of the world's first **skyscrapers** built in Chicago

Development of **first automobiles** by German engineers **Gottlieb Daimler** (1834–1900) and **Karl Benz** (1844–1929)

18 September Eastern Rumelia unites with **Bulgaria**

30 September British abolish Boer republic of **Stellaland**, adding it to Bechuanaland

November Third **Anglo–Burmese War** (to 1886) leads to British annexation of Burmese territory

1886

British troops of the Somersetshire Light Infantry cross a river in Burma, during the Anglo–Burmese War.

EMANCIPATION FINALLY ARRIVED FOR SLAVES IN CUBA in October 1886, after a long struggle. Although Britain had decided to end the slave trade in 1807 and abolish the practice of slavery in 1833, Spain and other European colonial powers did not follow suit. In 1817, the Spanish agreed a treaty with Britain to stop the slave trade – and then ignored it. With the loss of most of its Central and South American colonies, Spain turned to its remaining sugar islands of **Cuba** and **Puerto Rico** to refill its coffers. To this end, slavery not only continued, but increased over the course of the 19th century, although British anti-slave patrols tried to stop ships between the west coast of Africa and Havana. Despite their efforts, the numbers continued to rise. In 1840, around 14,500 slaves were brought to Cuba; by 1859 this number reached nearly 30,500.

By 1866, slave imports had fallen to just over 1,000 and the following year, the slave trade was finally outlawed by the Spanish legislature. However, this act did not free the considerable number of slaves on the island. Years of gradual abolition culminated in a royal **decree** that **emancipated the slaves** in 1886.

Meanwhile on 1 January, Britain annexed **Burma**, heralding a long period of insurgency.

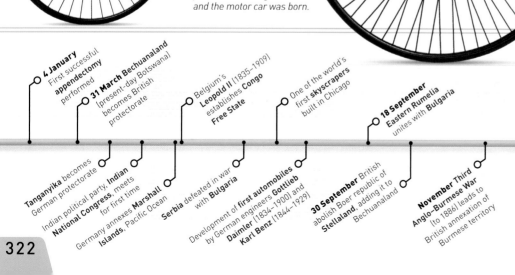

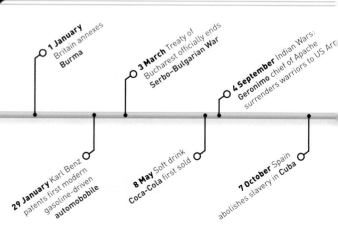

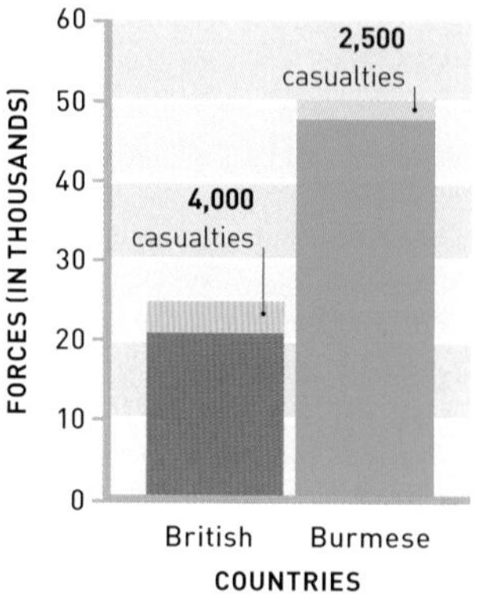

Third Burmese War
Although the war lasted a few weeks, the Burmese insurgency that followed lasted until 1899, claiming many more lives – as shown in this chart.

The annexation was the culmination of the **Third Anglo–Burmese War** in 1885, which had only lasted a few months. The war was triggered by Burmese king **Thibaw**'s negotiations with France over a political alliance and the construction of a railway line to the Indian border. Britain was unable to air its concerns as Thibaw refused a visit from the British envoy. Britain had already annexed Lower Burma after the previous war (see 1852) and the British decided to react by now seizing **Mandalay** and northern Burma. Thibaw was deposed and the territory was annexed to India, giving Britain control of the former kingdom. Although this marked the end of the official war, there was a sporadic guerrilla campaign by the Burmese which would continue to cause unrest in the region for another four years.

1 January Britain annexes **Burma**

29 January Karl Benz patents first modern gasoline-driven **automobobile**

3 March Treaty of Bucharest officially ends **Serbo–Bulgarian War**

8 May Soft drink **Coca-Cola** first sold

4 September Indian Wars: **Geronimo** chief of Apache surrenders warriors to US Arr

7 October Spain abolishes slavery in **Cuba**

1887

A crest belonging to Tsar Ferdinand I who was elected ruler of Bulgaria.

BULGARIA HAD BEEN CAUGHT UP in the wave of nationalism that swept through Europe in the earlier part of the 19th century (see 1848). Bulgaria's independence struggle – during which 15,000 Bulgarians were massacred by Turkish troops in 1876 – had attracted Europe's attention. A couple of years later a small Bulgarian principality was established and Britain and Austria-Hungary ensured Russia would not have influence there. By 1885, Bulgaria had merged with **Eastern Rumelia**, and after a coup d'état, the two states were unified. This altered the Balkan balance of power and Serbia declared war. The conflict was brief and peace was restored by 1886. On July 1887, **Prince Ferdinand** of Saxe-Coburg-Gotha (1861–1948) was elected ruler of Bulgaria.

Tsar Ferdinand I
Postage stamp, with Tsar Ferdinand. He was elected to the postion after political infighting led Bulgarians to look further afield for a leader.

1888

An engraving depicts slaves washing diamonds at a Brazilian mine.

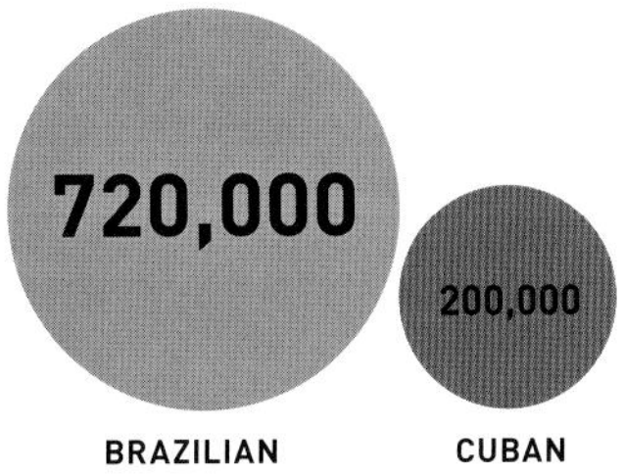

Slave population
At the time of their respective abolitions, Brazil and Cuba had large slave populations. Freedom was initially slow in coming to slaves.

BRAZIL, LIKE CUBA, CONTINUED TO MAKE USE OF SLAVES much later than other former colonies. In South America, the republics that emerged from the Spanish Empire had abolished slavery by the middle of the century. And like Spain, **Brazil** had been put under pressure by the British to end the trade, which eventually occurred in 1850. Over the next thirty years, growing **abolitionist sentiment** reached the highest level, as the emperor **Dom Pedro II** (1825–91) became sympathetic to these ideas. He was interested in the gradual abolition of slavery but was aware of the dangers of a slaveholder backlash. He had observed not only what had happened in Cuba, but also in the US Civil War (see 1861). In 1871, a gradualist measure known as the **Rio Branco Law**, which freed children born to slave mothers, was enacted. Later measures in 1885 freed slaves who were older than 65. Eventually, a **proclamation in May 1888** completely abolished slavery.

1889

" IF THERE BE A **GOD,** I THINK THAT WHAT HE **WOULD LIKE ME TO** DO IS **PAINT** AS MUCH OF **THE MAP OF AFRICA BRITISH RED** AS POSSIBLE… **"**

Cecil Rhodes, British politician, on colonization

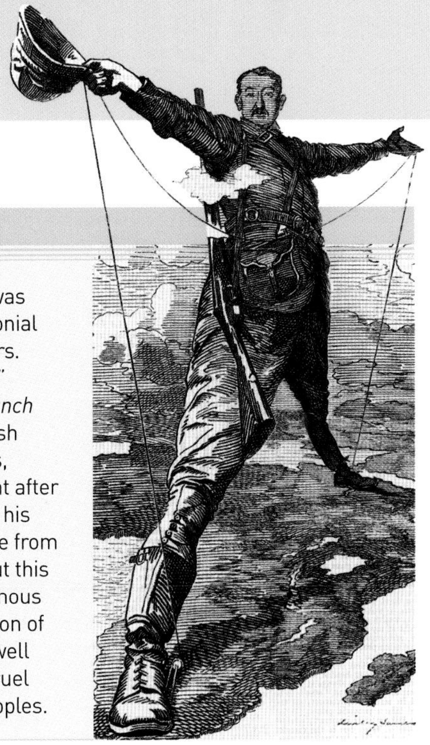

IN PARIS, ENGINEER GUSTAVE EIFFEL (1832–1923) DAZZLED the city and all of Europe with his **tower**, which was opened to the public on 31 March. Eiffel won a design contest to build the tower as part of the **International Exposition** of 1889 in honour of the centenary of the French Revolution. With its 300-m (984-ft) tower – twice the height of the Great Pyramid in Gaza – nothing like it had ever been seen. The tower attracted almost two million visitors in its first six months of opening.

Brazil, meanwhile, faced political upheaval as a military coup overthrew leader **Dom Pedro II**. The military, clergy, and aristocracy had been angered by some of Pedro's reforms and, although still popular with the public, he abdicated and a republic was declared.

Further north, in Panama, the canal project (see 1880) had collapsed, and work on it came to a halt. The **Compagnie Universelle du Canal Interocéanique** and the French public had lost faith in the enterprise as the death toll mounted and construction was plagued by endless problems.

In Africa, British rule was expanding apace as **Cecil John Rhodes** (1853–1902) – who had already established his reputation in the gold and diamond mines in South Africa – received a charter for his **British South Africa Company** in 1889. The company was expected to respect local law and beliefs. However, Rhodes's aim was to acquire territory in Southern Africa and continue the extraction of valuable minerals. Rhodes came to symbolize the excesses of **colonial greed**.

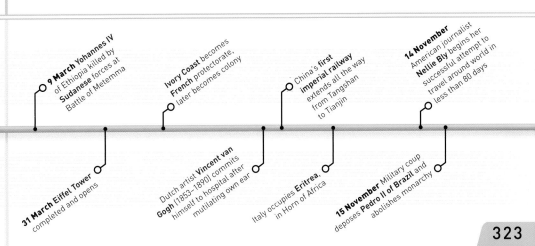

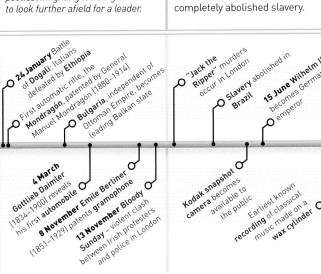

Eiffel Tower
Initially criticized by the Parisian public who thought it unsightly, the tower has come to be an iconic Parisian landmark.

IMPERIALISM

The late 19th century was a time of extensive colonial rule by European powers. "The Rhodes Colossus" (right) from an 1892 *Punch* magazine depicts British colonizer, Cecil Rhodes, straddling the continent after the announcemount of his proposed telegraph line from Cape Town to Cairo. But this was also a period infamous for European exploitation of natural resources, as well as the indifferent or cruel treatment of native peoples.

22,000

THE NUMBER OF WORKERS WHO **DIED DURING A FAILED ATTEMPT TO BUILD** THE **PANAMA CANAL**

24 January Battle of Dogali: Italians defeated by **Ethiopia**

4 March **Gottlieb Daimler** (1834–1900) reveals his first **automobile**

First automatic rifle, the **Mondragón**, patented by General Manuel Mondragón (1880–1914)

Bulgaria, independent of Ottoman Empire, becomes leading Balkan state

8 November **Emile Berliner** (1851–1929) patents **gramophone**

13 November **Bloody Sunday** – violent clash between Irish protesters and police in London

"Jack the Ripper" murders occur in London

Kodak snapshot camera becomes available to the public

Slavery abolished in **Brazil**

15 June **Wilhelm II** becomes German emperor

Earliest known **recording** of classical music made on a **wax cylinder**

9 March **Yohannes IV** of Ethiopia killed by **Sudanese** forces at Battle of Metemma

31 March **Eiffel Tower** completed and opens

Ivory Coast becomes **French** protectorate, later becomes colony

Dutch artist **Vincent van Gogh** (1853–1890) commits himself to hospital after mutilating own ear

China's **first imperial railway** extends all the way from Tangshan to Tianjin

Italy occupies **Eritrea**, in Horn of Africa

14 November American journalist **Nellie Bly** begins her successful attempt to travel around world in less than 80 days

15 November Military coup deposes **Pedro II of Brazil** and abolishes monarchy

THE IMPERIAL WORLD

THE ERA OF EUROPEAN COLONIAL EXPANSION ACROSS THE GLOBE

Throughout the 18th and 19th centuries the world witnessed a relentless European drive to control territories all over the globe. Colonies provided not only direct supplies of valuable natural resources, but also a theatre of conflict in which Europe's antagonisms were played out.

The Imperial Age saw Spain, Britain, France, Germany, Holland, Portugal, Italy, and to a lesser extent, Denmark and Sweden, scramble for territories. A country could lose colonies in one war, only to reclaim them later through trade in a wider political game. Colonies often started out as trading posts, in places such as India, but through political manoeuvring and exercising military might European countries began to take control. People living in the Americas, Africa, India, and Southeast Asia were often on the receiving end of racial prejudice and political oppression. Economic exploitation of colonial territories and their people also frequently occurred, as raw materials were exported out of the country, and slave labour was used. This situation persisted until after World War II, when many colonies around the world began to demand their independence (see pp.422–23).

EMPIRE BUILDING

In the 18th century, most colonial outposts were located along the world's coastlines, as settlements sprung up where ships stopped off. Trading posts grew into cities, often with European-style architecture to reflect the political changes. Over time, improvements in military power, transport, and health – tropical diseases killed thousands of Europeans – saw the spread of colonial rule throughout the 19th century. This was especially true for Britain and France. However, Spain, which had begun empire-building earlier and controlled large parts of Latin America at the beginning of the period, had lost almost all of its territories by the 1820s.

> **“ THE SUN NEVER SETS ON THE BRITISH EMPIRE. ”**

Popular saying coined during the early 1800s

Expansion
Following the example of Britain and the Netherlands, the small state of Belgium exploited the vast territory of the Congo, which was 76 times larger than Belgium.

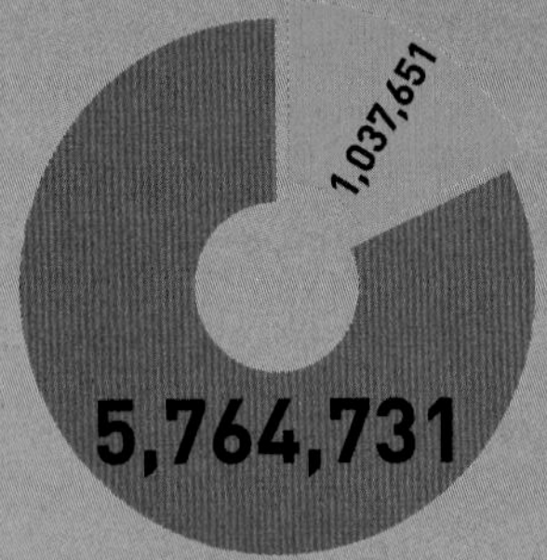

Colonial minority
Native Spaniards were in the minority in the Spanish colony of New Spain (Mexico and Central America). In 1810, they made up just under a fifth of the total population.

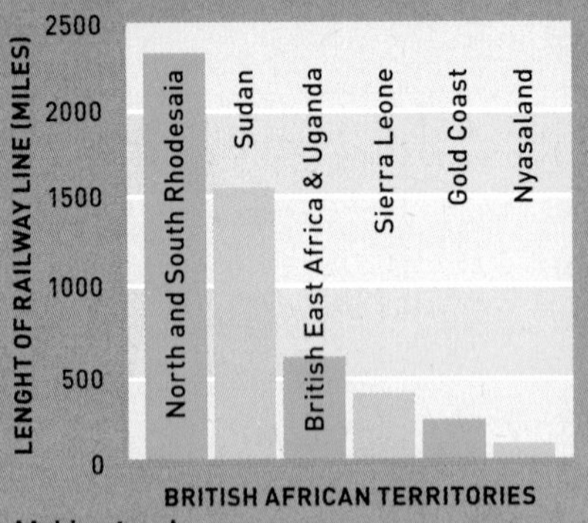

Making tracks
By 1914, the vast expanse of colonial British Africa was spanned by thousands of miles of railway track, opening the region up to trade and aiding communication between territories.

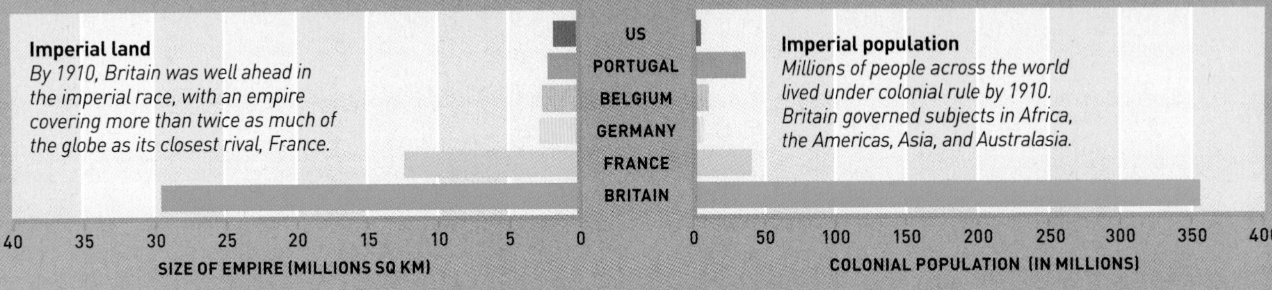

Imperial land
By 1910, Britain was well ahead in the imperial race, with an empire covering more than twice as much of the globe as its closest rival, France.

Imperial population
Millions of people across the world lived under colonial rule by 1910. Britain governed subjects in Africa, the Americas, Asia, and Australasia.

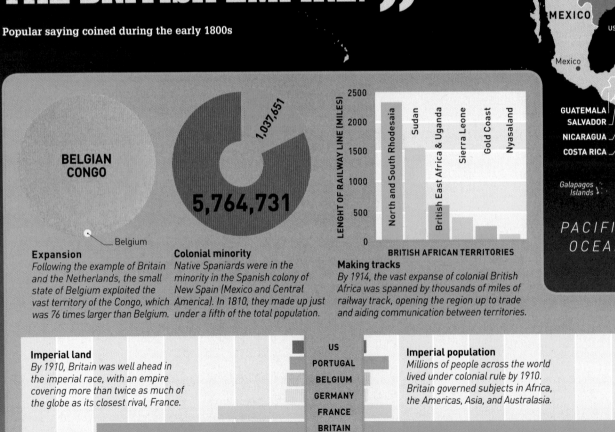

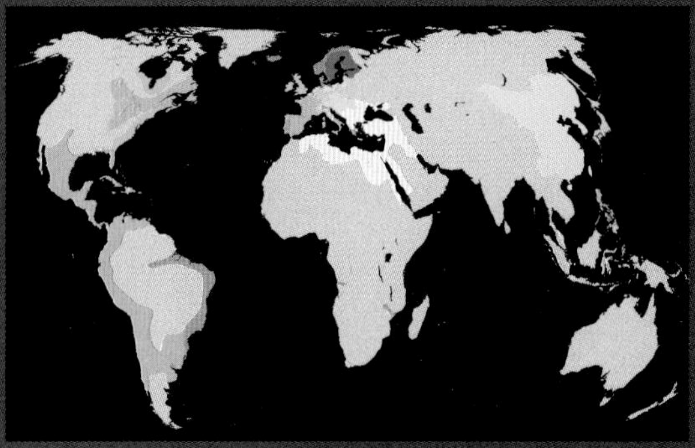

1700 In the 18th century, European expansion, with the exception of Spanish Central and South America, was mostly confined to port cities. Huge swathes of the world were under the control of the older Ottoman and Qing Empires in the East.

1800 A century later, Spain, France, and Britain had taken control of almost all of the Americas. The British had also made a series of incursions into India, as the Mughal Empire broke down, while also undertaking exploration into Africa.

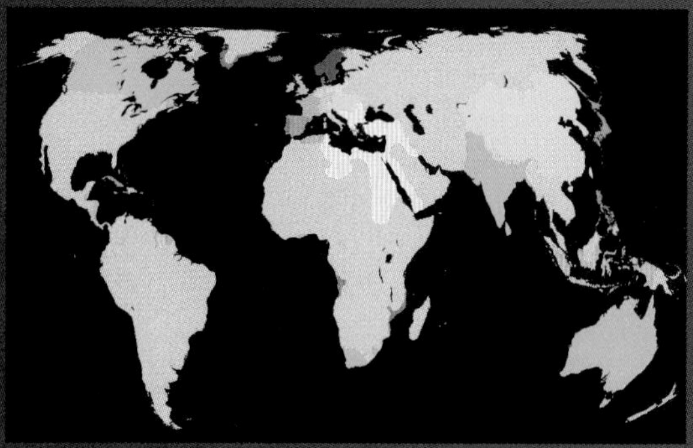

1850 By the middle of the 19th century, the world map had been reconfigured with the independence of Latin America. British and French attention had turned to the resource-rich lands of Africa, while the Dutch continued to expand into Southeast Asia.

1900 At the turn of the 20th century, European colonialism had reached across the globe. The "Scramble for Africa" in the 1880s saw the major powers jostling for territory and taking land from Africans. The US gained territories in the Caribbean and Southeast Asia.

1890

A coloured engraving depicts the massacre of Sioux Indians at Wounded Knee Creek, South Dakota, by US soldiers of the 7th Cavalry Regiment.

IN THE US, TENSIONS AND SPORADIC FIGHTING in the west between US troops and American Indiams had continued since the **Battle at Little Bighorn** (see 1876). In addition to this, American Indians faced increasingly harsh living conditions: poverty, disease, and crop failures were rife. By the 1880s, a new mysticism called the **Ghost Dance** had emerged among the **Sioux** people, based on the belief that an Indian messiah would come in 1891 and unite all the displaced native peoples. This new-found belief manifested in trances, dances, and a mass frenzy, which worried the US agents who oversaw the reservations. They attempted to stop the dances, and the Sioux people rebelled, with US army troops being called in by the end of the year.

The reservation of Wounded Knee Creek in South Dakota was the scene of a massacre on 29 December when around 150 American Indians – men, women, and children – were killed and 50 were wounded by US troops. During disarmament of the Sioux tribe a scuffle had broken out, and in the ensuing carnage around 25 US soldiers were also left dead, many due to friendly fire from US machine guns. This was the last major conflict between American Indians and the US Army, though poor relations persisted between the two groups.

In Europe, a small island off the North Sea coast of Germany, near the territory of Schleswig-Holstein, **Heligoland**, had formally come into British possession in 1814, having been seized by the Royal Navy seven years earlier. However, as Germany's European and African expansion continued, a deal was struck for Britain to hand over the island to Germany in exchange for the islands of **Zanzibar** and **Pemba**, near Tanzania's port of Tanga off the East African coast. Germany developed Heligoland into a large naval base.

Zanzibar was added to Britain's substantial territory in Africa, building on earlier deals struck with Germany, as well as claims made following the Berlin Conference (see 1885). In the following year, Britain formally established the **Nyasaland Districts Protectorate**. This became known as the "British Central Africa Protectorate" in 1893 and was then officially designated as "Nyasaland" in 1907. Part of this territory lay along Lake Nyasa and the Shire valley in present-day Malawi).

6:1 **Wounded Knee dead**
The massacre left 150 Sioux dead, while 25 troops from the US army were killed. A further 50 Sioux were wounded during the conflict.

Sioux weapon
A 19th-century style knife and beaded rawhide sheath, as carried by American Indian Sioux warriors.

1891

The Trans-Siberian railway during its construction in Russia.

9,310 KILOMETRES
THE DISTANCE BETWEEN MOSCOW AND VLADIVOSTOK ON THE TRANS-SIBERIAN RAILWAY

IN RUSSIA, CONSTRUCTION HAD BEGUN ON AN EXTENSIVE RAILWAY SYSTEM across its vast territory. The project was the idea of Alexander III (1845–94), and it was known as the **Trans-Siberian Railroad**. It stretched from Moscow to the port of **Vladivostok**, 9,198km (5,715 miles) to the east. Russia received permission from China to run tracks through parts of Manchuria, allowing the completion of a trans-Manchurian line by 1901. The work began from west and east ends and eventually met in the centre. By 1904, the sections linking Moscow and Vladivostok were connected and running. The railway facilitated the quicker movement of people through Russia and allowed for the further settlement of sparsely populated **Siberia**.

The Great Mosque of Djenne, Mali, was built after the French took control.

French in Africa
A postage stamp from French West Africa shows an illustration of a native mask. France managed to gain control of much of the region.

BRITAIN AND FRANCE WERE CONTINUING THEIR PUSH into West Africa. The British had secured ports along the coast, annexing Lagos in 1861. Lagos provided a key point from which to seize control of surrounding **Yorubaland**, situated around the lower parts of the Niger River, corresponding with much of modern southwest Nigeria. The British took advantage of existing internal divisions among Yoruba rulers, and in 1892, they overthrew the **Ijebu** government, part of the Yoruba political system.

Likewise, the French exploited divisions in the Muslim **Tukulor Empire** by signing treaties with its neighbours and building forts within Tukulor territory. By 1892, the French controlled much of the region around the Senegal River.

15 January **Pyotr Ilyich Tchaikovsky**'s *Sleeping Beauty* performed at St Petersburg, Russia

28 June **Cecil Rhodes'** British South Africa Company begins **colonization** of Southern African territory

1 July **Heligoland-Zanzibar** treaty between Britain and Germany

29 July Dutch post-Impressionist artist **Vincent van Gogh** dies two days after shooting himself (b.1853)

23 November **William III of Netherlands** dies; **Luxembourg** breaks away over succession to throne

29 December **Massacre at Wounded Knee** in which the US Army kills 150 Sioux including women and children

March Construction of the **Trans-Siberian Railway** begins (finishes 1917)

29 March **George Seurat** (1859–91) leading figure in **neo-Impressionist movement** dies

Malawi becomes a British protectorate

October Paleoanthropologist **Eugene Dubois** (1858–1940) finds first remains of ***Homo erectus***

7 January **Abbas II** becomes khedive of **Egypt** (to 1914)

19 May British defeat **Ijebu**, present-day Nigeria, with maxi[m] gun at River Yem[oji]

Dimitri Ivanovsky (1864–1920) discovers **viruses**

“ ALL THAT SEPARATES ... RACE, CLASS, CREED, OR SEX, IS INHUMAN, AND MUST BE OVERCOME. ”

Kate Sheppard, suffragist, in the pamphlet *Is it Right?*, 1892

ALTHOUGH FRANCE HAD MADE GAINS IN THE WEST AFRICAN INTERIOR, the coastal territories around the kingdom of **Dahomey** (present-day Benin) had proven difficult to subdue. In 1889, Britain had handed over to France the coastal city of **Cotonou** in Dahomey without consulting the Dahomeans. The result was the First Franco-Dahomean War (1889–90), which concluded with a treaty that ceded Cotonou and Porto Novo to France in exchange for payments to the king of Dahomey. However, tensions remained, and by 1892 another war had begun, this time over the issue of **slavery**. The king, Behanzin (1844–1906), was still allowing slave raids, despite the abolition of slavery. In addition, he attacked a French gunboat. France retaliated, this time with an army of French and Senegalese troops, and they overpowered the kingdom, bringing it under French control in 1893.

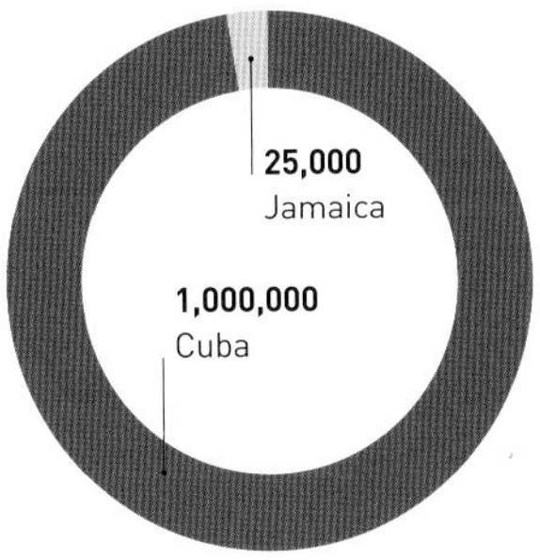

Sugar production in tonnes
In 1893, Cuba, then the dominant world sugar grower, produced 1 million tonnes of sugar, four times as much as Jamaica.

Halfway around the world, in the British colony of **New Zealand**, women won the right to vote. The push for women's **suffrage** was gaining momentum in many places, but these islands were the first to grant the right, after formidable efforts by suffragists and tireless campaigners, such as **Kate Sheppard** (1847–1934). Shortly after this act was passed, there was a general election in which 65 per cent of women cast their votes.

Meanwhile, **Cuba** was experiencing a sugar boom, with profits of $64 million in 1893. However, a US **tariff** the following year would cause profits to drop to $13 million by 1896.

Ruler of Dahomey
A painting of Behanzin, king of Dahomey (modern Benin), shows him holding symbols of kingship while surrounded by attendants.

An engraving showing the coronation ceremony of Emperor Nicholas II and the Empress Alexandra, who would be Russia's last ruling monarchs.

IN RUSSIA, AFTER THE DEATH OF ALEXANDER III, Nicholas II (1868–1918) became the next, and last, emperor of Russia. He presided over an increasingly troubled country, and would not be able to withstand the social **revolution** that engulfed Russia in the early 20th century.

Russia's neighbour, **China**, had become entangled in a local conflict in **Korea** that escalated into the **Sino-Japanese War**. The confrontation had started over an internal revolt in Korea. The monarch asked both nations for help, and both sent troops. Yet they also refused to leave once the rebellion was suppressed. Japan was allied with the modernizing government in Korea, while China backed the royal family. Tensions between China and Japan mounted and conflict broke out, with Japan declaring war on China on 1 August.

“ I AM NOT YET READY TO BE TSAR. I KNOW NOTHING OF THE BUSINESS OF RULING. ”

Tsar Nicholas II, on becoming ruler of Russia, 1894

In the Ottoman Empire, the **Christian Armenian** people were also caught up in the nationalist spirit of the time, and they tried to assert their independence. However, their efforts met with a particularly brutal **suppression**, ordered by Sultan Abdul Hamid II (1842–1918). This saw systematic massacres of Armenian people throughout the empire, resulting in the collapse of the independence movement a few years later. The death toll has been estimated to be around 250,000 Armenians killed out of a population of 2 million, between 1894 and 1897.

Sino-Japanese War
A painting of the Sino-Japanese War shows the Japanese forces conquering Jiuliancheng after defeating the Chinese at Pyongyang.

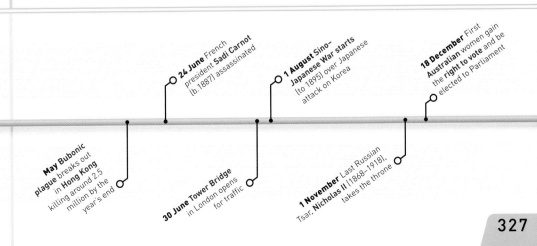

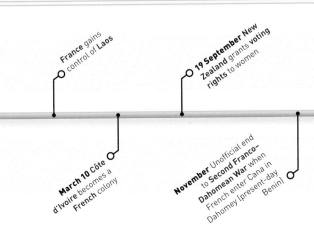

France gains control of **Laos**

March 10 Côte d'Ivoire becomes a French colony

19 September New Zealand grants **voting** rights to women

November Unofficial end to **Second Franco-Dahomean War** when French enter Cana in Dahomey (present-day Benin)

May Bubonic plague breaks out in **Hong Kong** killing around 2.5 million by the year's end

24 June French president **Sadi Carnot** (b.1887) assassinated

30 June Tower Bridge in London opens for traffic

1 August Sino-Japanese War starts (to 1895) over Japanese attack on Korea

1 November Last Russian Tsar, **Nicholas II** (1868–1918), takes the throne

18 December First **Australian** women gain the **right to vote** and be elected to Parliament

1895

“ EVERY DAY SEES **HUMANITY** MORE **VICTORIOUS** IN THE STRUGGLE WITH **SPACE AND TIME.”**

Guglielmo Marconi, Italian inventor

TECHNOLOGICAL DEVELOPMENTS WERE PROLIFERATING RAPIDLY all over the world. In Italy, physicist and inventor **Guglielmo Marconi** (1874–1937) invented a **wireless telegraph**. In his initial experiments, using a telegraph key to operate a **transmitter**, he was able to send electromagnetic waves in bursts that corresponded to **Morse code**. He then used a transmitter to ring a bell that had been placed 9m (30ft) away. He worked on the **receiving antennae** and by the end of the year he could transmit a signal 2.5km (1.5 miles). However, he found little enthusiasm for his work, so he went to Britain, where he patented the device the following year, and laid the foundation for **radio technology**. Meanwhile, German physicist **Wilhelm Conrad Röntgen** (1845–1923) had been experimenting with electric currents and cathode-ray tubes. The outcome was a type of radiation that allowed objects to **appear transparent** on photographic plates. Röntgen called this **X-radiation**, an early version of the modern X-ray.

In **Korea**, the clash between Japanese and Chinese forces (see 1894) came to an end after the **Chinese defeat** in Pyongyang, and subsequent naval victories by the **Japanese fleet**. China sued for peace on 12 February and the resulting **Treaty of Shimonoseki** – which had involved Russian, French, and German intervention – forced China to give up the island of **Formosa** (modern Taiwan) to Japan, as well as the nearby Pescadores (Penghu) Islands. China also had to recognize **Korean independence**, open more ports to Japanese trade, and pay a large indemnity.

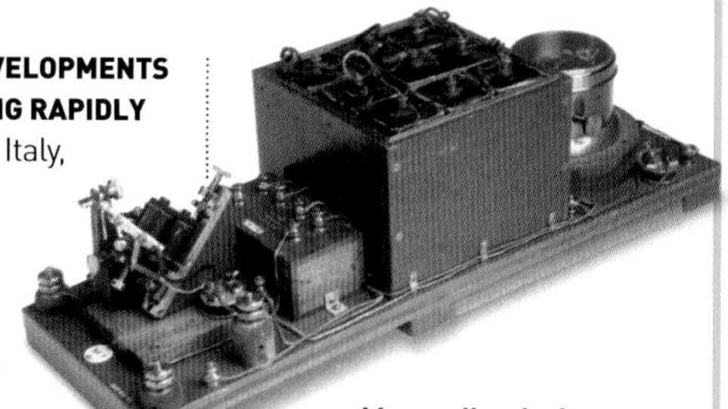

Marconi's wireless
The wireless telegraph (replica shown) developed by Guglielmo Marconi paved the way for the development of radio technology.

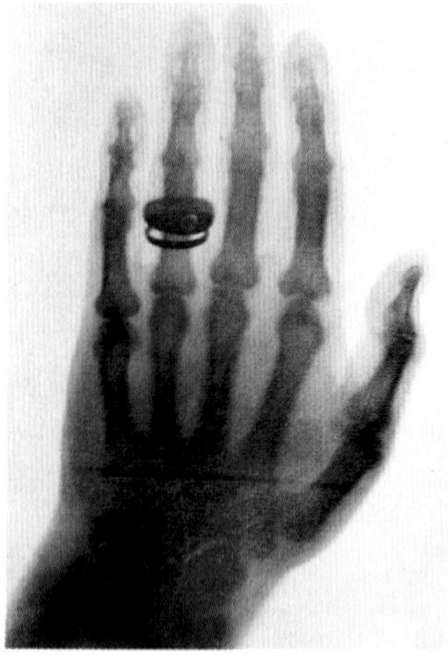

Early X-ray
One of the first X-ray photographs made by German professor Wilhelm Conrad Röntgen (1845–1923) captured a woman's hand with rings.

1896

This scene from the Italian invasion of Abyssinia in 1896 shows the Abyssinian forces routing the Italian troops.

GREECE SAW THE MODERN REBIRTH OF THE ANCIENT OLYMPIC GAMES, which was organized by an enthusiastic Frenchman, Baron **Pierre de Coubertin**. In 1890, he met **William Penny Brookes**, who had orchestrated a British Olympic Games in 1866. Coubertin and Brookes wanted to create an **international festival of modern sport**. After years of campaigning, Coubertin was finally able to organize the event in **Athens** from 6–15 April, which was a success. There were almost **300 contestants** competing in athletics, gymnastics, tennis, swimming, cycling, fencing, shooting, weightlifting, and wrestling, while **40,000 spectators** cheered them on. However, Brookes did not live to be present at the games, having died the previous year.

Meanwhile, **Italy** was trying to extend its reach in Africa with an invasion of the **Abyssinian Empire** (modern Ethiopia). Its previous attempt to annex the kingdom had ended in failure by 1889 (see 1872). Under the terms of the **Treaty of Uccialli**, Italy thought it had the right to establish a protectorate over **Abyssinia**, but this was contested.

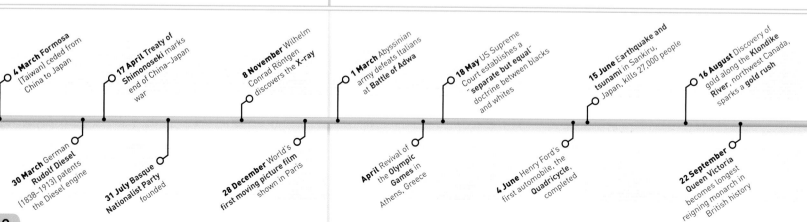

Olympic revival
The cover illustration for the April edition of Scribner's Magazine *celebrated the revival of the Olympic Games, being held in Athens, Greece. There were 43 events, in nine different sports.*

1896 OLYMPIC GAMES

- **43** THE NUMBER OF **EVENTS**
- **14** THE NUMBER OF **COUNTRIES**
- **241** THE NUMBER OF **ATHLETES**

By 1895, the disagreement between Italy and Abyssinian emperor **Menelik II** (1844–1913) had turned into an armed conflict. The turning point was the **Battle of Adwa** on 1 March 1896, at which 80,000 Abyssinians defeated 20,000 Italian soldiers.

7,000 THE NUMBER OF **ITALIANS KILLED** AT **ADWA**

4 March Formosa (Taiwan) ceded from China to Japan

30 March German **Rudolf Diesel** (1838–1913) patents the Diesel engine

17 April Treaty of Shimonoseki marks end of China–Japan war

31 July Basque Nationalist Party founded

8 November Wilhelm Conrad Röntgen discovers the **X-ray**

28 December World's **first moving picture film** shown in Paris

1 March Abyssinian army defeats Italians at **Battle of Adwa**

April Revival of the **Olympic Games** in Athens, Greece

18 May US Supreme Court establishes a **“separate but equal”** doctrine between blacks and whites

4 June Henry Ford's first automobile, the **Quadricycle**, completed

15 June Earthquake and tsunami in Sankiru, Japan, kills 27,000 people

16 August Discovery of gold along the **Klondike River**, northwest Canada, sparks a **gold rush**

22 September Queen Victoria becomes longest reigning monarch in British history

1897

A cartoon entitled "The concert of nations", in an 1897 edition of *Le Petit Journal*, satirizes the Thirty Days War, also known as the Greco–Turkish War.

ALTHOUGH THE TEN YEARS WAR HAD BEEN UNSUCCESSFUL (see 1868), many Cubans were unwilling to accept continued control by Spain. Leading the renewed cries for independence was the **Cuban Revolutionary Party**. It declared a republic in eastern Cuba and began a guerilla war, known as the **Cuban War of Independence**. Soldiers managed to reach **Havana** by the following year, although they were driven back. The US would end up getting involved when the **battleship *Maine* was blown up** in the Havana harbour (see 1898).

Trouble was brewing between **Greece** and the **Ottoman Empire** over the situation in **Crete**. There had been a brutal suppression of a Christian uprising on the island the year before, and Greece was determined to annex the territory. However, the **Thirty Days War** did not have the outcome Greece desired. When an armistice was agreed in August, it was forced to pay an **indemnity** and it lost part of the territory of **Thessaly**. The Turks withdrew their troops from Crete and the island was made an international protectorate.

JOSÉ MARTÍ (1853–95)

A writer, philosopher, journalist, and political theorist, José Martí became a key figure in the Cuban revolutionary struggle. He is considered a national hero for his planning and leadership during the Cuban War of Independence. He died on the battlefield at Dos Ríos, in the east of the island.

Meanwhile, Britain was undergoing a remarkable **boom in coal mining**. The level of coal production had doubled since the 1860s. The mining industry was also a major employer – in 1897 the number of **miners** in Britain was around 695,200, rising from about 216,200 in 1851.

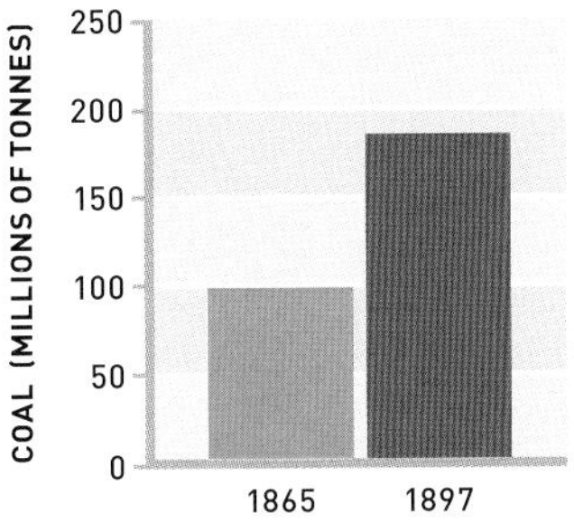

Coal mining in Britain
By 1897, Britain was the world leader in coal production. Its output of 200 million tonnes put it ahead of the US and Germany, who were also large coal producers.

1898

Four soldiers raise their rifles over the brush of San Juan Hill, Cuba, as they fight from trenches during the Spanish–American war.

WITH THE DESTRUCTION OF THE USS MAINE – blown up while docked in Havana's harbour – the **US** made the decision to go to **war against Spain**. Cuba's struggle for independence had already attracted much support in the US. The government blamed the *Maine* incident – in which **260 crew members were killed** – on Spain. Although Cuba and Spain had agreed an armistice on 9 April, the US began the **Spanish–American War** only a few weeks later, on 25 April. Battles were fought in two theatres: the Atlantic and the Pacific. US navy ships sailed into Manila Bay, in the **Spanish Philippines**, while another fleet made incursions into the southern harbour of Cuba, **Santiago**, where troops then disembarked. By 25 July, **Spain had capitulated**. It would pay a steep price for what the US Secretary of State John Hay (1838–1905) called "a splendid little war" in a letter to his friend and future US president **Theodore Roosevelt** (1858-1919), who had led the First Volunteer Cavalry (known as the "Rough Riders"). Under the terms of the **Treaty of Paris** of 10 December, Spain had to give up its remaining colonies, **allowing Cuba its independence**, and ceding Puerto Rico, Guam, and the Philippines to the US. However, the US continued to occupy Cuba, and the following year tried to exclude Cubans from governing, and disbanded the army. Around the same time the US also managed to annex the islands of **Hawaii**.

Hawaii annexed
In a contemporary illustration, Hawaiians in Honolulu receive news of their annexation by the US. The US would also take control of Guam and the Philippines.

Meanwhile, in **Egypt**, Britain and France became embroiled in the **Fashoda Incident**, which involved territorial disputes over their respective attempts at expansion in Africa. The British wanted to build a **railway linking Egypt and Uganda** while France wanted to continue its eastward drive into the **Sudan**. Although their troops met in Fashoda on 18 September, the situation did not escalate into war, as all sides wanted to **avoid battle**. Instead they decided that British, French, and Egyptian flags should fly over the fort that the French had occupied. Eventually, they agreed that their **boundaries** would be marked by where the **Nile and Congo rivers** divided.

1899

Cyclists of the Lancashire Fusiliers took part in the South African War.

HOSTILITIES BETWEEN THE BOERS AND BRITISH were once again heading toward conflict. They had already clashed in the **First Boer War** (see 1880). This time Boers were demanding that British troops protecting mining interests should withdraw from the **Transvaal**, but this request was ignored. So the South African Republic and the Orange Free State **declared war** on Britain in October. The **South African War** would last less than three years but, for the British, it would become the largest since the Napoleonic Wars, as its forces reached some 500,000 men. The war was fought across a **hostile terrain**, which the Boers – whose troops numbered less than 90,000 – could use to their advantage. The war became infamous because of the **treatment of Boer civilians**, who saw their farms burned and women and children put into **camps** where up to 25,000 died.

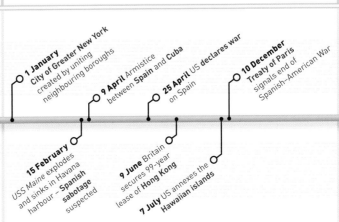

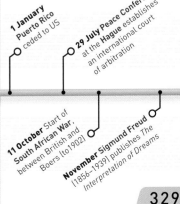

War medal
The Queen's South Africa Medal, awarded to military personnel who served in the war, is engraved with a Jubilee bust of Queen Victoria.

- **7 August Battle of Abu Hamed** sees British reconquer Sudan
- **29 August** The First Zionist **Congress** convenes in Basle, Switzerland
- **20 September** Greece and Turkey sign **peace treaty**, ending Thirty Days War
- **10 October Cuba** becomes **autonomous** but not fully independent from Spain
- **1 January City of Greater New York** created by uniting neighbouring boroughs
- **15 February** USS Maine explodes and sinks in Havana harbour – **Spanish sabotage** suspected
- **9 April** Armistice between **Spain and Cuba**
- **25 April** US declares war on Spain
- **9 June** Britain secures 99-year lease of **Hong Kong**
- **7 July** US annexes the **Hawaiian islands**
- **10 December Treaty of Paris** signals end of Spanish–American War
- **1 January Puerto Rico** ceded to US
- **29 July Peace Conference** at the **Hague** establishes an international court of arbitration
- **11 October** Start of **South African War**, between British and Boers (to 1902)
- **November Sigmund Freud** (1856–1939) publishes *The Interpretation of Dreams*

1900

This illustration shows the storming of Beijing by the international force which arrived to fight the anti-Western attacks during the Boxer uprising.

THE GROWING PRESENCE OF WESTERNERS – especially Christian missionaries – in China was starting to cause public anger. This eventually erupted into the **Boxer Rebellion**, which was a peasant uprising that aimed to eject all foreigners from China. The group behind the attacks had earlier founded a secret society known as the "Righteous and Harmonious Fists", hence the sobriquet "Boxer". Members of the group were also found among the Qing court, and so the movement's violent attacks on foreigners and Chinese converts to Christianity were officially sanctioned. An international **relief force** of 2,100 troops from Britain, France, Italy, Germany, Russia, Japan, and the US was eventually sent to the port of Tianjin in June 1900, but the Boxers continued to burn down churches and kill Christians. After the international troops seized several forts, the empress dowager, **Tz'u Hsi** (1835–1908), ordered all foreigners to be killed, and many foreign ministers were murdered. After the arrival of reinforcements, the international force made its way to Beijing, which it captured. The empress dowager fled, and a truce was negotiated with the imperial princes in September 1901. This put an end to the violence and provided for reparations to be made. While these events were taking place, the **Russians** took the opportunity to occupy southern **Manchuria**, which bordered southern Russia.

In Africa, mining began in **Katanga**, a southern region of the present-day Democratic Republic of the Congo. The discovery of rich **copper** deposits – as well as other minerals, including zinc, cobalt, and tin – led to the rapid establishment by Europeans of mining infrastructure, such as railway lines, and towns began to spring up in this region. As mining companies proliferated, Katanga was soon one of the most highly industrialized areas of the Congo, but the many Africans employed performed the dirty and dangerous work in the mines for very little pay.

Meanwhile, in West Africa, British troops faced a rebellion by the **Asante**, which took eight months to subdue. Unrest in the **Gold Coast** region continued throughout the following decade as Africans continued to resist British rule.

Across the Atlantic, in the US, decades of **immigration** had caused the country's population to nearly double. There were around 35.5 million people living in the US in 1870 and by 1900 that number had reached more than 75 million. Much of this growth had been in **urban areas** – some 40 per cent of the population were living in cities rather than settling in rural communities.

Going underground
A Metro sign built into a lamp post in Paris, France. The first underground trainline was opened in Paris in 1900.

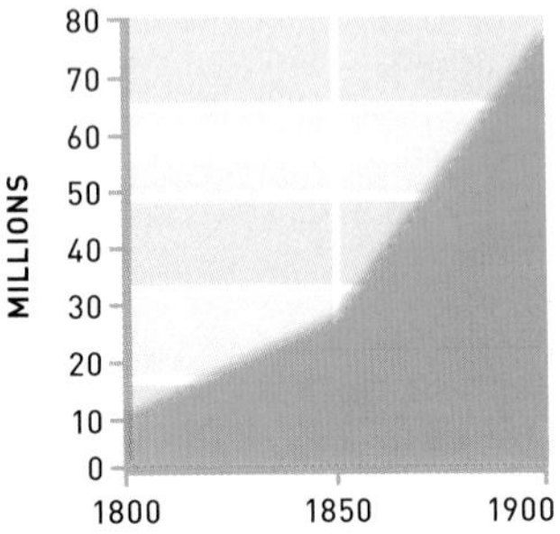

Growing nation
Thanks to decades of immigration, the population of the US had soared, reaching more than 75 million by 1900.

1901

Queen Victoria's funeral procession makes its way through London.

THE MANY COLONIES THAT HAD BEEN FOUNDED IN AUSTRALIA – Victoria, New South Wales, Queensland, South Australia, Western Australia, and Tasmania – ushered in a new era on 1 January, after the drafting and approval of the **constitution** and official establishment of the Commonwealth of Australia.

A few weeks later, Great Britain and its colonies mourned the loss of **Queen Victoria**, who died on 22 January. She had ruled over the nation and empire for 63 years, making her reign the longest by a British monarch. Her son, **Edward VII** (1841–1910), took the throne, and the largely peaceful – though very socially stratified – period under his rule was known as the **Edwardian era**.

Commonwealth stamp
This stamp showing Queen Victoria is from Australia, which brought its colonies into a federation the same year the monarch died.

1902

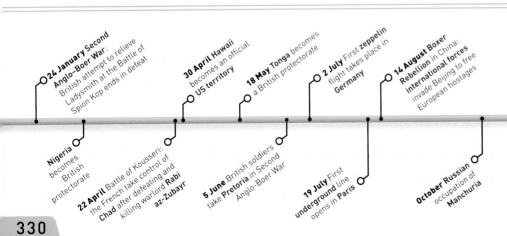

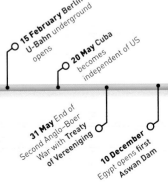

Prince Saud Ibn Abdul-Aziz, the first monarch of the modern Saudi state.

THE SOUTH AFRICAN, OR ANGLO-BOER, WAR between Boer settlers and the British ended on 31 May. The end of the war was hastened when the British adopted a "Scorched Earth" policy, which involved destroying crops and livestock to limit Boer supplies. The dispossessed Boer women and children were rounded up into concentration camps. Under the **Treaty of Vereeniging**, the Boers were forced to recognize British sovereignty in South Africa, ending the independence of the Orange Free State and the South African Republic. The whole territory was now under British control.

Meanwhile, **Ibn Saud** (*c.*1880–1953) recaptured the Saud dynasty's formal capital of Riyadh, after decades of civil war (see 1843). In 1901, Saud, who was living in Kuwait, set out to take back the territory he had been forced to leave by the rival Rashids. He and his men reached Riyadh in January 1902 and crept into town, waiting to ambush the Rashidi governor the following morning. Soon Saud had taken the city and the territory, with the help of a growing number of supporters. This became the kingdom of **Saudi Arabia** in 1932, and it remains under the Saud family's rule to the present day.

On the Caribbean island of Martinique, the violent eruption of **Mount Pelée** killed around 30,000 people and destroyed the port of Saint-Pierre on 8 May. The volcano had previously erupted in 1792 and 1851, but on nowhere near the scale of the 1902 eruption.

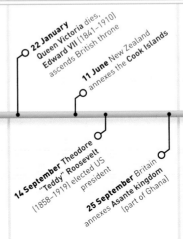

24 January Second Anglo-Boer War: British attempt to relieve Ladysmith at the Battle of Spion Kop ends in defeat

Nigeria becomes British protectorate

22 April Battle of Kousseri: the French take control of **Chad** after defeating and killing warlord **Rabi az-Zubayr**

30 April Hawaii becomes an official **US territory**

18 May Tonga becomes a British protectorate

5 June British soldiers take **Pretoria** in Second Anglo-Boer War

2 July First **zeppelin** flight takes place in **Germany**

19 July First **underground** line opens in **Paris**

14 August Boxer Rebellion in China: **international forces** invade Beijing to free European hostages

October Russian occupation of **Manchuria**

22 January Queen Victoria dies; **Edward VII** (1841–1910) ascends British throne

11 June New Zealand annexes the **Cook Islands**

14 September Theodore "Teddy" Roosevelt (1858–1919) elected US president

25 September Britain annexes **Asante kingdom** (part of Ghana)

15 February Berlin **U-Bahn** underground opens

20 May Cuba becomes independent of US

31 May End of Second Anglo-Boer War with **Treaty of Vereeniging**

10 December Egypt opens **first Aswan Dam**

The original 1903 aeroplane, designed by Wilber and Orville Wright, makes its first flight on 17 December 1903 in Kitty Hawk, North Carolina.

The French newspaper, *Petit Journal*, shows how the Russian sick and wounded were transported on skis during the Russo–Japanese war.

TWO BROTHERS IN THE US, WILBUR (1867–1912) AND ORVILLE (1871–1948) WRIGHT, became obsessed with the growing science of aviation and were determined to fly. They pumped the profits from their bicycle shop into their experiments and built a bi-plane. In the town of Kitty Hawk, on the coast of North Carolina, they began to conduct experiments. On the morning of 17 December, their work paid off when Orville made what is considered to be the **first successful flight** in an aeroplane that the pilot had complete control over (as opposed to earlier attempts with gliders). He travelled 60m (197ft) in 12 seconds. Later that day Wilbur flew 259m (850ft) in 59 seconds.

Further south, in **Panama**, the US had resurrected the idea of building a canal between the Atlantic and Pacific, the first attempt at which had failed more

Lion in the path
The United States publication, Judge, *depicts the Panama Canal as the "lion in the path" in this political cartoon.*

however, were intertwined with the infamous **Dreyfus Affair**. This was a scandal involving Alfred Dreyfus (1859–1935), a French officer who was accused of treason. Evidence came to light that cleared Dreyfus, but it was suppressed. Dreyfus was Jewish, and France became divided over the issue of **anti-semitism**. During the scandal, the sport newspaper *Le Vélo* supported Dreyfus. Angry advertisers decided to set up a rival periodical, *L'Auto-Vélo*, later called *L'Auto*. Cycling promoter Desgrange was hired as editor. However, *L'Auto*'s sales were initially poor, and so a race was organized to promote it. Desgrange devised a month-long cycling contest (though it was later shortened) which followed the route of Paris–Lyon–Marseille–Toulouse–Bordeaux–Nantes–Paris. On 1 July, 60 competitors set off. The event's first winner was Maurice Garin.

than a decade before (see 1889). The US wanted to purchase the assets of the former French holding company and begin construction, but talks with the **Colombian** government (which still controlled the isthmus) broke down. Soon after, in 1903, Panama, with the backing of the US, declared its **independence**. By 1904, Panama and the US had agreed on the terms of the Panama Canal Zone, in which the US would be permitted to exercise its jurisdiction until 1979, and work on the canal began.

In **France**, cyclist Henri Desgrange (1865–1940) organized a race that would become one of the most prestigious in the world: the **Tour de France**. Its roots,

12 SECONDS
THE DURATION OF THE WRIGHT BROTHERS' FIRST FLIGHT

JAPAN AND RUSSIA HAD BEEN COMPETING to expand their influence in Manchuria and Korea. Russia had built its Trans-Siberian railway (see 1891), which now had a line running into **Manchuria**, annexed during the Boxer crisis in China (see 1900). During this time, **Japan** had begun to build up its army and navy, and approached Russia in 1903 to suggest they recognize each other's mutual interests in these regions. The talks broke down on 6 February 1904, and three days later Japan attacked Russian warships, sinking two of them, and triggering the **Russo–Japanese War.** Japan then sent troops into Manchuria and Korea, forcing the Russians further north over the course of

Russo–Japanese War
This map shows the course of the conflict in which a victorious Japan drove Russia out of Manchuria, forcing Russia to give up its expansionist policy in the East Asia.

the year. A peace deal was brokered by US President, Theodore Roosevelt (1858–1919), and on 5 September a treaty was signed that forced Russia to leave Manchuria, cede part of the island of **Sakhalin** to Japan, and recognize Japan's interests in **Korea**, as well as grant fishing rights off the coast of Siberia. Japan's victory against Russia marked its emergence as a major world power.

In Africa, German troops were facing rebellions in their colonies. Revolts broke out in **German South West Africa** (Namibia), where the **Khoikhoi** people had risen up in 1903, followed by the **Herero** in 1904. Many Africans were rounded up and put into concentration camps, where the work conditions were so dire that more than half of the prisoners died. By the time Germany had suppressed the rebellion, in 1908, about 80 per cent of the Herero and 50 per cent of the Khoikhoi peoples had been killed, either in the course of the conflict or while interned in the camps.

KEY
- Japan
- Qing China
- to Russia 1897, to Japan 1905
- area leased to Japan 1895
- → Japanese advances 1904–05
- → route of Russian Baltic fleet
- ✕ Japanese victory, with date

Timeline:

June 11 Serbia's King Alexander Obrenović (b.1876) and Queen Draga (b.1864) are **assassinated**

29 September Prussia is first to require **drivers' licences** for automobiles

18 November Deal signed between US and Colombia to start on **Panama Canal** (canal opens in 1914)

4 November Panama declares **independence** from Colombia with US backing

17 December Inventor brothers Orville and Wilbur **Wright** make first flight at Kitty Hawk, North Carolina

12 January Herero Rebellion in German South West Africa begins

8 April Britain and **France** sign *Entente Cordial* paving way for peaceful relations ever since

8 February Russo–Japanese War (to 1905) begins when Japan sinks two Russian warships

9 May The *City of Truro* becomes the **first locomotive to exceed 100mph**, travelling from Plymouth to London in Britain

21 October Russo–Japanese War: **Dogger Bank** incident in which Russian fleet accidentally fires on British trawlers in North Sea

THE STORY OF THE CAR

FROM THE MODEL T TO HYBRIDS, CARS HAVE BEEN A DRIVING FORCE FOR CHANGE

Ford Model T

After thousands of years of slow transportation using ships, horses, or even travelling on foot, the development of the automobile revolutionized the way the world thought about distance and speed. Instead of spending days on a trip, people and goods could move hundreds of kilometres in a matter of hours.

Although the late 19th century witnessed many significant technological innovations in the realm of transport, such as the development of steamships, none would come close to having the widespread and immediate impact of the development and mass production of the car. Although automobile ownership was at first only the preserve of the wealthy, the US inventor Henry Ford was able to increase output and push down prices, so that by the 1920s many eager consumers could buy a car. This had a profound effect on the landscape as motorways sprang up, and by the 1950s, suburbs in the US were planned around the idea that residents would be driving.

Rolling off the assembly line
Workers on the assembly line at the Ford Motor Company assemble a Model T. Ford's innovative factories allowed the company to assemble millions of cars very quickly.

THE AGE OF THE AUTOMOBILE

Despite the subsequent problems – especially pollution and traffic jams – the love affair with the car has never ceased. Indeed, as people in developing countries become richer, they too want to be car owners. Now the challenge is to find more fuel-efficient and environmentally friendly ways to power cars, and more manufacturers are experimenting with other forms, such as hybrids (see panel, right). However, in spite of these issues, the automobile continues to be an integral part of transportation networks all over the world.

HYBRID CARS

Automobile engineers have long been trying to find ways to run cars on other fuels than petrol, including solar power and battery power. Hybrid cars combine a fuel engine with a battery engine, giving the driver better fuel consumption and producing less pollution.

> “ANY CUSTOMER CAN HAVE A CAR PAINTED **ANY COLOUR** THAT HE WANTS **SO LONG AS IT'S BLACK.**”
>
> Henry Ford, US industrialist, *My Life and Work*, 1922

15th century
Leonardo da Vinci's car
The Renaissance Italian designs the world's first self-propelled wagon.

Reconstructed da Vinci car

1769–70
The first true automobile
The French engineer Nicolas Cugnot builds a steam-powered vehicle that can reach speeds of up to 3kph (2mph).

Cugnot's Fardier

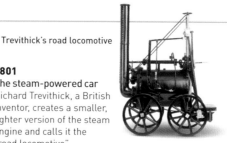

1801
The steam-powered car
Richard Trevithick, a British inventor, creates a smaller, lighter version of the steam engine and calls it the "road locomotive".

Trevithick's road locomotive

1860
The coal-gas engine
Belgian Jean-Joseph Étienne Lenoir invents a two-stroke internal-combustion engine fired by coal gas.

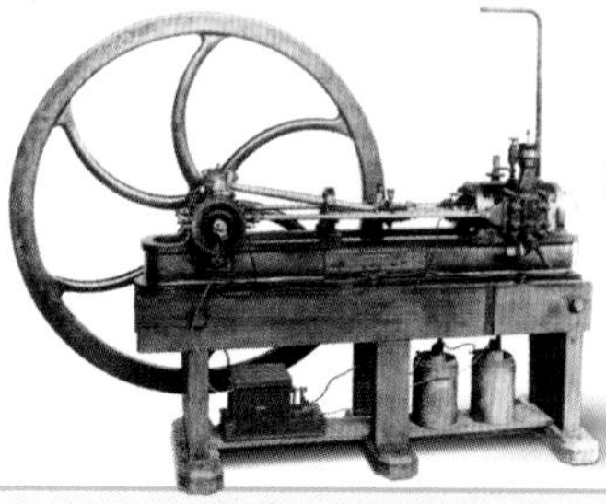

Lenoir gas engine

1867–77
The four-stroke Otto engine
The German inventor Nikolaus August Otto patents his four-stroke internal-combustion engine.

Otto engine

1885
Internal combustion improves
The Germans Karl Benz and Gottlieb Daimler separately develop practical cars with internal-combustion engines.

Benz three-wheeler

1913 Ford Model T

Henry Ford's design classic has many of the features found in today's cars. As well as being relatively cheap, it was sufficiently robust and reliable to withstand the rough roads of the US at the time.

1885–86
The four-wheeled car
Gottlieb Daimler makes improvements to the engine and adds a fourth wheel to the body, producing the first modern car.

1889–90
Front-mounted engines
René Panhard and Émile Levassor of France are the first to build entire cars for sale and to put the engine at the front.

Panhard et Levassor Dos-a-Dos

1890s–early 1900s
Early electric cars
Not all cars are developed with petrol engines. Some 28 per cent were using electricity by 1900.

1903–30
The Ford Model T
The US car manufacturer Henry Ford begins production of the mass-market Model T. By 1927, some 15 million cars have been produced, thanks to Ford's moving assembly lines.

1930s
Volkswagen's "compact car"
Developed in Germany, the "people's car" marks the rise of the affordable, fuel-efficient car.

Volkswagen Beetle

1940s–50s
The rise of the luxury car
Brands such as Rolls Royce and Cadillac become bywords for the most luxurious cars for sale.

Rolls Royce Silver Dawn

1997–present
Hybrid cars
Car makers look for cleaner, cheaper ways to fuel cars.

Toyota Prius

1905

“ THE ETERNAL MYSTERY OF THE WORLD IS ITS COMPREHENSIBILITY. ”

Albert Einstein, in the *Franklin Institute Journal*, March 1936

German-born Albert Einstein became one of the world's most famous scientists after the development of his Special Theory of Relativity.

IN RUSSIA, DISCONTENT WITH THE TSAR, NICHOLAS II, had been growing, and there were calls for a constitutional monarchy. This was compounded by the humiliating defeat in the Russo–Japanese War (see 1904). **Protests** spread around the country. In February, Nicholas promised to set up an **elected assembly**, but this did nothing to stop the unrest. Finally, the military joined in, and June saw a mutiny by the crew of the **battleship *Potemkin***. By October, Nicholas promised a constitution and an elected legislature, but this was insufficient for the protesters, who organized themselves into **soviets** (revolutionary councils). One of the leaders, **Leon Trotsky** (1879–1940), was jailed. Although the protests continued, anti-revolutionary forces finally suppressed what became known as the **Russian Revolution of 1905**. The following year, Nicholas implemented reforms, the **Fundamental Laws**, which included the creation of an elected legislature, or **Duma**.

In **Switzerland**, the German physicist **Albert Einstein** (1879–1955) had received his doctorate and international acclaim for his publications. The most influential was known as the **Special Theory of Relativity**, which explained the relationship between mass and energy in the equation $E=mc^2$. In 1921 he would receive a Nobel Prize for his scientific contributions.

In **India**, the British viceroy Lord Curzon (1859–1925) was facing increased nationalist opposition. He decided to **partition** the province of **Bengal**, joining East Bengal and Assam, with a capital in Dhaka. This move was attacked as an attempt to stifle the **nationalist movement**, which had strong support throughout Bengal.

Film poster
The film Battleship Potemkin *(1925), made by the Russian director Sergei Eisenstein, dramatized the 1905 mutiny of the ship's crew.*

1906

The ruins of the San Francisco City Hall after the 1906 earthquake.

SAN FRANSISCO EARTHQUAKE

25,000 BUILDINGS **DESTROYED**
450–700 PEOPLE **DIED**
$350 MILLION OF **DAMAGE**

SITUATED ON ONE OF THE WORLD'S MOST ACTIVE FAULT LINES – the San Andreas, which runs for 1,300km (810 miles) – the city of **San Francisco** is susceptible to **earthquakes**. By 1906, people in the growing city were used to the earth moving – there had been recorded quakes in 1836, 1865, 1868, and 1892 – but nothing had been done to make the city of 400,000 people better prepared. On 18 April, San Francisco bore the brunt of what was later estimated to be a **7.8 magnitude earthquake**, while people as far afield as Los Angeles and Nevada also felt shaking. The quake only lasted less than a minute, but it **wreaked damage** that would take years to repair, as buildings collapsed and many caught fire throughout the city.

In India, the **All India Muslim League** was established – initially with the support of the British government – with the aim of protecting the rights of Muslims. Some 3,000 delegates attended its first meeting on 30 December. By 1913 it had joined the growing call for **self-rule in India**.

1907

Life for Romanian peasants was harsh and many wanted land reform.

PEASANT UNREST THAT HAD BEEN SPREADING throughout the countryside in **Romania** culminated in a **revolt** in 1907. This was fuelled by land issues, as the peasants were forced into **exploitative contracts**, meaning many farmers had to live in poverty. As the rioting spread through villages, up to **10,000 people were killed** before it was suppressed by the military.

In Southeast Asia, **Cambodia** had clawed back some of its western provinces from Thailand due to **French pressure**. By 1863, France had established a strong presence in Cambodia, eventually restricting the Cambodian king's powers and installing a governor. This paved the way for **colonization** by the French, but angered Cambodian nationalists. The resistance was quelled by 1907.

The French in Thailand
A 19th-century French gun boat, armed with a Hotchkiss Cannon, patrols the waters of the Chao Phraya River in Bangkok, Thailand.

22 January Bloody Sunday massacre of 500 Russian demonstrators at the Winter Palace, St Petersburg

31 March Start of the **First Moroccan Crisis** in which Germany challenges France's dominance in Morocco

4 April Earthquake in **Kangara**, India, kills 20,000

15 May Las Vegas founded in the US

27 May The Japanese fleet destroys the Russian fleet at the **Battle of Tsushima** in the Russo-Japanese War

30 June Special Theory of Relativity published by German physicist **Albert Einstein** (1879–1955)

7 June Norway gains independence

16 October Partition of Bengal and nationalist agitation in India

18 April Great San Francisco earthquake almost destroys the city

23 August US troops appear in **Cuba** at request of ousted president

30 December Foundation of **All India Muslim League**

March Peasant revolt in **Romania** against feudal laws

15 March Nineteen women elected to Finnish parliament

25 July Korea becomes a protectorate of **Japan**

31 August Creation of **Triple Entente**, an alliance between Britain, France, and Russia

1908

An engraving in the Italian newspaper *La Domenica del Corriere*, from February 1908, depicts the assassination of Charles I, king of Portugal. He was murdered during a period of increased calls for a republican government.

PORTUGAL WAS CONVULSED BY REVOLUTION following the assassination of its king, **Charles I** (1863–1908), in February. Already a highly unpopular monarch, he made matters worse by deciding to appoint his own prime minister – **bypassing parliament** in the process. Events took a violent turn on 1 February when Charles and his eldest son, Lúis Filipe, were shot while they were travelling in a carriage in Lisbon. Charles was succeeded by his son, **Manuel II** (1889–1932), who managed to survive on the throne for just a couple of years before being overthrown (see 1910).

In Africa, the **Congo Free State** (see 1884) was abolished and Belgium's government established the **Belgian Congo**. The Free State had been run by a private company with Belgian **King Leopold II** (1835–1909) ruling over it personally. Africans working in the Free State provided the company with valuable **rubber and ivory**. However, reports over the appalling labour conditions led to an **international outcry** and calls for reforms. Belgium's answer to these demands was to make the territory an **official colony** and rule it from Brussels, ensuring the continued supply of Congolese products. But the brutal conditions persisted, and the **population dropped** from an estimated 20–30 million in 1884 to around 8.5 million by 1911.

Meanwhile, **Austria–Hungary** also reconfigured its colonial relationships – in its case with **Bosnia–Herzegovina**, which it had already occupied (see 1878). It had become worried about the implications of the **Young Turk Revolution** under way in the neighbouring Ottoman Empire (see 1909). Austria–Hungary was concerned that its power in the Balkans might be undermined because, technically, Bosnia–Herzegovina was still under Ottoman suzerainty and one of the Young Turks' aims was to reclaim the territory. After securing **Russia's** support, Austria–Hungary **annexed Bosnia–Herzegovina**. This move immediately angered nearby **Serbia**, which called for a section of Bosnia–Herzegovina that would give it access to the Adriatic Sea. Russia was soon caught in the middle of what would later be known as the **Bosnian Crisis**. At first it sought to secure some concessions for Serbia, but it later bowed to the demands of Austria–Hungary and its allies. During this period, **Bulgaria's Prince Ferdinand** (see 1887) – whose role as leader was not yet recognized by Russia and many other European countries – took advantage of the crisis to proclaim **Bulgarian independence** from the faltering Ottoman empire.

The Austro-Hungarian Empire
In 1908, Austria–Hungary was eager to assert its control over the Balkan states of Bosnia and Herzegovina in order to prevent the Ottoman Empire from taking the territory.

1909

> **“** ONE DAY MY **MORTAL BODY** WILL TURN TO DUST, BUT THE TURKISH REPUBLIC **WILL STAND FOREVER. ”**

Mustafa Kemel Ataturk, first president of Turkey, 1926

Sultan Mehmed V
The 35th Ottoman sultan, Mehmed V (1844–1918) was effectively a puppet for the Young Turks' Committee of Union and Progress.

FOLLOWING THE SUCCESSFUL REBELLION BY THE YOUNG TURKS the previous year, in 1909 the **Committee of Union and Progress** – the group's political wing – had taken control of the levers of power within the **Ottoman Empire** – something they would maintain for the next couple of years, despite internal disputes. The Young Turks had wanted to force the sultan to **restore the constitution**, and once this was accomplished Abdul Hamid II (r.1876–1909) ruled as a constitutional monarch, though only briefly – he was deposed on 27 April. They then proceeded to make his brother, **Mehmed V** (r.1909–1918), the new sultan.

Many of the Young Turks had been students and members of the Ottoman intelligentsia and they organized themselves while living in Europe and British-controlled Egypt. Although they were initially seen as "liberal", many of their policies were considered repressive, especially elsewhere in the empire. Much of the anger lay in the Young Turks' **nationalism**, which meant they wanted to push a **Turkish identity** at the expense of the many large ethnic groups throughout the Ottoman world, such as the Arabs and Slavs. However, they did implement some **progressive reforms**, such as secularizing the legal system and improving education, including allowing women better access to schooling. They also wanted to limit the amount of **foreign influence** throughout the empire in areas such as Bosnia–Herzegovina (see 1908).

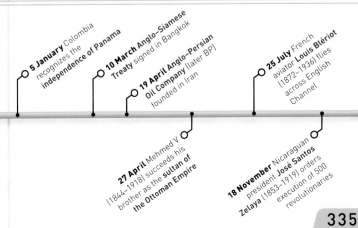

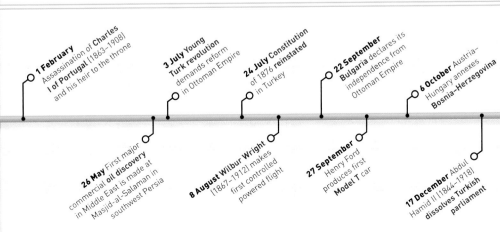

MUSTAFA KEMEL ATATURK (1881–1938)

Having been involved with the Young Turk Revolution of 1908, Mustafa Ataturk led the Turkish national movement in the Turkish War of Independence. When the Republic of Turkey was established in 1923 he became its first president.

1 February Assassination of **Charles I of Portugal** (1863–1908) and his heir to the throne

26 May First major commercial **oil discovery** in Middle East is made at Masjid-al-Salaman in southwest Persia

3 July Young Turk revolution demands reform in Ottoman Empire

24 July Constitution of 1876 **reinstated** in Turkey

8 August Wilbur Wright (1867–1912) makes first controlled powered flight

22 September Bulgaria declares its independence from Ottoman Empire

27 September Henry Ford produces first **Model T** car

6 October Austria–Hungary annexes **Bosnia–Herzegovina**

17 December Abdul Hamid II (1844–1918) **dissolves Turkish parliament**

5 January Colombia recognizes the **independence of Panama**

10 March Anglo–Siamese Treaty signed in Bangkok

19 April Anglo–Persian Oil Company (later BP) founded in Iran

27 April Mehmed V (1844–1918) succeeds his brother as the **sultan of the Ottoman Empire**

25 July French aviator **Louis Blériot** (1872–1936) flies across English Channel

18 November Nicaraguan president **José Santos Zelaya** (1853–1919) orders execution of 500 revolutionaries

> **“** IT’S BETTER TO **DIE UPON YOUR FEET** THAN TO **LIVE UPON YOUR KNEES!** **”**
>
> **Emiliano Zapata, leader during the Mexican Revolution**

Emiliano Zapata was one of the leaders involved in the fight to oust Porfirio Díaz from office and put in place a revolutionary government led by Franscisco Madero. Zapata was instrumental in organizing guerrilla troops.

A CENTURY AFTER ITS FIRST REVOLUTION (see 1810), Mexico was once again caught up in the throes of political change. Liberal reformers had begun to resent **Porfirio Díaz**’s political machine (see 1876) and the **Regeneration movement** was formed. Members of the group were often jailed, and the publication of their newspaper was suppressed. In 1906, they published a manifesto calling for a **one-term presidency** and reforms to land – the return of land confisicated by the Díaz regime to its rightful owners – and education. Díaz eventually allowed the development of an opposition, and other groups emerged. However, Díaz jailed one popular presidential candidate, **Francisco Madero** (1873–1913), on the eve of the 1910 election, reneging on his promise for fair elections. Madero escaped to Texas and began to **organize an uprising** for 20 November, the anniversary of the previous Mexican revolution. It was not a large rebellion, but involved small towns being attacked by pockets of **guerrilla groups**, which the army was able to suppress. However, by the following year, the revolutionary militias – many of them peasant farmers – led by **Francisco “Pancho” Villa** (1877–1932) and **Emiliano Zapata** (1879–1919) stepped up their attacks against the army. Díaz surrendered his office under the **Treaty of Ciudad Juarez**, and by November 1911 Madero was installed as president. However, he now came in for attacks from the right and the left as groups splintered from the revolutionary movement. This **political fighting spilled over into violence**, with warfare continuing for decades.

In East Asia, **China invaded Tibet** once again, trying to assert its claim to rule the territory. This invasion came after British attempts to occupy Lhasa in 1904, which were fuelled by fears that Tibet could fall under the influence of Russia. This was followed by a 1907 **treaty between China and Britain** that recognized China’s sovereignty over Tibet. Tibet did not consider it valid, and the Tibetans were able to use the **revolution** that began in China the following year (see 1911) as an opportunity to drive out the Chinese.

For nearby **Korea**, the consequences of the Russo–Japanese war (see 1904) had severe ramifications. It had allowed Japan to use the peninsula for military operations and in the resulting **Treaty of Portsmouth**, in 1905, Korea was made a **Japanese protectorate**, and by 1910 had been officially annexed.

Casa Mila
Designed by the Catalan architect Antoni Gaudi (1852–1956), Barcelona’s iconic Casa Mila was constructed between 1905 and 1910.

Imperial officials flee from Tientsin during the Chinese Revolution, which precipitated the end of the Qing dynasty, rulers of China since the 1600s.

6000
THE NUMBER OF **DIAMONDS** IN GEORGE V’S **CROWN**

EVENTS IN CHINA TOOK A DRAMATIC TURN AS THE QING DYNASTY – which had been in power for more than 260 years – faced a rebellion. Despite its longevity, many Chinese always considered the ruling **Manchu** as foreigners. They were also resentful at the **growing number of Westerners**, who had been permitted to move inland from the port cities. The 20th century had been full of unrest for China (see 1900) and this continued to grow as **revolutionary groups** began to form around the country. In October, a revolutionary plot was uncovered and the members arrested and executed. Soldiers in **Wuchang** who knew of the plot decided to push forward with a revolt; they led a **mutiny** on 10 October, which soon spread throughout the country, and the rebels **declared China a republic**. They were met with little resistance because many officials accepted that the Manchus’ days were numbered. In the US, exiled revolutionary leader **Sun Yat-sen** (1866–1925) had heard about the events in China and returned home. He was elected **provisional president** of the country, although prime minister **Yuan Shikai** (1859–1916) had been given full power by the imperial court. The two struck a deal, though Yuan would try to make himself **emperor** in 1915; his efforts ended in failure three months before he died in 1916.

Meanwhile, in **India**, the British were trying to display their colonial might with an enormous **durbar**, or assembly, in Delhi. This was to mark the visit of **King George V and Queen Mary**. During the visit, the king announced that the **colonial capital would be moved from Calcutta to Delhi**. Around the same time, the unpopular policy of **partition in Bengal** was ended (see 1905), and the territory was reunited. Over the following years,

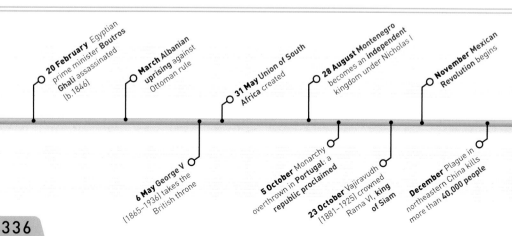

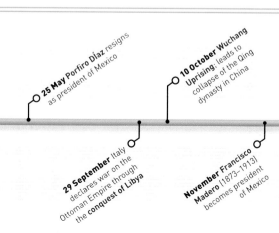

Sun Yat-sen
The cover of the magazine Je sais tout *shows a picture of Sun Yat-sen, president of the Chinese Republic.*

20 February Egyptian prime minister **Boutros Ghali assassinated** (b.1846)

March Albanian uprising against Ottoman rule

6 May George V (1865–1936) takes the British throne

31 May Union of South Africa created

28 August Montenegro becomes an **independent** kingdom under Nicholas I

5 October Monarchy overthrown in **Portugal**; a **republic proclaimed**

23 October Vajiravudh (1881–1925) crowned Rama VI, **king of Siam**

November Mexican **Revolution** begins

December Plague in northeastern China kills more than **40,000 people**

25 May Porfirio Díaz resigns as president of Mexico

29 September Italy declares war on the Ottoman Empire through the **conquest of Libya**

10 October Wuchang Uprising; leads to collapse of the Qing dynasty in China

November Francisco Madero (1873–1913) becomes president of Mexico

An illustration of General Lyautey, the French governor of Morocco.

A photograph captures the moment when suffragist campaigner Emily Davison is trampled by George V's horse at Epsom on Derby Day.

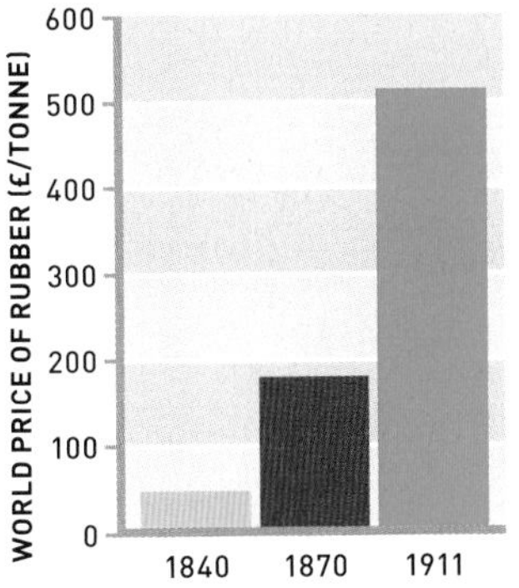

Rubber boom
Technological innovations, especially the tyres used on the increasingly popular motor car, fuelled a rise in the use – and price – of rubber.

a new part of Delhi was built, with a monumental **Viceroy's house** and government buildings designed by the leading British architect **Edwin Lutyens** (1869–1944). However, such displays did little to quell the growing nationalist sentiment.

In Europe, **Marie Curie** (1867–1934), a Polish-born French scientist, won her second **Nobel Prize**, this time in the category of chemistry for her work on **radioactivity**. She and her husband, Pierre (1859–1906), had been the recipients of the 1903 Nobel Prize for Physics.

In 1911, the world **price of rubber** was beginning to soar, fuelled by its use in **new technologies**, especially in the production of automobile tyres. Rubber came from the sap of trees that grew in the forests of Brazil, Southeast Asia, and West Africa.

THE OTTOMAN EMPIRE FACED FURTHER UPHEAVAL with the **First Balkan War**. The conflict ended with the Turks losing Albania, which became independent, and Macedonia, which was to be shared among the Balkan allies (see 1913).

In March 1912 **Morocco** was established as a French **protectorate** under the **Treaty of Fez**. The year before the new sultan **Abd al-Hafiz** (*c.*1875–1937), besieged in his palace, had asked the French to help him suppress internal dissent.

THE TREATY OF LONDON OF 1913 OFFICIALLY SIGNALLED THE END of the First Balkan War. However, the Balkan League – Serbia, Bulgaria, Montenegro, and Greece – that had challenged the Ottoman Empire soon started to disintegrate. Bulgaria attacked Serbia in June because of a disagreement over the **division of Macedonia**, although the fighting ended a couple of months later with a **Serbian–Greek alliance**. Greece and Serbia would receive most of Macedonia with Bulgaria only receiving a small part. This internal division opened a vacuum for the Turks. The **Young Turk government** in charge of the Ottoman Empire was not satisfied with the outcome of the **Treaty of London** and it mounted another invasion, this time recapturing Adrianople (modern Edirne) on 20 July. However, by this point it had lost almost all of its Balkan territory.

In Britain, the **suffragist battle** to give women the right to vote (see panel, left) took a violent turn as campaigner **Emily Davison** (1872–1913) threw herself in front of King George V's horse during the Epsom Derby in June. The horse, Anmer, struck Davison's chest and she was knocked down and remained unconscious for four days, until she died of her injuries on 8 June. It remains unclear if her intention was to commit suicide. A public funeral was held for her in London on 14 June.

By 1913, **Henry Ford** (1863–1947), the head of the US Ford Motor Company, which he set up in 1903, had sold nearly **250,000 Model T cars**. Although other companies were making cars, they were far too expensive for average consumers. Ford wanted to make them more affordable and so began production of the basic **Model T**. He also developed new and more efficient production techniques through the use of moving **assembly lines** that he had installed in his Michigan factory. This improvement meant that a completed chassis (car body) could be made in just over an hour and a half, while his competitors took hours longer.

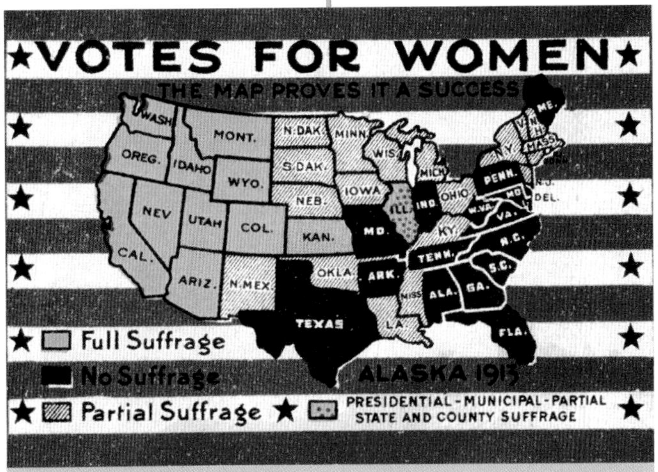

WOMEN'S RIGHT TO VOTE

By the early 20th century, the fight for women to be given the vote had gained pace all over the world. Australia had followed New Zealand (see 1893) by giving women suffrage in 1902. In northern Europe, Finland had introduced the women's right to vote in 1906, while Norway followed in 1913. While, women suffragists in Britain would have to wait until after World War I, countries such as Russia and the US (see above – states with full suffrage are gold) also began to peel back voting restrictions around this time.

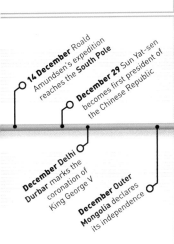

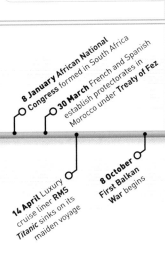

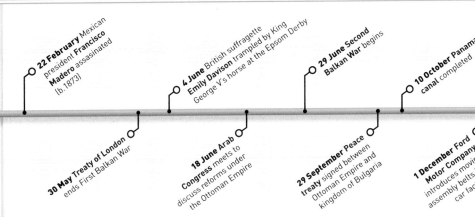

Coup d'etat
An illustration from Le Petit Journal *depicts the murder of Nazim Pasha, Ottoman minister of war, during the First Balkan War.*

> **" HISTORY IS MORE OR LESS BUNK.** IT'S TRADITION. **"**

Henry Ford, US industrialist, in an interview in the *Chicago Tribune*, 25 May 1916

- **14 December** Roald Amundsen's expedition reaches the **South Pole**
- **December Delhi Durbar** marks the coronation of King George V
- **December 29** Sun Yat-sen becomes first president of the Chinese Republic
- **December Outer Mongolia** declares its independence
- **8 January African National Congress** formed in South Africa
- **30 March** French and Spanish establish protectorates in Morocco under **Treaty of Fez**
- **14 April** Luxury cruise liner **RMS Titanic** sinks on its maiden voyage
- **8 October First Balkan War** begins
- **22 February** Mexican president **Francisco Madero** assassinated (b.1873)
- **30 May Treaty of London** ends First Balkan War
- **4 June** British suffragette **Emily Davison** trampled by King George V's horse at the Epsom Derby
- **18 June Arab Congress** meets to discuss reforms under the Ottoman Empire
- **29 June Second Balkan War** begins
- **29 September Peace treaty** signed between Ottoman Empire and kingdom of Bulgaria
- **10 October Panama canal** completed
- **1 December Ford Motor Company** introduces moving assembly belts into car factories

7

TECHNOLOGY AND SUPERPOWERS

1914–2011

Technological progress brought the wonders of space flight and the Internet, but radical projects to transform society failed. Despite two World Wars, human population quadrupled, creating new economic and environmental challenges.

1914

Young German men cheer as they march down Pariser Platz in Berlin. Many Germans reacted enthusiastically to being called up for war.

Raising the Stars and Stripes
American soldiers raise the flag over the Mexican port of Veracruz. The occupation cost 17 American lives and lasted for six months.

EARLY IN THE YEAR, ATTENTION WAS FOCUSED ON CENTRAL AMERICA. In January, the first ship completed its passage through **the Panama Canal**. This amazing feat of American engineering cost around $300 million to construct and claimed the lives of around 4,000 workers.

In April, the US intervened in **Mexico's civil war** by sending a force of Marines to **occupy the port of Veracruz**, which prevented the Mexican President Victoriano Huerta receiving arms shipments from Germany. The US held the port for six months, contributing to Huerta's fall from power in July.

Meanwhile, Europe began its descent into war. **World War I was sparked** by the assassination of Archduke Franz Ferdinand (1863–1914), heir to the Austro-Hungarian throne, and his wife Sophie. They were shot on 28 June during an official visit to Sarajevo in Austrian-ruled Bosnia. The fatal shots were fired by 19-year-old Bosnian Serb, Gavrilo Princip. **The Austrian government blamed Serbia for the assassinations.** Assured of Germany's full support by Kaiser Wilhelm II (1859–1941), on 23 July the Austrians sent an ultimatum to Serbia. Its demands were intended to be so humiliating that Serbia would reject them, giving the Austrians a pretext for military action. Although the Serbians were prepared to make concessions, Austria–Hungary declared war on 28 July. In response, Russia began mobilizing its army in support of Serbia.

Within a week, **all the major European powers were at war**. Brushing aside last-minute peace initiatives by Germany's Kaiser Wilhelm and Russia's Tsar Nicholas II (1868–1918), German military chiefs insisted that **Germany declare war on Russia**. Since their military plans demanded a swift victory in the west as a prelude to defeating Russia in the east, Germany also **declared war on France**. Germany did not want to fight the British, but in order to invade France they needed to send an army through Belgium, whose neutrality was guaranteed by Britain. On 4 August, after German troops had crossed the Belgian frontier, **Britain declared war on Germany**. Although many people privately regarded the onset of war with dismay, it was greeted by cheering crowds. The traditionally anti-militarist and internationalist **German Social Democrat Party** rallied to the war effort, convinced Germany had to defend itself against Russian conquest. In France, most previously anti-militarist radicals and socialists adhered to the ***union sacrée*** (sacred union), which called for a political truce with pro-war parties and vetoed any strike action. In the UK, **Ulster Protestant paramilitaries**, who had been on the verge of an armed rebellion against the British government's plans for Irish Home Rule, and their Catholic opponents, the **Irish Volunteers**, volunteered en masse for the British Army.

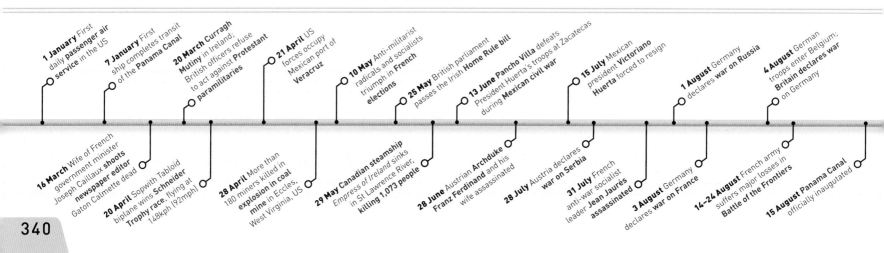

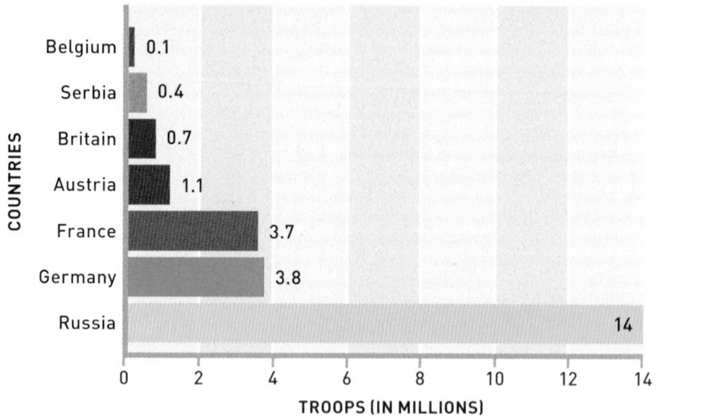

Army sizes at the outbreak of war
Russia's army was huge, but it was poorly equipped and badly organized. Britain had a relatively small army, and depended on its navy for defence.

1 January First daily **passenger air service** in the US

7 January First ship completes transit of the **Panama Canal**

16 March Wife of French government minister Joseph Caillaux **shoots newspaper editor** Gaton Calmette dead

20 March Curragh Mutiny in Ireland; British officers refuse to act against **Protestant paramilitaries**

20 April Sopwith Tabloid biplane wins **Schneider Trophy race**, flying at 148kph (92mph)

21 April US forces occupy Mexican port of **Veracruz**

28 April More than 180 miners killed in **explosion in coal mine** in Eccles, West Virginia, US

10 May Anti-militarist radicals and socialists triumph in **French elections**

25 May British parliament passes the Irish **Home Rule bill**

29 May Canadian steamship *Empress of Ireland* sinks in St Lawrence River, **killing 1,073 people**

13 June Pancho Villa defeats President Huerta's troops at Zacatecas during **Mexican civil war**

28 June Austrian **Archduke Franz Ferdinand** and his wife assassinated

15 July Mexican president **Victoriano Huerta** forced to resign

28 July Austria declares **war on Serbia**

31 July French anti-war socialist leader **Jean Jaurés assassinated**

1 August Germany declares **war on Russia**

3 August Germany declares **war on France**

4 August German troops enter Belgium; **Britain declares war** on Germany

14–24 August French army suffers major losses in **Battle of the Frontiers**

15 August Panama Canal officially inaugutated

British men queue outside the recruitment office in Southwark Town Hall, London. Thousands of men from all sections of society volunteered for army service.

> **"** THE **PLUNGE** OF CIVILIZATION **INTO** THIS **ABYSS OF BLOOD** AND **DARKNESS...** IS TOO **TRAGIC FOR** ANY **WORDS. "**
>
> **Henry James, American author**, 4 August 1914

In continental Europe, millions of men were called up and dispatched by train to the frontiers, while a much smaller force of British regular soldiers was sent to France as the **British Expeditionary Force (BEF)**. Lord Kitchener (1850–1916), the British secretary for war, launched a drive to recruit volunteers. The response was overwhelming, with three-quarters of a million British men enlisted by the end of September. Most people expected a short war with high casualties, and at first this expectation seemed justified.

German troops surged into Belgium, adopting an official policy of "Schrecklichkeit" (frightfulness). They committed atrocities against the Belgian population – in the worst incident 674 civilians were massacred at Dinant – and laid waste the historic city of Louvain, burning its famous university library.

The **BEF experienced its first action at Mons**. Unable to resist the German onslaught, the British and French were driven back **toward Paris**. Meanwhile, the French launched their own offensive along the eastern French–German border, but they suffered heavy losses for no gain. By the beginning of September the situation was desperate for the British and French armies. The Germans were also forced to change their tactics, abandoning their plan to advance to the west of Paris, and instead marching to the east of the city. French army commander General Joseph Joffre (1852–1931) launched a **counter-offensive at the Marne**, while troops from Paris – some of whom were carried to the front in buses and taxis – attacked the German flank. The German army was forced to retreat, their hopes of a swift victory in ruins.

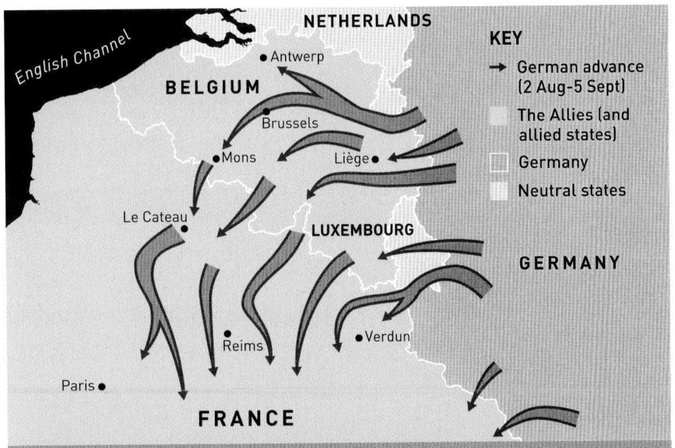

GERMAN INVASION OF FRANCE

The German war plan, devised in 1906 by then chief of staff Count Alfred von Schlieffen, assumed that, if attacked on two fronts, France would concentrate its forces along its eastern border. The bulk of the German army was to advance through Belgium and Luxembourg, encircling the French armies. The aim was to defeat the French in six weeks, before the Russians could enter the fray.

Refugees flee Belgium
Roads in Belgium were lined with refugees like these, carrying whatever possessions they could, and fleeing from the advancing German army.

250,000

THE **TOTAL NUMBER** OF **BRITISH, FRENCH,** AND **GERMAN CASUALTIES** AT THE **FIRST BATTLE OF YPRES**

On the Eastern Front the Russians mobilized more quickly than Germany had anticipated, but as they advanced into East Prussia the Russian First and Second Armies were crushed at the **Battles of Tannenberg and the Masurian Lakes**. The victorious German General Paul von Hindenburg (1837–1934) and his chief of staff General Erich Ludendorff (1883–1918) became national heroes.

On the Western Front, from September through to November, a series of battles were fought northward into Flanders (see pp.467–47). They culminated in the encounters known collectively as the **First Battle of Ypres**. With neither side able to inflict a decisive blow, the armies dug trenches along a line that was to remain broadly unchanged for three years.

Meanwhile, **the war was widening into a global conflict**. Ottoman Turkey joined in on the side of Germany, declaring a jihad (Muslim holy war) against the British Empire. British troops from India landed in Turkish-ruled Iraq and seized Basra, while Japan joined the Allies and fought for control of the German concession in China. In Africa, British troops invaded German East Africa and South African forces attacked German Southwest Africa – they also put down a revolt by the Boers, who had sided with the Germans.

At **Christmas, widespread fraternization** between opposing troops along the Western Front appalled generals, who feared their men would lose the will to fight, but the war continued. By the end of the year around half a million French and German troops were dead, and a third of the British men who had arrived in France in August had been killed.

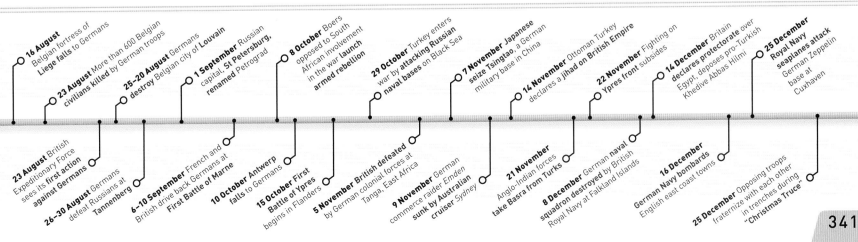

Recruitment poster
British War Secretary Lord Kitchener's face adorned recruitment posters that called for volunteers to join up and fight.

16 August Belgian fortress of **Liège falls** to Germans

23 August British Expeditionary Force sees its **first action against Germans**

23 August More than 600 Belgian **civilians killed** by German troops

25–20 August Germans **destroy** Belgian city of **Louvain**

26–30 August Germans defeat Russians at **Tannenberg**

1 September Russian capital, **St Petersburg, renamed Petrograd**

6–10 September French and British drive back Germans at **First Battle of Marne**

8 October Boers opposed to South African involvement in the war **launch armed rebellion**

10 October Antwerp falls to Germans

15 October First Battle of Ypres begins in Flanders

29 October Turkey enters war by **attacking Russian naval bases** on Black Sea

5 November British defeated by German colonial forces at Tanga, East Africa

7 November Japanese seize Tsingtao, a German military base in China

9 November German commerce raider *Emden* **sunk by Australian cruiser** *Sydney*

14 November Ottoman Turkey declares a **jihad on British Empire**

21 November Anglo-Indian forces **take Basra from Turks**

22 November Fighting on **Ypres front** subsides

8 December German naval **squadron destroyed** by British Royal Navy at Falkland Islands

14 December Britain **declares protectorate** over Egypt, deposes pro-Turkish Khedive Abbas Hilmi

16 December German Navy bombards English east coast towns

25 December Royal Navy seaplanes attack German Zeppelin base at Cuxhaven

25 December Opposing troops fraternize with each other in trenches during **"Christmas Truce"**

A submarine embarks on a mission in the Atlantic. German U-boats terrorized the seas, attacking both naval and merchant shipping at will.

A German airship taking off from its base for a bombing raid on London.

AT THE START OF 1915, THE GREAT POWERS OF EUROPE remained locked in a war for which they had been unprepared. The fighting had exhausted munition supplies, and so to continue the war the combatants had to **vastly expand their armaments industries.** Governments became aware that the war would be won, or lost, as much in the factories as on the front line. Britain set up a new Ministry of Munitions, and in Russia the tsarist government set up a special War Industries Committee. The French, meanwhile, had to recall conscripts from the trenches to work in factories, their production problems accentuated by the German occupation of industrial areas of northeast France.

Chemical warfare
Before the advent of the gas mask, troops, such as these French soldiers, protected themselves from a gas attack in any way they could.

On the **Western Front**, the **stalemate continued** along a double line of trenches that stretched from the Channel to the Swiss border. Generals assumed that sufficient numbers of men and shells hurled against these defences would achieve a breakthrough, but they were wrong.

The British attempted their first offensive of the trench war at **Neuve Chapelle** in March, with Indian troops leading the assault and the Canadian Expeditionary Force fighting for the first time. They gained a mere 2km (1.2 miles) of ground for 11,000 casualties. The Germans had a similar experience attacking at **Ypres** in April, and the French suffered in repeated offensives throughout the year. Mass offensives led only to mass casualties – **over 300,000 British and French losses** in the autumn Champagne-Loos offensive. On the Eastern Front, the fighting was far more mobile, and the **Russians were forced to retreat** from Poland and Lithuania.

In an attempt to break the deadlock on the Western Front, the Germans **used poison gas for the first time** at Ypres in April, releasing lethal chlorine to drift across to the Allied trenches. The first victims were French colonial troops on 22 April, followed two days later by soldiers of the First Canadian Division. But German troops failed to take advantage of the initial impact of the gas; Allied soldiers quickly discovered means of protection, and the Allies also adopted gas as a weapon against the Germans.

WOMEN AT WAR

A shortage of manpower meant that women were recruited into a range of jobs traditionally reserved for men. By 1918, around a third of the 1.7 million workers in French munitions factories were women, and they constituted over half of the total German industrial workforce. Women also replaced men as agricultural labourers, for example in the British Women's Land Army.

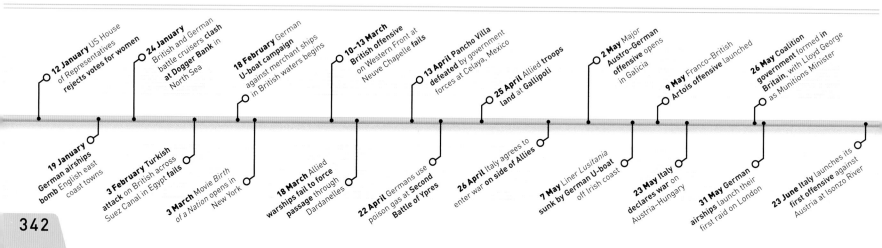

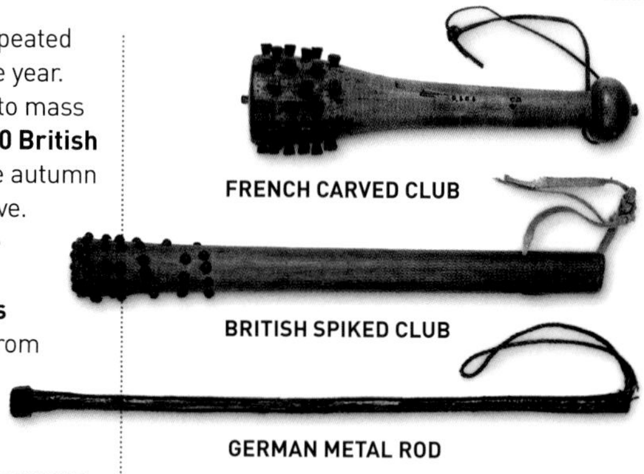

Savage attacks
Soldiers raiding enemy trenches often carried primitive weapons for close-quarters combat. As well as clubs like these, they used trench knives, knuckle dusters, and even spades in savage melees.

On 26 April, **Italy signed the Treaty of London**, committing it to enter the war on the side of Britain and France. Before the war, Italy had been an ally of Germany and Austria–Hungary, so this was a diplomatic coup for the Western Allies. Italy duly declared war on Austria on 23 May, and the fighting on the **Italo–Austrian Front** quickly descended into the same static stalemate as on the Western Front.

While stalemate persisted on the ground, **war in the air developed on a substantial scale**. Slow-moving aircraft flew over enemy trenches taking reconnaissance photographs and engaged in small-scale bombing missions, while nimbler fighter aircraft intercepted them.

Away from the battlefield, Germany's Zeppelin and Schütte-Lanze airships embarked on the **world's first long-range bombing campaign**, with Britain as their main target. German Navy airship commander Captain Peter Strasser believed that Britain could be "overcome by means of airships... through increasingly extensive destruction of cities, factory complexes, dockyards...". This was, in reality, far beyond the airships' capacity, but from 31 May onward **night raids** on London and other major cities still managed to cause many civilian casualties and forced Britain to divert resources from the Western Front to **home defence**.

At sea, Germany responded to an ongoing blockade of its ports by the British Royal Navy by attempting to impose its own blockade on Britain through the use of submarines. From February **German U-boats** were authorized to attack merchant shipping in British home waters without warning. On 7 May, the Cunard liner ***Lusitania***, bound from New York to Liverpool with almost 2,000 passengers and crew on board, was torpedoed off southern Ireland by the submarine *U-20*. More than 1,200 people were drowned, including 128 Americans citizens. The attack provoked anti-German riots in British cities and a hostile response in the US. After the

12 January US House of Representatives **rejects votes for women**

19 January German airships bomb English east coast towns

24 January British and German battle cruisers **clash at Dogger Bank** in North Sea

3 February Turkish attack on British across Suez Canal in Egypt **fails**

18 February German **U-boat campaign** against merchant ships in British waters begins

3 March Movie *Birth of a Nation* opens in New York

10–13 March British offensive on Western Front at Neuve Chapelle **fails**

18 March Allied **warships fail to force passage** through Dardanelles

13 April Pancho Villa defeated by government forces at Celaya, Mexico

22 April Germans use poison gas at **Second Battle of Ypres**

25 April Allied **troops land** at **Gallipoli**

26 April Italy agrees to enter war **on side of Allies**

2 May Major **Austro-German offensive** opens in Galicia

7 May Liner *Lusitania* **sunk by German U-boat** off Irish coast

9 May Franco-British **Artois offensive** launched

23 May Italy declares war on Austria–Hungary

26 May Coalition government formed **in Britain**, with Lloyd George as Munitions Minister

31 May German airships launch their first raid on London

23 June Italy launches its **first offensive** against Austria at Isonzo River

British troops on the Western Front are silhouetted against the sky, wearing the steel Brodie helmets that were first introduced in October 1915.

sinking of another passenger liner, *Arabic*, off Iceland on 19 August, the **Germans felt obliged to curtail U-boat attacks in the Atlantic to avoid provoking the US** into entering the war.

TAKE UP THE SWORD OF JUSTICE

Fighting a just war
This British recruitment poster uses the sinking of the Lusitania *as propaganda to prove the justice of the Allied cause.*

Seeking an alternative to the costly stalemate on the Western Front, Britain and France devised a plan to **crush Germany's ally Turkey**. British and French warships were to sail through the Dardanelles Straits into the Sea of Marmara, bringing the Turkish capital, Constantinople, under their guns. When the naval attack was made on 18 March, however, three battleships were sunk and consequently it was decided that the Dardanelles Straits should be seized before the navy could pass through.

Allied forces landed at Gallipoli on 25 April, including a large contingent of the Australian and New Zealand Army Corps (**ANZAC**). Faced with tough Turkish resistance on difficult terrain, they failed to break out of their landing zones. Renewed landings at **Suvla Bay** in August achieved no greater success. Trench warfare, similar to that in France but with conditions exacerbated by heat and disease, quickly developed. By the time the operation was abandoned in January 1916, the Allied forces had suffered almost a quarter of a million casualties.

Success at Gallipoli was a boost to Turkish morale, which was much needed after the Turkish Third Army had been virtually destroyed fighting the Russians in the Caucasus earlier in the year. Claiming that the Armenian population of eastern Turkey was collaborating with the Russians, the Turks embarked on a **mass deportation of Armenians** from the war zone. The deportation, which was accompanied by widespread massacres, has since been interpreted as an **act of genocide**. Between 800,000 and 1.5 million Armenians are thought to have died as a result of Turkish action.

The second half of 1915 was also marked by the terrible **sufferings of Serbian troops and civilians**. Serbia stoutly resisted Austrian offensives throughout the first year of the war, but in October 1915 its army collapsed in the face of a combined attack by the Germans, Austrians, and Bulgarians. Britain and France landed troops at **Salonika in Greece**, intending to aid the Serbs, but they were too late. Serbia was overrun, and as many as 200,000 Serbians died in a winter retreat through Kosovo into Albania.

While these awful events played out in Europe, **Hollywood** was establishing itself as the centre of movie production. Director D.W. Griffith's civil war epic *Birth of a Nation* was a runaway box office success. With the racist Ku Klux Klan as its heroes, Griffith's masterpiece provoked protests from African Americans and triggered race riots, but with a running time of three hours and ten minutes its ambition surpassed that of any previous film. Less controversially, British actor **Charlie Chaplin** blended slapstick comedy with pathos to achieve stardom in *The Tramp*.

> “... ACROSS THE RIDGES OF THE **GALLIPOLI PENINSULA** LIE SOME OF THE **SHORTEST PATHS** TO A **TRIUMPHANT PEACE.**”

Winston Churchill, First Lord of the Admiralty, urging the case for a renewed offensive at Gallipoli, 5 June 1915

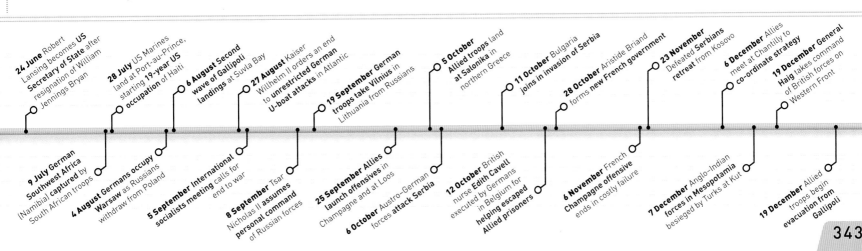

The ANZACS at Gallipoli
An Australian soldier carries a wounded colleague at Gallipoli. More than 26,000 Australians were killed or wounded in the campaign.

- **24 June** Robert Lansing becomes **US Secretary of State** after resignation of William Jennings Bryan
- **9 July German Southwest Africa** (Namibia) **captured** by South African troops
- **28 July** US Marines land at Port-au-Prince, starting **19-year US occupation** of Haiti
- **4 August Germans occupy Warsaw** as Russians withdraw from Poland
- **6 August Second wave of Gallipoli landings** at Suvla Bay
- **27 August** Kaiser Wilhelm II orders an end to **unrestricted German U-boat attacks** in Atlantic
- **5 September International socialists meeting** calls for end to war
- **8 September** Tsar Nicholas II **assumes personal command** of Russian forces
- **19 September German troops take Vilnius** in Lithuania from Russians
- **25 September Allies launch offensives** in Champagne and at Loos
- **5 October Allied troops** land **at Salonika** in northern Greece
- **6 October** Austro-German forces **attack Serbia**
- **11 October** Bulgaria **joins in invasion of Serbia**
- **12 October** British nurse **Edith Cavell** executed by Germans in Belgium for **helping escaped Allied prisoners**
- **28 October** Aristide Briand **forms new French government**
- **6 November** French **Champagne offensive** ends in costly failure
- **23 November** Defeated **Serbians retreat** from Kosovo
- **6 December** Allies meet at Chantilly to **co-ordinate strategy**
- **7 December** Anglo-Indian **forces in Mesopotamia** besieged by Turks at Kut
- **19 December General Haig** takes command of British forces on Western Front
- **19 December** Allied troops begin **evacuation from Gallipoli**

THE GREAT WAR

THE CONFLICT THAT CHANGED THE NATURE OF WAR FOREVER

World War I (Aug 1914–Nov 1918) was also known as the Great War. Although it was a global conflict, the focus was Europe, where the Central Powers – Germany, Austria-Hungary, and Turkey – fought an alliance led by France, Britain, and Russia. The US entered the war on the Anglo-French side in 1917.

From the outset, the decisive arena of conflict was Germany's Western Front. The Germans invaded neutral Belgium and Luxembourg, overcoming Belgian resistance at Liege and Antwerp. French and British forces were driven into retreat southward after clashes at Mons and Charleroi. At the Marne, however, French commander General Joseph Joffre rallied his forces for a counter-offensive and the Germans were pushed back.

After a desperate struggle at Ypres in autumn 1914, the rival armies dug into trenches that stretched from the North Sea to Switzerland. Massive resources were committed to offensives – by the Germans at Verdun and by the Western Allies at the Somme – without breaking the stalemate. Up to 1918, only a voluntary withdrawal by the Germans to the fortified Hindenburg Line significantly changed the position of the armies.

From March 1918 a series of large-scale German offensives broke through Allied defences and advanced the front line toward Paris. But, aided by the arrival of US troops, the Allies halted the Germans at the Marne. A successful British offensive at Amiens in August initiated the "Hundred Days", a series of advances that pushed the fighting back close to the German border.

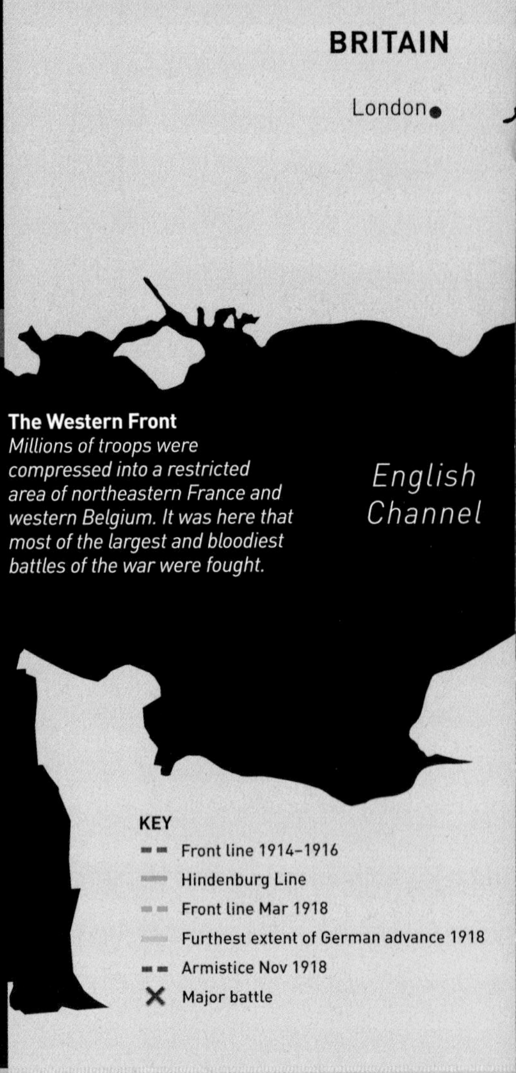

The Western Front *Millions of troops were compressed into a restricted area of northeastern France and western Belgium. It was here that most of the largest and bloodiest battles of the war were fought.*

A WAR ON ALL FRONTS

On the Eastern Front, Germany and Austria-Hungary faced the forces of the Russian Empire. From the battle of Tannenberg in August 1914, the German Army established an ascendancy over the Russians, but the Austro-Hungarians enjoyed no such superiority, suffering defeat in the Russian Brusilov offensive in 1916. Revolution in Russia in 1917 led to the country's exit from the war, and a humiliating peace treaty with Germany signed at Brest-Litovsk in March 1918.

The entry of the Turkish Ottoman Empire into the war as an ally of Germany in autumn 1914 spread the conflict to the Middle East. An Anglo-French bid to attack the Turkish capital, Constantinople, failed dismally at Gallipoli.

Bulgaria also joined the Central Powers, helping to crush Serbia in 1915 and Romania the following year. Allied troops based at Salonica in northern Greece from 1915 remained largely passive until the final months of the war, when their advance northward in September 1918 helped deliver a decisive blow to the collapsing Central Powers.

THE EASTERN FRONT Fought mostly in East Prussia, Poland, and Galicia, the war between Russia and the Central Powers brought Russia to political and military collapse. Peace terms enabled Germany to occupy Russian territory.

KEY
- Front line 1914–15 (limit of Russian advance)
- Limit of Austro-German advance 1915–16
- Brusilov offensive 1916
- Armistice line Dec 1917
- German penetration into Russia by 1918
- Major battle

THE BALKANS Serbia resisted attacks by Austria-Hungary, but was overrun once Germany and Bulgaria joined in. The Allies landed troops at Salonica and Gallipoli, and many retreating Serbs joined the Allies at Salonica.

KEY
- Salonican front Sep 1918
- Austrian, German, and Bulgarian advance 1915
- Retreating Serbs 1915
- Allied offensive Sep 1918
- Romanian offensive Aug–Sep 1916

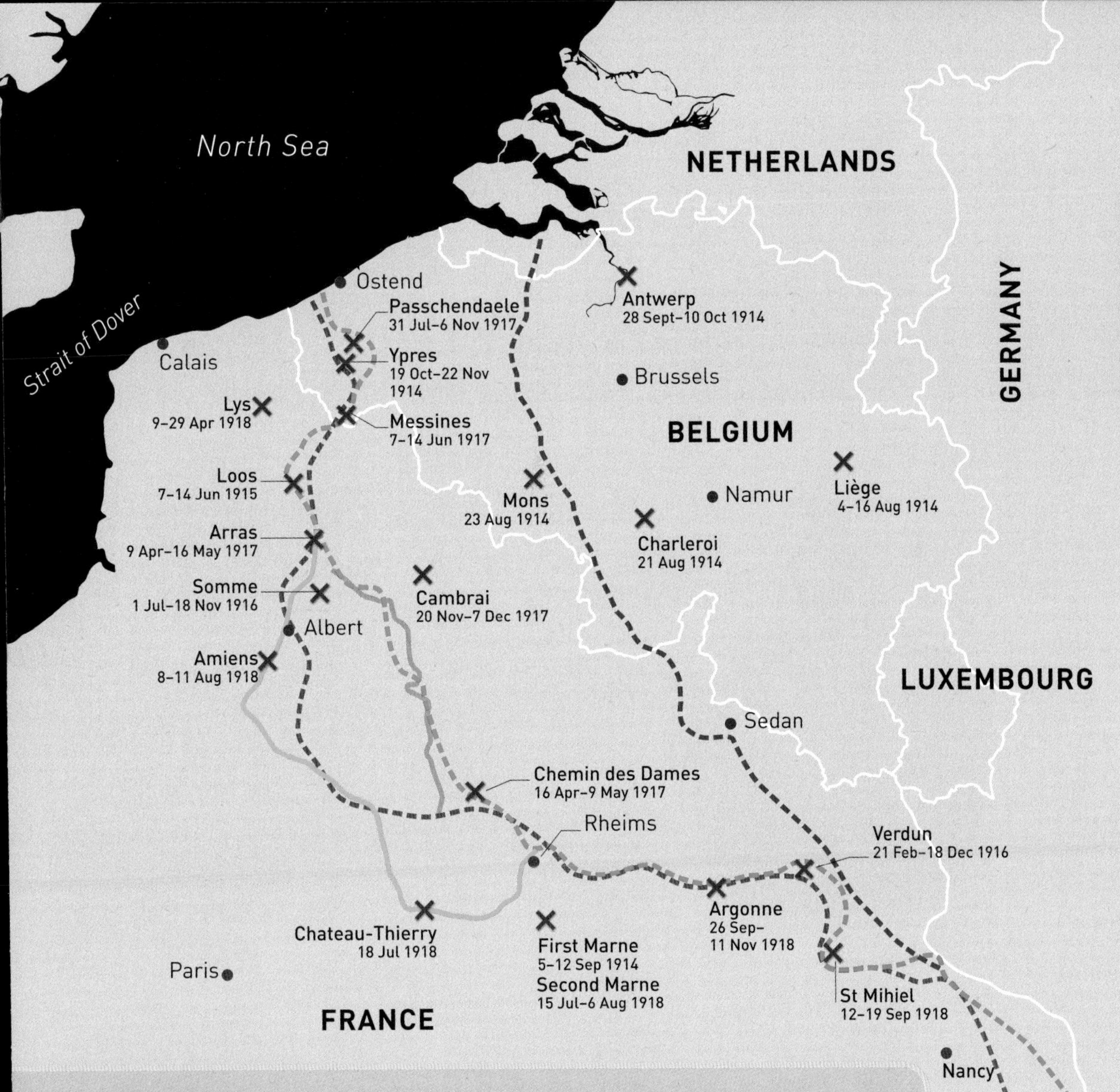

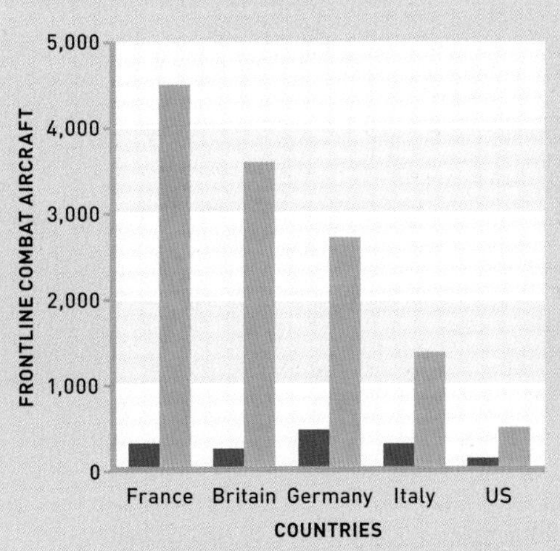

War in the skies
Military aviation expanded massively through the war. In August 1914, around 500 aircraft were deployed by all combatants combined. By the end of the war some 12,000 military aircraft were in action at the front.

KEY
- 1914
- 1918

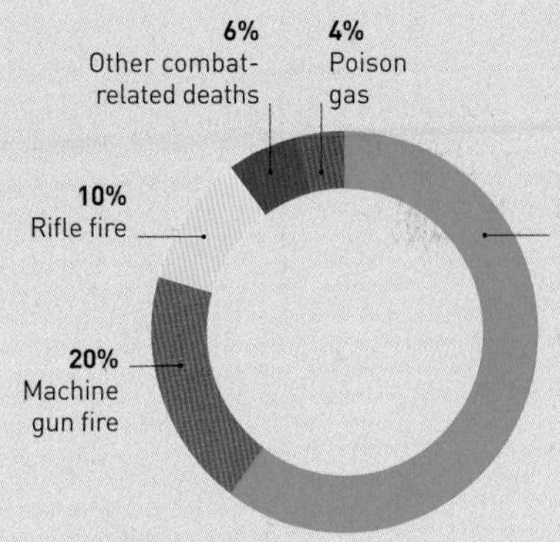

War casualties
The total military death toll in World War I was around 9.7 million. Germany suffered the heaviest loss at over 2 million, followed by Russia (1.8 million), and France (1.4 million).

Central Powers advance Sep 1916 –Jan 1917

Major battle

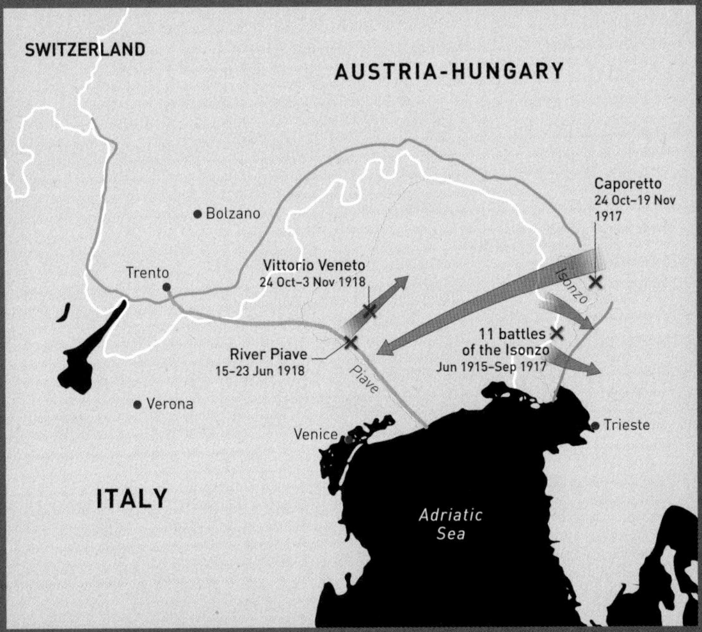

THE ITALIAN FRONT An ally of Germany and Austria-Hungary before the war, Italy remained neutral in 1914, and the following year entered the conflict on the side of Britain and France. A series of ineffective Italian offensives on the mountainous border with Austria at the Isonzo River were followed by headlong retreat after a crushing defeat at the battle of Caporetto. With British and French reinforcements, the Italians held firm at the River Piave in summer 1918.

KEY
- Italian advance
- Austro-German advance
- Allied offensive
- Front line Sep 1917
- Front line Dec 1917–Oct 1918
- Major battle

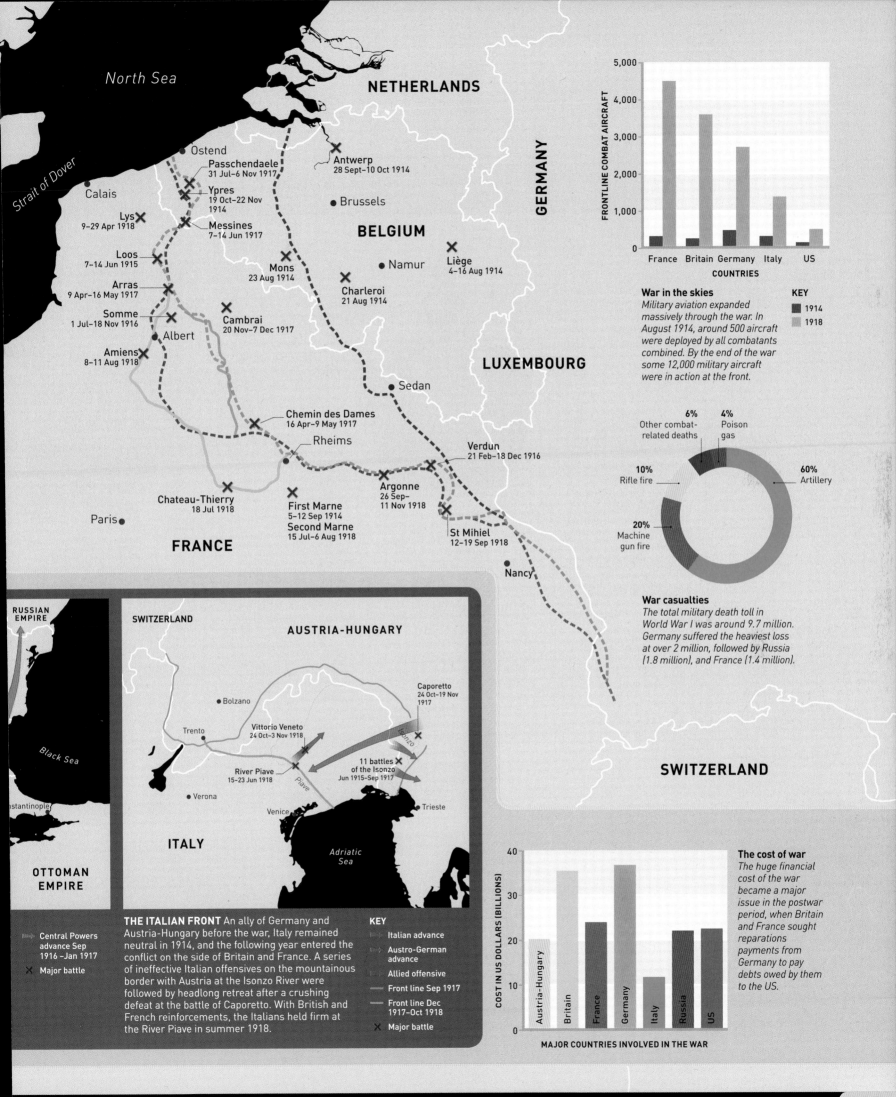

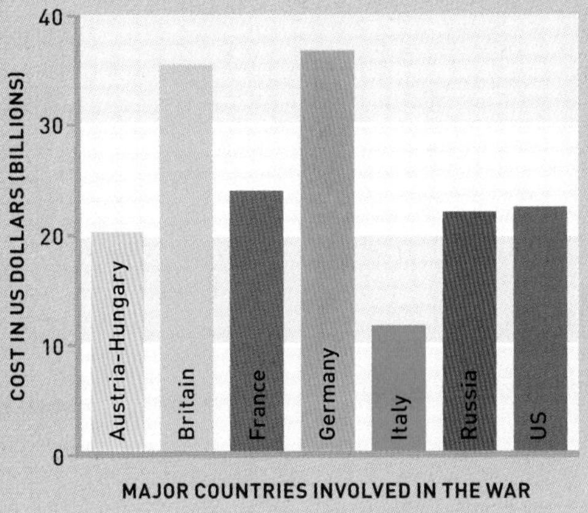

The cost of war
The huge financial cost of the war became a major issue in the postwar period, when Britain and France sought reparations payments from Germany to pay debts owed by them to the US.

1916

This Irish Republican barricade was set up across Townsend Street in Dublin during the Easter Rising to delay the advance of British troops fighting to retake the city.

A YEAR OF BATTLES OF UNPRECEDENTED SCALE opened with a German offensive against the French city of **Verdun** in February (see pp.344–45). German commander-in-chief Erich von Falkenhayn (1861–1922) aimed to "bleed the French army white" by drawing it into costly combat. The French reacted as he had hoped by sending reinforcements to be decimated by the German heavy guns. German losses also mounted up, as French resistance stiffened under the inspirational leadership of General Philippe Pétain (1856–1975). Repeated **German offensives** continued until mid-July, after which **French counteroffensives** succeeded into December. Little territory changed hands and both sides suffered around 400,000 casualties.

Meanwhile, the US was fighting a war on a quite different scale. In March, Mexican general **Pancho Villa** (1878–1923), the flamboyant leader of one of the revolutionary armies engaged in Mexico's ongoing civil war, made a **cross-border raid into the US**. His attack on Columbus, New Mexico, was rebuffed by the US Cavalry. The provocation was too great for the US to ignore, and President Woodrow Wilson (1856–1924) ordered General John Pershing (1860–1948) to lead an expedition into Mexico. Around 5,000 US troops fought engagements with both Villa supporters and Mexican government forces before withdrawing in January 1917.

Bandit leader
Originally a bandit chief, Pancho Villa became a key figure in the Mexican Revolution and Mexico's clash with the US in 1916.

Britain suffered a **military disaster** in the spring in Mesopotamia (Iraq), then part of the Turkish Ottoman Empire. The area had been occupied by British forces from India. From December 1915, Anglo-Indian troops had been **under siege by Turkish forces at Kut-al-Amara**, between Basra and Baghdad. Relief forces failed to fight their way through to Kut, so, facing starvation, they were forced to surrender. Taken prisoner, the British and Indian soldiers endured terrible hardship, less than half surviving captivity.

Prussian *wappen*, or helmet plate

German helmet
The German spiked Pickelhaube helmet was replaced in the course of 1916 by the metal Stahlhelm, which provided better protection.

This disaster was offset by the **Arab revolt against Turkish rule**. Encouraged by Britain, Hussein bin Ali, Sharif of Mecca (1854–1931), launched an uprising in June. Arab forces defeated the Turkish garrisons of Mecca, Medina, and other towns in the Hejaz, and Hussein proclaimed himself Sultan of the Arabs. The British sent **T.E. Lawrence** (1888–1935), a junior officer in Cairo, to act as adviser to Hussein's son Feisal, the most active leader of the revolt. Between them, Lawrence and Feisal organized an effective military force. They used guerrilla tactics to push for the liberation of Arabs throughout the Turkish-ruled Middle East.

In April, **Britain faced a revolt against its rule in Ireland**. The Irish Republican Brotherhood sought German support for a nationalist uprising, but Germany's attempt to supply rifles to the rebels was intercepted by the British. **Republicans** still went ahead with the **uprising on Easter Monday**, occupying key buildings in Dublin, and proclaiming a Provisional Government of the Irish Republic. The British sent troops to Dublin, and after five days of fighting the rebels surrendered. Fifteen republican leaders were executed after a secret trial by a British military court. Although few Irish had supported the rebellion, the executions stimulated a wave of pro-Republican sentiment.

At the end of May, the German High Seas Fleet and the Royal Navy's Grand Fleet met in the **Battle of Jutland** in the North Sea. The British spotted a sortie by the German fleet and sent a far superior naval force to attack it. German Admiral Reinhard Scheer (1863–1928) was caught by surprise, but British Admiral John Jellicoe (1859–1935) failed to profit from the advantage. The German warships were able to make a fighting withdrawal to port, while inflicting heavier losses than they suffered. Despite a disappointing performance, the Royal Navy had confirmed its superiority – it was the German fleet that had retreated.

In June, General Aleksei Brusilov (1853–1926) mounted **Russia's most successful offensive** of World War I, almost destroying the Austrian army in Galicia. The Austrians were only rescued by the arrival of German troops to support them. Brusilov's initial success was based on subtle tactics – surprise and the rapid movement of shock troops to exploit breakthroughs.

Unfortunately, the British did not learn from their Russian allies. On 1 July, General Douglas Haig

GENERAL DOUGLAS HAIG (1861–1928)

Cavalry officer Douglas Haig performed well as a corps commander in the first year of World War I. As British army commander-in-chief, his assaults on German defences at the Somme in 1916 and Passchendaele in 1917 resulted in huge losses. In 1918, Haig held firm in the face of the formidable German spring offensives, then presided over a string of British victories.

9 January Allies complete evacuation from **Gallipoli**

24 January Military Service Act introduces conscription in Britain

16 February Russian Caucasus offensive **seizes Erzurum** from Turkey

21 February Germans launch offensive against French at **Verdun**

25 February French General **Philippe Pétain** takes control of defence of Verdun

6 March Newton Baker appointed **US war secretary**

9 March Mexican general **Pancho Villa** raids Columbus, New Mexico

9 March Germany **declares war** on Portugal after Portuguese seize German ships

14 March US General **John Pershing** leads punitive expedition into Mexico

24 April In Dublin, Irish nationalists stage **uprising against British** rule

29 April Irish **rebels surrender** to British army in Dublin

30 April Anglo-Indian force in Kut surrenders to Turks

3–12 May British **execute** leaders of suppressed Dublin Easter uprising

14 May Austria launches **Trentino offensive** against Italy

16 May Sykes–Picot agreement plans postwar division of Middle East between Britain and France

31 May–1 June British and German fleets clash in inconclusive **battle of Jutland**

3 June US Congress approves **National Defense Act**, expanding armed forces

4 June Russian **Brusilov offensive** begins in Galicia

5 June Sharif Hussein declares Arab independence from Turkish rule, launching **Arab Revolt**

7 June At Verdun, French strong point of **Fort Vaux** falls to Germans

> **“ SUCCESS WILL COME TO** THE SIDE THAT HAS THE **LAST MAN STANDING. ”**
>
> **General Philippe Pétain**, 1916

French soldiers arriving at Verdun in eastern France. The standard tour of duty at the front was eight days – all a man could be expected to stand.

launched a massive offensive at **the Somme** (see pp.344–45). Rather than destroy enemy defences, the eight-day artillery bombardment had alerted the Germans to an imminent attack. British troops marched forward in lines, because the generals believed their conscripted troops were incapable of executing more intelligent tactics, and were mown down by German machine guns. Almost 20,000 men were killed, the **heaviest losses ever experienced by the British army** in a single day's fighting. Haig kept the men fighting for five months, introducing tanks as soon as this new weapon was available, and allowing his subordinates to experiment with varied tactics including night attacks. But there was no breakthrough, and the only result was attrition – a gradual wearing down of the armies.

By the second half of 1916, the strain of two years of warfare had left countries with the option of either ratcheting up their war effort or seeking a path to peace. In August, Germany changed its leadership. General Paul von Hindenburg (1847–1934) and his Quartermaster-General Erich Ludendorff (1865–1937) were given supreme command of the German army and control of the entire German war effort. In order to wring every drop of productivity out of German industry they created a state-directed economy that has been dubbed "**war socialism**". By contrast, their Austrian allies were losing their will to fight. The death of Emperor Franz Josef I (1830–1916) in November marked the beginning of the **end of the Austrian Empire**. His successor, Charles I (1887–1922), was desperate for a way out of the war.

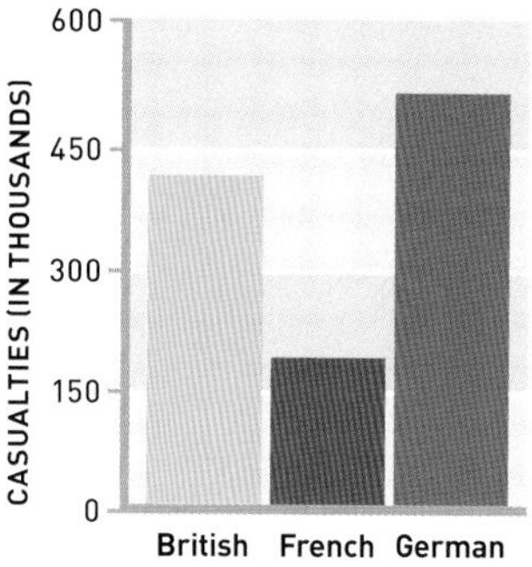

Casualties of the Somme offensive
The Somme was one of the bloodiest battles of the war. Between 1 July and 18 November over a million men were killed or wounded.

The collective madness of the battlefield provoked an **influential art movement** that gave itself the nonsense name **Dada**. Dadaists such as Hugo Ball and Hans Arp gathered at the Cabaret Voltaire in Zurich, in neutral Switzerland, and advocated a crazy anti-art that satirized a world afflicted by mass slaughter. Their anarchic works rejected the social order that legitimized war.

A more rational spokesman for peace was **President Woodrow Wilson, elected for a second term** of office in November. As the man who had kept the US out of the European war, Wilson put himself forward as a peacemaker. He issued a "**peace note**" that called on combatant countries to state their war aims as a prelude to ceasefire negotiations. Germany's civilian government came up with its own "peace offer", but the country's military leaders would not permit any of the concessions that might have made peace a practical possibility.

The **Russian Empire** was desperate for an end to the fighting, and its tsarist regime was leaking popular support. In December, court conspirators assassinated Grigori **Rasputin** (1869–1916), an hirsute "holy man" whose hold over the tsar's wife had become a public scandal. The assassination was widely welcomed, but it could not halt the tsarist **government's slide toward collapse**.

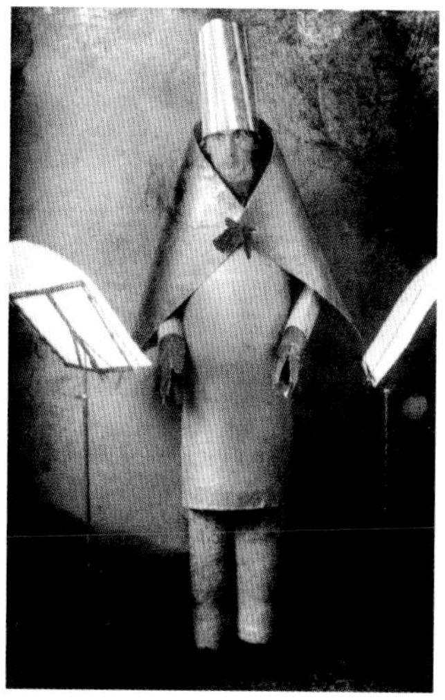

Performing artists
Leading Dada artist Hugo Ball performing at Cabaret Voltaire, which he founded in 1916. Dadaists protested against the war.

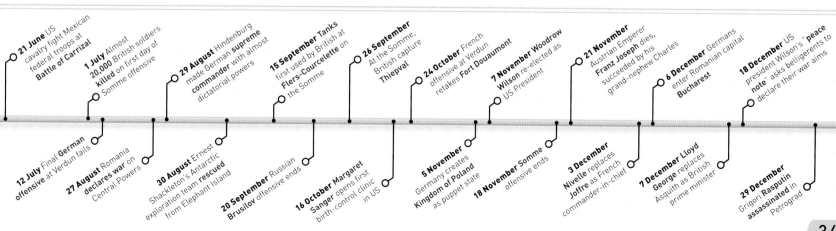

Going over the top
British soldiers prepare to attack during the Battle of the Somme, leaving the relative shelter of the trench for exposed ground.

21 June US cavalry fight Mexican federal troops at **Battle of Carrizal**

1 July Almost 20,000 British soldiers **killed** on first day of Somme offensive

12 July Final **German offensive** at Verdun fails

27 August Romania **declares war** on Central Powers

29 August Hindenburg made German **supreme commander** with almost dictatorial powers

30 August Ernest Shackleton's Antarctic exploration team **rescued** from Elephant Island

15 September Tanks first used by British at **Flers-Courcelette** on the Somme

20 September Russian **Brusilov** offensive ends

26 September At the Somme, British capture **Thiepval**

16 October Margaret Sanger opens first birth-control clinic in US

24 October French offensive at Verdun retakes **Fort Douaumont**

5 November Germany creates **Kingdom of Poland** as puppet state

7 November Woodrow Wilson re-elected as US President

18 November Somme offensive ends

21 November Austrian Emperor **Franz Joseph** dies, succeeded by his grand-nephew Charles

3 December Nivelle replaces **Joffre** as French commander-in-chief

6 December Germans enter Romanian capital **Bucharest**

7 December Lloyd George replaces Asquith as British prime minister

18 December US president Wilson's "**peace note**" asks belligerents to declare their war aims

29 December Grigori **Rasputin assassinated** in Petrograd

Armed workers and soldiers taking part in the overthrow of Russia's Provisional Government by the Bolsheviks in Petrograd. They established a communist revolutionary regime.

ON 9 JANUARY, GERMAN KAISER WILHELM II (1859–1941) approved the decision of his military commanders to engage in **unlimited submarine warfare**. The Germans knew that this would mean sinking American merchant vessels and would probably bring the neutral US into the war, but they believed they could sink enough ships to force Britain to sue for peace and make US intervention ineffectual. When an American cargo ship, the *Housatonic*, was sunk by a U-boat on 3 February off the Scilly Isles, the US broke off diplomatic relations with Germany.

Anticipating US entry into the war, German foreign minister Arthur Zimmermann decided to offer Mexico an alliance, encouraging them to fight to regain Texas, New Mexico, and Arizona from the US. A **telegram from Zimmerman** detailing this plan was intercepted, decoded by British intelligence, and passed to the US government. When it was published in the US press it caused a sensation, stoking anti-German feeling already ignited by the U-boat campaign.

Propaganda poster
New York's Mayor's Committee on National Defense declared 19 April "Wake Up America Day", and publicized it with this poster.

VLADIMIR ILYICH LENIN (1870–1924)

Born into Russian minor gentry, Vladimir Ilyich Ulyanov became a Marxist activist, adopting the name "Lenin". Living in exile in Western Europe, he led the Bolsheviks from 1903. Returning to Russia in 1917, he was determined to radicalize the revolution through a Bolshevik seizure of power. Once in control he ruthlessly stamped out all opposition, and founded the world's first communist state.

On 2 April, US president Woodrow Wilson (1856–1924) asked Congress to vote for a war "to make the world safe for democracy". Four days later the **US declared war on Germany**, keeping independence of action by not formally allying itself with Britain and France. The slow process of building and equipping a mass conscript army began.

While the US was entering the war, Russia was caught up in revolutionary turmoil. A momentous sequence of events was triggered by food riots, strikes, and a mutiny of soldiers in Petrograd (St Petersburg). On 15 March, **Tsar Nicholas II (1868–1918) abdicated** and a Provisional Government was established by politicians from the Duma (Russian parliament). Committees set up by workers and soldiers, known as "soviets", created a competing focus of political power. On 16 April, **Vladimir Ilyich Lenin** (see panel, left), leader of the extremist Bolshevik Party, returned to Petrograd from exile in Switzerland. Lenin sought to radicalize the revolution by proposing an end to the war and "all power to the soviets".

The dominant personality in the Provisional Government, moderate socialist **Alexander Kerensky** (1881–1970), was committed to continuing the war. The failure of the campaign he launched on 1 July, known as the **Kerensky Offensive**, was followed by widespread mutinies in the army at the front and desertion. Attempts to suppress the Bolsheviks failed. The Provisional Government survived a coup attempt, but on 7 November it succumbed to an armed takeover organized by Lenin's associate, **Leon Trotsky** (1879–1940). Lenin set up a **revolutionary government** of People's Commissars and proclaimed a unilateral armistice.

Meanwhile, on the Western front stalemate and slaughter continued. At the start of the year newly appointed French commander-in-chief Robert Nivelle (1856–1924) promised a crushing onslaught that would win the war in days. When the **Nivelle Offensive** was launched in mid-April, however, it proved no more successful than previous offensives. The disappointment was bitter. There were widespread mutinies and the French army threatened to disintegrate. Hastily appointed to replace Nivelle, General Philippe Pétain (1856–1951) restored order with a mixture of concessions and punishments, and ruled out any further French offensives.

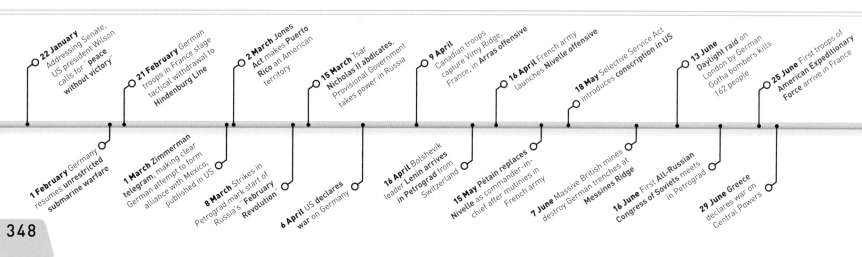

22 January Addressing Senate, US president Wilson calls for "**peace without victory**"

1 February Germany resumes **unrestricted submarine warfare**

21 February German troops in France stage tactical withdrawal to **Hindenburg Line**

1 March Zimmerman telegram, making clear German attempt to form alliance with Mexico, published in US

2 March Jones Act makes **Puerto Rico** an American territory

8 March Strikes in Petrograd mark start of Russia's "**February Revolution**"

15 March Tsar **Nicholas II abdicates**, Provisional Government takes power in Russia

6 April US **declares war** on Germany

9 April Canadian troops capture Vimy Ridge, France, in **Arras offensive**

16 April Bolshevik leader **Lenin arrives in Petrograd** from Switzerland

16 April French army launches **Nivelle offensive**

15 May Pétain replaces Nivelle as commander-in-chief after mutinies in French army

18 May Selective Service Act introduces **conscription in US**

7 June Massive British mines destroy German trenches at **Messines Ridge**

13 June Daylight raid on London by German Gotha bombers kills 162 people

16 June First **All-Russian Congress of Soviets** meets in Petrograd

25 June First troops of **American Expeditionary Force** arrive in France

29 June Greece declares war on Central Powers

> **“** THE **WORKERS’** AND **PEASANTS’** GOVERNMENT… **PROPOSES** TO ALL **WARRING PEOPLES… NEGOTIATIONS** LEADING TO A JUST, **DEMOCRATIC PEACE. ”**
>
> **Lenin**, 8 November 1917

These British Mark IV tanks are transported to the Cambrai offensive. They carry bundles of wood to fill the trenches, so that they can drive across them.

The British army remained committed to an offensive strategy. In the second half of the year General Douglas Haig (1856–1951) began **a new push at Ypres** (see pp.344–345), hoping to break through to the ports where German U-boats were based. Haig's offensive ran into persistent bad weather that reduced the battlefield to a sea of mud. The offensive persisted into November, until British and Canadian troops reached **Passchendaele**, the village that finally gave its name to the battle.

The mud in Flanders rendered tanks, an increasingly important element of British weaponry, inoperative. On harder ground at **Cambrai** in November, massed tanks helped British forces advance 6km (4 miles) in one day – three times the distance achieved at Passchendaele in three months. Any celebrations were premature, however, as a German counter attack soon retook most of the lost ground.

3 THE NUMBER OF **CREW** THAT FLEW AND OPERATED A **GERMAN GOTHA BOMBER**

The long stalemate between Italy and Austria–Hungary ended when German troops were transferred to the Italian front in October. At the **Battle of Caporetto**, an Austro-German offensive drove Italian forces into retreat. A line was stabilized in November behind the Piave River, just 30km (19 miles) from Venice (see p.345).

From June, civilians living in Paris and London were subjected to sporadic **air attacks by German Gotha bombers** and even larger "R-planes". These fixed-wing aircraft were faster and more difficult to shoot down than the German airships (see 1915), although defence by anti-aircraft guns and fighter aircraft soon forced them to attack exclusively by night. Physical damage and casualties were not great, but the psychological impact of these raids was considerable, as citizens were driven to hide underground in cellars and subway stations.

Dawn breaks at Passchendaele
Dead and wounded soldiers lie in the muddy desolation of the battlefield in the Ypres salient, where the battle of Passchendale was fought.

In all combatant countries war weariness and worsening conditions made it hard for governments to maintain solidarity. Food shortages and socialist sentiments, excited by the revolutionary uprising in Russia, led to widespread **strike action in German factories**. The German Reichstag (parliament) passed a resolution calling for peace negotiations in July, but it had no control over the military-dominated German government.

In France, scandals and strikes rocked the political system through the summer and autumn, but the appointment of the fiercely pro-war Georges Clemenceau (1841–1929) as prime minister in November stiffened resolve.

The British royal family, meanwhile, found it prudent to change their name from the Germanic Saxe-Coburg and Gotha to Windsor.

The British public was cheered in December by the **capture of Jerusalem from Turkey**. This military success gave practical importance to the previous month's **Balfour Declaration**, which expressed British government support for Zionist aspirations to "a national home for the Jewish people in Palestine". Britain's Arab allies, fighting alongside the British army against the Turks, had not been consulted.

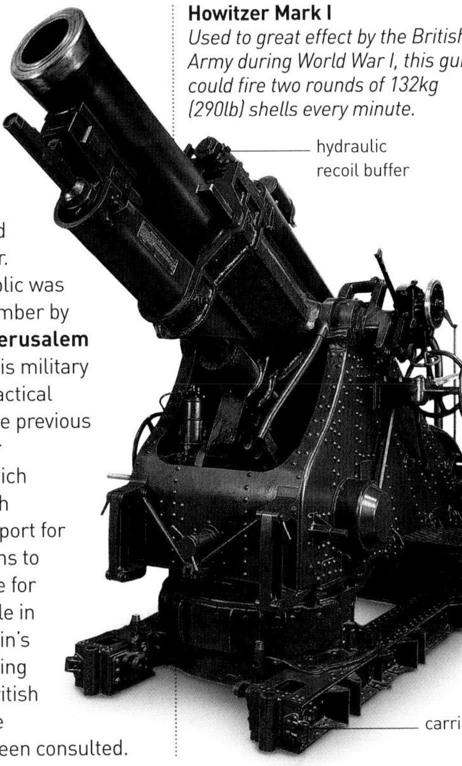

Howitzer Mark I
Used to great effect by the British Army during World War I, this gun could fire two rounds of 132kg (290lb) shells every minute.

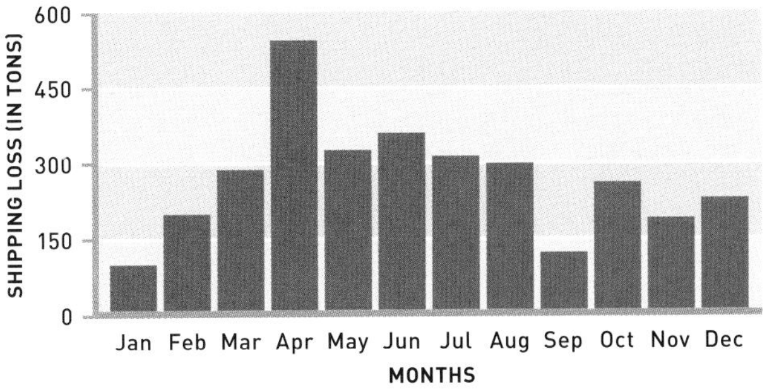

British merchant shipping losses to U-boats
German unrestricted submarine warfare increased attacks on merchant ships from February to April. The adoption of a convoy system in May reduced sinkings to a sustainable level.

1 July Russians launch **Kerensky offensive** in Galicia

16–20 July Russian government **cracks down on Bolsheviks** after disturbances in Petrograd

17 July British royal family changes name to **Windsor**

19 July German Reichstag passes **"peace resolution"**

20 July Corfu Declaration – Serbs, Croats, and Slovenes agree to create **Yugoslavia**

20 July Kerensky becomes head of **Russian Provisional Government**

31 July British launch offensive in **Ypres sector**

14 August China declares war on **Central Powers**

1 September Successful German offensive launched at **Riga**

9 September Attempted coup by Russian commander-in-chief Kornilov fails

15 October Margarethe Zelle, known as **Mata Hari**, executed in France as German spy

24 October Italian army suffers shattering defeat at **Caporetto**

2 November Balfour Declaration commits Britain to a homeland for Jews in Palestine

6 November British and Canadian troops capture **Passchendaele Ridge at Ypres**

7 November Lenin's **Bolsheviks seize power** in Petrograd

20 November Massed tanks cause short-lived British breakthrough at **Cambrai**

5 December General **Sidonio Pais** takes power in **Portugal** in military coup

6 December Over 2,000 people die when munitions **ship explodes** in port at Halifax, Nova Scotia

9 December British take **Jerusalem** from Turks

20 December Bolshevik government founds **Cheka secret police organization**

22 December Bolsheviks open **peace negotiations** with Germany at **Brest-Litovsk**

Revolutionary hero
DATE UNKNOWN
In this painting for a poster from the 1917 Revolution period, Lenin appears in front of the battleship *Aurora*, which was used in the Bolshevik seizure of power.

Red horsemen
*c.*1920
The 1917 revolution was followed by the Russian Civil War, between the Bolsheviks and the "White" armies led by tsarist officers. This poster is dedicated "to the peoples of the Caucasus Red Army".

SOVIET PROPAGANDA

ART FOR THE FURTHERANCE OF COMMUNIST POLITICAL IDEOLOGY AND REVOLUTIONARY IDEALS

For the communists who seized power in Russia in November 1917, art had to serve the socialist revolution and disseminate its ideology. Propaganda mobilized the populace in support of the regime and pilloried its enemies.

During the early phase of communist rule, many avant-garde artists believed their revolutionary ways of making art would accord with the political revolution. However, under the dictatorship of Joseph Stalin, from the late 1920s Soviet artists were required to depict workers and peasants in a heroic-realist style, their images reflecting the supposed happiness and progress of communist life.

Modernist poster
1919
Avant-garde artist El Lissitzky produced this Civil War poster. His red wedge represents the communist Red Army beating the anti-communist White armies.

The Revolution needs you
1928
The labour force underwent radical reorganization under the communists. This poster urges Soviet citizens to become members of workers' co-operatives.

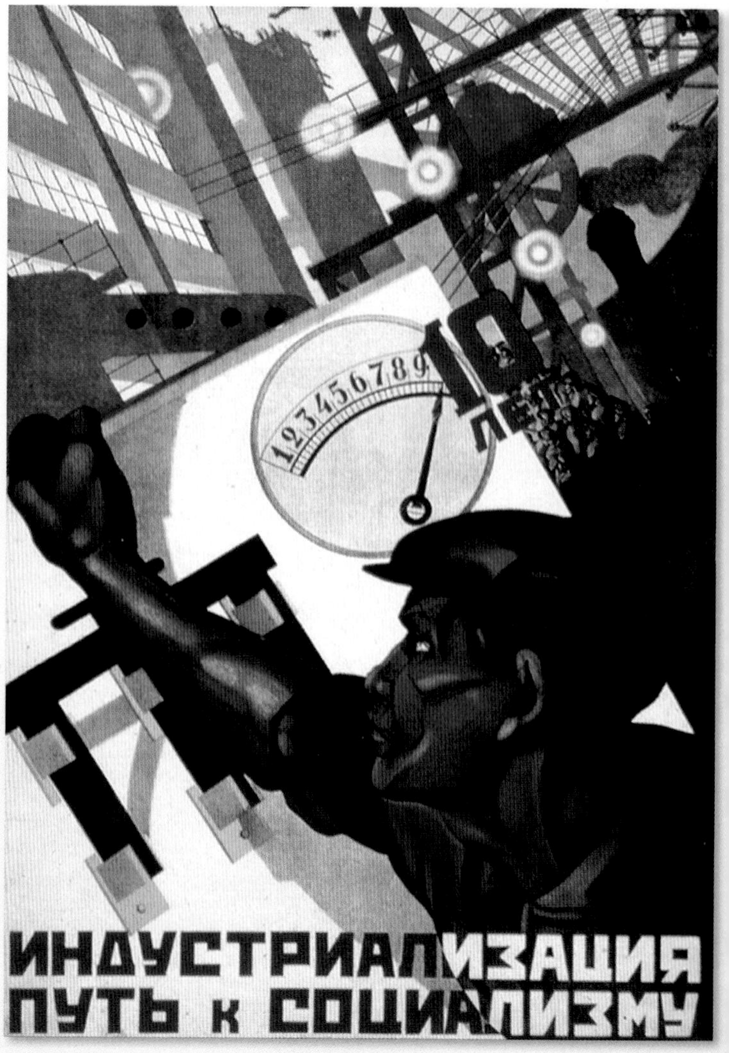

Rapid industrialization
1928
The communist leadership launched an industrialization drive in the late 1920s. Workers are compelled to increase production by this poster.

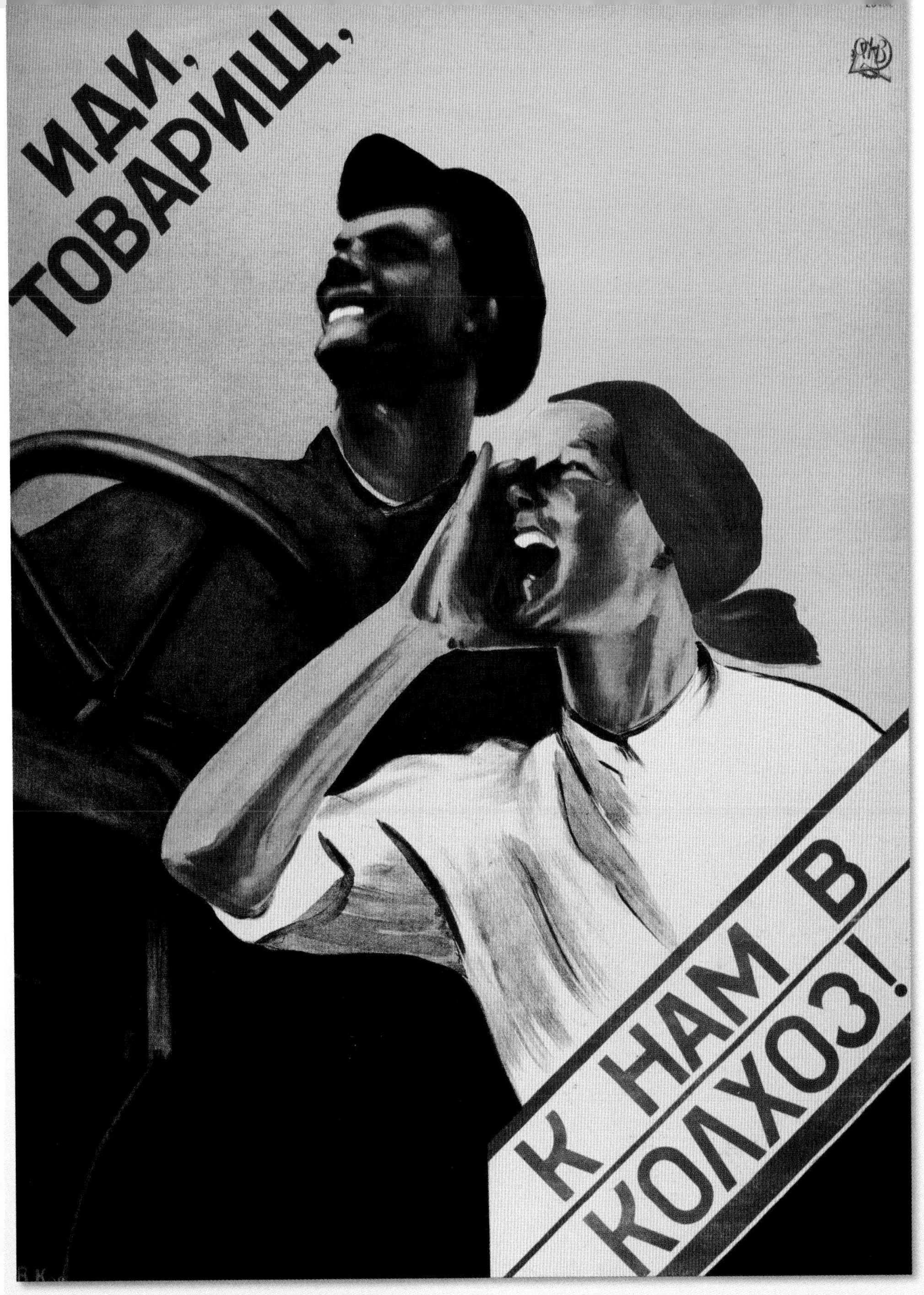

Collectivization
1930
A tractor driver and peasant woman call on their comrades to join a collective farm during Stalin's brutal drive to abolish private farms.

grand schemes to rebuild Moscow were derailed by World War II

Life under Stalin
1930s
Celebrating the unity and strength of the Soviet people under the banner of Stalin, this poster proclaims: "Onward to the heights of joy and happiness of mankind".

Military strength
1940s
A poster of the World War II era depicts bomber aircraft and a Soviet airman displaying the obligatory optimism of any communist citizen portrayed in Stalinist art.

Commemorating victory
1940s
The slogan on this poster commemorating the Soviet victory in World War II says: "Having won the war, the soldier has brought spring".

pig-like capitalist being held up

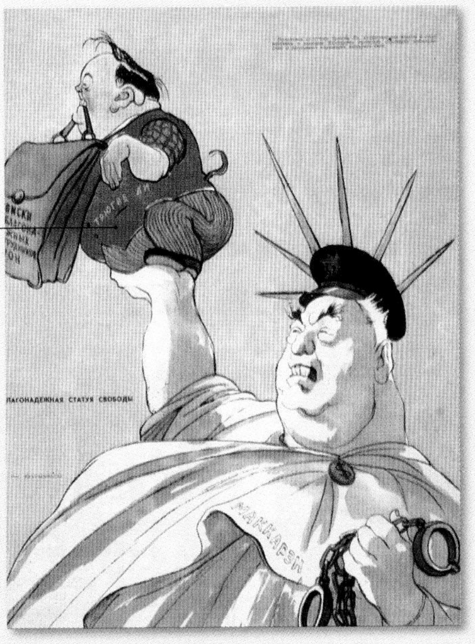

Cold War propaganda
1950s
This anti-American poster from the Cold War caricatures the Statue of Liberty, portraying the US as bloatedly capitalist and militaristic.

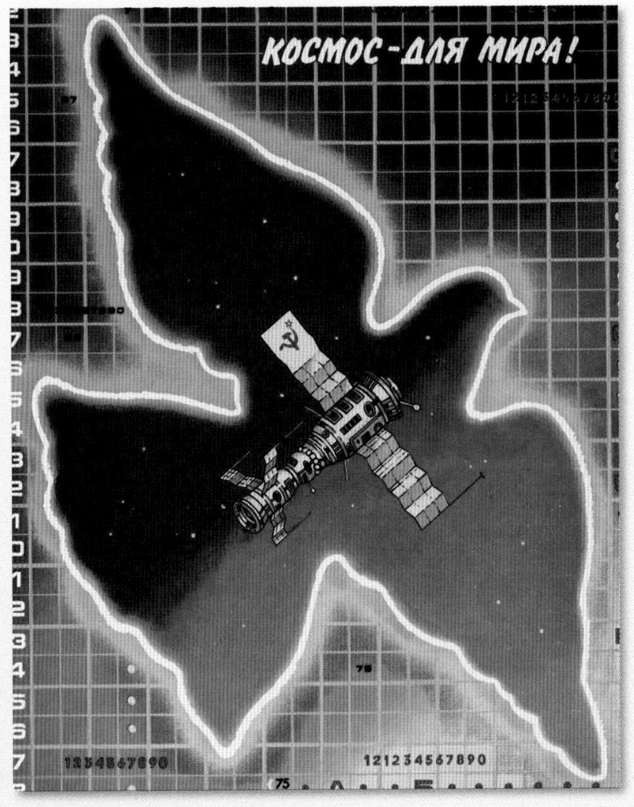

Peace and progress
1970s
A Salyut space station is superimposed on a dove of peace in this poster from the era of "peaceful coexistence" with the capitalist world.

1918

German prisoners of war in France – in the last three months of the war 363,000 German soldiers were captured by the advancing Allies.

ALTHOUGH THE US ENTERED WORLD WAR I IN APRIL 1917, at the start of 1918 its Expeditionary Force in Europe was still not ready for combat. Despite this, in anticipation of victory, US President Woodrow Wilson announced a **14-point programme** for a just and durable peace. His proposals included freedom of the seas and free trade, general disarmament, self-determination for European peoples who did not have their own nation-states, and an international organization to guarantee new borders against aggressors. Germany would have to hand back the territory it had occupied during the war as well as Alsace–Lorraine, which was taken from France in 1871.

The Germans had quite different ideas, however. In March, they used their military dominance over the newly installed Bolshevik government (see 1917) to impose punitive peace terms on Russia through the **Treaty of Brest-Litovsk**, which marked Russia's exit from World War I. With Poland, Ukraine, Belarus, Finland, and the Baltic States nominally independent as client states of Germany, the treaty deprived Russia of about a third of its pre-war population. The German military authorities then set about ruthlessly exploiting resources in the eastern regions they now controlled.

The humiliating treaty did not bring peace to Russia, which was already slipping into civil war. Determined to concentrate all the power in Bolshevik hands, **Lenin forcibly dispersed a democratically elected Constituent Assembly** in January – the Bolsheviks had won only 25 per cent of votes cast. His regime faced opposition from groups as diverse as rival socialist revolutionaries, tsarist generals, Ukrainian anarchists, and Don Cossacks. Lenin survived an assassination attempt in August, but throughout the year ever larger areas of Russia fell out of his followers' control.

Meanwhile, relieved of the need to fight a war on two fronts, Germany attempted to win a decisive victory in the west before American manpower could irreversibly tip the balance. On 21 March, the **Spring Offensive or "Kaiserschlacht"** struck the British line on the Somme front.

An initial bombardment by 9,000 guns and mortars, with munitions including 2 million gas shells, prepared the way for an infantry attack spearheaded by German Stormtroopers, many armed with flamethrowers. More than 20,000 British troops surrendered on the first day of the offensive, and by 25 March the leading German units had advanced 65km (40 miles). **The stalemate that had lasted on the Western front since 1914 was at an end.**

In early April, the Germans opened a fresh offensive at Lys in Flanders. In an emotional appeal to his troops, British commander General Douglas Haig (1861–1928) declared: "With our backs to the wall and believing in the justice of our cause, each one of us must fight on to the end." More practically, the French general **Ferdinand Foch (1851–1929) was appointed Supreme Commander** to co-ordinate the operations of the Allied armies, including US troops. Although the Allies made further retreats and remained on the defensive until July, the Germans failed to achieve the decisive success they needed.

One victim of the fighting in April was Germany's most renowned air ace, Manfred von Richthofen (1892–1918). **The "Red Baron" was shot dead** by ground fire while engaged in a dogfight with Canadian pilot Roy Brown over the Allied lines. His death symbolized the exhaustion of Germany's war effort. Richthofen's fighter wing, known to the British as the "Flying Circus", had an impressive reputation in combat and the Baron himself was credited with 80 "kills". But the German pilots were overwhelmed by the sheer number of allied aircraft – British and French factories built 55,000 aircraft in 1918 alone.

By June, over a **million American soldiers were in France**, under the command of General John Pershing (1860–1948). Their contribution was vital to stabilizing the Allied line in the face of German offensives. The fighting qualities of the US

MURDER OF THE RUSSIAN ROYAL FAMILY

After abdicating in 1917, Tsar Nicholas II, his wife, four daughters, and only son were sent to Siberia, where they lived in reasonable comfort. But in April 1918 the family was moved to Ekaterinburg in the Urals and placed under close guard by local Bolsheviks. On the night of 16–17 July Bolshevik secret police had the entire family shot in a cellar, along with their doctor and servants. Their bodies were buried and not discovered until 1991.

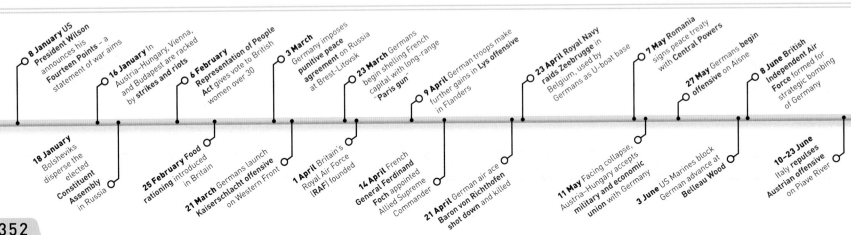

Poster of a German aircraft
A German poster advertising an exhibition of items captured in the air war. Most World War I aircraft were made of canvas and wood.

- **8 January US President Wilson** announces his **Fourteen Points** – a statement of war aims
- **16 January** In Austria-Hungary, Vienna, and Budapest are racked by **strikes and riots**
- **18 January** Bolsheviks disperse the elected **Constituent Assembly** in Russia
- **6 February Representation of People Act** gives vote to British women over 30
- **25 February Food rationing** introduced in Britain
- **3 March** Germany imposes **punitive peace agreement** on Russia at Brest-Litovsk
- **21 March** Germans launch **Kaiserschlacht offensive** on Western Front
- **23 March** Germans begin shelling French capital with long-range **"Paris gun"**
- **1 April** Britain's Royal Air Force **(RAF)** founded
- **9 April** German troops make further gains in **Lys offensive** in Flanders
- **14 April** French **General Ferdinand Foch** appointed Allied Supreme Commander
- **21 April** German air ace **Baron von Richthofen shot down** and killed
- **23 April Royal Navy raids Zeebrugge** in Belgium, used by Germans as U-boat base
- **7 May Romania** signs peace treaty with **Central Powers**
- **11 May** Facing collapse, Austria-Hungary accepts **military and economic union** with Germany
- **27 May** Germans **begin offensive** on Aisne
- **3 June** US Marines block German advance at **Belleau Wood**
- **8 June British Independent Air Force** formed for strategic bombing of Germany
- **10–23 June** Italy **repulses Austrian offensive** on Piave River

> **“ I HOPE WE MAY ALL SAY THAT THUS, THIS FATEFUL MORNING, CAME TO AN END ALL WARS. ”**
>
> **David Lloyd George, British Prime Minister**, 11 November 1918

British soldiers, an American sailor, and a Red Cross nurse celebrate the signing of the armistice on 11 November, ending four years of mass slaughter.

Marines particularly impressed their German enemies – a German reference to the Marines as "Devil Dogs" stuck as a nickname for the Corps.

The **turning point** was an **attack at Amiens** on 8 August, spearheaded by Australian and Canadian infantry, and supported by massed British and French tanks. Described by the German general Erich Ludendorff (1865–1937) as "the black day of the German army", it initiated the "Hundred Days" of relentless Allied offensives, with large-scale use of tanks and aircraft.

In September, Pershing achieved his ambition of commanding an independent US operation – the capture of the **St Mihiel salient**. This was followed by a combined American and French offensive in the **Argonne forest**, the costliest single battle in American history with 117,000 US casualties.

On 29 September, with their Hindenburg Line defences breached and their ally Bulgaria on the point of surrender, the **Germans sought an armistice**. They approached President Wilson (1856–1924), hoping to make a deal with the US, but Wilson aligned himself with the British and French who insisted that Germany should surrender. Although German troops were still putting up a stubborn defence, and there were not yet any Allied troops on German soil, the country was disintegrating from within. A mutiny in the German navy at the end of October was followed by strikes and socialist uprisings in major cities, where food shortages had fuelled political discontent.

Germany's main allies, Turkey and Austria–Hungary, stopped fighting. On 9 November, the Social Democrat Philipp Scheidemann declared Germany a republic, and Kaiser Wilhelm II (1859–1941) fled to the Netherlands. Two days later a German delegation **signed an armistice** in a railway carriage in the Compiègne forest. The guns fell silent at 11 a.m. on 11 November.

50 MILLION PEOPLE DIED IN THE FLU PANDEMIC OF 1918–19

Peace celebrations erupted in London, Paris, and other Allied cities, but even in the victor countries the reaction was muted by the memory of the millions that had died. There were no celebrations in the collapsed empires destroyed by the conflict – Germany, Austria, Russia, and Turkey – which faced an uncertain future amid political turmoil.

Meanwhile, a global pandemic of "**Spanish Flu**" was at its peak. One of the worst natural disasters in human history, the spread of the disease was probably aided by large-scale movements of troops and by the weakened immune systems of populations suffering from malnutrition. The disease killed more than 50 million people.

Troop numbers and deaths
Around 65 million men fought in World War I, of whom 8.5 million died. Germany suffered the highest number of casualties.

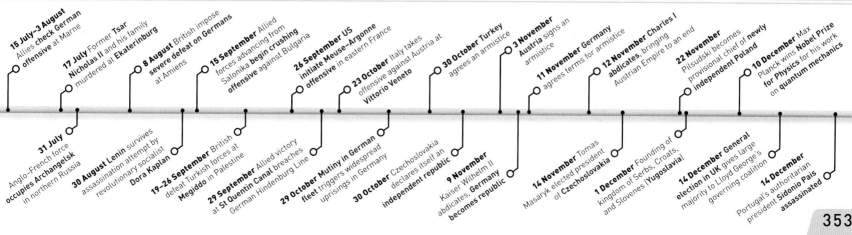

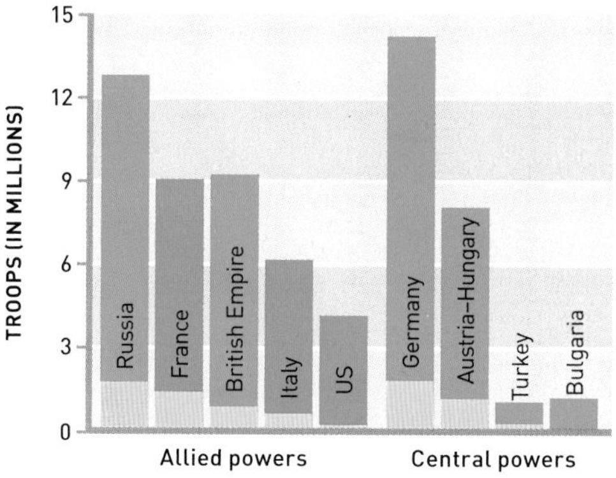

Signing the armistice
The Allied delegation, led by Marshal Foch, photographed outside the railway carriage at Compiègne where the armistice was signed.

- **15 July–3 August** Allies check German offensive at Marne
- **17 July** Former Tsar Nicholas II and his family murdered at Ekaterinburg
- **31 July** Anglo-French force **occupies Archangelsk** in northern Russia
- **8 August** British impose **severe defeat on Germans** at Amiens
- **30 August Lenin** survives assassination attempt by revolutionary socialist **Dora Kaplan**
- **15 September** Allied forces advancing from Salonika **begin crushing offensive** against Bulgaria
- **19–26 September** British defeat Turkish forces at **Megiddo** in Palestine
- **26 September US initiate Meuse-Argonne offensive** in eastern France
- **29 September** Allied victory at **St Quentin Canal** breaches German Hindenburg Line
- **23 October** Italy takes offensive against Austria at **Vittorio Veneto**
- **29 October Mutiny** in German **fleet** triggers widespread uprisings in Germany
- **30 October** Czechoslovakia declares itself an **independent republic**
- **30 October Turkey** agrees an armistice
- **3 November Austria** signs an armistice
- **9 November** Kaiser Wilhelm II abdicates, **Germany becomes republic**
- **11 November Germany** agrees terms for armistice
- **12 November Charles I abdicates**, bringing Austrian Empire to an end
- **14 November** Tomas Masaryk elected president of **Czechoslovakia**
- **22 November** Pilsudski becomes provisional chief of **newly independent Poland**
- **1 December** Founding of kingdom of Serbs, Croats, and Slovenes **(Yugoslavia)**
- **10 December** Max Planck wins **Nobel Prize for Physics** for his work **on quantum mechanics**
- **14 December General election in UK** gives large majority to Lloyd George's governing coalition
- **14 December** Portugal's authoritarian president **Sidonio Pais assassinated**

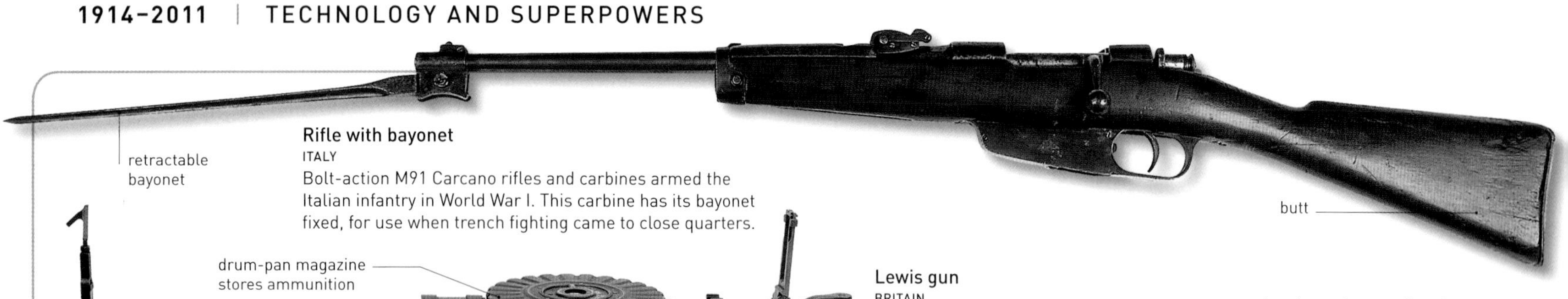

Rifle with bayonet
ITALY
Bolt-action M91 Carcano rifles and carbines armed the Italian infantry in World War I. This carbine has its bayonet fixed, for use when trench fighting came to close quarters.

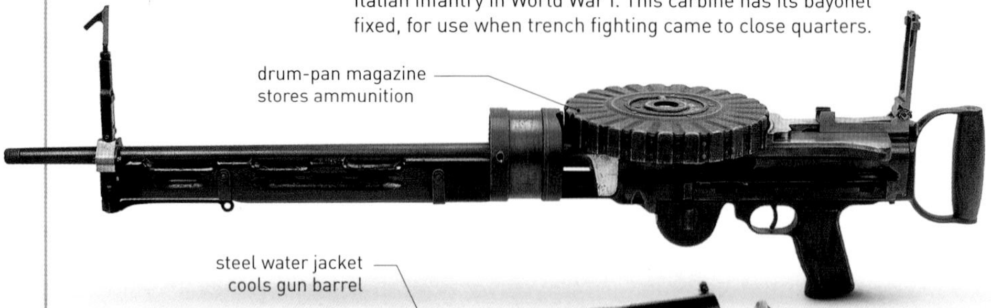

Lewis gun
BRITAIN
Originally an American design, the Lewis gun was adopted by the British Army as its standard light machine gun in 1915. It armed aircraft and tanks, as well as infantry.

Maxim machine gun
GERMANY
The German Army's heavy machine gun, the Maschinengewehr '08, was derived from the gun invented by American Hiram Maxim in 1884. It could fire 400 rounds a minute.

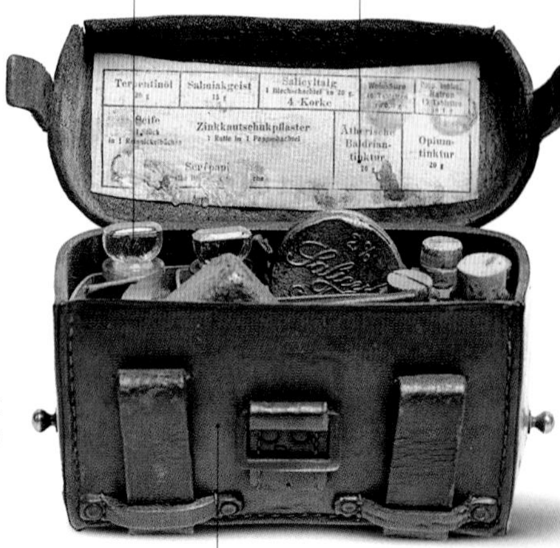

First-aid pouch
GERMANY
German medical orderlies carried a pouch containing basic painkillers and antiseptics, such as iodine, to treat wounded men before they were sent to dressing stations.

WORLD WAR I

MASS-PRODUCED WEAPONRY ALLOWS THE SLAUGHTER OF MILLIONS

World War I has been described as "industrial warfare" as manpower and economic resources of industrialized states were mobilized for fighting. Modern firearms provided armies with firepower on an unprecedented scale.

Formidable defensive systems of trenches, barbed wire, and machine-gun posts made offensive operations costly and tended to lead to stalemate. Weapons used in trench warfare ranged from grenades and flamethrowers to homemade clubs and knives. From 1916, the first slow and unreliable tanks made their appearance. Aircraft added a new dimension to warfare, carrying out reconnaissance and bombing, and strafing ground targets.

Artillery shells
FRANCE
Artillery ammunition in World War I ranged from shrapnel to high-explosive and gas shells. These shells were fired by the French 75-mm field gun.

Howitzer
BRITAIN
Howitzers such as this 6-inch British gun were effective in trench warfare because they sent a shell in a high trajectory, dropping onto the concealed enemy.

Officer's compass
BRITAIN

A compass was vital on a night patrol or raid. Without it, soldiers could lose their way in the no man's land betweed the trenches, rendered featureless by shelling.

Stereoscopic periscope
GERMANY

Soldiers in trenches used periscopes to keep watch on the enemy line. Snipers quickly picked off men who exposed their heads above the parapet.

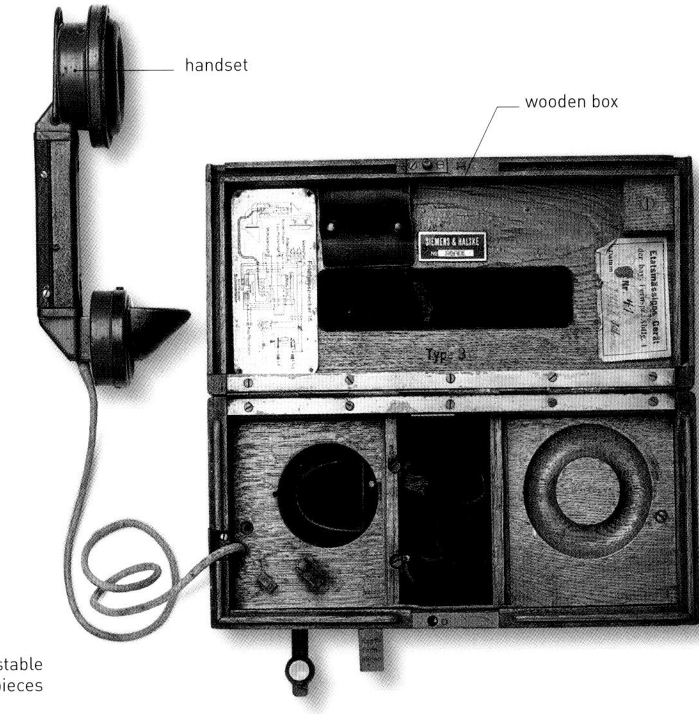

Field telephone
GERMANY

Although radios were also used, field telephones were the main communications link in trench warfare. When telephone cables had been ripped up by shellfire, runners carried messages to the front line by hand.

Gas mask
GERMANY

Effective masks were developed that protected the eyes and face from contact with poison gas and, through a filter respirator, neutralized the gas for breathing.

Folding shovel
ITALY

For an infantryman, a shovel was essential equipment, needed to dig trenches or temporary shelters. This folding shovel was used by Italian alpine troops.

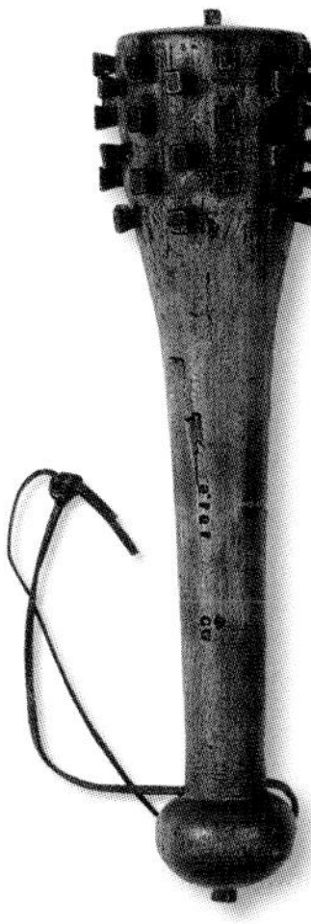

Nail club
BRITAIN

Primitive wooden clubs, with nails or other metal objects at the striking end, were used by soldiers on both sides as a silent, deadly weapon in trench raids.

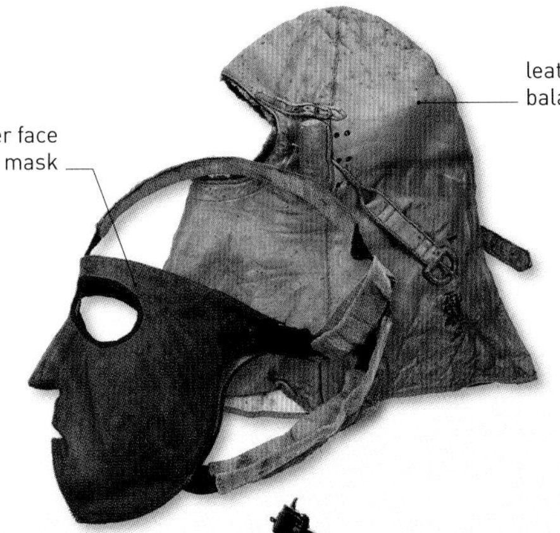

Aviator's headgear
BRITAIN

Flying in open cockpit aircraft, many aviators in World War I wore leather balaclavas and face masks to protect themselves against the cold and wind.

Turkish bayonet and grenade
TURKEY

The Turkish Army in World War I had some obsolete equipment, such as swords and bayonets, but also state-of-the-art German-supplied weaponry such as fragmentation grenades.

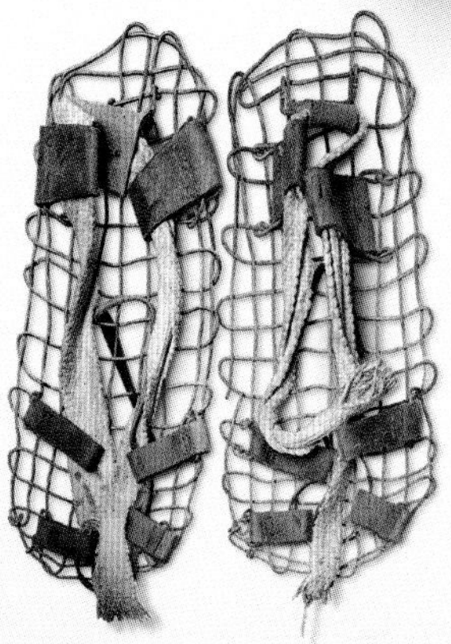

Desert shoes
BRITAIN

British troops fighting against the Turks in the Palestine campaign sometimes wore wire sand shoes over their army boots to facilitate marching on desert sands.

Tank helmet
BRITAIN

British tank crews found that when bullets struck their armoured vehicle, metal shards flew inside the hull. Helmets protecting the head and face were swiftly adopted to limit injuries.

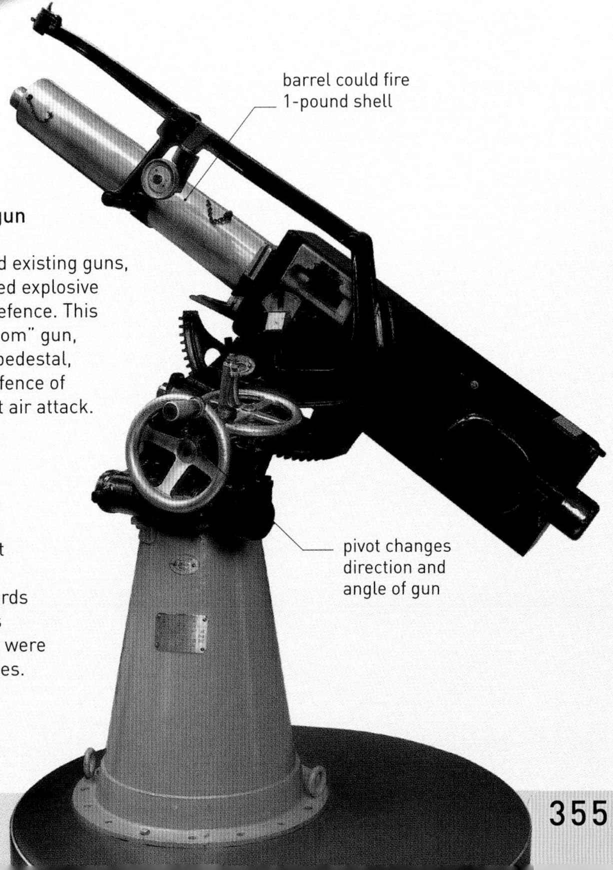

Anti-aircraft gun
BRITAIN

Armies adapted existing guns, firing time-fused explosive shells for air defence. This British "pom-pom" gun, mounted on a pedestal, was used in defence of London against air attack.

The "Big Four" – David Lloyd George, Vittorio Orlando, Georges Clemenceau, and Woodrow Wilson – meet amiably at the Paris Peace Conference.

IN JANUARY 1919, LEADERS OF THE VICTOR COUNTRIES FROM WORLD WAR I met for a peace conference in Paris. US President Woodrow Wilson's liberal idealism was the focus for popular hopes that a new and better world would be built on the ruins of the old. Wilson was one of the **"Big Four"** who dominated the proceedings in Paris, the others being French prime minister Georges Clemenceau (1841–1929), British prime minister David Lloyd George (1863–1945), and Italian prime minister Vittorio Orlando (1860–1952). Each European leader had his own agenda, inevitably dominated by issues of national self-interest. Wilson's idealism expressed itself in an agreement to create a **League of Nations**, which was to provide "collective security" against aggression and replace war by the negotiated settlement of disputes, but Clemenceau believed the best guarantee for the future peace of France was in a permanent weakening of Germany.

Defeat in war had reduced Germany to a state of economic and social collapse. In January, communist revolutionaries, known as **the Spartacists**, tried to imitate the success of the Bolsheviks in Russia (see 1917) by staging an uprising in Berlin. The **attempted revolution** was crushed by the army and right-wing paramilitary Freikorps; the two most prominent Spartacist leaders, Karl Liebknecht and Rosa Luxembourg, were captured and killed. In February, an elected assembly, sitting in the city of Weimar, set about drawing up a constitution for an impeccably democratic republic, but on the streets of Germany **extremism of right and left continued to flourish**. In the southern German state of Bavaria communists proclaimed a Soviet regime in April, only to be crushed by the army and Freikorps in May.

With Germany in no position to resume hostilities, the victorious Allies were able to impose peace terms in the **Versailles Treaty** without negotiation. Germany lost all its colonies and substantial territory in Europe. The European territorial loss consisted largely of areas needed to form the **new state of Poland**, and Alsace-Lorraine, which Germany had taken from France during the Franco-Prussian War (see 1870). Tight restrictions were placed on German armed forces and the Rhineland was demilitarized.

The Germans were also required to make reparations payments, which were justified by the assertion that Germany had been guilty of starting the war. The **"war guilt" clause** outraged Germans more than any other part of the treaty. The crew of the German High Seas Fleet – interned since the armistice at **Scapa Flow** in the Orkney Islands north of Scotland – scuttled their vessels as an act of defiance. But left with no choice German delegates signed the treaty, in the Hall of Mirrors at the Palace of Versailles, on 28 June.

While peace was being formalized in Western Europe, **civil war raged in Russia**, as Lenin's Bolshevik government fought for survival against various "White" counter-revolutionary armies. The Whites had the backing of foreign powers, who landed intervention forces at ports around Russia – US and Japanese at Vladivostok, French at Odessa, and British at Murmansk and Arkhangelsk – but these foreign interventions were half-hearted and mostly short-lived. The Bolshevik People's Commissar for War, **Leon Trotsky** (1879–1940), created a mass Red Army by conscripting peasants at gunpoint, and subjecting them to harsh discipline. Fighting between the

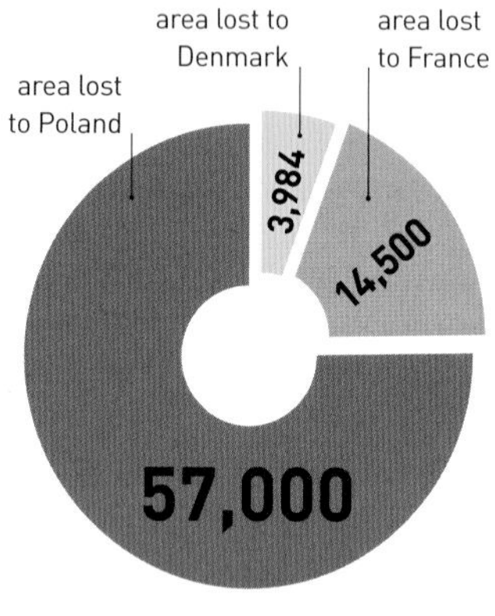

German loss of territory
After World War I Germany lost 13 per cent of its territory. Most went to the new state of Poland, while France regained Alsace-Lorraine.

Russian Red Army cap badge
The hammer-and-plough insignia from the Civil War period symbolizes the union of industrial workers and peasants in the revolutionary cause.

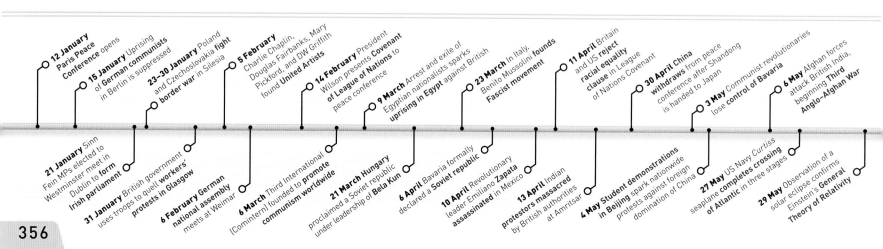

Revolutionary leader
Trotsky's organizational and leadership skills were essential to Bolshevik success in Russia. He is seen here addressing troops of the Red Army.

12 January Paris Peace Conference opens

15 January Uprising **of German communists** in Berlin is suppressed

21 January Sinn Fein MPs elected to Westminster meet in Dublin to **form Irish parliament**

23–30 January Poland and Czechoslovakia **fight border war** in Silesia

31 January British government uses troops to quell **workers' protests in Glasgow**

5 February Charlie Chaplin, Douglas Fairbanks, Mary Pickford, and DW Griffith found **United Artists**

6 February German national assembly meets at Weimar

14 February President Wilson presents **Covenant of League of Nations** to peace conference

6 March Third International (Comintern) founded to **promote communism worldwide**

9 March Arrest and exile of Egyptian nationalists sparks **uprising in Egypt** against British

21 March Hungary proclaimed a Soviet republic under leadership of **Bela Kun**

23 March In Italy, Benito Mussolini **founds Fascist movement**

6 April Bavaria formally declared a **Soviet republic**

10 April Revolutionary leader Emiliano **Zapata assassinated** in Mexico

11 April Britain and US **reject racial equality clause** in League of Nations Covenant

13 April Indian **protestors massacred** by British authorities at Amritsar

30 April China withdraws from peace conference after Shandong is handed to Japan

3 May Communist revolutionaries lose **control of Bavaria**

4 May Student demonstrations in Beijing spark nationwide protests against foreign domination of China

6 May Afghan forces attack British India, beginning **Third Anglo-Afghan War**

27 May US Navy Curtiss seaplane **completes crossing of Atlantic** in three stages

29 May Observation of a solar eclipse confirms Einstein's **General Theory of Relativity**

> **“** WE’VE HAD A **TERRIBLE VOYAGE...** THE **WONDER** IS **WE ARE HERE** AT ALL. **”**
>
> **John Alcock, officer in the British RAF,** after flying nonstop across the Atlantic, 15 June 1919

John Alcock and Arthur Whitten Brown in the plane they flew on the first non-stop transatlantic flight from Newfoundland in Canada to Ireland.

Red and White armies was vicious, and accompanied by massacres and atrocities on a vast scale.

In the midst of this mayhem Russia hosted a congress in Moscow to found the **Third International**, known as Comintern. Its aim was to promote the spread of communist revolution worldwide; its effect was to split the international socialist movement, forcing people on the political left to choose between social democracy and revolutionary communism.

The vision of an imminent world revolution had some credibility at a time when radical workers’ and anti-colonial movements were challenging the established authority in many countries.

Outside Russia, it was only **in Hungary** that **communists** established a national government in 1919. The collapse of the Austro-Hungarian Empire was a disaster for Hungary, which faced the loss of two-thirds of its pre-war territory to Czechoslovakia, Romania, and Yugoslavia. The communist **Bela Kun** (1886–1938) took power in March, launching military offensives against Czechoslovakia and Romania. He followed the Bolshevik example by forming a Red Army and exercising a reign of terror against his opponents, but after 133 days in power he was defeated by the Romanians. Admiral Miklós Horthy’s counter-revolutionary National Army marched into Budapest to suppress the communists with another reign of terror. In 1920, Horthy took power in Hungary as “Regent”.

In **Italy**, people of all political persuasions were disgusted with their country’s limited share in the spoils of victory. Orlando was forced to resign as prime minister on his return from the Paris Peace Conference, after failing to secure either Dalmatia or the port of Fiume (Rijeka) for Italy. In September, Gabriele D’Annunzio (1863–1938), a flamboyant right-wing nationalist poet and aviator, seized Fiume with a band of armed followers. He held the port-city, ruling as dictator of the Regency of Carnaro, until he was driven out by the Italian Navy after a peace deal between Italy and Yugoslavia in November 1920, which made Fiume a Free State.

Italians enter Fiume *Gabriele D’Annunzio’s nationalist legionnaires salute the flag of the short-lived Regency of Carnaro in Fiume, now the Croatian city of Rijeka.*

Meanwhile, **Britain was facing opposition to its rule in India**. The British were committed to a promise made during World War I to grant the Indians a measure of self-government, but they suspended civil liberties in a crackdown on what were described as “anarchical and revolutionary crimes”. On 13 April, British officer General Reginald Dyer (1864–1927) ordered troops to fire on an unarmed crowd of protestors at the Jallianwalla Bagh, a public garden in Amritsar, Punjab. At least 379 people were killed. Although the British government condemned the killings and dismissed General Dyer, the **Amritsar massacre** caused widespread outrage in India and increased pressure for independence.

Despite the world’s troubles, technological and scientific progress continued. On 14 June, British pilot Captain John Alcock (1892–1919) and his navigator Lieutenant Arthur Whitten Brown (1886–1948) took off from St John’s in Newfoundland to attempt the **first non stop flight across the Atlantic**. After a perilous 16 hours 27 minutes their Vickers Vimy bomber aircraft landed nose-down in a bog in Galway, Ireland. Their feat won them a hero’s welcome in London, but Alcock’s triumph was short-lived, as he was killed in an air crash just six months later.

At the time when Alcock and Brown made their famous flight, British scientists were analysing the results of an expedition sent to the African island of Principe to observe a solar eclipse. The expedition was intended to test the validity of the **General Theory of Relativity**, a revolutionary concept in physics formulated during World War I by Albert Einstein (1879–1955). In September, it was announced that the observations did indeed confirm Einstein’s theory, fundamentally changing the notions of time and space that had underpinned Isaac Newton’s view of the universe.

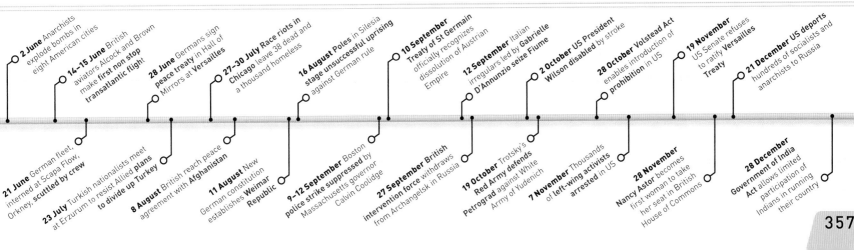

ALBERT EINSTEIN
(1879–1955)

Einstein was born to Jewish parents in southern Germany. In 1905, he published his Special Theory of Relativity, which was followed by the General Theory of Relativity in 1915. His theories revolutionized understanding of the relationship between time, space, matter, and energy. From the 1920s Einstein was fêted worldwide, but chose exile in the US, away from Hitler’s Germany.

- **2 June** Anarchists explode bombs in eight American cities
- **14–15 June** British aviators Alcock and Brown make **first non stop transatlantic flight**
- **21 June** German fleet, interned at Scapa Flow, Orkney, **scuttled by crew**
- **28 June** Germans sign **peace treaty** in Hall of Mirrors at **Versailles**
- **23 July** Turkish nationalists meet at Erzurum to resist Allied **plans to divide up Turkey**
- **27–30 July Race riots in Chicago** leave 38 dead and a thousand homeless
- **8 August** British reach peace agreement with **Afghanistan**
- **11 August** New German constitution establishes **Weimar Republic**
- **16 August** Poles in Silesia **stage unsuccessful uprising** against German rule
- **9–12 September** Boston **police strike suppressed** by Massachusetts governor Calvin Coolidge
- **10 September Treaty of St Germain** officially recognizes dissolution of Austrian Empire
- **12 September** Italian irregulars led by **Gabrielle D’Annunzio seize Fiume**
- **27 September British intervention force** withdraws from Archangelsk in Russia
- **2 October US President Wilson disabled** by stroke
- **19 October** Trotsky’s **Red Army defends Petrograd** against White Army of Yudenich
- **28 October Volstead Act** enables introduction of **prohibition** in US
- **7 November** Thousands of **left-wing activists arrested** in US
- **19 November** US Senate refuses to ratify **Versailles Treaty**
- **28 November Nancy Astor** becomes first woman to take her seat in British House of Commons
- **21 December US deports** hundreds of socialists and anarchists to Russia
- **28 December Government of India Act** allows limited participation of Indians in running their country

“WHAT HAVE I GOT FOR IRELAND? SOMETHING SHE HAS WANTED THESE LAST 700 YEARS.”

Michael Collins, Irish revolutionary leader, 1921

As the agitation for Irish independence mounts, an angry crowd of protestors in Dublin try to force a street barricade manned by British soldiers.

GERMANY REMAINED IMMERSED IN THE TURMOIL that had followed defeat in World War I (see 1919). In March, units of the nationalist paramilitary Freikorps occupied Berlin and declared the Weimar Republic overthrown. As conservative politician Wolfgang Kapp attempted to form a government, Weimar ministers called for a **nationwide general strike** to resist the Freikorps "putsch". Workers walked out, factories and transport shut down, and within days the Kapp regime had collapsed.

The Weimar government reluctantly engaged in talks with the victorious Allies over **implementation of the Versailles peace treaty** (see 1919). Germany began disbanding much of its armed forces and paying war reparations in kind, through deliveries of coal to France and large numbers of cattle, sheep, and horses to France and Belgium.

Further east, war continued to rage. The Bolsheviks triumphed over the White generals in the Russian Civil War. Asserting Bolshevik authority over Ukraine and Belarus brought the Red Army into conflict with the Poles. After some early success against Polish forces, the **Red Army invaded Poland**. Led by General Józef Piłsudski (1867–1935), the Poles mounted a counter-offensive outside Warsaw that crushed the Red Army. Lenin (see 1917) was forced to end the war on Polish terms.

The terms imposed on the Ottoman sultan by the victorious Allies in the Treaty of Sevres meant **breaking up the Turkish empire**. In April, General Mustafa Kemal (1881–1938), the Turkish hero of Gallipoli (see 1915), headed a nationalist parliament in opposition to the sultan and began a war to win control of what he regarded as Turkish national territory – much of which had been given to Greece by the Allies.

The year saw the beginning of prohibition in the US. The **18th Amendment** to the Constitution banned the manufacture and sale of "intoxicating liquors", a move that had little influence on alcohol consumption, but provided a massive boost to organized crime. The more momentous **19th Amendment**, ratified in August, guaranteed American women the vote on equal terms with men.

The US did not take part in the initiation of the **League of Nations**. This international body – dedicated to the peaceful resolution of disputes and the collective deterrence of aggression – was the brainchild of American president Woodrow Wilson, but the US Congress

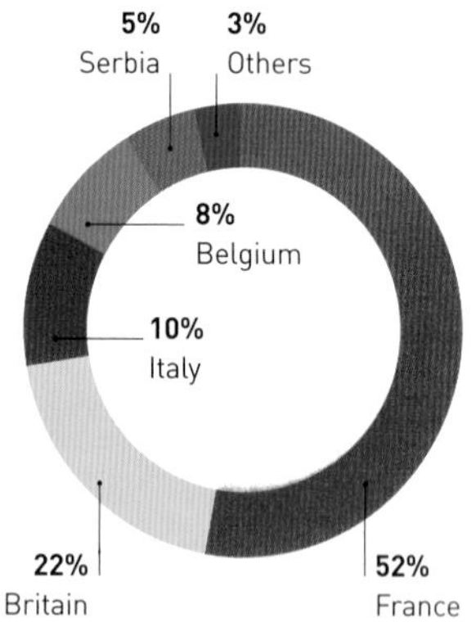

Dividing up reparations
The Allies agreed to divide up German reparations payments after a complex calculation of the losses they had suffered during World War I.

Victory for suffrage
This magazine cover celebrates the passing of the 19th amendment to the US Constitution, which gave women voting rights.

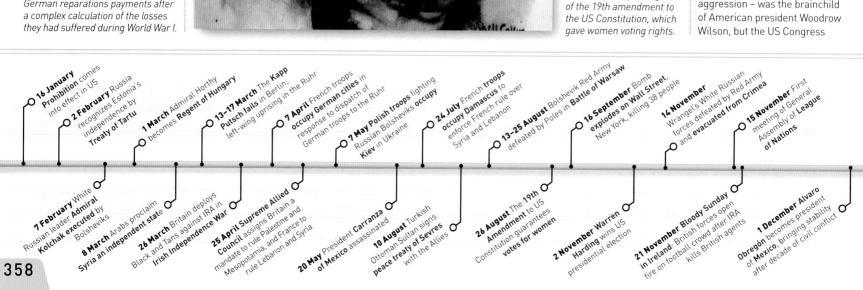

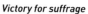

Polish Cross of Valour
This military decoration was introduced by Poland during the war with Bolshevik Russia in 1920 to recognize Polish deeds of heroism.

- **16 January Prohibition** comes into effect in US
- **2 February** Russia recognizes Estonia's independence by **Treaty of Tartu**
- **7 February** White Russian leader **Admiral Kolchak executed** by Bolsheviks
- **1 March** Admiral Horthy becomes **Regent of Hungary**
- **8 March** Arabs proclaim **Syria an independent state**
- **13–17 March** The **Kapp Putsch fails** in Berlin; left-wing uprising in the Ruhr
- **26 March** Britain deploys Black and Tans against IRA in **Irish Independence War**
- **7 April** French troops **occupy German cities** in response to dispatch of German troops to the Ruhr
- **25 April Supreme Allied Council** assigns Britain a mandate to rule Palestine and Mesopotamia, and France to rule Lebanon and Syria
- **7 May Polish troops** fighting Russian Bolsheviks **occupy Kiev** in Ukraine
- **20 May** President **Carranza of Mexico** assassinated
- **24 July** French **troops occupy Damascus** to enforce French rule over Syria and Lebanon
- **10 August** Turkish Ottoman Sultan signs **peace treaty of Sevres** with the Allies
- **13–25 August** Bolshevik Red Army defeated by Poles in **Battle of Warsaw**
- **26 August** The 19th **Amendment** to US Constitution guarantees **votes for women**
- **16 September** Bomb **explodes on Wall Street**, New York, killing 38 people
- **2 November Warren Harding** wins US presidential election
- **14 November** Wrangel's White Russian forces defeated by Red Army and **evacuated from Crimea**
- **15 November** First meeting of General Assembly of **League of Nations**
- **21 November Bloody Sunday in Ireland**: British forces open fire on football crowd after IRA kills British agents
- **1 December Alvaro Obregón** becomes president **of Mexico**, bringing stability after decade of civil conflict

5 MILLION
THE ESTIMATED **NUMBER OF PEOPLE** WHO **DIED** IN THE **RUSSIAN FAMINE** OF **1921**

Russian famine victims receive food from a relief train. The US played a leading role in the international effort to feed the starving.

refused to ratify it. Representatives of 41 countries attended the League's first General Assembly in Geneva in November, but neither Germany nor Russia was among them.

Meanwhile, **war had broken out in Ireland**, where Britain was resisting the declaration of an Irish Republic. British World War I veterans were recruited into two new units, the Black and Tans and the Auxiliaries, to fight the Irish Republican Army (IRA). On 21 November, in an operation planned by IRA intelligence chief **Michael Collins** (1890–1922), the IRA killed 13 people in Dublin. The Auxiliaries responded the same afternoon by firing into a Gaelic football crowd, killing 14 people.

In the same month, on the second anniversary of the armistice ending World War I, Britain and France each **buried an Unknown Soldier**. The French soldier was entombed at the Arc de Triomphe in Paris, and the British soldier in Westminster Abbey in London. It was intended to commemorate all those who had given their lives, irrespective of rank or social class.

The last major event of the year was the accession of **General Alvaro Obregón** (1880–1928) as president of **Mexico**. Obregón had been one of the chief players in the civil conflicts that had torn the country apart since the Mexican Revolution (see 1910). His armed overthrow of President Venustiano Carranza (1859–1920) gave Obregón the chance to establish a relatively stable government.

IN 1921, RUSSIA experienced one of the most **destructive famines** of the 20th century. Years of warfare and revolution had laid waste to the Russian countryside, which was compounded by drought in the Volga region. As hundreds of thousands died of starvation and disease, Lenin's Bolshevik government reluctantly appealed for foreign relief. The most prominent participant in the **international humanitarian effort** was the American Relief Administration, led by future US president Herbert Hoover (1874–1964). Despite the distribution of food aid to around 10 million people, millions died by the time the famine abated the following year.

The **Bolsheviks** continued to impose the will of their party upon their devastated country. In March, workers, soldiers, and sailors rebelled at the naval fortress of Kronstadt, demanding free elections, freedom of speech, and the right of peasants to own land and cattle. The **rebellion** was crushed by Bolshevik forces, but faced with popular discontent and economic devastation the Bolsheviks had to retreat from some of the communist measures they had adopted. **Lenin's New Economic Policy** (NEP) allowed a limited capitalist market economy. Once peasants were permitted to sell their produce at a profit, the rural economy quickly recovered and food supplies were assured.

Division of Ireland
Northern Ireland, with a mainly Protestant population, was separated from southern Ireland, which became the Irish Free State.

Despite the tribulations of the Russian Bolshevik government, its example continued to stimulate the foundation of Communist parties across the world. This included the **Communist Party of China**, which held its founding congress in Shanghai in July.

In Ireland, Britain attempted to fulfil its pre-World War I commitment to **Irish Home Rule** (see 1914). To appease the Irish Protestants the country was divided. Home Rule parliaments were established in Dublin and Belfast, and both parts remained within the United Kingdom. This was accepted by the Protestants, but rejected by Irish Republicans. **Negotiations** opened in London, and on 6 December the Irish delegation agreed to accept the **division of Ireland** in return for Dominion status within the British Commonwealth. Southern Ireland became the **Irish Free State**, but many Irish Republicans were outraged by the compromises in the Anglo-Irish Treaty, which led to civil war (see 1922).

MAO ZEDONG (1893–1976)

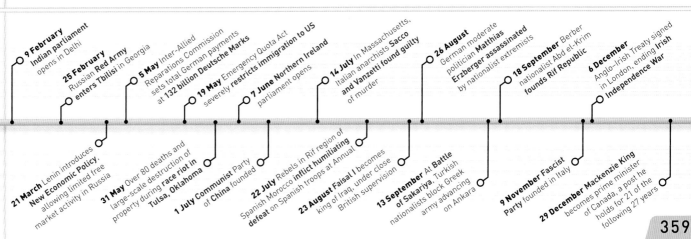

The son of a farmer, Mao helped to found the Chinese Communist Party in 1921. He developed the idea of basing a revolution on support from peasants, rather than industrial workers. From 1949 he ruled Communist China as party chairman. His radical policies, including the Great Leap Forward in 1958 and the Cultural Revolution of the 1960s, caused vast disruption and loss of life.

Britain also had **troubles at home**. A brief post-war economic boom was followed by the collapse in demand for products from many of the country's traditional industries, such as coalmining and shipbuilding. By June, more than **2 million people were unemployed**. For the men who had fought in World War I, it was a bitter irony to find themselves queuing for unemployment benefit.

In the US, racism and anxieties about political subversion were rife. In **Tulsa**, Oklahoma, the most destructive **race riot** in American history saw most of the African-American section of the town destroyed in white attacks. Support for the white supremacist Ku Klux Klan rose rapidly, and concerns about the racial make-up of the US population were reflected in tight limits on foreign immigration. **The Emergency Quota Act** linked the right of entry to country of origin, blocking mass immigration from southern and eastern Europe. Asians were entirely excluded.

The assumption of white racial superiority suffered a severe blow in **Morocco**, which the **French and Spanish** had casually divided into "spheres of influence". Spanish troops attempting to control the mountainous Rif region were surrounded and massacred by local **Berbers** at the Battle of Annual in July. The Berber leader Abd el-Krim declared the region an **independent Rif republic**, but it succumbed to a combined French and Spanish counter-attack four years later.

22 December Congress of Soviets adopts ambitious **plan for electrification** in Russia

23 December Government of Ireland Act **creates separate parliaments** for northern and southern Ireland

30 December French Communist Party founded at Tours congress

9 February Indian parliament opens in Delhi

25 February Russian **Red Army enters Tbilisi** in Georgia

21 March Lenin introduces **New Economic Policy**, allowing limited free market activity in Russia

5 May Inter-Allied Reparations Commission sets total German payments at **132 billion Deutsche Marks**

19 May Emergency Quota Act severely **restricts immigration to US**

31 May Over 80 deaths and large-scale destruction of property during **race riot in Tulsa, Oklahoma**

7 June Northern Ireland parliament opens

1 July Communist Party of China founded

14 July In Massachusetts, Italian anarchists **Sacco and Vanzetti found guilty** of murder

22 July Rebels in Rif region of Spanish Morocco **inflict humiliating defeat** on Spanish troops at Annual

23 August Faisal I becomes king of Iraq, under close British supervision

26 August German moderate politician **Matthias Erzberger assassinated** by nationalist extremists

13 September At **Battle of Sakariya**, Turkish nationalists block Greek army advancing on Ankara

18 September Berber nationalist Abd el-Krim **founds Rif Republic**

9 November Fascist Party founded in Italy

6 December Anglo-Irish Treaty signed in London, ending **Irish Independence War**

29 December Mackenzie King becomes prime minister of Canada, a post he holds for 21 of the following 27 years

1922

Demonstrators gather on the streets of Delhi to protest against the arrest of Indian nationalist leader, Mohandas Gandhi.

> **“** …ONE SHOULD BE **FREE TO GIVE** THE FULLEST **EXPRESSION TO HIS DISAFFECTION** SO LONG AS HE **DOES NOT CONTEMPLATE,** PROMOTE, OR **INCITE VIOLENCE. ”**
>
> **Mohandas Gandhi**, in a statement during his trial, 18 March 1922

FOUR YEARS AFTER THE CONCLUSION OF THE "WAR TO END WAR", serious progress was made towards a more peaceful future. Meeting in the US in February, the world's five major naval powers – Britain, France, Italy, Japan, and the US – signed **the Washington Treaty**, limiting the size of their navies. The same conference also called for an end to the military use of poison gas and banned submarine attacks on merchant shipping. It was the first effective arms limitation agreement between major powers. Britain sacrificed most, accepting naval parity with the US after long domination of the world's oceans, but the treaty was most controversial in Japan, where nationalists objected to naval inferiority to Britain and America.

Another hopeful sign of the flowering of peace was the **development of international air travel in Europe**. Small, noisy, uncomfortable aircraft had begun scheduled flights between European cities, exploiting the surplus of trained pilots and aircraft manufacturing capacity left over from the war. Navigation was primitive, and most pilots simply followed roads or railways. This resulted in the **first commercial air disaster** in April, when a passenger aircraft flying from London to Paris met an aircraft following the same route in the opposite direction.

In the **Middle East**, Britain faced intractable problems reorganizing the territories it had inherited from the Ottoman Empire. The immigration of Jews to Palestine (see panel, above), which Britain was committed to allowing, led to **clashes between Jews and Arabs** that the British could not control.

In another former Ottoman territory, **Egypt**, Britain faced determined nationalist opposition to the protectorate it had established in 1914. Unable to agree a settlement, in February Britain unilaterally **declared Egypt independent**, while retaining the right to station troops there.

A more positive side effect of the British presence in Egypt was the discovery by British archaeologists of **the tomb of Tutankhamun**. The Earl of Carnarvon (1866–1923) and Egyptologist Howard Carter (1874–1939) entered the tomb to find unparalleled treasure, including a gold face mask and jewel-studded chariots. Carnarvon's death the following year inspired a myth, "the curse of the tomb", that magnified the impact of the discovery.

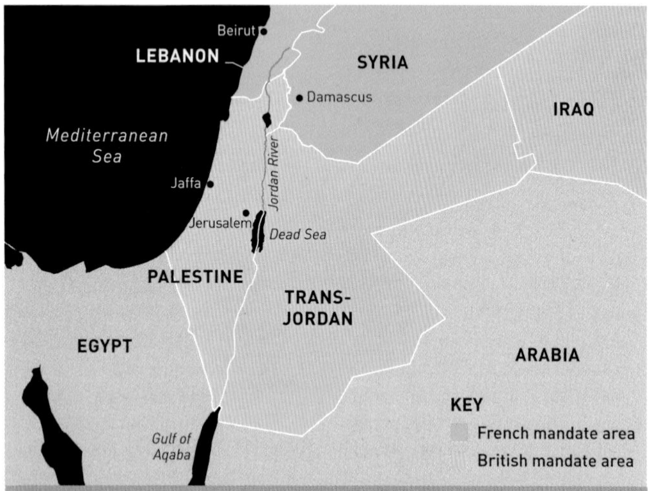

THE BRITISH MANDATE FOR PALESTINE

Former territories of the Ottoman Empire were divided between Britain and France, an arrangement legalized by League of Nations mandates. In accordance with the Balfour Declaration (see 1917), Britain had agreed to allow Jewish settlement in Palestine, but had also given wartime promises to the Arabs. In 1922, it divided its Palestinian mandate territory along the line of the Jordan River. Jewish settlement was allowed to the west, and to the east Transjordan would remain purely Arab land.

In India, nationalist opposition to British rule had found a leader in **Mohandas Gandhi** (1869–1948). Winning the support of the peasant masses for the Indian National Congress independence movement, he organized a nationwide campaign of civil disobedience, including a boycott of British goods. Although Gandhi advocated strict nonviolence, his campaign generated widespread disturbances, including the massacre of 23 police officers at Chauri Chaura in February. **Gandhi was arrested** by the British authorities in March and sentenced to six years prison, of which he served only two.

Implementation of the **Anglo-Irish Treaty** in southern Ireland (see 1921) led to a vicious **civil war**. Michael Collins (1890–1922), head of a provisional Irish Free State government in Dublin, was opposed by anti-Treaty republicans. In April, the Irish Republican Army (**IRA**) occupied Dublin's Four Courts building. After a lengthy standoff, in June Collins used artillery loaned by Britain to bombard the Four Courts, and retake the building. On 22 August, Collins was killed in an ambush on a country road in County Cork. More numerous and better armed, the Free State troops had crushed most opposition by the time the treaty came into effect on 6 December. The Protestant northern province of Ulster remained part of the United Kingdom.

In **Turkey**, nationalists led by **Mustafa Kemal** (1881–1938) were at **war with Greece**, which aspired to create a "Greater Greece" including Constantinople and much of western Anatolia. In August, a Turkish offensive at Dumlupinar drove the Greeks into retreat. The predominantly Greek city of Smyrna (Izmir) was occupied by pursuing Turkish

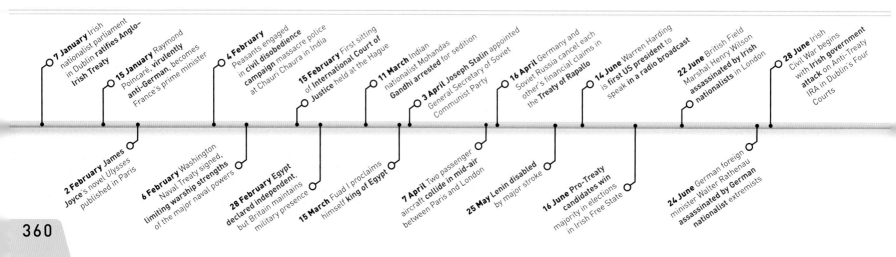

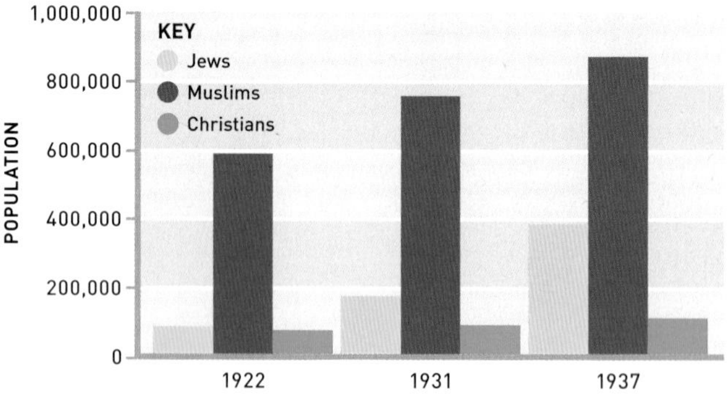

Population growth in Palestine
Through immigration, the proportion of Jews in Palestine increased rapidly. This provoked a violent reaction from the Muslim majority.

7 January Irish nationalist parliament in Dublin **ratifies Anglo-Irish Treaty**

15 January Raymond Poincaré, **virulently anti-German**, becomes France's prime minister

2 February James Joyce's novel *Ulysses* published in Paris

4 February Peasants engaged in **civil disobedience campaign** massacre police at Chauri Chaura in India

6 February Washington Naval Treaty signed, **limiting warship strengths** of the major naval powers

15 February First sitting of **International Court of Justice** held at the Hague

28 February Egypt **declared independent**, but Britain maintains military presence

11 March Indian nationalist Mohandas **Gandhi arrested** for sedition

15 March Fuad I proclaims himself **king of Egypt**

3 April Joseph Stalin appointed General Secretary of Soviet Communist Party

7 April Two passenger aircraft **collide in mid-air** between Paris and London

16 April Germany and Soviet Russia cancel each other's financial claims in the **Treaty of Rapallo**

25 May Lenin disabled by major stroke

14 June Warren Harding is **first US president** to speak **in a radio broadcast**

16 June Pro-Treaty candidates win majority in elections in Irish Free State

22 June British Field Marshal Henry Wilson **assassinated by Irish nationalists** in London

24 June German foreign minister Walter Rathenau **assassinated by German nationalist** extremists

28 June Irish Civil War begins with **Irish government attack** on Anti-Treaty IRA in Dublin's Four Courts

Benito Mussolini mingles with his Fascist Blackshirt paramilitaries in Rome after being appointed prime minister by the Italian king in October.

> **“ EITHER** THE **GOVERNMENT** WILL BE **GIVEN TO US OR WE** SHALL **SEIZE IT** BY MARCHING ON ROME. **”**
>
> **Benito Mussolini**, 24 October 1922

forces and devastated by fire. Britain contemplated intervening against the Turks, but in an **armistice** agreed at **Mudanya** in October both the European powers and Greece accepted the Turkish military victory. Under the agreed peace terms there was a large-scale exchange of people, with over a million Greeks expelled from Turkey and half a million Turks forced to leave Greece. Abandoned Greek villages in western Turkey still bear witness to this human tragedy. **The Republic of Turkey was founded** the following year, with Mustafa Kemal as its first president.

1922 was the year when **Benito Mussolini** (1883–1945) achieved power in Italy. Since the end of World War I, Italy's ruling class had been intimidated by waves of militant action, with socialist workers occupying factories and peasants taking over large estates. In this troubled situation, Mussolini founded the *fasci di combattimento*, a **nationalist militia** that attacked socialists and seized power by force in some Italian towns. In October, Mussolini threatened to lead his **Fascist** followers in a "March on Rome" unless he was made head of government. Italy's king, Victor Emmanuel III (1869–1947), eventually gave in and Mussolini assumed office as prime minister. Once in control, Mussolini began dismantling Italy's system of parliamentary democracy.

As Mussolini was muscling his way to power, the **first national radio broadcasting company** was being established in Britain. Like the early radio stations that were starting up in the US, the British Broadcasting Company (later Corporation) was financed by manufacturers of radio sets, eager to create a market for their products. And it worked; by March 1923, daily broadcasts of concerts, news, and talks had attracted 125,000 people to buy licences from the Post Office for their "wirelesses". The US would not have a major broadcasting network until the formation of the National Broadcasting Company (NBC) in 1926.

New **modernist trends in literature** were prominent in 1922. Irish writer James Joyce's novel *Ulysses*, published in Paris in February, broke all literary conventions, but its language and subject matter ensured that it was banned as obscene in countries with tighter censorship rules than France. The more decorous American expatriate poet T.S. Eliot caused a sensation with his long and obscure poem *The Waste Land*, which came with notes to help the reader follow its numerous literary allusions. Experimentation was also rife in **the movies**, from German director F.W. Murnau's expressionist horror movie *Nosferatu* to American filmmaker Robert Flaherty's groundbreaking documentary *Nanook of the North*.

Russia was entering a period of relative tranquillity, after the upheavals of revolution and civil war. At the year's end the former Russian Empire was reconstituted as the **Union of Soviet Socialist Republics** (USSR), but by then the founder of the world's first communist state, **Vladimir Lenin** (see 1917) had been disabled by a stroke. Despite this he dictated a document, later known as **"Lenin's Testament"**, that was critical of several of his colleagues. In particular it warned against the rudeness and intolerance of **Joseph Stalin** (1978–1953), newly installed as the Soviet Communist Party's General Secretary, and proposed that he be removed from his post. After Lenin's death, knowledge of the document was restricted to a communist inner circle, and action against Stalin was never taken.

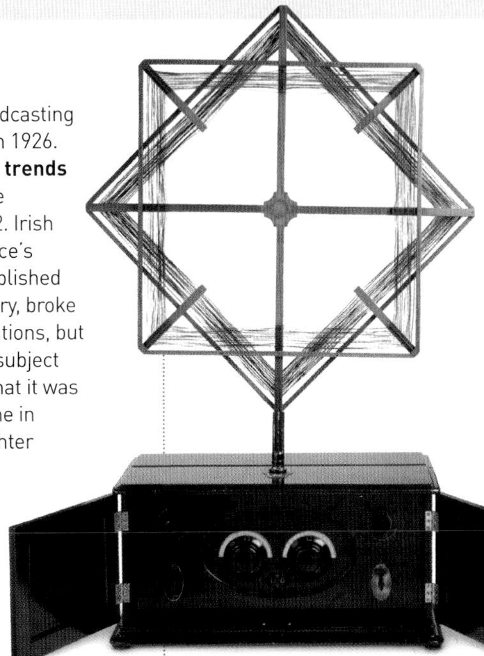

Early airwaves
Early radio sets were often impressive-looking pieces of equipment. This one, from 1925, has an unusual, star-shaped aerial.

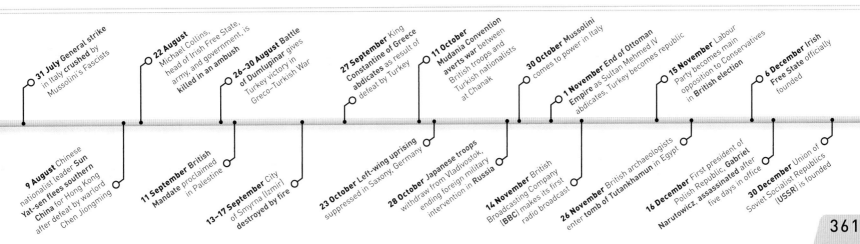

"Father of the Turks"
Mustafa Kemal, the founder of the Turkish Republic, talks with camel drivers during the Turko-Greek War. He later took the name Ataturk.

- **31 July General strike** in Italy **crushed** by Mussolini's Fascists
- **9 August** Chinese nationalist leader **Sun Yat-sen flees southern China** for Hong Kong after defeat by warlord Chen Jiongming
- **22 August** Michael Collins, head of Irish Free State, army, and government, is **killed in an ambush**
- **26–30 August Battle of Dumlupinar** gives Turkey victory in Greco-Turkish War
- **11 September British Mandate** proclaimed in Palestine
- **13–17 September** City of Smyrna (Izmir) **destroyed by fire**
- **27 September** King **Constantine of Greece abdicates** as result of defeat by Turkey
- **11 October Mudania Convention averts war** between British troops and Turkish nationalists at Chanak
- **23 October Left-wing uprising** suppressed in Saxony, Germany
- **28 October Japanese troops** withdraw from Vladivostok, ending foreign military intervention in **Russia**
- **30 October Mussolini** comes to power in Italy
- **1 November End of Ottoman Empire** as Sultan Mehmed IV abdicates, Turkey becomes republic
- **14 November** British Broadcasting Company **(BBC)** makes its first radio broadcast
- **15 November** Labour Party becomes main opposition to Conservatives in **British election**
- **26 November** British archaeologists enter **tomb of Tutankhamun** in Egypt
- **6 December Irish Free State** officially founded
- **16 December** First president of Polish Republic, **Gabriel Narutowicz, assassinated** after five days in office
- **30 December** Union of Soviet Socialist Republics **(USSR)** is founded

1923

Officers of Spain's Guardia Civil stand by debris from a bomb explosion in Barcelona during the disturbances preceding the seizure of power by de Rivera.

“WE HAVE **REASON ON OUR SIDE** AND, **THEREFORE, FORCE,** THOUGH **SO FAR** WE HAVE **USED FORCE WITH MODERATION.**”

Miguel Primo de Rivera, Spanish dictator, September 1923

IN 1922, THE GERMAN GOVERNMENT had declared itself unable to pay war reparations, which were due to the victorious Allies in gold Marks. The French, led by fiercely anti-German prime minister Raymond Poincaré (1860–1934), were determined to take action. In January 1923, **French and Belgian troops occupied the Ruhr**, Germany's industrial heartland. The German government responded by encouraging passive resistance – strikes stopped production in mines and factories.

The occupation triggered **hyperinflation**, and a collapse in the value of the German Mark. Inflation was already out of control before the Franco–Belgian occupation, but the German government's decision to print banknotes to pay striking Ruhr workers was fatal. By the summer, the Mark was almost worthless. The exchange rate against the US dollar rose hourly, and eventually reached 5.72 trillion Marks to the dollar. By the time inflation peaked, savings of 68,000 Marks would buy no more than a postage stamp. In contrast, those who owed money had their debts eradicated. In August, **Gustav Stresemann** (1878–1929), a respected German politician, formed a **coalition government**, and the following month called off passive resistance in the Ruhr. In November, the Mark was replaced by the **Rentenmark**, knocking 12 zeros off the old currency and restoring public confidence.

The chaotic state of Germany tempted a minor political extremist, **Adolf Hitler** (see panel, right), to make a bid for power in the **Munich Putsch** on 8–9 November. Hitler had made himself leader of the Nationalist Socialist Party (Nazis). He had also won powerful allies, including war hero General Erich Ludendorff (1865–1937). Hitler planned to use the Bavarian capital, Munich, as the base for a "March on Berlin" in imitation of Mussolini's "March on Rome" (see 1922). But, at the last moment, Bavarian leaders opposed the putsch. Hitler and Ludendorff were confronted by the army and police on the streets of Munich. After a brief gunfight, the attempted revolt disintegrated. Hitler was arrested two days later and charged with high treason (see 1924).

Worthless paper money
The collapse of the German currency resulted in the printing of 500 million Mark notes. Smaller notes were so worthless they were use to light stoves.

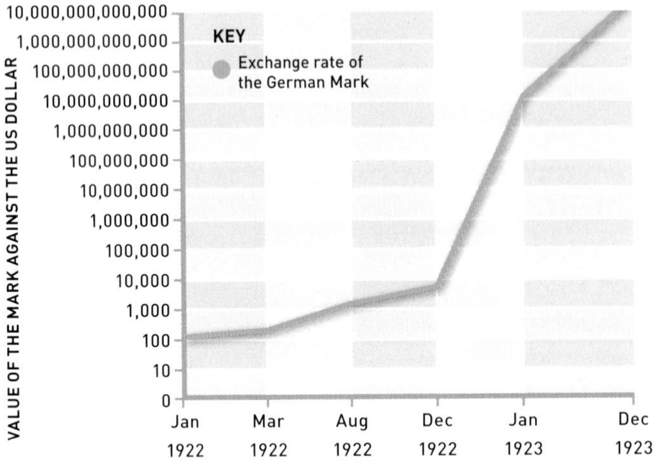

German hyperinflation
The value of the Mark against the US dollar reflects the acceleration of German inflation. Ten years earlier a dollar had been worth 2.3 Marks.

While Hitler's attempted coup failed, **in Spain General Primo de Rivera** (1870–1930) succeeded in seizing power. In the aftermath of the Spanish defeat by Abd el-Krim's Berbers at Annual (see 1921), the Spanish parliament had launched an investigation into the army and Spain's King Alfonso XIII (1886–1941) to apportion blame. Primo de Rivera dismissed parliament and established a **military dictatorship** under the king. Sadly, his desire to end Spain's economic problems and bitter political divisions proved far beyond his power or ability.

A more successful military man was Turkey's Mustafa Kemal (1881–1938), later known as Ataturk. Victorious in the war against Greece (see 1922), **Kemal formally founded the Turkish Republic** in October. He embarked upon a series of radical reforms designed to turn Turkey into a modern secular state. He banned traditional dress, abolished the Muslim caliphate system of government, and replaced Arabic script with the Roman alphabet.

In **Japan**, one of the worst natural disasters of the century struck on 1 September. Known as the **Great Kanto earthquake**, a tremor measuring 7.9 on the Richter scale **devastated Tokyo** and the surrounding area. The quake started fires that were whipped up by high winds into

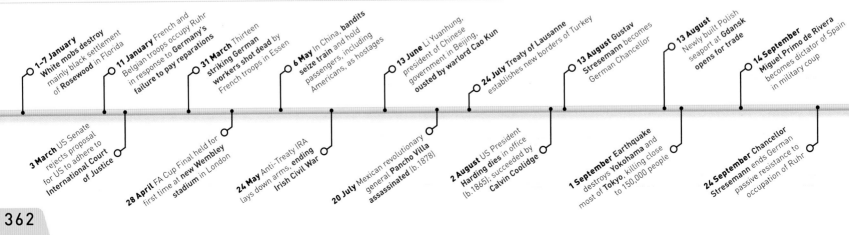

ADOLF HITLER
(1889–1945)

Born in Austria, Hitler fought in the German army in World War I. An inspired orator, he won mass support for his National Socialist (Nazi) Party from the late 1920s. From 1933, he established a ruthless dictatorship that resulted in the Holocaust (see 1942). His expansionist policies caused a war in 1939 that finally led to the destruction of his Reich.

1–7 January **White mobs destroy** mainly black settlement of **Rosewood** in Florida

11 January French and Belgian troops occupy Ruhr in response to **Germany's failure to pay reparations**

3 March US Senate rejects proposal for US to adhere to **International Court of Justice**

31 March Thirteen **striking German workers shot dead** by French troops in Essen

28 April FA Cup Final held for first time at **new Wembley stadium** in London

6 May In China, **bandits seize train** and hold passengers, including Americans, as hostages

24 May Anti-Treaty IRA lays down arms, **ending Irish Civil War**

13 June Li Yuanhung, president of Chinese government in Beijing, **ousted by warlord Cao Kun**

20 July Mexican revolutionary general **Pancho Villa assassinated** (b.1878)

24 July Treaty of Lausanne establishes new borders of Turkey

2 August US President **Harding dies** in office (b.1865); succeeded by **Calvin Coolidge**

13 August Gustav Stresemann becomes German Chancellor

13 August Newly built Polish seaport at **Gdansk opens for trade**

1 September Earthquake destroys **Yokohama** and most of **Tokyo**, killing close to 150,000 people

14 September Miguel Primo de Rivera becomes dictator of Spain in military coup

24 September Chancellor **Stresemann** ends German passive resistance to occupation of Ruhr

Tokyo in ruins after the earthquake of 1923. More than 140,000 people were killed in the disaster, which destroyed half a million buildings.

Queen Mary, wife of King George V, visits the Empire Exhibition at Wembley, mounted to inspire enthusiasm for Britain's imperial glory.

a firestorm. A tsunami up to 10m (30ft) high struck coastal districts, including the port of Yokohama. The death toll was estimated to be close to 150,000.

At this time, the US appeared as a beacon of prosperity in a dark world. President Warren Harding (1865–1923) died in office and was succeeded by his vice-president, **Calvin Coolidge** (1872–1933). Coolidge became notorious for his placid complacency, describing the US as enjoying "a state of contentment seldom before seen". Indeed, the US was becoming the **world's first modern consumer society**, producing nine out of ten of the world's automobiles.

African-American jazz musicians provided the soundtrack to this era of prosperity. Concentrated in the northern cities, such as Chicago and New York, jazz was popularized by the new medium of radio. New York's Harlem district became the centre of an African-American cultural explosion, in literature as well as music, and the **Cotton Club opened** there in 1923. It became one of the most famous venues for live jazz, but black people were only admitted as performers.

Despite its problems, Germany was still culturally vibrant. The **Bauhaus** crafts and design school was founded by architect Walter Gropius (1883–1969) in 1919, rejecting the traditional artist's hostility to modern technology and mass production. By the time of its first major exhibition in 1923, its mission was to bring functional modernist aesthetics to the everyday world, from the design of apartment buildings and electrical appliances to tubular-steel chairs and typography.

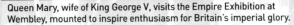

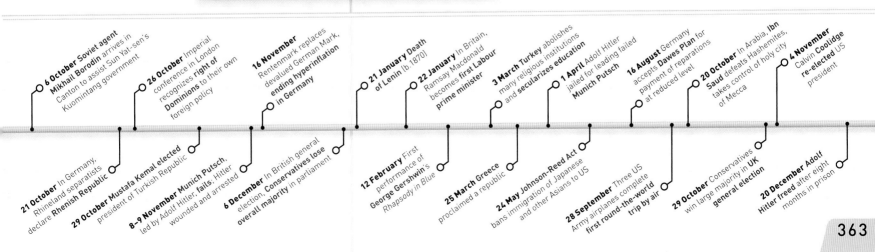

The Bauhaus exhibition
Joost Schmidt, a teacher at the Bauhaus, designed the poster for the 1923 exhibition, which linked modern art to industrial technology.

VLADIMIR ILYICH LENIN (1870–1924), founder of the Soviet Union, died of a massive stroke on 22 January. Hundreds of thousands filed past his body in Moscow's Hall of Columns. Largely at Stalin's insistence, Lenin's body was embalmed and placed on permanent display; his brain was removed for study by Soviet scientists, who were tasked with discovering "the substance of his genius". Lenin statues were erected across the Soviet Union, and the city of Petrograd was renamed Leningrad in his honour.

In **Britain**, the **Labour Party**, led by Ramsay Macdonald (1866–1937), enjoyed its first **brief spell in government**. Despite Macdonald's moderation, the presence of socialists in government was a shock to the British establishment. When an election was called in October, a letter, purportedly sent by Soviet Comintern chief Grigory Zinoviev, was leaked to the press. It was used to accuse Labour of being soft on communism, and contributed to their election defeat.

The **British Empire Exhibition**, held at Wembley in London from April, was a conscious attempt to promote the imperial idea as a source of strength and security in a troubled world. Its opening was the first occasion that a British monarch, George V (1865–1936), made a speech on the radio.

Political and economic conditions in Germany began to recover from postwar chaos, with the help of the US. **The Dawes Plan**, named for American banker and politician Charles G. Dawes, arranged for the withdrawal of French and Belgian troops from the Ruhr (see 1923), and for German payment of reparations with the help of US loans.

Meanwhile, Nazi leader Adolf **Hitler was put on trial** for his attempted Munich Putsch (see 1923). Seizing the opportunity to make political speeches in court, he became a national celebrity. He was found guilty of high treason, but given a lenient five-year prison sentence of which he served less than a year. During his time in Landsberg prison, he dictated the first volume of ***Mein Kampf*** (*My Struggle*), a statement of his political beliefs.

Meanwhile, in Italy the murder of socialist parliamentary deputy Giacomo Matteotti (1885–1924) drew attention to the lawless violence underpinning **Benito Mussolini's** Fascist government (see 1922). Matteotti was presumed to have been killed by **Fascist Blackshirts**. Opposition deputies withdrew from parliament in protest, opening the way for Mussolini to move more swiftly toward a single-party dictatorship.

900,000

THE NUMBER OF **PEOPLE** WHO **FILED PAST LENIN'S BODY** AS IT LAY **IN STATE** FOR **FOUR DAYS**

6 October Soviet agent Mikhail Borodin arrives in Canton to assist Sun Yat-sen's Kuomintang government

21 October In Germany, Rhineland separatists declare **Rhenish Republic**

26 October Imperial conference in London recognizes **right of Dominions** to their own foreign policy

29 October Mustafa Kemal elected president of Turkish Republic

8–9 November Munich Putsch, led by Adolf Hitler, **fails**; Hitler wounded and arrested

16 November Rentenmark replaces devalued German Mark, **ending hyperinflation** in Germany

6 December In British general election, **Conservatives lose overall majority** in parliament

21 January Death of Lenin (b.1870)

22 January In Britain, Ramsay Macdonald becomes **first Labour prime minister**

12 February First performance of **George Gershwin's** *Rhapsody in Blue*

3 March Turkey abolishes many religious institutions and **secularizes education**

25 March Greece proclaimed a republic

1 April Adolf Hitler jailed for leading failed **Munich Putsch**

24 May Johnson-Reed Act bans immigration of Japanese and other Asians to US

16 August Germany accepts **Dawes Plan** for payment of reparations at reduced level

28 September Three US Army airplanes complete **first round-the-world trip by air**

20 October In Arabia, **Ibn Saud** defeats Hashemites, takes control of holy city of Mecca

29 October Conservatives win large majority in **UK general election**

4 November Calvin **Coolidge re-elected** US president

20 December Adolf Hitler freed after eight months in prison

THE STORY OF FLIGHT

FROM HOT-AIR BALLOONS TO SUPERSONIC JETS, FLIGHT HAS COME A LONG WAY

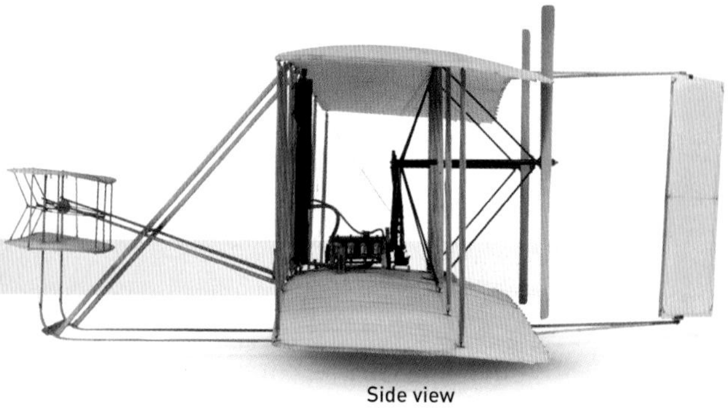

Side view

Until the 20th century, human flight was an area of experiment for enthusiasts. Ascents in balloons sparked the first flying craze but had little practical effect. In the 19th century, engineers calculated the forces involved in winged flight and experimented with gliders, but it was the arrival of petrol engines that made powered flight practicable.

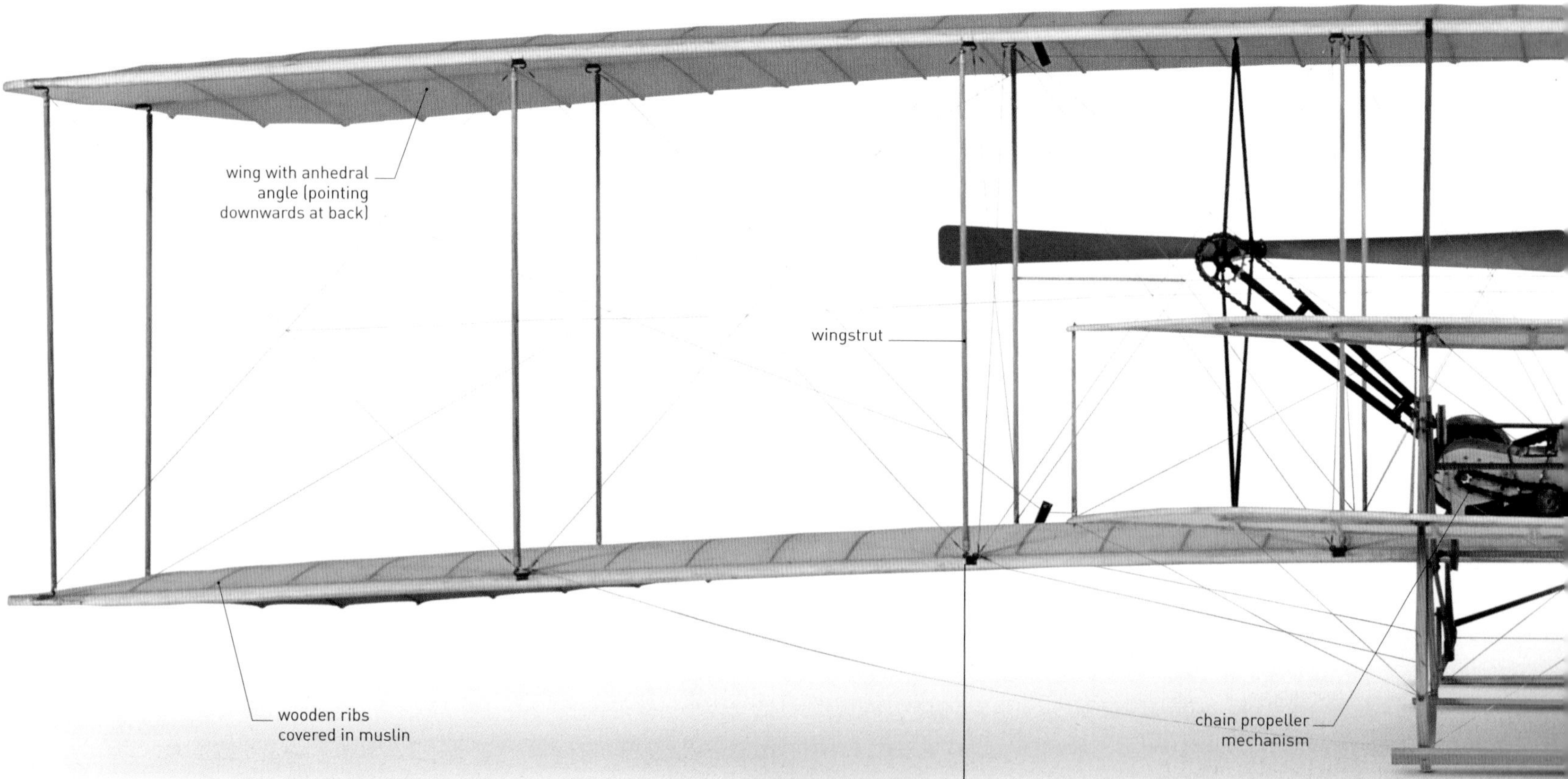

c.1485–1510
Leonardo's flying machine
Early concepts of human flight, like those sketched by Leonardo da Vinci, are based on bird flight but are technically impractical.

Da Vinci's ornithopter

1783
Hot-air balloon
French brothers Joseph and Etienne Montgolfier complete the first manned flight in a hot-air balloon.

Montgolfier balloon

1852
First powered flight
Frenchman Henri Giffard attaches a steam engine to a balloon filled with coal gas; powered flight begins.

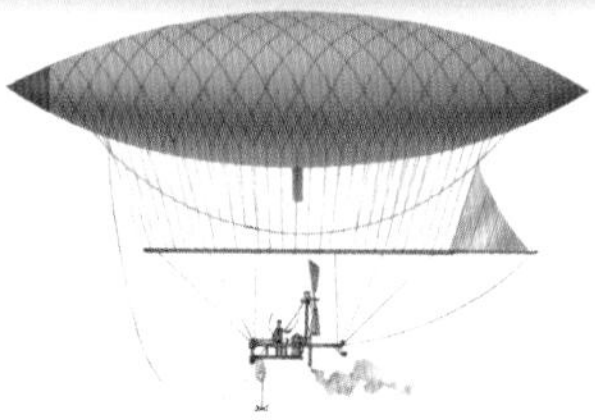

Giffard's airship

1900
First Zeppelin flight
On 2 July, German pioneer Ferdinand von Zeppelin's LZ-1 successfully takes to the skies.

Zeppelin airship

1903
The Wright Flyer
On 17 December, the Wright brothers complete the first sustained, controlled flight in a powered, heavier-than-air machine at Kill Devil Hills, North Carolina, US.

1909
Long-distance flight
On 25 July, Frenchman Louis Blériot flies across the English Channel from France to England.

Louis Blériot

1914
Aircraft in warfare
Use of aircraft for combat transforms aviation; tens of thousands of aircraft are mass-produced for the first time.

1919
Airlines progress
The first scheduled international passenger air service is inaugurated between London and Paris; the first airlines are set up.

“ WE COULD NOT UNDERSTAND THAT THERE WAS ANYTHING ABOUT A **BIRD THAT COULD NOT BE BUILT** ON A LARGER SCALE. ”

Orville Wright (1873–1948), American aviation pioneer

American brothers Orville and Wilbur Wright made the first viable powered winged aircraft by attaching an engine to a glider in 1903. They solved the problem of controlling an aircraft in flight and by 1905 had a machine that would stay airborne until its fuel ran out. In the beginning, airships outperformed winged aircraft, but they were slow and fatally accident-prone. Successors to the Wright brothers showed that winged aircraft had astounding potential for increase in size, range, and speed. By the 1930s, high-performance aircraft could exceed 640kph (400mph), while the development of flying instruments improved safety. Long-distance flying feats made pilots heroes in the 1920s and 1930s. But, by the 1940s, the same flights were available to paying passengers in the comfort of pressurized cabins. Jet engines carried aircraft performance to supersonic speed and altitudes at the edge of space. Rocket technology then propelled humans into space itself. From the 1970s, falling prices turned flight into a worldwide mass transport system and made it accessible to the majority. Air travel had bridged distances and shrunk the world.

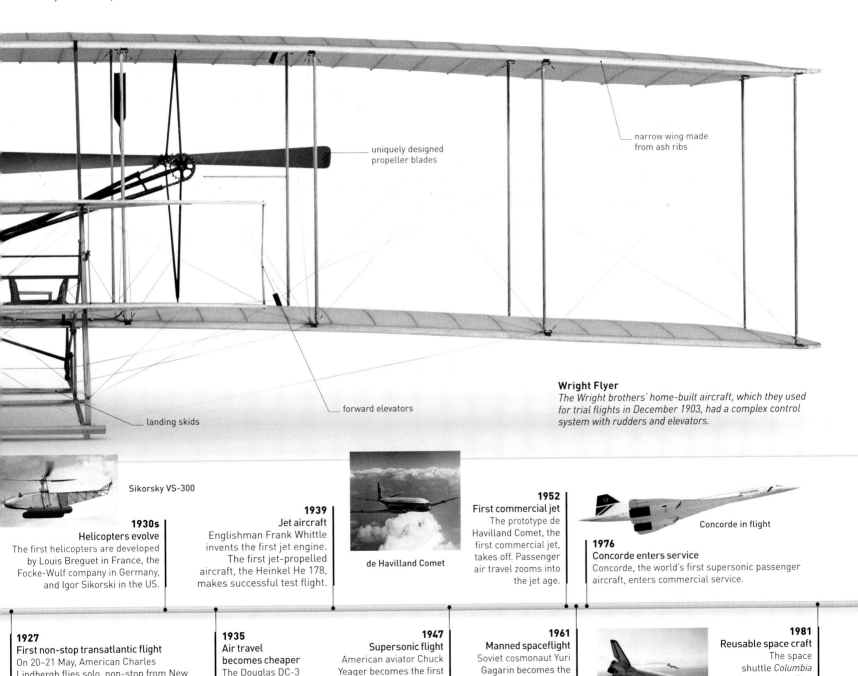

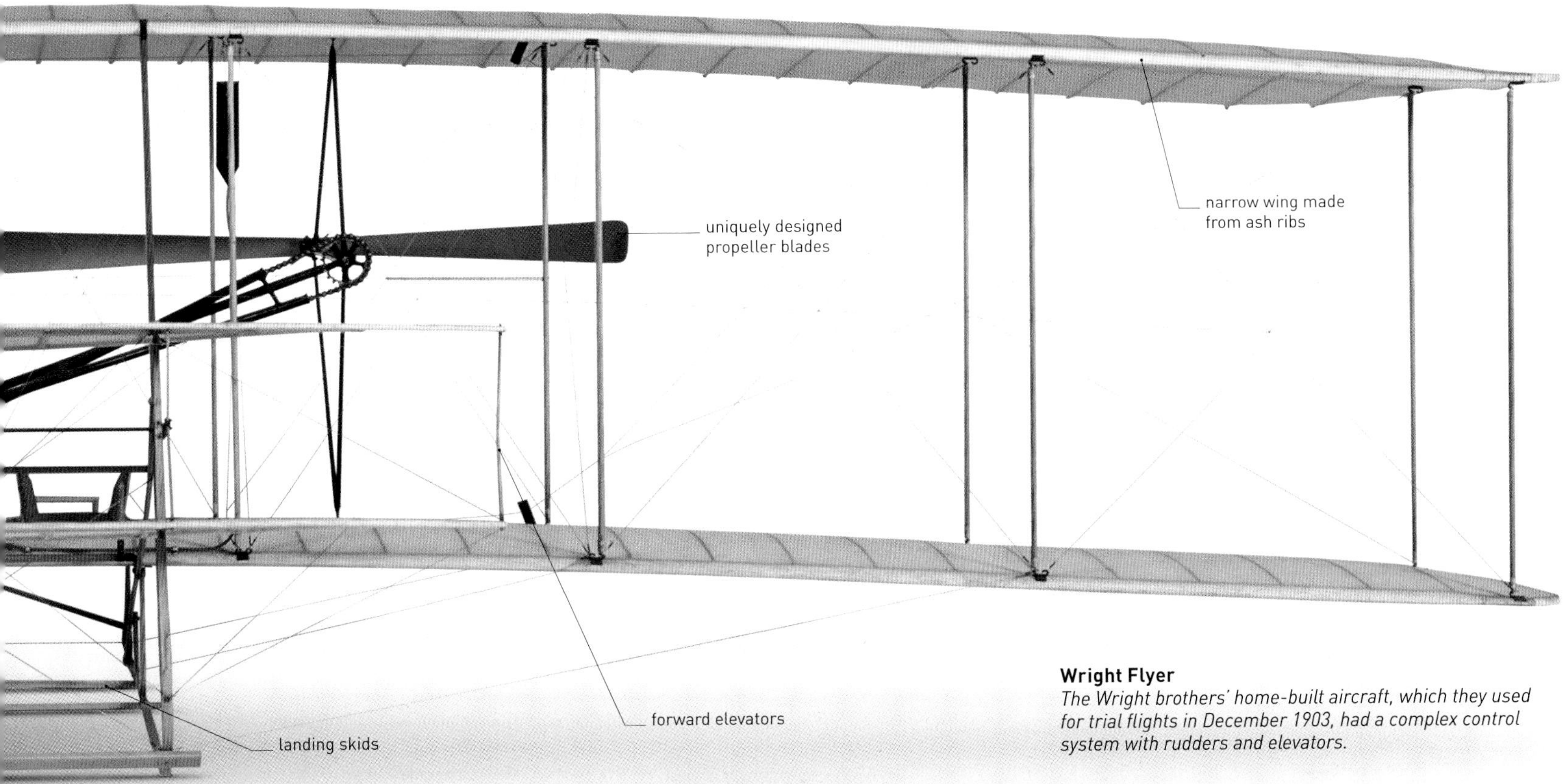

Wright Flyer
The Wright brothers' home-built aircraft, which they used for trial flights in December 1903, had a complex control system with rudders and elevators.

Sikorsky VS-300

1927
First non-stop transatlantic flight
On 20–21 May, American Charles Lindbergh flies solo, non-stop from New York to Paris in a single-engine monoplane.

Spirit of St Louis

1930s
Helicopters evolve
The first helicopters are developed by Louis Breguet in France, the Focke-Wulf company in Germany, and Igor Sikorski in the US.

1935
Air travel becomes cheaper
The Douglas DC-3 passenger aircraft makes flight cheaper and more viable.

1939
Jet aircraft
Englishman Frank Whittle invents the first jet engine. The first jet-propelled aircraft, the Heinkel He 178, makes successful test flight.

de Havilland Comet

1947
Supersonic flight
American aviator Chuck Yeager becomes the first to pilot the rocket-powered Bell X-1, the first aircraft to break the sound barrier.

1952
First commercial jet
The prototype de Havilland Comet, the first commercial jet, takes off. Passenger air travel zooms into the jet age.

1961
Manned spaceflight
Soviet cosmonaut Yuri Gagarin becomes the first man in space, orbiting the Earth in his Vostok spacecraft.

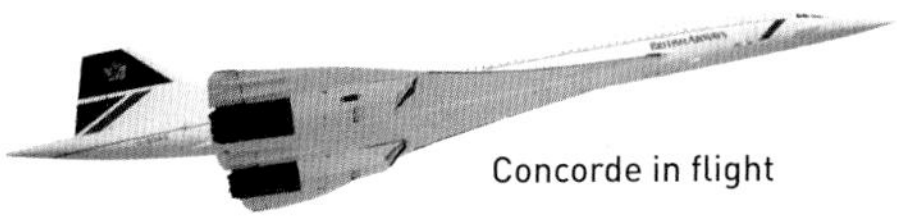

Concorde in flight

1976
Concorde enters service
Concorde, the world's first supersonic passenger aircraft, enters commercial service.

Space shuttle *Columbia*

1981
Reusable space craft
The space shuttle *Columbia* becomes the first shuttle to be launched into Earth's orbit, on 12 April.

1925

“ THE BEST OF AMERICA DRIFTS TO PARIS. ”

F. Scott Fitzgerald, American author

American dancer and singer Josephine Baker was described by writer Ernest Hemingway as “the most sensational woman anyone ever saw”.

PARIS REASSERTED ITS CLAIM as the world leader in taste and style with the **International Exhibition of Modern Industrial and Decorative Arts**. The exhibition gave a name – **Art Deco** – to the design trend toward angular shapes, abstract patterns, exuberant African, Aztec, and Egyptian motifs, and materials such as chromium and ivory. Art Deco soon set the style for everything from scent bottles and skyscrapers to ocean liners and movie theatres.

Less noticed at the time was a small exhibition of works in a Parisian gallery by artists calling themselves “**Surrealists**”. The group, which included the Catalan artist **Joan Miró** (1893–1983) and the American **Man Ray** (1890–1976), were dedicated to the exploration of dreams and unconscious impulses to subvert everyday reality. Over the following decade Surrealism was to become a major international art movement.

Man Ray was one of **a host of American expatriates** who **flocked to Paris** in the mid-1920s, lured by the vibrant cultural scene, and the favourable exchange rate. American writers based in the city included Gertrude Stein (1874–1976), Ernest Hemingway (1899–1961), and F. Scott Fitzgerald (1896–1940), whose classic work *The Great Gatsby* was published in 1925. African-American erotic dancer **Josephine Baker** (1906–1975) became a star of Parisian nightlife, performing at the Theatre des Champs-Elysées. For their part, the French took an adoring interest in American jazz.

Surrealist style

Harlequin's Carnival exemplifies the playful, anarchic style developed in the 1920s by Joan Miró, a Spanish Catalan artist living in Paris.

Back in the US, in Dayton, Tennessee, biology teacher **John Scopes was put on trial** for teaching Darwin's Theory of Evolution. Scopes was backed by the American Civil Liberties Union to test Tennessee's newly passed Butler Act, which had outlawed the teaching of evolution. Christian fundamentalists brought in former US Secretary of State William Jennings Bryan to act for the prosecution, and after a trial that enthralled America, Scopes was **found guilty**, although the verdict was later quashed.

The general world **political and economic outlook** was better than at any time since World War I. In April, Britain's Chancellor of the Exchequer, Winston Churchill, returned his country's currency to the pre-war **Gold Standard**. This set the value of sterling artificially high, creating problems for British exporters, but it was an important gesture toward the restoration of international financial stability.

In December, **the Locarno Pact was signed**. This was a series of treaties designed to restore normal peacetime relations between Germany and the victor states of World War I. The agreement depended on the relationship established between the German and French foreign ministers, Gustav Stresemann and Aristide Briand, and opened the way for Germany's admission to the League of Nations in 1926.

1926

Reza Khan Pahlavi on his throne after being appointed shah of Iran. His aim was to modernize his country along secular Western lines.

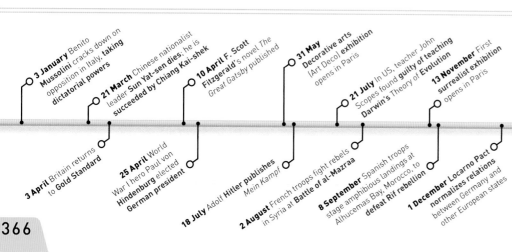

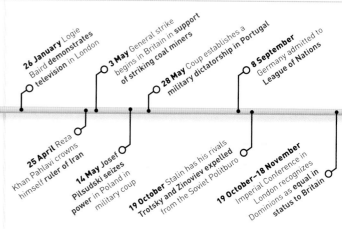

The first television camera

Logie Baird gave the first demonstration of television using a mechanical system with a spinning disk as the scanner.

IN JANUARY 1926, SCOTTISH ENGINEER JOHN LOGIE BAIRD (1888–1946) made the **first** demonstration of a **television transmission** in a loft in London's Soho district. Fifty members of the Royal Institution saw the indistinct, but recognizable moving image of a face.

In May, Britain experienced its only **General Strike**. This nationwide industrial stoppage, in support of coal miners, paralyzed transport networks and docks, and closed down newspapers and factories. The British government responded by mobilizing troops and recruiting volunteers to maintain essential services. After nine days the unions backed down and ordered a return to work.

In **Poland**, the nation's military hero **Marshal Jozef Pilsudski** (1867–1935) **led a coup d'état** in May, in reaction against the unstable parliamentary government. Pilsudski declined the presidency, but effectively took dictatorial powers.

In Iran, another military strongman, **Reza Khan Pahlavi** (1878–1944), **established a new dynasty** by crowning himself as shah on 25 April; his intention was to modernize his country. The Pahlavi dynasty he founded ruled in Iran until the 1970s.

160 MILLION

THE NUMBER OF **WORKING DAYS LOST TO STRIKES** IN THE **UK** IN **1926**

3 January Benito **Mussolini** cracks down on opposition in Italy, **taking dictatorial powers**

21 March Chinese nationalist leader **Sun Yat-sen dies**; he is **succeeded by Chiang Kai-shek**

3 April Britain returns to **Gold Standard**

10 April F. Scott Fitzgerald's novel *The Great Gatsby* published

25 April World War I hero Paul von **Hindenburg** elected **German president**

31 May Decorative arts (Art Deco) **exhibition** opens in Paris

18 July Adolf **Hitler publishes** *Mein Kampf*

21 July In US, teacher John Scopes found **guilty of teaching Darwin's Theory of Evolution**

2 August French troops fight rebels in Syria at **Battle of al-Mazraa**

8 September Spanish troops stage amphibious landings at Alhucemas Bay, Morocco, to **defeat Rif rebellion**

13 November First **surrealist exhibition** opens in Paris

1 December Locarno Pact **normalizes relations** between Germany and other European states

26 January Logie Baird **demonstrates television** in London

25 April Reza Khan Pahlavi crowns himself **ruler of Iran**

3 May General strike begins in Britain in **support of striking coal miners**

14 May Josef **Pilsudski seizes power** in Poland in military coup

28 May Coup establishes a **military dictatorship in Portugal**

8 September Germany admitted to **League of Nations**

19 October Stalin has his rivals **Trotsky and Zinoviev expelled** from the Soviet Politburo

19 October–18 November Imperial Conference in London recognizes Dominions as **equal in status to Britain**

"I OWNED THE WORLD THAT HOUR AS I RODE OVER IT..."

Charles Lindbergh, American aviator

Aviator Charles Lindbergh poses alongside the *Spirit of St Louis*, the aircraft in which he achieved the first non-stop flight from New York to Paris.

IN MAY 1927, 25-YEAR-OLD CHARLES LINDBERGH (1902–1974) **flew solo across the Atlantic**, a feat that made him the most famous American alive. The offer of a cash prize for the first non-stop flight between New York and Paris had stimulated feverish competition. On 8 May, famous French war aces Charles Nungesser and François Coli attempted the flight from Paris; they set off westward over the Atlantic and were never seen again. Such dramas had wrought excitement to a high pitch when the unknown Lindbergh, an airmail pilot, took off from Roosevelt Field on 20 May aboard a custom-built monoplane. Not only did he succeed in reaching **Paris in 33 hours and 30 minutes**, but he did it alone. Lindbergh was mobbed on landing in France and the mixed blessing of celebrity accompanied him for the rest of his life. His achievement stimulated the rapid growth of commercial aviation in the US.

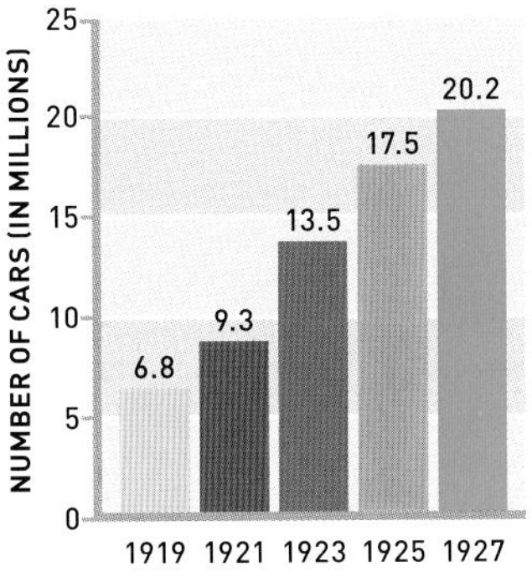

Car ownership in the US
In the eight years from 1919 to 1927 the number of cars on America's roads tripled. Five-sixths of the world's automobiles were in the US.

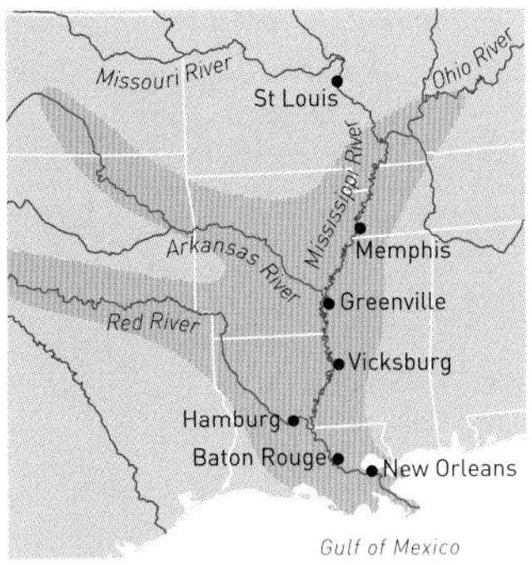

The Great Mississippi Flood
Following months of heavy rain, the Mississippi broke its levees in spring 1927, submerging a vast area of land (in purple) and killing 246 people.

America's upbeat mood was ripe for the world's **first modern consumer boom**, which was built around the purchase of cars and electrical goods. By 1927, there was one car for every six Americans – enough to ensure that even quite modest families might aspire to a Model T Ford. Levels of saving were high, and many chose to invest their spare cash in the rising stock market.

Not everything was as positive, however. **Falling prices for agricultural goods** were hitting rural areas worldwide, and the US, with almost half its population working the land, was not immune. Farm owners were heavily in debt and farm workers were badly paid.

The terrible conditions experienced by many rural workers was highlighted in April 1927 by the **Great Mississippi Flood**, which was the worst flood disaster in American history. Many of its victims were black and very poor; ill-treated and neglected in refugee camps after the disaster, many thousands of them swelled the movement of African-Americans from the south to new lives in northern cities.

Two of the greatest works in cinema history were released in 1927: Fritz Lang's futuristic *Metropolis* and Abel Gance's historical epic *Napoleon*. But these hugely ambitious silent movies were upstaged by the success of Al Jolson (1886–1950) in a sound film, *The Jazz Singer*. A new era of "**talkies**" had arrived.

Second only to the Lindbergh flight in media coverage in 1927 was the controversy surrounding the **execution of the anarchists** Ferdinando **Sacco** and Bartolomeo **Vanzetti**. Italian immigrants dubiously convicted of a murder in Massachusetts in 1920, their case became a focus of protests by liberals and socialists, and their execution by electric chair on 23 August provoked riots in a number of cities across the world.

Meanwhile, in the Soviet Union, **Leon Trotsky** (1879–1940) was expelled from the central committee of the ruling Communist Party in November, along with his allies Grigori Zinoviev and Lev Kamenev. Once favourite to succeed Lenin (1870–1924) as Soviet leader, Trotsky had been ruthlessly outmanoeuvred by the party's General Secretary Joseph Stalin (1878–1953). Accused of "factionalism", Trotsky was sent into internal exile in Kazakhstan the following January and finally **expelled from the Soviet Union** in February 1929. Zinoviev and Kamenev submitted to Stalin, but he had them executed in 1936.

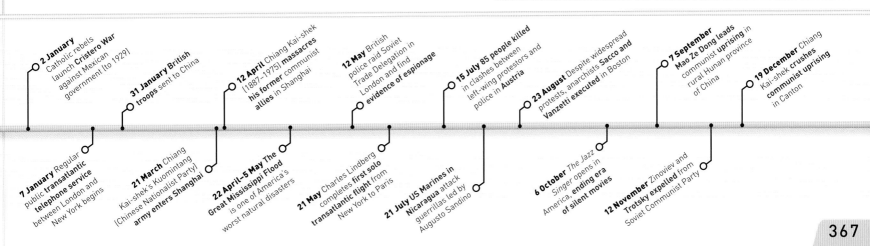

First feature-length "talkie"
The first successful full-length sound feature film, The Jazz Singer, *took $2.6 million at American box offices and made Jolson a household name.*

2 January Catholic rebels launch **Cristero War** against Mexican government (to 1929)

7 January Regular public **transatlantic telephone service** between London and New York begins

31 January British troops sent to China

21 March Chiang Kai-shek's Kuomintang (Chinese Nationalist Party) **army enters Shanghai**

12 April Chiang Kai-shek (1887–1975) **massacres his former** communist **allies** in Shanghai

22 April–5 May The **Great Mississippi Flood** is one of America's worst natural disasters

12 May British police raid Soviet Trade Delegation in London and find **evidence of espionage**

21 May Charles Lindberg completes **first solo transatlantic flight** from New York to Paris

15 July 85 people killed in clashes between left-wing protestors and police in **Austria**

21 July US Marines in Nicaragua attack guerrillas led by Augusto Sandino

23 August Despite widespread protests, anarchists **Sacco and Vanzetti executed** in Boston

7 September Mao Ze Dong leads communist **uprising** in rural Hunan province of China

6 October *The Jazz Singer* opens in America, **ending era of silent movies**

12 November Zinoviev and **Trotsky expelled** from Soviet Communist Party

19 December Chiang Kai-shek **crushes communist uprising** in Canton

Bacteriologist Sir Alexander Fleming surrounded by test tubes in his laboratory. Fleming discovered the antibiotic properties of penicillin in 1928.

IN THE SOVIET UNION, JOSEPH STALIN (1878–1953) began radical **economic and social reform**. Abandoning the compromise of Vladimir Lenin's New Economic Policy (see 1921), Stalin launched a **Five-Year Plan** to transform the Soviet Union into a major industrial country. He cracked down on businessmen and successful peasants who had made money out of the revolution. Hundreds of "bourgeois experts" – people, such as engineers, who had been valued for their skills rather than their involvement in the revolution – were arrested and **convicted of sabotage**.

In China, Chiang Kai-shek (1887–1975), leader of the nationalist **Kuomintang** (National People's Party), was close to establishing his rule over the entire country. The warlords who ruled different areas of China either became his allies or were defeated by his army. In June, Kuomintang forces took Beijing, and in October Chiang Kai-shek formally established a national government, but he still faced resistance. Former allies of the Kuomintang, the **communists** suffered heavy losses when Chiang Kai-shek turned against them in 1927. Forced out of the cities they continued their struggle in remote rural areas – a large area of mountainous Jiangxi and Fujian provinces came under the control of the communist leader Mao Zedong (see 1921).

Political violence was also widespread elsewhere. In Yugoslavia, hostility between Croats and Serbs led to the **killing of Croatian Peasant Party leader Stjepan Radić (1871–1928)**. He was shot by a Montenegrin Serb political opponent in the Yugoslav parliament on 20 June, and died later of his wounds. With his realm torn apart by nationalist passions, the following year Yugoslavia's King Alexander I (1888–1934) banned political parties and assumed dictatorial powers.

In Mexico, **General Alvaro Obregón** (1880–1928), the dominant figure in his country's politics since 1920, was **assassinated** after being elected president for a second term. His killer, José de León Toral, was a member of the **Catholic Cristero** movement that had launched an armed rebellion in response to the Mexican government's anti-clerical policies. The desire for stability after the shock of Obregón's assassination led to the formation of the **National Revolutionary Party**, which, under a variety of names, dominated Mexican politics for more than 70 years.

In Germany, stability seemed to have been achieved after the chaotic post-World War I period. In elections to the Reichstag in May, Adolf Hitler's extremist **Nazi Party won less than three per cent of the popular vote**, compared with almost 30 per cent for the moderate Social Democrats. Under the German Republic's rigorous proportional representation system, the Nazis' minimal support gained them 12 seats in parliament.

In August, Germany was one of the original signatories of an agreement for "the renunciation of war as an instrument of national policy". This supremely optimistic document, commonly known as the **Kellogg-Briand Pact** after US Secretary of State Frank B. Kellogg (1856–1937) and French Foreign Minister Aristide Briand (1862–1932), obliged states to only resort to war in self-defence. Within a year it had been signed by all the world's major powers.

Of more practical consequence was the **discovery of penicillin**. Scottish scientist Alexander Fleming (1881–1955) accidentally discovered the antibiotic mould in contaminated specimen dishes, but the development of penicillin for medical use was the work of other scientists in the 1940s.

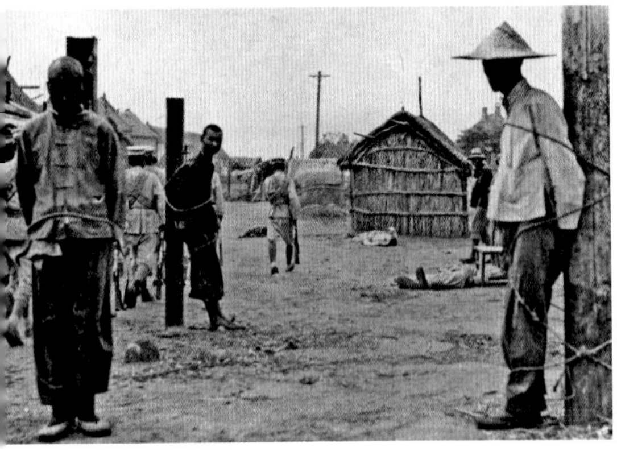

Chinese suffering
Prisoners taken during fighting between Chinese nationalist forces and those of the northern warlord Zhang Zuolin.

JOSEPH STALIN
(1878–1953)

Born Josif Dzhugashvili, in Georgia, Stalin joined Lenin's Bolsheviks in 1903. After Lenin's death he cleverly outmanoeuvred other leading Bolsheviks to achieve dictatorial power by 1929. He ran a ruthless police state that murdered millions of its citizens, yet he presided over the country's transformation into a major industrial power and led it to victory over Nazi Germany in 1945.

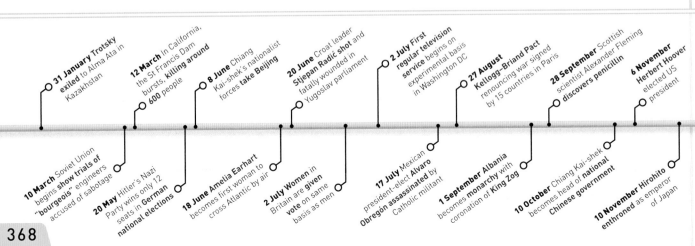

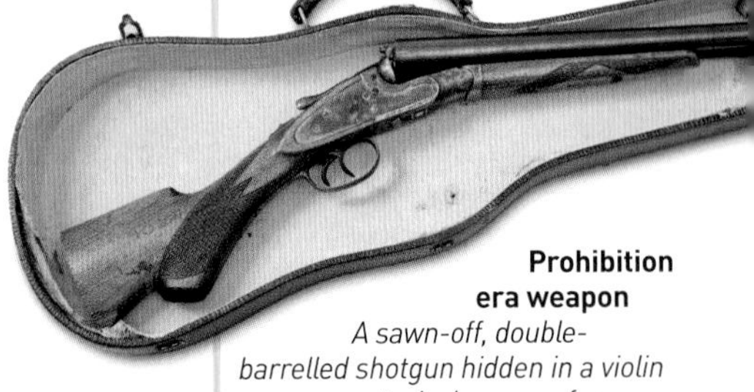

Prohibition era weapon
A sawn-off, double-barrelled shotgun hidden in a violin case was a typical weapon for an American gangster of the 1920s.

ON 14 FEBRUARY, SEVEN PEOPLE WERE SHOT DEAD in a garage on Chicago's North Side. The perpetrators of the **St Valentine's Day Massacre** were probably members of the gang headed by **Al Capone** (1899–1947), a prominent figure in organized crime. The victims belonged to the rival gang of Bugs Moran. Both Capone and Moran drew their main income from bootlegging – the illegal trade in alcoholic drinks that flourished under prohibition (see 1920). The massacre focused public outrage on the crime and violence that was rife in American cities. The authorities were forced to take action, which led to the arrest and imprisonment of Capone on charges of tax evasion in 1931.

On 4 March, Republican **Herbert Hoover** (1874–1964) was inaugurated as US president. His arrival in office coincided with a high point of complacency about US economic progress. Through the 1920s the US had become the world's first automobile-owning society, with 26 million cars on the road by 1929. Optimism and easy credit drove share prices on Wall

31 January Trotsky exiled to Alma Ata in Kazakhstan

10 March Soviet Union begins **show trials of "bourgeois"** engineers accused of sabotage

12 March In California, the St Francis Dam bursts, **killing around 600** people

20 May Hitler's Nazi Party wins only 12 seats in **German national elections**

8 June Chiang Kai-shek's nationalist forces **take Beijing**

18 June Amelia Earhart becomes first woman to cross Atlantic by air

20 June Croat leader **Stjepan Radić shot** and fatally wounded in Yugoslav parliament

2 July Women in Britain **are given vote** on same basis as men

2 July First regular television service begins on experimental basis in Washington DC

17 July Mexican president-elect **Alvaro Obregón assassinated** by Catholic militant

27 August Kellogg-Briand Pact renouncing war signed by 15 countries in Paris

1 September Albania becomes **monarchy** with coronation of **King Zog**

28 September Scottish scientist Alexander Fleming **discovers penicillin**

10 October Chiang Kai-shek becomes head of **national Chinese government**

6 November Herbert Hoover elected US president

10 November Hirohito enthroned as emperor of Japan

5 January King Alexander takes control of Yugoslavia, **abolishing parliamentary constitution**

11 February Lateran Treaty agreed between Mussolini's Italian government and Vatican

Herbert Hoover being sworn in as US president. His inauguration speech foresaw "the day when poverty will be banished from this nation".

> **"** ANY **LACK OF CONFIDENCE IN** THE **ECONOMIC FUTURE OF** THE **UNITED STATES** IS **FOOLISH. "**
>
> **President Herbert Hoover,** in a speech after the stock market crash, 15 November 1929

Street in an apparently endless upward curve – about 30 million Americans had some form of stock market investment. In the prevailing mood, it was easy for the president to view problems in the economic scene – the ruin of small farmers through falling crop prices and poverty-line wages of many urban workers – as temporary problems that could be overcome.

Moviegoing was one boom area of the US economy. **Hollywood** had become the centre of film production, and its "Big Five" studios churned out hundreds of movies a year. The **film industry** was going through a technological revolution, with the transition from silent to sound movies. It was also becoming intensely conscious of its status and image. The Academy of Motion Picture Arts and Sciences made its **first annual "Oscar"** awards in 1929, awarding Best Picture to the war film *Wings* – the only silent movie to win the accolade.

In Italy, **Benito Mussolini's** (1883–1945) Fascist regime achieved a diplomatic triumph in signing the **Lateran Treaty** with Pope Pius XI. Since the unification of Italy in 1871 there had been an unresolved dispute between the Italian state and the papacy, with successive popes regarding themselves as "prisoners" in the Vatican. The Lateran Treaty recognized the **Vatican City** as an **independent state** and acknowledged Catholicism as Italy's official religion. Unofficially it assured the Fascist regime the support of the Catholic Church.

Another attempt was made to draw a line under World War I when the wartime Allies set up a committee, headed by American industrialist Owen Young, to reconsider **German reparations payments**. Accepting that the Dawes Plan (see 1924) had fixed payments too high, the **Young Plan** made proposals for Germany to pay a reduced annual sum until 1988. Although the deal was accepted by the German government, it was denounced by conservative nationalists and by the Nazis. They forced a referendum on reparations, which they described as "the enslavement of the German people". Although only 14 per cent of voters backed it, the referendum campaign significantly raised Hitler's political profile in Germany.

The long shadow cast by World War I was also evident in a **wave of anti-war books**. They included American writer Ernest Hemingway's novel *A Farewell to Arms*, British poet Robert Graves's (1895–1985) war memoir *Goodbye to All That*, and *All Quiet on the Western Front*, written by German novelist Erich Maria Remarque (1898–1970). Presenting war as a futile waste of human lives, they captured the popular mood of the time.

By far the most important event of the year, however, was the **Wall Street Crash**. In September, the share rise faltered. By 23 October, shares prices were falling, and the following day, "Black Thursday", the **market dropped** in a stampede of selling. In vain, President Hoover assured the American public that "the fundamental business of the country" was "on a sound and prosperous basis", but the selling of shares went on, and there were further sharp falls. Speculators who had bought shares on credit were ruined, as were thousands of modest individuals who had entrusted their life savings to the market. Experts spoke of a temporary "market correction", and Hoover took action to stimulate the economy and create jobs, but the crash was the start of a long-lasting collapse in share prices, and the signal for the start of a **worldwide depression**.

Winning film
The first movie to win the Academy Award for Best Picture was Wings, *a silent film about World War I fighter pilots, staring actress Clara Bow.*

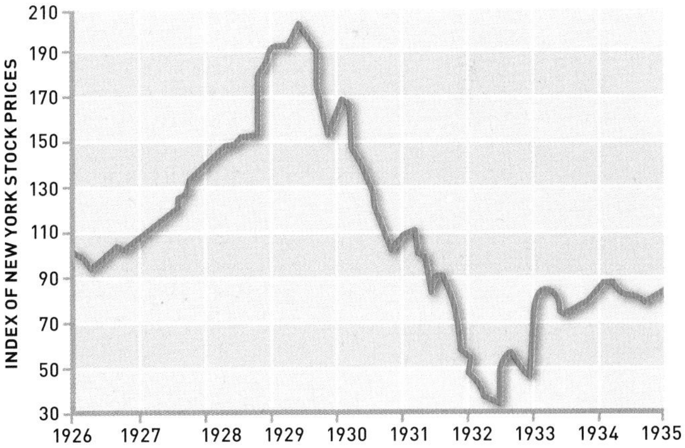

Wall Street index
Share prices on the New York stock exchange experienced a speculative boom in the 1920s, which was followed by an unstoppable collapse.

- **14 February** Seven killed in **St Valentine's Day Massacre** – the result of gang warfare in Chicago
- **4 March** Herbert Hoover **inaugurated** as US President
- **8 April** Indian revolutionaries explode bomb in corridors of **Legislative Assembly in Delhi**
- **16 May** First Academy Awards (**"Oscars"**) ceremony takes place
- **8 June** Labour government takes power in Britain under **Ramsay Macdonald**
- **21 June** US-brokered truce ends **Cristero War** in Mexico
- **8–29 August** German airship *Graf Zeppelin* **flies around world**
- **16 August Riots** break out **in Palestine** setting Arabs against Jews
- **31 August Young Plan** for German payment of reparations finalized
- **5 September** French Prime Minister Aristide Briand proposes a **United States of Europe**
- **24 September** US Army pilot James Doolittle makes **first "blind flight"** using instruments only
- **28 September In India, marriage** of girls under 14 banned by **Sarda Act**
- **3 October Gustav Stresemann**, architect of Germany's improved relations with France, **dies** (b.1878)
- **24–29 October** Share prices fall dramatically in **Wall Street crash**
- **31 October Lord Irwin**, British viceroy of India, declares that India will eventually receive dominion status
- **7 November Museum of Modern Art** opens in Manhattan
- **17 November** Nikolai **Bukharin**, Stalin's last opponent in Soviet government, **expelled from Politburo**
- **29 December** All-India Congress **demands immediate independence** from Britain

> **“ WE ARE 50 OR 100 YEARS BEHIND THE ADVANCED COUNTRIES. WE MUST MAKE GOOD THIS DISTANCE IN TEN YEARS. ”**

Josef Stalin, in a speech to the first All-Union Conference of leading personnel of Socialist Industry, 4 February 1931

Unemployed men waiting for food handouts in New York during the Depression. There was no federal unemployment benefit or welfare in the US.

IN THE EARLY MONTHS OF 1930, THE SOVIET UNION was thrown into turmoil by the mass **collectivization of agriculture** – the replacement of privately owned peasant farms with large, state-run farming practices. In the eyes of dictator Joseph Stalin (see 1928), who wanted to transform the Soviet Union into a modern industrial state, small-scale peasant agriculture was an obstacle to be ruthlessly swept aside – both inefficient and tainted with anti-socialist self-interest. The peasants, however, were ferociously attached to their land and farm animals, and when communist officials were sent to villages to organize collective farms, they met **widespread resistance**. Peasants slaughtered their animals rather than hand them over to the state, and attacked the communists with stones and clubs. The authorities responded with **mass arrests of "kulaks"** – better-off peasants – and troublemakers. By March it was announced that 14 million Soviet farms had been collectivized, but the chaos it created was so disruptive to food production that Stalin had to order a pause in the campaign.

It was no coincidence that the following month an agency known as the **Gulag was set up** to run a system of forced labour camps across the Soviet Union. Of about one million peasants arrested in the early 1930s, hundreds of thousands ended up in Gulag camps, providing slave labour to drive the developing Soviet economy.

Collectivization failed to produce an increase in agricultural output, and the vision of vast Soviet prairies farmed by tractors and mechanical harvesters remained largely a fantasy; instead there was famine (see 1933). But it did stimulate a mass movement of peasants to the cities, where they found work on construction sites and in factories. **Soviet industrial projects**, many using Gulag prison labour, developed on a vast scale, while the rest of the world plunged into an economic recession.

In **India** the wily and charismatic Mohandas Gandhi (see panel, right) was mounting a campaign of **civil disobedience** against British rule. Gandhi dramatized his opposition to the government salt monopoly by staging a march from Ahmedabad to the Indian Ocean. Setting out on 12 March, he reached the sea on 6 April, and scooped up a handful of salt water in public defiance of the government's ban on unlicensed salt gathering. Although Gandhi advocated strict non-violence, the **Salt March triggered riots** that redoubled after his arrest on 5 May. Despite this, the British remained committed to gradually extending India's limited self-government.

The exploits of adventurous **aviators** continued to fascinate the public, as they had done through the 1920s. Pilots became national heroes through pioneering **long-distance flights**. In May, Jean Mermoz (1901–36), who was employed by the French Aéropostale air mail company, made the first **postal flight across the South Atlantic**, flying a float plane non-stop from Dakar in West Africa to Natal in Brazil. This completed an unbroken airmail link that stretched from France to Chile. Meanwhile, the British cheered as **amateur pilot Amy Johnson** (1903–41) flew solo from Croydon in England to Darwin, Australia in a second-hand De Havilland Gipsy Moth biplane. The journey, which took 19 days, was especially remarkable since she had never even flown across the English Channel.

This amateur triumph of British aviation stood in stark contrast with the fate of an expensive government project, the **R101 airship**. On its maiden voyage in October, *R101* was intended to

MOHANDAS GANDHI
(1869–1948)

Known as Mahatma ("Great Soul"), Gandhi was born into a privileged Indian family and studied law in London. His first campaigns of non-violent civil disobedience were in South Africa. Returning to India in 1915 he led the opposition to British rule, although many nationalists rejected his non-violence. In 1948 he was assassinated by Hindu extremists, outraged by his conciliatory attitude toward Muslims.

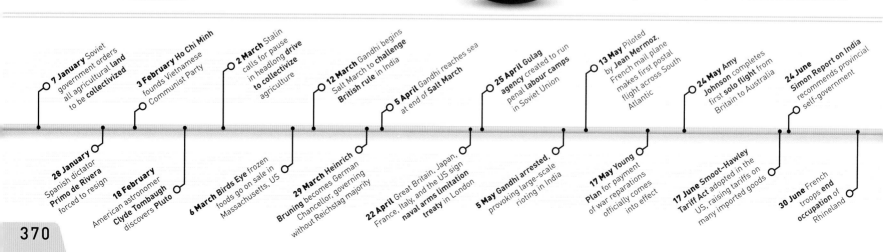

Soviet tractor
By the 1930s the Soviet Union was manufacturing its own tractors. There were about 200,000 tractors in the Soviet Union by 1934.

- **7 January** Soviet government orders all agricultural **land** to be **collectivized**
- **28 January** Spanish dictator **Primo de Rivera** forced to resign
- **3 February Ho Chi Minh** founds Vietnamese Communist Party
- **18 February** American astronomer **Clyde Tombaugh** discovers **Pluto**
- **2 March** Stalin calls for pause in headlong **drive to collectivize** agriculture
- **6 March Birds Eye** frozen foods go on sale in Massachusetts, US
- **12 March** Gandhi begins Salt March to **challenge British rule** in India
- **29 March Heinrich Bruning** becomes German Chancellor, governing without Reichstag majority
- **5 April** Gandhi reaches sea at end of **Salt March**
- **22 April** Great Britain, Japan, France, Italy, and the US sign **naval arms limitation treaty** in London
- **25 April Gulag** agency created to run penal **labour camps** in Soviet Union
- **5 May Gandhi arrested**, provoking large-scale rioting in India
- **13 May** Piloted by **Jean Mermoz**, French mail plane makes first postal flight across South Atlantic
- **17 May Young Plan** for payment of war reparations officially comes into effect
- **24 May Amy Johnson** completes first **solo flight** from Britain to Australia
- **17 June Smoot–Hawley Tariff Act** adopted in the US, raising tariffs on many imported goods
- **24 June Simon Report on India** recommends provincial self-government
- **30 June** French troops **end occupation** of Rhineland

The burnt-out wreckage of British airship *R101* lies in a field outside Beauvais in northern France. Britain's Air Secretary was killed in the crash.

Famous flight
British aviatrix Amy Johnson after her solo flight from England to Australia. Pilots were among the leading celebrities of the time.

carry the British Secretary of State for Air and other dignitaries from England to India. The badly designed craft only reached northern France, where it crashed in bad weather, killing 48 of 54 people on board.

By far the worst disaster of 1930, however, was the **collapse of the world economy**. In the US, at the start of the year, most commentators believed that, in the wake of the stock market crash (see 1929), the country was facing a temporary and modest economic downturn. In May, **President Herbert Hoover** (1874–1964) reassured Americans that they had "now passed the worst". Instead, unemployment continued to rise, bread lines became a common sight, farmers began to go bankrupt in large numbers, and over 1,300 US **banks failed** during the year. The US unwisely sought relief for its farmers and unemployed workers through blocking imports. The **Smoot–Hawley Tariff Act**, which became law in June, placed heavy duties on thousands of imported goods. When the US's trading partners retaliated, the world was set on course for a disastrous reduction in overall levels of trade.

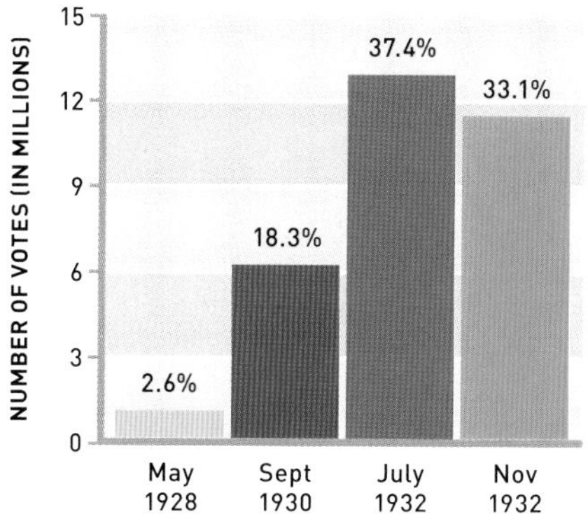

Nazi vote in federal elections 1928–1932
A minority extremist party in 1928, the Nazi party grew to be the largest single party by summer 1932. They peaked at 37.4 per cent of votes cast.

In **Germany**, economic crisis triggered political extremism and the **collapse of democratic government**. In March, the governing coalition fell apart because the Social Democrats would not agree to cuts in unemployment benefit. Heinrich Brüning (1855–1970), leader of the Centre Party, formed a government without majority support in the Reichstag. He dissolved parliament in July, calling a general election against a background of massive unemployment. Adolf Hitler's Nazi Party mounted a spectacular and violent election campaign, blaming all of Germany's problems on the Versailles Treaty (see 1919). The **Nazis increased their seats** in the Reichstag from 12 to 107, becoming the second largest party in the country. Brüning responded to a polarized Reichstag by ignoring it and clinging to power, ruling by Emergency Decree.

Many observers outside Germany were disturbed by the growing support for Hitler's aggressive nationalist extremism. France showed its lack of trust in a peaceful future by beginning construction of formidable defensive fortifications along its border with Germany. In the pursuit of absolute security, **the Maginot Line** consumed most of France's defence budget during the 1930s.

South American countries were especially vulnerable to the Depression because of their role as suppliers of food and raw materials to the industrialized US and Europe. Many experienced **political upheavals** as economic conditions worsened. In **Argentina**, a military coup ushered in a decade of political conflict and government corruption. In **Brazil**, an army revolt brought Getúlio Vargas (1882–1954) to power in November. Vargas installed a populist dictatorship that pushed for the industrialization of Brazil and suppressed political dissent, while introducing social welfare measures for the poor.

In Japan, radical nationalists, including many army and navy officers, believed the answer to **Japan's economic problems** lay in military conquest. The civilian government of prime minister **Osachi Hamaguchi** (1870–1931) outraged them further by seeking cuts in military spending to help offset a budgetary deficit. On 14 November, Hamaguchi was shot at Tokyo station by a member of a nationalist secret society. He never recovered, and died nine months later. It was an ominous sign of the Japanese militarists' determination to pursue their own aggressive expansionist policies.

Japanese assassination
Japanese Prime Minister Hamaguchi after being shot by a nationalist extremist at Tokyo station. He died the following year.

18 July German chancellor Bruning **dissolves Reichstag**, ruling by emergency decree

28 July In **Canada**, Conservatives defeat governing Liberal Party in **federal election**

30 July Uruguay defeats Argentina in **first football World Cup final**

5 August US census estimates country's population as **122.7 million**

22 August Peru's president **Augusto Leguia** overthrown in military coup

6 September Jose Felix Uriburu takes power in coup in Argentina

8 September Special session of **Canadian parliament** convened to respond to **rising unemployment**

14 September Hitler's **Nazi Party wins** 107 seats in elections to German Reichstag

5 October British **airship** *R101* **crashes** in France on maiden voyage

17 October US president Herbert Hoover establishes **Committee for Unemployment Relief**

2 November Haile **Selassie crowned** emperor of Ethiopia

3 November Getulio Vargas takes power in Brazil after military revolt

4 November Chiang Kai-shek triumphs over rival Chinese generals in **Central Plains War**

12 November First Round Table Conference on **future of India** opens in London

14 November Japanese premier **Hamaguchi Yuko shot** by nationalist extremists

2 December US president Hoover asks Congress for $150 million for projects to **stimulate employment**

8 December Indian nationalists assassinate British Inspector General of Prisons in Calcutta

16 December Trade unions declare **general strike** in Spain

1931

> **“** THE **CAPITALIST CHAIN** IS AGAIN **THREATENING TO BREAK** AT THE WEAKEST LINK. **SPAIN** IS **NEXT IN ORDER. ”**

Leon Trotsky, Russian revolutionary,
speaking on the revolution in Spain, January 1931

Demonstrators in Madrid celebrate the revolution of April 1931 that overthrew the Spanish monarchy. Among the new reforms was women's right to vote.

Scaling new heights
Photographer Lewis Hine documented the casual risks taken by workers during construction of the Empire State Building.

ON 14 APRIL 1931, KING ALFONSO XIII OF SPAIN (1886–1941) abdicated and fled into exile, after his supporters were defeated in municipal elections. The victors in this bloodless revolution, a coalition of moderate republicans and socialists, set up a provisional government headed by Niceto Alcalá-Zamora (1877–1949). The departure of the king and **founding of Spain's Second Republic** gave the urban and rural poor, as well as nationalists in the Basque country and Catalonia, hope, but army officers, landowners, industrialists, and the Catholic hierarchy were adamantly opposed to change. Spain was on the path to civil war.

In New York on 1 May the **Empire State Building was officially opened**. Standing 443m (1,454ft) tall to the top of its spire, it surpassed the Art Deco Chrysler Building, which had been the **world's tallest building** for just 11 months. Begun in 1929, at the height of the US stock market boom, the Empire State Building expressed the boundless optimism of the time. But its completion also came against a background of farm bankruptcies and rising unemployment.

Meanwhile, the world economic recession took a sharp turn for the worse through a major **European banking crisis**. In May, Austria's largest bank, the Creditanstalt, failed, and by July many major German banks also faced collapse. German Chancellor Heinrich Brüning proposed a customs union between Germany and Austria, and suggested Germany might renege on payment of war reparations. France's hostile response was to refuse to help prop up the German financial system. Germany and Austria were forced to take emergency measures to block foreigners from withdrawing funds.

Britain had made substantial loans to German banks – money that was now frozen. As a **crisis loomed**, financial experts advised **Ramsay Macdonald's** (1886–1937) **Labour government** to cut expenditure to balance the budget. In August, proposals to cut unemployment benefit and government employee pay provoked a mass resignation by Labour ministers. Macdonald stayed as prime minister, forming a coalition National Government with the other two main parties, the Conservatives and the Liberals. A Royal Navy strike over pay at Invergordon panicked foreign investors and triggered a run on the pound, reducing the value of sterling by a quarter.

The most ominous event of the year was **Japanese aggression against China**. On 18 September, Japanese army officers guarding the South Manchurian Railway carried out an attack on the tracks, which they blamed on the Chinese. This "**Mukden incident**" provided the pretext for the Japanese **military occupation of Manchuria**. The occupation was condemned by the League of Nations as an act of aggression, but the Japanese refused to withdraw. The following year Japan set up a puppet government in Manchuria under **Pu Yi** (1906–67), China's last emperor, who had been deposed in 1912.

From September to December a Round Table **Conference on the future of India** was held in London. The Indian National Congress, the principal Indian nationalist movement, was

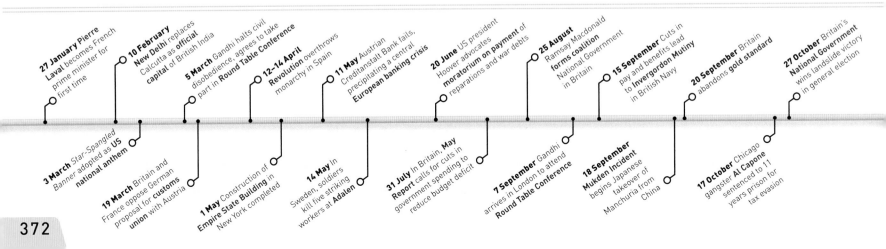

Occupation of Manchuria
Korea became a Japanese colony in 1910. In 1931, the Japanese extended into Manchuria, which became the puppet state of Manchukuo.

KEY
- Japanese Empire 1930
- Japanese sphere of influence 1930
- Japanese conquests 1931–3

27 January Pierre Laval becomes French prime minister for first time

10 February New Delhi replaces Calcutta as **official capital** of British India

3 March *Star-Spangled Banner* adopted as **US national anthem**

5 March Gandhi halts civil disobedience, agrees to take part in **Round Table Conference**

19 March Britain and France oppose German proposal for **customs union** with Austria

12–14 April Revolution overthrows monarchy in Spain

1 May Construction of **Empire State Building** in New York completed

11 May Austrian Creditanstalt Bank fails, precipitating a central **European banking crisis**

14 May In Sweden, soldiers kill five striking workers at **Adalen**

20 June US president Hoover advocates **moratorium on payment** of reparations and war debts

31 July In Britain, **May Report** calls for cuts in government spending to reduce budget deficit

25 August Ramsay Macdonald **forms coalition** National Government in Britain

7 September Gandhi arrives in London to attend **Round Table Conference**

15 September Cuts in pay and benefits lead to **Invergordon Mutiny** in British Navy

18 September Mukden Incident begins Japanese takeover of Manchuria from China

20 September Britain abandons **gold standard**

17 October Chicago gangster **Al Capone** sentenced to 11 years prison for tax evasion

27 October Britain's **National Government** wins landslide victory in general election

American pilot Amelia Earhart arrives in England after her historic solo transatlantic flight in a Lockheed Vega monoplane.

Japanese troops in Manchuria
The Japanese occupation of the northern Chinese province of Manchuria can be seen as their first step towards World War II.

represented by **Mohandas Gandhi** (1869–1948). He had negotiated a pact with the British Viceroy of India, Lord Irwin, to suspend the civil disobedience campaign (see 1930). The conference was not a success, however, and on his return to India Gandhi resumed his non-violent campaign against the British.

In contrast with the British treatment of India was the passage of the **Statute of Westminster** by the British parliament in December. This law **recognized full equality** between Britain and the dominions – Australia, New Zealand, Canada, South Africa, the Irish Free State, and Newfoundland. For them the British Empire had truly become a Commonwealth of Nations.

42 THE NUMBER OF **STATES WON BY ROOSEVELT IN** THE **1932 US ELECTIONS**

THE PEAK YEAR OF THE GREAT DEPRESSION saw declining output and sharply reduced levels of trade bring **mass unemployment** to the world's leading industrial nations. At least 13 million Americans, around 3 million Britons, and more than 5 million Germans were unemployed. In Europe, national unemployment benefit schemes helped the jobless to survive, but in the US, where only piecemeal local welfare schemes existed, unemployment led to abject poverty. Thousands became homeless, living in shanty towns ironically called "**Hoovervilles**" after the US president.

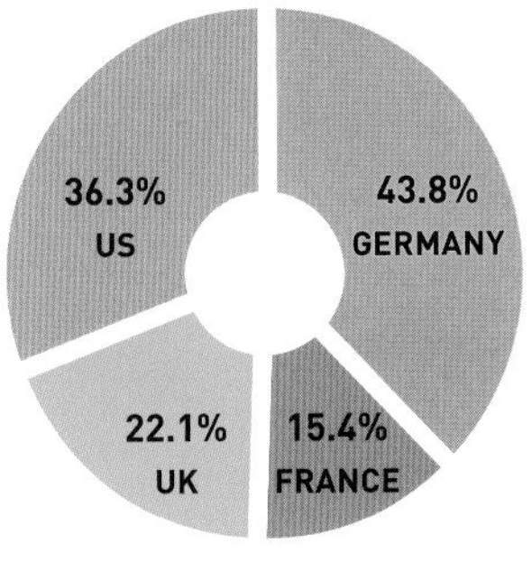

Industrial unemployment
German industrial workers had the worst unemployment rate at the peak of the depression, closely followed by the US.

In Ireland, **Éamon de Valera (1882–1975)** became president after an election victory for his Fianna Fàil party in March. As a republican who had taken part in the Easter Rising (see 1916) and had led the Irish Republican Army (IRA) in the Irish Civil War (see 1922), De Valera was renowned for his anti-British sentiments. He revoked the Oath of Allegiance to the British crown and entered into a **trade war with Britain** that damaged both countries.

In Germany, Nazi leader Adolf Hitler (1889–1945) suffered frustration in his campaign to win power through the democratic process. He stood for president in the spring elections, but was eventually beaten by the incumbent Paul von Hindenburg (1845–1934). Although in elections to the Reichstag the **Nazis were the largest single party**, they continued to be excluded from government. Ignoring the Reichstag, Hindenburg installed a conservative clique in power.

There was relief from the grim news of the Depression when American pilot Amelia Earhart (1897–1937) became the **first woman to fly solo across the Atlantic**. Taking off from Newfoundland in Canada on the morning of 20 May – the fifth anniversary of Charles Lindbergh's famous flight (see 1927) – she landed in a field in Northern Ireland 14 hours and 56 minutes later.

The US presidential election was held in November, against a background of bank failures, farm bankruptcies, and rising unemployment. Herbert Hoover's inability to halt his country's slide into the Depression gave him little hope against the Democratic challenger, and former governor of New York, **Franklin D. Roosevelt** (see 1933). During his campaign Roosevelt promised "a new deal for the American people". He won with 57.4 per cent of the popular vote, but what Roosevelt actually intended to do about the Depression remained unclear.

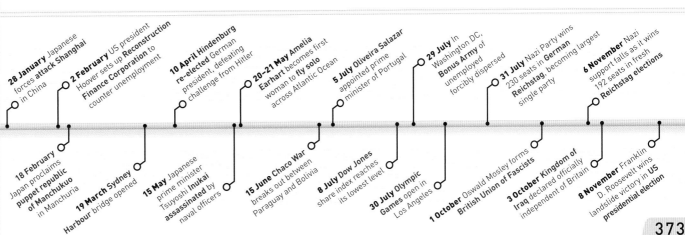

THE BONUS ARMY

In summer 1932, more than 20,000 unemployed World War I veterans gathered in Washington DC to demand payment of a "bonus" promised by the government in recognition of their military service. They established a shanty town within sight of the Capitol and vowed to stay until the money was paid. Their protest attracted widespread sympathy from Americans distressed at mass unemployment, but President Hoover refused to pay out. On 28 July, infantry, cavalry, and tanks were deployed to attack the protesters' camp and disband the Bonus Army.

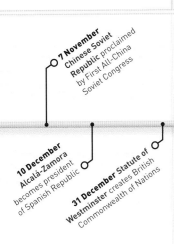

7 November Chinese Soviet Republic proclaimed by First All-China Soviet Congress

10 December Alcalá-Zamora becomes president of Spanish Republic

31 December Statute of Westminster creates British Commonwealth of Nations

28 January Japanese forces **attack Shanghai** in China

2 February US president Hoover sets up **Reconstruction Finance Corporation** to counter unemployment

18 February Japan proclaims **puppet republic of Manchukuo** in Manchuria

19 March Sydney Harbour bridge opened

10 April Hindenburg re-elected German president, defeating challenge from Hitler

15 May Japanese prime minister Tsuyoshi **Inukai assassinated** by naval officers

20–21 May Amelia Earhart becomes first woman to **fly solo** across Atlantic Ocean

15 June Chaco War breaks out between Paraguay and Bolivia

5 July Oliveira Salazar appointed prime minister of Portugal

8 July Dow Jones share index reaches its lowest level

29 July In Washington DC, **Bonus Army** of unemployed forcibly dispersed

30 July Olympic Games open in Los Angeles

31 July Nazi Party wins 230 seats in **German Reichstag**, becoming largest single party

1 October Oswald Mosley forms **British Union of Fascists**

3 October Kingdom of Iraq declared officially independent of Britain

6 November Nazi support falls as it wins 192 seats in fresh **Reichstag elections**

8 November Franklin D. Roosevelt wins landslide victory in **US presidential election**

THE STORY OF COMMUNICATION

ELECTRICITY TRIGGERS A REVOLUTION IN BROADCASTING AND PERSONAL COMMUNICATION

Instant worldwide communication has become a defining characteristic of the modern world. Until 200 years ago, most long-distance messages could travel no faster than the horse or ship carrying them. It was the advent of electricity in the 19th century that transformed communications.

In the 18th century, the French navy developed a system for transmitting orders between ships using semaphore flags. From the 1790s, semaphore was used on land, with lines of stations relaying coded messages using large signalling devices, each visible to the next station in the chain. From the 1830s, the development of electric telegraph replaced this medium. American Samuel Morse produced a robust and practical system, a simple on-off key generating a code that was transmitted along a wire. By the 1860s, telegraph wires spanned continents, and underwater cables enabled almost instant communication across oceans.

In the late 19th and early 20th centuries, the invention of the telephone enabled electronic transmission of speech. The discovery that radio waves could transmit sound opened the new possibility of broadcasting. From the 1920s, "wireless sets", providing entertainment and news, became a common feature of households. Television, however, did not become a mass medium until the 1950s.

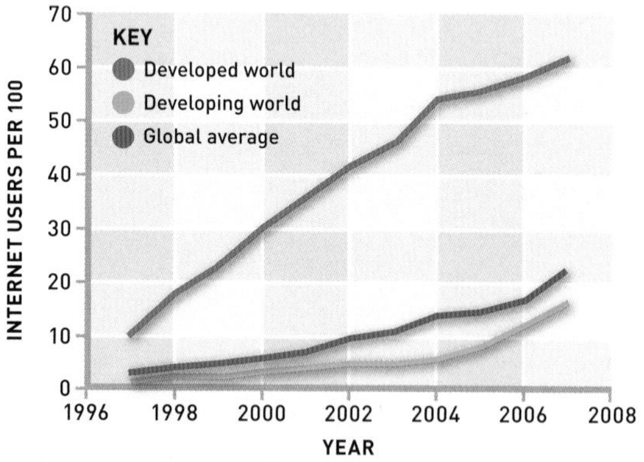

The rise of the Internet
The increase in Internet usage in developed countries was dramatic between 1997 and 2007, but access remained available only to a minority in the developing world.

THE INFORMATION AGE

Several lines of development revolutionized communications after World War II, creating the "Information Age". The advent of transistors made electronic goods smaller and cheaper, and advances in rocket technology allowed satellites to be placed in space, enabling global access to communication networks. The triumph of digital technology and microprocessors from the 1980s made computers almost universal. The potential flow of information worldwide was effectively limitless.

Long-distance call
Alexander Graham Bell initiates the first telephone link between New York and Chicago in 1892. By then, New York was already linked to Boston and Philadelphia.

Prehistory
Smoke signals
Fire allows smoke signals to be sent over considerable distances. However, this method is limited to a simple set of prearranged messages.

Sumerian tablet

3100–2500 BCE
Cuneiform writing
Writing is a giant step forward in communication. Mesopotamian cuneiform script is inscribed on clay tablets.

2900–2350 BCE
Carrier pigeons
Pigeons are used to carry messages in ancient Egypt and Persia. They will continue to be used by armies in World War I and World War II.

1st–2nd centuries
Letters by courier
Letters are written on papyrus or on wood in the Roman Empire. The Vindolanda tablets from Roman Britain include a birthday invitation.

Vindolanda tablet

17th century
Newspapers
Newspapers, which disseminate information to a large public, develop in 17th-century Europe. The development of the printing press contributes to their growth.

The London Post

1784
Mail coaches
Britain introduces four-horse coaches that are faster than passenger-carrying stagecoaches to carry post between major cities.

1791–95
Visual telegraphy
French inventor Claude Chappe pioneers a semaphore system that allows coded messages to be transmitted by chains of relay stations.

Chappe telegraph

Morse receiver

1837
Electric telegraphy
American inventor Samuel Morse develops the electric telegraph in the US. British Railways uses an electric telegraph.

“THAT’S **AN AMAZING INVENTION,** BUT WHO WOULD EVER WANT TO USE ONE OF THEM?”

Rutherford B. Hayes, US President, to Alexander Graham Bell after a demonstration of the telephone, 1876

Early table telephone
Made of metal, the Ericsson table telephone dates from 1890. It combined the transmitter and receiver into a single handset. The handle cranked a generator that rang a bell at the telephone exchange to contact the operator.

Penny Black

1837–40
Postage stamp
Britain introduces a low, uniform rate for postage, paid by buying an adhesive stamp.

1850s–60s
Transatlantic cable
Telegraph cables laid across the Atlantic seabed allow messages to be exchanged between Europe and North America in minutes.

1870s
The telephone
Inventors, including American Alexander Graham Bell, demonstrate early telephones in the US. The first telephone exchanges in North America and Europe date from 1878.

Early 1900s
Radio
Wireless telegraphy and sound transmission developed, leading to radio broadcasting.

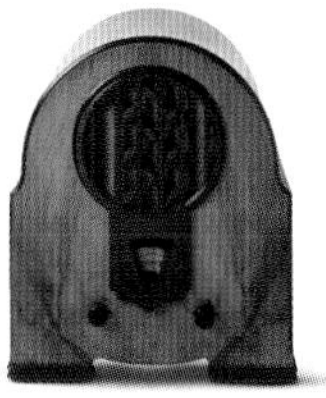
Wireless

1920s
Airmail
The carrying of mail by aircraft, initiated on a small scale before World War I, becomes important, transforming delivery times on long-distance routes.

1920s–30s
Television
Transmission of moving images leads to public television broadcasting, though few people own televisions until the 1950s.

1960s
Communication satellites
Telstar enables the first live transatlantic television broadcast in 1962.

Telstar

Late 20th century
The Internet
Global computer networks create instant communication through email.

Apple iPhone

Early 21st century
Mobile communication
Mobile phone usage becomes a mass phenomenon in the first decade of the 21st century.

" ... THROUGH GOD'S POWERFUL AID, WE HAVE BECOME ONCE MORE TRUE GERMANS. "

Adolf Hitler, German chancellor, 1933

Adolf Hitler being greeted by his followers at the annual Nazi Party rally at Nuremberg in September 1933 – it was a celebration of his rise to power.

Reichstag fire
A Dutch communist was executed for causing the fire at the German parliament building, but many believe the Nazis were responsible.

IN GERMANY, AT THE END OF JANUARY, after backroom negotiations with the conservative clique of politicians and army officers surrounding the president Paul von Hindenburg (1847–1934), Nazi leader **Adolf Hitler (1889–1945)** was invited to become **Chancellor** (head of government). The conservatives believed they would have Hitler under their control, since only three members of the coalition government were Nazis. Hitler, however, celebrated his appointment as if it was a revolutionary **seizure of power**.

On 28 February the **Reichstag building in Berlin burned down**. The fire was blamed on a Dutch communist called Marinus van der Lubbe. It provided a pretext for an **Emergency Decree** that gave the government and its police almost limitless powers. The Nazis fell short of a majority in elections five days later, but on 23 March, with the support of the nationalist and Catholic parties, Hitler won a parliamentary vote for an **Enabling Act** that **transferred all authority** from the Reichstag to his government. The German parliament had voted for its own destruction; Hitler soon banned all other political parties, and created a **single-party state**.

The consequence of Nazi rule soon became evident. The first improvised **concentration camps** opened in March; in April a one-day nationwide **boycott of Jewish businesses** was enforced; and in May the German Student Association organized the **burning of books** described as "un-German". These highly publicized acts were just the beginning. As the protection of the law was withdrawn from communists, socialists, and Jews, hundreds of **opponents** of the regime were **murdered** and thousands tortured and beaten.

Nazi violence troubled many Germans, but support for the regime was guaranteed by a sharp turnaround in the economy and the rapid disappearance of mass unemployment. This was partly achieved through ambitious public works programmes, most prominently the building of a network of autobahns (motorways), that provided employment. There was also a **restoration of confidence**, through the Nazis' projected image of Germany as united, powerful, and dynamic.

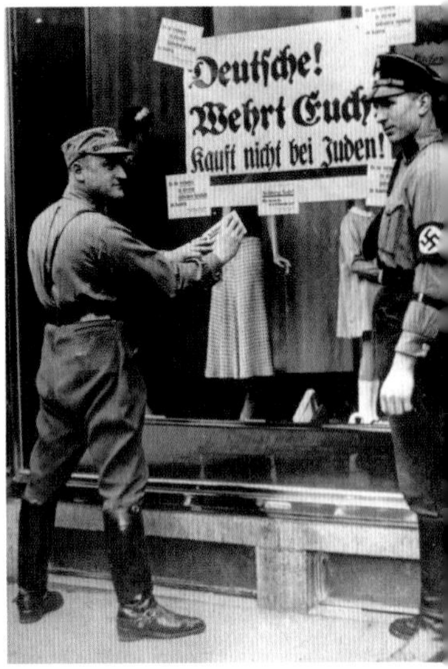

Jewish boycott
A Nazi Stormtrooper, accompanied by an elite Schutzstaffeln (SS) soldier, posts a notice on a Jewish shop window – "Don't buy from Jews!".

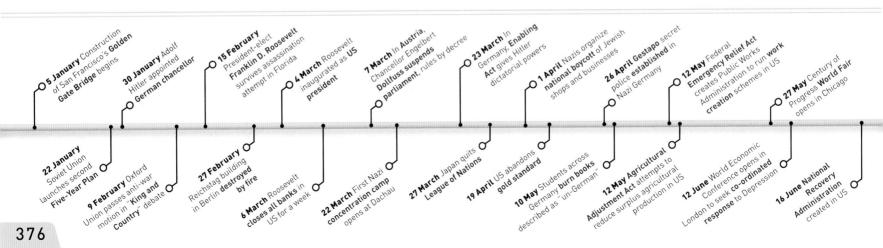

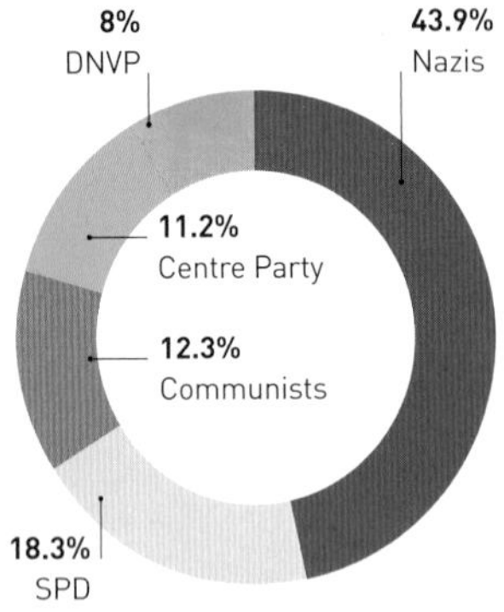

German election results
The Reichstag election of March 1933 showed stubborn support for the communists and the socialist SPD despite intimidation.

The US also found a strong, new leader in the person of President **Franklin D. Roosevelt** (see panel right). In his inauguration speech on 4 March, Roosevelt told Americans that "the only thing we have to fear is fear itself". He immediately applied this principle to the tottering US banking system. **On 6 March every bank in the US was closed.** The president announced that banks would not reopen until the federal authorities had established they

5 January Construction of San Francisco's **Golden Gate Bridge** begins

22 January Soviet Union launches second **Five-Year Plan**

30 January Adolf Hitler appointed **German chancellor**

9 February Oxford Union passes anti-war motion in "**King and Country**" debate

15 February President-elect **Franklin D. Roosevelt** survives assassination attempt in Florida

27 February Reichstag building in Berlin **destroyed by fire**

4 March Roosevelt inaugurated as **US president**

6 March Roosevelt **closes all banks** in US for a week

7 March In **Austria**, Chancellor Engelbert **Dollfuss suspends parliament**, rules by decree

22 March First Nazi **concentration camp** opens at Dachau

23 March In Germany, **Enabling Act** gives Hitler dictatorial powers

27 March Japan quits **League of Nations**

1 April Nazis organize **national boycott** of Jewish shops and businesses

19 April US abandons **gold standard**

26 April Gestapo secret police **established** in Nazi Germany

10 May Students across Germany **burn books** described as "un-German"

12 May Federal **Emergency Relief Act** creates Public Works Administration to run **work creation** schemes in US

12 May Agricultural Adjustment Act attempts to reduce surplus agricultural production in US

27 May Century of Progress **World Fair** opens in Chicago

12 June World Economic Conference opens in London to seek **co-ordinated response** to Depression

16 June National Recovery Administration created in US

“I PLEDGE MYSELF TO A NEW DEAL FOR THE AMERICAN PEOPLE.”

Franklin D. Roosevelt, at his nomination acceptance speech, 1932

Young women in Florida having their backs decorated with the Blue Eagle of the National Recovery Administration, a major plank of Roosevelt's New Deal.

were solvent. Americans accepted Roosevelt's assurance that the banks were now safe and came forward to deposit their savings – a confidence trick that worked.

Through the frenetic first 100 days of his administration, Roosevelt pushed through a raft of legislation to fulfil his promise of a "**New Deal**". The measures were neither entirely coherent nor uniformly successful. The wages of federal employees were cut. Farmers were paid to leave land fallow and slaughter animals, to raise farm prices. The **National Recovery Administration** pressured businesses to raise wages and prices, to increase profitability and consumer demand. The Tennessee Valley Authority brought electricity and modernization to one of the most economically backward regions in the US. Most popular were direct work creation schemes such as those organized by the **Civil Works Administration**. These ranged from important construction projects to "boondoggles" – futile jobs to keep men employed.

Above all, Roosevelt's personal leadership had a dramatic effect on American morale. His warm-hearted radio broadcasts, known as "**fireside chats**", convinced many Americans that they truly had a friend in the White House.

The British, meanwhile, were desperate to restore international free trade, and to end the slide toward protectionism and devalued currencies. When a **World Economic Conference** assembled in London, however, Roosevelt insisted on the right of the US to manipulate its own exchange rate and to deploy tariffs in its national interest.

FRANKLIN D. ROOSEVELT (1882–1945)

Franklin Delano Roosevelt entered politics as a Democrat before World War I. As governor of New York from 1928 he led efforts to provide relief for the unemployed. Elected president four times, from his first presidential campaign in 1932 he transformed American politics by attracting the votes of labour unions, ethnic minorities, and African-Americans. His New Deal policies won him enduring popularity, reinforced by his leadership during World War II.

4.4 YEARS
THE AVERAGE **LIFE EXPECTANCY** OF **A MALE CHILD BORN IN UKRAINE** IN **1933**

The conference failed and, in the absence of international co-operation, all the countries that attended continued to pursue aggressive nationalist policies, blocking the overall recovery of the world economy.

While capitalist countries struggled with the Depression, the communist **Soviet Union** seemed immune to such problems. Hidden from the outside world, its people suffered a different catastrophe. While Soviet propaganda celebrated rising output, in 1932–33 **famine gripped the Ukraine** and other grain-producing areas, killing millions of the rural population. It mainly came about as the result of the collectivization of agriculture (see 1930). But the scale of the disaster was vastly increased by Stalin's insistence on forcibly extracting grain from starving rural areas to feed cities.

At a time of widespread distress and upheaval, it was perhaps ironic that the **Chicago World's Fair**, opening in May, celebrated a "Century of Progress". The American public loved the fair's celebration of the onward march of technology, but not everything was devoted to "progress". The burlesque dancer Sally Rand was a major hit with her "fan dance", so too was the arrival of 24 Italian flying boats commanded by marshal of the Italian Air Force Italo Balbo, and a visit from the German airship *Graf Zeppelin*.

The Chicago Fair's emphasis on achievements in the air was timely, for this was the year in which the technology of **air travel** reached a critical turning point. The introduction of the all-metal, streamlined, monoplane **Boeing 247** airliner, which was capable of cruising at over 241kph (150mph), transformed journey times. The 247 could carry 10 passengers coast-to-coast across the US in just 20 hours. The Douglas Aircraft Company responded with the **DC-1** and **DC-2**, which shaved a further two hours off a transcontinental scheduled flight. Air travel was still expensive though and remained a form of transport used only by the well off.

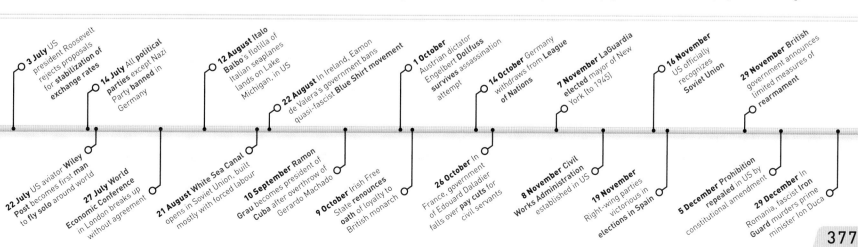

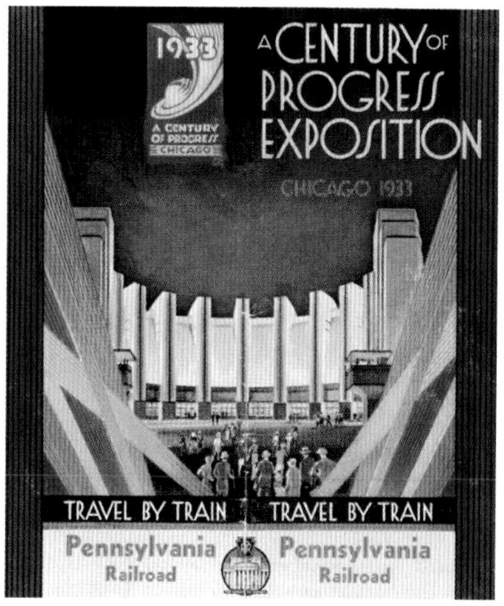

World's Fair programme
The 1933 Chicago World's Fair, staged on the shore of Lake Michigan, took the theme of science, technology, and industry.

A **strange incident** occurred in January 1933. The game of **cricket**, the playing of which was one of the ritual bonds holding together the British Commonwealth, **led to a diplomatic crisis**. The English team touring **Australia** adopted intimidating "**bodyline**" tactics, their fast bowler Harold Larwood aiming deliveries at the Australian batsmen's chests and heads. After two Australian players were injured at Adelaide, Australian protests went to government level. Intervention by the **British foreign office**, keen to maintain good relations with an assertive Commonwealth state, ensured that the unapologetic Larwood never played Australia again.

3 July US president Roosevelt rejects proposals for **stabilization of exchange rates**

14 July All **political parties** except Nazi Party **banned** in Germany

22 July US aviator **Wiley Post** becomes **first man to fly solo** around world

27 July World Economic Conference in London breaks up without agreement

12 August Italo **Balbo**'s flotilla of Italian seaplanes lands on Lake Michigan, in US

21 August White Sea Canal opens in Soviet Union, built mostly with forced labour

22 August In Ireland, Eamon de Valera's government bans quasi-fascist **Blue Shirt movement**

10 September Ramon **Grau** becomes president of **Cuba** after overthrow of Gerardo Machado

9 October Irish Free State **renounces oath** of loyalty to British monarch

1 October Austrian dictator Engelbert **Dollfuss survives** assassination attempt

14 October Germany withdraws from **League of Nations**

26 October In France, government of Edouard Daladier falls over **pay cuts** for civil servants

7 November LaGuardia **elected** mayor of New York (to 1945)

8 November Civil Works Administration established in US

16 November US officially recognizes **Soviet Union**

19 November Right-wing parties victorious in **elections in Spain**

29 November British government announces limited measures of **rearmament**

5 December Prohibition repealed in US by constitutional amendment

29 December In Romania, fascist **Iron Guard** murders prime minister Ion Duca

> **“** VERY **FEW** OF THESE **PANIC-MONGERS HAVE** ANY PERSONAL **KNOWLEDGE OF** THE **COUNTRIES** THAT ARE ALREADY **UNDER BLACKSHIRT GOVERNMENT. ”**
>
> **Lord Rothermere,** *Daily Mirror,* 22 January 1934

Black-shirted paramilitaries of Oswald Mosley's British Union of Fascists give the Nazi salute. Mosley was inspired by the example of Mussolini and Hitler.

IN A YEAR DOMINATED BY POLITICAL VIOLENCE and assassinations, the **French Third Republic** was rocked by the **Stavisky affair**. A crooked financier, Alexandre Stavisky committed suicide on 8 January, after the collapse of a dishonest investment scheme. The right-wing press accused leading French politicians of profiting from Stavisky's fraudulent deals. On 6 February, various nationalist and anti-Semitic groups assembled in Paris, intending to march on the Chamber of Deputies and overthrow the allegedly corrupt Republic. In a night of **street fighting** between thousands of demonstrators and police, 15 people were killed and many more injured. The attempt to force the government to resign failed, and the **Republic survived**.

In the US, the public was distracted from the woes of the **Depression** by the exploits and violent deaths of outlaws and gangsters. **Bonnie Parker** and **Clyde Barrow** led a gang that robbed banks, stores, and gas stations, roving from Texas to Minnesota. Their shoot-outs with police and narrow escapes were reported with feverish excitement in the press. Parker and Barrow were finally **ambushed and shot dead** by police at Bienville Parish, Louisiana, on 23 May 1934, sealing the legend of "Bonnie and Clyde". Another "most wanted" criminal was the gangster **John Dillinger**. Arrested in January, he escaped from custody, but was tracked down by federal investigation chief J. Edgar Hoover. On 22 July, Dillinger was gunned down by federal agents as he left the Biograph Theater, a movie house in Chicago.

Bonnie and Clyde *American outlaw Bonnie Parker playfully targets her partner-in-crime Clyde Barrow. This photo was on a reel of film found by police in 1933.*

Another man to die by the bullet in 1934 was **Sergei Kirov**, the Communist Party boss in Leningrad and a close associate of Soviet dictator **Joseph Stalin**. On 1 December, a man walked up behind Kirov in a corridor outside his office and shot him in the back of the neck. The **assassination** was blamed on Leonid Nikolaev, an expelled party member with a grudge, but suspicions persist that Stalin may have arranged the assassination himself. Whatever the truth, the Soviet dictator used Kirov's death to pass a **new anti-terrorist law**, which was later used to justify the **arrest and execution** of hundreds of thousands of people.

In Germany, on 30 June–1 July, Adolf Hitler confirmed his hold on power by a massacre, known as the **Night of the Long Knives**. The main target of the killings was the leadership of the SA (Sturmabteilung or Stormtroopers). These paramilitaries had provided the muscle for Hitler's rise to power, but now the disorderly street-fighters had become an embarrassment. SA chief **Ernst Röhm** was one of the hundreds that were killed. He was **arrested** early on the morning of 1 July by Hitler, who was accompanied by SS guards. Röhm was asked to kill himself, but refused and was **shot without trial** by the leader of the SS, Theodor Eicke. As well as the SA leadership, scores of individuals who had criticized the Nazi regime were also murdered.

In **Austria**, a Nazi attempt to seize power failed. The Austrian chancellor **Engelbert Dollfuss** had established an authoritarian single-party state. In February, Dollfuss suppressed a left-wing uprising in Vienna, using artillery against the socialists' stronghold in the Karl Marx Hof housing estate. He also banned the Austrian Nazi Party. In July, the Nazis attempted an armed coup, probably intending to achieve the unification of Austria with Nazi Germany. Although Dollfuss was killed, the coup failed. **Kurt Schuschnigg**, a member of Dollfuss's party, succeeded him as chancellor.

Britain was a relative haven of tranquillity, but even there **fascism** was on the rise. Former Labour minister Oswald Mosley had founded the **British Union of Fascists** (BUF) in 1932, hoping to turn Britain into an authoritarian state under his rule. In June 1934, Mosley staged a rally at Olympia in London that degenerated into a brawl as BUF paramilitaries fought with anti-fascist protestors. Such political violence had little appeal for the British, who were also alienated by the fascists' links with the Nazis – Hitler was a guest at Mosley's wedding. Although it enjoyed the backing of some national newspapers, the BUF remained a minority party without significant electoral support.

Ethiopian tribal warriors gather to fight for their emperor, Haile Selassie.

THROUGH THE FIRST HALF OF THE 1930S, parts of the US and Canada were swept by giant dust storms as topsoil blew off land ruined by a combination of persistent drought and intensive farming. The worst of these "**black blizzards**" occurred in April 1935, affecting a vast area of the plains of Kansas, Oklahoma, Texas, New Mexico, and Colorado. The **Dust Bowl** created by this

> **850 MILLION TONNES**
> THE ESTIMATED **AMOUNT OF TOPSOIL BLOWN OFF** THE **SOUTHERN PLAINS** OF THE **US BY DECEMBER 1935**

ecological disaster could no longer support small farmers, who were forced to migrate in their thousands. Many of them found their way to migrant camps in California, where they were exploited as casual labour.

Meanwhile, President Roosevelt's administration was pressing ahead with a raft of reforms often referred to as the **Second New Deal**. These policies were more radical than

- **8 January** Death of financier Alexandre Stavisky precipitates **political crisis in France**
- **1 February** Austrian Chancellor Dollfuss **bans all political parties** except his own Fatherland Front
- **6–7 February** Right-wing extremists **attempt coup** in Paris
- **21 February** Nicaraguan guerilla leader **Augusto Sandino** assassinated
- **24 March** Degree of **self-government** for US-controlled Philippines
- **29–30 June** Hitler has many opponents murdered on **Night of the Long Knives** in Germany
- **22 July** US gangster **John Dillinger** mortally wounded by police in Chicago
- **25 July** In Austria, **Dollfuss killed** but attempted Nazi seizure of power fails
- **30 July** Kurt **Schuschnigg** becomes chancellor of Austria
- **2 August** German president **Hindenburg dies**, opening way for Hitler to become Führer
- **6 October** Uprisings in Asturias and Catalonia **shake Spanish Republic**
- **9 October King Alexander** of Yugoslavia **assassinated** on state visit to France
- **16 October** Chinese communists retreat from Jiangxi province, begin **Long March**
- **1 December** Stalin's associate Sergei **Kirov assassinated** in Leningrad
- **1 December Lázaro Cárdenas** becomes president of Mexico
- **19 December** Japan renounces **Washington Treaties** limiting naval armaments
- **13 January Saarland** chooses to become part of Germany
- **17 January** Leading Soviet **communists**, including Kamenev and Zinoviev, **convicted** of complicity in Kirov's murder
- **16 March** Hitler introduces conscription in Germany in open **defiance of Versailles Treaty**

1,345 THE NUMBER OF **OFFICERS AND CREW ABOARD** THE **SS NORMANDIE**

BENITO MUSSOLINI (1883–1945)

Benito Mussolini imposed his authoritarian, militaristic rule on Italy from 1922 to 1943. His Fascist state was widely admired, but dreams of conquest led to military adventures and an alliance with Nazi Germany. Unwisely leading his country into World War II, he was deposed as the Allies invaded Italy in 1943 and eventually killed by partisans.

Roosevelt's original New Deal (see 1933), favouring labour unions over big business and the poor over the rich. The **Wagner Labor Relations Act** placed the government on the side of workers who went on strike to gain union rights. The **Social Security Act** provided federal pensions for the elderly and subsidies for state-run unemployment and sickness benefit schemes. Such measures, financed by higher taxes on the rich, were denounced as socialist by most US newspapers and their millionaire owners, but **confirmed Roosevelt's popularity** with the bulk of the American people.

In the **civil war** raging in **China**, communist guerrillas escaped destruction by the forces of Chiang Kai-shek's Nationalist government through a series of **strategic withdrawals** to remote areas of the north and west. During the **Long March** from Jiangxi to Shaanxi, a journey of around 10,000km (6,200 miles), **Mao Zedong** asserted himself as the foremost communist leader. In December 1935, Mao declared that the Long March had been "a manifesto, a propaganda force... proclaiming to the world that the Red Army is an army of heroes". But for the time being these "heroes" remained hunted rebels.

Long March survivors
Chinese communists of the First Front Army arrive at Yan'an in Shaanxi province at the end of the strategic retreat known as the Long March.

In Germany, Hitler's Nazi regime formalized its anti-Semitism through the **Nuremberg Laws** in September. Jews were deprived of German citizenship and, by the **Law for the Protection of German Blood and German Honour**, marriage and extramarital sexual relations between Jews and non-Jews were banned. A problem in the application of **anti-Semitic legislation** was identifying to whom it applied, since Jewish Germans had been intermarrying with non-Jewish Germans for generations. The Nuremberg Laws formally defined a Jew as a person with three or four Jewish grandparents.

Worried by Hitler's plans to expand German forces, Britain and France sought to enrol Italian Fascist dictator **Benito Mussolini** as an ally against Germany. This policy was wrecked by Mussolini's imperialist ambitions in Africa. In October, troops from Italy's east African colonies, Eritrea and Italian Somaliland, **invaded** the independent African state of **Ethiopia**. Ethiopian Emperor **Haile Selassie** was able to raise a large army, and although his forces were poorly equipped, they put up stout resistance. Ethiopia was a member-state of the League of Nations (see 1919). The League denounced Italy as an aggressor and called for economic sanctions. The British and French governments concocted a peace plan that would have given Mussolini a large chunk of Ethiopian territory. When news of the deal leaked out, public opinion in the democracies was outraged. British foreign secretary Samuel **Hoare** and French prime minister Pierre **Laval** were forced to resign, economic sanctions against Italy went ahead, and **Mussolini** was **pushed into the arms of Hitler**.

Despite the continuing effects of the economic Depression and the world's grave political problems, there were many **signs of technological progress**. The Hoover Dam was the most spectacular of a series of dam projects that would provide electric power and irrigation for large areas of the US. For those who could afford it, **luxury travel** – stylish ocean liners and intercontinental air travel – **flourished**. For the masses who could not afford this kind of luxury, there was always the cinema. The movie *Top Hat* marked the peak of the Hollywood musical, Fred Astaire and Ginger Rogers transporting viewers into a magical world of wealth and glamour.

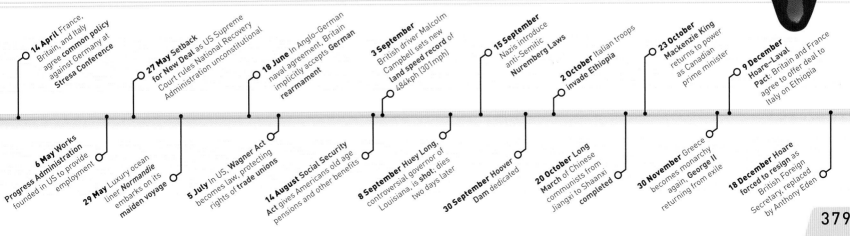

Luxury liner
The Normandie *was the largest, fastest, and most luxurious of the liners plying the Atlantic. Its interior was a riot of Art Deco features.*

14 April France, Britain, and Italy agree **common policy** against Germany at **Stresa Conference**

6 May Works Progress Administration founded in US to provide employment

27 May Setback for New Deal as US Supreme Court rules National Recovery Administration unconstitutional

29 May Luxury ocean liner ***Normandie*** embarks on its **maiden voyage**

18 June Anglo-German naval agreement, Britain implicitly accepts **German rearmament**

5 July In US, **Wagner Act** becomes law, protecting rights of **trade unions**

14 August Social Security Act gives Americans old age pensions and other benefits

3 September British driver Malcolm Campbell sets new **land speed record** of 484kph (301mph)

8 September Huey Long, controversial governor of Louisiana, is **shot**; dies two days later

15 September Nazis introduce anti-Semitic **Nuremberg Laws**

30 September Hoover Dam dedicated

2 October Italian troops **invade Ethiopia**

20 October Long March of Chinese communists from Jiangxi to Shaanxi **completed**

23 October Mackenzie King returns to power as Canadian prime minister

30 November Greece becomes monarchy again, **George II** returning from exile

9 December Hoare–Laval Pact: Britain and France agree to offer deal to Italy on Ethiopia

18 December Hoare forced to resign as British Foreign Secretary, replaced by Anthony Eden

22 THOUSAND THE NUMBER OF GERMAN TROOPS THAT MARCHED INTO RHINELAND

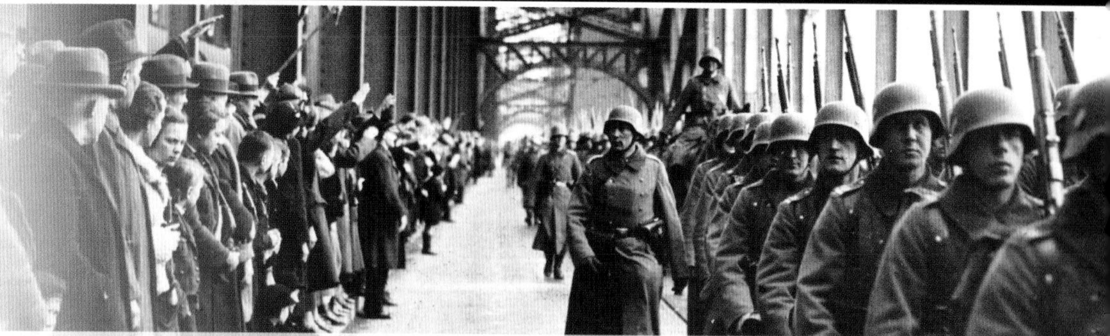

German troops march across a bridge into the demilitarized Rhineland. Hitler feared a military response by the Western democracies that never came.

EUROPE HAD BEGUN TO SLIDE inexorably down the slope toward a **major war**. On 7 March, Hitler sent troops into the Rhineland, a part of Germany that had been demilitarized under the terms of the Locarno Pact (see 1925). The operation was perfectly stage-managed, the marching soldiers greeted by cheering crowds and women throwing flowers. However, behind the scenes Hitler and his generals were racked by nervous tension. **German rearmament** was still in its early stages and the German army could not have resisted if France had opted for a military response, but strong public opinion and domestic issues inhibited a stronger stand. By doing nothing, the Western allies showed they would not act to uphold international agreements.

The **British and French** nonetheless embarked on **expansion of their armed forces** in response to developments in Germany. In Britain, Conservative leader Stanley Baldwin had won a general election in 1935 partly due to his promise to limit rearmament. Despite having a mandate for military expansion, Baldwin continued to proceed cautiously.

The main focus was on achieving an effective defence of Britain against attack by the **German Luftwaffe** (air force). Two days before Hitler's occupation of the Rhineland, a new fighter aircraft, the **Supermarine Spitfire**, made its maiden flight. RAF Fighter Command was created on 1 May, responsible for air defence. It was to be equipped with the Spitfire and the Hawker Hurricane, also then under development.

The importance of air power was demonstrated in the **conquest of Ethiopia** by Fascist Italy (see 1935). Italian aircraft were used to deliver poison gas onto Ethiopian troops, contributing to the defeat of Emperor Haile Selassie and the occupation of Addis Ababa in May. **Selassie fled to exile** in Britain. The following month he made a memorable speech at the League of Nations, ending with the ominous prophecy: "It is us today; it will be you tomorrow".

Confronted with the successes of Fascism and Naziism, the Soviet-controlled **Comintern** (Communist International) had decided that communist parties should seek to form "**Popular Front**" alliances with social democrat and centre parties. This policy bore fruit in France in May, when the Popular Front, led by socialist **Léon Blum**, won a large majority in parliamentary elections. At the same time, a workers' strike had led to the occupation of factories and department stores across France. Blum's first act as prime minister was to settle the strike by negotiating the **Matignon agreements**, which gave workers improved conditions including a 40-hour week and paid holidays. Struggling to maintain the support of communists on one side and centrist radicals on the other, however, the Blum government was soon bogged down in economic problems and the diplomatic dilemma posed by the outbreak of civil war in Spain.

A Popular Front of communists, socialists, republicans, and anarchists won **Spanish elections** in February. The Popular Front government promised sweeping land reforms and autonomy for **Catalonia**, but events soon ran out of their control, with peasants seizing large estates and anti-clerical attacks on convents and churches. On 13 July, José Calvo Sotelo, a leading anti-Popular Front politician, was murdered by socialist militants. Four days later, **Nationalist army** officers based in Spanish Morocco launched a **military uprising**. Resisted by hastily armed socialist and anarchist militias, and a large proportion of the Spanish armed forces, the revolt failed across much of Spain – Madrid, the Basque country, and Catalonia remained in Republican hands. When German and Italian aircraft began to ferry General Francisco Franco's **Army of Africa** from Morocco into southern Spain, the military revolt turned into civil war.

At first, a rapid Nationalist victory appeared probable. While Germany and Italy provided men, tanks, and aircraft to support the rebels, France and Britain adopted

Workers unite
Armed workers trample on Nazi and Fascist symbols in this Spanish Civil War poster. Communists were initially a minority in the Republican camp.

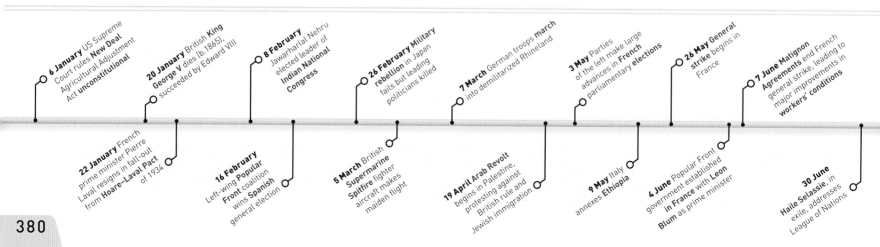

The Spanish Civil War
Crossing from Spanish Morocco, Nationalist troops advanced north. The Republicans held on to Madrid in desperate fighting.

KEY
- Republican zone
- Nationalist gains
- Initial Nationalist zone

- **6 January** US Supreme Court rules **New Deal** Agricultural Adjustment Act **unconstitutional**
- **20 January** British **King George V** dies (b.1865), succeeded by Edward VIII
- **22 January** French prime minister Pierre Laval resigns in fall-out from **Hoare–Laval Pact** of 1934
- **8 February** Jawarharlal Nehru elected leader of **Indian National Congress**
- **16 February** Left-wing **Popular Front** coalition wins **Spanish** general election
- **26 February Military rebellion** in Japan fails but leading politicians killed
- **5 March** British **Supermarine Spitfire** fighter aircraft makes maiden flight
- **7 March** German troops **march** into demilitarized Rhineland
- **19 April Arab Revolt** begins in Palestine, protesting against British rule and Jewish immigration
- **3 May** Parties of the left make large advances in **French** parliamentary **elections**
- **9 May** Italy annexes **Ethiopia**
- **26 May General strike** begins in France
- **4 June** Popular Front government established **in France with Leon Blum** as prime minister
- **7 June Matignon Agreements** end French general strike, leading to major improvements in **workers' conditions**
- **30 June Haile Selassie**, in exile, addresses League of Nations

“IF YOU DON’T TRY TO WIN YOU MIGHT AS WELL HOLD THE OLYMPICS IN SOMEBODY’S BACKYARD.”

Jesse Owens, US athlete, at the Olympic Games, 1936

US athlete Jesse Owens stands on the podium after winning the long jump at the Berlin Olympics. German silver medal winner Luz Long gives the Nazi salute.

a neutral stance, leaving only the Soviet Union to back the Republic. Franco’s Army of Africa advanced inexorably on Madrid, carrying out massacres along the way.

Meanwhile, Comintern was recruiting volunteers from many European countries and North America to fight in Spain. The first of these **International Brigades** played a vital role in the defence of Madrid in November. The Nationalist advance was halted and Madrid remained Republican.

In the highly charged political atmosphere of 1936, the holding of the summer **Olympic Games** in **Berlin** – agreed before the Nazis came to power – was inevitably a propaganda coup for Hitler. He seized the opportunity to present the Third Reich in a favourable light. The Olympics were staged on an unprecedentedly lavish scale with impeccable efficiency. Germany topped the medal table, but black American athlete **Jesse Owens** attracted most attention by winning four gold medals in sprint events and the long jump. Hitler was accused of snubbing Owens because his success ran counter to Nazi theories of Aryan racial superiority. Owens himself felt more insulted by the lack of congratulations from Roosevelt.

The Berlin Olympics were the occasion for the **first live TV broadcasts**. Seventy hours of fuzzy black-and-white coverage were shown in special viewing rooms around the city, as well as picked up by a handful of private TV sets. Later in the year, the BBC began the first regular high-definition television service, broadcast from Alexandra Palace in London.

In the autumn, two events occurred that would enter Britain’s political mythology. The **Jarrow Crusade** was a march by 200 cloth-capped jobless workers from a Depression-blighted shipbuilding town on the Tyne River. Jarrow had 70 per cent unemployment. The workers sought to publicize its plight by presenting a petition to parliament in Westminster. Their 450-km (280-mile) journey took almost a month, attracting sympathetic coverage in the press. Its effect was zero, but it became for the British a symbol of the era of mass unemployment.

On 4 October, the black-shirted **British Union of Fascists** (BUF) staged a march through a predominantly Jewish area of London’s East End. There they clashed with anti-fascists in what became known as the **Battle of Cable Street**. The march was abandoned. This humiliation for the BUF was followed by a government ban on political uniforms. British fascism never regained its momentum.

In the US, **Roosevelt** (see 1933) won a landslide victory in the presidential elections in November, securing a second term and confirming the popularity of his New Deal policies.

Three weeks after Roosevelt’s re-election, a further critical step toward a new world war was taken when Germany and Japan signed the **Anti-Comintern Pact**. Explicitly an agreement to resist communist subversion, the pact was aimed against the Soviet Union. It created an ideological link between the Nazis and an increasingly militaristic Japan.

On 16 November, Britain’s king **Edward VIII** (1894–1972) informed Prime Minister Stanley Baldwin that he intended to marry American divorcee **Mrs Wallis Simpson**. Political opinion was solidly behind Baldwin, who told the king that he must choose between Simpson and the throne. **Edward abdicated** and his brother, Albert, inherited the throne as George VI (1895–1952).

GENERAL FRANCISCO FRANCO (1892–1975)

Franco was a career officer who commanded the Spanish Foreign Legion in Morocco in the 1920s. A Catholic monarchist, he joined the military uprising against the Republic in July 1936 and was recognized as sole leader of the Nationalist rebels in September. After victory in the Civil War in 1939 he imposed a harsh dictatorship. He kept Spain neutral in World War II and remained in power until his death in 1975.

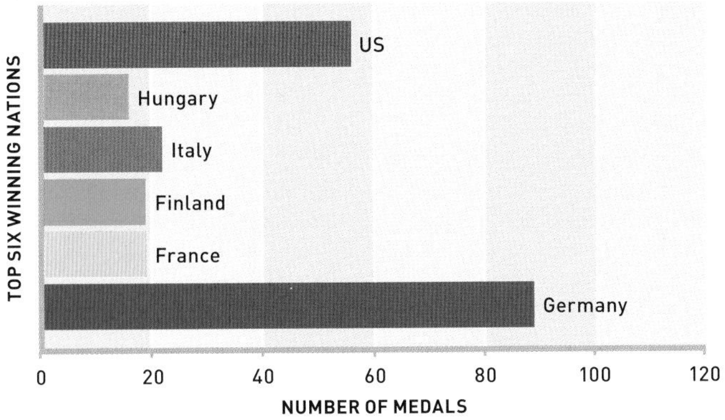

1936 Olympic Games medal tally
The most successful countries in the 1936 Berlin summer Olympics were Germany and the US. The Soviet Union and Spain were among countries that did not take part.

Marconiphone television receiver
Early televisions like this one made by Marconi were luxury products – the Marconiphone sold in Britain for 60 guineas, equivalent to about £3,000 ($4,500) today.

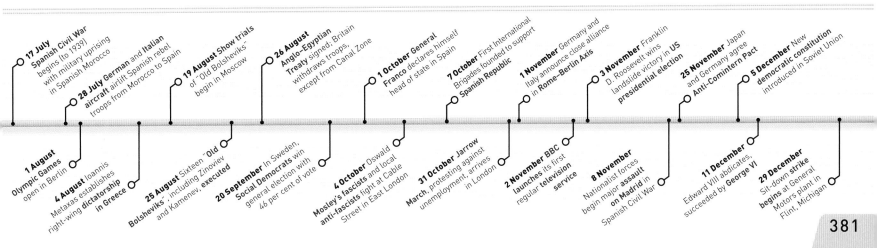

325
THE NUMBER OF DAYS EDWARD VIII REIGNED AS KING BEFORE HE ABDICATED

17 July **Spanish Civil War** begins (to 1939) with military uprising in Spanish Morocco

28 July German and **Italian aircraft** airlift Spanish rebel troops from Morocco to Spain

1 August **Olympic Games** open in Berlin

4 August Ioannis Metaxas establishes right-wing **dictatorship in Greece**

19 August Show trials of “Old Bolsheviks” begin in Moscow

25 August Sixteen “**Old Bolsheviks**”, including Zinoviev and Kamenev, **executed**

26 August **Anglo-Egyptian Treaty** signed; Britain withdraws troops, except from Canal Zone

20 September In Sweden, **Social Democrats** win general election with 46 per cent of vote

1 October General Franco declares himself head of state in Spain

4 October Oswald **Mosley’s fascists** and local **anti-fascists** fight at Cable Street in East London

7 October First International Brigades founded to support **Spanish Republic**

31 October Jarrow March, protesting against unemployment, arrives in London

1 November Germany and Italy announce close alliance in **Rome–Berlin Axis**

2 November BBC launches its first regular **television service**

3 November Franklin D. Roosevelt wins landslide victory in **US presidential election**

8 November Nationalist forces begin major **assault on Madrid** in Spanish Civil War

25 November Japan and Germany agree **Anti-Comintern Pact**

5 December New **democratic constitution** introduced in Soviet Union

11 December Edward VIII abdicates, succeeded by **George VI**

29 December Sit-down **strike begins** at General Motors plant in Flint, Michigan

George VI at his coronation in Westminster Abbey on 12 May. He ascended the throne following the abdication of his brother, Edward VIII.

> “I SEE **ONE THIRD** OF A NATION **ILL-HOUSED, ILL-CLAD, ILL-NOURISHED.**”

Franklin D. Roosevelt, American president, in his inauguration speech, 20 January 1937

THE YEAR BEGAN WITH FRANKLIN D. ROOSEVELT starting his second term in office as US president. In his inauguration speech on 20 January, Roosevelt drew attention to **persistent poverty** in America. He pledged to end this injustice, denouncing "heedless self-interest" as bad morals and bad economics. The president's **radical policies** brought him into conflict with the Supreme Court, while across America a wave of **sit-down strikes** pitted workers against their employers. As the number of jobless more than doubled between 1936 and 1938, it was not obvious that Roosevelt's approach was working. This period was ironically dubbed "Roosevelt's Depression".

For Britain and its empire, this was a year of change. In May the country saw a **new king crowned**, George VI (1895–1952), and a new prime minister in Downing Street, Neville Chamberlain (1869–1940). In Ireland, a referendum in July approved a proposal for a new constitution. The **Irish Free State became Eire** (Ireland in Gaelic), and in effect a fully independent country although officially still a dominion of the British Commonwealth. British India took another step toward self-government with implementation of the **India Act**, but the limited powers of its elected assembly fell far short of satisfying Indian nationalists. The British also failed to find a solution to the problem in **Palestine**, and their proposal to split it between the Jews and Arabs was rejected by both sides.

In Spain, the ongoing civil war (see 1936) was progressing badly for the Republican Loyalists. Political divisions, with Communists determined to suppress anarchists and Trotskyists, nullified the courage and determination of their military efforts. The Nationalist rebels continued to enjoy the support of German and Italian forces, especially in the air. On 26 April, the Basque town of **Guernica** became famous worldwide when, on a busy market day, it was devastated by aircraft of the German Condor Legion. Estimates of the death toll varied from 300 to 1,700. Graphically described by journalists who visited the town in the wake of the attack, the event focused **fears about aerial bombardment**, specifically the impact of the German Luftwaffe in any future war between the major powers.

In an increasingly divided world, art and literature were becoming politicized. **Prominent writers went to Spain**, either to fight in the Civil War (mostly on the Republican side) or as war tourists and journalists. Among these were George Orwell and W.H. Auden from Britain, Ernest Hemingway from the US, and André Malraux from France. The most famous response to the bombing of Guernica was Pablo Picasso's painting, which was first exhibited in the Spanish Republic's pavilion at the Paris International Exhibition in summer 1937.

The **Paris Exhibition** also featured grandiose Nazi German and Soviet Russian pavilions, both using monumental sculpture to trumpet the glories of their rival political systems. The Nazis also took the extraordinary decision to mount a show of the art they despised, displaying confiscated

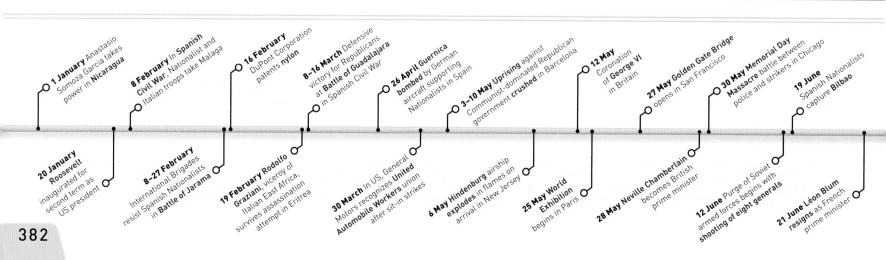

Picasso's vision of war
In response to the German bombing of the Basque town of Guernica, Pablo Picasso painted this large mural in support of the Spanish Republicans. It was displayed at the 1937 Paris Exhibition.

> “AT 2A.M. **TODAY** WHEN I VISITED THE **TOWN,** THE WHOLE OF IT WAS A **HORRIBLE** SIGHT, **FLAMING FROM END TO END.**”

George Steer, British journalist, reporting the bombing of Guernica for *The Times*, 27 April, 1937

- **1 January** Anastasio Somoza Garcia takes power in **Nicaragua**
- **20 January** Roosevelt inaugurated for second term as US president
- **8 February** In **Spanish Civil War**, Nationalist and Italian troops take Malaga
- **8–27 February** International Brigades resist Spanish Nationalists in **Battle of Jarama**
- **16 February** DuPont Corporation patents **nylon**
- **19 February Rodolfo Graziani**, viceroy of Italian East Africa, survives assassination attempt in Eritrea
- **8–16 March** Defensive victory for Republicans at **Battle of Guadalajara** in Spanish Civil War
- **30 March** In US, General Motors recognizes **United Automobile Workers** union after sit-in strikes
- **26 April Guernica bombed** by German aircraft supporting Nationalists in Spain
- **3–10 May Uprising** against Communist-dominated Republican government **crushed** in Barcelona
- **6 May Hindenburg** airship **explodes** in flames on arrival in New Jersey
- **12 May** Coronation of **George VI** in Britain
- **25 May World Exhibition** begins in Paris
- **27 May Golden Gate Bridge** opens in San Francisco
- **28 May Neville Chamberlain** becomes British prime minister
- **30 May Memorial Day Massacre** battle between police and strikers in Chicago
- **12 June** Purge of Soviet armed forces begins with **shooting of eight generals**
- **19 June** Spanish Nationalists capture **Bilbao**
- **21 June Léon Blum resigns** as French prime minister

“... THERE’S **FLAMES, NOW,** AND THE **FRAME IS CRASHING TO THE GROUND...** OH, THE HUMANITY... ”

Herbert Morrison, Chicago news reporter, as he watched the *Hindenburg* crash, 6 May 1937

The German Zeppelin airship *Hindenburg* exploding into a fireball while docking at Lakehurst in New Jersey. The cause of the disaster remains uncertain.

paintings by modernists and Jews at a “**Degenerate Art**” exhibition in Munich, to be laughed at by the German public.

Meanwhile, under the dictatorship of Joseph Stalin (1878–1953), the Soviet Union had begun the **Great Terror**. The Soviet regime had always been ruthless toward those it defined as enemies – for example, peasants who resisted collective agriculture (see 1930) – but now the unbridled power of the secret police was turned against the leadership of the Soviet armed forces, and of the ruling party itself. The process began in 1936, with the arrest, trial and execution of “**Old Bolsheviks**” – men who had participated in the 1917 Revolution. While arrests of Old Bolsheviks continued through 1937, other people also came under suspicion. Between 1937 and 1939 almost half the senior army commanders were executed, imprisoned, or sacked. Although the fate of the Soviet elite attracted most attention, Stalin’s reign of terror spread through the entire population. At least 680,000 people were killed during the **Great Purge**, and some historians believe the real figure could even be closer to 2 million.

In summer 1937 gradual **Japanese encroachment on Chinese territory** erupted into full-scale war. Japanese and Chinese forces clashed at the Marco Polo Bridge outside Beijing in July, and the following month large-scale fighting developed in Shanghai. **Chiang Kai-shek**’s Chinese Nationalist forces put up much stiffer resistance than the Japanese expected, inflicting around 50,000 casualties on the invaders, but they were forced to abandon the city. The Japanese then advanced on the Chinese Nationalist capital, **Nanking**, which they took in December. Nanking’s civilian population was subjected to a brutal attack by Japanese troops, while thousands of surrendered Chinese soldiers were also killed. This massacre, witnessed by Christian missionaries and other Western observers, shocked public opinion in the US and solidified the sympathy of the US government for the Chinese. US hostility to Japan’s actions in China was the **first step on the path to the Pacific War** (see 1941).

Elsewhere, the year was marked by **air disasters**. German airships had begun scheduled transatlantic passenger flights. On 6 May, the airship ***Hindenburg***, with 97 passengers and crew on board, burst into flames as it docked at Lakehurst, New Jersey. Within seconds the fire had spread through its hydrogen-filled gasbag. Remarkably, only 35 people were killed, but the disaster brought an abrupt end to the brief era of luxury airship travel. Two months later, America’s most famous woman pilot, **Amelia Earhart** (1887–1937), took off from New Guinea with co-pilot Fred Noonan for the Pacific leg of an attempted **round-the-world flight**. Their aircraft was never seen again.

Worker and peasant
This giant sculpture, by Vera Mukhina, dominated the Soviet pavilion at the World’s Fair in 1937. It is an example of Socialist Realist style.

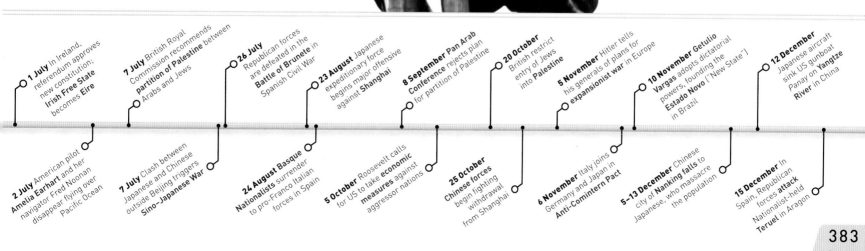

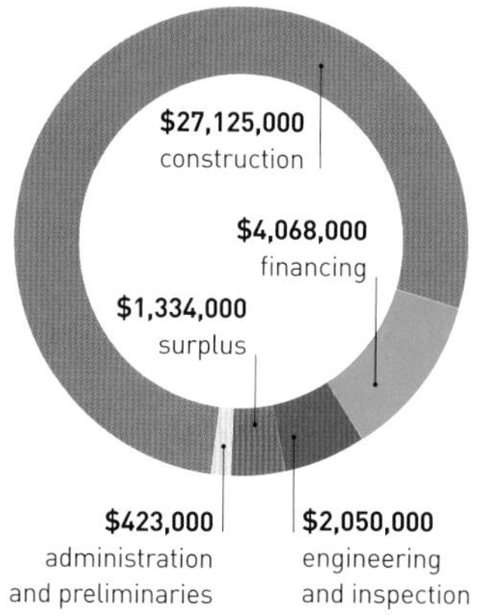

Golden Gate Bridge building costs
The original budget for building San Francisco’s Golden Gate Bridge was $27 million, but the actual building costs totalled $35 million.

Technology continued to progress throughout the year, culminating in the race for the first successful **trials of turbojet engines**, between Frank Whittle in Britain and Hans von Ohain in Germany. Whittle won, but the Germans forged ahead with development of a jet aircraft – Ohain’s engine powering the first jet flight in August 1939.

Another marker for progress was the opening of the **Golden Gate Bridge** in San Francisco. At 1,280m (4,200ft), its central span was the longest of any suspension bridge in the world, a record that stood until it was surpassed by the Verrazano-Narrows Bridge in New York in 1964.

1 July In Ireland, referendum approves new constitution; **Irish Free State** becomes **Eire**

2 July American pilot **Amelia Earhart** and her navigator Fred Noonan disappear flying over Pacific Ocean

7 July British Royal Commission recommends **partition of Palestine** between Arabs and Jews

7 July Clash between Japanese and Chinese outside Beijing triggers **Sino-Japanese War**

26 July Republican forces are defeated in the **Battle of Brunete** in Spanish Civil War

23 August Japanese expeditionary force begins major offensive against **Shanghai**

24 August Basque Nationalists surrender to pro-Franco Italian forces in Spain

8 September Pan Arab Conference rejects plan for partition of Palestine

5 October Roosevelt calls for US to take **economic measures** against aggressor nations

20 October British restrict entry of Jews into **Palestine**

25 October Chinese forces begin fighting withdrawal from Shanghai

5 November Hitler tells his generals of plans for **expansionist war** in Europe

6 November Italy joins Germany and Japan in **Anti-Comintern Pact**

10 November Getulio Vargas adopts dictatorial powers, founding the **Estado Novo** (“New State”) in Brazil

5–13 December Chinese city of **Nanking falls** to Japanese, who massacre the population

12 December Japanese aircraft sink US gunboat Panay on **Yangtze River** in China

15 December In Spain, Republican forces **attack** Nationalist-held **Teruel** in Aragon

British prime minister Neville Chamberlain (right) visited Nazi Germany for the Munich Conference on 28 September.

WALT DISNEY'S REWORKING OF THE FAIRY TALE OF SNOW WHITE and the Seven Dwarfs marked the transition of animated movies from cartoon shorts aimed primarily at children to a major strand in film culture. Dismissed in advance as "Disney's Folly", *Snow White* was an immediate hit, briefly holding the record for the **highest-grossing movie** of all time before being overtaken by *Gone with the Wind* (see 1939). The ability of Hollywood to manufacture universally appealing, mass-market films, along with the influence of American **big-band** "swing" dance music, was laying the foundations for a US-dominated, **international popular culture**.

All was not well with the **US economy**, however. A sharp **rise in unemployment** in 1938 drew attention to the fact that President Roosevelt's New Deal (see 1933) had failed to solve the economic problems of the US Depression.

Animated feature
Walt Disney's Snow White and the Seven Dwarfs *was the first feature-length, animated movie to be released worldwide, in 1938.*

By comparison, although pockets of high unemployment persisted in Britain, the **British economy** was performing well in the late 1930s, with high levels of house building, burgeoning production of consumer goods – from cars to vacuum cleaners – nationwide electrification, and growth in high-tech industries such as aircraft manufacturing. A symbol of **Britain's technological success** was the performance of the streamlined A4 Pacific-class locomotive *Mallard*. On 3 July it reached 203kmph (126mph), setting a **world speed record** for a steam engine that has never been surpassed.

The year's first major international crisis came in March, with the German **annexation of Austria** – the **Anschluss** ("unification"). Hitler had been applying mounting pressure on the government of Austrian Chancellor Kurt Schuschnigg (1897–1977) to back the Nazi movement inside Austria. When Schuschnigg attempted to hold a **referendum on Austrian independence**, Hitler forced his resignation and launched an **invasion**. German troops crossed the border unopposed; Hitler was greeted in Vienna by cheering crowds. The annexation was accompanied by widespread attacks by Nazis on Austria's large Jewish population.

Although the unification of Germany and Austria was a major **breech of the Versailles Treaty** (see 1919), Britain and France made no attempt to intervene. Instead, British prime minister **Neville Chamberlain** embarked upon an active policy of

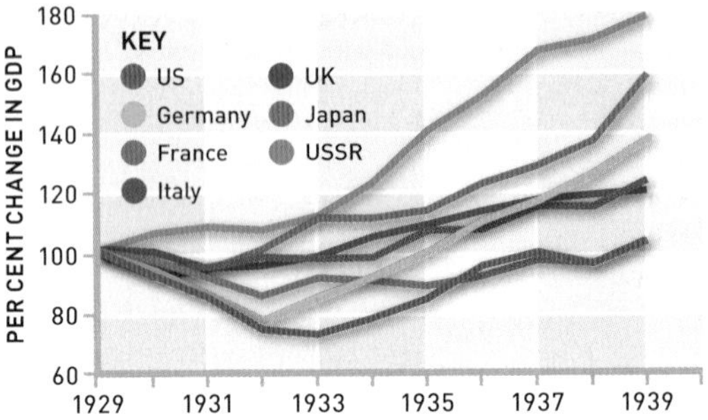

Economic growth
The Soviet Union achieved high economic growth in the 1930s. Japan and Germany also recovered well from the Depression.

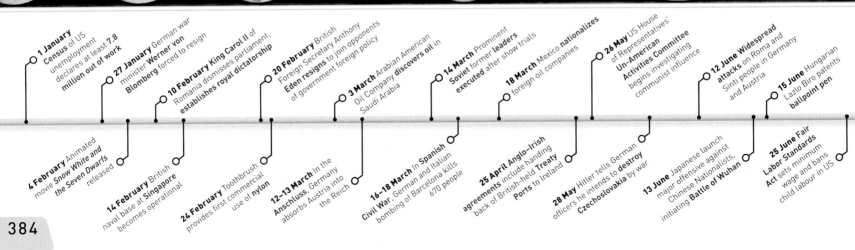

1 January Census of US unemployment declares at least **7.8 million out of work**

27 January German war minister **Werner von Blomberg** forced to resign

4 February Animated movie ***Snow White and the Seven Dwarfs*** released

10 February King Carol II of Romania dismisses parliament, **establishes royal dictatorship**

14 February British naval base at **Singapore** becomes operational

20 February British Foreign Secretary Anthony **Eden resigns** to join opponents of government foreign policy

24 February Toothbrush provides first commercial use of **nylon**

3 March Arabian American Oil Company **discovers oil** in Saudi Arabia

12–13 March In the **Anschluss**, Germany absorbs Austria into the Reich

14 March Prominent **Soviet** former **leaders executed** after show trials

16–18 March In **Spanish Civil War**, German and Italian bombing of Barcelona kills 670 people

18 March Mexico **nationalizes** foreign oil companies

25 April Anglo-Irish agreements include handing back of British-held **Treaty Ports** to Ireland

26 May US House of Representatives' **Un-American Activities Committee** begins investigating communist influence

28 May Hitler tells German officers he intends to **destroy Czechoslovakia** by war

12 June Widespread attacks on Roma and Sinti people in Germany and Austria

13 June Japanese launch major offensive against Chinese Nationalists, initiating **Battle of Wuhan**

15 June Hungarian Lazlo Biro patents **ballpoint pen**

25 June Fair Labor Standards Act sets minimum wage and bans child labour in US

“I BELIEVE IT IS **PEACE FOR OUR TIME.**”

British prime minister Neville Chamberlain, on his return to London from the Munich Conference, 30 September 1938

Arab prisoners are guarded by a British soldier in the Old City of Jerusalem during the suppression of the revolt against Britain's rule in Palestine.

"**appeasement**", based on the belief that a durable peace could be secured by settling Germany's "legitimate claims". Attention focused on the German minority in Czechoslovakia, concentrated in the **Sudetenland** area. Hitler stirred up unrest among the Sudeten Germans, while ordering his generals to prepare for an invasion of Czechoslovakia. The British and French governments were desperate to avoid war, but were committed to defending the Czechs. In September, Chamberlain embarked on an unprecedented diplomatic initiative, flying twice to Germany for **face-to-face talks with Hitler**. Although Britain pressured the Czech government into making major concessions, this only made Hitler raise his demands.

10,000,000

THE APPROXIMATE **ADDITION TO** THE **GERMAN POPULATION** BY THE **ANNEXATIONS** OF **AUSTRIA** AND **SUDETENLAND**

War seemed inevitable, and military preparations were under way in Britain and France when, on 28 September, Italian dictator **Benito Mussolini** proposed a **four-nation conference**. Hitler accepted and met the French premier Édouard Daladier (1884–1970), Chamberlain, and Mussolini at Munich. A deal was struck that preserved peace at the expense of Czechoslovakia, which had to **hand over the Sudetenland** to Germany. Chamberlain and Daladier were greeted as heroes when they returned home, the British and French people profoundly relieved to have avoided war. Conservative MP Winston Churchill (1874–1965) was among the minority who **denounced the Munich agreement**, calling it "a defeat without a war".

Post-Munich optimism only lasted until November, when **Kristallnacht** ("the Night of Broken Glass") provided graphic evidence of the extremist nature of the Nazi regime.

Steam record holder
Designed by Nigel Gresley, the steam locomotive Mallard *was a masterly fusion of form and function. It achieved an enduring world speed record.*

Night of broken glass
A shopkeeper clears up shattered glass from a looted Jewish shop in the wake of attacks on German and Austrian Jews in November.

The assassination of a German diplomat by a Jew in Paris served as a pretext for Nazi-orchestrated attacks on Jewish homes and businesses across Germany and Austria. Synagogues were burned down and sacred objects desecrated; 30,000 Jewish men were rounded up and taken to concentration camps, where beatings and torture were routine.

Those countries still committed to democracy and freedom expressed **outrage at Nazi anti-semitism**, but they were not keen to provide a home for Jews now desperate to escape Nazi persecution. At an **international conference** on the issue held at Evian in July, the Australian representative T. W. White stated bluntly: "As we have no racial problem, we are not desirous of importing one". Britain agreed to accept a limited number of Jewish children, without their parents, and the US maintained its existing barriers to immigration. **Jews were trapped** because, although the Nazis were ready to let them leave, they had nowhere to go.

One potential destination for Jews from Europe was **Palestine**, which was recognized by the British as a site for a **Jewish homeland** (see 1917). But the British were struggling with an armed uprising by **Palestinian Arabs** who were **bitterly opposed** to the expansion of Jewish settlement. In an attempt to defuse the situation, Britain imposed tight limits on Jewish immigration.

The high pitch of anxiety in the world at the time became evident when a radio broadcast induced **mass panic** in the US. Orson Welles's radio version of the alien-invasion classic ***The War of the Worlds*** was broadcast by CBS at Halloween. The news bulletin format convinced millions of Americans that a genuine invasion by Martians was underway. When genuinely frightened listeners finally understood their mistake, there was widespread anger.

3 July British locomotive *Mallard* sets **world speed record**

6 July Evian Conference on **refugees** reveals that no one wants to accept Jews fleeing Naziism

15 July US entrepreneur Howard Hughes completes **round-the-world flight** in 91 hours

25 July Spanish Republican forces launch offensive on **the Ebro**

4 August British mission arrives in Prague to seek solution of crisis over **Sudeten Germans**

15 September British Prime Minister **Chamberlain** flies to meet **Hitler** at **Berchtesgaden** over Sudetenland crisis

22 September Chamberlain flies to Germany for a second time, as **Hitler raises** his **demands**

29–30 September Munich Conference keeps peace in Europe at expense of Czechoslovakia

4 October In France, **Popular Front alliance** of left and centre breaks down

19 October British government **abandons** plans for partition of **Palestine**

21 October Japanese troops **occupy Canton** in China

27 October Chiang Kai-shek withdraws his forces to Chungking in southwest China

30 October Orson Welles's *War of the Worlds* radio broadcast causes **mass hysteria**

9–10 November On **Kristallnacht**, attacks are carried out by Nazis against Jews across **Germany** and **Austria**

16 November In Spain, Battle of the **Ebro ends in defeat** for Republicans

1 December Slovakia becomes an autonomous state

2 December First **Kindertransport** of Jewish children from Germany arrives in Britain

15 December US provides **financial backing** for **Chiang Kai-shek**'s war against Japanese

1939

Spanish women in Madrid, celebrating the victory of Franco's Nationalists in the country's civil war. Defeated opponents of Franco faced harsh oppression.

BY 1939 MILITARY DICTATORSHIPS WERE SPREADING ACROSS EUROPE. Only a handful of countries, chiefly Britain and France, maintained a liberal democratic system. In the spring, General Francisco Franco's **Nationalists triumphed in the Spanish Civil War**, occupying the surviving Republican strongholds of Barcelona and Madrid. Tens of thousands of Franco's enemies were executed. Others fled into exile, and many were interned in camps in France. Meanwhile, Italy's dictator Benito **Mussolini** (1883–1945) had **annexed Albania**, and driven out its monarch, King Zog (1895–1961).

More threatening for the peace of Europe was German Führer Adolf Hitler's **occupation of Prague**. The Munich agreement (see 1938) had left Czechoslovakia a defenceless state, and the Germans encouraged Slovakian nationalists, who were resentful of Czech domination, to declare independence. In March, **Hitler's troops marched unopposed into Prague**, turning the Czech lands of Bohemia and Moravia into a German "protectorate". After Hungary annexed the east, Czechoslovakia ceased to exist as a country.

> " WHEN STARTING AND WAGING **WAR** IT IS **NOT RIGHT THAT MATTERS, BUT VICTORY.** "
>
> **Adolf Hitler, military and political leader of Germany**, 30 January 1939

The German occupation of Prague forced the leaders of the Western democracies to acknowledge the ruthlessness of Nazi expansionism. It was obvious **Poland was to be the next target**. Believing a threat of force would deter Hitler, the British and French gave the Poles a guarantee of military support, but Hitler was not deterred. In April he began military planning for an invasion of Poland.

Desperate Jews tried to flee the expanding area coming under Nazi control, but many countries refused to let them in. Among the more fortunate were those rescued by the **Kindertransport** scheme that arranged for almost 10,000 unaccompanied **Jewish children** to find **refuge** in Britain. Adults were not allowed to accompany them, however, and many of the children never saw their parents again.

While all eyes were focused on Europe, the **Soviet Union was fighting an undeclared war with Japan** in Asia. Throughout the summer, clashes occurred along the border between Mongolia, a Soviet client state, and Japanese-occupied Manchuria. Soviet General Georgy Zhukov's hard-fought victory at the battle of Khalkhin Gol decided the outcome. This defeat influenced the Japanese to pursue naval-led expansion in the Pacific and Southeast Asia, rather than further land conquests in East Asia.

Anticipating a war with Germany, Britain and France unenthusiastically pursued

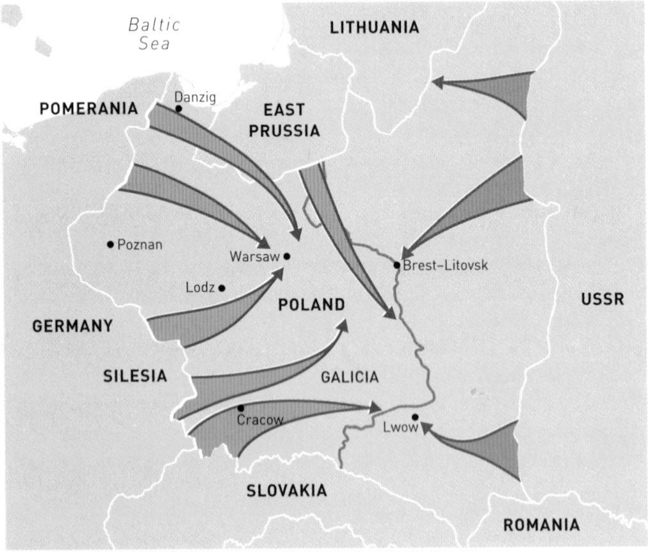

Invasion of Poland
German forces invaded Poland from East Prussia, Germany, and Slovakia on 1 September. With Nazi agreement, the Soviets occupied eastern Poland.

KEY
→ German advance/operation
→ Soviet advance
— German/Soviet demarcation line in Poland

EVACUATION OF THE CITIES

At the start of September, Britain and France began to evacuate civilians from danger areas. Expecting air attacks, the British evacuated 1.5 million children from large cities, along with mothers with babies and young children. The French carried out mass evacuations from the border provinces of Alsace and Lorraine in eastern France. Germany did not carry out mass evacuations until heavy bombing began in 1942.

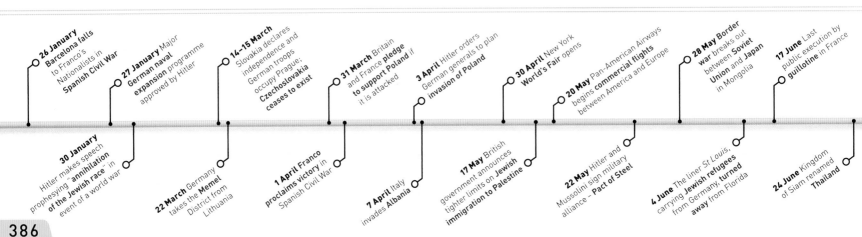

World War II British gas mask
All British civilians were issued with gas masks, for protection against poison gas air attacks. This brightly-coloured mask is for a child.

- **26 January Barcelona falls** to Franco's Nationalists in **Spanish Civil War**
- **27 January German naval expansion** programme approved by Hitler
- **30 January** Hitler makes speech prophesying "**annihilation of the Jewish race**" in event of a world war
- **14–15 March** Slovakia declares independence and German troops occupy Prague; **Czechoslovakia ceases to exist**
- **22 March** Germany takes the **Memel** District from Lithuania
- **31 March** Britain and France **pledge to support Poland** if it is attacked
- **1 April Franco proclaims victory** in Spanish Civil War
- **3 April** Hitler orders German generals to plan **invasion of Poland**
- **7 April** Italy invades **Albania**
- **30 April** New York **World's Fair** opens
- **17 May** British government announces tighter limits on **Jewish immigration to Palestine**
- **20 May** Pan-American Airways begins **commercial flights** between America and Europe
- **22 May** Hitler and Mussolini sign military alliance – **Pact of Steel**
- **28 May Border war** breaks out between **Soviet Union** and **Japan** in Mongolia
- **4 June** The liner *St Louis*, carrying **Jewish refugees** from Germany, **turned away** from Florida
- **17 June** Last public execution by **guillotine** in France
- **24 June** Kingdom of Siam renamed **Thailand**

During the period known as the "phony war", preparations for conflict in suburban Britain often seemed bizarre, with no real enemy to fire at.

a military alliance with the Soviet Union – a country they disliked and distrusted. No-one anticipated a deal between Hitler and the Soviet leader Joseph Stalin, but on 23 August the Soviet and German foreign ministers, Vyacheslav Molotov (1890–1986) and Joachim von Ribbentrop (1893–1946), signed a Non-Aggression Treaty, known as the **Molotov–Ribbentrop Pact**, which included a provision to divide Poland between them.

German forces invaded Poland on 1 September. Two days later, unable to escape their commitment to the Poles, the **British and French governments declared war on Germany**. Australia, New Zealand, Canada, and South Africa followed. Britain brought India into the war without consulting its elected representatives, while **Ireland** and the **US** declared their **neutrality**. Much to Hitler's annoyance, Italy also declared itself neutral. The war was greeted by all countries with fear and resignation. There were no cheering crowds in Berlin, London, or Paris.

36

THE NUMBER OF **DAYS GERMANY** TOOK TO **OVERRUN POLAND**

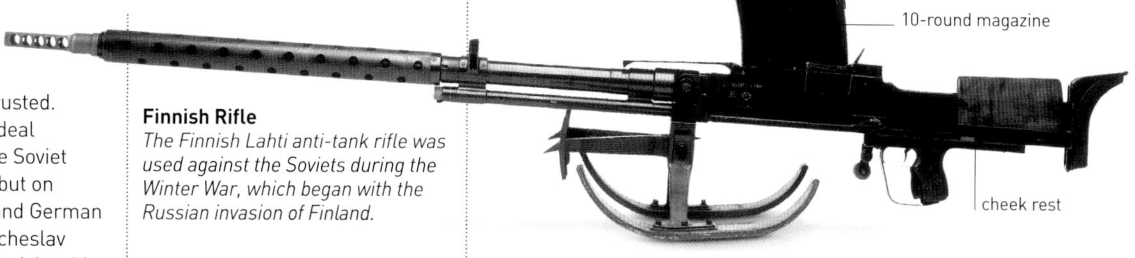

Finnish Rifle
The Finnish Lahti anti-tank rifle was used against the Soviets during the Winter War, which began with the Russian invasion of Finland.

The **destruction of Poland** was achieved with breathtaking speed. German troops reached the outskirts of Warsaw within a week. The Poles fought with courage and tenacity – Germany sustained more than 40,000 casualties – but once Soviet troops moved in from the east all was lost. **Warsaw surrendered** on 28 September, and the fighting stopped a week later. Dividing the country between them, the Soviets and Nazis set about imprisoning and massacring Poles in large numbers.

Throughout the autumn the Germans began confining Poland's Jews to **ghettos**, a major step toward the Holocaust (see 1942). Hitler had already signed an order in Germany at the start of the war for the killing of people with incurable mental disabilities. Over **70,000 German mental patients were murdered** by lethal injections or gassing, before the operation was suspended in August 1941.

With Poland crushed, the Western democracies entered the period known as the "**phony war**". After the fall of Poland the British and French rejected a peace offer from Hitler, but the troops they assembled in France remained passive. The lack of military action was a relief to the British and French governments. German air attacks and massive civilian casualties had been expected, but did not occur.

The only dramatic action in Britain's war against Germany was at sea. In October, the German Navy's U-boat *U-47* penetrated the defences of Britain's main naval base at Scapa Flow, in the Orkney Islands off Scotland, and **sank the battleship *Royal Oak***. British morale was raised two months later when the German battleship ***Graf Spee*** was driven by British cruisers to take refuge in the neutral port of Montevideo in Uruguay, where the Germans scuttled it.

At the end of November, the **Soviet Union** launched an **attack on Finland**. **The Winter War** revealed severe deficiencies in the organization, equipment, and leadership of the Soviet Red Army. By the end of the year, the Finns still held their Mannerheim Line defences, and the Soviets had suffered heavy losses.

Movie attendance
Movies of the late 1930s achieved extraordinary ticket sales. Around 80 million movie tickets were sold in the US every week.

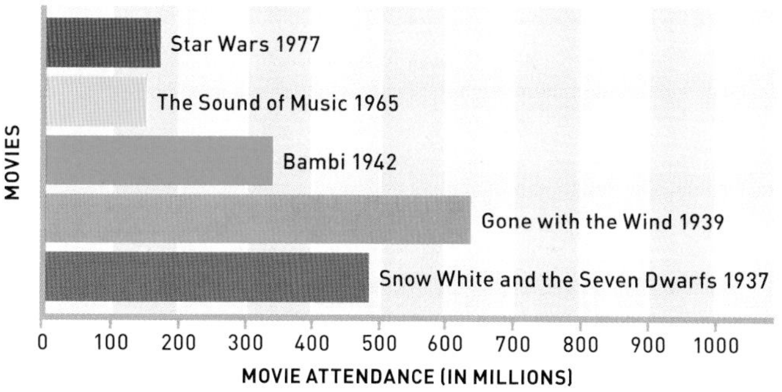

Remaining neutral, the US seemed a world away from the blacked-out cities of Europe. The **New York World's Fair**, opened in April, taking "The World of Tomorrow" as its theme. Around 44 million visitors came to see such novelties as nylon stockings and colour photography.

Hollywood was enjoying a **golden era**, with classic releases including *Gone With the Wind*, *The Wizard of Oz*, and *Stagecoach*. Grand picture palaces, some of which could accommodate more than 4,000 customers, were filled. The American economy was poised for a decisive upturn as an **amendment to the Neutrality Act** allowed US factories to equip the British and French war effort.

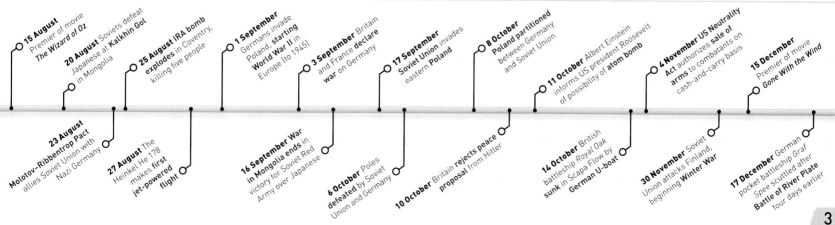

Off to see the Wizard
Julie Garland played Dorothy in the 1939 movie The Wizard of Oz – perfect fantasy entertainment for hard and dangerous times.

15 August Premier of movie ***The Wizard of Oz***

20 August Soviets defeat Japanese at **Kalkhin Gol** in Mongolia

23 August **Molotov–Ribbentrop Pact** allies Soviet Union with Nazi Germany

25 August IRA bomb **explodes** in Coventry, killing five people

27 August The Heinkel He 178 makes **first jet-powered flight**

1 September Germans invade Poland, **starting World War II** in Europe (to 1945)

3 September Britain and France **declare war** on Germany

16 September War **in Mongolia ends** in victory for Soviet Red Army over Japanese

17 September **Soviet Union** invades eastern **Poland**

6 October Poles **defeated** by Soviet Union and Germany

8 October **Poland partitioned** between Germany and Soviet Union

10 October Britain **rejects peace proposal** from Hitler

11 October Albert Einstein informs US president Roosevelt of possibility of **atom bomb**

14 October British battleship ***Royal Oak*** **sunk** in Scapa Flow by **German U-boat**

4 November **US Neutrality Act** authorizes **sale of arms** to combatants on cash-and-carry basis

30 November Soviet Union attacks Finland, beginning **Winter War**

15 December Premier of movie ***Gone With the Wind***

17 December German pocket battleship *Graf Spee* scuttled after **Battle of River Plate** four days earlier

German expansion
Between September 1939 and August 1942 Nazi German forces conquered most of mainland Europe, seizing control of an area from Norway to Crete, and from France to the Black Sea. Britain remained free of German domination, but was subjected to air attacks. Nazi U-boats also preyed on Britain's shipping lanes.

THE WAR IN EUROPE

THE ALLIED BATTLE TO TURN BACK THE TIDE OF NAZI CONTROL

The German invasion of Poland in September 1939 provoked Britain and France to declare war on Germany. At first the Germans won an astonishing series of victories, but from 1942 onward they were overwhelmed by the combined strength of the US, the Soviet Union, and Britain.

After the rapid defeat of Poland in April 1940, the Germans invaded Denmark and Norway. Their devastating campaign swiftly overran the Netherlands, Belgium, and France – British Forces escaped from Europe through an evacuation from Dunkirk in France. The German Luftwaffe failed to overcome the RAF in the Battle of Britain in summer 1940, but British cities were subjected to nightly bombing raids during the Blitz.

The entry of Italy into the war in June 1940 spread the fighting to the Mediterranean and North Africa. Needing to rescue Italian forces from defeat, the German army swept south to Crete and also intervened in North Africa. Hitler's invasion of the Soviet Union in June 1941 brought German forces to the gates of Moscow and Leningrad, but the German drive eastward came to a catastrophic end at Stalingrad in late 1942.

Defeated in North Africa, the Germans then faced an Allied invasion of Italy. In summer 1944 the Allies landed in Normandy and broke out to liberate France and Belgium. A final German counterattack in the Ardennes was repulsed, and Germany was finally invaded from east and west.

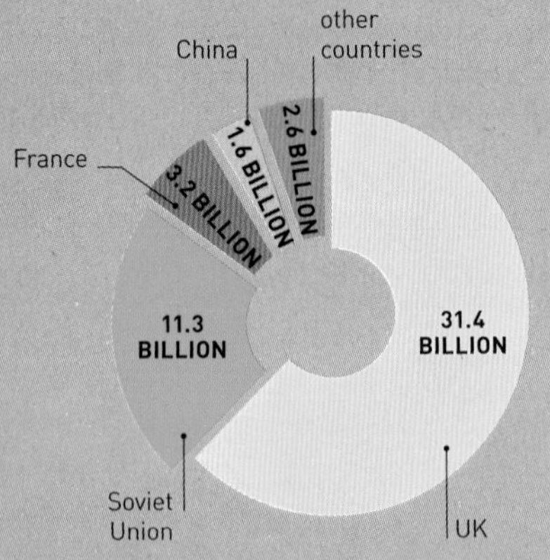

US lend-lease
The US provided its Allies with vast quantities of war equipment and supplies, under the lend-lease scheme. Britain and the Soviet Union were the major beneficiaries.

EUROPE IN 1942 By 1942 Nazi Germany dominated mainland Europe. Its allies and satellites included Italy, Hungary, Bulgaria, Slovakia, Croatia, and Vichy France. Greater Germany expanded before and during the war to include Austria, French Alsace-Lorraine, and much of Poland (which ceased to exist as a state in October 1939). Although the Nazis found some willing collaborators, their ambition to found a "New Order" in Europe eventually came to nothing.

Allied offensives
The tide of war turned with the British victory at El Alamein in North Africa, and the Soviet triumph at Stalingrad. Italy surrendered in 1943 after the Allies landed, and after the Normandy invasion on D-day in 1944, Germany was crushed between Soviet forces advancing from the east and the Western Allies attacking from the west.

KEY
- Frontiers 1937
- Frontiers Nov 1942
- Greater German Reich
- German occupation
- Axis satellite
- Italy and Italian occupied territory
- Finnish territory
- Neutral
- Allied territory

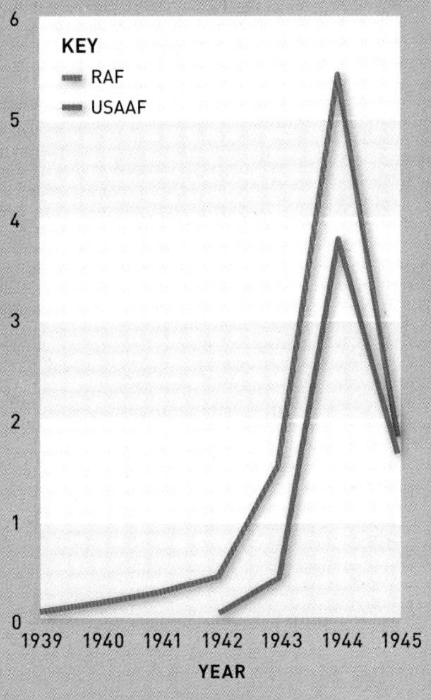

Stategic Allied bombing in Europe
RAF Bomber Command and the US Army Air Force carried out a sustained, large-scale bombing campaign on mainland Europe. The Allies dropped 2.7 million tonnes of bombs, killing around 500,000 people. The US bombed industrial objectives by day, while the RAF attacked cities by night.

THE IRON CURTAIN After World War II, Eastern European countries that were occupied by the Soviets were placed under communist governments. In Yugoslavia an independent communist regime refused Soviet tutelage. The divide between communist east and capitalist west, which ran down the middle of Germany, was dubbed the Iron Curtain.

KEY
- Soviet territory
- Soviet-dominated communist states by 1949
- Members of NATO 1949
- Independent communist state
- Iron Curtain in 1949
- Cities divided into zones of occupation

Allied soldiers form queues on the beach at Dunkirk, France, awaiting boats to carry them to England. German air attacks harassed the evacuation.

> **"** WE SHALL **FIGHT THEM ON THE BEACHES…** WE SHALL FIGHT **IN THE FIELDS** AND **IN THE STREETS,** WE SHALL FIGHT **IN THE HILLS;** WE SHALL **NEVER SURRENDER. "**
>
> **Winston Churchill, British prime minister,** addressing Parliament on 4 June 1940

United Commonwealth
A British propaganda poster shows men from the dominions and colonies united in the war effort. Even in 1940 Britain did not "stand alone".

ALTHOUGH BRITAIN AND FRANCE WERE AT WAR WITH GERMANY, the only fighting in Europe in early 1940 was between the **Soviet Union** and **Finland** (see 1939). The British and French governments, both strongly anti-communist, planned to send an expeditionary force to aid the Finns. Troops were assembled, but Soviet military successes led Finland to seek peace in March. In France, the failure to help the Finns led to the fall of the government of **Edouard Daladier**, who was replaced as prime minister by **Paul Reynaud** (1878–1966).

Also in March, Soviet dictator **Joseph Stalin** (see 1928) **approved the killing** of all Polish officers who had fallen into Soviet hands through the occupation of western Poland (see 1939). Most of the region's educated elite – doctors, lawyers, and teachers – were also murdered. Some 22,000 victims were buried in **mass graves** in Katyn Forest and elsewhere. In June, when the Soviet Union occupied the Baltic states – Lithuania, Latvia, and Estonia – tens of thousands more people were executed or deported to labour camps. Stalin's ruthless reach extended as far as Mexico, where his exiled rival **Leon Trotsky** had found refuge. In August, Trotsky was killed by Ramon Mercader, an agent of Stalin's secret police.

On 4 April, British prime minister **Neville Chamberlain** announced that Hitler had "missed the bus" by failing to launch a major offensive as **British rearmament accelerated**. Five days after this complacent speech, German forces **occupied Denmark** and **invaded Norway**. Britain and France sent troops and warships to aid the Norwegians but could not prevent a German victory. Norway's King Haakon VII was evacuated to Britain with his government to continue the fight from exile.

In Britain, the disastrous campaign in Norway destroyed confidence in the Chamberlain government. On 10 May, **Winston Churchill** became prime minister at the head of a broad coalition.

On the same day, **German forces** invaded the **Netherlands**, **Belgium**, and **Luxembourg**. After Rotterdam was heavily bombed, the Dutch forces surrendered to avoid further destruction. Dutch Queen Wilhelmina defiantly set up a government-in-exile in London.

Allied troops in northern France advanced into Belgium to meet the German offensive. The Germans unexpectedly delivered a powerful thrust **through the Ardennes region into France** and broke through the French defences at Sedan. Fast-moving German formations of tanks and motorized infantry supported by Stuka dive-bombers drove northward to reach the Channel coast and cut off the Allied forces in Belgium. The Allies established a defensive perimeter around the **port of Dunkirk** and a remarkable escape operation was mounted. Between 26 May and 4 June, 338,000 Allied troops were evacuated by sea before Dunkirk fell to the Germans.

Belgian **King Leopold III** (1901–83) **surrendered** on 28 May, overruling his government's wish to continue fighting.

The French army was driven into retreat, allowing the Germans to **occupy Paris** on 14 June. France was also attacked by Italy, Mussolini belatedly entering the war to pick up some of the spoils of German victory. The French government, along with much of the population, fled to the southwest. In Bordeaux, a new government was formed under the defeatist Marshal Pétain (1856–1951). **General Charles de Gaulle**, a junior minister under Reynaud and a serving army officer, escaped to Britain and

WINSTON CHURCHILL (1874–1965)

Churchill led an adventurous life as a soldier and war correspondent before entering politics. As First Lord of the Admiralty in World War I he was blamed for the Gallipoli disaster. A backbench MP during the 1930s, he opposed the appeasement of Hitler. In 1939, he returned to the Admiralty before becoming prime minister in May 1940. He led Britain through the war but lost the 1945 general election.

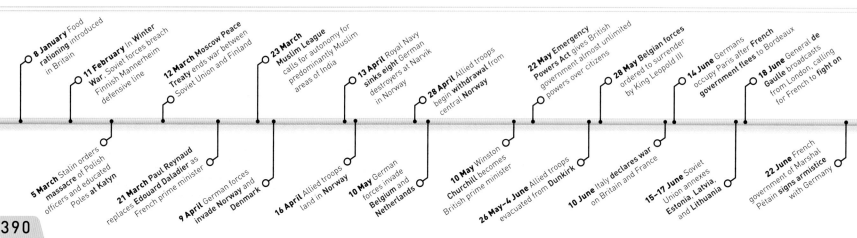

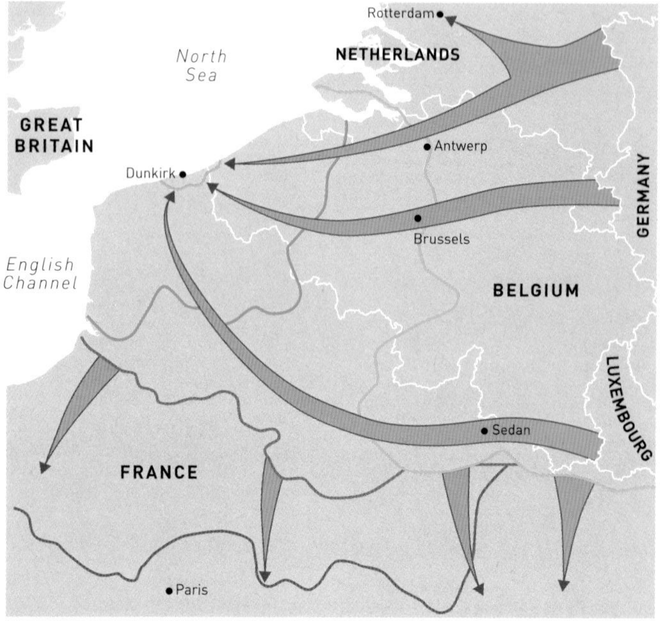

Battle of France
After the Dunkirk evacuation of the Allied forces, German troops advanced into central and western France.

KEY
- German advance
- Allied front line 16 May
- Allied front line 21 May
- Allied defensive line 28 May
- Allied front line 4 Jun
- Allied front line 12 Jun

8 January Food **rationing** introduced in Britain

11 February In Winter **War**, Soviet forces breach Finnish Mannerheim defensive line

5 March Stalin orders **massacre** of Polish officers and educated Poles **at Katyn**

12 March Moscow Peace Treaty ends war between Soviet Union and Finland

21 March Paul Reynaud replaces **Edouard Daladier** as French prime minister

23 March Muslim League calls for autonomy for predominantly Muslim areas of India

9 April German forces **invade Norway** and **Denmark**

13 April Royal Navy **sinks eight** German destroyers at Narvik in Norway

16 April Allied troops land in **Norway**

28 April Allied troops begin **withdrawal** from central **Norway**

10 May German forces invade **Belgium** and **Netherlands**

10 May Winston **Churchill** becomes British prime minister

22 May Emergency Powers Act gives British government almost unlimited powers over citizens

26 May–4 June Allied troops evacuated from **Dunkirk**

28 May Belgian forces ordered to surrender by King Leopold III

10 June Italy **declares war** on Britain and France

14 June Germans occupy Paris after **French government flees** to Bordeaux

15–17 June Soviet Union annexes **Estonia**, **Latvia**, and **Lithuania**

18 June General **de Gaulle** broadcasts from London, calling for French to **fight on**

22 June French government of Marshal Pétain **signs armistice** with Germany

German troops march down the Champs Elysées after the occupation of Paris in June 1940. The French capital was an open city and taken without fighting.

“ FRANCE HAS **LOST THE BATTLE,** BUT FRANCE HAS **NOT LOST THE WAR.** ”

Charles de Gaulle, French General, 18 June 1940

launched an emotional plea for continued resistance, but few heeded the call. Pétain sought an **armistice**, which was **agreed on 22 June**. At Hitler's insistence, the armistice was signed in the same railway carriage in which the 1918 armistice had been signed.

German troops occupied the north and west of France. Pétain established a regime in the town of **Vichy** that held responsibility for all of France, although policy in the occupied part had to be agreed with the Germans. Taking almost dictatorial powers as head of state, he affirmed conservative principles of religion, patriotism, and the family. The **Vichy French collaborated** on some points with the Nazis, introducing their own anti-Semitic laws.

In **Britain**, Churchill quashed defeatism. He encouraged a popular **mood of defiance** with his broadcast speeches and pushed through radical measures to stiffen resistance. These ranged from the internment of aliens to the creation of the **Home Guard** militia to resist German invasion.

Since the British refused to negotiate a peace deal, Hitler began preparing a cross-Channel invasion. In August, the Luftwaffe began a sustained air campaign over southern England, initiating the **Battle of Britain**. British air defences were well prepared, with radar early warning stations linked to command centres that co-ordinated a response by Spitfire and Hurricane fighters.

449

THE NUMBER OF **GERMAN BOMBERS INVOLVED IN** THE **10 HOUR RAID ON** THE BRITISH CITY OF **COVENTRY**

Despite this, RAF Fighter Command was hard pressed as waves of bombers with fighter escort attacked airfields, radar stations, and aircraft factories. It was a relief for the RAF when the Luftwaffe switched to **bombing London** from early September. On 15 September, attacked by over 1,000 German aircraft, the British shot down 60 for the loss of 28 of their own. Such figures meant that Germany could not win the command of the air needed to cover an invasion.

German invasion plans were abandoned in October, but from autumn 1940 until May 1941, British cities were **subjected to the Blitz**, a series of night raids by Luftwaffe bombers that caused heavy casualties – more than 40,000 civilians were killed – and widespread destruction. Contrary to pre-war predictions, however, the raids brought neither social breakdown nor the collapse of morale. British stoicism under fire won many admirers in the neutral US.

Going underground
During the Blitz, thousands of Londoners spent the night in Underground stations to shelter from the bombing.

In 1940, **Franklin D. Roosevelt** stood for and won a third term in office. Before the election, Roosevelt had made his hostility to Nazi Germany and Japan clear. He had begun rearmament and introduced a measure of conscription, but he was aware of the antiwar feeling among people in the US. In a "fireside chat" on radio, Roosevelt told Americans their country was to become the "**arsenal of democracy**", its factories providing the arms for Britain to fight the Axis.

Supermarine Spitfire
The Spitfire, the RAF's most famous fighter aircraft of World War II, could match the performance of the German Messerschmitt 109.

3 July British sink French warships at **Mers el-Kebir**, Algeria

10 July French National Assembly meeting at Vichy gives Pétain **exceptional powers**

10 July Battle of Britain begins with clashes between **RAF** and **Luftwaffe** over the Channel

15 August Luftwaffe and RAF begin **large-scale combat** over southern England

16 August British government decides to reinforce its army in **North Africa** to combat Italians

21 August Trotsky dies in Mexico, **assassinated** by an agent of Stalin

2 September US gives Britain 50 obsolete destroyers **in exchange for bases**

4 September America First Committee founded to campaign for keeping US out of war

7 September First mass Luftwaffe **bombing raid** on London

15 September Major combat between German **Luftwaffe and RAF**

16 September US introduces first peacetime **conscription** in its history

27 September Italy, Germany, and Japan sign **Tripartite Treaty**

12 October Hitler abandons plans for **invasion of Britain**

23 October Hitler meets Franco at Hendaye, but **Spain remains neutral**

28 October Italians invade Greece

5 November In US presidential election, **Roosevelt wins** unprecedented **third term**

11–12 November Aircraft from British carrier *Illustrious* **attack Italian fleet** at Taranto

23 November Romania adheres to **Tripartite Treaty**, joining Axis powers

9 December British launch offensive against Italians in **North African desert**

29–30 December City of London suffers **heavy damage** from German incendiary bombs

German tanks and infantry, belonging to Erwin Rommel's Afrika Korps, advance across Libya during the hard-fought campaign in North Africa.

" DON'T FIGHT A BATTLE IF YOU DON'T GAIN ANYTHING BY WINNING. "

Erwin Rommel, German Field Marshal and commander of the Afrika Korps, in his war diaries *Infanterie Greift An*, 1937

THE ENTRY OF FASCIST ITALY INTO WORLD WAR II IN JUNE 1940 extended the war into the Mediterranean and North Africa, where Italy had colonies, including Libya. Early in 1941, British Commonwealth forces, advancing from Egypt, captured the Libyan port of Tobruk and took 130,000 Italian prisoners. In response, Hitler sent General (later Field Marshal) Erwin Rommel (1891–1944) to North Africa with an armoured force – the Afrika Korps – to rescue his fascist ally. Rommel soon pushed the British back and placed Tobruk under siege, while German aircraft based in Sicily attacked British shipping and bombed the island of Malta, a vital British naval base.

The Italian army also attempted an **invasion of Greece** in 1940, but once again the Germans had to step in. Axis forces invaded **Yugoslavia** in April, which was rapidly defeated and dismembered, creating an **independent Croatia** under the rule of the fascist **Ustaše movement**.

German troops pressed south into Greece, which was swiftly overrun. British Commonwealth forces attempted to defend the **Greek island of Crete**, but it fell to the Germans after an initial assault by paratroopers.

For Hitler, the Mediterranean was merely a sideshow. He had already set in motion preparations for an **invasion of the Soviet Union**, codenamed **Operation Barbarossa**. Nazi intentions were genocidal. Hitler told his generals to plan "a war of annihilation". Special SS death squads, known as **Einsatzgruppen**, were detailed to follow the armies and kill communists and Jews in occupied territory. Nazi administrators anticipated the extermination of 30 million Soviet citizens to free up food supplies for Germany.

Launched on 22 June, Operation Barbarossa was warfare on a vast scale. Hitler had assembled more than **4 million troops**, including a million from his Axis allies. At first the invasion was an overwhelming success. In a series of encirclements, around 3 million Soviet soldiers were taken prisoner. The invaders reached the gates of Leningrad and thrust toward Moscow, but the **Axis advance** slowed with the autumn rains and eventually **ground to a halt in the snow.** The Soviets launched furious, often suicidal, counterattacks to drive the enemy back from the outskirts of Moscow. For the first time Germany had failed to achieve a lightning victory.

In the Baltic republics (Estonia, Latvia, and Lithuania), Belarus, and Ukraine, much of the population **initially welcomed the Germans** as liberators from Stalinist rule. However, few maintained their enthusiasm once they experienced the brutality of Nazi rule. In Leningrad, placed under siege by German and Finnish forces, thousands died every day, mostly from starvation. Almost all the **prisoners of war** captured by the Axis were **executed or perished** from starvation and neglect.

The Jews suffered worst. At **Babi Yar**, outside the Ukrainian capital Kiev, more than 30,000 Jewish people were murdered in two days. The Nazis also began systematic killing of Jews in Poland, using gas vans at an extermination centre at Chelmno.

Throughout 1941, Britain fought on against the Nazis, ignoring a bizarre **peace initiative by**

Airborne operation
The Germans used paratroopers to great success in their invasion of Greece at Corinth, and in the subsequent attack on Crete.

German parachute badge
German paratroopers, like airborne forces all over the world, were considered to be an elite, a status reflected in their stylish badge.

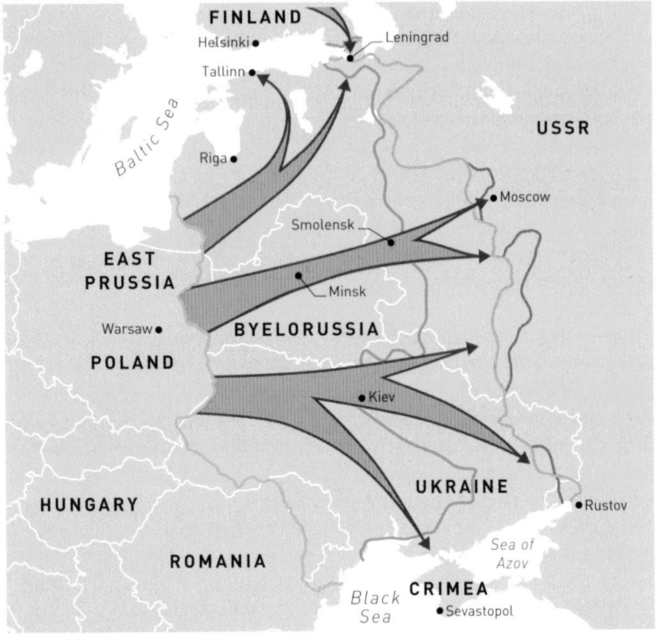

Operation Barbarossa
The Axis invasion of the Soviet Union made great progress in the second half of 1941. It inflicted heavy losses on Soviet forces, but failed to achieve the quick victory that Hitler needed.

KEY
- German/Axis advances
- Front line 21 June 1941
- Front line 1 Sept 1941
- Front line 15 Nov 1941
- Front line 5 Dec 1941

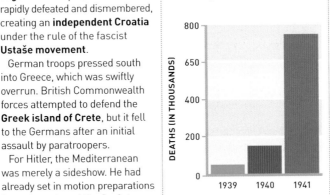

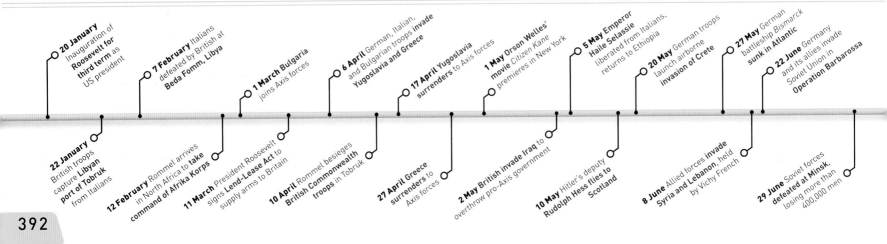

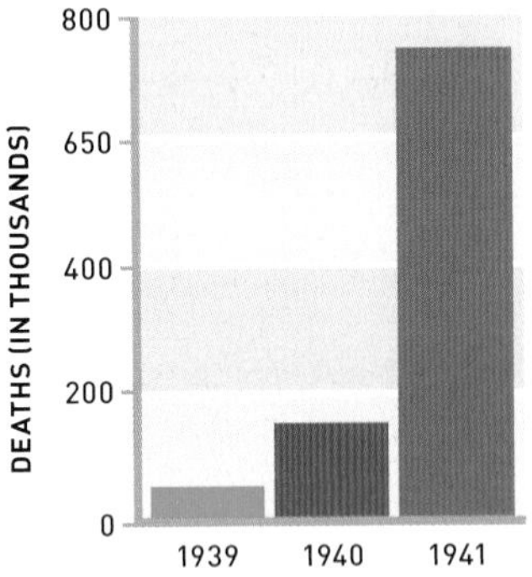

Axis war casualties
The casualties suffered by Germany and its Axis allies rose dramatically between 1939 and 1941, as the war widened its grip on Europe.

20 January Inauguration of **Roosevelt for third term** as US president

22 January British troops capture **Libyan port of Tobruk** from Italians

7 February Italians defeated by British at **Beda Fomm, Libya**

12 February Rommel arrives in North Africa to **take command of Afrika Korps**

1 March Bulgaria joins Axis forces

11 March President Roosevelt signs **Lend-Lease Act** to supply arms to Britain

6 April German, Italian, and Bulgarian troops **invade Yugoslavia and Greece**

10 April Rommel besieges **British Commonwealth troops** in Tobruk

17 April Yugoslavia surrenders to Axis forces

27 April Greece surrenders to Axis forces

1 May Orson Welles' movie *Citizen Kane* premieres in New York

2 May British invade Iraq to overthrow pro-Axis government

5 May Emperor Haile Selassie liberated from Italians, returns to Ethiopia

10 May Hitler's deputy **Rudolph Hess flies to Scotland**

20 May German troops launch airborne **invasion of Crete**

27 May German battleship *Bismarck* **sunk in Atlantic**

8 June Allied forces **invade Syria and Lebanon**, held by Vichy French

22 June Germany and its allies invade Soviet Union in **Operation Barbarossa**

29 June Soviet forces **defeated at Minsk**, losing more than 400,000 men

Battleships *USS West Virginia* and *USS Tennessee* are engulfed in smoke and flames during the surprise Japanese raid on Pearl Harbor.

> “THAT THE **PEARL HARBOR ATTACK** SHOULD HAVE SUCCEEDED IN ACHIEVING **SURPRISE SEEMS** A **BLESSING FROM HEAVEN.**”
>
> Hideki Tojo, Japanese Prime Minister

Hitler's Deputy Führer Rudolf Hess (1894–1987). On 10 May, Hess parachuted into rural Scotland, convinced that he could persuade the British government to ally itself with Germany. Instead, he was arrested and remained a prisoner for the rest of his life.

The chief threat to Britain at this stage in the war lay in the **Battle of the Atlantic** – German attempts to cut off the country's seaborne supplies of food and war material. In May, the German battleship *Bismarck* sortied into the Atlantic. After sinking the Royal Navy battle cruiser *HMS Hood*, *Bismarck* was tracked down, halted by torpedoes dropped from Swordfish aircraft, and then sunk by British battleships.

1,000,000

THE NUMBER OF LENINGRAD'S **RESIDENTS** THOUGHT TO HAVE **DIED DURING** THE **SIEGE**

The British and Canadian navies were less successful at protecting merchant convoys against **German submarines**, however, and losses were soon mounting. The British people felt the effect of this in reduced food rations.

Britain did not hesitate to ally itself with the **Soviet Union**, despite Prime Minister Winston Churchill's (see 1940) strong dislike of Soviet communism. But the British really needed the US to enter the war.

President Roosevelt (see 1933) made no pretence of neutrality. In March, he introduced **Lend-Lease** to supply Britain with military equipment paid for by the US government. American shipyards and factories benefited greatly from this, as did American workers with plentiful and well-paid jobs. Later in the year, free military aid from the US was extended to the Soviet Union.

In August, Roosevelt and Churchill met at Placentia Bay in Newfoundland, Canada, where they agreed the **Atlantic Charter**, a statement of joint war aims embodying liberal democratic principles. American warships were already escorting convoys in the eastern Atlantic, and in October a US destroyer was sunk by a German torpedo, but Roosevelt felt he lacked the popular support needed for a declaration of war.

Roosevelt's dilemma was resolved by the Japanese. The US opposed Japan's expansion into Asia, and after Japanese troops entered French Indochina in July **Roosevelt imposed an oil embargo**. Since Japan was entirely dependent on imported oil, its government had the choice of abandoning its military ambitions or fighting a war with the US.

Following a plan advocated by Admiral Isoroku Yamamoto, on 7 December, Japanese carrier aircraft delivered **a surprise attack** on the American naval base at Pearl Harbor in Hawaii. The raid sank or damaged 18 warships and destroyed around 300 aircraft, which severely damaged the US Pacific fleet. Other Japanese forces invaded the Philippines and the British colony of Malaya.

The shock of the raid on Pearl Harbor ensured popular American support for war with Japan, but not with Germany. To the relief of both Churchill and Roosevelt, Hitler chose to declare war on the US in support of his Japanese allies. At the **Arcadia Conference** in Washington at the end of the year, **Britain** and the **US** agreed a **military strategy** that gave priority to defeating the Germans. The two countries also agreed to unify their military command under the Combined Chiefs of Staff.

Fighting in the snow
A German soldier experiencing the Russian winter during the invasion of the Soviet Union. Axis forces were ill-equipped to cope with the conditions.

ISOROKU YAMAMOTO (1884–1943)

In the 1930s, Japanese Admiral Isoroku Yamamoto became a leading advocate of naval air power. As naval commander-in-chief he was the architect of the raid on Pearl Harbor in 1941. He was killed in April 1943 when his aircraft, identified by American intelligence, was shot down over Bougainville Island in the Pacific.

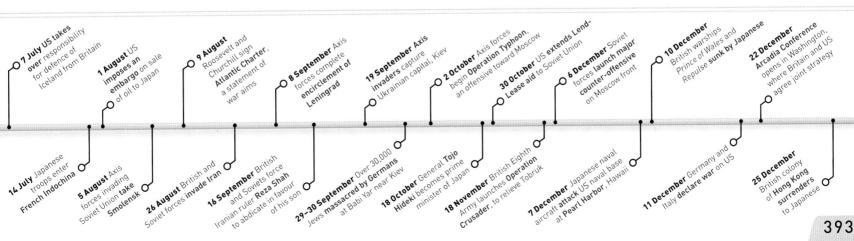

Pearl Harbor badge
The slogan "Remember Pearl Harbor" was widely used in the US to inspire patriotic support for the war against the Japanese.

- **7 July US takes over** responsibility for defence of Iceland from Britain
- **14 July** Japanese troops enter **French Indochina**
- **1 August** US **imposes an embargo** on sale of oil to Japan
- **5 August** Axis forces invading Soviet Union **take Smolensk**
- **9 August** Roosevelt and Churchill sign **Atlantic Charter**, a statement of war aims
- **26 August** British and Soviet forces **invade Iran**
- **8 September** Axis forces complete **encirclement of Leningrad**
- **16 September** British and Soviets force Iranian ruler **Reza Shah** to abdicate in favour of his son
- **19 September Axis invaders** capture Ukrainian capital, Kiev
- **29–30 September** Over 30,000 Jews **massacred by Germans** at Babi Yar near Kiev
- **2 October** Axis forces begin **Operation Typhoon**, an offensive toward Moscow
- **18 October** General **Tojo Hideki** becomes prime minister of Japan
- **30 October** US **extends Lend-Lease aid** to Soviet Union
- **18 November** British Eighth Army launches **Operation Crusader**, to relieve Tobruk
- **6 December** Soviet forces **launch major counter-offensive** on Moscow front
- **7 December** Japanese naval aircraft **attack** US naval base at **Pearl Harbor**, Hawaii
- **10 December** British warships *Prince of Wales* and *Repulse* **sunk by Japanese**
- **11 December** Germany and Italy **declare war** on US
- **22 December Arcadia Conference** opens in Washington, where Britain and US agree joint strategy
- **25 December** British colony of **Hong Kong surrenders** to Japanese

WAR IN THE PACIFIC

THE ALLIES DEFEAT IMPERIAL JAPAN IN THE PACIFIC

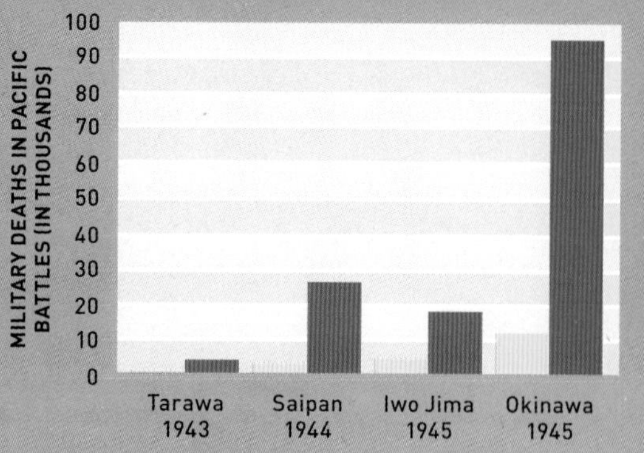

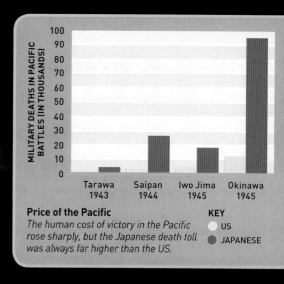

Price of the Pacific
The human cost of victory in the Pacific rose sharply, but the Japanese death toll was always far higher than the US.

KEY
US
JAPANESE

At war with China since 1937, the Japanese decided in 1941 to take a gamble that, if successful, would secure them an empire in Asia and the Pacific. On 7 December, they attacked the US base at Pearl Harbor in Hawaii, and launched an invasion of the Philippines and European colonies in Southeast Asia.

The British and Dutch colonies in Southeast Asia proved easy prey for Japan – the British base at Singapore fell with virtually no resistance. Within five months, the Japanese had reached the border of British India in Burma. Australia seemed threatened, but Japan's southward push was checked by a clash with US aircraft carriers at the Battle of the Coral Sea. A new phase of the war began with an ambitious thrust by the Japanese navy against Midway Island, which led to heavy losses. From August 1942, the most intense fighting focused around Guadalcanal, which the US eventually held. It was not until 1944 that the US had built up sufficient strength for a sustained advance. The Japanese navy was routed at the battles of the Philippine Sea and Leyte Gulf, while the seizure of the Mariana Islands brought the Japanese within range of US bomber aircraft. In August 1945, defeated in Burma and Okinawa, facing a Soviet invasion of Manchuria, and the destruction of cities by atom bombs, the Japanese surrendered.

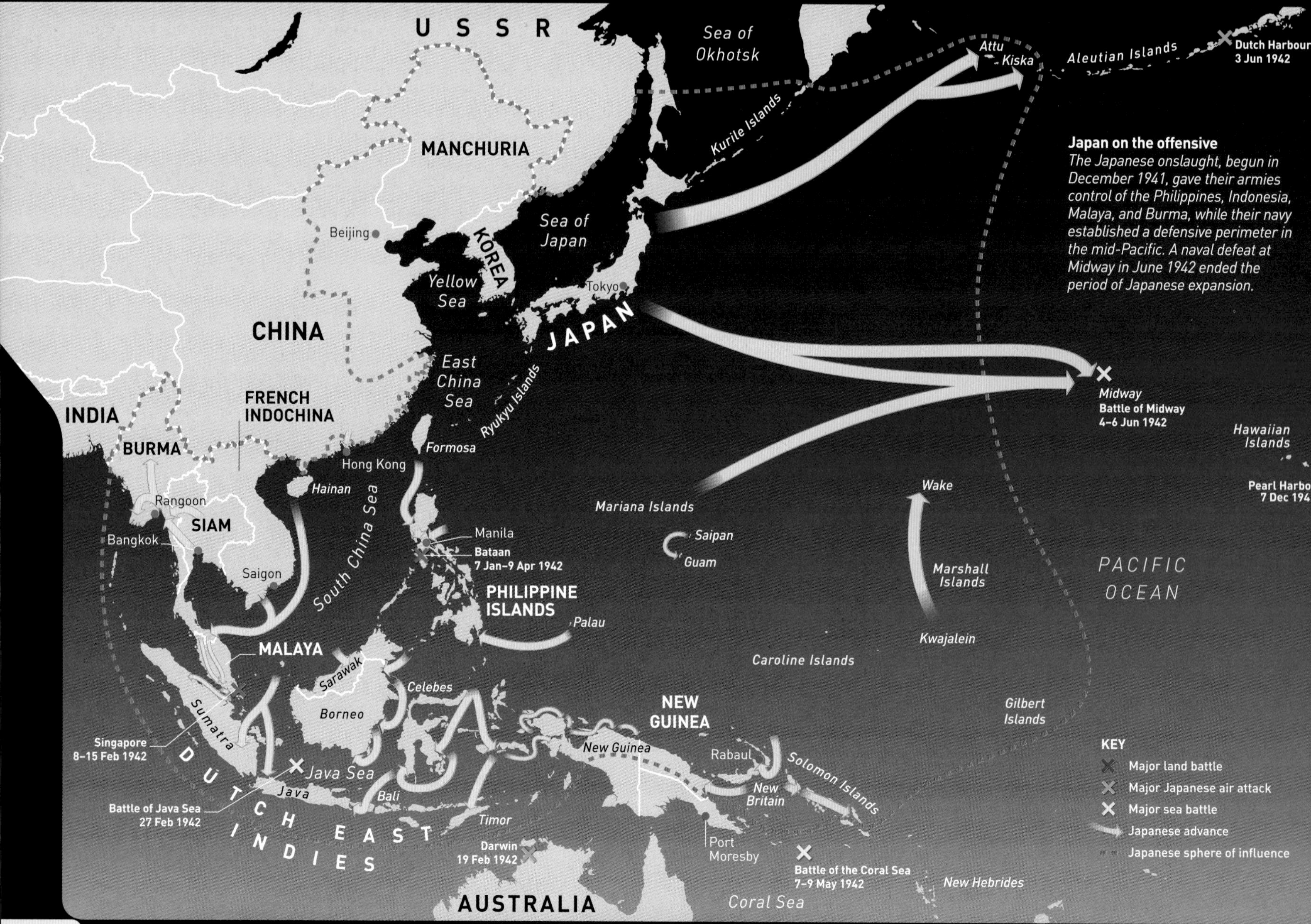

Japan on the offensive
The Japanese onslaught, begun in December 1941, gave their armies control of the Philippines, Indonesia, Malaya, and Burma, while their navy established a defensive perimeter in the mid-Pacific. A naval defeat at Midway in June 1942 ended the period of Japanese expansion.

KEY
Major land battle
Major Japanese air attack
Major sea battle
Japanese advance
Japanese sphere of influence

City	Number of raids	Percentage of city destroyed
Tokyo	5	50%
Nagoya	4	31%
Kobe	2	56%
Osaka	4	26%
Yokohama	2	44%
Kawasaki	1	33%

The Big Six
Between 10 March and 15 June 1945, six major Japanese cities, including Tokyo and Kobe, were decimated by heavy US bombing raids.

3:2 **Burma campaign**
Sixty per cent (three in five) of the Japanese troops who fought in the Burma campaign in 1942–45 lost their lives. Total Japanese casualties numbered around 200,000, compared with the 71,000 British and British Indian men who were killed and wounded.

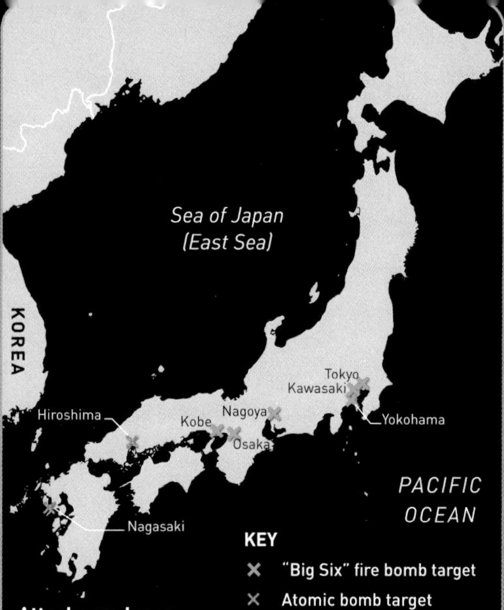

Attacks on Japan
Taking off from bases in the Mariana Islands, US B-29 Superfortress bombers devastated Japanese cities with incendiary devices from March 1945. The dropping of atom bombs on Hiroshima and Nagasaki (6 and 9 August 1945) was followed by Japanese surrender.

> **"** I REALIZE THE **TRAGIC SIGNIFICANCE** OF THE **ATOM BOMB**... WE THANK GOD IT HAS COME TO US INSTEAD OF OUR **ENEMIES... "**

US president Harry S. Truman, 9 August 1945

Allied counterattack
The US army led a fightback against the Japanese in the southwest Pacific, from New Guinea to the Philippines. In the Central Pacific, the US navy and marines spearheaded a thrust from the Gilbert Islands to the Marianas. The loss of Okinawa in June 1945 placed Japan under imminent threat of an Allied invasion.

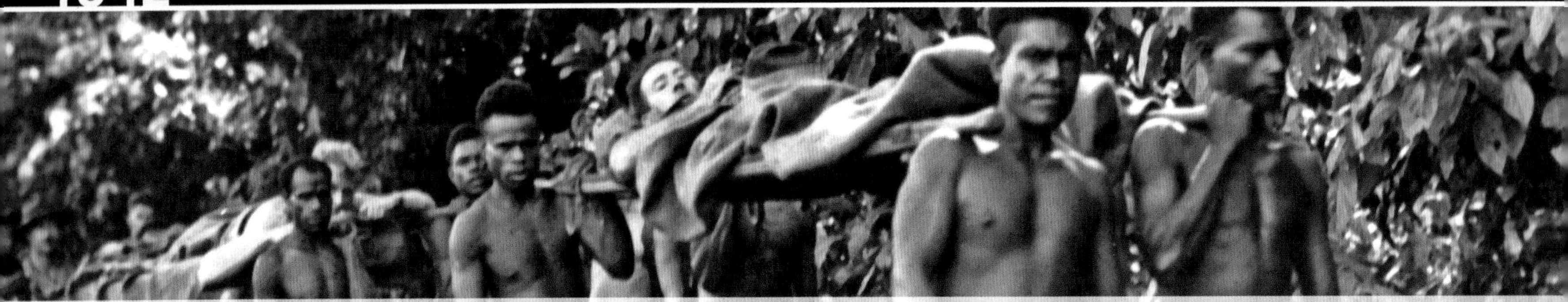

Wounded Allied soldiers are carried through the jungle by New Guineans. The harsh environment was as deadly an enemy as the Japanese.

ON 20 JANUARY 1942, SS GENERAL REINHARD HEYDRICH (1904–1942) chaired a conference at Wannsee, a suburb of Berlin. The purpose of the meeting was to brief German civil servants and foreign ministry officials on plans to systematically **deport Jews** en masse from every country in Europe. The Jews were to be transported to camps – chiefly in Poland – from which, it was made clear, none would return.

Meanwhile, a Japanese tide of conquest flowed across Southeast Asia. **The fall of Singapore**, a major British base that was surrendered to the Japanese in February after token resistance, was a blow to the prestige of the British Empire. About 80,000 British, Australian, and Indian troops were taken prisoner.

Determined resistance by American and Filipino soldiers on the Bataan peninsula in the **Philippines** ended in April. Large numbers of the troops died as prisoners of the Japanese on the brutal **Bataan Death March** – a 100-km (62-mile) trek that was forced upon the malnourished and disease-ridden men.

As the Japanese advance swept over Dutch-ruled Indonesia and British-ruled Burma, Australians worried that their country might be next. An **attack** by Japanese naval aircraft on the **port of Darwin** in Northern Australia in February caused over 500 casualties, and Japanese midget submarines penetrated Sydney Harbour at the start of June. In a sharp change of attitude, Australia began to look on the US, rather than Britain, as its chief military ally.

Amid intense anti-Japanese feeling, in February President Roosevelt signed **Executive Order 9066**, which allowed Japanese Americans living in the western United States to be deported to **internment camps**. About 120,000 ethnic Japanese were interned during the war.

As the United States geared up for total war, the **fight back against Japan** began. The naval battles in the Coral Sea in May and at Midway in June were duels between aircraft carriers, fought without the Japanese and American fleets coming within sight of each other. The **Coral Sea** encounter brought neither side decisive advantage, but **Midway** was a disaster for the Japanese Navy, which lost four aircraft carriers to American dive-bombers and torpedo aircraft.

The American victory at Midway was a turning point, but far from decisive in itself. When **American forces landed on Guadalcanal** in the Solomon Islands in August, the Japanese responded with ferocious determination, landing their own troops to counterattack and initiating a series of naval battles in which both sides suffered heavy losses. In **New Guinea, Australian troops** played a leading role in fighting in hostile jungle terrain.

In **India**, the British faced a political as well as a military challenge. With Japanese troops threatening an invasion from Burma, in August Mohandas Gandhi (1869–1948) and other National Congress leaders launched the **Quit India Movement**, demanding full independence. Their campaign of civil disobedience was ruthlessly repressed by the British authorities, and more than 100,000 Indians were arrested, including Gandhi. Some Indian nationalists joined **Subhas Chandra Bose's Indian National Army**, which fought alongside the Japanese, but far more fought for Britain: around 2.5 million Indians volunteered for the British army.

“ I CAME OUT OF BATAAN AND I SHALL RETURN. ”

General Douglas MacArthur, US commanding officer, after his escape to Australia following defeat in Bataan, 20 March 1942

THE HOLOCAUST

The Nazis murdered people from many groups, including Slavs, homosexuals, and gypsies, but their treatment of the Jews was without parallel. By 1942 they had embarked upon the total extermination of European Jews. To achieve this "final solution", the Nazis transported Jews to purpose-built camps equipped with gas chambers. Most were killed within hours of arrival, but some were kept alive and used as slave labour. About 6 million Jews were murdered, two-thirds of Europe's Jewish population.

Nazi death camps
The Germans built death camps, mostly in occupied Poland, expressly for the killing of Jews. There were many other concentration camps in which tens of thousands died.

KEY
• Nazi extermination camp

2 January Japanese forces **capture Manila**, in the Philippines

20 January At **Wannsee Conference**, German officials plan extermination of Jews

15 February British **surrender Singapore** to Japanese

19 February Japanese aircraft attack town of Darwin, in Australia's Northern Territory

19 February US President Roosevelt signs executive order **authorizing internment** of Japanese Americans

27 February Japanese navy defeats Allied fleet at **Battle of Java Sea**

8 March Japanese troops **capture Rangoon** in Burma

27–28 March British Commandos raid Normandie dock at St Nazaire in Occupied France

9 April American and Filipino troops **surrender to Japanese** in Bataan Peninsula, in the Philippines

15–29 April Many American and Filipino prisoners of war die on **Bataan death march**

18 April Carrier-launched American bombers attack Japan in **Doolittle Raid**

8 May Japanese and American aircraft carriers clash in **Battle of the Coral Sea**

12–28 May Soviet forces **suffer massive losses** in failed counter-offensive at Kharkov

26 May–11 June Free French troops resist Axis tanks in North African desert at **Bir Hakeim**

27 May Nazi **Reinhard Heydrich fatally wounded** by British-trained Czech agents in Prague

30–31 May Cologne is target of first "thousand bomber raid" by **RAF Bomber Command**

4–7 June US carriers inflict heavy losses on Japanese at naval **Battle of Midway**

17 June Roosevelt approves initial $90 million budget for **Manhattan Project** to develop atomic bomb

26 June Axis forces **retake Tobruk** in Libya after Rommel's victory at Gazala

Soviet infantry fight amid the ruined buildings of Stalingrad. German defeat in the city was a decisive turning point in World War II.

Naval power
US Navy dive-bombers fly over Midway Island in the Pacific. This was the location of a decisive duel between American and Japanese aircraft carriers in June 1942.

In the **desert war in North Africa**, after suffering repeated defeats at the hands of Field Marshal Erwin Rommel (1891–1944), the British Eighth Army, commanded by General Bernard Montgomery (1887–1976), won a great offensive victory at **Alamein** in October–November.

As Rommel's Axis army retreated westward across Libya, Allied forces, including a large contingent of American troops commanded by General Dwight D. Eisenhower (1890–1969), landed in French North Africa during **Operation Torch**. Opposition from French colonial forces loyal to the Vichy government (see 1940) was easily overcome, leaving Rommel trapped between armies to his east and west. The Germans responded by extending their military occupation of France to the Vichy-ruled area.

The war being fought in the **Soviet Union** (see 1941) came to its climactic turning point at the **Battle of Stalingrad**. The eastward advance of Axis forces had continued through most of the year, reaching the Caucasus by July and threatening the vital oilfields of Azerbaijan. Hitler insisted his troops capture the city of Stalingrad – of symbolic importance because of its name. German soldiers entered the city in September, but the Soviets defended it street-by-street amid the ruined buildings. In November, Soviet General Giorgi Zhukov (1896–1974) masterminded a counterattack. Striking from north and south, his armies encircled the Axis forces, trapping a quarter of a million men inside Stalingrad. Ordered by Hitler to stay and fight, by the end of the year they were starving, freezing, and short of ammunition. The German commander, Field Marshal Friedrich Paulus, was among the 90,000 men who lived to surrender the following February – and one of only a handful who then survived Soviet imprisonment.

Yank tank
American-built Grant tanks were supplied to the British in North Africa. This one was used by General Montgomery as an observation post.

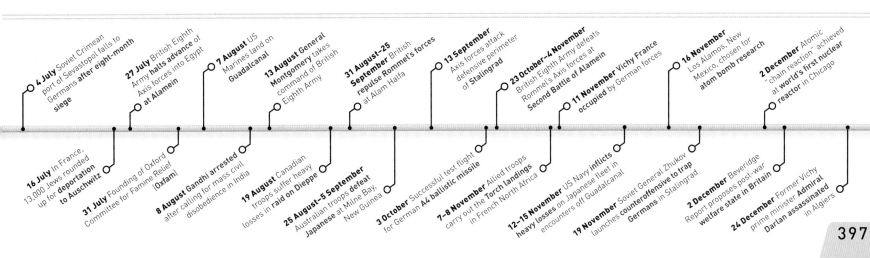

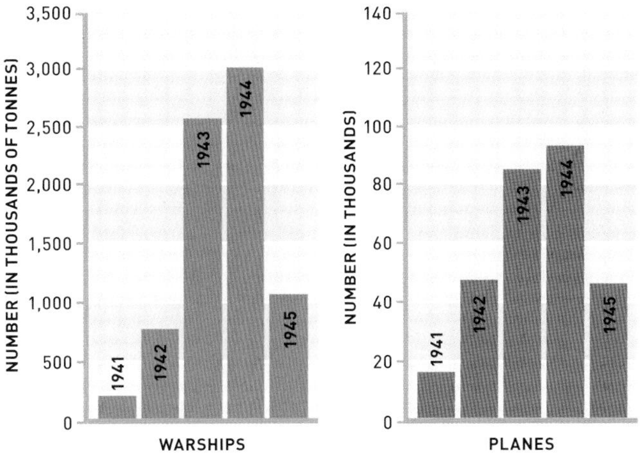

American industrial miracle
The output of US factories and shipyards soared during World War II. The number of workers employed in shipbuilding alone rose from around 100,000 in 1940 to 1.7 million late in the war.

4 July Soviet Crimean port of Sevastopol falls to Germans **after eight-month siege**

16 July In France, 13,000 Jews rounded up for **deportation to Auschwitz**

27 July British Eighth Army **halts advance** of Axis forces into Egypt **at Alamein**

31 July Founding of Oxford Committee for Famine Relief **(Oxfam)**

7 August US Marines land on **Guadalcanal**

8 August Gandhi arrested after calling for mass civil disobedience in India

13 August General Montgomery takes command of British Eighth Army

19 August Canadian troops suffer heavy losses in **raid on Dieppe**

31 August–25 September British **repulse Rommel's forces** at Alam Halfa

25 August–5 September Australian troops **defeat Japanese** at Milne Bay, New Guinea

13 September Axis forces attack defensive perimeter of **Stalingrad**

3 October Successful test flight for German **A4 ballistic missile**

23 October–4 November British Eighth Army defeats Rommel's Axis forces at **Second Battle of Alamein**

7–8 November Allied troops carry out the **Torch landings** in French North Africa

11 November Vichy France **occupied** by German forces

12–15 November US Navy **inflicts heavy losses** on Japanese fleet in encounters off Guadalcanal

16 November Los Alamos, New Mexico, chosen for **atom bomb research**

19 November Soviet General Zhukov launches **counteroffensive to trap Germans** in Stalingrad

2 December Atomic "chain reaction" achieved at **world's first nuclear reactor** in Chicago

2 December Beveridge Report proposes post-war **welfare state in Britain**

24 December Former Vichy prime minister **Admiral Darlan assassinated** in Algiers

1943

US President Roosevelt and British Prime Minister Churchill meet at Casablanca in January to discuss the conduct of the war.

French Resistance fighters pose for a group portrait. The Resistance carried out acts of sabotage, gathered intelligence, and mounted guerrilla warfare operations.

IN JANUARY 1943, Franklin D. Roosevelt met British prime minister **Winston Churchill** for a conference in **Casablanca**, Morocco, which set the future course of World War II in Europe. Britain persuaded the US to **plan for an invasion of Sicily**, knowing this meant an invasion of northern France would have to be postponed until 1944. The Allied leaders also agreed that their air forces would mount a combined bomber offensive against Germany. At the end of the conference, Roosevelt announced that the Allies would **accept nothing less than the "unconditional surrender"** of their enemies.

The surrender of Axis forces at Stalingrad (see 1942) in February was a massive setback for Germany, but the Germans remained in occupation of most of Europe. In many places, **armed resistance movements** contested the occupation. A turning point for the **resistance in France** was the decision in 1943 to conscript French men to work in German factories. To avoid forced labour, thousands of young men slipped away to form guerrilla bands in remote rural regions.

Casablanca
The general release of the film Casablanca *was timed to take advantage of the widely reported* Casablanca *Conference.*

Resistance movements were plagued by political divisions. In the **Balkans**, partisans led by the communist **Tito** (see panel, below) fought hard against the Germans, but were also actively hostile to the Chetnik guerrillas, led by Serb nationalist and monarchist **Draza Mihailovic**. In France, Resistance leader **Jean Moulin** strove to unite rival factions, but in May he was arrested, tortured by Gestapo chief Klaus Barbie, and died in captivity.

Spring 1943 brought the climax of the struggle against German U-boats known as the **Battle of the Atlantic**. In March, the Allies lost 260,000 tonnes of merchant shipping to German submarine attacks and there seemed a real risk that Britain's lifeline of seaborne supplies would be severed. German U-boats operated in groups known as "wolf packs", co-ordinated by radio. But then, a combination of factors, including increased use of aircraft on ocean patrols, intelligence from decrypted German naval messages, and the equipping of convoy escorts with improved radar and radio direction-finding equipment, tilted the balance against the submarines. By May, **U-boat losses** were so high that submarine commander Admiral Karl Dönitz had to withdraw his forces from the Atlantic. The U-boat offensive was never to regain its momentum.

By far the heaviest land fighting of 1943 was on **Germany's eastern front**. Despite the disaster at Stalingrad, Axis forces were able to mount a successful counteroffensive at **Kharkov** in the spring. This left the Soviets holding an exposed bulge of territory, or salient, at **Kursk**. German generals planned to attack from north and south to trap the Soviet forces inside the salient and destroy them. But deputy supreme commander **Georgi Zhukov** anticipated the German offensive and prepared a formidable defensive system. The forces assembled at Kursk were huge – the two sides together totalled over 2 million men, with more than 6,000 tanks and 5,000 aircraft. The Axis onslaught began on 5 July, initiating the **largest tank battle in history**. Soviet losses were heavy, but after four days the Axis offensive had stalled and the Red Army launched a counterattack. The Germans organized a fighting withdrawal but the tide of the war in the east had turned for good.

While the battle of Kursk was at its height, the Western Allies mounted a **large-scale invasion of Sicily**. US and British armies were put ashore and advanced around opposite sides of the island, receiving little opposition from Italian forces who quickly surrendered. The campaign turned into a race between US general **George S. Patton** and British general **Bernard Montgomery**. Patton was first to reach Messina, but between them the two armies allowed most of the Axis forces to escape to mainland Italy.

The loss of Sicily was a fatal blow to the Italian dictator Benito Mussolini. After **a vote of no confidence** from the **Fascist Grand Council**, Mussolini was dismissed by King Victor Emmanuel III (1869–1947) and arrested. His replacement,

> **" GERMANY IS A FORTRESS, BUT IT IS A FORTRESS WITHOUT A ROOF. "**
>
> **Franklin D. Roosevelt, US President,** 1944

Soviet badge
This badge was awarded to Soviet tank crewmen during World War II. The Soviets lost around 5,000 tanks at Kursk in summer 1943.

JOSIP BROZ TITO (1892–1980)

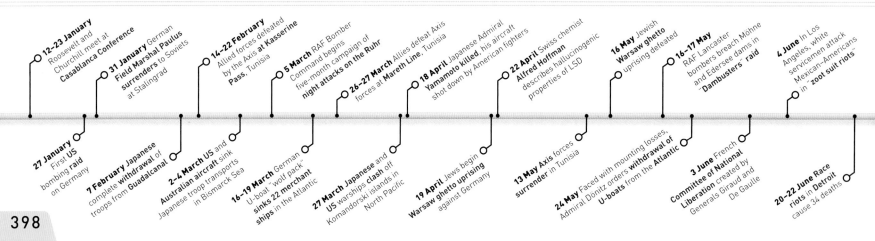

Born in Croatia, Josip Broz adopted the name Tito as a communist activist in the 1930s. After the German occupation of Yugoslavia in 1941, Tito led a guerrilla movement that took control of the country in 1945. He made Yugoslavia a communist state, but resisted the dominance of the Soviet Union. He remained Yugoslav president until his death.

- **12–23 January** Roosevelt and Churchill meet at **Casablanca Conference**
- **27 January** First **US bombing raid** on Germany
- **31 January** German **Field Marshal Paulus surrenders** to Soviets at Stalingrad
- **7 February** Japanese complete **withdrawal** of troops from **Guadalcanal**
- **14–22 February** Allied forces defeated by the Axis **at Kasserine Pass**, Tunisia
- **2–4 March US** and **Australian aircraft** sink Japanese troop transports in Bismarck Sea
- **5 March** RAF Bomber Command begins five-month campaign of **night attacks on the Ruhr**
- **16–19 March** German U-boat "wolf pack" **sinks 22 merchant ships** in the Atlantic
- **26–27 March** Allies defeat Axis forces at **Mareth Line**, Tunisia
- **27 March Japanese** and **US** warships **clash** off Komandorski islands in North Pacific
- **18 April** Japanese Admiral **Yamamoto killed**, his aircraft shot down by American fighters
- **19 April** Jews begin **Warsaw ghetto uprising** against Germany
- **22 April** Swiss chemist **Alfred Hoffman** describes hallucinogenic properties of LSD
- **13 May Axis** forces **surrender** in Tunisia
- **16 May** Jewish **Warsaw ghetto** uprising defeated
- **16–17 May** RAF Lancaster bombers breach Möhne and Edersee dams in **"Dambusters" raid**
- **24 May** Faced with mounting losses, Admiral Dönitz orders **withdrawal of U-boats** from the **Atlantic**
- **3 June** French **Committee of National Liberation** created by Generals Giraud and De Gaulle
- **4 June** In Los Angeles, white servicemen attack Mexican-Americans in **"zoot suit riots"**
- **20–22 June Race riots** in **Detroit** cause 34 deaths

Men of the US Coast Guard cutter *Spencer* watch the explosion of a depth charge that sank a German U-boat in the Atlantic on 17 April.

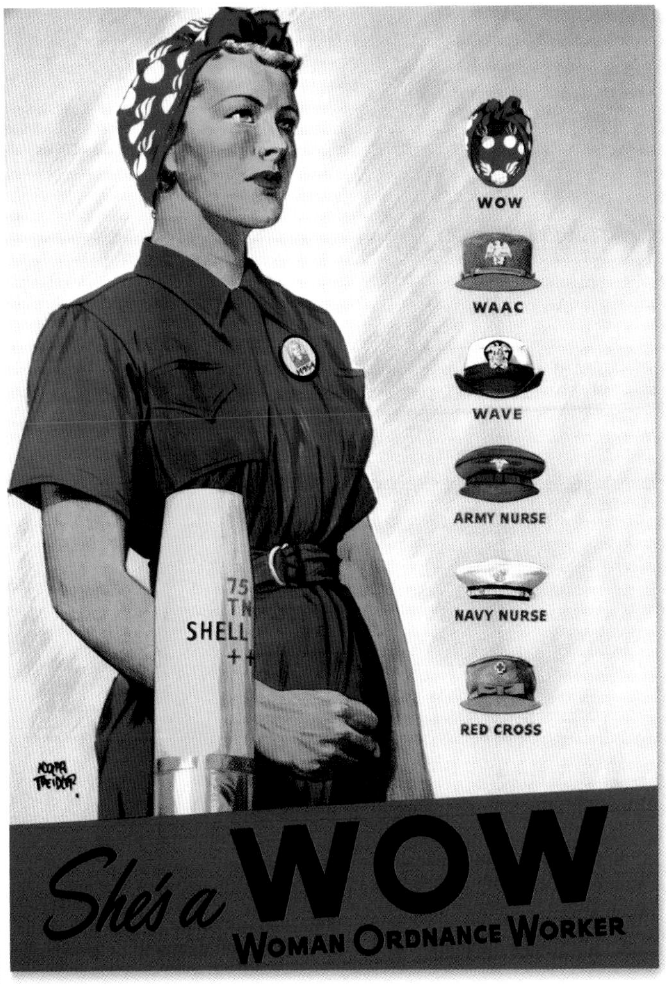

Women at war
A US poster suggests that working in munitions factories can be as glamorous as joining the various uniformed women's services.

Marshal Pietro Badoglio (1871–1956), signed an armistice with the Allies in early September. But the Germans had time to take over key positions in Italy and defend the peninsula against Allied invasion forces. German paratroopers rescued Mussolini from captivity. They set him up as ruler of a puppet **Italian Social Republic**, which was founded in the town of Salo. As Allied forces fought their way northward from Naples toward Rome, the **Badoglio government joined the Allies**, declaring war on Germany.

Germany came under **heavy air attack** through 1943. RAF Bomber Command, equipped with the new Lancaster bomber, achieved a spectacular success in the "**Dambusters**" raid in May. Using "bouncing bombs", Lancasters made a low-level night attack on four Ruhr dams, breaching two of them. In July, bombers saturated the port city of **Hamburg** with incendiary devices. In hot, dry weather conditions, separate fires blended into a single immense firestorm. More than 37,000 people were killed, most of them civilians.

While the RAF bombed Germany by night, the **US Army Air Force** began a **daylight bombing campaign**. The US bombers, bristling with guns, were expected to fight off attacks by German aircraft and drop bombs on targets using technologically advanced bombsights. In practice, the B-17s and B-24s suffered alarmingly heavy losses and precision bombing proved hard to achieve under combat conditions.

The **impact of bombing** on the German civilian population was huge. Apart from the casualties, hundreds of thousands were made homeless and there were severe food shortages. Over **two million children** were **evacuated** from the cities. Many factories were relocated underground to avoid the bombing.

Flying fortress
The crew of an American Eighth Air Force B-17 Flying Fortress at a base in England prepare for a bombing mission over Germany. The Eighth Air Force lost 26,000 men between 1942 and 1945.

The shortages experienced by German civilians were replicated, in greater or lesser degree, in all European countries, including neutral Spain. In Britain, labour shortages led to the **conscription of women for work** in civil defence, military auxiliary services, factories, and in agriculture. In the US, women workers were employed in heavy industrial jobs traditionally reserved for men.

Black workers also took jobs that in peacetime were reserved for whites. This led to **racial tensions** that **erupted into rioting** in Detroit in June. White and black mobs clashed, and 34 people were killed before federal troops restored order.

One of the worst tragedies of 1943 was the **Bengal famine** that killed more than a million people in British India. Responsibility for this catastrophe is disputed, but Prime Minister Churchill refused to allow shipping space, which prevented food from reaching the starving.

In Asia, 60,000 Allied prisoners of war (POWs) and almost 200,000 Asian labourers were **forced to build a railway** from **Thailand** to supply Japanese troops in **Burma**. Around 16,000 POWs and 90,000 Asian workers died while they were building it.

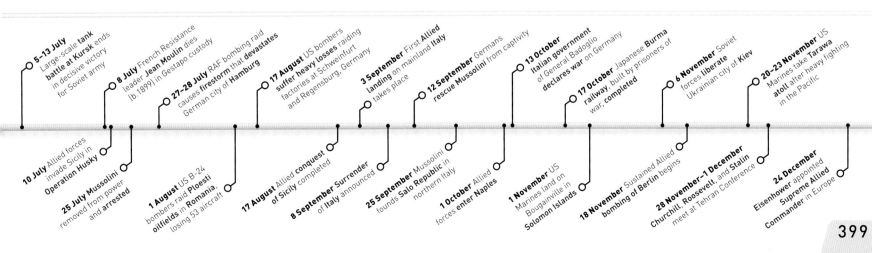

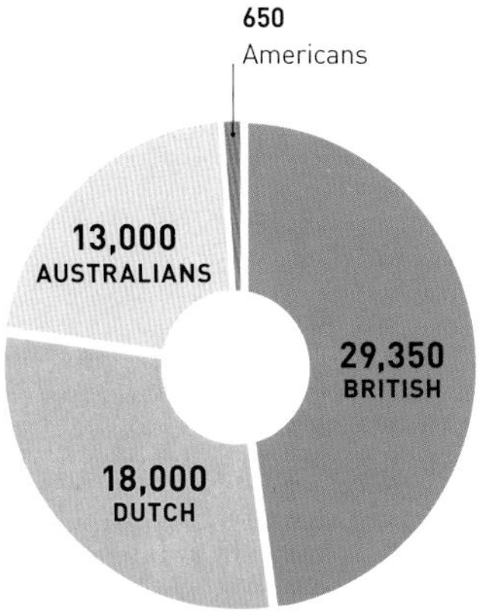

Building the Burma Railway
Alongside Asian forced labourers, chiefly British, Australian, and Dutch prisoners of war were used by the Japanese to build the railway.

5–13 July Large-scale **tank battle at Kursk** ends in decisive victory for Soviet army

8 July French Resistance leader **Jean Moulin** dies (b.1899) in Gestapo custody

10 July Allied forces invade Sicily in **Operation Husky**

25 July Mussolini removed from power and **arrested**

27–28 July RAF bombing raid causes **firestorm** that **devastates** German city of **Hamburg**

1 August US B-24 bombers raid **Ploesti oilfields** in **Romania**, losing 53 aircraft

17 August US bombers **suffer heavy losses** raiding factories at Schweinfurt and Regensburg, Germany

17 August Allied **conquest of Sicily** completed

3 September First **Allied landing** on mainland **Italy** takes place

8 September Surrender of Italy announced

12 September Germans **rescue Mussolini** from captivity

25 September Mussolini founds **Salo Republic** in northern Italy

1 October Allied forces **enter Naples**

13 October Italian government of General Badoglio **declares war** on Germany

17 October Japanese **Burma railway**, built by prisoners of war, **completed**

1 November US Marines land on Bougainville in **Solomon Islands**

6 November Soviet forces **liberate** Ukrainian city of **Kiev**

18 November Sustained Allied **bombing of Berlin** begins

20–23 November US Marines take **Tarawa atoll** after heavy fighting in the Pacific

28 November–1 December Churchill, Roosevelt, and **Stalin** meet at Tehran Conference

24 December Eisenhower appointed **Supreme Allied Commander** in Europe

American soldiers wade ashore from a landing craft during the invasion of Normandy on 6 June. The landings began the liberation of Occupied France.

150,000 THE NUMBER OF **ALLIED TROOPS** THAT **LANDED ON** THE **NORMANDY BEACHES**

9,000 THE NUMBER OF **ALLIED CASUALTIES** DURING THE LANDINGS

IN EARLY 1944 THERE WAS HEAVY FIGHTING IN ITALY as German troops blocked the Allied advance on Rome. In January, Allied seaborne landings at **Anzio**, behind the Germans' defensive Gustav Line, failed to break the deadlock. In February, Allied commanders decided to bomb the medieval abbey at Monte Cassino, a key point in the Gustav Line, but this much-criticized act of desecration was also ineffectual. **Monte Cassino eventually fell to the Polish infantry** in May, allowing Rome to be liberated the following month.

In the spring, British Indian troops withstood a Japanese attempt to invade northeast India from Burma. The **Japanese offensive** was so successfully repulsed that Allied forces were able to mount their own offensive to retake much of Burma later in the year. With the Quit India movement (see 1942) also suppressed, the British had reasserted their authority over the subcontinent.

Meanwhile, Allied preparations for an **invasion of Occupied France** turned southern England into an armed camp. Operation **Overlord**, was commanded by General Dwight D. Eisenhower (1890–1969). The Allies chose Normandy as the target for their invasion. Postponed because of bad weather, the **Normandy landings** took place on 6 June, referred to as **D-Day**.

During the night, 18,000 airborne troops landed by parachute or glider behind the German coastal defences. At dawn, a fleet of 5,000 ships carrying around 130,000 soldiers arrived off shore. It was the **largest amphibious operation in history**. Three of the five landing beaches, codenamed **Sword**, **Juno**, and **Utah**, were taken with relative ease by British, Canadian, and US troops, but the British at **Gold** beach and especially the Americans at **Omaha** beach suffered substantial losses before securing ground.

Burma Star
This military medal was awarded to British and Commonwealth soldiers for service in the Burma campaign between 1941 and 1945.

Two ingenious innovations, the **Mulberry floating harbour** and the Pluto undersea oil pipeline, allowed supplies to reach Allied forces once ashore. A gruelling struggle ensued to break out of Normandy, and German resistance was not overcome until August.

Meanwhile, **Adolf Hitler** (1889–1945) survived an **assassination attempt**. A plot was mounted by patriotic German officers and officials to overthrow the Führer and seek peace with the Western allies. On 20 July, Colonel Claus Schenk von Stauffenberg (1907–1944) carried a bomb in his briefcase to a meeting at Hitler's headquarters at Rastenburg, East Prussia. He placed the bomb under a table at which Hitler was sitting. It exploded, devastating the room and killing four people, but the **dictator survived unscathed**. Stauffenberg and some of the other leading conspirators were shot by firing squad; thousands more were arrested and tortured, many suffering lingering deaths. Field Marshal Erwin Rommel (1891–1944) was also implicated in the plot, but he was permitted to commit suicide.

The breakout of Allied forces from Normandy in August (see p.389) led rapidly to the **liberation of Paris**. After French Resistance fighters began an uprising in the city on 19 August, General Charles de Gaulle's Free French forces, fighting as part of Eisenhower's Allied armies, raced for Paris. A column of French tanks reached central Paris on 25 August.

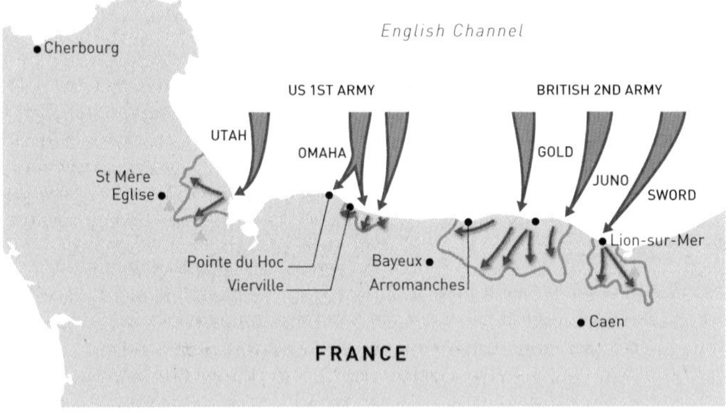

D-Day Landings
The Allies landed on five Normandy beaches – Sword, Juno, Gold, Utah, and Omaha. Allied troops also parachuted in behind enemy lines.

KEY
→ Allied landing/advance
▼ Allied parachute landing
— Allied front line 7 June 1944

22 January Allied forces **land at Anzio**, behind Gustav Line, in Italy

27 January Soviet forces **retake Leningrad**

15 February US bombers destroy abbey of **Monte Cassino** on Gustav Line

17 February US Marines land on Eniwetok in **Marshall Islands**

20–25 February US and British bombers attack German aircraft factories in Big Week

23 February Stalin orders **mass deportation** of Chechens and Ingush **to central Asia**

7 March Japanese launch an offensive from **Burma** (Myanmar) into northwest India

19 March German troops occupy Hungary to stop **Hungarian peace negotiations** with Allies

4 April British Indian forces resist Japanese at **Kohima**

18 April Japanese begin major offensive in China, **Operation Ichi-Go**

21 April French Provisional Government recognizes French **women's right to vote**

28 April Over 700 Americans **killed during rehearsal** for Normandy landings

5 May Gandhi released from prison because of poor health

9 May Soviet forces retake Black Sea port of **Sevastopol**

15 May Germans begin **deportation** of Hungarian Jews **to Auschwitz**

17 May Polish troops drive Germans out of Monte Cassino

4 June Rome falls to Allies

6 June Invasion of Normandy begins with **D-Day landings**

13 June First **German V1 flying bombs** launched against England

15 June US Marines and infantry begin landing on Saipan in **Mariana Islands**

19 June Japanese naval aviation suffers massive losses at **battle of Philippine Sea**

22 June Soviet Army launches **Operation Bagration** to drive Axis forces from Belarus

Soldiers of US 7th Armored Division patrol the snowy Belgian town of St Vith, a site of fierce fighting during the German Ardennes offensive in December.

> **“... AN OPERATION OF THE MOST EXTREME DARING.”**
>
> **General Alfred Jodl, Chief of Operations** on Hitler's counteroffensive

As the Germans withdrew, the celebrations in Paris began, and so too did **reprisals against alleged collaborators**. Around 9,000 French people were summarily executed and tens of thousands subjected to public humiliation – for example, women were paraded with shaved heads – before **De Gaulle formed a provisional government** and restored order.

Liberation of Paris
Parisians celebrate the liberation of their city, and welcome the return of General de Gaulle to France as leader of the Free French.

At the beginning of August the **Polish resistance movement** staged an uprising against the Germans in Warsaw. The Soviet Red Army had almost reached the city, after pushing westward through the summer, but Stalin had no desire to help the Poles, who were mostly anti-Russian and anti-communist. The Red Army stopped short of Warsaw, and did little for two months while the Polish uprising was crushed by Nazi troops. Several hundred thousand Poles were killed. After the survivors surrendered in early October, the Germans destroyed Warsaw.

In the west in September, with the Allies in control of most of Belgium, British general Bernard Montgomery (1887–1976) devised a plan to end the war quickly by an **airborne invasion of the occupied Netherlands**. British, US, and Polish paratroopers attempted to seize and hold a series of bridges that would allow Allied tanks to advance into northern Germany. The last bridge at **Arnhem** was not taken, however, and the operation failed leaving the Netherlands to suffer a harsh winter under the Nazis.

The US **offensive in the Pacific** gathered momentum through the year (see pp.394–95). Outnumbered and militarily outclassed, the Japanese fought with suicidal determination. In the battle for the **island of Saipan** between 15 June and 9 July, almost the entire garrison of 30,000 Japanese soldiers were killed. The Japanese Imperial Navy was almost wiped out in two great battles – the **Philippine Sea** in June, and **Leyte Gulf** in October.

Facing near certain death in unequal combat with superior US forces, some Japanese naval pilots mounted "**kamikaze**" suicide attacks, deliberately crashing their aircraft into US warships. These tactics proved so effective that they were adopted as a form of mass attack, using hundreds of virtually untrained rookie pilots.

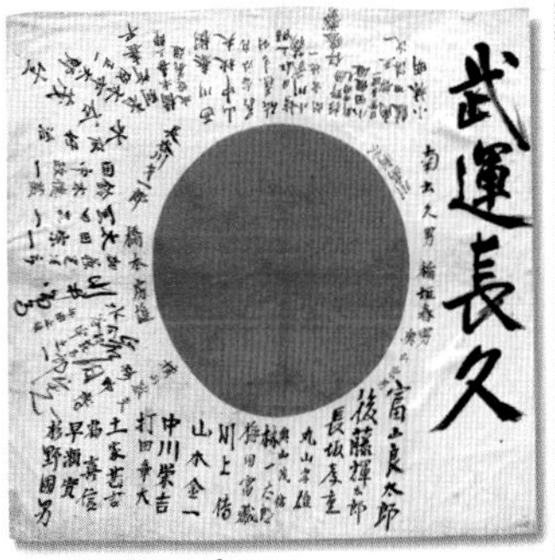

Prayer for safety
For good luck, some Japanese servicemen carried their national flag with a special prayer written on it, asking for a safe return.

Facing defeat in Europe, Hitler put his faith in secret weapons. The first jet aircraft, the German **Messerschmitt 262**, entered the conflict, but failed to reverse the mounting dominance of Allied air forces. The **V1 flying bombs** launched against London caused heavy casualties, but had no decisive effect, nor did the **V2 rockets**, the world's first ballistic missiles. Around 3,000 V2s were launched, mostly at London and Antwerp. They arrived without warning and there was no defence against them, but they were inaccurate, and failed to have the impact Hitler desired.

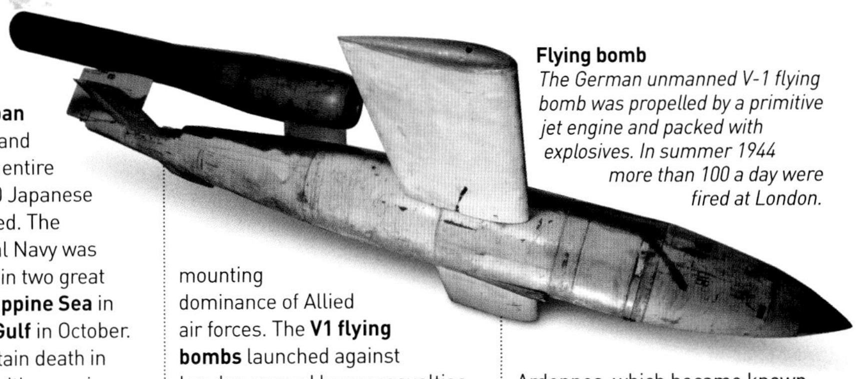

Flying bomb
The German unmanned V-1 flying bomb was propelled by a primitive jet engine and packed with explosives. In summer 1944 more than 100 a day were fired at London.

In December, the German Führer made his last gamble with a surprise offensive in the Ardennes, which became known as the **Battle of the Bulge**. German tanks broke through the US front line and headed for Antwerp. Stiffening resistance, especially by US airborne troops at Bastogne, was followed by a well-organized Allied counter-attack. The German tanks ran out of fuel, and improved weather allowed Allied aircraft to strike in support of ground forces. Hitler's last throw of the dice had failed.

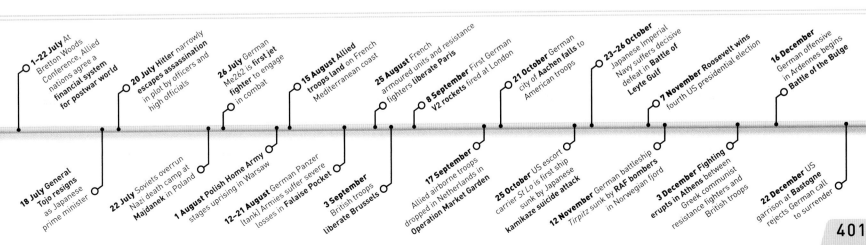

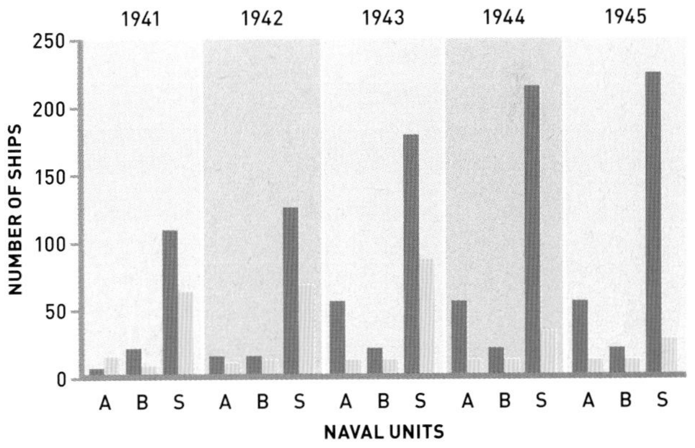

US and Japanese naval strengths
A combination of vastly productive US shipyards and heavy Japanese losses enabled the US to win naval dominance in the Pacific.

- **1–22 July** At Bretton Woods Conference, Allied nations agree a **financial system for postwar world**
- **18 July General Tojo resigns** as Japanese prime minister
- **20 July Hitler** narrowly **escapes assassination** in plot by officers and high officials
- **22 July** Soviets overrun Nazi death camp at **Majdanek** in Poland
- **26 July** German Me262 is **first jet fighter** to engage in combat
- **1 August Polish Home Army** stages uprising in Warsaw
- **15 August Allied troops land** on French Mediterranean coast
- **12–21 August** German Panzer (tank) Armies suffer severe losses in **Falaise Pocket**
- **25 August** French armoured units and resistance fighters **liberate Paris**
- **3 September** British troops **liberate Brussels**
- **8 September** First German **V2 rockets** fired at London
- **17 September** Allied airborne troops dropped in Netherlands in **Operation Market Garden**
- **21 October** German city of **Aachen falls** to American troops
- **25 October** US escort carrier *St Lo* is first ship sunk by Japanese **kamikaze suicide attack**
- **23–26 October** Japanese Imperial Navy suffers decisive defeat in **Battle of Leyte Gulf**
- **7 November Roosevelt wins** fourth US presidential election
- **12 November** German battleship *Tirpitz* sunk by **RAF bombers** in Norwegian fjord
- **3 December Fighting erupts in Athens** between Greek communist resistance fighters and British troops
- **16 December** German offensive in Ardennes begins **Battle of the Bulge**
- **22 December** US garrison at **Bastogne** rejects German call to surrender

Party member
GERMANY
This membership book, dated 15 July 1937, certified that the holder was a member of the Nazi party, the ruling party in Germany during World War II.

Yellow star
GERMANY
From September 1941, all Jews in the German Reich were forced to wear a yellow star with *Jude* (German for "Jew") written on it.

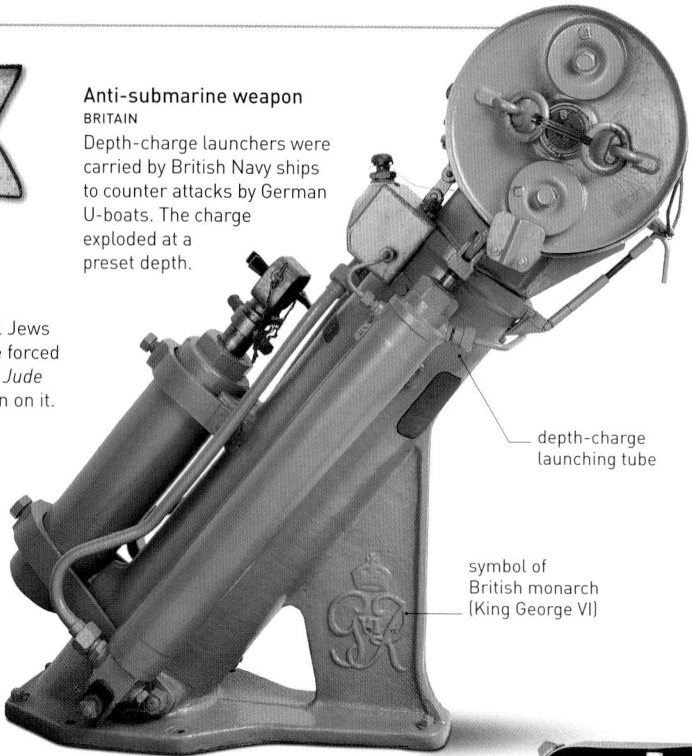

Anti-submarine weapon
BRITAIN
Depth-charge launchers were carried by British Navy ships to counter attacks by German U-boats. The charge exploded at a preset depth.

French Canadian poster
CANADA
This poster, addressed to Canada's French-speaking population, appeals for naval volunteers to join the fight against German U-boats.

SS dagger
GERMANY
Ceremonial daggers were issued to all members of the Nazi elite SS. The blade bears the SS motto *Meine Ehre heißt Treue* ("My Honour is Loyalty").

WORLD WAR II

A GLOBAL CONFLICT THAT INVOLVED NOT ONLY MILITARY PERSONNEL BUT ALSO CIVILIANS

World War II cost more lives than any other conflict in human history. Battle was joined on land, at sea, and in the air, with weapons ranging from the bolt-action rifle to the atomic bomb.

World War II involved more than 100 million military personnel and most nations of the world. As well as being the most widespread war in history, it was also marked by mass casualties among civilians, who were subjected to large-scale aerial bombardment, massacre by German and Japanese soldiers and security forces, and the dropping of atomic bombs on Japan.

Cipher machine
US
The M-209 was a mechanical cipher machine that provided swift and basic encryption, providing sufficient security for use on the battlefield.

Lee Enfield bolt-action rifle
BRITAIN
This rifle, which fired .303 cartridges from a 10-round magazine, was the standard British and Commonwealth infantry rifle in both World Wars.

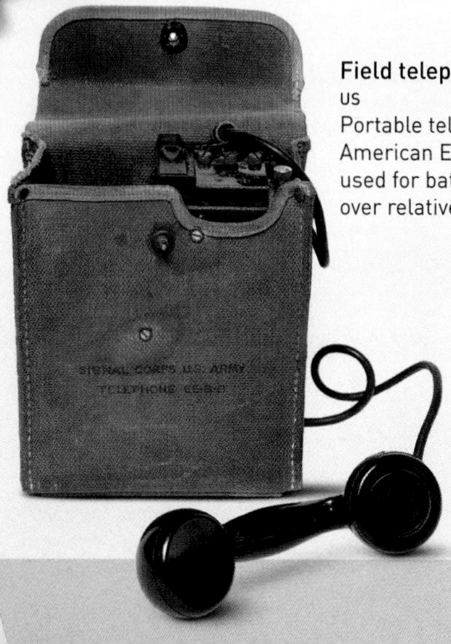

Field telephone
US
Portable telephones, such as the American EE8 shown here, were used for battlefield communication over relatively short distances.

Prayer card
JAPAN
This wooden prayer card belonged to a Buddhist Japanese serviceman. Troops of all nations sought comfort in religion and in superstition.

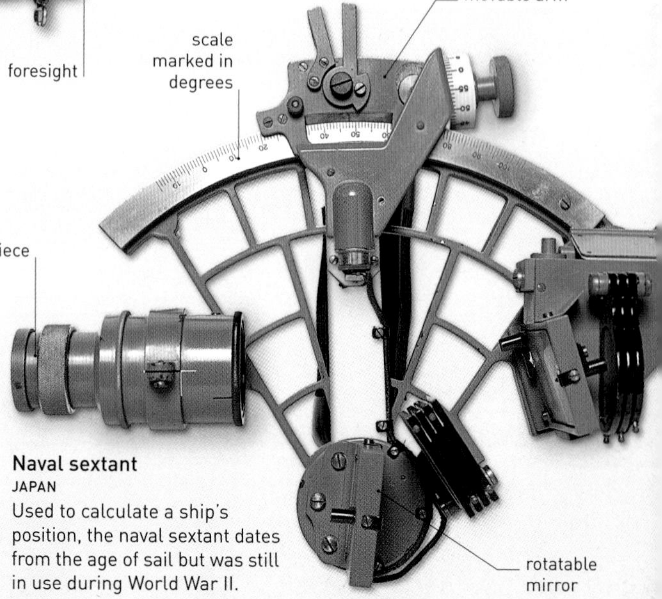

Naval sextant
JAPAN
Used to calculate a ship's position, the naval sextant dates from the age of sail but was still in use during World War II.

Suicide pill
BRITAIN
The British sent agents into Nazi-occupied Europe to liaise with local resistance fighters. Each agent carried a suicide pill to swallow if captured.

Sniper rifle
USSR
The Soviet Red Army made extensive use of snipers, especially in the Battle of Stalingrad. They used a standard-issue Mosin-Nagant infantry rifle fitted with a telescopic sight.

Improvised boots
GERMANY
German troops invading the USSR in 1941 were not equipped to face the Russian winter. Some made straw boots to protect against frostbite.

Blackout poster
GERMANY
A dramatic poster calls on German citizens to observe blackout regulations during air raids. The slogan says "The enemy sees your light! Make it dark!"

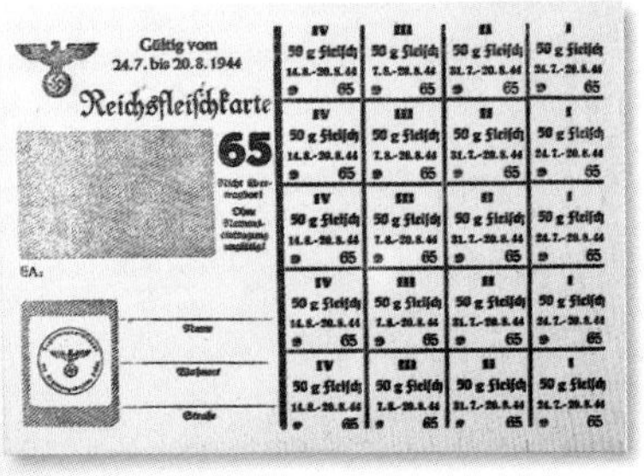

Civilian ration card
GERMANY
Shortages of food, fuel, and other essentials led most combatant countries to introduce rationing. This German ration card is for meat.

Desert headgear
NEW ZEALAND
The Long Range Desert Group, set up by the British, was initially formed of New Zealanders. They found Arab-style headgear a good defence against desert conditions.

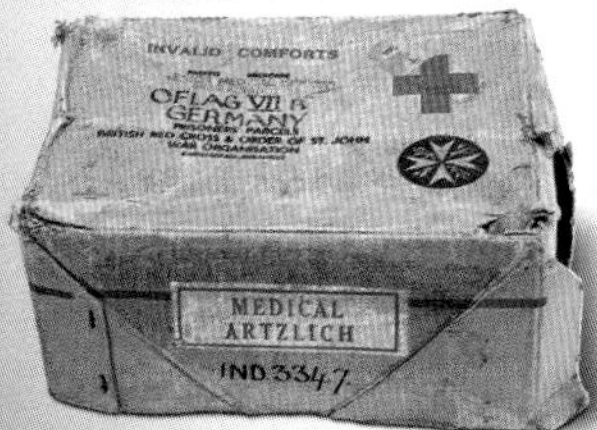

Red Cross parcel
BRITAIN
Prisoners of war received Red Cross food parcels. As a result, by the end of the war, Allied POWs were better fed than their captors.

Anti-tank mine
GERMANY
This Teller mine had a fuse activated by the pressure of tank tracks. Over three million of these mines were made in World War II.

Enigma cipher machine
GERMANY
The Germans believed messages encrypted by Enigma were secure but, with the help of an early electromechanical computer, Allied code-breakers cracked the code.

Nuclear relic
JAPAN
This melted glass bottle shows the extreme heat generated by the US atom bomb that destroyed Hiroshima on 6 August 1945.

Exuberant Londoners celebrate on Victory in Europe (VE) Day, 8 May, after the announcement of the final unconditional surrender of German forces.

“THIS IS **YOUR VICTORY!** IT IS THE **VICTORY OF** THE CAUSE OF **FREEDOM IN EVERY LAND.**”

Winston Churchill in an address to the crowds in London, 8 May 1945

IN FEBRUARY 1945, JOSEPH STALIN, FRANKLIN ROOSEVELT, AND WINSTON CHURCHILL met for the last time at a conference at **Yalta** in the Crimea. Stalin agreed to hold democratic elections in Poland – a promise he did not intend to keep. To aid the Soviet troops invading Germany from the east, the Western leaders agreed to step up bombing of German rail centres, including **Dresden**. On the night of 13–14 February, Britain's RAF dropped explosive and incendiary bombs on Dresden, causing a firestorm that destroyed the city's historic centre and killed some 25,000 people.

There was little pity for the Germans, as the **liberation of the death camps** exposed Nazi crimes. The major extermination centres, including **Auschwitz**, were liberated by the Soviet Red Army. The Western Allies met their most graphic experience of Nazi barbarity at **Belsen**, a concentration camp in Saxony. Liberating the camp in mid-April, British troops found thousands of prisoners dying of starvation, mistreatment, and disease, and bodies dumped in mass graves or left unburied. Cinema newsreel footage of Belsen convinced most people that the war against Germany had been justified.

Landing on Iwo Jima
American Marines are pinned down by Japanese fire on a beach of the volcanic island of Iwo Jima during the landings on 19 February.

The **human cost** of the war with Japan **continued to mount**. In February–March, US Marines suffered 26,000 casualties capturing the island of **Iwo Jima**, a volcanic rock in the Pacific defended to the death by an 18,000-strong Japanese garrison.

The **American invasion** of the much larger **Okinawa Island**, launched in April, resulted in a bloodbath. Japanese soldiers as usual fought to the death and tens of thousands of the island's civilian population also died, many by suicide. The Allied fleet offshore was battered by **mass kamikaze attacks** (see 1944).

Meanwhile, American B-29 bombers began the **systematic destruction of Japanese cities**. An incendiary raid on Tokyo on 9–10 March killed at least 80,000 people.

President Roosevelt did not live to see the defeat of Germany and Japan. The news of his **death** on 12 April came as a shock to the American people. The inexperienced **Harry S. Truman**, vice-president for less than three months, took over at the White House, facing formidable responsibilities.

The Allies had agreed that the Soviet Union should have the honour of **capturing Berlin**, and the heavy casualties that went with it. Hitler was determined to fight to the end, although much of the defence of Germany had devolved upon adolescents and the elderly. While American and Soviet troops advancing across Germany from west and east met amicably at the Elbe River, the Red Army fought street by street to take Berlin. As the Soviets drew near to his bunker, on 30 April **Hitler shot himself**. By then, former Italian dictator **Benito Mussolini** was also dead, **executed** by communist partisans.

Dresden in ruins
Inhabitants of the German city of Dresden attempt to cope with the aftermath of Allied bombing that created a firestorm in the city.

11.5 MILLION THE ESTIMATED NUMBER OF “DISPLACED PERSONS” IN EUROPE IN 1945

- **12 January** Soviet troops **resume offensive** in Poland and eastern Germany
- **22 January** F.D. **Roosevelt** inaugurated for **fourth term** as US president
- **27 January** Soviet Red Army **liberates** Auschwitz–Birkenau **death camp**
- **30 January** *Wilhelm* **Gustloff sunk** in the Baltic by a Soviet submarine, drowning 9,400 German refugees
- **3 February** US troops begin **battle to retake** Philippine capital **Manila**
- **4–11 February** Roosevelt, Churchill, and Stalin meet at **Yalta**
- **13–14 February Dresden destroyed** by Allied bombing
- **19 February** US Marines land on island of **Iwo Jima**
- **7 March US troops seize bridge** over Rhine at Remagen
- **8 March** Josip Broz **Tito** establishes provisional government in **Yugoslavia**
- **9–10 March** American air raid on **Tokyo** causes **firestorm** that kills around 80,000 people
- **1 April** US troops land on **Okinawa**
- **12 April** US President **Roosevelt dies**; he is succeeded by **Harry S. Truman**
- **15 April** Allied troops liberate **Belsen** and **Buchenwald** concentration camps
- **25 April** Soviet and American troops meet at the **Elbe River**
- **28 April** Benito **Mussolini** and his mistress **killed** by Italian partisans
- **30 April Hitler commits suicide** in Berlin
- **2 May** Soviet forces complete **victory** in battle for **Berlin**
- **7–8 May** Final **German surrender** ends war in Europe
- **5 June Allied Control Council** formally takes **power in Germany**
- **26 June United Nations Charter** signed by representatives of 50 countries

A formally dressed Japanese delegation prepares to sign the surrender papers on board the American battleship USS *Missouri* in Tokyo Bay on 2 September.

Raising the red flag
Taken by a Red Army photographer, this photo reconstructs the moment when soldiers raised the Soviet flag on the Reichstag building in Berlin.

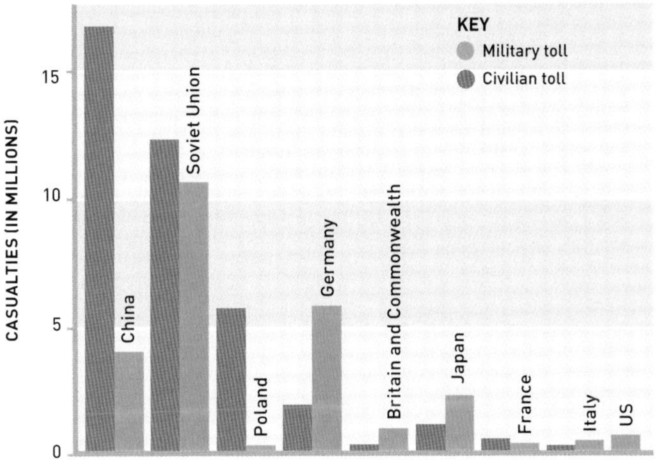

World War II casualties
More civilians than servicemen died in World War II. The Soviet Union and Germany had the heaviest military death tolls. Poland lost one in five of its population, including most Polish Jews.

His body and that of his mistress Clara Petacci were hung upside down from meat hooks in a Milan petrol station.

The **surrender of German forces** was complete by **8 May**, sparking heartfelt victory celebrations in Allied countries. Although war continued with Japan, the British Labour Party withdrew from the wartime coalition to fight a general election against the Conservatives led by Churchill. To general astonishment, **Labour** won a **landslide victory**, their promise of a welfare state and democratic socialism outweighing the popular appeal of Churchill's war record.

On 16 July, the New Mexican desert was lit up by the **world's first atomic explosion**. This was the culmination of the top-secret **Manhattan Project**, a feat of science and engineering that had cost America $2 billion, spent on presidential authority without Congressional approval. The explosion produced temperatures higher than those at the core of the sun.

The successful atomic test coincided with the gathering of Allied leaders for a conference at Potsdam, a Berlin suburb. Although differences between the Western Allies and the Soviet Union were growing, Stalin agreed to join in the war on Japan. At the end of the conference the Allies issued the **Potsdam Declaration**, calling on Japan to surrender immediately or face "prompt and utter destruction". The **Japanese government rejected the call to surrender** as "of no important value".

Preparations for dropping atom bombs on Japanese cities were well advanced even before the first atomic test. The first bomb was dropped on **Hiroshima** as soon as it was ready and weather conditions permitted (see panel, right). Three days later, on 9 August, a second bomb devastated the city of **Nagasaki**, killing at least 35,000 people. The **Soviet invasion of Manchuria** was a further shock to Japan.

Since June, the Japanese government had been split between those who wanted a negotiated peace and militarists insisting on a fight to the death. On 10 August **Emperor Hirohito intervened** decisively **in favour of the peace faction**. The Japanese agreed to **surrender** if the status of the emperor was guaranteed. Although Truman refused to offer any such assurance, on 15 August Hirohito told his people the war had developed "not necessarily to Japan's advantage", and that he was making peace.

The **war had ended** with unexpected suddenness. Dealing with the **aftermath** of devastated cities, broken economies, occupied enemy countries, refugees ("displaced persons"), and war criminals posed almost as great a challenge as the war itself.

HIROSHIMA

The American B-29 bomber, *Enola Gay*, piloted by Colonel Paul Tibbets, took off from Tinian Island in the Marianas at 2.45 on the morning of 6 August carrying an atom bomb. It dropped the bomb on the Japanese port-city of Hiroshima at 8.15. Heat, light, and the explosion killed some 70,000 people instantly. The lingering effects of radiation raised total deaths to an estimated 140,000.

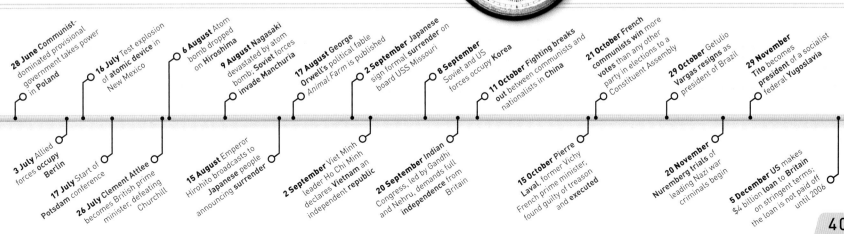

Time of death
A pocket watch retrieved from the body of a citizen of Hiroshima records the exact moment when the atom bomb exploded above the city.

28 June Communist-dominated provisional government takes power in **Poland**

3 July Allied forces **occupy Berlin**

16 July Test explosion of **atomic device** in New Mexico

17 July Start of **Potsdam** conference

26 July Clement Attlee becomes British prime minister, defeating Churchill

6 August Atom bomb dropped on **Hiroshima**

9 August Nagasaki devastated by atom bomb; **Soviet** forces **invade Manchuria**

15 August Emperor Hirohito broadcasts to **Japanese** people announcing **surrender**

17 August George Orwell's political fable *Animal Farm* is published

2 September Japanese sign formal **surrender** on board USS Missouri

2 September Viet Minh leader Ho Chi Minh declares **Vietnam** an independent **republic**

8 September Soviet and US forces occupy **Korea**

20 September Indian Congress, led by Gandhi and Nehru, demands full **independence** from Britain

11 October Fighting breaks out between communists and nationalists in **China**

15 October Pierre Laval, former Vichy French prime minister, found guilty of treason and **executed**

21 October French communists win more **votes** than any other party in elections to a Constituent Assembly

29 October Getulio **Vargas resigns** as president of Brazil

20 November Nuremberg trials of leading Nazi war criminals begin

29 November Tito becomes **president** of a socialist federal **Yugoslavia**

5 December US makes $4 billion **loan** to **Britain** on stringent terms; the loan is not paid off until 2006

Jewish refugees make their way to Palestine. Thousands attempted this journey before Britain stopped allowing illegal entry into Palestine.

REPRESENTATIVES OF 51 NATIONS BEGAN THE YEAR BY FORMING the **United Nations (UN) General Assembly**, the successor to the League of Nations (see 1919). Its aims were to provide a forum for the nations of the world and to **uphold peace and security**.

The peace after World War II was short-lived, as relations between **Western allies** and the **Soviet Union** continued to cool. In March, **Winston Churchill** summed up the threat of communism in a speech that described an "**iron curtain**" falling across Europe.

The Soviet Union tightened its grip on Europe by creating "**satellite states**". **Communist governments** were set up in Czechoslovakia, Bulgaria, Albania, Poland, Romania, and Hungary. In France and Italy, communist parties narrowly missed seizing control.

Tensions increased in **India** following Britain's declaration that India would gain **independence** after the war. The leader of the Muslim League, **Muhammad Ali Jinnah** (1876–1948), demanded a **separate Muslim state**, while Hindus opposed this idea. On 16 August, Jinnah declared a **Direct Action Day**, a mass protest against British proposals for an all-India government. Violent fighting erupted and thousands died. In response, **Mohandas Karamchad Gandhi** (1869–1948) began a campaign for reconciliation between Hindus and Muslims.

The US granted **independence** to the **Philippines** in July, though the gift had strings attached: the **US kept sovereignty** over several military bases, the Philippine economy was dependent on US markets, and a "parity" clause gave US citizens equal economic rights with Filipinos.

The drive for liberation in **Africa** continued with the establishment of the **Pan-African Federation** by **Kwame Nkrumah**, from Ghana, and **Jomo Kenyatta**, from Kenya. They aimed to promote African unity and end racial discrimination.

In **Palestine**, conferences were held to resolve the growing crisis of admitting **Jewish refugees into Palestine**, but no agreement was reached. The problem was compounded in August, when boats carrying refugees were blocked by **British warships**. Britain told the US it would no longer allow illegal entry into Palestine, igniting a diplomatic war.

Civil war resumed in China, having been suspended during the world war. The communist leader **Mao Zedong** (1893–1976) declared war on the ruling Kuomintang nationalist party and its leader **Chiang Kai-shek** (1887–1975).

France remained determined to hold onto its colonies in Indochina, beginning one of the longest **guerrilla wars** in history. In November, clashes intensified between the Viet Minh, led by **Ho Chi Minh** (1890–1969), and the Far East Expeditionary Corps, led by France. **The First Indochina War**, involving the rebellion of Vietnam, Cambodia, and Laos against France, was declared on 19 December (see 1954).

The Argentine former secretary of labour, **General Juan Domingo Perón** (1895–1974), was installed as president of Argentina on 4 June. With strong working-class support and military backing, he promised **social security** and **higher wages**.

Technicians at the University of Pennsylvania began operating the **first practical electronic digital computer**. The machine was first used for military purposes. It occupied 167 sq m (1,800 sq ft), had 18,000 vacuum tubes, and weighed almost 50 tonnes.

> “ AN **IRON CURTAIN** HAS **DESCENDED** ACROSS **THE CONTINENT.** ”
>
> **Winston Churchill, British politician,** 5 March 1946

Dead Sea Scrolls
The discovery of the Dead Sea Scrolls was one of the most important archaeological finds of the century. The scrolls are fragments of manuscripts of the Old Testament.

The division of post-war Europe
After the war, Britain, France, and the US occupied West Germany, while the Soviet Union controlled East Germany. Lithuania, Latvia, Moldavia, and Estonia were absorbed into the USSR.

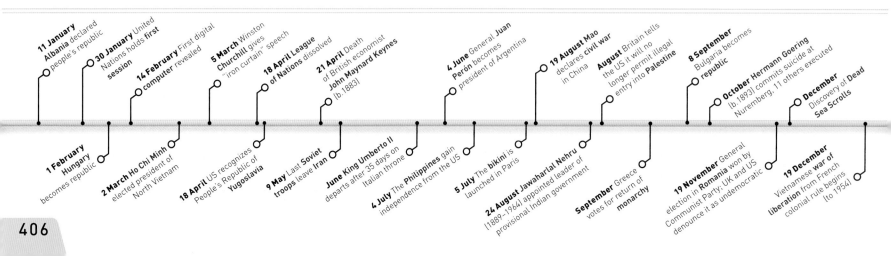

Juan Perón
Fiercely nationalistic, anti-US, and anti-communist, Perón pledged a "Third Way" between capitalism and communism.

11 January Albania declared people's republic

30 January United Nations holds **first session**

1 February Hungary becomes republic

14 February First digital **computer** revealed

2 March Ho Chi Minh elected president of North Vietnam

5 March Winston **Churchill** gives "iron curtain" speech

18 April League of Nations dissolved

18 April US recognizes People's Republic of **Yugoslavia**

21 April Death of British economist **John Maynard Keynes** (b.1883)

9 May Last Soviet **troops leave Iran**

June King Umberto II departs after 35 days on Italian throne

4 June General **Juan Perón** becomes president of Argentina

4 July The **Philippines** gain independence from the US

5 July The **bikini** is launched in Paris

19 August Mao declares **civil war** in China

24 August Jawaharlal Nehru (1889–1964) appointed leader of provisional Indian government

August Britain tells the US it will no longer permit illegal entry into **Palestine**

September Greece votes for return of **monarchy**

8 September Bulgaria becomes **republic**

October Hermann Goering (b.1893) commits suicide at Nuremberg, 11 others executed

19 November General election in **Romania** won by Communist Party; UK and US denounce it as undemocratic

December Discovery of **Dead Sea Scrolls**

19 December Vietnamese **war of liberation** from French colonial rule begins (to 1954)

The UN General Assembly in session in Central Hall, London. The General Assembly is the only part of the UN where all members have equal representation.

LORD LOUIS MOUNTBATTEN WAS APPOINTED THE LAST VICEROY of India to oversee the **end of British imperial rule**. He believed that the only way forward for the country was to **partition** it, dividing it in two parts based on the religion of those areas. In July, the British passed the **Indian Independence Act**, dividing the Raj into **India** (Hindu and Sikh) and **Pakistan** (Muslim), leaving Kashmir to determine its own fate. Pakistan was split into **East** and **West Pakistan**, with India separating the two areas. On 14 August, Pakistan gained independence, and **Muhammad Ali Jinnah** became its first governor-general. The next day an **independent India** was born. Partition set off waves of violence and displaced millions of Hindus and Sikhs who had lived in what was now Pakistani territory, as well as Muslims who lived in newly Indian territory.

The rulers of **Kashmir** were left with a momentous decision: to become independent, or to join India or Pakistan. In October, **war broke out between India and Pakistan** after Pakistan supported a Muslim insurgency in Kashmir. India agreed to a request for armed assistance from Kashmir's **maharaja**, in return for the accession of Kashmir to India once the hostilities between India and Pakistan ceased (see 1949).

After six years of war, **Britain**'s status had diminished, and the **US** emerged as the only power capable of matching the **Soviet Union**. The "**Truman Doctrine**" was established on 12 March, when Winston Churchill requested US aid in **Greece**, where a **civil war** had broken out between communists and the royalist government. In response, 400 million dollars were sent to Greece to help end the **communist threat**. President Truman's doctrine pledged support to all states struggling to uphold democracy against the threat of communism.

With fears that all of Europe could fall to communist regimes, the US secretary of state **George Marshall** (1880–1959) introduced a plan to help Europe's shattered economies recover from the war, helping victors and vanquished alike. The European Recovery Program, or **"Marshall Plan"**, provided fuel, raw materials, loans, food, and machinery, aiming to help kick-start economic growth.

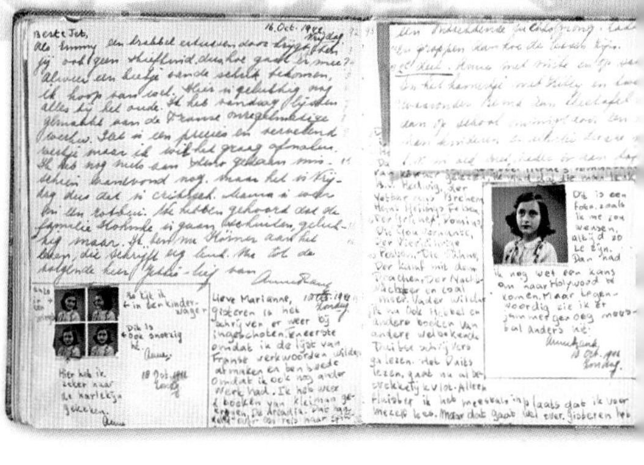

Anne Frank's diary
The publication of Het Achterhuis (The Secret Annex) *on 5 June introduced Anne Frank, a young Jewish girl whose diary chronicled her years hiding from the Nazis in Amsterdam during World War II.*

The **crisis in Palestine** (see 1946) continued to worsen as Britain referred the situation to the UN. A plan was devised to partition the area into **separate Jewish and Arab states**. The UN General Assembly agreed to this resolution on 29 November, but it was unpopular with Arabs.

While the British organized their withdrawal from the region, Arab and Jewish communities clashed and **terrorist attacks** intensified (see 1948).

The partition of India
Partition split the former British Raj into two separate new states: India and Pakistan. Pakistan was formed of two territories, 1,700km (1,050 miles) apart.

Uprooted by partition
Partition caused the largest mass migration in history – around 10 million people were displaced. These Sikh refugees are leaving the Muslim section of the Punjab.

25 January Death of **Al Capone**, US gangster (b.1899)

4 March Britain and France sign historic **50 year alliance**

6 February Poland becomes **communist republic**

10 March The US, Britain, France, and Russia meet to discuss the **future of Germany**

12 March President Truman offers his "**Truman Doctrine**" to countries threatened by communism

7 April Death of **Henry Ford**, motorcar pioneer (b.1863)

3 May Japan establishes a **constitutional democracy**

5 June Marshall Plan offered to Europe

20 July Dutch launch major military **offensive in Indonesia** (to 1949)

7 August Thor Heyerdahl crosses the Pacific Ocean on his raft **Kon-Tiki** and arrives in the Tuamotu Islands after 101 days

14 August British **rule in India ends**

29 August US scientists announce discovery of **plutonium fission**, offering the possibility of nuclear energy

1 September Communists win power in **Hungary**

18 September Central Intelligence Agency **(CIA)** formed in USA

4 October Death of **Max Planck**, German physicist (b.1858)

14 October US test pilot Chuck Yeager becomes first man to break **sound barrier**

27 October India and Pakistan at war (to 1949)

16 November British troops begin to **withdraw from Palestine**

29 November UN General Assembly votes to **partition Palestine**

23 December The **transistor** first demonstrated

30 December King Michael of Romania **forced to abdicate** by pro-Moscow government

1948

Mohandas Gandhi lies in state after his assassination by a Hindu fanatic who blamed him for the partition of India.

THE CROWNING ACHIEVEMENT OF MOHANDAS GANDHI (b.1868) was realized when **India won independence** in 1947. However, the concessions he made to Muslims led to his assassination by a **Hindu fanatic** who blamed him for the partition of India, even though Gandhi had bitterly opposed the splitting up of the subcontinent. The news of **Gandhi's assassination** had a profound effect throughout the world, and a state of mourning was declared in India.

South Africa held May elections that saw the **National Party** take power from Jan Smuts' United Party. **Dr D.F. Malan** (1874–1959) became prime minister, and formed the first government dominated by **Afrikaners**. Immediately after the election, the government began institutionalizing **segregation.** Malan believed that Africans threatened the prosperity and purity of the Afrikaner culture.

Segregation sign
Under apartheid, separate residency areas were created, and social contact between different races was strictly prohibited.

He based his policy on a system that became known as **apartheid** and enforced a racial hierarchy privileging white South Africans (see 1994).

Anti-colonial sentiment grew in the **Malay Peninsula** after World War II. Groups of guerrillas took to the jungle, led by communist fanatic **Chin Peng** (b.1924). In February, there were terrorist attacks on European settlers, and later an "emergency" was declared.

All-Korean elections had been called for in 1948, but **Kim Il Sung** (1912–94), the leader of North Korea, persuaded the **Soviets** not to allow the UN north of the **38th parallel** (the boundary between the northern zone of the Korean Peninsula, occupied by the USSR, and the southern zone, controlled by US forces), believing he could not possibly win a free election. As a result, a month after the South was granted independence as the **Republic of Korea**, on 15 August, the **Democratic People's Republic of Korea** (DPRK) was proclaimed, with Kim as premier. On 12 October, the Soviet Union declared Kim's regime the only lawful government on the peninsula. By 1949, **North Korea** was a fully-fledged **communist dictatorship**.

The UN had devized a plan to split **Palestine** into Jewish and Arab nations, but it was not adhered to when the **state of Israel** was proclaimed by its first prime minister, **David Ben-Gurion**, on 14 May. The last British troops withdrew on

Plan for Palestine
The UN General Assembly proposed to split Palestine into Jewish and Arab states, with Jerusalem under international administration.

15 May. Five **Arab armies** from Jordan, Egypt, Syria, Lebanon, and Iraq immediately invaded the new Jewish state but were repulsed. The Israeli army crushed pockets of resistance and extended its borders in what became known as the **first Arab–Israeli War** (see 1949). The realization that the Israeli nation might survive increased anti-Israeli and anti-Jewish sentiment throughout the Arab world.

The **Organization of American States** (OAS) came into being on 30 April. Its members were the independent states of North and South America. They pledged to **fight communism**, increase security, and aid economic growth.

Harry Truman (1884–1972) had steered the US through the end of World War II and the beginning of the Cold War. However, he was not expected to win the **1948 presidential election** against the Republican Thomas E. Dewey, due to his pro-civil rights policies, which had alienated many southern Democrats. As the campaign continued, he won the following of the people and was re-elected in one of the biggest **election upsets** in history.

In **Britain**, the debate over free healthcare had been ongoing since the 19th century. After Labour's election victory in 1945, **Aneurin Bevan** (1897–1960) presented a plan to provide free healthcare to all for the first time. Bevan formally launched the **National Health Service** (NHS) on 5 July.

With World War II over, the Olympic committee (IOC) could once again select a nation to host the **Olympic Games**. London was chosen, but six years of war had left Britain with shortages of food and clothing, and the 1948 celebrations became known as the **"Austerity Games"**. These Olympics saw the **first defection** from the communist East to the West when the head of the Czechoslovakian gymnastics team, **Marie Provaznikova**, refused to return home.

Czechoslovakia had been moving towards democracy after World War II, but the Soviets did not intend to allow any state within their sphere of influence to become a democracy. **Communists**, supported by the Soviets, carried out a **coup in Prague**, in February. The Czech president, **Edvard Beneš** (1884–1948), was removed from

DAVID BEN-GURION (1886–1973)

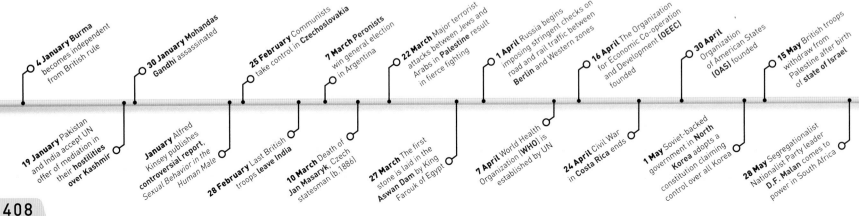

The founder of the state of Israel, Ben-Gurion was born in Poland and emigrated to Palestine in 1906. He became an active supporter of the struggle for an independent Jewish state and was expelled from Palestine in 1915 due to his nationalist activities. During World War II, he helped Jews fleeing from the Nazi holocaust. Ben-Gurion retired from politics in 1970.

4 January Burma becomes independent from British rule

19 January Pakistan and India accept UN offer of mediation in their **hostilities over Kashmir**

30 January Mohandas Gandhi assassinated

January Alfred Kinsey publishes **controversial report**, *Sexual Behavior in the Human Male*

25 February Communists take control in **Czechoslovakia**

28 February Last British troops **leave India**

7 March Peronists win general election in Argentina

10 March Death of **Jan Masaryk**, Czech statesman (b.1886)

22 March Major terrorist attacks between Jews and Arabs in **Palestine** result in fierce fighting

27 March The first stone is laid in the **Aswan Dam** by King Farouk of Egypt

1 April Russia begins imposing stringent checks on road and rail traffic between **Berlin** and Western zones

7 April World Health Organization (**WHO**) is established by UN

16 April The Organization for Economic Co-operation and Development **(OEEC)** founded

24 April Civil War in **Costa Rica** ends

30 April Organization of American States **(OAS)** founded

1 May Soviet-backed government in **North Korea** adopts a constitution claiming control over all Korea

15 May British troops withdraw from Palestine after birth of **state of Israel**

28 May Segregationalist Nationalist Party leader **D.F. Malan** comes to power in South Africa

“ I KNOW OF **NO OTHER MAN** IN OUR TIME, OR INDEED **IN RECENT HISTORY**, WHO SO CONVINCINGLY DEMONSTRATED THE **POWER** OF THE **SPIRIT** OVER **MATERIAL THINGS.** ”

Sir Stafford Cripps, British statesman, on Gandhi, 1948

Harry Truman holds up a newspaper that prematurely announced Thomas Dewey had won the election.

power and replaced by the leader of the Czech communist party, **Klement Gottwald** (1896–1953; see 1989). This was a tense period in Czechoslovakia. **Jan Masaryk**, the Czech foreign minister, had tried to assure the Soviets that a democratic Czechoslovakia posed no security threat. However, he had been in favour of accepting aid from the **Marshall Plan** (see 1947), which Stalin refused to endorse. On 10 March, the Czech government reported that Masaryk had committed suicide. Despite suspicions that the communists had murdered Masaryk, nothing was proven.

Berlin was divided into **four zones** after World War II, under an agreement between Britain, France, the US, and Russia (see 1961). Berlin as a whole was an enclave within Soviet-occupied East Germany. The Soviets were determined to force Western powers out of Berlin and, in the **first crisis of the Cold War**, cut road and rail links between the city and the West in June. The Allies responded to the "**Berlin Blockade**" by organizing a massive **airlift** to supply the people of Berlin, and the blockade was lifted in May 1949.

The end of World War II brought **mass movements of refugees** as millions of displaced people fled or were expelled from Eastern Europe. Many were treated brutally and found it hard to assimilate. In response, the UN adopted the **Universal Declaration of Human Rights**, which guaranteed a "right to seek and to enjoy in other countries asylum from persecution", as well as the Convention on the Prevention and Punishment of the Crime of Genocide.

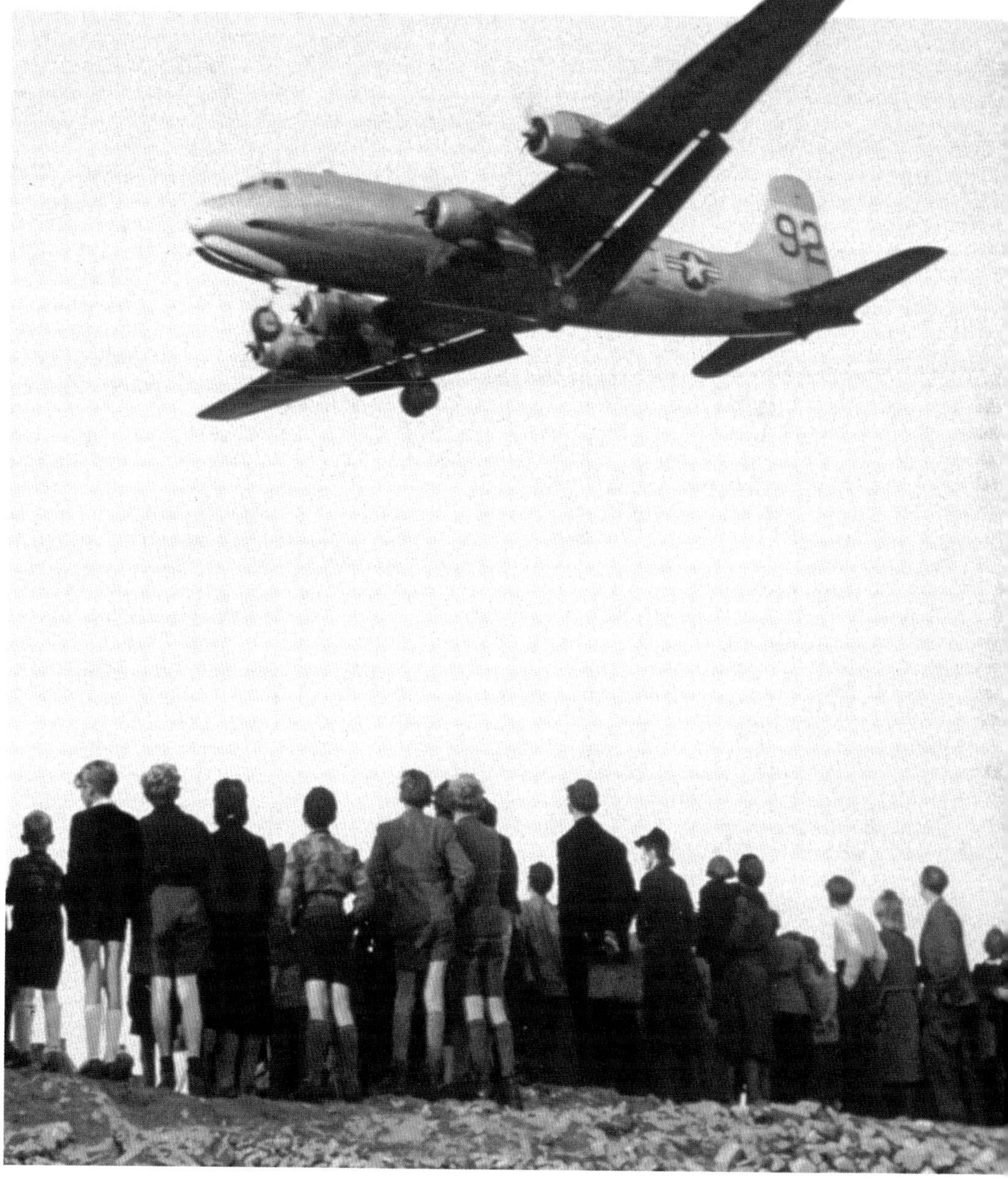

The Berlin Airlift
A crowd of Berliners watch a Douglas C-54 Skymaster plane carrying vital supplies to the Allied sectors of the city.

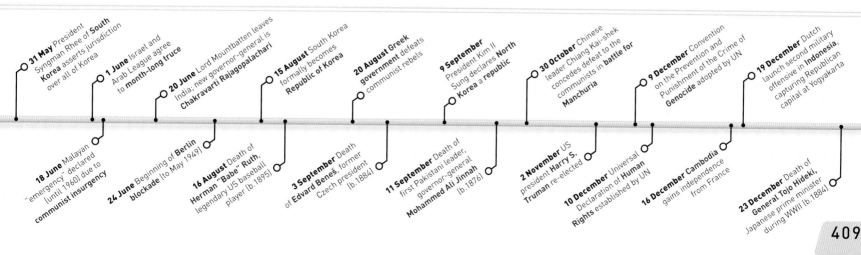

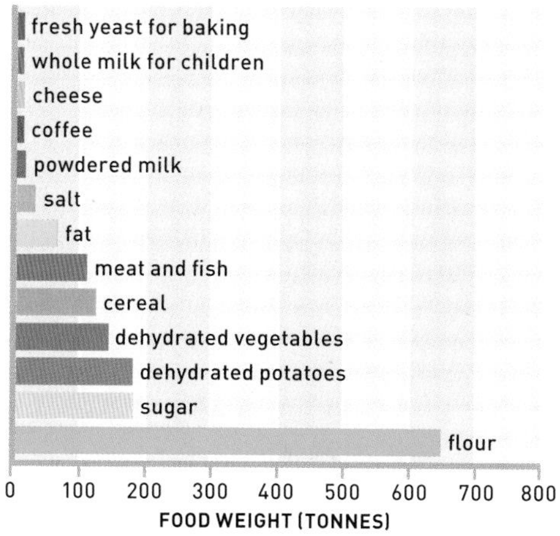

Feeding Berlin
At the height of the Berlin blockade, one plane reached Berlin every 30 seconds. This graph shows the quantity of food that was flown in daily to sustain Berlin's 2 million citizens.

31 May President Syngman Rhee of **South Korea** asserts jurisdiction over all of Korea

1 June Israel and Arab League agree to **month-long truce**

18 June Malayan "emergency" declared (until 1960) due to **communist insurgency**

20 June Lord Mountbatten leaves India; new governor-general is **Chakravarti Rajagopalachari**

24 June Beginning of **Berlin blockade** (to May 1949)

15 August South Korea formally becomes **Republic of Korea**

16 August Death of **Herman "Babe" Ruth**, legendary US baseball player (b.1895)

20 August Greek government defeats communist rebels

3 September Death of **Edvard Beneš**, former Czech president (b.1884)

9 September President Kim Il Sung declares **North Korea a republic**

11 September Death of first Pakistani leader, governor-general **Mohammed Ali Jinnah** (b.1876)

30 October Chinese leader Chiang Kai-shek concedes defeat to the communists in **battle for Manchuria**

2 November US president **Harry S. Truman** re-elected

9 December Convention on the Prevention and Punishment of the Crime of **Genocide** adopted by UN

10 December Universal Declaration of **Human Rights** established by UN

16 December Cambodia gains independence from France

19 December Dutch launch second military offensive in **Indonesia**, capturing Republican capital at Yogyakarta

23 December Death of **General Tojo Hideki**, Japanese prime minister during WWII (b.1884)

“ …A **ROOF** STRETCHING **OVER** THE **ATLANTIC OCEAN.** ”

Ernest Bevin, British foreign secretary, describing the North Atlantic Treaty

At the signing of the North Atlantic Treaty in Washington DC, on 4 April, US president Harry S. Truman gave an address on its significance.

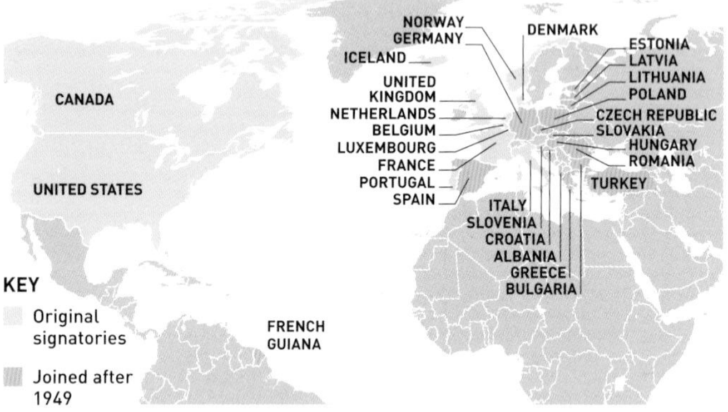

NATO alliance
This map illustrates the 12 nations that originally signed up to NATO in 1949. The alliance enabled the US to keep military bases in Europe.

A TRUCE WAS REACHED IN THE ARAB–ISRAELI WAR (see 1948), bringing an end to eight months of hostilities. The Israelis referred to it as their "**War of Independence**", while the Arabs called it "*Al Naqba*", or "**The Catastrophe**". The Arab states negotiated separate armistice agreements. Egypt was the first to sign on 24 February, followed by Lebanon, Jordan, and Syria. The agreement established a line between Israel and the Jordanian-held West Bank, which became known as the **Green Line**.

Representatives of Belgium, Britain, Canada, Denmark, France, Iceland, Italy, Luxembourg, the Netherlands, Norway, Portugal, and the US met in Washington DC, in April, to sign an historic treaty that established the **North Atlantic Treaty Organization**, or **NATO**. The alliance was intended for **mutual defence**; countries promised to develop their capacity to resist armed attack, and to consult one another when any of the countries was threatened. The treaty also provided that member countries would try to **settle disputes by peaceful means**.

The **Soviet Union** stunned the West by exploding its **first atomic bomb**, on 29 August, at a remote test site in Kazakhstan. Named "**First Lightning**", its development was facilitated by US spies, such as Julius and Ethel Rosenberg, and British spy Donald Maclean, who had passed technological secrets to the Soviets (see 1951). The loss of nuclear supremacy led US president Harry Truman to order the development of the much more powerful **hydrogen bomb**.

The **Berlin Airlift** (see 1948) by the Western Allies had aided solidarity with the West German leaders. On 23 May, the western occupied zones were united to form the **Federal Republic of Germany**. West Germany held the first free elections since 1932, and the Christian Democrats under **Dr Konrad Adenauer** (1876–1967) won a small majority.

In July, the Vatican issued the ***Acta Apostolicae Sedis*** under Pope Pius XII, which effectively **excommunicated Catholics** who collaborated with or supported the Communist Party. The decree represented a significant counteroffensive by the Holy See in a **religious Cold War** against the communist regime, following the persecution of Catholics in communist states.

On Easter Monday, 18 April, Eire became the **Republic of Ireland**, following the bill of 1938. It meant Ireland had officially broken free of allegiance to the British crown. In May, the British Parliament approved a bill continuing the status of Northern Ireland as a part of Great Britain; six northern Irish counties had shown a majority in favour of remaining British in the **Northern Ireland General Election** held on 19 February.

The **Fourth Geneva Convention** was adopted in August. It brought together the elements of the previous three Geneva Conventions of 1864, 1906, and 1929, and added rules to protect civilians during war. It came in response to **Nazi atrocities** during World War II and the practise of "total war". The international treaty governed the **treatment of civilians during wartime**, including hostages, diplomats, spies, bystanders, and civilians in territory under military occupation.

Civil war in China (see 1946) drew to an end in 1949. Beiping was taken by the communists and its name changed back to **Beijing**, and between April and November, most major cities passed to communist control with minimal resistance. **Mao Zedong** (see 1921) proclaimed the founding of the **People's Republic of China** on 1 October, and in December, Chiang Kai-shek and his Nationalist troops fled from the mainland to the island of Formosa (Taiwan), naming **Taipei** the **temporary capital of China**.

The Dutch finally gave up their struggle over **Indonesia** in December and conceded independence after four years of warfare. **President Ahmed Sukarno** (1901–70), who had co-operated with the Japanese during the war and had emerged as the strongest national leader, was faced with the task of welding all the separate regions into a **united nation** under a new constitution, with **Jakarta** as the capital of the Republic. On 26 September 1950, Indonesia was **admitted to the UN** (see 1965).

New **7-inch vinyl records** (also called 45s) were introduced in the US by record company RCA on 10 January. With its format of one song per side, the "**single**" was perfect for rock 'n' roll, and it went on to revolutionize the **pop music business**. In the first year of production, RCA pressed more than **25 million** 45s.

People's Republic
Following the proclamation of the People's Republic of China, propaganda posters showed a smiling Chairman Mao Zedong encouraging his people to build a new, prosperous country.

1 January Java, Indonesia, comes under Dutch control
1 January End of Indo-Pakistani war over Kashmir when ceasefire arranged by UN
10 January New **7-inch vinyl records** became available in the US
20 January President Truman's **inauguration** is first to be **televised** across America
1 February Hungary declared a people's republic
18 February Army leaders in Argentina attempt to force **Eva Perón** out of office (in office 1946–52)
24 February Truce signed between Israel and Egypt
4 April Twelve nations sign the **North Atlantic Treaty**
8 April US, Britain, and France reach agreement about future of **West Germany**
18 April Eire is proclaimed the **Republic of Ireland**
12 May Stalin lifts blockade of Berlin
23 May Democratic West Germany is born
26 May Shanghai falls to communist troops
28 June Last US combat soldiers leave **Korea**
29 June Dutch troops depart from **Jakarta**
19 July Laos becomes independent
27 July World's first jetliner, de Havilland Comet, makes maiden flight
1 August Dutch agree to a **ceasefire in Indonesia**
29 August USSR tests its first **atomic bomb**
2 September Third **Cannes Film Festival** opens
1 October Mao Zedong declares China a **Communist Republic**
7 October Stalin establishes **German Democratic Republic** in East Germany
November Britain launches major offensive in **Malaya** to flush out communist rebels
19 November Coronation of **Rainier III**, 30th ruling Prince of **Monaco**
8 December Nationalist government of China moves its capital to **Taipei, Formosa** (Taiwan)
13 December Capital of Israel moved from Tel Aviv to **Jerusalem**
16 December Ahmed Sukarno elected first president of **Republic of Indonesia**

The civil war in Korea quickly escalated and drew in troops from across the world under UN command, including these British machine gunners.

> **WE SHALL LAND AT INCHON, AND I SHALL CRUSH THEM.**
>
> **Douglas MacArthur, US General**, 1950

AFTER NEARLY 100 YEARS OF BRITISH RULE, India became a **republic** on 26 January. India had been managing its own affairs since the partition in 1947, but this day marked the official cutting of all ties. In a formal ceremony, **president Rajendra Prasad** (1884–1963) took the oath of office and a new constitution came into force.

Emblem of India *India adopted this emblem, taken from a sculpture called* Lion Capital of Ashoka, *after it became a republic. The words "truth alone triumphs" are inscribed in Devanagari script.*

Since it was first created as **Transjordan** after World War I, the **Hashemite Kingdom of Jordan** faced problems arising from its disputed status, weak economy, and artificial frontiers. On 24 April, King Abdullah of Jordan (1882–1951) **annexed Arab Palestine** to create an expanded kingdom, to the fury of his Arab neighbours. The annexed territory included East Jerusalem and **doubled Jordan's population**.

South Africa, with its oppressive apartheid laws (see 1948), began to witness **increasing racial tension**. Whites and blacks were segregated on a large scale, and **identity cards** specifying a person's race were introduced. On 1 May, a **general strike** was held protesting against all discriminatory laws. **Police opened fire** in the Alexandra Township, killing 18 people and wounding 30.

A year after communists had assumed power in **China** they invaded neighbouring **Tibet**. The military assault took place in October, and by April 1951, Tibet's leaders claimed to have been strong-armed into signing a treaty, known as the **"Seventeen Point Agreement"**, which gave China control over Tibet's external affairs and allowed **Chinese military occupation**.

Anti-communist witch-hunter **Senator Joseph McCarthy** launched a "red scare" crusade in America on 9 February, claiming that the US State Department was harbouring 205 communists. His claims were never substantiated, but many lost their jobs and their reputations (see 1954).

In June, a **new crisis** divided former wartime allies in **Korea**. Split into a Soviet-occupied northern zone and an American-occupied southern zone, once these two powers had withdrawn, the **north** – still backed by the USSR – **invaded the south**. The US, determined not to appease the Russians, provided the main contingent for a **United Nations army** that went to the support of the South Koreans. Within four months, the UN force had driven deep into North Korea; only the intervention of **China** saved North Korea from collapse (see 1953).

> **COMMUNISM IS A HAMMER WHICH WE USE TO CRUSH THE ENEMY.**
>
> Mao Zedong, 1950

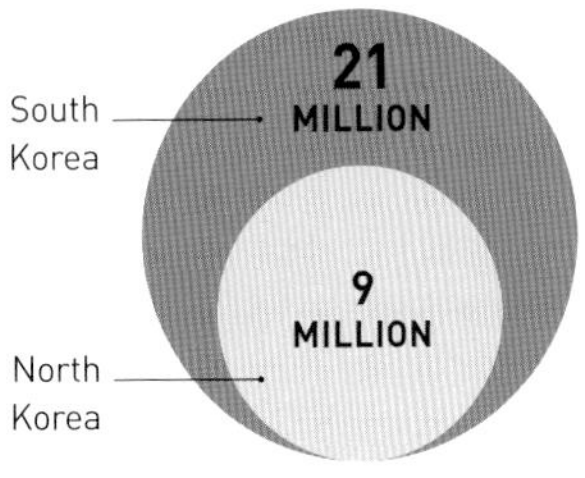

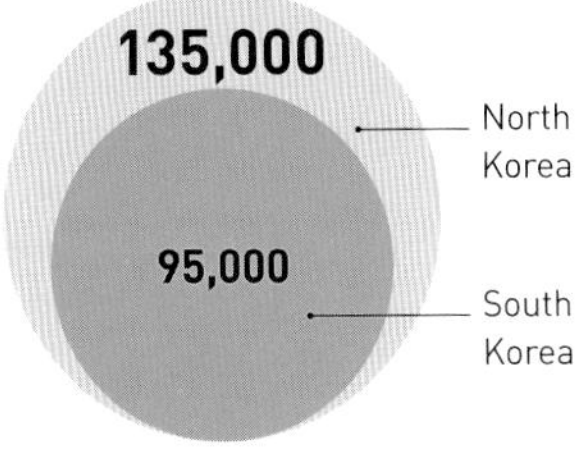

Korean population and army *Despite having less than half the population of South Korea in 1950, North Korea's army was superior in size and much better equipped.*

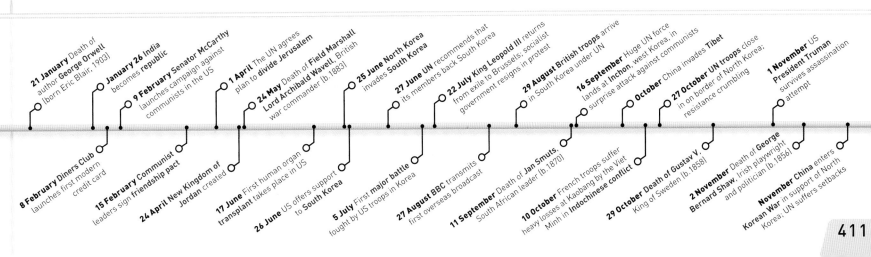

McCARTHYISM

Named for senator Joseph McCarthy (1908–57), McCarthyism became synonymous with the hunt for communists in US public life during the 1950s. The triumph of communism in Eastern Europe and China provoked a severe crisis in the US. Fears of a worldwide communist conspiracy resulted in a campaign against people suspected of communist leanings. McCarthy held senate hearings to "out" communists, and so-called "anti-American" books were removed from public libraries.

The **first human organ transplant** took place on 17 June at the Little Company of Mary Hospital in Illinois, US. A kidney from a dead body was used to replace a damaged kidney. Although it was later rejected, the transplant gave the patient's remaining kidney time to recover.

German-born physicist **Albert Einstein** (see 1919), who had become actively involved in advocating nuclear disarmament and civil rights, published ***"On the Generalized Theory of Gravitation"*** in April's *Scientific American*. In this paper, he attempted to unify **gravity** and **electro-magnetism** in a way that led to a new understanding of **quantum mechanics**.

The first **modern credit card**, which could be used at a variety of stores, was introduced in the US by Diners Club on 8 February. It was established mostly for businessmen to use for travel and entertainment expenses. Cardholders had up to 60 days to pay in full. Merchants were quick to accept the card because they found that **customers** who used a credit card **usually spent more** if they were able to "charge it".

- **21 January** Death of author **George Orwell** (born Eric Blair, 1903)
- **January 26 India** becomes **republic**
- **8 February Diners Club** launches first modern credit card
- **9 February Senator McCarthy** launches campaign against communists in the US
- **15 February Communist** leaders sign **friendship pact**
- **1 April** The UN agrees plan to **divide Jerusalem**
- **24 April New Kingdom of Jordan** created
- **24 May** Death of **Field Marshall Lord Archibald Wavell**, British war commander (b.1883)
- **17 June** First human organ transplant takes place in US
- **25 June North Korea invades South Korea**
- **26 June** US offers support to **South Korea**
- **27 June UN** recommends that its members back South Korea
- **5 July** First **major battle** fought by US troops in Korea
- **22 July King Leopold III** returns from exile to Brussels; socialist government resigns in protest
- **27 August BBC** transmits first overseas broadcast
- **29 August British troops** arrive in South Korea under UN
- **11 September** Death of **Jan Smuts**, South African leader (b.1870)
- **16 September** Huge UN force lands at **Inchon**, west Korea, in surprise attack against communists
- **October** China invades **Tibet**
- **10 October** French troops suffer heavy losses at Kaobang by the Viet Minh in **Indochinese conflict**
- **27 October UN troops** close in on border of North Korea; resistance crumbling
- **29 October** Death of **Gustav V**, King of Sweden (b.1858)
- **1 November** US **President Truman** survives assassination attempt
- **2 November** Death of **George Bernard Shaw**, Irish playwright and politician (b.1856)
- **November China** enters **Korean War** in support of North Korea; UN suffers setbacks

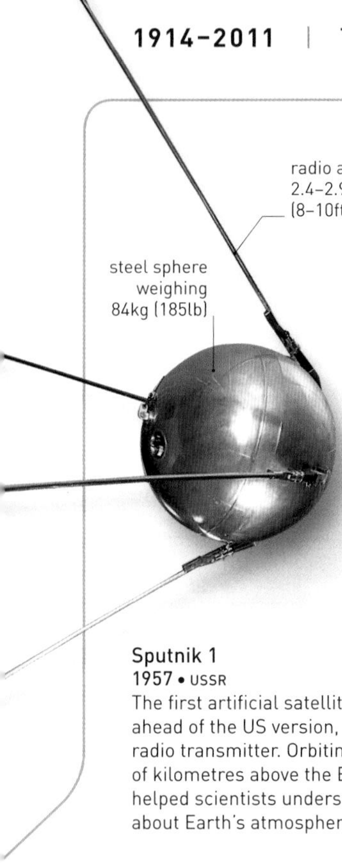

radio antennae 2.4–2.9m (8–10ft) long

steel sphere weighing 84kg (185lb)

Sputnik 1
1957 • USSR
The first artificial satellite, launched ahead of the US version, contained a radio transmitter. Orbiting hundreds of kilometres above the Earth, it helped scientists understand more about Earth's atmosphere.

Gagarin Poster
1961 • USSR
This Soviet poster shows a beaming Yuri Gagarin, who made history as the first man in space aboard Vostok I.

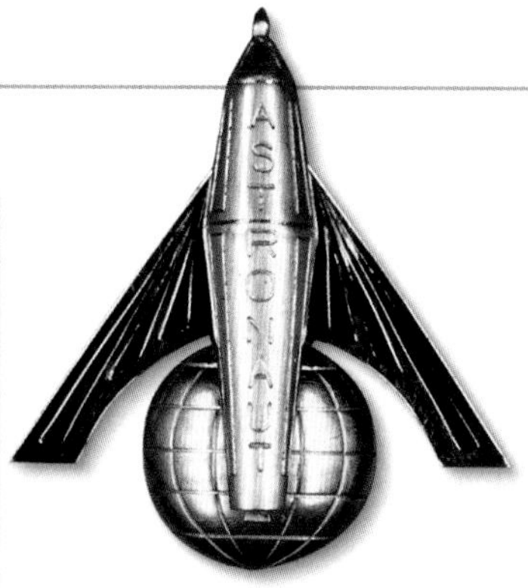

Marine award
1962 • US
John Glenn, the first American to orbit the Earth, was awarded a special medal by the US Marine Corps to commemorate the event. Alan Shephard had become the first American in space in the previous year.

Cosmonaut's suit
1965 • USSR
Soviet Alexsei Leonov was the first man to walk in space, in March 1965. His suit, the Berkut, came with a backpack life-support system.

seal connects helmet to suit

suit includes an airtight insulation layer

pressure gauge

insulated gloves with rubber fingertips to assist grip

THE SPACE RACE

TWO SUPERPOWERS COMPETE TO PROVE THEIR TECHNOLOGICAL MIGHT

Two nations dominated the race to explore space in the 1960s – the US and USSR. What had begun as a search for long-range missiles became a battle for international prestige, which neither wanted to lose.

In 1957, the Soviet Union stunned the US when it launched Sputnik 1 into orbit. Then, in 1961, Soviet cosmonaut Yuri Gagarin became the first human to orbit the Earth. It looked like the US was lagging behind. But after the creation of the Apollo programme, the US eventually won the ultimate prize: Neil Armstrong and Buzz Aldrin stepped onto the lunar surface on 21 July 1969, marking the beginning of a new era in space exploration.

Moon rock
1969
Collected by Apollo 11 astronauts, Moon rock resembled volcanic lava found on Earth, suggesting that the Moon was once molten.

Scoop

Brush

Sample testing kit
1969 • US
The crew of Apollo 11 took special tools and containers with them to collect rocks, soil, and dust from the lunar surface to return to Earth.

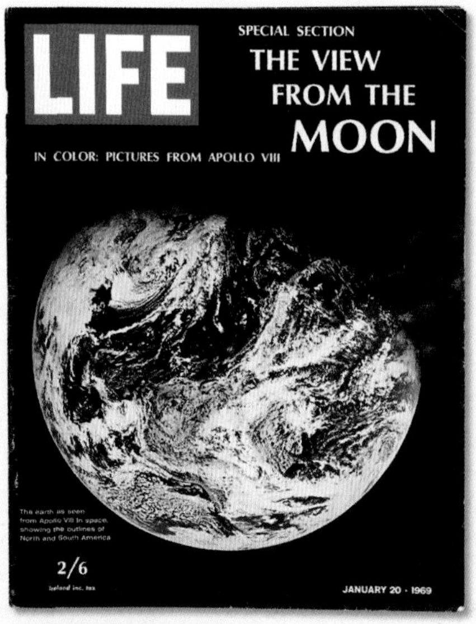

***Life* magazine**
20 January 1969 • US
Images from the Apollo 8 mission appeared on the front cover of *Life* magazine, such was the interest in space exploration. The Apollo 8 crew were the first to orbit the Moon.

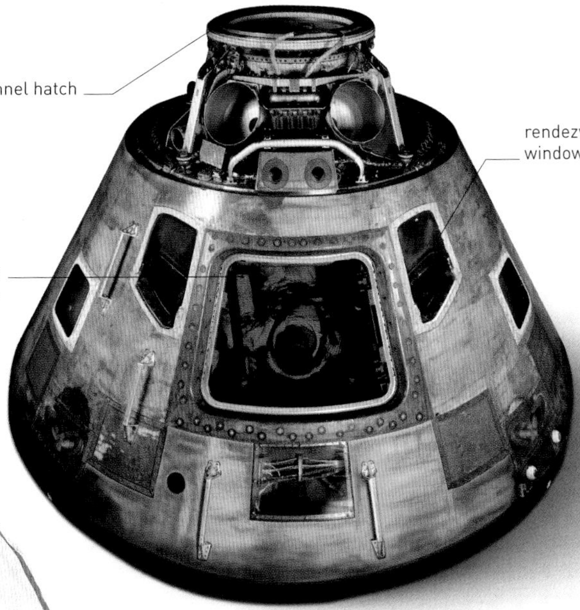

Apollo 10 command module
1969 • US
This module, carrying three crew, went into orbit around the Moon in a rehearsal for the Apollo 11 mission that landed on the Moon two months later.

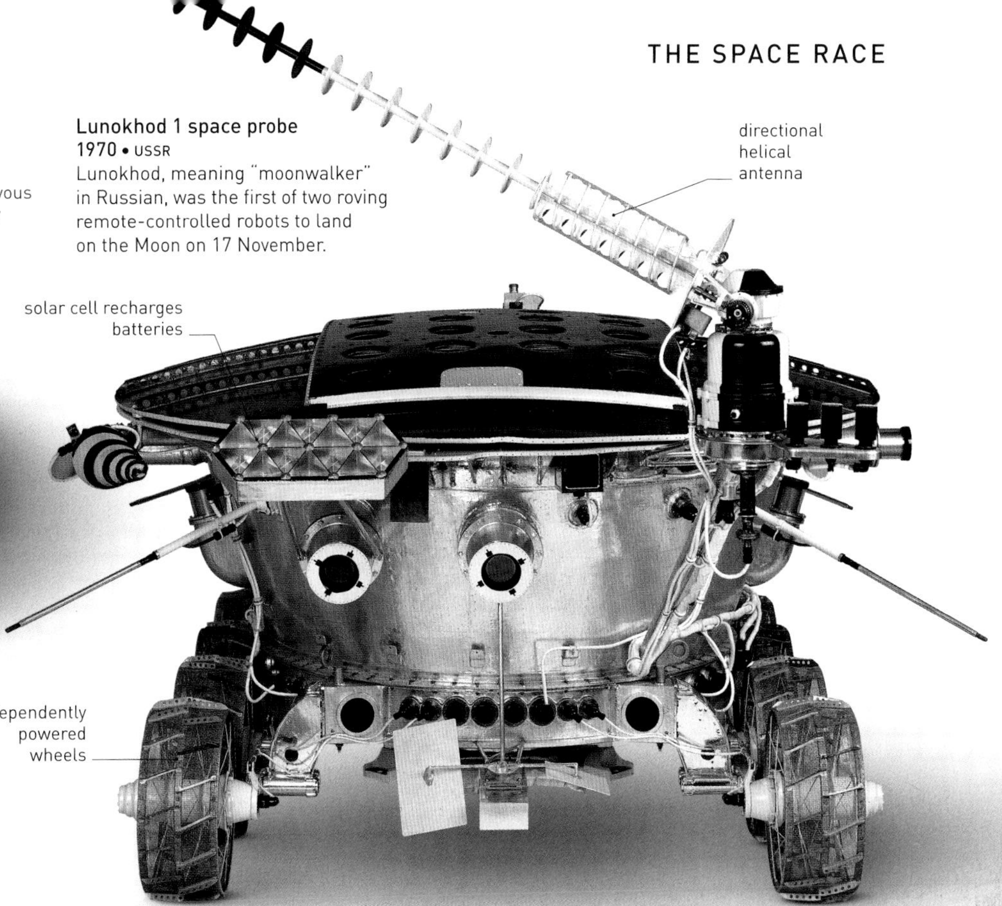

Lunokhod 1 space probe
1970 • USSR
Lunokhod, meaning "moonwalker" in Russian, was the first of two roving remote-controlled robots to land on the Moon on 17 November.

Apollo patch
1969 • US
An eagle carrying an olive branch perches on the lunar surface in the Apollo 11 patch, which was designed by the crew.

Mir patch
DATE UNKNOWN • USSR
This is the official mission patch for the Russian Space Station Mir programme. The word "Mir" appears in Cyrillic.

Space food tray
DATE AND PROGRAMME UNKNOWN
This food tray is magnetic to combat low gravity, with metal cutlery and Velcro fastenings to secure shrink-wrapped food packages and liquid.

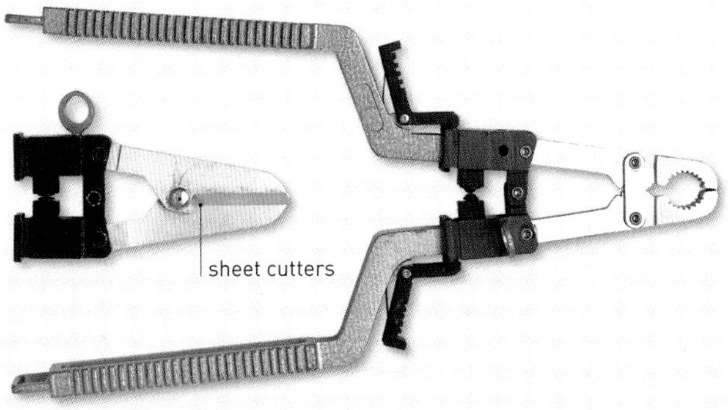

Space tools
DATE AND PROGRAMME UNKNOWN
Special tools were designed to help astronauts collect specimens. Because bulky space suit gloves made grasping difficult and tiring, tool handles were thicker than normal.

Granma
¡UN CUBANO EN EL COSMOS!
TRIPULACION CONJUNTA SOVIETICO-CUBANA
YURI ROMANENKO Y ARNALDO TAMAYO CIRCUNDAN LA TIERRA EN LA SOYUZ-38
EL HISTORICO DESPEGUE SE PRODUJO AYER
A LAS 3 Y 11 DE LA TARDE, HORA DE CUBA
¡VIVA LA AMISTAD SOVIETICO-CUBANA!

Cuban newspaper
1980 • CUBA
During the space race, astronauts from many communist countries, such as Cuba, went into space as crew members on Soviet spacecraft.

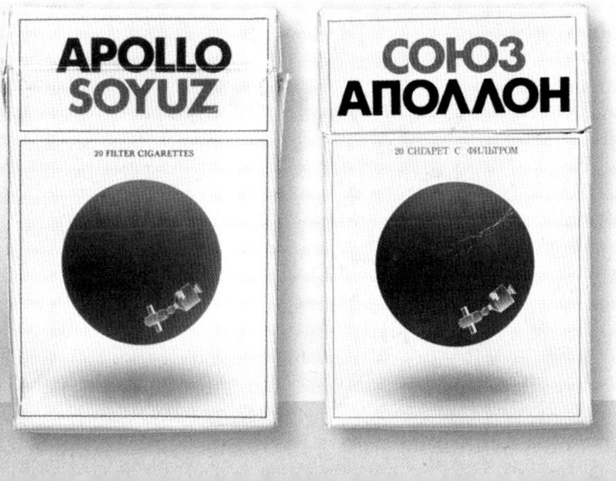

Commemorative cigarettes
1975 • US AND USSR
These cigarettes were made to celebrate the Apollo–Soyuz mission in 1975, when craft from the US and USSR docked together in space. The packets were printed in both English and Russian.

1951

“ IT HAD TO BE. ”

Julius Rosenberg, convicted spy, on his death sentence, 1951

EGYPT RENOUNCED ITS 1936 TREATY THAT GRANTED BRITAIN a lease on the Suez base, in October. Britain refused to withdraw and a guerilla war began in the **Suez Canal Zone**.

In March, the Iranian government nationalized its oil industry, which had been dominated by the **Anglo-Iranian Oil Company**. Britain responded with a **worldwide embargo** on Iranian oil.

A new era dawned in **nuclear power** when the first nuclear power plant, in Idaho, produced around 100 kW of power – enough for four 100 watt light bulbs.

Fears about the **spread of communism** deepened as **Julius and Ethel Rosenberg** were accused of stealing information from the US for the Soviets. British Foreign Office officials **Guy Burgess** and **Donald Maclean** disappeared on 28 May – it was later found out that they had **defected** to the Soviet Union.

The Rosenbergs awaiting trial
Americans Julius and Ethel Rosenberg were found guilty of smuggling atomic secrets to the Soviet Union.

1952

Thousands of suspected Mau Mau activists in Kenya were arrested following open revolt against British rule.

INDOCHINA PROVED VOLATILE THROUGHOUT THE YEAR. In April, the French launched a big push to smash the **Viet Minh resistance** northwest of Saigon. In October, another French operation targeted Viet Minh supply bases.

A **peace treaty** that **Japan** had signed in San Fransisco, US, in 1951 went into effect on 28 April, making the country an **independent state** again.

On 27 May, **East Germany** closed its border with **West Germany**. A 10-m (30-ft) wide "**control strip**" was dug along the border.

King George VI of Britain died on 6 February. His daughter, **Elizabeth**, was officially proclaimed queen two days later.

Opposition to British rule led to the **Mau Mau Rebellion** in **Kenya**. The Mau Mau were an anti-colonial insurgent army. They began raiding white-settler farms, and by the end of the year the British had declared a state of emergency.

The **European Coal and Steel Community** came into being in July. Comprised of six nations, it created a "**common market**" for coal and steel, and laid down the foundations for the future European Union.

50
THOUSAND
THE NUMBER OF **AFRICANS** WHO DIED IN THE **MAU MAU UPRISING**

EVA PERON (1919–52)

Maria Eva Duarte de Perón, or "Evita", played a crucial role in helping her husband, Juan Perón, become Argentinian president. She was idolized by the poor, and began many programmes of social welfare and reform. She died of cancer aged 32.

A **military coup in Egypt** headed by Colonel Gamal Abdal Nasser's **Committee of Free Officers** seized control of the government in July. Egypt became a republic in 1953.

The first atomic bombs had been dropped on Hiroshima and Nagasaki in 1945. The much more powerful **hydrogen bomb**, or H-bomb, was tested by the US on 1 November.

The world's first successful use of a **mechanical heart** was announced in the US, on 3 July. The **Dodrill–GMR** machine kept blood circulating for 50 minutes during open-heart surgery.

1953

STALIN'S POLICIES WERE BECOMING INCREASINGLY ANTI-SEMITIC. At the end of 1952, he told his Politburo that all Jews were sympathetic to America. On 13 January, nine doctors were arrested for conspiring to murder prominent figures in the Soviet armed forces. Six of them were Jews. These accusations were met by reactions of foreboding in Western Europe. The doctors were freed after **Stalin died** of a stroke in March.

Stalin's death led to a major **power struggle** in the Kremlin where a moderate coalition, headed by **Georgi Malenkov** (1902–88), took over. His moderate policies became unpopular and **Lavrenty Beria** (1899–1953), who had been the head of Stalin's secret police, tried to gain power. Beria was **charged with treason** and was then shot in the back of a lorry, in what seems to have been a summary **assassination**.

Hillary and Norgay
Edmund Hillary and Sherpa Tenzing Norgay become the first to successfully reach the summit of Mount Everest, the highest point on Earth, during the British Everest Expedition of 1953.

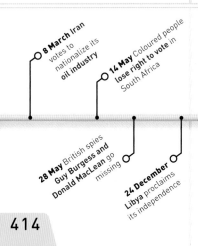

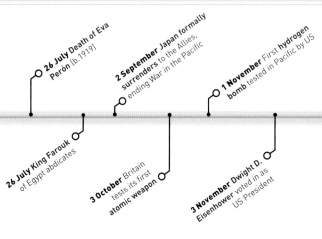

- **8 March** Iran votes to nationalize its **oil industry**
- **28 May** British spies **Guy Burgess and Donald MacLean** go missing
- **14 May** Coloured people **lose right to vote** in South Africa
- **24 December Libya** proclaims its independence
- **26 July** Death of Eva Perón (b.1919)
- **26 July King Farouk** of Egypt abdicates
- **2 September** Japan formally **surrenders** to the Allies, ending War in the Pacific
- **3 October** Britain tests its first **atomic weapon**
- **1 November** First **hydrogen bomb** tested in Pacific by US
- **3 November Dwight D. Eisenhower** voted in as US President
- **1 January** China's first **five year plan**, an economic development initiative, begins
- **3 January Samuel Beckett's** play *Waiting For Godot* premieres in Paris
- **14 January Josip Tito** elected Yugoslav president
- **5 March** King Norodom Sihanouk proclaims **independence for Cambodia**
- **5 March** Death of **Joseph Stalin**, Russian leader (b.1879)
- **25 April** James D. Watson and Francis Crick discover **DNA**
- **8 April Jomo Kenyatta**, Mau Mau leader, arrested and jailed
- **29 May Everest conquered** by Edmund Hillary and Tenzing Norgay

The Indochinese conflict lasted eight years, ending in 1954. This photograph shows French forces evacuating Hanoi.

DNA

A scientific breakthrough was made in 1953, when the blueprint of life, DNA (deoxyribonucleic acid), was mapped out by James Watson and Frances Crick. DNA is the hereditary material that contains the coded information needed to build and maintain all living organisms. Watson and Crick proposed a model for DNA called a double helix. It explained heredity, and led to the development of an entire biotechnology industry.

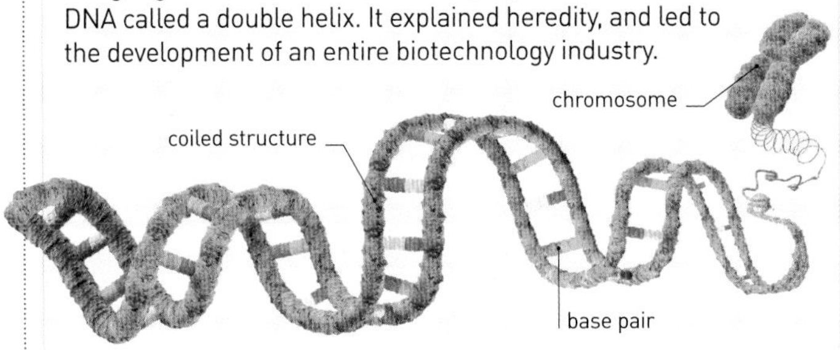

War in Korea (see 1950) ended when an **armistice** was signed on 27 July, but a state of suspended hostility remained. The **Republic of Korea** (South) and the **Democratic People's Republic of Korea** (North) chose not to sign the peace treaty.

Mount Everest, the world's highest mountain, was first climbed on 29 May, by New Zealander **Edmund Hillary** (1919–2008) and the Nepalese Sherpa **Tenzing Norgay** (1914–86). They stayed only 15 minutes at the summit as they were low on oxygen.

A new "absurdist" play, *Waiting for Godot* by **Samuel Beckett** premiered at the Theatre de Babylone in Paris on 5 January. Critics were at once divided over its merits.

FRENCH RULE IN INDOCHINA CAME TO AN END ON 21 JULY. Laos and **Cambodia** became independent, while Vietnam was divided into **North Vietnam**, with a communist government, and **South Vietnam**. In all three non-communist states, communist guerrilla movements sprang up.

Senator **Joseph McCarthy** intensified his campaign to root out communists (see 1950). He set his sights on the US army and made unsubstantiated allegations against them. This led to his being censored by the Senate on 2 December. Public support dwindled, and McCarthy's reign of fear ended.

A **vaccine for Polio** was tested in a huge field trial in the US, in April. The trials were successful, and a **nationwide vaccination** scheme was started the following year.

ISRAELI FORCES CONDUCTED A SURPRISE RAID on the Egyptian-held **Gaza Strip** in February. The raid was the largest of its kind against Arab forces since the end of the First Arab–Israeli War in 1949 (see 1956).

Under its **apartheid** legislation, the South African government forcibly evicted 60,000 black people from **Sophiatown**, in February, to make it a white-only suburb. The **African National Congress** (ANC), an anti-apartheid organization, responded with a day of prayer.

The Friendship, Cooperation and Mutual Assistance Treaty, known as the **Warsaw Pact**, was signed on 14 May. The treaty set up a military alliance of communist states to **counter NATO** in the West.

The **Soviet Union** ended its occupation of **Austria**, which had been ongoing since the end of World War II, on condition that Austria remained neutral. The **Austrian State Treaty** was signed on 15 May, re-establishing Austria as an independent sovereign state. It joined the UN the same year.

Juan Perón's position as president of Argentina was weakened by the death of his wife and a quarrel with the Roman Catholic Church. He was **overthrown** in a coup on 19 September, and exiled to Paraguay.

There was a turning point in the **Civil Rights movement** on 1 December, when **Rosa Parks** broke Alabama race laws by refusing to move to the back of a bus. Thousands boycotted the bus company in protest.

In the West, by the mid-1950s, **teenagers** stood out as a distinct group with interests, musical tastes, and their own fashions. This led to disapproval from adults who feared **juvenile delinquency**. New slang was condemned, dances were closed, and some institutions banned the wearing of jeans.

ROSA PARKS (1913–2005)

Rosa Parks made history when she refused to give up her seat on a bus for a white man. Her arrest mobilized a boycott of the bus system, which ended segregation on Montgomery's buses. The boycott also brought international attention to the civil rights cause. Parks remained committed to her cause, and was a symbol of the struggle for civil rights until her death in 2005, aged 92.

Eastern alliance

The Warsaw Pact united the Eastern Bloc in a similar alliance to NATO. The signatories were Albania, Bulgaria, Czechoslovakia, East Germany, Hungary, Poland, and the USSR.

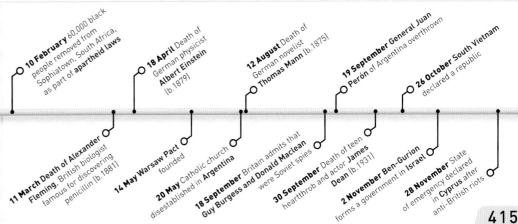

18 June After coup in Egypt the previous year, its army proclaims a **new republic**

19 June Julius and Ethel Rosenberg executed for espionage

27 July End of the Korean War (began 1950)

18 April Colonel Nasser becomes Egyptian prime minister

19 July Elvis Presley releases his first single

21 July Indochina War ends

2 December Senator Joseph McCarthy censored by US Senate

10 February 60,000 black people removed from Sophiatown, South Africa, as part of **apartheid laws**

11 March Death of Alexander Fleming, British biologist famous for discovering penicillin (b.1881)

18 April Death of German physicist **Albert Einstein** (b.1879)

14 May Warsaw Pact founded

20 May Catholic church disestablished in **Argentina**

12 August Death of German novelist **Thomas Mann** (b.1875)

18 September Britain admits that **Guy Burgess and Donald Maclean** were Soviet spies

19 September General Juan Perón of Argentina overthrown

30 September Death of teen heartthrob and actor **James Dean** (b.1931)

26 October South Vietnam declared a republic

2 November Ben-Gurion forms a government in **Israel**

28 November State of emergency declared in **Cyprus** after anti-British riots

1956

“ WHAT COULD WE DO? THERE WAS A REIGN OF TERROR. ”

Nikita Krushchev, on Stalin, 25 February 1956

Nikita Krushchev, photographed during an eight-day visit to London. Khrushchev's "de-Stalinization" of the USSR prompted a thaw in the Cold War.

Chevrolet Bel Air Convertible
The 1956 Chevy was just what the American public wanted – it was fast, big, and affordable. It soon became a classic symbol of the American Dream.

THE US CIVIL RIGHTS MOVEMENT experienced a turbulent time this year when a black student began attending the University of Alabama. White community members attacked African-Americans, and the activities of the **Ku Klux Klan**, an organization of white supremacists, increased.

Morocco declared its **independence** from France on 2 March, although Spain retained control of Ceuta and Melilla on the coast. Border disputes with Algeria led to fighting in 1963.

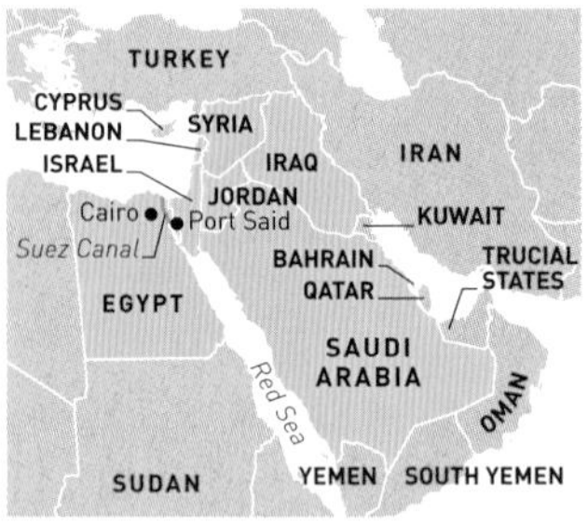

KEY
Areas affected by the Suez Crisis

The Suez Crisis
The Suez Canal was a vital trading route from the Mediterranean to the Red Sea. It was especially important for the shipment of oil.

Riots erupted in **Cyprus**, in March, after British authorities deported **Archbishop Makarios**, leader of the **campaign to unify Cyprus with Greece**. He was accused of fostering terrorism.

Egypt's **President Nasser** nationalized the **Suez Canal** on 26 July. Britain and France had shares in the Suez Canal Company, and met with Israel in October to conclude a secret agreement that Israel should attack Egypt, providing a pretext for an Anglo-French invasion of the Suez Canal Zone. On 29 October, **Israel invaded the Sinai Peninsula**. The US pressured Israel to withdraw, and UN forces were stationed along the Egyptian–Israeli border. The Anglo-French assault was launched on 5 November. International criticism forced a ceasefire and then a withdrawal. Tensions remained high between Egypt and Israel following the crisis, which became known as the **Second Arab–Israeli War**.

Nikita Khrushchev, Communist Party First Secretary of the Soviet Union, **denounced Stalin** as a "brutal despot" in a speech on 25 February. This outraged Stalinists, but led to the prospect of a **thaw in relations** with the US. In Eastern Europe it had a dramatic effect on raising expectations for change.

The **Hungarian Revolution**, in October, led to the formation of a liberal government and **Imre Nagy**, a moderate, became prime minister. On 3 November, Nagy announced a plan to withdraw from the Warsaw Pact (see 1955). The next day, Warsaw Pact **troops invaded**, crushed the rebellion, and **re-established control**.

1957

The Soviets began the "Race for Space" with the launch of the world's first satellites, Sputnik I and II – an achievement celebrated by this poster.

KASHMIR WAS FORMALLY INCORPORATED INTO INDIA on 26 January, defying a UN ruling. It was granted **special status** under India's constitution, which ensured, among other things, that non-Kashmiri Indians could not buy property there. Pakistan strongly objected (see 1917, 1965).

Ghana became the first black African country to gain its **independence** from colonial rule on 6 March. The first prime minister, Dr **Kwame Nkrumah** (1909–72), initiated ambitious development programmes and spearheaded the political advancement of Africa.

The **Treaty of Rome** was signed on 25 March. It set up the **EEC** (European Economic Community) and provided for the countries' social and economic programmes. It also gave ex-colonies free trade with the EEC, and made them eligible for aid.

The suppression of communist guerillas in **Malaya** had been a constant source of concern to Britain (see 1948). Eventually, Britain realized that this situation could not be resolved by military means, and made constitutional advances that culminated in the **independence of the Malayan Federation** on 31 August.

President Sukarno of Indonesia had struggled to maintain a parliamentary democracy since independence in 1945. On 14 March, he decided to dispense with parliament and imposed **martial law**. On 3 December, Sukarno nationalized Dutch businesses; two days later he expelled all Dutch nationals.

The **Space Age** began on 4 October, when Russia launched its **Sputnik I** satellite into orbit. It was followed a month later by **Sputnik 2**, which carried a dog called **Laika**.

European Economic Community
This map shows the composition of the EEC at its inception in 1957, when six countries signed the Treaty of Rome.

- **25 February Nikita Khrushchev** gives **anti-Stalin speech** to Communist Party
- **2 March Morocco** gains independence
- **10 March** Renewed anti-British **riots** in **Cyprus**
- **18 April Nikita Khrushchev** and **Premier Bulganin** of the Soviet Union visit Britain
- **29 June Riots** break out in **Poland** against communism
- **26 July** President Nasser of Egypt **nationalizes Suez Canal**
- **14 August Death of Bertolt Brecht**, German playwright (b.1898)
- **26 October–5 November Hungarian revolution** against Soviet domination
- **29 October** Israel attacks Sinai Peninsula; **Second Arab–Israeli War**
- **5 November** Joint **Anglo-French attack** on Suez Canal zone
- **8 November UN imposes ceasefire** on allies in Suez Canal zone
- **14 January Death of Humphrey Bogart**, US actor (b.1899)
- **26 January Kashmir** joins India
- **6 March Ghana** becomes independent
- **25 March Treaty of Rome** paves way for the European Economic Community **(EEC)**
- **2 May** Death of US Senator **Joseph McCarthy**, renowned for McCarthyism (b.1908)
- **7 August Nikita Khrushchev** visits East Germany
- **31 August Malaya** becomes independent
- **25 September** Desegregation takes place in **Little Rock, Arkansas**, US; black children attend school
- **4 October** Soviets are first in space with launch of **Sputnik I**

1958

Elvis Presley, seen here singing to an adoring young crowd, joined the US Army and set sail for Germany, putting a temporary halt to his extraordinary career.

MAO ZEDONG, FOUNDER OF THE PEOPLE'S REPUBLIC OF CHINA, initiated a programme of reform in 1958 that would ultimately kill millions. The "**Great Leap Forward**" was intended to rapidly industrialize China's rural economy. However, Mao's scheme plunged the country into one of the worst famines in history. At least 35 million people were worked, starved, or beaten to death in the following four years.

35 MILLION
THE **NUMBER OF DEATHS** IN THE **GREAT LEAP FORWARD**

The **Middle East** felt the repercussions of the **Suez Canal crisis** this year (see 1956). In February, Egypt and Syria merged to form the **United Arab Republic**. Pro-Western regimes in the Middle East saw the union as a threat to their security, and Iraq and Jordan formed a loose union. In July, a **civil war** broke out in Lebanon between the predominantly Christian and strongly pro-Western regime of **President Camille Chamoun** and the **Muslim Socialist National Front**. On 14 July, a group of Iraqi Free Officers led by Brigadier Abdul Karim Qasim captured power in Baghdad in a savage **military coup**. King Faisal II, the regent Abdul Illah, and Prime Minister Nuri al-Said were murdered.

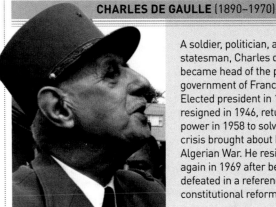

CHARLES DE GAULLE (1890–1970)

A soldier, politician, and statesman, Charles de Gaulle became head of the provisional government of France in 1944. Elected president in 1945, he resigned in 1946, returning to power in 1958 to solve the crisis brought about by the Algerian War. He resigned again in 1969 after being defeated in a referendum on constitutional reform.

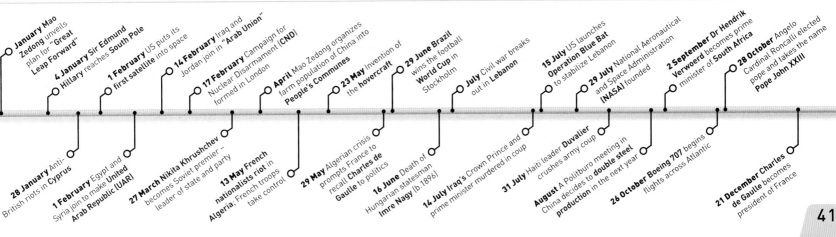

鋼
以鋼为綱.全面跃进
YI GANG WEI GANG QUAN MIAN YUE JIN

Great Leap Forward
This propaganda poster urges workers to make more steel as part of Mao Zedong's "Great Leap Forward", an attempt to modernize China.

The Iraqi coup threatened to **destabilize Western control** over the Middle East and its oil resources. To counter this, within 48 hours of the Baghdad coup the US sent a battalion of marines into Lebanon in **Operation Blue Bat**, to help prop up the tottering regime of President Chamoun. Tensions eased, and the US withdrew its forces on 25 October without a shot being fired.

French wars in Indochina, civil war in Algeria, and a series of unstable governments led to the recall of **General Charles De Gaulle** (see panel, above) to French politics. He demanded special powers for six months to restore order, and to draft a new constitution for a **Fifth Republic** – submitted to the French public in a referendum on 28 September. De Gaulle won an **easy victory to become president** on 21 December, 12 years after he had relinquished power.

Russia's success in launching a satellite in 1957 spurred the Americans into forming **NASA**, the North American Space Agency. On 29 July, President Eisenhower signed the **National Aeronautics and Space Act**, and NASA opened formally three months later.

Elvis Presley had become a huge star with a series of chart-topping records, and this year would prove to be pivotal. On 20 January, he began work on his fourth motion picture, *King Creole*. Then, at the height of what seemed a promising career, Presley was **conscripted into the army**, and in September he set sail for Germany. Billboard noted a drop in sales of his records and Elvis's army years would mark a clear line between the old Elvis and the new.

- **January Mao Zedong** unveils plan for **"Great Leap Forward"**
- **4 January Sir Edmund Hillary** reaches **South Pole**
- **28 January** Anti-British riots in **Cyprus**
- **1 February** US puts its **first satellite** into space
- **1 February** Egypt and Syria join to make **United Arab Republic (UAR)**
- **14 February** Iraq and Jordan join in **"Arab Union"**
- **17 February** Campaign for Nuclear Disarmament (**CND**) formed in London
- **27 March Nikita Khrushchev** becomes Soviet premier – leader of state and party
- **April** Mao Zedong organizes farm population of China into **People's Communes**
- **13 May French nationalists riot** in **Algeria**; French troops take control
- **23 May** Invention of the **hovercraft**
- **29 May** Algerian crisis prompts France to recall **Charles de Gaulle** to politics
- **29 June Brazil** wins the football **World Cup** in Stockholm
- **16 June** Death of Hungarian statesman **Imre Nagy** (b.1896)
- **July** Civil war breaks out in **Lebanon**
- **14 July Iraq's** Crown Prince and prime minister murdered in coup
- **15 July** US launches **Operation Blue Bat** to stabilize Lebanon
- **29 July** National Aeronautical and Space Administration **(NASA)** founded
- **31 July** Haiti leader **Duvalier** crushes army coup
- **August** A Politburo meeting in China decides to **double steel production** in the next year
- **2 September Dr Hendrik Verwoerd** becomes prime minister of **South Africa**
- **26 October Boeing 707** begins flights across Atlantic
- **28 October** Angelo Cardinal Roncalli elected pope and takes the name **Pope John XXIII**
- **21 December Charles de Gaulle** becomes president of France

1959

“A REVOLUTION IS NOT A BED OF ROSES.”

Fidel Castro, prime minister of Cuba from 1959–76

THE RACE BETWEEN THE US AND USSR TO SEND A MAN INTO SPACE accelerated in 1959. On 2 January, the Soviets launched the first spacecraft to escape Earth's orbit and reach the Moon, **Luna 1**. The US also had its first successful mission this year, when the **Juno 2** rocket sent the **Pioneer 4** probe towards the Moon. **Luna 2** was launched on 12 September, and on 7 October, pictures taken by **Luna 3** gave mankind its first look at the **far side of the Moon**.

Cuba had been ruled by a **series of dictators**, culminating in the corrupt regime of **Fulgencio Batista** (r.1940–44 and 1952–59). A group of revolutionaries led by law student **Fidel Castro** took up arms and set up a base in the Sierra Maestra mountains, provoking Batista to indiscriminate repression. Batista's regime collapsed, and **Castro took over** – he was sworn in as prime minister on 16 February. A "honeymoon" period with the US soon ended as Cuba became a **totally socialist state**.

In **Vietnam**, northern guerrillas under **Ho Chi Minh** (1890–1969) attacked the southern army in March. Ho Chi Minh aimed to unite Vietnam under communist rule. The US, seeking to stop the spread of communism, trained the **Army of the Republic of Vietnam** (ARVN) and provided advisors to South Vietnam. On 8 July, two Americans were killed by Viet Minh troops. These were the first American deaths in the **Vietnam War**.

The **Dalai Lama**, the spiritual leader of Tibet, fled his country on 31 March and **escaped to India** with his ministers. This came after widespread **open rebellion against Chinese rule** within Tibet, which had culminated in a full uprising. Thousands were reported killed as **China suppressed the revolt**. Over the next few months, an estimated 80,000 Tibetans fled to India.

Anti-apartheid riots continued in South Africa. Those in the township of **Sharpeville** resulted in the deaths of 70 demonstrators, and the **African National Congress** (ANC, see 1994) was banned. These events prompted **worldwide condemnation** of South Africa's apartheid policies. When the British prime minister **Harold Macmillan** visited the South African parliament in February 1960, he made a speech highlighting the "**wind of change**" which he believed would bring independence for black Africans.

FIDEL CASTRO (1926–)

Fidel Castro was jailed for his revolutionary activities in Cuba in 1953. After his release he went into exile, but returned in 1956. He was Cuban prime minister from 1959–76 and the first communist head of state in the Americas. His relations with the US were originally good, but speedily deteriorated. Although still a prominent figure, he retired as president in 2006.

VW Beetle
Produced by the German company Volkswagen, the Beetle survived the war and decorated Beetles became a symbol of peace around the world.

1960

John F. Kennedy and his wife, Jacqueline, smile from the back of an open-top car during Kennedy's inauguration celebrations.

THE STRAIN ON DIPLOMATIC TIES BETWEEN CHINA AND THE USSR became public in June, at the congress of the Romanian Communist Party, when **Nikita Khrushchev** and China's **Peng Zhen** clashed openly. The Soviets were alarmed with China's "**Great Leap Forward**" (see 1958), while the Soviets reneged on their earlier commitment to help China develop nuclear weapons, and were seen as too conciliatory to the West. At a meeting in November, the Chinese delegation clashed with the Soviets again, but eventually a compromise was reached, preventing a formal split.

The **Belgian Congo** became independent on 30 June, ushering in a period of turmoil. It was renamed the **Federal Republic of Congo**, with Joseph Kasavubu as president, and Patrice Lumumba – a socialist – as prime minister. In July, the province of Katanga declared independence and asked for Belgian help – Belgium sent an invasion force in response, causing Kasavubu to **appeal to the UN**. In September, Kasavubu dismissed Lumumba as prime minister, and in December he was arrested. **Lumumba was murdered** the following year.

In September, the major oil-exporting countries outside the communist bloc set up the Organization of the Petroleum Exporting Countries (**OPEC**). They combined to fix oil prices by controlling supply (see 1973).

The **laser** was first operated on 16 May. A device that emits an intense beam of light, it was invented by the US physicist **Theodore Maiman** (1927–2007). It drew the attention of scientists around the world and led to **advances** in engineering, medicine, and technology.

The influential civil rights activist **Martin Luther King** (1929–1968) rose to international prominence in the early 1960s. King was arrested in Atlanta, Georgia, during a "sit-in" on 19 October. He was sentenced to a four-month term in prison. Presidential candidate **John F. Kennedy** (1917–1963) intervened to secure King's release after eight days in jail.

John Fitzgerald Kennedy was elected as 35th President of the US in November. He narrowly defeated the Republican candidate Richard Nixon after some fiercely contested television debates.

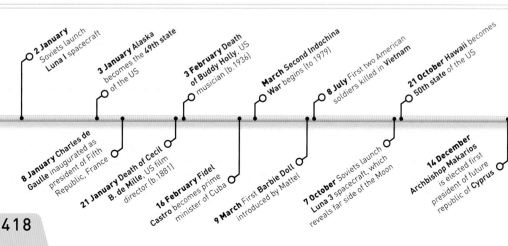

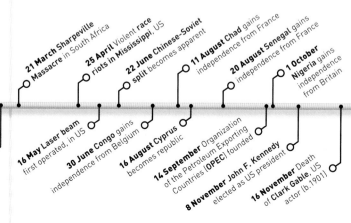

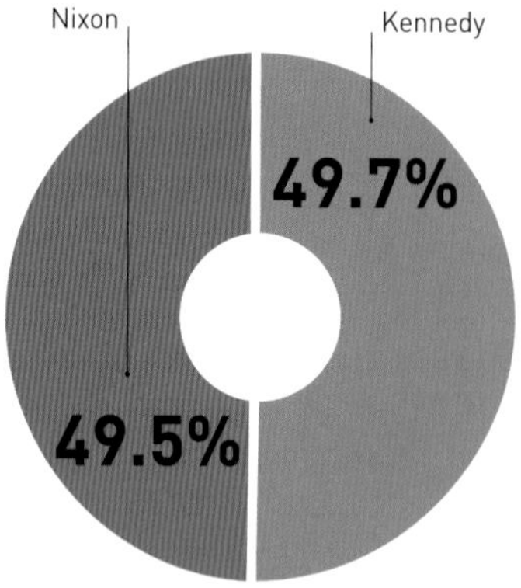

Race for the White House
The presidential race between Nixon and Kennedy was incredibly tight. Kennedy beat Nixon by less than 1 per cent – just 118,574 votes.

- **2 January** Soviets launch Luna I spacecraft
- **3 January Alaska** becomes the **49th state** of the US
- **8 January Charles de Gaulle** inaugurated as president of Fifth Republic, France
- **21 January Death of Cecil B. de Mille**, US film director (b.1881)
- **3 February Death of Buddy Holly**, US musician (b.1936)
- **16 February Fidel Castro** becomes prime minister of Cuba
- **March Second Indochina War** begins (to 1979)
- **9 March** First **Barbie Doll** introduced by Mattel
- **8 July** First two American soldiers killed in **Vietnam**
- **7 October** Soviets launch **Luna 3** spacecraft, which reveals far side of the Moon
- **21 October Hawaii** becomes **50th state** of the US
- **14 December Archbishop Makarios** is elected first president of future republic of **Cyprus**
- **21 March Sharpeville Massacre** in South Africa
- **25 April** Violent **race riots in Mississippi**, US
- **16 May Laser beam** first operated, in US
- **22 June Chinese-Soviet split** becomes apparent
- **30 June Congo** gains independence from Belgium
- **11 August Chad** gains independence from France
- **16 August Cyprus** becomes republic
- **20 August Senegal** gains independence from France
- **14 September** Organization of the Petroleum Exporting Countries (**OPEC**) founded
- **1 October Nigeria** gains independence from Britain
- **8 November John F. Kennedy** elected as US president
- **16 November** Death of **Clark Gable**, US actor (b.1901)

Paratroopers hold back a crowd of French nationals angry at news of self-determination for Algeria.

First man in space
Yuri Gagarin is pictured here in the cockpit of his spacecraft, Vostok 1. His groundbreaking first flight into space lasted 1 hour 45 minutes.

THE PORTUGUESE LUXURY PASSENGER LINER SANTA MARIA was hijacked in January while sailing in West Indian waters. The hijackers were **Iberian leftists** who opposed the Portuguese government and the fascist regime in Spain. The 900 people on board were released after 11 days.

The Soviet Union scored a victory in the **space race** when **Yuri Gagarin** (1934–68) became the first man to be launched into space. He **orbited the Earth** just once on 12 April, travelling at more than 27,000 km per hour (17,000 miles per hour) in his **Vostok 1** spacecraft.

In 1960, the Russians had scored a triumph by winning the allegiance of **Fidel Castro**, the newly installed dictator of Cuba (see panel, opposite). Washington responded in April by financing 1,500 anti-communist exiles in the ill-fated "**Bay of Pigs**" expedition. This badly conceived attempt at invasion on the southern coast was immediately repulsed (see 1962).

One of **John F. Kennedy's** first proposals as US president was the establishment of a **Peace Corps** to help in developing nations. The aim was for young people to take one or two years **working abroad** as teachers, healthcare workers, or advisors in Africa, Asia, and South America.

Worldwide action to conserve the **natural world** was put in place on 29 April, in Switzerland. The "**Morges Manifesto**" became the blueprint for the first global green organization, the World Wildlife Fund (**WWF**). The organization's headquarters were established in Switzerland, and national offices were gradually set up across the world, starting with Britain, in November. South America's first ever **National Park** was also established this year, in Brazil. The government created the 2.3 million hectare (5.6 million acre) **Xingu National Park** to resettle the indigenous people of Brazil, as their lands were taken over and developed. Seventeen tribes were settled in the new park.

South Africa focused on its anti-British policies and won the vote for **independence** on 31 May. It became a republic and left the Commonwealth. In the same year, **Nelson Mandela** (b.1918) headed the ANC's new military wing, and launched a sabotage campaign.

President Charles de Gaulle called for **self-determination in Algeria** (see 1954), but the atmosphere between France and Algeria remained murderous. French settlers living in Algeria reacted with outrage, and France braced itself for civil war. On 17 October, thousands of **Algerians converged on Paris** to protest against repressive measures taken against them. About 10,000 people were arrested and **hundreds were killed**.

Berliners found themselves living in a physically divided city on 13 August, as troops in East Germany closed the border between **East and West Berlin**. Barbed wire fences up to 2m (6ft) high were erected. Within days, these were replaced by concrete blocks, and the **wall became permanent** (see 1989).

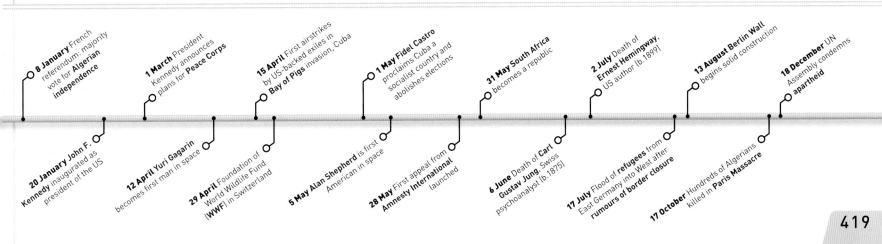

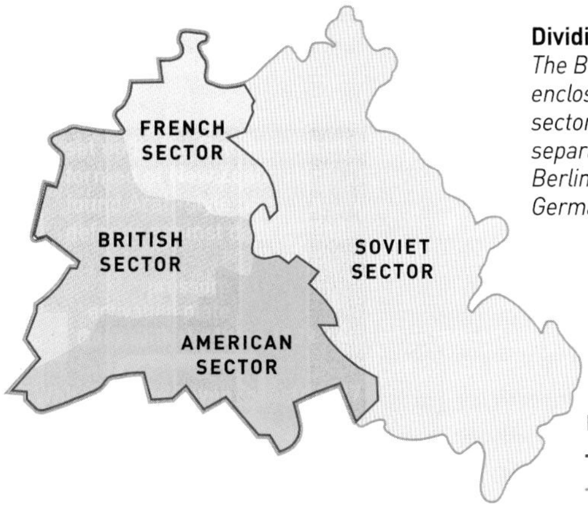

Dividing wall
The Berlin Wall enclosed the three sectors of West Berlin, separating it from East Berlin and East Germany.

KEY
— Berlin Wall
— Berlin city limits

- **8 January** French referendum: majority vote for **Algerian independence**
- **20 January John F. Kennedy** inaugurated as president of the US
- **1 March** President Kennedy announces plans for **Peace Corps**
- **12 April Yuri Gagarin** becomes first man in space
- **15 April** First airstrikes by US-backed exiles in **Bay of Pigs** invasion, Cuba
- **29 April** Foundation of World Wildlife Fund (**WWF**) in Switzerland
- **1 May Fidel Castro** proclaims Cuba a socialist country and abolishes elections
- **5 May Alan Shepherd** is first American in space
- **28 May** First appeal from **Amnesty International** launched
- **31 May South Africa** becomes a republic
- **6 June** Death of **Carl Gustav Jung**, Swiss psychoanalyst (b.1875)
- **2 July** Death of **Ernest Hemingway**, US author (b.1899)
- **17 July** Flood of **refugees** from East Germany into West after **rumours of border closure**
- **13 August Berlin Wall** begins solid construction
- **17 October** Hundreds of Algerians killed in **Paris Massacre**
- **18 December** UN Assembly condemns **apartheid**

1962

Soviet missiles are displayed at a parade in Havana. The US came close to confrontation with the Soviet Union over the establishment of Soviet nuclear installations on Cuba.

> “WE’RE **EYEBALL TO EYEBALL** AND THE **OTHER FELLOW** JUST **BLINKED.**”

Dean Rusk, US Secretary of State, on the Cuban crisis in 1962

PRESIDENT CHARLES DE GAULLE OF FRANCE reached an agreement with Algerian nationalists in March to proceed with Algerian independence. **The Organization Armée Secrète** (OAS), a secret organization of army officers who wanted Algeria to remain a French colony, launched a wave of bomb attacks across Paris and made repeated attempts on De Gaulle’s life. **Algeria** gained **independence** from France on 3 July, after a referendum held in January backed the move. It brought an end to eight years of civil unrest and guerrilla warfare. French officials estimated it had cost 350,000 lives; Algerian sources put the figure at 1.5 million.

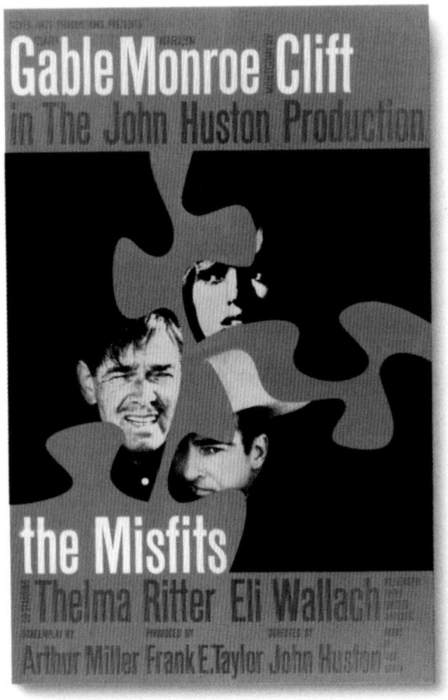

Marilyn Monroe
At the time of her death Marilyn Monroe was a huge star who had appeared in 29 movies. The Misfits was her last film.

Telstar, the world’s **first communication satellite**, was launched on 10 July from Cape Canaveral. In the early hours of 11 July, live transatlantic television pictures were sent from Maine in the US to Goonhilly in Cornwall, England.

The US was back in the news when screen idol **Marilyn Monroe**, was found dead in her Los Angeles apartment on 5 August. She was 36 years old. There was much speculation about the cause of her death; the coroner reported a “probable suicide”, but many believed she had accidentally overdosed on sleeping tablets.

Meanwhile, **Nelson Mandela** – leader of Umkhonto we Sizwe, the armed wing of the African National Congress (ANC) – was arrested on 5 August after 17 months on the run. Convicted of sabotage, he was **jailed for five years** on 7 November.

Jamaica became **independent** within the British Commonwealth on 6 August, with **Alexander Bustamante** (1884–1977) of the Jamaica Labour Party as prime minister. He would oversee several years of growth under his moderately conservative government.

The people of Berlin were not celebrating any such freedom after the construction of the **Berlin Wall** (see 1961). **Peter Fechter**, an 18-year-old German bricklayer, became one of the first victims of the Berlin Wall’s border guards after he was shot trying to cross from East to West Berlin.

In Britain, Liverpool-based rock band **The Beatles** finally signed with the record company EMI on 4 June. They had previously auditioned for several record companies, but despite the enthusiasm of their manager, Brian Epstein, they had been turned down. “**Love Me Do**”, their first single, was released on 5 October, and spent 18 weeks in the charts.

In the US, concerns were growing over the alliance of **Cuba** and the **USSR**. The installation of Soviet missiles on Cuba had reduced the warning time of a nuclear attack on the US from 15 minutes to two. In October, **President Kennedy** ordered a blockade of the island to prevent the arrival of more missiles, and delivered an ultimatum to the Russian leader, **Nikita Khrushchev**, to remove existing missiles. The world was on the brink of nuclear war, but Khrushchev finally backed down. This incident became known as the **Cuban Missile Crisis**.

India and **China** were fighting their own battle in a short but bloody **border war** over their claims to the Aksai Chin Plateau, on India’s northeast frontier. Chinese troops advanced into India on 20 October, but declared a ceasefire on 21 November.

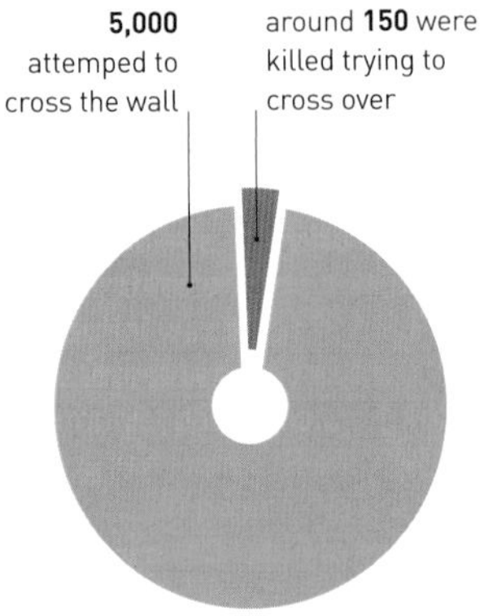

Crossing the Berlin Wall
Many people made desperate attempts to escape over the Berlin Wall from East to West Germany between 1961 and 1989.

1963

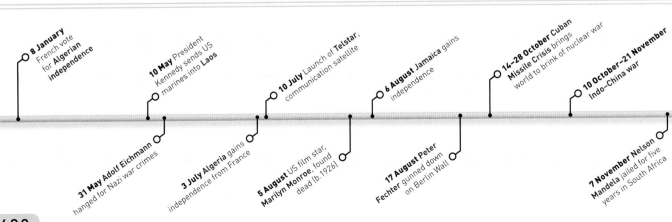

Martin Luther King Jr salutes the crowd from the Lincoln Memorial.

THE 1960S SAW THE REKINDLING of the women’s liberation movement. **Betty Friedan** (1921–2006) identified some of the frustrations felt by American housewives in her book *The Feminine Mystique*, which was published in February, and helped to start a **“second wave” of feminism** in the US.

In another display of unity, the heads of states of 32 African countries signed a charter on 25 May, setting up the **Organization of African Unity** (OAU). Their aims were to promote African solidarity, end colonialism, and to co-ordinate the economic, political, health, scientific, defence, and cultural policies of the members. The conference, hosted by **Haile Selassie** of Ethiopia, also planned to support African freedom fighters by supplying arms, training, and military bases.

Kenya, an early member of the OAU, became the 34th African nation to achieve independence. **Jomo Kenyatta** (1894–1978) was elected leader of the Kenya African National Union after nine years in prison, and won the national election in May. Kenyatta became prime minister and led Kenya from self-government to **full independence** on 12 December.

In Europe, US **president John F. Kennedy** made a morale-boosting **speech in Berlin** on 26 June. In it he offered solidarity to the citizens of West Germany, who were alarmed at the construction of the Berlin Wall. Thousands gathered in

8 January French vote for **Algerian independence**

10 May President Kennedy sends US marines into **Laos**

31 May Adolf Eichmann hanged for Nazi war crimes

3 July Algeria gains independence from France

10 July Launch of **Telstar**, communication satellite

5 August US film star, **Marilyn Monroe**, found dead (b.1926)

6 August Jamaica gains independence

17 August Peter Fechter gunned down on Berlin Wall

14–28 October Cuban Missile Crisis brings world to brink of nuclear war

10 October–21 November Indo–China war

7 November Nelson **Mandela** jailed for five years in South Africa

13 January Military coup in **Togo**

29 January Death of US poet **Robert Frost** (b.1874)

19 February Publication of Betty Friedman’s **The Feminine Mystique**

23 April Death of Israeli president **Yitzhak Ben-Zvi** (b.1884)

> **“** WE **CANNOT WALK ALONE...** WE CANNOT **TURN BACK...** I **HAVE** A **DREAM TODAY! ”**

Martin Luther King Jr
speaking at a rally in 1963

SECOND WAVE OF FEMINISM

The “first wave” of feminism addressed legal obstacles, such as votes for women, while the second focused on sexuality and family. Simone de Beauvoir’s *Le Deuxième Sexe* defined the woman’s movement and exploded the myth that women were second class citizens.

front of the Rathaus Schöneberg (City Hall) to hear him speak. In a strongly defiant message to the Soviets, Kennedy described West Berlin as a symbol of freedom. His speech dashed any hopes held by Moscow that the allies would abandon West Berlin.

Relations between East and West were still strained following the **Cuban Missile Crisis** (see 1962). The incident had raised worldwide concerns about nuclear contamination, which led to talks about a treaty to ban **nuclear testing** in the atmosphere, space, and under water. The **Test Ban Treaty** was signed in Moscow by the foreign ministers of the Soviet Union, the US, and Britain on 5 August. It was ratified by the US Senate on 24 September and came into force on 11 October.

Meanwhile, the **campaign for racial equality** in the US moved a step closer to victory on 28 August. A crowd of over 250,000 civil rights protestors gathered at the Lincoln Memorial for a mass “**March on Washington**” for jobs and freedom. Many leading figures spoke, including **Martin Luther King Jr** who famously stated “**I have a dream**”, while predicting a day when the promise of freedom and equality for all would become a reality in the US.

Another historical day for the US was 22 November, when president John F. **Kennedy was assassinated** as he travelled through Dealey Plaza, Dallas, in a open top car. Texas governor John Connally was also injured. Both of their wives, who were with them, were unharmed. Secret Service agents immediately stormed the School Book Depository building, where shots had been heard, and found a rifle with a telescopic lens. Just under an hour later, a policeman approached **Lee Harvey Oswald** and was shot dead. Oswald was arrested and charged with the murder of the policeman and Kennedy’s assassination.

Travelling back to Washington D.C. on board the presidential plane, *Air Force I*, Vice President **Lyndon B. Johnson** was sworn in as the 36th US president. Kennedy’s **funeral** took place on 25 November. The world’s reaction to the news was one of overwhelming shock.

Two days after Kennedy’s assassination, Lee Harvey Oswald, the man charged with the murder, was shot and killed. Oswald, a former marine, was being transferred from police headquarters to jail. He was surrounded by police and journalists. In the melee, **Jack Ruby**, a Dallas nightclub owner, stepped forward and shot Oswald. He later stated that he had done it “for Jackie Kennedy”. The murder was filmed and seen live on televisions across the US. Oswald had denied he was responsible for Kennedy’s death, which fuelled conspiracy theories. In an attempt to investigate the truth, the **Warren Commission** was set up on 29 November to examine the facts.

Kennedy funeral
Over one million people lined the route of Kennedy’s funeral procession, which ended at Arlington National Cemetery. Millions more watched it on TV.

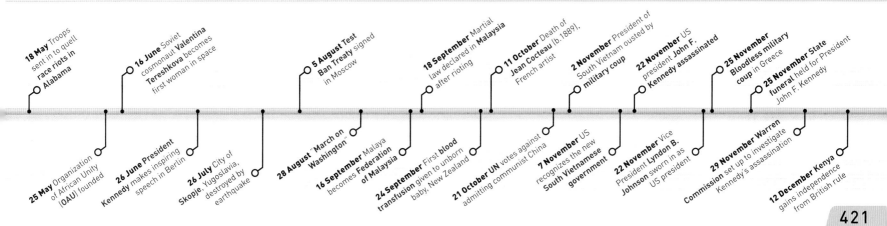

> **“** ALL **FREE MEN...** ARE **CITIZENS** OF **BERLIN. ”**

John Fitzgerald Kennedy, 26 June 1963

18 May Troops sent in to quell **race riots in Alabama**

25 May Organization of African Unity (OAU) founded

16 June Soviet cosmonaut **Valentina Tereshkova** becomes first woman in space

26 June President **Kennedy** makes inspiring speech in Berlin

26 July City of **Skopje**, Yugoslavia, destroyed by earthquake

5 August Test Ban Treaty signed in Moscow

28 August “**March on Washington**”

16 September Malaya becomes **Federation of Malaysia**

18 September Martial law declared in **Malaysia** after rioting

24 September First **blood transfusion** given to unborn baby, New Zealand

11 October Death of **Jean Cocteau** (b.1889), French artist

21 October UN votes against admitting communist China

2 November President of South Vietnam ousted by **military coup**

7 November US recognizes the new **South Vietnamese government**

22 November US president **John F. Kennedy assassinated**

22 November Vice President **Lyndon B. Johnson** sworn in as US president

25 November Bloodless military coup in Greece

25 November State funeral held for President John F. Kennedy

29 November Warren Commission set up to investigate Kennedy’s assassination

12 December Kenya gains independence from British rule

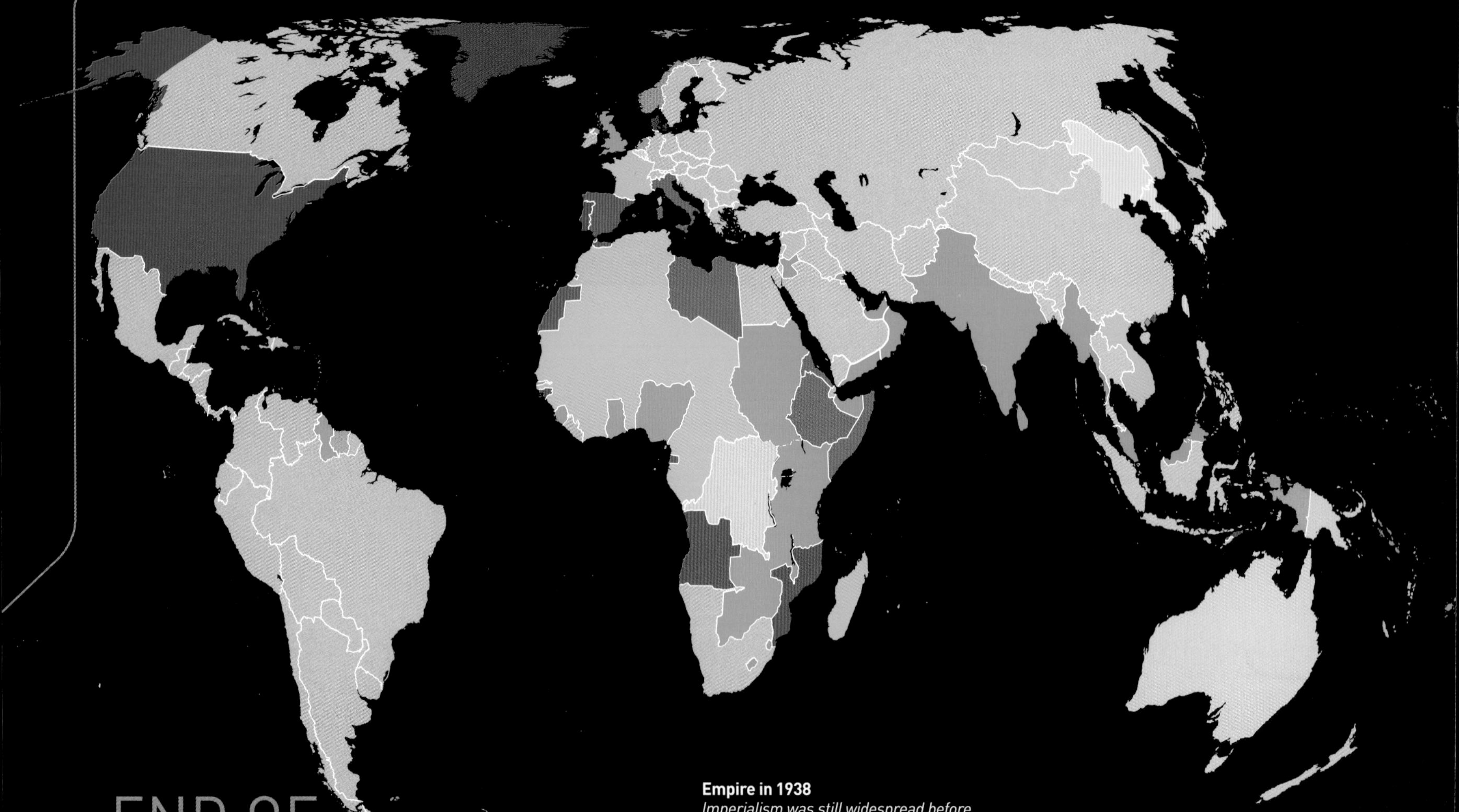

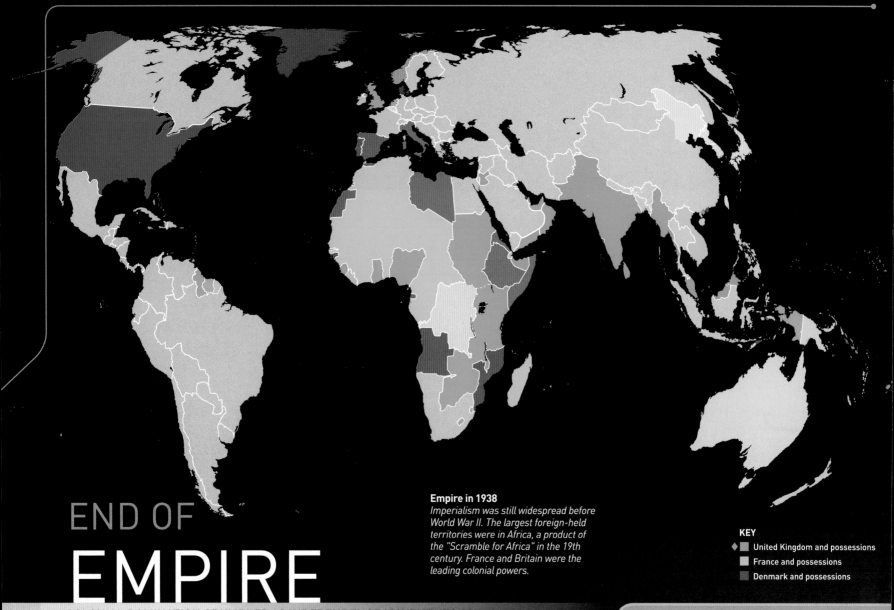

Empire in 1938
Imperialism was still widespread before World War II. The largest foreign-held territories were in Africa, a product of the "Scramble for Africa" in the 19th century. France and Britain were the leading colonial powers.

KEY
- United Kingdom and possessions
- France and possessions
- Denmark and possessions

END OF EMPIRE

COLONIAL DOMINATION CRUMBLES AS INDEPENDENCE MOVEMENTS GROW

Up until World War II, empires belonging to Britain, France, Belgium, Portugal, and the Netherlands stretched back centuries. At the end of the war the political landscape had changed significantly, and there was mounting opposition and challenge to imperial rule. In the modern world, almost all that is left of the European empires is a sprinkling of islands.

By 1945, the empires of Italy, Germany, and Japan had collapsed. The British Empire emerged from the war relatively unscathed, but it was the British who made the first move to end colonialism when they granted India independence in 1947. However, change was slow. In the mid-1950s the globe was still circled by British possessions.

Despite a widespread belief that imperialist nations had a responsibility to protect their people from communism, many were crippled by post-war austerity and, increasingly, discontent arose among their populations. Nationalist movements flourished, supported by Soviet Russia, and encouraged by the US. This clash of ideologies complicated the transition to independence; civil war often filled the vacuum.

The last fling of the imperial dice for France and Britain came with the Suez Crisis in 1956. The French were being defeated in Indochina and were engaged in a brutal civil war in Algeria, while Britain was trying to put down rebellions in Cyprus, Kenya, and Malaya. When Egyptian president Nasser nationalized the Suez Canal, it was a further blow to British imperial powers. British and French troops invaded, but suffered a humiliating climb down (see 1956). The dismantling of colonies in Africa followed: France had to give up Algeria, and Belgium the Congo. But the wealth of their past rulers was not inherited by the new nations, and many former colonies struggled with foreign intervention, corruption, and poverty.

MODERN OVERSEAS TERRITORIES

Overseas territories are countries that often have a degree of autonomy, but do not possess full political independence or sovereignty as a state. Many colonies fought for self-rule after World War II, but several of them rejected independence. Some overseas territories, for example, are too small and lack the resources to survive as viable independent countries. Others, such as French Guiana in the Caribbean, which is ruled by France, and the Falkland Islands in the South Atlantic, which are ruled by Britain, are of special strategic or economic importance to the states that control them, so are not easily relinquished.

AUSTRALIA	Ashmore and Cartier Islands
	Heard Island and the McDonald Islands
	Christmas Island
	Coral Sea Islands
	Cocos (Keeling) Islands
	Norfolk Island

Spain and possessions
Portugal and possessions
Netherlands and possessions
Norway and possessions
Belgium and possessions
Italy and possessions
Australia and possessions
US and possessions
Japan and possessions
1960 Date of independence

Modern imperialism
The world today looks very different: colonies in the West Indies, Africa, and Asia have gained independence. France is now the leading colonial power.

UNITED KINGDOM	Anguilla
	Bermuda
	British Indian Ocean Territory
	British Virgin Islands
	Cayman Islands
	Falkland Islands
	Gibraltar
	Guernsey
	Jersey
	Isle of Man
	Montserrat
	Pitcairn Islands
	Saint Helena
	South Georgia and the South Sandwich Islands
	Turks and Caicos Islands

DENMARK	Faroe Islands
	Greenland

NEW ZEALAND	Cook Islands
	Niue
	Tokelau

FRANCE	Bassas da India
	Clipperton Island
	Europa Island
	French Guiana
	French Polynesia
	French Southern and Antarctic Islands
	Glorioso Islands
	Guadelope
	Juan de Nova Island
	Martinique
	Mayotte
	New Caledonia
	Réunion
	Saint Pierre and Miquelon
	Tromelin Island
	Wallis and Futuna

THE NETHERLANDS	Aruba
	Netherlands Antilles

NORWAY	Bouvet Island
	Jan Mayen
	Svalbard

THE US	American Samoa
	Baker Island
	Guam
	Howland Island
	Jarvis Island
	Johnston Atoll
	Kingman Reef
	Midway islands
	Navassa Island
	Northern Mariana Islands
	Palmyra Atoll
	Puerto Rico
	Virgin Islands
	Wake Island

DISPUTED TERRITORIES	Antarctica
	Gaza Strip
	Parcel Islands
	Spratly Islands
	West Bank
	Western Sahara

Nelson Mandela was among eight men sentenced to life imprisonment during the Rivonia Trial – they left the court with their fists raised in defiance.

"NOTHING IS MORE IMPORTANT THAN **INDEPENDENCE** AND **FREEDOM."**

Ho Chi Minh, president of North Vietnam, on a propaganda poster during Vietnamese war

THE YEAR BEGAN WITH INCREASING TENSION between Greek and Turkish Cypriots. In March, the UN sent 7,000 troops into **Cyprus** to try to keep the peace. Strong diplomatic pressure finally brought an end to the violence on 10 August.

On 27 May, **Jawaharlal Nehru** – the first prime minister of an independent India, and regarded by many as the founder of modern India – died, aged 74. Gathering in mile-long queues, 250,000 men, women, and children filed past his body to pay their respects.

In South Africa, **Nelson Mandela**, a prominent figure of the **anti-apartheid** struggle, was jailed for life on 12 June. During the trial, Mandela and other members of the **African National Congress** (ANC, see 1994) admitted trying to bring down the government.

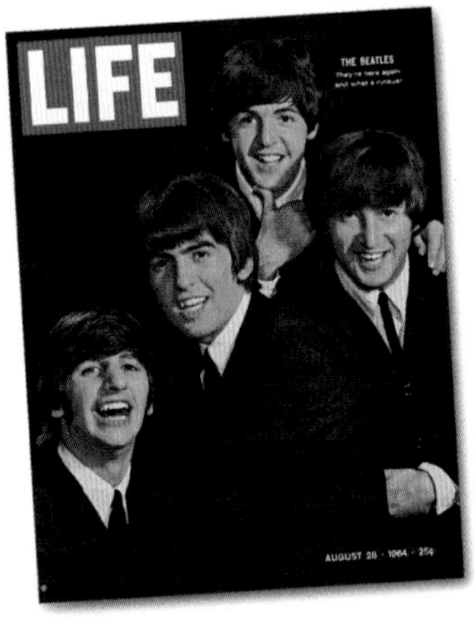

Beatlemania begins
The Beatles took the US by storm in 1964. Their faces were splashed across newspapers and magazines as their tour of 23 cities sold out.

Meanwhile, race equality in the US took a more positive turn when the **Civil Rights Bill** became law on 2 July. The bill created equal rights for all, regardless of race, religion, or colour. The signing was witnessed by civil rights campaigner **Martin Luther King Jr**, who had emerged as the symbolic leader of the worldwide struggle for civil rights. At 35, he became the youngest man to receive the **Nobel Peace Prize** for his work.

In Vietnam, the US was adamant that **South Vietnam** should not fall to the communists. On 7 August, US president Johnson received approval from Congress to **"take all necessary action"** against the communist regime in North Vietnam. As a result the war escalated, but it was largely kept from the American public, and in November Johnson won a landslide victory (see 1965).

Capturing the American public's attention, the **Warren Report**, investigating the assassination of Kennedy (see 1963) was released on 28 September. It asserted that there had been no conspiracy, and concluded that gunman Lee Harvey Oswald had acted alone.

In the East, Nikita **Khrushchev**, leader of the Soviet Union, "retired" in October, having been in power since 1958. His policies had become increasingly unpopular and he was voted out of office.

The Beatles made it big this year, sparking a hysteria known as "Beatlemania". Appearing on US TV in February, by April their singles occupied all top five spots on the *Billboard* Hot 100 chart.

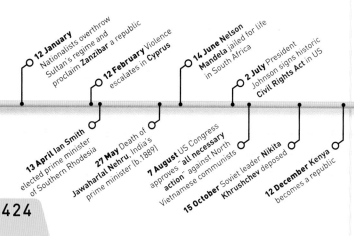

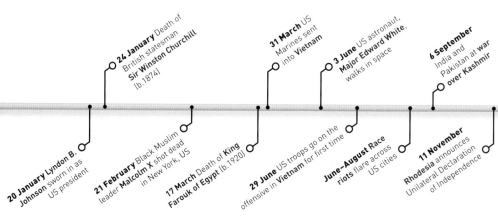

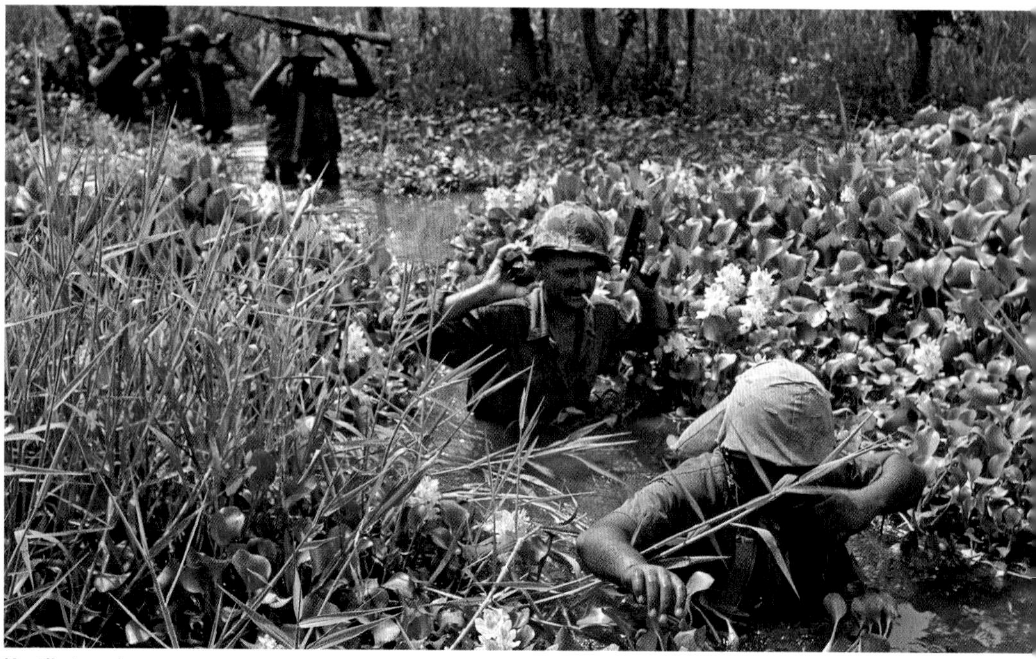

Hostile terrain
The US army was technologically superior in Vietnam, but struggled with unfamiliar territory such as the swamp that these marines are wading through.

ON 18 FEBRUARY, THE GAMBIA ACHIEVED INDEPENDENCE from British rule. Dawda Kairaba Jawara became the first prime minister, and was knighted the following year. By contrast, **Southern Rhodesia**, led by prime minister Ian Smith, announced a **Unilateral Declaration of Independence** on 11 November. Britain declared this action illegal, and through the UN most countries applied **economic sanctions** against Southern Rhodesia.

In **Vietnam**, the conflict was escalating. President Johnson ordered Operation Rolling Thunder, a massive **bombing campaign against North Vietnam**, and in March the first American ground troops landed in South Vietnam. By June they were fighting alongside South Vietnamese forces against the **Viet Cong**.

Back in the US, racial tension was at boiling point. Following the arrest of a black man for drink driving, Watts, a suburb of Los Angeles, erupted into violent **race riots**. Some blamed the heat wave, while others pointed the finger at police brutality.

In September **India** launched an **invasion of West Pakistan**, following covert operations by Pakistan across the ceasefire line. Since the ceasefire line had been established in 1949, both countries had laid claim to **Kashmir**. After three weeks of fighting, they agreed to a **UN ceasefire**.

President **Sukarno** of **Indonesia** barely survived an attempted coup in November. **General Suharto**, commander of the army's strategic reserve, emerged the victor in the power struggle.

Meanwhile, the lights went out in the US on 9 November during the biggest **blackout** in US history. More than 30 million people in the northwest were left without electricity, which was caused by human error.

12 January Nationalists overthrow Sultan's regime and proclaim **Zanzibar** a republic

12 February Violence escalates in **Cyprus**

13 April Ian Smith elected prime minister of Southern Rhodesia

27 May Death of **Jawaharlal Nehru**, India's prime minister (b.1889)

14 June Nelson Mandela jailed for life in South Africa

2 July President Johnson signs historic **Civil Rights Act** in US

7 August US Congress approves **"all necessary action"** against North Vietnamese communists

15 October Soviet leader **Nikita Khrushchev** deposed

12 December Kenya becomes a republic

20 January Lyndon B. Johnson sworn in as US president

24 January Death of British statesman **Sir Winston Churchill** (b.1874)

21 February Black Muslim leader **Malcolm X** shot dead in New York, US

17 March Death of **King Farouk of Egypt** (b.1920)

31 March US Marines sent into **Vietnam**

3 June US astronaut, **Major Edward White**, walks in space

29 June US troops go on the offensive in **Vietnam** for first time

June–August Race riots flare across US cities

6 September India and Pakistan at **war over Kashmir**

11 November Rhodesia announces Unilateral Declaration of Independence

1966

The Black Panthers, a black nationalist group based in Oakland, California, argued for working class unity. Here supporters hold up copies of Mao Zedong's *Little Red Book*.

WITH INCREASED FIGHTING IN VIETNAM, 1966 SAW THE US launch its **largest offensive** against the Viet Cong in Operation Crimp, to capture the Viet Cong's Saigon area headquarters. By the end of 1966, the number of US troops in Vietnam had reached 385,000, amid **increased public protests** about the war.

Pakistani and **Indian** leaders met more peacefully in January at Tashkent in Uzbekistan to sign a declaration agreeing to resolve their dispute (see 1965) by **peaceful means**. Shortly afterwards, Lal Bahadur Ahastri, prime minister of India, died of a heart attack. He was succeeded by Indira Gandhi, daughter of Nehru.

In **Northern Ireland**, violence erupted following the 50th anniversaries of the Battle of the Somme and the Easter Rising – symbolic dates for Protestants and Catholics respectively. The murder of two Catholics by a "loyalist" terror group called the **Ulster Volunteer Force** (UVF) sparked more riots in May and June. The UVF was banned, but the cycle of sectarian killings, known as **the Troubles**, had begun.

The shock assassination of **Hendrik Verwoerd**, prime minister of South Africa and the architect of apartheid, raised queries about the future of South Africa. He was stabbed to death on 6 September by Dimitri Tsafendas, who claimed not enough was being done for whites.

Race continued to be a dominant issue in the US, with **race riots** occurring in many cities throughout the mid-1960s. Student radicals were becoming impatient with Martin Luther King's strategy of non-violence, and in June, activist Stokely Carmichael popularized the term "**Black Power**". In October he formed the **Black Panther Party**, combining traditional civil rights slogans with Marxist rhetoric, and the language of black separatism.

State of play in Vietnam
This map shows North and South Vietnam in 1964, divided by a demilitarized zone. In 1966 the North Vietnamese crossed the zone and one of the largest battles to date broke out near Dong Ha.

The Little Red Book
Full of Mao's quotations, this book added to his cult and had a profound impact on the masses during the Chinese Cultural Revolution.

In August, Chinese communist leader Mao Zedong launched the **Cultural Revolution**, aiming to purge the country of "impure" elements. One-and-a-half million people died and much of the country's cultural heritage was destroyed. In September 1967, with many Chinese cities on the verge of anarchy, Mao sent in the army to restore order.

By the end of 1966, the decade known as the "**Swinging Sixties**" – so called because of the collapse of social taboos relating to race, sex, and gender – was in full flow. It was epitomized by rock music, photography, and fashion, with London and youth culture at its heart.

1967

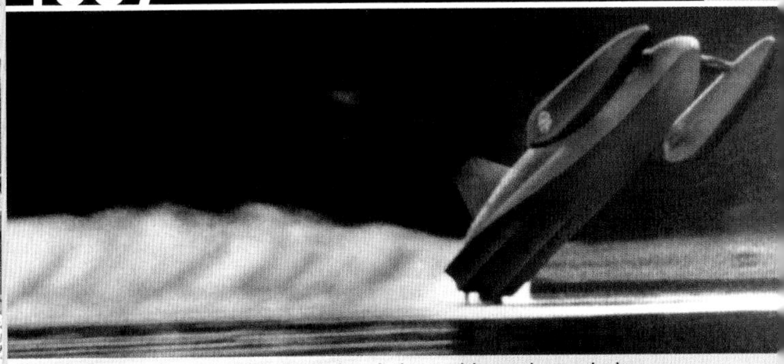

Donald Campbell was attempting to break the world speed record when his speedboat *Bluebird* crashed, killing him instantly.

THE YEAR BEGAN WITH THE TRAGIC DEATH OF DONALD CAMPBELL, who was killed on 4 January at Coniston Water in the Lake District, England, while attempting to break his own **water speed record**. He was travelling at more than 480kph (300mph) when his boat flipped.

Tensions were running high in the Middle East after Egypt asked for UN forces in the Sinai to be removed. The Israelis responded with a **pre-emptive attack**, which ended after six days with Israel in control of Sinai, Gaza, the West Bank, the Golan Heights, and Jerusalem.

Meanwhile, in Bolivia, **Ernesto "Che" Guevara** (see panel, right) was captured and shot dead, on the Bolivian president's orders, on 9 June. Guevara was in Latin America helping guerrilla groups.

More interested in saving lives, South African surgeon Christiaan Barnard conducted the **first heart transplant** on 3 December. Although the patient died later of pneumonia, the procedure was a great step forward for medicine.

In Europe, Nicolae **Ceausescu** became premier of **Romania** on 9 December, defying the Soviets by establishing diplomatic relations with Germany.

In **Greece**, after army officers seized power on 21 April, a counter coup by King Constantine II failed, and he fled to Rome.

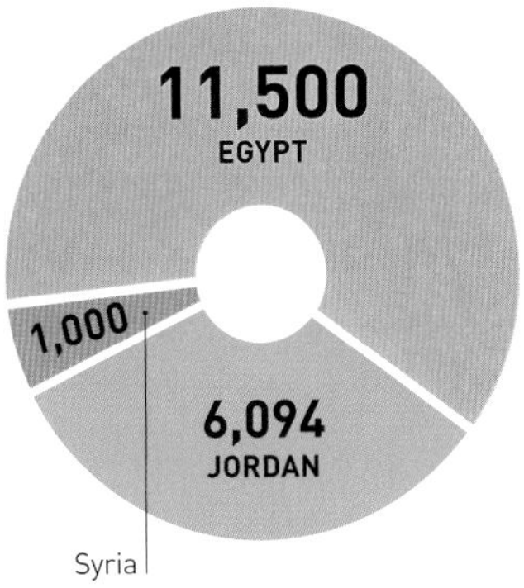

Casualties in the Six-Day War
Israel won a decisive victory in the Six-Day War between Israel, Egypt, Jordan, and Syria, with 759 casualties. Arab losses, in contrast, were high.

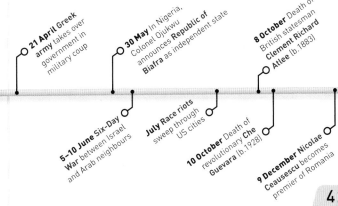

CHE GUEVARA (1928–67)

Ernesto "Che" Guevara was born in Argentina in 1928, and became involved in the opposition to Juan Peron. He travelled extensively through Latin America, where he saw poverty and social injustice that helped forge his radical political views. Che became an associate of Fidel Castro, and played a role in the fight for Cuba. He left Cuba to help revolutionaries abroad, and was executed in Bolivia.

- **10 January** Agreement signed between **India and Pakistan**
- **11 January** Death of Swiss sculptor **Alberto Giacometti** (b.1901)
- **16 January** Nigerian government overthrown in military coup led by **Major Chukwuma Nzugwa**
- **19 January Indira Gandhi** becomes Indian prime minister
- **11 August Malaysia and Indonesia** end three years of bush warfare
- **13 August** Chairman Mao announces a **Cultural Revolution** across China
- **6 September** South African prime minister **Dr Hendrik Verwoerd** assassinated (b.1901)
- **15 October Black Panther movement** formed in Oakland, California, US
- **1 November** Viet Cong shell Saigon
- **8 November Ronald Reagan** elected as governor of California
- **30 November** Barbados gains independence from Britain
- **15 December** Death of US animator **Walt Disney** (b.1901)
- **21 April Greek army** takes over government in military coup
- **30 May** In Nigeria, Colonel Ojukwu announces **Republic of Biafra** as independent state
- **5–10 June Six-Day War** between Israel and Arab neighbours
- **July Race riots** sweep through US cities
- **8 October** Death of British statesman **Clement Richard Atlee** (b.1883)
- **10 October** Death of revolutionary **Che Guevara** (b.1928)
- **9 December Nicolae Ceausescu** becomes premier of Romania

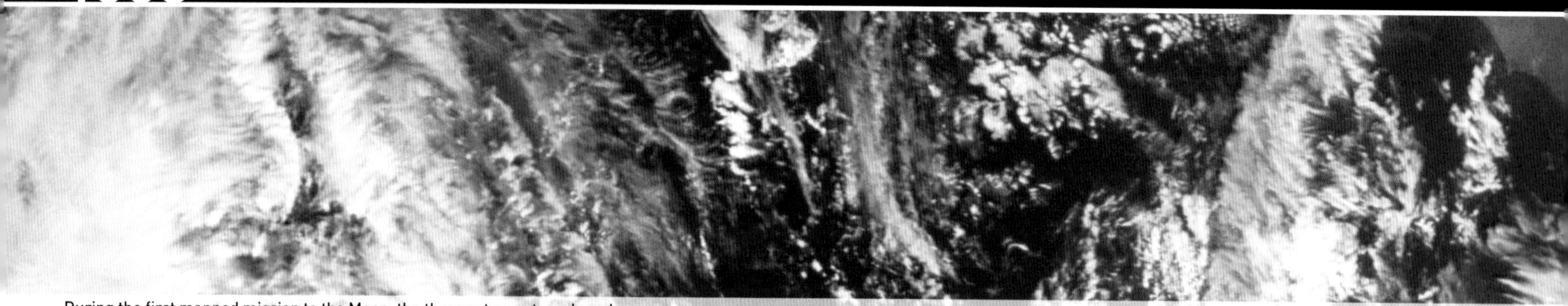

During the first manned mission to the Moon, the three astronauts on board Apollo 8 beamed back images of Earth as a planet in space.

THE MY LAI MASSACRE IN VIETNAM SENT SHOCK WAVES through the US political establishment. My Lai lies in the South Vietnamese district of Son My, an area where the **Viet Cong** were deeply entrenched. On 16 March, **US troops**, who had been on a "search and destroy" mission to root out communist fighters, **killed more than 500 Vietnamese civilians** in cold blood, many of them women and children. The massacre helped to **turn public opinion** against the Vietnam War, although the story was not made public until the following year.

By 1968, the Vietnam War was costing the US $66 million a day. **Protests against the war escalated** as people questioned the US's role in the conflict. Vivid news reports showed horrific civilian casualties. On 28 August, during the Democratic national convention in Chicago, **10,000 antiwar protesters gathered** and were confronted by 26,000 police and national guardsmen. The event was covered live on network TV.

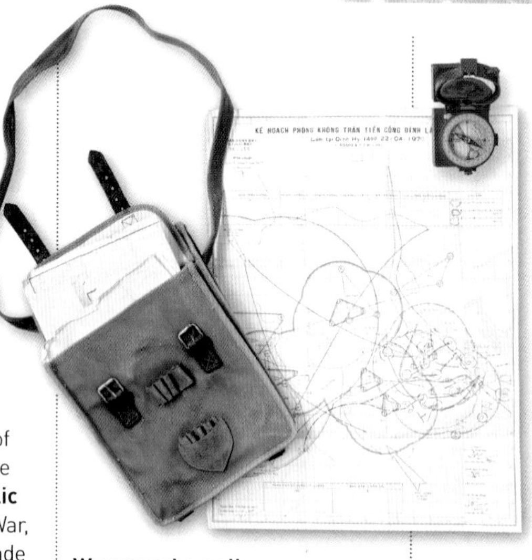

War paraphernalia
A Chinese compass, a map case, and a map with enemy bases marked on, formed the basic kit for Vietcong militia during the Vietnam War.

On 4 April, the African-American civil rights leader **Martin Luther King Jr** (see panel, right) was assassinated in the southern US city of Memphis, Tennessee. King was shot on the balcony of his hotel as he was preparing to lead a march of sanitation workers **protesting against low wages**. The day before his assassination, he delivered his famous speech, "I have seen the mountain top ..." in Memphis, which seemed to predict his end, "... **I've seen the promised land**. I may not get there with you".

King's death sparked **widespread race riots** across the US that cost dozens of lives and led to damage worth millions of dollars. It hastened the process of "**white flight**" from the inner cities that left many American downtowns virtually abandoned. **James Earl Ray**, a petty criminal, was convicted of King's murder and sentenced to 99 years in prison.

Senator Robert Kennedy (1925–68), increasingly opposed to the Vietnam War, struggled over his decision to challenge the Democratic party's incumbent president, **Lyndon Johnson**. His younger brother, Edward (Teddy), was against it; his wife, Ethel, urged him on. Many feared he would suffer the same fate as his brother John, who had been assassinated in 1963. He **announced his candidacy** on 16 March, and two weeks later Johnson dropped out of the race. America was a wounded nation, reeling from the war and inner-city riots. Kennedy based his presidential election campaign on **inequality and social justice**.

On 5 June, **Robert Kennedy was shot** in a Los Angeles hotel after giving a victory speech to celebrate his win in the California Primary. A **Palestinian immigrant**, **Sirhan Sirhan**, fired at Kennedy as he was being escorted through the kitchen pantry of the Ambassador Hotel. Robert Kennedy's **support for Israel** was believed to have prompted the attack. He died the following day. His death, coming 63 days after that of Martin Luther King Jr, made 1968 one of the most **volatile and traumatic**, years in US history.

On 6 November, Republican **Richard Nixon** (1913–94) emerged victorious in the US **presidential election**. He had based his campaign on rising crime and claimed he would restore law and order. It was a dramatic comeback; Nixon was Dwight D. Eisenhower's vice-president and lost the presidential race to John F. Kennedy in 1960.

Enoch Powell (1912–98), a British right-wing politician, made a hugely **controversial speech** on 20 April, in which he warned the government against opening the "floodgates" to **black immigrants**. He called for an immediate reduction in immigration, and viewed the future with foreboding. Quoting the Roman poet Virgil, he said, "... like the Roman, I seem to see the river Tiber foaming with much blood". His speech caused a **storm of protest**, and ended Powell's political ambitions.

Elsewhere in Europe, **France** experienced student **riots**, mass **protests**, and **strikes** throughout May, which brought the country

200,000

THE NUMBER OF WARSAW PACT TROOPS THAT **INVADED CZECHOSLOVAKIA**

MARTIN LUTHER KING JR (1929–68)

A leading African-American civil rights campaigner in the US, Martin Luther King Jr rose to prominence in 1955, when he led a boycott of buses in Montgomery, Alabama, in protest against the state's transport segregation laws. In this, and his subsequent campaigns, he insisted on non-violence. King was awarded the Nobel Peace Prize in 1964. Four years later, he was assassinated by a white gunman in Memphis, Tennessee.

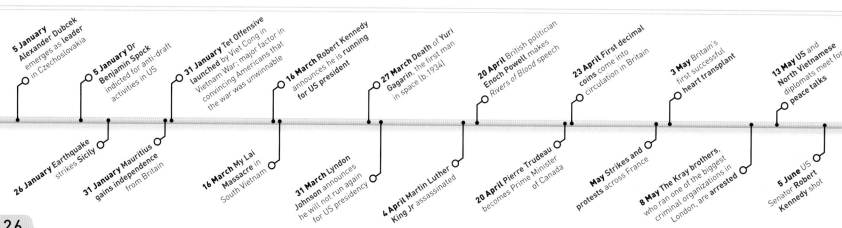

PHOTO

5 January Alexander Dubcek emerges as leader in Czechoslovakia

5 January Dr Benjamin Spock indicted for anti-draft activities in US

26 January Earthquake strikes Sicily

31 January Tet Offensive launched by Viet Cong in Vietnam War; major factor in convincing Americans that the war was unwinnable

31 January Mauritius gains independence from Britain

16 March Robert Kennedy announces he is **running for US president**

16 March My Lai Massacre in South Vietnam

27 March Death of **Yuri Gagarin**, the first man in space (b.1934)

31 March Lyndon Johnson announces he will not run again for US presidency

4 April Martin Luther King Jr assassinated

20 April British politician **Enoch Powell** makes *Rivers of Blood* speech

20 April Pierre Trudeau becomes Prime Minister of Canada

23 April First decimal coins come into circulation in Britain

May Strikes and protests across France

3 May Britain's first successful **heart transplant**

8 May The Kray brothers, who ran one of the biggest criminal organizations in London, are **arrested**

13 May US and **North Vietnamese** diplomats meet for **peace talks**

5 June US Senator **Robert Kennedy** shot

“THANK YOU **APOLLO 8.** **YOU SAVED 1968.**”

Anonymous telegram received by Frank Borman, after the success of the Apollo 8 mission

to its knees. It began as a series of student protests that broke out at universities in Paris, following confrontations with administrators and police. Further police action inflamed the situation, leading to a **general strike** by over 10 million workers across France – roughly two-thirds of the workforce. The government came close to collapse; President Charles de Gaulle (1890–1970) called for new parliamentary elections on 23 June. Although De Gaulle won the election, the Paris riots were regarded as a **cultural and social revolution**.

Troops from five **Warsaw Pact countries** (see 1955) stormed into **Czechoslovakia** on 20 August to seize control and restore communism to the country. During an eight-month period that became known as the **Prague Spring**, the incumbent prime minister Alexander Dubcek had made **substantial reforms**, including freedom of speech. He was arrested, and his government replaced with a **repressive regime** (see 1989). The invasion drew condemnation from around the world. Jan Palach, a Czech student, **burned himself to death** in protest over the Soviet occupation. An estimated 500,000 gathered to watch his funeral procession.

On 7 September, a prominent gathering of women disrupted the staging of **Miss America**, a long-standing **beauty pageant** held at Atlantic City's convention hall. The protest was organized by the **New York Radical Women** (NYRW), a group active in the civil rights and antiwar movements. They attacked the pageant's beauty standards as racist – no black woman had ever made it to the final. The demonstrators brandished signs that read "**Women's Liberation**", and threw bras into bins as a sign of protest, which began the myth that feminists "burn their bras".

Americans, finally, had cause to rejoice at the end of the year when **Apollo 8**, the first manned craft to **orbit the moon**, was launched into space on 21 December. Live pictures of the lunar surface were beamed back to Earth. The crew, Frank Borman, James Lovell, and William Anders, returned on 27 December as **national heroes**.

150 WOMEN PROTESTERS

52 BEAUTY CONTESTANTS

Beauty and backlash
The glamorous contestants appearing in the Miss America Pageant, in Atlanta, were outnumbered three to one by the protestors.

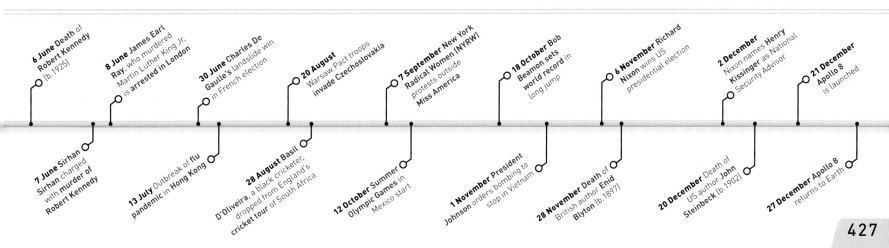

Protest in Paris
When French strikers took to the streets in May, the country was on the verge of revolution. The largest rallies were held in Paris.

6 June Death of **Robert Kennedy** (b.1925)

7 June Sirhan Sirhan charged with **murder of Robert Kennedy**

8 June James Earl Ray, who murdered Martin Luther King Jr, is **arrested in London**

13 July Outbreak of **flu pandemic** in **Hong Kong**

30 June Charles De Gaulle's landslide win in French election

20 August Warsaw Pact troops **invade Czechoslovakia**

28 August Basil D'Oliveira, a black cricketer, dropped from England's **cricket tour** of South Africa

7 September New York Radical Women (NYRW) protests outside **Miss America**

12 October Summer **Olympic Games** in Mexico start

18 October Bob Beamon sets **world record** in long jump

1 November President Johnson orders bombing to stop in Vietnam

6 November Richard **Nixon** wins US presidential election

28 November Death of British author **Enid Blyton** (b.1897)

2 December Nixon names **Henry Kissinger** as National Security Advisor

20 December Death of US author **John Steinbeck** (b.1902)

21 December **Apollo 8** is launched

27 December **Apollo 8** returns to Earth

THE STORY OF GENETICS

THE SEARCH FOR THE BLUEPRINT OF LIFE AND THE MECHANISM OF HEREDITY

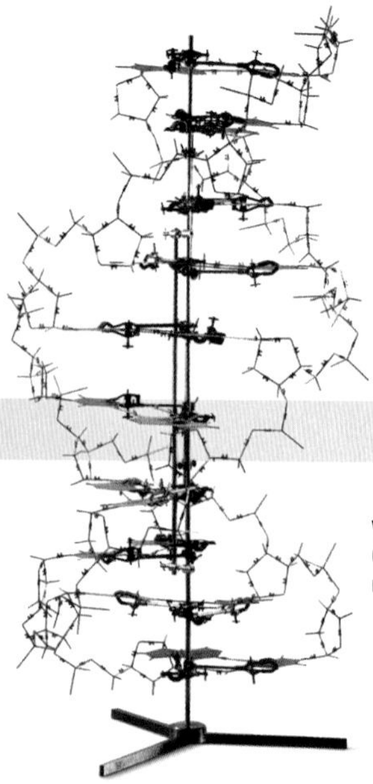

Watson and Crick's DNA model

For thousands of years, humans have wondered how characteristics are inherited, but it was not until the 19th century that scientists began to understand the fundamental mechanisms. Now, the knowledge that DNA carries genetic information has provided insight into the basis of life itself.

One of the earliest theories of heredity was that of the ancient Greek Hippocrates, who proposed that elements from all of the body became concentrated in semen, which then made a human in the womb containing the characteristics of both parents. Charles Darwin later called this mechanism of inheritance "pangenesis".

It was not until the 19th century that the basic rules of heredity were discovered, by the Austrian monk Gregor Mendel. At about the same time, the Swiss scientist Friedrich Miescher extracted from the cell nucleus a substance he called "nuclein" (now known as DNA). In the early 20th century, American biologist Thomas Hunt Morgan's experiments with fruit flies confirmed that genes reside on chromosomes. However, it was still thought that protein, not DNA, was the substance that transmits inherited traits.

THE SIGNIFICANCE OF DNA

In the 1940s, Oswald Avery, Colin MacLeod, and Maclyn McCarty discovered that DNA is the hereditary molecule in most organisms and is the chemical basis of genetic information. In the early 1950s, Maurice Wilkins and Rosalind Franklin discovered that DNA has a helix shape, and in 1953, these findings were put together by Francis Crick and James Watson in their double-helix model of DNA. The Human Genome Project went further, mapping all the human genes.

GENETIC CODE

A gene is a portion of DNA containing information for making a specific protein (comprising a specific sequence of amino acids). This is encoded as an "alphabet" of bases: A (standing for adenine), C (cytosine), G (guanine), and T (thymine). These are arranged into "words" (codons) of three letters; each codon corresponds to a particular amino acid. In a cell, a gene's codon sequence is translated into a sequence of specific amino acids, making the specific protein coded for by that gene.

> “**YOU,** YOUR JOYS AND YOUR SORROWS, YOUR MEMORIES AND AMBITIONS, YOUR SENSE OF PERSONAL IDENTITY AND FREE WILL, **ARE … NO MORE THAN THE BEHAVIOUR OF… NERVE CELLS AND … MOLECULES.**”

Francis Crick, *The Astonishing Hypothesis: The Scientific Search for the Soul,* 1994

c.460–375 BCE
Hippocrates' pangenesis hypothesis
Hippocrates devises the theory that hereditary material collects from throughout the body and reassembles inside the womb to form human life.

Hypocrates

1663–65
Cells first described
English scientist Robert Hooke coins the term "cell" to describe the microscopic units he observed while examining a section of cork with an early compound microscope.

Robert Hooke's microscope

1859
Theory of natural selection
Charles Darwin publishes *The Origin of Species,* in which he puts forward his theory that the fittest organisms survive and pass on their traits.

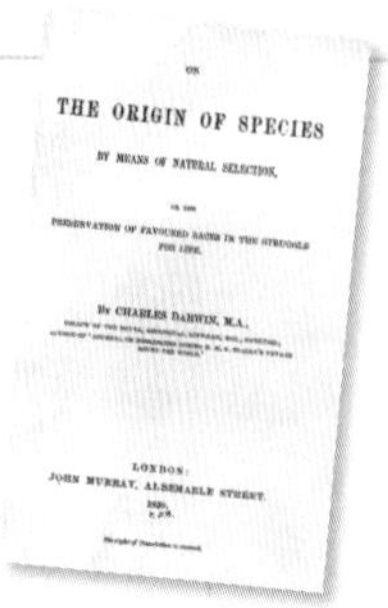

THE ORIGIN OF SPECIES

The Origin of Species

1863
Gregor Mendel
Experimenting with peas, Austrian monk Gregor Mendel finds that traits, such as whether peas are round or wrinkled, are passed on by independent units, later called genes.

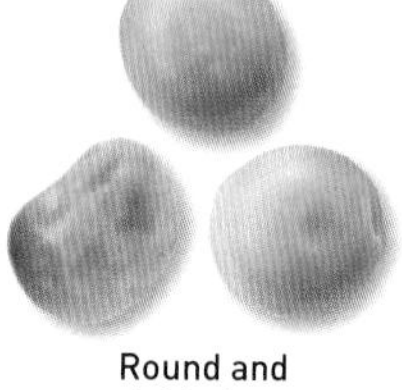

Round and wrinkled peas

c.1868–69
Nuclein discovered
Swiss scientist Friedrich Miescher discovers a substance he calls "nuclein" in the nuclei of white blood cells. Later called nucleic acid, nuclein is now known as DNA.

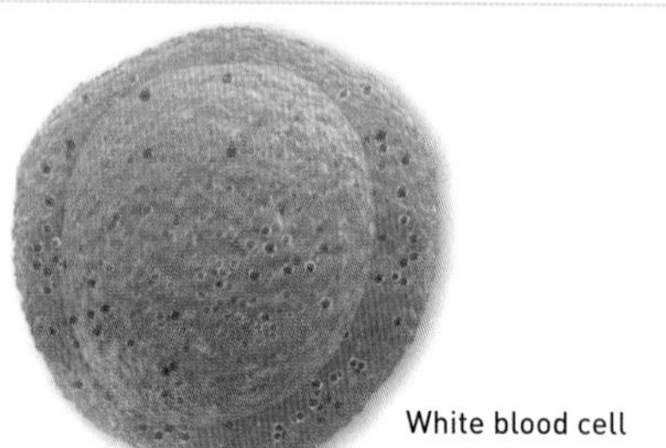

White blood cell

1880s
Meiosis discovered
Meiosis, the process of cell division that produces gametes (sex cells), is described in the early 1880s. Its significance for inheritance is elucidated in the 1890s by German biologist August Weismann.

1888
Chromosomes discovered
German anatomist Heinrich Waldeyer notices that the central part of the cell (the nucleus) sometimes contains thread-like bodies, for which he coins the term "chromosomes".

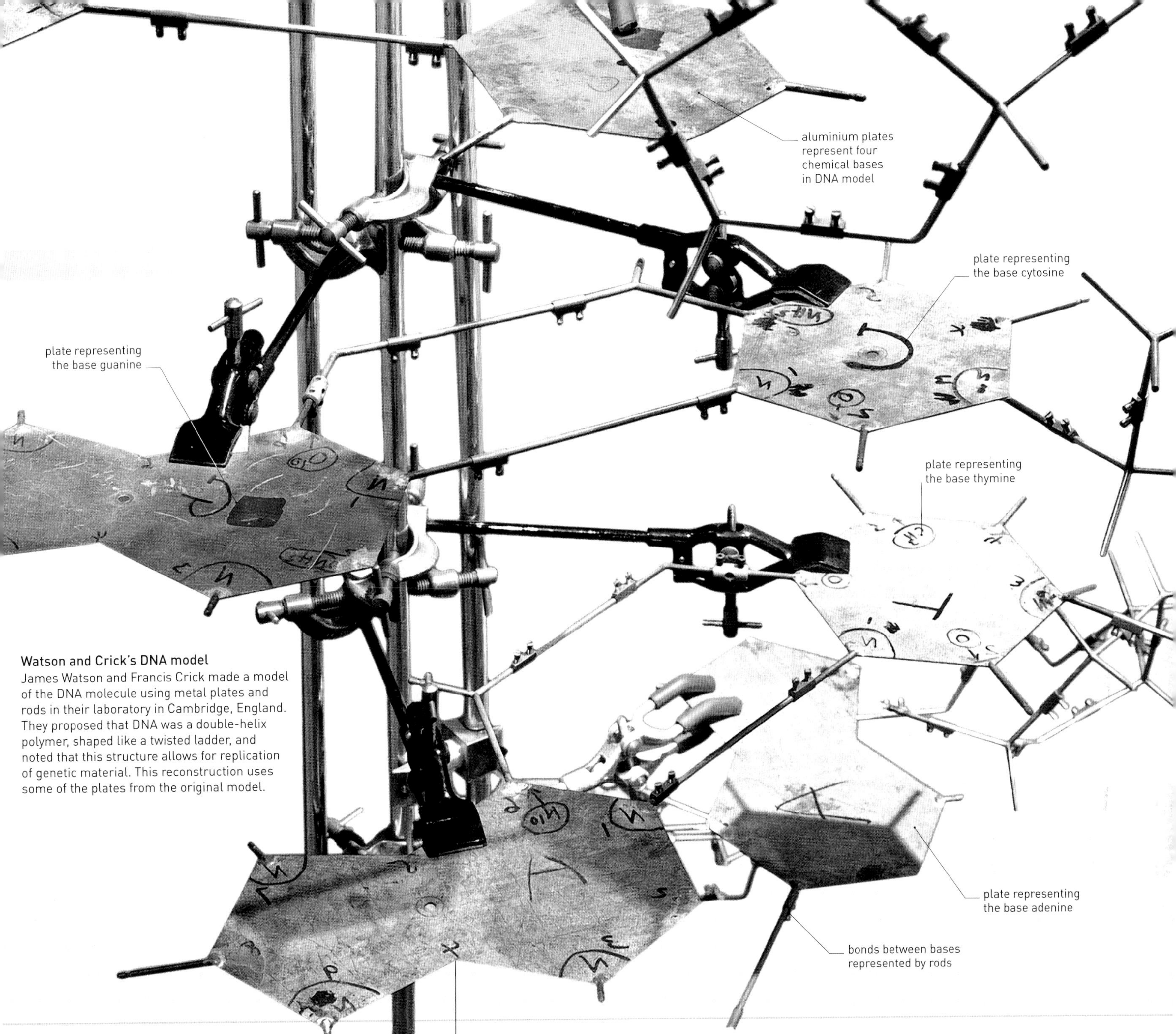

Watson and Crick's DNA model
James Watson and Francis Crick made a model of the DNA molecule using metal plates and rods in their laboratory in Cambridge, England. They proposed that DNA was a double-helix polymer, shaped like a twisted ladder, and noted that this structure allows for replication of genetic material. This reconstruction uses some of the plates from the original model.

1905
Sex chromosomes identified
American geneticists Nettie Stevens and E.B. Wilson independently identify the XY chromosome sex-determination system: males have XY and females have XX sex chromosomes.

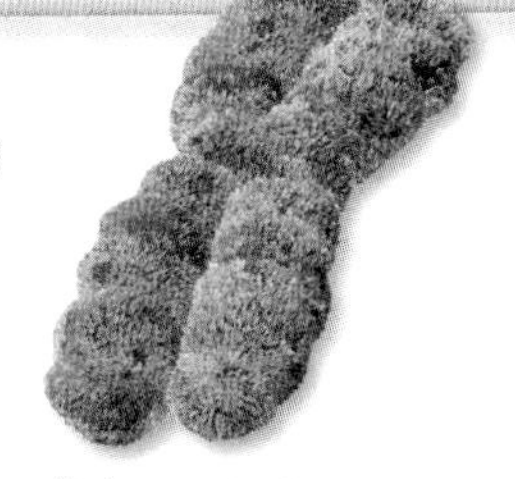
X chromosome

Early 20th century
Role of chromosomes in heredity
Working with fruit flies, American geneticist Thomas Hunt Morgan establishes that genes controlling heredity are positioned along chromosomes, and links the inheritance of a specific trait with a particular chromosome.

1940–44
DNA identified as genetic messenger
Using *Streptococcus pneumoniae* bacteria, American scientists Oswald Avery, Colin MacLeod, and Maclyn McCarty discover that DNA is the hereditary material in most living organisms.

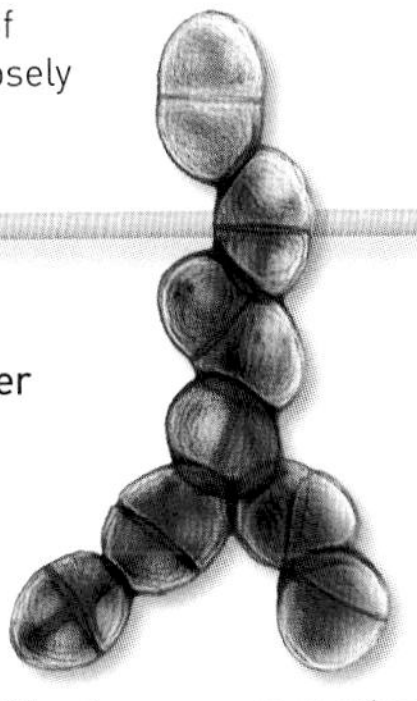
Streptococcus pneumoniae

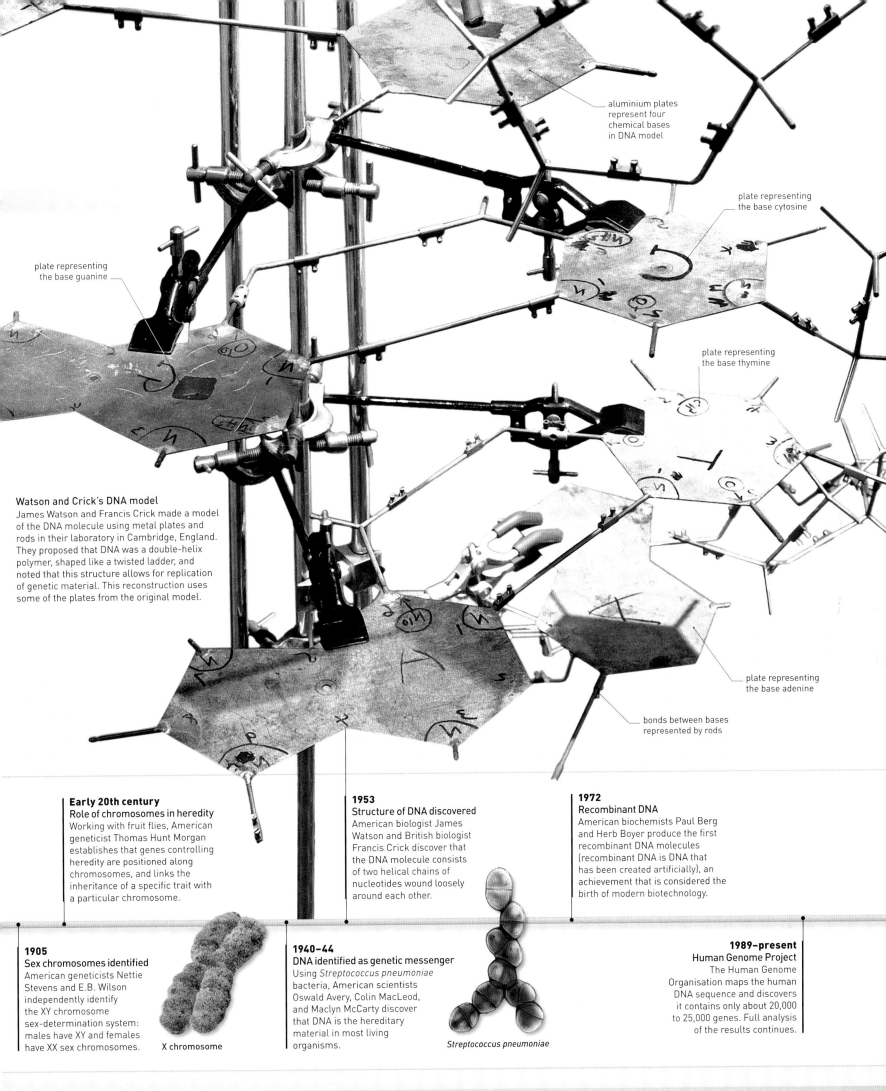

1953
Structure of DNA discovered
American biologist James Watson and British biologist Francis Crick discover that the DNA molecule consists of two helical chains of nucleotides wound loosely around each other.

1972
Recombinant DNA
American biochemists Paul Berg and Herb Boyer produce the first recombinant DNA molecules (recombinant DNA is DNA that has been created artificially), an achievement that is considered the birth of modern biotechnology.

1989–present
Human Genome Project
The Human Genome Organisation maps the human DNA sequence and discovers it contains only about 20,000 to 25,000 genes. Full analysis of the results continues.

1969

2 January **Violence flares** on the streets of **Londonderry**, Northern Ireland

3 February Yasser Arafat (1929–2004) becomes leader of the **Palestine Liberation Organization (PLO)**

13 February Human **egg fertilized** in test tube for the first time by Robert Edwards

March 2 Anglo-French **Concorde** makes **maiden flight**

10 March James **Earl Ray** pleads guilty to the murder of **Martin Luther King** and is jailed for life

17 March Golda Meir (1898–1978) becomes premier of Israel

19 March British troops invade island of **Anguilla** in the Caribbean

28 March Death of US Commander and former president **General Dwight Eisenhower** (b.1890)

28 April Charles De Gaulle (1890–1970) resigns as President of France

May 1 Major **James Dawson Chichester-Clark** becomes new prime minister of Northern Ireland

8 June Spain closes its land border with **Gibraltar** (to 1985)

30 June Nigeria bans relief aid to Biafra during civil war

1 July Prince Charles invested as **Prince of Wales**

“THAT’S **ONE SMALL STEP** FOR [A] **MAN, ONE GIANT LEAP** FOR **MANKIND.**”

Neil Armstrong, on first setting foot on the Moon, on 21 July 1969

This photograph shows hijacked planes that were set on fire by Palestinian militants belonging to Popular Front for the Liberation of Palestine (PFLP).

YASSER ARAFAT (1929–2004), A PALESTINIAN FREEDOM FIGHTER, became the leader of the **Palestine Liberation Organization (PLO)** in February. He had formed the radical group **Al-Fatah** in the late 1950s, which was merged with the Popular Front for the Liberation of Palestine (PFLP) to form the PLO.

In Libya, **Mu’ammar al-Gaddafi** (b.1940) led a group of army officers to depose King Idris (1890–1983) on 1 September, in a bloodless coup, and established the **Libyan Arab Republic**.

Nigeria banned food aid from the Red Cross to the breakaway state of **Biafra**, bringing millions of people to the brink of **starvation**. Biafra accused Nigeria of using starvation and genocide to win the civil war (1967–70), and pleaded for help from the world.

On 14 August, **Britain sent troops into Northern Ireland** following three days of violence in the predominantly Catholic bogside area of **Londonderry**. Although intended to be a brief intervention, the troops remained after the **violence intensified**.

Willy Brandt (1913–92) was sworn in as the **Chancellor of West Germany** on 21 October, becoming the first Socialist politician to lead a German government since 1930.

***Eagle* returns**
Apollo 11's lunar module Eagle, *holding astronauts Neil Armstrong and Buzz Aldrin, makes its way back to the command module.*

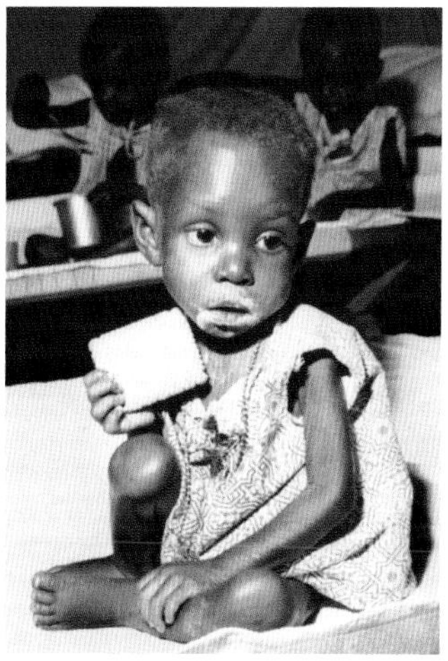

Biafra starves
A child suffers the effects of hunger and malnutrition during the Biafran blockade. Pictures of the famine garnered worldwide sympathy.

Concorde, the supersonic airliner, made its **maiden flight** in March. Piloted by Andre Turcot, the Anglo-French plane took off from **Toulouse** in France; it reached 3,050m (10,000ft), and was in the air for 27 minutes.

Elsewhere in Europe, Beatle **John Lennon** (1940–80) and his wife **Yoko Ono** spent **two weeks in bed**, drawing the world’s attention to peace. They spent the first week at the Hilton Amsterdam, in March, and the second at the Queen Elizabeth Hotel in Montreal, where the song *Give Peace a Chance* was recorded, in May.

Large-scale **music festivals** were held in Europe and the US during a summer that epitomized the **hippie movement**. The British band The Rolling Stones played a free concert at Hyde Park, London; the American musician, Bob Dylan (b.1941), performed the headline act at the **Isle of Wight Festival**, England; and up to 400,000 turned up at **Woodstock**, New York.

Millions marched across the US on 15 October to protest against the **Vietnam War**. In Washington DC, 250,000 people gathered to participate in **anti-war rallies** and hear activists speak.

On 21 July, **Neil Armstrong** (b.1930) and **Edwin Aldrin** (b.1930) took man’s **first steps on the moon** from their spacecraft *Apollo 11*. Millions watched this televised event that represented a **symbolic victory** for the US over the USSR during the Cold War.

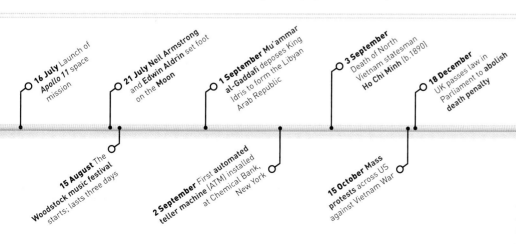

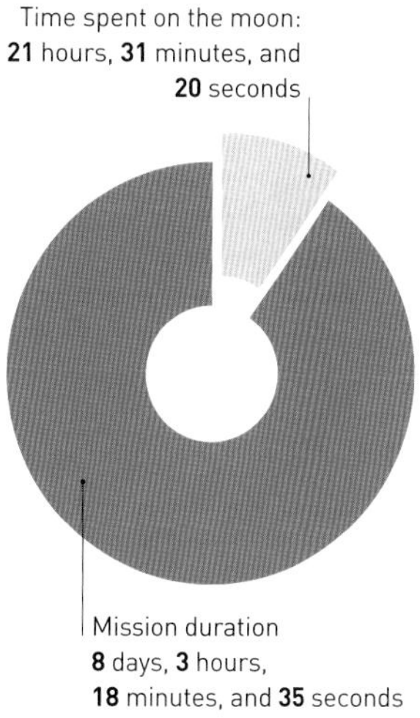

The lunar mission
The prime mission objective of Apollo 11 *was stated simply as: “perform a manned lunar landing and return”.*

IN CAMBODIA, THE HEAD OF STATE, PRINCE NORODOM SIHANOUK (b.1922) was overthrown by **General Lon Nol** in a **coup**, on 18 March. Lon Nol claimed to have support from the US. In April, **President Richard Nixon** (1913–94) ordered US troops and B-52 bombers into **Cambodia** to destroy North Vietnamese and Vietcong sanctuaries and supplies.

In early September, **Palestinian militants** forced two planes to fly to the Jordanian desert, where the hijackers **blew up the aircraft** after releasing most of the hostages. A third plane was flown to **Cairo** and was also blown up. After 24 days of talks, the remaining **hostages were freed** in exchange for seven Palestinian prisoners. On 16 September, fighting broke out between Jordanian troops and PLO guerrillas. Egyptian President **Gamal Abdel Nasser** (b.1918) **brokered a settlement** on 27 September. However, **Nasser died** of a heart attack a day later. He had become the most powerful figure in the Middle East while **attempting to unify Arab nations.**

A **catastrophic cyclone** hit East Pakistan (modern Bangladesh) on 12 November. The **Bhola Cyclone** was the **deadliest ever recorded**, with up to 500,000 casualties. Alleging neglect and lack of help from West Pakistan, the Bengalis went on to vote for Sheikh Mujibur Rahman’s **Awami League**, which demanded autonomy from West Pakistan in the following elections (see 1971).

Elections were held in Chile on 4 September, and **Salvador Allende’s Marxist coalition** was elected. Allende instituted a programme of sweeping **nationalization and reforms**.

In April, the German pharmaceutical company **Grünenthal** pledged to pay DM 100 million to **thalidomide victims**. Thalidomide, a drug given to pregnant women for nausea, was withdrawn in 1961 after nearly 10,000 babies were born with **major disabilities**.

Charles De Gaulle (b.1890), who led the French resistance to the Nazi occupation during World War II and became the President of liberated France, **died** on 9 November. His funeral was held on Armistice Day, 11 November.

The Beatles, the most famous music band in the world, split when Paul McCartney (b.1942) announced his decision to leave in April. The **group officially disbanded** on 31 December.

500 **THOUSAND** THE NUMBER **KILLED** IN THE **CYCLONE** IN **BANGLADESH**

16 July Launch of *Apollo 11* space mission

15 August The **Woodstock music festival** starts; lasts three days

21 July Neil Armstrong and **Edwin Aldrin** set foot on the **Moon**

2 September First **automated teller machine** (ATM) installed at Chemical Bank, New York

1 September Mu’ammar al-Gaddafi deposes King Idris to form the Libyan Arab Republic

3 September Death of North Vietnam statesman **Ho Chi Minh** (b.1890)

15 October Mass protests across US against Vietnam War

18 December UK passes law in Parliament to **abolish death penalty**

12 January Civil war between **Nigeria and Biafra ends**

2 March Rhodesia (modern Zimbabwe) **becomes a republic**

23 January First **Boeing 747** arrives at Heathrow airport, London

19 June Edward Heath becomes prime minister of Britain

30 April US sends troops to **Cambodia**

28 September Death of **Egyptian president Nasser** (b.1889)

27 July Death of former Portugese leader **Antonio Salazar** (b.1889)

November 9 Death of General Charles De Gaulle (b.1890)

19 October Major oil find in the North Sea

December Anti-government **riots rock Poland**

1971

1972

“ I AM **NOT** A **POLITICIAN,** BUT A **SOLDIER.** ”

Idi Amin, in his first speech to the Ugandan nation, January 1971

British troops remove civil rights protestors from Londonderry, Northern Ireland, after the army opened fire on demonstrators during “Bloody Sunday”. Among the 13 civilians killed were seven teenagers.

IN UGANDA, GENERAL IDI AMIN SEIZED POWER from President Milton Obote in a **military coup** on 25 January, while the president was out of the country attending the Commonwealth conference in Singapore (see 1979).

Sierra Leone, in West Africa, and **Qatar**, in the Middle East, formally achieved independence from Britain in this year.

In March, a **civil war** broke out between **Pakistan** and its dominion, **East Pakistan** (modern Bangladesh). Nearly nine million **refugees** fled to India. In December, Indian troops entered East Pakistan, following a **surprise attack on Indian airfields**. There was also heavy fighting in **Kashmir**. In a campaign lasting only 13 days, Indian troops crushed Pakistani forces in the east. On 20 December, the independent state of **Bangladesh** was born (see 1972).

In **Northern Ireland**, the **Provisional IRA** stepped up its campaign against British security forces (see 1969). In August, the Northern Ireland government introduced **internment without trial** to stop the growing violence.

On 15 September, a small team of activists set sail from Vancouver, Canada, on the ship *Phyllis Cormack* to protest against US nuclear tests in **Alaska**. They later adopted the name **Greenpeace**.

The **Walt Disney World** resort officially opened near Orlando in Florida, USA, on 1 October. It featured Adventureland, Fantasyland, Frontierland, Liberty Square, and Tomorrowland.

IDI AMIN (1925–2003)

Idi Amin became known as the “Butcher of Uganda”. After seizing power in 1971, he ruled by terror – an estimated 300,000 people died during his reign. His behaviour was both barbaric and eccentric: famously, he declared himself the “King of Scotland”. Idi Amin’s rule ended in 1979 after he was ousted by troops from neighbouring Tanzania then forced to flee the country.

On 25 October, **China’s admission to the UN** boosted the country’s international status. The US president, Richard Nixon (1913–94), sent his national security adviser, **Henry Kissinger** (b.1923), to China for secret talks. Kissinger also began talks with the **USSR** which led to a number of formal agreements, including one regarding **access to Berlin**.

BRITISH MINERS WALKED OUT ON NATIONAL STRIKE on 9 January after refusing a government pay offer. All 289 pits across the country were closed. On 19 February, they agreed to a **new pay deal** and returned to work on 25 February.

On 30 January, British troops opened fire on demonstrators in **Londonderry**, Northern Ireland, **killing 13 people** and injuring 14. The marchers were protesting against the policy of internment without trial. This day came to be known as “**Bloody Sunday**”.

In the largest attack on mainland Britain since “**The Troubles**” (see 1966), the **IRA** bombed the 16th Parachute Brigade headquarters at Aldershot, Hampshire, on 22 February, killing seven civilians.

President Nixon flew to China in February and met **Mao Zedong** (1893–1976), marking a new **cordiality in US–China relations**. In May, Nixon paid a state visit to **Moscow** to sign 10 agreements, the most important of which were the nuclear arms limitation treaties known as SALT I.

On 8 June, South Vietnamese planes dropped a **napalm bomb** on **Trang Bang**, which was under North Vietnamese occupation. Napalm was an incendiary liquid that burned everything it touched. Images of **burned civilians** were shown around the world and increased pressure on the US to withdraw from Vietnam.

The prime ministers of India and Pakistan, **Indira Gandhi** (1917–84) and **Zulfikar Ali Bhutto** (1954–79), signed the **Simla Agreement** in July, in the wake of the 1971 war. The agreement reiterated the promises for peaceful negotiations made in **Tashkent** (see 1966).

The terrorist group **Black September**, a faction of the Palestine Liberation Organization (PLO), took members of the **Israeli team** hostage during the **Summer Olympics** at Munich, West Germany. They later **killed 11 athletes**, launching a new era of international terrorism.

New horizons

For the Munich Olympics, leading artists made 35 posters, including the one shown below. Their aim was to erase the memory of the 1936 games, held during Hitler’s reign.

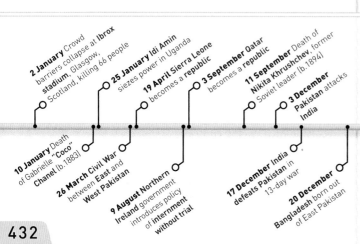

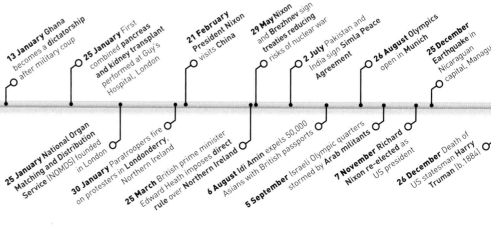

- **2 January** Crowd barriers collapse at **Ibrox stadium**, Glasgow, Scotland, killing 66 people
- **10 January** Death of Gabrielle **“Coco” Chanel** (b.1883)
- **25 January Idi Amin** siezes power in Uganda
- **26 March Civil War** between **East** and **West Pakistan**
- **19 April Sierra Leone** becomes a **republic**
- **9 August Northern Ireland** government introduces policy of **internment without trial**
- **3 September Qatar** becomes a **republic**
- **11 September** Death of **Nikita Khrushchev**, former Soviet leader (b.1894)
- **3 December Pakistan** attacks **India**
- **17 December India** defeats **Pakistan** in 13-day war
- **20 December Bangladesh** born out of East Pakistan
- **13 January** Ghana becomes a **dictatorship** after military coup
- **25 January** First combined **pancreas and kidney transplant** performed at Guy’s Hospital, London
- **25 January National Organ Matching and Distribution Service** (NOMDS) founded in London
- **30 January** Paratroopers fire on protesters in **Londonderry**, Northern Ireland
- **21 February President Nixon** visits **China**
- **25 March** British prime minister Edward Heath imposes **direct rule** over **Northern Ireland**
- **29 May Nixon** and **Brezhnev** sign **treaties reducing** risks of nuclear war
- **2 July** Pakistan and India sign **Simla Peace Agreement**
- **6 August Idi Amin** expels 50,000 Asians with British passports
- **26 August Olympics** open in **Munich**
- **5 September** Israeli Olympic quarters stormed by **Arab militants**
- **7 November Richard Nixon re-elected** as US president
- **25 December Earthquake** in Nicaraguan capital, Managua
- **26 December** Death of US statesman **Harry Truman** (b.1884)

“ THERE WILL BE NO WHITEWASH AT THE WHITE HOUSE. ”

Richard Nixon, US president, in a TV speech on Watergate, 30 April 1973

The White House, the official residence of the US President, was rocked by the Watergate scandal and the subsequent resignation of President Nixon.

ON 30 JANUARY, SEVEN MEN WERE CONVICTED of breaking into the Democratic Party's **Watergate** headquarters in Washington DC and **bugging** it. **President Nixon**, who had just been re-elected, continually denied any connection between Watergate and the **White House**. However, *Washington Post* reporters, **Bob Woodward** and **Carl Bernstein**, brought to light the president's involvement in the bugging, which would eventually lead to his **impeachment** and **resignation** from office (see 1974). Their work on the "**Watergate scandal**", helped by crucial information from the mysterious informant, "Deep Throat", led to the *Washington Post* being awarded the **Pulitzer Prize**.

Allende's reforms
The Chilean president's sweeping nationalization and reforms resulted in costly welfare schemes and economic chaos in the country.

In a landmark judgement referred to as the **Roe v. Wade** case, the supreme court **legalized abortions** in the US. The ruling came after Norma McCorvey, under the pseudonym "Jane Roe", challenged the criminal abortion laws in Texas.

The **Vietnam war** was officially over for the US, when it signed a **ceasefire agreement** in January after months of talks in Paris.

Britain, **Ireland**, and **Denmark** became fully-fledged members of the **European Economic Community** (EEC) in January, bringing the number of member states to nine. It was the first enlargement of the organization since its inception in 1957.

The **IRA** extended its **bombing campaign** in mainland Britain. On 8 September, there were bombs in Manchester city centre and at Victoria station, London. Two days later, explosions ripped through King's Cross and Euston stations. On 14 November, an IRA gang was **convicted of the bombings**.

In September, Chilean president **Salvador Allende** (1908–73) was killed in a coup led by his trusted ally **General Augusto Pinochet** (1915–2006), and backed by the **US**. Pinochet killed 3,000 supporters of the Allende regime, **shut the Chilean Parliament**, and banned all political activity. In 1974, he made himself president (see 1998).

In December, the Basque separatist movement, **ETA**, killed Spanish prime minister Admiral **Luis Carrero Blanco** in Madrid, in retaliation for the execution of Basque militants (see 1959).

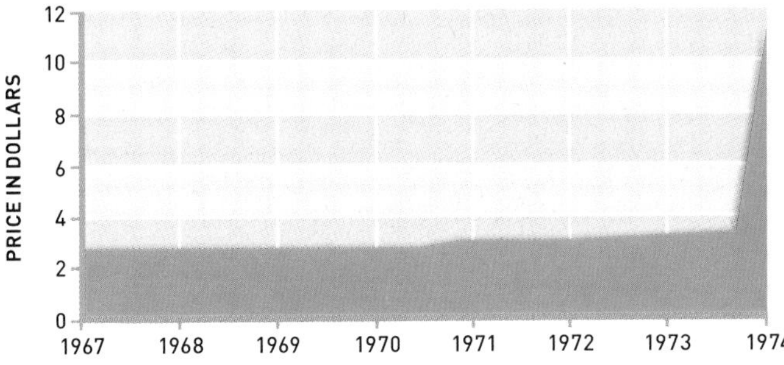

Costing dear
When OPEC shut off oil supplies to the western nations that had supported Israel, it sent prices shooting up from less than $3 a barrel to $11 in a matter of weeks.

Heavy fighting broke out between **Arab and Israeli forces** in what came to be known as the **Yom Kippur War**, in October. Egyptian forces broke the Israeli line on the eastern bank of the Suez Canal, and in the north, Syrian troops battled with Israeli defences along the **Golan Heights**, seized by Israel from Syria in 1967. A peace deal, signed on 11 November between Egypt and Israel, ended the strife. Following the war, the Arab oil-producing countries imposed an **oil embargo** on all the countries that had supported Israel. In October, **oil prices soared** around the world, from under $3 a barrel before the war to over $11 by early 1974.

THE POLITICS OF OIL

The Arab oil embargo caused global chaos. The Organisation of Petroleum Exporting Countries (OPEC) switched off supply at a time when the market was already starting to suffer shortages. The crisis revealed oil as a powerful political weapon. Countries in the Middle East were seen to have acquired control of a vital commodity, and Western nations were vulnerable because they relied on oil imports.

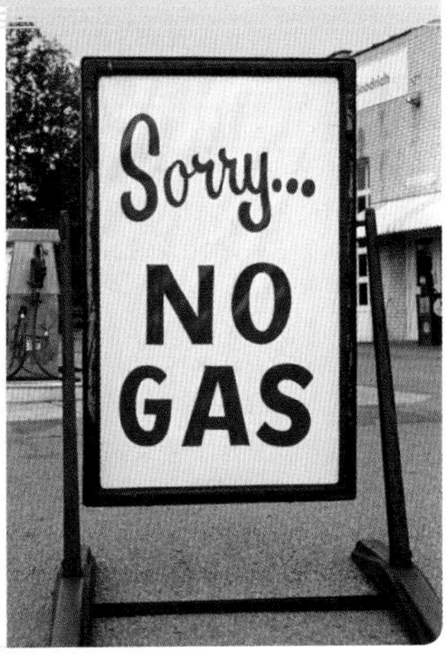

1974

Emperor of Ethiopia, Haile Selassie, had been crowned "King of Kings".

THE OIL EMBARGO OF 1973 HAD A DRASTIC EFFECT on the developed world, leading to a long-term recession. Unemployment and inflation soared, and **stock markets crashed** globally.

In Portugal, **General Antonio de Spinola** (1910–96) led a bloodless military coup, ending 50 years of dictatorship. Known as the **Carnation Revolution**, this event ushered in a new era of democracy in the country.

In Britain, the **IRA** attacked the Houses of Parliament on 17 June, the Tower of London in July, and a Guildford pub in October.

In July, **Turkish troops** invaded northern **Cyprus** following a coup in which **President Archbishop Makarios**, a Greek Cypriot, was deposed. The island was split in two parts, with Greek-Cypriots fleeing to the south and the Turkish community, to the north.

After years of war and famine in Ethiopia, **Emperor Haile Selassie** (1892–1975) was overthrown in a coup, on 12 September. General **Tafari Benti** (1921–77) became head of state.

In the US, the **Watergate** break-in (see 1973) was traced to a Nixon support group. In July, the Supreme Court ordered Nixon to turn over the **tape recordings** relating to the scandal. He was impeached, and **resigned from office** in August.

Disco, a genre of dance music that had started in the clubs of New York in the late 1960s, peaked at this time with new music, polyester suits, and films such as ***Saturday Night Fever***.

1 January Britain, Denmark, and Norway join **EEC**

22 January Former US President **Lyndon Johnson** dies (b.1908)

22 January Abortion becomes legal in US

23 January Ceasefire agreed in **Vietnam**

24 February Israel **shoots down** Libyan **passenger plane**

3 March IRA bombs central London

7 March Sheikh Mujibur Rahman is first prime minister of Bangladesh

26 March British playwright **Noel Coward** dies (b.1899)

29 March Last **US troops** leave **Vietnam**

April 4 World Trade Centre, world's tallest building, is built

8 April Death of artist **Pablo Picasso** (b.1881)

14 May *Skylab*, first US Space Station, is **launched**

17 May US Senate hears **Watergate** case

10 July Bahamas gains independence from Britain

11 September Chilean president, **Salvador Allende** assassinated (b.1908)

28 September Sydney Opera House opens in Australia

6 October Yom Kippur War begins

16 October OPEC declares **oil embargo** on Western nations

25 November Greek army seizes power in Athens

20 December Spanish prime minister **Blanco assassinated**

8 February Raymond Damadian develops **Magnetic Resonance Imaging** (MRI) in the US

2 April Death of **Georges Pompidou**, the president of France (b.1911)

20 July Turkey invades Northern **Cyprus**

8 August President **Nixon resigns** after Watergate scandal

1975 | 1976 | 1977

“VIETNAM WAS LOST IN THE LIVING ROOMS OF AMERICA, NOT ON THE BATTLEFIELDS OF VIETNAM.”

Marshall McLuhan, media commentator, writing at the end of the Vietnam War

Two punks kiss on the Kings Road in London. Punk rock emerged during the mid-70's as an angry expression of contempt for politics and society.

MARGARET THATCHER BECAME THE FIRST WOMAN to lead a political party in Britain on 11 February, when she won the Conservative Party vote.

In the Middle East, Saudi Arabia's **King Faisal** (1906–75) was **assassinated** by his nephew, Prince Faisal Ibu Musaed.

Prince Juan Carlos was sworn in as King of Spain, two days after dictator General Francisco Franco died on 20 November.

In April, the Cambodian capital, **Phnom Penh**, fell to the radical communist movement, the **Khmer Rouge**, led by **Pol Pot**. They transformed Cambodia into a communist, rural society. All inhabitants of cities were expelled to work in agricultural communes.

After almost two decades of fighting, the **Vietnam War** finally ended on 30 April as the government in Saigon surrendered to the **North Vietnam** forces. Saigon was renamed **Ho Chi Minh City** and the following year, North and South Vietnam were reunified.

Fall of Saigon
The North Vietnam troops (pictured) met little resistance in Saigon, but the final hours of America's presence were marked by chaos.

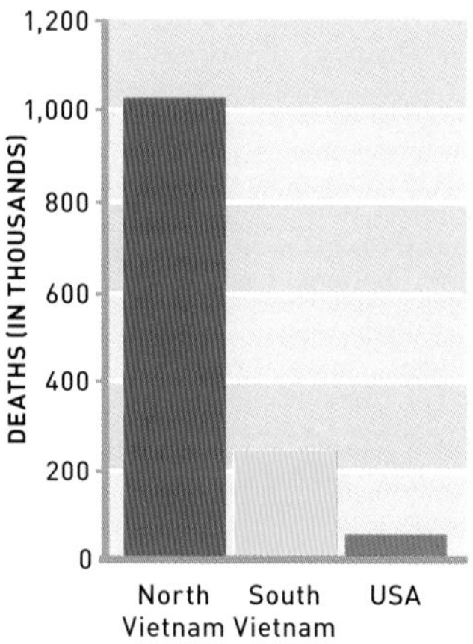

Vietnamese war casualties
More than one million North Vietnamese troops died, compared to around 220,000 from South Vietnam, and 58,000 from the US.

Mozambique became **independent** on 25 June, after a coup in Portugal ended colonial rule (see 1974). Four months later, **Angola** also gained its independence (see 1976).

Iraq stepped up its military pressure against **Kurdish rebels** in northern Iraq. The **Kurds** were **crushed** with the razing of Zakho and Qala Diza.

In **Lebanon**, Christian militia attacked a bus full of Palestinians in Beirut. This started a **civil war** that lasted for 15 years (see 1990).

This was a year of global terrorism, as **Arab terrorists** held **hostages** at Orly airport in Paris; a German left-wing group seized the **German Embassy** in Stockholm, Sweden; and South Moluccan terrorists took over the **Indonesian Embassy** in Amsterdam, the Netherlands.

In November, **oil** began to flow from the **North Sea** from sources that British Petroleum (BP) discovered six years earlier.

Microsoft was officially founded on 4 April by **Bill Gates** (b.1955) and **Paul Allen** (b.1953), starting the world of personal computing.

US Purple Heart
A US military decoration awarded to the wounded or killed, 351,794 Purple Hearts were awarded during the Vietnam War.

THE MARXIST PEOPLE'S MOVEMENT FOR THE LIBERATION OF ANGOLA (MPLA) took nominal control of the whole country by February, and the new **Angola People's Republic** was recognized. This was preceded by intense fighting that also involved the National Front for the Liberation of Angola (FNLA) and the Union for the Total Independence of Angola (UNITA).

Anti-apartheid protests in Soweto, **South Africa** turned violent on 16 June. Demonstrators clashed with police and more than 300 people were killed.

40–70 MILLION
THE NUMBER OF DEATHS CAUSED BY MAO'S REGIME

Mao Zedong (b.1893), the founder of the People's Republic of China, died of a heart attack on 9 September.

Syrian peacekeeping troops entered **Lebanon** on 9 June. In December, after more than 50 ceasefires had been violated, uneasy peace prevailed.

The **Seychelles gained independence** from Britain on 29 June, with James Mancham as president and France Rene as prime minister of the coalition.

THE ARCHBISHOP OF UGANDA, DR JANANI LUWUM (b.1922), was murdered on 16 February for being an Anglican, and for protesting against the excesses of **Idi Amin's regime** (see 1971).

Steven Biko (see panel, right), a prominent black rights leader in South Africa, **died in prison** on 12 September. He had been detained under the terrorism act. His death caused **international outrage** but an inquest cleared the police of any wrong doing.

In Pakistan, Zulfiqar Ali Bhutto's **Pakistan People's Party** (PPP) was accused of **vote rigging**. This prompted Army Chief General Mohammed Zia ul-Haq to depose Bhutto in a **military coup** on 4 July.

The right-wing **Menachem Begin** (1913–92) had a surprise win at the Israeli elections in May, ending 29 years of Labour rule. As premier, he initiated a **peace process** with Egypt (see 1979).

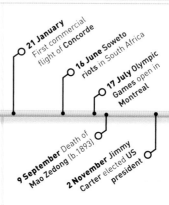

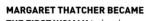

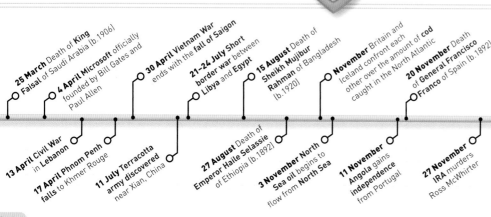

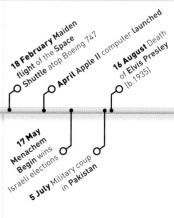

Fruit of knowledge
Apple Inc. computers went on sale this year. The distinctive logo – a rainbow-coloured apple with a bite taken out – symbolized knowledge.

25 March Death of **King Faisal** of Saudi Arabia (b.1906)

4 April Microsoft officially founded by Bill Gates and Paul Allen

13 April Civil War in **Lebanon**

17 April Phnom Penh falls to Khmer Rouge

30 April Vietnam War ends with the **fall of Saigon**

11 July Terracotta army discovered near Xian, China

21–24 July Short border war between **Libya** and **Egypt**

15 August Death of **Sheikh Mujibur Rahman** of Bangladesh (b.1920)

27 August Death of **Emperor Haile Selassie** of Ethiopia (b.1892)

November Britain and Iceland confront each other over the amount of **cod** caught in the North Atlantic

3 November North Sea oil begins to flow from **North Sea**

11 November Angola gains **independence** from Portugal

20 November Death of **General Francisco Franco** of Spain (b.1892)

27 November IRA murders Ross McWhirter

21 January First commercial flight of **Concorde**

16 June Soweto riots in South Africa

17 July Olympic Games open in **Montreal**

9 September Death of **Mao Zedong** (b.1893)

2 November Jimmy Carter elected **US president**

18 February Maiden flight of the **Space Shuttle** atop Boeing 747

April Apple II computer **launched**

17 May Menachem Begin wins Israeli elections

5 July Military coup in **Pakistan**

16 August Death of **Elvis Presley** (b.1935)

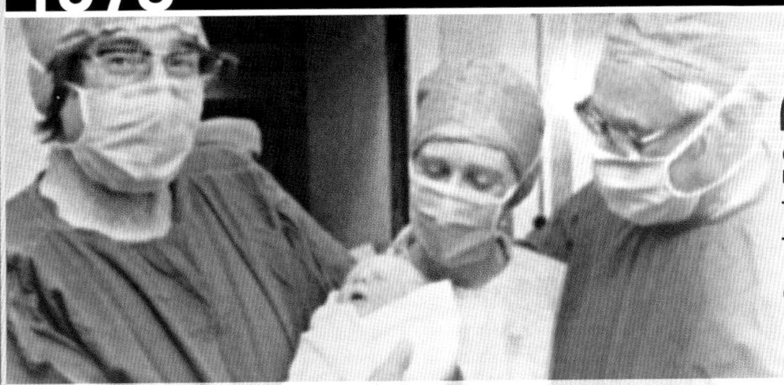

Dr Robert Edwards holds the world's first test tube baby, Louise Brown. It was a medical breakthrough fraught with controversy.

> **" ALL EXAMINATIONS** SHOWED THAT THE **BABY** IS **QUITE NORMAL. "**
>
> **Obstetrician Patrick Steptoe**, after the birth of Louise Brown

STEVEN BIKO (1946–77)

In 1968, Steve Biko was the first president and co-founder of the all-black South African Students' Organization (SASO), which aimed to raise black consciousness. The government banned him in 1973, but he continued to spread his word. On 18 August 1977, the police seized Biko, held him for 24 days, and tortured him to death. The *Rand Daily Mail* exposed their brutality.

Amnesty International, the human rights organization, won the **Nobel Peace Prize** for having "contributed to securing the ground for freedom, for justice, and thereby also for peace in the world". The movement proclaimed 1977 "**Prisoners of Conscience Year**". The following year Amnesty also received the United Nations Human Rights Award.

ISRAELI SOLDIERS CROSSED THE LEBANESE BORDER on 14 March, in Operation Litani. Thousands of **Palestinians fled** the area and hundreds died. Israel claimed Palestinian fighters were using southern Lebanon to mount attacks against civilian and military targets in Israel.

Demonstrators on the streets of **Tehran**, capital of Iran, had been shouting dissent all year, but in September, **protests grew** against the policies of Iran's supreme ruler, **Shah Mohammed Reza Pahlavi** (1919–80). The challenge stunned the Shah and his generals, and rioters were attacked. Many people were killed, and **martial law** was imposed in major cities.

Egyptian President **Anwar Sadat** (1918–81) arrived in Washington DC for talks with **President Jimmy Carter** (b.1924), in February. His visit represented a change in **Egyptian foreign policy** which had previously sought favour from the **Soviet Union**. Shortly after, Israeli Prime Minister **Menachem Begin** met President Carter. These initial talks paved the way for historic joint meetings at Camp David, Maryland, from 5–17 September. Here, both sides signed the **Camp David Peace Accord** for peace in the Middle East. Sadat and Begin later received the Nobel Peace Prize.

Cambodia was **invaded by Vietnam** on 25 December in a lightning assault. The Vietnamese forced out **Pol Pot's Khmer Rouge** regime, but the war that followed continued to be a major source of international tension. Pol Pot's army was not completely defeated; thousands of his troops fled to the **Thai–Cambodia border**, where they were able to build up their strength, and skirmishes forced the Vietnamese to stay in Cambodia for the next decade (see 1991).

Former Italian prime minister **Aldo Moro** was **kidnapped** in Rome on 16 March. The extreme left-wing **Red Brigade**, who wished to overthrow capitalist Italy, claimed responsibility and demanded that the trial of their leader, Renato Curcio, be stopped. The government refused, and eight weeks later, **Moro's body** was found in the boot of a car in Rome.

The oil tanker ***Amoco Cadiz*** ran aground on Portsall Rocks, three miles off the Brittany coast when its steering mechanism failed. The entire cargo of 1.6 million barrels spilled into the sea, causing an **oil slick** 30km (18 miles) wide and 130km (80 miles) long. Dozens of Breton **beaches were polluted**. Devastating scenes of marine animals covered in oil and dying were broadcast around the world.

The world's **first test tube baby** was born on 25 July. **Louise Brown** was born in Oldham, Lancashire, England, with the help of gynaecologist **Patrick Steptoe**, who had pioneered the technique along with **Dr Robert Edwards** (see 1969).

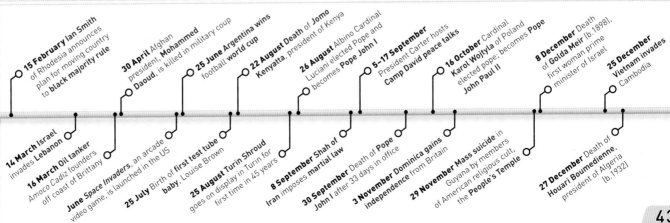

Khmer Rouge fighter
Under Pol Pot, Khmer Rouge soldiers, often teenagers, controlled Cambodia. They were responsible for killing over 1 million people.

12 September Death of anti-apartheid activist **Steven Biko** (b.1946)

18 November President Sadat of Egypt is first Arab leader to **visit Israel**

25 December Death of **Charlie Chaplin**, actor and director (b.1889)

15 February Ian Smith of Rhodesia announces plan for moving country to **black majority rule**

14 March Israel invades **Lebanon**

16 March Oil tanker *Amoco Cadiz* founders off coast of Brittany

30 April Afghan president, **Mohammed Daoud**, is killed in military coup

June Space Invaders, an arcade video game, is launched in the US

25 June Argentina wins football **world cup**

25 July Birth of **first test tube baby**, Louise Brown

25 August Turin Shroud goes on display in Turin for first time in 45 years

22 August Death of **Jomo Kenyatta**, president of Kenya

26 August Albino Cardinal Luciani elected Pope and becomes **Pope John I**

8 September Shah of Iran imposes **martial law**

5–17 September President Carter hosts **Camp David peace talks**

30 September Death of **Pope John I** after 33 days in office

16 October Cardinal **Karol Wojtyla** of Poland elected pope, becomes **Pope John Paul II**

3 November Dominica gains independence from Britain

29 November Mass suicide in Guyana by members of American religious cult, the **People's Temple**

8 December Death of **Golda Meir** (b.1898), first woman prime minister of Israel

25 December Vietnam invades Cambodia

27 December Death of **Houari Boumedienne**, president of Algeria (b.1932)

“IN ISLAM, THE LEGISLATIVE POWER AND COMPETENCE TO ESTABLISH LAWS BELONG EXCLUSIVELY TO GOD.”

Ayatollah Khomeini, from his lectures on Islamic Government

Iranian women holding posters of Ayatollah Khomeini show support for the Islamic Revolution. Mass demonstrations brought the country to a halt.

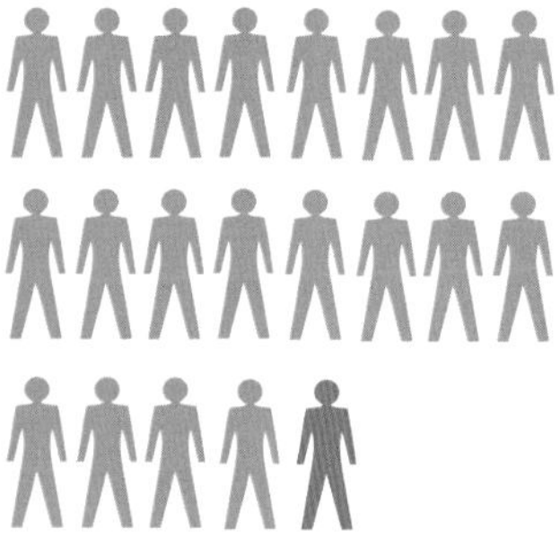

20:1 **War casualties** *Afghans paid a heavy price for the Soviet invasion – for every Soviet who was killed or wounded, 20 Afghan soldiers lost their lives.*

VIETNAMESE FORCES ENTERED CAMBODIA in 1978, in response to repeated border attacks by the **Khmer Rouge** (see 1978). On 7 January 1979, they seized the Cambodian capital of **Phnom Penh** and the Khmer Rouge were driven from power. **Pol Pot**, leader of the Khmer Rouge, fled to the jungle in Thailand and began a **guerrilla war** against a succession of Cambodian governments. On 2 April, Vietnamese forces discovered a **mass grave** in the northeast – this was the first of many mass graves from the Pol Pot era to be discovered. It became apparent that between 1975 and 1979 Pol Pot was responsible for the slaughter of more than 1 million people.

China viewed the Vietnamese attack on Cambodia as a serious provocation, and, on 17 February, Chinese forces **invaded Vietnam**. Casualties on both sides were high, and each side claimed to have won the upper hand.

When **Afghan communists** took power through a coup in 1978, they found themselves pulled three ways: between the **Soviets**, the **Americans**, and the Islamic regime in **Iran**. In March, a resistance group declared a **holy war** against the "godless" Marxist regime and killed Soviet citizens in Herat, western Afghanistan. In the countryside, revolt grew against repressive government initiatives, and the Afghan army faced total collapse. In light of this, the Soviet Union feared an Iranian-style **Islamist revolution**. Citing the 1978 Treaty of Friendship, the **Soviets invaded Afghanistan** on 24 December. In doing so, they were confident of military superiority. However, the US had been covertly training anti-government forces, the **Mujahideen** (warriors), and the Soviets were met with fierce resistance when they stormed into Kabul.

As the political situation in **Iran** deteriorated (see 1978), the **Shah** was forced into exile. **Ayatollah Ruhollah Khomeini** (1902–89), a Shi'ite Muslim cleric, returned from 15 years of exile to jubilant crowds, and the **Islamic Republic of Iran** was proclaimed on 1 April. Western influences were suppressed, and many who had been educated in the West fled the country. Young supporters of Ayatollah Khomeini, angered by America's long support of the Shah, took control of the US embassy in **Tehran**. They seized 63 hostages, and vowed not to release them until the US returned the Shah for trial. In response, **President Carter embargoed Iranian oil**. Female and non-US citizen hostages were released, and then a male hostage who became seriously ill, in 1980, but 52 Americans remained hostage until 1981.

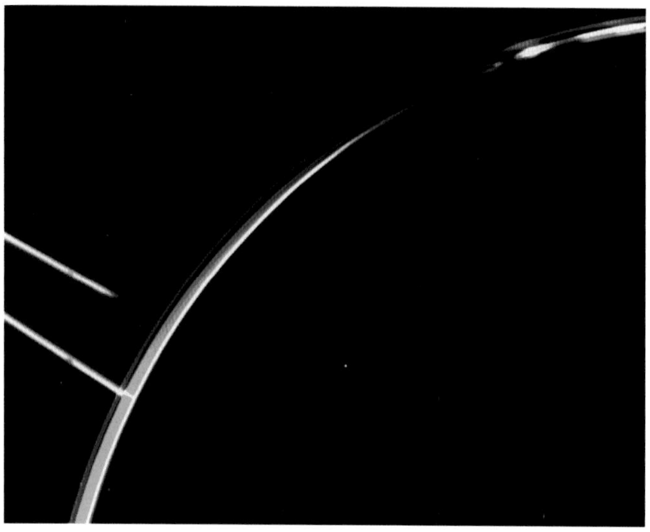

Rings of Jupiter
An image taken by NASA's Voyager 2 spacecraft shows Jupiter's ring system, never seen before, being bombarded by tiny meteorites.

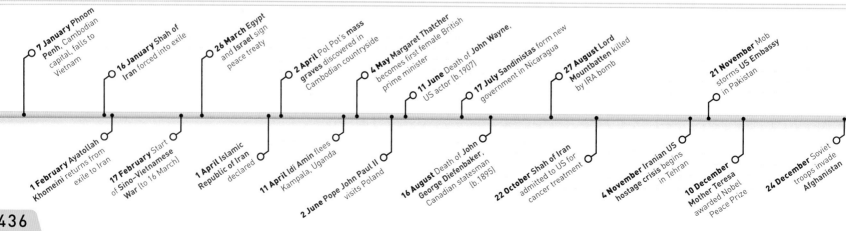

AK-47 Kalashnikov assault rifle
The AK-47 became an iconic weapon during the Soviet war in Afghanistan. Used by both sides, Kalashnikovs were cheap and readily available.

The left-wing **Sandinista National Liberation Front** succeeded in overthrowing the US-backed regime in the republic of **Nicaragua** and took the capital, Managua. This ended seven years of civil war against the **Somoza** government. The Sandinistas established a revolutionary government on 20 July, led by **Daniel and Humberto Ortega**.

Both the Irish Republican Army (**IRA**) and the Irish National Liberation Army (**INLA**) were active this year. On 30 March, shadow Northern Ireland secretary **Airey Neave** was killed by an INLA car bomb. On 27 August, **Lord Louis Mountbatten** (a member of the British royal family) was killed by an IRA bomb blast. Hours later, 18 soldiers were killed in booby-trap bomb explosions close to the border with the Irish Republic. The deaths unleashed a series of civilian killings.

Ugandan leader **Idi Amin** (1925–2003) was forced to flee the capital city of Kampala on 11 April as Tanzanian troops, along with exiles and the **Uganda National Liberation Front**, closed in. Two days later, Kampala fell and a coalition government took power. **Yusufu Lule** (1912–85), who had been driven into exile by Amin, became president. Amin escaped to Libya, leaving behind a country with its economy in tatters.

The **Sony Walkman** was launched in **Japan** on 22 June. The first Walkman featured a cassette player and the world's first lightweight headphones. It cost US$200, and sold out within a month.

- **7 January Phnom Penh**, Cambodian capital, falls to Vietnam
- **16 January Shah of Iran** forced into exile
- **1 February Ayatollah Khomeini** returns from exile to Iran
- **17 February** Start of **Sino-Vietnamese War** (to 16 March)
- **26 March Egypt** and **Israel** sign peace treaty
- **1 April Islamic Republic of Iran** declared
- **2 April** Pol Pot's **mass graves** discovered in Cambodian countryside
- **11 April Idi Amin** flees Kampala, Uganda
- **4 May Margaret Thatcher** becomes first female British prime minister
- **2 June Pope John Paul II** visits Poland
- **11 June** Death of **John Wayne**, US actor (b.1907)
- **17 July Sandinistas** form new government in Nicaragua
- **16 August** Death of **John George Diefenbaker**, Canadian statesman (b.1895)
- **27 August Lord Mountbatten** killed by IRA bomb
- **22 October Shah of Iran** admitted to US for cancer treatment
- **4 November Iranian US hostage crisis** begins in Tehran
- **21 November** Mob storms **US Embassy** in Pakistan
- **10 December Mother Teresa** awarded Nobel Peace Prize
- **24 December** Soviet troops invade **Afghanistan**

24 KILOMETRES

THE HEIGHT OF THE **ERUPTION COLUMN** IN **THE MOUNT ST HELENS** EXPLOSION

Mount St Helens in Washington State erupted, with a massive avalanche in May, and a cloud of ash that screened out all sunlight as far as 400km (250 miles) away.

ROBERT MUGABE WON A SWEEPING VICTORY on 4 March, becoming prime minister of **Rhodesia**. A Marxist guerrilla fighter, he was hated by Ian Smith's white-minority regime. On 18 April, Rhodesia became **Zimbabwe**.

Parts of **Africa** suffered extreme deprivation due to **famine** in 1980. Drought, cattle raiding, and a breakdown in civil order caused a food shortage. The **famine in Uganda** is regarded as one of the worst in history – 21 per cent of the population died.

Smallpox was declared **extinct** on 8 May by the World Health Organization, 21 years after the global eradication programme had begun. The last natural case of smallpox was in Somalia in October 1977. Around **300 million** people died from smallpox in the 20th century alone.

The **Iranian Embassy** in **London** became involved in a dramatic siege on 30 April, when six gunmen from a group opposed to **Ayatollah Khomeini** took over the building. They demanded the release of 91 Iranian political prisoners. The siege ended after a raid by the **Special Air Service** (SAS). Nineteen hostages were set free, but one died and two were injured in the cross-fire.

On 22 September, **Iraq** invaded **Iran** sparking a bitter eight-year war, which destabilized the whole region. By the end of October, **Khorramshahr**, the largest port in Iran, fell to Iraqi forces.

Under President Tito's grip (see 1943), **Yugoslavia** had achieved internal peace. **Tito's death**, on 4 May, combined with the decline of communist ideology, led to the weakening of Yugoslavia's unifying factors. Ethnic and nationalist differences flared, and individual republics began pushing for **independence**.

A huge bomb ripped through a railway station in **Bologna**, Italy, on 2 August, killing 85 people and injuring hundreds in one of the worst terrorist attacks in Italian history. **Right-wing extremists** were thought to be responsible.

Poland experienced a turning point with the **Gdansk shipyard strike**: the first political mass movement to emerge in the Soviet bloc. On 30 August, the Polish government reached an agreement with striking shipyard workers, led by **Lech Walesa**. It authorized the establishment of **Solidarity**, a new trade union free of communist control. Membership rapidly swelled to over 10 million.

Mount St Helens, a volcano in Washington State, northwest US, **violently erupted** on 18 May, spewing a huge cloud of ash. It triggered an earthquake measuring 5.2 on the Richter scale; the north face of the mountain collapsed, and 57 people died.

Ronald Reagan, a former Hollywood actor and Republican governor of California, won the **US presidential election** on 4 November, beating Jimmy Carter in a landslide victory. He would go on to serve two terms.

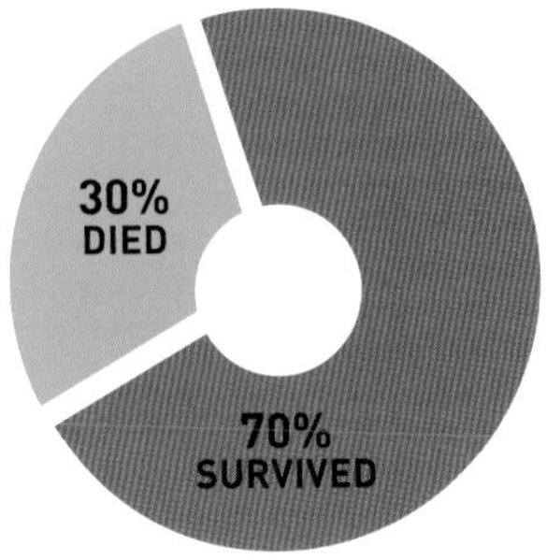

Smallpox eradication

A global vaccination campaign led to WHO declaring smallpox eradicated in 1980. Smallpox was a devastating illness, with a mortality rate of 30%.

Iran–Iraq War

An Iraqi soldier watches an oil refinery burn during the Iran–Iraq war. Oil fields and refineries were heavily targeted by both sides.

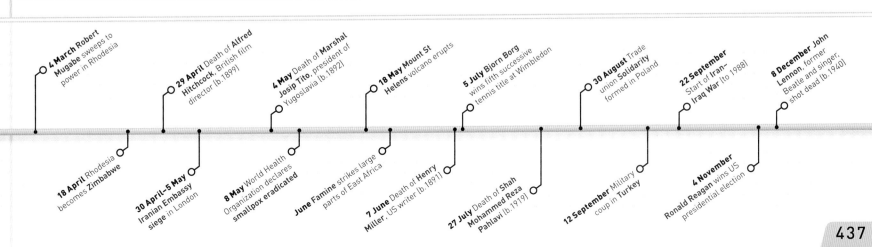

- **4 March Robert Mugabe** sweeps to power in Rhodesia
- **18 April** Rhodesia becomes **Zimbabwe**
- **29 April** Death of **Alfred Hitchcock**, British film director (b.1899)
- **30 April–5 May Iranian Embassy siege** in London
- **4 May** Death of **Marshal Josip Tito**, president of Yugoslavia (b.1892)
- **8 May** World Health Organization declares **smallpox eradicated**
- **18 May Mount St Helens** volcano erupts
- **June Famine** strikes large parts of East Africa
- **7 June** Death of **Henry Miller**, US writer (b.1891)
- **5 July Bjorn Borg** wins fifth successive tennis title at Wimbledon
- **27 July** Death of **Shah Mohammed Reza Pahlavi** (b.1919)
- **30 August** Trade union **Solidarity** formed in Poland
- **12 September** Military coup in **Turkey**
- **22 September** Start of **Iran–Iraq War** (to 1988)
- **4 November Ronald Reagan** wins US presidential election
- **8 December John Lennon**, former Beatle and singer, shot dead (b.1940)

Demonstrators carry a banner reading *Solidarność*, or "Solidarity", the name of the first non-communist Polish trade union.

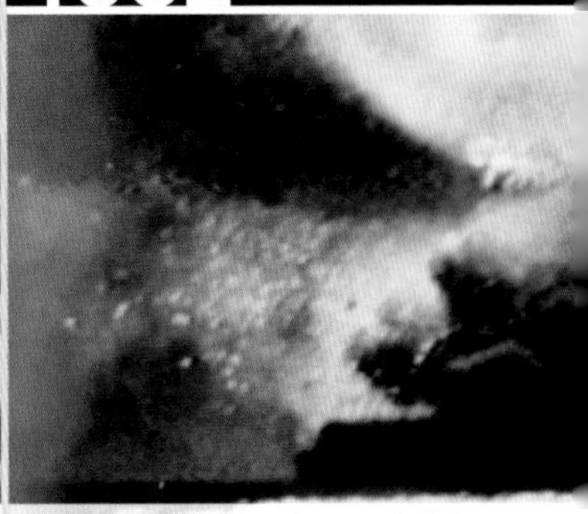

The frigate *HMS Antelope* exploded on 23 May, during the Falklands War.

FORMER ACTOR RONALD REAGAN BECAME THE 40TH PRESIDENT of the US on 20 January. Two months later he survived an assassination attempt by **John Hinckley**, who was obsessed with actress Jodie Foster, and believed an assassination of the president would impress her.

Pope John Paul II survived being **shot four times** on 13 May as he travelled through crowds in his "popemobile" in St Peter's Square, Rome. Police arrested Mehmet Ali Hagca, a Turkish citizen, who was sentenced to life imprisonment in July.

A **state of emergency** was declared in **Egypt** after **President Anwar Sadat** was assassinated at a military parade. A group calling itself the **Independent Organization for the Liberation of Egypt** said it carried out the attack. Vice-President Hosni Mubarak succeeded President Sadat as head of state.

> " IF WE RESIGN TODAY WE WILL BURY **OUR HOPES FOR FREEDOM** FOR MANY YEARS TO COME. SEVERAL THOUSAND PEOPLE **CANNOT OVERCOME TEN MILLION.** "
>
> **Solidarity, trade union**, message to the people of Poland, December 1981

On 20 January, **Iran** finally agreed to **release 52 American hostages**, who had been held for 444 days. This followed a guarantee from the US that it would release Iranian assets that had been frozen in American banks since the US embassy was seized in Tehran.

Iran also saw renewed political terrorism this year. The **Mujahidin**, a group of muslim fighters, mounted waves of **bombings and assassinations**. In August, both the new president **Ali Rajai** and the prime minister **Javad Bahonar** were killed. In October, **Ali Khamenei** was elected president in a landslide victory.

Spain was in turmoil after an attempted **right wing coup**, led by Lieutenant Colonel Antonio Tejero Molina (b.1932), who stormed the Spanish parliament along with 200 soldiers. Armed forces put down the coup on 23 February.

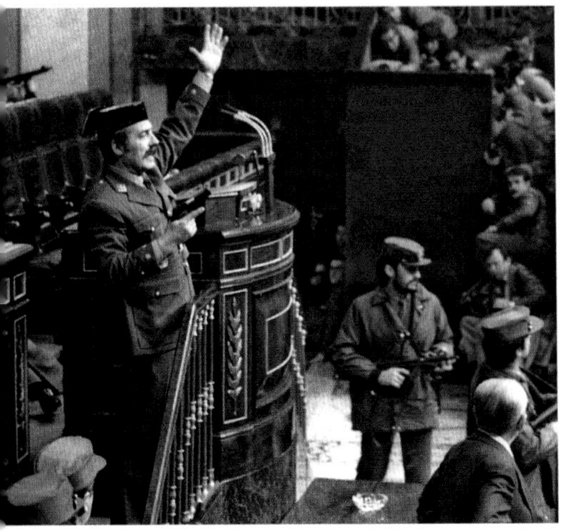

Spanish coup
Colonel Antonio Tejero stormed the Spanish parliament, firing shots into the air as he announced a military coup. The coup collapsed within hours.

Israel shocked the world by blowing up a **nuclear plant** near Baghdad, **Iraq**, on 7 June. They claimed it had the capability of making nuclear weapons to destroy Israel – Iraq denied this.

In the face of union protests, the **Polish government** declared a **state of emergency** on 13 December, and placed leaders of the **Solidarity** trade union under arrest. In response, members of Solidarity called for a **national strike** (see 1982).

Brixton, south London, erupted into **riots** on 11 April after a black man was arrested by police. The violence spread to other cities where there had been unrest due to poor relations between black communities and the police.

Columbia became the first **shuttle** to fly into space on 12 April. The maiden flight was piloted by veteran US astronauts **John Young** (b.1930) and **Robert Crippen** (b.1937), and heralded a new era in space exploration.

Bob Marley (b.1945), the international face of reggae music, died of cancer on 11 May. He was 36 years old. Bob Marley and the Wailers was the world's most recognized **reggae band**.

AIDS (see panel, below) came to the fore in June after the deaths of five men in Los Angeles. Previously, no cases had been reported outside the gay community; it became clear that the disease affected other groups. The unknown condition came to be named **Acquired Immune Deficiency Syndrome** (AIDS).

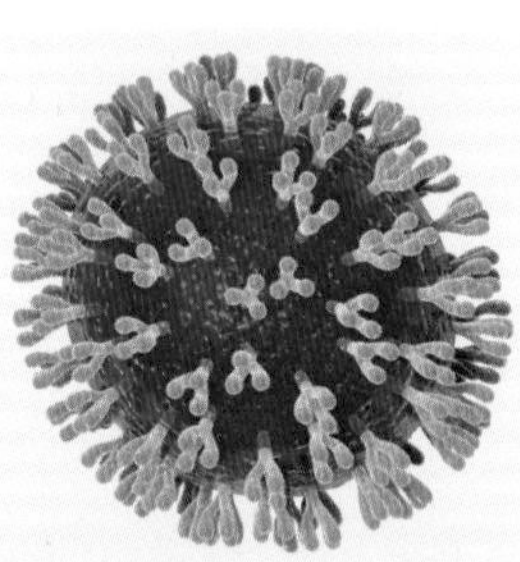

HIV VIRUS

HIV is a virus that causes Acquired Immune Deficiency Syndrome (AIDS), a disease of the immune system. The HIV virus was discovered in May 1983 by doctors at the Pasteur Institute in France. The isolation of the HIV virus meant that drugs could be developed that dramatically extended the life expectancy of those with AIDS, although no vaccine has yet been found. At least 28 million people worldwide have died from the disease; Africa has been the worst affected area.

ARGENTINA INVADED THE BRITISH TERRITORY of the **Falkland Islands** in the South Atlantic on 2 April. The sovereignty of the islands had long been disputed. British prime minister **Margaret Thatcher** (b.1925) sent a naval task force to liberate the islands. The subsequent conflict cost the lives of hundreds of Argentine and British servicemen, many of them through **missile attacks on navy warships**. The conflict ended on 14 June, when the commander of the Argentine garrison at **Port Stanley** surrendered to the British.

Iran launched **Operation Undeniable Victory** in March, as part of its war against Iraq (see 1980). This marked a major turning point, and Iran forced the Iraqis to retreat. Within a week, Iran succeeded in destroying a large

20 January Ronald Reagan (1911–2004) inaugurated as US president

20 January Iran releases American Embassy **hostages** after 444 days

4 February Prime minister Thatcher announces further plans to **privatize** nationalized British industries

23 February King Juan Carlos of **Spain** survives military coup

30 March President Reagan survives assassination attempt

12 April US space shuttle *Columbia* launched

5 May IRA prisoner **Bobby Sands** dies while on hunger strike

10 May François Mitterrand (1916–96) becomes president of France

30 May President **Ziaur Rahman** of Bangladesh assassinated (b.1936)

June Scientists identify the **AIDS** virus

29 July Wedding of **Prince Charles** to **Lady Diana Spencer** at St Paul's Cathedral, London

1 August MTV (Music Television) launched in US

5 August President and prime minister of **Iran** both **assassinated**

6 October President **Anwar Sadat** of Egypt assassinated (b.1918)

1 November Antigua and Barbuda gains independence

10 November Hosni Mubarak (b.1928) becomes new president of Egypt

8 January Spain calls off its siege of **Gibraltar**

25 March Nicaragua declares **state of emergency**

2 April Falkland War begins between Britain and Argentina

“A FLAGRANT VIOLATION OF INTERNATIONAL LAW.”

UN Security Council, on the US invasion of Grenada in 1983

2:5 **Falklands casualties** *During the Falklands War, which lasted 74 days, 255 British and 649 Argentine soldiers were killed. More than 11,000 Argentine soldiers were taken prisoner.*

part of three Iraqi divisions. Iranian president **Ali Khamenei** (b.1939) rejected an Iraqi offer of a ceasefire and sent thousands of young Iranians to their death in "**human-wave**" **attacks** that cleared the way for Iranian tanks. However, by the year's end, Iraq had been resupplied with new **Soviet arms**, and the ground war entered a new phase (see 1983).

King of pop
The dominant pop star of the 80s, Michael Jackson released the album Thriller *in 1982. It became, and remains, the best-selling album of all time.*

Israel invaded **Lebanon** on 6 June, in an attempt to wipe out **guerrilla positions** on Israel's northern border. By 15 September, the Israeli army occupied West Beirut. From 16–18 September the **Phalangists**, loyal to Israel, killed hundreds of Palestinians in refugee camps. Defence minister **Ariel Sharon resigned** after an Israeli inquiry stated he had failed to act to prevent the massacre.

The **IRA** continued their campaign against British rule in Northern Ireland by exploding **two bombs** in London parks. The first, at **Hyde Park**, killed four soldiers from the Household Cavalry. Horses were also slain. The second, placed underneath the bandstand in **Regents Park**, killed seven soldiers.

Israel attacks Lebanon
Many cities were bombarded by heavy artillery during the Israeli invasion of Lebanon – an attempt to drive out the PLO.

Solidarity (see 1981), the Polish Trade Union Movement, was **banned by the Polish government** on 8 October. This was greeted by **international condemnation** and street protests. US President Ronald Reagan put pressure on Poland by imposing economic sanctions. **Lech Walesa** (b.1943), the Solidarity leader, was released after 11 months of internment on 12 November.

Leonid Brezhnev (b.1906), leader of the Soviet Union, died on 10 November. He had served as general secretary for 18 years. He was succeeded by **Yuri Andropov** (1914–84). During his leadership, Brezhnev had pushed for better relations with the West, and increased Soviet military and industrial strength, but living standards remained poor.

The world's **first test tube twins** were born in Manchester, England, on 28 April. The twins were conceived outside the womb after their mother underwent in-vitro fertilization (**IVF**).

ON 17 JANUARY, NIGERIA ANNOUNCED that it would **expel all resident aliens**. Over a million foreigners were forced out. The move was condemned abroad, but appeared popular in Nigeria.

Drought struck Ethiopia this year. Harvests failed and there were massive food shortages. The crisis was exacerbated by the communist government's military spending and censorship of the emerging crisis.

The **US embassy in Beirut** was hit by a suicide bomber on 19 April. The US government believed the attack was carried out by **Hezbollah**, a militant Islamic group. Later in the year, terrorists bombed the French and American peacekeeping headquarters in Beirut, with extensive loss of life.

In the **Iraq–Iran War**, Iraq had begun using **chemical weapons** – the blister agent mustard gas was deployed as Iraq fought back against attacks from the "human waves" of Iranian troops.

Vicious attacks were carried out against members of the **Tamil** ethnic group in **Sri Lanka** on 23 July. These followed a deadly ambush by **Tamil Tigers**, which killed 13 Sri Lankan soldiers. The year marked the start of **civil war**.

$20 BILLION THE PROPOSED **COST** OF **“STAR WARS”**

Secret hunger
A mother holds her child during the Ethiopian famine. The Ethiopian government initially hid the famine from the rest of the world.

The **Soviets** were accused of **shooting down a Korean airliner** on 1 September. They claimed the airliner flew into their airspace and did not respond to communication.

President Reagan had spearheaded a strategy to support **anti-communist insurgencies** bent on overthrowing Marxist regimes. In May, Reagan openly expressed support for the **Contras**, the Nicaraguan opposition to **Communist Sandinista** rule. In October, the US overthrew the Marxist government of **Grenada**.

On 23 March, President Reagan launched his **Strategic Defence Initiative** (SDI), an ambitious scheme to combat nuclear weapons in space. Reagan's SDI became known as "**Star Wars**".

- **25 April** British marines recapture **South Georgia** from Argentina
- **2 May** Argentine cruiser **Belgrano** sunk by British forces
- **25 May HMS Coventry** bombed during Falkland's conflict
- **6 June** Israel invades **Lebanon**
- **14 June Argentine** forces **surrender** to British, ending Falklands War
- **20 July IRA** bomb two London parks
- **31 August** PLO driven out of Beirut as **Yassir Arafat** leaves
- **8 October Solidarity**, the Polish trade union movement, is **banned**
- **10 November** Death of **Leonid Brezhnev**, Soviet leader (b.1906)
- **12 November Lech Walesa**, leader of Solidarity, **released** from internment
- **17 January Nigeria** announces it will expel all foreign workers
- **25 February** Death of **Tennessee Williams**, US playwright (b.1911)
- **23 March** President Reagan announces "**Star Wars**" initiative
- **14 April** President Reagan denies that sending covert aid to **Contra rebels in Nicaragua** is illegal
- **14 June** Thousands march against **General Pinochet**'s rule in Chile
- **21 July** Polish government lifts **martial law**
- **23 July** Civil war begins in **Sri Lanka**
- **1 September** Soviets shoot down **Korean airliner**
- **25 October Grenada** invaded by **US**
- **30 October Argentine** elections usher in new era of **democracy**

1984

Arthur Scargill, leader of the National Union of Miners (NUM), confronts a battalion of police during the British miners' strike, which lasted a year.

BRITISH COAL MINERS WENT ON STRIKE from 12 March over pay and pit closures. The dispute lasted an entire year.

Police constable Yvonne Fletcher was killed outside the **Libyan Embassy** in London during a demonstration on 17 April. Her death led to a **police siege** of the building. Subsequently, the UK expelled Libyan diplomats from the country.

On 19 December, **China** and **Britain** signed a treaty to transfer **Hong Kong**, a British colony, to Chinese rule in 1997.

An **IRA bomb** went off at the Grand Hotel, **Brighton**, on 12 October, targeting the British cabinet who had gathered for the **Conservative Party conference**. Prime Minister Margaret Thatcher (b.1925) had a narrow escape.

Major General Mohammed Buhari (b.1942) seized power in Nigeria in a bloodless **military coup** on 1 January, citing the government's corruption record.

Indira Gandhi (b.1917), the prime minister of India, was **assassinated** on 31 October. The killing was carried out by **Sikh extremists** in response to an attack on the Sikh shrine, the **Golden Temple of Amritsar**. Ghandi ordered the attack, known as **Operation Blue Star**, to remove Sikh separatists, who were thought to be amassing weapons at the temple. The operation resulted in up to **1,000 deaths**.

On 3 December, a **poison-gas leak** at the US-owned Union Carbide pesticide plant near **Bhopal**, India, became one of the worst industrial accidents in history.

The US president **Ronald Reagan** (1911–2004) declared the withdrawal of peacekeeping troops from the Lebanese capital of **Beirut**, on 7 February, following increased terrorist attacks.

Red ribbon
A symbol of solidarity for those suffering from HIV/AIDS, the Red Ribbon Foundation was formed in 1993 to promote awareness about the disease.

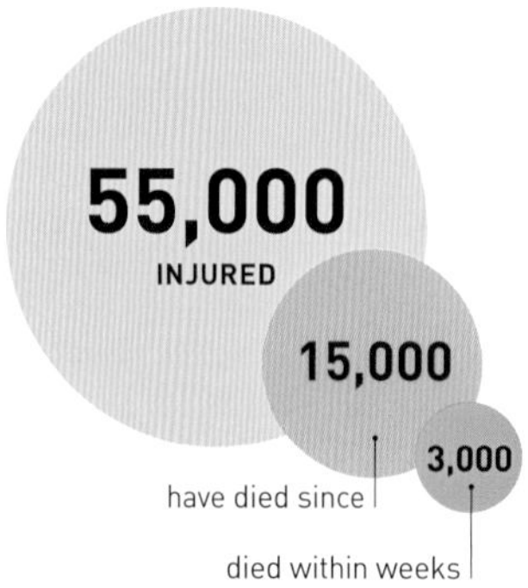

Bhopal gas victims
The Bhopal tragedy injured many thousands and killed 3,000 people within weeks. At least 15,000 are thought to have died subsequently.

Free in space
US astronaut Bruce McCandless floats free in space. He used a jet pack to fly nearly 91m (300 feet) away from the shuttle Challenger.

1985

Two billion viewers in 60 countries watched the Live Aid concerts.

TANCREDO NEVES (1910–85) WAS ELECTED PRESIDENT OF BRAZIL on 15 January, after 21 years of military rule. Democracy also returned to **Uruguay**, in March, and to **Bolivia**, in August.

On 25 May, hundreds died in attacks on Palestinian strongholds in **Beirut** by Syrian-backed **Shi'ite troops**. Prime minister **Shimon Peres** (b.1923) withdrew Israeli troops from Lebanon, but Israel held a 19km- (12 mile-) wide **security zone** in the south. Later in the year, on 7 October, Palestinian Liberation Organization (**PLO**) militants hijacked an Italian cruise liner, the *Achille Lauro*, demanding the release of **50 Palestinian prisoners** held in Israel. The

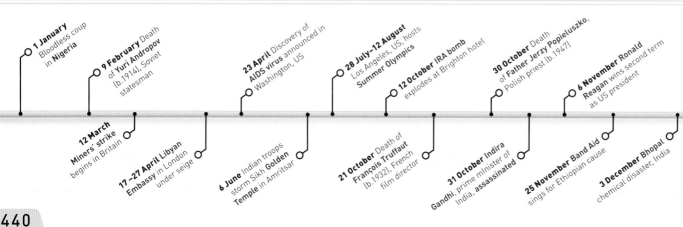

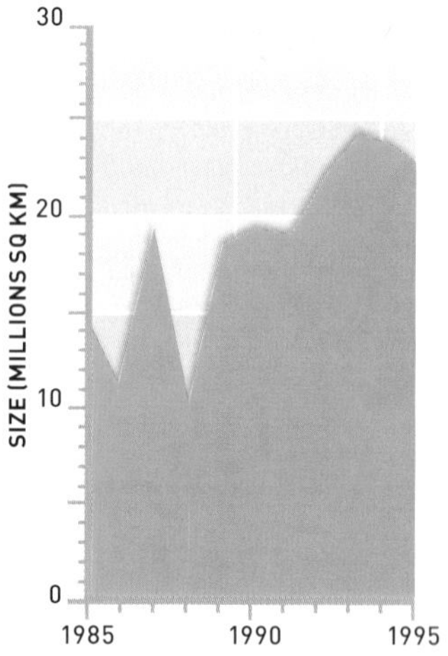

Hole in the ozone layer
This graph shows the average size of the hole in the ozone layer in each year from 1985–95. As a comparison, the area of Europe is about 10 million sq km (4 million sq miles).

1 January Bloodless coup in **Nigeria**

9 February Death of **Yuri Andropov** (b.1914), Soviet statesman

12 March Miners' strike begins in Britain

17–27 April Libyan Embassy in London under seige

23 April Discovery of **AIDS virus** announced in Washington, US

6 June Indian troops storm Sikh **Golden Temple** in Amritsar

28 July–12 August Los Angeles, US, hosts **Summer Olympics**

12 October IRA bomb explodes at Brighton hotel

21 October Death of **François Truffaut** (b.1932), French film director

30 October Death of **Father Jerzy Popieluszko**, Polish priest (b.1947)

31 October Indira Gandhi, prime mlnister of India, **assassinated**

6 November Ronald Reagan wins second term as US president

25 November Band Aid sings for Ethiopian cause

3 December Bhopal chemical disaster, India

15 January Brazil elects first civilian president in 21 years

4 February Siege of Gibraltar ends

5 February Terry Waite negotiates release of UK hostages held in Libya

11 March Mikhail Gorbachev (b.1931) becomes Soviet leader

May Scientists reveal depletion in **ozone layer**

The Russian space station *Mir* (peace) provides a home for visiting astronauts. The first crew arrived on 15 March.

crisis ended on 10 October, when the hijackers abandoned the liner in exchange for safe conduct.

The **Siege of Gibraltar** ended after 16 years, when the Spanish government opened the border, on 4 February. The dispute over the island's sovereignty continued.

British scientists discovered a **hole in the ozone layer** over Antarctica. Their findings, published in the May issue of *Nature*, rallied environmentalists.

Live Aid rocked the world in July with two huge concerts held simultaneously in London and Philadelphia to raise money for **famine relief in Ethiopia**.

MIKHAIL GORBACHEV
(1931–)

Mikhail Gorbachev became leader of the Soviet Union on 11 March 1985. He was the architect of glasnost (openness) and perestroika (restructuring). He built bridges with the West and renounced Stalinist ideas. He won the Nobel Peace Prize in 1990, but his policies led to the implosion of the Soviet Union.

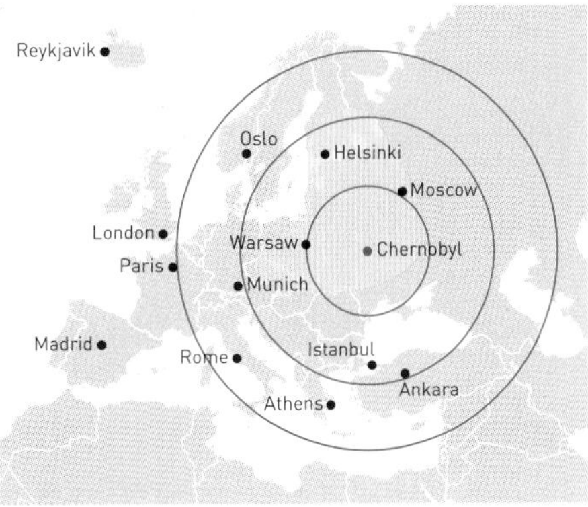

Nuclear fallout
Following the nuclear power plant accident at Chernobyl, radiation spread across Europe as far as Paris.

WITH THE IRAN–IRAQ WAR IN ITS SIXTH YEAR, Iran launched a surprise assault and **captured** the abandoned **Iraqi oil port of Faw** in February. Iraq was accused of using mustard gas in its efforts to hold off the attack.

"Irangate", a scandal involving US president **Ronald Reagan**, came to light in October in the US. The Reagan administration had been selling **arms to Iran** to secure the release of US hostages in Lebanon. The profits of the deal were used to fund **Contra rebels** fighting the Marxist regime in **Nicaragua**. Reagan survived, but his chief of staff, **Donald Regan** and national security adviser, **John Poindexter**, resigned.

US planes **bombed** military targets in **Tripoli**, Libya, on 15 April. President Reagan cited self-defence to justify the move. Days earlier, US soldiers had died in a **bomb attack** at the La Belle disco in West Berlin, believed to have been ordered by Libya.

John McCarthy (b.1956), a British journalist, was **kidnapped** by Islamic terrorists in Beirut, on 17 April. On the same day, three British hostages were killed in retaliation for Britain's support of the US bombing of Libya (see 1991).

Yemen experienced turmoil in January as power struggles within the **Yemen Socialist Party** (YSP) led to a **brutal war** between the north and south. Britain's Royal yacht, *Britannia*, helped to evacuate British citizens.

***Challenger* badge**
On 28 January, the American space shuttle Challenger *broke apart 72 seconds after take off, leading to the death of all seven crew members.*

The **Soviet Union** admitted to an accident at a nuclear power station in **Chernobyl**, Ukraine, on 26 April. The accident was the worst disaster in the history of nuclear power. It released a high level of **radioactive contamination**, which spread to Europe.

Mir, the Soviet space station, was launched on 20 February, as part of a **space city** to house cosmonauts. The first crew arrived on board the space station on 15 March.

On 12 June, **South Africa** imposed a **state of emergency** before the 10th anniversary of the black student uprising in **Soweto**. The government enforced curfews and banned television cameras from filming "unrest".

Ferdinand Marcos (1917–89) was forced to quit as **dictator of the Philippines** on 25 February, after the military and a tide of world opinion turned against him. **Corazon Aquino** (1933–2009), the first female leader of the country, was sworn in as his successor.

Nearly **50,000 students** gathered in Shanghai's **People's Square** on 21 December, urging for more social freedom. Students right across China held demonstrations in major cities demanding **democratic reforms**.

50,000
THE **NUMBER OF STUDENTS** WHO **MARCHED** IN SHANGHAI FOR **DEMOCRACY**

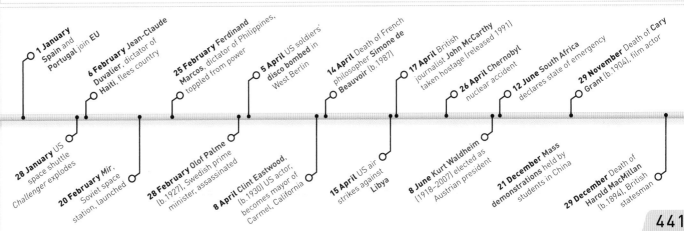

SWEDISH DEMOCRATS

Olof Palme led the Swedish Social Democratic Party from 1969. As prime minister he initiated major reforms and was an avid supporter of women's rights, healthcare, and welfare standards. His party was also a forerunner of green politics. He was accused of being pro-Soviet, which some thought led to his death in 1986.

Spain and **Portugal** joined the **European Union** (EU) on 1 January, taking its membership to 12. A new flag was also adopted as the official symbol of Europe.

The Australia Act, signed on 3 March, made Australian law **independent** of the British legal system. It also transferred control of Australian constitutional documents into Australian hands.

23 June Air India jumbo jet crashes into Irish Sea
13 July Live Aid concerts for Ethiopia in London and Philadelphia
3 September *Titanic* wreck found
13 November Volcano erupts in **Columbia**
15 November Anglo-Irish Treaty signed
11 December Unabomber claims first victim in 17-year mail-bomb campaign in US

1 January Spain and **Portugal** join **EU**
28 January US space shuttle *Challenger* explodes
6 February Jean-Claude Duvalier, dictator of **Haiti**, flees country
20 February *Mir*, Soviet space station, launched
25 February Ferdinand Marcos, dictator of Philippines, toppled from power
28 February Olof Palme (b.1927), Swedish prime minister, assassinated
5 April US soldiers' **disco bombed** in West Berlin
8 April Clint Eastwood, (b.1930) US actor, becomes mayor of Carmel, California
14 April Death of French philosopher **Simone de Beauvoir** (b.1987)
15 April US air strikes against **Libya**
17 April British journalist **John McCarthy** taken hostage (released 1991)
26 April Chernobyl nuclear accident
8 June Kurt Waldheim (1918–2007) elected as Austrian president
12 June South Africa declares state of emergency
29 November Death of **Cary Grant** (b.1904), film actor
21 December Mass demonstrations held by students in China
29 December Death of **Harold MacMillan** (b.1894), British statesman

Collapse of the USSR
After the collapse of the USSR, the former empire split into 15 new states. The independent governments formed a loose union: the Commonwealth of Independent States (CIS).

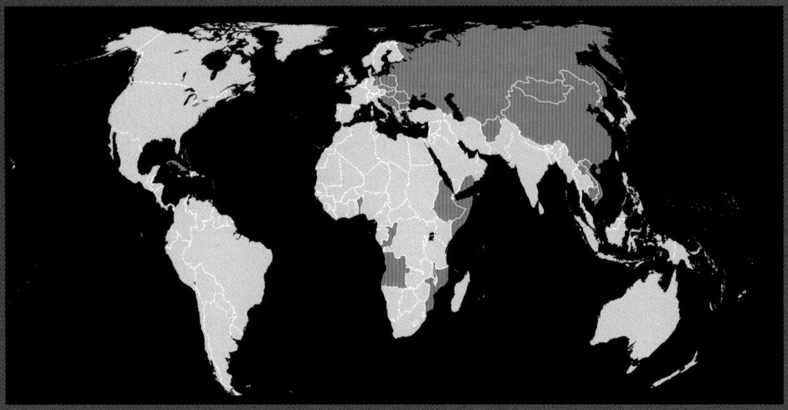

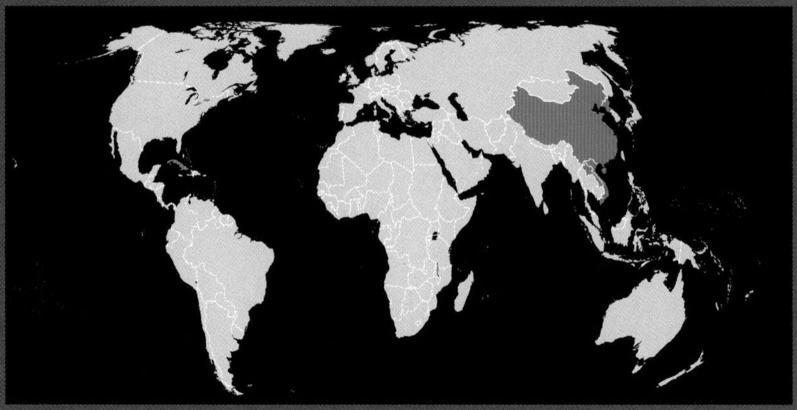

BEFORE Communist regimes could be found across the world at the high point of communist influence. After Soviet triumph in World War II, communism was embraced by one third of the world's population. Fear that it would spread further dominated the conduct of the Cold War.

AFTER Today, there are only five communist countries in the world. China remains one of the most prominent, while Laos, Vietnam, North Korea, and Cuba also have communist regimes. Communist parties still exist in many democratic nations.

COLLAPSE OF THE SOVIET UNION

THE RAPID DISINTEGRATION OF THE SOVIET STATE SHOCKED THE WORLD

In March 1985, Mikhail Gorbachev became leader of a stagnating Soviet Union. He realized that the Soviet Bloc needed radical reforms, and tried to modernize socialism. The result was the total disintegration of the USSR, which transformed the map of Europe and brought about a new world order.

Mikhail Gorbachev was a popular choice for leader. He introduced two new concepts, glasnost and perestroika – meaning openness and restructuring – and championed a more liberal, dynamic society. Although Gorbachev's popularity was affirmed when he withdrew troops from Afghanistan, non-Russian minority groups throughout the USSR agitated for independence. In July 1989, Gorbachev announced that countries within the Warsaw Pact (see 1955) could determine their own futures in openly contested elections.

East and Central Europe responded to Gorbachev's greater freedoms: in 1989 Poland elected to end communist rule; Hungary opened its borders with the West; and the Berlin Wall was torn down. When Gorbachev did not respond with force, Czechoslovakia and Romania broke free, followed by Ukraine and Armenia in 1990, and then Turkmenistan and Tajikistan in 1991.

To outsiders, Gorbachev was a hero. He won a Nobel Peace Prize and was feted by foreign leaders. But at home, living standards fell and he wrestled with deep economic problems. Gorbachev struggled to hold the empire together as his ministers deserted him and the clamour for independence in the Baltic States became overwhelming. In July 1991, Boris Yeltsin was elected president of Russia and emerged as a champion of reform when he saved Gorbachev from a coup by hard-line opponents in August. That same month, Yeltsin ordered the Soviet Communist Party to cease its activities in Russia. The Soviet Union faced oblivion when Ukraine, Russia, and Belarus secretly planned to form a new union. His position untenable, on Christmas Day 1991, Gorbachev resigned as Soviet president. Of the 15 remaining Soviet republics, 12 became sovereign states, and the USSR passed into history.

THE RISE AND FALL OF COMMUNISM

Communism was one of the most powerful political movements of the modern world, inspiring great thinkers and guerrilla fighters alike. It was supposed to offer ordinary people freedom from want and oppression and it united Western critics of the capitalist system.

The great experiment, which began with the seizure of the Winter Palace in Petrograd in 1917 ended in 1989–91, as the Berlin War was torn down and the empire of the USSR came apart. China, Cuba, Vietnam, and North Korea still call themselves communist, yet the consensus is that, without the Soviet Union to hold it together, communism is at a dead end.

> “UPON THE **SUCCESS** OF **PERESTROIKA** DEPENDS THE FUTURE OF **PEACE.**”
>
> **Mikhail Gorbachev, Soviet statesman,** 1987

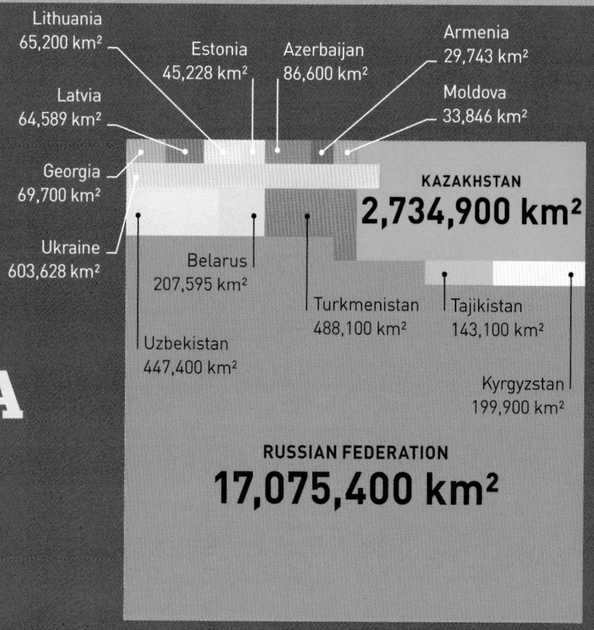

Soviet dissolution
Territory that once belonged to the Soviet Union now forms a number of new states – by far the largest is the Russian Federation.

1987

The New York Stock Exchange crash on "Black Monday" saw the Dow Jones drop more than 500 points.

500 BILLION DOLLARS THE **DECLINE** IN THE **VALUE** OF QUOTED **SHARES** ON **BLACK MONDAY**

5 BILLION THE **WORLD POPULATION** IN **1987**

IN JULY, THE WORLD POPULATION REACHED FIVE BILLION. This was double what it was in 1950, and a **billion higher** than in 1974. The population of the world was growing at a rate of **220,000 people a day**. Much of the growth was seen in parts of the world least able to sustain it. The concern about the social and economic impact of population growth led to 11 July being known as the **Day of Five Billion**. Thereafter, 11 July became **World Population Day**.

Terry Waite (b.1939), special envoy to the Archbishop of Canterbury, travelled to Lebanon, in January, to seek the **release of hostages** from Western countries, including the journalist **John McCarthy** (see 1986). However, he himself was **captured by militants** and held in **Beirut** (see 1991).

In May, **France** was forced to pay $8.6 million to **Greenpeace** for the sinking of their flagship, ***Rainbow Warrior***. The vessel, which was to lead a Greenpeace flotilla protesting against **French nuclear testing** in the Pacific, had been sunk by an explosion on 10 July 1985, in **Auckland harbour**, New Zealand. A photographer, Fernando Pereira, was killed in the blast. The incident provoked an **international scandal** and led to the cooling of relations between New Zealand and France. Two **French secret agents**, implicated in the bombing, were imprisoned. France paid $6.5 million to New Zealand as **compensation** and for returning its agents to French jurisdiction.

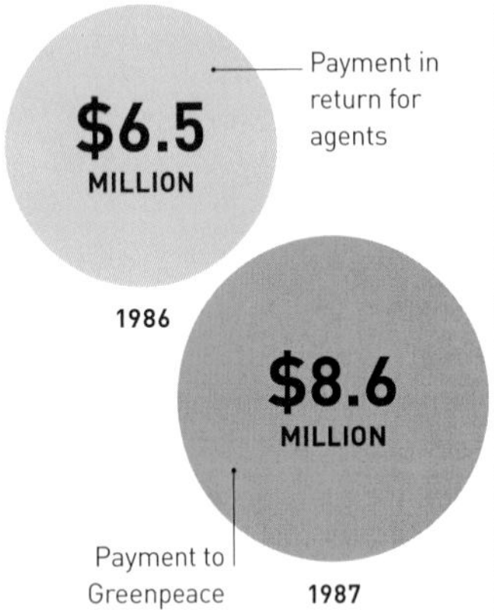

French compensation
France paid New Zealand $6.5 million to return its agents. It also paid $8.6 million to Greenpeace for the sinking of its ship, Rainbow Warrior.

On 20 March, the drug azidothymidine (**AZT**) was approved by the US Food and Drug Administration. It was the first antiretroviral drug made specifically to combat **HIV/AIDS**. While AZT could not cure AIDS, it proved that the disease could be managed, and that HIV was not a death sentence.

On 19 October, the **Dow-Jones average** in the US declined by 22.6 per cent – the **largest** single-day **percentage drop** in its history. The next day, the London Stock Exchange saw £50 billion wiped off its share values.

Stock markets around the globe also **plummeted**. The crash was triggered by fears about the weak dollar and the **US trade deficit**. It was aggravated by news of the US retaliating against Iranian attacks in the Persian Gulf by bombing an oil rig. "**Black Monday**", as it came to be known, was almost twice as bad as the crash of 29 October 1929.

Margaret Thatcher (b.1925) **visited Moscow** in March. It was the first official visit by a British prime minister in 12 years, and marked the **normalization of British–Soviet ties**. During the talks, **Mikhail Gorbachev** (b.1931), the Soviet premier, condemned the Brezhnev doctrine and called the "**Iron Curtain**" archaic, suggesting more liberal policies towards Eastern Europe. The next month, Gorbachev visited Prague, Czechoslovakia, and implied that the Eastern Bloc countries could be **independent**.

In December, the leaders of the **USSR and US signed a treaty** to reduce the size of their ground-based nuclear arsenal. Known as the **Intermediate-range Nuclear Forces (INF) Treaty**, its aim was to reverse the nuclear arms race by destroying all medium- and short-range nuclear weapons in Europe, capable of hitting targets at ranges of 500–5,500km (300–3,000 miles). This was the first time the superpowers had agreed to **reduce** their massive **nuclear arsenals**.

Negotiating freedom
Terry Waite became a familiar figure in Lebanon. As a church envoy, he made many missions to negotiate the release of hostages held by Islamic militant organizations.

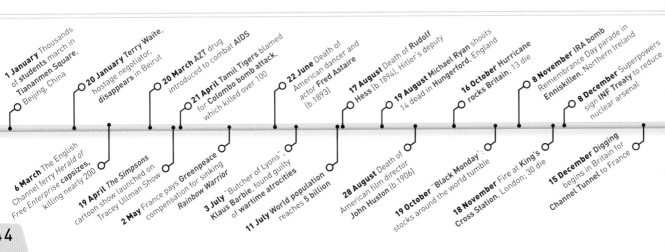

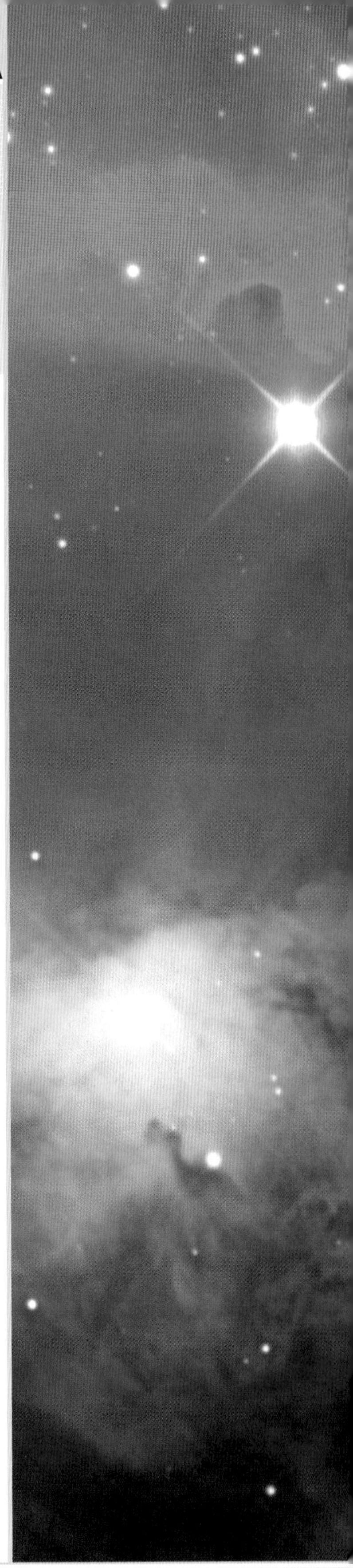

1 January Thousands of **students** march in **Tiananmen Square**, Beijing, China

20 January Terry Waite, hostage negotiator, **disappears** in Beirut

6 March The English Channel ferry *Herald of Free Enterprise* **capsizes**, killing nearly 200

20 March AZT drug introduced to combat **AIDS**

19 April *The Simpsons* cartoon show launched on Tracey Ullman Show

21 April Tamil Tigers blamed for **Colombo bomb attack**, which killed over 100

2 May France pays **Greenpeace** compensation for sinking ***Rainbow Warrior***

22 June Death of American dancer and actor **Fred Astaire** (b.1893)

3 July "Butcher of Lyons", **Klaus Barbie**, found guilty of **wartime atrocities**

11 July World population reaches **5 billion**

17 August Death of **Rudolf Hess** (b.1894), Hitler's deputy

19 August Michael Ryan shoots 14 dead in **Hungerford**, England

28 August Death of American film director **John Huston** (b.1906)

16 October Hurricane rocks Britain; 13 die

19 October "**Black Monday**": stocks around the world tumble

8 November IRA bomb Remembrance Day parade in **Enniskillen**, Northern Ireland

18 November Fire at **King's Cross Station**, London; 30 die

8 December Superpowers sign **INF Treaty** to reduce nuclear arsenal

15 December Digging begins in Britain for **Channel Tunnel** to France

15 January Israeli soldiers clash with Palestinians outside **Temple Mount**, East Jerusalem

15 January Death of **Sean McBride** (b.1904), Amnesty International co-founder

6 March IRA gang shot dead in Gibraltar by **SAS**

16 March Iraq drops **chemical bombs** on Kurdish town of Halabja

1 April Stephen Hawking publishes *A Brief History of Time*

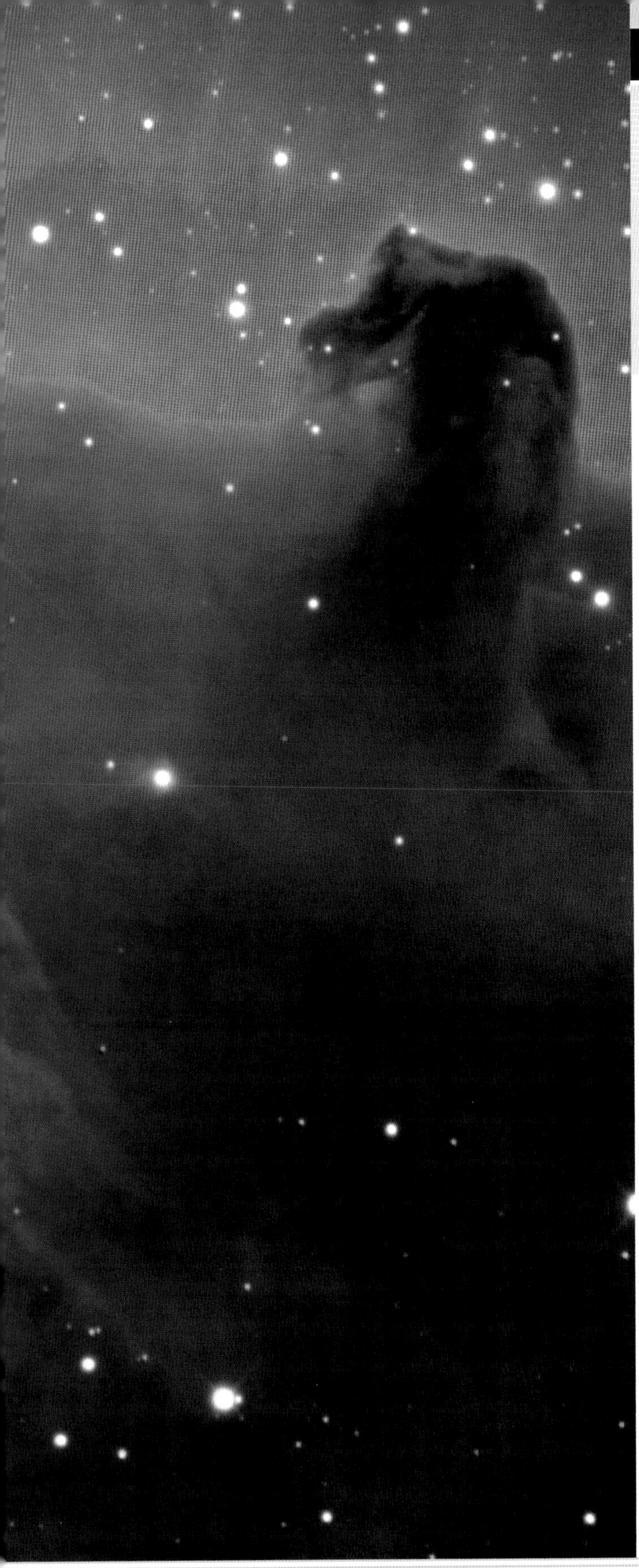

1988

“ READ MY LIPS, NO NEW TAXES. ”

George Bush, accepting the Republican presidential nomination in New Orleans, 18 August 1988

THREE MEMBERS OF THE IRISH REPUBLICAN ARMY (IRA) were shot dead by the Secret Air Service (**SAS**) in Gibraltar, on 6 March. The IRA was planning to **detonate a bomb** during a "change of guard" ceremony in the British territory. The event was to be attended by the 1st Battalion Royal Anglian Regiment, following a tour of Northern Ireland. The incident led to a **wave of violence** in Belfast.

This year saw the first documented use of **chemical weapons** in the Iran–Iraq war, when Iraq dropped bombs containing **mustard gas and nerve agents** on the Kurdish city of **Halabja** in Iraq, in March. Between 3,000 and 5,000 civilians died, and many more suffered long-term health problems. The massacre is known as "**Bloody Friday**" (see 2010).

On 8 August, a UN-arranged **ceasefire** ended the **Iran–Iraq war** (see 1980). Lasting eight years, the war resulted in more than **1 million casualties**.

Throughout 1988, Palestinian Arabs of the **Gaza Strip** and **West Bank** continued a mass uprising against Israeli occupation of Palestinian territories. Known as "**intifada**", it took the form of general strikes, boycott of Israeli products, demonstrations, and use of **petrol bombs**. On 14 November, the Palestine Liberation Organization (**PLO**) accepted the "**two-state solution**" (see 1947), officially recognizing Israel's right to exist.

On 2 December, **Benazir Bhutto** (see panel, below) was sworn in as **Pakistan's first female prime minister**. At 35, she also became the youngest leader of a world nation (see 2007).

Mikhail Gorbachev's **perestroika** (economic and political reforms), and **glasnost** (open debate), played a key role in ending the Cold War (see 1948). In a dramatic speech to the UN, on 7 December, Gorbachev announced unilateral **arms and troop reductions**, and withdrawal of forces from Eastern Europe.

On 21 December, **Pan Am flight 103** crashed at **Lockerbie**, Scotland, killing all 259 passengers and crew, and 11 on the ground. Evidence of a **bomb** instigated a huge investigation. Two **Libyan intelligence agents** were linked to the bombing, although it took over 11 years to bring them to trial.

George Bush (b.1924) became the first US vice president since 1836 to win the **presidential election**. On 8 November, he claimed a comfortable victory over democrat **Michael Dukakis**.

South Africa's border war with Namibia and Angola had been ongoing since 1966. South Africa was under intense pressure from the international community to **grant Namibia independence**. They agreed to do this, but only if **Cuba** removed its troops from **Angola**. Initially the UN rejected this proposal, but on 22 December the participants met in New York where a **bilateral agreement** was signed by Cuba and Angola, and a **tripartite accord**, by Angola, Cuba, and South Africa.

In April, Stephen Hawking (b.1942) published ***A Brief History of Time***, a story of the Universe from the "**Big Bang**". The most popular science book ever, it was translated into 40 languages and sold more than **10 million copies**.

Horsehead nebula
The resumption of shuttle flights, in 1988, meant that NASA's Hubble Space Telescope programme was back on track. Hubble would produce stunning images of the universe.

BENAZIR BHUTTO (1953–2007)

Benazir Bhutto set up the Pakistan People's Party (PPP) in London after her father, Zulfikar Ali Bhutto, was assassinated in 1979. She returned to Pakistan in 1986 and served as prime minister from 1988–90 and 1993–96. Benazir was exiled in 1999 on corruption charges, but returned in 2007 for fresh elections. Two months later, she was assassinated in a suicide attack.

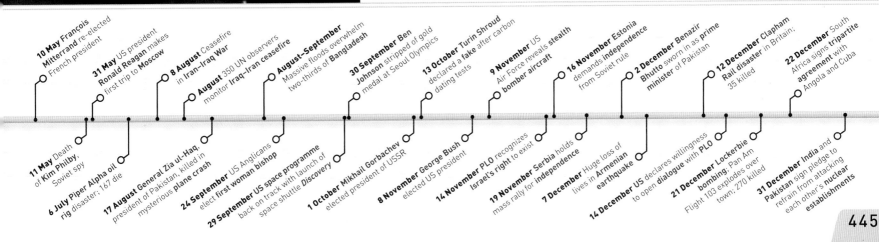

- **10 May François Mitterrand** re-elected French president
- **11 May** Death of **Kim Philby**, Soviet spy
- **31 May** US president **Ronald Reagan** makes first trip to **Moscow**
- **6 July Piper Alpha oil rig** disaster; 167 die
- **8 August** Ceasefire in **Iran–Iraq War**
- **17 August General Zia ul-Haq**, president of Pakistan, killed in mysterious **plane crash**
- **August** 350 UN observers monitor **Iraq–Iran ceasefire**
- **August–September** Massive floods overwhelm two-thirds of **Bangladesh**
- **24 September** US Anglicans elect **first woman bishop**
- **29 September US space programme** back on track with launch of space shuttle ***Discovery***
- **30 September Ben Johnson** stripped of gold medal at Seoul Olympics
- **1 October Mikhail Gorbachev** elected president of USSR
- **13 October Turin Shroud** declared a **fake** after carbon dating tests
- **8 November George Bush** elected US president
- **9 November** US Air Force reveals **stealth bomber aircraft**
- **14 November PLO** recognizes **Israel's right** to exist
- **16 November Estonia** demands **independence** from Soviet rule
- **19 November Serbia** holds mass rally for **independence**
- **2 December Benazir Bhutto** sworn in as **prime minister** of Pakistan
- **7 December** Huge loss of lives in **Armenian earthquake**
- **12 December Clapham Rail disaster** in Britain; 35 killed
- **14 December** US declares willingness to open **dialogue** with **PLO**
- **21 December Lockerbie bombing**; Pan Am Flight 103 explodes over town; 270 killed
- **22 December** South Africa signs **tripartite agreement** with Angola and Cuba
- **31 December India** and **Pakistan** sign pledge to refrain from attacking each other's **nuclear establishments**

Thousands gather during the Velvet Revolution in Czechoslovakia, a bloodless uprising that saw the overthrow of the communist government on 29 December.

IN SOUTH AFRICA, F.W. DE KLERK (B.1936) WAS ELECTED LEADER of the **National Party** on 2 February. The party had governed the country since 1948 on the principle of **apartheid**. However, De Klerk was more willing than his predecessors to modernize the political system. On 15 August, the incumbent president, P.W. Botha (1916–2006) suffered a stroke and **De Klerk took over**. Klerk began **releasing prominent black leaders** who had been imprisoned, including Walter Sisulu, a close friend of Nelson Mandela (b.1918), one of the the leaders of the African National Congress (ANC).

On 14 February, **Ayatollah Khomeini** (1902–89), the spiritual leader of Iran, issued a *fatwa*, or decree, calling for the death of author **Salman Rushdie** (b.1947) and the publishers of his book, *The Satanic Verses*. The book was considered to be a **blasphemy against Islam**. Rushdie was forced into hiding, under armed guard, to protect his life (see 1998).

Later in the year, on 3 June, **Khomeini died** in Tehran. His death was **mourned by millions**. Eight people were killed in the stampede and hundreds more injured while approaching the body to pay obeisance. The incumbent president, Ali Khamenei became Supreme Leader of Iran.

Vietnam promised to withdraw its troops from Cambodia by the end of September, a decade after invading the country (see 1979). In a declaration made on 5 April, Vietnam also urged the world to ensure that the **Cambodian civil war** was truly over and that Khmer Rouge leader **Pol Pot** (see 1973) would never be allowed to return to power again.

Making a stand
The figure of a lone man in front of army tanks in Tiananmen Square, China, became a poignant symbol of the protests.

In China, a **demonstration** held in **Tiananmen Square**, Beijing, ended in **bloodshed** on 4 June, after civilians were killed by the People's Liberation Army. Tanks were lined up in the streets to confront protestors, mainly students, who had been stationed there for seven weeks. The crowds, which swelled to more than 100,000, called for economic and political reform in the country.

Almost a decade after they had stormed the country, **Soviet troops withdrew** from Afghanistan in February. They left the economy in ruins. Many Afghans had fled, and **civil war continued** as the Mujahideen (Persian for "warriors") pushed to overthrow President Najibullah's Soviet-backed government (see 1992).

On 17 April, **Solidarity**, Poland's free trade union movement, was **legalized** after a ban of seven years. It grew into a political movement, and in elections held on 5 June, **Solidarity won** an overwhelming majority. After 45 years, **communist rule in Poland ended**. Solidarity formed a new non-communist government in the former Eastern Bloc. On 12 September, Tadeusz Mazowiecki became prime minister.

Tiananmen Square massacre
The Chinese Army shot dead nearly 3,000 of the 100,000 demonstrators who protested in Tiananmen Square in Beijing.

By the start of 1989, communist regimes had ruled Eastern Europe for 45 years. By the end of the year they had all been routed by extraordinary **public uprisings**. Following the election of Solidarity in Poland, Hungary's rulers published a **plan for independence**. A **coup in Bulgaria** brought down party leader Todor Zhivkov. On 28 November, the **Czechoslovak communist regime surrendered** to the people. A month later, Václav Havel became President of the Czechoslovak Republic in the non-violent **Velvet Revolution**. In Romania, the incumbent president, **Nicolae Ceausescu** was removed from office and **shot** in December.

Erich Honecker, leader of the German Democratic Republic, entered 1989 confident that the reforms in neighbouring countries would not affect his country, but protests grew. The Hungarian government demolished the electric fence along the Austrian frontier, part of the **Iron Curtain** – the heavily guarded border between the countries of the Eastern Bloc and the rest of Europe. By September, when the **border controls were lifted**, 60,000 East Germans were in Hungary waiting to pour through to the West. On 2 October, a **huge protest calling for reform** gathered in Leipzig, and decided

COLD WAR ESPIONAGE

Espionage epitomized the Cold War. Intelligence gathered by electronic devices, satellites, and spies was used for military information and technology. The US Central Intelligence Agency (CIA), the Soviet KGB, and East German secret police, or *Stasi* (see badge, right), spent decades spying on the enemy and undermining rivals through covert action.

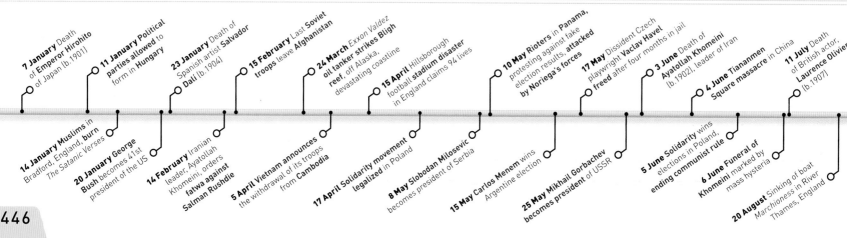

7 January Death of **Emperor Hirohito** of Japan (b.1901)

11 January Political parties allowed to form in **Hungary**

14 January Muslims in Bradford, England, **burn** *The Satanic Verses*

20 January George Bush becomes 41st president of the US

23 January Death of Spanish artist **Salvador Dalí** (b.1904)

14 February Iranian leader, Ayatollah Khomeini, orders **fatwa against Salman Rushdie**

15 February Last **Soviet troops** leave **Afghanistan**

24 March *Exxon Valdez* **oil tanker strikes Bligh reef**, off Alaska, devastating coastline

5 April Vietnam announces the withdrawal of its troops from **Cambodia**

15 April Hillsborough football **stadium disaster** in England claims 94 lives

17 April Solidarity movement legalized in Poland

8 May Slobodan Milosevic becomes president of Serbia

10 May Rioters in **Panama,** protesting against fake election results, **attacked by Noriega's forces**

15 May Carlos Menem wins Argentine election

17 May Dissident Czech playwright **Vaclav Havel freed** after four months in jail

25 May Mikhail Gorbachev becomes president of USSR

3 June Death of **Ayatollah Khomeini** (b.1902), leader of Iran

4 June Tiananmen Square massacre in China

5 June Solidarity wins elections in Poland, **ending communist rule**

6 June Funeral of Khomeini marked by mass hysteria

11 July Death of British actor, **Laurence Olivier** (b.1907)

20 August Sinking of boat *Marchioness* in River Thames, England

“ WE HAVE BEEN **TOO LONG IN DARKNESS.** ONCE ALREADY WE HAVE **BEEN IN THE LIGHT,** AND WE **WANT IT AGAIN. ”**

Alexander Dubcek, Czechoslovakian leader, 1989

Huge crowds demonstrate for the end of communist rule in Hungary. The Republic of Hungary was proclaimed on 23 October, marking a new era in Europe.

The Wall falls
An East German border guard peers through a hole in the Berlin Wall, brought down in 1989, a potent symbol of the end of communism.

to keep meeting every Monday until their demands were met. On 9 October, the army refused to fire on the crowds. Honecker was ousted from office on 18 October.

After the fall of Honecker's regime, the leader of the East Berlin communist party, Günter Schabowski, announced on 9 November that the **border with West Berlin would be opened** for "private trips abroad". That night, 50,000 East Berliners rushed to the Berlin Wall (see 1961). The guards let them pass. The crowds were met by ecstatic West Berliners on the other side. The next morning, they started **bringing the wall down**.

On 3 December, the US and the USSR met in Malta and declared the **end of the Cold War**. At a joint news conference held on board the Soviet cruise ship, *Maxim Gorky*, President George Bush (b.1924) and President Mikhail Gorbachev (b.1931) announced plans for **substantial reductions in weapons** in Europe. Praised by those outside the USSR, internally it placed Gorbachev's position as Soviet leader at risk (see pp.442–43).

Kosovo, an autonomous province of Serbia, had been clamouring for independence since the death of Josip Tito (see 1980). There was increasing **ethnic tension between Serbs and Albanians** for control of the province. Serbs argued that they were being persecuted by the majority Albanians. When **Slobodan Milosevic** became president of Serbia on 8 May, he used this alleged persecution as a justification for **stripping Kosovo of its autonomy** and became a champion of Serbian nationalism.

On 20 December, **US troops invaded Panama** in a bid to oust dictator Manuel Noriega. Over 200 civilians died in the fighting. A new government, headed by Guillermo Endara, was installed.

In New York, **Wall Street suffered a crash** on Friday 13 October, as a failed buyout of United Airlines caused share values to plummet. It was the second largest drop of the Dow Jones industrial average, a stock market index, in history, and became known as the **"Friday-the-13th mini-crash"**.

The US launched *Galileo*, an **unmanned probe to Jupiter** and its moons, aboard the space shuttle *Atlantis* on 18 October. At a cost of $1.5 billion, *Galileo* reached its final destination in 1994 after taking detailed images of Venus and the asteroid belt on the way.

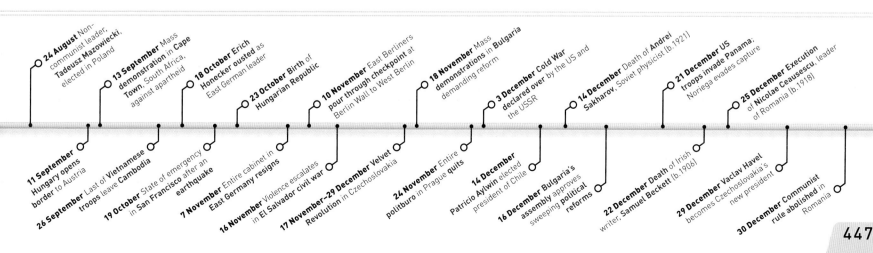

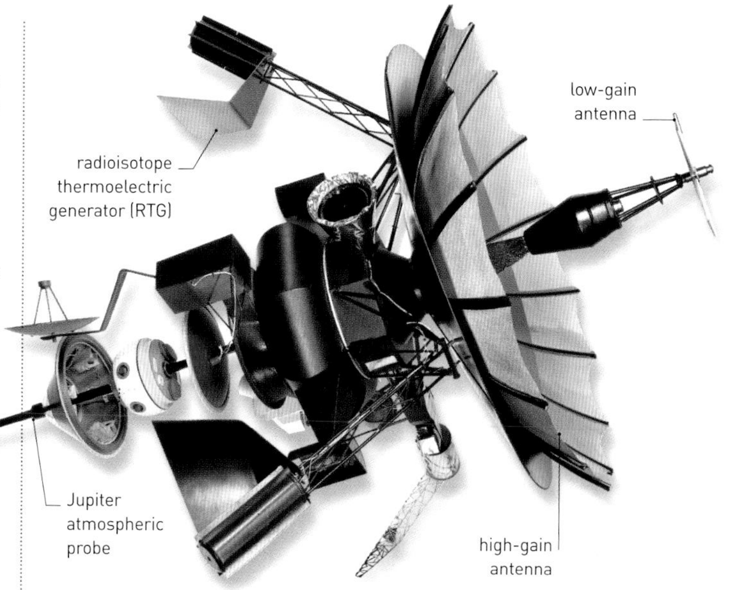

Galileo space probe
Named after astronomer Galilei Galileo, the probe travelled a distance of more than 4.5 billion km (nearly 3 billion miles), circling Jupiter 34 times.

24 August Non-communist leader, **Tadeusz Mazowiecki,** elected in Poland
11 September Hungary opens border to Austria
13 September Mass **demonstration** in **Cape Town**, South Africa, against apartheid
26 September Last of Vietnamese **troops leave Cambodia**
18 October Erich Honecker ousted as East German leader
19 October State of emergency in **San Francisco** after an **earthquake**
23 October Birth of **Hungarian Republic**
7 November Entire cabinet in **East Germany resigns**
10 November East Berliners **pour through checkpoint** at Berlin Wall to West Berlin
16 November Violence escalates in **El Salvador civil war**
17 November–29 December Velvet Revolution in Czechoslovakia
18 November Mass **demonstrations** in **Bulgaria** demanding reform
24 November Entire politburo in Prague **quits**
3 December Cold War declared over by the US and the USSR
14 December Patricio Aylwin elected president of Chile
14 December Death of **Andrei Sakharov**, Soviet physicist (b.1921)
16 December Bulgaria's assembly approves sweeping **political reforms**
21 December US troops invade Panama; Noriega evades capture
22 December Death of Irish writer, **Samuel Beckett** (b.1906)
25 December Execution of **Nicolae Ceausescu**, leader of Romania (b.1918)
29 December Vaclav Havel becomes Czechoslovakia's new president
30 December Communist rule abolished in Romania

1990

“ I GREET YOU IN THE NAME OF **PEACE, DEMOCRACY,** AND **FREEDOM.** **”**

Nelson Mandela, ANC leader

Nelson Mandela and his wife Winnie punch the air in a victory salute after his release from Victor Verster prison. He was held in captivity for 27 years.

THE 30-YEAR BAN ON THE AFRICAN NATIONAL CONGRESS (ANC) in South Africa was lifted by President De Klerk on 2 February. This started the long process of **dismantling the apartheid system**. In sweeping reforms, De Klerk also announced that the outlawed South African Communist Party and the Pan-Africanist Congress would be allowed to resume legal political activities.

Nine days later, **Nelson Mandela** (b.1918), the leader of the ANC, **walked free** after spending **27 years in jail**.

Neighbouring **Namibia** became the 47th African country to **gain independence** after 25 years of struggle against South African rule. Sam Nujoma was elected as the first president in March.

In Central America, **free elections** were held **in Nicaragua** on 25 February. National Opposition Union, a coalition of political parties backed by US funding, defeated the left-wing Sandinistas. Violeta Chamorro (b.1929) became the first female president of Nicaragua.

In the Persian Gulf, **Iraq invaded Kuwait** on 2 August. The invasion was preceded by border disputes between the two countries, and Iraq's inability to repay money borrowed from Kuwait during the Iraq–Iran War (1980–88). On 8 August, Iraqi leader **Saddam Hussein** (1937–2006) announced that **Kuwait had become a part of Iraq**. World leaders condemned the invasion. Soon after, allied forces led by the US were sent to the Gulf (see 1991).

On 23 August, Saddam Hussein appeared on television with **Western hostages**, mostly of British origin, captured in Iraq. He denied accusations that he was using these hostages as "human shields" against a potential US-led coalition attack.

Further north, Soviet troops were ordered into Baku, Azerbaijan, on the evening of 19 January to put down a separatist movement by **Azerbaijani nationalists**. The next day, thousands of Azerbaijanis set fire to their Communist Party membership cards.

Germany was reunited on 3 October, nearly a year after the fall of the Berlin Wall (see 1989). Helmut Kohl (b.1930) was elected as the first chancellor of the reunified nation.

On 1 December, the **Channel Tunnel**, the world's longest undersea rail tunnel linking Britain with France, came a step closer to completion. The construction workers drilled through the final section of rock to join the two halves of the tunnel.

LECH WALESA (1943–)

One of the founding members of Poland's Solidarity trade union movement, Lech Walesa was awarded the Nobel Peace Prize in 1983. In 1990, he became Poland's first post-communist president. He failed to gain a second term in office, as he had alienated voters with his erratic leadership style.

War zone
Kuwait, a small oil-rich Arab nation, was annexed by neighbouring Iraq. The seven-month-long occupation ended after military intervention by US-led forces in Operation Desert Storm, a largely air offensive.

1991

A man tries to put out a fire at an oil well in Burhan, Kuwait. Iraqi troops had set alight more than 600 oil fields during their occupation of the country.

ON 13 JANUARY, SOVIET TROOPS STORMED INTO LITHUANIA to suppress dissident nationalists. In the crackdown, 14 people were killed and more than 500 injured. Protestors had gathered to protect a TV station after a broadcast called for people to defend government buildings from the Soviet troops.

On 13 June, **Boris Yeltsin** (1931–2007) became the first popularly elected president of Russia, inflicting a heavy defeat on the Communist Party. The win gave him a power base to challenge the incumbent leader of the Soviet Union, Mikhail Gorbachev (b.1931).

A **military coup** attempted to remove Gorbachev from power when he was on holiday in August. Yeltsin organized a resistance and the coup collapsed on 21 August. Subsequently, Yeltsin ordered the **Communist Party of the Soviet Union to end its rule** in Russia.

The **USSR disintegrated** into **15 separate countries** as the world looked on in amazement. On 8 December, heads of three of the Soviet Union's 15 republics, Russia, Ukraine, and Belarus, met to disband the Soviet Union and form a new union, the **Commonwealth of Independent States**. On 21 December, eight others joined it. After four days, Mikhail Gorbachev announced he was resigning as Soviet president; **the USSR was no more**.

Yugoslavia was also breaking up – **Slovenia and Croatia declared independence** in June. Serban president Slobodan Milosevic sent troops to both regions to stop them from seceding. The city of Vukovar in eastern Croatia was devastated after a three-month siege by Serbs, which ended in November.

In **Northern Ireland**, the main political parties held an **historic meeting** on 18 June to discuss the future of the province. Northern Ireland had suffered years of sectarian violence and there was an overwhelming public desire to end bloodshed.

Peace talks were also held on the **Middle East** between Arabs and Israelis in Spain, on 30 October. It was the first time in over 40 years that Israel had sat down with all its Arab neighbours to discuss peace.

Elsewhere, the **United Nations** (UN) **issued an ultimatum** to Saddam Hussein to withdraw Iraqi troops from Kuwait by 15 January

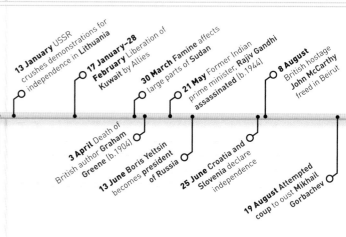

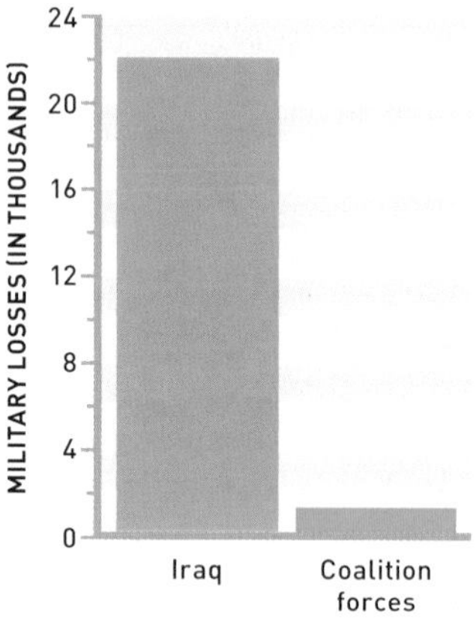

Iraq–Kuwait war casualties
The superiority of coalition forces is starkly illustrated by the disproportionately heavy losses inflicted on the Iraqi military.

- **19 January** Soviet troops crush protestors seeking independence in **Azerbaijan**
- **2 February** South Africa lifts ban against **African National Congress** (ANC)
- **11 February** ANC leader **Nelson Mandela freed**
- **25 February** Free elections held in **Nicaragua**
- **21 March** Namibia gains independence
- **31 March** Poll tax riots in London
- **2 August** Iraq invades **Kuwait**
- **24 August** Irish hostage, **Brian Keenan, released** by Islamic extremists in Lebanon
- **3 October** Germany is reunited
- **27 November** John Major ousts Margaret Thatcher as prime minister of Britain
- **9 December** Lech Walesa becomes **president of Poland**
- **13 January** USSR crushes demonstrations for independence in **Lithuania**
- **17 January–28 February** Liberation of **Kuwait** by Allies
- **3 April** Death of British author **Graham Greene** (b.1904)
- **30 March** Famine affects large parts of **Sudan**
- **13 June Boris Yeltsin** becomes **president of Russia**
- **21 May** Former Indian prime minister, **Rajiv Gandhi assassinated** (b.1944)
- **25 June Croatia and Slovenia** declare independence
- **8 August** British hostage **John McCarthy** freed in Beirut
- **19 August Attempted** coup to oust **Mikhail Gorbachev**

Residents of Sarajevo, Bosnia, duck sniper shots at a peace march during the Bosnian War as radical Serbs open fire on them.

The division of Yugoslavia
After 72 years, Yugoslavia disappeared from the map of Europe after war and political upheaval led to the formation of six independent countries.

(see 1990). He refused to comply, and on 17 January, the US and coalition forces launched "**Operation Desert Storm**", also known as the **First Gulf War** (1990–91). Kuwait was liberated after five weeks.

The First Gulf War left Saddam Hussein vulnerable in Iraq. There were **anti-government uprisings by Shi'ite Muslims** in the south of the country and by **Kurds** in the north. During March and April, thousands of people were killed as Saddam crushed the revolts.

In India, **Rajiv Gandhi** (b.1944), the former prime minister, was **assassinated** on 21 May. He was killed by a bomb in the town of Sriperumbudur while campaigning with his party for the forthcoming elections. A female suicide bomber from Liberation Tigers of Tamil Eelam (LTTE), a guerilla group in Sri Lanka also known as the "**Tamil Tigers**", was later found to have been responsible.

On 8 August, **John McCarthy**, a British journalist held hostage by an Islamic extremist group in Lebanon, was **released after five years in captivity** (see 1986). Later in the year, fellow British hostage Terry Waite, and Americans Terry Anderson and Tom Sutherland were also freed.

THE IDEA OF A UNITED EUROPE CAME CLOSER TO REALIZATION when leaders of 12 European countries signed the **treaty on European Union** and the **Maastricht Final Act** on 7 February. It heralded common citizenship, and common economic and defence policies.

The break up of Yugoslavia continued as **Bosnia and Herzegovina declared independence** on 3 March. Serbs living in Bosnia, however, resisted the move. **War broke out** and the Yugoslav army under Slobodan Milosevic attacked the Muslim population of Bosnia. The capital, Sarajevo, came under siege from Bosnian Serbs. Supplies became short and people struggled for survival (see 1996).

UN PEACEKEEPING

United Nations Peacekeeping emerged out of World War II as a way to place military personnel between warring countries or communities to stop fighting. UN forces were first used as an observer to monitor the armistice between Israel and the Arab states in 1948. Its role has grown substantially since then: supervising elections, checking human rights, clearing land mines, and intervening in failed states. By 1992, UN Peacekeeping forces had made 26 interventions worldwide.

6,000
THE NUMBER OF **BOSNIANS** AND **CROATS HELD IN** OMARSKA **DEATH CAMP**

In August, footage of **Serbian prison camps**, showing starving men behind barbed-wire fences, sparked outrage around the world. The camps, mostly in Bosnia, were part of Serbia's "**ethnic cleansing policy**" that called for the removal of other ethnic groups from Serb-dominated communities.

On 20 December, **Slobodan Milosevic was re-elected** as Serbian president. Prime minister Milan Panic called for fresh elections, citing fraud. After nine days, Panic lost a parliamentary vote of no confidence.

Algerian president **Mohammed Boudiaf** was **assassinated** on 29 June at a rally in Annaba. Boudiaf had been instrumental in the Algerian uprising against France (see 1958). He had recently returned from exile to help the government combat the Islamic Salvation Front, a fundamentalist party, whom many believed was responsible for the assassination.

US Marines waded onto the shores of **Somalia** on 9 December. Somalia was **stricken by famine**, but extortion and looting prevented foreign aid from getting through. The US-led operation aimed to hold Mogadishu's airport to enable supplies to be airlifted to starving locals.

The **Los Angeles police department** was accused of **racism and excessive force** after a video of four policemen savagely beating a black man, **Rodney King**, was broadcast in 1991. The officers were acquitted in a trial, triggering **race riots** on 29 April, which led to 55 casualties.

On 4 November, Democrat **Bill Clinton** (b.1946) **beat George Bush** (b.1924) in the US presidential elections. Clinton promised to lift the US out of economic stagnation.

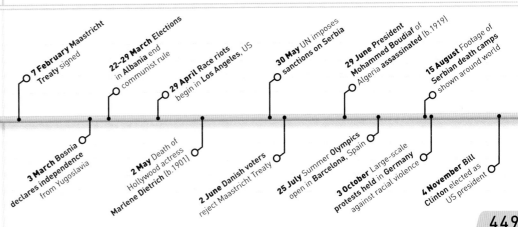

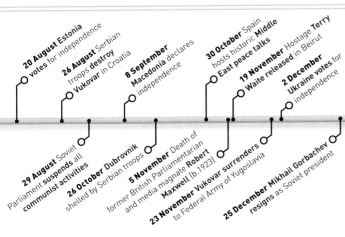

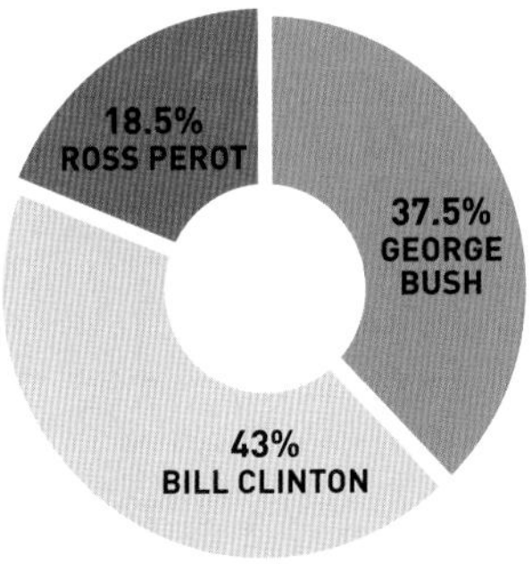

Clinton's victory
Bill Clinton became the 42nd president of the US by beating opponents Ross Perot and George Bush.

- **20 August Estonia** votes for independence
- **26 August** Serbian troops **destroy Vukovar** in Croatia
- **29 August** Soviet Parliament **suspends all communist activities**
- **8 September Macedonia** declares independence
- **26 October Dubrovnik** shelled by Serbian troops
- **30 October** Spain hosts historic **Middle East peace talks**
- **5 November** Death of former British Parliamentarian and media magnate **Robert Maxwell** (b.1923)
- **19 November** Hostage **Terry Waite released** in Beirut
- **23 November Vukovar surrenders** to Federal Army of Yugoslavia
- **2 December Ukraine votes** for independence
- **25 December Mikhail Gorbachev** resigns as Soviet president
- **7 February Maastricht Treaty** signed
- **3 March Bosnia declares independence** from Yugoslavia
- **22–29 March Elections** in Albania end communist rule
- **29 April Race riots** begin in **Los Angeles**, US
- **2 May** Death of Hollywood actress **Marlene Dietrich** (b.1901)
- **30 May** UN imposes **sanctions on Serbia**
- **2 June Danish voters** reject Maastricht Treaty
- **29 June President Mohammed Boudiaf** of **Algeria assassinated** (b.1919)
- **25 July** Summer **Olympics** open in **Barcelona**, Spain
- **15 August** Footage of **Serbian death camps** shown around world
- **3 October** Large-scale **protests held in Germany** against racial violence
- **4 November Bill Clinton** elected as US president

1993

Prague, famed for its architecturally diverse castle district shown above, became the capital of the newly formed Czech Republic. The castle is the official seat of the Czech head of state.

THE SINGLE MARKET CAME INTO FORCE across European Union (EU) countries in January. It gave greater freedom to citizens of member states to live and work in other EU countries and paved the way for a single currency, **the Euro**.

On 1 January, **Czechoslovakia was split into Slovakia and the Czech Republic**, dissolving the 74-year-old federation. The creation of the Czech Republic, with its capital in Prague, and Slovakia, with its capital in Bratislava, became known as the "Velvet Divorce" following the Velvet Revolution (see 1989).

Russian president **Boris Yeltsin** (1931–2007) faced mounting opposition to his **"shock therapy"** programme of reforms, which he had initiated in 1992. The measures were aimed at loosening the state's grip on the economy and moving towards a market-driven model, but they were widely regarded as being capitalist and "Western". The Russian parliament tried to impeach Yeltsin, who responded with a decree **dissolving the parliament** on 21 September.

Under increasing pressure from his political opponents, Yeltsin ordered parliamentarians to vacate the parliament building. When they refused, Yeltsin ordered the army to seize the building.

A series of **bomb blasts rocked** India's financial capital **Mumbai** (formerly Bombay) on 12 March, killing 257 people and injuring 713 others. They were carried out by an underworld crime syndicate.

The **Irish Republican Army** (IRA) exploded a **massive bomb** in the **City of London**, the economic heart of the English capital, on 24 April. This came a month after an IRA blast in Warrington, which killed two children. Later in the year, on 15 December, the leaders of Northern Ireland and Britain signed a peace declaration, aiming to end violence in the province.

Moves towards peace were also underway between **Israel** and the Palestine Liberation Organization (**PLO**). They signed the **Oslo Accords** in Washington, D.C. in the presence of the US president Bill Clinton (b.1946) in September. Aimed at mutual recognition, the accords were preceded by secret talks between the two parties, encouraged by the Norwegian government.

On 19 April, a **siege** at the headquarters of a US religious sect, the Branch Davidian, near Waco, Texas killed at least 70 people, including its leader, **David Koresh**, when it ended in a fire. The Federal Bureau of Investigation (FBI) had surrounded the building since February, when four agents with the Bureau of Alcohol, Tobacco, and Firearms (ATF) were killed while trying to arrest Koresh for illegally possessing firearms.

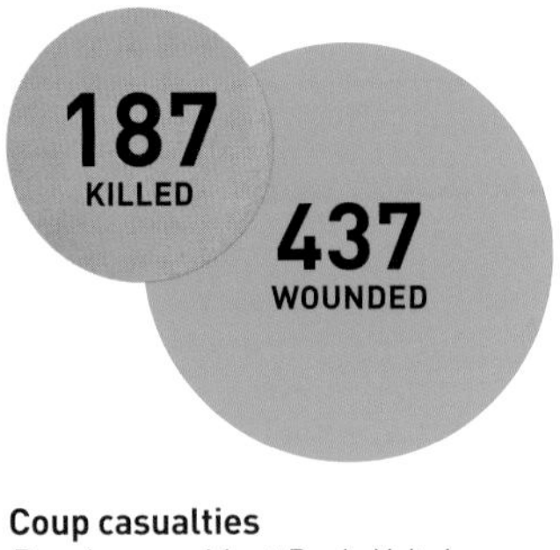

Coup casualties
Russian president Boris Yeltsin seized absolute authority by storming the parliament in Moscow, ending a rebellion by hardline opponents.

Mostar Bridge
A 16th-century bridge spanned the Neretva River for 427 years before it was destroyed during the fighting between Croats and Muslims.

1994

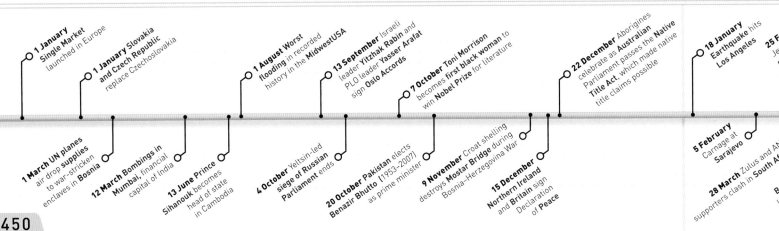

Refugees flee the civil war in Rwanda and head for refugee camps in Zaire.

IN SOUTH AFRICA, ZULUS AND AFRICAN NATIONAL CONGRESS (ANC) supporters clashed on 28 March – more than 18 people were killed. The Zulus were responding to calls by their leaders to boycott the forthcoming national elections. The elections went ahead, and on 10 May, **Nelson Mandela** became **South Africa's first black president** after more than three centuries of white rule. His party, the ANC (see panel, opposite), won 252 of the 400 seats in the **first democratic elections** in South Africa's history.

Elsewhere in Africa, the president of Rwanda, **Juvenal Habyarimana** (b.1937), a Hutu, was killed when his **plane was shot down** above Kigali airport on 6 April. The incident catalyzed a **mass genocide**. Between April and June, about **800,000 Rwandans were killed**, most of them Tutsis killed by Hutus.

On 1 July, PLO chairman **Yasser Arafat** (1929–2004) returned to the **Gaza Strip** after **27 years in exile**. It marked the start of the enactment of the Declaration of Principles agreed at the Oslo Accords, signed in Washington D.C. the previous year (see 1993).

Israel and **Jordan** signed a historic peace deal on 26 October, **ending 46 years of war**. US president Bill Clinton witnessed the treaty between Israeli prime minister Yitzhak Rabin (1922–95) and King Hussein at a ceremony in Wadi Araba, on the Israel–Jordan border.

On 31 August, the **IRA declared a ceasefire** after 25 years of

1 January **Single Market** launched in Europe

1 January Slovakia and Czech Republic replace Czechoslovakia

1 March UN planes air drop **supplies** to war-stricken enclaves in **Bosnia**

12 March Bombings in Mumbai, financial capital of India

13 June Prince Sihanouk becomes head of state in Cambodia

1 August Worst flooding in recorded history in the **MidwestUSA**

13 September Israeli leader **Yitzhak Rabin** and PLO leader **Yasser Arafat** sign **Oslo Accords**

4 October Yeltsin-led **siege of Russian Parliament** ends

7 October Toni Morrison becomes **first black woman** to win **Nobel Prize** for literature

20 October Pakistan elects **Benazir Bhutto** (1953–2007) as prime minister

9 November Croat shelling destroys **Mostar Bridge** during Bosnia-Herzegovina War

15 December Northern Ireland and **Britain** sign Declaration of **Peace**

22 December Aborigines celebrate as **Australian** Parliament passes the **Native Title Act**, which made native title claims possible

18 January Earthquake hits **Los Angeles**

5 February Carnage at **Sarajevo**

25 February Jewish extremists **gun down 30 Palestinian** worshippers in **Hebron**

28 March Zulus and ANC supporters clash in **South Africa**

28 March Silvio Berlusconi becomes Italian prime minister

> **“...THE GREATEST FAILURE OF THE WEST SINCE THE 1930s.”**

Richard Holbrooke, US Assistant Secretary of State,
on the Bosnian crisis

armed struggle against British rule in Northern Ireland. The ceasefire indicated the IRA's willingness to enter into **peace talks** on the political future of the province. The Irish prime minister, Albert Reynolds, asked loyalist paramilitaries to toe the same line. However, loyalists were suspicious of this declaration and feared that Northern Ireland's position in Great Britain would be threatened, but in the end, on 13 October, they announced their own ceasefire.

War continued in Bosnia and Herzegovina, and on 5 February, a marketplace in downtown **Sarajevo was devastated** by a mortar bomb, killing 68 people and injuring a further 200. The international community condemned the atrocity, which was believed to have been carried out by Serbians.

On 11 December, Russian president Boris Yeltsin ordered troops into the **rebel region of Chechnya** to prevent it from breaking away from the country. This Muslim-dominated region had **declared its independence** from Moscow three years before under the leadership of General Dzhokhar Dudayev.

On 19 September, the **US led an invasion force in Haiti** to bring the military junta to an end and restore democracy under President Aristide, exiled three years earlier. No shots were fired.

On 6 May, **Queen Elizabeth** (b.1926) of Britain and **President Francois Mitterrand** (1916–96) of France formally **opened the Channel Tunnel**. Linking England and France, the tunnel took eight years to build.

MS Estonia, a car and passenger ferry, **sank in the Baltic Sea** on 28 September – 852 passengers died, half of whom were Swedes.

Eurostar's maiden run
The high-speed rail service, Eurostar, which travels through the Channel Tunnel, linking England and France, made its maiden voyage in 1994.

Brazil's Samba Boys
Marcio Santos of Brazil holds the FIFA World Cup trophy to celebrate victory. Brazil, known as the Samba Boys, beat Italy in the final.

An investigation into the accident found that stormy weather, poor maintenance, and high speed contributed to the disaster.

Millions watched in horror as the Formula One racing champion, **Ayrton Senna**, ploughed off the track at the San Marino Grand Prix, on 1 May, in a **fatal crash**. A state funeral was held in his home city of São Paulo. Senna was a national hero in Brazil and had given millions to help the country's underprivileged children.

AFRICAN NATIONAL CONGRESS

Founded in 1912 with the aim of increasing the rights of black South Africans, the African National Congress (ANC) came to power in 1994, when Nelson Mandela was elected president of South Africa. The ANC still enjoys majority support, but is troubled by internal power struggles between Thabo Mbeki and Jacob Zuma, the two successors of Mandela, and the challenges of poverty and AIDS.

THE CITY OF KOBE IN JAPAN WAS DEVASTATED BY AN EARTHQUAKE on 17 January. Measuring 7.2 on the Richter scale, it resulted in hundreds of deaths and over 13,000 injuries.

Barings, a British investment bank, was **declared bankrupt** after an employee, Nick Leeson, risked huge amounts of money on the Nikkei, the Japanese stock market index. The index collapsed after the Kobe earthquake.

On 20 March, **Turkey launched** a major **military offensive**, involving 35,000 troops, against the **Kurds** in northern Iraq. This was an attempt to pursue rebel Turkish Kurds who had fled into the region and prevent them from setting up permanent bases there. The Kurds had been engaged in an armed struggle for a separate homeland since 1984 and had grievances over the lack of rights for Kurds within Turkey.

The Ebola scare
An outbreak of Ebola occurred in 1995 in Zaire. Of the 315 cases identified, 254 died, giving a fatality rate of 81 per cent.

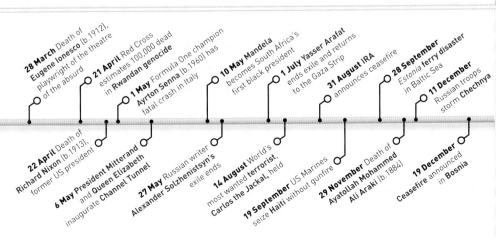

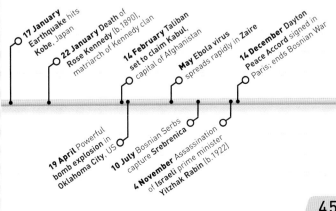

Oklahoma bombing
A massive truck bomb exploded in front of the Alfred P. Murrah Federal Building in Oklahoma City, US, on 19 April. It was felt 48km (30 miles) away.

The Turkish government hold the separatist **Kurdistan Worker's Party (PKK)** responsible for more than 30,000 deaths over the course of the conflict. Repeated military operations by Turkey against the PKK have not proved effective and the conflict continues.

A powerful **bomb exploded in Oklahoma City**, US, on 19 April, killing 168 people. Timothy McVeigh, a Gulf War veteran, was convicted of the attack. The bombing was in reaction to the government's handling of the **Waco siege** (see 1993).

Srebrenica, a Muslim enclave and UN-designated safe haven, was **overrun by Bosnian Serbs** on 10 July and "ethnically cleansed". In December, the leaders of Bosnia, Serbia, and Croatia signed the **Dayton Peace Accord** in Paris, bringing three years of war in Bosnia to an end.

- **28 March** Death of **Eugene Ionesco** (b.1912), playwright of the theatre of the absurd
- **21 April** Red Cross estimates 100,000 dead in **Rwandan genocide**
- **22 April** Death of **Richard Nixon** (b.1913), former US president
- **1 May** Formula One champion **Ayrton Senna** (b.1960) has fatal crash in Italy
- **6 May President Mitterand** and **Queen Elizabeth** inaugurate **Channel Tunnel**
- **10 May Mandela** becomes South Africa's first black president
- **27 May** Russian writer **Alexander Solzhenistsyn's** exile ends
- **1 July Yasser Arafat** ends exile and returns to the Gaza Strip
- **14 August** World's most wanted **terrorist**, **Carlos the Jackal,** held
- **31 August IRA** announces ceasefire
- **19 September** US Marines seize **Haiti** without gunfire
- **28 September** *Estonia* **ferry disaster** in Baltic Sea
- **29 November** Death of **Ayatollah Mohammed Ali Araki** (b.1884)
- **11 December** Russian troops storm **Chechnya**
- **19 December Ceasefire** announced in **Bosnia**

- **17 January Earthquake** hits **Kobe**, Japan
- **22 January Death** of **Rose Kennedy** (b.1890), matriarch of Kennedy clan
- **14 February Taliban set to claim Kabul**, capital of Afghanistan
- **19 April** Powerful **bomb explosion** in **Oklahoma City**, US
- **May Ebola virus** spreads rapidly in **Zaire**
- **10 July** Bosnian Serbs capture **Srebrenica**
- **4 November** Assassination of **Israeli** prime minister **Yitzhak Rabin** (b.1922)
- **14 December Dayton Peace Accord** signed in Paris; ends Bosnian War

THE GROWTH OF THE EU

1957 The Treaty of Rome is signed, establishing the European Economic Community (EEC), with six members.

1973 The Treaty of Accession: Denmark, Ireland, and the United Kingdom join the EU, giving nine member states.

1981 Greece becomes the 10th member of the EU. It had applied to join in 1975, after the restoration of its democracy.

1986 Spain and Portugal join the EU. The Single European Act is signed in 1987, aiming to create a single market.

1995 Austria, Finland, and Sweden join the EU, bringing membership of the EU up to 15 countries.

THE EUROPEAN UNION

FROM THE RUINS OF WAR, A CONTINENT UNITED

Europe emerged from World War II impoverished, war weary, and politically unstable. Born of a desire for peace and unity that would make another European war unthinkable, in 1957 six European countries joined in economic union. Since then, the European Union has grown substantially.

The modern age of the European Union (EU) began in 1987 with the Single European Act, an attempt to further unify Europe and create a "single market" for trade. The EU works toward increased co-operation in areas such as the environment, transport, and employment. European citizenship and the introduction of the euro, a common currency, have made it easier to work, travel, and do business with other member states, and the EU has become the largest economy in the world. Supporters of enlargement of the EU highlight this, and the benefits of political stability. Critics worry about immigration issues, the economic burden of supporting poorer countries, and the huge bureaucracy needed to run the organization.

17

THE NUMBER OF **COUNTRIES** WITH **THE EURO** AS THEIR OFFICIAL CURRENCY

People of Europe
The EU has over half a billion people, which is 7.3 per cent of the world's population. It is less than half the size of the US, but its population is over 50 per cent larger.

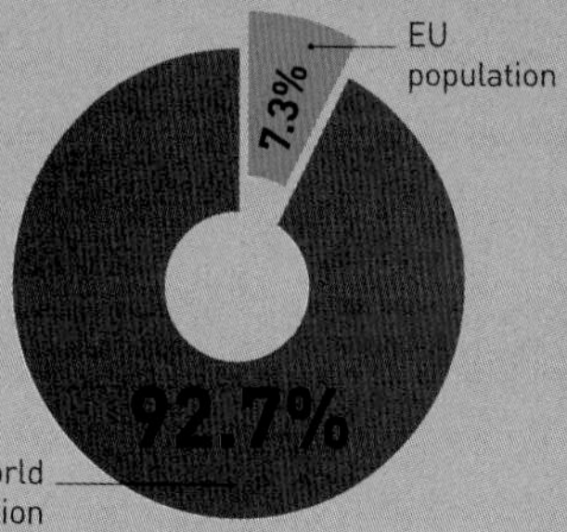

3:4 **City living**
The EU has a mainly urban population, with 75 per cent living in cities rather than in the countryside. By contrast, only around 45 per cent of Africa's population lives in cities.

Population comparison
The population of the EU is the world's third largest after China and India.

> **"EUROPE** IS THE FORCE THAT PREVENTS HATE FROM **BEING ETERNAL.** WE MUST OPEN OUR **HEARTS** TO THIS NEW **EUROPE."**

Jean-Pierre Raffarin, French prime minister, 2004

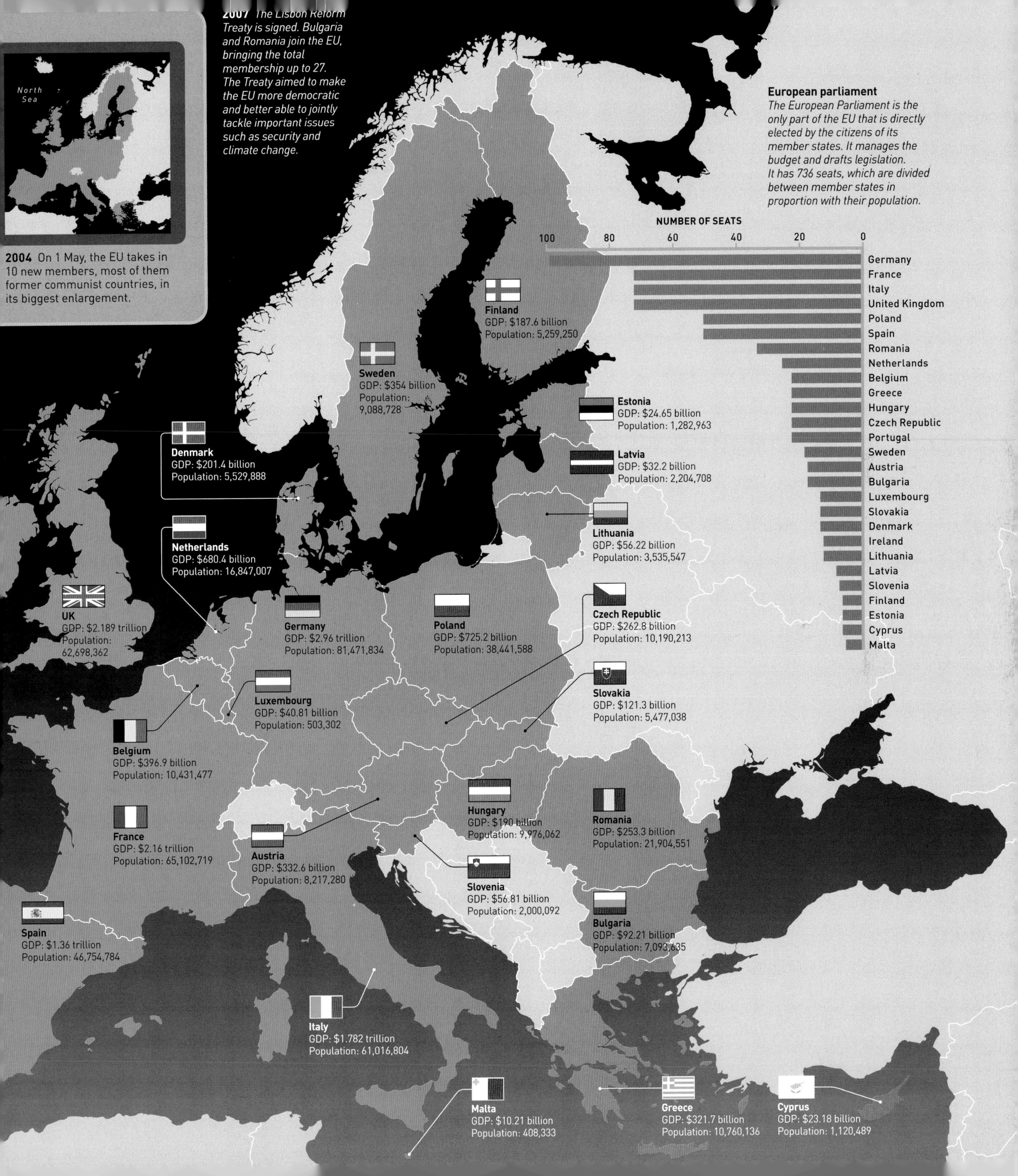

North Sea
2007 The Lisbon Reform Treaty is signed. Bulgaria and Romania join the EU, bringing the total membership up to 27. The Treaty aimed to make the EU more democratic and better able to jointly tackle important issues such as security and climate change.
2004 On 1 May, the EU takes in 10 new members, most of them former communist countries, in its biggest enlargement.
European parliament
The European Parliament is the only part of the EU that is directly elected by the citizens of its member states. It manages the budget and drafts legislation. It has 736 seats, which are divided between member states in proportion with their population.
NUMBER OF SEATS
100
80
60
40
20
0
Germany
France
Italy
United Kingdom
Poland
Spain
Romania
Netherlands
Belgium
Greece
Hungary
Czech Republic
Portugal
Sweden
Austria
Bulgaria
Luxembourg
Slovakia
Denmark
Ireland
Lithuania
Latvia
Slovenia
Finland
Estonia
Cyprus
Malta
Finland GDP: $187.6 billion Population: 5,259,250
Sweden GDP: $354 billion Population: 9,088,728
Estonia GDP: $24.65 billion Population: 1,282,963
Denmark GDP: $201.4 billion Population: 5,529,888
Latvia GDP: $32.2 billion Population: 2,204,708
Lithuania GDP: $56.22 billion Population: 3,535,547
Netherlands GDP: $680.4 billion Population: 16,847,007
UK GDP: $2.189 trillion Population: 62,698,362
Germany GDP: $2.96 trillion Population: 81,471,834
Poland GDP: $725.2 billion Population: 38,441,588
Czech Republic GDP: $262.8 billion Population: 10,190,213
Slovakia GDP: $121.3 billion Population: 5,477,038
Luxembourg GDP: $40.81 billion Population: 503,302
Belgium GDP: $396.9 billion Population: 10,431,477
Hungary GDP: $190 billion Population: 9,976,062
Romania GDP: $253.3 billion Population: 21,904,551
France GDP: $2.16 trillion Population: 65,102,719
Austria GDP: $332.6 billion Population: 8,217,280
Slovenia GDP: $56.81 billion Population: 2,000,092
Bulgaria GDP: $92.21 billion Population: 7,093,635
Spain GDP: $1.36 trillion Population: 46,754,784
Italy GDP: $1.782 trillion Population: 61,016,804
Malta GDP: $10.21 billion Population: 408,333
Greece GDP: $321.7 billion Population: 10,760,136
Cyprus GDP: $23.18 billion Population: 1,120,489

1996

Dolly the sheep, the first mammal to be cloned from an adult animal's DNA, in her pen at the Roslin Institute in Edinburgh, Scotland.

CHECHNYAN REBEL LEADER Salman Raduyev was shot on 6 March and reported dead (he had in fact disappeared abroad for medical treatment). A **ceasefire** was signed between Russia and Chechnya (see 1994) on 31 August.

Romanian elections were won by the Romanian Democratic Convention, bringing 48 years of communist rule to an end.

Civil war began in **Afghanistan**, when Taliban rebels seized Kabul on 27 September, forcing hundreds to flee the war-torn city.

The Kurdish civil war continued, and Iraq seized a city inside the Kurdish "safe haven" protected by US-led troops on 31 August. In response, America launched **Operation Desert Strike**, firing missiles at Iraqi military targets.

17

THE NUMBER OF **MONTHS** THE **IRA CEASEFIRE** LASTED

The **IRA** (Irish Republican Army) exploded a bomb in the Docklands area of East London on 10 February, ending a 17-month ceasefire (see 1994), which had tried to enable both sides to find a solution to Northern Ireland's political problems.

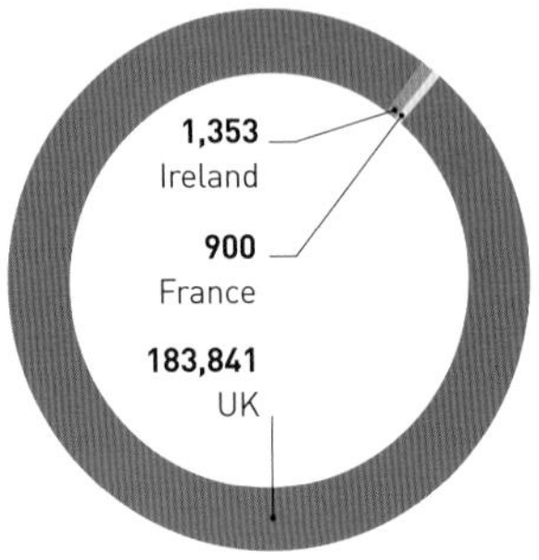

BSE cases
Bovine spongiform encephalopathy, or "mad-cow disease", caused a major health scare in Europe. Most cases of BSE occurred in the UK.

US president **Bill Clinton** won another term in office on 6 November. When Clinton reshuffled his cabinet on 12 December, **Madeleine Albright** became the first female American Secretary of State.

Science fact met science fiction when **Dolly**, a sheep, was born on 5 July in Edinburgh, Scotland. Dolly was the first mammal to be **cloned** from an adult cell.

Online shopping
The online auction site eBay boomed in 1996 with clever technology and a forum for rating buyers and sellers. It is now a global phenomenon.

1997

$1,835,300,000

THE GROSS **REVENUE EARNED** AT THE **BOX OFFICE** BY THE FILM **TITANIC**

VIOLENCE IN ZAIRE ESCALATED in February, intensifying the misery of Rwandan–Hutu refugees who had fled there to escape the civil war in Rwanda. In April, rebel soldiers, mainly Tutsis, sealed off camps in eastern Zaire, where refugees were trapped in appalling conditions. Thousands were massacred. The government of Zaire collapsed on 3 April, and **Etienne Tshisekedi** (b.1932) became prime minister of the new government. As the violence escalated 56,000 Zaireans fled into Tanzania.

Albania was consumed by anarchy during March and April, as law and order collapsed. When government insurgents began nearing the capital Tirana, those loyal to President Sali Berisha armed civilians in Tirana, opening up stores of guns and ammunition. The result was chaos, and foreign nationals were urged to leave.

Hong Kong was handed back to the Chinese authorities on 1 July after 150 years of British rule. The new chief executive, **Tung Chee Hwa**, formulated a policy based on "one country, two systems," to preserve Hong Kong's role as a capitalist centre in Asia.

Diana, Princess of Wales, died in a car crash on 31 August in a Paris underpass. The news of her death was greeted with unprecedented scenes of mourning around the world.

Iraq refused to allow UN **weapons inspectors** entry in October. The inspectors had been sent in the aftermath of the 1991 Gulf War with a remit to destroy Iraq's nuclear, biological, and chemical weapons arsenal. This action provoked a **diplomatic crisis** which was defused by a Russian-brokered compromise.

In Japan, the **Kyoto Protocol** was signed on 11 December. It committed industrialized nations to reducing emissions of greenhouse gases, principally carbon dioxide, in an attempt to combat **global warming**.

The film *Titanic*, about the ill-fated voyage of the famous passenger liner that sank in 1912, was premiered in December. At the time, it was the most expensive film ever made, but also the most successful, grossing over $1.8 billion. It also won 11 Academy Awards (Oscars).

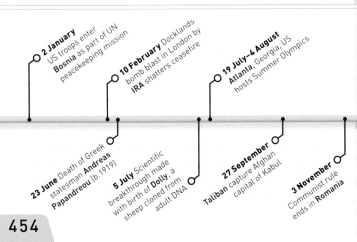

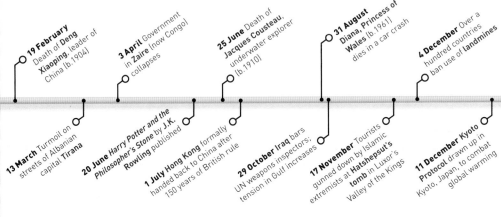

Guggenheim museum
This museum in Bilbao, Spain, designed by US architect Frank Gehry, was opened on 18 October.

2 January US troops enter **Bosnia** as part of UN peacekeeping mission

10 February Docklands bomb blast in London by **IRA** shatters ceasefire

23 June Death of Greek statesman **Andreas Papandreou** (b.1919)

5 July Scientific breakthrough made with birth of **Dolly**, a sheep cloned from adult DNA

19 July–4 August **Atlanta**, Georgia, US hosts Summer Olympics

27 September **Taliban** capture Afghan capital of Kabul

3 November Communist rule ends in **Romania**

19 February Death of **Deng Xiaoping**, leader of China (b.1904)

13 March Turmoil on streets of Albanian capital **Tirana**

3 April Government in **Zaire** (now Congo) collapses

20 June ***Harry Potter and the Philosopher's Stone*** by **J.K. Rowling** published

25 June Death of **Jacques Cousteau**, underwater explorer (b.1910)

1 July **Hong Kong** formally handed back to China after 150 years of British rule

31 August **Diana, Princess of Wales** (b.1961) dies in a car crash

29 October **Iraq** bars UN weapons inspectors; tension in Gulf increases

17 November Tourists gunned down by Islamic extremists at **Hatshepsut's tomb** in Luxor's Valley of the Kings

4 December Over a hundred countries ban use of **landmines**

11 December **Kyoto Protocol** drawn up in Kyoto, Japan, to combat global warming

1998

Bill Clinton hugs White House intern Monica Lewinsky the day after his re-election in 1996. The image was later said to be evidence of their relationship.

IN JANUARY, US PRESIDENT BILL CLINTON became the centre of a scandal involving his relationship with a former White House intern, **Monica Lewinsky**. Clinton was already implicated in a sexual harassment case and was being investigated by independent counsel Kenneth Starr. The president denied the relationship. In December, he became only the second president in US history to be **impeached** (Andrew Johnson was the first, in 1868). Clinton was charged with committing perjury in front of a grand jury, but acquitted the following year.

A devastating **earthquake** hit northern **Afghanistan** on 4 February. It killed an estimated 4,000 people, and left around 30,000 homeless.

The **Good Friday Agreement** was signed on 10 April. It marked a major breakthrough in the Northern Ireland **peace process**. A referendum held in Northern Ireland and the Republic of Ireland on 22 May was overwhelmingly in favour of the accord.

Pol Pot, former Khmer Rouge ruler of Cambodia (see 1978), died on 15 April. The Khmer Rouge had deposed him as leader and sentenced him to life imprisonment in 1997.

Eritrean and **Ethiopian** border clashes turned into a full-scale war in May. Both countries, among the poorest in the world, spent millions on sophisticated weaponry.

India and **Pakistan** went nuclear this year. India performed underground nuclear explosions on 12 May near the Pakistani border; Pakistan responded by carrying out its own tests on 28 May.

Japan officially entered a **recession** on 12 June. It was the first time its economy had shrunk in 12 years. The news caused global stock markets to slump.

US missiles pounded targets in **Afghanistan** and **Sudan** on 20 August, in retaliation for the bombing of US Embassies in Tanzania and Kenya earlier in the month. America said one target was a base for **Osama Bin Laden**, founder of the Islamic extremist organization **al-Qaeda**.

General Pinochet, former Chilean dictator (see 1973), was arrested in London on 16 October by police acting on behalf of Spain, who alleged Pinochet had committed atrocities against Spanish citizens. Pinochet was deemed too ill for extradition and released in 2000.

On 1 May, Saddam Hussein wrote an open letter to the UN Security Council threatening "grave consequences" if sanctions against Iraq were not lifted. The attempts by **UN weapons inspectors** to verify the weapons arsenal in Iraq ended on 16 December, when the Iraqis refused to co-operate. US and British air strikes on Iraq, known as **Operation Desert Fox**, began hours later.

6.1
THE **MAGNITUDE** OF THE **AFGHANISTAN EARTHQUAKE**

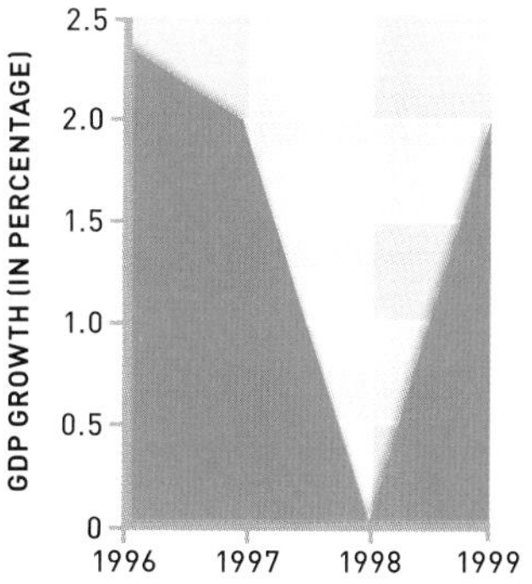

Recession in Japan
Japan's recession was at its worst in 1998. It was caused by a drop in exports, weak domestic demand, and a fall in property prices.

1999

Police confront demonstrators at the WTO conference in Seattle, northwest US. The protests were against large corporations and globalization.

A SINGLE EUROPEAN CURRENCY, the **Euro**, was launched on 1 January. Eleven European Union member states decided to adopt the Euro, which became a full economic currency in 2002.

The international community accused President Slobodan Milosevic of "**ethnic cleansing**" when 45 ethnic Albanians were found dead, apparently executed by Serbs. Kosovo peace talks ended without agreement on 23 February and a week later NATO forces announced they would escalate their **bombardment of Yugoslavia**. The purging of Albanians by Serbian troops increased, and half a million Albanians fled Kosovo. Milosevic agreed to withdraw his troops on 9 June, in response to unrelenting NATO bombing.

Thabo Mbeki won the South African presidential elections on 2 June, succeeding Nelson Mandela. He faced huge economic and social challenges, including the terrible impact of HIV/AIDS.

East Timor, in Southeast Asia, asked for intervention from international troops after a complete breakdown in law and order in September. This followed a referendum, which voted for independence from Indonesia. Anti-independence Timorese rebels, supported by the Indonesian military, killed an estimated 1,400 Timorese, and 300,000 people fled to neighbouring West Timor.

A military coup in **Pakistan** on 12 October brought to power **General Pervez Musharraf** (b.1943), who took the role of "chief executive". The international community condemned the coup and many nations imposed sanctions against Pakistan.

The **World Trade Organization** (WTO) held a **conference** in Seattle, US, late in the year, which was delayed by protesters campaigning for environmental issues and against globalization. Demonstrators clashed with police before being dispersed.

NASA lost contact with its **Mars Polar Lander** shortly before its planned entry into the Martian atmosphere. The failure of the mission was blamed on a software error.

Macau reverted from Portuguese to Chinese rule on 20 December, after 442 years of Portuguese control. Macau was the last remaining colonial state in Asia. **Edmond Ho Hau-wah** (b.1955), a banker, became leader of the new government.

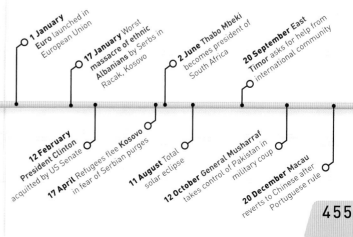

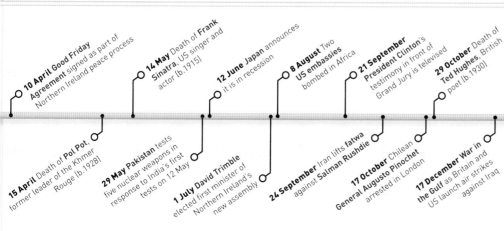

Solar eclipse
A total solar eclipse occurred on 11 August 1999. It was watched by over 350 million people in Asia and Europe.

10 April Good Friday Agreement signed as part of Northern Ireland peace process

15 April Death of **Pol Pot**, former leader of the Khmer Rouge (b.1928)

14 May Death of **Frank Sinatra**, US singer and actor (b.1915)

29 May Pakistan tests five nuclear weapons in response to India's first tests on 12 May

12 June Japan announces it is in recession

1 July David Trimble elected first minister of Northern Ireland's new assembly

8 August Two **US embassies** bombed in Africa

21 September President Clinton's testimony in front of Grand Jury is televised

24 September Iran lifts **fatwa** against **Salman Rushdie**

17 October Chilean **General Augusto Pinochet** arrested in London

29 October Death of **Ted Hughes**, British poet (b.1930)

17 December War in the Gulf as Britain and US launch air strikes against Iraq

1 January Euro launched in European Union

17 January Worst **massacre of ethnic Albanians** by Serbs in Racak, Kosovo

12 February President Clinton acquitted by US Senate

17 April Refugees flee **Kosovo** in fear of Serbian purges

2 June Thabo Mbeki becomes president of South Africa

11 August Total solar eclipse

20 September East Timor asks for help from international community

12 October General Musharraf takes control of Pakistan in military coup

20 December Macau reverts to Chinese after Portuguese rule

A trader despairs at the fall of the Nasdaq Stock Market and the New York Stock Exchange when the dot-com bubble burst. The Nasdaq never fully recovered.

Millennium celebrations
Fireworks explode in a spectacular display over Sydney Harbour Bridge and Opera House as Australia welcomed in the new millennium.

IN JANUARY, THE UN WAR CRIMES TRIBUNAL in The Hague sentenced five Bosnian Croat militiamen to 25 years in prison for a 1993 murder spree that emptied a Bosnian village of all its Muslim inhabitants during the Bosnian War (1992–95).

Opposition supporters from Serbia stormed the Yugoslav parliament building in Belgrade on 5 October using a **bulldozer**, proclaiming **Vojislav Kostunica** as the new Yugoslav president after discrepancies in September elections caused outrage. President **Milosevic** announced his resignation the next day.

In 1991, **Denmark** and **Sweden** agreed to build a bridge connecting the two countries. The 16-km (10-mile) long **Oresund Link** – running between the Danish capital, Copenhagen, and the Swedish port of Malmo – was opened to traffic this year.

In March, stock markets around the world crashed when internet companies began to fail and the **dot-com bubble**, caused by speculative investment into internet-based companies, **burst**.

Anti-globalization **protestors** descended on Prague in September during meetings between the **World Bank** and the **International Monetary Fund**. The police presence was huge, and more than 600 people were injured in riots.

The first crew arrived at the **International Space Station** in November, with NASA astronaut Bill Shepherd as commander.

Israel announced its withdrawal from South Lebanon in May, 22 years after occupying it. The occupation had become unpopular with the Israeli electorate.

North and **South Korea** held a summit in June, the first since the peninsula was divided in 1945. The South Korean president Kim Dae-jung received the **Nobel Peace Prize** for his efforts.

More than 800 followers of a **Ugandan cult** known as the Restoration of the Ten Commandments of God died in their churches in March. It is uncertain whether they committed mass suicide or were murdered by the leaders of the cult.

The year ended in bloodshed as a series of terrorist bombs went off on 30 December in the **Philippines**. They became known as the **Rizal Day bombings** because of the national holiday celebrated on this day.

2:1 **First crew of ISS**
The International Space Station received its first crew in 2000. The crew was composed of three men: two Russians and one American.

- **10 March Dot-com boom** climaxes before crash
- **24 May** Israel announces its withdrawal from **South Lebanon**
- **12–14 June Talks** between North and South Korea
- **25 July** Concorde **Air France flight 4590** crashes killing all on board
- **5 August** Death of British actor **Sir Alec Guinness** (b.1914)
- **12 August** Russian **submarine** *Kursk* **destroyed** by its own torpedo – all 118 crew killed
- **5 October Bulldozer Revolution** in Belgrade
- **6 October** Slobodan Milosevic resigns as Yugoslav president
- **30 December Rizal Day bombings** in Philippines

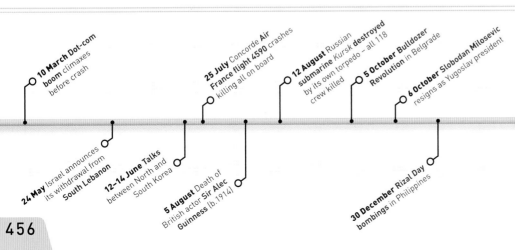

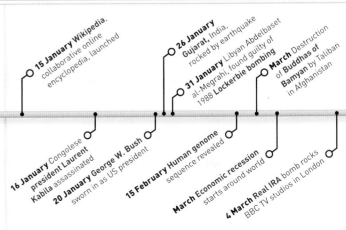

George W. Bush was elected president of the US in 2001. Here he shakes hands with Al Gore, the defeated Democrat candidate, outside the US Capitol in Washington.

$11 BILLION THE AMOUNT OF **MONEY LOST** BY **ENRON SHAREHOLDERS**

THE REPUBLIC OF MACEDONIA WAS ON THE BRINK OF WAR in March, as ethnic Albanian rebels demanding equal rights clashed with government forces. In August, NATO announced it would send a **peacekeeping force** to this former Yugoslavian republic.

The **US** experienced an unprecedented day of terror on **11 September**, when 19 al-Qaeda terrorists hijacked four passenger airlines. Two flew into the twin towers of the **World Trade Centre**, another into the **Pentagon**. The fourth crashed into a field near Pittsburgh. Nearly 3,000 people were killed. These events left America, and the world, in a profound state of shock. The devastating impact of what became known simply as **"9/11"**, September 11, prompted President Bush to declare a **"war on terror"**. NATO met the day after the attacks, offering full support and invoking a Cold War-era treaty clause that stated when one member is attacked; all members are attacked.

Only a week after 9/11, letters were mailed to several news offices and two Democratic US Senators containing **anthrax** spores. Five people died and a further 17 were infected. The suspect committed suicide.

In October, the US and Britain launched attacks on targets in **Afghanistan**, where **Osama Bin Laden** (1957–2011), head of the militant Islamic organization al-Qaeda, was believed to be hiding. Operation "**Enduring Freedom**" aimed to remove the Taliban regime and replace it with a democratic government.

Large parts of the world were tipped into **recession** after the 9/11 terror attacks, and many in the business community were mourning deceased colleagues. Economic problems worsened when **Enron**, an American power-trading company, went bust in December in the world's biggest corporate collapse.

In December, **Argentina** plunged into financial ruin. The government announced that its foreign debt could not be paid back and billions of dollars in government spending would be cut.

Another attempted terrorist attack occurred towards the end of the year. **Richard Reid**, a British passenger flying from Paris to Miami, was caught trying to light a fuse protruding from his **shoe**. Reid, an Islamic

- **15 January Wikipedia**, collaborative online encyclopedia, launched
- **16 January** Congolese president **Laurent Kabila** assassinated
- **20 January George W. Bush** sworn in as US president
- **26 January Gujarat**, India, rocked by earthquake
- **31 January** Libyan Abdelbaset al-Megrahi, found guilty of 1988 **Lockerbie bombing**
- **15 February Human genome** sequence revealed
- **March** Destruction of **Buddhas of Bamyan** by Taliban in Afghanistan
- **March Economic recession** starts around world
- **4 March Real IRA** bomb rocks BBC TV studios in London

“ **PEACEFUL** TRANSFER OF AUTHORITY IS **RARE** IN HISTORY, YET **COMMON** IN OUR COUNTRY. WITH A **SIMPLE OATH,** WE AFFIRM OLD TRADITIONS, AND MAKE **NEW BEGINNINGS.** ”

George W. Bush, opening his inaugration speech, 20 January 2001

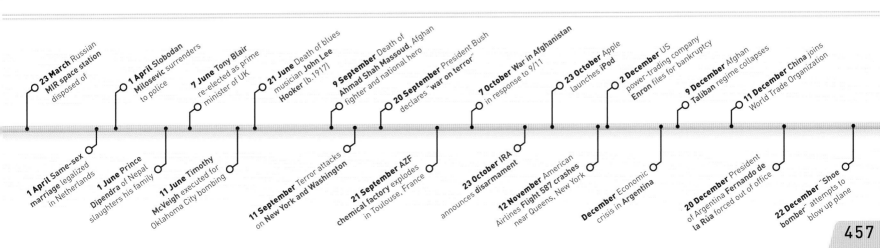

fundamentalist and supporter of al-Qaeda, was sentenced to life imprisonment.

As the terrorist threat from al-Qaeda took centre stage, the **Irish Republican Army** (IRA) made an historic announcement. On 23 October, it stated that it had begun to **disarm** and had put some of its weapons "beyond use."

In India, the state of **Gujarat** was rocked by an **earthquake** on 26 January, which registered 7.9 on the Richter scale. More than 20,000 people died and 400,000 homes were destroyed.

The free online encyclopedia "**Wikipedia**" was launched on 15 January by Jimmy Wales and Larry Sanger. By the end of the year, it held more than 20,000 articles in 18 languages. Articles are written by volunteers and can be edited by anyone.

The **Human Genome Project** (HGP) aimed to identify all the genes in the human body. In February, the HGP published its first draft: a 90 per cent complete sequence of all three billion base pairs in the human genome.

US technology company, **Apple**, had high hopes for its new digital music player, the **iPod**, which was launched on 23 October. The device could store hundreds of music tracks, yet was around the same size as a pack of cards.

Terror attack
Hijacked United Airlines Flight 175 crashed into the South Tower of the World Trade Centre, and exploded, killing hundreds of people.

23 March Russian **MIR space station** disposed of

1 April Same-sex marriage legalized in Netherlands

1 April Slobodan Milosevic surrenders to police

1 June Prince Dipendra of Nepal slaughters his family

7 June Tony Blair re-elected as prime minister of UK

11 June Timothy McVeigh executed for Oklahoma City bombing

21 June Death of blues musician **John Lee Hooker** (b.1917)

9 September Death of **Ahmad Shah Massoud,** Afghan fighter and national hero

11 September Terror attacks on **New York and Washington**

20 September President Bush declares "**war on terror**"

21 September AZF **chemical factory** explodes in Toulouse, France

7 October War in Afghanistan in response to 9/11

23 October Apple launches **iPod**

23 October IRA announces **disarmament**

12 November American Airlines **Flight 587 crashes** near Queens, New York

2 December US power-trading company **Enron** files for bankruptcy

December Economic crisis in **Argentina**

9 December Afghan **Taliban** regime collapses

11 December China joins World Trade Organization

20 December President of Argentina **Fernando de la Rúa** forced out of office

22 December "**Shoe bomber**" attempts to blow up plane

2002

Members of a Chechen militant group speak to journalists inside a theatre in Moscow, during a stand-off with Russian troops.

THE EURO BECAME LEGAL TENDER at the start of the year when 12 countries in the **Eurozone** (see 1999) abolished their individual currencies.

Slobodan Milosevic, the former Yugoslav president, went on **trial** on 12 February, charged with **crimes against humanity**. He chose to defend himself, and the trial faced many delays due to his ill-health. Milosevic died in 2006, before the trial was completed.

President George W. Bush of **America** and President Vladimir Putin of **Russia** agreed to cut numbers of nuclear warheads by two-thirds each in the **Treaty of Moscow**, signed on 24 May.

In Moscow, a gang of heavily armed **Chechen militants** besieged a theatre on 23 October, and threatened those inside if Russia did not withdraw from Chechnya. Russian special forces pumped gas into the building before engaging the rebels in a gun battle – 118 people were killed.

A **nightclub** on the Indonesian island of **Bali** became the target of a terrorist attack in which more than 200 people died.

Common currency
A new currency for 12 members of the European Union, the Euro, was launched in January 2002. It has since become secure as global tender.

Members of a violent Islamist group, **Jemaah Islamiyah**, were convicted of the attack.

US-led forces began the first large-scale campaign against the **Taliban** in Afghanistan – **Operation Anaconda** began in March.

The US journalist **Daniel Pearl** was kidnapped in January in Karachi, Pakistan. Pearl was investigating extremist Muslim groups. His ransom demanded the release and return to Pakistan of prisoners from Guantanamo Bay, a US prison camp in Cuba. Pearl's body was found in May.

India and **Pakistan** came close to war in May, following a major terrorist attack on the Indian parliament in 2001, which India claimed was carried out by Pakistan-based militant groups fighting Indian rule in **Kashmir**, north India. Both countries positioned troops either side of the international border with Kashmir.

Tamil rebels signed a **ceasefire** with the Sri Lankan government in February as part of a Norwegian-led initiative that ended 19 years of civil war.

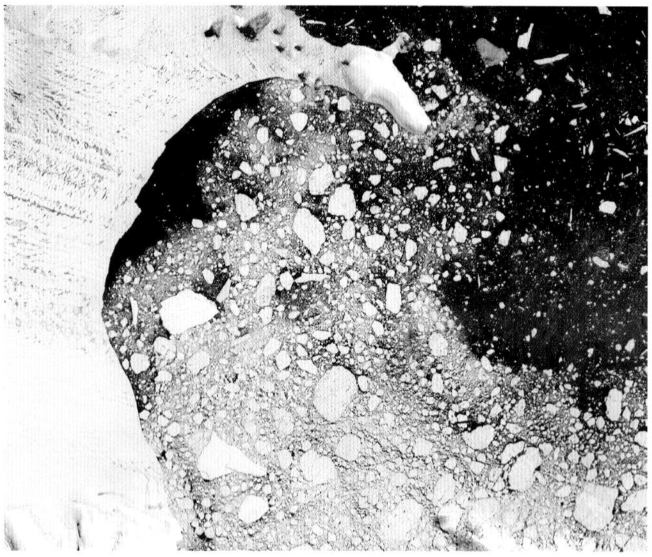

Meltdown
A massive chunk of Antarctica's Larsen ice shelf broke up in 2002 – it lost a total of about 3,250 sq km (1,255 sq miles).

Sierra Leone in West Africa emerged from a decade of civil war with the help of a strong diplomatic and military presence from Britain, its former colonial ruler.

The 26-year civil war in **Angola** ended in April when a **ceasefire** was agreed between the Angolan Army and UNITA (National Union for the Total Independence of Angola). The civil war had been ongoing since independence from Portugal in 1975.

The **African Union** replaced the Organization of African Unity in July. The new union was intended to reflect the different challenges facing the continent.

> **“WE, …TRUE OWNERS** OF THIS LAND, **SHALL NOT BUDGE,** THE **LAND IS OURS.”**
>
> **Robert Mugabe, president of Zimbabwe,** December 2002

Robert Mugabe, president of Zimbabwe, ordered white farmers to leave as part of his policy on land redistribution to the black populace. The declaration was defied by many farmers.

US millionaire **Steve Fossett** became the first person to fly a balloon solo non-stop around the world. He completed the journey on 2 July in 13 days and 12 hours.

2003

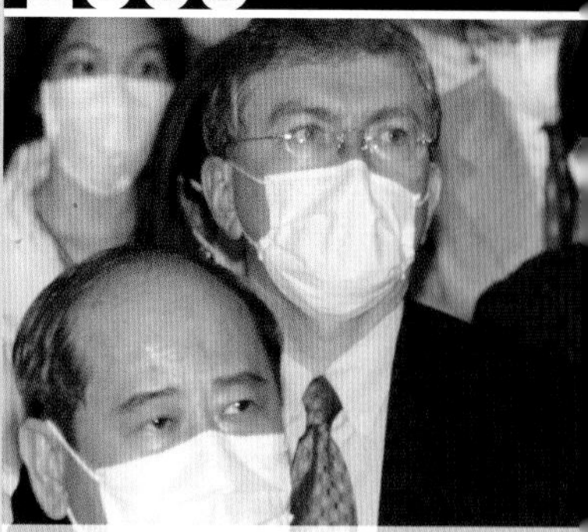

THE BEGINNING OF THE YEAR was marred by tragedy when the US space shuttle ***Columbia*** **disintegrated** as it re-entered the Earth's atmosphere. All seven crew members were killed. An investigation confirmed that a heat shield had malfunctioned on take-off, causing it to break up upon re-entry.

The last commercial flight of **Concorde**, the supersonic aircraft, was made in October. Concorde was given an emotional farewell at Heathrow airport in London, England. It had flown for 27 years but spiraling costs and dwindling ticket sales led to its demise.

Yugoslavia voted to end its existence in February, becoming **Serbia** and **Montenegro**. The Yugoslavian Federation had existed for 74 years, but had lost its other four republics in

Speedy exit
The supersonic airliner Concorde retired in 2002. Concorde was an international icon and epitomized the advance of modern technology.

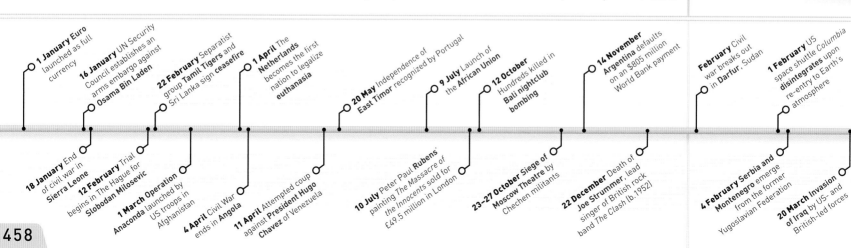

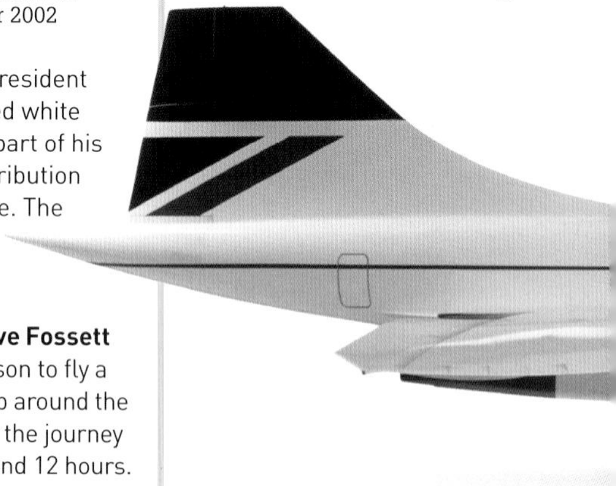

1 January Euro launched as full currency

16 January UN Security Council establishes an arms embargo against **Osama Bin Laden**

18 January End of civil war in **Sierra Leone**

12 February Trial begins in The Hague for **Slobodan Milosevic**

22 February Separatist group **Tamil Tigers** and Sri Lanka sign **ceasefire**

1 March Operation Anaconda launched by US troops in Afghanistan

1 April The Netherlands becomes the first nation to legalize **euthanasia**

4 April Civil War ends in **Angola**

11 April Attempted coup against **President Hugo Chavez** of Venezuela

20 May Independence of **East Timor** recognized by Portugal

9 July Launch of the **African Union**

10 July Peter Paul **Rubens'** painting *The Massacre of the Innocents* sold for £49.5 million in London

12 October Hundreds killed in **Bali nightclub bombing**

23–27 October Siege of **Moscow Theatre** by Chechen militants

14 November Argentina defaults on an $805 million World Bank payment

22 December Death of **Joe Strummer**, lead singer of British rock band *The Clash* (b.1952)

February Civil war breaks out in **Darfur**, Sudan

1 February US space shuttle *Columbia* **disintegrates** upon re-entry to Earth's atmosphere

4 February Serbia and Montenegro emerge from the former Yugoslavian Federation

20 March Invasion of Iraq by US- and British-led forces

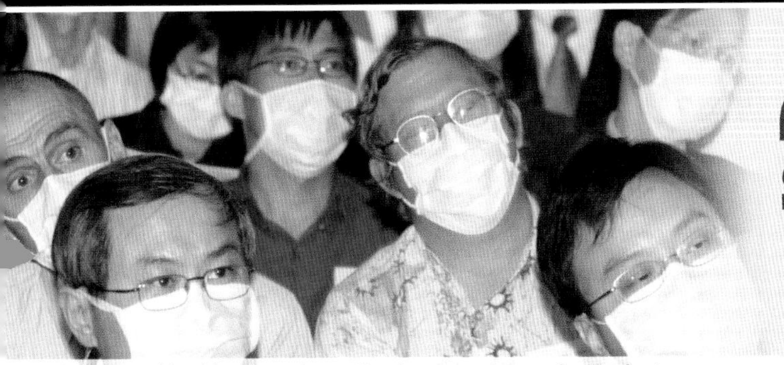

Doctors and healthcare workers attend a symposium on Severe Acute Respiratory Syndrome (SARS) in Hong Kong.

“WE HAVE **CONQUERED** THE **SARS EPIDEMIC** IN 2003.”

Wen Jiabao, Premier of China

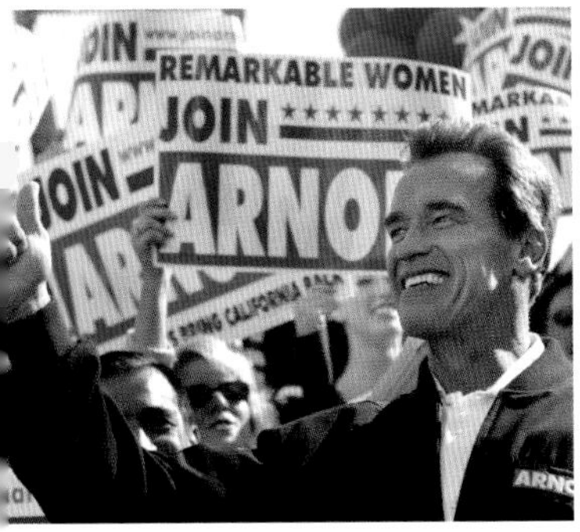

Star power
Arnold Schwarzenegger, former movie star, greets supporters during his election campaign for governor of California in the US in 2003.

a series of bloody conflicts throughout the 1990s.

The treaty establishing a Constitution for Europe was approved in June. It aimed to create a consolidated **constitution** for the **European Union** (EU). It was to replace the existing European Union treaties with a simplified single text, and would create an EU president and foreign minister.

Arnold Schwarzenegger, a former actor famous for playing the“Terminator” in Hollywood movies, became **governor of California**, US, in October.

Istanbul, Turkey, was rocked by two **bombs** on 20 November, which targeted the British consulate and the headquarters of the British-owned HSBC bank. The explosions claimed 60 lives and were linked to **al-Qaeda**.

Iraq’s regime crumbled on 20 March when US-led troops invaded and toppled Saddam Hussein’s government. They argued that Iraq was hiding **weapons of mass destruction** (WMD). This triggered years of civil conflict in Iraq between rival religious factions. The war was hugely controversial and many questioned its legality. As Western troops began losing their lives, extensive media coverage fanned the flames of public discontent. **Mass protests** were held all over the world.

Neighbouring Iran ended the year with an **earthquake** in the southeast, which devastated the ancient city of **Bam**. On the UNESCO list of World Heritage Sites, the city was more than 2,000 years old. The earthquake killed more than 26,000 people. The US offer of aid helped improve relations between the two nations.

Civil war erupted in the western region of **Darfur**, Sudan, as rebels rose up against the government, claiming the region was being neglected by the authorities in the capital, Khartoum. So far in this civil war, an estimated 200,000 people have died, and 2.5 million have fled to refugee camps.

A virus made headlines around the world and caused considerable panic. **Severe Acute Respiratory Syndrome** (SARS) is a disease found in humans, which is highly infectious and can be fatal. In 2003, an outbreak spread from China to 37 other countries. Governments took rigorous measures to contain the virus.

Camera phones, which can make calls and take photographs, came into their own this year. They had a profound social impact. Used for surveillance, news gathering, but also enabling voyeurism, they ignited debates about privacy. Some countries banned their use.

Fall from grace
A statue of Saddam Hussein in Baghdad, Iraq is toppled from its plinth by Iraqi civilians, aided by US marines.

2.5 MILLION THE NUMBER OF **PEOPLE** WHO FLEW WITH **CONCORDE**

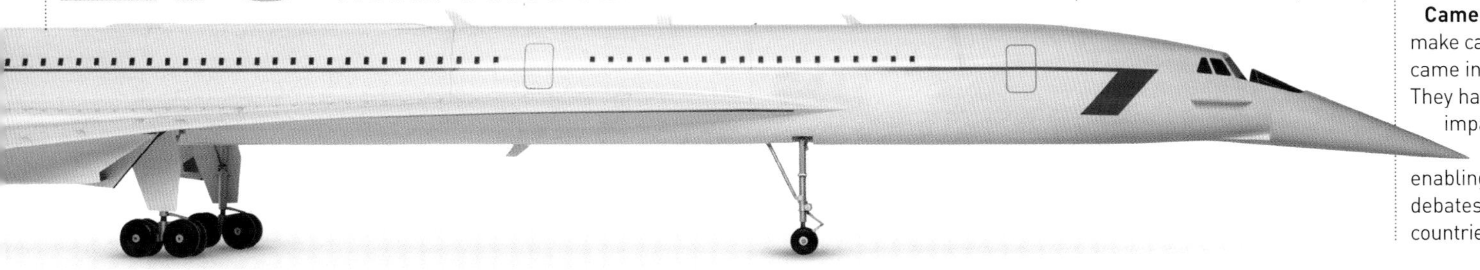

- **9 April Saddam Hussein’s** regime collapses in Iraq
- **14 April Human Genome Project** to map the human gene completed
- **28 April** US technology company Apple launches **iTunes Music Store**
- **12 May** Huge car bomb explodes in **Riyadh**, capital city of Saudi Arabia
- **25 May Nestor Kirchner** becomes president of **Argentina** defeating Carlos Menem
- **June–August** 40,000 die across Europe in record-breaking **heat wave**
- **5 July** WHO declares that **SARS** outbreak is contained
- **27 July** US cyclist **Lance Armstrong** claims 5th Tour de France
- **14 August** Parts of US and parts of Canada suffer **major blackout** due to power surge
- **16 August** Death of former Ugandan dictator **Idi Amin** (b.1925)
- **10 September Anna Lindh**, foreign minister of Sweden, fatally stabbed while shopping
- **12 September** Death of US musician **Jonny Cash** (b.1932)
- **14 September** In referendum **Sweden** rejects adopting Euro
- **28 September Power cuts in Italy** affect 56 million people
- **8 October Arnold Schwarzenegger** becomes Governor of California
- **15 October** China launches first manned space mission, **Shenzhou 5**
- **19 October Mother Teresa** beatified by Pope John Paul II
- **24 October Concorde** makes last commercial flight
- **15 and 20 November** Two bomb attacks in **Istanbul**, Turkey
- **5 December** Bomb blast on commuter train, **Russia**
- **13 December Saddam Hussein** captured
- **22 December** Earthquake hits **San Simeon**, California, US
- **23 December** Huge earthquake in Iran devastates city of **Bam**

2004

Afghan citizens in Kabul wait in line to vote at the Jaffaria Mosque, in the first presidential elections since the overthrow of the Taliban government.

THE NEW AFGHAN CONSTITUTION was signed in the capital Kabul on 26 January. **Hamid Karzai**, leader of the transitional government, was officially declared the winner of Afghanistan's presidential election on 3 November. The result of the election had been delayed due to an investigation into voting irregularities.

In April, the CBS news programme "Sixty Minutes" broadcast shocking images in the US showing abuse of prisoners at **Abu Ghraib** in Iraq by members of the US military police. President George W. Bush issued an apology. **Bush was re-elected** for a second term as US president on 2 November. He portrayed himself as a strong leader in a time of war.

On 29 October, Arabic TV station **al-Jazeera** aired a video in which **Osama Bin Laden** threatened fresh attacks on the US. The video was Bin Laden's clearest statement of responsibility for the terror attacks of 9/11.

US and Iraqi forces stormed into western areas of Fallujah, **Iraq**, a rebel stronghold, early on 8 November. The aim was to put an end to guerrilla control of the Sunni Muslim city.

The **European Union** (EU) grew on 1 May, as ten more countries joined. It was the largest single enlargement in its history. Many of the new member states were former Eastern Bloc countries.

Chechen president **Akhmad Kadyrov** died in an explosion at a stadium in Grozny, the capital of Chechnya, on 9 May. The assassination, during a parade, was thought to be the work of Islamic militants.

Trouble continued in Chechnya when **separatists** stormed a school in **Beslan**, North Ossetia, on 1 September. They held children and staff hostage for three days – hundreds of hostages died, including 186 children.

Beslan crisis
A group of armed Chechen separatists took more than 1,000 people hostage at a Russian school – 331 died, many of them children.

Spain also experienced terrorist attacks when explosions tore through three **Madrid** train stations on 11 March, killing 191. **Al-Qaeda** claimed responsibility.

The Summer **Olympic Games** were held in **Athens**, Greece, birthplace of the ancient games, for the first time since 1896. The US won the most medals – 103 in total.

An **earthquake** under the Indian Ocean near the Indonesian island of Sumatra on 26 December unleashed a series of killer waves, **tsunami**, that sped across the sea. More than 200,000 people died and millions made homeless in 11 countries, making this the most destructive tsunami in history.

Wave of destruction
Tsunami waves travelled 1,600 km (1,000 miles) across the Indian Ocean in only 90 minutes. They caused a massive amount of damage.

2005

An aerial view of New Orleans in the aftermath of Hurricane Katrina, in which 80 per cent of the city was flooded.

YASSIR ARAFAT DIED IN 2004, and the leader of the Palestine Liberation Army, **Rawhi Fattouh**, became interim president of the Palestinian Authority. Under Palestinian law he held the post for 60 days until elections were held. **Mahmoud Abbas** became the new president on 6 January. Abbas and the Israeli prime minister, Ariel Sharon, announced a **ceasefire** on 8 February. It was seen as the best chance for peace in the region for many years.

The former Lebanese prime minister **Rafik Hariri** was killed by a suicide bomb in west Beirut on 14 February. Hariri had been planning to make a comeback in forthcoming elections. He had called on Syria to cease its involvement in Lebanese affairs – Syria denied any involvement in his death. The assassination put further pressure on **Syria** to remove their troops from Lebanon. On 26 April, they announced that they had withdrawn. This was regarded as an historic day in the Middle East.

Former leader of Iraq, **Saddam Hussein**, went on **trial** in October, nearly two years after his capture, for atrocities he carried out during his rule. He refused to acknowledge the authority of the court trying him, and claimed that he was not guilty. Hussein was sentenced to death and executed in 2006.

Four explosions ripped across **London** on 7 July. Co-ordinated

“ IT'S TOTALLY WIPED OUT. ”

George W. Bush, US president, surveying the damage to New Orleans, 31 August 2005

EXTREME WEATHER

Weather became increasingly wild in the 2000s. Hurricane Katrina (pictured) in 2005 was only one of an unprecedented series of hurricanes and tropical storms. Other weather phenomena included record levels of rainfall, melting icecaps, and severe drought, all contributing to increased concerns about the prospect of global warming. The forecast is for more extreme weather, disrupting lifestyles, making animal species extinct, and threatening human lives.

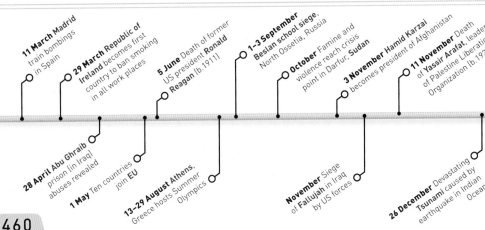

11 March Madrid train bombings in Spain

29 March Republic of Ireland becomes first country to ban smoking in all work places

28 April Abu Ghraib prison (in Iraq) abuses revealed

1 May Ten countries join **EU**

5 June Death of former US president **Ronald Reagan** (b.1911)

13–29 August Athens, Greece hosts Summer Olympics

1–3 September Beslan school siege, North Ossetia, Russia

October Famine and violence reach crisis point in Darfur, **Sudan**

3 November Hamid Karzai becomes president of Afghanistan

November Siege of **Fallujah** in Iraq by US forces

11 November Death of **Yassir Arafat**, leader of Palestine Liberation Organization (b.1929)

26 December Devastating **Tsunami** caused by earthquake in Indian Ocean

6 January Mahmoud Abbas becomes leader of PLO

8 February Israel–Palestine ceasefire

February Youtube launched

14 February Rafik Hariri, former Lebanese prime minister, assassinated (b.1944)

16 February Kyoto Protocol comes into force

26 April Syria withdraws troops from **Lebanon**

7 July London hit by four terrorist bombs on transport system

29 August Hurricane Katrina blasts New Orleans, US

terrorist attacks struck three underground trains and a double-decker bus, killing 52 people, and injuring several hundred more. The four suicide bombers, all British men, were backed by **al-Qaeda**.

Weeks after the al-Qaeda attack on the London transport system, the **provisional IRA** – the paramilitary wing of the Irish Republican Army – announced it was **ceasing its armed campaign** on 28 July. Two months later there was a verification statement from the independent arms decommissioning body that the IRA had put all its weapons beyond use.

The **Kyoto accord** came into force seven years after it was first agreed (see 1997). It aimed to curb the air pollution blamed for global warming. The US, the world's top polluter, did not sign up, as the protocol was not thought to be in the best interest of the American economy.

Hurricane Katrina hit New Orleans in the US, on 29 August causing unprecedented destruction. The hurricane also battered large swathes of the Louisiana and Mississippi coastlines, leaving two oil rigs adrift in the Gulf of Mexico and causing damage estimated at £14.4bn ($26bn).

YouTube, a video-sharing website, was launched in February and soon grew into one of the most popular websites on the internet. After only a year 100 million videos were being viewed every day.

2006

> **"FUTURE GENERATIONS** MAY WELL ASK THEMSELVES, **WHAT WERE OUR PARENTS THINKING?"**
>
> **Al Gore, US politician,** *An Inconvenient Truth*, 2006

THE BASQUE SEPARATIST GROUP ETA declared a permanent **ceasefire** on 22 March. They aimed to pursue independence for the Basque region through a **democratic process**.

Montenegro became a sovereign state on 3 June after a **referendum** in which just over 55 per cent of the populace voted for **independence**. It meant the end of the former Union of Serbia and Montenegro, created only three years earlier from the former Yugoslavia (see 2003).

Iran announced that it had produced the **enriched uranium** needed to make nuclear fuel. It insisted this was for generating nuclear power, but the West was concerned that Iran was making a nuclear bomb.

Power generator
The building of the world's largest hydroelectric installation, the Three Gorges Dam, was completed in 2006, in China.

Another nuclear power, **North Korea**, announced it had tested a **nuclear weapon** on 9 October, provoking severe international condemnation.

Construction began on the **Freedom Tower** in New York on 26 April. The skyscraper was to replace the twin towers destroyed in the 9/11 attacks (see 2001).

Seven **bombs** exploded on the suburban railway of **Mumbai**, India, on 11 July. Over 200 lost their lives. Tension between India and Pakistan increased when evidence suggested that the Pakistani intelligence agency was involved in the attacks.

The **Three Gorges Dam** in China was completed on 20 May. At 2.3km (1.4 miles) long, it is one of the world's largest dams, and one of the most controversial public works in modern times. The dam was engineered to prevent flooding along the **Yangtze River**, but had a huge social and ecological impact.

2007

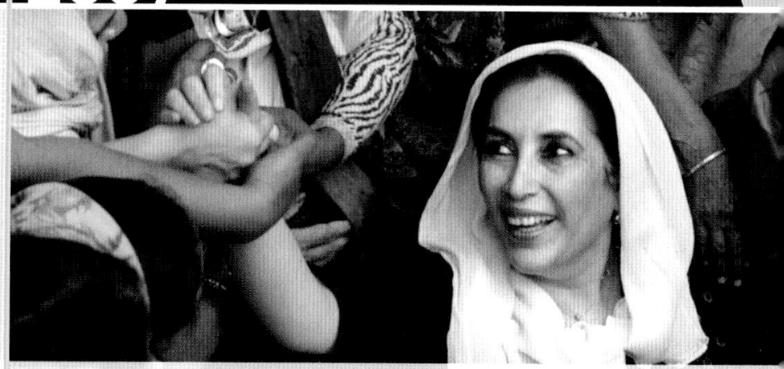

Former prime minister of Pakistan, Benazir Bhutto, campaigning in Karachi before elections.

BULGARIA AND ROMANIA joined the **European Union** on 1 January. They took the membership of the group from 25 to 27 member states.

Direct rule over **Northern Ireland** by London officially ended on 8 May. Democratic Unionist Party leader **Ian Paisley** and Sinn Fein's **Martin McGuinness** were sworn in as first and deputy first ministers of the new executive.

Iranian forces captured 15 British sailors on 23 March. The sailors were accused of entering Iranian waters and were held prisoner for 11 days.

Nawaz Sharif, former prime minister of Pakistan, returned home from exile in August, vowing to end the "dictatorship" of President Musharraf. Within weeks he was deported to Saudi Arabia.

Another former leader of Pakistan, **Benazir Bhutto**, was assassinated on 27 December during a political rally. Islamist militants were thought to be responsible.

> **"I PUT MY LIFE IN DANGER** AND CAME HERE BECAUSE I **BELIEVE MY COUNTRY** TO BE IN DANGER."
>
> **Benazir Bhutto, Pakistani politician,** in a speech shortly before her assassination

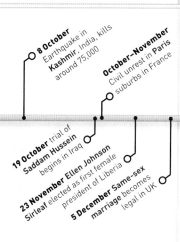

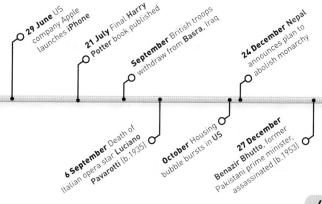

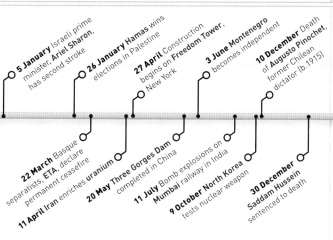

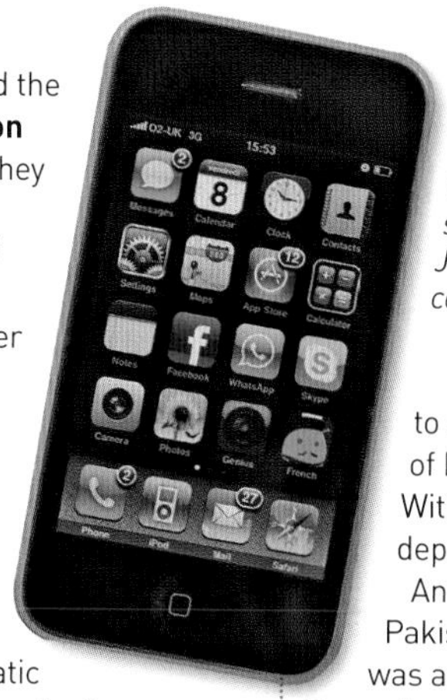

iPhone
A new type of multi-media phone, the iPhone connects to the internet via a touch screen. It was launched in January by US technology company Apple.

On 24 December, **Nepal** announced that it would abolish its monarchy after elections, which were to be held in 2008. Some parties had refused to serve in government until Nepal became a republic.

A major scientific breakthough was made when the first **artificial sperm** was created in April. It was grown from human bone marrow samples in a laboratory in Newcastle, England.

The mysterious **dark matter** that makes up a quarter of the Universe was revealed in May by a 3D map made by the **Hubble telescope**. It helped explain how the universe was formed.

The final book in the **Harry Potter** series by J.K. Rowling was released on 21 July. *Harry Potter and the Deathly Hallows* became the fastest selling book of all time.

- **8 October** Earthquake in **Kashmir**, India, kills around 75,000
- **19 October** trial of **Saddam Hussein** begins in Iraq
- **October–November** Civil unrest in **Paris** suburbs in France
- **23 November Ellen Johnson Sirleaf** elected as first female president of Liberia
- **5 December Same-sex marriage** becomes legal in UK
- **5 January** Israeli prime minister, **Ariel Sharon**, has second stroke
- **26 January Hamas** wins elections in Palestine
- **22 March** Basque separatists, **ETA**, declare permanent ceasefire
- **11 April** Iran enriches **uranium**
- **27 April** Construction begins on **Freedom Tower**, New York
- **20 May Three Gorges Dam** completed in China
- **3 June Montenegro** becomes independent
- **11 July** Bomb explosions on **Mumbai** railway in India
- **9 October North Korea** tests nuclear weapon
- **10 December** Death of **Augusto Pinochet**, former Chilean dictator (b.1915)
- **30 December Saddam Hussein** sentenced to death
- **29 June** US company Apple launches **iPhone**
- **21 July** Final **Harry Potter** book published
- **6 September** Death of Italian opera star **Luciano Pavarotti** (b.1935)
- **September** British troops withdraw from **Basra**, Iraq
- **October** Housing bubble bursts in **US**
- **24 December Nepal** announces plan to abolish monarchy
- **27 December Benazir Bhutto**, former Pakistani prime minister, assassinated (b.1953)

9.69 SECONDS

USAIN BOLT'S RECORD IN THE 100M SPRINT

Usain Bolt became the fastest man on Earth when he sprinted his way to a new 100m world record at the Summer Olympics in Beijing.

THIS WAS THE YEAR OF "BLACK MONDAYS" in the world of **finance**. On Monday 21 January, the London Stock Exchange experienced a dramatic fall in overall value. On Monday 15 September, the US investment firm **Lehman Brothers** declared **bankruptcy**, and on the US stock market the Dow Jones Industrial Average lost 4.4 per cent of its value. On Monday 29 September, there was a seven per cent drop in the Dow.

BARACK OBAMA (1961–)

Democrat Barack Hussein Obama made history when he was elected to the White House as the 44th President of the US. Born in Hawaii, he is the first African-American to hold the office, and gained admirers for his relaxed charm and stirring oratory. However, his first year met with fierce opposition as he attempted to change America's healthcare system, tackle climate change, and reach new agreements on nuclear disarmament.

The Australian prime minister **Kevin Rudd** (b.1957) made an official **apology** for years of mistreatment inflicted on the country's **Aboriginal** people on 13 February. He singled out the "Stolen Generations" – mixed-race children who were forcibly removed from their families under a government-sanctioned policy of white assimilation.

On 7 January, New Jersey became the first northern state in the US to apologize for its part in the slave trade. It prohibited the importation of slaves after 1786, but was the last northern state to emancipate them.

Democrat **Barack Obama** won the US presidential election on 4 November, becoming the first African-American president, and winning 52.5 per cent of the popular vote. Obama's main rival was Republican **John McCain**.

Cuba's leader, **Fidel Castro**, **retired** after half a century on 19 February. He had not appeared in public since undergoing stomach surgery. Castro's brother, **Raul**, became president.

Pakistan's president **Pervez Musharraf** bowed to intense pressure and **resigned** on 18 August ahead of impeachment proceedings. He launched a passionate defence of his record.

India suffered a series of co-ordinated **terrorist attacks** on 28 November across the city of **Mumbai** – 166 people were killed. India blamed the attacks on Pakistan-based militant groups and the attacks derailed peace talks between the two nations.

Kosovo declared **independence** from Serbia on 17 February, but the legitimacy of this was disputed. Kosovo's bid to be recognized as Europe's newest country was the latest episode in the dismemberment of the former **Yugoslavia**, 17 years after its dissolution began.

Radovan Karadzic, Europe's most wanted man, was **arrested** on 21 July. The former Bosnian Serb leader had been on the run for 12 years, facing charges of genocide.

South Ossetia became the focus of a **war** between Russia and Georgia in August when it tried to **break away** from Georgia. Georgia launched a full military offensive to try and reconquer the region, which lead to violent clashes with Russia. After Georgia's troops were ejected, Russia withdrew and recognized South Ossetia's independence.

Irish voters plunged the **EU** into disarray on 13 June by **rejecting** the **Lisbon Treaty**, which was designed to bring more European integration. All European member states had to ratify the treaty for it to go into force in 2009. It had been approved by 18 countries, but Ireland was the only one to put the treaty to a public vote.

Usain Bolt sprinted into history with a world record-breaking run on 16 August at the Summer **Olympics** held in **Beijing**, China. Bolt, from Jamaica, ran the 100m final in a time of 9.69 seconds, breaking his own record of 9.72 seconds set earlier in 2008. The decision to pick Beijing as the host for the Summer Olympics of 2008 was controversial, as critics cited China's record of human rights violations. The event became a source of enormous national pride for China.

Twenty years in the making, the world's largest "atom smasher", the **Large Hadron Collider**, built near Geneva, Switzerland, was started on 10 September. It was designed to look at the "big bang" and other mysteries of the Universe.

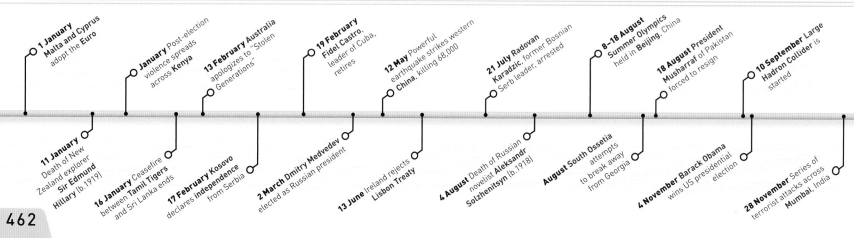

The Hadron collider at CERN
The most intricate machine ever built, it is hoped that the Large Hadron Collider will unravel the mystery of how the Universe began.

- **1 January** Malta and Cyprus adopt the **Euro**
- **11 January** Death of New Zealand explorer **Sir Edmund Hillary** (b.1919)
- **January** Post-election violence spreads across **Kenya**
- **16 January** Ceasefire between **Tamil Tigers** and Sri Lanka ends
- **13 February** Australia apologizes to "Stolen Generations"
- **17 February** Kosovo declares **independence** from Serbia
- **19 February** **Fidel Castro**, leader of Cuba, retires
- **2 March** Dmitry Medvedev elected as Russian president
- **12 May** Powerful earthquake strikes western **China**, killing 68,000
- **13 June** Ireland rejects **Lisbon Treaty**
- **21 July** Radovan **Karadzic**, former Bosnian Serb leader, arrested
- **4 August** Death of Russian novelist **Aleksandr Solzhenitsyn** (b.1918)
- **August** South Ossetia attempts to break away from Georgia
- **8–18 August** Summer Olympics held in **Beijing**, China
- **18 August** President **Musharraf** of Pakistan forced to resign
- **10 September** Large **Hadron Collider** is started
- **4 November** Barack Obama wins US presidential election
- **28 November** Series of terrorist attacks across **Mumbai**, India

173

THE NUMBER OF **DEATHS** IN THE VICTORIA **BUSH FIRES**

BP workers lay an oil absorbent boom near a wildlife refuge off the Gulf of Mexico to stop the spread of oil from the Deepwater Horizon platform disaster.

FOLLOWING AIR STRIKES THE PREVIOUS YEAR, Israeli troops invaded Gaza in early January. Israel claimed it was in an attempt to stop **Hamas**, the main Islamic resistance movement, from firing rockets into Israel. A ceasefire was declared and Israeli troops withdrew from Gaza by the end of January.

Right-wing activists in the US calling themselves the **Tea Party** roared onto the political scene this year, demanding fiscal responsibility and lower taxes.

American car giants **General Motors** and **Chrysler** both filed for **bankruptcy** in 2009, as the ongoing financial crisis took its toll on industries around the world.

Zimbabwe's opposition leader **Morgan Tsvangirai** (b.1952) was sworn in as prime minister in a unity government with President Robert Mugabe on 11 February. This power-sharing deal was designed to put an end to the ongoing political violence in Zimbabwe.

The **Copenhagen climate summit** was held in December. Five nations, including China and the US, agreed to attempt to limit global temperature rises. Some critics were disappointed, as they thought that the agreement did not go far enough.

Swiss tennis player **Roger Federer** won the men's tennis final at Wimbledon in July; it was his 15th Grand Slam win, and made him the most successful men's tennis player in Grand Slam history.

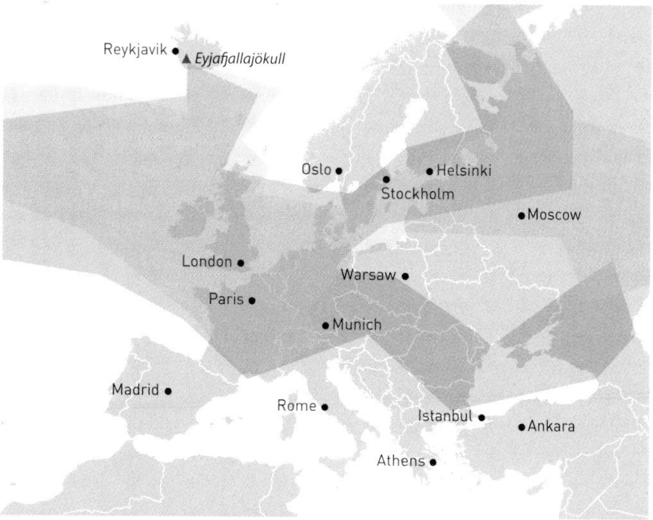

Spread of volcanic ash in Europe
The constantly shifting high-altitude cloud of volcanic ash from Eyjafjallajökull, Iceland, caused travel chaos as European airspace was closed.

KEY
19th April 0000 GMT
19th April 0600 GMT

AN EARTHQUAKE DEVASTATED the Haitian capital **Port au Prince** on 12 January. It measured 7 on the Richter scale, and around 230,000 people died. Many were housed in badly constructed buildings.

An **Icelandic volcano**, dormant for two hundred years, erupted near the Eyjafjallajökull glacier on 14 April. It sent clouds of ash soaring as high as 11,000m (36,000ft), disrupting air traffic in Europe, and delaying millions of air passengers across the world.

The **US** experienced an **environmental disaster** in April when the BP-owned **Deepwater Horizon** oil rig exploded and sank. Around four million barrels of **oil** were pumped into the Gulf of Mexico and 11 men were killed.

At the **UN climate summit** held in Cancun, Mexico, a new fund was agreed, to give money to developing countries trying to tackle the consequences of climate change.

Poland was plunged into mourning when President Lech Kaczynski, his wife Maria, and other senior Polish figures were killed in a **plane crash** in Russia on 10 April.

The global recession continued, and the **Greek economy** faced the threat of bankruptcy. On 2 May, the International Monetary Fund (IMF) agreed a €110 billion loan for Greece, on the condition that **austerity** measures were enforced. **Ireland** asked the European Union for a **rescue finance** package on 21 November, after seven days of denying it needed a bailout for its banking system. People across Europe held **demonstrations** on 29 September, protesting at austerity measures made by their governments. They were particularly angry at the vast sums of money that had been used to rescue **banks**.

The world held its breath in late November as **North Korea** bombarded a South Korean island near a disputed maritime border, leaving two soldiers dead. The clash was one of the most serious since the end of the Korean War (see 1950). War was not declared but tensions continued to simmer.

Burma's military regime released pro-democracy leader **Aung San Suu Kyi** (see panel, below) on 13 November.

The imprisoned Chinese dissident, **Liu Xiaobo**, won this year's **Nobel Peace Prize**. The ceremony was boycotted by China, who launched an unprecedented campaign against the award.

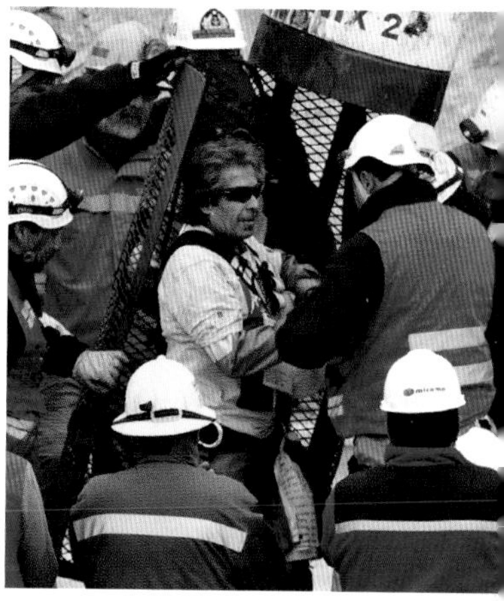

Chilean rescue
A Chilean miner is helped to the surface after being trapped underground for 10 weeks following the collapse of the San Jose mine.

On 5 August, 33 **Chilean miners** were trapped underground following a cave-in. They spent 69 days in the mine and the world became transfixed by their ordeal and successful rescue, which was completed on 14 October.

AUNG SAN SUU KYI (1945–)

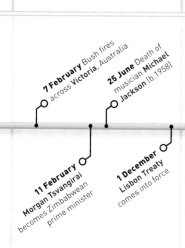

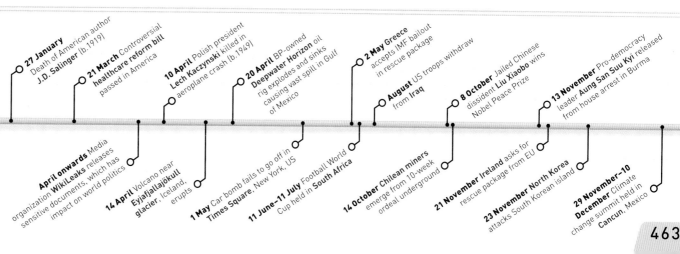

Burmese opposition leader Aung San Suu Kyi spent most of the pervious 20 years under house arrest, due to her efforts to bring democracy to Burma. Her tireless determination to stand for non-violent resistance in the face of a brutal military regime inspired the world. She was released from house arrest in 2010 and called for "national conciliation."

7 February Bush fires across **Victoria**, Australia

11 February Morgan Tsvangirai becomes Zimbabwean prime minister

25 June Death of musician **Michael Jackson** (b.1958)

1 December Lisbon Treaty comes into force

27 January Death of American author **J.D. Salinger** (b.1919)

21 March Controversial **healthcare reform bill** passed in America

April onwards Media organization **WikiLeaks** releases sensitive documents, which has impact on world politics

10 April Polish president **Lech Kaczynski** killed in aeroplane crash (b.1949)

14 April Volcano near **Eyjafjallajökull glacier**, Iceland, erupts

20 April BP-owned **Deepwater Horizon** oil rig explodes and sinks causing vast spill in Gulf of Mexico

1 May Car bomb fails to go off in **Times Square**, New York, US

2 May Greece accepts IMF bailout in rescue package

11 June–11 July Football World Cup held in **South Africa**

August US troops withdraw from **Iraq**

8 October Jailed Chinese dissident **Liu Xiaobo** wins Nobel Peace Prize

14 October Chilean miners emerge from 10-week ordeal underground

13 November Pro-democracy leader **Aung San Suu Kyi** released from house arrest in Burma

21 November Ireland asks for rescue package from EU

23 November North Korea attacks South Korean island

29 November–10 December Climate change summit held in **Cancun**, Mexico

Prince William, second in line to the British throne, kisses his bride, Catherine Middleton, on the balcony of Buckingham Palace following their wedding at Westminster Abbey on 29 April.

EXTRAORDINARY EVENTS ACROSS THE MIDDLE EAST led to what became known as the "**Arab Spring**". It began when a man in Tunisia burned himself to death in December 2010 in protest at his treatment by police. This led to pro-democracy rebellions, which erupted across the **Middle East**. After days of protests, Tunisian president Zine el Abidine Ben Ali promised more jobs while vowing to punish rioters. On 9 January, protestors clashed with police and there were calls for the president to resign. A few days later he fled to Saudi Arabia.

Riots began in **Algeria** over food prices and unemployment. A man burned himself to death in an apparent echo of events in Tunisia that sent new shockwaves across North Africa. Anti-government activists announced a "day of anger" in Egypt, and there were calls for **President Mubarak** (b.1928) to resign. In response, Mubarak shut down mobile phone and internet networks and then appointed his first ever vice president in an attempt to calm things down. Eventually, after 18 solid days of mass protest, **Mubarak surrendered power** to the army on 11 February and flew out of Cairo.

The uprising in Egypt led to an upsurge of **violent protests** against repressive regimes in **Yemen**, **Jordan**, **Morocco**, **Oman**, and **Iran**. On 16 February, protests erupted in Libya's second largest city, **Benghazi**, following the arrest of a human rights campaigner. The uprising against **Colonel Muammar Gaddafi** (b.1942) developed into an armed conflict pitting rebels against government forces. A NATO-led coalition with a UN mandate to protect civilians also became involved. The country's coastal cities became roughly split between pro-Gaddafi forces

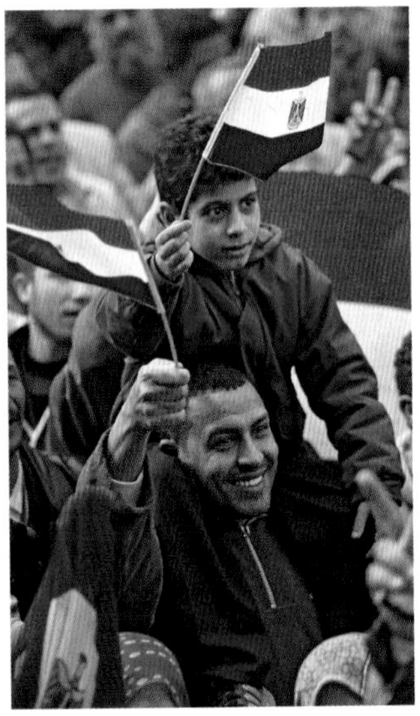

Revolution in Egypt
An Egyptian man and boy celebrate the resignation of Egyptian President Hosni Mubarak in Tahir Square, Cairo after weeks of protests.

controlling the capital, Tripoli, and the west, and rebels controlling Benghazi in the east.

The wave of popular unrest also hit **Syria**, where the government began a violent crackdown on civilian dissenters. **President Assad** (b.1965) promised reform on 16 April, but the death toll rose and scores of prominent intellectuals and activists went into hiding. Syrians demanded greater political freedom, an end to corruption, and the lifting of an emergency law in place for nearly 50 years.

There was cautious optimism in two African nations this year as they struggled to end years of bloody conflict. In January, the **Sudanese voted in a referendum** to split the country between north and south and form a new state. However, within months of the poll a wave of violence spread across southern Sudan as its army clashed with rebel militia. These rebel groups accused the government of plotting to stay in power indefinitely, not representing all tribal groups, and neglecting development in rural areas. This led to fears that **Southern Sudan** would fail as a country before it had even got started.

The **Ivory Coast** held elections in 2010. A high turnout fostered the belief that the country's post-civil war division might come to an end. The Constitutional Council named incumbent president **Laurence Gbagbo** the winner, but the electoral commission named **Alassane Ouattara**, who was immediately recognized by the UN, US, and the EU. Gbagbo fought to stay in power and there was fierce fighting between the two sides. The UN sent in troops, and on 5 April launched air attacks on Gbagbo's positions. Under the auspices of the UN, French helicopters attacked Gbagbo's palace on 9 April and he was arrested two days later. Ouattara

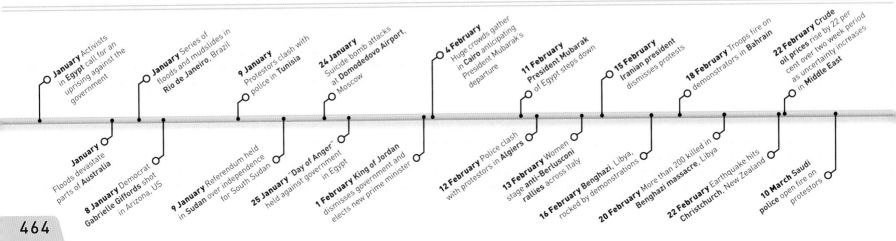

Broken city
A family walks past cars upturned by the tsunami in Japan. A massive 8.9 magnitude earthquake hit Sendai, the capital of the Miyagi Prefecture.

became president, but inherited a country politically and militarily divided, half destroyed by civil war, and with an economy starved of investment.

A series of **natural disasters** struck around the globe during the first few months of the year, causing unprecedented damage and destruction. Brisbane, **Australia**, resembled a muddy lake in January following catastrophic **flooding**, with debris from houses and businesses washed away down the Brisbane River. The floods spread to other parts of Queensland – more than 200,000 people in 20 towns and cities were affected.

Torrential rain caused deadly mudslides and **flooding in Brazil** in one of its deadliest natural disasters on record. Almost 500 people were killed across three cities north of Rio de Janeiro.

On 22 February, a huge **earthquake** ripped apart the centre of **Christchurch**, one of New Zealand's biggest cities. The quake, measuring 6.3 on the Richter scale, hit at the height of the working day and killed an

January Activists in **Egypt** call for an uprising against the government

January Floods devastate parts of **Australia**

January Series of floods and mudslides in **Rio de Janeiro**, Brazil

8 January Democrat **Gabrielle Giffords** shot in Arizona, US

9 January Protestors clash with police in **Tunisia**

9 January Referendum held in **Sudan** over independence for South Sudan

24 January Suicide bomb attacks at **Domodedovo Airport**, Moscow

25 January **"Day of Anger"** held against government in Egypt

1 February **King of Jordan** dismisses government and elects new prime minister

4 February Huge crowds gather in **Cairo** anticipating President Mubarak's departure

11 February **President Mubarak** of Egypt steps down

12 February Police clash with protestors in **Algiers**

13 February Women stage **anti-Berlusconi rallies** across Italy

15 February **Iranian president** dismisses protests

16 February **Benghazi**, Libya, rocked by demonstrations

18 February Troops fire on demonstrators in **Bahrain**

20 February More than 200 killed in **Benghazi massacre**, Libya

22 February Earthquake hits **Christchurch**, New Zealand

22 February **Crude oil prices** rise by 22 per cent over two week period as uncertainty increases in **Middle East**

10 March **Saudi police** open fire on protestors

2 BILLION THE NUMBER OF PEOPLE WHO WATCHED THE BRITISH ROYAL WEDDING

estimated 181 people. It was the worst disaster in New Zealand in 80 years.

Japan experienced its most powerful **earthquake** since records began on 11 March. Measuring 9.0 on the Richter scale, the earthquake struck the northeast coast, causing a massive **Tsunami**. A wall of water racing inland swept away cars, ships, and buildings. The official death toll was 14,000, but many thousands were missing and the cost to human life is not yet fully known. A **state of emergency** was declared at a **nuclear power plant** in Fukushima, where pressure exceeded normal levels, leading to worldwide concerns about a nuclear disaster. By May, the plant showed little sign of calming down, and officials announced a complete cold **shutdown** by the end of the year.

The world was suffering from a **financial hangover** in 2011, as austerity measures began to bite. A bailout package given to Ireland and Greece in 2010 had been intended to stop their **Euro debt crisis** from spreading to the rest of Europe, but whispers of a **bailout in Portugal** were enough to put stocks on shaky ground, and raise fears that Spain was also in trouble. A bailout for Portugal was awarded on 17 May. Eurozone ministers met in the same month to staunch the market's anxieties about **Greece, Portugal, and Ireland**, amid concerns that these countries would be unable to meet the repayments on their loans.

Elizabeth Taylor
One of the Hollywood greats, British born American actress Elizabeth Taylor died on 23 March at the age of 79.

The future of the **single currency** looked **uncertain**. But it was not all gloom for the euro, as Germany and France saw their economies grow.

Terrorism struck again in the heart of **Russia**, as two suicide bombers blew themselves up at Domodedovo Airport in Moscow, on 24 January, devastating the international arrivals hall and killing dozens of people. They were believed to be Islamist militants from the North Caucasus.

Italy grappled with problems of a different sort as its leader, **Silvio Berlusconi** (b.1936), who had shown a knack for surviving charges of corruption, faced new charges in February of having sex with an underage girl. The scandal, combined with the poor state of the country's finances, lost Berlusconi his key supporters.

The bitter debate over the **Tea Party movement** (see 2009) in the US and its inflammatory right wing rhetoric was reignited when Democratic Congresswoman **Gabrielle Giffords** was shot in the head during a public meeting in Tuscon, Arizona. Six people were killed in the attack on 8 January, but Giffords survived.

President Obama continued to have a tough time exerting his authority, and budget cuts, on a reluctant Congress. Bickering between Republicans and Democrats was intense, and Republicans pushed for even greater cuts. The US Congress finally passed a budget bill in April that would cut $38.5 billion in government spending over the rest of the fiscal year. Obama's attempts to spotlight positive initiatives were swamped by the crush of news from Japan, Egypt, and Libya.

Criticism of Obama's leadership was overshadowed by the news that **Osama Bin Laden** (b.1957), the leader of al-Qaeda and the most hunted man in the world, had been **killed** on 1 May in a fire fight with US forces in Pakistan. The news sparked an outpouring of emotion across America, but led to immediate fears of retaliation. Retaliation was, indeed, swift. The Pakistani Taliban carried out a double **suicide bombing** on 13 May that killed 80 recruits at a military training centre in the northwest of the country.

A shaken world
The earthquake in Japan was the fifth largest since records began – this graph shows the magnitude of the ten biggest earthquakes in history.

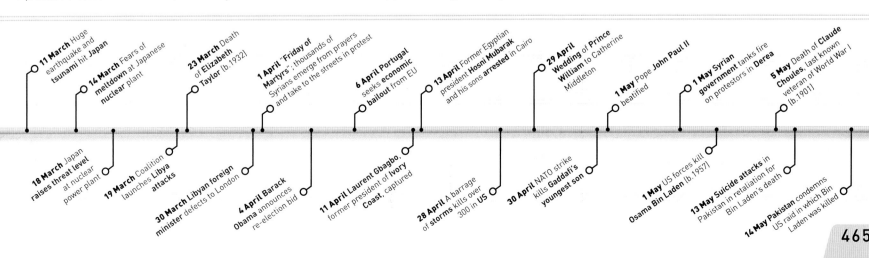

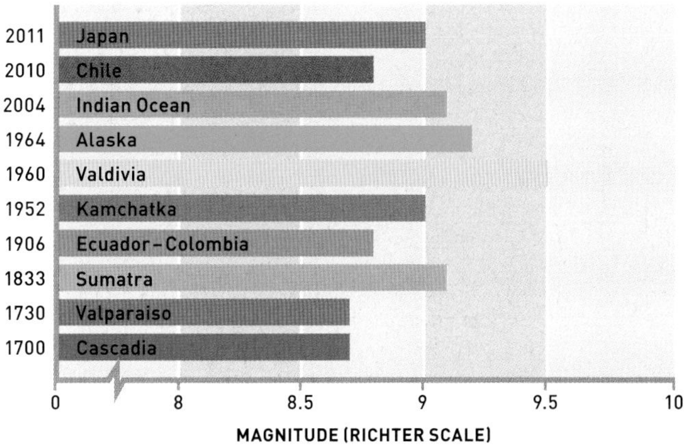

Death of Bin Laden
Osama Bin Laden, hunted for three decades, made headline news around the world after his death at the hands of US special forces.

Only days after the dramatic events of Osama Bin Laden's death, the world's last known combat veteran of World War I, **Claude Choules**, died peacefully in Australia aged 110. He had served in both World Wars. Conflict shaped his life, and he became a staunch pacifist. His death marked the moment the Great War passed from living memory into the history books.

- **11 March** Huge earthquake and **tsunami** hit **Japan**
- **14 March** Fears of **meltdown** at Japanese **nuclear** plant
- **18 March** Japan **raises threat level** at nuclear power plant
- **19 March** Coalition launches **Libya attacks**
- **23 March** Death of **Elizabeth Taylor** (b.1932)
- **30 March Libyan foreign minister** defects to London
- **1 April "Friday of Martyrs"**; thousands of Syrians emerge from prayers and take to the streets in protest
- **4 April Barack Obama** announces re-election bid
- **6 April Portugal** seeks **economic bailout** from EU
- **11 April Laurent Gbagbo,** former president of **Ivory Coast,** captured
- **13 April** Former Egyptian president **Hosni Mubarak** and his sons **arrested** in Cairo
- **28 April** A barrage of **storms** kills over 300 in **US**
- **29 April Wedding** of **Prince William** to Catherine Middleton
- **30 April** NATO strike kills **Gaddafi's youngest son**
- **1 May** Pope **John Paul II** beatified
- **1 May** US forces kill **Osama Bin Laden** (b.1957)
- **1 May Syrian government** tanks fire on protestors in **Derea**
- **5 May** Death of **Claude Choules,** last known veteran of World War I (b.1901)
- **13 May Suicide attacks** in Pakistan in retaliation for Bin Laden's death
- **14 May Pakistan** condemns US raid in which Bin Laden was killed

THE GLOBAL ECONOMY

AN INCREASING DIVIDE BETWEEN RICH AND POOR

The world is richer than ever, strengthened by international alliances and technology, but there is still widespread poverty. Wars continue to be fought, and even developed nations can be devastated by natural disasters.

There are currently almost 7 billion people living on the planet, three times the population of 1900. The fate of each person depends on where they live, and the distribution of the world's wealth has changed little since World War II. Many high-income countries are in the northern hemisphere, with the world's poorest in sub-Saharan Africa. The six wealthiest countries account for more than half the world's Gross Domestic Product (GDP) – the value of all the goods and services a country produces – while over half the world's population live on less than $2.50 a day.

The countries of Western Europe and North America have well-established business sectors, with multinational corporations selling products globally. The nations of Africa and Central America have a smaller range of industries, and many depend on trading a single commodity. But this is slowly changing, and the economies of countries such as Mexico, Brazil, and India are growing rapidly.

THE US

Although the US is the wealthiest country in the world, it is home to only 5.2 per cent of the world's population. Forty-one per cent of the world's millionaires live in the US, but it also has the highest level of total household debt.

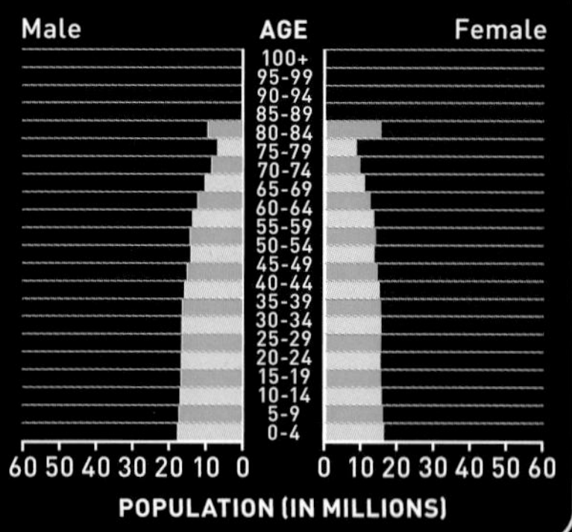

Interdependent world
The economies of the world are based on a vast range of industries, and populations range from 800 (Vatican City) to over a billion (India and China). No countries are fully self-supporting, however, and they all depend on trade with other countries to fully meet their needs.

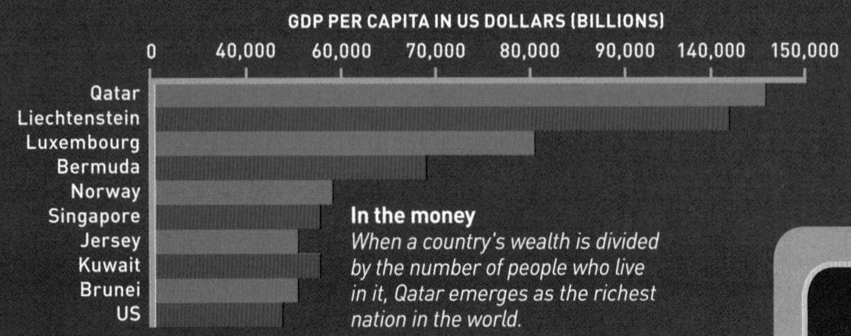

In the money
When a country's wealth is divided by the number of people who live in it, Qatar emerges as the richest nation in the world.

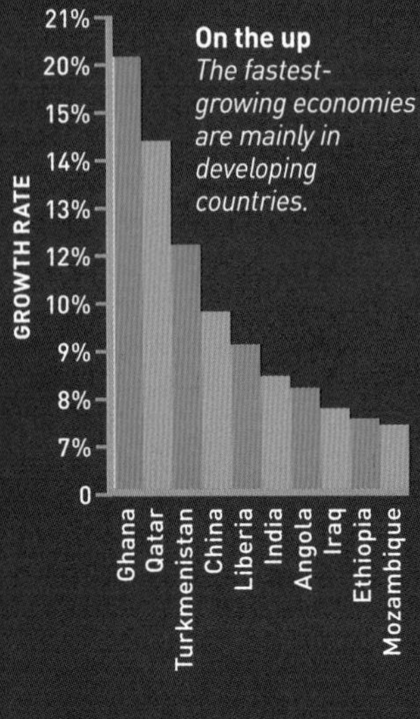

On the up
The fastest-growing economies are mainly in developing countries.

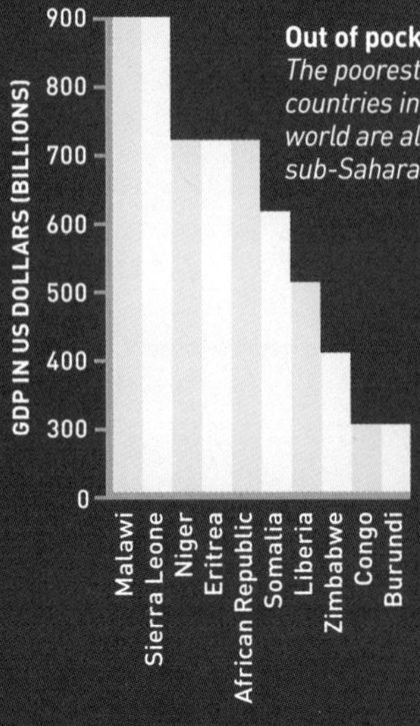

Out of pocket
The poorest countries in the world are all in sub-Saharan Africa.

BRAZIL

Brazil has the largest economy in South America, and the ninth largest in the world. Well-established agriculture, mining, and service sectors have helped create a healthy economy, and Brazil is also rich in natural resources. Huge gaps remain between rich and poor, however.

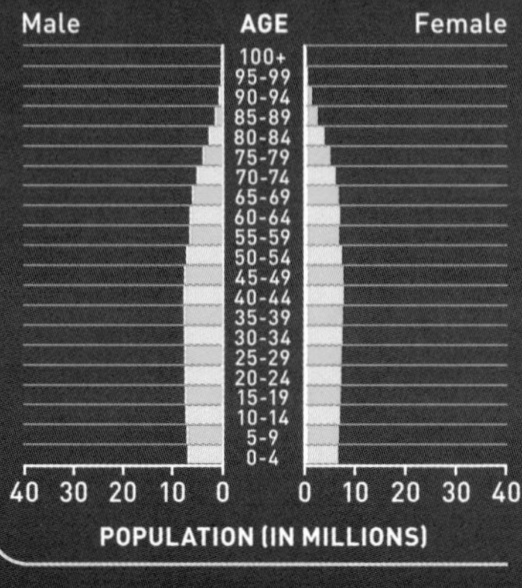

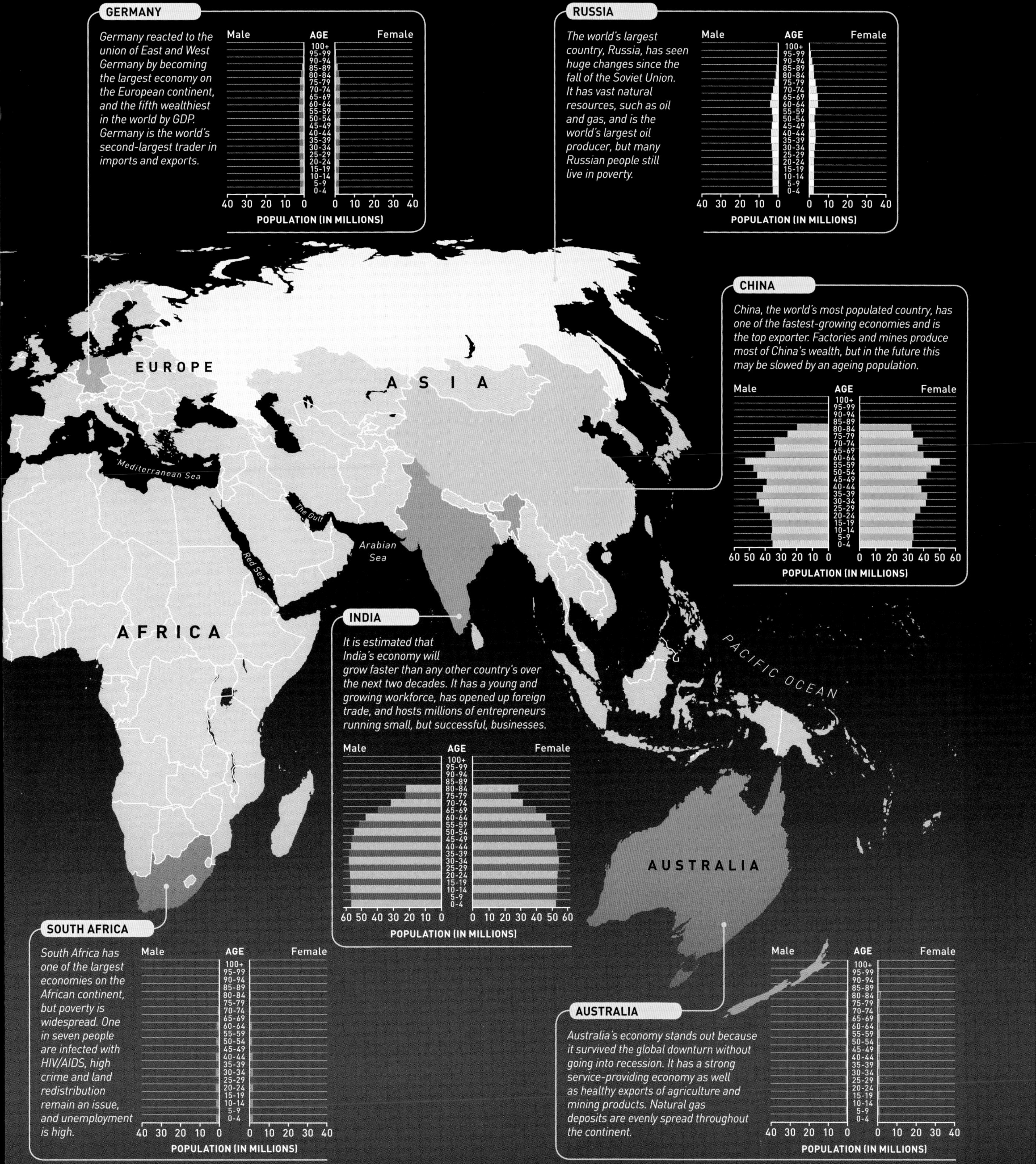

GERMANY

Germany reacted to the union of East and West Germany by becoming the largest economy on the European continent, and the fifth wealthiest in the world by GDP. Germany is the world's second-largest trader in imports and exports.

RUSSIA

The world's largest country, Russia, has seen huge changes since the fall of the Soviet Union. It has vast natural resources, such as oil and gas, and is the world's largest oil producer, but many Russian people still live in poverty.

CHINA

China, the world's most populated country, has one of the fastest-growing economies and is the top exporter. Factories and mines produce most of China's wealth, but in the future this may be slowed by an ageing population.

INDIA

It is estimated that India's economy will grow faster than any other country's over the next two decades. It has a young and growing workforce, has opened up foreign trade, and hosts millions of entrepreneurs running small, but successful, businesses.

SOUTH AFRICA

South Africa has one of the largest economies on the African continent, but poverty is widespread. One in seven people are infected with HIV/AIDS, high crime and land redistribution remain an issue, and unemployment is high.

AUSTRALIA

Australia's economy stands out because it survived the global downturn without going into recession. It has a strong service-providing economy as well as healthy exports of agriculture and mining products. Natural gas deposits are evenly spread throughout the continent.

DIRECTORY

RULERS AND LEADERS

Whether leadership is achieved through heredity, democracy, or sheer brute force, leaders make decisions that determine how history will judge their time in power. Great leaders have been the salvation of their people, while weak leaders have been responsible for bringing mighty empires to their knees.

EGYPTIAN PHARAOHS

Ancient Egyptian history is divided up into a number of major periods: the Old Kingdom (2686–2181 BCE); the Middle Kingdom (2040–1650 BCE); and the New Kingdom (1550–1070 BCE), with "Intermediate" periods between them and a Late Period (747–332 BCE) at the end. Within these time periods, a large number of dynasties ruled Egypt, from the 1st Dynasty (3100–2890 BCE) even before the Old Period, reaching the 26th Dynasty (664–525 BCE), which ended with Egypt's conquest by the Persian ruler Cambyses. Apart from a brief period when native Egyptian rulers regained power, Egypt remained part of the Persian Empire until 332 BCE, when it was conquered by Alexander the Great. In 30 BCE, it became part of the Roman Empire.

PERIOD	DYNASTY	NOTABLE PHARAOHS
Early Dynastic Period (3100–2686 BCE)	1st Dynasty (3100–2890 BCE)	Narmer (*c.*3100 BCE) Menes (*c.*3000 BCE) Den (*c.*2950 BCE)
	2nd Dynasty (2890–2686 BCE)	Peribsen (*c.*2700 BCE)
Old Kingdom (2686–2181 BCE)	3rd Dynasty (2686–2613 BCE)	Djoser (2667–2648 BCE)
	4th Dynasty (2613–2494 BCE)	Snefru (2613–2589 BCE) Khufu (Cheops) (2589–2566 BCE) Menkaure (Mycinerus) (2532–2503 BCE) Shepseskaf (2503–2498 BCE)
	5th Dynasty (2494–2345 BCE)	Userkaf (2494–2487 BCE) Sahure (2487–2475 BCE) Nyuserre (2445–2421 BCE) Djedkare (2414–2375 BCE) Unas (2375–2345 BCE)
	6th Dynasty (2345–2181 BCE)	Teti (2345–2323 BCE) Pepi I (2321–2287 BCE) Merenre (2287–2278 BCE) Pepi II (2278–2184 BCE)
First Intermediate Period (2181–2040 BCE)	7th and 8th Dynasties (2181–2125 BCE)	Numerous ephemeral kings, as central authority collapsed
	9th and 10th Dynasties (at Kerakleopolis) (2160–2025 BCE)	Power struggle between minor rulers of Upper and Lower Egypt
	11th Dynasty (at Thebes) (2125–2040 BCE)	Intef II (2112–2063 BCE)
Middle Kingdom (2040–1650 BCE)	11th Dynasty (all Egypt) (2040–1985 BCE)	Mentuhotep II (2040–2004 BCE) Mentuhotep III (2004–1992 BCE) Mentuhotep IV (1992–1985 BCE)
	12th Dynasty (1985–1795 BCE)	Amenemhet I (1985–1955 BCE) Senwosret I (1965–1920 BCE) Amenemhet II (1922–1878 BCE) Senwosret III (1874–1855 BCE) Amenemhet IV (1808–1799 BCE)
	13th Dynasty (1795–*c.*1650 BCE)	Minor rulers
	14th Dynasty (*c.*1750–*c.*1650 BCE)	Minor rulers
Second Intermediate Period (1650–1550 BCE)	15th Dynasty (Hyksos) (1650–1550 BCE)	Apophis (*c.*1585–*c.*1542 BCE)
	16th Dynasty (1650–1550 BCE)	Minor Hyksos rulers contemporary with the 15th Dynasty
	17th Dynasty (at Thebes) (1650–1550 BCE)	Kamose (1555–1550 BCE)
New Kingdom (1550–1069 BCE)	18th Dynasty (1550–1295 BCE)	Ahmose (1550–1525 BCE) Amenhotep I (1525–1504 BCE) Tuthmosis I (1504–1492 BCE) Tuthmosis II (1492–1479 BCE) Tuthmosis III (1479–1425 BCE) Hatshepsut (1473–1458 BCE) Amenhotep II (1427–1400 BCE) Tuthmosis IV (1400–1390 BCE) Amenhotep III (1390–1352 BCE) Amenhotep IV/Akhenaten (*c.*1352–1336 BCE) Smenkhare (1338–1336 BCE) Tutankhamun (1336–1327 BCE) Ay (1327–1323 BCE) Horemheb (1323–1295 BCE)
	19th Dynasty (1295–1186 BCE)	Ramesses I (1295–1294 BCE) Seti I (1294–1279 BCE) Ramesses II (1279–1213 BCE) Merneptah (1213–1203 BCE)
	20th Dynasty (1186–1070 BCE)	Ramesses III (1184–1153 BCE) Ramesses V (1147–1143 BCE) Ramesses XI (1099–1069 BCE)
Third Intermediate Period (1069–747 BCE)	21st Dynasty (1069–945 BCE)	Smendes (1069–1043 BCE) Psusennes I (1039–991 BCE) Osorkon I (984–978 BCE) Psusennes II (959–945 BCE)
	22nd Dynasty (945–715 BCE)	Shoshenq I (945–924 BCE) Osorkon II (874–850 BCE) Shoshenq III (825–773 BCE) Osorkon V (730–715 BCE)
	23rd Dynasty (*c.*818–715 BCE) 24th Dynasty (727–715 BCE)	Competing lines of lesser rulers at Hermopolis Magna, Leontopolis, and Tanis
Late Period (747–332 BCE)	25th Dynasty (Nubia and all of Egypt) (747–656 BCE)	Piye (747–716 BCE) Shabaqa (716–702 BCE) Taharqa (690–664 BCE)
	26th Dynasty (664–525 BCE)	Psammetichus I (664–610 BCE) Apries (589–570 BCE) Amasis (570–526 BCE) Psammetichus III (526–525 BCE)

ROMAN EMPERORS

In 27 BCE, Octavian, on becoming Rome's first emperor, renamed himself Gaius Julius Caesar Augustus. From then on, emperors took the honorific title Augustus. Until 286, this was normally a title unique to one person, but there were periods of joint rule, usually when the succession was disputed or the nominated heir was too young to rule alone. However, the emperor Diocletian instigated a different system, the Tetrarchy, under which four individuals ruled the empire, two as Augustus and two as Caesar – a kind of "junior emperor". This persisted (with some variations) until 395, when the eastern and western portions of the empire split from each other permanently.

NAME	REIGN
Augustus	27 BCE–14 CE
Tiberius	14–37
Gaius Caligula	37–41
Claudius	41–54
Nero	54–68
Galba	68–69
Otho	69
Vitellius	69
Vespasian	69–79
Titus	79–81
Domitian	81–96
Nerva	96–98
Trajan	98–117
Hadrian	117–38
Antoninus Pius	138–61
Marcus Aurelius	161–80
Lucius Verus (co-Augustus)	161–69
Commodus	180–92
Pertinax	193
Didius Julianus	193
Septimius Severus	193–211
Caracalla (co-Augustus 198–211)	198–217
Geta (co-Augustus)	209–11

»

NAME	REIGN
Macrinus	217–18
Diadumenianus (co-Augustus)	218
Elagabalus	218–22
Alexander Severus	222–35
Maximinus Thrax	235–38
Gordian I and Gordian II	238
Pupienus and Balbinus	238
Gordian III	238–44
Philip I	244–49
Philip II (co-Augustus)	247–49
Decius	249–51
Herennius Etruscus (co-Augustus)	251
Trebonianus Gallus	251–53
Hostilianus (co-Augustus)	251
Volusianus (co-Augustus)	251–53
Aemilianus	253
Valerian	253–60
Gallienus (co-Augustus 253–60)	253–68
Claudius Gothicus	268–70
Quintillus	270
Aurelian	270–75
Tacitus	275–76
Florian	276
Probus	276–82
Carus	282–83
Numerian	283–84
Carinus (co-Augustus 283–84)	283–85
Diocletian	284–305

NAME	REIGN
Maximian (Caesar 285–86, co-Augustus 286–305)	286–305
Constantius I Chlorus (Caesar 293–305, co-Augustus 305–06)	305–06
Galerius (Caesar 293–305, co-Augustus 305–11)	305–11
Severus (Caesar 305–06, co-Augustus 306–07)	306–07
Licinius	308–24
Maximin Daia (Caesar 305–10, co-Augustus 310–13)	310–13
Constantine I (Augustus 306, Caesar 306–07, co-Augustus 307–24)	306–37
Constantine II (Caesar 317–37, co-Augustus 337–40)	337–40
Constantius II (Caesar 324–37, co-Augustus 337–50)	337–61
Constans (Caesar 333–37, co-Augustus 337–50)	337–50
Julian (Caesar 355–60)	360–63
Jovian	363–64
Valentinian I (co-Augustus)	364–75
Valens (co-Augustus)	364–78
Gratian (co-Augustus)	367–83
Valentinian II (co-Augustus)	375–92
Theodosius I (co-Augustus 379–92)	379–95

WESTERN EMPIRE

NAME	REIGN
Honorius	395–423
Constantius III (co-Augustus)	421
Valentinian III	424–55
Petronius Maximus	455
Avitus	455–56
Majorian	457–61
Libius Severus	461–65
Anthemius	467–72
Olybrius	472
Glycerius	473–74
Julius Nepos	474–75
Romulus Augustulus	475–76

EASTERN EMPIRE

NAME	REIGN
Arcadius	395–408
Theodosius II (co-Augustus 405–08)	405–50
Marcian	450–57
Leo I	457–74
Zeno (deposed)	474–75
Basiliscus	475–77

BYZANTINE EMPERORS

After 395, the eastern half of the Roman Empire was never ruled by the same emperor as the western portion. The eastern emperors continued to rule from Constantinople after the fall of the western Roman Empire in 476, and are referred to after that date as Byzantine emperors (from "Byzantium", the ancient Greek name for a town on the site of Constantinople).

NAME	REIGN
Zeno	477–91
Anastasius	491–518
Justin	518–27
Justinian	527–65
Justin II	565–78
Tiberius II	578–82
Maurice	582–602
Phocas	602–10
Heraclius	610–41
Heraclonas	641
Constantine III	641
Constans II	641–68
Constantine IV	668–85
Justinian II (deposed)	685–95
Leontius	695–98
Tiberius III	698–705
Justinian II (restored)	705–11
Philippicus	711–13
Anastasius II	713–15
Theodosius III	715–17
Leo III the Isaurian	717–41
Constantine V Copronymos	741–75
Leo IV	775–80
Constantine VI	780–97
Irene (Empress)	797–802
Nicephorus I	802–11

NAME	REIGN
Stauracius	811
Michael I	811–13
Leo V the Armenian	813–20
Michael II	820–29
Theophilus	829–42
Michael III	842–67
Macedonian Dynasty	
Basil I the Macedonian	867–86
Leo VI ("the Wise")	887–912
Alexander	912–13
Constantine VII Porphyrogenitus	912–59
Romanus I Lecapenus (co-Emperor)	919–44
Romanus II	959–63
Nicephorus II Phocas	963–69
John I Tzimisces	969–76
Basil I "the Bulgar Slayer"	976–1025
Constantine VIII (co-emperor to 1025)	976–1028
Romanus III Argyrus	1028–34
Michael IV the Paphlagonian	1034–41
Michael V Calaphates	1041–42
Constantine IX Monomachus	1042–55
Zoe (co-ruler as Empress)	1042–50

NAME	REIGN
Theodora (sole ruler as Empress)	1055–56
Michael VI Stratioticus	1056–57
Comnenid Dynasty	
Isaac I Comenus	1057–59
Ducid Dynasty	
Constantine X Ducas	1059–67
Romanus IV Diogenes	1068–71
Michael VII Ducas	1071–78
Nicephorus III Botaniates	1078–81
Comnenid Dynasty	
Alexius I Comnenus	1081–1118
John II	1118–43
Manuel I	1143–80
Alexius II	1180–83
Andronicus I	1183–85
Angelid Dynasty	
Isaac II Angelus	1185–95
Alexius III	1195–1203
Isaac II (restored)	1203–04

NAME	REIGN
Alexius IV (co-Emperor)	1203–04
Alexius V Mourzouphlos	1204
Lascarid Dynasty	
Theodore I Lascaris	1204–22
John III Vatatzes	1222–54
Theodore II	1254–58
John IV	1258–61
Palaeologid Dynasty	
Michael VIII (to 1261 as Emperor of Nicaea)	1259–82
Andronicus II	1282–1328
Michael IX (co-Emperor)	1293–1320
Andronicus III	1328–41
John V	1341–76
John VI (co-Emperor)	1347–54
Andronicus IV	1376–79
John V (restored)	1379–91
Manuel II	1391–1425
John VII (regent)	1399–1402
John VIII	1425–48
Constantine XI	1448–53

OTTOMAN EMPERORS

NAME	REIGN
Osman I	1299–1326
Orkhan	1326–59
Murad I	1359–89
Bayezid I	1389–1403
Suleiman (rival claimant)	1403–10
Mehmed (rival claimant to 1410)	1403–21
Murad II	1421–44
Mehmed II	1444
Murad II (restored)	1444–51
Mehmed II (restored)	1451–81
Bayezid II	1481–1512
Selim I the Grim	1512–20
Suleiman I the Magnificent	1520–66
Selim II	1566–74
Murad III	1574–95
Mehmed III	1595–1603
Ahmad I	1603–17
Mustafa I	1617–18
Osman II	1618–22
Mustafa I (restored)	1622–23

NAME	REIGN
Murad IV	1623–40
Ibrahim	1640–48
Mehmed IV	1648–87
Suleiman II	1687–91
Ahmad II	1691–95
Mustafa II	1695–1703
Ahmad III	1703–30
Mahmud I	1730–54
Osman III	1754–57
Mustafa III	1757–74
'Abdul Hamid I	1774–89
Selim III	1789–1807
Mustafa IV	1807–08
Mahmud II	1808–39
'Abdul-Majid I	1839–61
'Abdul-'Aziz	1861–76
Murad V	1876
'Abdul-Hamid II	1876–1909
Mehmed V	1909–18
Mehmed VI	1918–22
'Abdul-Majid II (caliph)	1922–24

RULERS OF THE HOLY ROMAN EMPIRE

NAME	REIGN
Charlemagne	800–14
Louis I	814–40
Lothair I	840–55
Louis II	855–75
Charles II	875–77
Charles III	884–87
Guy of Spoleto	891–94
Lambert of Spoleto	894–96
Arnulf	896–99
Louis III	899–911
Berengar I	915–24
Ottonian Saxon Dynasty	
Conrad I of Franconia	911–18
Henry I the Fowler	919–36
Otto I the Great	962–73
Otto II	973–83
Otto III	996–1002
Henry II of Saxony	1014–24
Salian Frankish Dynasty	
Conrad II of Franconia	1027–39
Henry III	1046–56
Henry IV	1084–1105
Henry V	1111–25

NAME	REIGN
Supplingburger Dynasty	
Lothair III	1133–37
Hohenstaufen Dynasty	
Conrad III	1138–52
Frederick I Barbarossa	1155–90
Henry VI	1191–97
Philip of Swabia	1198–1208
Guelph Dynasty	
Otto IV of Saxony	1209–15
Hohenstaufen Dynasty	
Frederick II	1215–50
Conrad IV	1250–54
William of Holland	1254–56
Alfonso X of Castile	1267–73
Rudolf I of Habsburg	1273–91
Adolf of Nassau	1292–98
Albert I of Austria	1298–1308
Henry VII	1312–13
Louis IV of Wittelsbach	1328–47
Charles IV of Luxemburg	1347–78
Wenzel of Luxemburg	1378–1400
Rupert II of the Palatinate	1400–10
Sigismund of Luxemburg	1433–37

RULERS OF THE HOLY ROMAN EMPIRE (CONTINUED)

NAME	REIGN
Habsburg Dynasty	
Albert II	1437–39
Frederick II of Styria	1440–93
Maximilian I	1493–1519
Charles V	1519–56
Ferdinand I	1556–64
Maximilian II	1564–76
Rudolf II	1576–1612
Matthias	1612–19
Ferdinand II of Styria	1619–37
Ferdinand III	1637–58
Leopold I	1658–1705
Charles VI	1711–40
Wittelsbach Dynasty	
Charles VII of Bavaria	1742–45
Habsburg–Lorraine Dynasty	
Francis I	1745–65
Joseph II	1765–90
Leopold II	1790–92
Francis II	1792–1806

EMPERORS OF AUSTRIA

NAME	REIGN
Francis (Holy Roman Emperor Francis II)	1804–35
Ferdinand	1835–48
Franz Joseph	1848–1916
Charles	1916–18

KINGS OF PRUSSIA

NAME	REIGN
Frederick I	1701–13
Frederick William I	1714–40
Frederick II the Great	1740–86
Frederick William II	1786–97
Frederick William III	1797–1840
Frederick William IV	1840–61
William I (from 1871 German Emperor)	1861–71

EMPERORS OF GERMANY

NAME	REIGN
William I (King of Prussia)	1871–88
Frederick	1888
William II (Kaiser Wilhelm)	1888–1918

PRESIDENTS AND CHANCELLORS OF GERMANY

CP Centre Party, **CDU** Christian Democratic Union, **FDP** Free Democratic Party, **GPP** German People's Party, **MSP** Majority Socialist Party, **NSP** National Socialist Party (Nazi), **SDP** Social Democratic Party

UNITED GERMANY (1919–45)

NAME	TERM
PRESIDENTS (FROM 1919)	
Friedrich Ebert (MSP)	1919–25
Walter Simons	1925
Paul von Hindenburg	1925–34
(Führer) Adolf Hitler (NSP)	1934–45
(Führer) Karl Dönitz (NSP)	1945
CHANCELLORS	
Otto von Bismarck	1871–90
Leo von Caprivi	1890–92
Chldowig Hohenlohe-Schillingfurst	1894–1900
Bernhard von Bülow	1900–09
Theobald von Bethman-Hollweg	1909–17
Georg Michaelis	1917
Georg von Hertling	1917–18
Prince Max von Baden	1918
Friedrich Ebert (MSP)	1918–19
Philipp Scheidemann (MSP)	1919
Gustav Bauer (MSP)	1919–20
Hermann Müller (MSP)	1920
Konstantin Fehrenbach (CP)	1920–21
Karl Wirth (CP)	1921–22
Wilhelm Cunto	1922–23
Gustav Streseman (GPP)	1923
Wilhelm Marx (CP)	1923–25
Hans Luther	1925–26
Wilhelm Marx (CP)	1926–28
Hermann Müller (SDP)	1928–30
Heinrich Brüning (CP)	1930–32
Franz von Papen (CP)	1932
Kurt von Schleicher	1932–33
Adolf Hitler (NSP)	1933–45
Joseph Goebbels (NSP)	1945

GERMAN DEMOCRATIC REPUBLIC (DDR, 1949–90)

NAME	TERM
PRESIDENTS	
Wilhelm Pieck	1949–60
Walter Ulbricht	1960–73
Willi Stoph	1973–76
Erich Honecker	1976–89
Egon Krenz	1989
Manfred Gerlach	1989–90
Sabine Bergmann-Pohl	1990
PRIME MINISTERS	
Otto Grotewohl	1949–64
Willi Stoph	1964–73
Horst Sindermann	1973–76
Willi Stoph	1976–89
Hans Modrow	1989–90
Lother de Maiziere (CDU)	1990
GENERAL SECRETARIES OF COMMUNIST PARTY (SUP)	
Walter Ulbricht	1950–71
Erich Honecker	1971–89
Egon Krenz	1989

FEDERAL REPUBLIC OF GERMANY (1945–1990, REUNITED WITH DDR FROM 1990)

NAME	TERM
PRESIDENTS	
Theodor Heuss (FDP)	1949–59
Heinrich Lübke (CDU)	1959–69
Gustav Heinemann (SDP)	1969–74
Walter Scheel (FDP)	1974–79
Karl Carstens (CDU)	1979–84
Richard von Weizsäcker (CDU)	1984–94
Roman Herzog (CDU)	1994–99
Johannes Rau (SDP)	1999–2004
Horst Köhler (CDU)	2004–10
Christian Wulff (CDU)	2010–
CHANCELLORS	
Konrad Adenauer (CDU)	1949–63
Ludwig Erhard (CDU)	1963–66
Kurt-Georg Kiesinger (CDU)	1966–69
Willy Brandt (SDP)	1969–74
Walter Scheel (FDP)	1974
Helmut Schmidt (SDP)	1974–82
Helmut Kohl (CDU)	1982–98
Gerhard Schröder (SDP)	1998–2005
Angela Merkel (CDU)	2005–

KINGS OF FRANCE

After the fall of Rome, a number of barbarian groups vied for power in Gaul. The Franks, led by the Merovingian ruler Childeric, emerged victorious, uniting France under Childeric's son Clovis. On Clovis's death, his kingdom was partitioned between his four sons and their descendants until Pepin, the first of the Carolingians, was anointed king of all the Franks by Pope Zachary in 751.

NAME	REIGN
Merovingian Dynasty	
Childeric I	c.457–81
Clovis I	481–511
Theoderic I (Rheims)	511–34
Chlodomir (Orléans)	511–24
Childebert (Paris)	511–58
Chlotar I (Soissons)	511–61
Theudebert I (Austrasia)	534–48
Theodebald (Austrasia)	548–55
Charibert I (Paris)	561–67
Guntram (Burgundy)	561–92
Sigebert (Metz)	561–75
Chilperic I (Soissons)	561–84
Childebert II (Austrasia)	575–95
Chlotar II (Soissons; sole king 613–23)	584–629
Theudebert II (Austrasia)	595–612
Theoderic II (Burgundy; Austrasia 612–13)	595–613
Dagobert I (Austrasia 623–34, Neustria 629–39)	623–39
Charibert II (Aquitaine)	629–32
Sigebert II (Austrasia)	634–59
Clovis II (Neustria and Burgundy)	639–57
Dagobert II (Austrasia)	659–61
Chlotar III (Neustria)	657–73
Childeric II (Austrasia)	661–75
Theoderic III (Neustria; Austrasia)	673–90
Dagobert II (Austrasia)	676–79
Clovis III	690–954
Childebert III	685–711
Dagobert III	711–15
Chilperic II (Neustria)	715–21
Chlotar IV (Austrasia)	718–19
Theoderic IV	721–37
Childeric III	743–51
Carolingian Dynasty	
Pepin the Short	751–68
Charlemagne (Charles I)	768–814
Carloman (co-ruler)	768–71
Louis I the Pious	814–40
Charles II the Bald	840–77
Louis II the Stammerer	877–79
Louis III	879–82
Carloman II	879–84
Charles the Fat	884–87
Odo	887–98
Charles III the Simple	898–923
Robert I	922–23
Raoul	923–36
Louis IV	936–54
Lothair	954–86
Louis V	986–87
Capetian Dynasty	
Hugh Capet	987–96
Robert II the Pious	996–1031
Henry I	1031–60
Philip I	1060–1108
Louis VI the Fat	1108–37
Louis VII the Young	1137–80
Philip II Augustus	1180–1223
Louis VIII	1223–26
Louis IX the Saint	1226–70
Philip III the Bold	1270–85
Philip IV the Fair	1285–1314
Louis X	1314–16
John I	1316
Philip V	1316–22
Charles IV the Fair	1322–28
House of Valois	
Philip VI the Fortunate	1328–50
John II the Good	1350–64
Charles V the Wise	1364–80
Charles VI	1380–1422
Charles VII	1422–61
Louis XI	1461–83
Charles VIII	1483–98
House of Valois-Orléans	
Louis XII	1498–1515
House of Valois-Angoulême	
Francis I	1515–47
Henry II	1547–59
Francis II	1559–60
Charles IX	1560–74
Henry III	1574–89
House of Bourbon	
Henry IV of Navarre	1589–1610
Louis XIII	1610–43
Louis XIV	1643–1715
Louis XV	1715–74
Louis XVI	1774–92
French Republic	1792–1804
First Empire	
Napoleon I (Bonaparte)	1804–14,1815
House of Bourbon	
Louis XVII	1814–15, 1815–24
Charles X	1824–30
House of Bourbon–Orléans	
Louis-Philippe	1830–48
Second French Republic	1848–52
Second Empire	
Napoleon III	1852–70

DUKES OF NORMANDY

After the 9th century, much of France was controlled by rulers independent of French kings, notably the Dukes of Normandy, who ruled an area of northwestern France from 911 until the 13th century.

NAME	REIGN
Rolf Ganger	911–32
William I	932–42
Richard I	942–96
Richard II	996–1027
Richard III	1027–28
Robert I	1028–35
William II (I of England)	1035–87
Robert II	1087–1106
Henry I (of England)	1106–35
Stephen	1135–44
Geoffrey of Anjou	1144–50
Henry II (of England)	1150–89
Richard IV (I of England)	1189–99
John (of England)	1199–1204

PRESIDENTS AND PRIME MINISTERS OF FRANCE

CP Centre Party, **DA** Democratic Alliance, **DR** Democratic Resistance, **DUR** Democratic Union for the Fifth Republic, **IRP** Independent Republican Party, **PRM** People's Revolutionary Movement, **RA** Republican Alliance, **RFR** Rally for the Republic, **RSP** Radical Socialist Party, **SP** Socialist Party, **RSU** Radical Socialist Union, **UMP** Union for a Popular Movement, **UNR** Union for the New Republic

PRESIDENTS (SINCE 1871)

NAME	TERM
Adolphe Thiers	1871–73
Patrice MacMahon	1873–79
Jules Grevy	1879–87
François Sadi-Carnot	1887–94
Jean Casimir-Périer	1894–95
François Faure	1895–99
Emile Loubet	1899–1906
Armand Fallières	1906–13
Raymond Poincaré	1913–20
Paul Deschanel	1920
Alexandre Millerand	1920–24
Gaston Doumergue	1924–31
Paul Doumer	1931–32
Albert Le Brun	1932–40
Philippe Pétain	1940–44
Vincent Auriol (SP)	1947–54
René Coty (IRP)	1954–59
Charles de Gaulle (UNR, DUR)	1959–69
Alain Poher (CP)	1969
Georges Pompidou (DUR)	1969–74
Valérie Giscard d'Estaing (IRP)	1974–81
François Mitterand (SP)	1981–95
Jacques Chirac (RFR/UMP)	1995–2007
Nicolas Sarkozy (UMP)	2007–

PRIME MINISTERS

NAME	TERM
Adolphe Thiers	1871–73
Patrice MacMahon	1873–74
Ernest de Cissey	1874–75
Louis Buffet	1875–76
Jules Dufaure	1876
Jules Simon	1876–77
Albert de Broglie	1877
Gaëtan de Rochebouet	1877
Jules Dufaure	1877–79
William Waddington	1879
Charles de Freycinet	1879–80
Jules Ferry	1880–81
Léon Gambetta	1881–82
Charles de Freycinet	1882
Charles Duclerc	1882–83
Armand Fallières	1883
Jules Ferry	1883–85
Henri Brisson	1885–86
Charles de Freycinet	1886
René Goblet	1886–87
Maurice Rouvier	1887
Pierre Tirard	1887–88
Charles Floquet	1888–89
Pierre Tirard	1889–90
Charles de Freycinet	1890–92
Emile Loubet	1892
Alexandre Ribot	1892–93
Charles Dupuy	1893
Jean Casimir-Périer	1893–94
Charles Dupuy	1894–95
Alexandre Ribot	1895
Léon Bourgeois	1895–96
Jules Meline	1896–98
Henri Brisson	1898
Charles Dupuy	1898–99
René Waldeck-Rousseau	1899–1902
Émile Combes	1902–05
Maurice Rouvier	1905–06
Ferdinand Sarrien	1906
Georges Clemenceau	1906–09
Aristide Briand (SP)	1909–11
Ernest Monis	1911
Joseph Caillaux	1911–12
Raymond Poincaré	1912–13
Aristide Briand (SP)	1913
Louis Barthou	1913
Gaston Doumergue (RSP)	1913–14
René Viviani	1914–15
Aristide Briand (SP)	1915–17
Alexandre Ribot	1917
Paul Painlevé	1917
Georges Clemenceau	1917–20
Alexandre Millerand	1920
Georges Leygues	1920–21
Aristide Briand (SP)	1921–22
Raymond Poincaré	1922–24
Frédéric François-Marsal	1924
Eduoard Herriot (RSP)	1924–25
Paul Painlevé	1925
Aristide Briand (SP)	1925–26
Edouard Herriot (RSP)	1926
Raymond Poincaré	1926–29
Aristide Briand (SP)	1929
André Tardieu	1929–30
Camille Chautemps (RSP)	1930
André Tardieu	1930
Théodore Steeg (RSP)	1930–31
Pierre Laval	1931–32
André Tardieu	1932
Edouard Herriot (RSP)	1932
Joseph Paul-Boncour (RSU)	1932–33
Edouard Daladier (RSP)	1933
Albert Sarraut (RSP)	1933
Camille Chautemps (RSP)	1933–34
Edouard Daladier (RSP)	1934
Gaston Doumergue (RSP)	1934
Pierre Flandin (DA)	1934–35
Ferdinand Bouisson (SP)	1935
Pierre Laval	1935–36
Albert Sarraut (RSP)	1936
Léon Blum (SP)	1936–37
Camille Chautemps (RSP)	1937–38
Léon Blum (SP)	1938
Edouard Daladier (RSP)	1938–40
Paul Reynaud (RA)	1940
Philippe Pétain	1940–42
Pierre Laval	1942–44
Charles de Gaulle	1944–46
Félix Gouin (SP)	1946
Georges Bidault (PRM)	1946
Léon Blum (SP)	1946–47
Paul Ramadier (SP)	1947
Robert Schuman (PRM)	1947–48
André Marie (RSP)	1948
Robert Schuman (PRM)	1948
Henry Queuille (RSP)	1948
Georges Bidault (PRM)	1948–50
Henri Queuille (RSP)	1950
René Pleven (DR)	1950–51
Henri Queuille (RSP)	1951
René Pleven (DR)	1951–52
Edgar Faure (RSP)	1952
Antoine Pinay (IRP)	1952–53
René Mayer (RSP)	1953
Joseph Laniel (IRP)	1953–54
Pierre Mendès-France (RSP)	1954–55
Christian Pineau (SP)	1955
Edgar Faure (RSP)	1955–56
Guy Mollet (SP)	1956–57
Maurice Bourges-Maunoury (RSP)	1957
Félix Gaillard (RSP)	1957–58
Pierre Pflimlin (PRM)	1958
Charles de Gaulle (UNR)	1958–59
Michel Debré (UNR)	1959–62
Georges Pompidou (UNR)	1962–68
Maurice Couve de Murville (UNR)	1968–69
Jacques Chaban-Delmas (DUR)	1969–72
Pierre Messmer (DUR)	1972–74
Jacques Chirac (DUR)	1974–76
Raymond Barre	1976–81
Pierre Mauroy (SP)	1981–84
Laurent Fabius (SP)	1984–86
Jacques Chirac (RFR)	1986–88
Michel Rocard (SP)	1988–91
Edith Cresson (SP)	1991–92
Pierre Bérégovoy (SP)	1992–93
Edouard Balladur (RFR)	1993–95
Alain Juppé (RFR)	1995–97
Lionel Jospin (SP)	1997–2002
Jean-Pierre Raffarin (UMP)	2002–05
Dominique de Villepin (UMP)	2005–07
François Fillon (UMP)	2007–

KINGS AND QUEENS OF SPAIN

The northern Spanish kingdoms of Castile and Leon were joined by marriage in 1037 and were formally united in 1230. In 1469, Isabella of Castile married Ferdinand of Aragon, and when both succeeded to their respective thrones, they united their domains to form the kingdom of Spain.

KINGS AND QUEENS OF CASTILE-LEON

NAME	REIGN
Ferdinand I	1037–65
Sancho II	1065–72
Alfonso VI	1065–1109
Urraca	1109–26
Alfonso VII	1126–57
Sancho III (Castile)	1157–58
Ferdinand II (Leon)	1157–88
Alfonso VIII (Castile)	1158–1214
Alfonso IX (Leon)	1188–1230
Henry I (Castile)	1214–17
Ferdinand III (Castile, Leon from 1230)	1217–52
Alfonso X the Wise	1252–84
Sancho IV	1284–95
Ferdinand IV	1295–1312
Alfonso XI	1312–50
Peter the Cruel	1350–66
Henry II	1366–67
Peter the Cruel (restored)	1367–69
Henry II (restored)	1369–79
John I	1379–90
Henry III	1390–1406
John II	1406–54
Henry IV	1454–74
Isabella	1474–1504
Joanna	1504–16
Philip I	1504–06
Ferdinand V (II Of Aragon)	1506–16

KINGS OF ARAGON

NAME	REIGN
Ramiro I	1035–63
Sancho	1063–94
Peter I	1094–1104
Alfonso I	1104–34
Ramiro II	1134–37
Petronilla	1137–62
Alfonso II	1162–96
Peter II	1196–1213
James I the Conqueror	1213–76
Peter III	1276–85
Alfonso III	1285–91
James II	1291–1327
Alfonso IV	1327–36
Peter IV	1336–87
John I	1387–95
Martin	1395–1410
Ferdinand	1412–16
Alfonso V	1416–58
John II	1458–79
Ferdinand II (V of Castile)	1479–1516

KINGS AND QUEENS OF UNITED SPAIN

NAME	REIGN
Habsburg Dynasty	
Charles I	1516–56
Philip II	1556–98
Philip III	1598–1621
Philip IV	1621–65
Charles II	1665–1700
Bourbon Dynasty	
Philip V	1700–24
Luis	1724
Philip V (restored)	1724–46
Ferdinand VI	1746–59
Charles III (of Naples)	1759–88
Charles IV	1788–1808
Ferdinand VII	1808
House of Bonaparte	
Joseph Bonaparte	1808–13
Bourbon Dynasty	
Ferdinand VII (restored)	1813–33
Isabella II	1833–68
House of Savoy	
Amadeus of Savoy	1870–73
First Spanish Republic	1873–74

KINGS AND QUEENS OF SPAIN (CONTINUED)

NAME	REIGN
Bourbon Dynasty	
Alfonso XII	1874–85
Alfonso XIII	1886–1931
Second Spanish Republic	1931–39
Francoist Spain	1939–75
Bourbon Dynasty	
Juan Carlos	1975–

PRIME MINISTERS OF SPAIN

CP Conservative Party, **LP** Liberal Party, **LRP** Left Republican Party, **PP** Popular Party, **RP** Radical Party, **SP** Socialist Party, **PSOE** Spanish Socialist Workers' Party, **UDC** Union for the Democratic Centre

NAME	TERM
Francisco Cea Bermudez	1833–34
Francisco Martínez de la Rosa	1834–35
Conde de Toreno	1835
Juan Alvarez Mendizábal	1835–36
Manuel Isturiz y Montero	1836
José Calatrava	1836–37
Eusebio Bardaji y Azara	1837
Conde de Ofalia	1837–38
Duc de Frias	1838
Evaristo Pérez de Castro	1838
Isidro Alaix	1838–40
Antonio González y González	1840
Valentin Ferraz	1840
Modesto Cortazar	1840
Duc de Vitoria	1840–41
Antonio González y González	1841–42
José Rodil y Gallaso	1842–43
Joaquín López	1843
Alvaro Gómez Becera	1843
Joaquin López	1843
Salustiano de Olozaga	1843
Luiz González Bravo	1843–44
Duc de Valencia	1844–46
Marqués de Miraflores	1846
Francisco Isturiz y Montero	1846–47
Duc de Sotomayor	1847
Joaquín Pacheco y Gutiérrez	1847
Florencio García Gómez	1847
Duc de Valencia	1847–50
Juan Bravo Murillo	1850–52
Federico Roncali	1852–53
Francisco de Lersundi Ormaechea	1853
Luiz Sartorius	1853–54
Fernando Fernández de Córdoba	1854
Angel de Saavedra	1854–55
Duc de Victoria	1855–56
Leopoldo O'Donnell y Joria	1856
Duc de Valencia	1856–57
Francisco Armero y Peñaranda	1857–58
Francisco Isturiz y Montero	1858
Leopoldo O'Donnell y Joria	1858–63
Marqués de Miraflores	1863–64
Lorenzo Arrazola	1864
Alejandro Mon	1864
Duc de Valencia	1864–65
Leopoldo O'Donnell y Joria	1865–66
Duc de Valencia	1866–68
Luiz González Bravo	1868
José Gutiérrez de la Ocncha	1868
Francisco Serrano y Dominguez	1868–69
Juan Prim y Prets	1869–70
Juan Topete y Carballa	1870–71
Serrano y Dominguez	1871
Manuel Ruiz Zorilla	1871
José Malcampo y Monge	1871
Praxedes Sagasta	1871–72
Juan Topete y Carballa	1872
Manuel Ruiz Zorilla	1872–73
Marqués de Sierra Bullones	1874
Praxedes Sagasta	1874
Antonio Cánovas del Castillo	1874–75
Joaquín Jovellar	1875
Antonio Cánovas del Castillo	1875–79
Arsenio Martínez-Campos	1879
Antonio Cánovas del Castillo	1879–81
Praxedes Sagasta	1881–83
José de Posada Herrera	1883–84
Antonio Cánovas del Castillo	1884–85
Praxedes Sagasta	1885–90
Antonio Cánovas del Castillo	1890–92
Praxedes Sagasta	1892–95
Antonio Cánovas del Castillo	1895–97
Marcelo de Azcarraga y Palmero	1897
Praxedes Sagasta	1897–99
Francisco Silvela y Le-Vielleuze	1899–1900
Marcello de Azcarraga y Palmero	1900–01
Praxedes Sagasta	1901–02
Francisco Silvela y Le-Vielleuze	1902–03
Raimundo Fernández de Villaverde (CP)	1903
Antonio Maura y Montaner (CP)	1903–04
Marcello de Azcarraga y Palmero (CP)	1904–05
Raimundo Fernández de Villaverde (CP)	1905
Eugene Montero Ríos	1905
Segismundo Moret y Prendergast (CP)	1905–06
José López Dominguez (LP)	1906
Segismundo Moret y Prendergast (LP)	1906
Marqués de la Vega de Armijo (LP)	1906–07
Antonio Maura y Montaner (CP)	1907–09
Segismundo Moret y Prendergast (LP)	1909–10
José Canalejas y Mendez (LP)	1910–12
Conde de Romanones (LP)	1912
Marqués de Alhucemas (LP)	1912–13
Eduardo Dato y Iradier (CP)	1913–15
Conde de Romanones (LP)	1915–16
Marqués de Alhucemas (LP)	1916–17
Eduardo Dato y Iradier (CP)	1917
Marqués de Alhucemas (LP)	1917–18
Antonio Maura y Montaner (CP)	1918
Marqués de Alhucemas (LP)	1918
Conde de Romanones (LP)	1918–19
Antonio Maura y Montaner (CP)	1919
Joaquín Sánchez de Toca	1919
Manuel Allende Salazar	1919–20
Eduardo Dato y Iradier (CP)	1920–21
Gabino Bugallal Araújo	1921
Manuel Allende Salazar	1921
Antonio Maura y Montaner (CP)	1921–22
José Sánchez Guerra (CP)	1922
Marqués de Alhucemas (LP)	1922–23
Miguel Primo de Rivera y Orbaneja	1923–30
Damaso Berenguer y Fuste	1920–31
Juan Bautista Azmar-Cabanas	1931
Niceto Alcala Zamora	1931
Manuel Azaña y Diéz (LRP)	1931–33
Alejandro Lerroux y García (RP)	1933
Diego Martínez Barrio (RP)	1933
Alejandro Lerroux y García (RP)	1933–34
Ricardo Samper Ibáñez	1934
Alejandro Lerroux y García (RP)	1934–35
Joaquín Chapaprieta y Terragosa	1935
Manuel Portela Valladares	1935–36
Manuel Azaña y Diéz (LRP)	1936
Santiago Cásares Quiroga	1936
Diego Martínez Barrio	1936
José Giral y Pereira	1936
Francisco Largo Caballero (SP)	1936–37
Juan Negrin (SP)	1937–39
Francisco Franco Bahamonde	1939–73
Luis Carrero Blanco	1973
Torcuatro Fernández Miranda	1973–74
Carlos Arias Navarro	1974–76
Fernando de Santiago y Díaz	1976
Adolfo Suárez González (UDC)	1976–81
Leopoldo Calvo-Sotelo y Bustelo (UDP)	1981–82
Felipe González Marquez (PSOE)	1982–96
José María Aznar López (PP)	1996–2004
Luis Rodríguez Zapatero (PSOE)	2004–

KINGS OF SARDINIA

NAME	REIGN
Victor Amadeus II	1718–30
Charles Emmanuel III	1730–73
Victor Amadeus III	1773–96
Charles Emmanuel IV	1796–1802
Victor Emmanuel I	1802–21
Charles Felix	1821–31
Charles Albert	1831–49
Victor Emmanuel II (from 1861 King of Italy)	1849–61

KINGS OF ITALY

NAME	REIGN
Victor Emmanuel II (of Sardinia)	1861–78
Umberto I	1878–1900
Victor Emmanuel III	1900–46
Umberto II	1946

PRESIDENTS AND PRIME MINISTERS OF ITALY

AP Action Party, **FI** Forza Italia, **DC** Christian Democratic Party, **PRI** Italian Republican Party, **PSI** Italian Socialist Party, **PLI** Italian Liberal Party, **Ulivo** Olive Tree, **DS** Left Democrats, **PP** Popular Party, **PL** People of Freedom

PRESIDENTS

NAME	TERM
Enrico de Nicola	1947–48
Luigi Einaudi	1948–55
Giovanni Gronchi (DC)	1955–62
Antonio Segni (DC)	1962–64
Cesare Merzagora	1964
Giuseppe Saragat (DC)	1964–71
Giovanni Leone (DC)	1971–78
Amintore Fanfani	1978
Alessandro Pertini (DC)	1978–85
Francesco Cossiga (DC)	1985–92
Oscar Scalfaro (DC, PP)	1992–99
Nicola Mancino	1999
Carlo Azeglio Ciampi	1999–2006
Giorgio Napolitano (DS)	2006–

PRIME MINISTERS

NAME	TERM
Camille Cavour	1861
Bettino Ricasoli	1861–62
Urbano Rattazzi	1862
Luigi Farina	1862–63
Marco Minghetti	1863–64
Alfonso la Marmora	1864–66
Bettino Ricasoli	1866–67
Urbano Rattazzi	1867
Luigi Menabrea	1867–69
Giovanni Lanza	1869–73
Marco Minghetti	1873–76
Agostini Depretis	1876–78
Benedetto Cairoli	1878
Agostini Depretis	1878–79
Benedetto Cairoli	1879–81
Agostini Depretis	1881–87
Francesco Crispi	1887–91
Marchese di Rudini	1891–92
Giovanni Giolitti	1892–93
Francesco Crispi	1893–96
Marchese di Rudini	1896–98
Luigi Pelloux	1898–1900
Giuseppe Saracco	1900–01
Giuseppe Zanardelli	1901–03
Giovanni Giolitti	1903–05
Alessandro Fortis	1905–06
Sidney Sonnino	1906
Giovanni Giolitti	1906–09
Sidney Sonnino	1909–10
Luigi Luzzatti	1910–11
Giovanni Giolitti	1911–14
Antonio Salandra	1914–16
Paolo Boselli	1916–17
Vittorio Orlando	1917–19
Francesco Nitti	1919–20
Giovanni Giolitti	1920–21
Ivanoe Bonomi	1921–22
Luigi Facta	1922
Benito Mussolini	1922–43
Pietro Badoglio	1943–44
Ivanoe Bonomi (PLI)	1944–45
Ferrucio Parri (AP)	1945
Alfredo de Gasperi (DC)	1945–53
Giuseppe Pella (DC)	1953–54
Amintore Fanfani (DC)	1954
Mario Scelba (DC)	1954–55
Antonio Segni (DC)	1955–57
Adone Zoli (DC)	1957–58
Amintore Fanfani (DC)i	1958–59
Antonio Segni (DC)	1959–60
Fernando Tambroni (DC)	1960
Amintore Fanfani (DC)	1960–63
Giovanni Leone (DC)	1963
Aldo Moro (DC)	1963–68
Giovanni Leone (DC)	1968
Mariano Rumor (DC)	1968–70
Emilio Colombo (DC)	1970–72
Giulio Andreotti (DC)	1972–73
Mariano Rumor (DC)	1973–74
Aldo Moro (DC)	1974–76
Giulio Andreotti (DC)	1976–79
Francesco Cossiga (DC)	1979–80
Arnaldo Forlani (DC)	1980–81
Giovanni Spadolini (DC)	1981–82
Amintore Fanfani (DC)	1982–83
Benedetto Craxi (PSI)	1983–87
Amintore Fanfani (DC)	1987
Giovanni Goria (DC)	1987–88

NAME	TERM
Ciriaco de Mita (DC)	1988–89
Giulio Andreotti (DC)	1989–92
Giuliano Amato (PSI)	1992–93
Carlo Azeglio Ciampi	1993–94
Silvio Berlusconi (FI)	1994–95
Lamberto Dini	1995–96
Romano Prodi (PP)	1996–98
Massimo D'Alema (DS)	1998–2000
Giuliano Amato (Ulivo)	2000–01
Silvio Berlusconi (FI)	2001–06
Romano Prodi (Ulivo)	2006–08
Silvio Berlusconi (PL)	2008–

KINGS AND QUEENS OF ENGLAND

NAME	REIGN
House of Wessex	
Egbert	802–39
Ethelwulf	839–55
Ethelbald	855–60
Ethelbert	860–66
Ethelred I	866–71
Alfred the Great	871–99
Edward the Elder	899–925
Athelstan	925–39
Edmund	939–46
Edred	946–55
Edwy	955–59
Edgar	959–75
Edward the Martyr	975–78
Ethelred II the Unready	978–1013
House of Denmark	
Sweyn Forkbeard	1013–14
House of Wessex	
Ethelred II (restored)	1014–16
Edmund Ironside	1016
House of Denmark	
Canute	1016–35
Harold I Harefoot	1035–40
Harthacnut	1040–42
House of Wessex	
Edward the Confessor	1042–66
Harold II Godwinson	1066
House of Normandy	
William I the Conqueror	1066–87
William II Rufus	1087–1100
Henry I	1100–35
Stephen	1135–41
Matilda	1141
Stephen (restored)	1141–54
House of Plantagenet	
Henry II of Anjou	1154–89
Richard I the Lionheart	1189–99
John	1199–1216
Henry III	1216–72
Edward I	1272–1307
Edward II	1307–27
Edward III	1327–77
Richard II	1377–99
House of Lancaster	
Henry IV Bolingbroke	1399–1413
Henry V	1413–22
Henry VI	1422–61
House of York	
Edward IV	1461–70
House of Lancaster	
Henry VI (restored)	1470–71
House of York	
Edward IV (restored)	1471–83
Edward V	1483
Richard III	1483–85
House of Tudor	
Henry VII	1485–1509
Henry VIII	1509–47
Edward VI	1547–53
Mary I	1553–58
Elizabeth I	1558–1603
House of Stuart	
James I (VI of Scotland)	1603–25
Charles I	1625–49
Commonwealth (Republic)	1649–60
House of Stuart	
Charles II	1660–85
James II	1685–88
William III	1689–1702
Mary II (co-ruler)	1689–94
Anne (of Great Britain from 1707)	1702–14

KINGS AND QUEENS OF SCOTLAND

NAME	REIGN
House of Alpin	
Kenneth MacAlpin (of Dalriada)	843–58
Donald I	858–62
Constantine I	862–77
Aed	877–78
Eochaid	878–89
Donald II	889–900
Constantine II	900–42
Malcolm I	942–54
Indulf	954–62
Dubh	962–66
Culen	966–71
Kenneth II	971–95
Constantine III	995–97
Kenneth III	997–1005
Malcolm II	1005–34
House of Dunkeld	
Duncan I	1034–40
Macbeth	1040–57
Lulach	1057–58
Malcolm III Canmore	1058–93
Donald III Bane	1093–94
Duncan II	1094
Donald III Bane (restored)	1094–97
Edgar	1097–1107
Alexander I	1107–24
David I	1124–53
Malcolm IV	1153–65
William the Lion	1165–1214
Alexander II	1214–49
Alexander III	1249–86
Margaret of Norway	1286–1300
House of Balliol	
John Balliol	1292–90
House of Bruce	
Robert I the Bruce	1306–29
David II	1329–71
House of Stuart	
Robert II	1371–90
Robert III	1390–1406
James I	1406–37
James II	1437–60
James III	1460–88
James IV	1488–1513
James V	1513–42
Mary I (Queen of Scots)	1542–67
James VI (I of England from 1603)	1567–1625

KINGS AND QUEENS OF GREAT BRITAIN

NAME	REIGN
House of Hanover	
George I	1714–27
George II	1727–60
George III	1760–1820
George IV	1820–30
William IV	1830–37
Victoria	1837–1901
House of Saxe-Coburg-Gotha	
Edward VII	1901–10
House of Windsor	
George V	1910–36
Edward VIII	1936
George VI	1936–52
Elizabeth II	1952–

PRIME MINISTERS OF THE UNITED KINGDOM

C Conservative, **Lib** Liberal, **Lab** Labour, **W** Whig

NAME	TERM
Robert Walpole	1721–42
Earl of Wilmington (Spencer Compton)	1742–43
Henry Pelham	1743–46
Earl of Bath (William Pulteney)	1746
Henry Pelham	1746–54
Duke of Newcastle (Thomas Pelham-Holles)	1754–56
Duke of Devonshire (William Cavendish)	1756–57
Earl of Waldegrave (James Waldegrave)	1757
Duke of Newcastle	1757–62
Earl of Bute (John Stuart)	1762–63
George Grenville	1763–65
Marquis of Rockingham (Charles Wentworth)	1765–66
Earl of Chatham (William Pitt the Elder)	1766–68
Duke of Grafton (Augustus Fitzroy)	1768–70
Baron North (Frederick North)	1770–82
Marquis of Rockingham	1782
Earl of Shelburne (William Petty-Fitzmaurice)	1782–83
Duke of Portland (William Cavendish-Bentinck)	1783
William Pitt (the Younger)	1783–1801
Henry Addington	1801–04
William Pitt (the Younger)	1804–06
Lord Grenville (William Grenville)	1806–07
Duke of Portland	1807–09
Spencer Perceval	1809–12
Earl of Liverpool (Robert Jenkinson)	1812–27
George Canning	1827
Viscount Goderich (Frederick Robinson)	1827–28
Duke of Wellington (Arthur Wellesley) (C)	1828–30
Lord Grey (Charles Grey) (W)	1830–34
Viscount Melbourne (William Lamb) (W)	1834
Duke of Wellington (C)	1834
Robert Peel (C)	1834–35
Viscount Melbourne (W)	1835–41
Robert Peel (C)	1841–46
Lord John Russell (W)	1846–52
Earl of Derby (Edward Stanley) (C)	1852
Earl of Aberdeen (George Hamilton-Gordon) (W)	1852–55
Viscount Palmerston (Henry Temple) (W)	1855–58
Earl of Derby (C)	1858–59
Viscount Palmerston (W)	1859–65
Lord John Russell (W)	1865–66
Earl of Derby (C)	1866–68
Benjamin Disraeli (C)	1868
William Gladstone (Lib)	1868–74
Benjamin Disraeli (C)	1874–80
William Gladstone (Lib)	1880–85
Marquis of Salisbury (Robert Cecil) (C)	1885–86
William Gladstone (Lib)	1886
Marquis of Salisbury (C)	1886–92
William Gladstone (Lib)	1892–94
Earl of Rosebery (Archibald Primrose) (Lib)	1894–95
Marquis of Salisbury (C)	1895–1902
Arthur Balfour (C)	1902–05
Henry Campbell-Bannerman (Lib)	1905–08
Herbert Asquith (Lib)	1908–16
David Lloyd George (Lib)	1916–22
Andrew Bonar Law (C)	1922–23
Stanley Baldwin (C)	1923–24
Ramsay MacDonald (Lab)	1924
Stanley Baldwin (C)	1924–29
Ramsay MacDonald (Lab)	1929–35
Stanley Baldwin (C)	1935–37
Neville Chamberlain (C)	1937–40
Winston Churchill (C)	1940–45
Clement Attlee (Lab)	1945–51
Winston Churchill (C)	1951–55
Anthony Eden (C)	1955–57
Harold MacMillan (C)	1957–63
Alexander Douglas-Home (C)	1963–64
Harold Wilson (Lab)	1964–70
Edward Heath (C)	1970–74
Harold Wilson (Lab)	1974–76
James Callaghan (Lab)	1976–79
Margaret Thatcher (C)	1979–90
John Major (C)	1990–97
Anthony Blair (Lab)	1997–2007
Gordon Brown (Lab)	2007–10
David Cameron (C)	2010–

RULERS OF RUSSIA

NAME	REIGN
RURIKID DYNASTY	
Princes of Moscow	
Daniel	1283–1303
Yuri	1303–25
Ivan I	1325–40
Simeon the Proud	1340–53
Ivan II	1353–59
Grand Princes of Moscow–Vladimir	
Dmitri Donskoi	1359–89
Vasili I	1389–1425
Vasili II the Blind	1425–62
Ivan III the Great	1462–1505
Vasili III	1505–33
Tsars of Russia	
Ivan IV the Terrible (Tsar from 1547)	1533–84
Feodor I	1584–98
GODUNOV DYNASTY	
Boris Godunov	1598–1605
Feodor II	1605
Dimitri II	1605–06
SHUISKII DYNASTY	
Vasili IV	1606–10
ROMANOV DYNASTY	
Michael	1613–45
Alexei	1645–76
Feodor III	1676–82
Ivan V	1682–96
Peter I the Great (Emperor from 1721)	1696–1725
Catherine I	1725–27
Peter II	1727–30
Anna	1730–40
Ivan VI	1740–41
Elizabeth	1741–62
Peter III	1762
Catherine II the Great	1762–96
Paul I	1796–1801
Alexander I	1801–25
Nicholas I	1825–55
Alexander II	1855–81
Alexander III	1881–94
Nicholas II	1894–1917

LEADERS OF THE SOVIET UNION AND RUSSIAN FEDERATION

After the establishment of the USSR in 1923, the country had heads of state and heads of government, but real power resided in the leadership of the Soviet Communist Party. Some Soviet leaders combined several roles, but their powerbases always lay within the Communist Party.

OHR Our Home is Russia, **UR** United Russia

SOVIET UNION (USSR, 1923–91)

HEADS OF STATE

NAME	TERM
Mikhail Kalinin	1922–46
Nikolai Svernik	1946–53
Marshal Kliment Voroshilov	1953–60
Leonid Brezhnev	1960–64
Anastas Mikoyan	1964–65
Nikolai Podgorny	1965–77
Leonid Breznhev	1977–82
Vasili Kuznetsov	1982–83
Yuri Andropov	1983–84
Konstantin Chernenko	1984–85
Vasili Kuznetsov	1985
Andrei Gromyko	1985–88
Mikhail Gorbachev	1988–91

HEADS OF COMMUNIST PARTY

NAME	TERM
Vladimir Lenin	1923–24
Joseph Stalin	1924–53
Georgi Malenkov	1953
Nikita Khrushchev	1953–64
Leonid Brezhnev	1964–82
Yuri Andropov	1982–84
Konstanin Chernenko	1984–85
Mikhail Gorbachev	1985–91

HEADS OF GOVERNMENT

NAME	TERM
Vladimir Lenin	1923–24
Alexi Rykov	1924–30
Vyacheslav Molotov	1930–41
Joseph Stalin	1941–53
Georgi Malenkov	1953–55
Nikolai Bulganin	1955–58
Nikita Khrushchev	1958–64
Alexi Kosygin	1964–80
Nikolai Tikhonov	1980–85
Nikolai Ryzkov	1985–91
Valentin Pavlov	1991

RUSSIAN FEDERATION (SINCE 1991)

PRESIDENTS

NAME	TERM
Boris Yeltsin	1990–99
Vladimir Putin	1999–2008
Dmitry Medvedev	2008–

PRIME MINISTERS

NAME	TERM
Ivan Silayev	1990–91
Boris Yeltsin	1991–92
Yegor Gaidar	1992
Dr Viktor Chernomyrdin (OHR)	1992–98
Sergei Kiriyenko	1998
Dr Viktor Chernomyrdin (OHR)	1998
Yevgeni Primakov	1998–99
Sergei Stepashin	1999
Vladimir Putin	1999–2000
Mikhail Kasyanov	2000–04
Viktor Khristenko	2004
Mikhail Fradkov	2004–07
Viktor Zubkov	2007–08
Vladimir Putin (UR)	2008–

EMPERORS OF CHINA

China was united by Qin Shi Huangdi, the First Emperor, in 221 BCE. However, the collapse of the Han Dynasty in 220 CE was followed by three centuries of disunity during which the country was sometimes split into as many as 17 kingdoms. China was reunited by the Sui in 589, but after the collapse of their successors, the Tang, in 907, the country was once more divided during the Five Dynasties and Ten Kingdoms period (907–60). The Song reunited China in 960, but they lost control of the north of the country in 1126. Final reunification came under the Mongol Yuan dynasty in 1279.

NAME	REIGN
Qin Dynasty	
Qin Shi Huangdi	221–210 BCE
Er Shi	210–207 BCE
Western Han Dynasty	
Gaodi	206–195 BCE
Huidi	195–188 BCE
Lu Hou (Regent)	188–180 BCE
Wendi	180–157 BCE
Jingdi	157–141 BCE
Wudi	141–87 BCE
Zhaodi	87–74 BCE
Xuandi	74–49 BCE
Yuandi	49–33 BCE
Chengdi	33–7 BCE
Aidi	7–1 BCE
Pingdi	1 BCE–6 CE
Ruzi	7–9
Hsin Dynasty	
Wang Mang	9–23
Eastern Han Dynasty	
Guang Wudi	25–57
Mingdi	57–75
Zhangdi	75–88
Hedi	88–106
Shangdi	106
Andi	106–25
Shundi	125–44
Chongdi	144–45
Zhidi	145–46
Huandi	146–68
Lingdi	169–89
Xiandi	189–220
Period of Disunity	220–581
Sui Dynasty	
Wendi	581–604
Yangdi	604–17
Gongdi	617–18
Tang Dynasty	
Gaozu	618–26
Taizong	626–49
Gaozong	649–83
Zhongzong	684
Ruizong	684–90
Wu Zetian	690–705
Zhongzong (restored)	705–10
Ruizong (restored)	710–12
Xuangzong	712–56
Suzong	756–62
Daizong	762–79
Dezong	779–805
Shunzong	805
Xianzong	805–20
Muzong	820–24
Jingzong	824–27
Wenzong	827–40
Wuzong	840–46
Xuanzong	846–59
Yizong	859–73
Xizong	873–88
Zhaozong	888–904
Aidi	904–07
Five Dynasties and Ten Kingdoms Period	907–60
Northern Song Dynasty	
Taizu	960–76
Taizong	976–97
Zhenzong	998–1022
Renzong	1022–63
Yingzong	1064–67
Shenzong	1068–85
Zhezong	1086–1101
Huizong	1101–25
Qinzong	1126
Southern Song Dynasty	
Gaozong	1127–62
Xiazong	1163–90
Guangzong	1190–94
Ningzong	1195–1224
Lizong	1225–64
Duzong	1265–74
Gongzong	1275
Duanzong	1276–78
Bing Di	1279
Yuan Dynasty	
Shizu (Kublai Khan)	1279–94
Chengzong (Temur Oljeitu)	1294–1307
Wuzong (Khaishan)	1308–11
Renzong (Ayrbarwada)	1311–20
Yingzong (Shidebala)	1321–23
Taiding (Yesun Temur)	1323–28
Wenzong (Tugh Temur)	1328–29
Mingzong (Khoshila)	1329
Wenzong (restored)	1329–32
Shundi (Toghon Temur)	1332–68
Ming Dynasty	
Hongwu	1368–98
Jianwen	1399–1402
Yongle	1403–24
Hongxi	1425
Xuande	1426–35
Zhengtong	1436–49
Jingtai	1449–57
Zhengtong (restored)	1457–64
Chenghua	1464–87
Hongzhi	1487–1505
Zhengde	1505–21
Jiajing	1521–67

NAME	REIGN
Longqing	1567–72
Wanli	1572–1620
Taichang	1620
Tianqi	1620–27
Chongzhen	1628–44
Qing Dynasty	
Shunzhi	1644–61
Kangxi	1661–1722
Yongzheng	1722–35
Qianlong	1735–96
Jiajing	1796–1820
Daoguang	1820–50
Xianfeng	1850–61
Tongzhi	1861–75
Guangxu	1875–1908
Puyi	1908–11

LEADERS OF THE PEOPLE'S REPUBLIC OF CHINA

After the victory of Mao Zedong's Communist Party in the Chinese Civil War in 1949, the leader of the Party occupied the pre-eminent role in China's government. China retained a president with largely ceremonial powers, and a prime minister who in theory headed the government, but these officials were firmly subordinate to the will of the Communist Party leadership.

HEADS OF STATE

NAME	TERM
Mao Zedong	1949–59
Liu Shaoqi	1959–68
Dong Biwu	1968–75
Position vacant	1975–83
Li Xiannian	1983–87
Yang Shangkun	1987–93
Jiang Zemin	1992–2003
Hu Jintao	2003–

HEADS OF COMMUNIST PARTY

NAME	TERM
Mao Zedong	1945–79
Hua Guofeng	1979–81
Hu Yaobang	1981–87
Zhao Ziyang	1987–89
Jiang Zemin	1989–2002
Hu Jintao	2002–

PRIME MINISTERS

NAME	TERM
Zhou Enlai	1949–76
Hua Guofeng	1976–80
Zhao Ziyang	1980–87
Li Peng	1987–98
Zhu Rongji	1998–2003
Wen Jiaobao	2003–

RULERS OF INDIA

The Indian subcontinent has seen the rise and fall of many kingdoms and empires. The Mauryan Empire encompassed almost all of South Asia; the Gupta Empire formed a wide band across northern India; and the Chola Empire stretched across Southeast Asia. At their heights, the Muslim Delhi Sultanate and Mughal Empire controlled virtually all of modern India and Pakistan.

MAURYA EMPIRE (321–180 BCE)

NAME	REIGN
Chandragupta Maurya	321–297 BCE
Bindusara	297–272 BCE
Ashoka	272–232 BCE
Dasaratha	232–224 BCE
Samprati	224–215 BCE
Salisuka	215–202 BCE
Devadharma	202–195 BCE
Satamdhanu	195–187 BCE
Brihadratha	187–180 BCE

GUPTA INDIA (*c.*275–550)

NAME	REIGN
Gupta	*c.*275–300
Ghatotkacha	*c.*300–20
Chandragupta I	*c.*320–50
Samudragupta	*c.*350–76
Chandragupta II	*c.*376–415
Kumaragupta	*c.*415–55
Skandagupta	*c.*455–67
Kumaragupta II	*c.*467–77
Budhagupta	*c.*477–95
Chandragupta III	*c.*495–500
Vainyagupta	*c.*500–15
Narasimhagupta	*c.*515–30
Kumaragupta III	*c.*530–40
Vishnugupta	*c.*540–50

CHOLA INDIA (*c.*846–1279)

NAME	REIGN
Viyayalaya	*c.*846–71
Aditya I	*c.*871–907
Parantaka I	907–53
Rajaditya I (co-ruler)	947–49
Gandaraditya	953–57
Arinjaya (co-ruler)	956–57
Parantaka II	957–73
Aditya II (co-ruler)	957–69
Madurantaka Uttama	973–85
Rajaraja I	985–1016
Rajendra I	1016–44
Rajadhiraja I	1044–54
Rajendra II	1054–64
Raja Mahendra (co-ruler)	1060–63
Virarajendra	1064–69
Adirajendra	1069–70
Rajendra III Kulottunga Chola	1070–1122
Vikrama Chola	1122–35
Kulottunga Chola II	1135–50
Rajaraja II	1150–73
Rajadhiraja II	1173–79
Kulottunga III	1179–1218
Rajaraja III	1218–46
Rajendra IV	1246–79

DELHI SULTANATE (1206–1526)

NAME	REIGN
Slave Mamluk Dynasty	
Aibak	1206–10
Aran Shan	1210–11
Iltutmish	1211–36
Firuz Shah	1236
Radiyya Begum	1236–40
Bahram Shah	1240–42
Mas'ud Shah	1242–46
Mahmud Shah	1246–66
Balban	1266–87
Kai-Qubadh	1287–90
Kayumarth	1290
Khalji Dynasty	
Firuz Shah II	1290–96
Ibrahim I	1296
Muhammad I	1296–1316
'Umar	1316
Mubarak I	1316–20
Khusraw	1320
Tughluqid Dynasty	
Tughluq I	1321–25
Muhammad II	1325–51
Firuz Shah III	1351–88
Tughluq II	1388–89
Abu Bakr	1389–90
Muhammad III	1390–94
Sikandar I	1394
Mahmud II	1394–13
Daulat Khan Lodi	1413–14
Sayyid Dynasty	
Khidr Khan	1414–21
Mubarak II	1421–34
Muhammad IV	1434–45
Alam Shah	1445–51
Lodi Dynasty	
Bahlul Lodi	1451–89
Sikandar II	1489–17
Ibrahim II	1517–26
Mughal Dynasty	
Babur	1526–30
Humayun	1530–40
Surid Dynasty	
Shir Shah Sur	1540–45
Islam Shah	1545–53
Muhammad 'Adil	1553–55
Ibrahim III	1555
Sikandar III	1555–56
Mughal Emperors	
Humayun (restored)	1555–56
Akbar I the Great	1556–1605
Jahangir	1605–27
Shah Jahan I	1628–58
Aurangzeb	1658–1707
Azam Shah	1707
Bahadur Shah I	1707–12
'Azim-ush-Sha'n	1712
Jahandar Shah	1712–13
Farrukhsiyar	1713–19
Rafi' ud-Darajat	1719
Shah Jahan II	1719
Nikusiyar	1719
Muhammad Ibrahim	1719–48
Ahmad Shah	1748–54
Alamgir II	1754–59
Shah Alam II	1759–88
Baidar Bakht	1788
Shah Alam II (restored)	1788–1806
Akbar II	1806–37
Bahadur Shah II	1837–58

PRESIDENTS AND PRIME MINISTERS OF INDIA

BJP Bharatiya Janata Party, **CP** Congress Party, **CIP** Congress I (Indira) Party, **LD** Lok Dal, **JD** Janata Dal, **JDS** Janata Dal (Secular), **JP** Janata Party, **JSP** Janata Secular Party

PRESIDENTS

NAME	TERM
Dr Rajendra Prasad	1950–62
Dr Sarvapali Radhakrishnan	1962–67
Dr Zakir Husain	1967–69
Sri Vaharagiri Venkata Giri	1969
Muhammad Hidayat Ullah	1969
Sri Vaharagiri Venkata Giri	1969–74
Fakhruddin 'Ali Ahmad	1974–77
Basappa Danappa Jatti	1977
Neelam Sanjiva Reddy	1977–82
Gian Zail Singh	1982–87
Rameswar Venkataraman	1987–92
Dr Shankar Dayal Sharma	1992–97
Sri Kocheril Raman Narayanan	1997–2002
Dr Awul Abdul Kalam	2002–07
Pratibha Patil	2007–

PRIME MINISTERS

NAME	TERM
Jawaharlal Nehru (CP)	1947–64
Gulzarilal Nanda (CP)	1964
Lal Bahadur Shastri (CP)	1964–66
Gulzarilal Nanda (CP)	1966
Srimati Indira Gandhi (CP)	1966–77
Morarji Ranchhodji Desai (JP)	1977–79
Charan Singh (JSP)	1979–80
Srimati Indira Gandhi (CIP)	1980–84
Rajiv Gandhi (CIP)	1984–89
Vishvant Pratap Singh (JD)	1989–90
Sadanand Singh Shekhar (JDS)	1990–91
Pamulaparpi Narasimha Rao (CIP)	1991–96
Atal Bihari Vajpayee (BJP)	1996
Haradanhalli Dewe Gowda (JD)	1996–97
Inder Kumar Gujral(JD)	1997–98
Atal Bihari Vajpayee (BJP)	1998–2004
Dr Manmohan Singh (CIP)	2004–

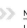

RULERS OF JAPAN

Japanese tradition dates the accession of the country's first emperor, Jimmu Tenno, to 660 BCE, but archaeological discoveries have indicated he is more likely to have ruled around 40 CE. Over time, Japan's emperors lost power to influential military families, and from 1185 to the 19th century real power was wielded by a series of military warlords (shoguns), including the Tokugawa family, who held the post of shogun for over 250 years until the restoration of the emperor's powers in 1867.

EMPERORS

NAME	REIGN
Yamato Period (c.40 BCE–710 CE)	
Jimmu	40–10 BCE
Suizei	10 BCE–20 CE
Annei	20–50
Itoki	50–80
Kōshō	80–110
Kōan	110–40
Kōrei	140–70
Kōgen	170–200
Kaika	200–30
Sujin	230–58
Suinin	258–90
Keikō	290–322
Seimu	322–55
Chūai	355–62
Ojin	362–94
Nintoku	394–427
Richū	427–32
Hanzei	432–37
Ingyō	437–54
Ankō	454–57
Yūryaku	457–89
Seinei	489–94
Kenzō	494–97
Ninken	497–504
Buretsu	504–510
Keitai	510–27
Ankan	527–35
Senka	535–39
Kimmei	539–71
Bidatsu	572–85
Yōmei	585–87
Sushun	587–92
Suiko (Empress)	593–628
Jomei	629–41
Kōgyoku (Empress)	642–45
Kōtoku	645–54
Saimei (Kōgokyu restored)	655–61
Tenji	661–72
Kobun	672
Temmu	672–86
Jitō (Empress)	686–97
Mommu	697–707
Nara Period (710–784)	
Gemmei (Empress)	707–15
Genshō (Empress)	715–24
Shōmu	724–49
Kōken (Empress)	749–58
Junnin	758–64
Shōtoku (Kōken restored)	764–70
Kōnin	770–81
Heian Period (784–1185)	
Kammu	781–806
Heizei	806–09
Saga	809–23
Junna	823–33
Nimmyō	833–50
Montoku	850–58
Seiwa	858–76
Yōzei	876–84
Kōkō	884–87
Uda	887–97
Daigo	897–930
Suzaku	930–46
Murakami	946–67
Reizei	967–69
En'yū	969–84
Kazan	984–86
Ichijō	986–1011
Sanjō	1011–16
Go-Ichijō	1016–36
Go-Suzaku	1036–45
Go-Reizei	1045–68
Go-Sanjō	1068–73
Shirakawa	1073–87
Horikawa	1087–1107
Toba	1107–23
Sutoku	1123–42
Konoe	1142–55
Go-Shirakawa	1155–58
Nijō	1158–65
Rokujō	1165–68
Takakura	1168–80
Antoku	1180–85
Kamakura Period (1186–1333)	
Go-Toba	1183–98
Tsuchimikado	1198–1210
Juntoku	1210–21
Chūkyō	1221
Go-Horikaw	1221–32
Shij	1232–42
Go-Saga	1242–46
Go-Fukakusa	1246–60
Kameyama	1260–74
Go-Uda	1274–87
Fushimi	1287–98
Go-Fushimi	1298–1301
Go-Nijō	1301–08
Hanazono	1308–18
Southern Court (1336–92)	
Go-Daigo	1318–39
Go-Murakami	1339–68
Chōkei	1368–83
Go-Kameyama	1383–92
Northern Court (1336–92)	
Kōgon	1331–33
Kōmyō	1336–48
Sukō	1348–51
Go-Kōgon	1352–71
Go-En'yū	1371–82
Muromachi Period (1392–1573)	
Go-Komatsu	1382–1412
Shōkō	1412–28
Go-Hanazono	1428–64
Go-Tsuchimikado	1464–1500
Go-Kashiwabara	1500–26
Go-Nara	1526–57
Ōgimachi	1557–86
Tokugawa Period (1603–1867)	
Go-Yōzei	1586–1611
Go-Mizunoo	1611–29
Meishō	1629–43
Go-Kōmyō	1643–54
Go-Sai	1655–63
Reigen	1663–87
Higashiyama	1687–1709
Nakamikado	1709–35
Sakuramachi	1735–47
Momozono	1747–62
Go-Sakuramachi (Empress)	1735–47
Go-Momozono	1771–79
Kōkaku	1780–1817
Ninkō	1817–46
Kōmei	1846–67
Modern Japan (1867–)	
Meiji	1867–1912
Taishō	1912–26
Shōwa (Hirohito)	1926–89
Akihito	1989–

SHOGUNS

NAME	REIGN
Kamakura Shogunate	
Minamoto Yoritomo	1192–95
Yoriie	1202–03
Sanemoto	1203–19
Kujō Yoritsune	1226–44
Yoritsugu	1244–52
Munetaka	1252–66
Koreyasu	1266–89
Hisaaki	1289–1308
Morikuni	1308–33
Ashikaga Shogunate	
Ashikaga Takauji	1338–58
Yoshiakira	1359–67
Yoshimitsu	1369–95
Yoshimochi	1395–1423
Yoshikazu	1423–25
Yoshinori	1429–41
Yoshikatsu	1442–43
Yoshimasa	1449–74
Yoshihisa	1474–89
Yoshitane	1490–93
Yoshizumi	1495–1508
Yoshitane (restored)	1508–22
Yoshiharu	1522–47
Yoshiteru	1547–65
Yoshihide	1568
Yoshiaki	1568–73
Tokugawa Shogunate	
Tokugawa Ieyasu	1603–05
Hidetada	1605–23
Iemitsu	1623–51
Ietsuna	1651–80
Tsunayoshi	1680–1709
Ienobu	1709–12
Ietsugu	1713–16
Yoshimune	1716–45
Ieshige	1745–60
Ieharu	1760–86
Ienari	1787–1837
Ieyoshi	1837–53
Iesada	1853–58
Iemochi	1858–66
Yoshinobi	1867–68

PRIME MINISTERS OF JAPAN

DP Democratic Party, **JNP** Japan New Party, **JRP** Japan Renewal Party, **LDP** Liberal Democratic Party, **LP** Liberal Party, **SP** Socialist Party

NAME	TERM
Ito Hirobumi	1885–88
Kuroda Kiyotaka	1888–89
Yamagata Aritomo	1889–91
Matsukata Masayoshi	1891–92
Ito Hirobumi	1892–96
Matsukata Masayoshi	1896–97
Kuroda Kiyotaka	1897
Matsukata Masayoshi	1897–98
Ito Hirobumi	1898
Okuma Shigenobu	1898
Yamagata Aritomo	1898–1900
Ito Hirobumi	1900–01
Saionji Kimmochi	1901
Katsura Taro	1901–06
Saionji Kimmochi	1906–08
Katsura Taro	1908–11
Saionji Kimmochi	1911–12
Katsura Taro	1912–13
Yamamoto Gonnohyoe	1913–14
Okuma Shigenobu	1914–16
Terauchi Matsakate	1916–18
Hara Takashi	1918–21
Uchida Yasuya	1921
Takahashi Korekiyo	1921–22
Kato Tomosabura	1922–23
Yamamoto Gonnohyoe	1923–24
Kiyoura Keigo	1924
Kato Takaaki	1924–26
Wakatsuki Reijiro	1926–27
Tanaka Giichi	1927–29
Hamaguchi Osachi	1929–31
Wakatsuki Reijiro	1931
Inukai Takashi	1931–32
Takahashi Korekiyo	1932
Saito Makoto	1932–34
Okada Keisuke	1934–36
Goto Fumio	1936
Hirota Koki	1936–37
Hayashi Senjuro	1937
Konoye Fumimaro	1937–1939
Hironuma Kiichiro	1939
Abe Nobyaki	1939–40
Yonai Mitsumasa	1940
Konoye Fumimaro	1940–41
Tojo Hideki	1941–44
Koiso Kuniaki	1944–45
Suzuki Kantaro	1945
Naruhiko Higashikini	1945
Shidehara Kiuro	1945
Yoshida Shigeru (LP)	1946–47
Katayama Tetsu (SP)	1947–48
Ashida Hitoshi (DP)	1948
Yoshida Shigeru (LP)	1948–54
Hatoyama Ichiro (LDP)	1954–56
Ishibashi Tanzan (LDP)	1956–57
Kishi Nobusuke (LDP)	1957–60
Ikeda Hayato (LDP)	1960–64
Sato Eisaku (LDP)	1964–72
Tanaka Kakuei (LDP)	1972–74
Miki Takeo (LDP)	1974–76
Fukuda Takeo (LDP)	1976–78
Ohira Masayoshi (LDP)	1978–80
Ito Masayoshi (LDP)	1980
Suzuki Zenko (LDP)	1980–82
Nakasone Yasuhiro (LDP)	1982–87
Takeshita Nobaru (LDP)	1987–89
Uno Sosuke (LDP)	1989
Kaifu Toshiki (LDP)	1989–91
Miyazawa Kiichi (LDP)	1991–93
Hata Tsutomu (JNP)	1993–94
Murayama Tomiichi (JNP)	1994–96
Hashimoto Ryutaro (LDP)	1996–98
Obuchi Keizo (LDP)	1998–2000
Mori Yoshiro (LDP)	2000–01
Koizumi Jun'ichiro (LDP)	2001–06
Abe Shinzo (LDP)	2006–07

»

NAME	REIGN	NAME	REIGN
Fukuda Yasuo (LDP)	2007–08	Hatoyama Yukio (DP)	2009–2010
Aso Taro (LDP)	2008–09	Kan Naoto (DP)	2010–

INCA EMPERORS

NAME	REIGN	NAME	REIGN
Manco Capac	*c.*1100	Tupac Yupanqui	1471–93
Sinchi Roca	unknown	Huayna Capac	1493–1526
Lloque Yupanqui	unknown	Huascar	1526–32
Mayta Capac	unknown	Atahuallpa	1530–33
Capac Yupanqui	*c.*1200	Tupac Hualpa	1533
Inca Roca	unknown	Manco Inca Yupanqui	1533–45
Inca Yupanqui	unknown	Sayri Tupac	1545–60
Viracocha	unknown	Titu Cusi Yupanqui	1560–71
Inca Urco	1438	Tupac Amaru	1571–72
Pachacuti	1438–71		

AZTEC EMPERORS

NAME	REIGN	NAME	REIGN
Acampichtli	1372–91	Tizoc	1481–86
Huitzilihuitl	1391–1415	Ahuitzotl	1486–1502
Chimalpopoca	1415–26	Moctezuma II Xocoyotzin	1502–20
Itzcoatl	1426–40	Cuitlahuac	1520
Moctezuma I Ilhuicamina	1440–68	Cuauhtemoc	1520–21
Axayacatl	1468–81		

PRESIDENTS OF THE UNITED STATES

F Federalist, **DR** Democratic Republican, **D** Democratic, **R** Republican, **W** Whig, **NU** National Union

NAME	TERM	NAME	TERM
George Washington	1789–97	Benjamin Harrison (R)	1889–93
John Adams (F)	1797–1801	Grover Cleveland (D)	1893–97
Thomas Jefferson (DR)	1801–09	William McKinley (R)	1897–1901
James Madison (DR)	1809–17	Theodore Roosevelt (R)	1901–09
James Monroe (DR)	1817–25	William Howard Taft (R)	1909–13
John Quincy Adams (DR)	1825–29	Woodrow Wilson (D)	1913–21
Andrew Jackson (D)	1829–37	Warren G. Harding (R)	1921–23
Martin Van Buren (D)	1837–41	Calvin Coolidge (R)	1923–29
William Henry Harrison (W)	1841	Herbert Hoover (R)	1929–33
John Tyler (W)	1841–45	Franklin D. Roosevelt (D)	1933–45
James Knox Polk (D)	1845–49	Harry S. Truman (D)	1945–53
Zachary Taylor (W)	1849–50	Dwight D. Eisenhower (R)	1953–61
Millard Fillmore (W)	1850–53	John F. Kennedy (D)	1961–63
Franklin Pierce (D)	1853–57	Lyndon B. Johnson (D)	1963–69
James Buchanan (D)	1857–61	Richard Nixon (R)	1969–74
Abraham Lincoln (R)	1861–65	Gerald Ford (R)	1974–77
Andrew Johnson (D/NU)	1865–69	James ("Jimmy") Carter (D)	1977–81
Ulysses S. Grant (R)	1869–77	Ronald Reagan (R)	1981–89
Rutherford B. Hayes (R)	1877–81	George H. W. Bush (R)	1989–93
James A. Garfield (R)	1881	William ("Bill") Clinton (D)	1993–2001
Chester A. Arthur (R)	1881–85	George W. Bush (R)	2001–09
Grover Cleveland (D)	1885–89	Barack Obama (D)	2009–

PRIME MINISTERS OF CANADA

CP Conservative Party, **LP** Liberal Party, **PCP** Progressive Conservative Party, **UP** Unionist Party

NAME	TERM	NAME	TERM
John Alexander MacDonald (LP)	1867–73	Lester Pearson (LP)	1963–68
Alexander MacKenzie (LP)	1873–78	Pierre Trudeau (LP)	1968–79
John Alexander MacDonald (CP)	1878–91	Joseph Clark (PCP)	1979–80
John Abbott (CP)	1891–92	Pierre Trudeau (LP)	1980–84
John Thompson (CP)	1892–94	John Turner (LP)	1984
MacKenzie Bowell (CP)	1894–96	Brian Mulroney (PCP)	1984–93
Charles Tupper (CP)	1896	Kim Campbell (PCP)	1993
Wilfred Laurier (LP)	1896–1911	Jean Chrétien (LP)	1993–2003
Robert Borden (CP, UP)	1911–20	Paul Martin (LP)	2003–06
Arthur Meighen (UP)	1920–21	Stephen Harper (CP)	2006–
W. Mackenzie King (LP)	1921–26		
Arthur Meighen (UP)	1926		
W. MacKenzie King (LP)	1926–30		
Richard Bennett (CP)	1930–35		
W. MacKenzie King (LP)	1935–48		
Louis St Laurent (LP)	1948–57		
John Diefenbaker (PCP)	1957–63		

PRESIDENTS AND PRIME MINISTERS OF SOUTH AFRICA

ANC African National Congress, **LP** Labour Party, **NP** National Party, **NPP** National People's Party, **SAP** South African Party, **S** Solidarity, **UP** United Party

PRESIDENTS

NAME	TERM	NAME	TERM
Charles Swart	1961–67	Marais Viljoen	1979–84
Jozua Naudé	1967–68	Pieter Botha	1984–89
Jacobus Fouché	1968–75	Frederik de Klerk	1989–94
Jan de Clerk	1975	Nelson Mandela (ANC)	1994–99
Nicolaas Diederich	1975–78	Thabo Mbeki (ANC)	1999–2008
Marais Viljoen	1978	Kgalema Motlanthe (ANC)	2008–09
B. Johannes Vorster	1978–79	Jacob Zuma (ANC)	2009–

PRIME MINISTERS

NAME	TERM	NAME	TERM
Louis Botha (SAP)	1910–19	Charles Swart	1958
Jan Smuts (SAP)	1919–24	Hendrik Verwoerd (NP)	1958–66
James Barry Herzog (NP/UP)	1924–39	Ebenhezer Dönges	1966
Jan Smuts (UP)	1939–48	B. Johannes Vorster (NP)	1966–78
Daniel Malan (NP)	1948–54	Pieter Botha (NP)	1978–84
Johannes Strijdom (NP)	1954–58		

PRIME MINISTERS OF AUSTRALIA (SINCE 1901)

ALP Australian Labour Party, **CP** Country Party, **LPA** Liberal Party of Australia, **NP** National Party, **UAP** United Australia Party

NAME	TERM	NAME	TERM
Edmund Barton	1901–03	Arthur Fadden (CP)	1941
Alfred Deakin (LPA)	1903–04	John Curtin (ALP)	1941–45
John Watson	1904	Francis Forde	1945
George Reid	1904–05	Joseph Chifley (ALP)	1945–49
Alfred Deakin (LPA)	1905–08	Robert Menzies (LPA)	1949–66
Andrew Fisher (ALP)	1908–09	Harold Holt (LPA)	1966–67
Alfred Deakin (LPA)	1909–10	John McEwan (CP)	1967–68
Andrew Fisher (ALP)	1910–13	John Gorton (LPA)	1968–71
Joseph Cook	1913–14	William MacMahon (LPA)	1971–72
Andrew Fisher (ALP)	1914–15	E. Gough Whitlam (ALP)	1972–75
William Hughes (ALP, NP)	1915–23	Malcolm Fraser (LPA)	1975–83
Stanley Bruce (NP)	1923–29	Robert Hawke (ALP)	1983–91
James Scullin (ALP)	1929–32	Paul Keating (ALP)	1991–96
Joseph Lyons (UAP)	1932–39	John Howard (LPA)	1996–2007
Earl Page (CP)	1939	Kevin Rudd (ALP)	2007–10
Robert Menzies (UAP)	1939–41	Julia Gillard (ALP)	2010–

PRIME MINISTERS OF NEW ZEALAND

Lab Labour Party, **Lib** Liberal Party, **NP** National party, **RP** Reform Party, **UP** United Party

NAME	TERM	NAME	TERM
Henry Sewell	1856	William Hall-Jones (Lib)	1906
William Fox	1856	Joseph Ward (Lib)	1906–12
Edward Stafford	1856–61	Thomas MacKenzie (Lib)	1912
William Fox	1861–62	William Massey (RP)	1912–25
Alfred Domett	1862–63	Francis Bell (RP)	1925
Frederick Whitaker	1863–64	Joseph Coates (RP)	1925–28
Frederick Weld	1864–65	Joseph Ward (UP)	1928–30
Edward Stafford	1865–69	George Forbes (UP)	1930–35
William Fox	1869–72	Michael Savage (Lab)	1935–40
Edward Stafford	1872	Peter Fraser (Lab)	1940–49
George Waterhouse	1872–73	Sidney Holland (NP)	1949–57
William Fox	1873	Keith Holyoake (NP)	1957
Julius Vogel	1873–75	Walter Nash (Lab)	1957–60
Daniel Pollen	1875–76	Keith Holyoake (NP)	1960–72
Julius Vogel	1876	John Marshall (NP)	1972
Harry Atkinson	1876–77	Norman Kirk (Lab)	1972–74
George Grey	1877–79	Hugh Watt (Lab)	1974
John Hall	1879–82	Wallace Rowling (Lab)	1974–75
Frederick Whitaker	1882–83	Robert Muldoon (NP)	1975–84
Harry Atkinson	1883–84	David Lange (Lab)	1984–89
Robert Stout	1884	Geoffrey Palmer (Lab)	1989–90
Harry Atkinson	1884	Michael Moore (Lab)	1990
Robert Stout	1884–87	James Bolger (NP)	1990–97
Harry Atkinson	1887–91	Jenny Shipley (NP)	1997–99
John Balance (Lib)	1891–93	Helen Clark (Lab)	1999–2008
Richard Seddon (Lib)	1893–1906	John Key (NP)	2008–

HISTORY IN FIGURES

HOMININS

Modern humanity's most distant ancestors were ape-like creatures living in Africa millions of years ago. Our own species, Homo sapiens, only appeared about 150,000 years ago.

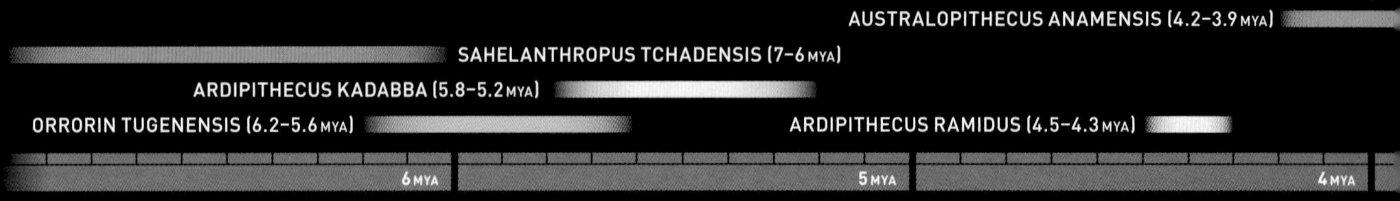

LARGEST CITIES

The greatest cities of the ancient world still had comparatively small populations. The development of more effective sanitation systems then allowed cities such as Rome to grow to almost 500,000 in the 1st century BCE, a figure scarcely matched until after the Industrial Revolution of the 19th century.

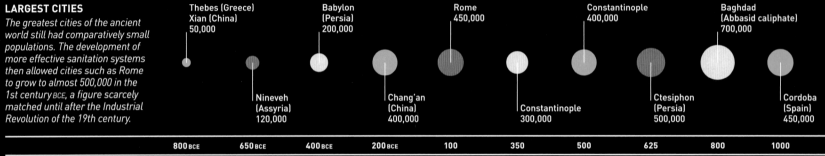

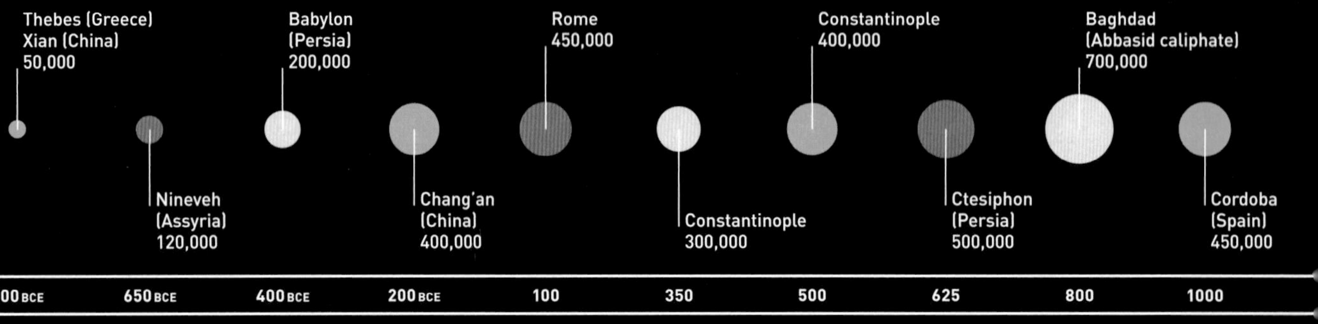

WORST WARS BY CASUALTY FIGURES

Although World War II was the world's worst war in terms of casualties, many older conflicts were astonishingly bloody considering the smaller armies of the time and the lower populations of the countries in which they were fought.

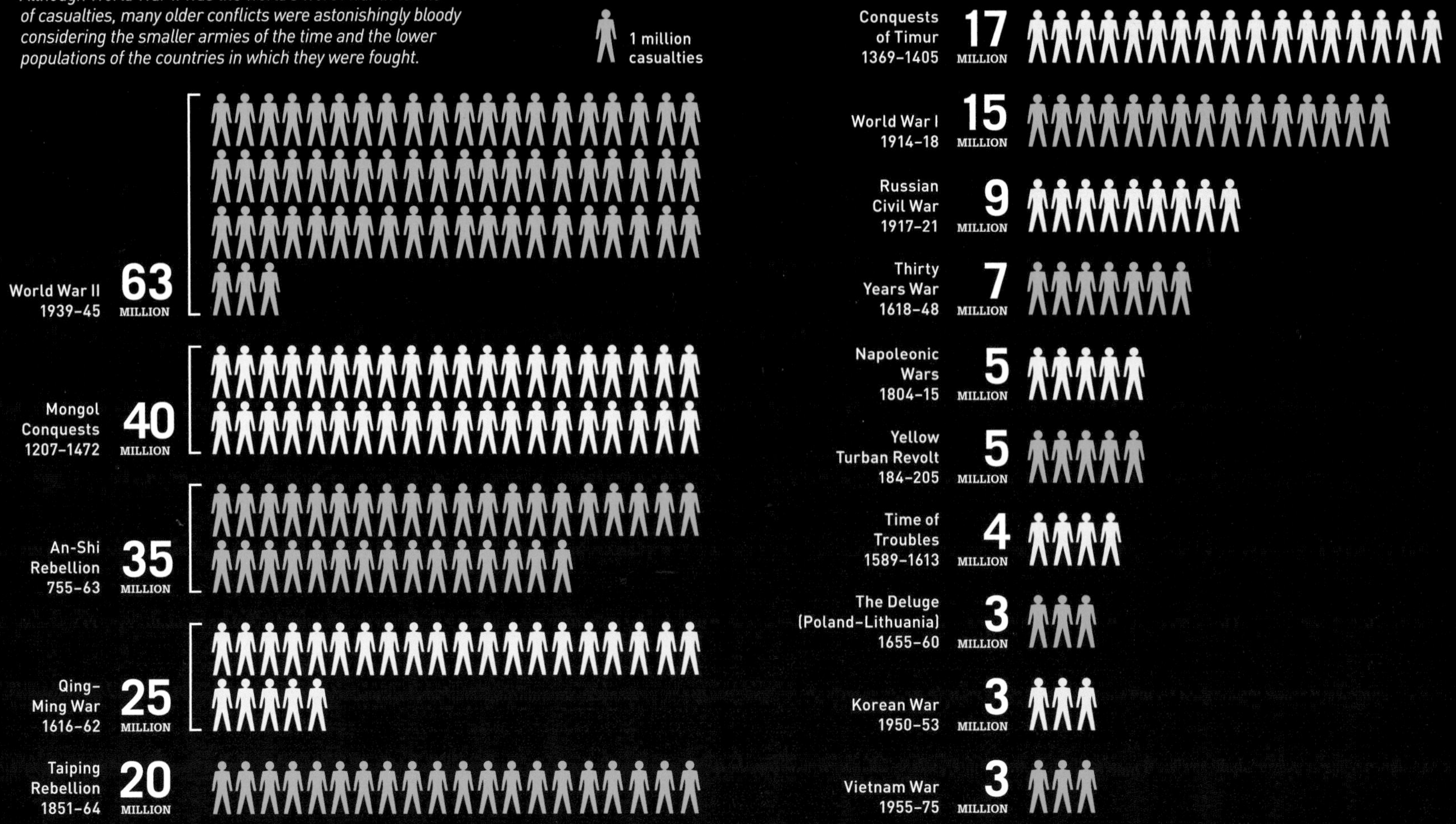

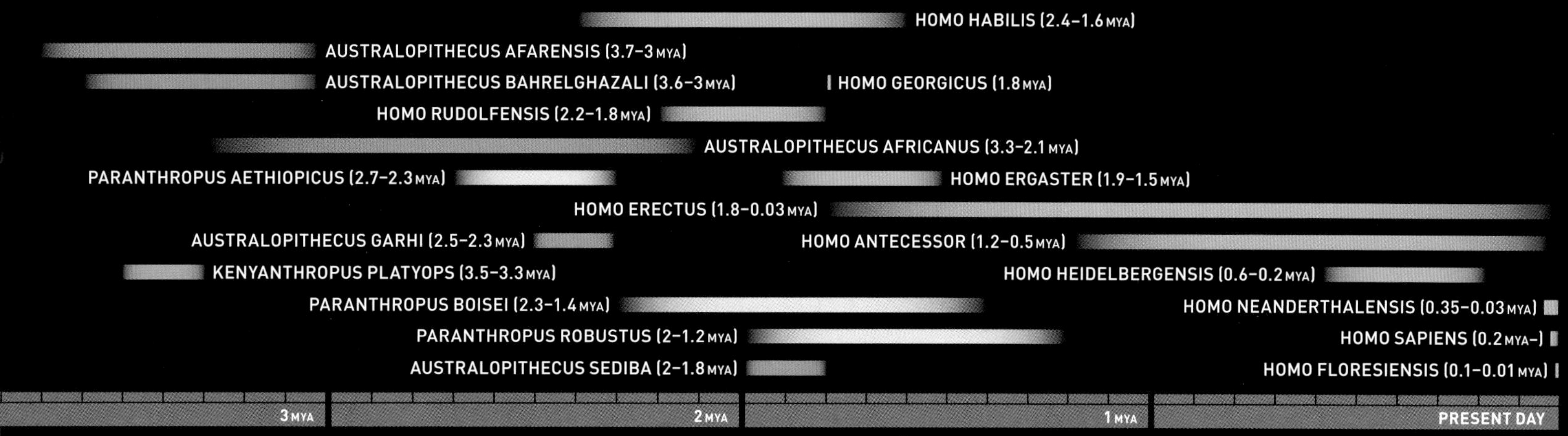

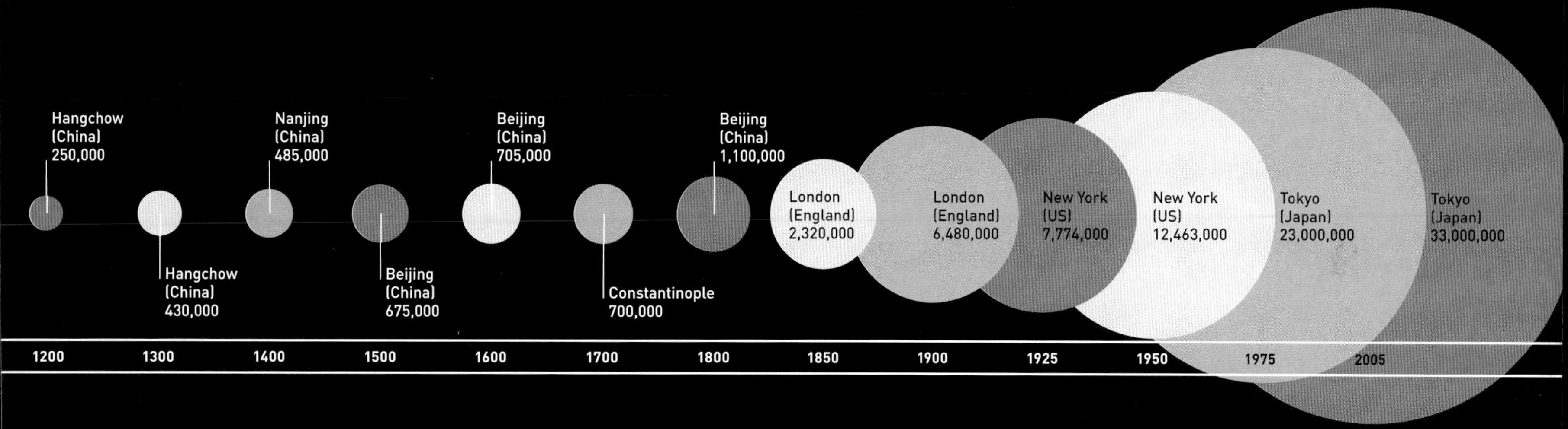

LONGEST-REIGNING DYNASTIES

Although the lifespan of a ruling dynasty has seldom been more than a few hundred years, in exceptional cases a ruling house has held power for more than a thousand, while in Japan the Yamato dynasty has survived for more than 2,500 and still rules today.

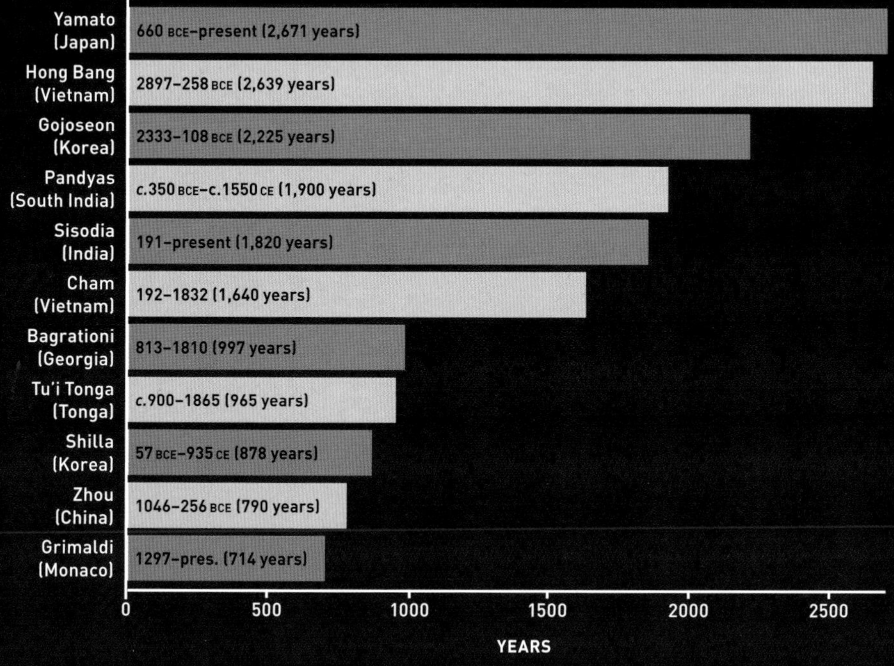

LONGEST-REIGNING MONARCHS

Some monarchs have had astonishingly long reigns. Although in general this meant they came to the throne as small children and initially exercised little power, those who enjoyed a long reign often brought a period of power and prosperity to their country.

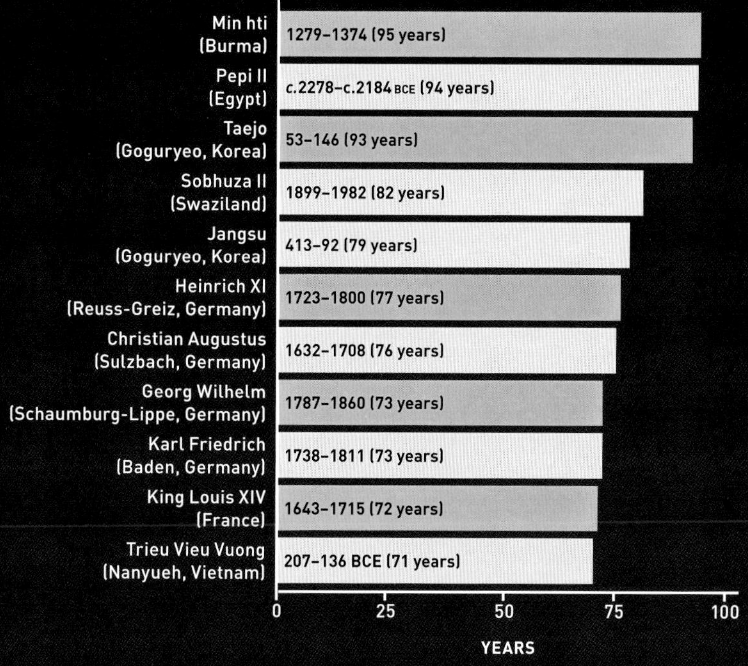

WARS

The human story is one of conflict. Disputes over territory, religion, and governance have escalated into war throughout history, and while the stories of great battles and great commanders make compelling reading, the tragic consequences of war should never be forgotten.

MAJOR WARS

WAR	DATE	OPPOSING FORCES
Greek–Persian Wars	490–448 BCE	Coalition of Greek city-states including Athens and Sparta v. Persia
Peloponnesian War	431–404 BCE	Athens and allies v. Sparta and allies
Alexander the Great's Conquests	334–323 BCE	Macedonia v. Persian Empire
First Punic War	264–241 BCE	Rome and allies v. Carthage and allies
Second Punic War	218–202 BCE	Rome and allies v. Carthage and allies
Third Punic War	149–146 BCE	Rome and allies v. Carthage and allies
First Roman Civil War	49–44 BCE	Julius Caesar v. Pompey the Great
Second Roman Civil War	33–31 BCE	Octavian (Augustus) v. Mark Antony
Byzantine–Seljuk Wars	1064–71, 1110–17, 1158–76	Byzantines v. Seljuk Turks
The Crusades	1095–1272	Various Western European Christian armies v. Muslim states of the eastern Mediterranean and Egypt
Mongol Conquests	1206–1405	Mongols v. various European and Asian peoples
Hundred Years War	1337–1453	English (and Burgundians) v. French
Onin War	1467–77	Yamana clan v. Hosokawa clan
The Italian Wars	1494–95, 1521–25, 1526–30, 1535–38, 1542–44	Italian city-states and Holy Roman Empire v. French and Italian allies
Wars of Japanese Unification	1560–1603	Oda Nobunaga, Toyotomi Hideyoshi, Tokugawa Ieyasu and allies v. opposing *daimyo* (warlord) clans
Eighty Years War (The Dutch Revolt)	1568–1648	Dutch v. Philip II of Spain and allies in southern Netherlands
War of the Three Kingdoms (The English Civil War)	1642–51	Charles I and Royalists v. Parliamentarians
The Thirty Years War	1618–48	Imperial Catholic alliance v. mainly Protestant powers plus France
The Great Northern War	1700–21	Sweden v. Denmark, Saxony, Poland–Lithuania, Russia
The Seven Years War	1756–63	Britain and Prussia v. France, Austria, Russia, Saxony, Sweden
American Revolutionary War	1775–83	Britain v. American colonists (and French allies)
French Revolutionary Wars	1792–1802	France v. varying coalitions including Britain, Austria, Prussia, Russia
The Napoleonic Wars	1803–15	France v. varying coalitions including Britain, Austria, Prussia, Russia
Crimean War	1853–56	Russia v. Ottoman Turkey, Britain, France
The Indian Mutiny	1857–58	British v. native Indian forces
American Civil War	1861–65	The Union v. the Confederacy
Franco-Prussian War	1870–71	France v. Prussia
Taiping Rebellion	1850–64	Chinese central (Qing) government v. Taiping rebels
Boer Wars (South African Wars)	1880–81, 1899–1902	British v. Boers (Afrikaners)
Balkan Wars	1912–13	(First) Bulgaria, Greece, Serbia, Montenegro v. Ottoman Turkey (Second) Bulgaria v. Turkey, Serbia, Greece, Romania
World War I	1914–18	Entente (Britain, France, Italy, Russia, US, and others) v. Central Powers (Germany, Austro-Hungary, and others)
Russian Civil War	1918–21	Bolsheviks v. "White" Russians
Spanish Civil War	1936–39	Nationalists v. Republicans
World War II	1939–45	Allies (British, French, and others) v. Axis (German, Japanese, Italians to 1943, and others)
Chinese Civil War	1945–49	Communists v. Nationalists (Kuomintang)
Korean War	1950–53	North Koreans and Chinese v. South Koreans and UN force (including Americans, Australians, and British)
French Indochina War	1946–54	French v. Vietnamese nationalists (Viet Minh)
Arab–Israeli Wars	1948–73	Israel v. Egypt, Syria, Jordan, Lebanon, Iraq, and Palestinians
Vietnam War	1961–75	South Vietnamese, Americans, and Australians v. North Vietnamese (Viet Cong)
Iran–Iraq War	1980–88	Iraq v. Iran
Gulf Wars	1990–91, 2003	Iraq v. international coalition led by US
Afghanistan War	2001–	US-led coalition v. Taliban

EXPLORERS

The "discoveries" of many early explorers were actually of lands that had thriving indigenous societies, which often led to disastrous results. Yet we can still admire the imagination and tenacity of those who risked their lives journeying into territory completely unknown to them.

NOTABLE EXPLORERS

NAME	LIVED	ORIGIN	EXPEDITIONS/DISCOVERIES
Hanno	Active 5th century BCE	Carthage	Sailed down the west coast of Africa (*c.*470 BCE)
Erik the Red	*c.*950–1002	Norway	Explored the coast of Greenland (985)
Leif Eriksson	Active 11th century	Norway	Discovered Vinland, part of North America (*c.*1000)
Marco Polo	1254–1324	Italy	Travelled extensively in China and along the Silk Road (1275–92)
Ibn Battuta	*c.*1304–68	Morocco	Explored the Sahara, Arabia, India, Central Asia, China, and Southeast Asia
Dinís Diaz	Active mid-15th century	Portugal	Discovered the Cape Verde islands off the west coast of Africa (1445)
Bartolomeu Dias	*c.*1450–1500	Portugal	Rounded Africa's Cape of Good Hope (1488)
Vasco da Gama	*c.*1469–1524	Portugal	Sailed round Africa's Cape of Good Hope and reached India (1497–98)

»

NAME	LIVED	ORIGIN	EXPEDITIONS/DISCOVERIES
Christopher Columbus	1451–1506	Italy	Discovered the Americas, landing in the Bahamas (1492); discovered the mainland of South America (1498)
John Cabot	c.1450–99	Italy	Discovered mainland North America (1497)
Pedro Alvarez Cabral	c.1467–1520	Portugal	Discovered Brazil (1500)
Amerigo Vespucci	1454–1512	Italy	Explored the coastline of South America (1501)
Afonso de Albuquerque	1453–1515	Portugal	Reached India via Zanzibar (1503–04)
Vasco Núñez de Balboa	1475–1519	Spain	First European to navigate the South Sea (Pacific Ocean), from Panama (1513)
Juan Ponce de Leon	c.1460–1521	Spain	Discovered Florida (1513)
Hernán Cortes	1485–1547	Spain	Led the conquest of the Aztec Empire in Mexico (1518–22)
Ferdinand Magellan	c.1480–1521	Portugal	Explored the Philippines; partially circumnavigated the globe (1520–21)
Francisco Pizarro	1475–1541	Spain	Led the conquest of the Inca Empire in Peru (1530–33)
Jacques Cartier	1491–1557	France	Explored the Gulf of St Lawrence and St Lawrence River (1535–36)
Francisco Vásquez de Coronado	1510–54	Spain	Led the first major expedition to the southwest of the modern United States (1540–42)
García López de Cárdenas	Active 1540s	Spain	Reached the Grand Canyon in 1540
Martin Frobisher	c.1535–94	England	Reached the Frobisher Strait (Canada) while searching for the Northwest Passage (1576)
Francis Drake	c.1540–96	England	Circumnavigated the globe (1580)
John Davis	c.1550–1605	England	Explored Greenland, discovered the Davis Strait (1585) while searching for the Northwest Passage
Willem Barents	1550–97	Netherlands	Searched for the Northeast Passage (1594–97)
Walter Raleigh	1552–1618	England	Undertook numerous voyages to America; attempted, unsuccessfully, to found a colony in Virginia (1584)
Cornelis de Houtman	1565–99	Netherlands	Led first Dutch expedition to the East Indies; sailed the south coast of Java (1598)
Samuel de Champlain	1567–1635	France	Explored the St Lawrence River (1603); founded Quebec (1608)
Henry Hudson	c.1565–1611	England	Discovered Hudson Bay (Canada) (1610)
William Baffin	1584–1622	England	Explored Baffin Bay, part of the Northwest Passage (1616)
Abel Tasman	1603–c.1659	Netherlands	Reached New Zealand and Tasmania (1642)
William Dampier	1651–1715	England	Crossed the Pacific Ocean (1683)
Vitus Bering	1681–1741	Denmark	Explored Siberia (1733–41)
James Bruce	1730–94	Britain	Explored the Blue Nile; claimed to have found the source of the Nile (1768–74)
James Cook	1728–79	Britain	Mapped the New Zealand and Australian coasts (1769); made first Australian landfall, at Botany Bay, New South Wales (1770)
Antoine Bruni d'Entrecasteaux	1739–93	France	Surveyed the South Pacific (1791–93)
Mungo Park	1771–1806	Britain	Explored the Niger River (1795–96)
George Bass	1771–1803	Britain	Explored the coastline of southeastern Australia (1795–98)
Friedrich Alexander von Humboldt	1769–1859	Germany	Explored modern Venezuela and the Orinoco River (1799–1800)

NAME	LIVED	ORIGIN	EXPEDITIONS/DISCOVERIES
Matthew Flinders	1774–1814	Britain	Circumnavigated Australia (1801–03)
Meriwether Lewis	1774–1809	US	Led the first transcontinental expedition across the US (1804–05)
William Clark	1770–1838	US	Co-leader of expedition with Lewis (above)
Fabian von Bellingshausen	1778–1852	Estonia	Early explorer of the Antarctic (1819–21)
Alexander Gordon Laing	1793–1826	Britain	First European to reach Timbuktu, in Mali (1826)
William Edward Parry	1790–1855	Britain	Made an early attempt to reach the North Pole overland (1827)
James Clark Ross	1800–62	US	Made an extensive exploration of the Antarctic, discovering the Ross Sea and Ross Ice Shelf (1841)
John Franklin	1786–1847	Britain	Searched for the Northwest Passage; never returned from his expedition (1847)
Richard Francis Burton	1821–90	Britain	Travelled in Arabia and reached Medina and Mecca (1853)
David Livingstone	1813–73	Britain	Discovered the Victoria Falls on the Zambezi River (1855)
Robert O'Hara Burke	1820–61	Ireland	Led an ill-fated expedition to explore the Australian interior (1860–61)
Henry Morton Stanley	1841–1904	Britain	Undertook voyages down the Congo (1874)
Fridtjof Nansen	1861–1930	Norway	Crossed Greenland (1888)
Sven Hedin	1865–1962	Sweden	Explored Central Asia and discovered lost cities in the Taklamakan desert (1893–97)
Salomon Andrée	1854–97	Sweden	Attempted to balloon over the Arctic; disappeared during the flight (1897)
Otto Nordenskjöld	1869–1928	Sweden	Spent the winter in Antarctica (1901–03)
Francis Younghusband	1863–1942	Britain	Led an expedition that reached Lhasa in Tibet (1903–04)
Aurel Stein	1862–1943	Hungary	Explored Central Asia and located an ancient complex at Dunhuang (1906–08)
Robert Peary	1856–1920	US	Claimed to have reached North Pole (1909)
Roald Amundsen	1872–1928	Norway	First man to reach the South Pole (1911)
Robert Falcon Scott	1868–1912	Britain	Lost out to Roald Amundsen in the race to reach the South Pole (1911–12)
Ernest Shackleton	1874–1922	Britain	Led an expedition to cross Antarctica, but became stranded for four months on Elephant Island (1914)
Richard Byrd	1888–1957	US	Completed the first overflight of the North Pole (1926)
Vivian Fuchs	1908–99	Britain	Completed the first land crossing of the Antarctic continent (1958)
Wilfred Thesiger	1910–2003	Britain	Intrepid traveller who twice crossed the Empty Quarter of Arabia
Jacques-Yves Cousteau	1910–97	France	Marine ecologist who dedicated his life to deep-water oceanic exploration
Thor Heyerdahl	1914–2002	Norway	Sought to prove theories of prehistoric migration by sea with long voyages on rafts built from natural materials
Edmund Hillary	1919–2008	New Zealand	Completed the first ascent of Mount Everest in the Himalayas (1953)
Yuri Gagarin	1934–68	USSR	Vostok 1 (12 April 1961); first man in space, and first to orbit the Earth
Alan Shepard	1923–98	US	Freedom 7 (5 May 1961); first American in space and later fifth man to walk on Moon
Gherman Titov	1935–2000	USSR	Vostok 2 (6 August 1961); youngest person in space at 25 years old, and second man to orbit the Earth
Valentina Tereshkova	b.1937	USSR	Vostok 6 (16 June 1963); first woman in space
Alexei Leonov	b.1943	USSR	Voskhod 2 (18 March 1965); first tethered spacewalk

NOTABLE EXPLORERS (CONTINUED)

NAME	LIVED	ORIGIN	EXPEDITIONS/DISCOVERIES
Neil Armstrong	b.1930	USA	Apollo 11 (20 July 1969); first man to walk on the Moon
Vladimír Remek	b.1948	Czechoslovakia	Soyuz 28 (2 March 1978); first person in space from a country other than the USA or USSR
Sigmund Jähn	b.1937	German Democratic Republic	Soyuz 31 (26 August 1978); first German in space
Jean-Loup Chrétien	b.1938	France	Soyuz T-11 (24 June 1982); first French person in space
Ulf Merbold	b.1941	Germany	STS-9 28 (November 1983); first ESA astronaut, second German in space
Rakesh Sharma	b.1949	India	Soyuz T-11 (3 April 1984); first Indian in space
Sultan Salman al Saud	b.1956	Saudi Arabia	STS-56 (17 June 1985); first Arab (and first Muslim) in space
Mamoru Mori	b.1948	Japan	STS-47 (12 September 1992); first Japanese person in space
Valeri Polyakov	b.1942	Russia	Soyuz TM-18 (8 January 1998); longest space flight at 437 days
John Glenn	b.1921	US	STS-95 (29 October 1998); oldest person in space at 77 years old – previously flew on Friendship 7 in 1962
Dennis Tito	b.1940	US	Soyuz TM 32 (28 April 2001); first "space tourist"
Yang Liwei	b.1965	China	Shenzhou 5 (15 October 2003); first Chinese person in space
Sergei Krikalev	b.1958	Russia	Soyuz TMA-6 (11 October 2005); reached most time spent in space (803 days 9 hours 39 minutes)

INVENTIONS AND DISCOVERIES

The modern world is very different from the world of our ancestors. Over the course of human existence, basic human needs – from the need to survive to the urge to obtain knowledge – have produced tens of thousands of inventions and discoveries. These have transformed both the way we function and the way we think, and have made us distinct from the rest of the animal kingdom.

NOTABLE INVENTIONS AND DISCOVERIES

INVENTION/DISCOVERY	DATE	ORIGINATOR	PLACE OF ORIGIN
Stone tools	c.2.75 MYA	Early humans	Africa
Control of fire	c.400,000 YA	Early humans	Africa
Boat	c.50,000 YA	Early migrants	Australasia
Mining	c.40,000 YA	Paleolithic humans	Europe
Permanent shelters	c.28,000 YA	Paleolithic humans	Eastern Europe
Pottery vessels	c.14,000 BCE	Jomon people	Ancient Japan
Farming	c.10,000 BCE	West Asian peoples	Mesopotamia
Irrigation	c.5000 BCE	West Asian peoples	Mesopotamia
Horse domestication	c.4500 BCE	Andronovo culture	Europe/Asia
Plough	c.4000 BCE	Sumerian people	Mesopotamia
Wheeled transport	c.3500 BCE	Sumerian people	Sumer
Silk weaving	c.3500 BCE	Chinese peoples	Ancient China
Writing	c.3300 BCE	Sumerian people	Sumer/Egypt
Calendar	c.3000 BCE	Babylonians	Babylonia
Papyrus scroll	c.2600 BCE	Imhotep (attributed)	Ancient Egypt
Plumbing	c.2500 BCE	Indus Valley civilization	Indus (Pakistan)
Law code	c.1755 BCE	King Hammurabi	Babylonia
Alphabet	14th century BCE	Semitic people (slaves of the Egyptians)	Ancient Egypt
Magnetism	c.1000 BCE	Thales of Miletus (attributed)	Ancient Greece
Coinage	c.600 BCE	Lydian people	Ancient Turkey
World map	6th century BCE	Babylonians	Babylonia
Planetary models	c.360 BCE	Eudoxus of Cnidus	Ancient Greece
Rotation of the Earth	c.350 BCE	Heraclides Ponticus	Ancient Greece
Steel production	c.200 BCE	Han dynasty	India/China
Compound pulley	c.200 BCE	Archimedes	Ancient Greece
Encyclopaedia	77	Pliny the Elder	Roman Empire
Paper	c.105	Cai Lun	Ancient China
Compass	250	Chinese peoples	Ancient China
Concept of zero/decimal system	c.590–650	Brahmagupta	India
Astrolabe	c.800	Muhammad al-Fazari	Arabia
University	859	Fatimah al-Fihri	Morocco
Star chart	c.1000–50	Abu Rayhan Biruni	Persia
Pendulum	c.1000	Ibn Yunus	Egypt
Magnifying glass	c.1021	Ibn al-Haytham	Persia
Moveable type	c.1045	Bi Sheng	China
Mechanical clock	1088	Su Song	China
Algebra	1202	Fibonacci	Italy
The scientific method	c.1220–35	Robert Grosseteste	England
Printing press	c.1445	Johannes Gutenburg	Germany
Terrestrial globe	c.1490	Martin Behaim	Bohemia
Sun-centred Universe	1503–43	Copernicus	Italy
Compound microscope	c.1595	Hans Lippershey, Zacharias Janssen	Netherlands
Laws of planetary motion	1609–19	Johannes Kepler	Germany
Newspaper	1609	Johann Carolus	Germany
Refracting telescope	1609	Galileo Galilei	Italy
Mechanical calculator	1642	Wilhelm Schickard	Germany
Barometer	1643	Evangelista Torricelli	Italy
Atmospheric pressure	1647–48	Blaise Pascal	France
Microscopic life	1673	Antoni van Leeuwenhoewk	Netherlands
Laws of motion	1687	Sir Isaac Newton	England
Seed drill	1701	Jethro Tull	England
Steam piston engine	1712	Thomas Newcomen	Britain
Marine chronometer	1735	John Harrison	Britain
Lightning rod	1752	Benjamin Franklin	US
Watt steam engine	1776	James Watt	Britain
Oxygen	1777	Antoine Lavoisier	France
Hot air balloon	1783	Montgolfier brothers	France
Threshing machine	1786	Andrew Meikle	Britain
Battery	1800	Alessandro Volta	Italy
Bicycle	1818	Karl Drais	Germany
Permanent photography	c.1820	Joseph Nicéphore Niépce	France
Braille alphabet	1821	Louis Braille	France
Electric motor	1821	Michael Faraday	Britain

INVENTION/DISCOVERY	DATE	ORIGINATOR	PLACE OF ORIGIN
Programmable computer	1822	Charles Babbage	Britain
Electromagnet	1823	William Sturgeon	Britain
Internal combustion engine	1826	Samuel Morey	US
Water turbine	1827	Claude Burdin, Benoît Fourneyron	France
Steam locomotive	1829	George Stephenson	Britain
Electrical generator	1831	Michael Faraday	Britain
Refrigerator	1834	Jacob Perkins	US/Britain
Vulcanization of rubber	1837	Charles Goodyear	US
Polystyrene	1839	Eduard Simon	Germany
Undersea telegraph cable	1858	Charles Wheatstone	Britain
Theory of evolution	1859	Charles Darwin	Britain
Pasteurization	1862	Louis Pasteur, Claude Bernard	France
Laws of heredity	1866	Gregor Mendel	Austria
Dynamite	1867	Alfred Nobel	Sweden
Periodic Table	1869	Dmitri Mendeleev	Russia
Telephone	1876	Alexander Graham Bell	Britain
Phonograph	1877	Thomas Edison	US
Incandescent light bulb	1878	Joseph Wilson Swan	Britain
Automobile	1885	Karl Benz	Germany
Petrol engine	1886	Gottlieb Daimler	Germany
Wireless communication	1893	Nikolai Tesla	Austria–Hungary
Radio telegraph	1895	Guglielmo Marconi	Italy
Cinematography	1895	Auguste & Louis Lumière	France
Radium	1898	Marie & Pierre Curie	Poland/France
Quantum theory	1900	Max Planck	Germany
Rigid dirigible airship	1900	Ferdinand Graf von Zeppelin	Germany
Aeroplane (controlled powered flight)	1903	Wright brothers	US
Conditioned reflexes	1904	Ivan Pavlov	Russia
Theory of relativity	1905	Albert Einstein	Switzerland
Bakelite plastic	1909	Leo Baekeland	Belgium
Stainless steel	1913	Harry Brearley	Britain
Structure of the atom	1913	Niels Bohr	Denmark
Television	1925	John Logie Baird	Britain
Law of the expanding universe	1929	Edwin Hubble	US
Nylon	1935	Wallace Carothers	US
RADAR	1935	Robert Watson-Watt	Britain
Jet engine	1937	Frank Whittle	Britain
Ball-point pen	1938	László Bíró	Hungary
Nuclear reactor	1942	Enrico Fermi	Italy /US
Aqualung	1943	Jacques Cousteau, Emile Gagnan	France
Atomic bomb	1945	J. Robert Oppenheimer	US
Photosynthesis	1946	Melvin Calvin	US
Commercial jet airliner	1948	Vickers	Britain
Radiocarbon dating	1949	Willard Libby	US
Big Bang theory	1949	George Gamow, Ralph Alpher, Robert Herman	US
Structure of DNA	1953	Francis Crick, Rosalind Franklin, James D. Watson	Britain/US
Communications satellite	1958	Kenneth Masterman-Smith	US
LASER	1960	Theodore H. Maiman	US
Plate tectonics	1967	Dan McKenzie	Britain
Microprocessor	1969	Intel	US
E-mail	1971	Ray Tomlinson	US
Genetic modification	1973	Stanley Norman Cohen, Herbert Boyer	US
Personal computer	1973	Xerox PARC	US
Mobile telephone	1973	Martin Cooper (Motorola)	US
Compact disc	1980	Philips Electronic/ Sony Corporation	Netherlands/ Japan
World Wide Web	1990	Tim Berners-Lee	Britain
Global Positioning System	1995	US Department of Defense	US
Genetic cloning	1996	Ian Wilmut, Keith Campbell	Britain
Portable media player	2001	Apple	US

PHILOSOPHY AND RELIGION

The earliest enquiries into the nature and meaning of life come from the founders of the great Eastern religions. Since their time, Western philosophers have journeyed to the outer limits of thought and understanding, posing questions that challenge our most fundamental beliefs.

Originating from almost every corner of the globe, the world's great faiths are as diverse as its cultures. Some have their origin in prehistoric times, yet the 20th century saw the emergence of several new religions that have attracted followers in their millions.

GREAT THINKERS

NAME	LIVED	ORIGIN	IDEAS/KEY WORK
Siddhartha Gautama (Buddha)	c.563–483 BCE	India	Founder of Buddhism as a path to achieving nirvana (spiritual enlightenment) and thus release from the earthly cycle of reincarnation.
Lao Tzu	Active 6th century BCE	China	Founder of Daoism, concerning an individual's approach to life. *Dao De Jing*.
Confucius	551–479 BCE	China	Founder of Confucianism: social harmony is promoted via social conventions and practices.
Pythagoras	c.550–c.500 BCE	Greece	Polymath interested in esoteric knowledge (that he made available to only a few initiates) and the mystical power of numbers.
Socrates	c.469–399 BCE	Greece	One of the founders of Western philosophy, to whom this quote is attributed: "A life unexamined is not worth living". No surviving writings.
Plato	c.427–347 BCE	Greece	A pupil of Socrates; argued that everything we perceive is a mere shadow of its abstract, ideal Form. *The Republic* (c.360 BCE).
Aristotle	384–322 BCE	Greece	Wide-ranging philosopher with a special interest in logical classification. *Metaphysics* (350 BCE).
Plotinus	205–270	Greece / Roman Empire	Founder of Neoplatonism, a development of Plato's original ideas. *Enneads* (c.253–70).
St Augustine of Hippo	354–430	North Africa/ Roman Empire	Transmitted Platonism through Christian theology. *The City of God* (413–26).

GREAT THINKERS (CONTINUED)

NAME	LIVED	ORIGIN	IDEAS/KEY WORK
St Thomas Aquinas	1225–74	Italy	Greatest Medieval religious philosopher. *Summa Theologiae* (1259–69).
Niccolò Machiavelli	1469–1527	Italy	Argued that the state should promote the common good, irrespective of any moral evaluation of its acts. *The Prince* (1513).
Francis Bacon	1561–1626	England	Recognized that scientific knowledge could procure power over nature. *Novum Organum* (1620).
Thomas Hobbes	1588–1679	England	Father of English political philosophy, the study of how societies are organized. *Leviathan* (1651).
René Descartes	1596–1650	France	Overturned Medieval and Renaissance scholasticism. *Meditations* (1641).
Baruch Spinoza	1632–77	Netherlands	One of the most important 17th-century Rationalists, arguing that knowledge of the world can be gained through reason. *Tractatus Theologico-Politicus* (1670).
John Locke	1632–1704	England	Proponent of empiricism, the view that all knowledge of anything that actually exists must be derived from experience. *Treatises of Government* (1690).
Gottfried Wilhelm Leibniz	1646–1716	Germany	Mathematican and rationalist philosopher. *Monadology* (1714).
George Berkeley	1685–1753	England	Great empiricist who developed an idealist metaphysical system, maintaining that reality ultimately consists of something non-material. *Principles of Human Knowledge* (1710).
David Hume	1711–76	Britain	Leading sceptic of metaphysics, the philosophy concerned with the ultimate nature of what exists. *Treatise of Human Nature* (1734–37).
Jean-Jacques Rousseau	1712–78	Switzerland	Proponent of the sovereignty of the citizen body. *The Social Contract, or Principles of Political Right* (1762).
Immanuel Kant	1724–1804	Germany	Sought to establish the authority of reason by critical examination. *Critique of Pure Reason* (1781).
Thomas Paine	1737–1809	Britain	Governments must respect the natural rights of their citizens. *The Rights of Man* (1791–92).
G. W. F. Hegel	1770–1831	Germany	Most influential of the German Idealists. *The Phenomenology of Spirit* (1807).
Karl Marx	1818–83	Germany	Radical social theorist and philosopher of Communism. *Das Kapital* (1867).
Arthur Schopenhauer	1788–1860	Germany	Espoused transcendental idealism, the belief that human experience of things consists of how they appear to us. *The World as Will and Representation* (1818).
Søren Kierkegaard	1813–55	Denmark	A forerunner of Existentialism, stressing the individual's unique position as a self-determining agent. *Concluding Unscientific Postscript to Philosophical Fragments* (1846).
Friedrich Nietzsche	1844–1900	Germany	Rejected religious and metaphysical interpretations of the human condition in favour of the principle of the "Superman". *Thus Spake Zarathustra* (1883–85).
Bertrand Russell	1872–1970	Britain	Founder of analytic philosophy, emphasizing clarity and argument. *Principia Mathematica* (1910–13).
Ludwig Wittgenstein	1889–1951	Austria	Most prominent analytical philosopher. *Tractatus Logico-Philosophicus* (1921).
Jean-Paul Sartre	1905–80	France	Leader of the Existentialist movement, which focused on the totality of human freedom. *Being and Nothingness* (1943).

MAJOR WORLD FAITHS

NAME	PLACE/DATE	ADHERENTS	FOUNDER	TEXT
Chinese traditional religion	Unknown, prehistoric	400 million	Indigenous	n/a
Hinduism	India, prehistoric	900 million	Indigenous	The Vedas, Upanishads, and Sanskrit epics
Shinto	Japan, prehistoric	3–4 million	Indigenous	*Kojiki, Nihon-gi*
Voodoo	West Africa, unknown	8 million	Indigenous	n/a
Judaism	Israel, *c.*1300 BCE	15 million	Abraham; Moses	Hebrew Bible; Talmud
Zoroastrianism	Iran, 6th century BCE	200,000	Zoroaster	The Avesta
Daoism	China, *c.*550 BCE	20 million	Lao Tzu	*Dao De Jing*
Jainism	India, *c.*550 BCE	4 million	Mahavira	Mahavira's teachings
Buddhism	Northeast India, *c.*520 BCE	375 million	Siddhartha Gautama (Buddha)	Pali canon, Mahayana sutras
Confucianism	China, 6th/5th centuries BCE	5–6 million	Confucius	The Four Books and Five Classics
Christianity	Israel, *c.*30	2,000 million	Jesus Christ	The Bible (Old and New Testaments)
Islam	Saudi Arabia, revealed in 7th century	1,500 million	n/a; Muhammad is Prophet	The Qu'ran (scripture); Hadith (tradition)
Sikhism	Punjab, India, *c.*1500	23 million	Guru Nanak	Adi Granth (Guru Granth Sahib)
Church of Jesus Christ of Latter-Day Saints (Mormons)	New York, 1830	13 million	Joseph Smith	The Bible; *Book of Mormon*
Tenrikyo	Japan, 1838	1 million	Nakayama Miki	*Mikigaurata, Ofudesaki, Osashizu*
Baha'i Faith	Tehran, Iran, 1863	5–7 million	Baha'u'llah	Writings of Baha'u'llah
Church of Christ (Scientist)	New York, USA, 1879	Up to 400,000	Mary Baker Eddy	The Bible; *Science and Health with Key to the Scriptures*
Cao Dai	Vietnam, 1926	8 million	Ngo Van Chieu	Cao Dai Canon
Rastafari	Jamaica, 1930s	1 million	Haile Selassie I	*Holy Piby*
Family Federation for World Peace and Unification	South Korea, 1954	3 million (official figure)	Sun Myung Moon	*Sun Myung Moon, the Divine Principle*
Wicca	1950s, but based on ancient beliefs	1–3 million	Gerald Gardner	n/a
Falun Gong	China, 1992	10 million	Li Hongzhi	Writings of master Li, including *Zhuan Falun*

CULTURE AND LEARNING

From the poets, sculptors, and painters of the ancient world to the commentators and conceptual artists of the 21st century, the work of writers and artists provides an invaluable insight into the thoughts and aspirations of these the great civilizations of the past. In Europe, from the 11th century, and in the succeeding centuries on other continents, the talents of many of these people were nurtured in the universities that sprang up as conduits for the transmission of learning.

POETS, PLAYRIGHTS, AND NOVELISTS

Literature gives us a special insight into the past. Though the plots of novels and plays may be invented, the characters speak and behave in ways that reflect the preoccupations, social mores, and artistic conventions of their time, and in many works, a fictional chain of events plays out against a rich background of verifiable historical happenings.

NAME	LIVED	ORIGIN	GENRE	NOTABLE WORKS
Homer	8th century BCE	Ancient Greece	Poet	*Odyssey* (8th century BCE)
Aeschylus	*c.*525–456 BCE	Ancient Greece	Playwright	*Seven Against Thebes* (*c.*467 BCE)
Sophocles	*c.*496–406 BCE	Ancient Greece	Playwright	*Antigone* (*c.*442 BCE)
Euripides	*c.*484–406 BCE	Ancient Greece	Playwright	*Medea* (*c.*431 BCE)
Aristophanes	*c.*448–388 BCE	Ancient Greece	Playwright	*The Frogs* (*c.*405 BCE)
Valmiki	*c.*400–200 BCE	Ancient India	Poet	*Ramayana* (*c.*400–200 BCE)
Virgil	70–19 BCE	Roman Empire	Poet	*Aeneid* (*c.*29–19 BCE)
Ovid	43 BCE–*c.*17 CE	Roman Empire	Poet	*Metamorphoses* (8 CE)
Murasaki Shikibu	*c.*978–1014	Japan	Novelist	*The Tale of Genji* (*c.*1001–10)
Dante Alighieri	1265–1321	Italy	Poet	*Divine Comedy* (*c.*1321)
Petrarch	1304–74	Italy	Poet	*Canzoniere* (1327–68)
Geoffrey Chaucer	1343–1400	England	Poet	*The Canterbury Tales* (1387–1400)
Miguel de Cervantes	1547–1616	Spain	Novelist/ poet/ playwright	*Don Quixote* (1605)
William Shakespeare	1564–1616	England	Playwright/ poet	*Romeo and Juliet* (*c.*1591–95)
John Milton	1608–74	England	Poet	*Paradise Lost* (1667)
Molière	1622–73	France	Playwright	*Le Misanthrope* (1666)
Jean Racine	1639–99	France	Playwright	*Phèdre* (1677)
Jonathan Swift	1667–1745	Ireland	Novelist/ essayist	*Gulliver's Travels* (1726)
Xueqin Cao	*c.*1715–63	China	Novelist	*Dream of the Red Chamber* (1791)
Johann Wolfgang von Goethe	1749–1832	Germany	Novelist/ playwright	*Faust* (1808)
William Wordsworth	1770–1850	Britain	Poet	*The Prelude* (1799)
Jane Austen	1775–1817	Britain	Novelist	*Pride and Prejudice* (1813)
John Keats	1795–1821	Britain	Poet	*Endymion* (1818)
Alexander Pushkin	1799–1837	Russia	Poet/ novelist	*Eugene Onegin* (1828)
Honoré de Balzac	1799–1850	France	Novelist	*La Comédie Humaine* (1827–47)
Alexandre Dumas	1802–70	France	Novelist	*The Three Musketeers* (1844)
Victor Hugo	1802–85	France	Novelist	*Les Misérables* (1862)
Ralph Waldo Emerson	1803–82	US	Essayist/ poet	*The Conduct of Life* (1860)
Hans Christian Andersen	1805–75	Denmark	Novelist	*Fairy Tales* (1835–37)
Henry Longfellow	1807–82	US	Poet	*Hiawatha* (1855)
Charles Dickens	1812–70	Britain	Novelist	*Great Expectations* (1860–61)
Ivan Turgenev	1818–83	Russia	Novelist/ playwright	*Fathers and Sons* (1862)
George Eliot	1819–80	Britain	Novelist	*The Mill on the Floss* (1860)
Fyodor Dostoyevsky	1821–81	Russia	Novelist	*Crime and Punishment* (1866)
Walt Whitman	1819–92	US	Poet	*Leaves of Grass* (1855–89)
Gustave Flaubert	1821–80	France	Novelist	*Madame Bovary* (1857)
Henrik Ibsen	1828–1906	Norway	Playwright	*Peer Gynt* (1867)
Leo Tolstoy	1828–1910	Russia	Novelist	*War and Peace* (1865–69)
Mark Twain	1835–1910	US	Novelist	*Huckleberry Finn* (1885)
Thomas Hardy	1840–1928	Britain	Novelist	*Tess of the d'Urbervilles* (1891)
Henry James	1843–1916	US	Novelist	*The Bostonians* (1886)
August Strindberg	1849–1912	Sweden	Playwright	*The Dance of Death* (1901)
George Bernard Shaw	1856–1950	Ireland	Playwright	*Man and Superman* (1903)
Joseph Conrad	1857–1924	Poland	Novelist	*Heart of Darkness* (1902)
Anton Chekhov	1860–1904	Russia	Playwright	*The Cherry Orchard* (1904)
Rabindranath Tagore	1861–1941	India	Poet/ playwright	*Gitanjali, Song Offerings* (1912)
Edith Wharton	1862–1937	US	Novelist	*The Age of Innocence* (1920)
William Butler Yeats	1865–1939	Ireland	Poet	*The Wild Swans at Coole* (1917)
Marcel Proust	1871–1922	France	Novelist	*Remembrance of Things Past* (1912–27)
Robert Frost	1874–1963	US	Poet	*Mountain Interval* (1916)
Thomas Mann	1875–1955	Gemany	Novelist	*Death in Venice* (1913)
Hermann Hesse	1877–1962	Germany	Novelist	*The Glass Bead Game* (1945)
James Joyce	1882–1941	Ireland	Novelist	*Ulysses* (1922)
Virginia Woolf	1882–1941	Britain	Novelist	*Mrs Dalloway* (1925)
Franz Kafka	1883–1924	Czech Republic	Novelist	*The Metamorphosis* (1916)
D.H. Lawrence	1885–1930	Britain	Novelist/ poet	*Sons and Lovers* (1913)
Ezra Pound	1885–1972	US	Poet	*The Cantos* (1915–62)
T.S. Eliot	1888–1965	US/Britain	Poet/ playwright	*The Waste Land* (1922)
Karel Capek	1890–1938	Czech Republic	Playwright	*R.U.R.* (1920)
Boris Pasternak	1890–1960	Russia	Novelist	*Doctor Zhivago* (1957)
Mikhail Bulgakov	1891–1940	Russia	Novelist	*The Master and Margarita* (1928)
William Faulkner	1897–1962	US	Novelist	*The Sound and the Fury* (1929)
Bertolt Brecht	1898–1956	Germany	Playwright	*Mother Courage* (1938)
Federico García Lorca	1898–1936	Spain	Playwright	*The House of Bernarda Alba* (1936)
Ernest Hemingway	1899–1961	US	Novelist	*The Old Man and the Sea* (1952)
Jorge Luis Borges	1899–1986	Argentina	Novelist	*Labyrinths* (1953)
Vladimir Nabokov	1899–1977	Russia/US	Novelist	*Lolita* (1958)
John Steinbeck	1902–68	US	Novelist	*The Grapes of Wrath* (1939)
George Orwell	1903–50	Britain	Novelist	*Nineteen Eighty-Four* (1949)
Samuel Beckett	1906–89	Ireland	Playwright/ novelist	*Waiting for Godot* (1954)

»

POETS, PLAYRIGHTS, AND NOVELISTS (CONTINUED)

NAME	LIVED	ORIGIN	GENRE	NOTABLE WORKS
W.H. Auden	1907–73	Britain	Poet	*The Sea and the Mirror* (1944)
Naguib Mahfouz	1911–2006	Egypt	Novelist	*The Cairo Trilogy* (1956–57)
Albert Camus	1913–60	France	Novelist	*The Plague* (1947)
Saul Bellow	1915–2005	Canada	Novelist	*Humboldt's Gift* (1975)
Arthur Miller	1915–2005	US	Playwright	*Death of a Salesman* (1946)
Alexander Solzhenitsyn	1918–2008	Russia	Novelist	*One Day in the Life of Ivan Denisovich* (1962)
Iris Murdoch	1919–99	Britain	Novelist	*The Sea, The Sea* (1978)
Yukio Mishima	1925–70	Japan	Novelist	*The Sea of Fertility* (1965–70)
Dario Fo	1926–	Italy	Playwright	*Accidental Death of an Anarchist* (1970)
Gabriel Garcia Marquez	1928–	Colombia	Novelist	*One Hundred Years of Solitude* (1967)
Milan Kundera	1929–	Czech Republic	Novelist	*The Unbearable Lightness of Being* (1984)
Harold Pinter	1930–2008	Britain	Playwright	*The Birthday Party* (1958)
Toni Morrison	1931–	US	Novelist	*Beloved* (1987)
V.S. Naipaul	1932-	Trinidad	Novelist	*A House for Mr. Biswas* (1971)
Philip Roth	1933–	US	Novelist	*Portnoy's Complaint* (1972)
Wole Soyinka	1934–	Nigeria	Playwright/poet	*A Dance of the Forests* (1960)
Seamus Heaney	1939–	Ireland	Poet	*Door into the Dark* (1969)
Margaret Atwood	1939–	Canada	Novelist/poet	*The Handmaid's Tale* (1985)
Peter Carey	1943–	Australia	Novelist	*Oscar and Lucinda* (1988)

PAINTERS AND SCULPTORS

All of the great civilizations, from Egypt to Greece and Rome, from ancient China to India and Medieval Europe, have produced works of art of great power. It is only later, around the 9th century CE, that we begin to know the names of some of these artists. In almost all societies, religious scenes were an important part of the output, as well as portraits that flattered the rulers and the aristocracy. Landscapes and rural scenes have also delighted artistic patrons through the ages. In the modern era, artists, free from patronage, have pursued their own often shocking agendas.

NAME	LIVED	ORIGIN	NOTABLE WORKS
Exekias	c.550–525 BCE	Greece	*Achilles and Ajax Playing in a Game*
Phidias	c.480–420 BCE	Greece	*Frieze of the Parthenon*
Praxiteles	Active c.350 BCE	Greece	*Cnidian Aphrodite*
Gu Kaizhi	c.345–406	China	*Admonitions of the Instructress to the Court Ladies*
Yan Liben	c.600–73	China	*Imperial Sedan Chair*
Wu Daozi	c.710–c.760	China	*Flying Demon*
Han Gan	c.720–c.780	China	*Shining Night of Light*
Lu Hong	Active early 8th century	China	*Ten Views from a Thatched Lodge*
Zhang Xuan	Active 714–42	China	*Ladies Preparing Newly Woven Silk*
Guanxiu	832–912	China	*The Arhat Pindola*
Huang Quan	903–65	China	*Sketches of Birds and Insects*
Li Cheng	919–67	China	*A Solitary Temple amid Clearing Peaks*
Huang Jucai	933–c.993	China	*Pheasant and Small Birds by a Jujube Shrub*
Dong Yuan	d.962	China	*Summer Mountains*
Juran	Active c.960–85	China	*Distant Mountain Forests*
Zhang Zeduan	Mid-11th century	China	*Peace Reigns over the River*
Guo Xi	c.1020–90	China	*Early Spring*
Li Gonglin	1049–1106	China	*Pasturing Horses*
Wang Shen	Late 12th century	China	*Serried Hills over a Misty River*
Li Di	c.1100–c.97	China	*Shrike on a Winter Tree*
Ma Yuan	c.1190–1224	China	*Bare Willows and Distant Mountains*
Lian Kai	13th century	China	*The Sixth Ch'an Patriarch Chopping Bamboo*
Qian Zuan	c.1235–1307	China	*Dwelling in the Floating Jade Mountains*
Cimabue	c.1250–1302	Italy	*Madonna Enthroned*
Zhao Mengfu	1254–1322	China	*Autumn Colours on the Qiao and Hua Mountains*
Nicola Pisano	c.1258–84	Italy	*Pulpit of the Baptistry of Pisa Cathedral*
Giotto di Bondone	c.1267–1337	Italy	*Life of St Francis*
Huang Gongwang	1269–1354	China	*Dwelling in the Fuchun Mountains*
Wu Zhen	1280–1354	China	*Stalks of Bamboo by a Rock*
Ni Zan	1301–74	China	*Six Gentlemen*
Wang Meng	1308–74	China	*Dwelling in the Qinghai Mountains*
Muto Shi	14th century	Japan	*Portrait of Muso Soseki*
Taiku Josetzu	Active 1405–23	Japan	*Hyonen-zu*
Donato de Niccolo (Donatello)	1386–1466	Italy	*David*
Fra Angelico	1387–1455	Italy	*Annunciation*
Jan van Eyck	c.1395–1441	Belgium	*Wedding Portrait*
Paolo Uccello	1397–1475	Italy	*The Battle of San Romano*
Rogier van der Weyden	c.1400–64	Flemish	*Deposition*
Fra Filippo Lippi	c.1406–69	Italy	*Tarquinia Madonna*
Piero della Francesca	c.1415–92	Italy	*Nativity*
Sesshu Toyo	1420–1506	Japan	*Autumn Landscape*
Shen Zhou	1427–1509	China	*Lofty Mount*
Giovanni Bellini	c.1430–1516	Italy	*Agony in the Garden*
Hans Memling	c.1430–1494	Netherlands	*Mystic Marriage of St Catherine*
Andrea Mantegna	c.1431–1506	Italy	*The Triumph of Caesar*
Sandro Botticelli	1445–1510	Italy	*Mystic Nativity*
Hieronymus Bosch	c.1450–1516	Netherlands	*Christ Crowned with Thorns*
Leonardo da Vinci	1452–1519	Italy	*Mona Lisa*
Lu Ji	Active c.1500	China	*Egret, Eagle, and Falling Lotus Flowers*
Mathias Grünewald	c.1460–1528	Germany	*Isenheim Altarpiece*
Wen Zhengming	1470–1559	China	*The Peach Blossom Spring*
Albrecht Dürer	1471–1528	Germany	*The Four Apostles*
Michelangelo Buonarotti	1475–1564	Italy	*David*
Lucas Cranach (the Elder)	1472–1553	Germany	*Rest on the Flight into Egypt*
Jan Gossaert	c.1478–1533	Belgium	*Adoration of the Magi*
Kano Montonobu	1476–1559	Japan	*Landscape with Waterfall and Crane*
Raffaello Sanzio da Urbino (Raphael)	1483–1520	Italy	*Sistine Madonna*
Tiziano Vecelli (Titian)	c.1487–1576	Italy	*The Tribute Money*
Hans Holbein (the Younger)	c.1497–1543	Germany	*The Ambassadors*

NAME	LIVED	ORIGIN	NOTABLE WORKS
Jacobo Robusti Tintoretto	c.1487–1576	Italy	*Last Supper*
Sukei Sesson	c.1504–1589	Japan	*Landscape and Boat in Stormy Weather*
Pieter Bruegel (the Elder)	c.1525–69	Flemish	*The Peasant Dance*
Kaiho Yushio	1533–1615	Japan	*Peonies*
Pieter Paul Rubens	1577–1640	Belgium	*Adoration of the Magi*
Hasegawa Tohaku	1539–1610	Japan	*Pine Trees*
El Greco	1541–1614	Spain	*The Burial of Count Orgaz*
Kano Eitoku	1543–1590	Japan	*Crane and Pine Tree*
Dong Qichang	1555–1636	China	*Autumn Mountains*
Hon-Ami Koetsu	1558–1637	Japan	*Flowers of the Four Seasons*
Kano Sanraku	1559–1635	Japan	*Plum Tree and Pheasant*
Michelangelo Merisi da Caravaggio	1573–1610	Italy	*Deposition*
Tawaraya Sotatsu	1576–1643	Japan	*Deer and Calligraphy*
Frans Hals	1580–1666	Netherlands	*Laughing Cavalier*
José Ribera	1591–1652	Spain	*The Martyrdom of St Bartholomew*
Nicolas Poussin	1593–1665	France	*Worship of the Golden Calf*
Gianlorenzo Bernini	1598–1680	Italy	*The Ecstasy of St Teresa*
Diego Velasquez	1599–1660	Spain	*The Water Carrier*
Anthony van Dyck	1599–1641	Belgium	*Charles I of England*
Claude Lorrain	1600–82	France	*Embarkation of St Ursula*
Harmensz Rembrandt van Rijn	1606–69	Netherlands	*The Night Watch*
Hongren	1610–64	China	*Monumental Landscape*
Bartolomé Esteban Murillo	1617–82	Spain	*Virgin and Child*
Jan Vermeer	1632–75	Netherlands	*Woman with a Water Jug*
Wang Hui	1632–1717	China	*The Kangxi Emperor's Southern Inspection Tour*
Tao-Chi	1641–c.1717	China	*Landscape*
Ogata Korin	1658–1716	Japan	*White Plum Blossoms in the Spring*
Antoine Watteau	1684–1721	France	*The Pilgrimage to Cythera*
Giovanni Battista Tiepolo	1696–1770	Italy	*The Finding of Moses*
William Hogarth	1697–1764	England	*Rake's Progress*
Giovanni Antonio Canal (Canaletto)	1697–1768	Italy	*A Regatta on the Grand Canal*
Joshua Reynolds	1723–92	Great Britain	*The Three Graces*
Ikeno Taiga and Yosa Buson	1723–76, 1716–83	Japan	*The Ten Conveniences and the Ten Pleasures*
Thomas Gainsborough	1727–88	Britain	*The Blue Boy*
Maruyama Okyo	1733–95	Japan	*Nature Studies*
Francisco de Goya	1746–1828	Spain	*The Naked Maja*
Jacques-Louis David	1748–1825	France	*The Rape of the Sabines*
Utamaro Kitagawa	1753–1806	Japan	*Book of Insects*
William Blake	1757–1827	Britain	*Divine Comedy*
Katsuhika Hokusai	1760–1849	Japan	*The Great Wave*
Caspar David Friedrich	1774–1840	Germany	*The Cross in the Mountains*

NAME	LIVED	ORIGIN	NOTABLE WORKS
Joseph Mallord William Turner	1775–1851	Britain	*Juliet and her Nurse*
John Constable	1776–1837	Britain	*The Haywain*
Jean-August-Dominique Ingres	1780–1867	France	*Odalisque*
John James Audubon	1785–1851	US	*Birds of America*
Theodore Gericault	1791–1824	France	*The Raft of the Medusa*
Ichiyu-sai (Ando) Hiroshige	1797–1858	Japan	*Landscape at Shono*
Eugène Delacroix	1798–1863	France	*Liberty Leading the People*
Edwin Landseer	1802–73	Britain	*Monarch of the Glen*
Gustave Courbet	1819–77	France	*Burial at Ornans*
Edouard Manet	1823–83	France	*Déjeuner sur l'Herbe*
William Holman Hunt	1827–1910	Britain	*Light of the World*
Dante Gabriel Rosetti	1828–82	Great Britain	*Beata Beatrix*
John Everett Millais	1829–96	Britain	*Order of Release*
Camille Pissarro	1830–1903	France	*The Harvest*
James Abbott McNeill Whistler	1834–1903	US	*The Artist's Mother*
Hilaire-Germain-Edgar Degas	1834–1917	France	*La Danseuse au Bouquet*
Alfred Sisley	1839–99	Britain	*Flood at Port Marly*
Paul Cézanne	1839–1906	France	*Bathers*
Auguste Rodin	1840–1917	France	*The Kiss*
Claude Monet	1840–1926	France	*Waterlilies*
Pierre-Auguste Renoir	1841–1919	France	*Luncheon of the Boating Party*
Paul Gauguin	1848–1903	France	*Ta Matete*
Vincent van Gogh	1853–90	Netherlands	*Road with Cypresses*
John Singer Sargent	1856–1925	US	*Carnation, Lily, Lily, Rose*
Georges Seurat	1859–91	France	*Sunday Afternoon on the Grande Jatte*
Walter Richard Sickert	1860–1942	Britain	*Ennui*
Gustav Klimt	1862–1928	Austria	*Mosaic mural for the Palais Stoclet in Brussels*
Edvard Munch	1863–1944	Norway	*The Scream*
Henri de Toulouse-Lautrec	1864–1901	France	*At the Moulin Rouge*
Akseli Gallen-Kallela	1865–1931	Finland	*Lake Keitele*
Wassily Kandinsky	1866–1944	Russia	*Improvisations with Colour*
Henri Matisse	1869–1954	France	*Odalisque*
Piet Mondrian	1872–1944	Netherlands	*Composition*
Paul Klee	1879–1940	Switzerland	*Twittering Machine*
Jacob Epstein	1880–1959	Britain	*Memorial for Oscar Wilde*
Ernst Ludwig Kirchner	1880–1938	Germany	*Street Scene*
Pablo Picasso	1881–1973	Spain	*Guernica*
Georges Braque	1882–1963	France	*Vase of Anemones*
Edward Hopper	1882–1967	US	*Nighthawks*
Max Beckmann	1884–1905	Germany	*The Night*
Amedeo Modigliani	1884–1920	Italy	*Portrait of Madame Zborowski*

PAINTERS AND SCULPTORS (CONTINUED)

NAME	LIVED	ORIGIN	NOTABLE WORKS
Diego Rivera	1886–1957	Mexico	*Creation*
Oskar Kokoschka	1886–1980	Austria	*View of the Thames*
Georgia O'Keeffe	1887–1986	USA	*Cityscapes of New York*
Marcel Duchamp	1887–1968	France	*Fountain*
Marc Chagall	1887–1985	France	*Calvary*
Giorgio de Chirico	1888–1978	Italy	*Nostalgia of the Infinite*
Paul Nash	1889–1946	Britain	*Dead Sea*
Egon Schiele	1890–1918	Austria	*The Artist's Mother Sleeping*
Giorgio Morandi	1890–1964	Italy	*Still Life*
Man Ray	1890–1978	US	*The Rope Dancer Accompanies Herself with her Shadows*
Max Ernst	1891–1976	Germany	*The Elephant Celebes*
George Grosz	1893–1959	Germany	*Suicide*
Joan Miró	1893–1983	Spain	*Harlequin's Carnival*
Henry Moore	1898–1986	Britain	*Recumbent Figure*
René Magritte	1898–1967	Belgium	*This is not a Pipe*
Alberto Giacometti	1901–66	Switzerland	*Tall Figures*
Mark Rothko	1903–70	US	*Green on Blue*
Salvador Dali	1904–89	Spain	*The Persistence of Memory*
Willem de Kooning	1904–97	US	*Woman Series*
Frida Kahlo	1907–54	Mexico	*The Frame*
Francis Bacon	1909–92	Britain	*Three Studies at the Base of a Crucifixion*
Jackson Pollock	1912–56	USA	*Autumn Rhythm*
Sidney Nolan	1917–92	Australia	*Themes from the Career of Ned Kelly*
Roy Lichtenstein	1923–97	US	*Whaam!*
Andy Warhol	1930–87	US	*Campbell's Soupcans*
David Hockney	b.1937	Britain	*Mr and Mrs Clark and Percy*
Antony Gormley	b.1950	Britain	*Angel of the North*
Ai Weiwei	b.1957	China	*Sunflower Seeds*
Liu Xiadong	b.1963	China	*Three Gorges: Newly Displaced Population*

THE WORLD'S OLDEST UNIVERSITIES

UNIVERSITY	COUNTRY	DATE OF FOUNDATION
Bologna	Italy	1088
Oxford	England	*c.*1167
Modena	Italy	1175
Vicenza	Italy	1204
Cambridge	England	1209
Salamanca	Spain	1218
Padua	Italy	1222
Naples	Italy	1224
Siena	Italy	1246
Lisbon	Portugal	1290
Madrid	Spain	1293
Lérida	Spain	1297
La Sapienza	Rome, Italy	1303
Coimbra	Portugal	1308
Perugia	Italy	1308
Pisa	Italy	1343
Charles	Prague, Czech Republic	1347
Perpignan	France	1350
Pavia	Italy	1361
Jagiellonian	Poland	1364
Vienna	Austria	1365
Heidelberg	Germany	1385
Universidad Michoacana de San Nicolás de Hidalgo	Mexico	1540
Harvard	Massachusetts, US	1636
Fourah Bay College	Sierra Leone	1827
Calcutta	India	1857
Sydney	Australia	1850

DISASTERS

Few civilizations have been immune to the effects of natural disasters, which have sometimes killed hundreds of thousands, or even, in the case of plagues, many millions of people. Disasters such as the eruption of Pompeii, the Antioch earthquake of 526 CE and the Black Death caused huge loss of life, but modern societies are no less vulnerable, as evidence by the loss of life in the 2004 Indian Ocean and 2011 Japanese tsunamis.

EARTHQUAKES

PLACE	DATE	MAGNITUDE	DEATHS	DESCRIPTION
Sparta, Greece	464 BCE	7.2	*c.*20,000	Led to revolt of helots and contributed to the outbreak of the Peloponnesian War
Rhodes, Greece	226 BCE	Unknown	Unknown	Destroyed the Colossus of Rhodes
Crete and Eastern Mediterranean	365	9.0	Unknown	Widespread destruction in Crete and North Africa
Antioch (Turkey)	526	8.0	250,000	Partial destruction of the city
Lebanese coast	551	7.5	30–50,000	Widespread destruction in Beirut, Tyre, Tripoli, and other coastal cities
Aleppo, Syria	1138	9.0	200–250,000	Partial destruction of city
Eastern Mediterranean	1201	7.6	Unknown	Caused famines in which more than a million people died
Shaanxi, China	1556	8.3	830,000	Most destructive earthquake in China's history
Peru	1687	8.7	5,000	Severely damaged Lima, destroyed port of Pisco
Lisbon, Portugal	1755	8.7 and tsunami	80,000	Destroyed most of city
Ecuador and Peru	1797	7.3	40,000	Widespread destruction in Quito and Cuzco
Arica, Chile	1868	8.5	25,000	Destroyed a number of towns, including Arica and Arequipa
San Francisco	1906	7.9	3,000	Widespread destruction in San Francisco, partly caused by fire
Valparaiso, Chile	1906	8.2	4,000	Destruction of most of Valparaiso
Ningxia, China	1920	7.8	250,000	Total destruction in Haiyuan County
Kanto, Japan	1923	7.9	125,000	Most deadly earthquake in Japanese history
Ancash, Peru	1970	7.9	75,000	Worst natural disaster in Peruvian history
Tangshan, China	1976	7.5	240,000–255,000	Largest 20th-century earthquake by death toll
Armenia	1988	6.9	25,000	Destruction of city of Spitak (many deaths caused by substandard building design)
Western Turkey	1999	7.6	18,000	Partial destruction of city of Izmit; many substandard buildings collapsed
Bam, Iran	2003	6.6	27,000	Ancient mud-brick city of Bam destroyed
Indian Ocean	2004	9.2 and tsunami	230,000	Widespread devastation along Indian Ocean coastlines
Kashmir, Pakistan	2005	7.6	75,000	Widespread damage around Muzaffarabad
Sichuan, China	2008	8.0	70,000	Deadliest Chinese earthquake since Tangshan (1976)
Haiti	2010	7.0	316,000	Widespread damage in Port-au-Prince; worst death toll in western hemisphere
Northeast Japan	2011	9.0 and tsunami	*c.*18,000	Widespread damage around Sendai; caused emergency at Fukushima Nuclear Power Plant

VOLCANIC ERUPTIONS

VOLCANO NAME	DATE	DESCRIPTION
Vesuvius (southern Italy)	79	Destroyed cities of Pompeii and Herculaneum
Oraefajökull (Iceland)	1362	"Glacier burst" devastated coastal communities and covered northern Iceland in ash
Mount Etna (Sicily)	1669	Worst eruption in modern times, destroying a dozen villages
Lanzarote (Canary Islands)	1730–36	Longest recorded eruption in the Canary Islands, burying communities in the west
Laki (Iceland)	1783	Produced largest flow of lava ever recorded
Tambora, Sumbawa, (Indonesia)	1815	Effects of volcanic ash aerosol caused the "year without a summer" and crop failures and famines in many countries
Krakatoa (Indonesia)	1883	Caused much of island of Krakatoa to sink, killing 35,000 people, The volcanic aerosol produced beautiful sunsets worldwide for several months
Montagne Pelée (Martinique)	1902	Destroyed the town of Saint-Pierre.
Mount St Helens (Washington State, USA)	1980	Destroyed 300km (185 miles) of roads.
Nevada del Ruiz (Colombia)	1985	Mud flow destroyed town of Magdalena, killing 23,000 people.
Pinatubo (Philippines)	1991	Expelled 10 times as much material as Mount St Helens, but mass evacuations meant only 200–300 people died.
Eyjafjallajökull (Iceland)	2010	Volcanic ash cloud grounded aviation in much of Europe

FLOODS

PLACE	DATE	DESCRIPTION
England	48	Flooding of River Thames caused 10,000 deaths
England, and Netherlands coastline	1099	Severe winter storm caused floods that killed 100,000 and created the Goodwin Sands, Kent
Netherlands and Germany	1218	North Sea storm surge killed 100,000
Belgium, Netherlands, Denmark	1287	Severe storms caused floods, killing 50–80,000
Denmark, Netherlands, northern Germany	1362	Widespread coastal floods killed 100,000
Western England	1606	Tsunami in the Bristol Channel killed 3,000
China	1887	Floods along the Yellow River broke dikes, drowning 900,000
Central China	1931	Flooding of Yellow, Yangtze, and Huai rivers killed up to 3,000,000
Guatemala	1949	Hurricane caused floods, killing 40,000
Bangladesh	1974	Heavy monsoon rains caused floods, killing 29,000
China	1975	Failure of the Banqiao Dam, Henan Province, led to floods and deaths of 86,000; worst dam failure in history
Pakistan	2010	Floods submerged one-fifth of the country, killing 2,000
Australia	2010–11	River surges killed 35 and devastated several towns in Queensland

FAMINES

PLACE	DATE	DESCRIPTION
Central America	*c.*800–900	Drought and famine caused collapse of Classic Maya civilization
China	875–884	Famine sparked the Huang Zhao rebellion, which fatally undermined the Tang dynasty
Japan	1229–32	The Kangi famine, worst in Japanese history
Northern Europe	1315–17	"The Great Famine" killed up to 10 per cent of the population (partly through effects of disease on a weakened population)
India	1406–17	The Durga Devi famine in Maharashtra killed many thousands over a 12-year period
Russia	1601–03	Worst famine in Russian history, killed up to 2 million – one-third of the population
India	1630–32	Severe famine in the Deccan led to around 2 million deaths
Prussia	1708–11	Famine killed 250,000 (around two-fifths of the population)
Bengal, India	1769–73	Worst famine in Indian history killed 10 million
Ireland	1845–49	Potato blight caused severe famine and death of 1 million
Iran	1870–71	"The Great Persian Famine" killed 1.5 million and led to many nomadic tribes becoming sedentary
Ethiopia	1888–92	"The Great Ethiopian Famine"; pest killed 90 per cent of cattle; locust and caterpillar plagues ate most crops; one-third of population perished
Ukraine	1932–33	The "Holodomor"; Soviet collectivization and industrialization policies caused famine that killed 4 million
China	1959–61	"The Great China Famine", the worst in Chinese history, killed 30 million
Ethiopia	1984–85	Failure of rains caused famine, killing up to 1 million

EPIDEMICS AND PLAGUES

PLACE	DATE	DESCRIPTION
Greece	430–427 BCE	Early description of plague symptoms during epidemic at Athens
Mediterranean world	165–180	The Antonine Plague killed up to 5 million, one-third of the population of the Roman Empire, severely weakening the military might of the Roman army
Mediterranean world	541–542	Plague of Justinian killed 40 per cent or more of population
Worldwide	1348–50	The Black Death killed around 30 million people
India	1630–32	Severe famine in the Deccan led to around 2 million deaths
India	1817	First recorded outbreak of cholera in Bengal
India	1907	Outbreak of bubonic plague killed 1.5 million
Worldwide	1918–19	Spanish influenza killed 50 million, the worst recorded natural disaster

GLOSSARY

Terms defined elsewhere in the glossary are in *italics*.

abolitionism
Advocacy of the abolition of slavery.

absolutism
A theory of the state where a country's ruler or government is regarded as possessing an **absolute authority**: that is, an authority that is not dependent on the consent of the people being governed.

accession
The point at which a monarch begins their reign.

agrarian
Relating to land and its cultivation. The term **agrarianism** relates to political movements aimed at promoting the interests of agriculture and rural life.

allies/Allied
People or countries working together. In World War I and World War II, the Allies or Allied forces were the countries fighting against Germany.

anarchy
In its original meaning, absence of government; also used for a condition of public disorder. Politically, **anarchism** is a movement or ideology that believes in the abolition of government as an ideal for society.

anticlericalism
Opposition to the influence of churches and other religious organizations in society. In some (mainly *Catholic*) countries such as France, Spain, and Italy it has been an important political force.

antisemitism
Antagonism and hostility towards Jewish people.

apartheid
The policy of racial *segregation* formerly followed in the Republic of South Africa, or policies elsewhere that resemble this.

armistice
A truce or cessation of hostilities.

authoritarian
Term applied to leaders or governments who exercise power with little or no regard for *democracy* or other constraints.

autocracy
A form of political rule where all power is concentrated in one person (the **autocrat**). Unlike the similar term *dictator*, the word autocrat is often applied to a powerful king or emperor.

Axis
The alliance between Germany and Italy (and later Japan) before and during World War II; also these countries considered collectively (Axis forces or Axis domination).

bilateral
Involving two governments (or other organizations), especially with reference to treaties and agreements. Compare *multilateral*.

bloc
A group of countries that act together in matters of international relations.

bourgeois
Originally a member of the French middle classes, now often used disparagingly for a supporter of the capitalist system (see *capitalism*), or simply for a person with conventional views. In *Marxist* theory, the **bourgeoisie** are the class of capitalists.

buffer state
A smaller country lying between two more powerful rival countries. The presence of a buffer state is considered useful in decreasing tension between the rival countries.

Byzantine Empire
The mainly Greek-speaking Christian Empire that was a continuation of the eastern Roman Empire and lasted for around 1,000 years, until its conquest by the Ottoman Turks in 1453.

Caliphate
In Islamic (see *Islam*) culture this is a political/religious institution in which a chosen individual, the **caliph**, is regarded as a successor to the Prophet Muhammad, and thus able to confer political legitimacy on individual rulers across the Islamic world. Once powerful rulers themselves, caliphs later became mainly figureheads, although the Ottoman rulers of Turkey continued to claim the title until the 20th century.

Calvinism
A strict form of Protestantism named after the 16th-century religious reformer John Calvin. **Calvinist churches** are usually *Presbyterian* in organization.

capitalism
A way of organizing society that favours the activity of **capitalists**: private individuals or organizations who accumulate wealth (**capital**), especially in the form of the buildings and equipment that are necessary to produce goods and services. These businesses generate employment, while also providing profits for the capitalists.

Catholic
A term that originally meant inclusive or all-embracing, so that the **Catholic Church** originally meant the whole of the Christian Church. After various splits over the centuries, the Catholic Church is now the organization of churches that owes its allegiance to the pope in Rome, thus it is also called the Roman Catholic Church.

charter
A written grant of rights or similar legal document.

city-state
A self-governing, independent city.

classical/Classical
Relating to the civilizations of ancient Greece and Rome and their achievements (the **Classical Period**) or to later artistic and cultural movements that emulated the values of this period. The term classical can also be applied to the high point of any civilization or culture, and can be used with other shades of meaning, such as "possessing timeless value".

client state
A country that is dependent on another larger country for trade, protection, etc.

coalition
A formal arrangement in which two or more different groups agree to act together, such as when different political parties come together to form a government.

Cold War
The period of hostility between the West and the communist countries dominated by the former USSR. The Cold War lasted from shortly after World War II until the collapse of *communism* in Eastern Europe in 1989.

collective
Organized in common; taken together as a whole.

colonialism
The practice and policy of acquiring foreign colonies, often with the implication that this involves cultural domination and exploitation.

commonwealth/Commonwealth
The term commonwealth originally meant "the common good". With an initial capital, Commonwealth refers either to the government of Britain in the years following the execution of Charles I, or to the (British) Commonwealth of Nations, the association set up to maintain links between countries of the former British Empire. The word also occurs in the full official names of several countries and US states.

commune
A community of people who aim at sharing everything in common.

communism
(**1**) Any society based on the principles of mutual help, in which property is not owned by individuals, but is held in common. (**2**) More specifically, political movements or governments inspired by or claiming to act in the name of the political and philosophical doctrines of Karl Marx (see *Marxist*).

Congress
In the US Constitution, the body forming the legislative arm of the federal government (see *federal system*). It comprises two elected assemblies, the House of Representatives (or Lower House) and the Senate (or Upper House).

conservative/Conservative
Various social and political meanings, including: caution in accepting change; respect for traditional values and authority; support for free-market *capitalism* and opposition to government intervention; membership of a particular political party, such as the Conservative Party in the United Kingdom.

consul
One of the two highest officials in the Roman republic, who each held power for only one year.

Counter-Reformation
The period of revival in the *Catholic* Church following the Protestant *Reformation*, involving both internal reforms and active opposition to *Protestantism*.

coup
Short for coup d'etat, the sudden illegal seizing of power by a small group.

Crusades
Military expeditions organized by the papacy in the *Medieval period*, initially with the aim of gaining control of the "Holy Land" (Palestine) from Islamic powers (see *Islam*).

Danegeld
A tax raised in Anglo-Saxon England to pay off and defend against Danish invaders. It later became a general land tax.

decimal system (army)
The principle of organization of Genghis Khan's Mongol army, with a hierarchy of military units that contained between 10 and 10,000 men.

demagogue
A politician whose power base relies on stirring up the emotions of the people of a country through charismatic and emotional speeches, often in opposition to established authority.

democracy
A political system in which the people of a country control their government. **Direct democracy**, which operated in ancient Athens, allowed citizens to decide policy by direct votes. Most democracy is **representative democracy**, with the people electing politicians to represent them. Democracy has often been popular with groups that are excluded from voting, such as women and non-property owners.

denomination
A body of religious believers sharing a common faith and organization and having a recognized name; most commonly applied to sections within the Christian Church – for example, Baptists and Methodists.

dependency
A subordinate territory that does not form an integral part of the country which has overall control of it.

despotism
An *autocracy*, especially one that is headed by a king or emperor. An **enlightened despot** is one who is seen as ruling for the benefit of the people rather than for him/herself. Also refers to the exercise of power itself by the ruler.

detente
The lessening of tension between two countries; used especially for the time when tension was decreasing between the US and the former USSR.

devaluation
The lowering in value of one country's currency compared with other currencies.

diaspora
The members of a particular ethnic group (see *ethnicity*) who are living away from their land of origin. It was originally used with reference to the Jews.

dictator
Originally an official in ancient Rome who was given sweeping powers for a short period during a time of national emergency. Now used for any person who rules a country alone and with no effective restrictions on their individual power. The word is not normally applied to hereditary kings or emperors, unlike the similar terms autocrat and despot (see *autocracy* and *despotism*).

dissolution
In general, this means the process of dissolving or separating into constituent parts. The **Dissolution of Parliament** is the official end of a parliament before a general election is held to elect new representatives. The **Dissolution of the Monasteries** was the disbanding of monasteries and other religious institutions in 16th-century England during the reign of Henry VIII.

dominion/Dominions
(**1**) The right to govern or control. (**2**) Any territory owing allegiance to a particular ruler or government. (**3**) A term formerly used, especially the plural (Dominions), for the larger self-governing territories within the British Empire, especially Canada and Australia.

dynasty
A royal family that rules over a country for several generations.

Eastern Bloc
The communist (see *communism*) countries of eastern Europe during the *Cold War* period.

ecclesiastical
Relating to the Church or to the clergy.

ecumenical
Relating to: (**1**) the whole of the Christian Church; (**2**) movements aimed at reuniting different branches of the Church.

ethnicity
Characteristics and features associated with belonging to a particular ethnic group, which may be defined purely by culture or with reference to biological or racial characteristics.

evangelical
Relating to: (**1**) the Christian Gospels; (**2**) Protestant (see *Protestantism*) doctrines that emphasize personal salvation by faith; (**3**) religious movements that actively go out to preach to and convert others (to **evangelize**).

excommunication
The action taken by a religious organization of cutting off an individual from communication or membership of the organization, and/or from taking part in its rites.

fascism
Originally, the ideology of the political movement led by Benito Mussolini, who was in power in Italy between 1922 and 1943. Fascist doctrines were *authoritarian*, anti-democratic (see *democracy*), and anti-communist (see *communism*); they emphasized subjection of the individual to the state and tended to glorify war and *nationalism*. The term **fascist** is now used loosely for any ideology or attitude seen as authoritarian or intolerant.

fatwa
In *Islam*, a pronouncement, especially by a cleric, that gives an opinion and/or seeks to direct an action.

federal system
Any political system where there is an overall central government (**federal government**), but with many areas of decision-making being carried out by regional governments – for example, governments of provinces or states; the division of powers between the federal and regional governments is normally guaranteed by a constitution.

feudalism
The elaborate social system that grew up in *Medieval* Europe, where each nation was conceived of as a "pyramid", with a monarch at the top. Each level of society was entitled to claim rights from, but also obliged to undertake duties to, those "above" and "below" in the hierarchy.

fiefs
Lands held on condition of service offered to a superior lord under the feudal system (see *feudalism*).

free trade
Trading of goods and services between countries without restrictions, such as quota limits or taxes on imported goods. See also *protectionism*.

fundamentalism
A strict belief in all the traditional teachings of a given religion.

genocide
The systematic extermination of a racial or ethnic group (see *ethnicity*).

globalization
The process by which improved communications and international links have resulted in ideas, cultures, labour markets, and ways of life becoming increasingly widespread and/or interconnected globally.

gnosticism
Any of various religious ideologies and movements that emphasize the acquiring of secret or mystical knowledge as a way to salvation. Gnosticism was widespread in early Christianity, but came to be regarded as heretical (see *heresy*) by the Church.

Gothic
(**1**) Relating to the Goths, a Germanic tribe that invaded the Roman Empire in the 3rd and 4th centuries CE; (**2**) A style of European architecture that flourished from the 13th to 16th centuries, and was characterized by distinctive pointed windows and other features. Most of the great *Medieval* cathedrals were built in this style.

Greek Church
The branch of the Christian Church associated with the (Greek-speaking) *Byzantine Empire*, in which church services were conducted in Greek. See also *Orthodox Church*.

guerrilla warfare
Warfare where the fighters operate in small irregular units, often without uniforms or an official army structure.

guild
A *Medieval* mutual-aid association. Craftsmen and merchants in towns were often organized into guilds, and individuals were often only allowed to practise their trade if they belonged to the guild of that particular trade.

hegemony
A situation in which a powerful country exerts a significant influence over its less powerful neighbours.

heresy
Usually a minority belief or tendency within a given religion that is regarded as unacceptable or even evil by other adherents to the religion. A **heretic** is a person regarded as heretical.

Holy Roman Empire
An empire set up in Western Europe in *Medieval* times, whose territory was centred on modern-day Germany. Both connected to and forming a rival to the papacy, it increasingly took the form of a loose collection of states. The emperor of the Holy Roman Empire held little power by the time it was formally abolished by Napoleon in 1806.

hominin
A member of the biological group that includes humans and their extinct ancestors and relatives, back to the point at which they split from the line leading to chimpanzees.

Huguenots
Historical term for French Protestants (see *Protestantism*), whose history of persecution led many to emigrate and settle in other countries.

humanist
(**1**) A Latin or Greek scholar, especially of the *Renaissance* period. The work of Renaissance humanists involved the rediscovery of classical texts and their human-centred values, as opposed to the emphasis on God and theology of the *Medieval period*. (**2**) A person who advocates an ethical approach to human life that does not involve belief in a god or gods.

imperialism
Originally the system of government or rule in an empire. Now, more particularly, the attitudes of mind that supported the acquisition of distant territories by 19th-century Western powers.

Iron Curtain
Term for the barrier between the USSR-dominated communist countries (see *communism*) of Eastern Europe and the non-communist West during the *Cold War*.

Islam
A monotheistic (single-god) religion established in the 7th century CE in Arabia by the Prophet Muhammad. Islam means "submission" (to God). The two main branches of Islam, **Sunni** and **Shi'ite**, differ in the authority and legitimacy they ascribe to different members of the Prophet's family after his death.

Islamism
A tendency within *Islam* that aims to establish Islamic law and values in societies worldwide.

isolationism
A policy of isolating a country from international disputes, especially by not taking part in alliances. The term is particularly associated with certain periods of Chinese, Japanese, and US history.

Jacobin
A member of the extreme revolutionary group during the French Revolution.

Jacobite
In British history, a supporter of the claims of the Stuart monarchs to regain the throne, after James II (Jacobus in Latin) was forced to flee and abdicate the British throne in 1689.

Jesuit
A member of the Society of Jesus, an organization founded in 1534 within the *Catholic* Church, which played a leading role in the *Counter-Reformation*. It continues to be active in education and in the spreading of Catholic doctrine.

jihad
A struggle or war undertaken on behalf of the Islamic faith (see *Islam*).

judiciary
A collective term for the judges holding office in a particular country.

khedive
A title used mainly by the rulers of Egypt from 1867 to 1914, who were nominally subject to the authority of the Ottoman (Turkish) Empire, but in practice were largely independent.

knight
A feudal rank (see *feudalism*) that combined a high status in society with obligations to undertake military service.

league
An association between individuals or states for mutual protection, or for furthering common interests.

legion
A fighting unit of the Roman army consisting of 3,000–6,000 men.

legislature
The institution(s) of government that are responsible for passing laws.

Levant
The region of the eastern Mediterranean and the territories bordering it.

liberalism
A political movement or philosophy that emphasizes individual freedom, as well as supporting forms of government that are answerable to the people (contrast *absolutism*). The term **economic liberalism** means support for free-market *capitalism*. In the US, **liberal** often implies a left-wing stance that supports increased governmental intervention and spending on social welfare.

mandate
A legal command or commission, especially a commission in which a country was authorized by the former League of Nations to govern a particular territory in the interests of its inhabitants. See also *trusteeship*.

manifesto
A written declaration of policy and aims, especially one issued by a political party or movement.

Marxist
Term applied to a variety of doctrines that trace their origin to the German-born philosopher and social thinker Karl Marx. Marx himself believed that he had discovered laws of history which proved that eventually *capitalism* would collapse and be replaced by *communism*.

Medieval period
The period from approximately 600 to 1450 CE in Europe, from the end of the western Roman Empire to the *Renaissance*.

mercenary
A soldier who fights for other nations for money.

missionary
A representative of a particular religion who travels to another country, region, or culture with the aim of converting people to his or her religion.

Monophysitism
The belief that Jesus Christ has only one nature (with his divine nature absorbing his human nature), rather than having two separate natures. A minority view in the Christian Church, it is upheld mainly by the Coptic Church and other churches with their roots in the ancient Near East.

multilateral
Involving three or more governments (or other organizations), especially with reference to treaties and agreements. Compare *bilateral*.

nation
(**1**) An independent country. (**2**) A people defined by shared historical, cultural, and linguistic ties, whether constituting a single independent country or not.

nationalism
A political attitude of strong support for the interests and future of one's nation.

nationalization
The taking of private property into public ownership by the state, especially on a large scale, such as an entire industry.

NATO
North Atlantic Treaty Organization, an international military alliance of Western powers established in 1949.

Nazism
The doctrines of the National Socialist (Nazi) party, in power in Germany under Adolf Hitler 1933–45. Nazism was similar to *fascism*, but in addition was racist, believing in the supremacy of a supposed "Aryan" race of which the German people were allegedly the "purest" representatives. See also *totalitarianism*.

neoclassicism
Any cultural movement in which styles or ideals of a *classical* period are revived. More specifically, an 18th-century movement in European art and literature, which was inspired by renewed interest in the values of ancient Greek and Roman art.

neocolonialism
The situation in which a powerful, developed country has influence over a less developed country (especially a former colony) in ways that are seen as similar to aspects of actual *colonialism*.

oligarchy
A political system where a few powerful, and often rich, individuals combine to rule a country. The former Republic of Venice is a historic example. Many former communist countries (see *communism*) were also effectively oligarchies, with communist party officials monopolizing power.

order (religious)
In the Christian Church, a body of people adhering to a particular rule or way of life that is often set down by an individual founder – orders of monks, for example. The phrase "**in orders**" means occupying a clerical position, such as priest or bishop.

Orthodox Church
A major group of Christian Churches that descend from a split with the Western (*Catholic*) Church that occurred in 1054 CE. Prominent in Eastern and southeastern Europe, it includes several different traditions and national Churches.

Outremer
The *Medieval* French states set up in the Near East after the *Crusades*.

overlord
A lord who is superior to other lords or rulers, especially within the feudal system (see *feudalism*).

pacifism
Opposition to all war.

papal bull
An order or edict issued by a pope on a matter of importance.

peasant
A worker on the land, especially an agricultural labourer or small farmer.

pharaoh
Title of the ruler of ancient Egypt, who was traditionally seen as both a king and a god.

pilgrimage
A journey undertaken for religious reasons to a shrine or other sacred site.

plebiscite
A referendum, especially on a major constitutional issue.

pogrom
An organized massacre, especially one carried out against the Jews in Eastern Europe in the late 19th and early 20th centuries.

polity
A form of government and political organization.

populist
Generally a critical term for a politician whose power base comes from successfully appealing to the general public, without necessarily being respected by other politicians. It is often implied that a populist simply tells people what they want to hear.

Praetorian prefect
A high administrative office in the Roman Republic and Empire, deriving originally from the headship of the state bodyguards – the Praetorian Guard.

pre-Colombian
Relating to the cultures of the Americas before their contact with European explorers and conquerors.

Presbyterians
Members of various *Protestant* Churches that do not have a hierarchy of bishops, but are run by **presbyters** (elders) elected by church congregations.

proletariat
A collective term for working-class wage earners who do not possess their own capital (see *capitalism*); often contrasted with *bourgeoisie* (see *bourgeois*) in *Marxist* theory.

protectionism
The policy of defending the industries of a country by creating barriers to foreign competition, for example restricting imports.

protectorate
A colony in which the emphasis is on the colonizing power being responsible for defence and foreign affairs for the benefit of the people of the territory.

Protestantism
Any of the forms of Christianity resulting from the *Reformation* of the 16th century and afterwards, in which allegiance is no longer offered to the pope in Rome.

puppet state
A country that, though nominally independent, is actually under the control of another country.

purge
A term, usually associated with totalitarian systems (see *totalitarianism*), for the expulsion of people from an organization who are regarded as undesirable by the organization's leadership.

Puritanism
Originally a movement within the Church of England in the 16th and 17th centuries that pressed for further changes to Church organization and doctrine, going beyond the split from the *Catholic* Church that had occurred under Henry VIII. The term was later applied to religious groups with similar views outside the Church of England, and then eventually to any way of thinking that was seen as disapproving of pleasure and indulgence.

putsch
A violent attempt to overthrow a government.

recession
A reduction in the economic activity of a country, though less serious than a depression. A recession is often defined as having occurred when economic output has declined for two successive three-month periods.

Reformation
The Christian reform movement of the 16th century, in which many churches and individuals broke from the Western (*Catholic*) Church headed by the pope in Rome.

Renaissance
A cultural phase of European history, centred on Italy in the 15th and early 16th centuries, that involved the rediscovery of the cultural achievements of ancient Greece and Rome. This in turn became the inspiration for new ideas in literature and the creation of new artworks.

reparations
A term that came into use after World War I for payments made by the defeated countries to the victors, regarded as being in recompense for their aggression. An older term for the same thing is **indemnity**.

republic
Any country not headed by a hereditary king, prince, or emperor. Modern republics are usually headed by presidents, and range from democratic regimes to dictatorships.

republicanism
(**1**) Support for a *republic* as the preferred form of government. (**2**) Beliefs and values associated with the Republican Party in the US. (**3**) In Irish contexts, support for the complete independence of Ireland from the UK.

restoration/Restoration
The restoring of a previous state of affairs. In British history, the Restoration refers to the return of the British monarchy in 1660, after the Civil War and *Commonwealth*, and the years following this.

Roman Church
The Western branch of the Christian Church, which developed under the leadership of the pope in Rome, and in which church services are, or were, conducted in Latin. See also *Catholic*, *Greek Church*.

Romantic Movement
A many-sided cultural and artistic movement in Europe that reached its peak in the early 19th century. It included an increased appreciation of nature and an emphasis on feelings and emotions in contrast to reason.

royal minority
The period when the monarch of a country is still a child (a minor).

satrap
A provincial governor in the ancient Persian Empire; also, a subordinate ruler generally.

scholasticism
The approach to reasoning and knowledge that is characteristic of centres of higher education during the Christian *Medieval period*.

sect
A religious group or organization that holds distinctive or non-standard beliefs. The term is often used to imply that the views held are doubtful, or even heretical.

sectarian
Displaying hostile attitudes to people from a different social grouping, especially those adhering to a different denomination of the same religion.

secular
Non-religious.

segregation
Separation, in particular separation of one race from another within a racist or *apartheid* social system.

self-determination
Situation in which a people or nation are able to choose their own government, or to govern themselves.

Senate
(**1**) The assembly that acted as the main ruling body in ancient Rome (eventually losing most of its powers to the emperors). (**2**) The upper legislative house of the US *Congress*, or of other legislatures that are similarly organized.

serf
A *peasant* living in a condition of semi-slavery, with no right to leave the land of the landowner for whom he or she works.

shogun
A hereditary commander-in-chief in Japan. For various periods in Japanese history, shoguns, rather than the emperor, held the real power.

social democracy
Formerly another term for *socialism* or *communism*. In modern usage it refers to a moderate form of socialism that is compatible with democracy and *liberalism*.

socialism
Term used for a variety of left-wing ideologies and movements that all involve some government intervention in society and the economy, with the aim of redistributing wealth for the common good. Socialist movements have ranged from the moderate and democratic to revolutionary communist movements (see *democracy* and *communism*).

sovereignty
Complete legitimate authority over a given territory.

soviet
One of the many elected councils that operated at all levels of society in the former USSR. **Soviet Union** is another name for the USSR.

Soviet Bloc
Another name for the *Eastern Bloc*.

speculation
An economic term for the buying and selling of shares, or other tradeable assets, for the purpose of making a profit if the price rises or falls in the way that the speculator predicts.

state
(**1**) An independent country. (**2**) A self-governing region within a country. (**3**) The governmental apparatus of a country.

stock exchange
An organization that allows trading in shares of companies, government bonds, and other financial assets.

suffrage
The right to vote, especially in a public election. A **suffragist** is an advocate of the right to vote; especially, in many cases, the rights of women.

sultan
A title, equivalent to king or emperor in some *Islamic* contexts and cultures (see *Islam*).

suzerainty
Feudal overlordship (see *overlord*). Also, the supremacy of one state over a less powerful one.

synod
A church council or assembly.

technocrat
(**1**) A member of a technical elite. (**2**) Someone who regards political problems as being best approached by seeking technical solutions, rather than via ideologies or value judgements.

tetrarchy
A governing arrangement in parts of the Roman Empire whereby a region was divided into four subdivisions, each with its own ruler (**tetrarch**). Also the name for the district ruled by a particular tetrarch.

theocracy
Rule by a priest or a priesthood.

tithe
A tax imposed for the upkeep of the Church, especially in the *medieval period*, usually consisting of one-tenth of the agricultural produce of a given piece of land.

totalitarianism
A form of *authoritarian* rule in which the government aims to control the details of individual people's lives and thoughts, treating individual freedom as unimportant compared with the state.

trade union
An association of workers, formed to advance their economic interests and to provide mutual support.

tribune
A title for various officials in ancient Rome. A tribune of the people was one of two (later more) officials appointed to protect the rights of the common people against the nobility. A military tribune was an officer attached to a *legion*.

triumph
An official victory procession in ancient Rome.

trusteeship
Situation in which a territory is administered by a particular country on behalf of the United Nations, for the benefit of the territory's inhabitants. See also *mandate*.

tsar
The title of the former emperors of Russia. A female tsar, or a tsar's wife, is a **tsarina**.

usurp
To seize power from another in a manner regarded as wrongful.

Utopia
An imaginary, ideal world. The name, meaning "nowhere", comes from the title of a book by Sir Thomas More, published in 1516. The word **Utopian** has come to be applied to any impracticably idealistic scheme.

vassal In the feudal system (see *feudalism*), a person holding land from a superior, in return for offering them allegiance; also used more generally for a servant or subordinate.

viceroy
A person who governs as the deputy of a monarch in a colony, region, or province.

Viet Cong
The political and military organization that carried out guerrilla warfare and other activities during the Vietnam War. Although it claimed to be an independent rebel movement within the then non-communist South Vietnam, in fact it was largely controlled by communist North Vietnam (see *communist*).

Zionist
A supporter of the creation of an independent state for the Jewish people. Also, following the creation of Israel in 1948, a strong supporter of Israel's continued existence as a Jewish state.

INDEX

Page numbers in **bold** indicate main treatments of a topic; numbers in *italic* refer to illustrations.

A

H

I

J

K

L

M

P

T

U

V

W

X

Y

Z

ACKNOWLEDGMENTS

Dorling Kindersley would like to thank the following people: Irene Lyford for proof reading; Jonny Burrows, Philip Fitzgerald, Spencer Holbrook, Clare Joyce, Maxine Pedliham, Hugh Schermuly, and Jackie Swan for design assistance; Steve Crozier for colour work; Amy Smith and Jen Allison at the Ure Museum, Reading University; Rachel Grocke and Helen Armstrong at Durham University Oriental Museum; Catherine Harvey at Hastings Museum; Gary Ombler for photography.
DK India would like to thank Dharini, Sreshtha Bhattacharya, Archana Ramachandran, Anita Kakar, and Vineetha Mokkil for editorial assistance; Pooja Verma, Ira Sharma, Priyabrata Roy Chowdhury, and Niyati Gosain for design assistance.

The publisher would like to thank the following for their kind permission to reproduce their photographs:

(Key: a-above; b-below/bottom; c-centre; f-far; l-left; r-right; t-top)

© 1982 MJJ Productions, Inc.: Used by permission. Photographer: Dick Zimmerman 439ca.
Courtesy of 3M: 282cr.
akg-images: British Library, London 222bl, 232tr; CDA / Guillemot 188-189t, 192cl, 206tc, 218cr; DEA Picture Library 188cl; François Guénet 77t; Joseph Martin 200tl; Nimatallah 208-209b, 223b; North Wind Picture Archives 292tc; Ru-ssian Picture Service 319tl, 351tl; Sotheby's 233tr; Yvan Travert 137tr; Tretjakov Gallery 235r, 309tr, 318t; Ullstein Bild 334br; World History Archive / IAM 28cr, 154cb, 186bl; Erich Lessing 40cl, 108tc, 182fbr, 183t.
Alamy Images: AAA Photostock 193cl; Nir Alon 301cr; Ayhan Altun 94-95t, Ancient Art & Architecture Collection Ltd 41t, 70c, 146c; Antiques & Collectables 240br, 244bc; Arco Images GmbH 25t; Art Directors & TRIP 36-37t, 78l, 213tr; The Art Archive 30bl, 34tl, 35br, 36c, 41cr, 48tl, 64bc, 65c, 72b, 92t, 112c, 114tc, 116tc, 138cl, 142tc, 143cl, 156cl, 160cl, 170bl, 171b, 182cb, 192b, 193c, 194-195t, 195tr, 195cl, 196tl, 201tr, 201c, 206-207t, 211cl, 216crb, 218tl, 220tc, 226cr, 234tr, 242tr, 259tl, 272cl, 273tr, 284tc, 288tl, 292tr, 294ca, 296tl, 302-303tc, 304tr, 313tc, 332clb, 335tl, 358bl, 402ftr, 410crb, 411cra; The Art Gallery Collection 7tl, 18cra, 50tl, 68tr, 80cl, 102cl, 114cl, 114c, 129cr, 143c, 159c, 179tr, 181tc, 196ca, 201tl, 202tc, 212tl, 238cl, 265tc, 285c; ASP Religion 131tl; Authors Image 142bl; Greg Balfour Evans 114tl; Peter Barritt 137tl; Paul Bevitt 282clb; Anders Blomqvist 35tr; BrazilPhotos.com 224-225t; Vlad Breazu 80b; CBW 65bl; Charistoone-Images 149tr; B. Christopher 41cl; Classic Image 329tr; Dennis Cox 153tr; Stephen Coyne 116cl; Craig Joiner Photography 26-27t; CuboImages srl 76b; Gianni Dagli Orti / The Art Archive 312br, 318cra; DBI Studio 326cra; Dinodia Photos 225b; Michael Doolittle 333br; EmmePi Travel 177tr; Eye Ubiquitous 19cra; Stuart Forster 149b; Robert Fried 169cr; GL Archive 334tl; Globuss Images 26tl; Tim Graham 153tc; Spencer Grant 332cra; Mike Greenslade 284-285t; Sonia Halliday Photographs 116-117t; Mark Harmel FAP 283crb; Hemis 279tr; Peter Horree 34ca, 52c; Imagebroker 132tl; ImageClick, Inc. 127tr; Images and Stories 195c; Interfoto 27bl, 55bl, 94cr, 99t, 147b, 153b, 159tr, 167ca, 170-171t, 211b, 212tr, 220tl, 229bl, 267tr, 323tl; Hanan Isachar 139tl; F. Jack Jackson 248tl; Martin Jenkinson 70-71t; Jon Arnold Images / Demetrio Carrasco 7ftr; Wolfgang Kaehler 34-35t; LatitudeStock 151br; Lebrecht Music and Arts Photo Library 185c, 207tr, 225tr, 234br, 289ca, 364cb; David Lyons 88cl; Celia Mannings 288tc; Mary Evans Picture Library 51b, 98c, 99cr, 157tl, 163cr, 181tr, 232tl, 240bl, 259tc, 261tc, 306t, 318br, 323cr, 330tc, 364clb; Steven May 330br; John Mitchell 305tr; Carver Mostardi 136tl; Niday Picture Library 222tc, 303tr; North Wind Picture Archives 126tc, 150c, 211tr, 224br, 244cr, 270tr, 277tl, 285tc, 301tc, 321tr, 322tl, 329ca; B O'Kane 147tl; Oasis / Photos 12 336br; Olivier Parent 73cr; David Paterson 245t; PhotoEdit 454clb; Photos-12 150tr, 329tl; Pictorial Press Ltd. 197tl, 220-221t, 295cra, 296tc, 414clb; Pictures Colour Library 118c; Paris Pierce 320tr; Mark Pink 140-141t; Pink Sun Media 215tr; PjrStudio 88tc; Niels Poulsen DK 239br; The Print Collector 31br, 112tr, 151tr, 162tl, 166c, 175ca, 194bl, 251bc, 289crb, 305b, 313cra; Prisma Archivo 319br; Prisma Bildagentur AG 249tr; Ria Novosti 143tl, 207bl; Rolf Richardson 163tc; Robert Estall Photo Agency 109tc; Robert Harding World Imagery 108-109t; Robert Preston Photography 92bl; Russ Images 146b; Kumar Sriskandan 365bl; Stock Montage, Inc. 206c; Homer Sykes Archive 434-435t; Vintage Power and Transport / Mark Sykes 332crb; Giovanni Tagini 194tc; TAO Images Limited 120t; The Natural History Museum 216fclb; TTL Images 152c; V&A Images 136cr, 280tc; Ivan Vdovin 323bl; Visions of America, LLC 220bl; Janine Wiedel Photolibrary 425tl; Pete M. Wilson 296tr; World History 4-5, 65tr, 113tl, 176tl, 252t, 278tl, 309tc, 320tl, 326tr, 327bl, 415cra.
www.BibleLandPictures.com 21tr, 40tl, 64c.
Ancient Art & Architecture Collection: 148b; Prisma 100tl.
The Art Archive: Bibliothèque Nationale Paris 62cl, British Library 196b; Cathedral of Santiago de Compostela / Gianni Dagli Orti 127c; Edinburgh University Library 146tr, Galleria d'Arte Moderna Rome / Alfredo Dagli Orti 71br; Genius of China Exhibition 27cr; Musée du Louvre Paris / Gianni Dagli Orti 94cl; Musée Guimet Paris / Gianni Dagli Orti 99b; Museum of the City of New York, Gift of Rita and Murray Hartstein (inv 96.13.1) 210tr; Naval Museum Genoa / Alfredo Dagli Orti 205tr; Royal Horticultural Society / Eileen Tweedy 257tl; V&A Images 259crb.
Bibliothèque Nationale De France, Paris: 154crb;
The Bridgeman Art Library: 103r, 143tr, 184tr, 253tr, 264cra, 269cr, 271tr, 374bc; Archives Charmet 157tr, 167tr, 208bl, 236cr, 253cl, 277tr, 288tr, 328tr; Art Gallery of New South Wales, Sydney 319tr; Ashmolean Museum, University of Oxford, UK 40cr, 243t; Bibliothèque de l'Institut de France 205bc; Bibliothèque Nationale, Paris 6ftr, 129tl, 130cl, 140tl, 152tc, 156tr; Bildarchiv Steffens Henri Stierlin 40tr; Bonhams, London 314tl; William Bradley 273cr; Bristol City Museum and Art Gallery, UK 297ca; © British Library Board. All Rights Reserved 118tc, 132tc, 141cla, 200tr, 272tr, 301tl; Brooklyn Museum of Art, New York, USA 169cb; Brooklyn Museum of Art, New York, USA/ Gift of K. Thomas amd Sharon Elghanayan 110-111t; Burgos Cathedral, Burgos, Spain 175tr; Byzantine / Prado, Madrid, Spain 112tc; Chester Beatty Library, Dublin 220br; Chicago History Museum 312bl; Chiostro dei Morti, Santissima Annunziata, Florence 149tl; Christie's Images 243tl; City of Edinburgh Museums and Art Galleries, Scotland 264tr; English Heritage Photo Library 72tl; Giraudon 50-51t, 102tl, 102-103t, 115cl, 187r; Harappan 26bl; Index 88tr; Indian School 68cl; Patrick Lorette Giraudon 295tl; Louvre, Paris 189b; Massachusetts Historical Society, Boston, MA, USA 236c; Ministere des Affaires Etrangeres, Paris, France / Flammarion Giraudon 218bl; Mucha Trust 119tr; Musée de la Presse, Paris / Giraudon 337tl; Museo Histórico Nacional, Buenos Aires, Argentina / Index 312tl; National Gallery, London 205br; National Museums of Scotland 316tr; Palacio del Senado, Madrid, Spain 141tc; Palazzo Ducale, Venice, Italy, Cameraphoto Arte Venezia 156tl; Peabody Essex Museum, Salem, Massachusetts 300tc; Peter Newark Historical Pictures 151tl; Peter Newark Military Pictures 196tr; Private Collection 257crb; Private Collection / Heini Schneebeli 203br; Private Collection / The Stapleton Collection 204bl; RIA Novosti 224c; The Royal Collection © 2011 Her Majesty Queen Elizabeth II 229t; Science Museum, London, UK 154br; Sumy Art Museum, Sumy, Ukraine 168tl; The Board of Trinity College, Dublin, Ireland 29bl; Professor Ernest Tristram 67tl; Universitetskaya Naberezhnaya, St. Petersburg, Russia / Bernard Cox 244tl; Victoria & Albert Museum, London 198bl; Wallace Collection, London 214bl; Courtesy of the Warden and Scholars of New College, Oxford 131b; © Trustees of the Watts Gallery, Compton, Surrey 301tr.
The Trustees of the British Museum: 2, 6tc, 8b, 25c, 27tr, 54bl, 64t, 67c, 87bl, 93c, 108tl, 149cr, 176-177b, 257clb.
ChinaFotoPress: 30cr.
Corbis: 7tc, 7r, 89cl, 186br, 205bl, 222tl, 238bl, 252br, 256tc, 278clb, 282bl, 284ca, 330tl, 346bl, 348cla, 350tr, 373cla, 393cra, 404c, 414ca, 426t, 439cra, 441tr, 444-445, 450t, 456cla, 457c, 459tl, 459cla, 460clb; Mike Agliolo 238crb, Albright-Knox Art Gallery / © Successió Miró 2011, 366bl; Alinari Archives 357cla; Paul Almasy 88bc, 128bl, 213c; Amanaimages 192tl; Mladen Antonov, 455cra; H. Armstrong Roberts / ClassicStock 433crb; Tony Arruza 161cr; Arte & Immagini 205tc; 237cl; Asian Art & Archaeology, Inc. 105br, 138tl; Atlantide Phototravel 87cr; Maher Attar / Sygma 444clb; Nathan Benn 21cb, 21bc; Bettmann 29bc, 47c, 65br, 68c, 87t, 139tr, 175cr, 176cl, 201cr, 208tc, 210cr, 225tl, 229br, 264tl, 266tr, 267clb, 278tr, 278crb, 289tl, 289tr, 300tl, 306cra, 308b, 309bc, 315tl, 328bl, 329tc, 329cla, 334tc, 340clb, 342tl, 343br, 350bc, 358tr, 360tl, 362bl, 363tl, 365clb, 366tr, 369tl, 370-371t, 371crb, 375br, 377tr, 378bl, 381tr, 391cra, 393tl, 397l, 399t, 400tl, 404bl, 407t, 412tr, 419t, 421crb, 428cb, 430, 433cl, 446ca; Stefano Bianchetti 228tr, 374cr; Bernard Bisson / Sygma 447tr; Brooklyn Museum 30-31t, 126cr, 241bl; Henri Bureau, 437cb; Alexander Burkatovski 41bl; Burstein Collection 66t, 127cl, 180c, 191c, 227cr; Car Culture 333bl; Charles Caratini 450-451t, Jacques M. Chenet, 440-441t; Christie's Images 163tr, 240tl; Elio Ciol 95ca, 105bl; Pierre Colombel 46-47t, 105t; Christopher Cormack 266tc; Marco Cristofori 152tl; Gianni Dagli Orti 28bl, 45b, 46cr, 49tc, 50c, 53cr, 57cr, 61tl, 62-63t, 259tr, 314b; Keith Dannemiller 158tl; David J. & Janice L. Frent Collection 337clb; Araldo de Luca 73bl, 77b, 81bl, 86cr, 89cr, 91cr, 374bl; Leonard de Selva 374br; Destinations 207tc; Dennis di Cicco 183bl; DPA / Agentur Voller Ernst / Yevgeny Khaldei 404-405; Richard Dudman / Sygma 435r; EFE 386t, 406t, 427cb; Anatoly Maltsev / EPA 118bl, EPA 226b, 462cr; Waltraud Grubitzsch / EPA 29cl; Patrick Escudero / Hemis 67tr; Dominique Faget, 438-439cb; Najlah Feanny-Hicks, 454tl; Fine Art Photographic Library 180b; Werner Forman 69b, 83b, 156b, 238clb; Michael Freeman 129cl, 236bl; The Gallery Collection 6tl, 17crb, 17br, 47br, 54bc, 61cra, 124tc, 128tr, 142tl, 158-159b, 184c, 197cr, 204tc, 204bc, 205cl, 210bl, 218tr, 261tr, 287tr, 295cb, 303br, 312-313tc; Christel Gerstenberg 362clb; Karie Hamilton, 455tr; Blaine Harrington II 287tl; Ron Haviv / VII, 449tr; Gavin Hellier / JAI 215c, Hemis / Tuul 142tr; Heritage Images 117bc, 132-133t, 185bl; Jon Hicks 73tc; Historical Picture Archive 46tl, 60tl, 108tr, 304tl, 304tc, 323tc; Hoberman Collection 204tr; Angelo Hornak 101cr, 199ca, 199bc, 199br; Hulton-Deutsch Collection 260tl, 335br, 341tl, 342bc, 343tr, 364br, 406crb; Mimmo Jodice 64br; Dewitt Jones 126tl; Mark Karrass 63tr; Karen Kasmauski 405bc; Alain Keler / Sygma 436tr; Keystone 340t; Lebrecht Authors / Lebrecht Music & Arts 130tl; Lebrecht Music & Arts 202-203t, 246t; Danny Lehman 52-53t; Charles & Josette Lenars 93t; Diego Lezama Orezzoli 269tl; Philippe Lissac / GODONG 150b; Yi Lu 174-175tl; Frank Lukasseck 115tr, Rick Maiman, 456tl; Luis Marden / National Geographic Society 287cb; John Marian / Transtock 333bc; Francis G. Mayer 52cr, 63cl, 211tl; Ulli Michel / Reuters 448tc; Momatiuk - Eastcott 28cl; David Muench 70tl, 206bl; NASA 458bl; NASA / Science Faction 55crb; National Gallery - London 280tl, 280tr, 281tl, 281clb, 283br, 284tl, 284tr, 284crb, 285tr, 292tl, 293tr, 296-297t, 297tr, 297cb; Michael Nicholson 57cb, 350tl, 350bl, 351bl, 351br, 380cl; Richard T. Nowitz 203tr; Christine Osborne 130tc; Nigel Pavitt / JAI 8-9; Jacques Pavlovsky / Sygma 434ca; Philadelphia Museum of Art 327br; PictureNet 265tr; Matthew Polak, 451cla; Radius Images 174c; Enzo & Paolo Ragazzini 182crb; Vittoriano Rastelli 80tr; Carmen Redondo 72-73tc, 200bl; Reuters

108b, 171tr, 183br; Bertrand Rieger / Hemis 126-127t; Robert Harding World Imagery 224tl; Royal Ontario Museum 90bl, 236-237t; David Rubinger 408crb; Michael Runkel / Robert Harding World Imagery 182br; Brendan Ryan /Gallo Images 12-13t; Rykoff Collection 416tr; Sakamoto Photo Research Laboratory 37br, 66b; Michael T. Sedam 82tc; Paul Seheult / Eye Ubiquitous 83cl; Smithsonian Institution 116bc, 259cra; Hubert Stadler 124tl; Stapleton Collection 86tl, 159tc, 160-161t, 214tl, 260tr, 288cb; State Hermitage Museum, St Petersburg 238bl, 327tr; George Steinmetz 147tc; Keren Su 117tr, 136tr, 461clb; Summerfield Press 153tl, 161tr; Swim Ink 2, LLC 301cla, 328cra, 343cla, 351cr, 390cla, 399l; Frédéric Soltan / Sygma 147tr, 160tc, 270tl, Sygma 2-3, 351tr; Homer Sykes 115tc; Luca Tettoni 104b, 137cl; The Art Archive 63br, 95tc, 120cl, 131tr, 150cr, 160tl, 162-163t, 166tr, 173crb, 189tr, 193tl, 200c, 211cr, 214tr, 228tl, 246cr; The Print Collector 112tl; Arthur Thévenart 166clb; Travelasia / Asia Images 157br; Peter Turnley 438tl, 446t, 448ca; Underwood & Underwood 352cra, 356br, 361tl; US Air Force 460-461t; Ruggero Vanni 45t, 77cr, 117tc; Sandro Vannini 24bc, 40bl, 56ca, 75br; Brian A. Vikander 58cla; Nik Wheeler 83tl, 126cb; Roger Wood 84bl; Adam Woolfitt 77cl, 132bc, 157c.
Dorling Kindersley: 412tl; The American Museum of Natural History 291crb; The Board of Trustees of the Armouries 48ca, 139c, 160cr, 168-169b, 217bl, 242br, 306b, 306cb, 402cb, 436cra, 438cr, 440cra; Ashmolean Museum, Oxford 135cr; Sarah Ashun 425ca; Bayerische Verwaltung der staatlichen Schlösser, Gärten und Seen 256crb; BFI Stills, Posters and Designs 334bl; Birmingham Museum and Art Galleries 144tr; British Airways 365crb; By permission of The British Library 28bc, 173clb; The Trustees of the British Museum 20tc, 25b, 28t, 29clb, 48tr, 48cb, 48crb, 48bl, 48br, 49tr, 49bl, 54tl, 54ca, 54cb, 54br, 59cl, 65cr, 84tl, 84tc, 84cra, 84bc, 84br, 84ftr, 85tc, 85tr, 85br, 92br, 108ca, 109cr, 122r, 123cl, 134r, 140-141b, 145tc, 162b, 198bc, 204tl, 216cl, 216clb, 216cb, 279cra, 290tr, 317crb, 374cb, 406cra; © CONACULTA-INAH-MEX. Authorized reproduction by the Instituto Nacional de Antropología e Historia 111r, 113c, 119tc, 119br, 144tc, 144cra, 144c, 144cr, 144br, 145c, 145cl, 145cr, 145b, 170t; Captain Cook Birthplace Museum, Middlesbrough Council 269cra; Andrew L Chernack 434cb; City Palace Museum, Jaipur 198br; Joe Cornish 286crb; Courtesy of the Charlestown Shipwreck and Heritage Centre, Cornwall 251bl; Courtesy of the RAF Museum, Hendon 355cr, 355crb; Andy Crawford 383c, 413tr, 413cb, 447cra; Danish National Museum 115cr, 119ca, 122tl, 122tr, 122cr, 123tr, 123tc, 123c, 123cra, 123cr; The Eden Camp Museum, Yorkshire 374crb, 375crb, 375bc, 386crb; English Civil War Society 198c; English Heritage 112bl; Ermine Street Guard 85ca, 85cr, 216br; Bob Gathany 412bl, 416ca; Steve Gorton 413bl, 413bc, 413br; Ellen Howdon 291cra; Wilberforce House, Hull City Museums 208bc; Imperial War Museum, Duxford 459b; Imperial War Museum, London 217br, 349cra, 356bl, 354tr, 354cla, 355tl, 355tc, 355tr, 355bl, 355bc, 355br, 397cr, 402tl, 402cr, 402bl, 402br, 402ftl, 403tl, 403l, 403tr, 403cra, 403c, 403crb, 403br, 403fcrb; Prem Kapoor 411cla; Colin Keates 298clb; James Mann 418clb; Jamie Marshall 82cl, 98tl, 219b, 299crb; Mary Rose Trust, Portsmouth 55cb, 55clb; Andrew McRobb 250bc; Judith Miller 190br, Judith Miller / Bath Antiquities Centre 124cl, Judith Miller / Kevin Conru 148c, Judith Miller / Lyon and Turnbull Ltd. 313b, Judith Miller / Sloan's 29c, 190tr, 316tl, 316tc, Judith Miller / VinMagCo 412br, Judith Miller / Wallis and Wallis 134clb; The Ministry of Defence Pattern Room, Nottingham 387ca; Museo Archeologico Nazionale di Napoli 79c; Museu da Cidade, Lisbon 256cl, 257tr; Courtesy of the Museum of English Rural Life, The University of Reading 250cb, 251clb; Museum of London 20bl, 20br, 21bl, 21br, 21fbr, 28cr; Museum of Mankind Museum of Mankind / The Trustees of the British Museum 21cr; Museum of the Revolution, Moscow 370clb; Royal Museum of Scotland 144-145t; NASA 412cl, 440l, 275bc; National Maritime Museum, London 124-125b, 135tr, 182ca, 198tl, 198tc 275bc; National Motor Museum, Beaulieu 332bl, 354bl, 354bc; National Museum, New Delhi 199tr, 199tc, 199cl, 199cr, 247bl; Trustees of the National Museums of Scotland 215br, 252ca; National Railway Museum, York 384-385b; Natural History Museum 12cr, 13cr, 54clb; New York City Police Museum 368cra; Gary Ombler 268cra, 290tl, 290tc, 290c, 290cr, 290bl, 290ca, 290cra, 290bc, 290fbl, 291tl, 291tc, 291tr, 291ca, 291ca/2, 291cr, 291bl, 291ftl, 291ftr, 375bl, 391cb, 392c, 398crb, 402cla, 402bc, 403cb, 449c; Gary Ombler / Collection of Jean-Pierre Verney 354tl, 354tc, 355ca, 355cl; Opera di S. Maria del Fiore di Firenze 150tl; Pitt Rivers Museum, Oxford 20ca, 326c, 145cra; Pitt Rivers Museum, University of Oxford / David King 20cb, 20bc, 64cl; Martin Plomer 401cb; Rob Reichenfeld 256tl; Alex Robinson 271tl; Rough Guides 133tr, 141tr, 433tc; Royal Green Jackets Museum, Winchester 329crb; Courtesy of the Science Museum, London 123br, 134c, 182tr, 207br, 238cb, 250-251, 268cl, 274t, 274bl, 296cr, 298cb, 298crb, 298bl, 298-299c, 299cb, 299bl, 299bc, 318bl, 328cla, 332cb, 361cra, 428bl, 413tl; Dave Shayler / Astro Info Service Ltd 413c; Shuttleworth Collection, Bedfordshire 364tr, 364-365c; Spink and Son Ltd, London 358cra; James Stevenson 412-413, 413cl, 413cr; Jane Stockman 283bc; Harry Taylor 253cra; Universitets Oldsaksamling 123bl, 123bc; University Museum of Archaeology and Anthropology, Cambridge 20tr, 20-21ca, 21tl, 21cra, 144bl, 145tr; Lorenzo Vecchia 250bl; Jean-Pierre Verney 342cra, 346ca; Vietnam Rolling Thunder 426cla, 426ca, 428clb, 428bc; Vikings of Middle England 122bc, 122br; Wallace Collection, London 198tr, 198cla, 216-217, 217crb, 233b, 266cla; Matthew Ward 400ca, 401cra; Warwick Castle, Warwick, 17bc, 132cl, 132cr, 303cra; York Archaeological Trust for Excvation and Research Ltd 28br; Michel Zabe 144tl.
Dreamstime.com: Seregal 130tr.
Éditions Gallimard: Simone de Beauvoir, Le Deuxième Sexe I Les Faits et Les Mythes, 1949 421cl.
John Frost Historical Newspapers: 426crb.
Getty Images: Sylvester Adams 78-79t; AFP 86tr, 284clb, 347tr, 370cra, 420-421t, 424tl, 444tl, 451c, 458t, 463cr, 463b, 464-465c, 465cr; Alterndo Images 243b; Altrendo Travel 91t; Marilyn Angel Wynn / Nativestock.com 70bl; Apic / Hulton Archive 331tr, 335cra, 337cra, 347cra, 363b; Edward A. Armitage 94tl; Arthur Barrett / Hulton Archive 337tr; Allan Baxter 454-455cb; Pietro Benvenuti 286tl; Bloomberg 396cl, 398tl, 398tr, 398clb, 399cra, 400-401b, 401tl, 456-457t, 459cra, 460tl, 460crb, 461tr, 462cl; Bridgeman Art Library 101c, 180-181t, 184tl; Sisse Brimberg 16-17t; Bronze Age 19crb; Father Browne / Universal Images Group / Hulton Archive 186-187t, 189cl, 209tr, 300tr, 315tr; Michelangelo Buonarroti 178; Buyenlarge 331cla; Central Press / Hulton Archive 302tl, 321b, 359cra, 362tl, 363tr, 380tr, 381cl; Philippe Chery 60cb; Manuel Cohen 51cr, 336bl; Cosmo Condina 111tr; Cover 373t, 373cr, 376tr, 379tl, 382b; De Agostini Picture Library 34cl, 34-35c, 37bl, 56t, 100ca, 110bl, 175clb, 232cl, 294clb, 385tr; DEA / W.Buss 168-169t; DEA / A. Jemolo 44bl; DEA / G. Dagli Orti 26cr, 44bc, 56-57t, 76ca, 120c, 250br; DEA / L. Pedicini 250fbr, 258t, 258cl, 259clb; Danita Delimont 83tr, 223tl; Patrick Dieudonne 18-19t; Dinodia Photos / Brand X Pictures 307cl; Macduff Everton 81t, 104t; Gamma-Keystone 286tr, 293tl, 293ca, 293clb, 296clb, 299clb, 353br, 371ca, 372-373t, 392clb, 397t, 405t, 410tr, 431cla; Gamma-Rapho 407cra, 408t, 408clb, 409cr, 417t, 417cra, 418ca, 425tr, 432tr, 437tl, 438-439t, 441cl, 462t, 463t, 464c, 464-465t, 465cl; Kenneth Garrett 44-45t; Giraudon 102cr; Deborah Lynn Guber 67b; Henry Guttmann / Hulton Archive 349tr; Hulton Archive 58bl, 118cr, 136tc, 179cr, 188b, 193tr, 202tl, 222tr, 223tr, 228b, 229c, 237t, 244cl, 248tr, 280br, 301bl, 305tc, 314tr, 320cla, 326tc, 330tr, 334tr, 336tr, 342tr, 342cla, 346t, 404tl; Imagno 261cla, 267cra, 269cb, 372l; Imagno / Austrian Archives 279cb; Islamic School 46b; Jean I. Juste 179tl; Keystone-France / Gamma-Keystone 332cl, 341cra, 346cr, 366tc; Michael Langford 270clb; Gottfried Lindauer / The Bridgeman Art Library 300cla; London Stereoscopic Company / Hulton Archive 315br; Michael Melford 81cr, 120-121t, 138cr, 142c, 148tl; Nakshi 209br; National Archive / Newsmakers 331tl; New York Daily News 353tr, 356t; National Geographic 69t, 315ca; Nativestock / Marilyn Angel Wynn 227bl, 376cl; New York Daily News Archive 367tr; Richard T. Nowitz 89tr; Panoramic Images 90tr; Per-Anders Pettersson 376cra; 377cra, 377clb, 432cr, 433tr, 448-449t, David Poole 128tl, 435tc, 435cla; Popperfoto 269ftl, 309cl, 341bl, 347bl, 348t, 348bl, 371tr, 383tr, 390clb, 393clb, 396t, 398ca, 411tl, 414-415t, 419c, 431tr; Emile Prisse d'Avennes 286cb; Rischgitz / Hulton Archive 322tr; Roger Viollet 225tc, 405cr; Science & Society Picture Library / NMeM / Kodak Collection 319cla; DEA / M. Seemuller 54crb, Frank Siteman 24t; Sports Illustrated 451cra, 451clb; SSPL 180-181b, 225cl, 261crb, 265ca, 268tl, 268cr, 270cra, 271tc, 272tc, 274bc, 275cl, 275cr, 275cb, 275bl, 276tl, 276cl, 276cr, 282c, 282br, 283t, 283cb, 293crb, 366cra, 378tl, 412tc, 440tl, 428tr; Keren Su 36tl; SuperStock 188tr, 267tl, 368tl, 368cr; David Sutherland 79tr; Jane Sweeney 113tr, 256tr; The Bridgeman Art Library 39bl, 59br, 114-115t, 130cr, 131c, 132tr, 140c, 158tr, 161tc, 168cl, 176-177t, 184bl, 185t, 186t, 192tr, 193br, 197br, 219t, 221c, 226-227t, 232br, 233cr, 247t, 248b, 249cr, 274clb, 304ftr; Time & Life Pictures 58-59t, 120-121b, 218br, 235tl, 257tc, 265tl, 277cla, 280clb, 382t, 384t, 385cra, 386cra, 387t, 387crb, 390tl, 391tl, 407br, 409tr, 415tr, 418tr, 424cra, 424clb, 432cla, 445crb; Time & Life Pictures / Mansell 236tl, 241tl, 313cla, 321tl, 348br; Topical Press Agency / Hulton Archive 336tl, 357tr, 359tr, 361bl, 368bl; Travel Ink 69cl; Roger Viollet 101t, 272crb, 352t, 352bl, 357cr, 362cra, 379cla, 392tl, 425cra; Art Wolfe 233tl.
Robert Hooke, Micrographia, London 1665: Ant from Scbem. XXXII and p203 222cra.
International Instituut voor Sociale Geschiedenis (http://www.iisg.nl/): Take steel as the key link for a leap forward in all fields, Tianjin People's Fine Arts Publishing House, 1958; offset, 53 x 77 cms, inv. nr. BG E12 / 530 417bl.
Riccie Janus: 461cr.
David King Collection: 350br, 351bc.
The Kobal Collection: Paramount 369bl; Warner Bros 367br.
Library Of Congress, Washington, D.C.: 266tl, Battelle Memorial Institute / 126770pu, 155br.
Magnum Photos: Rene Burri 420t; Steve McCurry 447l.
Mary Evans Picture Library: 287tc; AISA Media 234c; Alinari Archives, Florence 160-161b; IBL Collections 247cr; Suddeutsche Zeitung 170br, 203bl.
Moviestore Collection: 420b; Disney 384ca.
NASA: 365br, 441cb; GSFC / JPL, MISR Team 245cl.
National Maritime Museum, Greenwich, London: 238bc, 238br, 379cr; Ministry of Defence Art Collection 238tr, 239c.
NRAO / AUI / NSF: 183bc.
David Parfitt: 251crb.
Photolibrary: Wayne Fogden 125tr; Erwin Bud Nielsen 155crb; Sites & Photos 56-57b.
Press Association Images: 416tc; AP / Zoran Bozicevic 438clb, 450clb.
Rex Features: 455tl;
Royal Geographical Society: Alfred Gregory, 414crb.
The Royal Bank of Scotland Group: © 2011 65bc.
Giovanni Sarbia: 90c.
Photo Scala, Florence: 269tc; BPK, Bildagentur fuer Kunst, Kultur und Geschichte, Berlin 212b; Heritage Images 110cr; The Metropolitan Museum of Art / Art Resource 182fbl, 195br; Vorderasiatisches Museum, Staatliche Museen zu Berlin 31cl; White Images 154bc, 155tl.
Science Museum / Science & Society Picture Library: 55br, 155bl, 183cl, 214br, 222br, 239bl, 239bc, 251cr, 253bl, 269ftr, 299cr, 332br, 365cb, 381crb, 429t.
Science Photo Library: Martin Bond 275crb; Jean-Loup Charmet 282bc; Eye of Science 429bc; John Greim 283bl; NASA 436clb; Science Source 208tr.
Courtesy of The Schøyen Collection, Oslo and London: 154clb, 154bl.
Socialdemokraterna (www.socialdemokraterna.se): 441cra.
SuperStock: De Agostini 55cr; Science and Society 233cl, 332bc, 375cl.
TopFoto.co.uk: The Granger Collection 125cla, 182bl, 264clb, 272tl, 272ca, 307tl, 307tc, 308t, 326tl; Public Record Office / HIP 300bc; RIA Novosti 294tl; World History Archive 271cb.
US Naval History & Heritage Command: Admiral Isoroku Yamamoto, Imperial Japanese Navy, (1884-1943) Official portrait, by Shugaku Homma, 1943 (inv NH 79462-KN) 393cb.
Werner Forman Archive: Biblioteca Nacional, Madrid 127tc.
Wikipedia: 65cl; Apple Inc. (http://en.wikipedia.org/wiki/File:Apple_Computer_Logo_rainbow.svg) 434crb; Courtesy of the Rare Book Room/Andreas Vesalii, De Humani

corporis fabrica p184-185, printed Johannes Oporinus c1543 282crb.

Endpaper Front: Alamy Images: Imagebroker. **Endpaper Back:** Getty Images Andy Caulfield. **Jacket images:** Front and back: **Alamy Images:** Art Directors & TRIP (Sikh Khanda), Lebrecht Music and Arts Photo Library (Churchill), (Napoléon), LOOK Die Bildagentur der Fotografen GmbH (Tutankhamun), Religion UK / Alan King (Celtic cross); **The Bridgeman Art Library:** English Heritage Photo Library (William I), Kunsthistorisches Museum, Vienna (Salt cellar); **Corbis:** (Elizabeth I), (Henry VIII), Bettmann (Martin Luther King), (Nightingale), (Shakespeare), The Gallery Collection (Queen Victoria), The Print Collector (Nelson); **Dorling Kindersley:** The Trustees of the British Museum (Celtic brooch), The Trustees of the British Museum (Emperor Tiberius), The Trustees of the British Museum (Eye of Horus), Courtesy of the Royal Artillery Historical Trust (Gattling gun), National Maritime Museum, London (Sextant), St Mungo, Glasgow Museums (Shiva), Jewish Museum, London (Torah), Imperial War Museum, London Imperial War Museum, London / By kind permission of The Trustees of the Imperial War Museum, London (Tank), Judith Miller / Wallis and Wallis (Vase), Museum of the Moving Image, London (Gramophone), Science Museum, London (Steam engine), (Tea-maker), (Telescope), Wallace Collection, London (Battle-axe), (Mace), (Sword), Michel Zabe (Aztec gold); **Getty Images:** (Aung San Suu Kyi), (Lincoln), AFP (Gandhi), Hulton Archive (Catherine The Great), The Bridgeman Art Library (Scarab); **National Maritime Museum, Greenwich, London:** (Astrolabe);

Back: **Dorling Kindersley:** Natural History Museum, London (Venus);

Spine: **Alamy Images:** Lebrecht Music and Arts Photo Library (Napoléon); **Dorling Kindersley:** Science Museum, London (Telescope), The British Museum (Eye of Horus), The Wallace Collection, London (Mace); **Getty Images:** Hulton Archive (Catherine the Great).